THE BUILDINGS OF ENGLAND

FOUNDING EDITOR: NIKOLAUS PEVSNER

YORKSHIRE WEST RIDING
LEEDS, BRADFORD AND THE NORTH

PETER LEACH AND NIKOLAUS PEVSNER

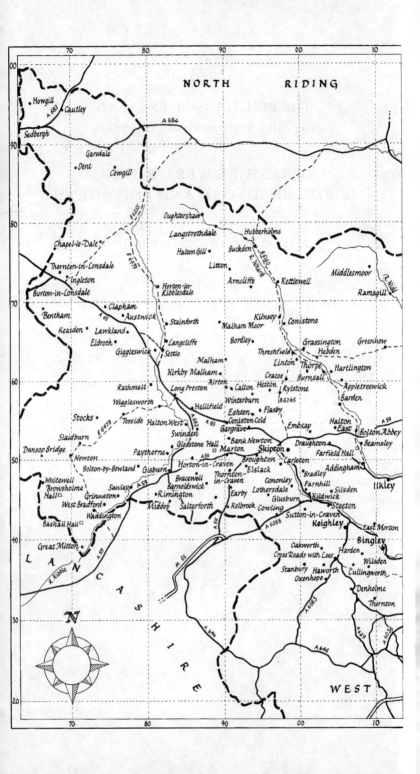

Yorkshire West Riding
Leeds, Bradford and the North

BY

PETER LEACH

AND

NIKOLAUS PEVSNER

WITH CONTRIBUTIONS FROM

JOHN MINNIS

RICHARD POLLARD

SUSAN WRATHMELL

AND

CHRISTOPHER WILSON

THE BUILDINGS OF ENGLAND

YALE UNIVERSITY PRESS
NEW HAVEN AND LONDON

YALE UNIVERSITY PRESS
NEW HAVEN AND LONDON
302 Temple Street, New Haven CT 06511
47 Bedford Square, London WC1B 3DP
www.pevsner.co.uk
www.lookingatbuildings.org
www.yalebooks.co.uk
www.yalebooks.com
for
THE BUILDINGS BOOKS TRUST

Published by Yale University Press 2009
Reprinted with corrections 2014
2 4 6 8 10 9 7 5 3

ISBN 978 0 300 12665 5

Printed in China
through World Print
Set in Monotype Plantin

TO GILLIAN

CONTENTS

CONTENTS

LIST OF TEXT FIGURES AND MAPS

Every effort has been made to contact or trace all copyright holders. The publishers will be glad to make good any errors or omissions brought to our attention in future editions.

MAPS

PHOTOGRAPHIC ACKNOWLEDGEMENTS

We are grateful to English Heritage and its photographer Bob Skingle for taking most of the photographs in this volume (© English Heritage Photo Library) and also to the sources of the remaining photographs as shown below. We are grateful for permission to reproduce them as appropriate.

Martin Charles, Architectural Photography: 116
Churches Conservation Trust/Boris Baggs: 25
Churches Conservation Trust: 85
Elain Harwood: 123
English Heritage (NMR): 4, 12, 51, 59, 80, 83, 86, 87, 94, 95, 100, 101, 109, 115, 118
English Heritage (Photo Library): 11, 88
Peter Leach: 9, 38, 77
Leeds City Council: 113
Les McLean: 110
National Trust Photographic Library/Andrew Butler: 32

MAP REFERENCES

The numbers printed in italic type in the margin against the place names in the gazetteer of the book indicate the position of the place in question on the index map (pp. ii–iii), which is divided into sections by the 10-kilometre reference lines of the National Grid. The reference given here omits the two initial letters which in a full grid reference refer to the 100-kilometre squares into which the county is divided. The first two numbers indicate the *western* boundary, and the last two the *southern* boundary, of the 10-kilometre square in which the place in question is situated. For example, Aberford (reference 4030) will be found in the 10-kilometre square bounded by grid lines 40 (on the *west*) and 50, and 30 (on the *south*) and 40; Yeadon (reference 2040) in the square bounded by the grid lines 20 (on the *west*) and 30, and 40 (on the *south*) and 50.

The map contains all those places, whether towns, villages, or isolated buildings, which are the subject of separate entries in the text.

FOREWORD

This volume is the first of two which are the successors to Nikolaus Pevsner's *Yorkshire: The West Riding*, first published exactly half a century ago in 1959 and slightly expanded in a second edition of 1967. It covers, broadly, the northern half of the West Riding; but in the local government reorganization of 1974 the Ridings were done away with as administrative entities, and a definition of the area in terms of the current dispensation is more complicated. About two-thirds of it lies within the present county of North Yorkshire; a little less than a quarter – but four-fifths of the population – in the area of the 1974 metropolitan county of West Yorkshire; and the rest has been hived off to Lancashire and Cumbria. Authorship also presents some complexities. The gazetteer entry on Leeds, developed from the *Leeds* city guide in this series, is by Susan Wrathmell, John Minnis and Richard Pollard, with an Introduction by Charles O'Brien and contributions on individual buildings by Derek Linstrum, Janet Douglas, Elain Harwood, Christopher Webster, Anthony Wells-Cole and Stuart Wrathmell. Richard Pollard also carried out preliminary work on parts of the outer neighbourhood of Leeds and on Knaresborough, and the entries for Aldborough, Boroughbridge and a score of places in the Tadcaster–Wetherby area are based on a draft text by him, finished by Charles O'Brien. The account of Ripon Cathedral is by Christopher Wilson. The specialist contributors to the Introduction are Alison Armstrong, Neil Redfern and Blaise Vyner, and the section on post-1918 buildings is by Charles O'Brien.

Particular thanks are due to those who have permitted and facilitated access to buildings – owners and occupiers, custodians and administrators acting on their behalf, incumbents, ministers, churchwardens and church secretaries. Their hospitality and generosity with their time are greatly appreciated: they are of course too numerous to list individually, and to single out a few would be invidious. It must however be emphasized that description of a building in the text does not in any way imply that it is open to the public.

Many people have kindly passed on information from their researches, answered queries or helped with expert comment etc. Glyn Coppack gave valued assistance on Fountains Abbey, Maurice Taylor answered many questions about Ripon Cathedral, and Rochelle Ramey of Field Archaeology Specialists Ltd and the late Andor Gomme both made available their respective analyses of Markenfield Hall. Arnold Pacey of the

Yorkshire Vernacular Buildings Study Group provided data on a range of buildings in Airedale and Wharfedale, Karen Lynch contributed her findings on Harewood House and estate, and Pauline Ford information on buildings in Keighley and Shipley; Colum Giles discussed textile mills, and Alan Clough communicated his knowledge of Glusburn model village. Geoffrey Brandwood passed on many gleanings about C19 churches culled from contemporary newspapers, Robert Finnigan and John Chappell provided data on Roman Catholic churches, John Hughes reported his discoveries about Edmund Sharpe, and Christopher Webster volunteered information on R. D. Chantrell not published in his monograph and on several other matters. Michael Swift supplied a copy of his database on Victorian stained glass in the Ripon diocese, and other information on stained glass came from Michael Kerney, Ruth Cooke and Philip Collins. Elizabeth Coatsworth communicated the latest thinking on Anglo-Saxon sculpture, and Geoffrey Fisher provided a commentary on C17 monuments. Karen Evans carried out research on request at the RIBA. Others who should be mentioned are Patrick Farman, Claire Gapper, Richard Hewlings, Colin Stansfield, Aidan Turner-Bishop, Sandra Wedgwood, Roger White, Heather Beaumont, Edward Bishop, Maurice Colgan, Ian Dewhirst, Barbara Gent, Jim Godfrey, Elspeth Griffiths, Malcolm Neesam, Roger Pyrah, Barry Rawson, the late James Wales, Dennis Warwick and Susan Wrathmell.

Information has also been provided by the National Trust at Malham Tarn, the Yorkshire Dales National Park Authority, Harrogate Borough Council, the City of Bradford Metropolitan District Council, Lancashire County Council, the Highways Agency and the Department of Transport. Of librarians and archivists, thanks go in particular to Robert Frost and Janet Senior at the Yorkshire Archaeological Society, and also to the staff of the West Yorkshire Archives Service at Leeds and Bradford, the North Yorkshire Record office at Northallerton, King's Manor Library, University of York, the Local Studies departments of the City Libraries at Leeds and Bradford, and the libraries at Harrogate, Keighley and Skipton.

In addition, the authors of the Leeds entry wish to reiterate their thanks to the following for information and advice: the conservation team of Leeds City Council; Kevin Grady, Director of Leeds Civic Trust; David Boswell (Bedford & Kitson), Colin Dews (Methodist churches), Roger Shaw and Charles Sewell (churches by Geoffrey Davy), Helen and Andy Guy (industrial archaeology), Chris Hammond and Robert Sladdin (Leeds University campus); and Peter Baker, Peter Brears, Stephen Burt, Ann Clark, Michael Devenish, Arthur Hopwood, Freda Matthews, Colin Price and Joan Newiss. They also wish to thank the staff of the Leeds Library, the Leeds Museum Service and the West Yorkshire Archaeology Service; and the Brotherton Library, University of Leeds, and the Leeds Metropolitan University Library for kind permission to use their facilities.

Funding to support research has been provided by the Leverhulme Trust, the Buildings Books Trust and Nicolas Hawkes, and expenses for the maps and text figures were met by the C. J. Robertson Trust. Another special note of thanks is to the late Tom Wesley, Josephine Wesley and Susan Bailey for making appointments for some of the visits, and to Tom and Josephine Wesley for checking early versions of the text for the city centres of Leeds and Bradford for changes on the ground. At Yale University Press, Bridget Cherry at the outset of the project inspired by example and guided the first steps; and subsequently Charles O'Brien as editor has not only been a nonpareil of calmness and supportive encouragement in frequently trying circumstances, but as noted above has contributed substantially to the text itself. The production editor was Sophie Kullmann, the picture researcher Louise Glasson, the copyeditor Bernard Dod, the proofreader Charlotte Chapman and the indexer Judith Wardman. The commissioning editor was Sally Salvesen. The county map and those of outer Leeds and Bradford were drawn by Reg Piggott, the other maps and plans by Alan Fagan. Most of the photographs were taken by Bob Skingle of English Heritage.

Finally, the greatest debt of gratitude, reflected in the dedication, is to my wife, for her unfailing moral support and many-facetted practical assistance over the many years of research and writing: after the rigours of that regime we both now look forward to living in less extraordinary times. As to the outcome, in his Foreword to *Yorkshire: The West Riding* in 1959, contrasting his experience with that of an earlier writer, Pevsner commented that he could not 'regard the result of my travels with "pure complacency"'; and complacency remains entirely foreign to the enterprise. The architectural wealth of the West Riding has meant that the application throughout the greater part of Pevsner's own principles of selective inclusion and discriminating brevity has been an essential discipline without which the volume would have grown to an uncontrollable size; but as always the authors and publishers will be glad to receive notice of any errors.

Peter Leach
2009

INTRODUCTION

The West Riding of Yorkshire was the largest of England's historic counties, and so it follows that the area covered in this volume is still large by average county standards* – a sixty-mile-long band of terrain extending from the outskirts of York to the edge of the Lake District, with the cities of Leeds and Bradford located towards its s boundary. Unsurprisingly, it is an area full of contrasts. One image is the urbanized one of the cities and their hinterland of tight-knit mill towns and villages pushing into the Pennines – the N half of the former textile zone of the West Riding, which also extends s to Wakefield, Halifax and Huddersfield. Another is of the still sparsely populated Yorkshire Dales to the NW** – Ruskin's 'truly wonderful country', its beauties and curiosities admired by tourists since the C18, which has long had a symbiotic relationship with the more industrialized parts of the West Riding as a place of escape and recreation (*see* J. B. Priestley's *English Journey*, 1933). A third might embrace the World Heritage Site of Fountains Abbey and Studley Royal on the gentler E Pennine margin, the nearby cathedral town of Ripon and spa town of Harrogate, and the opulently agricultural 'broad acres' beyond, forming part of the Vale of York.

So the fundamental contrast in the configuration of the LANDSCAPE is between the upland two-thirds of the centre and w – running across virtually the whole width of the Pennines – and the lowland third to the E. The former is a land of bare open moors and fells, steep-sided valleys and drystone-walled pastures; the latter flat or nearly so, crossed by the meandering lower reaches of the rivers Wharfe and Nidd. But the division between the two areas is indistinct, the Pennine margins dipping imperceptibly into the plain, and geologically the upland zone is by no means uniform. A broad swathe on the E side, from the head of Nidderdale through the buffer zone of Ilkley Moor, between lower Wharfedale and Airedale, to the 'Brontë country' sw of Keighley, is classic Millstone Grit territory, where the moors are heather-clad and boggy with black peat, and the weathered crags are similarly dark; but underlying the two cities are the rocks of the Coal Measures, and E from Leeds was deep

---

* 954,700 acres (381,880 hectares) (cf. e.g. 1,201,850 (480,740) for the whole of historic Lancashire, 638,278 (255,311) for Derbyshire). The population in 2001 was 1,426,000.
** Or rather of their s and w parts – Wharfedale, Nidderdale, Ribblesdale, Dentdale etc. – as this area correspondingly continues N into the North Riding.

1

mining country, the N tip of the Yorkshire coalfield. To the NW, from upper Wharfedale as far as Ingleton and Dent, the gritstone gives way to the distinctive karst country formed by the silvery-grey Carboniferous Limestone, with bare upland terraces of limestone 'pavement' alternating with the grass and long 'scars' on the valley sides, all culminating in the Three 'Peaks' of Craven – Ingleborough, Whernside and Penyghent – flattish-topped fells capped by patches of the gritstone. S of this area, running W from Skipton, is the lower gently rolling countryside of the Aire Gap, overlooked on the S side by Pendle Hill across the border in Lancashire; and beyond that the border country of the Forest of Bowland, a Pennine outlier. Then in the far NW the landscape changes again, to the rounded grassy Howgill Fells behind Sedbergh, which geologically have more in common with the fells of the Lake District than with the rest of the Pennines.

Regarding the pattern of SETTLEMENTS, there is some topographical linkage with the Roman era, at Aldborough which occupies the site of a Roman town, at Tadcaster and Ilkley, which are built over those of a lesser settlement and a legionary fort respectively, and perhaps at Leeds where there may have been another fort; while Leeds and Otley, as well as Ripon, appear to have been particularly significant centres in Anglo-Saxon times. Towns where the right to hold a market had been established in the Middle Ages are quite numerous (although not all the sites so designated grew into real urban entities). They include Leeds, Bradford and Keighley within the urbanized textile zone; a handful, notably Knaresborough and Skipton, which developed alongside a royal or baronial castle; and two, Ripon and Otley, which were promoted by the Archbishops of York. During the C18 and C19, in addition to the predominantly textile-based expansion of existing towns, there also developed a number of other specialist centres – spa towns at Ilkley and Boston Spa as well as Harrogate, the upmarket dormitory at Ilkley, brewing at Tadcaster. Villages are inevitably variegated. One feature, common in the upland but also present in the lowland, is a pattern in the medieval period of very large parishes, containing several settlements served by a single parish church – sometimes supplemented by chapels of ease, of medieval or C17 origin, or later by additional churches of the C19. A more recent phenomenon is the model village. There are two notable examples of the agrarian kind, Harewood and Ripley; then more characteristically three of the industrial variety, including pre-eminently the famous Saltaire, the area's second World Heritage Site.

p. 679 As to BUILDING MATERIALS, remains of early timber framing are quite widespread, but beyond that the upland–lowland division is once again fundamental, the upland being overwhelmingly an area of building in stone, the lowland largely, although not exclusively, one of brick (so while Bradford is a city of the former, much of Leeds, nine miles further E towards the junction of the two zones, is of the latter). But the building stones themselves are more diverse than they might seem to be at first sight; and so a more detailed look at the geology of the area is now required.

GEOLOGY AND BUILDING STONES

BY ALISON ARMSTRONG AND PETER LEACH

In addition to the rocks of the Carboniferous period – Carboniferous Limestone etc., Millstone Grit and the Coal Measures – the northern West Riding has strata from both earlier and later eras in the geological record, the whole presenting a chronological sequence which runs broadly from NW to E. In the NW sector the pattern is complicated by two great geological fractures, the Dent fault running N–S and the Craven faults running W–E. The oldest rocks are those of the ORDOVICIAN and SILURIAN periods – mainly dark slates and shales, purple and green – which form the Howgill Fells, to the W of the Dent fault, and are also exposed in two smaller patches further S, close to the Craven faults, one at Ingleton (probably Ordovician) and the other near Horton-in-Ribblesdale (mainly Silurian). The Howgill shales have been used in the Sedbergh area for rough rubble walling, e.g. at Sedbergh parish church – combined with imported sandstone for the dressings – and in a coursed version for some C19 buildings, but were unsuited for use as freestone and have not been worked extensively. But the slates and flags of Ingleton and of Helwith Bridge near Horton were more significant, quarried commercially from at least the C18 to the early C20 and widely used in the W Dales and beyond: 'Ingleton slate' is referred to in the building accounts for Gisburne Park and Malham Tarn House in 1775-7. In addition to roofing and flooring, particular uses and products included rainwater tanks and dairy shelving – still to be found in some Dales farmhouses – gateposts and stall partitions for animals; while some thicker flaggy sandstones, similar to Millstone Grit, have been used locally for walling.

The neighbouring CARBONIFEROUS LIMESTONE group, of both the uplands and the lower country to the S of the Craven faults as far as lower Ribblesdale and the Bowland Forest, divides vertically into two parts, the lower mainly composed of the massive Great Scar Limestone itself, the upper shading into a regular repetitive sequence of limestones, shales and buff flaggy sandstones known as the YOREDALE BEDS, which creates the characteristic stepped profile of some of the valley sides. The Great Scar Limestone and its equivalents, frequently taken from the naturally occurring outcrops rather than actual quarries, have been used throughout their locality for rubble and drystone walling – sometimes combined with erratic boulders deposited by Ice Age glaciers – and occasionally in earlier buildings for quoins and rough doorheads. Again, however, they are not well suited for freestone use – many of these walls were originally rendered – and by the late C17 the Yoredale sandstones were preferred for the accompanying dressings and frequently for walling also, although they usually had to be quarried further afield, high on the valley sides or hilltops. The Folly at Settle (1670s) has a front elevation apparently of Yoredale sandstone with dressings of Millstone Grit – which was also available nearby

p. 694

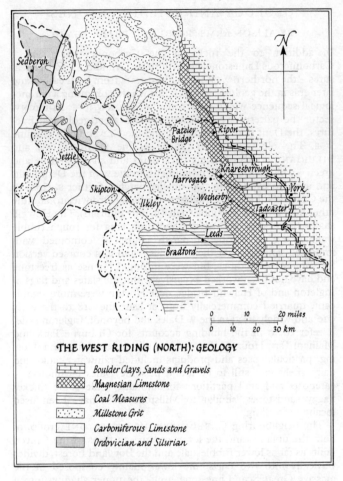

Geological map of the northern West Riding and surrounding area

– but a back wall of limestone rubble. The Yoredale sandstones also provided the flags or 'grey slates' which are still the predominant roofing material of the Dales. The building account for Hemplands Farmhouse at Conistone (1686–7) records that slates were brought from Hard Rake in Waldendale (North Riding) – but it was only in the late C18 that exploitation on a significant scale for roofing and flooring was begun, so many existing slate roofs must have replaced thatch. Still in the Yoredale Beds, certain of the fossiliferous limestones have been exploited as a source of a quite different material, polishable 'marble' for interior use. 'Nidderdale Marble' was quarried from a small outcrop on a grange of Fountains Abbey near Pateley Bridge, and used in the manner of Purbeck Marble in the C13 parts of the abbey;* while the black 'Dent Marble', used as flooring in Dent parish church, was worked in several small quarries in Dentdale by the early C19 and achieved a nationwide popularity in Victorian times as a material for fireplace surrounds.

Above the Carboniferous Limestone group comes the MILL-STONE GRIT, the hard, coarse sandstone which is the most characteristic building stone of the area, its geological zone extending from the E Pennine margins to an outlying block S of the Craven fault, running into Bowland. It is far from uniform – colours range from greys to browns and yellows, and the occasional soft pink – and different qualities can occur within a single quarry. The best is massively thick-bedded, and capable of being worked as freestone and even ashlar; other strata are more uneven and could only be used for rubble walls; while a little is finer and fissile, suitable for flooring and roofing. The history of its use is lengthy: gritstone was quarried by the Romans at Thorner, NE of Leeds, for building in York. In the Middle Ages the pattern of use generally appears to have been more localized – the stone for Fountains Abbey for example was from quarries, still discernible, immediately adjoining the site, while Embsay Moor and its neighbourhood provided that for Bolton Abbey and Skipton Castle – but production evidently expanded with the stone building of the C17: East Riddlesden Hall at Keighley (c. 1648) is one of many buildings which show the high-quality detail that could be imposed on this material. But the really large-scale exploitation belongs to the C19, when the strength of the stone and its availability in very large blocks made it an excellent material for the new industrial buildings and in particular for the new components, such as engine beds, brought into being by mechanization; while its resistance to sea water led to a worldwide use in the underwater parts of dock basins. Particularly favoured strata were the Rough Rock of the upper Millstone Grit, known locally as Bramley Fall Stone, which outcrops to the W and NW of Leeds – the material *inter alia* of Kirkstall Abbey, the Euston Arch and parts of the London docks – and the 'Brontë freestone' from Haworth Moor, which was exported to Manchester; while other important quarries included Hangingstones on Ilkley Moor and Scot Gate Ash in Nidderdale. A number in the area still remain active, including several in the neighbourhood of Keighley.

In the COAL MEASURES round Leeds and Bradford, further bands of sandstone suitable for building alternate with coal seams, ironstone and other shales. The Coal Measures sandstones** are generally less coarse than the Millstone Grit, and a little of it is soft and prone to 'honeycomb' weathering, but otherwise it presents a similar picture – similar in its range of colours (grey, buff, yellow and orange) and in the extent of its

18, 27–8

38

12

---

*Most of it has been robbed out.
**A complication is the trade name 'York Stone', which in its strict sense denotes just these Coal Measures sandstones quarried in the West Riding, but which has also been applied to all West Riding Carboniferous sandstones, or even more loosely to any sandstone from the whole county.

popularity during the C19, for the same and complementary reasons. Hard and available in very large blocks – up to ten tons in weight – it was the source of the fine smooth ashlar with crisp carved detail still to be found, for example, in the surviving parts of the C19 centre of Bradford, while the more fissile strata provided the paving slabs, kerbs and copings which were exported throughout the country and beyond. Notable strata are the Elland Flags, which were intensively quarried in the uplands W of Bradford, in the neighbourhood of Thornton; the adjacent Gaisby Rock, quarried at the famous Bolton Woods Quarries on the N side of the city, which were greatly expanded after 1867; and the 'Morley Blue' – actually orange when weathered – from SW of Leeds. At Allerton and Idle Moor, respectively on the W and N edges of Bradford, the Elland Flags were mined underground.

E of all this, running N–S along the W edge of the Vale of York, is a band of MAGNESIAN LIMESTONE of the Permian period. Apart from where the river Nidd cuts through it at Knaresborough, and to a lesser extent where the Wharfe crosses it at Wetherby, it is barely discernible as a landscape feature; and beyond it the solid geology dips below the glacial boulder clays, sands and gravels of the central Vale. The stone is strikingly pale – white, cream or lightest grey – and fine-grained with a distinctive crystalline character, and although it is not of the most durable the best strata have been quarried as a building material over a long period and used well beyond its geological confines. The Romans worked it near Tadcaster for use in York; and in the Middle Ages the same locality provided stone not only for York Minster and other major buildings in the city but also for those of the East Riding beyond, including the Beverley Minster. Closer to hand, it is the stone of Markenfield Hall (c. 1290–1310), the early C16 nave of Ripon Cathedral and many of the village churches of the Vale; while in the C18 and C19 on the limestone belt itself it was used more inclusively, as either ashlar or rubble, for a whole range of domestic buildings. Boston Spa, Bramham and Wetherby furnish good examples.*

Alternatives to local building stone were twofold. One was brick from suitable local clays, both in the Vale of York and on the Coal Measures, and in the later C19 fired clay and terracotta provided a medium for mass-producing decorative details at a fraction of the cost of masonry. The other was the use of IMPORTED STONES from other parts of Britain, made possible by the improvements in transport from the late C18 on. Amongst the most widely used were roofing slates from NW England, the green-grey Westmorland and the 'Lancashire blue', which were imported by rail to the industrial towns – and are also conspicuous in Nidderdale, which was linked to the railway network in 1862. In addition, granite paving setts were brought by rail from Mountsorrel in Leicestershire, Shap in Cumbria, and Aberdeen; and Leeds, strategically placed on the canal network, became an entrepôt for the polished marbles and granites which decorate

---

*A further product of the limestone belt is the mineral gypsum which was extracted for making plaster, and plaster attic floors are a feature of some houses in the Ripon area.

many C19 commercial and civic buildings. During the early and mid C20 the practice developed further – perversely so in a county so rich in good building stone – in the choice of stone as a cladding material on concrete- and steel-framed buildings. The popularity of Portland stone during the 1920s and 1930s was reflected in its use for the war memorials at Skipton and Ilkley (1921 and 1922), the Leeds Civic Hall (1931–3) and the Parkinson Building at Leeds University (begun 1936); and at the Bradford Central Library the fashion persisted as late as the 1960s. The late C20 and early C21 have seen something of a revival in the use of local materials, but frequently only in the form of cladding in 'reconstituted' stone. ¹¹⁸

Finally, a word about QUARRYING and FINISHING techniques, particularly in relation to the sandstones and the huge size of the blocks which were obtained. During the C19 quarrying remained a labour-intensive industry dependant on the use of crowbars, wedges and jibs to extract the blocks. Skilled banker-hands would then cut or split these into smaller sections using just a few wedges and a hammer, and flag fettlers trimmed split stones into standard-sized paving flags. After *c.* 1860 powered frame saws were used to slice the blocks into slabs – although the long straight door and window surrounds of the mid C19 found in a number of locations suggest that some mechanized sawing may have been in use earlier – and in the later C19 the use of powered cranes facilitated the extraction of stone from greater depths than hitherto. Quarry masons dressed wall stone and finished sills and lintels to a smooth surface, but carved work was done in masons' yards, in the C19 often sited near railways. Different styles of stone finish were produced using a variety of masons' punches and wide-bladed chisel-like implements. Rough dressing using a punch can be seen on many gritstone quoins from the C17 to the C19, while the 'broached ashlar' specified for Addingham church in 1756 is a typical fine finish on coarse gritstone, with a light pecking on squared wall stones executed with a broaching pick. The Georgian 'broad tool', a very wide chisel, was used to produce a neat horizontal and vertical tooling which could be extended across both lintels and jambs, often framed by chisel-drafted margins; and the narrower 'boaster' of the later C19 was used to execute a fine finish consisting of rows, or drafts, of diagonal tooling. 'Pitch-faced' or 'rock-faced' stone, exhibiting the scalloped gouges of the pitching tool, is a coarser finish frequently found on the massive blocks used in late C19 railway viaducts and textile mills.

PREHISTORIC AND ROMAN ARCHAEOLOGY

BY NEIL REDFERN AND BLAISE VYNER

The earliest human activity in the northern West Riding may have occurred in the UPPER AND LATE UPPER PALAEOLITHIC (*c.* 25,000 to 10,000 years ago) when small groups of hunters engaged in intermittent seasonal activity through landscapes which varied from birch woodland to scrub and tundra and supported mammoth, brown bear and wild horse. Evidence of early hunter-gatherer activity, and of its northward extension through England, is provided by an antler harpoon from Victoria Cave, Settle, dating from 11,000 years ago. The warmer climate during the MESOLITHIC, from perhaps 8500 B.C., encouraged more extensive hunting and gathering by nomadic people, and they appear to have made particular use of the river valleys through the Pennine uplands where flint artefacts (tools) and the waste from their manufacture are widely distributed, occasionally in association with pits and hearths, notably at Green Crag and Green Crag Slack on the SW flank of Wharfedale between Ilkley and Burley, and on the uplands of Baildon Moor, a distribution which also extends westwards along Airedale. To the N, on the limestone uplands around Malham Tarn the location of seasonal camps is marked by extensive concentrations of microlithic barbs and points, made from imported flint.

Occupation and use of these Mesolithic sites continued into the NEOLITHIC. In common with adjoining areas of the Pennine uplands, however, monuments of this period are hardly found in the West Riding, a reflection perhaps that hunting and gathering was still favoured after the introduction of agriculture in this period. Excavations in advance of the upgrading of the A1 near Wetherby and further N across the River Ure at Marton-le-Moor (North Riding) have revealed a number of PITS (suggesting periods of fixed settlement) containing fruit and grains as well as artefacts, dated to 3700–3520 B.C. On the Coal Measures, E of Leeds, a pit containing Grooved Ware at Swillington Common, and a group of early Neolithic flints at Garforth, raise the possibility that Neolithic activity was more widespread across the area. FUNERARY SITES likely to belong to the late fourth millennium B.C. include a long cairn on Bradley Moor, near Skipton, and the Giant's Grave, a chambered cairn at Pen-y-Ghent Gill, Halton Gill. Of the latter little is visible above ground but excavations in 1936 showed evidence of several human burials in cists. The principal monumental evidence for the Neolithic, however, is to be found in the major river valleys as they run into the Vale of York. In the West Riding the middle reach of the River Ure is of paramount importance. Here, on the S side or the river, near Boroughbridge, are the Devil's Arrows, an alignment of three (once four) huge STANDING STONES, the tallest standing 22 ft (6.9 metres) high. They are set on a NNW–SSE alignment shared by the general arrangement of a larger complex of monuments that extends eleven miles NW into the North Riding via Marton-le-Moor, Cana Barn and Hutton Moor and concludes with the henges at Thornborough, built in the earlier part of the third millennium B.C. These monuments were probably constructed at various times during the Neolithic, although, like the other river-valley monuments, they remain largely unexcavated and the sites in the West Riding have all been lowered by ploughing. Another henge has been identified to the S on the

Wharfe near Newton Kyme, again significantly sited near the lowest fording point of the river and a location later chosen by the Romans for a fort. An assemblage of pottery found beneath a Bronze Age barrow at North Deighton also points to the general location of a monument complex by the river Nidd, and it is probable that the stones of the Devil's Arrows were brought from the vicinity of Plompton Rocks, also on the s side of the Nidd. The location of monument complexes on rivers (cf. Newton Kyme and Ferrybridge on the Aire, West Riding South) bears close comparison with contemporary complexes on the major rivers to the N (e.g. Thornborough on the Ure and Catterick on the Swale). It appears from the evidence of distinctive artefacts that these were the locations of social gatherings for people who travelled long distances, probably with herds of cattle. These people can have been only semi-sedentary – there are no known remains of Neolithic houses in the West Riding, nor any direct evidence for arable agriculture. The distribution of sites suggests that the Neolithic population was concentrated around these monument complexes bordering the western side of the Vale of York and in E Yorkshire. The paucity of monuments elsewhere – there is a single-entrance henge enclosure unusually sited on high ground overlooking the valley of the Wharfe at Yarnbury near Grassington – suggests that the principal movement of people to the Vale of York monument complexes was from the E, and then to the N and, perhaps, s. But there is evidence that the Pennine valleys provided a link between E Yorkshire and the NW in the presence of artefacts made from stone imported from the Lake District and in particular the famous axe factory site at Langdale (Cumbria). More significant is the remarkable mid-Pennine concentration of 'rock art' – natural rocks bearing carved, or more accurately, pecked, designs which include single and multiple CUP-AND-RING MARKS and sinuous linear trails (traditionally considered to be of Early Bronze Age date; research is now suggesting an earlier Neolithic origin to this tradition). They are found principally on Baildon Moor and Ilkley Moor and on the moors to the N (*see* Beamsley and Low Snowden). Although this distribution of the 'rock art' appears to be defined by the larger rivers, closer inspection shows that it is more nearly related to the headwaters of the smaller tributary becks. On Ilkley Moor excavation has found an association between decorated rocks and assemblages of flint and later Neolithic Grooved Ware pottery, with associated radiocarbon dates in the earlier half of the third millennium B.C. Some of the flint is of a distinctive type, derived from the coast of E Yorkshire, and reinforces the evidence for links between E and W through the river valleys. The absence of earthwork monuments such as those seen in the Vale of York, however, suggests that only small numbers of people may have been involved in cross-Pennine travel.

A number of limestone caves in Craven were used for shelter and ritual purposes in the LATER NEOLITHIC AND EARLY BRONZE AGE (*c.* 2500–2000 B.C.), but activity during this period continued to be associated principally with the monuments along

the Magnesian Limestone ridge in the E. But there are also a few
STONE CIRCLES and RING CAIRNS, mostly found in the Craven
uplands, e.g. the paired circles at Fancarl Top (Appletreewick)
and Threshfield, and the Twelve Apostles on Ilkley Moor. From
around 2000 B.C. date some individual and grouped BURIAL
MOUNDS. They survive as earthwork mounds on the Millstone
Grit and, more especially, on the limestone uplands. Most have
been robbed in antiquity, there are few records, and few therefore are described in the gazetteer. A circular kerb of limestone
boulders in Langstrothdale may be an example of this type of
monument. A barrow at Rylstone contained a burial wrapped in
a woollen cloth and placed in a wooden coffin. Excavation of the
Apron Full of Stones cairn (Thornton-in-Lonsdale) recovered a
cremation burial and a scatter of flints. Burial mounds were
established at and around the Boroughbridge monument complexes, although most of these sites have long been reduced by
arable agriculture. At Garforth, a burial in a collared urn is one
of the few records of Early Bronze Age burials from the Coal
Measures. At Stanbury a collared urn containing the cremated
remains of a young man together with grave goods which
included a stone mace-head may once have been set within a
mound.

Evidence for middle and LATER BRONZE AGE activity, ritual
or settlement, in the northern West Riding is hard to find, as it
is in the North Riding – there was certainly a population here,
but it was not one which favoured the use of pottery, a tradition
which endured through the subsequent Iron Age and into the
Romano-British period. Just a few pottery sherds of possible Late
Bronze Age date have been recovered from pits at Garforth.
Others are associated with a circular stone foundation at Comb
Scar (Malham Moor), the dating of which suggests that some of
the round-house foundations and earthwork field banks on the
limestone uplands of Craven and further N in the Dales may
be of Later Bronze Age date. Slight earthworks on the Millstone
Grit uplands may also be of this period, as at Clayton Wood,
Cookridge (Leeds), where a rubble-banked enclosure with a pos-
sible hut circle inside has associated vertical stone slab field walls.

Amongst the slight evidence for the EARLIER IRON AGE are
HILL-FORTS, constructed probably in the fifth century B.C. and
including Ingleborough (Ingleton) and Barwick-in-Elmet (E of
Leeds). Ingleborough is one of the most impressive sites in Yorkshire and among the highest hill-forts in England. A truncated
conical hilltop, about 15 acres (6 hectares) in area, is encircled
by a stone rampart which encloses twenty circular hut foundations. There is no evidence that these exposed locations were
permanently occupied and it is probable that the hill-forts mark
the location of tribal gathering places that may never have had
to be defended. Indeed, recent research at Ingleborough now
suggests that it should be considered a sanctuary site rather than
a hill-fort. For the LATER IRON AGE, perhaps from early in the
C3 B.C., the eastern areas of the West Riding exhibit a greatly
increased range of sites associated with intensified agriculture,

particularly along the Magnesian Limestone ridge and adjoining areas of the Coal Measures on the eastern flank of the Pennines. The majority of the sites, having been ploughed flat, are now known only from cropmarks and are not described in the gazetteer. SETTLEMENTS are characterized by enclosures with round-houses and associated with pits which sometimes contain whole or partial human and animal skeletons. The settlements then became the focus of a bounded landscape with large fields reached by droveways edged by ditches. Similar sites have occasionally been found on the Coal Measures and on the clays of the Vale of York. Still surviving as considerable earthwork monuments are the Aberford Dykes which stretch for several miles E and W of the village of Aberford. Excavations undertaken as part of the construction of the M1–A1 Link Road has led to the consideration that these are of Iron Age origin and possibly associated with defence against the Roman expansion N in the C1 A.D. Arable agriculture is suggested by 'four-posters' – the post-holes of rectangular structures, thought to be granaries, often associated with charred grain. Subdivision of the large fields into smaller enclosures, and the extension of the field systems, took place in the Late Iron Age and, probably, the Romano-British period. Away from the arable areas of the West Riding, in the Pennines, pastoral farming dominated, probably without many field boundaries. Iron Age settlement in these areas was based on sub-rectangular enclosures.

The ROMANO-BRITISH period starts late in the West Riding and northern England as a whole. By the time of the Roman Conquest in 43 A.D. the area was part of the tribal domain of the Brigantes, a loose-knit confederacy of tribes whose territory extended across most of Yorkshire and northern England. Under their queen, Cartimandua, they became a client state of Rome, and in the early years of Roman occupation provided a stable frontier to the north of England, obviating the need for a Roman military presence. The population was slow to adopt Roman ways and Roman influence was probably felt most keenly in new taxation, until, that is, Cartimandua was overthrown by her consort, Venutius. The queen was rescued by the Romans, but Venutius was left to control Brigantia as a rebel state and Roman military intervention was initiated by Petillius Cerealis, who became governor of Britain in A.D. 71. In the West Riding the FORTS at Adel, Ilkley and Elslack controlled the trans-Pennine routes along the Aire and the Wharfe, while forts at Roecliffe (known from aerial photography and geophysical survey) and Newton Kyme, on the crossing of the River Wharfe, were part of a chain which extended up the Vale of York. The initial forts were operational for perhaps twenty years, attracting in that time civilian settlement around them and encouraging the development of local commerce. Apart from extracting taxation in the form of grain, hides and other animal products, the Roman military presence would have demanded considerable supplies of stone, timber, iron and lead. In the West Riding lead was a particularly important resource: one of three lead ingots found near Greenhow between Upper Wharfedale and Upper Nidderdale bore the name of the Emperor Trajan, dating to 81 A.D., and this demonstrates the rapid development of the industry.

The Roman administration consolidated an existing network of routes to create a ROAD SYSTEM, such as the line of Dere Street which picked up earlier N–S communication routes through the Vale of York. Although the system fell into desuetude following the collapse of Roman administration by 410 A.D., it is largely followed by the roads of today as again illustrated by Dere Street and the alignment of the A1. At Aldborough, soon after the military subjugation of the early 70s A.D., the Romans established a small town – *Isurium Brigantium* – to be a capital, unique in the West Riding as an urban development. Little is known of the detail of the town, which is assumed to have had a forum and, probably, other appurtenances such as a bath house, theatre and temples, but it is notable for containing a number of houses with mosaic pavements. A defensive earthen bank was constructed probably in the C2, with a town wall constructed in the C3, to which were later added artillery bastions. Tadcaster (Calcaria) has been suggested as a Roman settlement but little physical evidence has been found to support this suggestion. Aside from the military presence, it appears that the rural population continued to live as they had before, many Iron Age SETTLEMENTS continuing in occupation probably throughout the Roman period, acquiring Romanized styles of pottery and other artefacts and occasionally adopting Roman ways more wholeheartedly. At Dalton Parlours (Collingham), a series of conjoined enclosures contained round-houses which were established during the later Iron Age. Part of the settlement was later overlain with a pair of Roman-style buildings provided with mosaic floors and heating, contained within walled courtyards. These were occupied over the period approximately 200 to 370 A.D. and were associated with a pair of sunken-floored buildings with rounded ends which may represent a Romanized style of lower-status buildings. Recent excavation has revealed a very similar sunken-floored structure next to the A1 at Wetherby. As with the developed Iron Age settlements, Romanized settlement seems confined to the Pennine flanks, with a villa at Gargrave on the W and North Stainley, with others in North Yorkshire, to the E. The end of Roman administration early in the C5 A.D. brought the end of urban and villa settlement, settlement and economy reverting to the Iron Age traditions which in the West Riding had never fully been abandoned.

THE MIDDLE AGES

For the purpose of this account the Middle Ages run from the time of St Wilfrid in the C7 to the mid C16 and in some respects further still, a period too long for any common themes to emerge except perhaps the recurrence of disasters. The Norman Conquest was followed by William the Conqueror's 'harrying of the North' in 1069–70, which was focused particularly on Yorkshire; and although opinions have differed as to the condition of the county as a whole in the following decades, it is unsurprising that little of the post-Conquest building in the northern West Riding can be ascribed with confidence to earlier than the mid C12. The area then suffered heavily from the Scottish incursions after the battle of Bannockburn in 1314, and some of the building projects of the second quarter of the C14 can possibly be interpreted as works of reconstruction; but in the wake of the Black Death of 1349 there appears to have been no such recovery, and during the second half of the C14 major building activity seems to have come to a virtual standstill. On the positive side, however, the contribution from the mid C12 on of monasticism – or, specifically, of the new Cistercian order – had been outstanding; and the northern West Riding, together with the adjoining North Riding, form the most rewarding area in the country for the study of the Cistercians' architecture. By the C15 the monastic architectural patrimony was largely complete, but there was then a new round of parish church rebuilding and enlargement, particularly in the W of the area – the so-called 'Pennine Perpendicular'. As to its causes, it seems unlikely that it can be attributed to economic factors alone – a supposed prosperity deriving from the wool and cloth trades – and other more generalized influences must have played a part, such as a diversion of the lay architectural patronage previously absorbed by the monasteries and the space-consuming character of much late medieval religious practice, with its focus on masses for the dead and the formation of religious fraternities. Regarding secular building, of castles there are perhaps fewer than might be expected, although feudal magnates – de Lacy, de Mowbray, Percy, Clifford – were by no means lacking; but fortified and semi-fortified houses, the coming type by *c.* 1300, are quite well represented, a reflection doubtless of chronically turbulent times.

Anglo-Saxon architecture and sculpture

The earliest and most important surviving structure, which ranks high amongst early Anglo-Saxon monuments in England, is the crypt of St Wilfrid's church at Ripon, built in the 670s. It is very similar to that of its sister church at Hexham (Northumberland), and was evidently intended for the display of relics to pilgrims. Otherwise there is a complete little church at Kirk Hammerton – although now attached to a larger C19 building – of W tower, nave and chancel, perhaps C8 and C10–11; the greater part of another at Bardsey, including a W tower built over a W porch, C9–10 and C11; and certain amounts of fabric at Collingham, Bramham and perhaps Guiseley, Otley and Newton Kyme. More numerous are the remains of carved CROSSES, which mainly appear to have been funerary memorials. The forms of carving are interlace patterns and, on the more ambitious pieces, figural scenes. Most are of the C10, but the most important are earlier, p. 339 C8 and C9: three cross-shafts at Ilkley, one with a figure of Christ p. 616 enthroned; two possibly related pieces at Otley, one evoking parallels with the Ruthwell and Bewcastle crosses, the other with splendid dramatic beasts; and two at Collingham, with similar motifs. The most ambitious later example is the Weland cross at Leeds.

Norman parish churches

Over forty parish churches and chapels in the area, mainly in its E half, retain significant quantities of Norman fabric *in situ*, and over a dozen more retain reused features, most commonly a doorway or a font. Precise dating is rarely possible, but a broad chronology can be established. Herringbone masonry, of *c.* 1100, is found at Kippax and Barwick-in-Elmet, the former quite large-scale but on a simple plan, of nave, chancel and W tower, the latter perhaps originally similar but much altered; and other Early Norman work – tower, nave W wall and chancel arch – is at Leathley. Then of the early C12 is the N arcade at Bardsey, with cylindrical piers and heavy scalloped capitals, cut through the Saxon wall. From the mid C12, *c.* 1150–60, come three of the 9 most rewarding churches, at Adel on the edge of Leeds, and 7 Healaugh and Wighill, further E towards York. Adel is of the common small type, consisting of nave and short narrower chancel (Copgrove, Moor Monkton and Stainburn are other examples). Healaugh also has a W tower, and both it and Wighill have a later C12 N aisle. Their special feature is the sumptuous p. 483 CARVED DECORATION applied to their doorways – part of a 8 larger group, centred on York – and at Adel and Healaugh to the chancel arches also, with extensive figural SCULPTURE evidently from a regional 'school'. Some of the subjects have precedents in SW France, and the proprietor of Adel church, Holy Trinity Priory at York, was a daughter house of the abbey of Marmoutier near Tours. The main non-figural motifs are the ubiquitous zigzag, both single and double, and beakhead. Of components to which no very meaningful date can be given, the surviving chancel at Farnham is especially pleasing, although without any ornamental display. TOWERS are not uncommon but also always plain, the best perhaps at Bramham. Other good doorways are at e.g. Bardsey, East Ardsley, Goldsborough and Kirkby Malzeard, all but the last re-set. Arcades are at Guiseley and Kirk Deighton – one each, both with stout quatrefoil piers.

With the Late Norman or TRANSITIONAL phase, after *c.* 1175, one reaches firmer ground, and it is clear that much of the C12 work belongs to this period. That applies to the majority of schemes providing aisles. The most ambitious, although much 10 rebuilt in the C19, is at Spofforth, with a full complement of two five-bay arcades and chancel arch. Curiosities of planning are Long Marston and the rough upland Horton-in-Ribblesdale, the former with one aisle, the latter with two, but both with nave and chancel in one. Other late C12 arcades, in addition to Healaugh and Wighill, are at e.g. Bilton-in-Ainsty (two), Bardsey (s), Bramham and Linton (one each). Piers are mainly cylindrical: at Healaugh and Wighill they are quatrefoil, at Spofforth cylindrical in one arcade and quatrefoil in the other, and at Horton-in-Ribblesdale a mixture of cylindrical and octagonal. Also of this phase are the little single-cell churches at Askham Bryan and Askham Richard, the former with an elaborate doorway; and another of the nave-and-chancel type, at Lotherton. The characteristic detail includes waterleaf and other leaf-form capitals (e.g. Askham Bryan, Askham Richard, Bardsey s arcade, Bilton-in-Ainsty, Healaugh (priest's doorway and arcade), Long Marston, Lotherton, Spofforth); keeled mouldings, responds and arcade lobes (Healaugh priest's doorway, Long Marston, Lotherton, Spofforth, Wighill arcade); and waterholding bases (Linton). There is even the occasional pointed arch, in the s arcade at Bardsey and the chancel arches at Spofforth and Linton. But by this time architectural style had moved on much more emphatically elsewhere in the area.

Great churches, monastic and collegiate

Of the monastic and other ORDERS, chronological priority goes to the Augustinian canons, who were established at Embsay, near Skipton, in 1120 before moving to Bolton, in Wharfedale, c. 1154. Then came the Cistercians, at Fountains in 1132/3, Barnoldswick in 1147 – moving to Kirkstall in 1152 – and Sawley in 1148, followed by Cistercian nuns at Syningthwaite (Bilton-in-Ainsty) in 1155 and in the late C12 at Esholt. The monasteries were closely related, Kirkstall founded from Fountains and Sawley from Newminster in Northumberland, which was another of Fountains' daughter houses. Meanwhile, a Benedictine nunnery had been established at Nun Monkton and a Cluniac one at Arthington, both c. 1150; and a second Augustinian house was to follow at Healaugh in 1218. Of the CISTERCIAN ABBEY CHURCHES, little remains at Sawley – always a poor foundation – but those of Fountains and Kirkstall are exceptionally well pre- 11–13 served. The dates of the C12 building campaigns are very close, Fountains and Sawley both begun c. 1150, Kirkstall just a few years later, and all probably completed during the 1170s; but a complication in the chronology is that the present church at Fountains is the third on the site, preceded first by a timber building and then by a first stone church, begun c. 1136, of both of which a little is known by excavation. Sawley and the second church at Fountains were evidently both of an early Cistercian type represented also by Waverley (Surrey), c. 1128, the first Cistercian house in England, and by the C12 church at Tintern (Gwent), c. 1131, consisting of an unaisled straight-ended chancel, transepts with straight-ended E chapels separated by solid walls, and an unaisled nave. The present Fountains, and p. 259

p. 506–7 Kirkstall – together with the slightly earlier church at Rievaulx, in the North Riding – represent the next stage, the 'Bernardine' type of the second church at Clairvaux, begun in 1135, with E parts much as before but on a much larger scale, and a long aisled nave; and with the plan came some important structural devices adopted by the Cistercians from the early C12 Romanesque of their Burgundian homeland (e.g. at Fontenay, 1139–47, the earliest surviving Cistercian church in France), notably pointed arches and pointed tunnel vaults. One theme at Fountains and Kirkstall is the way in which the austere uniform prescriptions of the order – powerfully implemented at Rievaulx – were progressively diluted by an admixture of more luxurious Anglo-Norman forms. A particular case is that of towers, originally forbidden under the Cistercian statutes but provided over the crossing at both churches: after 1157 lantern towers were in effect permitted, but it is not entirely clear that Fountains' met even that condition. Another is the form of the nave arcade piers, big cylinders at Fountains but at Kirkstall, a little later, tellingly more elaborate, a sort of cross between an Anglo-Norman compound pier (e.g. Durham) and a type of clustered pier which the Burgundian Cistercians had used in chapter houses but not in churches; and these are accompanied in the aisles at Kirkstall by ribbed vaults, again in the tradition of Durham, rather than the Burgundian tunnel vaults.

The prevalence of pointed arches, particularly in conjunction with ribbed vaulting, inevitably introduces the question of the advent of GOTHIC. The massiveness of Fountains and Kirkstall is far from that,* but an unambiguous manifestation of the style did appear in the area at an early date only a few miles from Fountains, in the rebuilt collegiate church of Ripon (cathedral since 1836). This was begun by Archbishop Roger of York probably c. 1175 and perhaps completed under his successor, Geoffrey Plantagenet, c. 1200, and is therefore contemporary with that other salient of early French Gothic influence in England, the E arm of Canterbury Cathedral. The critical first 17 phase was the choir, which appears in many respects to have been a copy of Roger's choir at York Minster, begun c. 1160. Little of it remains unaltered, but enough to establish its character: not only a consistent use of pointed forms, but an open airiness with wide arcade arches on slender piers, and French-style rib-vaults in the aisles. The effect would have been even more persuasive if the intended rib-vault over the main vessel had been executed. But as Professor Wilson explains, there are also some Cistercian features, notably the clustered piers – although now completely transformed from the heaviness of Kirkstall's. Of the later parts, p. 657 the curious unaisled nave – echoing that of the C11 York Minster – had a striking internal elevational system with alternating wide and narrow bays and an arcaded wall passage to the tall middle stage, but only fragments of it survive.

---

*But Pevsner in 1959 considered that the conjunction established for Kirkstall 'a position in English architectural history very close to the threshold from Romanesque to Gothic'.

The internal elevation of the Ripon choir was to be highly influential elsewhere in the North but not, apparently, in the West Riding; and the late C12 work at two further great churches is still in a TRANSITIONAL mode. At Nun Monkton, the handsome and instructive W portal of *c.* 1175 combines an ornate round-arched doorway with double zigzag and keeled mouldings, water-leaf and just pre-stiff-leaf capitals, pellet decoration and a trefoil-headed niche. At Bolton Abbey a phase of work of *c.* 1170–90 – providing, *inter alia*, a Cistercian-style straight-ended presbytery and Cistercian-style transeptal chapels – runs from Late Norman intersected blind arcading in the presbytery to waterholding bases in the crossing and pointed blind arcading with leaf capitals against the nave wall. But from the early C13 on there is a distinguished series of undertakings in mature EARLY ENGLISH style. It begins with the new E arm at Fountains Abbey, first an aisled presbytery, *c.* 1210–20, and then beyond it the beautiful Chapel of Nine Altars of *c.* 1220–30, a p. 262 full-height E transept. A quite austere design by cathedral, if not by Cistercian, standards, its main decorative motif was the extensive use of 'Nidderdale Marble' quarried on one of the abbey's outlying estates, culminating in the eight detached shafts (now robbed out) which surrounded the slim octagonal 50-ft (15-metre) piers of the transept. Then probably of the 1230s is the twin-towered W front at Ripon, a composition with, in Pevsner's 15 words, a classic 'clarity and balance' which he regarded as rare in E.E. façades; and of about the same date will be the upper stage of the aisleless nave at Nun Monkton, in which the theme p. 610 of the Ripon nave interior is memorably redeployed, now with much dogtooth and nailhead. Of the mid C13 is the corresponding completion of the nave at Bolton Abbey, with an ornate dog-tooth-encrusted W front – mostly covered by an uncompleted p. 134 Perp W tower – of the sort that Pevsner condemned as 'disjointed'; but the S flank strikes a different note, with tall two-light windows with transoms and plate tracery, and again a wall passage behind.

Thereafter the pace slackens. The GEOMETRICAL phase is represented by the rebuilt E end at Ripon, begun *c.* 1286. It is of 16 the 'cross-sectional' form common in the North, with tracery details very similar to those of the late C13 parts of York Minster, particularly the chapter house – i.e. strongly influenced by French Rayonnant – but an internal treatment of the clerestory in the adjoining bays recalling the Angel Choir at Lincoln. Of the mid-C14 DECORATED there are the rebuilt E parts of Bolton 18 Abbey – the presbytery still unaisled – with a huge E window but most of the flowing tracery unfortunately lost, and the sedilia at Ripon, in instructive contrast to its surroundings of a few decades earlier;* but of the new E arm at Sawley, aisled and again 'cross-sectional' at the E end, only footings remain.

---

* There was also a timber vault over the choir, destroyed in the C17, bosses from which were reused in *Scott*'s restoration.

As to PERPENDICULAR, much of the period is a blank but there
were major repairs at Ripon after 1450 and then a final flurry of
activity from the late C15 on. The sequence begins with the
CHOIR STALLS at Ripon, dated 1489 and 1494, with elaborate
canopies – carefully restored by *Scott* – and an uncommonly full
and varied set of MISERICORDS. They were followed by the
PULPITUM there, *c.* 1500, echoing that at York (and still remembering Dec in some details), and then most substantially by the
new nave of 1503–20 – again acknowledging York, this time the
E arm. There are also early C16 roofs at Ripon and Bolton.
Alongside these are the projects for prodigy TOWERS at the three
foremost monasteries: Abbot Huby's famous one at Fountains,
c. 1500; the heightening of the crossing tower at Kirkstall in
1509–28 – the rivalry with Fountains still apparently potent – and
the W tower at Bolton begun in 1520. The unfinished state of the
last is an apposite comment on the times.

Monastic buildings

The buildings at Fountains are the most complete in Britain,
those at Kirkstall not far behind, and together they give an extraordinarily vivid picture of a large Cistercian establishment. One
is impressed both by the orderliness and logic of the standardized plan, developed from the existing Benedictine model, and
by the careful siting, pragmatically exploiting the presence of
running water to provide services ranging from fishponds for
food to drainage under the latrines. As with the churches, virtually everything was done by *c.* 1230, and the inner core of claustral ranges by earlier than that; and the question of architectural
style again merits attention. At Kirkstall the core was completed
by *c.* 1180 and almost all of it is in the same style as the church,
powerfully reinforcing the sense of austere rigour; but at Fountains the building history was more extended and the position
more complicated. The chapter house and parlour, of the 1160s,
and the guesthouses, perhaps of the 1170s, are in a Transitional
style quite different from the contemporary work on the church,
with rib-vaulting and foliage capitals, while the refectory and the
memorable undercroft of the W range, both probably of *c.* 1200,
mark the arrival of a fully Gothic mode. The phase of the Chapel
of Nine Altars, *c.* 1230, was then represented by the infirmaries
at both establishments and the Abbot's Lodging at Kirkstall.
Regarding the other houses in the area, at Sawley and Bolton the
remains are largely reduced to footings but they are instructive
nonetheless: at Bolton the chapter house was polygonal – a
cathedral rather than a monastic form – and the handsome C14
gatehouse stands entire, as the nucleus of Bolton Hall.
Some individual components survive much altered at Healaugh
and Syningthwaite (*see* Bilton-in-Ainsty).

Parish churches, C13 and C14

The tally of EARLY ENGLISH work is quite limited. Just one entirely new church can be identified, at Barnoldswick, and little of that remains recognizable. At Knaresborough there was evidently a substantial rebuild, at Sedbergh the completion of a scheme begun in the C12 – both churches much altered later – and at Goldsborough the start of a complete rebuilding which continued into the C14. Otherwise there are enlargements, usually the addition of an aisle – e.g. Bramham, Kirkby Malzeard – the aisle itself usually widened later, at Guiseley a transept, at Collingham and Newton Kyme the E extension of the chancel. There are TOWERS at Knaresborough (lower stage) and Woodkirk, at Great Ouseburn a belfry stage. The high points are the crossing at Knaresborough from the beginning of the period, *c.* 1200, a sumptuous transept arch there of a few decades later, and the Guiseley transept at the end, *c.* 1260–75, with bar-traceried S window and arch responds with a cluster of detached shafts. Piers are still mostly cylindrical, but at Bramham the arcade form appears which was to be all but universal during the later Middle Ages, with octagonal piers and double-chamfered arches. Round arches still persist occasionally, e.g. at Sedbergh. Other attractive details are the curious two-directional piscina at Kippax, and the trefoil-headed priest's doorway at Newton Kyme.

In a mirror image of the great church history, the GEOMET-RICAL and DECORATED phases saw a slightly higher level of activity. Complete or virtually complete rebuildings, in addition to Goldsborough, are at Great Mitton and Whixley, *c.* 1300–10, and Long Preston and Walton – a particularly attractive example – *c.* 1340–50; and evidently substantial ones, subsumed in later work to a greater or lesser extent, were at Kildwick and Skipton, both *c.* 1300 on, Bradford (now cathedral) after 1327 and Aldborough, *c.* 1330–50. Enlargements by the addition of aisles are now numerous, e.g. Calverley, Methley, Swillington. The sequence of events can be followed through the evolution of TRACERY designs. The Geometrical forms of the late C13 are found at e.g. Knaresborough (N chapel) and Goldsborough, the latter's including spheric triangles; simple Y and intersecting tracery at e.g. Great Mitton; and the cusped intersecting type at Whixley, interrupted in the larger windows by an encircled cinquefoil or sexfoil. Of the flowing tracery of mature Dec the commonest form is reticulation, e.g. at Walton. More fanciful designs are rare – examples are at Calverley (E window), Linton (W), and a particularly pleasing re-set window at Skipton, with mouchettes and daggers within a reticulated mesh – but a significant innovation is the straight-headed window more usually associated with the Perp style which is present by the mid C14: the lights are frequently ogee-headed, e.g. Walton etc. The commonest pier form is now the octagonal, but in the earlier part of the period quatrefoil piers appear occasionally – e.g. Kildwick,

22   Skipton, Whixley – while at Bradford there is a variant form with
      a continuous undulating section, the shafts alternating with
      concave quadrants. The few towers include a curiously planned
      one at Long Preston, the lower part largely solid with two small
      vaulted spaces.

Perp parish churches

So to the predominant phase of church building, at least as far
as the upland centre and w of the area are concerned. The total
rebuilds range from Giggleswick and Slaidburn in the far w to
Harewood in the neighbourhood of Leeds. The little church at
Cowthorpe is a special case, built on a new site to replace one
which was inconveniently distant from the village. External trans-
p. 150   formations and major enlargements include Bradford, Kildwick,
20   Skipton and – further to the E –Tadcaster: Knaresborough gained
an impressive new nave. The amount of activity was the more
marked in that it was not spread evenly over the whole late
medieval period: Harewood can be dated to *c.* 1410, but most of
the area's Perp is of the mid C15 or later and much of it after
1500. The idea of a Pennine regional style, however, needs to be
treated with caution. While the churches of the upland zone do
appear to have much in common, this is due to such factors as
the prevalence of the same unmistakeable building stone –
Millstone Grit – a certain sturdiness of form, and the rather
unvarying detail: the near-universal straight-headed windows to
aisle flanks and clerestories, now with simple arched lights,
cusped or uncusped, and the arcades of octagonal piers and
double-chamfered arches. A more positively distinctive regional
group is found only in the w, in Craven and the Sedbergh area.
Its characteristics are long low proportions on buildings with a
full complement of aisles, chapels and clerestories; and the
absence of a structural division between nave and chancel. The
classic examples – some the result of complete rebuilding, some
of remodelling and enlargement – are Bolton-by-Bowland, Dent,
Kildwick, Kirkby Malham, Skipton and Slaidburn. To them may
be added Giggleswick and Sedbergh, which have the chancel
slightly lower than the nave but no chancel arch; while most of
the smaller churches in the area also show some of the same characteristics. As to the origins of the type, the extent of the Perp
changes at Kildwick and Skipton makes it impossible to say
whether the C14 churches there were also longitudinally undivided, but the similar form of C12 Horton-in-Ribblesdale raises
the possibility that it has a long history in the area.

Turning to individual components, TOWERS are now very
common, perhaps the quintessential Perp feature throughout the
whole of the West Riding, whether as part of a rebuilding –
usually but not invariably the last part to be built – or as an addition. (Spires on the other hand are very rare, confined to just
three on the Magnesian Limestone belt – Aberford, Bramham
and Kirk Deighton – together with the occasional lead-covered

spike). The best examples are at Tadcaster and Kirk Deighton in the E, Bradford and Bolton-by-Bowland further W. A curiosity is p. 150 the turret at Cowthorpe, resting on two buttresses which join at the top to form an arch. But otherwise the area's towers are not strongly characterized, neither specially tall nor short, ornate nor plain. This is borne out by an interesting near-identical group from the mid C15 mainly to the E and NE of Leeds – Barwick-in-Elmet, Guiseley, Rothwell, Swillington, Thorner, Whitkirk – the only really distinguishing feature of which is their corbelled-out battlemented parapets. Other typical additions, alongside the aisles and chapels, are clerestories and PORCHES, of which there is a group with ribbed tunnel-vaults (Calverley, Kirkby Malham, Methley, Swillington, Whitkirk etc.). On detail there is not much to add, individual touches being largely confined to little remi-niscences of Dec – e.g. on the towers at Giggleswick and Kirk Deighton – or, in a small group of churches in Craven and the NW – Bolton-by-Bowland, Dent, Gisburn, Kildwick, Sedbergh – of an even earlier period, in the form of E windows resembling a set of stepped lancets. Finally a few ROOFS should be mentioned, nothing spectacular but of sound quality. Those at Bradford, Methley and Skipton are very low-pitched, with moulded tie- 22 beams and short kingposts flanked by a little timber tracery (cf. Bolton Abbey). At Barnoldswick and Kildwick they are steeper and have tie-beam and arched-brace trusses alternating, and cusped windbraces. Slaidburn's and Great Mitton's have arch-braced collars, Addingham's tie-beams and kingposts. Timber-panelled ceilings survive at Aldborough, Rothwell and Methley.

Parish church fittings and furnishings, and church monuments

Of fittings, the most numerous and chronologically diffuse cate-gory is that of FONTS, but few show much artistic ambition. Almost half are Norman, most elementally plain but an excep-tion is that at Ingleton, with intersected arcading occupied by biblical figures. A few are C13 and C14, then rather more are Perp, mainly octagonal, some with concave sides, the best that at Bolton-by-Bowland. With these should be mentioned the spec-tacular late medieval font cover at Bradford, a filigree timber spire (cf. Almondbury, Halifax and Selby, West Riding South). A few simple parclose screens survive, mainly in the W of the area, together with two ROOD SCREENS, both very late: one at Skipton of 1533, straightforward enough by SW standards, the 22 other at Hubberholme, dated 1558 – i.e. Marian – and still with a rood loft;* but screen and loft do not go together and it is not quite clear what the dated work consisted of. Of medieval STAINED GLASS there is very little. The main examples are two windows assembled in the C19, at Methley, of C15 saints and

---

*It is signed by the carpenter *William Jake*. The apparently contemporary work on the church itself is very roughly done, but still Perp as far as it is anything.

angels, and Calverley, of more miscellaneous fragments, C14 and
C15. Otherwise, there is some Dec canopy work at Aldborough,
re-set in the C19, and smaller fragments at e.g. Gisburn, Nether
Poppleton, Tadcaster, Waddington. Of other items by far the most
important is the unique C15 EASTER SEPULCHRE at Cowthorpe,
of timber, moveable, a chest under a gabled canopy. Three
Craven churches, Bracewell, Broughton and Kirkby Malham,
have curious crudely executed IMAGE NICHES attached to
arcade piers or responds. Late medieval BENCH ENDS, reused in
C19 stalls, survive at Little Ouseburn, Woodkirk and the chapel
of St Mary Magdalen at Ripon. Other woodwork is represented
by the traceried Perp doors at Healaugh and the chapel at
Hazlewood Castle; IRONWORK by the door hinges at Leathley
and Aldborough, C12 and C14 respectively. In the churchyard at
Ripley is the base of a PENITENTIAL CROSS, with recesses for
kneeling.

The MONUMENTS present a more consistently rewarding area
of study, pride of place going to those of alabaster from the C15
and C16, of which there is a particular wealth. At Harewood there
are no fewer than six, the largest number in any English parish
church, all of the highest quality, commemorating members of
the Gascoigne, Ryther and Redman families. The dates of death
run from 1419 to 1529. All are of the same type, with paired
recumbent effigies on tomb-chests with various permutations of
angels, weepers and canopies round the sides, but were evidently
the work of different workshops, the earliest probably from the
celebrated one at Chellaston, Derbyshire. At Methley there are
two more, that of Sir Robert Waterton (†1425) and his wife especially fine and very similar to one of the Redman tombs. Others
are at Ripon Cathedral (Sir Thomas Markenfield, †1487, and his
wife) and Allerton Mauleverer (†1468), the latter with the effigies only surviving; while that of Sir Robert Scargill and his wife
at Whitkirk (Leeds), executed c. 1550 but still entirely Perp, continues the tradition to the end of the period. The same type of
monument from the pre-alabaster era is represented by those of
Sir Thomas Ingilby II (†1381) and his wife at Ripley and Sir
Thomas Markenfield (†c. 1390) and his wife at Ripon Cathedral.
From an earlier period again, the first half of the C14, comes a
group of effigies of CROSS-LEGGED KNIGHTS, the best at Goldsborough (Sir Richard de Goldsborough IV and V, †1308 and
†c. 1333), and Hazlewood Castle (possibly Sir William and Walter
Vavasour, †1313 and †1315); while two at Allerton Mauleverer are
of oak rather than freestone. Of other types, mention should be
made of the small early C14 slab at Moor Monkton with a relief
figure partly visible through a quatrefoil and half-quatrefoil;
and that of Sir Ralph Pudsey (†1468) and his wives at Bolton-
by-Bowland, a large limestone slab on which the figures of
the subjects and their numerous children are delineated two-
dimensionally, in the manner of ornamental brasses. Actual
BRASSES are few. The best surviving is the 6-ft (2-metre) figure
of William de Aldeburgh, c. 1360, at Aldborough, a particularly
interesting one that of Sir John Mauleverer (†1400) and his wife

26

25

p. 590

p. 139

at Allerton Mauleverer, which is an engraved plate rather than the usual cutout. The elaborate brass of Sir Bryan Rouclyff (†1494) and his wife at Cowthorpe, with a model of the church he had founded, has been mutilated, and that of Henry Clifford first Earl of Cumberland (†1542) and his wife at Skipton, set on a tomb-chest, survives only in the form of a C19 replica.

A word should be added about the settings of monuments. The effigy of Sir Richard de Goldsborough IV at Goldsborough and the Waterton monument at Methley occupy correspondingly handsome tomb-arches between the chancel and a chapel, another de Goldsborough tomb (†1504) is similarly housed in an arch between a chapel and the E end of the nave, and at Harewood and Ripley simpler tomb-arches were provided at the E end of both nave arcades as a part of the design of the church. The two monuments at Hazlewood and a late C14 effigy of a knight at Walton are all set in ornamented tomb-recesses; and similar features, mainly also C14, are found at several other places, the best in the S chapel at Knaresborough, en suite with the elaborate sedilia, piscina and image niche.

Medieval secular buildings

By far the best CASTLE is Skipton, both a fortress and a magnate's palace. The compact D-shaped core, with close-set round towers, was probably built c. 1190–1220 by William de Fors I and II, replacing an earlier structure; and the later parts, military and domestic, were added by the Cliffords in the early C14 and c. 1500 on. One which should outrank this in terms of status is the royal castle of Knaresborough, with its sumptuous residential tower built in 1307–12 for Edward II, but it was reduced to a fragment after the Civil War. Otherwise there are various motte-and-bailey type earthwork structures, mainly of the C12, the best preserved at Barwick-in-Elmet (de Lacy), Burton-in-Lonsdale (de Mowbray) and Sedbergh. The FORTIFIED and SEMI-FORTIFIED HOUSES are of several different types. The classic example, and one of the earliest, is Markenfield Hall (licence to crenellate 1310 but probably begun c. 1290), which has an L-shaped main block, with hall on the upper floor, set at one corner of a moated rectangular enclosure; but the big traceried windows perhaps belie a serious defensive intent. At Hazlewood Castle (licence to crenellate 1290, altered) the core is a hall block apparently of very similar form, and at the Percy family's Spofforth Castle (licence 1308) the well-detailed hall range, also raised on an undercroft, represents a rebuilding of an earlier house, presumably unfortified; but in both cases the defensive outer perimeter, assuming there was one, has been lost. But the most sophisticated example is Harewood Castle (licence to crenellate 1367), a compact intricately planned tower house (cf. Langley Castle, Northumberland) but with the hall – complete with elaborate buffet recess – on the ground floor; and the beautifully situated Barden Tower, c. 1500, is a later version of

27–8
p. 705

29
p. 584

p. 326

p. 298

p. 24
1

Harewood Castle, buffet.
Engraving, 1859

the same type. Houses developed in contrasting ways from a solar
tower are Hellifield Peel, where an attached hall range was later
dispensed with and the tower enlarged to form a tower house
proper; and Bolling Hall, Bradford, where the corresponding
ranges were gradually rebuilt and extended. Ripley Castle, a
house apparently of the mid C15 defended just by a gatehouse
and perimeter wall, gained a strong solar tower as late as 1555.

Of stone-built UNFORTIFIED HOUSES, there are fragmentary
early survivals at Massey Garth, Spofforth (c. 1200), and at
Spofforth Old Rectory and Grassington Old Hall, late C13 with

plate-traceried windows. Probably of the C14 are the carcase of Farnhill Hall, a single range with four little battlemented turrets, superficially fortified-looking; the cross-passage area of Ilkley Manor House, with two shouldered-arched doorways into the service end; and the Old Court House at Ripon, a two-storey range with common rafter roof, which may be a remnant of the Archbishop of York's palace there. Probably the best surviving example is Calverley Old Hall, *c.* 1490 but succeeding earlier buildings, a simple hall and cross-wing but on a quite large scale, much altered but retaining its fine hall roof – arched-brace trusses plus one with a tie-beam, probably a spere-truss – and a similar roof and charming screened gallery in the chapel. Its near-contemporary is the Old Vicarage at Tadcaster, a smaller version of a similar plan-type, thoroughly restored; and perhaps of the same period is the enigmatic medieval fabric at Wigglesworth Hall, the main component of which is another good roof, of crown-post type. A contrastingly cosmopolitan Early Tudor manner was represented by Thomas Darcy's Temple Newsam, Leeds, of *c.* 1500, with diaper-patterned brickwork much of which survived the C17 remodelling. 30

Mention of the roofs at Calverley Old Hall etc. leads to the subject of TIMBER-FRAMED BUILDING, to the traditions of which the roofs belong. A fair amount survives, almost all in the centre and E of the area, but mostly in a quite degraded state and encased in later stone or brick. A few fragments are possibly as early as the C14, notably the three service-end doorways at Baildon Hall, but most belong to the period from the later C15 to the later C16, and in the lowland zone the tradition continues further, until the mid C17.* As to its forms, walling is generally quite plain, with none of the ornamental features found in e.g. South Lancashire and Cheshire – straightforward close-studded box framing frequently with curved wind-braces, but with jetties in the towns only. Roofs are mainly of either the common rafter type or that with kingpost trusses, notionally the 'lowland' and 'upland' forms respectively but in practice overlapping extensively in their distribution. Perhaps the most illuminating example overall in terms of domestic planning is Home Farm at Scriven, a 'Vale of York' yeoman's house of *c.* 1500, with common rafter roof, full-length rear outshut and until *c.* 1600 an open hall probably with a fire-bay; while a more ambitious one, probably a little later – and wholly cased in stone – is Royds Hall, Low Moor, Bradford, of hall-and-cross-wings plan with the open hall still undivided. The finest individual component surviving is the ornamented early C16 arched-brace roof at Fold Farm, Kettlewell, which is similar to some of the arched-brace church roofs and to that at Horbury Hall near Wakefield (West Riding South); and particularly interesting earlier survivals are the hall at Cad Beeston Manor House, Leeds, datable to 1421, the parlour wing at Scotton Old Hall and a gatehouse in Kirkgate, Ripon, which was probably that of the archbishops' palace, all of 31

p. 686

---

*Three examples in Knaresborough are datable to *c.* 1610–25 by documentary evidence.

which have crown-post roofs of a type usually associated with the
City of York. At Bashall Hall there is a partly timber-framed
lodgings range of *c.* 1600, with external first-floor gallery.
Surviving examples of CRUCK construction are few and none
apparently earlier than the C16, the most complete probably Red
Gables at Ilkley.

Finally there are a few medieval aisled BARNS (the timber-
framed walls again mainly rebuilt in stone), the best that at
Bolton Abbey, of *c.* 1518, the roof with kingpost trusses
alternating with subsidiary collars. At nearby Barden there are
two barns with cruck trusses.

ELIZABETHAN AND
SEVENTEENTH CENTURY

The particular feature of this period is the distinctive stone-built
C17 architecture of the Pennine region, represented by large
numbers of handsome houses of mainly moderate size. To some
extent the phenomenon can be related to the growth of the
Pennine woollen textile industry which in the early C18 was
described by Daniel Defoe in a famous passage of his *Tour
through England and Wales*, but it is too widespread to be wholly
explained by that and appears to be a case where the broader
concept of an early modern 'Great Rebuilding' is applicable. For
the most part these houses constitute the first generation of
secular building in stone below feudal magnate level, replacing
timber-framed structures, and occasionally the process itself is,
as it were, preserved in the fabric, the walls encasing fragments
of an earlier timber frame. Like their stone-built counterparts in
other areas of the country they may appear markedly conservative in some of their forms and details, and so the theme of a
Renaissance-influenced style and its dissemination runs in counterpoint to this one. The latter is also played out primarily in the
field of domestic architecture, but C16 and C17 country houses
more conventionally defined were never very numerous in the
area and have been much affected by demolition and alteration.
On the other hand C17 religious buildings are by no means
absent, a reflection doubtless partly of the relatively thin spread
of medieval provision in some areas and partly of the early
strength of Nonconformity.

Elizabethan and Jacobean country houses

As elsewhere in the country, political uncertainty (e.g. the
Northern Earls' Rebellion, 1569) appears to have discouraged
activity until the later years of Elizabeth's reign, when the story
began with two grand many-turreted courtyard houses, built for
different branches of the Savile family: Methley Hall, begun

c. 1588, and the even larger Howley Hall near Morley of *c.* 1590. Both have been demolished, the latter in the early C18, the former in 1963. Then came a group all of *c.* 1600, smaller but no less sophisticated, generally tall and compact. Chief amongst them is Fountains Hall, built by the recusant hunter Sir Stephen Proctor and persuasively attributed to *Robert Smythson* – a dramatic half-H with affinities to his Wollaton Hall, including an ingenious solution to that characteristic Elizabethan conundrum, reconciling a central entrance and a traditional great hall. The others, all a little further W, are of interest *inter alia* as providing a possible point of departure for the C17 Pennine style: they are Broughton Hall, Weston Hall, Myddleton Lodge at Ilkley, and Friars Head at Winterburn. Broughton was totally remodelled in the C18 and C19 but retains traces of another feature associated with Robert Smythson, the transverse hall (cf. Hardwick Hall, Derbyshire). Weston Hall has also been greatly altered but has in the grounds an exceptionally lavish three-storey banqueting house; and Myddleton Lodge, compactly planned as the term 'lodge' implies at this time, is the first fully developed double pile in the northern West Riding. At Friars Head, the precisely proportioned symmetrical front incorporates what are probably the first examples in the region of a type of truncated-ogee-headed window – its origins apparently related to those of Elizabethan shaped gables – which was to become a characteristic motif of Pennine architecture. With these can be placed Guiseley Rectory, dated 1601, more simply detailed but presenting the symmetrical Elizabethan scheme of a central porch and gabled end bays.

Moving into the Jacobean phase, the Red House at Moor Monkton, begun in 1607, was largely demolished in the C19 apart from the chapel (*see* below), leaving as the main survival the remodelled Temple Newsam, of after 1622 for the London merchant and courtier Sir Arthur Ingram. The house is U-shaped, with an elaborate stone porch, and a flat roof surrounded by a balustrade incorporating an inscription in large cut-out letters. That links it to perhaps the most interesting aristocratic project of the earlier C17, the ornamental remodelling of the outer gatehouse at Skipton Castle, *c.* 1629 for Henry Clifford, which included also the creation of an allegorical shell-work grotto redolent of the courtly world of Isaac de Caux and Inigo Jones. The tally is completed by Goldsborough Hall of *c.* 1625, another tall gabled double pile still entirely in the Jacobean manner; but an exceptional undertaking of the mid C17 can also be mentioned here, Lady Anne Clifford's restorations of Skipton Castle and Barden Tower in 1657–9, following respectively a parliamentary slighting and years of neglect. The motive for these activities was evidently the glorification of her Clifford ancestors and her connection with them rather than any precocious appreciation of medieval architecture in itself; but the simple traditional style of her buildings is the more noteworthy in that, as Countess of Pembroke, she had been mistress of Wilton House when de Caux's s front was built.

Of INTERIOR FITTINGS and decoration perhaps the most
notable survivals are the staircases at Myddleton Lodge, Goldsborough Hall and the Red House. The first is of the 'cage' type,
with continuous moulded newel posts round a narrow open well,
and vertically symmetrical balusters; the second has the same
components but on a spacious dog-leg plan; and the third, made
in 1637 and now in the chapel, has a selection of heraldic beasts
on the newel posts. Big ornate stone fireplaces with bas-relief
overmantel panels survive at Fountains Hall and Goldsborough
Hall, and at Weston one with an arcaded timber overmantel.
At Ripley Castle there are two good-quality decorative plaster
ceilings; but both plasterwork and woodwork are better
represented in the smaller houses.

C17 Pennine houses

These are the houses of the minor gentry, and the substantial
yeoman farmers and clothiers. A consistent distinction between
gentry and non-gentry house-types is not always discernible, but
in Craven at least a useful indicator is that the former are frequently built tall, with a full attic storey (cf. Friars Head etc.)
whereas the latter generally are not. Other general characteristics
are a tendency to informality of composition, rejecting the
rigours of strict symmetry, the long persistence of multiple-light
mullioned windows, and a scarcity of conventional Renaissance
ornament. Distinctiveness lies not only in the nature of the building materials – the low pitch of roofs and gables reflecting the
weight of the gritstone roofing slabs – but in certain curiosities
of planning and above all in what Pevsner called the houses'
'grossly fanciful' detail. The quality of the buildings is apparent
in the ordinary walling as well as the dressings, typically of regular
coursed stone rather than rubble, but also in the standard of
accommodation: it is noticeable that longhouses, common
amongst the C17 farmhouses of Cumbria and the North York
Moors, are virtually absent here, although there is some evidence
of their earlier existence in the area. As to dating a little more
precisely, stone-built ranges which were doubtless added to
timber-framed houses survive from the decades either side of
1600 in at least two cases (Upper Headley, Thornton, 1589; Dean
House, Allerton, Bradford, 1605); and then there is a group of
buildings of hybrid construction, with external walls of stone but
some internal structural components still of timber (e.g. High
Stead, Ilkley, 1596; East End, Norwood, before 1625). The fully
developed type was evidently established at both gentry and non-
gentry levels by the 1620s – e.g. Swinsty Hall, by 1627; Frogden
House, Bierley, Bradford, 1625 – but its heyday was in the second
half of the C17, from the 1660s to the 1690s, and elements of the
style persisted in some places until well into the C18.

Now for some specifics. With regard to PLANNING, one can
take as a starting-point the traditional hall-and-cross-wings form,
but it is observable that the accommodation within it was not

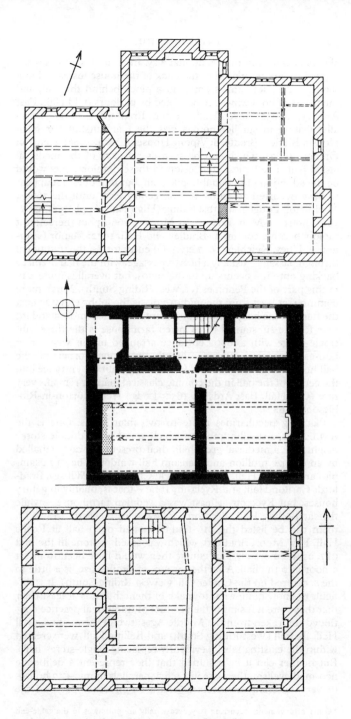

C17 Pennine houses, comparative plans: (top to bottom)
Bradford, Heaton, Royds Hall *c.* 1671; Airton, Vipont House, 1666;
Keighley, Utley, Manor Farmhouse, 1677

always arranged in the traditional way. In a number of cases the service rooms are placed at the back of the house instead of in a service 'end', sometimes partly in a block behind the hall, and the fronts of both wings are occupied by parlours (Old Hall, East Ardsley, c. 1652; Royds Hall, Heaton, Bradford, c. 1671). A parallel feature in smaller houses was the rear outshut (Frogden House, Bierley, Bradford; Vipont House, Airton, 1666; Menston Grange, 1672), which can be seen as a legacy of the medieval aisled hall. The logical conclusion to these developments would be the adoption of the double-pile plan, but that does not appear to have occurred at gentry or non-gentry level until the 1660s, Myddleton Lodge notwithstanding (High Hall, Appletreewick, c. 1667; house in Main Road, East Morton, 1669); but thereafter it rapidly became common (Bradley Old Hall, 1672; Manor Farmhouse, Utley, Keighley, 1677 etc.). Of entry forms, the traditional through passage – usually a hearth passage, with the hall fireplace backing onto it – occurs up to the 1670s, but overall is quite rare in this part of the Pennines (cf. West Riding South). Much more common, at least from the mid C17 on, is the lobby entry against the flank of the hall, or housebody, fireplace: the almost standard type for the substantial C17 Craven farmhouse is the three-unit single range with a lobby entrance arranged in this way. Other houses have the entrance directly into one corner of the hall/housebody (e.g. Kildwick Hall, c. 1655); but the entrance into the centre of the hall in the coming classical manner remains very rare (Old Hall, East Ardsley, 1652; Lodge Hall, Horton-in-Ribblesdale, 1687).*

Planning peculiarities relate to two main areas. One is the HALL itself, a small number of which are of up to double-storey height, like a medieval great hall, their presence always signalled by an outsize mullion-and-transom hall window. The C17 examples are at High Hall, Appletreewick; Chapel Fold, Wibsey, Bradford; Carlton Hall; and Ryecroft, Tong – that is, mainly in gentry houses, but Ryecroft at least was a yeoman farmhouse – while that at Bolling Hall, Bradford, followed in the early C18. With them can be listed the C16 timber-framed open hall at Royds Hall, Low Moor, Bradford, which was cased in stone in the mid C17, as the more obvious course then would have been to insert a floor into the hall. A further group, of similar size, is a little to the S, centred on the Calder valley (West Riding South). It is difficult to know quite what to make of them, but it is at least clear that they were not simply the product of traditional practice continued unbroken from the Middle Ages: two of them, at Oakwell Hall, Birstall (West Riding South) and Bolling Hall, were created within the existing fabric, evidently replacing single-storey halls. But neither can it be assumed that they represent a deliberate neo-medievalism: there are just a few parallels in mid-C17 houses of very different architectural character in other parts of the

*Other arrangements occurring very occasionally are entrances in the gable-end rather than at the front (Vipont House, Airton; Ivy House, Harden, 1676); and, on the E Pennine margins, semi-subterranean vaulted dairies projecting at the rear (East End, Norwood).

country (e.g. Lees Court, Kent), and they should perhaps be seen in the same light as the progressive developments in planning referred to above. The other peculiarities, largely confined to Craven farmhouses, are focused on some of the two-storey PORCHES which are a common C17 Pennine feature. One group has the entrance in the side of the porch instead of the front (e.g. Lower Hardacre, Clapham, 1664; Woodhead, Lothersdale, 1673; Ivy Cottage, Buckden, 1705), an arrangement which together with the size of some of the porches suggests that they had a function other than simply protecting the entrance to the house. Another has the house staircase either in a projection beside the porch instead of in the commoner position at the rear (Old Cotes, Arncliffe, c. 1650; Battle Hill, Austwick, 1673), or later within the porch itself (Kirkbeck, Bentham, after 1676; Manor House, Halton Gill, c. 1700; Sawyers Garth, Litton, 1714). Slightly more widespread is the curious practice of jettying the upper storey of the porch, as if it was timber-framed (Low Hall, Low Snowden; Horton Hall, Horton-in-Craven etc.).

That leads to the matter of the distinctive DETAIL of the houses. Its sources are frequently unclear, but apparently multifarious. The most characteristic item in this part of the Pennines, centred on Craven but not confined to it, is the ornamented doorhead or door lintel, the designs typically consisting of a recessed geometrical figure, usually accompanied by the date and the initials of the owner, on the lintel's face. They appear to start in the 1630s (e.g. Bentham, 1635) but most are of the 1660s on, with a final flurry in the first two decades of the C18 concentrated in the far w (Austwick, Bolton-by-Bowland, Sawley etc.). The motifs range from simple rectangles and semicircles to others of much greater complexity. A few of them are of apparently Gothic character – pointed blind arches – but they are exceptional and

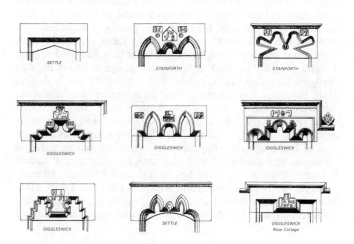

Comparative Pennine doorheads.

35, p. 694
38, p. 360
41

evidently all related to a single building of the 1670s, The Folly at Settle, which is very much a special case with elements also derived from Serlio and other pattern books.* A design at Stainforth (1697) recalls C17 enriched panelling. Another particularly striking feature is the wheel window, of which there are two at East Riddlesden Hall, Keighley (*c.* 1648), one at Lumb Hall, Drighlington, and smaller versions at Hartwith (1696) and Threshfield. They are outliers of a larger group in the Halifax area (West Riding South), where they start in the 1590s, and are probably to be explained as a species of Elizabethan 'device' rather than a literal Neo-Gothicism. The truncated-ogee-headed window, and its probable origins, have already been mentioned. It can be seen as a variant on the much more widely occuring stepped (or double-stepped) mullioned window, typically located in attic gables or the upper stages of porches, in which the central light is extended up further than the others. It is followed by flattened-ogee-headed doorways (Idle Old Chapel, Bradford, 1630; Bradley Old Hall, 1672), while the flattened and truncated ogee appears as one of the ornamented doorhead motifs (Settle, 1664, etc.). A further feature worthy of note is the persistence of arched lights in mullioned windows. In some locations, e.g. the Keighley area, they evidently represent a simple continuation of past practice, but at The Folly they are probably a conscious neomedievalism and in other cases (Bradley Old Hall etc.) they occur in approximations to Serliana, forming a variation on the stepped window. Then there are the occasional decorated hoodmould stops (Bolton-by-Bowland 1687, Esholt 1691); and the finials on the apexes and kneelers of gables which are a common feature of C16–17 stone building.

Much of the INTERIOR DECORATION remains wholly Elizabethan or Jacobean in character. That applies to the decorative plaster ceilings, of which there are several handsome examples with the usual geometrical patterns formed of narrow ribs, and enrichment of various kinds in the panels. The earliest, at Hawksworth Hall (1611) and Kildwick Grange (*c.* 1620?), both form segmental barrel vaults; others are at East Riddlesden Hall, Keighley (*c.* 1648), including one from a design in Serlio, Baildon Hall and Weetwood Hall, Leeds (mid C17); while one at Bolling Hall, Bradford, has strapwork-like bands rather than ribs. Less ambitious schemes – friezes, overmantels etc. – survive, sometimes fragmentarily, in a number of smaller houses, e.g. an overmantel dated 1697 at Conistone. The best staircase is perhaps that at Baildon Hall, with open well, enriched newels crowned by finials, and the typical mid-C17 vertically symmetrical turned balusters. That at The Folly has barley-sugar balusters, an early example; while at Swinsty Hall, Kildwick Hall and Lodge Hall, Horton-in-Ribblesdale the staircases are of stone, rising round a solid rectangular core. Amongst the schemes of panelling, timber

---

*Its impact in other respects on the architecture of the locality can be seen at e.g. Lodge Hall, Horton-in-Ribblesdale and Broxup House, Bolton-by-Bowland.

overmantels etc., mention should be made of the delightful hall screen at High Hall, Appletreewick (*c.* 1667), enriched with miniature balusters. Painted decoration on the other hand is very rare, the main survival beyond the Pennine zone at Home Farm, Scriven (*c.* 1600). Other fragments are at Hill Top, Malham; Oldfield House, Oakworth; and Lane House, Silsden, the last dated 1689.

Finally again, ROOFS, an area in which medieval practices were certainly continued. The finest are of arched-brace type, at Swinsty Hall, Great Mitton Hall, Bashall Hall and Park House, Paythorne; and simpler ones, with upper crucks, are at Friars Head, Winterburn (*see* above); Paget Hall, Gargrave; and Brimham Lodge, Hartwith (1661). The Manor House, Langcliffe (1678) has a remarkable structure with pendant king blocks. Also continuing older traditions are the numerous aisled BARNS, with arcades of timber, but the external walls now usually stone-built from the outset. Particularly good examples are those at Bank Newton and East Riddlesden Hall, Keighley.

Churches and chapels, and their furnishings

In comparison with the domestic buildings the number of churches and chapels is of course tiny, but there is much of interest here. The sequence again starts with a work from the end of the Elizabethan period, the Sherburne Chapel added to Great Mitton church in 1594. It is still entirely, and smartly, Perp – apart from a Renaissance tablet over the entrance and some odd little details on the arcade, while the arcade screen combines ogee-headed lights and Renaissance balusters. The outstanding example, and a building of national importance although much restored in the C19, is the new church of St John at Leeds built in 1632–4, founded and endowed by the Leeds clothier John Harrison to supplement the overcrowded parish church. The style this time is essentially Pennine Gothic, with the familiar straight-headed windows with arched lights; but the end windows and the bell-openings of the W tower were an odd quasi-Dec rather than Perp, and the original porch (dem. C18) had a round-headed entry and strapwork cresting. The main departure from medieval practice was in the plan, undivided longitudinally but with two naves of equal height and width rather than a nave and aisles. The special feature of the church is the furnishings – much rearranged in the C19 restorations but narrowly escaping a worse fate – notably the sumptuous screen the whole width of the building, with delicate tapering balusters and elaborate strapwork cresting, the similarly ornate pulpit and a complete set of ornamented pews. They were almost certainly the work of the Leeds joiner *Francis Gunby*, who executed the similar screen at Wakefield Cathedral (West Riding South).

Alongside this, CHAPELS of the early and mid C17 survive at Moor Monkton (*c.* 1621), Eldroth (before 1627), Idle, Bradford (1630), Bramhope (1649) and Chapel-le-Dale, and remnants of them at Low Moor, Bradford (1606) – incorporated into the church of 1836–7 – and Thornton (1612). The first was a private chapel attached to the Red House (*see* above) and most of the others were parochial chapels of ease; but the best-known, that at Bramhope, built by an 'ardent and unswerving Puritan', fell somewhere between the two. All are simple rectangles, most combining straight-headed mullioned windows on the flanks and an arched Jacobean Perp E window with crude panel tracery, Puritan Bramhope eschewing the latter. The Red House chapel again retains a range of C17 furnishings – pulpit, communion rail, screen, gallery, painted glass – as well as the staircase referred to above. Bramhope has its C17 pulpit. Then at the end of the century comes one C17 parish church rebuilding, at Fewston (1697), mainly in the classicizing style of that decade (*see* below) with cross-windows and an arcade with Tuscan columns, but again a C17 Perp E window.

As to FURNISHINGS elsewhere, the finest items of woodwork are the screen at Slaidburn, a simpler version of that at St John, Leeds, the medievalizing spire-like font covers at Calverley, Skipton, Methley and Long Preston – the last dated as late as 1726 – and the pulpit at Giggleswick (1680), with emblems of the twelve tribes of Israel. A pleasing C17 ensemble is at Barnoldswick, with three-decker pulpit still in its pre-Ecclesiological position halfway along the N wall, and extensive C17 pewing, some of it with ball finials at the pew-ends. Pulpits otherwise are not uncommon – that at Dent is dated 1614 – but generally a harmonious enrichment of interiors rather than individually remarkable. Of pews the best are at Kildwick and Kirkby Malham, dated 1633 and 1631 etc., with balustraded superstructures. Others are at e.g. Bolton-by-Bowland and Dent, some again with ball finials to the ends. Of fonts, that at Tosside is dated 1619, and then there is a post-Restoration trio near Leeds – Rothwell (1662), East Ardsley (1663) and Kippax (1663) – all very similar, with octagonal bowls, that at Kippax bearing the names of the churchwardens, Rothwell's with initials of churchwardens, vicar and king. Thornton's (1679) is similar on a smaller scale, while Farsley has a tiny portable font dated 1667. There is also a little painted glass, by the York glass painter *Henry Gyles*. The most important piece is his King David at Denton (1700), the others at Adel, Leeds (1681 and *c.* 1706), Aldborough (1700) and, fragments only, at Ripon (*c.* 1670).

Also of the later C17 is the notable group of early FRIENDS' MEETING HOUSES. The best-known is that at Brigflatts near Sedbergh (1675), wonderfully complete with mullioned windows, off-centre two-storey porch and galleried interior. Others are at Settle (1678), Farfield Hall (1689) – tiny and also untouched – Skipton (1693), Rawdon (1697, altered) and Airton (1700). Characteristic features of the gravely simple interiors are the elders' bench, usually across one end, and the women's chamber or gallery, screened by shutters. With these can be mentioned the Presbyterian Chapel at Winterburn, of 1703–4 (now a house), also still with mullioned windows.

Church monuments

These present a quite different narrative, of the spread of Renaissance forms largely uninfluenced by regional characteristics. The story can be taken up at the point where it ended in the Middle Ages, with the alabaster altar tomb carrying recumbent effigies, production of which was now centred on Burton-on-Trent. Those of Lord Wharton (†1568) and his two wives at Healaugh and Sir Richard Sherburne (†1594) and his wife at Great Mitton – the first of the excellent series of Sherburne monuments there – show just a slight movement towards Renaissance taste, in the form of the balusters framing the shields and mourners on the sides of the tomb-chest; while a later example, Robert Stapleton's at Wighill (†1634), has Ionic colonettes instead of balusters. The same format is handsomely represented in black and white marble by the monument to Sir John Savile (†1607) and his son (†1632) and daughter-in-law at Methley – again with Ionic colonettes – attributed to *William Wright* of Charing Cross; and examples in stone are at Knaresborough (Francis Slingsby, †1600, and his wife), with panelled pilasters; Ripley (Sir William Ingilby, †1617), with cartouche on the backplate; and Otley (Lord Fairfax, †1640, and his wife). But in the 1630s an entirely post-Jacobean style had appeared in memorable fashion in two further Slingsby monuments at Knaresborough, one definitely by *William Wright* and the second attributed to him. Both feature an upright figure: Sir Henry (†1634) is shown in his shroud, after the manner of Nicholas Stone's monument to John Donne in St Paul's Cathedral (1631), and his brother Sir William (†1638) standing in the classically derived cross-legged pose – its first appearance in English funerary sculpture.

Meanwhile, the type with paired kneeling figures in profile within an aedicule had appeared at Great Mitton (Richard Sherburne, †1629, and his wife), a single figure so presented at Nether Poppleton (†1620) and the less common kneeling figures placed frontally at Hazlewood Castle (Sir Thomas Vavasour, †1632, and his wife). A demi-figure angled slightly off the frontal is at Nether Poppleton (†1651), a frontal demi-figure in an oval frame at Kirk Deighton (†1656). Also at Nether Poppleton is a mid-c17 monument with a small frontal kneeling figure flanked by two standing. Monuments without sculpture include both traditional altar tombs (Otley, †1610; Skipton, †1605, executed 1654; Bilbrough, †1671) and the tablet to John Harrison of Leeds (†1656) in the church he founded (*see* above), framed by classical forms without Jacobean frills. Of BRASSES the only example requiring mention is that of the Lindley and Palmes families at Otley, dated 1593, a plate with a heraldic family tree.

A second high point comes at the end of the century, at two locations. In the monument to three generations of the Sherburne family at Great Mitton (†1668, 1689, 1690, 1693) the old theme of recumbent effigies on an altar tomb is beautifully reprised, the men crossing their legs in elegant reminiscence of c14 knights. It is by *William Stanton, c.* 1690: there is also a fine

relief (†1702) by him. At Whitkirk, Leeds, that to the second Viscount Irwin (†1688) by *John van Nost*, 1697, is an effective, fluent
rendering of the Renaissance type with semi-reclining effigy –
first seen in the area in an exceptionally inept version at Ripon
Cathedral (†1608) – here accompanied on the tomb-chest by
mourning wife at his head and baby daughter at his feet, against
a tall pedimented backplate. Lesser monuments of the later C17
include that of the Mallories, father and son (†1655, 1666), at
Ripon Cathedral, erected in 1678, with gadrooned sarcophagus;
the tablet and bust to John Thoresby (†1679) in Leeds parish
church, by *Andrew Carpenter*; and other tablets and cartouches
which by the 1690s are beginning to verge towards the Baroque.
In the churchyard of the United Reformed Church at Morley is
a remarkable series of grave-slabs, from the mid C17 on, with
much low-relief carving, and a late C17 mausoleum, a small cube
of mixed architectural style.

Public buildings

43   The outstanding item is Beamsley Hospital, the almshouses
founded in 1593 by the Countess of Cumberland: the design is
an Elizabethan conceit, circular with a chapel in the middle and
the lower rooms surrounding it. Otherwise little needs mention
here. The SCHOOLS reflect the unchanging nature of so much
C17 architecture in the area, so e.g. Burnsall (1602) and nearby
Threshfield (1674) present very much the same sort of scheme,
a two-storey range with mullioned windows and off-centre two-
storey porch not unlike a Pennine farmhouse. Of the same type
also is Earby (mid-C17), but Ilkley (1637) and Wilsden (1680) are
humbler, just a single storey. Only with the Boyle School at
55   Bolton Abbey (1700) does a more classicizing style appear (*see*
below), with cross-windows and a heavily rusticated doorway
crowned by a semicircular pediment. Two other buildings, the
Court House at Knaresborough Castle, of *c.* 1600, and the
former House of Correction at Ripon (1686), also reflect the lack,
as yet, of a distinctive form and vocabulary for their specific functions, the former – which retains its very plainly detailed courtroom – quite domestic-looking, with mullioned windows, the
latter of institutional rather than punitive appearance, the mullioned windows small and regularly placed. Of the several C17
BRIDGES surviving, particularly in the upland zone, the least
altered are at Ilkley (1674–6) and Barden (1676), both rebuildings after a flood in 1673. A few others, e.g. Settle, echo medieval
structural practice, with longitudinal ribs on the undersides of
the arches.

Post-Restoration classicism and the architecture of the 1690s

The progression is broadly from E to W and more narrowly from
brick to stone. In the BRICK zone to the E there are three major

landmarks. The first, built probably in the 1660s, is The Priory at Nun Monkton, which represents approximately the classical hipped-roofed block type of the mid C17, but in a Mannerist version, with a giant pilaster order (cf. Lees Court, Kent etc.) derived partly from Serlio and a few other quirky details. There is a staircase with fat balusters and panelled newel posts. The second is Ribston Hall, built *c.* 1674 for the soldier-diplomat Sir Henry Goodricke, which before alteration in the C18 presented a markedly French variant on the type, with steep pavilion roofs and a *cour d'honneur*. The third, Newby Hall, is the climax, built for the Newcastle coal magnate Sir Edward Blackett *c.* 1685–93 and just possibly the work of no less a figure than *Sir Christopher Wren*. Much admired at the time, it presents the fully up-to-date version – the big red brick block now three-storeyed with a flat roof and balustrade, and sash windows, as opposed to timber cross-windows, from the outset – and set the scene for the changes in the architecture of the area in the early C18.

Alongside these is a quite extensive supporting cast: the situation is as follows. At Thorpe Underwood there is a house all of brick with shaped gables still of Jacobean type, mullioned windows and diagonally-set chimneystacks; and at Lofthouse one which is the brick equivalent of the houses of hybrid construction in the upland zone, with internal structure of timber. Then at The Priory there is an outbuilding range with brick rustication (cf. Archbishop Frewen's work at Bishopthorpe Palace, West Riding South, 1662, and e.g. Wilberforce House, Hull, *c.* 1660); and the same detail appears at Old Thornville, Cattal, along with

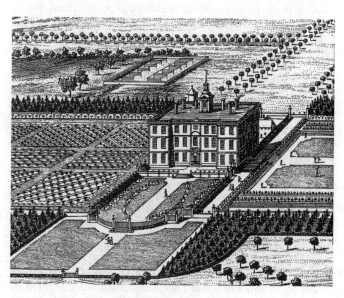

Newby Hall.
Engraving by J. Kip and L. Knyff, 1707

a Dutch gable. The latter feature also occurred at Boroughbridge
Hall, but the house has been altered beyond recognition and the
only other examples are from the end of the century, on a cottage
at Arkendale and, apparently datable to 1693, at the back of a
house in High St Agnesgate, Ripon. This also has the best surviving interior fittings of the late C17 in the area, including a staircase with enriched inverted brackets at the foot and several
56   corner fireplaces, two of them with painted overmantels. Meanwhile, further examples of the hipped-roofed post-Restoration
type appeared at e.g. Whixley Hall (c. 1680) and Long Marston
Hall (largely burned down in the C18); then on a smaller scale at
the Old Rectory at Barwick-in-Elmet (before 1695) and its near-
54   twin at Methley, and particularly at Austhorpe Hall on the edge
of Leeds (1694). The Old Rectories have fronts of five bays:
Austhorpe's is of seven, still with its timber cross-windows,
together with quoins, and a pediment over the centre bay.

By that date similar ideas had also reached the STONE districts
of the centre and w, where the 1690s were a period of marked
architectural change. The characteristic details are cross-
windows, frequently with exaggeratedly steep pediments, and
oval windows set vertically. The first dated example is the wing
p. 360   added to East Riddlesden Hall, Keighley, in 1692, where the ovals
are in three little gables with ball finials; and other examples of
the same style are the wings at Paper Hall and Bolton Old Hall,
both in Bradford, and a range at Old Harden Grange, Bingley
(1704). More ambitious versions, demolished or wholly remodelled in the C18, were a range at Bierley Hall, Bradford, and
p. 103   Arthington Hall (1697), the former with shaped gables crowned
by urns, the latter an exotically detailed composition to rival The
Folly at Settle of twenty years earlier; but the combination of
shaped gable and cross-windows still survives in additions at
Linton Hall, in Wharfedale, of c. 1700. Of yeoman houses more
generally, two examples of the three-unit sort with off-centre
lobby entry, done in the new style, are at Cullingworth and
Wilsden; but more significant is the emergence of a slightly
smaller type which then continues well into the C18. This is
similar to the Old Rectories above except that the roof-ends are
gabled, not hipped: a double pile with symmetrical cross-
windowed five-bay front, and increasingly with the entrance
leading directly into a corner of the housebody rather than a
lobby, and the staircase aligned on it at the back. A point of
departure is provided by e.g. Cragg House, Addingham Moorside (1695) and Eldwick Hall, Bingley (1696), double piles with
not-quite-central lobby entries and the fronts therefore still not
quite symmetrical, and still with mullioned windows – and the
latter with a mixture of classicizing and non-classicizing detail.
53   The type is almost complete at Trench Farm, Baildon (1697),
with smart symmetrical front but irregular at the back; then, it
appears, completely so at Clock House, Manningham, Bradford
(1699) and a house in Banks Lane, Riddlesden, Keighley (1700),
both altered. Undated examples are Castley Hall, Scale House
at Rylstone and the Manor House at Spofforth.

THE GEORGIAN ERA

'Here are Several Gentlemen in these Parts of the World,
that are possess'd with the Spirit of Building'

Sir John Vanbrugh's oft-quoted comment, written at Castle
Howard (North Riding) in 1721, serves to introduce the first of
the period's two main themes: the sense that this was when the
West Riding as a whole quickly rejoined the architectural main-
stream. The 'Several Gentlemen' are part of that both as patrons
and occasionally as designers: alongside them is a quite comprehensive sequence of London-based architects – although Vanbrugh himself is not among them – representing all the phases
of Georgian architecture; but all of them appear only briefly, and
quantitatively it is the work of local practitioners that is dominant. The second theme, belonging to the second half of the
period, is the Industrial Revolution and its architectural consequences; and while the first was developed primarily, but not
exclusively, through the now well-represented medium of the
country house, the second is reflected in a wide range of building types, not just the specifically industrial. The two themes are
intertwined: some of the new industrialists' villas are architecturally indistinguishable from country houses, and while industrial expansion had a particular impact in the growth of towns,
many of the mills themselves were in the country.

Country houses

The account begins immediately, in the first decade of the C18,
with two houses which present parallels to the English BAROQUE
style rather than the style itself. The first, Tong Hall (1702–4),   p. 40
the *chef d'oeuvre* of the Wakefield lawyer-architect *Theophilus
Shelton*, is a scaled-down version of the Newby Hall type but dra-
matized, with a heavy cornice and the pedimented centre half a
storey taller than the rest. The second, Bramham Park   60, p. 206
(*c.* 1705–10), is one of the area's grandest, probably designed by
the owner himself, *Robert Benson*, later first Lord Bingley – long,
low and markedly unornamented, but built up impressively in
stages on the rising ground on the entrance side and set in even
more remarkable grounds. Of the same decade is Esholt Hall
(1706–10), a finely detailed example of the hip-roofed late C17
type. These were followed, on a generally smaller scale, by Bar-
rowby Hall (1718–20) by *William Etty* of York, the leading local
craftsman-architect of the early C18 (*see* below); Farfield Hall
(1728), with giant fluted pilasters and decoration derived from
Chatsworth; and Gisburne Park (1728–36), plain apart from a
Baroque doorcase hinting at the decoration within; and then in
the 1730s in a more conventional pattern-book style by Sleningford Park, North Stainley, and North Stainley Hall, two-and-a-
half-storey boxes. In a more rustic mode, retaining more of a
regional character and still with cross-windows, are Mewith

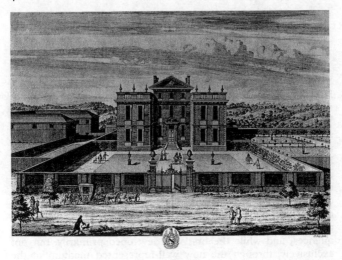

Tong Hall.
Engraving by J. Kip and L. Knyff, 1707

Head Hall, Bentham (1708), with raised centre section recalling
Tong; Dougill Hall, Hartwith (1722) and Stone Gappe,
Lothersdale (1725, altered *c.* 1800), both of two-and-a-half
storeys; and Currer Hall, Beamsley, across the Wharfe from
Farfield Hall, with giant pilasters but oddly disposed.

The first full-dress PALLADIAN country house in the area
was Kirby Hall, Little Ouseburn (dem.), by *Roger Morris, Lord
Burlington,* and the client Stephen Thompson, built in 1747–52,
a design with affinities to Morris's Marble Hill; but Lord Burlington himself had estates – and much of his political power base –
in the northern West Riding, and several of the inner circle of
Palladian architects were employed here well before that. They
include *Colen Campbell* and *Morris* in the grounds at Studley
Royal by the late 1720s (*see* below), possibly *William Kent* likewise at Lord Burlington's own *pied-à-terre* at Bolton Abbey in the
early 1730s, and *Henry Flitcroft* at Swillington House *c.* 1738
p. 285 (dem.); and they were perhaps followed by *Isaac Ware* at Grantley Hall *c.* 1750. The next generation is represented by *James
Paine,* who lived in the southern West Riding for a brief period
at the beginning of his career and subsequently obtained a good
number of commissions there. In the North he did rather less,
but the tally includes one interesting early work, Kirkstall Grange
on the edge of Leeds (1752), and one of his very finest, Stockeld
p. 720 Park (1758–63), a dramatic triple-pedimented composition with
62   a spectacular staircase within. By *c.* 1760, however, the dominant
figure was one of the most famous of Georgian provincial architects, *John Carr* of York. Born at Horbury near Wakefield (West
Riding South) into a family of masons and quarry-owners and
himself a stonemason by training, his success was based on a

reputation for all-round competence and what the C18 called 'good taste'. His first recorded undertaking was the erection of Kirby Hall to Morris's and Lord Burlington's design, one of his first as an architect in his own right was Thorp Arch Hall (1749–56), and his largest country house – one of the prime commissions of the mid C18 in the whole country, secured still quite early in his career – was Edwin Lascelles's Harewood House (1759–71). Of his later houses in the area one might single out Denton Hall (1772–8), where he attempted something of the spatially variegated interior planning developed by Paine and Sir Robert Taylor; the elegant Farnley Hall (1786–90) – one of his best – and the reconstruction of Arthington Hall (c. 1790), where he provided a remarkable staircase to set alongside Paine's at Stockeld. p. 300–1 p. 240

Of the many other country houses of the later C18 four can be mentioned here: Halton Place by the London architect *John Crunden* (1770), a simplified version of Paine's tripartite formula; two demolished works by better-known colleagues, *Wyatt*'s Wetherby Grange (1784) and *Holland*'s Allerton Mauleverer (1788); and, perhaps the most interesting, the rebuilding of Ripley Castle, begun in 1783 by another York architect, *William Belwood*. This is in a minimal GOTHIC style (but classical inside), a mode which is rare amongst the C18 country houses of the area: the only other example was the remodelling of Kippax Park (c. 1750, dem.) by Lord Burlington's clerk of works *Daniel Garrett*. But one famous name is still to appear, that of *Robert Adam*, and for that it is necessary to turn to the INTERIOR DECORATION of the houses. Those of the early C18 present a variety of options. Bramham Park has a monumental cubic entrance hall, with giant pilasters, and a similar one, now subdivided, was created at Whixley Hall by *Etty* in 1718. Several have enriched panelling and other high-quality woodwork, including an overmantel in the manner of Le Pautre and Marot at Tong, one with carving in the style of Grinling Gibbons at Whixley, and at Farfield – where there are also good compartmented ceilings – a particularly fine staircase. But the high point of this phase is the ebullient Baroque plasterwork in several rooms at Gisburne Park, of 1730–3 by the Italian stuccoists *Quadri* and *Vassalli*; and a ceiling of similar style but a few years later is at Carr Head Hall, Cowling.* The next stage is exemplified by the delicate proto-Rococo ceilings at Temple Newsam executed in 1738–45 by *Thomas Perritt* of York but probably designed by *Garrett*, together with a little good-quality mid-C18 decoration at North Stainley Hall and Grantley Hall. Then come the two schemes by *Adam*, both of them extended suites of interiors – his characteristic type of commission – executed by many of his regular team of artificers, including the plasterer *Joseph Rose* and the decorative artists *Biagio Rebecca* and *Antonio Zucchi*. At Harewood (1765–71), where he also proposed some modifications to Carr's

57 61 63

---

* *Vassalli* and *Quadri*, together with *Giovanni* and *Giuseppe Artari*, also worked in the 1730s at Parlington Hall, Aberford (dem.).

design for the house itself, the scheme was one of his most ambitious, encompassing over a dozen rooms, but many were altered
p. 601–2 in the C19. That at Newby Hall (1766–72) for the connoisseur
William Weddell – also done in conjunction with work by Carr
– is smaller but more successful, culminating in the excellent
sculpture gallery, a most persuasive evocation of Antiquity. The
style was copied immediately, notably by Carr himself at Ribston
Hall (c. 1775), Denton and Farnley.

Returning to exteriors, the principal mode of the early C19 was
a smooth post-Wyatt classical, either Tuscan or GRECIAN. Examples of the former are Rudding Park, begun 1807, and Copgrove
Hall, c. 1820 by *Pritchett & Watson* of York; of the latter the wings
58   added to Broughton Hall in 1809–11, and Ingleborough Hall,
Clapham (c. 1814), both by *William Atkinson*, Thomas Hope's
architect at The Deepdene. A correspondingly refined Regency
interior style appeared in *Wyatville*'s drawing room at Browsholme Hall (1805), and then at Rudding and Broughton in particular. Gothic is represented just by a wing at Bolton Hall – the
core of the house is the medieval gatehouse of Bolton Abbey –
by *Peter Atkinson Jun.* of York (1814); but an alternative was
p. 741 established in two interesting houses, Netherside Hall, Threshfield (1820–2) and Eshton Hall (1825–7), which are early works
of the Kendal architect *George Webster*, the leading practitioner in
the W part of the area during the second quarter of the C19. These
are pioneering examples of the scholarly JACOBEAN REVIVAL
style, and at Eshton there is even a hint of the local C17 manner.
So the Georgian story at the end runs almost in a full circle.

Of the GROUNDS, two schemes are of outstanding importance,
outshining most of the houses themselves. The first is Robert
60, p. 209 Benson's at Bramham, begun like the house c. 1705, which is one
of the best surviving examples in the country of the formal grand
manner of Le Nôtre and his followers, its creation involving in
some capacity first the Royal gardener *George London* and later
the young *John Wood*. Other formal designs include the Avenue
at Temple Newsam, laid out by *Etty* (1712). The second major
67   scheme is John Aislabie's Studley Royal,[*] begun c. 1719, where
formal elements are combined, extraordinarily effectively, with a
far from formal site in a narrow winding valley. The culminating
touch, the incorporation into the grounds of the ruins of Fountains Abbey in 1768, was due to Aislabie's son William, who had
previously (c. 1750) brought into being the Sublime woodland
pleasure ground at Hackfall, Grewelthorpe. Another of that type
is Daniel Lascelles's at Plompton, begun in 1755, dramatically
exploiting a series of gritstone outcrops. Of later, landscaped
parks the main example is at Harewood, partly the work of *Capability Brown* (c. 1772–80). A generation later *Repton* was consulted
there (1800–2), and laid out the grounds at Armley House, Leeds
(c. 1803; *see* below) and Oulton Hall (c. 1809). Many of the
schemes incorporate a characteristic complement of GARDEN
BUILDINGS. They include a handsome rotunda and other

[*] The house was demolished after a fire in 1946.

temples at Bramham, a banqueting house (*c.* 1727–30) and
temple (1730s) at Studley Royal, attributable to *Colen Campbell*
and *Roger Morris* respectively, and another banqueting house and
a Gothic tower at Hackfall; but some of the most memorable are
elsewhere – a rustic aqueduct at Bolton Abbey (*c.* 1732) possibly   68
by *William Kent*; an octagonal gazebo at Allerton Mauleverer
perhaps also by him; the delightful Gothic entrance lodges at
Gisburne Park by the owner *Thomas Lister*, first Lord Ribbles-   65
dale, and his agent (1775–7); and the triumphal arch at
Parlington Hall, Aberford, celebrating the American victory in   66
the War of Independence, by *Thomas Leverton* (1781–3). There is
also an excellent series of STABLE BLOCKS, the most substantial
of estate buildings. It starts with that at Studley Royal, 1729–30   64
by *Campbell* and *Morris*, and the smaller one at Bramham,
perhaps by *Wood*; and others are at e.g. Harewood (1755–8);
Kirby Hall, Plompton, Gledstone, Ribston and Denton, probably all by *Carr* – Gledstone's with a remarkable circular courtyard – and Newby Hall by *Belwood* (1777). With these can be
grouped MODEL FARMS, e.g. at Plompton, again by *Carr*
(*c.* 1760), the Home Farm complex at Harewood (*c.* 1763),
Parlington, Farnley, and Broughton (1816).

Other housing, rural and urban

Of early C18 YEOMAN houses, examples of the five-bay double
pile type established *c.* 1700 are Hollins Hill Farmhouse,
Guiseley (1720) and St Helens, Eshton (but both with their
cross-windows changed to sashes). The persistence of the
traditional C17 manner is shown by e.g. Kettlesing Grange,
Felliscliffe (1731) and Mould Greave, Oxenhope (1742); and
contrasting compromises between old and new are Colton
House, Burnsall (1723) and Brooksbank House, Great Horton,
Bradford (1746). In the Sedbergh area, where there are few signs
of major rebuilding before the end of the C17, a particular feature
is the wealth of internal woodwork – panelled partitions, staircases etc. – e.g. at High Oaks (1706) and Hollin Hill (1712),
Sedbergh, and Low Haygarth, Cautley (1728).

For middling Georgian TOWN HOUSES of the sort which will
have been widespread the best location now is probably Knaresborough, although some remain in other market towns. There is,
however, an interesting group which are rather grander and
detached. The earliest, e.g. the Manor Hall in Kirkgate, Bradford
(1705–7), similar in style to Esholt Hall, were demolished in the
C19. Surviving are Lord Burlington's 'New House' at Skipton,
now the Devonshire Hotel (1728–30), which has a little of the
character of a Palladian villa; Minster House, now the Deanery,
at Ripon, with panelling and fine staircase like those at Farfield
Hall; and Knaresborough House (*c.* 1768), perhaps by *Carr*; and
to these can be added the Old Hall at Ripon (1738), smaller and
plainer but with a little good-quality plasterwork in the manner
of *Cortese*. Then come the VILLAS built on the edges of towns by

merchants, industrialists etc., the main concentration of them unsurprisingly in the vicinity of Leeds (and now within the city). An early example, it appears, is Little Woodhouse Hall (*c.* 1741,

59 altered *c.* 1840 etc.), the grandest from the C18 nearby Denison Hall, 1786 by Carr's former assistant *William Lindley* for the merchant John Denison, with fine Adam-style interiors. A distingushed Grecian sequence follows, notably Armley

p. 566 House, as remodelled *c.* 1817 by *Robert Smirke* for the industrialist Benjamin Gott, and Gledhow Grove, *c.* 1835 by *John Clark* (*see* below): Roundhay Park Mansion, *c.* 1816 for the banker Thomas Nicholson, further from the town on a substantial estate, is perhaps halfway between a villa and a country house. At Bradford nothing survives earlier than *c.* 1830 – Bolton Royd, Manningham – but examples also occur on the edges of smaller towns, e.g. Anley House, Settle (*c.* 1818, Grecian) and Aireville Hall, Skipton (1836, Neo-Jacobean, perhaps by *Webster*), both for bankers; and Eastwood House, Keighley (1819).

Urban PLANNED DEVELOPMENT for housing during this period was almost entirely confined to Leeds, principally the formation from *c.* 1770 of a 'West End', centred on Park Square (laid out 1788), with seemly brick-built houses, some of them pedimented. The main developers were two carpenters, *John Cordingley* and *William Hargrave*. But there was an earlier, if rudimentary, hint of regular planning in the country, at the Moravian settlement of Fulneck, begun in 1746; and alongside this

69 can be placed the two model estate villages of Harewood (begun *c.* 1755) and Ripley (*c.* 1820–35), although both were built piecemeal on the site of the old village, not from scratch on a new one. Elements of planning can also be found occasionally in the field of industrial WORKERS' HOUSING. Cottages built for their workers by the owners of the new textile mills start to appear *c.* 1800, e.g. a row at Vale Mill, Cross Roads with Lees, and Iron Row, Burley-in-Wharfedale (*c.* 1820); and other early C19 developments survive particularly at Thornton – Cloggers Row (1806), South Square (1832) etc. – and Great Horton, Bradford, the latter including some of the very basic single-storey 'low houses'. Housing for handloom weavers, of the sort common further s in the Colne and Calder valleys (West Riding South), with a loomshop occupying the top floor, is rare here: Weavers Court, Armley, Leeds, is an example (late C18), but an alternative arrangement is represented by the Rookery at Addingham (*c.* 1805), two rows of back-to-back cottages with loomshops attached. A cottage of *c.* 1800 in Railton Yard, Sedbergh, has an external spinning gallery.

Churches and chapels

Churches of the C18 are not common, but no rarer than might be expected. The earliest and grandest is Holy Trinity, Leeds, 1722–7 by *William Etty* in the manner of James Gibbs, with

admirably sensitive Wren-style spire of 1839 by *R. D. Chantrell.**
The most remarkable is Allerton Mauleverer, 1745 for Richard   73
Arundell, friend of Lord Burlington and erstwhile Surveyor of
the King's Works, almost certainly by *John Vardy*, one of his
subordinates there. The style is a mixture of simplified Palladian,
proto-Neo-Norman, a little Gothick and a sort of C17 Revival;
the plan cruciform, with a central tower. A more conventional
Georgian country church mode, with nave, chancel and w tower,
is represented by Tong (1727) and Addingham (1757), the former
of which has a particularly well-preserved interior, complete with
three-decker pulpit, hierarchically graduated box pews, and w
gallery. Two more – Bierley, Bradford (1766) and Denton (1776)
– are by *Carr*, the former a Palladian box, the latter superficially
Gothic. More wholeheartedly in that style is Aldfield (1783),   74
small, T-shaped, with another well-preserved interior, covered by
a delightful plaster rib-vault. An interesting case is Kirkby
Overblow, which was extensively restored by the Rector between
1778 and 1802: also Gothic, with some of the detail surprisingly
good for the period. Then at the end of the century came Leeds's
fourth church, St Paul (1791–3, large, classical; dem. 1905).
Of C18 FURNISHINGS otherwise, the best are the three-decker
pulpit and complement of pews at Slaidburn, then the same
items at Weston.

In the early C19, after *c.* 1810, the position changes. Many more
were built, many – but not all – in the expanding towns and mill
villages, virtually all were Gothic and several of them were large
and serious, designed by architects who specialized in ecclesiastical commissions. The first example of that trend was Bradford's
second church, Christ Church (1813–15, dem. 1878), by *Thomas
Taylor*, a former assistant of James Wyatt who had established
himself at Leeds. By far the finest is *Rickman*'s at Oulton   75
(1827–9), one of his best, its form as well as its detail properly
medieval, with aisles, clerestory and full-length chancel. There is
even real vaulting. Others are e.g. Pudsey (1821–4) and Holy
Trinity, Ripon (1826–7), both again by *Taylor*, and Shipley
(1823–6) by *John Oates* of Halifax. Pudsey and Shipley are both
early Commissioners' churches, built under the Act of 1818, and
have the galleries and undeveloped chancels associated with their
kind; but both are unusually lavish compared with most of those
which followed. More typical is Idle, Bradford (1828–30), also by
Oates, a box-and-tower in simple lancet style with the galleries
on cast-iron supports.

The finest of the C18 NONCONFORMIST CHAPELS is again the
earliest surviving, the Moravian chapel at Fulneck (1746–8). It
approximates in monumental form to a characteristic early type
which is more accurately represented by a second Moravian
chapel, at Wyke (1775): a simple unadorned rectangle, wider than
it is deep, with two tall windows in the middle of the front and
doorways l. and r. Internally the pulpit is between the two windows

---

* The interior was much altered in 1883, the galleries removed etc.

and a gallery runs round the other three sides. By the early C19 the internal arrangement is reversed, with the pulpit against the back wall; and then more radically the proportions change, the rectangle becoming deeper than it is wide, usually with a gable or pediment to the front. Examples of the intermediate stage are the Congregational chapels at Grassington (1811), Tosside (1812–13) – with manse adjoining to one side, under the same roof – and Horton-in-Craven (1816); of the completed process the former Methodist chapel at Skipton (1811, interior altered), the Congregational chapel at Wyke (1824) and the Hall Green Baptist Chapel at Haworth (1824–5). The latter type provided the blueprint for most of the larger and more ornate chapels of the mid and later C19: the classic early example was *Joseph Botham*'s Brunswick Chapel, Leeds (1824–5, dem.), but a survivor of sorts from this period (exterior only) is the former Salem Congregational Chapel at Bradford (1834–6), with quirky Grecian façade. In addition, the sequence of Friends' Meeting Houses continues, e.g. at Grindleton (1777) and Bentham (1798); and there is a small group of early ROMAN CATHOLIC chapels and churches. The first, at Aberford (1793) and Bishop Thornton (1809), are very humble. The next step was the Catholic Emancipation Act of 1829, and an immediate post-Emancipation example, still more or less unobtrusively domestic-looking, is at Knaresborough, 1831 by *John Child*; but the story thereafter belongs to the Victorian period.

Funerary monuments

The list is headed by the Mausoleum of the Thompson family at Little Ouseburn, of 1743, possibly by *Roger Morris*, a pseudo-peripteral rotunda with a number of interesting details. The most ambitious otherwise start with a type continued from the late C17, with a semi-reclining effigy usually accompanied by mourning spouse. The first is Sir Walter Vavasour's (†1713) at Hazlewood Castle, with kneeling wife at his feet and two children at his head (cf. Viscount Irwin, †1688, at Whitkirk, above). Next comes Sir Edward Blackett (†1718) in Ripon Cathedral, by *John Hancock*, with two wives standing; and then two Savile monuments at Methley, *Scheemakers*'s to Charles Savile (†1741), with wife seated – the backplate unfortunately removed – and *Wilton*'s to the first Earl of Mexborough (†1778). Of other forms, at Long Marston there is a monument consisting of an obelisk and three busts (†1740), and at Goldsborough the excellent Byerley family memorial by *Wilton* again, c. 1766, an aedicule framing figures of Faith and Charity, with medallions of those commemorated.* A very fine NEOCLASSICAL monument is William Weddell's (†1792) in Ripon Cathedral, a half-rotunda based on the Choragic Monument of Lysicrates, with a bust by *Nollekens* within; and also by him is that to the ninth Viscount and Viscountess

*The monument to Sir John Gascoigne (†1723) by *Galilei* at Barwick-in-Elmet was destroyed in the C19.

Irwin at Whitkirk (1810), with a Grecian female figure bowed over
an urn. Then come the works of the Rome-based Yorkshireman
Joseph Gott, a pupil of Flaxman. By him are one in St Peter Leeds,
(†1828), a bust flanked by figures of soldiers; and those at
Armley, Leeds, to his relatives the industrialist Benjamin Gott
(†1839) – who had sent him to Rome in 1824 – and the latter's
son Benjamin junior (†1814). The son's is another variant on the
theme of a Grecian female with an urn, the father's once again
a semi-reclining figure – but in the almost obsessive accuracy of
costume details perhaps more Victorian than Neoclassical.

The lesser wall monuments present a more continuous stylistic progression, Baroque cartouches and aedicules succeeded by
Palladian and then Neoclassical panels and tablets. Putti appear
until the late C18, overlapping with portrait medallions – and
relief sarcophagi and urns – which all begin in the mid C18. Of
reliefs otherwise, there is a memorable man o' war (Admiral
Fairfax †1725) at Newton Kyme, and at Bradford Cathedral a
trophy of mathematical instruments by *Scheemakers*, to the math-
ematician Abraham Sharp (†1742); but most are from the 1790s
on. Specially pleasing is one by *Flaxman* (*c*. 1810), of a teacher   78
and two pupils, also at Bradford, and another by him is at
St Peter, Leeds (1811): one by *Westmacott*, a Raising of Lazarus
(†1821), is at Methley. Recurring themes are the female mourner
again (e.g. at Denton †1795 by *Robert Cooke*, Methley †1821 and
1828 by *Blore*, and Bradford †1833 again by *Gott*) and the dying
or weeping tree (Leeds Holy Trinity †1821, Haworth †1822,
Denton †1839, by *Leyland* of Halifax). Striking individual subjects are Eddystone lighthouse on the monument to the engineer
John Smeaton (†1792) at Whitkirk, Leeds, by *Cooke*, and the construction of the Leeds and Liverpool Canal on that of the canal
superintendent Joseph Priestley (†1817) at Bradford, by *William
Pistell*. Other London-based statuaries represented in the area
are *J. F. Moore* (Bradford †1767), the Fleming *John Devaere*
(Thornton-in-Craven †1778, 1784), *Coade & Co.* – i.e. Coade
stone – (Kirkby Overblow †1793), and *John Bacon Jun.*
(Bradford †1800). Of the local artificers, *John Carr* appears early
in his career as the maker of a pedimented Palladian panel,
without sculpture, at Otley (†1747); but the leading figures were
the three generations of the *Fisher* family of York, whose work
runs from the 1770s to the mid C19. Others are *Michael Taylor* of
York and *Skelton* of York. A curiosity is a tablet at Swillington
(†1771) in the form of a scroll unrolled against a Gothic tomb-
chest; and at the end of the period GOTHIC tablet designs,
usually in a form suggesting a miniature tomb-recess, begin to
appear, e.g. at Skipton (†1820) by the *Webster* firm of Kendal –
evidently pioneers of this development – and Otley (†1825).

Public buildings

The position broadly parallels that of the churches, except that
much more has been lost. From the early C18 there is a small

variegated group of particular interest. The first item is a solitary
work by *Hawksmoor*, a civic adornment rather than a building,
the obelisk erected in Ripon Market Place in 1702 (rebuilt 1781)
largely at the cost of John Aislabie of Studley Royal, which was
one of the earliest full-size obelisks in Britain. The second was
the Moot Hall at Leeds (1710, dem. 1827) by *William Etty*, more
or less Baroque, with giant pilasters. The third is the remarkably
monumental Fountain's Hospital (almshouses) at Linton of
c. 1725, the one work in the area decidedly in the style of
Vanbrugh, for which *Etty* – who became clerk of works at Castle
Howard in 1721 – is again a possible candidate as architect. But
apart perhaps from the series of cloth halls (for which *see* Commercial and industrial buildings, below) it was only at the turn
of the century that a real body of architecturally significant urban
public buildings began to appear. Before that, there are two quite
handsome early C18 SCHOOLS, at Sedbergh (1716) and Slaidburn
(1717), the former not in a local style, the latter with the usual
cross-windows: others show less ambition (e.g. Knaresborough,
1741) but that at Burnt Yates is an interesting case of architectural
conservatism, with mullion-and-transom windows as late as
1760. From the second half of the C18 the most important
loss is *Carr*'s General Infirmary at Leeds (1768–71, dem. 1893).
Survivors are the much-altered Parish Poorhouse at
Rothwell (1772) and the Old Town Hall at Skipton (1789).

The later series begins with *Wyatt*'s Town Hall at Ripon
(1799–1801), a town hall of the assembly room type. Those which
followed were mainly in the Grecian style, and included early
works by two architects from elsewhere who established practices
at Leeds, *R. D. Chantrell*, a pupil of Sir John Soane, and the Scot
John Clark; but most have been demolished. These include the
Court Houses at Leeds and Bradford (1811–13 and 1834–5), the
former by *Thomas Taylor*; the Leeds Philosophical Hall (1819–22)
and South Market (1823–4), by *Chantrell*; the Leeds Central
Market, by *Francis Goodwin* (1824–7); the Commercial Buildings
there – a sort of Exchange – by *Clark* (1826–9); and the Victoria
Baths (1832) and Spa Rooms (1835) at Harrogate, also by him.
Survivors are the Leeds Library, by *Thomas Johnson* of Leeds
(1808); the gatehouse and chapel of the former Woodhouse
Cemetery, Leeds (now St George's Fields), by *Clark* (1835); and,
altered out of recognition, *Goodwin*'s former Exchange Buildings
at Bradford (1826–8). In a different vein are the cell block of the
Ripon House of Correction, 1816 by the third *Lord Grantham*
(later, as Earl de Grey, first President of the Institute of British
Architects); and *Webster*'s Settle Town Hall – another set of public
rooms – in his hallmark Jacobean style (1832–3).

A further dimension, however, was the development of the
infrastructure of TRANSPORT. The great undertaking was the
Leeds and Liverpool Canal, in effect a W continuation, across
the Pennines, of the earlier (1704) Aire & Calder Navigation.
The E section, between Leeds and Gargrave, together with the
branch to Bradford (and the corresponding W part, from Liverpool to Wigan), were constructed *c.* 1770–7 by the engineer *John*

Longbotham of Halifax, the summit stretch *c.* 1790–1816 by *Robert Whitworth*. The engineering works include the famous Five Rise Locks at Bingley (1773–4). In addition a number of important 70 roads were turnpiked (e.g. the Keighley–Kendal, 1753) and many road BRIDGES were widened or rebuilt. Most of the latter lack a strongly individual character but some of those erected during the West Riding Bridges surveyorship of *Bernard Hartley Sen.* (1797–1834) are marked out by their vigorously textured masonry (e.g. Lower Hodder Bridge, Great Mitton, 1826). *Rennie*'s Wellington Bridge, Leeds (1817–19, widened), built for Benjamin Gott, is a single elliptical arch of 100 ft (30 metres) span. Newlay Bridge at Horsforth (1819) is of cast iron with a few Gothic details, made by *Aydon & Elwell* of Shelf.

Commercial and industrial buildings

Straddling the divide between public and commercial buildings were the CLOTH, or PIECE, HALLS for the buying and selling of cloth by clothiers and merchants, a feature of the pre-factory industrial system. At Leeds no fewer than five were built during the C18, the First, Second and Third White Cloth Halls (1711, 1756 and 1776–7), the Coloured Cloth Hall (1757) and the Irregulars' Hall (1793); and at Bradford one (1773). Of these the first Leeds hall, and part of the third, survive, although altered. Both were of quadrangular form, mainly single-storeyed: the Coloured Cloth Hall was similar but larger. Bradford's was a single range, of two storeys.

So to the early TEXTILE MILLS; and first a note on the area's textile industry generally during this period. There were three main pre-existing branches – 'woollen' (i.e. heavy wool cloth for coats, blankets etc.), worsted (lighter wool cloth) and linen – and alongside these cotton was introduced when mass industrialization effectively began in the 1780s. The worsted industry was centred on Bradford; the woollen further E, towards Leeds, and further S, in the Huddersfield area (West Riding South); cotton to the NW, in Craven; and linen at Leeds and in Nidderdale; but the distribution was not totally static, and in the early C19 the Keighley area largely shifted back from cotton to worsted manufacture. With regard to the main manufacturing processes, broadly, spinning was mechanized earlier than weaving, and cotton manufacture before wool and linen; but certain others, notably fulling – the vigorous washing of woollen cloth – had been mechanized since the Middle Ages. So most of the mills in the area built during this period were for spinning, and most of the earliest, of the 1780s and 1790s, were at least originally for cotton; but an important, if exceptional, development from the 1790s on, as yet limited to the woollen and linen branches, was the 'integrated' mill, in which all or most of the processes, whether mechanized or not, were brought together on a single site – the full 'factory system' which looks forward to the fully mechanized integrated mills of the Victorian period. As to the power source, the earliest mills were of course water-powered: many of them took the place of corn mills, and in a few cases corn mills were simply converted to textile manufacture without rebuilding. Steam power appeared in the 1790s, but there was no universal shift from the one source to the other. Many mills used both, and at some water power continued in use until the C20.

Many of the early mills have been lost, not just to C20 demolition but as a result of repeated C19 rebuilding and their extreme vulnerability to fire. Surviving C18 examples, all originally for cotton spinning, are Langcliffe Mill in Ribblesdale (1783), High Mill, Addingham (1788) – erstwhile neighbour to the first worsted spinning mill, Addingham Low Mill (1787, dem.) – and Ponden Mill, Stanbury (1791–2). Benjamin Gott's epoch-making Bean Ing Mills at Leeds (1792 etc.), an integrated steam-powered woollen mill, was demolished c. 1960; but the main surviving concentration of examples from the early C19 is in the city. Extensive buildings of 1806 on remain at Marshall's Mill (flax spinning, founded 1791); and Winker Green Mill, Armley (1825–36) is a smaller-scale counterpart to Bean Ing, with a workshop range for hand spinning and handloom weaving and a steam-powered main mill for fulling etc. Aireworth Mills at Keighley, a water-powered cotton spinning mill of 1787 rebuilt in 1808, was converted to worsted spinning in 1813 and equipped with power looms and steam power c. 1835. As to the buildings themselves, their pre-eminent characteristic was their extreme plainness, typically multi-storey ranges with many bays of close-set windows – although Bean Ing ran to a projecting pedimented centre on the main mill. The main refinement to appear during the course of this period was the system of FIREPROOF FLOOR CONSTRUCTION, with segmental brick vaults on cast-iron beams and columns, which had been pioneered at Ditherington Mill, Shrewsbury (1796–7). It was first used in Yorkshire in 1802–3 at Benyon's Mill, Leeds (flax spinning; from c. 1804–5 an integrated mill; dem.), which was built by the same engineer as

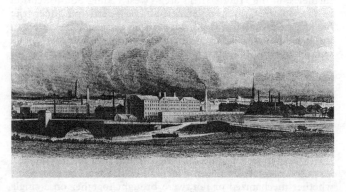

Leeds, Bean Ing Mills.
Engraving by C. Fowler, 1832

Ditherington Mill, *Charles Bage*, and for the same partnership; and then at e.g. Armley Mills, Leeds (1805–7), and Marshall's Mill – whose owner also had an interest in Ditherington Mill. Compromise measures were cast-iron columns supporting timber beams and floors, and iron plating on woodwork.

Of other buildings associated with the textile industry, there remain a substantial three-storey loomshop for handloom weavers (1817) at Addingham; a flax-dressing shop (1825) in Whiteley Yard, Knaresborough; and a few early examples of the characteristic WAREHOUSES for the storage and display of finished cloth – as opposed to those for the storage of raw materials – which already have more architectural enrichment than the mills themselves. They are the misleadingly named Piece 72 Hall at Addingham, a handsome little building of *c*. 1826 built by the same local entrepreneur as the loomshop, and a group in Piccadilly, Bradford, of the early 1830s. Other industries can be dealt with quickly. LEAD MINING and smelting in the late C18 and early C19 has left remains – of smelting mills, tunnel portals, watercourses etc. – on the moors particularly at Greenhow and above Grassington; elements of two late C18 IRON FOUNDRIES survive at Leeds (but nothing of their counterparts at Bradford); and of PAPER MILLS at Knaresborough (1770) and Keighley (1822). Returning to more agricultural matters, there are several water-powered CORN MILLS, the most substantial Thwaite Mill at Stourton, Leeds (1823–5).

VICTORIAN AND EDWARDIAN

Throughout much of the area this was the period of transformation, much of it driven by the continued expansion of the wool textile industry. Existing towns expanded vastly – the largest, Leeds and Bradford, turning into cities – and their centres were largely if not entirely rebuilt; villages grew into towns, and some completely new urban entities appeared. So the central architectural fact is the sheer quantity of material to be seen. With regard to the architects and their backgrounds, the position is broadly similar to that in Georgian times. There is an impressive roll-call of well-known London architects, but their contribution was mainly confined to churches and none of them produced a really large body of work in the area: rather it was the local representatives of a profession now burgeoning particularly in Leeds and Bradford who again obtained the lion's share of the commissions, and indeed the county appears to have gained a reputation in the London architecural press as terrain distinctly unwelcoming to outsiders. All this has implications for the question of regional character in architecture. Regional distinctiveness during this period lies in topography, the types of buildings erected – particularly those associated with industry, commerce and perhaps Nonconformity – building materials, and only lastly in architectural style; but the local architects perhaps had an advantage over their London rivals in relation to the effective combination of local materials and the modification of architectural vocabularies to respond to the specific requirements and conditions of the area.

Churches

There is a wide variation of quality, the best exceptionally fine, others no more than routine. The busiest periods appear to have been the 1840s and then the 1870s. Medieval styles, overwhelmingly Gothic, are universal. The story during the EARLY VICTORIAN phase has several strands. It starts emphatically with the rebuilding of the medieval parish church at Leeds (St Peter) in 1837–41 by *R. D. Chantrell* for the energetic High Church vicar the Rev. W. F. Hook. The scheme was just too early to reflect the teachings of Pugin and the Ecclesiologists – it has the long chancel (echoing the previous building) of which the latter would have approved, the galleries which they would not – but Chantrell's contribution more generally to the church architecture of the time is that in his mature churches he developed a relatively solid and scholarly Gothic mode largely without reference to those influences. Other examples are Christ Church, Skipton (1837–9), Denholme (1843–6) and St Andrew, Keighley (1846–8). Also from the 1830s are two Roman Catholic churches: St Stephen, Skipton, 1836–8 by *Richard Lane* of Manchester, which presents a development in the same direction as Chantrell's own, and St Anne, Keighley, 1838–40, a minor work by *Pugin* himself although much altered and enlarged. Another interesting initiative was *Salvin's* reconstruction of Arncliffe church (1841) for the Rev. William Boyd – a rural counterpart to Dean Hook, who desired for his church 'somewhat of a more ecclesiastical and religious character' – and then the quintessential Tractarian project was St Saviour, Leeds, 1842–5 by *J. M. Derick*, a lavishly appointed church in a poor part of the town, in the Ecclesiologists' favoured Middle Pointed, paid for by one of the founders of the Oxford Movement, Dr Edward Pusey.

Meanwhile, churches in an entirely pre-Ecclesiological manner continued to be built at least until the mid 1840s, some of them still more Georgian than Victorian in character, e.g. *J. P. Pritchett's* charming chapel at Brearton (1836). A group in the NW of the area – Cowgill (1837–8), Howgill (1838) and Stainforth (1839–41) – is by *Edmund Sharpe*, founder of the long-lived Lancaster practice which was subsequently Sharpe & Paley, later Paley & Austin etc. Another interesting architect of this phase was *R. H. Sharp* of York, whose works include the curious St John, Bowling, Bradford (1840–2), built by the Bowling Iron Co., which combines the usual lancet style with masonry vaulting and extensive use of cast iron, and one of the most memorable products of the short-lived NEO-NORMAN fashion of the 1840s, the little chapel at Roecliffe (1843–4), also vaulted. By far

80
p. 400

p. 353

the most ambitious of that group is another Roman Catholic
church, at Clifford (1845–9), built by *J. A. Hansom* to a design by   81
an artist named *Ramsay* but with an excellent later tower by
Goldie; and an exceptionally serious one is at Oxenhope, by
Ignatius Bonomi & J. A. Cory (1849). Others are St Thomas,
Farsley (*H. Rogerson*, 1839–41), St John, Keighley (*Walker
Rawstorne*, 1841–3) and Shadwell, Leeds (*Chantrell*, 1842).

Thereafter the course of events is more straightforward.
Regarding the work of LONDON ARCHITECTS, there is a very
early church by *Butterfield* at Cautley near Sedbergh (1845–7),
small, serious and unfussy; two from the 1850s by *G. G. Scott* –
Weeton (1851–2) and Bilton, Harrogate (1851–7), both sound
E.E. – and then, more important, his final church, All Souls,
Blackman Lane, Leeds (1876–80), also E.E. High Victorian
vigour first appeared in the small church at Blubberhouses (1856)
by the 'rogue' architect *E. B. Lamb*; next at *Norman Shaw*'s early
Holy Trinity, Bingley (1866–8, dem.), in the muscular manner of
his master G. E. Street; and reaches its splendid climax in *William
Burges*'s two sumptuous estate churches at Skelton (1871–6) and   85, p. 54
Studley Royal (1871–8), respectively for Lady Mary Vyner of   88
Newby Hall, and her son-in-law and daughter the first Marquess
and Marchioness of Ripon. A different effect, of power through
austerity, is provided at St Hilda, Leeds (1876–82), daughter
church of St Saviour, by the archaeologist-architect *J. T. Micklethwaite*. Then the Late Victorian phase begins with *Pearson*'s
Horsforth (1877–83) and St Michael, Headingley, Leeds   86
(1884–6), both major works in his careful refined E.E.; and
Norman Shaw's St Margaret, Ilkley (1878–9), which marks the
return to English Perp in the area. Later come *G. F. Bodley*'s St
Matthew, Chapel Allerton, Leeds (1897–9), with striking near-   90
detached tower, and *J. Oldrid Scott*'s finely detailed St Mark,
Harrogate (1898–1905). But the late C19 also presented some
other options. One is the Early-Christian-cum-Romanesque
basilica of St Aidan, Harehills, Leeds, 1889–94 by *R. J. Johnson*   87
& A. Crawford Hick – not London architects but not locals either
(they were based at Newcastle) and best mentioned here – of
austere brick without but richly appointed within, including
Brangwyn's famous mosaics (1916). Another is *T. G. Jackson*'s
Giggleswick school chapel (1897–1901), his celebrated exposition   89
of a cruciform Gothic church with a dome. The high level of
achievement was then maintained through the Edwardian period
in two churches by *Temple Moore*. St Wilfrid, Harrogate (begun
1904), is his masterwork, big, cruciform, once again in E.E. style,
handled throughout with unostentatious freedom; and St Wilfrid,   93
Bradford (1905), is an airy hall church of great beauty. A third,
St Margaret, Cardigan Road, Leeds (1907–9), was not completed
to his design but shows the master's hand clearly enough.

Of the LOCAL ARCHITECTS, the most important in the field
of church design was the Bradford practice which began *c.* 1846
as *Mallinson & Healey* and after the latter's death in 1863 and
Mallinson's departure was continued by Healey's sons as *T. H. &
F. Healey*. The firm makes an interesting study. Although rarely

Skelton, Christ the Consoler.
Engraving, 1878

startlingly original, they evidently kept abreast of the changes of
taste in ecclesiastical architecture throughout the period and
responded to them rapidly, and their best work is of excellent
quality. The elder Healey was a pupil of R. D. Chantrell, and from
the outset Mallinson & Healey were competent exponents of
the orthodox Ecclesiological manner, occasionally enlivened by
attractive individual details (e.g. St Matthew, Bankfoot, Bradford, 1848–9, etc.). The climax of this phase was All Saints, Little

Horton Green, Bradford (1861–4), a big and elaborate church after the manner of G. G. Scott; but their most creative period came with the second generation. From the mid 1860s on they produced a series of churches in a C13 Anglo-Norman style reminiscent of the work of the early 1860s of Pearson and James Brooks, with clean uncluttered outlines, plate tracery, in two cases smooth semicircular apses, and fine towers with spires. The best is St John, Great Horton, Bradford (1871–4); others are 82 St Barnabas, Heaton, Bradford (1864), and Thornton (1870–2). Then after *c.* 1880 this style alternates with Late Victorian free Dec and Perp with occasional Arts and Crafts details, but in similar compositions and with the series of good towers continuing (St Luke, Manningham, Bradford, 1880; St Luke, Harrogate, 1895–7, etc.).

A few others can be mentioned more briefly. Ecclesiological precepts were adopted at an early date by a little-known York architect, *A. H. Cates* (Markington, 1843–4; South Stainley, 1845), and a little more hesitantly by *Perkin & Backhouse* of Leeds (East Morton, 1849–50, etc.). In the mid-Victorian years, *W. H. Crossland*, a pupil of G. G. Scott who was based in Leeds *c.* 1864–70, was co-architect with Scott's 'friend and tormentor', the Leeds banking dynast *Edmund Beckett Denison* (later first Lord Grimthorpe) of the elegant St Chad, Far Headingley, Leeds (1868), but his other work in the area is less notable; while from *Paley & Austin* – effectively locals in the W of the area – there is one church of their High Victorian phase (Burton-in-Lonsdale, 1868–70, E.E.), but most of their work here was in restorations and schools (*see* below). The Bradford firm of *Andrews & Pepper*, not primarily associated with churches, produced two interesting essays in the C13 Anglo-French style – perhaps more consciously muscular than their counterparts by the Healey Brothers – Christ Church, Shipley (1868–9, unfinished), and St James, Bolton, Bradford (1876–7); but one of the area's finest Victorian churches, St Bartholomew, Armley, Leeds (1872–7), a great powerful cruciform mass in E.E. style with prominent crossing tower, 83 is also one of its puzzles, the sole large-scale work of the Leeds practice of *Walker & Athron*. Of later figures, *C. Hodgson Fowler* of Durham did some pleasant village churches (Burton Leonard, 1877–8; Bishop Monkton, 1878–9) and *W. Swinden Barber* of Halifax some larger, more austere ones (Drighlington, 1878–80; East Ardsley, 1880–1). In the early C20 significant contributors were *Connon & Chorley* of Leeds, e.g. at Winksley (1914–17), a free Perp reminiscence of Albi.

Meanwhile, the ROMAN CATHOLICS continued to employ a different range of architects. In the mid C19 the principal figures were the brothers *J. A.* and *C. F. Hansom*, and *George Goldie*. The younger Hansom did two minor churches in simple Puginian Dec style (Sicklinghall, 1849–54; Otley, 1850–1); his elder brother the massive Mount St Mary, Leeds (1853–7), neighbour and rival to Pusey's St Saviour,* and the theatrical French Gothic

---

*Completed in 1866 to a different design by *E. W. Pugin*.

St Wilfrid, Ripon (1860–2); and Goldie St Patrick, Bradford (1852–3, Dec), and St Robert, Harrogate (1872–3), starker, of brick, in early French Gothic again. Then from the 1870s there was a local architect of some ability concentrating almost exclusively on R.C. churches, *Edward Simpson* of Bradford. He started in the same French Gothic mode as his predecessors (St Mary, East Parade, Bradford, 1874–6), but then developed his own highly idiosyncratic version of C13 Gothic, e.g. St Joseph, Pakington Street, Bradford (1885–7). A further change of direction at the beginning of the C20 brings in the climax: St Anne's Cathedral, Leeds, by *J. H. Eastwood* and *S. K. Greenslade* (1901–4), a distinguished piece of Arts and Crafts Gothic to set alongside the churches of the period by Temple Moore.

Finally, a word about RESTORATIONS of medieval churches. There were over sixty such projects in the area, the largest numbers during the 1860s and 1870s, and the identities of the relative saints and sinners are not necessarily quite as might be expected. The most important scheme was of course one of *Scott*'s, at Ripon Cathedral (1862–72), which Professor Wilson refers to as 'one of [his] least controversial'; and there is indeed little about it that one need regret. At most of his others also (Farnham 1854, Goldsborough 1859, Whixley 1862, Long Marston 1869, Bilton-in-Ainsty 1869–71) the result is at least visually harmonious; but at Harewood (1862–3) the loss of C18 woodwork is immediately apparent in the chilliness of the interior. The other leading practitioners, also with seven schemes, were *Paley & Austin*. Post-medieval fittings, although not totally unscathed, generally fared better at their hands, and one scheme, at Kirkby Malham (1879–80), was markedly restrained overall; but two others at least – Little Ouseburn (1875), Giggleswick (1890–2) – were certainly invasive, the latter evidently the subject of some disagreement at the time. Two important churches, Bolton Abbey and Adel, received notably sympathetic restorations from *G. E. Street* (1866–7 and 1878–9); Hubberholme (1863) and Knaresborough (1871–2) more muscular ones from *Ewan Christian*, adviser to the Ecclesiastical Commissioners. Another difficult case was that of the C17 St John's church in Leeds, restored in 1866–8 by *Norman Shaw*, who had previously campaigned against its proposed demolition; but Shaw later referred to his 'dismal failures' there, and a further 'reparation' and re-restoration were carried out in 1884–8. But the worst damage was done by lesser figures, mainly local, and their clients, whose enthusiasm was evidently not matched by an awareness of actual medieval architecture, e.g. *J. W. Hugall* at Spofforth (1854), *John Varley* engineer of Skipton at Burnsall (1858–9) and Linton (1861), and *J. B. & W. Atkinson* of York at Ripley (1862).

Stained glass and other church furnishings, and church monuments

The quantity of STAINED GLASS is again vast and the quality even more varied – so a particularly selective approach is necessary – but here it is the manufacturers with a nationwide reach who dominate. One can start with that designed by *Pugin* at St Saviour, Leeds, and Bolton Abbey, made by *O'Connor* (*c.* 1845) and *Crace* (1853) respectively, all in scholarly c13 style, the colours glowing but not strident, and the scale of the figures finely judged. Otherwise the 1850s were marked by the ubiquity of *William Wailes's* work, the beginnings of the unaccountable popularity of *Capronnier* of Brussels, and a theatrical window at Sharow by *Hedgeland* (1853), partly after Raphael. The second high point comes with the foundation of *Morris & Co.* in 1861, for the area is particularly rich in glass from the firm's early and most interesting years. The earliest of all, of 1861 and 1862, was for private houses not for churches (*see* below), then in 1863–4 there followed the E and a chancel S window at Bradford Cathedral – unfortunately no longer in their original form – designed by *Morris* himself and a range of his associates: *Ford Madox Brown, Burne-Jones, Peter Paul Marshall, D. G. Rossetti* and *Philip Webb.* Other excellent examples are at e.g. Mill Hill Unitarian Chapel, Leeds (after 1865, *Morris* and *Ford Madox Brown* the designers); St Saviour, Leeds (1868–78, *Morris, Burne-Jones, Ford Madox Brown* and *G. J. Baguley*); Knaresborough (1872–3, mainly *Ford Madox Brown*); Nun Monkton – a particularly exquisite one (1873, *Burne-Jones* and *Morris*); and Tadcaster (1877, the same).

By then good-quality work from a wider range of mid- and Late Victorian manufacturers was beginning to appear. In the mid 1870s the little-known firm of *Saunders & Co.* provided glass to stand comparison with Morris's, for William Burges at Skelton and Studley Royal, from cartoons by *Fred Weekes.* Others were more prolific. Present from the early 1860s but producing important work later were *Clayton & Bell* (All Saints, Ilkley, 1861 and 1867; All Saints, Little Horton Green, Bradford, 1879; St John, Keighley, *c.* 1882, etc.); *Ward & Hughes,* with their nicely observed floral details (Arthington 1864, Aldborough 1865, Collingham 1880 etc.); and *Heaton, Butler & Bayne* (Ripon Cathedral *c.* 1860, Bramhope and East Ardsley *c.* 1881–1900 etc.). A little later were *Burlison & Grylls* (St Peter, Harrogate, 1876–1921, Giggleswick School Chapel *c.* 1900 etc.); *Shrigley & Hunt* of Lancaster (St James, Bolton, Bradford, 1876; Burton-in-Lonsdale 1909 etc.); *Powell & Sons* (Bingley 1890, designed by *Henry Holiday*; St Margaret, Ilkley, 1897–1919, etc.); and pre-eminently *C. E. Kempe,* together with his successors after 1907, *Kempe & Co.* (Drighlington 1878–1905: St Martin, Potternewton, Leeds, 1890–1921; Sedbergh School chapel 1898–1912; St Columba, Bradford, 1906–21, etc.). Standards were also maintained into the early c20 by e.g. *A. O. Hemming* (Aldborough 1907 etc.)* and Temple Moore's frequent associate *Victor Milner* (St Wilfrid, Harrogate, 1911–37). The main local firm, confusingly enough, was *Powell Bros.* of Leeds, prolific but rarely noteworthy.

*Also by Hemming are the murals (1913) at St Martin, Potternewton, Leeds (*Adams & Kelly,* 1879–81).

As to other furnishings, mention here can be confined to a reredos by *Pugin* (1842) in St Anne's Cathedral, Leeds, from the previous church; a full set – reredos, choir stalls, pulpit, lectern, pews, font and font cover, and organ case – at St John, Bentham, by *Shaw* and *Lethaby*, *c.* 1878–90 (the church had been rebuilt by *Shaw*); and a remarkable group in free Arts and Crafts Gothic by *Bromet & Thorman* of Tadcaster – panelling, screens and pulpit at Tadcaster (1906–15), panelling and screen at Bramham (*c.* 1910), reredos at Otley (1912). Regarding MONU-MENTS, the principal theme is the persistence of Neoclassical formulae long after the churches had shifted to Gothic. There is one of real quality, a relief by the little-known *Joseph Towne* at Rothwell (1842). In contrast to this is the BRASS to Elizabeth Tempest (†1845) in St Stephen, Skipton, designed by *Pugin* and executed by *Hardman*, and another good medieval-style brass is at Marton cum Grafton (†1899). A curiosity is the monument to the Egyptologist Charles Piazzi Smyth (†1900) and his wife at Sharow – a miniature pyramid.

Nonconformist churches and chapels

91 One of the finest anywhere is the United Reformed Church at Saltaire (1856–9), in opulent Italianate style with semicircular portico and domed cylindrical tower, built for Sir Titus Salt as part of his model industrial village by the leading Bradford firm of *Lockwood & Mawson* (*see* below); but it was always a unique design and by the time it was built an architect specializing in Nonconformist chapels, *James Simpson* of Leeds, had already appeared in the area, and his stock-in-trade was an Italianate of a more utilitarian, no-nonsense variety. Examples of his work are the former Temple Street Methodist Chapel at Keighley (1845–6) 92 and the Central Methodist Chapel at Morley (1860–1), the latter with galleried interior still little altered. Others in a similar mid-C19 mode include the Great Horton Methodist Chapel, Brad-ford, as enlarged in 1862 by *Samuel Jackson*, with temple front portico *in antis*; the former Sion Baptist Chapel at Bradford by *Lockwood & Mawson* again (1871–3); and the Methodist Chapel at Otley by *Edward Taylor* of York (1874). But by no means all Nonconformist chapels were in classical styles, as if to distinguish them unambiguously from the Anglican churches. A prominent early case of the use of Gothic is the Mill Hill Unitarian Chapel at Leeds of 1847 by *Bowman & Crowther*. Many more followed after *c.* 1860, ranging from the former Headingley Hill Congre-gational Church, Leeds, 1864–6 by *Cuthbert Brodrick* (*see* below) and *C. O. Ellison*'s former St John's Methodist Church, Man-ningham, Bradford (1878–9), both with tall spires, to *Garside & Pennington*'s free Perp Ben Rhydding Methodist Church at Ilkley (1909). On the other hand the very elaborate *fin-de-siècle* 'debased' Italianate or 'free classical' styles were never particu-larly common. Examples are the former Trinity Methodist Chapel at Pudsey, 1898–9 by *W. H. Dinsley*, and the Oxford Place

Methodist Chapel at Leeds as remodelled in 1896–1903 by *Danby & Thorp*. A charming instance of Art Nouveau inflexion is the former Methodist Assembly Hall at Ilkley, 1903–4 by *Adkin & Hill* of Bradford – with Gothic and classical details juxtaposed. The former Grange Congregational Chapel at Great Horton, Bradford, 1892 by *T. C. Hope*, presents a revival of the octagonal form recommended by John Wesley, in a mixture of Jacobean Gothic and Scottish Baronial.

Public buildings

The major civic projects such as TOWN HALLS provide some of the architectural high points of the period, their commissioning always an important public event which frequently generated much discussion and on occasion controversy. In the case of the two main centres, Leeds and Bradford, they also serve to introduce the practices with which their C19 architectural identities are particularly associated. At Bradford it is the partnership of *Lockwood & Mawson*, which was established in 1849 and quickly achieved an extraordinary near-monopoly of the town's biggest civic commissions. H. F. Lockwood, a native of Doncaster and a former pupil of the London architect P. F. Robinson, had, since the mid 1830s, been in practice in Hull: Mawson was from Leeds. Their strength was a more than competent Italianate, which was supplemented by efficiently derivative Gothic when required. The corresponding figure at Leeds is *Cuthbert Brodrick*, who was born in Hull and had been Lockwood's pupil there. He was also a classicist, but a much more gifted practitioner than his tutor, and although he did not achieve the same level of quantitative success as Lockwood & Mawson, his qualitative contribution to his respective *locus operandi* was even greater.

The best is mainly at the beginning of the sequence, and one item at the end. The start is *Lockwood & Mawson*'s St George's Hall, Bradford (1851–3), their first major commission, a grand public hall after the manner of Birmingham Town Hall (begun 1832), of approximate classical temple form now turned Italianate. But it was immediately eclipsed by *Brodrick*'s Leeds Town 95, p. 413 Hall (1852–8), which more ambitiously combines a public hall with a council chamber, courtrooms, a mayoral suite and municipal offices. This is one of the great C19 public buildings, drawing skilfully on ideas from both H. L. Elmes's St George's Hall at Liverpool and the French Neoclassical models Brodrick had studied on completing his pupilage, but also, as Pevsner noted, in the boldness and vigour of its detail hinting at an affinity with the English Baroque. After that, the 1860s produced only a few smaller fry, e.g. the pleasing Neo-Palladian town hall at Skipton by *J. D. Jee* of Liverpool. Then came another major one, *Lockwood & Mawson*'s at Bradford (1870–3), providing municipal and p. 60 judicial facilities which were previously deficient. Here, in the wake of Manchester Town Hall and the London Law Courts

Bradford, Town Hall.
Engraving, 1872

competition, the style is Gothic, the motive for the choice presumably a desire for contrast with what had been done at Leeds. The later C19 added two more, at Yeadon, 1879–80 by *William Hill* of Leeds – also Gothic, crudely done – and Morley, 1892–5 by *G. A. Fox* of Dewsbury, extraordinarily ambitious for the size of the town, a descendant of Leeds's via William Hill's at Bolton (Lancs.). From the Edwardian period are the louche mixed Renaissance Royal Hall at Harrogate, a multi-purpose auditorium by *Robert Beale* and *Frank Matcham* (1902–3);* the pretty Northern Renaissance Ilkley Town Hall by *William Bakewell* of Leeds (1906–8); and, much the most interesting, the addition to Bradford Town Hall by *Norman Shaw* and the City Architect *F. E. P. Edwards* (1905–9), in a clever mixture of styles, balancing the demands of continuity and contrast.

97

After the town halls comes a group of purpose-built MUNICIPAL OFFICES for various branches of local government. Pride of place goes to the former Municipal Buildings at Leeds, alongside the Town Hall – School Board and other offices, public library etc. – of 1878–84 by the Leeds architect *George Corson*, in a mixed Renaissance style harmonizing with their neighbour. Others are the former Poor Law Office at Bradford (now the Register Office) by *Andrews & Pepper* (1877, Italianate); the charming Free Renaissance former School Board Offices at Keighley, 1893 by *James Ledingham* of Bradford; and the Council Offices at Rothwell, also 1893. Of an iconic status similar to that of the town halls themselves are the two EXCHANGES at Leeds and Bradford, again by *Brodrick* and *Lockwood & Mawson* respectively. The former's Leeds Corn Exchange (1860–2) is as

94

*There was also an ambitious scheme for a Town Hall proper at Harrogate, by *H. T. Hare*, but only a small part of it was built (1904–6).

remarkable a building as his Town Hall, oval in plan (cf. the Halle du Blé at Paris, 1763–7), with North Italian diamond-faced rustication; but the latter's Wool Exchange at Bradford (1864–7), p. 155 notionally Venetian Gothic, is chiefly notable as the outcome of a particularly controversial architectural competition in which the unsuccessful contestants included William Burges and Norman Shaw. With regard to MARKETS, the only survivor of the characteristic type, of iron and glass behind perimeter ranges of brick or stone, is the City Markets complex in Leeds (*J. & J. Leeming*, 1904), but an important earlier example was *Lockwood & Mawson*'s Kirkgate Market at Bradford (1871–8, dem. *c.* 1970). The two cities each have one of *Sir Henry Tanner*'s GENERAL POST OFFICES, both prominently situated, Bradford's (1886–7, now offices) in French classical style, Leeds's (1896) Northern Renaissance. The (former) COURTHOUSES of the period are all relatively modest – e.g. one of *Charles Reeves*'s in palazzo style at Bradford (1859) – but Leeds has the big castle-style Armley Prison, 1843–7 by *Perkin & Backhouse*.

Now to SCHOOLS. Of the Anglican (or National) schools which were built in some numbers from the 1830s to the 1870s the early examples are mainly modest structures in a simple Gothic style, the later ones more ambitious. An unusually grand one for its date is Thornton's School at Burton-in-Lonsdale (1851–3), Tudor-collegiate. Several were built by *Mallinson & Healey* and *T. H. & F. Healey*, mainly in association with their churches, the best of the 1860s and 1870s in a domestic version of their C13 Gothic style of the time, e.g. Little Horton Green, Bradford (1863), Ilkley (1871–2); while another particularly attractive late example is *Paley & Austin*'s at Bolton-by-Bowland 98 (1874) in a Northern-accented Jacobean style. At Clifford there is a former Anglican convent school by *J. A. Hansom* (1847), at Oughtershaw at the head of Wharfedale a little school-cum-chapel in round-arched style (1857) which was probably designed by *Ruskin*. Then very well represented in the area are the non-denominational BOARD SCHOOLS built under the Education Act of 1870: Bradford in particular gained a reputation for the elaboration of its school buildings – designed by a number of local architects – but good examples are to be found more widely than that. The early ones are mostly Gothic like the church schools, the best of them – e.g. Barkerend (Bradford), by *Andrews & Pepper*, Whetley Lane (Bradford), by *T. H. & F. Healey*, both 1873–4 – continuing the Healeys' domestic version: a few others are Italianate (Drighlington, 1874–5 by *Lockwood & Mawson*; Shipley Central, 1876 by *Jackson & Longley*; Armley, Leeds, 1878 by the city School Board's own architect *Richard Adams*) or quasi-Jacobean (Pateley Bridge, 1875 by *Corson & Aitken*). Later the range includes versions of free classical or Free Renaissance (Beeston Hill, Leeds, 1880 by *Adams*; Great Horton, Bradford, 1884–6 by *Morley & Woodhouse*; two at Harrogate, by *T. E. Marshall*, 1895–7; Morley Victoria Road, 1898–9 by *T. A. Buttery & I. B. Birds*, etc.); while after the turn of the century there are occasional enlivening touches of Art Nouveau detail (Wyke, 1902–3 by *Adkin & Hill*; Lapage Street, Bradford, 1903 by *C. H. Hargreaves*). Most are single-storeyed, some with a tower, more or less fanciful (Pateley Bridge, Shipley Windhill (1885), Wyke, Lapage Street etc.), a few on the 'Prussian' plan with classrooms round a central hall. Taller blocks of the type associated with the London School Board's buildings are largely confined to inner-city Leeds and to the Higher Grade – i.e. secondary – schools (Leeds, 1889 by *Birchall & Kelly* – big, classical – Belle Vue and Hanson, Bradford, 1895–7 by *Hargreaves*, Free Renaissance again), but they also include the two at Harrogate, which are particularly close to the London schools. Leeds's grandest, Hillcrest (1906), was designed by the son of the London School Board's architect.

Of the grammar and public schools, the former Leeds Grammar School building is by *E. M. Barry*, 1858–9, Gothic; Ripon Grammar School, 1888–9 by *Corson*, Jacobean. But the specialists in the field locally were *Paley & Austin*, at Giggleswick School (1868–1900), Skipton Grammar School (1875) and Sedbergh School (1878–1907), mainly a serious simple Jacobean, partly Gothic, but in some parts at Sedbergh a more up-to-date collegiate Queen Anne. As to the institutions of HIGHER EDUCATION, the earliest in the area again had an ecclesiastical character – e.g. the former Ripon College, built as a training college for the diocese's schoolmistresses, 1860–2 by *J. B. & W. Atkinson* of York, and the former Congregationalist ministers' training college at Bradford (now Bradford University School of Management), 1874–7 by *Lockwood & Mawson*. In a reversal of the usual stereotypes, the former is Italianate, the latter Gothic. Then come the first buildings of what was to become Leeds University, 1879–94 by *Alfred Waterhouse*, and the Italianate Bradford College (originally Technical School), 1880–2 by *Hope & Jardine*. Later arrivals included the Leeds College of Art, 1901–3 by *Bedford & Kitson* (*see* below), and the former Bingley College (Teacher Training), 1909–11 by the West Riding County Architect *J. Vickers Edwards*. Bradford College and the Leeds College of Art both started as offshoots from a different kind of educational institution, characteristic of the time, their respective cities' MECHANICS' INSTITUTES; and a number of these also had buildings of remarkable ambition. An early one was the Bradford Institute's first, 1839–40 by *Perkin & Backhouse* (dem. *c.* 1960), which was succeeded by a larger building in 1870–1 by *Andrews & Pepper* (dem. 1974). Surviving examples are at e.g. Bingley, 1862–4 by *Waterhouse*; Leeds, 1865–8, the third of *Brodrick*'s great public buildings in the city; Otley, 1869–71 by *Charles Fowler* of Leeds; Pudsey, 1879–80 by *Hope & Jardine*; and Silsden, 1883 by *J. B. Bailey* and *W. H. Sugden*. Of Keighley's, 1868–70 by *Lockwood & Mawson*, which was one of the biggest, the dominant building of the town centre, only a part remains. It is indicative of the nature of these buildings that of the alternative uses to which they were put in the C20, in three cases – Otley, Pudsey and Silsden – it was as a town hall.

A role complementary to that of the Mechanics' Institutes was played by the PUBLIC LIBRARIES. At Leeds and Bradford the central libraries were incorporated into the Municipal Buildings and Kirkgate Market respectively (*see* above): most of the others belong to the decade after 1900 and exhibit the usual stylistic tendencies of that period. A particularly attractive example is Armley Branch Library, Leeds, 1901 by *Percy Robinson* in Flemish   100 Renaissance style; an eye-catching one is Keighley Library, 1902–4 by *McEwan & Swan* of Birmingham, Free Renaissance at its trickiest. Of ART GALLERIES the outstanding example, a major civic undertaking by any standards, is the Cartwright Hall   96 at Bradford, 1900–4 by *J. W. Simpson & E. J. Milner Allen* (previously designers of the Glasgow Art Gallery): grandiose Edwardian Baroque in fine Bradford sandstone.

Moving to different types of provision, first there are the former WORKHOUSES – typically in a simple classical style but some of the later ones Neo-Jacobean etc. Examples of the former are at Skipton, 1839 by *George Webster*, Bradford (now St Luke's Hospital), 1852, and Clayton (Bradford), 1858, both by *Lockwood & Mawson* – Bradford's in particular showing these architects' strength at a sort of functional simplified Italianate – of the latter Ripon (now Council Offices) and Leeds (now part of St James's Hospital), both by *Perkin & Backhouse*, 1858. So, many of the workhouses developed into HOSPITALS, alongside those which were purpose-built. By far the most important of the latter is *G. G. Scott*'s Leeds Infirmary, 1863–9, replacing Carr's, a landmark in the use of the Gothic style for secular public buildings in the area and one of the first hospitals in England of the pavilion type. Others are Cookridge Hospital, Leeds, 1868–9 by *Norman Shaw* – so almost contemporary with Scott's but totally different in mood, Home Counties Old English with jettied gables and tilehanging – the vast former High Royds Mental Hospital at Menston, 1884–8 by *J. Vickers Edwards*, an early example of the *echelon* plan; and the former Children's Hospital at Bradford, 1889–90 by *H. & E. Marten*, with an unusual circular ward wing. A specialist type of health facility is represented by the SPA BUILDINGS of Harrogate, from the jaunty octagonal Royal Pump   99 Room, 1842 by *I. T. Shutt*, son of a Harrogate hotel proprietor, to the more ponderous Royal Baths of 1894–7 by Londoners *Baggalay & Bristowe* – to which can be added the florid terracottafaced Spa Baths at neighbouring Ripon, 1904 by *S. Stead*. Alongside these go the PUBLIC BATHS of the industrial centres, surviving examples of which are the Central Baths at Bradford, by the baths specialist *A. H. Tiltman* and the City Architect *F. E. P. Edwards*, 1903–5, and Bramley Baths, Leeds, 1904 by *J. Lane Fox*, both again with touches of municipal Art Nouveau ornament.*

Other sanitary improvements included the provision of CEMETERIES. The most memorable are Undercliffe, Bradford,

---

* *Brodrick*'s Oriental Baths at Leeds (1866) were extensively altered in 1882 and demolished in 1969.

on an elevated site overlooking the city, laid out 1853–4 by the surveyor *William Gay*, and Lawnswood, Leeds (1875), the layout and the original buildings by *George Corson* assisted by *Gay*; but historically the most important, as a pioneering example of a municipal cemetery, is Beckett Street, Burmantofts, Leeds, 1845. Bradford's first municipal cemetery was Scholemoor (1860), laid out by the Borough Surveyor, *Charles Gott*. Of others, Bingley (1870) has an attractive picturesque layout, and a number more still also retain their chapels etc., of the same decade. Of PUBLIC PARKS, the biggest is Roundhay Park, Leeds, opened in 1873, with landscaping again by *Corson*; but Bradford has two earlier, Peel Park (1853) and Lister Park (1870). The most substantial of the works for improving WATER SUPPLY are further from the cities, in the catchment areas: Leeds Corporation's reservoirs in the Washburn Valley (Fewston, Lindley), 1871–87, and Bradford's, even more heroic, in Nidderdale (Ramsgill, Middlesmoor) begun in 1893 by the engineer *James Watson* but not completed until 1936.

Now TRANSPORT, which essentially means the railways; and the area is rich in excellent examples of RAILWAY ENGINEER-ING. The *locus classicus* is the Midland Railway's famous Settle–Carlisle line (1870–4, chief engineer *John Sidney Crossley*) – perhaps the most heroic (and hubristic) of all English railway undertakings – the most dramatic sections of which lie within the northern West Riding, epitomized by the magnificent Ribblehead Viaduct at Chapel-le-Dale. Previous development had been centred on Leeds, the early lines including the Leeds & Selby (1834), the North Midland's to Derby and so to London (1840), and the link to Bradford (1846); and one of the first to require substantial engineering works was the Leeds & Thirsk (1845–9, *Thomas Grainger* engineer), notably the Bramhope Tunnel, with its castellated portal, and nearby Wharfedale Viaduct (Castley). Another prominent viaduct, also by *Grainger*, is at Knaresborough (1851); while a feature of a different kind is the vaulted labyrinth of the 'dark arches' spanning the river Aire at Leeds, which was built as the substructure of the 'New' Station in 1864–9 (*T. E. Harrison* engineer). Of STATIONS themselves from the period, none survives at either Leeds or Bradford, but there is a reasonable tally of the smaller ones, including one of *G. T. Andrews*'s attractive Gothic offerings for George Hudson (Thorp Arch, 1847); the Palladian one at Ilkley by *J. H. Sanders* for the Midland Railway (1865); a number on the Settle–Carlisle, also by *Sanders*, e.g. Settle (1876); and the interestingly planned Hellifield, 1880 by *Charles Trubshaw*, again for the Midland.

Finally, a word about PUBLIC SCULPTURE. The most ambi-tious scheme is the ensemble in City Square, Leeds, of 1893–1903, its centrepiece an equestrian statue of the Black Prince by *Thomas Brock*, which is accompanied by allegorical figures and Leeds notables by *Alfred Drury* and others. The earli-est examples are Sir Robert Peel at Leeds and Bradford, 1852 and 1855 respectively, both by *W. Behnes*, and the Duke of Wellington at Leeds, 1854 by *Marochetti*. Other heroes of indus-try – and of campaigns to ameliorate its social effects – followed

106

2

107

in both places, the most grandiose individually the Sir Titus Salt monument in Bradford (1874), presumptuously similar to the Albert Memorial, the architecture by *Lockwood & Mawson*, the sculpture by *J. Adams-Acton*; and then there was a crop of Queen Victorias (Harrogate 1887 by *Webber*; Leeds 1903 by *George Frampton*; Bradford 1904 by *Drury*). In smaller towns there are Sir Mathew Wilson (first M.P. for the Skipton division) at Skipton, 1888 by *A. B. Joy*, and the first Marquess of Ripon, 1912 by *F. Derwent Wood*, at Ripon. Statuary in city centre sites has tended to be peripatetic, leading in Leeds to an effective concentration on Woodhouse Moor but in Bradford rather to dispersal in the suburbs.

Industrial and commercial buildings

One can start with the TEXTILE MILLS. Of the four main branches of the textile industry present in the early C19 the linen branch declined after 1850, but by then a small silk spinning and weaving branch was beginning to develop which in the northern West Riding was, like worsted, centred on Bradford; and the main concentration of mills from this period is in Bradford and its neighbourhood. Compared to those of the previous phase they tend to be larger and more regular, and more of them provided for integrated production; but most are still severely plain, with architectural detail in a simplified Italianate style typically focused on an entrance feature or the top of a staircase or privy tower. The main building forms resolve into two, the multi-storey range for spinning and warehousing, and single-storey sheds with north-light sawtooth roofs for weaving and preparatory processes. A technical development during the period was a move from shaft to rope or cable drive systems, which led to the appearance of the characteristic rope race bay adjoining the engine house.

Of individual examples three in particular stand out, representing three different branches of the industry. The first, from the beginning of the period (1838–43), is Temple Mill, Leeds, p. 555 which is actually a big weaving shed and an office block added to the existing Marshall's flax mill to create an integrated linen mill. Its immediately striking feature is its exceptional degree of architectural elaboration in a unique style, a scholarly Egyptian Revival – the architect was the Egyptologist *Joseph Bonomi Jun.*, curator of the Soane Museum – but equally significant was the interior form of the weaving shed (devised by the engineer *James Combe*), single-storeyed and top-lit, a pioneering example of the type. Next is Sir Titus Salt's mill at Saltaire, of 1850–3 by *Lock-* p. 680 *wood & Mawson* and the engineer *Sir William Fairbairn*. This is the pre-eminent integrated worsted mill, exceptional in its size and the clarity of its planning, the product of a single building campaign on a greenfield site, and the exemplar of industrial Italianate; while the New Mill, added in 1865–8, is one of a small 103 group in which the mill chimney is enjoyably dressed up as an

105 Italian campanile. The third is Manningham Mills, Bradford, Samuel Cunliffe Lister's integrated silk mill, mainly of 1870–3 by *Andrews & Pepper* – even bigger and grander than Saltaire Mill, with the most monumental of the campanile chimneys. Others to mention here are Whetley Mills, Bradford, 1863 etc. by *Milnes & France*, the corresponding epitome of a worsted spinning mill; the ornately detailed Dalton Mills, Keighley, 1866–77 by *W. Sugden* of Leek, with three spinning ranges, two engine houses and another curious chimney; and Ebor Mill, Haworth, enlarged 1887 by *W. & J. B. Bailey* of Keighley but originating in a water-powered spinning mill of the early C19 and developed gradually for steam-powered integrated working from *c.* 1850. Meanwhile, refinements in the use of water power were made at Glasshouses Mill (flax spinning), which had a large iron waterwheel designed by *Sir William Fairbairn* (1851), and at Dale End Mill, Lothersdale, which retains an even larger wheel, of iron and timber, installed ten years later. Of later examples, Becks Mill, Keighley (1907) was apparently the first electric-powered textile mill in Yorkshire; and Ardsley Mills, East Ardsley (1914), was built using the Hennebique system of reinforced-concrete construction, the frame fully exposed externally. Waterloo Mill, Silsden, retains the steam engine installed in 1916, in an impressively cyclopean engine house of the same date.

The complementary DISPLAY WAREHOUSES, located in both Bradford and Leeds, also developed greatly in size and grandeur. The main period of construction was from the 1850s to the 1870s but they continued to be built up to 1914. Leeds's are mainly in the Wellington Street area and show a lively variety of styles – Italianate, Gothic and even a little Moorish: the principal exponent was *George Corson*, from 1859 on. But Bradford has many more, including the whole warehouse zone known as Little Germany, developed from 1855, which remains remarkably intact; and they tend to be more homogeneous, mainly in a restrained palazzo style frequently enhanced by fine decorative ironwork. Particular features of their planning are corner entrances leading to handsome main staircases, and – presumably a measure to prevent premature disclosure of new products – private loading areas at the rear of the buildings, reached by cart entrances, rather than the taking-in doors onto the street of earlier warehouses. The leading architects in Little Germany were *Milnes & France*, but the first of the Bradford 'palace' warehouses, Milligan & Forbes's in Hall Ings (1852–3), is by *Andrews & Delaunay* and another of the most spectacular, 102 the Law Russell Warehouse in Little Germany, is by *Lockwood & Mawson* (1873–4). A type of industrial building unique to Leeds, however, was the CLOTHING FACTORY for the production of ready-made suits etc.; and a few survive including the extraor-104 dinary one in Moorish style on the S side of Park Square, built in 1878 by *Thomas Ambler* of Leeds for the pioneering entrepreneur John Barran.* Of other sectors also, the most substantial

* Only the façade survives, fronting a modern office block, St Paul's House.

survivals from this period are those of Leeds's ENGINEERING and METALWORKING industries – in particular *Thomas Grainger*'s railway depot buildings of the late 1840s for the Leeds & Thirsk, including a roundhouse and a half roundhouse; and the famous Tower Works – for the manufacture of pins for carding and combing machines – with its pair of brick Gothic campanile chimneys (1864–6 by *Thomas Shaw* and 1899 by *William Bakewell*) and engine house with portrait medallions designed by *Alfred Drury* (1899). Elsewhere, there is the impressive Hoffman LIMEKILN at Langcliffe, 1872–3, and the tall iron-work-crested John Smith's BREWERY at Tadcaster, 1883 by *Scamell & Colyer*.

108

Returning to the town and city centres and their commercial buildings, the first of the BANKS and Insurance Offices is the Grecian Craven Bank at Skipton of 1849 (now Barclays); and then come two in sumptuous palazzo style, the Leeds & Yorkshire Fire Assurance Co., 1852–5 by *W.B. Gingell* of Bristol, and the former Bradford Bank, 1858 by *Andrews & Delaunay*. Later p. 159 Italianate examples include the former Branch Bank of England in Leeds, 1862–4 by *P.C. Hardwick*; but Gothic was represented by *Scott*'s Beckett's Bank in Leeds, of 1863–7 (dem. 1965), and on a smaller scale by the Bradford Commercial Bank (now Natwest), 1867–8 by *Andrews & Pepper*. From the 1890s are two contrasting branches of the Yorkshire Penny Bank – in Infirmary Street, Leeds, by *Perkin & Bulmer* (1893–4), still Gothic, and Bradford by *James Ledingham* (1895–8), exuberant Free Renaissance – and two of *Waterhouse*'s Prudential Assurance offices (Leeds and Bradford), chiefly identifiable by their materials: granite, brick and Burmantofts terracotta (*see* below). Of the following decade is Atlas House, Leeds, insurance offices by *Perkin & Bulmer*, concrete-framed and entirely terracotta-faced. Regarding the broader run of MIXED-USE buildings, three episodes can be singled out. One is the redevelopment of Boar Lane, Leeds, 1869–76 by *Thomas Ambler*, a profuse mixture of Gothic, Italianate etc., the second the contemporary rebuilding of much of the commercial core of Bradford, centred on the Wool Exchange, by a number of local architects but once again more consistently Italianate overall. The third is the creation *de novo* of the commercial centre of Harrogate in the years from *c.* 1860, and in particular the buildings erected by the developer George Dawson to the designs of *J.H. Hirst* in a coarse but inventive Franco-Italianate style, e.g. Cambridge Crescent, 1867–8. p. 316 A special feature of Leeds is the famous series of SHOPPING ARCADES, all running off Briggate and exploiting the long narrow medieval burgage plots. They begin with the mildly Gothic Thornton's Arcade, of 1877–8 by *George Smith*, and culminate in the splendid County and Cross Arcades (now the Victoria 109 Quarter), 1898–1904 by *Frank Matcham*, in which extensive use was made of that characteristic building material of late Victorian Leeds, the highly coloured architectural faience made by the Leeds Fireclay Co. at Burmantofts – by the 1890s the largest clay-working company in the country.

Then there are the HOTELS, for which the obvious focus is
Harrogate: in spite of some changes there is still a whole procession, from the unshowily dignified White Hart of 1846, much
117   admired by Pevsner, to the spectacular towering Majestic,
1898–1900 by *G. D. Martin*, of red brick with dome and Flemish
gables. Alongside these goes the best of the 'hydropathic establishments' or 'hydros' of Ilkley, *Cuthbert Brodrick*'s grandly monumental palazzo-style Wells House of 1854–6. Of railway hotels
the main example is the Midland at Bradford, 1885 by *Charles
Trubshaw* – its rival close to the city's other terminus is the Victoria, 1867 by *Lockwood & Mawson* – but a curiosity is the former
hotel beside the (closed) Leeds & Thirsk line in open country at
Nidd near Knaresborough, a neat little classical box of *c.* 1849.
Of the same showy period as the Majestic is the Metropole at
Leeds, 1897–9 by *Connon & Chorley*, Loire style in red terracotta;
and two of the city's PUBS which are again notable for the lavish
use of Burmantofts faience, Whitelock's, off Briggate (1890s) and
The Garden Gate, Hunslet (1903). Of THEATRES the earliest surviving is the unpretentious City Varieties at Leeds, 1865 by *George*
p. 427   *Smith*; by far the finest the Leeds Grand, 1877–8 by *George Corson*
and *J. R. Watson*, conceived of as a high-mindedly 'noble temple
of the drama', the exterior in a curious quasi-medieval round-
arched style, the domed auditorium sumptuously decorated.
Others are at Harrogate and Bradford. There is one remarkably
well-preserved early CINEMA, the Hyde Park Picture House at
Leeds, 1914 by *T. Winn & Sons*.

Housing

During this period the COUNTRY HOUSE properly defined was
in decline as an architectural type, although there was a brief
flurry of activity at the beginning, in the 1840s and early 1850s
– in part a continuation from the Late Georgian phase – and then
a smaller final one in the years round 1900. The best products of
the former were the later works of *George Webster* in the W of the
area, in particular the picturesque Graeco-Italianate refacing of
Broughton Hall, 1838–50; the most substantial *Sir Charles Barry*'s
Italianate remodelling of Harewood House, 1842–50, and the
rebuilt Allerton Park, 1848–51 by *George Martin*, Gothic-cum-
112   Jacobean with a melodramatic full-height central hall. From the
latter are *C. E. Kempe*'s interior alterations at Temple Newsam,
Leeds (1889–97); *Temple Moore*'s Bilbrough Manor (1900–1) and
the York country-house architect *Walter Brierley*'s Thorpe Underwood Hall (1902–3), contrasting versions of domestic Neo-
Jacobean; and the plush Neo-Wren remodelling of Gargrave
House by *J. B. Dunn* of Edinburgh (1913–17). But the country
house story still had one further significant episode, in the interwar years (*see* below).

What came to take centre stage are the MANSIONS and VILLAS
of the commercial and industrial elites, occasionally also in the
country but more frequently in the expanding suburbs; but the

most ostentatious do not appear immediately. More typical of the Early Victorian period is the suburban villa of moderate size, of which a good collection is at Headingley Hill, Leeds, some still classical, others a little unexpectedly Gothic, e.g. Cumberland Priory (*c.* 1841), probably by *John Child*, and North Hill House (1846). Elsewhere in Leeds, Roundhay Hall, 1841–2 by *Samuel Sharp* for stuff merchant William Smith, concludes the city's early C19 sequence of larger Grecian villas; and an interesting scheme of early Victorian interior decoration is at Little Woodhouse Hall, by *W. R. Corson* and *E. la Trobe Bateman* with advice from *Owen Jones* (1847). Of middle-class terraced housing of the period there is more in Bradford, particularly the Manningham area, e.g. Peel Square (1851) and Apsley Crescent (1854–5), a shallow curve with the classical detail still solid and restrained. Of the smaller towns, Settle has a handsome Grecian terrace of *c.* 1840: at Skipton and Harrogate the terraces stay traditionally Georgian in character into the 1850s. The real 'brass castles' start at the end of that decade. One of the grandest – and one of the few by a non-local architect – was Titus Salt junior's Milner Field at Bingley, by *Thomas Harris* (1871–3, dem.). Surviving examples from the mid-Victorian years – Gothic, Italianate, or Neo-Jacobean – include Moor Park, Beckwithshaw, 1859 by *Andrews & Delaunay* for the Leeds ironfounder and railway contractor James Bray; Malsis Hall, Glusburn, *c.* 1862 etc. by *Samuel Jackson* for James Lund, textile manufacturer of Keighley; Lady Royd, Bradford, 1865 by *Milnes & France* for worsted spinner Henry Illingworth; Meanwood Towers, Leeds, 1867–73 by *E. W. Pugin* for Thomas Kennedy, textile machinery manufacturer; and Spenfield, Leeds, 1875 by *George Corson* for the banker James Walter Oxley. As to interiors, the most interesting work of the period was in more modest houses: the excellent very early *Morris* glass at Harden Grange, Bingley (1862) – now at Cliffe Castle Museum, Keighley – and Oakwood, Bingley (1865),* and a big chimneypiece by *Burges* also at Oakwood. Of other smaller villas, the characteristic spiky Gothic type of Ilkley – where development as a dormitory town for the middle classes of Leeds and Bradford began in earnest *c.* 1867 – first appears *c.* 1870, and the best of the Italianate ones at Harrogate are of similar date.

But the housing of the period which makes the most rewarding study is that of the Arts and Crafts-influenced DOMESTIC REVIVAL of the late C19 and early C20, which is well represented in the area over a range of types, from grand individual mansions to relatively modest speculative developments. The Shaw–Nesfield southern Old English style, with half-timbering and tile-hanging, which had first appeared in the area in Shaw's Cookridge Hospital of 1868–9 (*see* above), was quite widely adopted after *c.* 1880, first in developments on the Newton Park estate, Leeds of *c.* 1881 on by *Chorley & Connon* and a number of houses of the 1880s at Heaton, Bradford, by *James Ledingham*;

*The earliest of all was that installed in 1861 at Woodbank, Harden, since removed to an unknown location.

and then from the early 1890s on with particularly attractive results in the work of the Leeds architect *F. W. Bedford* (after 1897 *Bedford & Kitson*), who had worked in the office of Ernest George & Peto. Examples of his numerous Old English houses in the Leeds suburbs include Nos. 49–51 Cardigan Road, Headingley (1893), and Webton Court, Chapel Allerton (1902–3); while at Gledhow Manor (1903) the firm provided a persuasive essay in Neo-Georgian. Another development – already prefigured in the work of George Webster and then Paley & Austin (*see* above) but given a new impetus by Arts and Crafts ideas – was of a regional Pennine Revival style, using the local gritstone. A starting point is provided, perhaps ironically, by a pair of houses by non-local architects: *Norman Shaw*'s St John's, Ilkley, of 1878–9, which is a stone-built paraphrase of his Old English manner,* and Carr Manor, Leeds (1881), an early work of Shaw's former pupil, *E. S. Prior* – which was explicitly intended to be 'representative of a Yorkshire manor house of the 17th century', although as yet the image was rather generalized, without the characteristic details of a more precisely regional focus. A move in that direction can be detected in the alterations to Thornton Hall, of 1886; but the most convincing example in the northern West Riding comes in the next decade, the delightful Steeton Manor (formerly Currerwood), 1895 by *W. H. Sugden* of Keighley for worsted manufacturer Sir Swire Smith. Another practice producing houses of a broadly Arts and Crafts character was *Isitt, Adkin & Hill* of Bradford: at The Briery, Ilkley (1897), they combined a slate-hanging and roughcast Old English manner with Pennine Revival details and the occasional Art Nouveau flourish.

The new century brought a further group of works by London architects. The first was *Barry Parker*, of *Parker & Unwin*. His self-consciously pretty Foulis Cottage (*c.* 1900) must always have seemed out of place in industrial inner-city Bradford, but The Gables, Harrogate (1903–5), is another effective piece of Arts and Crafts Old English. The full-height living room lit by a double-transomed corner window recalls the work of Shaw and more particularly that of the second figure, *Sir Edwin Lutyens*; but at Heathcote, Ilkley (1906–7) – perhaps the most domineering of all the 'brass castles', for the Bradford wool merchant J. T. Hemingway – Lutyens famously abandoned his earlier Domestic Revival style in favour of a classical grand manner which contrasts quite deliberately with its surroundings. For the time being, however, Old English continued to have the last word, as in the palatial extensions to another industrialist's house, Whinburn Lodge at Keighley, by *Simpson & Ayrton* (1912–13): the Arts and Crafts phenomenon at its most – ironically – luxurious.

The contrast between all this and even the best of WORKERS' HOUSING could hardly be greater. The prime example is of course Sir Titus Salt's model industrial village of Saltaire, 1853–68 by *Lockwood & Mawson*, exceptional in its size and the range of its amenities – including a town-hall-like institute,

---

*Badly mauled *c.* 1955.

almshouses and hospital as well as chapels, schools and wash-house – and providing decent-quality through-terraced housing with back yards and properly clearable privies. Smaller later industrial settlements are Glasshouses in Nidderdale, c. 1855–75, and Glusburn near Keighley – with another elaborate institute – c. 1890–1902; and other millowners' developments of workers' housing are at e.g. Cannon Mill, Great Horton, Bradford, 1864–5 and Grove Mills, Keighley, c. 1890. What these should be compared to are the notorious BACK-TO-BACKS, which continued to be built in Bradford until the 1870s and in Leeds into the early C20; but by no means all were as bad as those which had contributed to the scandalous state of housing in both cities by the mid C19, the standard improving markedly during the second half of the century. Surviving examples in Leeds are Chapel Terrace and Square in Headingley, of c. 1850, and the streets known as 'The Harolds' in the Hyde Park area (c. 1880); in Bradford St Andrew's Villas, off Listerhills Road, 1864 by T. C. Hope, a superior type, in blocks of four with a little Gothic detail. The houses at Grove Mills, Keighley, are also an improved version of back-to-backs – 'through-by-lights', in which a narrow slice of each house runs right through the terrace. Early COUNCIL HOUSING is rarer than might be expected. Examples are the Faxfleet Street estate, 1902–4 (terraces) and the Longlands p. 202 estate, 1903–10 (tenements), both in Bradford. Finally, another work by *Parker & Unwin*, Nos. 197 and 199 Hookstone Chase, Harrogate (1902–3), is a pair of small cottage semis of the type built in their thousands, by councils and private developers alike, during the interwar years.

BUILDINGS SINCE 1918*

The interwar years

The First World War did not provide a decisive break with the years before 1914, and the activities of the Victorian and Edwardians in almost every area of building means that it is only from the late 1920s that there is much new work to note. What followed demonstrates the advent of new styles in architecture.

Associated with the war itself is the hangar at the former Bramham Moor airfield, opened in 1915 for the R.F.C. Otherwise it is appropriate to begin with WAR MEMORIALS. Some interesting variations to the conventions of the type are provided by *Lutyens*'s simple cross for the Leeds Rifles at St Peter, Leeds, a cenotaph with flaming urn by *J. J. Joass* at Ilkley, and *John Cassidy*'s memorial for Skipton, with a crouching figure breaking a sword at the base of a soaring triangular pillar topped by Victory. Figures of Peace-Victory are at Wetherby and Calverley, both by *L. F. Roslyn*, and *H. C. Fehr*'s memorial at Keighley.

*This chapter has been prepared by Charles O'Brien.

A similar figure originally adorned Fehr's memorial for Leeds city, which also has two fine statues in the style of the sculptor's earlier association with the 'New Sculpture' movement. But the masterpiece is the memorial for Leeds University by *Eric Gill*, with its ferocious relief of figures in contemporary dress, including a top-hatted pawnbroker, being flailed and driven out of the temple by Christ. It caused as much offence, for different reasons, as the infantrymen in attacking pose for the Bradford memorial.

Gill also contributed the Stations of the Cross (1921–4) at St Cuthbert, Manningham (Bradford), one of the few notable contributions to CHURCH ARCHITECTURE in the decade after the war, which also include furnishings and glass at Aberford, Harrogate and Lotherton (by *Comper*) and Drighlington (by *Sir Charles Nicholson*). The best and most ambitious set of fittings is at St Hilda, Leeds, installed over two decades, with excellent work by *Alfred Southwick* in the Gothic tradition. While some pre-war church building was carried over (St Wilfrid, Harrogate), it is the expansion of the suburbs around Leeds from the mid 1920s which caused the first great campaign of work since the Victorian period. Some looked directly back to the period before 1914, most notably *W. D. Caröe's* final church of St Mary, Hawksworth Wood (1932–5), in full-blown Arts and Crafts Gothic. The expense was borne by H. M. Butler of the Kirkstall Forge, so the craftsmanship is commensurately fine. A handful of works for the Nonconformists in the mid 1920s also held to earlier traditions with well-crafted interiors (South Parade Baptist Church, Headingley, and Lidgett Park Methodist, Roundhay), but increasingly the emphasis was on economy, partly prompting the vogue for Byzantine, Romanesque and early Christian styles which could be achieved in brick, steel and concrete and relied for effect on massing rather than expensive carved ornament and decoration. Two characteristic examples are St Philip, Osmondthorpe (1932–3) and St Cross on the Middleton Estate (1935). Both are by *F. L. Charlton* and were funded by the Church Forward Movement, founded in 1930 by Bishop Burroughs of Ripon to increase the number of Anglican churches on new estates. A comparable group, but in a more overtly stripped style, are the churches of 1937–9 by *Gribbon, Foggitt & Brown* (Venerable Bede, St John & St Barnabas, and St Augustine R.C.). A single gift from the Sunderland shipbuilder, Sir John Priestman, produced the two most important designs of this period, both in the E suburbs of Leeds: the mighty but plain French Romanesque-inspired church of the Epiphany (Gipton) by *N. F. Cachemaille-Day* and St Wilfrid (Halton), a late work by *A. Randall Wells* in a strikingly expressive and angular Gothic. These churches are also significant for giving greater prominence to the altar; going further, and a pioneer in this respect, is Our Lady, Heaton (Bradford) of 1935, built for the Roman Catholics and from the first planned around a central altar, the earliest such example in Britain. Sharing some of the architectural characteristics of these suburban churches but in a class of its own is the former Synagogue in Chapeltown Road, Leeds, built in 1929–32 by *J. Stanley Wright* in Art Deco-cum-Byzantine.

As in church architecture, the handsome provision of CIVIC AND PUBLIC BUILDINGS by the Victorians and Edwardians means only a handful of important undertakings during this period. Again, the story is dominated by events in Leeds. First comes the Civic Hall by *E. Vincent Harris*, 1931–3, which Pevsner   118 recognized as having 'originality and some courage, even the courage of naughtiness in the details', including memorably odd Wren-style towers and many borrowing from Lutyens's grand classical manner. Also firmly in the traditionalist camp, but again with a subdued grandeur, are *Lanchester, Lucas & Lodge*'s monumental additions to the University, one of the finest essays in stripped classicism of the period. After Leeds, other public buildings seem to be of relatively minor significance, most in the widely favoured Neo-Georgian or revival styles (Bingley Magistrates Court, 1928–9; Harrogate Municipal Buildings, 1931; Shipley Town Hall, 1931–2). The most interesting, but sadly much-altered, is Beckfoot School, Bingley, built as the County Secondary School in 1939–40 by *W. G. Newton*, with a very uncommon wedge-shaped plan.

The big local authorities were also concerned for the first time with the mass provision of PUBLIC HOUSING. Bradford had completed two schemes of council housing in the early years of the C20 (Faxfleet Street and the Longlands estate) and after the Addison Act of 1919 introduced subsidies erected over 7,000 homes, about one-third of all the new housing in the city up to 1939. Leeds, by contrast, was noticeably delinquent before the war and after 1918 built fewer houses than any other major industrial city (7,000 in eleven years) and continued to tolerate the building of back-to-backs. That was changed only after 1933, when the Labour-led Corporation appointed *R. A. H. Livett* as Architect and Director of Housing. For the most part the new estates in both cities are characterized by low-density layouts of two-storey houses. Some have semi-formal street patterns of curved and straight avenues, in other words the orthodox 'cottage estate' espoused by Raymond Unwin and seen across interwar Britain. The one scheme for which Leeds was distinguished among the English industrial cities was its vast group of flats at Quarry Hill, begun in 1938 on the E edge of the city centre. Built using a patented steel and concrete building system, it was conceived as a self-contained neighbourhood but completed without the necessary social amenities that had been an integral feature of the Continental housing schemes on which it was modelled (specifically the Karl Marx Hof, Vienna). By the 1970s it was ready for demolition.

There was, of course, also much PRIVATE HOUSING in the cities and towns but it is of a far more prosaic kind than in the Edwardian heyday. In one or two places earlier traditions continued, most spectacularly at Gledstone Hall, in Craven, one of the last great country houses by *Lutyens*, 1922–6, in a classical

French C18 manner, with gardens by *Jekyll*. His site architect, *Richard Jaques* of Burnley, designed a small house at Thornton-in-Craven in a nice Arts and Crafts-influenced style. As might be expected it is the Arts and Crafts Movement which carried on immediately after the war in the houses and villas of the wider area, e.g. Far Scar (Grassington), of 1920 by *Sir Edward Maufe* and his earlier Stonedene, Ilkley, of 1914. Also in Ilkley is Five Oaks, of 1929–30, which belongs to a small, and for England very early, group of villas in the area in the white-walled, flat-roofed Modernistic style of contemporary Continental architecture. The architect was *J. C. Procter* of Leeds; his White House, Ilkley, is exactly contemporary, Kirkby House at Kirkby Overblow followed in 1931, White Lodge, Adel (Leeds) in 1935. Of the same name and date, and now the best-preserved of this type, is White Lodge, Harrogate, designed by *Col. R. B. Armistead* for himself with fittings by *Betty Joel*.

Nothing yet has been said of COMMERCIAL BUILDINGS. The principal work was the reconstruction of the Headrow in Leeds, to a unified scheme by *Sir Reginald Blomfield*, begun in 1929. It was of an ambition and scale unique among the English cities of this period, even if the predominantly Neo-Georgian style creates little excitement. For jazzier tastes one looks to the interior of the Queen's Hotel, Leeds, fitted out by *W. Curtis Green* in the Art Deco associated with his work on London's Dorchester; the associated rebuilding of the station to its rear by *W. H. Hamlyn* is more subdued but equally elegant. At Bradford, Sunwin House, built for the Co-op in 1935–6, is the one building in the area to show an awareness of Continental developments, in this case the streamlined style imported to Britain by Erich Mendelsohn. Also in Bradford, the New Victoria cinema-theatre (now Odeon), by *W. Illingworth*, 1930, is an extravagant and large affair but it is the Harrogate Odeon of 1936, by the chain's regular architect *Harry Weedon*, that properly captures the *Zeitgeist*.

From 1945 to the mid 1970s

The Second World War brought little material damage to the area – enemy bombing was primarily directed at the major industrial cities in the southern West Riding. The commercial and trading centres of Bradford and Leeds (with the exception of nine raids on Hunslet and Kirkstall and the destruction of *Chantrell*'s Leeds Philosophical Society hall in the city centre) escaped largely unscathed. The effects of industrial decline were, as yet, unpronounced and Leeds in particular had grown prosperous between the wars on the back of its mass clothing industry. The priority in the cities was therefore to recommence work halted in 1939, principally slum clearance and expansion of HOUSING estates. The progress of these developments follows the national pattern: housing built at higher densities than before and mixed developments of different sizes and types of dwellings. Leeds had one of the most ambitious programmes among the English cities, driven by Karl Cohen, the Housing Committee Chairman, resulting in an unusual preoccupation with different building systems and non-traditional forms of construction (one of which was patented by the City Architect, *R. A. H. Livett*). This was mostly low-rise housing but from the mid-1950s Leeds also pioneered provision of high-rise flats (first with slabs at Saxton Gardens, 1957, then in increasingly mundane fashion with blocks of twelve storeys at Seacroft in 1962 and eventually up to seventeen storeys high on some suburban estates). Bradford operated on a smaller scale but erected a group of eight Y-plan towers, then a popular type, in Barkerend Road, and eight standard towers at Idle, both *c.* 1955. Taller varieties, typical of the mid 1960s, are at Keighley and Bingley.

In the light of its enthusiasm for towers, it is all the more surprising that from 1965 Leeds insisted on low-rise estates and the improvement of areas of the city through refurbishment of existing terraces and back-to-backs; an approach which was shortly taken up across England. New schemes of this era that reflect the changing priorities in Leeds are the private housing at Newton Garth, Potternewton, by *Derek Walker*, 1969, with two rows of terraces facing a communal garden, and nearby Town Street Housing of *c.* 1970 by the *City Architect*, as well as Potternewton Gardens by the *Yorkshire Development Group*,[*] 1973, a small mixed estate comfortably inserted among C19 terraces. Smaller schemes of infill that defer to their settings are Haworth's West Lane housing by the Keighley Borough Architect, *B. A. Waddington* (1967), that at Great Horton, Bradford, by the local firm, *John Brunton & Partners*, *c.* 1978, which is nicely grouped around the Congregational chapel, and the excellent scheme at Cononley by *Wales, Wales & Rawson*, 1978–9. Individual private houses of architectural merit are a less significant feature than in the pre-war period although at Alwoodley (Leeds) is Gould House, with a glass skin and external staircase, by *David Walker, John Attenborough & Bryn Jones*, 1967.

In the wider area, the role of the County Architect achieved new significance. *Hubert Bennett*, formerly the Borough Architect at Southampton, was appointed in 1945 and built up a massive staff before he became Architect to the London County Council in 1956.[**] The primary task was the building of new SCHOOLS. There were one hundred in all, mostly in an unchallenging Modernist style of snecked stone with plain pitched roofs (e.g. Ilkley and Bardsey primary schools, 1953 and 1954; Rawdon Primary, 1955, and Upper Wharfedale Secondary School of 1953). Much the most distinguished is Tadcaster Grammar School, 1957–60 by Bennett's successor, *A. W. Glover*, which is set in parkland at some distance from the town and incorporates Toulston Lodge, a C19 villa. A similar strategy was taken by *Scherrer & Hicks* of

Manchester at Oakbank School, Keighley, in 1961–4 but the
relationship between old and new there is less sympathetic and
the same firm's Rhodesway School, Allerton, Bradford (1960) is
a better example of their work. Of the same date and equally
characteristic is Benton Park School, Rawdon, by *Sir John Burnet
Tait Durrant & Partners*. The most impressive secondary school
was Salt Grammar School, Baildon, of 1960–5 by *Chamberlin,
Powell & Bon* (dem. 2008), with a quad, circular library and a
gymnasium under a row of barrel vaults, of the type familiar from
their competition design for Churchill College, Cambridge
(1959). The same firm produced the major achievement of this
period in their additions to LEEDS UNIVERSITY, planned in
1960, begun in 1963. This is the most important post-
war building in the area, a dense scheme for 10,000 students with
buildings linked in a continuous sequence on the sloping ground
between the C19 and interwar University, to the N, and the city
centre. An impressive and genuine urban character is achieved,
with much emphasis on vistas through the complex of elevated
decks, bridges and walkways. The buildings for the Leeds Central
Colleges (now Leeds Metropolitan University) by *Yorke, Rosenberg & Mardall*, 1955–69, were an altogether more modest affair,
now very substantially altered. The University at Bradford, established in 1966, is also a disappointment, given the excellent
topography of the site, but appears to have been the casualty of
a failure to fully implement the original masterplan by *Building
Design Partnership*, whose Chesham Building (1966–70) provides
a glimpse of what might have been.

The post-war housing, school and higher education programmes belong to the wider concern with REPLANNING, the
full effect of which is to be seen in the centres of Leeds and
Bradford. Each issued its own development plan: Leeds in
1951–5 promised (but did not realize) major rebuilding of the
civic centre, Bradford began work on its plan in the late 1950s,
sweeping away much of the Victorian city and replacing it with
banal PUBLIC AND COMMERCIAL BUILDINGS, by the City
Engineer *S. G. Wardley* and his successors (Library, Magistrates'
Court, Police Station etc.), and *Young & Engle*, who established
the dull architectural character of this period in Bradford with
their office block, Landmark House (1958–9). A characteristic
building type of the era, especially in areas where large sites
could be obtained, is the multi-functional structure as represented by the Merrion Centre in Leeds, 1962–4 by *Gillinson,
Barnett & Allen*, with its open-air shopping precinct combined
with dance hall, office tower etc., and the theatre/skating
rink/office slab (now Media Museum) in Bradford by *Seifert &
Partners*, 1963–5. The revision of the development plan for Leeds
in 1965–8, with an emphasis on comprehensive reconstruction of
the business and commercial areas and vertical segregation
of pedestrians and traffic, threatened more of the same. While
the worst excesses were avoided, there was much new office
building of a generally anonymous Modernism, the only clear
exceptions to which are the inverted ziggurat of the Bank of

England, King Street, by *Building Design Partnership*, 1969–71, and Lloyds Bank, Park Row, of 1972–7 by *Abbey Hanson Rowe*; both expensively finished. The period also produced some notable examples of indigestible Brutalism: the Highpoint office slab in Westgate, Bradford, 1972, and the Bradford & Bingley headquarters at Bingley, 1976, both by *John Brunton & Partners*. They perpetrated Bradford's similarly unfriendly Kirkgate Shopping Centre in 1974. This was one of the Arndale Centres, soon nationally renowned for their insensitivity to context. The first was at Crossgates, E of Leeds, opened 1967, a massive (9-acre; 3.6-hectare) site covered by low malls and car parks; another, at Headingley, Leeds, is typical in the inclusion of an overbearing tower. Of about the same time is Keighley's Airedale Shopping Centre, part of the town's wider redevelopment. Occasionally, the opportunity to build on a grand scale was exploited effectively, as shown by the Yorkshire Post offices and printworks in Leeds, of 1968–70 by the *John Madin Design Group* of Birmingham.

By now it will be understood that the subject of CHURCH BUILDING is much less significant in the decades after the war. The major work was the addition to Bradford Cathedral by *Edward Maufe*, although this failed to engage very successfully with the medieval fabric. New suburbs required new buildings but stylistic continuity was maintained with the pre-war years, and until the removal of controls in the mid-1950s designs were simple indeed. A break with the past is made by a trio of inexpensive churches for the Anglicans in Leeds by *Geoffrey Davy* of *Kitson, Parish, Ledgard & Pyman* (St David, Beeston; St James p. 550 & St Cyprian, Harehills; St Paul, Ireland Wood) of 1959–65. Preoccupied with developments in liturgical planning, they offer three different solutions to bringing congregation and priest closer together. *G. G. Pace*'s St Saviour, Girlington, Bradford, 122 1966, with its plain brick interior bridges the gap between the earlier C20 Gothic tradition and a spare Modernism; his pleasant chapel of 1961 at Scargill House conference centre, Kettlewell, should be noted also. The first overtly Modernist church for the Roman Catholics is St Nicholas, Gipton, 1960–1 by *Weightman & Bullen* but it too has a traditional bell-tower. Altogether tougher is the Brutalism of the Sacred Heart (R.C.; now Leeds Grand Mosque), by *Derek Walker*, 1963–5. Liturgical changes and the advent of centralized plans influenced the design of St Gregory the Great (R.C.), Swarcliffe, Leeds, by *L. A. G. Pritchard, Son & Partners*, 1969–70, with its hyperbolic paraboloid roof (and excellent furnishings by *Jerzy Faczynski* and *Adam Kossowski*), and *P. H. Langtry-Langton*'s St Margaret Clitherow (R.C.), Threshfield, whose low, pyramid roof structure is exposed as buttresses at the angles. Most radical of all is St Columba, Headingley, by *W. & J. A. Tocher*, 1964–6, with its powerful use of dark brick and glazing under an angular roof.

To close this account of the post-war decades, one should mention two very different kinds of buildings in rural settings; the control station at Chelker Reservoir and Pumping Station at

Lob Wood (Draughton), of 1978–80, in an updated Pennine vernacular, and the eerie cluster of spherical radomes at R.A.F. Menwith Hill on high ground near Darley.

The later C20 to the present

The last thirty years have been characterized by some broad and related themes: reactions against the unadventurous, institutional style of Modernism propagated up to the 1970s; opposition to the destruction of historic buildings and, in favour of reuse and (sometimes) sympathetic conversion; remaking of public spaces in urban areas and an associated boom of residential schemes in those places – reversing the trend of the C19 and C20; the design of new buildings that show sensitivity to context without (in the best examples) a resort to pastiche; and, in most recent times, the growing significance of sustainable architecture.

A small number of buildings commenced in the mid and later 1970s might now be regarded as forward-looking: the Richard Dunn Sports Centre, Bankfoot, Bradford, by the *City Architect's Department*, is an early example of the interest in visibly engineered structures while the Bradford Telegraph & Argus offices, by the *Robinson Partnership*, 1979–80, shows a debt to Foster's offices for Willis, Faber & Dumas, Ipswich, 1975, in the choice of a sleek, dark continuous glass curtain wall to enclose, and reveal, the printworks. In an entirely different vein, but indicative of the resurgence of the classical tradition in British architecture at this time is Newfield at Mickley, a Palladian country villa by *Erith & Terry*, 1979–81.

Stylistic transition during these years is quite well represented by the contrast between, for example, the Magistrates' Court in Skipton, 1971–3 by the *West Riding County Architect's Dept*, and the Combined Court Centre in Leeds, 1977–80 by the *Property Services Agency*, both of which are variations on an ahistoric Modernism, and the increasingly pompous manner of the courts at Harrogate, 1991, Bradford, 1989–92, and, especially, Leeds, 1994. Indeed, from the early to mid 1980s Leeds became synonymous with a renewed enthusiasm for local traditions – the so-called 'Leeds Look' recalling the Victorian and Edwardian eras in brick, terracotta and stone. It was to be found in a diversity of other buildings, from office buildings in Park Row, to the College of Art and Design at Woodhouse, the West Yorkshire Playhouse, 1985–90, and the monstrous Quarry House, 1993. The same kind of showiness, although unwedded to any tradition, is Harrogate's International Conference Centre, 1976–82 by *Morgan Bentley Ferguson Cale & Partners*. At the other end of the scale is the small but distinguished group of primary schools in the Bradford area, several designed by *Ron Furniss* of the City Architect's Department (e.g. Bowling and Manningham, 1982–91) in an attractive self-effacing manner with low roofs. Contemporary with the last of these is the city's

Technology College, with a plan divided by a central 'mall', a concept which gained much currency in schools after about 1980.

CONSERVATION AND REUSE of historic buildings also became an issue of major importance, aided by legislation. Early battles were fought, and nearly lost, for Boar Lane in Leeds, and in the 1980s the need to find new uses for many abandoned industrial buildings became acute. The Leeds Urban Development Corporation played a role after 1985 in reinvigorating buildings along the Aire intermingled with some new build of an appropriate if unimaginative character, but the concept of reuse as a tool for regeneration only really bore fruit from the mid 1990s, so much so that the conversion of former warehouses and mills into offices, flats and shops became a cliché, however well done. The results are often highly memorable, whether individually (the mill at Saltaire, brilliantly reused after 1986 as an arts centre etc. without significant physical change; Douglas Mill, Bowling, Bradford, 2004–5, by *Allen Tod Architects*; and Manningham Mills, Bradford, 2004–9 by *Latham Architects* and *David Morley Architects*) or as a group (Marshall's Mills and the Round Foundry as Holbeck Urban Village, Leeds, and the warehouses in Bradford's Little Germany). REFURBISHMENT of other buildings has taken place in the cause of economic regeneration or, to put it plainly, shopping. The chief beneficiaries in Leeds were the Victorian and Edwardian arcades, most of which were restored in exemplary fashion in the 1990s, culminating in the spectacular revival of *Matcham*'s County Arcade as Victoria Quarter. Here was also demonstrated, in the insertion of a glass curtain wall for the frontage of Harvey Nichols (by *Brooker Flynn Architects*), that sensitive infill need not mean copyism. The same lesson was given by *Dempster Thrussell & Rae* in their remodelling of Bradford's Wool Exchange in 1995–6, also for shops. Retail buildings in thrall to the past are Skipton's Craven Court shopping arcade, 1987, with a well-executed interior in Victorian style and, on a much larger scale, the grotesque pastiche of the Victoria Centre, Harrogate, 1991–2, which makes the error of adopting a neo-Palladian style entirely unrelated to its neighbours and compounds this with a skyline of statues in contemporary dress (later C20 public sculpture is weakly represented in the area as whole).

Here one might also mention some interesting changes made to CHURCHES beyond mere reordering, although the refurbishment of St Anne's R.C. Cathedral, Leeds, by *Buttress Fuller Alsop Williams*, 2005–6, is easily good enough to deserve attention in its own right. Major remodelling and new work is in shorter supply but includes St Augustine, Undercliffe, Bradford, 1987, and St Peter, Gildersome, 1989–92, both by *Ashfield Architects*, and the clever expansion of St Joseph's (R.C), Wetherby by *Pascal J. Stienlet & Son*. The Thornbury Centre, 1998–9 by *Allan Joyce Architects,* in the suburbs of Bradford, is a large complex in which the Anglican worship space is only one element. Many suburban buildings in the cities have been converted for secular use or, equally commonly, have been reused by other faiths as the populations of those areas have changed. From the early 1980s the established Muslim communities in Bradford and Leeds had begun to build anew, so that in several areas the most prominent building is the mosque, dominating streets of two-storey terraces just as churches did a century before. Architecturally, it must be said, they tend to be repetitive, e.g. brick with coloured trim, green domes etc. and without much sophisticated detailing.

The subject of HOUSING by local authorities ceases to be of any significance during this period, having been brought to a halt after 1979, leaving new build in this sector in the hands of housing associations. They were often more adept at bringing interest to small schemes than the monolithic councils. Some back-to-back terraces have been successfully refurbished (e.g. in Hyde Park and Burley, Leeds) and occasionally an opportunity has been taken to correct an earlier mistake, as in the development of Victoria Square in Skipton (1986 by *Wales, Wales & Rawson*), which reintroduced the character of yards behind the High Street that had been cleared in the 1930s. Some private housing has been provided through conversions, as noted above, but a great deal has been in the erection of new flats, especially in Leeds where a mania for towers of a superficially luxurious character has gripped the city. Some of the tallest have been for OFFICES, culminating with the appalling Bridgewater Place, rising to thirty-eight storeys high, in 2004–7. This should not detract attention from the number of good late C20 and early C21 buildings in the city, many of them by local firms: notably No. 1 City Square by *Abbey Hanson Rowe*, 1996–8 (cf. their Yorkshire Building Society offices in Bowling, Bradford); the Host New Media Centre by *Bauman Lyons*, 2001–2, and the Princes Square offices by the prolific *Carey Jones Architects*. National firms have had little of a look in but have made some striking contributions, including the Henry Moore Institute by *Jeremy Dixon & Edward Jones*, with *BDP*, 1989–93, and flats facing Brodrick's Corn Exchange, by *Allford Hall Monaghan Morris*, 2003–5, which manage to be entirely respectful without being too polite. Although Bradford has been the poorer relation during this period, it has the very fine Idle Medical Centre of 1993–4 by *VjQ Architects*, which recalls the abstract forms of earlier Modernism but is entirely harmonious with an area of predominantly C19 character.

At the beginning of the C21 much attention has been paid to the regeneration of PUBLIC SPACE, which began in Leeds with Millennium Square and the refurbishment of City Square, and was followed by Bradford's Centenary Square, in front of the town hall. Bradford, having deprived itself in the mid C20 of a rich dowry of Victorian buildings, required a comprehensive attempt at reform but much of its ambitious regeneration scheme of 2003, which included outlandish proposals from *Will Alsop* for the reflooding of the city's

canal, remain unrealized. Smaller benefits to INFRASTRUCTURE
are also worth noting, including the attractive cable-stayed footbridge over the Aire at Leeds, which made possible a continuous pedestrian route along the riverside, and the similar bridge
spanning the relief road at Bingley, both by *Ove Arup & Part-* 127
ners. The Bus Station at Keighley is a spirited job by *Watson &*
Batty of Guiseley, 2001–2; the same cannot be said of the Bradford Travel Interchange. Expansion of Leeds–Bradford Airport
(*see* Yeadon) since 1985 has made an unfortunate architectural
jumble of the crescent-shaped terminal of 1967–8 by *Norman &*
Dawbarn.

Some of the most important new buildings since the late
C20 have been entirely unconnected with the urban areas.
The Fountains Abbey Visitor Centre, 1987–92 by *Edward* 128
Cullinan, was a bold commission by The National Trust, and in
retrospect, helped to accustom many to the notion that an overtly
modern building could integrate sensitively with historic buildings and landscape through intelligent use of materials. On a
smaller scale, this confidence is also shown by the nicely crafted
Henshaws Arts and Crafts Centre at Knaresborough, 1999, but
the outstanding recent exemplar is the handsome Utopia Pavilion at Broughton Hall by *Hopkins Architects*, 2004–5. Some buildings of the late 1990s and the first decade of the new century
have also displayed a wider preoccupation with low energy use
and sustainability, ranging from self-build 'eco-houses' in the
suburbs of Leeds, to the Epicentre by *OSA*, 1998–9 at the Meanwood Valley Urban Farm, Leeds, and the Ecology Building
Society headquarters at Silsden, 2003, by *Hodson Architects*.
The latest example is the Innovate Green Office by *Rio Architects*
at Thorpe Park (Whitkirk, Leeds), 2004–7, a large commercial
building planned and constructed to produce minimal carbon
emissions.

To conclude, a brief note on some of the physical CHANGES
to the area which have taken place since Pevsner visited half a
century ago. Many will already be apparent from the previous
pages; but a central experience of the period has been the steep
decline of the textile industry from the 1960s on, and a little more
should be said about that. The most dramatic visual consequence
has been the loss of the forests of mill chimneys which used to
dominate the view of any of the industrial towns: surplus to
requirements, expensive to maintain and saddled with the negative connotations of industrial pollution, the chimneys have
frequently been dispensed with even when other parts of the mill
complex have been reused. But of the neighbouring buildings so
many have been cleaned that the soot-attracting qualities of
Millstone Grit have become a distant memory, and there is more
colour everywhere. Other changes are common to the country as
a whole. There are more (and far busier) roads, and fewer
railways; urban expansion has continued – although in general
at nothing like the same rate as in the first half of the C20 –
and the countryside has come to play host to commuters and

second-home owners. But in spite of institutional dismembering the sense of place remains strong, underlined rather than obscured by the area's diversity.

FURTHER READING

Given the West Riding's size and populousness it is not surprising that both the traditional GENERAL HISTORIES of the C18 and C19 and more modern studies have tended to focus on its component parts – towns and cities and their neighbourhoods, deaneries, wapentakes, individual valleys and even some of the big historic parishes – rather than on the county as a whole. So the earliest such work relating to the area is Ralph Thoresby's *Ducatus Leodinensis* of 1715, and this was followed by Gent's *Antient and Modern History of the Loyall Town of Ripon* (1733) and Hargrove's *History of the Castle, Town and Forest of Knaresborough* (1775 etc.). The only real exception is Thomas Allen's rather sketchy *New and Complete History of the County of York* (1828–31); and the lack is compounded by the incomplete state of the Riding's *Victoria County History*, with no detailed topographical volumes published (but vol. 3 (1913) contains a useful account of religious houses).

Two writers however can be considered as virtual county historians, for the northern West Riding at any rate. The first was Thomas Dunham Whitaker, Vicar of Whalley (Lancs.), one of the great figures of Georgian antiquarianism. His works on the area are *The History and Antiquities of the Deanery of Craven* (first edition 1805, second 1812, third, with additions by A. W. Morant, 1878, reprint 1973); his edition of Thoresby's *Ducatus Leodinensis* and his own companion volume, *Loidis and Elmete* (both 1816); and the posthumous *History of Richmondshire* (1823) – which takes in the area of Ingleton, Bentham etc. within the West Riding – a less thoroughly researched work than its predecessors but notable for its engravings after J. M. W. Turner. The second was Harry Speight, son of the manager of a Bradford dyeworks, whose more accessible but still well-researched accounts cover almost all the more rural parts of the area. They include *The Craven and North-West Yorkshire Highlands* (1892), *Nidderdale and the Garden of the Nidd* (1894, revised 1906 as *Nidderdale, from Nun Monkton to Whernside*), *Upper Wharfedale* (1900) and *Lower Wharfedale* (1902). Another work with a relatively wide topographical range which is useful for the present purpose is J. J. Sheahan, *History and Topography of the Wapentake of Claro* (1871); while the main county-wide DIRECTORIES are E. Baines's (1822) for the whole of Yorkshire and Kelly's (1901 etc.) for the West Riding. The principal antiquarian PERIODICAL is the *Yorkshire Archaeological Journal* (hereafter *Y.A.J.*), and a valuable series of monographs is published by the Thoresby Society.

Now the TOWN and CITY HISTORIES. For LEEDS, after Thoresby and Whitaker there is a compelling account of the city in the C19 in A. Briggs, *Victorian Cities* (1963) and two classic general studies, M. W. Beresford's *East End, West End* (1988), covering the period from 1684 to 1842, and S. Burt & K. Grady *The Illustrated History of Leeds* (2002), with a detailed bibliography. Also useful are D. Fraser, *A History of Modern Leeds* (1980), and for documentary sources A. Heap & P. Brears, *Leeds Describ'd* (1994). BRADFORD is well endowed with C19 histories, notably J. James's (1841 and 1866), a number by W. Cudworth, including *Round about Bradford* (1876), on the suburbs and hinterland, and *Historical Notes on the Bradford Corporation* (1881); and W. Scruton, *Pen and Pencil Pictures of Old Bradford* (1889). Of C20 works the most useful is D. James, *Bradford* (1990), again with well-judged bibliography. At HARROGATE the main C19 account is W. Grainge, *History and Topography of Harrogate and the Forest of Knaresborough* (1871); a detailed study of the town's development during the second half of the C19 is H. H. Walker, *Harrogate under the Improvement Commissioners* (1986); and briefer contributions include M. Neesam, *Harrogate, a History and Guide* (2001). For RIPON, following Gent there is J. R. Walbran, *A Guide to Ripon, Fountains Abbey . . . and several places of interest in their vicinity* (1862 etc.) – a guidebook (one of many) rather than a history as such but written by a respected antiquary – while of more recent studies perhaps the most significant here is W. Mackay, 'The Development of Medieval Ripon', *Y.A.J.* 54 (1982). At ILKLEY the C19 account is R. Collyer & J. Horsfall Turner, *Ilkley: Ancient and Modern* (1885), a detailed C20 one D. Carpenter, *Ilkley: the Victorian Era* (1986); and at SKIPTON the C19 history is W. H. Dawson's (1882) and modern works include D. Williams, *Medieval Skipton* (1981). Others are e.g. J. Horsfall Turner (1897) and H. Speight (1898) on Bingley; N. Scatcherd (1874) and W. Smith (1886) on Morley.

VILLAGE and PARISH HISTORIES are too numerous to list. Two informative early examples are both on Harewood, J. Jewel's of 1819 and J. Jones's of 1859, and from the mid C20 there are e.g. T. Brayshaw & R. M. Robinson, *A History of the Ancient Parish of Giggleswick* (1932), which covers the town of Settle, and H. S. Darbyshire & G. D. Lumb on Methley (Thoresby Society 1937). Alongside these one can note some of the early TRAVEL MEMOIRS – e.g. Celia Fiennes (1697), Defoe (1724–6), Torrington (1792) – and a few BIOGRAPHICAL STUDIES. Those of Lady Anne Clifford, restorer of Skipton Castle are by G. C. Williamson (1922) and R. T. Spence (1997), on Sir Titus Salt, creator of Saltaire, there is R. Balgarnie (1877), R. Suddards (ed.), *Titus of Salts* (1976), J. Reynolds, *The Great Paternalist: Titus Salt and the Growth of Bradford* (1983), and J. Styles, *Titus Salt and Saltaire* (1990).

For ARCHITECTURE there is again no general survey of the whole area, but here the agent of division is the local government reorganisation of 1974. The parts in the present county of West Yorkshire have Derek Linstrum's classic *West Yorkshire, Architects and Architecture* (1978), but there is no equivalent for the rest. LEEDS also has his *Historic Architecture of Leeds* (1969), a brief introduction with atmospheric photographs; and then *Leeds* in this series, by Susan Wrathmell, John Minnis and others (2005, reprinted with corrections 2007), which covers the city centre and selected suburbs – and contains a fuller bibliography including works on individual buildings – the text of which has been condensed and revised for this volume. For BRADFORD there are two brief accounts, J. Ayers, *Architecture in Bradford* (1973) and G. Sheeran, *The Buildings of Bradford* (2005). For a wider area but limited as to chronological range there is P. Ryder, *Medieval Buildings of Yorkshire* (1982).

A far greater wealth of material relates to individual building types and to ARCHITECTS, and they can be looked at together after first noting the general sources of information for the latter: Howard Colvin, *A Biographical Dictionary of British Architects 1600–1840* (4th edn 2008) and more schematically the RIBA *Directory of British Architects 1834–1914* (2nd edn 2001). One can start with the GREAT CHURCHES of the Middle Ages; and given the predominance of the Cistercian order that means with P. J. Fergusson, *Architecture of Solitude: Cistercian Abbeys in Twelfth-Century England* (1984) and D. Robinson (ed.) *The Cistercian Abbeys of Britain* (1998). With regard to the individual establishments, for Fountains there is first W. H. St John Hope's description in *Y.A.J.* 15 (1900), then the English Heritage Guidebook, by R. Gilyard-Beer & G. Coppack (1993), and G. Coppack, *Fountains Abbey: the Cistercians in Northern England* (2003). The first two churches are discussed in R. Gilyard-Beer & G. Coppack, 'Excavations at Fountains Abbey 1979–80: the early development of the monastery', *Archaeologia* 108 (1986); and the early C13 E arm in C. Wilson, 'The Early Thirteenth-Century Architecture of Beverley Minster: Cathedral Splendours and Cistercian Austerities', in P. R. Cross & S. D. Lloyd (eds), *Thirteenth-Century England* 3 (1989). For Kirkstall Abbey and Bolton Priory the respective accounts by W. H. St John Hope & J. Bilson (Thoresby Society 1907) and A. H. Thompson (Thoresby Society 1924) remain unsuperseded. The influence of Cistercian architecture on the C12 work at Ripon Cathedral is discussed in C. Wilson, 'The Cistercians as "Missionaries of Gothic" in Northern England', in C. Norton & D. Park (eds), *Cistercian Art and Architecture in the British Isles* (1986); and the C12 building is also examined in detail in M. F. Hearne, 'Ripon Minster: the Beginning of the Gothic style in Northern England', *Transactions of the American Philosophical Society* 73 (1983), and S. Harrison & P. Barker, 'Ripon Minster: an Archaeological Analysis and Reconstruction of the 12th-century Church', *Journal of the British Archaeological Association* 152 (1999).

Coverage of PARISH CHURCHES is again mainly localized. Exceptions are G. A. Poole, *The Churches of Yorkshire* (1844), a selection with a delightful series of engravings; and *The Yorkshire Church Notes of Sir Stephen Glynne* (ed. L. Butler, Y.A.S. Record Series 2007) – written mainly in the 1840s to 60s and perhaps more revealing with regard to Victorian tastes in ecclesiastical architecture than about the buildings themselves, but in the new edition supplemented by useful references to accounts of the individual churches. Then come J.R. Lunn, *Ecclesiology of the Rural Deanery of Boroughbridge* (1867) and *Ecclesiology of the Rural Deanery of Knaresborough* (1870), R.V. Taylor, *Churches of Leeds* (1875), covering a wide area round the city,* and W.A. Shuffrey, *The Churches of the Deanery of North Craven* (1914), all of which deal with churches of their own times as well as medieval ones and are informative on C19 restorations and embellishments. An invaluable modern work is P. Ryder, *Medieval Churches of West Yorkshire* (1993). Accounts of individual churches are again too numerous to list, but mention should be made of the well-researched series on several in the vicinity of Leeds, produced from the 1930s to the 1950s by the Y.A.S. librarian G.E. Kirk, and of a number in *Y.A.J.* throughout the C20. Moving on in time, Leeds has T. Friedman, *Church Architecture in Leeds* (1996), important for the C18, and J. Minnis & T. Mitchell, *Religion and Place in Leeds* (2007). For the C19 more generally one can start with M.H. Port, *Six Hundred New Churches* (1967), on the Commissioners' churches; but beyond that the most useful modern sources tend to be the studies of architects. Most relevant for this area are F. Beckwith on Thomas Taylor (Thoresby Society 1949); C. Webster on Chantrell (Thoresby Society 1991); A. Quiney on Pearson (1979); J.M. Crook on Burges (1981); A. Saint on Norman Shaw (1976) and G. Brandwood on Temple Moore (1997). An account of C19 church building and restoration in one small rural corner is P. Leach, 'Ecclesiology in Wharfedale: two Incumbents and their Churches', *Transactions of the Ancient Monuments Society* 43 (1999).

NONCONFORMIST CHAPELS are covered by C. Stell, *An Inventory of Nonconformist Chapels and Meeting Houses in the North of England* (1994), supplemented by D.M. Butler, *The Quaker Meeting Houses of Britain* (1999). With regard to ecclesiastically-related SCULPTURE, for the Anglo-Saxon period *see* W.G. Collingwood in *Y.A.J.* 23 (1915) and now E. Coatsworth (ed.), *Corpus of Anglo-Saxon Stone Sculpture in England: Western Yorkshire* (2008); for Romanesque R. Wood, 'The Romanesque Doorways of Yorkshire', *Y.A.J.* 66 (1994) etc.; and for the later medieval alabaster tombs P. Routh, *Medieval Effigial Alabaster Tombs in Yorkshire* (1976) etc. The post-medieval period is represented by M. Whinney, *Sculpture in Britain 1530–1830* (Pelican History of Art, 2nd edn. 1988), A. White, *A Biographical Dictionary of London Tomb Sculptors c.1560–c.1660* (Walpole Society 1999), and R. Gunnis, *Dictionary of British Sculptors 1660–1851* (2nd edn 1968). For C19 STAINED GLASS, M. Harrison, *Victorian Stained Glass* (1980) is a helpful introduction, and for individual manufacturers there are A.C. Sewter, *Stained Glass of William Morris and his Circle* (1974) and the Kempe Society's *Corpus of Kempe Stained Glass in the United Kingdom and Ireland* (2000).

---

*But unfortunately incomplete, arranged alphabetically by place and stopping after the letter L.

CASTLES require only a brief mention. On Skipton an important contribution is D. F. Renn, 'An Angevin Gatehouse at Skipton Castle', *Chateau Gaillard* 7 (1975), and well-documented accounts of several phases in the castle's history are provided in three short works by R. T. Spence (1991, 1994, 2002). A reconstruction by J. Goodall of the King's Tower at Knaresborough is in *Country Life* (17 January 2008). But for DOMESTIC ARCHITECTURE the material is abundant. One can begin with A. Emery, *Greater Medieval Houses of England and Wales* 1 (1996); then moving on to the late medieval and early modern minor gentry houses and yeoman farmhouses, there is one still invaluable classic, T. Ambler's *Old Halls and Manor Houses of Yorkshire* (1913) and two broadly complementary modern works, C. Giles, *Rural Houses of West Yorkshire 1400–1830* (1986) and B. Harrison & B. Hutton, *Vernacular Houses in North Yorkshire and Cleveland* (1984). The former includes an inventory of examples, the latter (covering a narrower social range) does not; but both are backed by an extensive archive of survey reports on individual buildings, the former's at the National Monuments Record Centre (English Heritage), the latter's (by members of the Yorkshire Vernacular Buildings Study Group) at the Yorkshire Archaeological Society. Particular aspects of the subject are also covered by B. Hutton, 'Timber framed Houses in the Vale of York', *Medieval Archaeology* 17 (1973), B. Hutton & J. Martin, *Doorways in the Dales* (1986), and P. Leach, 'Rose Windows and other Follies: Alternative Architecture in the Seventeenth-Century Pennines', *Architectural History* 43 (2000). For the grander COUNTRY HOUSES and their estates an informative snapshot of the position in the early C18 is provided by *Samuel Buck's Yorkshire Sketchbook* (Wakefield Historical Publications 1979). The relevant biographies of architects are P. Leach on Paine (1988), B. Wragg on Carr (ed. G. Worsley, 2000), E. Harris on Adam's interiors (2001), and (although marred by over-enthusiastic attributionism) A. Taylor on The Websters of Kendal (ed. J. Martin, 2004) – to which can be added J. Low on William Belwood, *Y.A.J.* 56 (1984) and P. Leach on 'Lord Burlington in Wharfedale', *Architectural History* 32 (1989). Regarding individual examples there are the usual articles in *Country Life*, while particularly substantial or otherwise significant studies include M. Mauchline, *Harewood House* (1992), Leeds Museums and Art Galleries, *Drawing from the Past: William Weddell and the Transformation of Newby Hall* (2005) and P. Smith, 'A House by Sir Christopher Wren? The second Newby Hall and its Gardens', *Georgian Group Journal* 16 (2008).

The industrialists' and merchants' VILLAS of the C19 are the main focus – its title notwithstanding – of A. Healey, *A Series of Picturesque Views of the Castles and Country Houses in Yorkshire* (1885), and the subject of G. Sheeran's analysis, *Brass Castles: West Yorkshire New Rich and their Houses 1800–1914* (1993). For suburban housing in general there is S. Muthesius, *The English Terraced House* (1982); for that of Leeds in particular C. Treen,

'The process of suburban development in North Leeds 1870–1914', in F. M. L. Thompson (ed.), *The Rise of Suburbia* (1982); F. Trowell, *Nineteenth-Century Speculative Housing in Leeds with special reference to the suburb of Headingley 1838–1914* (York University PhD thesis 1982); and D. Hall, *Far Headingley, Weetwood and West Park* (2000): for Bradford G. Sheeran, *The Victorian Houses of Bradford* (1990). The studies of architects are D. Boswell, *The Kitsons and the Arts* on Bedford & Kitson (York University PhD thesis, 1995), and C. Hussey (1950) and R. Gradidge (1981) on Lutyens. WORKERS' HOUSING is covered by L. Caffyn, *Workers' Housing in West Yorkshire 1750–1920* (1986) and the final chapter of C. Giles & I. Goodall, *Yorkshire Textile Mills 1770–1930* (1992), A. Ravetz, *Model Estate: planned housing at Quarry Hill* (1974) and M. Glendinning & S. Muthesius, *Tower Block: Modern Public Housing in England, Scotland, Wales and Northern Ireland* (1994). It is set in a wider context by S. D. Chapman, *The History of Working Class Housing* (1971), J. N. Tarn, *Five per cent Philanthropy* (1973) and J. A. Jowitt (ed.), *Model Industrial Communities in mid-Nineteenth Century Yorkshire* (1986).

With regard to PUBLIC BUILDINGS, K. Grady, *The Georgian Public Buildings of Leeds and the West Riding* (Thoresby Society 1989) and C. Cunningham, *Victorian and Edwardian Town Halls* (1987) are useful for Leeds and Bradford, and the relevant studies of architects are D. Linstrum, *Towers and Colonnades* (1999) on Brodrick, and C. Cunningham & P. Waterhouse on Waterhouse (1992). An interesting discussion is I. Webb, 'The Bradford Wool Exchange: Industrial Capitalism and the Popularity of Gothic', *Victorian Studies* (1976). For schools there is by M. Seaborne, *The English School* (1971 and 1977), supplemented by Bradford Corporation, *Education in Bradford since 1870* (1970); for transport M. Clarke, *The Leeds and Liverpool Canal* (1994) and *The Aire & Calder Navigation* (1999), G. Biddle, *Britain's Historic Railway Buildings: An Oxford Gazetteer of Sources and Sites* (2003) and R. Anderson & G. K. Fox, *Stations and Structures on the Settle & Carlisle Railway* (1986). For PUBLIC SCULPTURE see B. Read, *Victorian Sculpture* (1982) and S. Beattie, *The New Sculpture* (1983). The central text for INDUSTRIAL and COMMERCIAL BUILDINGS is C. Giles & I. Goodall, *Yorkshire Textile Mills 1770–1930* (1992), which again has an inventory of examples and is backed by an archive of reports at the National Monuments Record Centre. The textile warehouses in Bradford are examined in J. S. Roberts, *The Bradford Textile Warehouse 1770–1914* (Bradford University MSc thesis, 1976) and *Little Germany* (1977), and S. Varo, *A Mercantile Meander* (1989); aspects of Leeds's industrial development in G. Cookson, *Early Textile Engineers in Leeds 1780–1850* (Thoresby Society 1994). For lead mining *see* e.g. A. Raistrick, *Lead Mining in the Mid Pennines* (1973) and R. T. Clough, *The Lead Smelting Mills of the Yorkshire Dales and Northern Pennines* (1980); for banks J. Booker, *Temples of Mammon: the Architecture of Banking* (1990), for shops K. Morrison, *English Shops and Shopping* (2004).

Finally regarding other disciplines, a review of the ARCHAEOLOGY of the area is T. G. Manby, S. Moorhouse & P. Ottaway (eds), *The Archaeology of Yorkshire: an Assessment at the Beginning of the 21st Century* (2003) and a guide to a single aspect is J. D. Hedges (ed.), *The Carved Rocks on Rombalds Moor* (1986). For GEOLOGY *see* e.g. T. Waltham, *The Yorkshire Dales, Landscape and Geology* (2008), and F. G. Dimes & M. Mitchell, *The Building Stone Heritage of Leeds* (1996).

GAZETTEER

ABERFORD

Limestone village along the Roman road from Castleford to
Tadcaster – later part of the Great North Road – switchbacking
across the valley of the Cock Beck. A market charter was granted
in 1251. Parlington Hall, the seat of the Gascoigne family, was
1 m. to the SW.

ST RICARIUS. The only church in Britain dedicated to the C7
Frankish hermit St Riquier. Norman W tower heavily restored
in 1891 by *G. Fowler Jones & Son*. Two-light belfry openings
framed by a super-arch (cf. Bramham), late medieval parapet
and short spire (also cf. Bramham). The rest 1861–2 by *Salvin*,
apart from one small Norman window re-set in the chancel N
wall, and the walling of the E end, which had already been
rebuilt *c.* 1845. Dec style, the nave with a clerestory of small
trefoils. – SCULPTURE. Fragments of three Anglo-Saxon
crosses. Interlace patterns, late C9 or C10. – Large PAINTING
of the Crucifixion, round the chancel arch, by a parishioner,
1914. Very bad. – STAINED GLASS. E window by *Sir Ninian
Comper*, 1923; chancel N and S, S chapel S, and S aisle third from
E, by *Wailes*, 1862; S chapel E by *Ward & Hughes*, 1862; S aisle
W by *Michael O'Connor*, *c.* 1862; S aisle second from E by
Preedy, *c.* 1868; N aisle NE by *Clayton & Bell*, *c.* 1870.

At the entrance to the churchyard the MARKET CROSS, restored
1912. In the Main Street a little further N ABERFORD HOUSE,
mid-C18 with a handsome but curiously organized ashlar front,
with two identical pedimented doorways. The rhythm on the
ground floor is two windows, doorway, two windows, doorway,
two windows: on the first floor there are simply five windows,
one above each of the pairs below and one above each doorway.
Quoins, partly balustraded parapet. The explanation seems to
be that a house with a five-bay front centred on the r. doorway
was carefully extended to the l. in the same style a few decades
later. This is clearer at the back, where the extension is
expressed as a big canted bay, embracing an octagonal dining
room. The l. doorway at the front opens onto the service areas,
which include a large kitchen at a lower level behind a high
blank wall. N again, back on the other side of the street, THE
SWAN HOTEL, a coaching inn of the late C18, with segment-
headed archway between two canted bays, and extensive

Aberford, Gascoigne Almshouses.
Lithograph by A. McClure, c. 1845

stabling behind. Then the former WATER MILL, probably late
c18, with Gothick Y-traceried window in the gable-end and
pointed tailrace below; and behind it a house also with a
Gothick window. After that, across the beck, a little triangular
green with at its head FIELD HOUSE, late c18, ashlar, three
bays with pediment; and finally a short row of model cottages
of the Becca Hall estate (*see* below), dated 1865.

A number of outlying items.

R.C. CHAPEL (former), ⅜ m. s of the village, on the E side of the
old main road. A very early example, built in 1793 (Catholic
Relief Act 1791), the site provided by Sir Thomas Gascoigne
of Parlington Hall.* Simple three-bay rectangle with round-
headed windows. Former presbytery adjoining, perhaps
later. Then on the w side of the road the GASCOIGNE
ALMSHOUSES, a much more ambitious affair, 1843–5 by
George Fowler Jones for Mary and Elizabeth Gascoigne as a
memorial to their father and brothers. Now offices. Long
ashlar front in Perp Gothic style, with elaborate central tower,
many steeply pitched gables, and many outsize octagonal pinnacles. Projecting cross-wings with traceried windows, housing
the chapel (l.) and refectory (r.), the domestic intermediate
parts two-storeyed. Rib-vaulted porch in the tower, leading to
an entrance hall with contemporary stained glass. At the back,
office ranges added 1998–2004 by *Duncan Biggin*, in a busy
variety of materials. Third in this group, on the E side of the
road again, HICKLAM HOUSE, mid-c18 box, three bays and
two-and-a-half storeys, brick with stone quoins. (Venetian
screen at the half-landing of the staircase.)

PARLINGTON HALL, home of the Gascoignes from the early c18
to 1905, was largely demolished in 1952; but much of the
landscaped park and several subsidiary buildings remain, all

---

*The Gascoignes had been R.C. until Sir Thomas Gascoigne conformed in 1780.
In 1772 he had commissioned a design for a chapel and chaplain's house, in the
Gothick style, from *John Carr*.

evidently from the time of Sir Thomas Gascoigne (†1810). Chief amongst the latter is the TRIUMPHAL ARCH, ¼ m. N of the house at the head of the avenue running from the village, erected in 1781–3 to the design of *Thomas Leverton*. About 30 ft (9 metres) high, it famously carries on its frieze the inscription, in fine large letters, LIBERTY IN N AMERICA TRIUMPHANT MDCCLXXXIII – a statement of political dissent reflecting Sir Thomas Gascoigne's position as a follower of the second Marquess of Rockingham, advocate of colonial independence during the American War. It is of the Arch of Constantine type, with three openings, the central larger than the others, framed by Doric pilasters; but the idea is confined to two dimensions, the structure stage-set thin. Other components are the HOME FARM, ¼ m. WSW – brick, quadrangular – for which there is a variant design by *Carr*; the GARDEN HOUSE, between the arch and the hall, three-by-three bays; and a circular Gothick DEER SHED, ½ m. E, now ruinous, of 1802 by *William Lindley* of Doncaster. Also PIKE'S HEAD LODGE, facing the entrance to the avenue, on the W edge of the village in Cattle Lane, pyramid-roofed with cylindrical chimneys at each corner; a pedimented lodge E of the deer shed, on Parlington Lane; and beside the main road ½ m. S of the almshouses the HOOKMOOR LODGES, smaller pedimented pavilions, more vigorously detailed, with curious quatrefoil-plan gatepiers between. ⅝ m. SW of these, off the road to Garforth, PARK HOUSE, a complicated composition, partly mutilated, facing N across the park towards the site of Parlington Hall. Two-storey canted-bay centre between taller flanking bays, attached by short screen walls to pavilions similar to the Hookmoor Lodges, with quadrant screens beyond.

BECCA HALL, 1⅜ m. NW of the village. *c.* 1785 by *William Lindley* for William Markham, private secretary to Warren Hastings, much altered and extended. The 1780s house is of two storeys and five bays, with pediment over the three-bay centre. Of the early C19 will be the slightly taller one-bay attachments l. and r., the tetrastyle Doric porch, and a rear extension providing an enlarged staircase hall. The attachments have an awkward disposition of the floor levels – two main storeys and a mezzanine between – unrelated to those of the main block: tripartite windows under segmental relieving arches. Then come the single-storey canted bay windows flanking the porch, the Victorian plate glass etc. To the l. a pebbledashed service range perhaps incorporating part of an earlier house – see the big chimney-breast and a chamfered stone jamb inside – and attached to the back a brutally blank office wing of *c.* 1960, scheduled for demolition at the time of writing. Spacious early C19 cantilevered stone staircase, interior detail otherwise mainly *c.* 1860.

ABERFORD DYKES. Impressive bank-and-ditch linear earthwork, running for *c.* 1½ m. WNW of the village on the N side of the Cock Beck (Becca Banks and The Ridge) and *c.* 1 m. to the E, in two intersecting sections S of the beck (The Rein and South Dyke). Opinion is divided as to whether it is of Iron Age or Dark Age date – in the latter case in part associated with the Celtic kingdom of Elmet – and whether wholly defensive or partly a boundary marker.

0040

ADDINGHAM

Substantial village in the middle reaches of Wharfedale, with a long twisting main street. The site of the first worsted spinning mill, opened in 1787 (dem. 1973).

St Peter. The church stands within an Iron Age ditched enclosure on the bank of the Wharfe, at the E end of the village. At first sight it appears to be entirely of the C18, with W tower, three-bay nave and slightly lower chancel. This phase dates from 1757 and was executed by the mason *Joshua Breare*. Rather heavily detailed, in a generally pre-Palladian vein, with rustic quoins and round-headed windows. Nave and chancel doorways with triple keystones and blocked surrounds. But much of the medieval church remains also. Perp N aisle, with the usual low straight-headed windows, with uncusped arched lights, described as 'new' in 1547. Arcade inside of three bays with octagonal piers and four-centred, single-chamfered arches dying into them. Four-centre-headed, double-chamfered chancel arch with C18 responds. Handsome nave roof – which was propped while the S wall was rebuilt – with tie-beams and kingposts, and ornament including the coat of arms of the Vavasour family, medieval Lords of the Manor who also held the incumbency of the church between 1483 and 1510. Sacristy, chancel roof and deeply unfortunate Middle Pointed E window of 1858. – Font. C18, of baluster shape. – W gallery, on crude columns. 1757, made by *Thomas Guyer*, carpenter. – sculpture. Late Anglo-Saxon cross-shaft, with two small figures below an encircled cross. Interlace above and on the sides. – monuments. Classical tablets to Eliza Parr †1809 by *James Sherwood* of Derby, and William Cunliffe †1823 by *William Whitelaw* of New Road, London. – William Cunliffe Lister †1841. Gothic aedicule by *Francis Webster* of Kendal.

E of the church the former Rectory, 1808. Three-bay front with broad pediment. S of it a small one-arched footbridge carrying a footpath to the church over the little beck. Possibly C17. Beyond this in walled grounds Hallcroft Hall, a restrained hipped-roofed block of *c.* 1840. Deep modillioned eaves and Italianate porch. To the W, in Church Street, Fir Cottage, 1677, has a flattened-ogee-headed doorway (cf. Old Hall, Bradley); and then in the Main Street, the principal accents are the Mount Hermon Wesleyan Reform Chapel, 1861, with simple pedimented front, and

further on the former PIECE HALL, built *c.* 1826 for the Cock- [72]
shott family of cotton manufacturers and merchants for the
storage and display of cloth. Handsome ashlar façade with pediment and giant angle pilasters, a little like that of a Nonconformist chapel of the period, the building behind a
two-storeyed rectangle running back from the street. Two
earlier undertakings of John Cockshott are in streets off to the
N: THE ROOKERY, Bolton Road, *c.* 1805, two short rows of
back-to-back cottages with, originally, a communal loomshop
building for handloom weavers set at right angles against the
end of each row (one remains); and in CHAPEL STREET a
larger, three-storey LOOMSHOP built *c.* 1817, which in 1829
accommodated sixty-two cotton handlooms. Beyond this, in
the graveyard of the former Methodist chapel, the MAU-
SOLEUM of George Oates Greenwood †1845. Egyptian-cum-
Grecian style, with battered sides of banded masonry and
primitive pediments, crowned by a huge urn.

HIGH MILL, on the river ³⁄₈ m. NW. Cotton-spinning mill
built *c.* 1788, replacing a corn mill. Converted to worsted
spinning *c.* 1822 and to silk spinning 1869. Now housing.
Much altered three-storey range incorporating the wheelhouse
of the corn mill. Segment-headed millrace and tailrace entries
in the gable-ends.

At ADDINGHAM MOORSIDE, 1¼ m. SSW, several C17 farmhouses, including CRAGG HOUSE, 1695, small double pile
with central lobby entry and another flattened-ogee-headed
doorway. Segment-headed housebody fireplace flanked by a
spice cupboard dated 1698. Further W, HIGH HOUSE, 1697,
is of the same plan type but refronted in the C18, with an oval
panel over the entrance and unchamfered mullions. In
between, UPPER GATE CROFT, in origin one-storeyed and
perhaps a longhouse, of *c.* 1600. Raised and the porch added
c. 1700, the adjoining barn largely rebuilt C19. ½ m. SE of Cragg
House, the PIPER'S CRAG STONE, an outlier of the Bronze
Age carved rocks on Ilkley Moor (q.v.).
See also Farfield Hall.

AIRTON   9050

Dales village with a triangular green on which stands just one
cottage with its walled garden.

FRIENDS' MEETING HOUSE, at the E corner. 1700. Featureless
towards the road: on the other side a segment-headed doorway
under a hood on shaped brackets, and two-light mullioned
windows. Humble interior with elders' bench at the W end,
women's chamber to the E, screened by a partition with top-
hung shutters, with gallery over (cf. Skipton).

AIRTON MILL, beyond, beside the juvenile river Aire. Cotton
spinning mill, replacing a corn mill, now flats. Main part is the

'new mill', built in 1836, which was both water- and steam-powered but has lost its chimney. Three storeys and attic with bellcote on the s gable.

p. 29 VIPONT HOUSE, at the sw corner of the green. Dated 1666, a small proto-double pile. But it faces away from the village and has the entrance in the gable-end, into the rear outshut. Pigeon holes to the loft above the doorway.

SCOSTHROP MANOR, ¼ m. N. Hearth-passage house with two-storey ashlar-fronted porch dated 1686. The porch has ball finials to the gable, a stepped transomed window to the upper floor, and an ornamented doorhead with two semicircles. Altered 1905.

4060

ALDBOROUGH

A charming village centred on a wide triangular green and set on gently rising ground with views to the North York Moors. This is the site of the Roman cantonal *civitas* of the Brigantes tribe, with the name *Isurium Brigantum*. One of the most northerly towns of the empire, it may have been founded as a military camp in the late C1, perhaps succeeding a fort at Roecliffe when the main crossing of Dere Street over the River Ure was fixed about ½ m. N of the present village. A tile stamped LEG. IX HISP, the mark of the famous Ninth Legion (based at York from the 70s until the 120s) is in the Museum. The surviving built remains are no earlier than C2–C3, by which time this was a flourishing civil township and administrative centre. Its history from the departure of the Romans in the C5 is enigmatic until Domesday, where it is recorded as Burg, a royal property and the centre of Burgshire. A castle is recorded in the later C12. After the new bridge across the Ure was built at Boroughbridge (q.v.) ½ m. w, Burg became the Old Borough and declined in significance. Aldborough was a quintessential C18 pocket borough, controlled by the Duke of Newcastle, and until the Great Reform Act of 1832 returned two M.P.s – including Pitt the elder.

Remains of the ROMAN TOWN were uncovered as early as the C18; sporadic excavations were undertaken from the 1830s, notably in 1846 and 1848 by H. E. Smith who described all the finds in *Reliquiae Isurianae* (1852). By then a private museum had been established by Andrew Lawson, Lord of the Manor. More systematic work followed in the next century, which established the town's grid plan and the extent of its defences. The WALLS, built c. A.D. 200, were 1¼ m. in circumference and covered an area of 60 acres (cf. Londinium: 360 acres). The village occupies the s two-thirds of this area. The defences were over 8 ft (2.5 metres) thick and faced in coursed red sandstone, with an earthen rampart behind and – at the N end at least – a 13-ft (4-metre) ditch in front. For foundation the builders rammed large cobblestones, river pebbles, soil and sand into the blue clay to a depth of 5ft (1.5 metres). On this durable base the walls might have been raised to over 12ft (3.7 metres) high. In the C4 the defensive ditch was moved outwards to accommodate bastions, of millstone grit or white limestone, at each of the corners. Remains of three additional watch towers have also been uncovered. Of the original gates, two huge blocks of millstone grit, evidently brought from a distance, were excavated on the site of the N GATE, through which a cobbled road 30ft (9 metres) wide ran towards Dere Street and the Ure. The line of the N–S road through the town – the Via Praetoria – is partly preserved as the village street running uphill s of the church. It would have intersected with a lateral road although the present E–W street follows a slightly different line; Back Street represents the E street of the grid and no doubt was originally complemented by another street to the W. The manor presumably stands on the site of the W gate while the church occupies the position of a large public building, probably the forum-basilica (a range over 270ft (82m) long E–W was excavated in 1770). The position of the S gate is approximately marked by the museum (English Heritage) and the 'PROSPECT TOWER'. Built before 1852 (it is depicted in the handsome frontispiece to *Reliquiae Isurianae*), evidently for visitors to the recently excavated remains, it housed the museum after 1864. Originally square, with moulded crenellations enclosing the viewing platform, later extended. The broken fragments of the CITY WALL are to be seen to the W, in the captivating setting of a pinetum planted by Andrew Lawson, who oversaw the excavations *c.* 1850. Here one may wander along the lush paths and examine the lower courses of part of the wall at one's leisure, and in an evocative atmosphere. They extend over a distance of 300 yards, incorporating at intervals the remains of the watch towers, and take one to the deep, overgrown quarry from which the Roman masons derived their material. Further fragments are in the grounds of Aldborough Manor to the N (*see* below), where C19 excavations revealed the site of the baths and a hypocaust.

Aldborough was famous in former centuries for its MOSAICS, as Leland (1534) and Drake (1730) testify. Altogether twenty pavements, or fragments of pavements, have been found but practically all of them, alas, have vanished and only five are known to remain *in situ*. Most were found in the SW quarter of the town where the houses of the wealthy presumably stood and their quality is a measure of the town's prosperity. Two are still visible, housed in little pantile-roofed huts in a field to the N of the museum; one of these huts has bulgy rusticated walls of local red sandstone. Both floors are dated to the C2–C3. The first, discovered in 1832, depicts a lion sitting under a palm tree, the second, found in 1848, is in a near-perfect state of preservation and shows at its centre an eight-pointed star. Both have outer bands of guilloche pattern but the latter has an additional border of swastikas. A fragment of a third mosaic (early C4) from an apsidal-ended room in the same building is now in the museum. It shows part of a female figure, one of the Nine Muses (probably Thalia or Polyhymnia) of whom others survived at the time of its discovery in 1846. But its greatest significance is its Greek inscription (unique in Britain) 'Helicon', executed in blue glass, a material rarely used. More of the same scheme remains buried along with two others that lie beneath buildings in the village. One more is in Leeds City Museum, a large pavement depicting Romulus and Remus and the wolf. This was discovered near Aldborough Hall in 1842 but its crude execution has cast doubt on its authenticity. For some years it was used to pave a summerhouse in Boroughbridge.

St Andrew. Low and long. Nave and aisles are of *c.* 1330–60, see the two-light Dec windows of the aisles; the s aisle rebuilt with ashlar in 1827. Perp chancel, with fine E window (later renewed), short Perp w tower, Perp clerestory. Inside, four-bay arcades: octagonal piers, double-chamfered arches; hood-moulds with big headstops on the N side only. The arches intersect at their springing points with vertical pieces standing on the abaci. Good nave roof panelled with bosses and grotesque masks. *Salvin* restored and refurnished in 1864–5, adding the organ chamber and unblocking the w window. – PULPIT. With a C17 inscription, but mostly C19. – PANELLING around the chancel, C17, and brought from various places.– DOOR to the vestry. Possibly C14, with scrolly hinges. – SCULPTURE. Badly worn Roman relief figure, set atop other fragments. Believed to be Mercury; his staff was recognizable in the C17, but now worn away. – Wooden PANEL of Daniel in the Lion's den in high relief; Flemish, C16? BREAD SHELF. Handsome with pedimented top; C18. – CHARITY BOARD. One very large example, detailing the bequest of Mark Smithson (†1787; *see* his table tomb outside). – STAINED GLASS. In the N aisle windows, Dec canopies in settings composed by *John Barnett* of York, 1827 (motifs repeated in his N aisle E window of 1830). Quatrefoil top light of the second from the E by *Henry Gyles*, 1700. E window, 1843, and chancel SE, 1852, by *Wailes*. s aisle, E and first from E by *Kempe* (1885 and 1889), second from E by *Kempe & Co.*, 1909. Fourth from E by *A. O. Hemming*, 1907, with attractive details of birds and animals, and good colouring. Vibrant w window, the Good Shepherd, with fruiting vines, passion flowers etc; 1865, probably by *Ward & Hughes* (cf. chancel NW of the same date). – MONUMENTS. BRASS of William de Aldeburgh, *c.* 1360, the figure 6 ft (1.8 metres) long. – William Aldburgh †1627. A tiny empty frame consisting of slender columns, entablature and on top framed arms.

w of the church is the small Tudorbethan National School of 1830, now VILLAGE INSTITUTE. It overlooks a small green with the peculiar VILLAGE CROSS, which stood originally in Market (now Hall) Square at Boroughbridge (q.v.). Possibly C14. A slender shaft, heavily weathered, with four diagonal shafts and four spurs between, in three stages of decreasing height. The shafts of the second stage have crocketed capitals; on top of the final stage an ill-fitting crocketed capital, clearly not the original arrangement. Around this green an agreeable mix of mostly brick cottages, with some evidence of earlier structures, e.g. MANOR COTTAGE with close-studded first floor. W is the grander ALDBOROUGH MANOR, which was bought in 1825 by Andrew Lawson and remodelled by *R. H. Sharp c.* 1840. Three storeys to the street, with a bowed (former) porch under a two-storey bow window. Five-bay garden (now entrance) front. In the garden, in addition to the Roman remains, are fragments of an Anglo-Saxon CROSS-SHAFT, the upper parts of which are at Cundall (North Riding). A very good piece of the late C8–early C9, attributed to the Uredale Master and showing influence of Mercian traditions. One scene is interpreted as the Raising of Lazarus (cf. Masham, North Riding). S of the church is the spacious green known as THE SQUARE, on which is a maypole, and on the upper (S) side the C18 OLD COURT HOUSE, an utterly simple two-bay brick building with its gable-end to the green, against which steps rise to a platform in front of a blocked door. Here the hustings were held. In front are the stocks. To the E, two pretty mid-C19 cottages in a Tudor Revival style, similar in manner to extensions made to ALDBOROUGH HALL after 1834. This house, NE of the church, is probably *c.* 1628–9, when Arthur Aldburgh purchased the manor. Three big storeys plus attics, with many large mullioned-and-transomed windows. Twin gables to front and back and full-height gabled bays projecting from the centre on three sides. The bay on the S side possibly C19, when other substantial additions and alterations were made including a N wing – pieces salvaged from its demolition have been used to make up the N porch. (Spectacular late C17 oak staircase, from Lymore Hall, near Montgomery, dem. 1930s, introduced by Donald Hart (cf. Hazlewood Castle and the Bridge Inn, Walshford.) At second floor, extending W–E through the centre of the house, a passage with pretty low-relief flower designs to the ceiling. First-floor drawing room formed from two rooms and lined with raised-and-fielded pine panelling).

STUDFORTH HILL, SE of the line of the Roman wall. A knoll, probably the site of a Norman motte or ringwork, possibly the royal castle documented at Aldborough in 1158–75.

ALDFIELD   2060

ST LAURENCE. Chapel founded in the C14, rebuilt *c.* 1783. 74
T-shaped, with a 'transept' halfway along the N side, and a three-bay S flank with central entrance, opposite the transept. Pointed windows with Y-tracery: C19 Dec replacement at the E end. Over the doorway a sundial dated 1696. Very attractive

interior, perfectly preserved, with four-centred plaster ribbed vault. – Three-decker PULPIT on the s wall beside the entrance, and BOX PEWS all arranged to face it. – ALTAR RAIL with turned balusters, and ogee-headed CATECHISM BOARDS flanking the E window. – MONUMENTS. Caroline Mary Brooke †1814 and six siblings, by *Skelton* of York. Wall tablet with a high-relief sarcophagus. – Temperance Bury †1820, similar, by *R. King*.

ALLERTON MAULEVERER

4050

A variegated scatter of buildings just off the Great North Road. Ownership has been varied too. From the Mauleverers the estate passed in 1721 to Richard Arundell (†1759), friend of Lord Burlington, M.P. for Knaresborough and Surveyor of the King's Works; then later it went in rapid succession by purchase, first in 1786 to the Duke of York, brother of the Prince Regent, in 1789 to Colonel Thomas Thornton – who renamed it Thornville Royal – and in 1805 to the 17th Lord Stourton.

73   ST MARTIN. A very strange but not unattractive church, built in 1745 by Richard Arundell: a little of the fabric of its medieval predecessor was retained inside. The architect was almost certainly the Office of Works place-holder *John Vardy*, who the following year made (unexecuted) designs for a new house here for Arundell. The stylistic make-up is a mixture of Gothick, simplified Burlingtonian Palladian and what seems to be a proto-Neo-Norman – what the C18 would have called 'Saxon'; while the plan is equally noteworthy, cruciform with aisled nave and long chancel but with a tower over the W bay of the latter rather than the crossing. The W front sets the tone, the nave with a steep gable – the significance of which becomes apparent shortly – but the aisles presented as slightly projecting pavilions with open pediments on heavy antae: round-headed W doorway, matching windows to the aisles, but above the door a big oculus and two smaller round-headed windows of more overtly 'Norman' character. The aisle and chancel sides on the other hand have pointed windows, the transepts two-light windows with an attempt at plate tracery, and the E end a re-set Late Perp window of five lights. The most explicitly Neo-Norman element is the tower, with more of the smaller round-headed openings, an eyebrow-like stringcourse above them, and a pyramid roof. The interior is even more of a mix. The s nave arcade is of the C14, four bays with octagonal piers and no capitals, the N arcade is an C18 copy of it (leaving a short stretch of medieval masonry to the E), but the tower arches and the transverse arches in the aisles are straightforwardly round-headed classical. Most remarkable is the nave roof, elaborately hammerbeamed and at first sight apparently

a C17 survival, but clearly shown by the drawings for the 1745 rebuilding to be part of that phase.

COMMUNION RAIL. Apparently C17, with vertically symmetrical balusters. – PULPIT, BOX PEWS and BENCHES. All c. 1745 but in C17 style, like the roof, the pulpit a two-decker with sounding board. – FONT. Sturdy C18 baluster. – Large C18 PAINTING of Moses and Aaron with the Ten Commandments, over the W tower arch. Round-headed panels of the Creed and Lord's Prayer l. and r. – STAINED GLASS. By *William Peckitt* of York, 1756. In the tracery panels of the E window are Moses with the Commandments again, Calvary, Moses with two cherubs, Faith and Hope, and two views of the church. In the transepts N and S, heraldic quatrefoils. – MONUMENTS. Two wooden effigies of cross-legged knights, early C14, presumably members of the Mauleverer family. Exceptional survivals. – Brass of Sir John Mauleverer †1400, and his wife Eleanor. Small rectangular plate with the two figures engraved (cf. Aveley, Essex), rather than cut-outs as usual in England. Fine quality. – Sir John Mauleverer †1468, and his wife Alyson. Badly preserved alabaster effigies, without a tomb chest. – Mary Thornton, wife of Col. Thomas Thornton, †1800. Mausoleum-like structure, c. 5 ft (1.5 metres) high with Ionic columns to the front. Marble bas-relief sarcophagus on the wall above.

ALLERTON PARK. A disappointment, externally at least. The old house had been remodelled in 1788 for the Duke of York, apparently by *Henry Holland*, but was almost entirely replaced by the present one, built in 1848–51 for the 19th Lord Stourton by an obscure London-based architect called *George Martin* – a large, harshly detailed gritstone pile in an overblown Gothic-cum-Jacobean style, with polygonal turrets and pinnacles and occasional shaped gables. The principal features are a tall tower-cum-porte-cochère in the middle of the entrance front; a big rectangular lantern behind it, with elaborate Perp windows; and inside, the *clou* to the whole, a spectacular full-height central hall *à la* Wollaton, the lantern forming its clerestory. The hall's enrichments include hammerbeam roof trusses and a first-floor gallery, and at each end arches lead into top-lit subsidiary spaces, one occupied by an imperial staircase – the lower flight extending through the middle arch – the other with a huge Gothic fireplace. But the theatrical effect is dampened by hamfisted planning, the staircase coming up uncomfortably against a blank wall and the entrance from the porte cochère leading in not at one end but to one side. At the entrance, statues of Henry VII and Elizabeth of York, 1838–42 by *Charles Raymond Smith*, originally at Mamhead, Devon.

The surviving part of the earlier house forms a range running out from the E flank. The greater part of this is formed by the CHAPEL (R.C.) built by the 17th Lord Stourton c. 1807 – of rendered brick, cruciform (the transepts an early addition) and very plain, with minimal Gothic detail. But the first bay, next to the 1848 building, appears to be the SE corner of the house as remodelled by *Holland* – shorn of its upper two storeys – with a pedimented tripartite window which is shown in this position in a view of 1800. (The interior of the chapel, derelict at the time of writing, is similarly simple but pleasantly proportioned, with four-centred plaster rib-vault and deep W gallery.) E of the house the former STABLE BLOCK, traditionally said to have been built for the Duke of York and if so perhaps also by *Holland*. Quadrangular, of rendered brick, in a simplified Palladian manner rather short of distinguishing features (but for the oculi flanking the head of the entrance arch cf. the service ranges at Berrington Hall, Herefordshire). Nearby a rustic late C18 SUMMERHOUSE, with rough battlements and timber veranda.

TEMPLE OF VICTORY. A misleading name for the most distinguished piece of architecture here, a gazebo on an eminence NW of the house overlooking the Great North Road, which was in existence by 1770 and is presumably of the Arundell phase. A domed octagon absolutely in the manner of William Kent – almost a repeat of the temple at Shotover Park, Oxon and the banqueting houses at Carlton House, London, and Euston Park, Suffolk – it could well be by *Kent* himself, who was Arundell's ally in the Office of Works and designed interior fittings for his London house; or otherwise again by *Vardy* (who drew the Euston Park design).* Ashlar, of *piano nobile* and basement, with two of the cardinal sides stepped forward. Pedimented doorways to all the cardinal sides, those on the projecting ones within a relieving arch; one opening onto a perron, the others onto balconies. On the diagonals, niches and raised panels. Of the C18 landscaping of the grounds a series of LAKES survives, in existence in some form by 1770. Other park buildings include an early C19 cottage-style LODGE to the W.

APPLETREEWICK

In Wharfedale, a single short steep village street.

ST JOHN. At the top. Small single-cell church of 1898 constructed out of the stone, including the mullioned windows, from two C17 cottages previously on the site. Built as a chapel of ease of Burnsall, and designed by the rector, the *Rev. William Stavert*.

Opposite, but facing away from the street, is HIGH HALL, built in the 1660s by Thomas Craven (†1682), great-nephew of the famous Sir William Craven (*see* Burnsall): a datestone of 1667

---

*Another suggestion has been *James Paine*, who was known to Arundell and designed Serlby Hall, Notts., for his nephew, Lord Galway.

bearing Thomas's initials formerly existed in the remains, now lost, of the original porch. The house strikingly combines a neat, up-to-date rectangular plan-form with a traditional high great hall with screens passage and gallery – managed by making the front r. quarter of two storeys, with the hall below and the great chamber above, but the rest, although the same height, of three. As a result, the fenestration of the front is markedly asymmetrical. Splendid big double-transomed hall window of four-plus-four lights, that to the great chamber of four-plus-four lights with one transom, others of three-plus-three lights. In the middle, the present single-storey porch is an C18 replacement and too low for the building, but a patch of rebuilt masonry on the wall above it indicates that its predecessor rose the full height of the house. In the centre of the rear elevation a zigzag of five two-light windows lighting the staircase. The gable-ends to the big single roof again of later stonework; the original arrangement probably consisted of two parallel roofs running front to back. Many interior features. In the hall, a panelled screen with a band of miniature vertically symmetrical balusters on a level with the arched heads of the doorways, and full-size balusters of the same design to the gallery above. Big segment-headed fireplace. Beyond the screens passage a dog-leg staircase, with similar balusters, and behind the hall the kitchen, with another segment-headed fireplace. Smaller arched fireplaces in other rooms, in the great chamber a plaster frieze of enriched arcading, and in the chamber next to it a plaster overmantel of the Craven arms.

Lower down the street is MOCK BEGGAR HALL, dated 1696 on a fireplace and 1697 on the porch. An odd little façade, with a crude semicircular pediment over the porch doorway. To the r. of this the projecting gable-end of a barn wing, with a depressed-arched upper doorway – reached by external steps – surmounted by an owl hole and flanked by windows with ornamented lintels. Pigeon holes above. Inner doorway with the lintel dipping down towards the centre. The l. part of the building, and probably the roof-line of the porch, remodelled in the C18.

LOW HALL, ¼ m. W. C17 house refronted in 1868. Behind it an unusually handsome BARN, dated 1690. Segment-headed cart entrances with moulded imposts, pairs of doorways to the shippon end with stepped chamfers to the lintels. Other C17 farmhouses in the parish are WOODHOUSE FARM, 1 m. WNW, with a lean-to roofed rectangular projection to the housebody bay, and LANE HOUSE FARM, ¾ m. ENE, with a similar projection to the parlour end.

PARCEVALL HALL, 1 m. NE. 1671, restored and extended 1929 by *Sir William Milner* for himself. Now a Diocesan retreat. Gabled parlour cross-wing, three-plus-three-light windows to the housebody, parlour and parlour chamber and a stepped three-light window in the gable. Milner's addition is a wing at right angles to the rear in a matching style. Jekyll-influenced terraced GARDEN also laid out by him.

On FANCARL TOP, 2 m. NNE, a well-preserved Bronze Age
STONE CIRCLE, 26 ft (8 metres) in diameter, consisting of five
free-standing gritstones and a large inset boulder. ⅝ m. N
again, at GRIMWITH RESERVOIR, a small FIELD BARN with
raised cruck truss and heather thatch roof. A rare survival,
probably C17, partly rebuilt 1982 by the Yorkshire Water
Authority. On the moorland SE of the circle, beyond Parcevall
Hall, various Bronze Age 'cup-and-ring' ROCK CARVINGS,
northerly outliers of the concentration centred on Ilkley Moor
(q.v.). In the same area and further E, remains of LEAD
MINING.

ARKENDALE

ST BARTHOLOMEW. Engagingly bad, 1836 by *John Freeman* of
neighbouring Staveley, replacing an earlier chapel. Basic lancet
style in incongruous white brick, the narrow W tower crowned
by a top-heavy ashlar parapet stage with outsize corner pinnacles. Unaisled nave, one-bay chancel.
At the W edge of the village LONG COTTAGE, red brick with a
Dutch gable to each end. *c.* 1700.

ARNCLIFFE

A Dales village with an attractive village green. The church lies
away from this, beside the river Skirfare.

ST OSWALD. Sturdy Perp W tower with diagonal buttresses and
small finials. The body of the church rebuilt 1796, then reconstructed 1841 by *Salvin* for the Rev. William Boyd. The E third
of the C18 building was demolished and replaced by a new
chancel, the wide nave remodelled to match. Two-light Perp
windows with four-centre heads, offset buttresses, thin
traceried roof trusses. – SCREEN. 1894 by *William Tate*, an
assistant of Kempe. Arts and Crafts Gothic. – ROYAL ARMS.
1797 by *Poor Birket*, painter. In a Neoclassical frame. –
STAINED GLASS. E and chancel SW windows by *Wailes*, 1846–7;
nave NW and chancel SE by *Heaton, Butler & Bayne*, 1886 and
1895. – MONUMENTS. Thomas Foster of Nether Hesleden
†1778. Tablet surmounted by bas-relief urn. – Rev. Henry
Tennant †1779. Pedimented tablet.
OLD VICARAGE. Artisan Palladian. Three-bay front with well-
detailed Venetian windows in the flanking bays to ground and
first floors. 1770 for the Rev. Henry Tennant, Vicar of Arncliffe
1765–79. An inscription above the former front doorway gives
his name and the incomplete date MDCC(L)XX. New entrance
range to r. added 1836.

w of village green a former WATER MILL, now a house. Built late
C18 as a corn mill, converted to cotton spinning *c.* 1820. Nine
bays, two storeys.

OLD COTES, ¼ m. NW, across the river. Farmhouse with porch
dated 1650. In the l. angle between porch and house a staircase turret, an unusual position for this feature (but cf. Battle
Hill, Austwick: also the Manor House, Halton Gill and
Sawyers Garth, Litton). Stepped three-light window to porch
upper storey, other mullioned windows of two to five lights.
Extension at r. end 1914 replacing a barn.

On the hillside ½ m. S of the village the remains of an Iron Age
or Romano-British SETTLEMENT. Two large enclosures and a
number of rectangular and circular huts, the walls standing up
to 3 ft (1 metre) high.

ARTHINGTON   2040

ST PETER. 1864 by *Mallinson & Healey*, at the cost of William
Sheepshanks of Arthington Hall. Pleasingly robust C13 Gothic
with plate and Geometrical tracery. NW tower-porch with
stumpy broach spire, unaisled nave with transepts, chancel. –
Marble REREDOS, 1873 by *T. H. & F. Healey*, executed by
Farmer & Brindley, flanked by tile and marble wall panelling.
– STAINED GLASS. The best is the E window, 1864 by *Ward &
Hughes*. Also chancel N 1865 by *Hardman*; W window 1864 by
Clayton & Bell; S transept 1875 by *Capronnier*; N transept 1876
by *Lavers, Barraud & Westlake*; nave SE 1879 by *Heaton, Butler
& Bayne*; nave NE 1883 by *Ward & Hughes* again.

ARTHINGTON HALL. The product of three main phases: a large
house of fanciful design, under construction in 1697, reconstructed on a smaller scale probably *c.* 1790 and apparently by
Carr, perhaps after a fire, with additions and decorations of

Arthington Hall, before C18 reconstruction.
Engraving, C19

1876–8 by *Waterhouse*. Carr's building is a plain two-storey block of slightly uneasy proportions, nine bays wide with a broad five-bay centre the pediment of which was removed in the C19. Detail apparently reused from the C17 house is limited to some of the balustraded parapet, with fat square balusters, two Tuscan columns on pedestals set against the E side, and perhaps parts of some of the window surrounds. By Waterhouse are the masonry-framed conservatory in front of the entrance and a wing at the back. The most notable feature now is the remarkable staircase, an imperial stair in reverse with 'flying' upper flight, set in an oval well and executed in timber, with slim turned balusters (cf. Carr's earlier, rectangular staircase at Kirklees Hall (West Riding South), and Chambers's Navy Stair at Somerset House). The staircase is top-lit, in the middle of the house, but an oddity is that it faces sideways, onto a corridor, rather than towards the entrance hall. It received some attention from Waterhouse, presumably the decoration to the upper stage of the stairwell, with Ionic pilasters, and the dome. In one of the bedrooms a Campbellesque bed alcove, with segment-headed arch flanked by pilasters, apparently a mid-C18 survival from before the reconstruction. Drawing room with Neo-Adam ceiling in the Waterhouse wing. – E of the house the former STABLES, mid-C18, with pedimented centre.

No village but a few C18 estate COTTAGES along the main road. First a short row with big relieving arches, truncated by a lowering of the wall-head. Then one with Gothick quatrefoils in screen walls at each end.

THE NUNNERY, ¾ m. E. Handsome stone house of uncertain date, on the site of a priory of Cluniac nuns founded in the mid C12. The four-centre-headed doorway bears the date 1585 and initials identifiable as those of Thomas Brigge, who held the property then; but he was only a yeoman and 1585 is unusually early even for a minor gentry house of stone in the area. There was formerly also a C17 datestone with initials of a member of the would-be gentry Mitchell family who bought the estate in 1593, and they are more feasible candidates as the builders, in the early C17 – in which case the doorway is probably to be interpreted as a survivor from the pre-Reformation building, embellished by Brigge and retained by the Mitchells. The house is a three-storey range three rooms long, with central rear kitchen block between two-storey outshuts. Above the doorway a two-storey canted oriel (cf. Myddleton Lodge, Ilkley). Long low mullioned windows, of five-plus-five lights to the housebody and the chambers above it, four-plus-four to the r. parlour and the chambers above that, the lights all straight-headed. (Interior much altered mid C20, including the removal of the partition wall demarcating the hearth passage. Tudor-arched fireplace in the housebody and alongside it, against the front wall of the house, a stone spiral staircase. In the parlour beyond, a plaster ceiling with vine trails on the central beam, three diamond shapes with foliage and one oval.)

VIADUCT. *See* Castley.

ASKHAM BRYAN

ST NICHOLAS. Late Norman, small, with nave and chancel in one (cf. Askham Richard). Magnesian limestone, with a band of river stone on three sides. S doorway re-set in the C19 as the entrance to the S porch. Two orders of shafts, with waterleaf and ram's horn capitals. Three orders of arches, with point-to-point chevrons to the inner and outer, diamond fret to the middle. On the teeth of the chevrons, small low-relief leaves. The priest's doorway and the N and S windows renewed. In the E wall three tiny slit windows – framed by colonettes and roll moulding inside – and high up above them a vesica-shaped window with ball moulding, i.e. a C13 insertion. C19 W bell-cote. W gallery. – PULPIT and COMMUNION RAIL. Both C17.

In the village street, ASKHAM BRYAN HALL, *c.* 1847 by *J. B. & W. Atkinson*, a brick-built Grecian villa with oversailing hipped roof. In Chapel Lane a little former METHODIST CHAPEL, early C19. Two large windows with depressed-arch lintels and Gothick glazing bars.

COLLEGE OF AGRICULTURE, ½ m. S. 1936–9. Long Neo-Georgian brick range facing S. Three storeys, hipped roof.

ASKHAM RICHARD

ST MARY. Virtually a pair to Askham Bryan (q.v.), but extensively restored 1878–9 by *Atkinson & Demaine*, with the W wall rebuilt a short distance to the E. Nave and chancel in one. Porch of 1878–9 with a Norman-style doorway, a simplified copy of Askham Bryan's. Within the porch is the genuine late Norman S doorway. Two orders of shafts, waterleaf and scalloped capitals. Also an early Norman or possibly pre-Conquest doorway re-set in the W wall of the NW vestry, completely unmoulded except for plain cushion-like imposts, bulging laterally not frontally. – REREDOS, and painted decoration to the chancel ceiling. 1890, designed by *Temple Moore*. – SCULPTURE. A block with serpent design (E end of the nave, N side), probably Norman. – STAINED GLASS. W window by *Taylor & O'Connor* of London, 1878; chancel S by *Kempe*, 1879, with Virgin and Child; E windows by *Victor Milner*, 1903. – MONUMENT (churchyard, E). Elizabeth Berry, signed *Mylne* fecit 1770. Fluted and wreathed marble urn on a broken column. – COFFIN. Also in the churchyard. Stone, claimed to be Roman.

Attractive GREEN with pond, encircled by brick farmhouses and cottages and dominated at the N end by ASKHAM GRANGE, now a women's prison, built 1886 for Sir Andrew Fairbairn, a Leeds textile machinery manufacturer. Fussily Old English, with various gables and bay windows, bits of half-timbering and pargetted eaves, a turret and an oriel – and a very tall water

tower. Jacobean-style staircase hall with diamond-shaped
landing and pretty painted skylight. Ballroom wing of 1913
clumsily attached to the NW corner. Unsympathetic C20 accretions for the Prison Service.

AUSTWICK

Excellently situated amongst the limestone outworks building up
towards Ingleborough.

EPIPHANY. 1841, built as a chapel of ease of Clapham. Four-bay
lancet-style box. Apsidal-ended chancel added 1883. –
STAINED GLASS. Four windows in the chancel by *Lavers,
Barraud & Westlake*, 1887 and 1890.

At the NE end of the main street, BATTLE HILL, 1673, with the
unusual feature of a staircase turret in the angle between the
housebody and the two-storey porch (cf. Old Cotes, Arncliffe).
N of this TOWN HEAD FARM, small double pile of
c. 1700. Approximately central entrance and above it a gabled
attic dormer window of three stepped lights. Rear range of
rooms consisting of two short gabled wings and an outshut
containing the staircase between them (cf. Cowside,
Langstrothdale). Elsewhere two particularly elaborate doorheads, both incorporating an approximation to a pediment, at
THE CUDDY, 1712, N of the church, and HARDEN COTTAGE,
1719, near the SW end of the village.

SCHOOL, 1842, given by the Ingleby family of Austwick Hall.
Straight-headed windows (altered) under hoodmoulds.

At WHARFE, 1¼ m. NE, the so-called MANOR HOUSE, a
small house which never had that status, with porch dated
1715 on the simply ornamented doorhead. Massive chimney-
breast to r. In 1959 Pevsner described Wharfe as 'a close stone-
built hamlet, uncommonly attractive in its pre-motor-car
remoteness'.

BAILDON

Across the Aire from Shipley, the village greatly expanded down
the hillside in C19 and C20.

ST JOHN. 1847–8 by *Mallinson & Healey*, replacing a chapel of
ease of Otley, of C12 origin. E.E. style, with big S aisle. S tower
1928 by *F. H. Healey*. In the chancel a simple piscina, one of
several items reused from the old church. – FONT. Octagonal,
probably C14. – PULPIT. Convincing Jacobean style, incorporating C17 carved oak panels. – SCREEN. Of wrought iron, 1905.
– STAINED GLASS. W window 1849, probably by *Wailes*;

s aisle second from e by *Barnett* of York, also 1849; e window 1872 by *Heaton, Butler & Bayne,* designed by *Henry Holiday;* Nave N second from e by *Clayton & Bell,* 1875. – MONUMENTS. Thomas Butler †1745. Panel with crude broken pediment. – Paul Meyer †1768. Convex roundel in an elaborate finely carved surround.

MORAVIAN CHURCH, Browgate. 1868 by *Samuel Jackson* of Bradford. Simple rectangle with unchamfered two-light Gothic windows. w (ritual) gallery on iron columns.

BAILDON HALL, Hallfield Drive, s of the church. Gentry house of medieval origin. The oldest part, perhaps C14, is a timber-framed partition with three pointed doorways, between the lower end of the hall and the r. cross-wing – the textbook medieval arrangement. The rest of the wing is also timber-framed, probably of the late C15, cased in stone apparently in 1673 (datestone, no longer visible). Three bays, kingpost trusses. The line of the passage across the wing from the middle door in the C14 partition is marked by mortices in the ground-floor ceiling beams. On another, close-studded, partition graffiti dated 1618. Mullioned windows with arched lights to ground-floor front and back. Are they reused? Rest of the house rebuilt probably mid C17. Two-and-a-half storeys, with flat triple-gabled front, partly refenestrated. Transomed hall window originally of ten lights, truncated to seven. Attic windows also transomed, of two lights. Behind the hall, in a gabled turret projecting at the back, a handsome staircase with vertically symmetrical balusters and ornamented newels with ogee finials. In the parlour an elaborate plaster ceiling with a geometrical pattern of narrow ribs, little pendants etc. (cf. East Riddlesden Hall, Keighley), and contemporary panelling. On the ceiling frieze the initials of Francis Baildon (†1669).

BANK WALK HOUSE, Bank Walk, w of the church. Another timber-framed building, of *c.* 1500, cased in stone in the C17. Four bays, with a narrow rear aisle or outshut. Elements of four trusses remain, with tie-beams, kingposts, curved principal rafters and wind-braces. Plain altered exterior. A few other C17 houses in the village centre, including one in WESTGATE with inserted doorways dated 1715 and 1717. Also some of the early C18 to the SE in STATION ROAD (datestones of 1718, 1724 etc.), then further on a group of villas built by members of the Ambler family of Bradford industrialists. ROUNDWOOD GRANGE, Roundwood Road, 1898 for John Ambler, is by *Isitt, Adkin & Hill* of Bradford. Restrained stone-built Old English with gables and mullioned windows. N of it across the railway, WOODLANDS, 1899 for John's uncle George, in the same style and presumably by the same architects. s of it HOYLE COURT, Hoyle Court Road, 1912 for his brother Sam by *J. C. Procter* of Leeds. Domestic Neo-Wren, the garden front symmetrical with little fancy dormers. Elaborate staircase hall.

Towards SHIPLEY GLEN, 1¼ m. sw of the centre, TITUS SALT SCHOOL, Higher Coach Road, descendant of Sir Titus Salt's foundation at Saltaire (q.v.), the present building 2007–8 by

Anshen & Allen. It replaces that of 1960–65 by *Chamberlin, Powell & Bon* (dem. 2008), quadrangular, with a columned portico running through the S range, shell-concrete barrel vaults over the N. Further on TRENCH FARMHOUSE, 1697, with smart symmetrical five-bay front. Unchamfered cross-windows, half-elliptical-headed doorway with keystone, oculus above it, and rusticated quoins. Outshut and gabled wing at the back. For ROBERTS PARK *see* Saltaire.

Various Bronze Age CARVED ROCKS in the neighbourhood, outliers of the group on Ilkley Moor (q.v.), including two associated with the SOLDIER'S TRENCH, a fragmentary settlement enclosure on Bracken Hall Green, 1½ m. W of the centre.

BANK NEWTON

NEWTON HALL. Tall, compact C17 house, a single short range of three storeys and attic (cf. Paget Hall, Gargrave). Impressive SE gable-end, with mullioned windows of eight, seven, four and two lights, working upwards. Massive chimney-breast against the SW flank. Main rooms on ground and first floors have big moulded Tudor-arched fireplaces, the former also a timber panel of the Banke coat of arms. The NW half of the range is divided longitudinally on all floors by a post-and-panel partition. Lower, later NE wing. Very fine C17 aisled BARN close by. Five bays plus a separate storeyed bay at the SE end. Rubble walls. Aisle-posts on high padstones, kingpost roof trusses.

BARDEN

BARDEN TOWER. A large and impressive tower house beautifully situated in Wharfedale, mainly of *c.* 1500 for Henry Lord Clifford, the 'Shepherd Lord' (*see* Skipton). Repaired in 1657–9 by Lady Anne Clifford after it had 'layne ruinous' for some years, and a ruin once again since the late C18. Henry Clifford's house is evidently the central section of the present building. It was of three storeys with a symmetrical S elevation of three bays, the centre bay formerly a rectangular projection, the others with big three-light windows in hollow-chamfered surrounds. The stump of the l. flank of the projection retains the jamb of a similar window at first-floor level. In the bay to the l. also a four-centre-headed doorway. At the back was another projection, housing the staircase. The lower addition to the r., with plainer window details, is presumably of Lady Anne Clifford's time, but the full-height section to the l. is probably of the mid C16: archaeological evidence suggests that the latter replaced a wing extending further in that direction. Internally, a number of doorways and fireplaces remain, and a pair of four-centre-headed archways which opened into the front projection. A transverse wall in the central section, abutting against the largest of the fireplaces, will be part of Lady Anne Clifford's work.

Detached to the s is the CHAPEL block, built 1515–17 and again repaired by Lady Anne Clifford. Mullioned windows with three-centre-headed lights. The w front has a squat tower to the r., a two-storey domestic wing to the l., and a lower gabled section, representing the chapel itself, in the middle. The ground floor of the tower is the chapel porch, but the top storey was probably a belvedere or banqueting house, linked to the domestic accommodation, which extends over the w bay of the chapel, and also reached by an outside stair.

BARDEN BRIDGE. 'Repaired' in 1676, i.e. rebuilt as its predecessor had been 'overturned' by a flood in 1673. Three segmental arches, triangular cutwaters and refuges. ½ m. downstream an AQUEDUCT built in 1896 by the Bradford Corporation Water Works. Three half-elliptical arches, crenellated parapet and turret-like half-octagonal cutwaters.

At DREBLEY, 1¼ m. N, two BARNS each with three cruck trusses and traces of heather thatch beneath the corrugated iron cover. Rare survivors locally, perhaps C16.

BARDSEY   3040

ALL HALLOWS. Anglo-Saxon in substantial part: the w tower – tall, slender and unbuttressed – and much of the nave walling. But the tower is evidently of two phases, the lower part originally a w porch coeval with the nave (cf. Corbridge, Monkwearmouth): see the massive side-alternate quoins of the porch stage only, visible on the w face, and perhaps the hint of a gable above. The earlier fabric will be C9 or C10, the tower proper C11. On its s side a pair of two-light openings, one above the other, with mid-wall shafts and throughstone imposts, and on the other faces contemporary one-light counterparts. Also Dec straight-headed two-light bell-openings in the w and N sides, a Dec w window of similar design in the lower stage, and Perp corbelled-out parapet. Aisles, embracing the tower, were added in the C12 and then widened in the late C14, their width accentuating the tower's narrowness. The narrow Norman w windows remain, flanked by Dec two-light successors matching that in the tower – and the visible joint between the work of the two phases. In the s aisle also the re-set Norman s doorway, with two orders of colonettes, scalloped capitals, and to the arch an inner order of zigzag and an outer of beakheads. Chancel C14, replacing the Saxon one; N chapel 1521, with reused C14 windows; transeptal s chapel 1724, built by the first Lord Bingley (see Bramham Park) apparently as a family pew.

Nave and chancel heightened in 1806, extensive renewal and replacement of windows in a restoration of 1867.

Inside, the plain round-headed N and S doorways of the Saxon W porch can be seen, now opening into the aisles, with narrow windows above them. The nave is predominantly Norman in character. Three-bay arcades of different dates: the N early C12, with stout cylindrical piers, big square heavily scalloped capitals and unmoulded arches; the S of c. 1175–1200, with similar but slimmer piers, simply moulded capitals, two of them with small foliage-like volutes, and the arches pointed, although still unmoulded. Signs of blocked Saxon windows above the N arcade. Plain early C12 tower and chancel arches also cut through the Saxon walling, their predecessors presumably narrower; superimposed roof-lines, the lower Saxon, the upper Norman, visible above the tower arch. The chancel has a cusped lancet on each side and a cusped 'lowside' window below that to the S, all now opening into the N and S chapels, an unmoulded flattened-ogee-headed sedilia, probably C15, and a trefoiled piscina. Roofs 1913–14 by *Connon & Chorley*. – ARCHITECTURAL FRAGMENTS. Probably all C12, including part of an incised cross-head, zigzag etc. – Painted ROYAL ARMS, 1819. – MONUMENTS. Some small C17–C18 wall tablets, including Elizabeth Thorpe †1666, with strapwork and broken pediment. – SUNDIAL, in the churchyard, dated 1751. On a square pillar.

CASTLE HILL, N of the church. Large earthwork enclosure, probably late C12. Excavation in 1930 revealed evidence of a square masonry structure, perhaps a keep.

PRIMARY SCHOOL, a little further on. 1954 by *West Riding County Architect's Department* (County Architect *Hubert Bennett*). Brick and stone, stepping up a gentle slope.

OAK TREE COTTAGE, W of the church. Timber-framed range of c. 1600, the framing exposed to the first floor at the front, close-studded with straight braces. Two bays, perhaps originally longer, with hearth passage. C19 addition at the rear.

BARNOLDSWICK

Small mill town on the summit section of the Leeds and Liverpool Canal. The site of a short-lived Cistercian foundation – the predecessor of Kirkstall, to which the monks moved in 1152 – established from Fountains in 1147.

ST MARY-LE-GILL. In open country E of the town, at the end of a lane. The previous church, on a different site, had been taken over, and then demolished, by the Cistercians. Perp W tower, with date interpreted as 1524 on the S side. Battlements and flat SE stair-turret. Nave and chancel in one, with C13 E window of three stepped lancets, and another smaller lancet on the N side. Low full-length Perp S aisle under the same roof. Straight-headed windows with arched lights. Pleasing unimproved interior. Perp five-bay arcade with octagonal piers and double-chamfered arches. Roof with alternating tie-beams and arched braces, and cusped wind-braces between the rafters and the purlins. – PULPIT. A complete C17 three-decker, with sounding-board, set halfway along the N wall. – BOX PEWS. Mainly C17, some with ball finials on the ends. Churchwarden's pew at W end dated 1836. – FONT. A simple bowl. – Painted ROYAL ARMS and CATECHISM BOARDS, all early C19. – HEARSE SHED at the entrance to the churchyard. Dated 1814, with the names of the incumbent and churchwardens.

INDEPENDENT METHODIST CHAPEL, Walmsgate. 1892. Ornate pedimented façade, with segment-headed openings to the lower stage, round-headed above. Interior largely unaltered. Slightly raked floor with the pews curved, auditoriumwise. Apsidal-ended gallery with vigorously panelled front, on fluted Corinthian columns. Similarly detailed rostrum. – Adjoining SUNDAY SCHOOL, 1911.

Former BAPTIST CHAPEL, Walmsgate, opposite the above. 1797. Front, at right angles to the street, with Venetian windows and pedimented doorway.

BAPTIST CHAPEL, Manchester Road, 1975 by *Ferguson Smith & Associates*. Stark irregular heptagon, of blockwork and artificial stone, with asymmetrically pitched roof incorporating a long roof-light. On two levels, exploiting the steeply sloping site, with a meeting room below and the chapel above.

COATES HALL, Skipton Road. Double-pile block of *c.* 1700 with symmetrical triple-gabled front. Centre of three narrow bays, slightly projecting side sections of two, wider. Cross-windows. Oculi in the gables. Slightly later doorcase, too big for the available space, with crudely detailed coupled Composite columns and pediment.

In the town centre, a successful TOWN SQUARE was formed in 1990 in the grid of modest early C20 streets by removing one complete block. The older part is further W, around CHURCH STREET, with some very unpretentious early C19 houses. Of the former cotton-weaving mills, the surviving part of BANCROFT MILL, Gillians Lane, completed as late as 1920, is now a museum. The weaving shed and warehouse range have been demolished, leaving just the big engine house – still with working steam engine – the boiler house and the cylindrical brick chimney.

BARROWBY HALL
Austhorpe

3030

Front range of 1718–20 by *William Etty* for Arthur Ingram, a connection of the Ingrams of nearby Temple Newsam (Leeds).

Two storeys, seven bays, with lugged surround to the doorway, triple keystones to the windows, solid parapet. In front a terrace with steps aligned on the door, and at right angles l. and r. short screen walls and big panelled gatepiers. Further off, more remains of a formal layout, a dog-eared axial canal which was evidently once framed by an avenue (cf. the E avenue etc. at Temple Newsam, laid out by Etty in 1712). (Back part of the house dated 1677, with a gabled turret containing a staircase with turned balusters.) C19 service wing to r.

BARWICK-IN-ELMET

ALL SAINTS. Perp W tower of the local type with diagonal buttresses, corbelled-out parapet and crocketed corner pinnacles (cf. Rothwell, Thorner and Whitkirk (Leeds)), the lower half partly of Magnesian limestone, the rest of gritstone. It is datable to c. 1455–60 by inscriptions accompanying two statue niches on the W face. Only one of the statues survives, identified as Sir Henry Vavasour of Hazlewood Castle (q.v.) and dated 1455: he was the owner of limestone quarries and is shown carrying a block of stone. The other was the Rector, Richard Burnham (†1457), the inscription recording that he gave ten marks for the building of the tower: the bequest is stipulated in his will. Perp also the aisles, nave arcades – four bays, with the usual octagonal piers and double-chamfered arches – and clerestory. But the spacious nave and the short narrower chancel are both in principle of c. 1100, with some herringbone masonry (cf. Kippax), one Norman window on the N side of the chancel – now facing into the vestry – and in the nave massive E responds, those of the later arcades backing against them. So did the nave have transepts or even Anglo-Saxon-style *porticus*? A further puzzle is the ornate ogee-headed doorway between the chancel and the vestry, with an excessively thick heavy surround: is it C14, or a post-Reformation interpretation of Dec? The chancel arch is probably C14, the vestry of c. 1800, with Gothick sash windows. An extensive restoration of 1856 by *G. Fowler Jones* accounts for most of the other fenestration, and the roofs.

PULPIT. 1725. An attractive piece with a little inlay. – SCREEN. What appears to be part of a 'modern' – i.e. C17 – example referred to in 1856 is attached to the W nave wall above the tower arch. – SCULPTURE. Two fragments of Anglo-Saxon crosses, both probably C10. One with three figures, one large and two small, l. and r., possibly the Expulsion of Adam and Eve from Eden; the other with interlace and looser scrolls of broadly Viking character. – A (medieval?) statue of the Virgin in the vestry, found in 1898 during demolition of nearby cottages. – STAINED GLASS. E window by *Clayton & Bell*, 1867. –

N aisle E by *W. Furness*, 1858. Armorial glass still entirely pre-Victorian in character, installed by the Gascoigne family of Parlington Hall, Aberford, the inscription explains, following the removal of the monument to Sir John Gascoigne (†1723) 'which on the restoration of the church being commenced, was found to be too dilapidated to be repaired'. The monument was by *Alessandro Galilei*, executed in Florence in 1726: an armorial panel is preserved nearby. – N aisle second from E by *Burlison & Grylls*, 1912. – ROYAL ARMS of Queen Victoria, painted 1856. – MONUMENTS. John Gascoigne of Lasingcroft †1445. Grave-slab with incised cross and marginal inscription. – William Vevers †1744. Pedimented tablet.

OLD RECTORY, at right angles to the main street. Before 1695 for the Rev. Jordan Tancred. Five-bay brick-built box (now rendered), with hipped roof. Early C19 porch etc. (Good staircase with turned balusters.) Further W, behind the Methodist chapel, HALL TOWER HILL, earthwork of a motte-and-bailey castle of the de Lacy family (cf. Kippax), probably mid-C12, the circular motte well preserved, the bailey destroyed on the E side. It overlies the S part of a substantial Iron Age hill-fort, its bank and ditch best seen in the area to the N.

POTTERTON HALL, 1m. NNE. Hidden in a wooded hollow. Two C18 ranges of different dates, facing away from each other, forming an L-shape: now two houses. Both fronts ashlar. The earlier range is the W, of *c.* 1750. Front (W) of five bays and two-and-a-half storeys, with pilastered Doric doorcase, pediment and splayed architrave surround to the window above. Curious rusticated surrounds to the other windows. Excellent doorcases, cornices etc. inside, and at the back a top-lit cantilevered staircase with iron balusters. The S range was built *c.* 1787–8 for Thomas Wilkinson, perhaps by *William Lindley* (cf. Denison Hall, Little Woodhouse, Leeds, for Wilkinson's brother, John Denison), the front of two storeys and seven bays, smoothly elegant, with a pediment over the centre three and a Tuscan porch. Entrance hall with pilasters and coved ceiling, staircase *c.* 1975. To the E a plain service wing.

KIDDAL HALL, 1¼m. NNW beside the Leeds–York road. The late medieval house of the Ellis family, with elaborate bay window dated 1501, was partly dismantled in the 1920s and the best bits shipped to America.* It retains little sign of antiquity, patched up with a new front reusing some old stone; but some associated buildings remain, although also much altered. A long outbuilding range facing the road, attached to the house at right angles, is probably late C16 in origin: later segment-headed archway under a gable but on the courtyard (W) side three Tudor-arched doorways, one at first-floor level perhaps re-set. To the W what appears to have been a second house, probably early C17, now in agricultural use. L-shaped,

* Acquired by William Randolf Hearst, and last seen in a Bronx warehouse.

with similar doorways, massive internal chimney-breast, and raised cruck roof trusses. N of this a single-aisled BARN of the C16. Seven bays, with kingpost trusses. Some evidence of timber-framed walls, largely replaced in stone.

MORWICK HALL, 1⅞ m. W, S of the main road. Mid-C18 villa built by a mayor of Leeds, defaced by enlargement c. 1900. Now offices. The C18 house has five bays, two-and-a-half storeys, and pedimented three-bay centre, and was flanked by detached pyramid-roofed pavilions. The extension is on the E side only, over the site of the E pavilion, in the same style but with no attempt to maintain symmetry. At the same time the ground floor of the C18 front was pushed out slightly. Also a brutal addition to the surviving pavilion, and undistinguished office wings at the rear, c. 2000.

7040

BASHALL HALL

An uncommonly interesting house, of strangely disjointed and lopsided appearance, probably built in the mid C17 for Colonel William White (*see* Bishopthorpe Palace), who had married an heiress of the Talbots of Bashall, but reduced in size and otherwise altered c. 1700. It appears to have consisted of a broad principal range probably with three gables to front and back, and gabled cross-wings at each end, projecting to the front (S) only: the main range was of three storeys, of which the first floor was the most important, the wings a storey lower. Of this, the E wing has gone, apart from remains of its front and W return walls, and the l. section of the main range has been reduced a storey in height. The front wall of this section was partly rebuilt c. 1700, with a main doorway at first-floor level, reached by external steps, and a gable containing an oculus, the doorway crowned by a broken segmental pediment and flanked by tall windows in architrave surrounds. The other two front gables of the main range also received oculi to match, and perhaps just slightly later the first- and second-floor levels of the middle section were re-windowed, in three bays, the detail this time not matching. But the r. section retains its big mullion-and-transom windows to all three storeys and the front of the W wing has one of seven lights to the first floor and a mullioned window below. At the back the main feature is a large C17 canted bay window, with mullions and transoms, on the lowered section. Also a Tudor-arched doorway with stopped and chamfered jambs, not in its original position and serving as a window, and a big buttress near the NE corner perhaps reusing some earlier stonework.

Inside, the first floor of the reduced section is occupied by a single large room running across the building from front to back, and this appears to be an original feature – see the two symmetrically arranged Tudor-arched doorways in the W wall;

but presumably it was something other than the C17 hall – perhaps the great parlour – as the hall is more likely to have been in the central section. In the E wall a C17 Tudor-arched fireplace, moved from the W wing. In the central section there are now two rooms with early C18 fielded panelling, one above the other on the first and second floors, and behind them an early C18 staircase with twisted balusters; but the roof, with arch-braced trusses, again running from front to back and presumably intended to be seen, suggests the presence of another large transverse space, perhaps a second-floor great chamber. The first-floor rooms of the E section have C17 panelling.

Also some ancillary buildings of interest. N of the house what appears to have been a LODGINGS RANGE, probably of c. 1600, belonging to the previous house. Two storeys, the upper timber-framed to front and back, with an external gallery along the front. Several doorways opening onto the gallery, one ogee-headed; remains of timber mullioned windows at the back; big C17 transomed window in the E end. S of the house, a walled garden area with at the SW corner a handsome early C18 SUMMERHOUSE, quoined and pedimented and crowned by six big urns, and a BARN of the same period, with circular pitching holes and reused crocketed finials.

BEAMSLEY

0050

BEAMSLEY HOSPITAL. Almshouses founded 1593 by Margaret Countess of Cumberland and 'more perfectly finished' by her daughter Lady Anne Clifford c. 1650–60. The low front range, with a central segment-headed entrance arch surmounted by heraldic panels, is presumably Lady Anne's addition. Behind it, the original building is an Elizabethan conceit: circular, c. 30ft (9 metres) in diameter, with a circular core carried up as a lantern. This part is a chapel, the rooms encircling it ambulatory-wise and mostly opening off it. Three chimney-stacks disposed round the lantern, mullioned windows, conical roof with finial. In the chapel a circle of pews. [43]

BEAMSLEY HALL. An early C18 view shows a house of medieval origin, formerly the seat of the Clapham family; but the present smaller building, extensively altered in the C19, has nothing visible earlier than the C17. Mullion-and-transom windows on N side, square three-bay C19 addition to S. In the grounds a C17 aisled BARN. Five bays, with kingpost trusses.

CURRER HALL, on the hillside 1¼ m. SE of Beamsley Hall. Early C18 house with a number of surprising features. Double-pile plan, three rooms wide, the largest in the centre with the staircase behind. But the smartly detailed façade is oddly organized and unrelated to this, of four-plus-three bays flanked and separated by giant Doric pilasters. Cross-windows. Doorway, with lugged architrave surround ramped up to a point in the middle and segmental pediment over, in the centre bay of the r. part. So this leads into the r. room, not the centre one as one would expect. More good-quality stonework inside. In the centre room a big segment-headed fireplace with panelled jambs, doorcases of various designs, and even a barrel vault to the little lobby alongside the chimney-breast, leading to the l. room. Torus-moulded chimneypiece and doorcase in the r. room; and cantilevered staircase, with square newels and vertically symmetrical balusters of timber.

On moorland 1 m. E again, some Bronze Age 'cup-and-ring' ROCK CARVINGS (cf. Ilkley Moor).

BECKWITHSHAW
Pannal

ST MICHAEL. 1885–6 by *W. Swinden Barber* of Halifax. Dec, unaisled, with SW tower. – REREDOS. Stone arcade with bas-relief panels. – STAINED GLASS. E and W windows by *Kempe*, 1886 and 1888. Others 1892 by *C. E. Tute*.

MOOR PARK. Ornate stylistically promiscuous mansion, 1859 by *Andrews & Delaunay* of Bradford for James Bray, a Leeds iron-founder and railway contractor. Near-symmetrical front with debased Italianate central tower, the rest more or less Neo-Jacobean, with shaped gables. More correctly Italianate former stable block at the back. Jacobean-style staircase with elaborate coved ceiling. Now flats.

BENTHAM

Two settlements a mile apart, Lower Bentham to the W, beside the river Wenning, with the old parish church, and High Bentham to the E, a small market town.

LOWER BENTHAM

ST JOHN THE BAPTIST. Perp W tower. The body of the church largely rebuilt by *Norman Shaw*, 1876–8, in a complementary style. The arcades and clerestory of the short two-bay nave are entirely his, but the chancel arch and the arches to l. and r. of it, leading into the chancel chapels, are old work, as are much of the perimeter walling and some of the two-light straight-headed windows with cusped lights. – A full set of FITTINGS by *Shaw* and his associates. Contemporary with the rebuilding are the REREDOS, of Caen stone, carved by *Thomas Earp* and flanked by WALL TILES by *Maw*; the PULPIT, with linenfold panelling on a stone base; and the CHOIR STALLS and PEWS. Slightly later are the LECTERN, 1885, of brass, iron and wood; the elaborate ORGAN CASE, by *Shaw* and *Lethaby*, 1886, of teak with fretted pipe shades, carved by *Knox* of Lambeth; and the FONT and fanciful pinnacled FONT COVER, 1890 by *Lethaby*. – STAINED GLASS. W window and S chapel SW, 1878 by *Heaton, Butler & Bayne*, the former designed by *Henry Holiday*. E window and chancel S by *Powell & Sons*, c. 1890. S aisle W by *Shrigley & Hunt*, c. 1907. – SCULPTURE. Very primitive stone crucifix. Possibly C13.

Former RECTORY. 1884–5, also by *Shaw*. Now a school. Old English stone-built farmhouse style, but Wealden rather than Pennine. Front with gabled cross-wings and central porch, subtly asymmetrical. Many-gabled rear elevation partly jettied and rendered.

CALF COP CHAPEL (Friends' Meeting House), ⅝ m. NNE. 1798 (the date 1718 on the doorway commemorates a previous chapel). Gabled porch of tooled ashlar. To the l., two sash windows in tooled surrounds, lighting the meeting room, to the r. two smaller windows one above the other, the upper lighting the gallery. Meeting room has the usual panelled elders' bench, and a doorway below the gallery with entablature and fluted pilasters.

THE RIDDING, ¾ m. NW, well situated above the river. 1857 by *E. G. Paley*. Scottish Baronial, not large, with a tower at one corner with conical topped angle turrets and steep hipped roof. Crowstepped gables and rope mouldings.

KIRKBECK, ¾ m. SSE. Dated 1676 on the basket-arched doorway. Added porch to the r. of this, of two storeys and attic, containing the staircase (cf. the Manor House, Halton Gill). Off-centre entrance with ornamented lintel, first-floor window of three stepped round-headed lights.

HIGH BENTHAM

ST MARGARET. 1836–7, built at the cost of a local industrialist, Hornby Roughsedge. Lancet style with W tower and wide unaisled nave. Chancel and big S chapel added 1901–2 by *Austin & Paley*. – STAINED GLASS. E window and chapel E window by *Shrigley & Hunt*, 1903 and 1909.

In the town the principal accents are the pedimented and pilastered front of the former FRIENDS' MEETING HOUSE (now Community Centre) in the main street, 1864; the domed clock turret added in 1902 to the entirely plain PUBLIC HALL, 1877; and the schoolroom of the former GRAMMAR SCHOOL at the E end (now the Library), a little gabled box of 1897 with shouldered bellcote. The school had been founded 1726, rebuilt 1830. Also in the main street some simple decorated doorheads, including one of the type with two rectangular recesses, dated as early as 1635.

MEWITH HEAD HALL, 2¼ m. SE. Gentry house of the early C18. A date of 1708 on an outbuilding, with the initials of Ralph Baynes Esq. (†1729) and his wife, most probably applies to the house also. Double-pile block three rooms wide. Symmetrical front with gabled three-storey centre and two-bay, two-storeyed flanking sections. Tall central doorway with Doric pilasters and entablature, and bold segmental pediment. Cross-windows with unchamfered mullions and transoms, and architrave surrounds. Quoins. At the back more cross-windows, and two mullion-and-transom windows of three lights, possibly reused. To l. and r., matching outbuildings with their gable-ends in line with the front. Inside the house, early C18 bolection-moulded panelling to two rooms, and a segment-headed kitchen fireplace with a keystone. Excellent views to the N but the front faces S, into the hillside.

1060

BEWERLEY

Across the Nidd from Pateley Bridge.

BEWERLEY GRANGE CHAPEL, at the S end of the main street. Chapel of a grange of Fountains Abbey, probably built during the abbacy of Marmaduke Huby (1494–1526), whose motto appears on the E gable. A one-storey dwelling adjoins to the W, the two forming a single low range. In 1679 the chapel was converted into a school (a chapel again since 1965) and the W part of the range was built or rebuilt then as the schoolmaster's house. Straight-headed windows with four-centre-headed lights. C19 porch, with segment-headed entrance, probably reusing earlier stonework.

BEWERLEY OLD HALL, E of the chapel. Modest C17 block with some elaborate embellishments of c. 1700. Mullioned windows of three-plus-three lights. Central two-storey porch of the later phase, the lower stage with two Tuscan columns to the open front and a plaster ceiling with a large figure of a woman, said to be a saint. All the internal walls are panelled partitions, some of c. 1700, bolection-moulded, some earlier and re-set. Very big segment-headed C17 fireplace to the housebody. Of c. 1700 also the staircase, with turned balusters, and an excellent compartmented plaster ceiling in one of the upstairs rooms, with figures and coats of arms in diamond-shaped frames but a more traditional vine-scroll ornament on the soffits of the beams.

YORKE'S FOLLY, ¾ m. S, above the crags overlooking the valley. Mid-C18 eyecatcher built by the Yorke family of Bewerley Hall (dem. 1925). Two tall piers of masonry – originally there were three – suggesting a ruin of a Gothic church. E from the Old Hall, BEWERLEY HALL FARM, a model farm layout of 1870 for the Yorkes; and beyond it, beside the river, CASTLESTEAD, 1861–2 by *Corson & Aitken* of Manchester for George Metcalfe, proprietor of Glasshouses Mill (q.v.). Gables and a bulky tower.

At the N end of the village, GRASSFIELD HOUSE, now an hotel. Elegant ashlar villa of 1810. Five bays, with three-bay pedimented centre and Tuscan doorcase. Further on, the characteristic industries of Nidderdale are both represented. First FOSTER BECK MILL, former water-powered flax-spinning mill of *c.* 1860. Two-storey twelve-bay range with a big breast-shot water wheel, as tall as the building itself, against the gable-end, installed in 1904. Then upstream on the other side of the beck, the former HEATHFIELD LEAD-SMELTING MILL, now caravan site office, 1855 for John Yorke of Bewerley Hall. Rock-faced, with a gable at the front. A long condensing flue ran up the hillside behind.

See also Greenhow.

BILBROUGH

5040

ST JAMES. 1872–3 by *G. Fowler Jones*, in the Neo-Norman style with NW tower. Pevsner judged it 'truly hideous', the problem being the excessively large scale of the architectural detailing. The one remaining part of the medieval church is the Perp SE chapel, of two bays. – In it two MONUMENTS. John Norton, founder of the chapel. Big tomb-chest of *c.* 1500 with shields and quatrefoils, and indents for brasses. – Thomas, third Lord Fairfax, general of the New Model Army and victor of Naseby, †1671. Tomb-chest with, on two sides only, beautifully cut heraldic arms and luxurious foliage, separated by stumpy pilaster strips with cruder trophies. Black marble top. No effigy. – Gothic REREDOS, 1923 by *G. Fellowes Prynne*. From St Sampson, York, imported by *G. G. Pace* as part of his reordering of the chancel in 1970. – Also a medieval MENSA incorporated by him into a new altar table.

Two parallel streets. Several attractive houses along MAIN STREET, notably the mellow brick BILBROUGH GRANGE, opposite the church, dated 1755 on a rainwater head delightfully decorated with cherubs. Street elevation of two-plus-five bays with parapet, altered three-bay garden front facing W with the principal entrance. Excellent panelled rooms on both floors, and a good later staircase of cantilevered stone with iron balusters. Rusticated gatepiers. The so-called OLD MANOR HOUSE, E of the church, was not that at all, although over the former entrance at the back is a datestone of 1670 with the initials of General Fairfax. Whatever the house was, it is reduced to a cottage. Magnesian limestone. Mullioned windows, some renewed. Polygonal-sided chimneystacks to gable-end. The manor house of the Fairfaxes was to the W of the church. The present BILBROUGH MANOR, close to the site with extensive outlook to the W, is of 1900–1 by *Temple Moore* – not one of his very best works but nevertheless tempered by his skilled and scholarly hand. Large and long with roughcast walls, the main part frankly Neo-Jacobean with gables and large mullion-and-transom windows throughout, the service wing with sashes. Over the N entrance a large carved armorial panel of the C17. (On the S side another, dated 1595, from Steeton Hall, Colton, West Riding South, also a Fairfax house. Some good interiors.)

4040

BILTON-IN-AINSTY

ST HELEN. C12 church with nave and aisles under one roof, chancel, Perp S chapel and much Perp and C17 fenestration. Restored 1869–71 by *G. G. Scott*. W front with C19 double bell-cote, long Norman window and circular window above, both renewed. C12 also the S aisle W window (blocked), the S entrance (the porch itself rebuilt later) with colonnettes in two orders, waterleaf and scalloped capitals and chamfered arch, and the plain slightly chamfered S and N doorways (N blocked). The chancel's corbel table is visible inside. Perhaps a little later are the arcades of three bays. The piers are circular and quite slender, the arches round and double-chamfered, the capitals simply moulded, on the N side plain, on the S side with sparse pellets, billet mouldings and fleurs-de-lys. Chancel arch on double-chamfered responds with a heavy roll moulding flanked to the W and E by heavy chevron. The carving is C19; did Scott re-cut, restore, or imagine? – FONT. A plain bowl on octagonal stem. – COMMUNION TABLE. C17. – LECTERN. A wooden eagle, the body C17 or earlier, heavily restored by Scott after being rediscovered in use as a chopping board. – SOUTH DOOR. Dated 1633 with the initials RS in nails. – SCULPTURE. Various good fragments of Anglo-Saxon crosses. One has two figures standing side by side, another with very hieratically carved figures, perhaps the three Men in the Fiery Furnace or the Arrest of Christ; also a cross-head with a figure. – MONUMENT. Lady, early C14, N chancel aisle; a little defaced.

THE OLD VICARAGE, Church Street. Late C18. Brick with Gothick sashes. Its successor (now BILTON BROW) is early Victorian, attributed to *G. T. Andrews*.

BILTON HALL, ¼ m. W, set in the remnants of C18 landscape. A long evolution, possibly beginning in the C17, harmonized by render and renewed Georgian windows. Two storeys, eaves cornice and hipped roof. E and S fronts early C18, the S front the more recent: five bays with substantial doorcase. Later W front with three full-height canted bays. N wing

of *c.* 1865. (A fine symmetrical C18 STABLE range to
the N).

SYNINGTHWAITE PRIORY FARM, 1 m. SW. Of the Cistercian
NUNNERY of St Mary, founded in 1155 by Bertram Haget,
nothing remains but its refectory range, incorporated as the
rear wing of the old farmhouse. In the N side a re-set doorway
with one order of leaf capitals and one arch in which enriched
trellis overlies a roll moulding. Leaf motifs in the spandrels. To
the r. of this doorway are two smaller blank arches, part of the
laver. At first floor, outlines of tall round-arched windows –
blocked *c.* 1500 when a floor was inserted (the ground-floor
room has a ceiling with richly carved beams) and six-light mullioned windows introduced on the S side. The mullioned
windows of the N front and the chimneystack on the S are post-
Reformation alterations. The line of a MOAT can still be traced.

BINGLEY

The Airedale mill town of Bingley is probably best known to
readers of *The Buildings of England* as the site of *Norman Shaw*'s
fine early church of Holy Trinity which was demolished in 1974
– one of many demolitions and clearances in the S part of the
town during the 1960s and 70s – but Shaw's presence in the first
place is worth remarking, for during the 1860s Bingley was for a
short time a cynosure of the artistically innovative, with work by
a number of other figures of the coming generation – *Morris &
Co.*, *William Burges* and *Alfred Waterhouse* – as well as Shaw. The
principal agents in bringing this about were two local Ruskini-
ans, the textile manufacturer turned decorator John Aldam
Heaton, then resident at the nearby village of Harden, and the
Bradford banking magnate Alfred Harris, who was Holy Trinity's
main benefactor. As to the town more generally, in spite of a
market charter of the early C13 it is in essence a greatly overgrown village, with a single long main street sandwiched between
the fast-flowing river Aire on one side and the canal (1774), the
railway (1847) and now the Bingley relief road (2001–3) on the
other. The first (water-powered) textile mill, for cotton spinning,
was established *c.* 1792, but by 1830 there had been a wholesale
shift to worsted. Rapid expansion in the later C19 was mainly on
the hillside to the E – rigorously stratified, with back-to-back
terraces at the bottom, villas further up.

CHURCHES

ALL SAINTS. At the NW end of the town centre. Not large, of
rural rather than urban character. Short Perp W tower, the top

stage, with paired two-light Gothic bell openings, added 1739. Clerestory to the nave, with straight-headed windows of three lights, lower chancel said to have been rebuilt in 1518. Aisles, S chapel and E window all much renewed in restoration of 1870–1 by *T. H. & F. Healey*. N chapel more extensively restored at the same time by *Norman Shaw* but retaining a NE angle pilaster from a classicizing phase presumably of the C18. Perp four-bay nave arcades, with slender octagonal piers and double-chamfered arches; the same, in two bays, to the chancel, and similarly detailed chancel arch. Chunky kingpost roof to nave. The 'Ferrand Pew', a transept-like projection against the N aisle, 1834 by *Walker Rawstorne*, was replaced by a vestry in 1953. – SCREENS. N chapel parclose by *Shaw*, 1870, as part of his restoration. Stately Perp.* – Chancel screen and S parclose 1898, a less distinguished version of the same style. – FONT. 1881, also by *Shaw*. Ornate Perp design with a tabernacle-work timber cover. – SCULPTURE. A late Anglo-Saxon font bowl or cross base, square with some crude inter-lace and a runic inscription of uncertain meaning. Also a small fragment of a late Anglo-Saxon cross-shaft, with interlace. – STAINED GLASS. E window 1890 by *Powell & Sons*, designed by *Henry Holiday*. – N chapel E by *Morris & Co.*, 1873, designed by *Burne-Jones*. Three angels with long trumpets. – S aisle third from E, 1917 by *Kempe & Co.*; W window 1848. – MONU-MENTS. Many wall tablets including the following. Thomas Fell †1697, with crude segmental pediment. – David Leach †1752 and Thomas Leach †1763. Good-quality Baroque car-touches. – General William Twiss †1827 by *Timothy Butler*. Sar-cophagus with portrait roundel. Naturalistic lion below, turret and cannon above. – Walker Ferrand †1835 by *J. Gott*. With high-relief profile figure of Hope, her hands resting on an anchor. – Edward Ferrand †1837 by *Butler*, with shrouded sarcophagus. – Sarah Ferrand †1854, the same.

HOLY TRINITY. Although the church has gone, two related buildings by *Shaw* remain. The SCHOOL, by the churchyard in Trinity Place, is of 1871–2 with a wing at right angles added in 1879. Plainest Gothic in dark gritstone, the only visual clue to its authorship the tall clustered chimneystack. ¼ m. SSW, just off Bradford Road but facing away SW across the valley, is the former VICARAGE, now White Lodge, of 1873–4. Snecked stone, steeply pitched red tile roof with hips and half-hips. Prominent chimneys, sash and casement windows. Two big canted semi-dormers on the S front.

ST LAWRENCE, Otley Road, Eldwick. 1893 by *Armistead & Parkinson* of Bingley and Bradford. Tiny suburban church. Lancet style with fancy saddleback bellcote on the W gable.

SACRED HEART (R.C.), Crow Nest Road and Nethermoor View. 1877–80 by *Edward Simpson*. On a steeply sloping site, with the former school below the chancel and the presbytery adjoining

---

* The chapel is now occupied by the organ, and the STALLS which Shaw designed for it have been dispersed. Some are in the S chapel.

to one side. 'Not in any particular style of architecture' (Speight) but Gothic is the closest, with simplified wooden tracery to the plain pointed windows.

UNITED REFORMED CHAPEL (Congregational), Ferrand Lane. Totally plain rectangle of 1818 down a steep alley close to the river. Extended at one end 1845, with a two-storey basement cottage below, forebuilding at the other *c*. 1890. Interior refitted 1899 with gallery describing an elongated octagon.

INDEPENDENT METHODIST CHAPEL ('Ebenezer Christian Brethren'), Leonard Street. 1868. Four-bay pedimented front with two tiers of windows.

BAPTIST CHAPEL, Park Road. 1874–6 by *F. B. Payton* of Bradford. Basic Gothic with unbuttressed NW tower and stumpy slate-hung spire.

METHODIST CHURCH, Mornington Road. The big Gothic church of 1874 by *J. P. Pritchett Jun.*, with tall tower and spire, has been demolished. Some stonework details reused in the entrance front of its more utilitarian successor, 2002–3 by *Nuttall Yarwood* of Leeds.

CEMETERY, Bailey Hills. 1870. Attractive layout on a knoll overlooking the river, with winding paths and much thick evergreen planting. Two CHAPELS, informally sited, simple Gothic with octagonal bellcotes.

PUBLIC BUILDINGS

For MYRTLE GROVE (Council Offices), and neighbouring buildings in the town centre, *see* Perambulation. For COTTINGLEY TOWN HALL, *see* Outer Bingley.

MAGISTRATES COURT and POLICE STATION, Bradford Road. 1928–9. Domestic Neo-Georgian with hipped roof. Two storeys, nine-plus-three bays.

Former BINGLEY COLLEGE (Teacher Training), Lady Lane. Now flats, with bijou housing built over the grounds. 1909–11 by West Riding County Architect *J. Vickers Edwards*. Main building in intermittently ebullient Wrenaissance style, a three-storey half-H with domed clock-turret-cum-cupola. Also five former residential blocks arranged in a crescent, in a plainer version of the same manner, with mansard roofs.

GRAMMAR SCHOOL, Keighley Road. Oldest part first built in 1853 on a different site and rebuilt on the present one ten years later. Jacobean style, one storey, with shaped gables. Other buildings 1907, 1931 etc.

BECKFOOT SCHOOL (former County Secondary), Bradford Road. 1939–40 by *W. G. Newton*, much altered and expanded. Brick-built on a wedge-shaped plan. Spine containing full-height hall and gymnasium, terminating at the N end in a (defaced) portico with thin square pillars and pediment, somewhat colonial – or Swedish – looking. Rather trivial square clock turret over. Lower flat-roofed splayed classroom ranges to each side now swallowed up in the sea of later development.

BOARD SCHOOL, Mornington Road (Priestthorpe Primary School). 1876–7 by *Jackson & Longley* of Bradford. Gothic, altered, with a two-storey return wing to l.

COTTAGE HOSPITAL, Fernbank Drive. 1889. Modest single-storey block with gable. Additions 1911, 1924 etc.

RAILWAY STATION, Wellington Street. 1892 by the Midland Railway Co.'s architect *Charles Trubshaw*. Weak Free Renaissance with gables and sash windows.

70 FIVE RISE LOCKS, on the Leeds and Liverpool Canal. One of the great showpieces of canal engineering, designed by *John Longbotham* of Halifax, engineer to the canal company, and built in 1773–4. The contractors were *Barnabas Morvil, Jonathan Farrar* and *William Wild*, of Bingley, and *John Sugden* of Silsden. A continuous flight of five lock basins and six sets of lock gates, they contribute a rise of 59 ft (18 metres) – out of a total for the canal across the Pennines of 487 ft (148 metres) – over a distance of 320 ft (98 metres). Other structures, further SE, also by *Longbotham* are the THREE RISE LOCKS – three basins and four sets of gates – the TWO RISE LOCKS, and the DOWLEY GAP AQUEDUCT over the Aire, with seven low arches.

IRELAND BRIDGE, over the Aire. 1686, widened and repaired 1775. Five arches.

BECKFOOT BRIDGE, over Harden Beck. 1723, *Benjamin Craven* and *Joshua Scott*, masons. Of pedestrian or packhorse width only, one arch. The cost was £10.

127 FOOTBRIDGES over the relief road, at the Three Rise Locks and Britannia Street. 2001–3 by *Ove Arup & Partners* and contractors *Amec Civil Engineering Ltd*. The former of steel truss construction, the latter cable-stayed with a single pylon.

PERAMBULATION

The MAIN STREET has two focal points, one at each end. To the N is the area round the parish church, where a new road was made on the E side of the churchyard in 1904 leaving the OLD MAIN STREET to the W as the only part still retaining its domestic, small-town character. Modest houses mainly of the later C18 with just one, of three bays and two tall storeys, more polite than the rest. Also at the junction with Millgate the OLD WHITE HORSE INN, C17, much altered, with gabled cross-wing and some mullioned windows.

The other, towards the S end, is an open space on the W side created by demolitions in the 1960s, extending back as far as an attractive terrace overlooking the river. Dominating on the S side is the six-storey concrete ziggurat of the BRADFORD & BINGLEY former head office, 1976 by *John Brunton &*

Partners. To the E, across the street, the former LIBRARY, built as the Mechanics' Institute, 1862–4 by *Alfred Waterhouse.* Serious C13 Gothic but not large, the frontage just a tall gable-end with two tiers of windows. In the middle of the space, next to the lumpish ARTS CENTRE, 1974, are the MARKET HALL and BUTTER CROSS which were re-erected here in 1984. They originally stood in the Main Street a little to the N – side by side as now from *c.* 1820, when the cross had been moved from a position further N – and had been dismantled in 1888 for road widening and re-erected in Prince of Wales Park at the top of Park Road. The Market Hall is a low single storey of five bays with plain square piers and hipped roof, and is dated 1753 on the archway at the end towards the Butter Cross:* confusingly, a payment in the following year to *Thomas Lister* for 'building the Cross' probably relates to this building rather than the other, as it was later referred to as the 'Market House and Cross'. The Butter Cross consists of a tall shaft standing on a stepped base, surrounded by a square pyramid-roofed shelter with slightly taller square piers and the top of the shaft poking through the apex of the roof. The cross itself is allegedly medieval, at least in origin; the shelter presumably of *c.* 1820.

Off to the r. from here is the OLD FIRE STATION, 1902, now a bar, with an Art-Nouveau-detailed tower crowned by a fancy timber belvedere. And further back to the SW, behind the BATHS, 1927, is MYRTLE GROVE, a gentry house built 1770–2 by Johnson Atkinson Busfeild. The Town Hall from 1926, now Council Offices. Main block of two storeys and nine uniform bays, under a curiously over-emphatic hipped roof. Pedimented doorcase with Tuscan columns. Much altered recessed flanking wings, with pedimented centres and ball-finial-crested link bays. Interior exceedingly cut about from 1926 onwards. The grounds, in front, are a public park.

Running NE from a point on the Main Street between the two foci is PARK ROAD, first crossing the railway, relief road and canal and then heading uphill. Along the canal crowd some of the remaining TEXTILE MILLS. Prominent is BOWLING GREEN MILL (Damart) to the l., 1871. Boxy, storeyed range partly obscured by later addition, big shed at right angles, gabled engine house between them and massive square chimney with heavy bracketed top. On the r. side of the road, on the corner with Clyde Street, the former PARK ROAD TANNERY, of similar date. Four by seven bays and four storeys, the lower two with heavy Italianate detail but the top part, which included the leather-drying room, of weatherboarding between cast-iron columns. Then behind Bowling Green Mill the main block of the former BINGLEY MILL, also *c.* 1870, four storeys, restrained Italianate, with gabled ends and pyramid-roofed tower. Converted to flats and the rest of the site redeveloped as THE LOCKS housing

---

*A suggestion that the building was enlarged in 1753 but is otherwise older, is not convincing.

scheme, 1995–6 by the *Arthur Quarmby Partnership*. Gabled apartment blocks overlooking the canal, in a quasi-industrial idiom.

Further items in this direction are more scattered, amongst the suburbia. In Park Road on the r. the OLD VICARAGE ('Monks Barn'). Small early C18 front block with quoins, cross-windows – converted to plate-glass sashes on the two-bay front – and a doorway with architrave surround in the l. gable-end. C17 L-shaped complex behind and to l., with seven-light house-body window in the l. part. Some good interior features, including two staircases with turned balusters, one in the front block and one in the l. wing, and early C18 panelling. Then off to the l. at the end of Gawthorpe Drive is GAWTHORPE HALL, a substantial C17 Pennine gentry house apparently incorporating elements of an earlier building, altered mid C19 and later. It now appears as a rectangular block with flush elevations to front and back, each with five more or less variegated gables, the middle bay at the front containing the entrance; but until *c.* 1900 the second bay, to the l. of the entrance, was recessed, without a gable, and the entrance bay was a two-storey porch. So the house presumably began as a conventional hall range with cross-wings – the parlour wing to the l, the service to the r. – with the doubling in thickness of the service wing, to create the fifth bay, forming an early addition. Mullion-and-transom windows of three to seven lights – the largest, to the altered hall bay, are partly renewed, with their lights lengthened, but broadly represent what was there before. (Interior much changed in C19 but said to retain some C17 fireplaces and, remarkably, in the original part of the service wing a late medieval common rafter roof encased below the present one. Other roofs C17, with kingposts.)

Finally, ¼ m. further up again in Lady Lane, OAKWOOD (now an hotel), a villa of 1864 by *Knowles & Wilcock* of Bradford for textile merchant Thomas Garnett, with a chimneypiece by *William Burges* and splendid early stained glass by *Morris & Co.*, both of the following year. The link in this case was evidently Garnett's cousin the Rev. Charles Beanlands, founder-curate of St Michael, Brighton, where both Morris and Burges were employed. The house, not specially large, is in a simple domestic Gothic style, gently asymmetrical. The glass is in the mullioned-and-transomed staircase window, over the front door. St George in the centre, designed by *Burne-Jones*, flanked by figures of the Four Seasons, by *Morris* himself. Above are portrait roundels of Chaucer and of four Chaucerian heroines, the latter also from a set by *Burne-Jones*. Specially fine background quarries with flower patterns, in yellow, brown and violet, possibly by *Morris*, set within a green and yellow diagonal trellis. The chimneypiece, in the former dining room, carved by *Thomas Nicholls*, has a gabled overmantel with a prominent imp figure carrying a bracket. *Burges* also provided an even bigger and more elaborate chimneypiece for the drawing room and designed furniture for the house, but the former has been broken up and it is unclear how much of the latter was executed.

OUTER BINGLEY

1. North: Crossflatts and Micklethwaite

CASTLEFIELDS MILL, Castlefields Lane. Founded 1792 for cotton spinning. One early block remains, three storeys, six bays. The rest probably after 1892. Nearby, the mill-master's house, *c.* 1800, with a row of mill-workers' cottages attached. Plain three-storey rectangle with some Gothic glazing, the cottages, at right angles, of two storeys.

RYSHWORTH HALL, Keighley Road. In origin a timber-framed house of the early and mid C16, much altered and extended since. The earliest part is the three-bay putative hall range now buried in the middle of the building, the roof with closed king-post trusses at each end and an intermediate one of more unusual form, with a short kingpost on a collar supported by straight braces. Slightly later E cross-wing, with some close-studded framing visible inside and more kingpost trusses but rendered externally, as is the small infill block of uncertain date in front of the hall to the S, with a gable to match the wing. Below both gables are C19 canted bays. Meanwhile, in the C17 the wing had been extended to the N in stone, with a mullion-and-transom window, and in the early C18 a smart W cross-wing was built, with sash windows, eaves cornice and hipped roof. Later C19 entrance block between the two wings to the N. Good early C18 staircase in the W wing, with double-spiral balusters, and a panelled room of the same date in the N part of the E wing. On the framing some graffiti relating to the Bynns family, owners of the property from 1591 to 1672.

BRADFORD & BINGLEY HEAD OFFICE, beside the relief road. 1990–2 by the *John Brunton Partnership*. Four-storey block with big hipped roof, the first three storeys of coursed stone with heavy dressings, the top continuously glazed (cf. their earlier head office in the town centre).

MICKLETHWAITE GRANGE, in the hamlet on the hillside. 1695, an irregular L-shape. Front doorway (facing away from the road) with torus-moulded surround flanked by strips of banded masonry (cf. Eldwick Hall, below), an upright oval window above, and on the same axis a chimney with shallow blind arcading (cf. School Street, Steeton, 1710, and Stone Gappe, Lothersdale, 1725, etc.). On the S flank a doorway with lugged surround. Other windows mullioned, one at the back stepped.

2. East: Eldwick and Gilstead

ST LAWRENCE. *See* Churches.

ELDWICK HALL, Otley Road, beyond the built-up area. 1696. Double pile with slightly off-centre lobby entry – and the front therefore not quite symmetrical. Doorway with lugged archi-trave surround flanked by banded pilaster-strips (cf. Micklethwaite Grange), and above it a curious window of two arched lights in a flattened-ogee-headed frame. Flanking

windows mullioned-and-transomed, of four lights to the l., six
to the r. Stringcourse between the storeys, ramped up over the
door; another doorway, ogee-headed, in the r. flank, leading
to the kitchen. Acorn finials on the gable-ends. Pilastered
gatepiers at the front. A little further N, LOW HOUSE, 1731,
still with a simply ornamented doorhead.

MILNER FIELD. *Thomas Harris*'s muscular Gothic mansion of
1871–3 for Titus Salt Jun., son of the builder of Saltaire (q.v.),
has been demolished; but his NORTH LODGE in Primrose
Lane remains, in a melodramatically ruinous state. Tall and
compact, with a roguish conical-roofed turret and some
Caernarvon-arched openings.

Opposite the top of Primrose Lane, in GILSTEAD LANE, a much
altered C17 house of hybrid construction, externally of stone
with the remains of a timber arcade between the body of the
house and the rear outshut. Off the road back into the town,
overlooking the canal, three eleven-storey blocks of council
flats on the Bison system, 1966.

3. South: Cottingley

COTTINGLEY TOWN HALL, Main Street. Opened 1865, an
unusual little multi-purpose building, built to house the
mechanics' institute and village school and to serve as a non-
denominational (Protestant) chapel. Three-bay, two-storey
Italianate front with clock-turret-cum-bellcote over the centre.
Hall with round-headed windows behind.

In BRADFORD ROAD, by Cottingley Bridge, an C18 house of
seven bays with full-height entrance-cum-staircase hall in the
centre, and opposite an altered C17 double pile with gable-end
entry. Further E, BANKFIELD, now an hotel. Charmless
Jacobean-style industrialist's house of 1848 by *Andrews &
Delaunay*, enlarged 1871 by the same firm and totally swamped
by C20 additions.

4. West: St Ives and Harden Grange

Two houses associated with the Ferrand family who bought the
Harden Grange estate in 1636, the story complicated by swap-
ping of names. The present ST IVES, on the site of the original
Harden Grange, is a substantial but unremarkable building of
at least two phases in the early and mid C19, one of *c.* 1830 for
Walker Ferrand and one of *c.* 1854 onwards for William Busfeild Ferrand, with a Doric porte cochère on the entrance front.
But attached to it, as part of an odd group of structures at the
office end, is the truncated rump of the C17 house, known as
OLD HARDEN GRANGE. L-shaped with a doorway framed by
columns and entablature, and a heraldic panel above, all
evidently *ex situ*. On the lintel a verse attributed to George
Herbert. Beyond this is a range partly of 1680, with a pyramid-
roofed bellcote-like structure on the gable, and partly of 1704

(date in basement), with four little gables pierced by upright ovals (cf. the Starkie wing at East Riddlesden Hall, Keighley), former cross-windows below, and a chimney with blind arcading (cf. Micklethwaite Grange). Alongside are the remains of a C19 conservatory and in front of the 1704 part a funny late C18 garden feature, a row of pointed arches surmounted by crosses. In the wall at right angles a reused doorway dated 1584. Behind the range the former STABLES, 1900, Neo-Baroque-cum-Pennine Revival; and W and E of the house cottage-style LODGES with Y-tracery windows, one dated 1851.

The present HARDEN GRANGE, ½ m. downhill to the S, occupies the site of the original St Ives – the name allegedly derived from a putative monastery of St Heiv – which was the main seat of the family from 1712 until 1854; and it was then that the names of the properties were transposed. It had been rebuilt in 1759 by *James Paine* – his design was a plain version of his characteristic tripartite formula (cf. Stockeld Park) – and the kitchen block of that building was evidently incorporated into the existing house, which was erected by W. B. Ferrand *c.* 1859 and let to the Bradford industrialist Walter Dunlop. This is totally undistinguished architecturally but in 1862 Dunlop commissioned important early STAINED GLASS from *Morris & Co.* (now at Cliffe Castle Museum, Keighley) for the entrance hall. The subject was the story of Tristram and Isoude as told in Malory's *Morte d'Arthur*, the designs by *Rossetti*, *Burne-Jones* and *Morris* himself, together with *Arthur Hughes*, *Val Prinsep* and *Ford Madox Brown*. Beside the house a mid-C18 Palladian STABLE BLOCK, with pedimented centre, which there is no particular reason to associate with Paine. By the road another rustic LODGE.

See also Harden.

III

BIRKENSHAW
Gomersal

2020

ST PAUL. A Commissioners' church, 1829–31 by *Peter Atkinson Jun*. Thin lancet-style W tower with recessed spire, aisleless body with traceried windows, extended E by two bays in 1892–3. – STAINED GLASS. Garish E window 1865 by *R. B. Edmundson* (re-set 1892). – W entrance to the churchyard aligned on the tower. Flanking it the former NATIONAL SCHOOLS, two near-matching blocks, the l. 1838, the r. 1850. One storey, with hoodmoulds to the windows, altered.

BIRSTWITH

2050

ST JAMES. 1856–7 by *Rohde Hawkins* for Frederick Greenwood of Swarcliffe Hall. Conventional Dec, with W tower and broach spire. – REREDOS. 1883, with mosaic panels by *Powell & Sons*. Tiles to l. and r. 1907, also by them. – STAINED GLASS. E window by *Powell & Sons*, 1888; S aisle second from E, 1857 by *Clayton & Bell*; S aisle SW by *Hardman*, 1869; the rest *Ward & Hughes*, 1857–75.

SWARCLIFFE HALL, on rising ground W of the church. Now a school. 1848–50, also by *Rohde Hawkins*, for Greenwood's brother and predecessor Edwin. Enlarged 1866–7. Restrained Jacobean with many gables and a squat tower with spire.

NEW BRIDGE, over the Nidd, ½ m. NNW. 1822, perhaps reusing stone from the previous packhorse bridge. Elegant single span, the roadway only 6 ft (2 metres) wide.

BISHOP MONKTON

3060

ST JOHN. 1878–9 by *C. Hodgson Fowler* (cf. Burton Leonard), replacing a chapel of ease of Ripon rebuilt in 1822. Simple E.E. in Magnesian limestone. NW tower-porch with octagonal belfry stage and spirelet. – STAINED GLASS. E window 1885 by *Ward & Hughes*; W window 1889 by *Powell Bros.* of Leeds; chancel S 1900 by *Burlison & Grylls*; nave S (two) 1900 by *A. L. Moore*.

Village street with stream running alongside. In the NE part the former MECHANICS' INSTITUTE, 1859, a little brick building, originally single-storeyed, with a saddleback-roofed clock turret capped by a bellcote, over the central porch. Dormer windows added. ½ m. further E the former CORN MILL, now housing, of limestone, c. 1800. Three storeys, eleven bays.

BISHOP THORNTON

2060

ST JOHN. 1888. Small, free Dec, with octagonal bellcote. Of its predecessor, ½ m. N, 1825 by *John Oates* of Halifax, there remains the TOWER, with Y-tracery bell-openings. The rest dem. 1888.

ST SAVIOUR (R.C.). 1809. Humble oblong with round-headed windows.

BLUBBERHOUSES

1050

ST ANDREW. On steeply sloping ground above the main road. 1856 by *E. B. Lamb*, built as a chapel of ease of Fewston. The patron was Lady Louisa Frankland Russell of Thirkleby Hall in the North Riding, for whom Lamb also designed churches at Thirkleby and at Aldwark and Bagby in the same county. Not large, but with Lamb's usual low heavy contour and some of his other eccentricities. E.E. style. Thin NW tower with odd pyramidal spire, NW porch butting against it, short narrow N aisle. Complicated roof trusses on prominent corbels, two-bay arcade with a stumpy masonry pier carrying a timber aisle-plate instead of arches. – ALTAR RAIL. C17, with turned balusters. – PULPIT and fronts of the first row of PEWS, of C17 woodwork, said to have been brought from Thirkleby.

BLUBBERHOUSES HALL, N of the main road. c. 1856 for Lady Frankland Russell, possibly also by *Lamb*. An approximation to Pennine Jacobean, with some wilful details.

APPRENTICE HOUSE, Hardisty Hill, ½ m. N. Built c. 1800 by the proprietors of the West House Linen Mill at Fewston (dem.) to house 'apprentices' – that is, child labour from the workhouses. Three storeys, the ground-floor windows round-headed.

BOLTON ABBEY   0050

'The Abbey is placed, as most lovers of our English scenery know well, on a little promontory of level park land, enclosed by one of the sweeps of the Wharfe. On the other side of the river, the flank of the dale rises in a pretty wooded brow, which the river, leaning against, has cut into two or three somewhat bold masses of rock, steep to the water's edge, but feathered above with copse of ash and oak. Above these rocks, the hills are rounded softly upwards to the moorland; . . . the general impression upon the eye is that the hill is little more than twice the height of the ruins, or of the groups of noble ash trees which encircle them. One of these groups is conspicuous above the rest, growing on the very shore of the tongue of land which projects into the river, whose clear brown water, stealing first in mere threads between the separate pebbles of shingle, and eddying in soft golden lines towards its central current, flows out of amber into ebony, and glides calm and deep below the rock on the opposite shore . . . A little farther up the valley the limestone summits rise, and that steeply, to a height of twelve hundred feet above the river, which foams between them in the narrow and dangerous channel of the Strid. Noble moorlands extend above, purple with heath, and broken into scars and glens; and around every soft tuft of wood, and gentle extent of meadow, throughout the dale, there floats a feeling of this mountain power, and an instinctive apprehension of the strength and greatness of this wild northern land. It is to the association of this power and border sternness with the sweet peace and tender decay of Bolton Priory, that the scene owes its distinctive charm.' Thus Ruskin in *Modern Painters* (1856). How Romantic artists felt the scene so described can be seen in Turner's famous watercolour.

Bolton Priory, for it was a priory and never an abbey, was a house of Augustinian Canons founded *c.* 1154 by Alice de Romille. Her mother had endowed a priory at Embsay in 1120. Alice transferred it to Bolton – but not to commemorate her son's fatal jump across the Strid: the boy was still alive in 1154. Building began in earnest *c.* 1170, continuing until the mid C13, but incorporated parts of a structure either from the time of the foundation or already in existence by then. In the early C14 the establishment suffered from the incursions of the Scots and the canons were dispersed for a time, but the return to normality was marked by another major building campaign. Dissolved in 1539, the priory was acquired in 1541 by Henry Clifford, first Earl of Cumberland, whose family had been its hereditary patrons; and from the Cliffords the estate passed in the C17 to the Earls of Burlington – including in due course the architect – then in 1753 to the Dukes of Devonshire. Of the canons' church, the nave was retained in use as a place of worship, first as a chapel of ease of Skipton and then from 1864 as a parish church (St Mary and St Cuthbert) in its own right. The E parts meanwhile became a highly picturesque ruin, mainly still standing to wall-head height; and a few masonry courses of the living quarters also remain, made more eloquent by the results of Hamilton Thompson's excavations in 1923–4. The priory gatehouse, W of the church, became the nucleus of Bolton Hall, the occasional residence of the post-Dissolution owners.

The CHURCH is the product of four main building phases. That of *c.* 1170–90 provided a Cistercian-style straight-ended aisleless presbytery, the crossing, transepts with straight-ended E chapels also in the Cistercian manner, and the lower stage of the nave S wall. There was then a break, apparently because attention was switched to the domestic quarters, and it was only in the mid C13 that the nave, with N aisle, was continued to completion. In the mid C14 the presbytery and transepts were substantially rebuilt; and in 1520, as an inscription records, a W tower was begun but then left unfinished. Externally therefore the E parts appear almost entirely Dec, the PRESBYTERY still unaisled but lengthened a bay to the E. Huge E window, now deprived of its tracery; tall side windows, one on the S preserving its details: three lights and flowing tracery. In the TRANSEPTS the E chapels were reconstructed without the partition walls between them, and the innermost S chapel lengthened to the E. Base of a pier with eight attached demi-shafts in the S transept; two-bay arcade with octagonal pier and clerestory windows with reticulated tracery all surviving in the N, but decidedly less elegant than the presbytery details.

But the doorway between the S transept and the cloister to the W is of *c.* 1290 – see the pointed trefoil head with pierced spandrels – and earlier fabric remains within the presbytery and the crossing. In both the presbytery side walls a round-

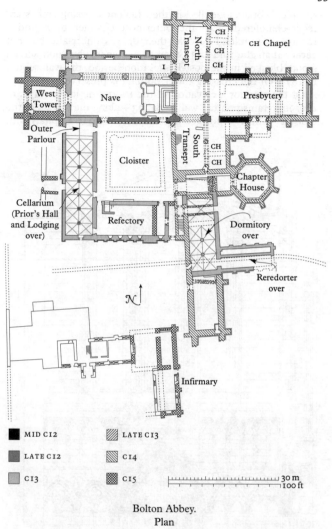

Bolton Abbey.
Plan

MID C12   LATE C13
LATE C12   C14
C13   C15

30 m
100 ft

headed arch of *c.* 1170 cut through rough walling of *c.* 1154 to connect with the inner transept chapels, then E of these intersected blind arcading also of *c.* 1170 – but according to Hamilton Thompson re-set in the C14 – with scalloped capitals of various designs (the shafts robbed out). In the added C14 E bay a tomb recess to the N and scanty remains of the sedilia to the S; and also on the S side, cutting through the blind arcading, a tomb arch with panelled jambs and soffit, and a doorway, which belonged to a chantry chapel of *c.* 1400, built continuing the line of the inner S transept chapel. In the CROSSING, the E piers are again of *c.* 1170, with scalloped capitals, the W ones slightly later, *c.* 1190 – see the waterholding base on the

NW pier – but remodelled in the C14. The crossing arches are triple-chamfered, with the outermost chamfer to N and S resting on moulded corbels: their date is uncertain, but not earlier than the mid C13. W archway, where the rood screen stood, blocked in the post-Dissolution period, the wall rebuilt in 1877. Of the crossing tower nothing is preserved.

Of the exterior S elevation of the NAVE, the lower stage, of *c.* 1190, retains pointed wall arcading – along the N walk of the cloister – and two pointed doorways flanking it. Capitals with

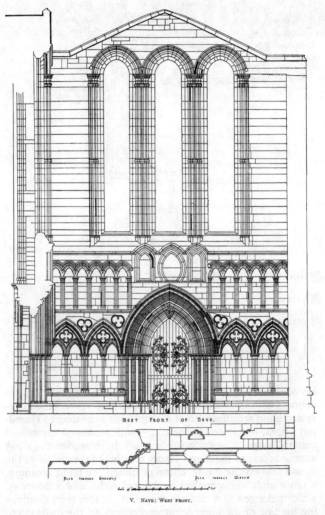

WEST FRONT OF NAVE.

PLAN THROUGH DOORWAY   PLAN THROUGH WINDOW

V. NAVE: WEST FRONT.

Bolton Abbey, mid-C13 west front.
Measured drawing, 1924

upright leaves, or scalloped, or plainly moulded, evidently related to those in the presbytery. The mid-C13 upper stage has six tall, closely set two-light windows with transoms – an unusual feature at the time – and plate tracery of small pointed quatrefoils. N elevation of four bays with simple C13 lancets to the clerestory, their heads linked by a string, Dec buttresses and three-light windows to the aisle, the tracery of the latter much renewed in the restoration of the parish church by *G. E. Street*, 1866–7. The climax and presumably the conclusion of the mid-C13 campaign is the W FRONT, the main part standing behind the early C16 W tower and framed by its tower arch, and only surviving because of the failure to complete the tower. Deeply splayed central portal with three orders of colonnettes and an arch with a large number of fine mouldings. To l. and r. of this are two blind arches of two lights each, with quatrefoils in the spandrels between the sub-arches and trefoils in the spandrels between the main arches. Above runs a small blind arcade of pointed trefoil-headed arches broken by the mouldings of the portal, over which is an odd group of two small blind arches flanking a vesica which is ruthlessly truncated at the foot. Above that a group of three tall lancet windows of even height. Much dogtooth everywhere. But as so often in E.E. work there is the strangest lack of congruity between this part and that fronting the aisle. The portal of the latter is narrow and flanked by even narrower blind lancet arches, one to each side, which disconcertingly reach higher than the main arch, and there is none of the blind tracery. Above is no more than a smaller version of the same motif. The only thing which nave and aisle have in common is the abundance of dogtooth.

As to the W TOWER itself, it is also extremely ornate, starting with two tiers of square panels containing wheel motifs. Deep angle buttresses, with cinquefoil-headed panels and heraldic statuary to the outer faces. W doorway with fine mouldings and shields in quatrefoils to the spandrels. Zone of niches and shields above, and tracery-headed panels to each side. Above again the inscription, and then the very tall window of five lights. Transom with panel tracery below it, the head also with panel tracery and divided by sub-arches in a two-plus-one-plus-two rhythm. Ogee hoodmould with crockets over, but nothing above that until 1982–5 when the tower was roofed, the window glazed and a bell-turret added, by *Neil Hartley*.

In contrast to all this is the restrained INTERIOR of the nave. Four-bay N arcade with two octagonal piers and a circular one between them, and triple-chamfered arches with thin hoodmoulds. Wall-shafts on small corbels just above the hoodmould stops, clerestory as outside. On the S side, deep window reveals pierced by a sill-level wall passage, and wall-shafts between alternate windows on corbels just below the sill. The only decorative enrichment is a little nailhead to the piers and the shafts, and some dogtooth to the clerestory string and the window hoodmoulds. Roof probably early C16, with moulded tie-beams and tracery above them, that to the aisle 1866–7 by *Street*. – CHANCEL ENCLOSURE also by *Street*. Low stone walls with trefoil-headed blind arcading, and *ambones* for pulpit and reading desk at the corners. – REREDOS. 1877. A series of traceried panels, structurally part of the rebuilt crossing arch wall, with naturalistic flower paintings by *George Bottomley* of Cross Hills. – STAINED GLASS. C14 fragments in the heads of the aisle windows. – Nave S, six windows designed by *A. W. N. Pugin*, 1850–2, and executed by *J. G. Crace*, 1853, for the sixth Duke of Devonshire. An important series based on C13 examples from Northern Europe. Scenes from the life of Christ in quatrefoil-shaped panels, six to a window, set within decorative borders of varied design. – Aisle NW by *Clayton & Bell*, 1877. Lively scenes.

DOMESTIC BUILDINGS. For the N walk of the cloister, *see* above. The W range, of *c.* 1200 and a little later – see the remaining bases of the circular piers – contained the outer parlour, the Cellarium to the S of this and the original prior's lodging over. It was markedly lofty, as the roof-line on the nave S wall shows. In the S range, early C13, the upper floor was the Refectory. A passage and vestibule at the N end of the E range led to the chapter house, which was octagonal, of *c.* 1370. S of the passage, the undercroft of the dormitory, with an octagonal pier, probably of the early C13, and a fragment of the C14 day stair rising from the SE corner of the cloister. As usual the reredorter or lavatory ran out at right angles to the dormitory to the E and was placed above a drain. The dormitory range was continued to the S by the C14 new prior's lodging. Immediately SW of this was an L-shaped building of the C15 which was probably the Infirmary. The W wall now forms the E end of the Old Rectory (*see* below), the E parts incorporated into a building known as the Boyle Room which was remodelled in the C19. At the N end of this a mullioned window of six trefoil-headed lights. To the SW of the Old Rectory a large fragment of a chimney and a fireplace, perhaps of *c.* 1500 and part of a guesthouse.

OLD RECTORY. Built in 1700 by the second Earl of Burlington as the Boyle School, in accordance with the will of his greatuncle the scientist Robert Boyle – apart from the E wall (*see* above) and perhaps some other fragments of masonry inside. Unsophisticated but approximately symmetrical S front. Crosswindows, most of them altered in the C19, to the ground floor, mullioned windows above, all in architrave surrounds. Central porch with heavily rusticated doorway crowned by a semicircular pediment, upright oval windows in the sides.

BOLTON HALL. In addition to the priory gatehouse, the building consists of a long lower range, probably of medieval origin, to the N and a shorter wing to the S. The gatehouse, built in the early C14, is of three storeys, with a rectangular staircase turret against the N wall, a corresponding garderobe projection against the S, diagonally set miniature angle turrets over the buttresses, and crenellated parapets. C15 mullioned windows, some of them renewed. Probably in the immediate post-Dissolution period the archways into the gateway passage were blocked to convert the passage into the main room of the house. The w wall incorporates a big C16 fireplace (another similar is on the top floor), that to the E a reused doorway of *c.* 1370 which Hamilton Thompson suggested came from the chapter house: the three-centre-headed windows flanking it were inserted in the 1760s. Halfway along, the passage has a cross-wall pierced by separate main and pedestrian arches (cf. Fountains Abbey etc.), both chamfered and round-headed. Both parts of the passage are covered by bluntly pointed barrel-vaults, with transverse and longitudinal ribs creating an effect of panelling, the ribs hollow-chamfered in the w part, more elaborately profiled to the E. In the E part of the passage an ogee-headed doorway on each side, that to the N leading to the spiral staircase.

The house was repaired for the third Earl of Burlington in 1726–7, and it was probably then that the panels of the barrel-vault were decorated with *grisaille* portraits of Roman emperors and empresses – now much faded – perhaps by *William Kent.* C19 alterations for the sixth Duke of Devonshire. s wing rebuilt 1814 by *Peter Atkinson Jun.* and *Matthew Phillips.* Gothic style matching the gatehouse (the canted bay window at the s end added 1875). N wing remodelled and extended in castellated style by *Sir Joseph Paxton* and *John Robertson* 1843–4. Drawing room in the s wing, with geometrical painted decoration, designed by *Pugin* and executed by *Crace, c.* 1846, to the panels of the ceiling.

Also a number of miscellaneous structures along the road. s of the Hall, the AQUEDUCT which carried the millrace of the adjoining water mill across the road is another putative contribution by *Kent.* Three half-elliptical-headed arches, roughly rusticated, the centre one larger than the others (the centre arch heightened slightly, and the wall-head raised, in the 1930s). The estate accounts suggest it was built for Lord Burlington in 1732, and the composition closely resembles one used by Kent for a number of rustic cascades, eg. at Chiswick. s of this a stretch of the priory PRECINCT WALL, with high battered coping, the regular buttresses robbed out; then the TEA HOUSE, the stump of an aisled barn turned into a picturesque C19 cottage (one kingpost truss inside), and beside it a row of C19 cottages with diagonally set chimneystacks. Could this be the work at Bolton Abbey carried out in the 1830s by *John Harper*? s again the aisled GREAT BARN, a very fine example, dated 1518 by dendrochronology. Nine bays, with the usual kingpost trusses and between them collars carrying subsidiary kingposts. Braces from the aisle-posts to the aisle-plates and the tie-beams and from the kingposts to the ridge pole. The walls were originally timber-framed, the present stone walling C19. N of Bolton Hall, the CAVENDISH MEMORIAL FOUNTAIN, erected 1886 in memory of Lord Frederick Cavendish, who was killed in Phoenix Park, Dublin in 1882.

68

Hexagonal Gothic pavilion with an open ogee crown, by *T. Worthington & J. G. Elgood* of Manchester.

BOLTON BRIDGE, ¾ m. s. Rebuilt in 1778. Two segmental arches.

BOLTON-BY-BOWLAND

7040

Attractive gently scattered village of the Ribble valley, with the church between two greens: a subsidiary settlement, Holden, is ⅝ m. w. The centre of a late flowering of the fanciful architectural detail of the Pennines, mainly after 1700, the best examples away from the village itself. Bolton Hall, the former seat of the Pudsey family, was demolished *c.* 1960.

ST PETER AND ST PAUL. Evidence from the C13 is a lancet at the w end of the s aisle, the priest's doorway, with sunken quadrant moulding, and the reused moulded components now forming the (straight-headed) main s doorway, including one with unfinished dogtooth ornament. Otherwise all Perp, but not uniform. Tall and handsome ashlar-faced w tower – the upper part rebuilt in 1852 – with diagonal buttresses, two tiers of two-light bell-openings, the upper Tudor-arched with very emphatic central mullions, a zone of pierced roundels above them, battlements and pinnacles. Equally smart is the Pudsey Chapel (s) of *c.* 1500, with battlemented parapet and big straight-headed windows. The rest – nave and chancel in one, with clerestory and narrow aisles – is rubble-built and less regular. E window of five tall stepped lancet lights under a four-centred arch (cf. Gisburn and Kildwick), the others straight-headed but smaller than on the chapel, some with cusped lights. Five-bay N and six-bay s arcades with octagonal piers and double-chamfered arches, apart from the far arch into the chapel which is heavily moulded. In the chancel N wall a fragment of a tomb recess. Restoration 1885–6 by *Paley & Austin*, their work including the nave roof and parapets.

FONT. A solid and impressive early C16 piece, with inscription soliciting prayers for the souls of Sir Ralph Pudsey, his wife Edwina and their son William (†1507), Rector of Bolton. The bowl a concave-sided octagon bearing coats of arms, on a base of the same profile. – PEWS. Dated 1694, rearranged 1886. Simple, with ball finials at the ends. – PULPIT. 1886, incorporating two Flemish Baroque relief panels, of the Annunciation and the Nativity. Behind it a panel from the former pulpit, dated 1703. – COMMUNION RAIL. 1704. Turned balusters, and a pair of ball finials flanking the gate. – SOUTH DOOR. Dated 1705. Closely and handsomely studded. – STAINED GLASS. E window 1876 by *Hardman*; w window by *Shrigley & Hunt*, *c.* 1885; three windows in the s aisle by *Kempe*, 1895 and 1899. – MONUMENTS, in the Pudsey Chapel. Sir Ralph Pudsey †1468 and his three wives. Very large slab of

Bolton-by-Bowland, St Peter and St Paul, monument
to Sir Ralph Pudsey †1468 and his three wives.

polished grey limestone, set on a tomb-chest of 1857. On it figures of husband, wives and below them their twenty-five children in three rows. The manner of representation is similar to that of monumental brasses, the figures flat with their outlines formed by cutting away the ground between them and other detail all incised. – Henry Pudsey †1509, the builder of the Pudsey Chapel, and his wife Margaret Conyers †1500. Brasses of two small kneeling figures, and coat of arms. – GATEPIERS to the churchyard, dated 1706, with ball finials.

CONGREGATIONAL CHAPEL, Holden. 1766–8. Round-headed windows. Interior altered *c.* 1882–4 etc. but the gallery retains an C18 panelled front. Former manse to l. added 1777, refronted 1909.

98 SCHOOL, at the E end of the village. 1874 by *Paley & Austin.* Pleasing composition in simple northern Jacobean style, with stepped mullion-and-transom windows and Westmorland slate roofs. The school house, with hipped-roofed canted bay window, forms a wing. Extension to N in similar mode, 1906 by *Austin & Paley.*

Also E of the church, the OLD COURTHOUSE, dated 1859 but incorporating earlier fabric, with two-storey porch, two storeys to the r. of it but three to the l. W of the church, in MAIN STREET, a Jacobethan model cottage and barn, dated 1835 on a big coat of arms, then on the l. a cottage with an elaborate ornamented doorhead of 1716, the design a development of one found in the Giggleswick area in the 1690s.

FOODEN HALL, ⅞ m. ESE. C17 with a short main range and a central two-storey gabled porch. Three-centre-headed doorway with moulded responds; transomed window above, of six lights to the front and two more to each side. To l. and r. of the porch, a mullioned window to the ground floor (five lights to the l., six to the r.) and a transomed window to the first. Lobby entry, and big segment-headed fireplace in the r. room. Deep outshut to the rear.

BOLTON PELE, ¾ m. SW. The name is misleading – a neat C17 farmhouse. Off-centre porch with a stepped three-light window to the upper stage (cf. Park House, Paythorne). Housebody window, r. of the porch, of three-plus-three lights. Fireplaces to all three main rooms.

BROXUP HOUSE, Holden. The earliest of the exotica, dated 1687. Doorhead with spiral decoration on two lobes (cf. Cromwell House, Long Preston); ground-floor windows to the r. under a continuous hoodmould with the stops also decorated with spirals; two transomed first-floor windows above these of the type incorporating a Serliana (cf. The Folly, Settle, 1670s); and over the doorway a vesica-shaped window again with ornamented stops to the hoodmould. Lobby-entry plan, with the housebody fireplace flanked by segment-headed doorways. Former service end to the l. remodelled in the C19 as a separate cottage.

STOOP LANE FARMHOUSE, ¾ m. NNW. Small double pile with central two-storey porch dated 1703, the upper stage again with the Folly-type window. Torus-moulded surround to the doorway. HIGHER HEIGHTS, 1⅜ m. WSW, follows the same formula but with the porch upper storey jettied.

ALDER HOUSE, 1⅜ m. WNW, the culmination of the group. Dated 1708 but perhaps incorporating some earlier masonry. Three-storey double pile, with a central three-storey gabled porch slightly jettied above the lowest stage. Ornamented doorhead similar to that in the village Main Street; above it a transomed three-light window making another variation on the Serliana theme, with the central lower light arched but the light over it also stepped up; and above that a stepped window with all three lights arched. Spiral stops to the hoodmoulds at all the stages. To l. and r. the windows are mullioned-and-transomed on the ground and first floors, conventional stepped to the second. On the N gable-end two of one light with shouldered heads, at the back a mixture of mullioned and cross-windows. Tudor-arched doorway within the porch; staircase against the rear wall with the lower flights of stone, the upper of oak, and turned balusters, some of them renewed. A little early C18 fielded panelling.

BORDLEY

9060

LAINGER HOUSE. 1673. Two-storey porch entered at the side, with a fanciful moulded doorhead and a stepped three-light window in the gable under an oddly shaped hoodmould. The house altered, originally it seems only one room wide with a lean-to rear outshut.

BOROUGHBRIDGE

3060

A Norman new town on the Great North Road (now by-passed), laid out in the C12 on the S bank of the River Ure following the building of the bridge, which superseded the earlier crossing ½ m. E (N of Aldborough, q.v.). The three long parallel streets of the medieval town are still evident as Bridge Street/Horsefair, High Street and Back Lane, and closing each end of High Street are squares, originally for the market (N) and chapel (S).

ST JAMES, Church Lane. 1852 by *Mallinson & Healey*. An honest Dec-style church with W tower and quatrefoil arcade piers. Re-set into the N wall of the vestry are extremely interesting ornate Late Norman ARCHITECTURAL FRAGMENTS. These were brought from the medieval chapel* but are unlikely either

---

* An engraving shows them set into the chapel's chancel S wall.

to have originated there or from a single scheme. Some are arranged into an arch, with beakhead decoration, the imposts and jambs composed of about a dozen small panels with figures and bits of foliage. The figures are very lively and a little comical. In addition, seven other fragments including one panel of the Crucifixion, with foliage beneath, and another of the Deposition. – STAINED GLASS. E window with *Wailes*'s monogram, dated 1852; S aisle second from E by the same firm. Five windows by *Ward & Hughes*, 1861–73: W window; S aisle E, first from E, and W; and chancel S. Clerestorey, a complete set of 1864 by *H. M. Barnett*.

The BOROUGH BRIDGE over the Ure is of three arches but its roadway is mostly of 1949 when it was widened; its downstream side (with triangular cutwaters) is possibly of 1562 but the upstream part with rounded ashlar piers appears to be of 1784, reputedly by *John Carr*. Into the C18 Boroughbridge was a major river port and coaching halt; its Georgian townscape is its most rewarding aspect, even if few buildings are individually notable. S of the Bridge, on BRIDGE STREET, however, is a nicely scaled elevation (now solicitors' offices) in the manner of Shaw or Nesfield, with a painted plaster frieze and Ipswich windows. Also some good Georgian houses, e.g. No. 3 with bow windows. The three-storey former THREE GREYHOUNDS HOTEL, with its impressive setting facing down Fishergate, is only superficially Georgian; its details are mostly due to late C20 restoration. Two-plus-three-plus-two bays with a pedimented centre. The cobbled former Market Square at the N end of High Street was the setting for the medieval cross (now at Aldborough), allegedly erected to commemorate the Battle of Boroughbridge in 1322. In its place the War Memorial with poor white marble figure of Faith. On the square's N side are gates to BOROUGHBRIDGE HALL, apparently C17 but so altered by the removal of Dutch gables and superimposed pilasters that it is unrecognizable. (Inside, early C17 panelling and turned balusters.) At the higher S end of the short HIGH STREET is the more spacious ST JAMES'S SQUARE. In the centre, on the site of the medieval chapel (dem. 1851), is the remarkable MARKET WELL, erected in 1875 in memory of Andrew Lawson of Aldborough Manor. An open octagonal structure raised on steps, with Doric columns on pedestals, a triglyph frieze, little brick gables to each side and a pretty cupola. The pedestals and columns look Late Georgian reused, but from where? The pump is in the form of a pedestal with an urn (renewed?). Modest Georgian buildings around the edges of the square, but also THE BLACK BULL pub (SW corner) which has inside substantial remains of a (C16–C17?) timber frame.

ORNHAMS HALL. 2 m. S. Designed by *J. B. Papworth*, and built in 1835. A modest stuccoed house with two façades and fine views, set in an equally modest landscaped park. Entrance façade, W. Three bays with tripartite windows l. and r. of a rather clumsy porch. N façade with a two-storey canted bay.

THE DEVIL'S ARROWS, ¼ m. WSW off Roecliffe Lane. A Late ³
Neolithic or Early Bronze Age stone row, comprising three
large and striking monoliths aligned NNW–SSE. They are of
undressed millstone grit, originally from an outcrop at Plompton Rocks, 8 m. S, the vertical grooves on their faces being the
result of weathering. They project 18 ft (5.5 metres), 21 ft (6.5
metres), and 22 ft (7 metres) above the ground and are buried
to an average depth of 5 ft (1.5 metres). The distance covered
by the monoliths is 570 ft (206 metres), and 6 ft (2 metres)
NNW of the central one is the site of a fourth stone, which in
the C16 Leland recorded as still standing. It is thought to have
been broken up in the early C17. The stones are probably to
be considered as part of the complex of Neolithic and Early
Bronze Age ceremonial monuments which extend N for over
11 m. and include the henges at Thornborough, Cana, and
Hutton Moor (*see Buildings of England: Yorkshire, The North
Riding*).

BOSTON SPA   *4040*

ST MARY, High Street. 1872–84 by *Walter Parkinson*, replacing a
chapel of 1814 by *Samuel Taite*. Of the local Magnesian limestone. Large, with W tower. Lancets. The arcades have round
piers, undersized foliate capitals and high arches with deep
chamfers. Angel corbels. – STAINED GLASS. N aisle, three
windows by *Ward & Hughes*, 1882–5; three more by *Clayton &
Bell*.
METHODIST CHURCH, Spa Lane. *J. B. & W. Atkinson*, 1846–7.
Italianate. Well preserved inside with gallery, box pews and
pulpit with organ behind. Pretty STAINED GLASS.
BRIDGE, across the Wharfe to Thorp Arch. Elegant structure of
five segmental arches. Built 1768–70: *John Gott* was paid £10
for plans.
The spa was discovered in 1744 but Thorp Spa (as it was known
into the C19) did not develop until 1753, when *Joseph Taite*, a
mason of Bramham, built the inn in the HIGH STREET that
developed into the ROYAL HOTEL (No. 182, by Church Street,
now a shop). Growth of the spa accelerated in the late C18 and
the long street still shows many handsome limestone-built Late
Georgian buildings. They are terraced, semi-detached, and
detached, some have bay windows and columned porches, and
there is a great deal of stabling. Of special note two larger
houses on the S side with low wings: BOSTON HOUSE (Nos.
212–14), five bays and three storeys with Doric porch and, r.,
pedimented stables, and BOSTON HALL (No. 218), two storeys
with an open-pedimented Doric doorcase. On the N side, set
back, is ST KITTS, a villa with a pedimented and slightly projecting centre. The most ambitious development, however, is
THE TERRACE to the E, also set back in grounds. Built as an

hotel *c.* 1790 by Kelita Kitchen, papermaker of Thorp Arch (q.v.). Three storeys over a basement, nine bays, the projecting outer ones with (altered) tripartite windows. Set back to the l. the former stable and carriage house range. Directly below, by the Wharfe, is a former BATH HOUSE (now housing), erected by the Spa Bath Co. in 1833–4. Canted bay overlooking the river.

BRACEWELL

ST MICHAEL. Norman S doorway with scalloped capitals (the shafts below missing), and unchamfered Norman chancel arch on scalloped corbels. Short nave and slightly narrower chancel under one roof, but the chancel has been heightened. On the S side, two straight-headed Perp windows to the nave, the ghost of a lancet window to the chancel. Perp N aisle and chapel, also under the same roof, with straight-headed windows with uncusped arched lights. Reused three-light reticulated window of *c.* 1330–50 to the W end. Unbuttressed W tower of two stages, the upper at least probably post-medieval. E window and other S windows C19. Two-bay arcades to aisle and chapel, with octagonal piers and double-chamfered arches. On the E respond of the nave arcade a crude trefoil-headed image niche (cf. Broughton, Kirkby Malham). Nave roof with tie-beams, collars and cusped windbraces. – PULPIT. C17. – FONT. Plain bowl with C17 cover. – STAINED GLASS. Medieval heraldic fragments in the aisle and chapel windows. – E window, 1854 by *Baillie & Mayer.*

SW of the church the unevocative remnant of the so-called KING HENRY'S PARLOUR, a late medieval house which was supposedly a retreat of Henry VI, now doing service as a barn. Traces of two straight-headed windows, each of two ogee-headed lights, are discernible.

BRADFORD

See also Esholt, Thornton, Tong, Wyke.

INTRODUCTION

'My good Yorkshire friends, you have asked me down here . . . that I might talk to you about this Exchange you are going to build: but . . . most simply and sorrowfully I have to tell you . . . that I do *not* care about this Exchange of yours – because *you* don't; and because you know perfectly well I cannot make you. Look at the essential conditions of the case . . . You are going to spend £30,000, which to you, collectively, is nothing; . . . but you think you may as well have the right thing for your money. You know there are a great many odd styles of architecture about; you don't want to do anything ridiculous; you hear of me, among others, as a respectable architectural man-milliner; and you send for me, that I may tell you the leading fashion; and what is, in our shops, for the moment, the newest and sweetest thing in pinnacles. p. 155

Now, pardon me for telling you frankly, you cannot have good architecture merely by asking people's advice on occasion. All good architecture is the expression of national life and character; and it is produced by a prevalent and eager national taste, or desire for beauty.

. . . It is long since you built a great cathedral; . . . but your rail-road mounds, vaster than the walls of Babylon; . . . your chimneys, how much more mighty and costly than cathedral spires! . . . your warehouses; your exchanges! – all these are built to your great Goddess of "Getting-on"; and she has formed, and will continue to form, your architecture, as long as you worship her; and it is quite vain to ask me to tell you how to build to *her*; you know far better than I.

. . . But, look strictly into the nature of the power of your Goddess; and you will find she is the Goddess – not of everybody's getting on – but only of somebody's getting on. This is a vital, or rather deathful, distinction.

Your ideal of human life . . . is, I think, that it should be passed in a pleasant undulating world, with iron and coal everywhere underneath it. On each pleasant bank of this world is to be a beautiful mansion . . . In this mansion are to live the favoured votaries of the Goddess; the English gentleman, with his gracious wife, and his beautiful family . . . At the bottom of the bank, is to be the mill . . . In this mill are to be in constant employment from eight hundred to a thousand workers, who never drink, never strike, always go to church on Sunday, and always express themselves in respectful language. Is not that . . . the kind of thing you propose to yourselves? It is very pretty indeed, seen from above; not at all so pretty, seen from below.'

Ruskin's lecture 'Traffic', delivered in Bradford in 1864, when the town was at the peak of its prosperity as the worldwide capital of the worsted textile industry, touches on more than one aspect of its C19 history. Its position then was the product of astonishingly rapid growth over just the previous three-quarters of a century. Population for the area of the borough – incorporated in 1847 – had been 13,000 in 1801, 26,000 in 1821, 67,000 in 1841, and 104,000 in 1851. In 1881 it was 183,000; in 1901, for a larger area, 280,000 (the 2001 figure for a similar one was 271,000).* Bradford's origins as a town, however, go back to the Middle Ages: a market charter was granted in 1251, a woollen trade appears to have been in existence by 1277, and the parish church, now the cathedral, is testimony to some later medieval prosperity. But in 1472 it ranked only eighth in importance in Yorkshire for its cloth trade, behind Halifax, Ripon, Leeds, Almondbury, Hull, Barnsley and Wakefield; and in the mid C18 it was still only a minor market town. A Piece Hall for the sale of cloth was built in 1773, but the reasons for the town's sudden success thereafter are not straightforward. Situated away from the main rivers, it always suffered from an inadequate water supply; and nor was it specially quick off the mark with the initial stages of mechanization: the first worsted spinning mill in the town – steam-powered from the outset – was not opened until 1800. Significant factors, doubtless, were first the opening of the Bradford Canal, a tributary of the Leeds and Liverpool, in 1774; and later, by the time of Ruskin's visit, its development as a mercantile as well as an industrial centre, with an export trade much of which was conducted by immigrant merchants from Germany. But, as at Leeds, other industries were also established alongside textiles,

---

*The borough of 1847 included the townships of Manningham, Horton and Bowling as well as Bradford itself. Bolton followed in 1873, Allerton, Heaton and Thornbury in 1882, Bierley, Eccleshill, Idle, Thornton and Tong in 1899. The area covered in this entry is that of the city prior to local government reorganization in 1974 – before which its boundaries had been unchanged for forty years – minus the four 'outermost' settlements, which have separate entries.

notably the ironworks at Bowling and Low Moor, founded in 1788 and 1789 respectively and originally exploiting ore deposits to the s of the town – their products ranging from railway lines, locomotive components and heavy armaments, to railings, gates and bedsteads.

The town – city since 1897 – occupies a hollow surrounded by tableland, its nucleus at the point where the Bradford Beck changed direction and was joined by tributary streams. To Pevsner – echoing a sentiment expressed in *The Builder* over fifty years earlier in 1898 – the most striking feature of the Victorian centre was 'the total absence of a plan', but that was not the whole story. The ancient streets formed an inverted Y, the serpentine line of Kirkgate and Church Bank running e towards Leeds, Ivegate and Bridge Street running se towards Wakefield and Westgate nw towards Keighley. At the junction, on sloping ground n of the beck, was the Old Market Place, and e of that on Kirkgate the manor house, Bradford Hall, built in 1705–7. The 'New' Street, later Market Street, running alongside the beck between Kirkgate and Bridge Street, was laid out c. 1783; and within the triangle of streets thus formed, which in due course became the centre's innermost hub, a New Market Place was established c. 1800. Surrounding this area there developed zones of the characteristic display warehouses – the public face of the textile industry – the wool warehouses mainly to the w, those for yarn and finished goods mainly to the e, close to the town's two railway termini (The Midland Railway, approaching via Shipley (n), arrived in 1846, the Lancashire & Yorkshire, approaching from the s, in 1850). The textile mills themselves were generally located further out again, with a major concentration along the Thornton Road to the w, following the line of the Bradford Beck and its attendant goit. The best suburbs were an area to the sw, towards Little Horton, then Manningham and Heaton, to the nw.

A watershed in the town's c19 development can, however, be detected c. 1850. Undertakings of the first half of the century included a small number of public buildings in simple classical style and several important new streets and roads, including the new turnpike to Leeds, s of the old one, opened in 1824, and its w counterpart, Thornton Road, opened in 1826. But very little of the town of this period survives, and the larger picture is indeed of an uncontrolled free-for-all, in which the pressures of factory-system industrialization and rapid population increase made the town a byword of urban squalor, appallingly polluted and overcrowded. In the second half, following incorporation of the borough and then the onset of the golden years of the 1860s and early 1870s, living conditions generally improved and a town more worthy of its economic standing was created. Better housing was built as the urban area expanded rapidly; and the centre was largely reconstructed, with a series of new civic amenities. The latter process was conditioned by the activities of the council's Street Improvement Committee – widening existing

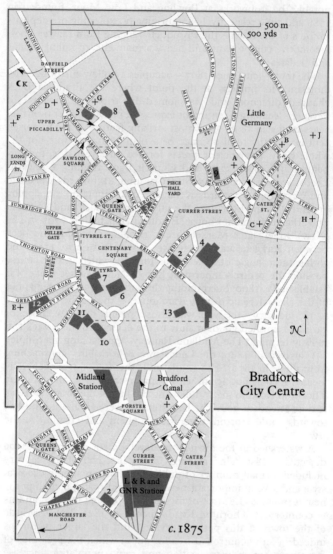

Bradford
City Centre

c. 1875

A Cathedral
B College Congregational Chapel (former)
C Eastbrook Methodist Hall (former)
D Friends' Meeting House (former)
E German Evangelical Church
F St Andrew's Presbyterian Chapel (former)
G Salem Congregational Chapel (former)
H Sion Baptist Chapel,
   now Amrit Sikh Temple
J St Mary (R.C) (see Barkerend, Laisterdyke
   and Thornbury)
K Central Mosque (see Manningham)

1   Town Hall
2   St George's Hall
3   Wool Exchange
4   Law Courts
5   County Court (former)
6   Magistrates Court
7   Central Police Station
8   Register Office
9   General Post Office
10 Central Library
11 National Media Museum
12 Central Baths
13 Metro Travel Interchange

streets and laying out new ones, and controlling the standard of development – so an element of planning, of a pragmatically piecemeal kind, was present. The result was rarely less than harmonious and dignified, the buildings predominantly although not exclusively Italianate in style, in the fine local sandstone ashlar.

As to individual examples, the key starting points were St George's Hall, 1851–3, and nearby the first of a new generation of warehouses – 'rivalling in size and splendour the famed palaces of Venice' in the eyes of the Bradford historian John James (1866) – which together established a new standard of monumentality. Then came the Wool Exchange in the 1860s – followed by much rebuilding in the inner core – and the Town Hall and the Markets complex in the 1870s. But a further aspect of the story is that all of these public buildings were the work of a single local architectural practice, that of *Lockwood & Mawson*, who achieved an extraordinary virtual monopoly of the town's major civic projects, largely through competitions held without professional assessors. In the Anglican ecclesiastical field a similar position was held, less controversially, by another Bradford firm, *T. H. & F. Healey* (previously *Mallinson & Healey*).* Another notable group of public buildings was the Board Schools – designed by a wider range of local architects: the author of the 1870 Education Act, W. E. Forster, was a Bradford M.P., and the town's School Board was a progressive body which quickly gained a reputation for the lavishness of its provision.

In the second half of the C20 the city suffered the dual misfortune first of a comprehensive city centre redevelopment scheme and then of massive economic decline, the latter affecting not only textiles – with the inevitable loss of many of the mills – but also more recently established industries. The redevelopment plan had its origins in the interwar period when a policy of replacing warehouses by shops and offices first took shape, was devised 1947–53 by the City Engineer *S. G. Wardley*, and implemented in part from 1959 onwards, across a swathe of the E and S parts of the centre from Forster Square to Little Horton Lane. The losses were severe, the wide new roads and draughty open spaces woefully at odds with the Victorian city's close-knit texture, and the replacement buildings mostly of mind-numbing banality. In 2003 the city council tried again, commissioning a new city centre regeneration masterplan from *Alsop Architects*. The proposals embrace *inter alia* the current orthodoxy of increased residential provision, but a 'big idea' of creating yet more open spaces and a bizarre description of the city centre as 'dispersed' suggest that not all the lessons from past mistakes have been learnt. Retention of the surviving monuments erected to Ruskin's 'Goddess of Getting-on' is now of course received wisdom; but whether the Goddess herself can be enticed back to the city, and with what results on the ground, remains to be seen.

---

*Many of the churches were built by a body called the Bradford Church Building Society, founded in 1859.

CITY CENTRE

PLACES OF WORSHIP

CATHEDRAL (ST PETER), Church Bank. The old parish church
of Bradford, raised to cathedral rank in 1919. Impressively
situated on rising ground E of the commercial core. The pre-
cathedral church is strongly Pennine in character, of coursed
gritstone and mainly Perp outside with earlier work within; but
extensive enlargements, of 1951–65 by *Sir Edward Maufe*, have
been not at all to its benefit architecturally. The sturdy W tower
now appears squeezed between two lumpish wings, and the
chancel and all but the outer walls of the N and S chancel
chapels were pulled down to make way for the new E arm.

The medieval nave is long and low. Aisles and clerestory with
four-centre-headed windows, parapets on the S side only until
the C19. The tower was added, it is said, in 1493–1508. Six-
light W window, paired two-light belfry openings, angle buttresses, panelled and battlemented parapet and eight
pinnacles. S chapel rebuilt 1615, the windows with a crude
Jacobean version of Perp tracery. S aisle and clerestory refaced,
and S porch rebuilt, 1832–3 by *John Clark* (in a manner 'worthy
of a railway viaduct engineer' according to Ruskin); restoration
1860–2 by *Mallinson & Healey*; aisle-height transepts, taller
vestry block N of the N chapel, and further restoration, 1898
by *T. H. & F. Healey*. The additions by *Maufe* are in a smooth
sandstone ashlar. The W wings are the Song Room (N), 1951–4,
and the cathedral offices (S), 1956–9. The E arm followed in
1958–63: choir and sanctuary with ambulatory, axial Lady
Chapel, N chapel with chapter house over. Minimalist Gothic,
with lantern tower over the choir and three-sided E apse.

Bradford, St Peter (now Cathedral) in the early C19.
Engraving by W. O. Gelder, 1828

On the s side also a bellcote in a sort of Italianate vernacular style. Sculpture by *Alan Collins*. SE porch 1963–5.

Inside, the nave arcades are of the C14, after a fire of 1327. Eight bays, with piers of deeply undulating section with four shafts connected by hollows. Moulded capitals of two different designs, and arches with the typical moulding of two sunk quadrants. The same arch details in the w bay, which was added when the tower was built. Triple-chamfered tower arch. Fine Perp nave roof (thatched until 1724), with moulded tie-beams, and kingposts and tracery above. Angel corbels, brackets above them and carved bosses all of 1860–2, as also is the chancel arch. In the N wall of the former N chapel the lower stages of a rood stair, and then round a corner to the l. a re-set C14 piscina. *Maufe*'s E parts have pointed arches without capitals. Further reordering 1987, including removal of his ungainly w organ case, under the tower, and blocking of the w ends of the aisles.

FONT COVER. A spectacular Late Gothic piece, tall with a crocketed spire above a filigree of buttresses and tracery (cf. Halifax, West Riding South). – BISHOP'S THRONE. 1935 by *Sir Charles Nicholson*. – SCULPTURE. Small square Anglo-Saxon piece with irregular interlace, probably from a C10 cross. Built into the wall beside the piscina. – Carved ROYAL ARMS of Queen Anne. – STAINED GLASS. The pre-Maufe chancel had two windows of outstandingly fine early glass by the *Morris* firm, the E window of 1863 and the s of 1864. The main designers, in addition to Morris himself, were *Ford Madox Brown*, *Burne-Jones*, *Peter Paul Marshall*, *D. G. Rossetti* and *Philip Webb*. Clearly and vigorously designed figures. The E window had seven lights, with Christ in Majesty (*Rossetti*), St Peter (*Marshall*) and the Agnus Dei (*Webb*) in the centre and Prophets, Evangelists and Patriarchs to each side. s window with a Pelican (*Webb*) and the Salvator Mundi (an isolated commission from *Albert Moore*) in the centre and Saints in the sidelights. The E window glass tactfully re-set 1964 as the three windows of the E apse. But five surplus angels (by *Morris*) were given to the Whitworth Art Gallery, Manchester. The figures from the s window re-set less satisfactorily 1990 in the w windows of the transepts and, artificially lit, in the N ambulatory. – w window by *Heaton, Butler & Bayne*, 1864. s transept sw and s centre by *Kempe*, 1898 and 1900, and SE by *Kempe & Co.*, 1924. s aisle third and fourth from w, and N transept NW and NE, by *Shrigley & Hunt*, 1898 and 1912. SE porch (formerly s chapel E) and s chapel s (i.e. s ambulatory) by *A. K. Nicholson*, 1911 and 1912. Pleasant sub-Morris manner.

MONUMENTS. A good series of wall tablets, the most notable as follows. John Smyth †1686, cartouche-like, with putti and skull. – Faith Sharp †1710, Baroque aedicule flanked by volutes, and John Midgley †1730, similar. – Isaac Hollings †1734, in high relief with volutes, broken pediment and urn. – William Swain †1737, enriched Palladian with a baseless pediment, and Mary Field †1750, the same. – Abraham Sharp

†1742 by *Scheemakers*. With a trophy of mathematical instruments at the base. – Faith Sawrey †1767 by *J. F. Moore*. High-relief sarcophagus with two putti on it, the whole in an aedicule. – Abraham Balme †1796, by *Flaxman* (executed *c*. 1810). With a delightful relief of a bearded teacher reading to a boy and a girl. – Nancy Stead †1806. Of marbled wood with fluted pilasters. – Mary Lister †1809 by *W. & R. Fisher* of York, and Samuel and Mary Hartley †1833 by *Joseph Gott*. Both with a kneeling female figure above the inscription. – Joseph Priestley †1817 by *William Pistell*. With a relief at the foot showing the construction of the Leeds and Liverpool Canal, of which Priestley was superintendent for nearly fifty years. – John Rand †1873 by *Matthew Noble*. Bas-relief profile bust in trefoil-headed niche. – Also a number of the common type with the inscription surmounted by a bas-relief urn, including Samuel Lister †1792 by *Stead* of York, William Northrop †1800 by *Bacon*, and Francis Rawson †1801 by *Taylor* of York. – Of the monument to William Sharp †1833 by *Gott* only a fragment remains, the inscription and a bas-relief portrait. Sharp was a well-known surgeon at St Bartholomew's Hospital, London, and the monument was erected by public subscription. It consisted of a free-standing figure of a Grecian maiden, her breasts bare, leaning over a pedestal which bore the portrait. But the maiden was removed as 'unsuitable', *c*. 1970.

For ENVIRONS *see* Public Buildings, former Post Office, and Perambulation 3, below.

COLLEGE CONGREGATIONAL CHAPEL (former). *See* Perambulation 3, below.

EASTBROOK METHODIST HALL, Leeds Road. 1902–4 by *W. J. Morley & Son* of Bradford, on the site of the Eastbrook Chapel, 1825 by *Joseph Botham*. Conversion to flats begun in 2006, after a long period of disuse. Always a very worldly looking building, both inside and out. Four-storey front in Anglo-French Renaissance style, with shops on the ground floor and offices above. A little copper dome over the entrance bay. The interior was redolent more of a theatre or a music hall than a chapel, a slightly elongated octagon with thin iron columns supporting half-elliptical arches and a dished ceiling, and a gallery front decorated with swags and cartouches.

FRIENDS' MEETING HOUSE (former). *See* Perambulation 1, below.

GERMAN EVANGELICAL CHURCH, Great Horton Road. A testimony to the importance of the German community in later C19 Bradford. The church was built as a Sunday School, *c*. 1860, and was acquired by the congregation in 1882. Low and modest in lancet style, but the slate-covered flèche on a canted projection turning the street corner was evidently added by the Germans. – STAINED GLASS. Three windows by *Powell Bros.* of Leeds.

ST ANDREW'S PRESBYTERIAN CHAPEL (former) and SALEM CONGREGATIONAL CHAPEL (former). *See* Perambulation 1, below.

SION BAPTIST CHAPEL, Shipley Airedale Road, now AMRIT SIKH TEMPLE. 1871–3 by *Lockwood & Mawson* in their best Nonconformist Italianate mode. Engaged three-bay Corinthian temple front, and matching outer and return bays framed by Corinthian antae. Two tiers of openings, the upper with oddly unemphatic pediments.

PUBLIC BUILDINGS

TOWN HALL, Centenary Square. 1870–3 by *Lockwood & Mawson*, their third competition success in a row for the town's major public buildings, a result which attracted sarcastic comment in the architectural press. Extension 1905–9 by *Norman Shaw* (*see* Wool Exchange, below) as consultant and the City Architect *F. E. P. Edwards*. A town hall of the municipal-administrative kind: the council had previously met in the old Fire Station House (dem.), and designs for purpose-built accommodation had been prepared by Lockwood & Mawson as early as 1851. p. 60 97

Their executed building occupies a shallow irregular site and its qualities are not best served by the open spaces which have been created round it. Richly textured but unvarying C13 Gothic style in sandstone ashlar (the architects also submitted an alternative classical version), with a number of features borrowed in particular from Burges's design for the London Law Courts. Long symmetrical façade with tall slim central tower (220 ft. (67 metres)) modelled on a Tuscan campanile. Picturesque polygonal corner towards Broadway. Two-light first-floor windows under arches with plate tracery, continuous arcade above punctuated by statues of kings and queens – and Oliver Cromwell – by *Farmer & Brindley*. The extension, which doubled the size of the building, is a truncated triangle in plan. Edwards, it seems, was responsible for the planning and Shaw for the elevations, in a clever mixture of styles. The main part of the front has quasi-Romanesque granite arches to the ground floor, a continuation of Lockwood & Mawson's arched fenestration to the first, tall Queen Anne windows with Gallic bow-fronted balconies to the second, and at the top two-storey dormers with Late French Gothic gables. But for the truncated corner he reverted to the heroic Old English style of Adcote, with a pair of many-transomed bay windows lighting the dining hall, and a big plain gable.

Inside, the respective contributions of Shaw and Edwards are less clear. The DINING HALL is thoroughly Shavian in manner, with a huge arched inglenook and a sculpted over-mantel representing Progress, executed by *H. M. Miller* of *Earp, Hobbs & Miller* of Manchester. The top-lit COUNCIL CHAMBER however is classical, cruciform under an intersecting barrel ceiling, but with Arts and Crafts plasterwork by *Ernest Gimson*. The main surviving interior of the Lockwood & Mawson phase is the COURTROOM, rigorously Gothic with blind arcading round the walls. The original council chamber, centrally placed behind the tower, was replaced by the present main staircase, giving direct access to the rooms in the extension. This was intended as part of the Shaw/Edwards scheme but not realized until 1913–14 to a new design by the then City Architect *W. Williamson*.

St George's Hall, Bridge Street. 1851–3 by *Lockwood & Mawson*, the first of their competition successes. Sir Titus Salt (*see* Saltaire) was one of the leading promoters of the project. A relative of Elmes's St George's Hall at Liverpool (1841–54) and more particularly of Hansom & Welch's Birmingham Town Hall (begun 1832), both in its function – a public hall for cultural events – and in its architecture, with the same Corinthian temple form but much more loosely applied, the detail turned Victorian Italianate instead of Neoclassical. Pediment at one end only, the giant columns attached instead of properly peripteral, and the rusticated podium grown disproportionately tall and elaborate, accommodating a mezzanine with big swagged consoles framing the windows. Terrace running along the Bridge Street elevation at mezzanine level, sensitively matching the original scheme, 1985 by the *City Architect's Department* (project architect *P. Mawson*). Relatively restrained interior, with flat ceiling above a shallow cove, two galleries on fluted cast-iron columns, and an apsidal end containing the organ, with case of 1856.

Wool Exchange, Market Street. The central symbol of C19 commercial Bradford, 1864–7 by *Lockwood & Mawson*. The most obviously ill-conducted of the competitions won by them: the defeated entrants included William Burges and Norman Shaw, both as exponents of the Advanced Gothic favoured by the promoters of Ruskin's intervention* (*see* Introduction). Triangular island site, previously occupied by an early C19 market house. The actual style is 'Venetian Gothic . . . freely treated', although a more immediate source was evidently G. G. Scott's unexecuted design for Halifax Town Hall (1856). Pointed arches, some with Geometrical tracery, to the ground floor, paired arched windows to the first and slightly smaller tripled ones to the second, all marked by polychrome voussoirs. Openwork arcaded cresting – the most 'Venetian' feature of the design – and big corbelled-out corner pinnacles. At the N end a tower, with the same big pinnacles, and a short fanciful spire. The ground floor forms an open porch, which originally extended into the adjoining part of the main block. On the tower, statues of Bishop Blaize, patron saint of woolcombers, and a medieval king, probably Edward III, by *James Tolmie*. In the arcade spandrels portrait medallions of thirteen notables. Towards Market Street: Cobden, Sir Titus Salt (*see* Saltaire), Stephenson, Watt, Arkwright, J. M. Jacquard (inventor

* Principally the banker Alfred Harris and the textile manufacturer John Aldam Heaton (*see* Bingley). Ruskin eventually recommended Waterhouse's Assize Courts in Manchester as a model.

Bradford, Wool Exchange.
Engraving, 1864

of the Jacquard loom), Gladstone, Palmerston. Towards Bank
Street: Raleigh, Drake, Columbus, Captain Cook, Anson. Part
of the rear (Hustlergate) elevation rebuilt as a glass curtain, as
part of a rehabilitation for retail use, 1995–6 by *Dempster Thrussell & Rae*. The main interior space is a well-lit central hall,
with tall columns of polished pink granite supporting a continuous lintel above which the 'heads' of the arcade form
clerestory windows with thin iron tracery. Steeply pitched
hammerbeam roof with dormers and iron details, big rose

windows in the end gables. At the N end a STATUE of Cobden, 1876 by *Timothy Butler*. Outer aisle on the Market Street side, the arcade with naturalistic foliage. Offices in the rest of the perimeter.

LAW COURTS, Drake Street. 1989–92 by *Napper, Collerton & Partners*. On the elevated site of the Lancashire & Yorkshire Railway Company's Exchange Station (1881–8). A large square block of smooth sandstone ashlar with a pitched slate roof, the upper stage projecting on cylindrical columns. Expensive-looking and facetiously detailed. The inside calmer and more rational, round an octagonal central courtyard with glazed walls. Eight identical courtrooms.

COUNTY COURT (former), Manor Row. 1859 by *Charles Reeves*, the County Court Surveyor. Set back from the street. Palazzo-style, quite modest, with two tiers of round-headed windows. To the r. the former CUSTOMS and EXCISE OFFICE, 1899, a slightly stiff ashlar-built version of Queen Anne.

MAGISTRATES' COURT, The Tyrls. 1969–72 by the *City Architect's Department*. A squat square on a podium next to the Town Hall, covering the site of the Chapel Lane Unitarian Chapel, 1867–8 by *Andrews & Pepper*. Also on the podium the CENTRAL POLICE STATION, 1972–4 by the same Department, obtrusively blocking the view towards the Town Hall from Morley Street.

REGISTER OFFICE, Manor Row. 1877 by *Andrews & Pepper*, built as the Poor Law Offices. Refined Italianate façade of three bays and three storeys, with pedimented two-storey frontispiece.

Former GENERAL POST OFFICE, Forster Square, in front of the cathedral tower. 1886–7 by *Sir Henry Tanner*. Now ST PETER'S HOUSE, part used as Council Offices. Mildly French classical, two storeys with a pair of taller pavilions, hipped and mansard roofs. At the back an extension at first-floor level facing the cathedral, bridging onto the high retaining wall of the church-yard – the outcome of a short-lived scheme to use the rest of the building as a museum – 1999–2000 by *Philip Lees & Associates*. Admirable in theory, with the entrance persuasively aligned on the cathedral W door, but in realization rather incongruous and cliché-ridden, in lightweight glass and steel with a trio of pointless butterfly roofs.

CENTRAL LIBRARY, Prince's Way. 1964–7 by the *City Architect's Department*. Heavy nine-storey block, Portland stone faced. Beside it the NATIONAL MEDIA MUSEUM, built as a theatre 1963–5 by *R. Seifert & Partners* in association with the City Architect. Converted to its present use in 1983, extension and new curved glass façade 1998–9 by *Austin-Smith: Lord*. At the back a grim high-rise office slab over a skating rink, part of the same 1960s development. In front a STATUE of J. B. Priestley, 1986 by *Ian Judd*. Bronze.

CENTRAL BATHS, Morley Street and Great Horton Road. 1903–5 by *A. Hessell Tiltman* but with modifications to the design by the City Architect *F. E. P. Edwards*. English Renaissance with Art Nouveau touches. The Morley Street elevation quite low, asymmetrical, stepping down the hill: two curly gables, but alternating with them ranges of shop units in a more emphatically Art Nouveau manner which are evidently Edwards's contribution, with rippling parapet copings and a pyramid-roofed bay with mushroom finial at the lower end. Further back an excellent chimneystack with attenuated classical detail to the crown. On the Great Horton Road side a big gabled feature but the rest heightened later. Iron roof trusses and arcading round the pool inside: in winter it could be converted into a public hall. Adjoining at the s end is the QUEEN'S HALL, 1914 by *W. Williamson* (City Architect). More conventionally Neo-Georgian. The auditorium originally intercommunicated with the baths through its proscenium arch.

METRO TRAVEL INTERCHANGE, Bridge Street. In reality just a bus station with markedly meagre provision for trains tacked on as an appendage. Passenger concourse *c.* 2001 by *Abbey Holford Rowe* – a rectangular shed with part-glazed roof – replacing a much larger and more distinguished scheme of 1973–7 by the *British Rail Architect's Department*, the extra space given over to commercial office blocks of repulsive blandness.

PERAMBULATIONS

1. Markets area

The heart of what remains intact of the city's Victorian commercial centre, an area of high townscape quality, is NEW MARKET PLACE, now a small pedestrianized space confined to the intersection of Bank Street, Hustlergate and Tyrrel Street, by the w corner of the Wool Exchange (*see* Public Buildings, above), but originally larger. To the w, on the NW side of TYRREL STREET with a narrow corner facing towards the intersection, THORPE BUILDINGS, former department store, 1871 by *Hope & Jardine* and at once eminently characteristic of the city, four storeys in unshowy and human-scale Italianate with intermittent superimposed orders. Behind is an intimate cul de sac formed by the w end of Hustlergate; and in QUEENSGATE, stepping up the hill, EXCHANGE CHAMBERS, *c.* 1850 but with the character of the earlier C19, quite plain with narrow round-headed windows. In front of that, again with a short end towards the Market Place, and its front running up Bank Street (*see* below), is BANK HOUSE, built as the Liberal Club 1876–7 by *Lockwood & Mawson*, a more festive but still restrained Italianate; and on the other corner, of Bank Street and HUSTLERGATE, the NATWEST BANK, built as the Bradford Commercial Bank 1867–8 by *Andrews & Pepper*, Gothic for once like the Wool Exchange opposite, with the spikiest angle tower and equally spiky gabled dormers but otherwise quite reasonably C13. Painted decoration to the coved ceiling of the banking hall.

The view from here E along Hustlergate is closed by a second NatWest Bank, formerly the Bradford District Bank, on another prominent corner at the NE end of Market Street: 1873 by *Milnes & France*, commercial Baroque in fine local ashlar with a giant order above the ground floor and a domed corner turret. But before that is reached, first No. 33 Hustlergate, 1880 also by *Milnes & France*, modest pilastered Italianate with beside it a delightful glimpse l. up PIECE HALL YARD – the Piece Hall, demolished in 1873, ran along the l. side – to the front of the former Public Rooms in Kirkgate (*see* below). Then in a violent change of scale LLOYDS BANK, 1920 by *James Young*, a tremendous Art Deco classical pile with polished granite ground floor and two tiers of giant pilasters above. Spacious banking hall with glazed central lantern, tactful alterations 1993. Finally PARKINSON'S BUILDINGS, 1877–8 by *Knowles & Wilcock*, another neat Italianate design with a little dormer feature over the centre. Back SW along MARKET STREET – effecting a circumnavigation of the Wool Exchange – of much patchier quality, the principal loss the Swan Arcade, 1877–81 by *Milnes & France*, replaced by the high-rise ARNDALE HOUSE, 1965 by *John Graham & Partners*. On the l. two more bank buildings, the HSBC (former Midland), 1926 by *T. B. Whinney*, an echo of the same formula; and No. 69, built as the Anglo-South American Bank, 1925 by *W. J. Morley & Son*, the conventional interwar City of London type, with giant columns high up. On the r. after the Wool Exchange the former BROWN & MUFF'S store, 1870 by *Knowles & Wilcock*, the back towards New Market Place C20. Now steeply up BANK STREET, with Bank House on the l. On the r., next to the Gothic bank, No. 28, *c.* 1865 apparently by *Andrews & Pepper*, an odd mixture of Gothic details to the ground floor and Quattrocento above; and then at the top corner the former TALBOT HOTEL, 1877–8 again by *Andrews & Pepper*, an extra-ordinary design with an Egyptian flavour among the classical, with incised ornament to the second floor, strange tapered pilasters and prominent block-like pediments to the third.

The street at right angles here is KIRKGATE, its W part wrecked by the KIRKGATE CENTRE, 1975 by *John Brunton & Partners*, brutally out of scale in dingily Brutalist pre-cast concrete, which replaced *Lockwood & Mawson*'s Kirkgate Market of 1871–8, an early example of the type with an iron and glass market hall and perimeter ranges containing shops. Ahead is Darley Street, laid out 1813–15, now the city's main shopping street (*see* below). On the N corner of the crossroads the former BRADFORD BANK (now Bradford & Bingley), the first of the prestige bank buildings in the town, 1858 by *Andrews & Delaunay*. Sumptuous palazzo style, rusticated with vermiculation below, engaged Corinthian columns above. Later extended by two bays along Darley Street and the first-floor windows altered, with flanking lights added and attic windows cut through the pediments. Good interior with Corinthian columns supporting an elaborate compartmented ceiling.

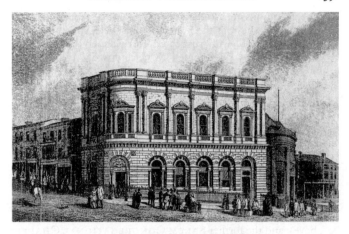

Bradford, Bradford Bank (former).
Engraving by J.H. Le Keux, *c.* 1865

Next to it in Kirkgate the former PUBLIC ROOMS (later called
the EXCHANGE BUILDINGS), originally 1826–8 by *Francis
Goodwin* in simple Grecian style but remodelled in the later
C19, when its two storeys were recast as three, and further
altered since. On the present façade the upper stages are
treated as a sort of applied temple front, with flat pilasters and
the cornice broken, late Roman-fashion, over the centre bay,
but Goodwin's design was quite different, a pilastered segmental bow. On the flank all that remains of his design is the
bay rhythm and the entrance portal with Greek Doric columns
in antis. The building contained a meeting room, a newsroom
and a subscription library. On the other side of the street, with
its entrance in Piece Hall Yard, the BRADFORD CLUB, 1877 by
Lockwood & Mawson in an effective simplified Gothic, vertically accented; and at the E end on the l. the former
BECKETT'S BANK, 1885 by *Milnes & France* in the same
manner as their Bradford District Bank, with fine wrought-iron
entrance gate. Opposite this, in CHEAPSIDE, the MIDLAND
HOTEL, 1885 by the Midland Railway Company's architect
Charles Trubshaw, bulkily asymmetrical in French Renaissance
style with domed octagonal turret and mansard roofs. Attached
to the r. the (reconstructed) SCREEN to the forecourt of their
Forster Square Station (dem.), rebuilt by Trubshaw 1884–90.
The present station is ⅛ m. further N.

Now back to the Public Rooms and up PICCADILLY, laid
out *c.* 1830 and built up 1830–4 with a series of WOOL WARE-
HOUSES by *James Richardby*, which together with the ROOMS
are now the main survivals from the early C19 in the city centre.
The street has been much altered but they still make quite a
noble show, in a plain Neoclassical style. On the r. Nos. 14–16
have added Art Nouveau ironwork to the recessed entrance,

Nos. 18–24 pilasters to the upper stage and a stepped parapet;
and then the best, at the junction with Duke Street, are Nos.
17–19, on the l., with rusticated entry under a pedimented
centre, and Nos. 36–8, dated 1833, confusedly asymmetrical
but with powerfully cyclopean detail. To the NE Duke Street
leads out into MANOR ROW, the continuation NW of Cheapside. First more warehouses but of the late C19 phase: much
bigger, with restrained Italianate details progressively sparser
as one goes up, and corner entrances. On the l. WILLEY'S
WAREHOUSE, c. 1884–5 by *Waugh & Isitt*, on the r. MANOR
BUILDINGS, 1892 by *Fairbank & Wall*, and Nos. 8–20, 1883
by *Rhodes Calvert*. Then a public and quasi-public phase. On
the l. YORK HOUSE, built as a club, 1866 by *Lockwood &
Mawson*, minimal Venetian Gothic, and the former County
Court and Customs and Excise Office (*see* Public Buildings,
above). On the r. the Register Office (*see* Public Buildings,
above), and the former SALEM CONGREGATIONAL CHAPEL,
1834–6, succeeded in 1888 by the Salem Chapel in Oak Lane,
Manningham (dem.) and since then used as offices. Quirky
simplified Neoclassical. Pediment with big plain antefixae, battered angle pilaster-strips. Single-storey Ionic portal added
1888 by *C. H. Hargreaves*. The rear also pedimented, with a full-
height segmental bow. After that – and SALEM STREET, with
a modest but complete domestic terrace of the 1850s – is a neat
two-storey commercial building of c. 1840, with banded rustication and pilasters; and opposite these a fragment of early C19
residential development, two detached villas and a pair of
semis.

Finally in this direction, the former YORKSHIRE PENNY
BANK, finest of the Bradford banks, 1895–8 by *James Ledingham*. On a prominent pointed corner site at the junction with
North Parade, facing away along Manningham Lane – the
sequence now bathetically disrupted by the inner ring road –
and marking the start of the city centre from the NW. Gor-
geously exuberant Free Renaissance. Segmental frontispiece
with three-bay loggia to the ground floor and another to the
second, spiral fluted colonnettes as mullions to the first-floor
windows and little corbelled-out polygonal turrets to each side.
Pedimented dormers and a crazy timber cupola with sloping
sides. Iron entrance gates drop into the pavement. Interior
retains plasterwork, marble dado, mahogany woodwork. From
here, first round the corner to the w, in FOUNTAIN STREET,
is the façade only of the former FRIENDS' MEETING HOUSE,
1876–7 by *Lockwood & Mawson*. 'Chaste, ample and substantial' (*Bradford Observer*). Originally there was a pediment over
its whole width. Then back along NORTH PARADE, with a picturesque *fin-de-siècle* sequence of commercial properties continuing on from the Yorkshire Penny Bank. Nos. 36–38, 1897
also by *Ledingham*, idiosyncratic Free Renaissance, each unit
gabled above a shallow two-storey segmental bow; DEVON-
SHIRE HOUSE, 1898, charming Art Nouveau fantasy on C15
chateau style, asymmetrical with serpentine balcony in front of

the gable window; Nos. 20–24, *c.* 1913, with occasional Art Nouveau details; and Nos. 14–18, 1897 by *Walker & Collinson*, similar to Nos. 36–38, with three pediment-capped gables and the first and second floors treated as a giant glazed arcade. Then by contrast CHURCH HOUSE, built as the Church Institute, 1871–3 by *Andrews & Pepper*, a tall emphatic five-bay façade in C13 French Gothic, with big plate-traceried windows to the main floor and gabled dormer above; and on the corner with Upper Piccadilly the former INSTITUTE FOR THE BLIND, 1867–8, grimly utilitarian Jacobean by *Knowles & Wilcock*.

At this point RAWSON SQUARE is reached, a small and rather tatty space partly on the site of Bradford's first C19 church, Christ Church, 1813–15 by *Thomas Taylor* (dem. 1879 for road widening), and almost all the best of this itinerary has been seen. The STATUE of Richard Oastler, 1867 by *John Birnie Philip*, which previously stood here has been moved to NORTHGATE, a few yards to the NW. Instigator of the Ten Hours Act, limiting the working hours of children in the mills, he is shown with a boy and a girl. At the W corner of the square the former MASONIC HALL, starved Gothic of 1876; and the former RAWSON HOTEL, 1899–1905 by *Hope & Jardine*, the surviving part of an extension to Rawson Market (*see* below), meagre mongrel Renaissance with a little dome.* To the E the former ROYAL HOTEL, 1887 by *Ledingham*, Flemish-cum-Jacobean with shaped gables. This stands at the top of DARLEY STREET, the upper part of which at least is reasonably intact. On the l. No. 48 is another Art Nouveau design; Nos. 34–36 built as the Bradford Dispensary, 1826–7 by *Peter Atkinson Jun.*, plainest Late Georgian and much altered, top storey added 1905. Opposite, Nos. 43–45, 1875 by *T. H. & F. Healey*, heavy Italianate. Then r. into GODWIN STREET, blighted by the Kirkgate Centre but on the r. the façade only of RAWSON MARKET, originally the provisions counterpart of Kirkgate Market, the first part 1871–5 by *Lockwood & Mawson*, the extension beyond *Hope & Jardine*'s of 1899–1905, all coarsely Franco-Italianate with banded pilasters. The rebuilding behind partly 1931, partly 2004. At the bend of the street r. again into WESTGATE, where there is now not much to see. At the corner, Nos. 29–31, 1871–2 by *Andrews & Pepper*, built as a department store, mixed Renaissance with the usual iron-crested pavilion roofs; then on the r. Nos. 50–54, louche Art Nouveau Jacobean of *c.* 1910; on the l. again, unavoidably, HIGHPOINT, 1972 by *John Brunton & Partners*, aggressive missile-silo-like office tower in vertically corrugated aggregate; but further on, on the r., the best thing here, the former ST ANDREW'S PRESBYTERIAN CHAPEL, 1849 by *Mallinson & Healey*. Handsome applied Tuscan temple front *in antis*. Three bays, with doorway and round-headed windows in deep chamfered reveals.

---

*The rest of the extension, to the W, with another dome at the far corner, replaced 1956–8 following bomb damage.

s from here, in an area of the inner city rather than the city centre proper, is the LONGLANDS ESTATE, early council housing built 1903–10 on a slum clearance site. Tenement blocks of two and three storeys with balcony access, the first of brick and render, U-shaped with the fronts facing outward, the others single ranges of stone with timbered gables. Modernized and re-windowed. s again is another area of wool warehouses, showing the last phase in their development. In GRATTAN ROAD, the WOOLSTON WAREHOUSE, 1904 by *Calvert*, its lower stages vigorously rusticated. Corner doorway with polished granite columns and in the pediment a high relief of a merino sheep, symbolizing the colonial wool trade. Downhill alongside it to SUNBRIDGE ROAD, formed by the town council in 1875–82 to improve access to the mills further w along Thornton Road: on the s side LA PLATA HOUSE/ STANDARD BUILDINGS of 1914, steel-framed, with glazed screens in giant round-headed arches and areas of banded brown and red sandstone. Now back E along Sunbridge Road towards the inner core. On the r. at the junction with Godwin Street SUNWIN HOUSE (former Co-op store), 1935–6 by *W.A. Johnson*, in the International Modern style of Erich Mendelsohn favoured by this architect, with glazed cylindrical corner turrets and long bands of fenestration. Opposite, TORDOFF'S BUILDINGS, 1889 with Art Nouveau gables, an early example of the style. From here a short diversion along Kirkgate leads to Nos. 1–3 UPPER MILLERGATE on the corner with Ivegate, engaging Italianate design of *c.* 1850, with pilasters and niches to the upper floor. Back in Sunbridge Road, on the s side QUEEN ANNE CHAMBERS, modest-sized, 1880 by *Waugh & Isitt* and one of the first examples of this style in Bradford. At the bottom of the hill on the l., Nos. 12–20, funny Gothic of *c.* 1880 with continuous tiers of Caernarvon-arched windows; then turning the corner into Tyrrel Street, close to the start of the perambulation, one of *Waterhouse*'s unmistakable PRUDENTIAL ASSURANCE buildings, 1895, in the company's favoured red brick. Approximate Loire chateau style with gabled dormers.

2. *Town Hall area*

The line of Sunbridge Road is continued SE by BRIDGE STREET. On the r. the shapeless open space in front of the Town Hall, formed in part by the demolition in 1974 of the Mechanics' Institute (1870–1 by *Andrews & Pepper*) and since 1997 called Centenary Square (*see* below), the centenary that of Bradford's city status. On the l. a final characteristic city-centre commercial block of the mid-Victorian rebuilding: four storeys, mainly Italianate of 1871 by *Knowles & Wilcock*, but with one narrow unit in Venetian Gothic. Beyond that a larger-scale city-centre group: first LANDMARK HOUSE, 1958–9 by *Young & Engle* (refurbished *c.* 2003), Bradford's inauspicious first experience of the post-war office block; then BRITANNIA HOUSE, 1929 by the City Architect *W. Williamson*, standard interwar classical with a copper dome over one corner; then St George's Hall (*see* Public Buildings, above); and finally the VICTORIA HOTEL, 1867 by *Lockwood & Mawson*, in a kind of round-arched Italian Trecento but with pavilions at each end formerly crowned by funny French domes. Its front faces the other way, towards the site of Exchange Station, now partly occupied by the Law Courts (*see* Public Buildings, above). Also nearby, adjoining St George's Hall to the NE, in HALL INGS, the BRADFORD TELEGRAPH & ARGUS building. It is in two parts. The first is one of the earliest and grandest of the mid-C19 display warehouses, 1852–3 by *Andrews & Delaunay* for the stuff merchants Milligan & Forbes. Opulent palazzo style: five storeys – the second the most emphasized, with projecting pediments to the close-set windows – and heavy top cornice. The other part, the printing hall (on the site of the old Court House, 1834–5,* dem. *c.* 1960), is one of the extremely few memorable modern buildings in the city centre, 1979–80 by the *Robinson Partnership*. The idea is simple, the front a sheer curtain of brown-tinted glass, curved at the corners, in daytime blandly screening the interior but at night dramatically transformed, dissolving into transparency to show the printing presses at work, illuminated like a piece of street theatre.

The area SW of St George's Hall, behind the Town Hall, represents the city centre of the 1960s and 1970s at its worst, so back to CENTENARY SQUARE. Beyond the Town Hall, opposite the Magistrates' Court and Police Station (*see* Public Buildings, above), a two-storey, crescent-shaped development of shops and bars, 2002–4 by *Panter Hudspith*, no obvious improvement on its eight-storey office-block predecessor of the 1970s. W again, at the junction of Thornton Road and PRINCE'S WAY – the latter a product of the post-war redevelopment scheme – the ODEON CINEMA, formerly the New Victoria, 1930 by *W. Illingworth*, brick and faience with two domes. Designed as a dual-purpose ciné-variety theatre with a capacity of over 3,000 people, and originally incorporating a ballroom and restaurant as well as dressing rooms, orchestra pit etc., but the interior now wholly altered. The domes repeat a theme from its neighbour to the S, the ALHAMBRA THEATRE, 1914 by *Chadwick & Watson* of Leeds for the impresario Francis Laidler, successfully modified and enlarged 1984–6 by *Renton Howard Wood Levin*. The 1914 building is in a coarsely detailed classical style, originally faced in white faience but long since painted over, and occupies a narrow wedge-shaped site. The apex of the triangle is formed by a domed rotunda with coupled columns – now housing the main staircase – further back are two domed turrets, and extending sideways to the r. of the rotunda is the 1980s foyer area, echoing the original

---

*There is conflicting evidence as to whether the architect was *Bernard Hartley II* or *James Richardby*.

vocabulary in glass and steel. The best part is the carefully restored auditorium, with domed ceiling, decoration by *de Jong* and painted tympana. s again, across the bottom of Morley Street in a little area of garden, the STATUE of Queen Victoria, 1904 by *Alfred Drury*, bronze, with plinth and the surrounding balustraded terrace by *J. W. Simpson*, architect of the Cartwright Hall (*see* Manningham, below). In front of this the WAR MEMORIAL, 1922, designed by the City Architect *W. Williamson*, an ashlar cenotaph flanked by bronze figures of two servicemen advancing, originally with fixed bayonets – the figures much criticized in Bradford at the time for their 'crude and mistaken symbolism'. Further back, facing onto Little Horton Lane, GLYDE HOUSE, 1861 by *Lockwood & Mawson*, built as the school of the Horton Lane Congregational Chapel (dem.). Jacobean style with shaped gables and loggia. Then the 1960s backdrop of the National Media Museum complex (*see* Public Buildings, above).

Finally, a short foray into the former industrial heartland along THORNTON ROAD. On the l., in QUEBEC STREET, is a mixed row of early C19 wool warehouses, two and three storeys; and a little further along on the r. SOHO WORKS, built as an iron foundry 1864 by *Milnes & France*, now flats. Compact plan with small central yard, storeyed mill ranges to front and r., the former with arched entry and loading doors in the narrow w end, lower forge building with round-headed windows behind to l.

3. Cathedral area and Little Germany

The area E and NE of Perambulations 1 and 2, as far as Forster Square, is at the time of writing one enormous demolition site, about to undergo a second round of comprehensive redevelopment having previously been cleared and redeveloped under the scheme of the 1950s. Before that it had contained, *inter alia*, a major concentration of warehouses,* including two of the finest, Titus Salt's (later Kassapian's), 1853 by *Lockwood & Mawson*, and McKean Tetley's, 1862 by *Eli Milnes*. FORSTER SQUARE itself was first created by the council's Street Improvement Committee in 1874–82 by clearance of a notorious slum adjoining the canal basin (closed 1867). It was then approximately triangular, its s side following the curve of Kirkgate and Well Street, but was re-formed to a quite different shape *c.* 1963. There is currently nothing to see apart from two survivals on the E side, the former Post Office (*see* Public Buildings, above) and next to it the GATEWAY AND STEPS to the Cathedral churchyard, 1882–3 by *Milnes & France*. Three-bay screen wall in Flamboyant Gothic behind which the steps rise to the churchyard round an open well, the lowest flight under

* On a grid of streets laid out 1835 by the surveyor *Thomas Dixon* on former water meadows – the Hall Ings – beside the Bradford Beck.

a rib-vault. The STATUE of W.E. Forster, 1890 by *J. Havard Thomas*, which stood in the middle of the square, has been removed temporarily.

To the SE, however, on sloping ground between Church Bank and Leeds Road, is LITTLE GERMANY, the one warehouse precinct in the city to survive substantially intact, developed 1855 onwards but incorporating some earlier streets. The name reflects the original preponderance of German export houses in the area, but most moved in from elsewhere in Bradford rather than settling here initially to form a compact foreign mercantile colony. A convenient starting point, immediately to hand, is the E side of WELL STREET, which forms a clear-cut W frontage to the area. At the N end, on the corner with Church Bank, No. 39, of 1867, is by *Milnes & France*, the leading warehouse designers, and an ideal introduction to their work: five storeys, in restrained but boldly modelled Italianate – battered plinth, continuous line of first-floor pediments, modillion cornice – with a canted corner entrance bay enclosing a handsome octagonal staircase, and a cart entrance leading into a private loading bay at the rear. Next No. 45, 1864 by the same architects, a slightly plainer prototype; then No. 47, 1855 by *Lockwood & Mawson*, one of the earliest warehouses in the area, with narrow frontage and quadrant corner; and Nos. 51–53, *c.* 1865, a striking exotic, Venetian Trecento with crocket capitals and a gable at each end of the symmetrical front. The last two are now wholly redeveloped internally, as offices, and the same applies to No. 4 CURRER STREET behind them, 1860 by *Lockwood & Mawson* for Nathan Reichenheim & Co., with another quadrant corner which contained one of the best warehouse staircases.

Another good group is along VICAR LANE, the ancient thoroughfare across the area, which was transformed by development into a narrow urban canyon. At the S end, next to Eastbrook Hall (*see* Places of Worship, above), Nos. 53–55 Leeds Road, 1859–62 by *Eli Milnes*: in two stages, the later with a tower and the detail untypically florid. Next a particularly ambitious pair, almost opposite each other, both by *Lockwood & Mawson*. On the r., at the corner with Aked Street, No. 62, 1871 for Thornton Homan & Co., with ornate pedimented first-floor windows, corner entrance portal bearing sculptural reference to the firm's American links, excellent ironwork grilles to the basement. On the l. the LAW RUSSELL WAREHOUSE (No. 63) of 1873–4, on a wedge-shaped site with all enrichment concentrated on the narrow canted corner, a spectacular composition of five superimposed orders against banded masonry crowned by a little Second Empire dome. Good iron gates and overthrow to the cart entrance along the l. flank, circular spiral staircase with enriched balusters. Then two more austere specimens, by *Milnes & France*: on the r. No. 64, 1867–8, of similar bulk to its neighbour; and on another wedge-shaped site where Vicar Lane bends to the l., No. 66, 1866–7, a good example of the second rank of warehouses, with

102

the usual canted entrance corner and especially enjoyable decorative iron gates to the cart entrance. Adjoining this is No. 6 Currer Street, 1857–8 for James and Leopold Reiss, an elegant design with the Vicar Lane front symmetrical about the cart entrance, another quadrant corner and the Currer Street elevation a concave curve following the street line. Finally in Vicar Lane, No. 72, 1860 by *Milnes*, a smaller type, just three storeys, but with an unusually exuberant treatment of the quadrant.

After that comes a sequence of more modest examples. In CURRER STREET on the r. Nos. 8 and 10, 1861 and 1862 by *Milnes*, the former built as a speculation by the architect, with his initials over the doorway. Via Cater Street to BURNETT STREET, continuing uphill the line of the lower part of Vicar Lane: at the corner No. 1, 1867 by *Milnes & France* in their familiar austere manner; then at the junction with Peckover Street a near-matching pair by *J. T. Fairbank*, Nos. 4–6 (l.) and No. 5 (r.), 1859–60; and the early PICKWICK HOUSE, 1855 also by *Fairbank*, a wool warehouse still with twelve-pane sash windows and taking-in doors onto the street. Further up on the r. No. 8, 1862 by *Andrews & Delaunay*, refined Italianate with long two-storey façade round the corner in Scoresby Street. Now SE along PECKOVER STREET, marred by a number of empty sites, to CHAPEL STREET, one of the earlier streets, formed *c.* 1825, which introduces a slightly wider variety of building types. On the corner No. 40, another handsome warehouse, 1860 by *Andrews & Delaunay* with simple linear decoration; and next to it No. 38, a repeat of the same formula by the same firm ten years later. Downhill on the r. the former QUAKER SCHOOL, 1831, four storeys, the top two added on conversion to a warehouse in 1884, the dour, much altered façade with central round-headed doorway; and further down on the l. a pair of modest terraced houses with Gothick windows, built for the ministers of the Eastbrook Methodist Chapel, 1825 by *Joseph Botham*. Uphill from Peckover Street No. 37 on the l., a late warehouse by *Milnes & France*, 1902 for Edelstein, Moser & Co., rationalized classical detail in common wallstone instead of the usual ashlar, on an iron and steel frame.

A final group is a little further along PECKOVER STREET, at the junction with East Parade. First, on the r., No. 46, 1870–1 by the Leeds architect *George Corson* for Heugh, Dunlop & Co., an exceptional design here, in Scottish Baronial style.* Beyond it No. 26 EAST PARADE, 1873 by *Milnes & France* for Behrens & Co., a massive rectangular block in their unshowily monumental palazzo manner, with good grilles and railings, staircase in slightly florid mixed Renaissance, and typical interior structure of timber beams on cast-iron columns; and on the corner opposite No. 61, the same date and architects for Delius & Co. – the family of the composer – again with attractive ironwork. Further up East Parade,

*Both the architect and the clients had Scottish connections.

No. 67, 1913 by *Mawson & Hudson*, with curved frontage and almost Art Deco detail; and then close to the inner ring road No. 99, a much degraded Late Georgian house absorbed into a mid-C19 industrial building: Venetian windows.

W of this Upper Park Gate emerges from Little Germany into BARKEREND ROAD and a different inner-city scene, with a group of grim eight-storey Y-plan blocks of flats, 1955–6, opposite. On the corner, the mutilated façade of the former COLLEGE CONGREGATIONAL CHAPEL, 1838–9 by *J. P. Pritchett*. Grecian style with segmental projecting centre and single flanking bays of which only one survives: pilasters over a banded ground floor, little pediments with antefixae. The rest replaced by a C20 industrial building. Further up, at the junction with the inner ring road, PAPER HALL, the only C17 house remaining close to the centre. Dated 1643, substantially restored 1980–94, now offices. Conventional plan of storeyed hall range, projecting cross-wings and two-storey porch next to the service wing. Stepped four-light windows in the wing gables, some mullion-and-transom windows elsewhere; but the fronts of the parlour wing and hall range remodelled *c.* 1700 with cross-windows, all apart from those above the hall crowned by excessively steep linked pediments, semicircular below and triangular above. Changed interior but a number of C17 fireplaces.

From further down Barkerend Road, by the E end of the Cathedral, STOTT HILL runs N, intact at the S end only. On the corner a detached Georgian house, three bays, altered; then on the l. the CATHEDRAL PARISH ROOM, 1891 by *T. H. & F. Healey*, Gothic, surprisingly modest; and on the r. the DIOCESAN OFFICE, 1932 by *T. Barker*, residual Gothic. N again, beyond an area of empty sites, in CAPTAIN STREET, the former PARISH CHURCH SCHOOL, 1872 by *Samuel Jackson*, also Gothic, two storeys with central tower and truncated spire. Below this, straddling the line of the former canal, is a further zone of wool and yarn warehouses, mainly of the later phases – including Nos. 37–41 BOLTON ROAD, 1912 by *James Ledingham*, one of the largest and most extraordinary, twenty-two bays in cream faience with mixed Renaissance details. From Bolton Road down Balme Street to the S end of CANAL ROAD, flanked by a pair on narrow wedge-shaped sites, with the acutest canted entrance corners and flatter detail than those of the mid C19: on the r. No. 18, 1898 by the ubiquitous *Milnes & France*, starting a whole row, 1903 etc., on this side; on the l. Nos. 15–17, 1905–7 by *Samuel Jackson*, with panelled vestibule and iron-balustraded staircase. Round the corner to the W are Nos. 14–22 MILL STREET, an earlier development by *Jackson*, 1871, on an unusual plan, three long plain ranges running back from the street (two of them now truncated) with loading yards between them. Street fronts treated as a trio of palazzo-style pavilions – the details of each differing slightly – the first of three bays but the other two forming semi-detached pairs of units. From here Forster Square is just to the S.

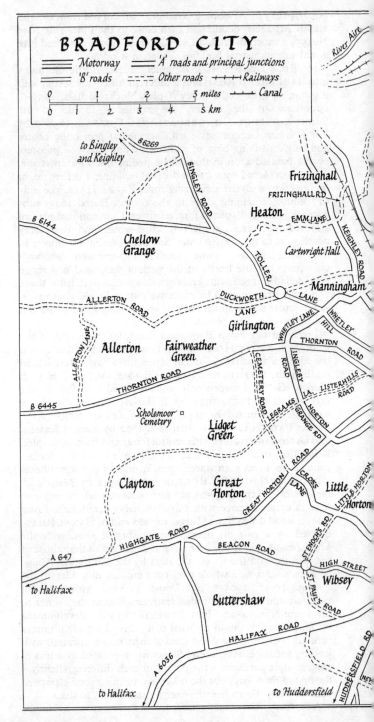

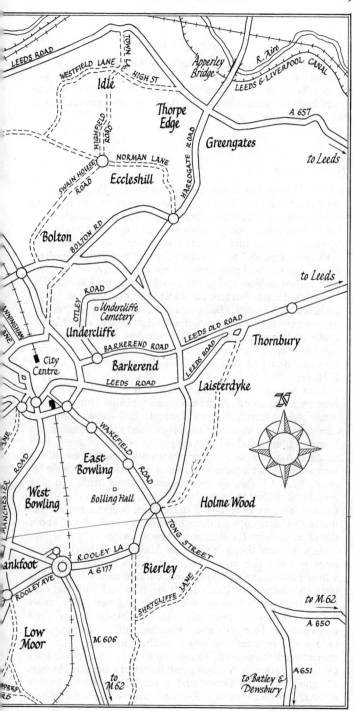

NORTH-WEST

Bradford's premier mid-C19 suburb, developed mainly from the 1850s to the 1870s with a few earlier villas interspersed, but also the location of the city's finest industrial building. This account covers both the suburb itself and the inner-city approach to it, along Manningham Lane.

Places of worship

St Luke, Victor Road, now Church of God of Prophecy. 1880 by *T. H. & F. Healey*. Free Perp, with dense meshes of Arts and Crafts-inspired tracery. Especially good almost detached NE tower (completed 1906) with a very effective juxtaposition of materials, a sheer unbuttressed coursed stone shaft rising to an elaborate octagonal belfry stage of ashlar and a stumpy slate-covered spire. No break between nave and chancel, SE vestry with canted corners and tall chimney. Quiet spacious interior. – Elaborate panel-traceried REREDOS of alabaster. 1891, designed by *T. H. & F. Healey* and executed by *Farmer & Brindley*. – STAINED GLASS. E window and N aisle NW by *Heaton, Butler & Bayne*, 1881 and 1888. W window and three in the S aisle by *Shrigley & Hunt*, 1912 and *c.* 1900–36. – Former SUNDAY SCHOOL to S, now Mosque. 1886 also by *T. H. & F. Healey*.

St Mary Magdalene, Wood Street. 1876–8 by *Edward Pearson Peterson* of Bradford. A dramatic and unusual church of the inner city, tall and stark in a simple E.E. style. Nave and chancel in one with a very steeply pitched roof, the aisles and E end entirely windowless. Vertiginous W end crowned by a pyramid-roofed bellcote. Bare stone walls inside. W bay of the nave at arcade level partitioned off as a parish room 1986–7 by *Wales, Wales & Rawson*, but creatively done with a timber version of a Gothic groin-vault. – ROOD, 1894, on a ROOD BEAM with carved vine-trail decoration. – WALL PAINTING, the Te Deum, occupying three blind arches in the E wall above the altar. 1889 by *Powell Bros.* of Leeds. Good.

St Paul, Church Street. 1846–8 by *Mallinson & Healey*. Quite large, in a rich E.E. style. Cruciform with a central tower, just a little pinched, and tall spire, made the more effective by the later alignment of St Paul's Road on the E end. Stiff-leaf capitals to the S porch doorway and the crossing piers. Outer aisles added *c.* 1856, the N originally with a double-pitch roof, the S cross-gabled. Fairly drastic alterations of 1971, the outer aisle roofs replaced by single pitches and the aisles and transepts partitioned off. – STAINED GLASS. E and W windows by *Wailes*, *c.* 1850. – A single small lancet of Christ in Majesty, designed by *D. G. Rossetti* and executed by *Morris & Co. c.* 1864, a smaller version of Rossetti's panel of the same subject

in the E window of Bradford Cathedral. Originally in the outer
N aisle W window but now displayed in an illuminated case on
the N side of the nave. – S transept E and S, and three S aisle
windows, by *Burlison & Grylls*, 1879, 1885 and 1900, the two
in the transept now obscured by partitioning. – Former
SCHOOL nearby in Ambler Street, 1861–2 by *Knowles &
Wilcock*. Gothic, two storeys, with turret, turning octagonal,
over the entrance.

ST CUTHBERT (R.C.), Wilmer Road. 1889–91 by *H. & E.
Marten*. Low and unassuming but with some quirky details,
the windows a mixture of free Perp and little lancets. Polygonal turrets flanking the W end, another at the junction of nave
and chancel. – STATIONS OF THE CROSS. 1921–4 by *Eric Gill*,
mainly after drawings by *Fr Desmond Chute*, for Fr John
O'Connor. Square bas-relief panels of Beer stone. – STAINED
GLASS. Six aisle lancets by *Leonard Walker*, 1930. – Mildly Arts
and Crafts PRESBYTERY adjoining.

GREENFIELD CONGREGATIONAL CHAPEL, Carlisle Road,
now Council Offices. 1875–6 by *Hope & Jardine*. A rather
approximate Quattrocento style, with superimposed pilaster
orders.

ST JOHN'S METHODIST CHURCH, Park View Road, now
UKRAINIAN R.C. 1878–9 by *C. O. Ellison*. Rock-faced Gothic,
large but overstretched. Tall tower and spire flanking the front
gable, the spire with small flying buttresses at the base. Gallery
on iron columns with foliage capitals. – STAINED GLASS.
Includes second and fourth pairs of lancets on each side by
Heaton, Butler & Bayne, 1901–13. – Big detached SUNDAY
SCHOOL of 1885–6 to the rear.

WESTGATE BAPTIST CHAPEL, Carlisle Road. 1899–1900 by
James Ledingham, replacing the old Westgate Chapel in the city
centre (dem.). Accomplished Art Nouveau Gothic. Characteristic panels of dense stylized foliage as hoodmould stops and
above the entrance, tapered finials on the roofs of the flanking
bays. Interior largely unaltered. Gallery and two tiers of iron
columns with foliage capitals. – Excellent WOODWORK,
notably the bulbous projecting PULPIT, with carved panels and
flanking steps with tapered newel-posts-cum-lamp-standards.
In front of it the COMMUNION RAIL with balusters pierced
with the tulip motif. – STAINED GLASS. Stylized fruit and
foliage motifs in gentle colours.

SYNAGOGUE, Bowland Street. 1881 by *T. H. & F. Healey*. Islamic
Revival style in brown and red banded sandstone. Two-light
windows, ornate doorways to l. and r., all with Saracenic-
arched heads. Cresting of oriental merlons. Little altered
interior in similar vein.

CENTRAL MOSQUE, Darfield Street. 1986–99 by *Neil Waghorne*.
Coursed stone rectangle with much Islamic-style carved decoration, and similarly ornate lead dome.

JAMIA MASJID HANFIA MOSQUE, Carlisle Road. 1982–92 by
A. Salam. Beige brick facing with concrete dressings, fibreglass
dome, minaret. Five-sided prayer hall.

Public buildings

96 CARTWRIGHT HALL (Art Gallery), Lister Park. 1900–4 by
    J. W. Simpson & E. J. Milner Allen, winners of the competition
    (assessed by Alfred Waterhouse) and previously designers of
    the Glasgow Art Gallery. It stands on the site of Manningham
    Hall, erstwhile home of Samuel Cunliffe Lister, builder of
    Manningham Mills (*see* below), who in 1870 had sold the
    house and grounds to the town council to form the public
    park. Subsequently, in 1898, Lister offered funds to erect a
    public building here as a memorial to Dr Edmund Cartwright,
    inventor of the first woolcombing machine, the choice of func-
    tion being left to the council. Effusive Neo-Baroque in fine
    sandstone ashlar over a rockily rusticated base, with slightly
    projecting cross-wings l. and r. and a prominent porte-cochère-
    cum-balcony in the middle, crowned by a pediment and tall
    cupola. At the back a broad apsidal projection flanked by
    domed turrets repeated from the Glasgow gallery. Extensive
    scheme of allegorical sculpture executed by *Alfred Broadbent*.*
    The grand manner is continued inside, with a full-height
    central sculpture gallery flanked by matching staircases. The
    other main galleries are in the cross-wings, the upper ones top-
    lit with a civic reception suite between them across the front.
    Marble STATUE of Cartwright here, by *H. C. Fehr*.
        Also in the PARK, near the SE corner, a STATUE of Lister,
    1875 by *Matthew Noble*. NW of this, aligned on the front of the
    Cartwright Hall, fine wrought-iron ENTRANCE GATES of 1904.
    At the NE corner the so-called NORMAN ARCH, 1883–9 by
    T. H. & F. Healey, a castellated entrance gatehouse in Arts and
    Crafts Gothic complete with portcullis. The name derives from
    its predecessor, a temporary 'Norman archway' set up in 1882
    at the time of a visit to Bradford by the Prince and Princess of
    Wales. Behind it the SIR TITUS SALT MONUMENT, 1874, a
    miniature Albert Memorial by *Lockwood & Mawson* with
    seated marble statue by *J. Adams-Acton*. It originally stood in
    front of the Town Hall and was moved to this position in 1896.
POLICE STATION, Lilycroft Road. 1993 by *Wakefield
    Metropolitan District Council Design Services Division*. Three-
    storey ashlar block with hipped slate roof. Fortress-like yard
    wall turning the corner with Heaton Road.
BRANCH LIBRARY, Carlisle Road. 1910 by *W. Williamson* (City
    Architect). Art Nouveau Jacobean, with enriched cartouches
    containing the names of literary figures. Segmental barrel
    ceiling inside (cf. Great Horton, Branch Library, below).
BATHS, Carlisle Road. 1903–4 by *A. Hessell Tiltman* and the City
    Architect *F. E. P. Edwards*. Mildly Art Nouveau classical, with
    symmetrical gabled front, squat chimneystack, and the same
    rippling copings as the same architects' Central Baths (*see* City
    Centre Public Buildings, above).

---

*Broadbent also worked as an assistant to George Frampton, who had supervised
a similar scheme at Glasgow.

GRAMMAR SCHOOL, Keighley Road. 1937–48 by *Petch & Fermaud*, successor to a building in the city centre (1872–3 by *Andrews & Pepper*, dem.). Large two-storey composition in simplified Neo-Tudor style, with gabled end pavilions and central gatehouse motif – that is, aesthetically out of date from the moment it was taken over. In the grounds CLOCK HOUSE, double pile of 1699, altered. Five-bay front – the windows Victorianized – with quoins, parapet and a semicircular attic gablet over the middle bay, containing an oculus. Also a re-set sundial dated 1657. Stepped mullioned windows in the gable-ends, central chimneystack with shallow blind arcading (cf. Micklethwaite Grange, Bingley, etc.).

LILYCROFT BOARD SCHOOL, Lilycroft Road. One of the first of the Board Schools, 1873–4 by *Hope & Jardine*. Elaborately ecclesiastical Gothic with Geometrical tracery, a long near-symmetrical range with turret and spirelet over one of the porches. Others are DRUMMOND ROAD, 1886–7, and GREEN LANE, 1899–1903, both by *E. P. Peterson*, plainer and more secular, with only vestigial Gothic details; and the former BELLE VUE HIGHER GRADE SCHOOL, Manningham Lane, 1895 by *C. H. Hargreaves*. Free Renaissance, a big tall symmetrical three-storey block with an approximation to a Pennine-style door lintel at the front (cf. Hanson School, Barkerend, below).

PRIMARY SCHOOLS of the later C20 are represented by a near-identical trio by the *City Architect's Department* (project architect *Ron Furniss*), built under the Bradford Schools Programme: ATLAS, Priestman Street, and MIRIAM LORD, Carlisle Road, both 1987, and WESTBOURNE, Skinner Lane, 1988–91. Single low open-plan classroom ranges under a very wide pitched roof with deep eaves and a trio of elongated dormers at the ridge. Beige or red brick (cf. Swain House, Bolton, and Newby, Bowling, below).

CHILDREN'S HOSPITAL (former), Welbury Drive. 1889–90 by *H. & E. Marten*. A most surprising building. Loosely Queen Anne style. Tall compact main block with two tiers of dormers. To the l. a two-storeyed ward wing of circular form, an early example of the type. Flat roof with iron railing round, forming a 'convalescent promenade', and central octagonal chimney the lower stage of which was surrounded by a glazed veranda. Ogee-roofed stair-turret. A balancing wing was intended to the r.

ST CATHERINE'S HOME, St Mary's Road. 1898 by *James Ledingham*. Restrained Jacobean with Mannerist central portal.

Textile mills

LUMB LANE MILLS, Lumb Lane. 1856–70 by *Lockwood & Mawson*, for James Drummond. Sophisticated epitome of the large-scale integrated worsted mill. The focus is the five-storey spinning mill, with sober Italianate detail including a pair of belvedere-topped privy towers on the w side. Fireproof construction and remarkable laminated arched roof trusses. Engine house at s e corner, partly in a return wing now reduced in height. Tall octagonal chimney with bracketed crown. Three-storey warehouse range parallel to the spinning mill, forming the street front. Weaving sheds reduced and altered.

105 MANNINGHAM MILLS, Heaton Road. 'Stupendous manufacturing pile' (W. Cudworth) built as an integrated silk mill for Samuel Cunliffe Lister mainly 1870–3 by *Andrews & Pepper*. Part conversion to residential use by Urban Splash, begun 2004, the first phase by *Latham Architects*, the second by *David Morley Architects*. On a commanding site above the suburb, its famous chimney an omnipresent feature of the Bradford townscape, it is wholly exceptional among the city's mills in both its size – an area of 16 acres – and its elaboration.

The most prominent elements, forming the s part of the complex, date from after a fire in 1871 which destroyed much of its predecessor, a worsted mill founded in 1838, and resulted in the adoption of a 'grand design'. They are the two great near-matching multi-storey ranges – the spinning mill (E) and the warehouse (w) – the boiler house forming the N end of the yard between them, the chimney N of the warehouse, and the Lily Shed, built as a combing shed, E of the mill. Mill and warehouse of six storeys and forty-one and forty-five bays long respectively. Robust if slightly impure Italianate style, with tall panelled parapets masking the top floor and the corner bays breaking forward. Privy turrets on the courtyard sides. Fireproof construction with concrete vaults on ornamented cast-iron columns. The mill has a prominent staircase tower on the E flank crowned by steeply pitched pavilion roof with iron cresting, and engine house within its N end; the slightly less elaborate warehouse a wide doorway at the s end leading to an internal loading bay. The Lily Shed has an ornamental perimeter wall to s and E, with battered rusticated plinth, a pavilion at the corner, and along the E (Heaton Road) elevation the main entrance to the complex – a broad round-headed doorway surmounted by Lister's coat of arms – aligned on the mill staircase tower. Inside, the north-light roofs have cast-iron trusses in the s part, timber in the N, on the usual iron columns. The monumental boiler house, reconstructed internally 1931–2, is crowned by a big bellcote; while the chimney, 249 feet (75 metres) high, completed in 1873, is the most direct Italianate reference, an industrialized sandstone version of the campanile of St Mark's in Venice.

N of the multi-storey ranges is a confused area of sheds, dyehouse etc. incorporating fragments of the pre-1870 buildings but entirely remodelled in the 1870s and later. E of this, next to the Lily Shed, is a weaving shed built in 1870 before the fire. Its E front consists of an office building – with Quattrocento windows to the first floor and end bays projecting under steep hipped roofs – flanked by stretches of walling which establish the system then used further s. North-light roofs on cast-iron columns. N again, across Beamsley Road, is North Mill, the SE quarter of which – a weaving shed – is part of *Andrews & Pepper's* work of 1871–3. The same elevational treatment to the E. Extended further N 1885 by *T. G. Andrews*; dyehouse, boiler house etc. to W 1880s and later.

Perambulation

The start of the approach along MANNINGHAM LANE, across the inner ring road from the former Yorkshire Penny Bank (*see* City Centre, Perambulation 1, above), is not encouraging, more post-urban than suburban. Soon on the r. a piquant jux-taposition, of HALLFIELD HOUSE (Christian Science Church), a mutilated Grecian villa of 1836, and the CON-NAUGHT ROOMS (former Masonic Hall), one of the few sur-vivors here of a city-centre scale, 1926–8 by *Ross & Briggs* of Bradford. Heavy giant order to the first and second floors, with Doric pilasters at the corners, Ionic half-columns flanking the centre. Pedimented entrance flanked by shopfronts, bracketed entablature with attic windows in the frieze. (Banqueting hall with balconies and music gallery, panelling and coffered ceiling.) Then at right angles on the l. ELDON PLACE, a plain ashlar three-storey terrace stepping up the slope, 1845 by *James Richardby*. Across the top ELDON TERRACE, two and three storeys; and behind that, facing the other way onto Lumb Lane, PEEL SQUARE, 1851. This is not a square but a shallow half-H, but an unusually architectonic scheme for Bradford at this date. Two storeys, with a pediment over the centre four bays, the bays adjoining also emphasized, by a blocking course, and the corners to the side ranges turned by a concave bay. Chunky pedimented doorcases, recessed panels below the windows, eaves cornice. Reached from Eldon Place via HALL-FIELD ROAD, more modest terraces with some stylistically promiscuous detail, 1862–6 by *T. C. Hope* mainly for the Hall-field Building Club.

Back in Manningham Lane, and on the l. between two face-less modern blocks the narrow entrance to HANOVER SQUARE, *c.* 1850, admirably rehabilitated 1990 by *Allen Tod Architects* for the British Historic Buildings Trust. Not strictly speaking a square either but a wedge shape, closed at the broader (W) end where the corners are again concave curves. Several gabled projections, vaguely Tudor windows with round-headed lights, but cornices on brackets to the doorways. Now a longer gap, and then still on the l. the former BELLE VUE HOTEL, 1874, simplified French chateau style with mansard roof and projecting cylindrical balconied corner; the former Belle Vue School (*see* Public Buildings, above); and BELLE VUE PLACE, *c.* 1840, another three-storey ashlar terrace at right angles to the road. Banded rustication to the ground floor, Tuscan doorcases alternately pedimented. After that, however, Manningham itself is reached and a more

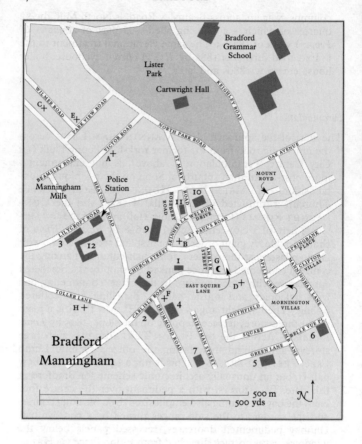

A St Luke
B St Paul
C St Cuthbert (R.C.)
D Greenfield Congregational Chapel
   (former)
E St John's Methodist Church,
   now Ukrainian R.C.
F Westgate Baptist Chapel
G Jamia Masjid Hanfia Mosque
H St Chad
   (see Girlington and Thornton Road)

1 Library
2 Baths
3 Lilycroft Board School
4 Drummond Road Board School
5 Green Lane Board School
6 Belle Vue Higher Grade School (former)
7 Atlas Primary School
8 Miriam Lord Primary School
9 Westbourne Primary School
10 Children's Hospital (former)
11 St Catherine's Home
12 Bradford Tradesmen's Homes

consistent suburban character established, with some trees
along the road and the buildings set further back. On the l. an
area laid out for development in 1854 by the surveyor *Joseph
Smith*, the first and best result APSLEY CRESCENT, 1854–5,
along the w edge of the site. Two storeys, ashlar, mainly a
shallow curve but turning more tightly at the s end, with
effective restrained detail similar to that of Peel Square.
In the streets leading to it, e.g. MORNINGTON VILLAS,

semi-detached villa pairs of 1857 onwards, Italianate and Gothic, mainly by *Samuel Jackson*; and onto Manningham Lane modest Italianate terraces, one 1865 by *T. C. Hope*. On the other side of Manningham Lane two *culs-de-sac*, CLIFTON VILLAS and SPRING BANK PLACE, with more detached and semi-detached villas of the 1850s and 1860s, again mainly Italianate; and further down the slope ROSE MOUNT, 1849–51 by *Andrews & Delaunay*, gaunt Jacobean with shaped gables.

Next comes Manningham Lane's brief climax. On the r., first BOLTON ROYD, set back in wooded grounds, a Grecian villa of *c.* 1830 perhaps by *Francis Goodwin* (*see* Public Rooms, City Centre, Perambulation 1, above): a similar design appears in his *Domestic Architecture* (1833). Rectangular two-storey bay windows flanking a Doric porch. Addition to l., 1862, with mansard roof, extensive C20 additions at the back. After this an area of mainly Gothic villas of the 1860s and 1870s, detached and semi-detached, erected by various building clubs on what had been the Bolton Royds estate, including MOUNT ROYD, 1863–4 probably by *Lockwood & Mawson*, four semi-detached pairs in simple gabled quasi-Gothic with decorative bargeboards, overlooking a wooded dell. At the far NE corner of the estate at the foot of OAK AVENUE two later interpolations in quirky Queen Anne style, 1889 by *H. & E. Marten*. Meanwhile on the l. side of Manningham Lane are two three-storey terraces, the first BLENHEIM TERRACE, 1865 by *Samuel Jackson*, unremarkable Italianate, the other 1873 by *T. C. Hope*, weaker; and at right angles between them ST PAUL'S ROAD, laid out *c.* 1874 aligned on the earlier St Paul's church (*see* above) and creating an effect of large-scale formal planning otherwise absent from the area. On one side another undistinguished terrace by *Hope*, 1874. N from here is LISTER PARK (*see* Public Buildings, above), with further terraces and villas of the 1850s onwards facing onto it on the w side in NORTH PARK ROAD.

Further w, in the neighbourhood of St Paul's church, are a few reminders of the pre-Victorian settlement, including, to the N of the church in ROSEBERY ROAD, a fragment of the C17 MANOR HOUSE: a cross-wing with altered mullioned windows and the stump of a hall range, the latter largely a C19 rebuild reusing earlier material but retaining some roof timbers *in situ*. Another C17 house to the SE, in ASHDOWNE PLACE off East Squire Lane. S of this, off Lumb Lane, SOUTHFIELD SQUARE, a long rectangle with modest houses of the 1850s and 1860s, the s side uniform, the N not; and to the w, in CARLISLE ROAD – the suburb's main street, with Library and Baths (*see* above) – also the former MARLBOROUGH CINEMA, 1921 by *T. Patrick*, painted brick with corner cupola. Uphill w of the church, off the w side of HEATON ROAD, the BRADFORD TRADESMEN'S HOMES, almshouses of 1867 etc. by *Milnes & France*. Four detached ranges round a rectangular green, the s an addition of 1878. Crude Gothic with half-hipped dormers. In the middle of the N range a chapel-cum-meeting room with projecting canted front and STAINED GLASS by *Camm Bros* of Smethwick, 1872–8.

HEATON

ST BARNABAS, Ashwell Road. 1864 by *T. H. & F. Healey* for the Bradford Church Building Society (N aisle 1895–6). Early French Gothic with plate tracery windows (cf. the same architects' St John, Great Horton, below). Triple-gabled w end, no clerestory. SE tower with broach spire, semicircular apse. Cylindrical arcade piers with crocket capitals. – STAINED GLASS. Apse windows and s aisle SW by *Kempe*, 1888 and 1890; N aisle second from W and s aisle third from W by *Kempe & Co.*, 1919 and 1933; N aisle NE by *Powell Bros.* of Leeds, 1895.

ST MARGARET, Shipley Fields Road, Frizinghall. 1895–6 by *H. & E. Marten* (chancel 1904). Suburban Perp with occasional tricky details. Hall-church form, big SW porch with pyramid roof. Polygonal turrets framing the nave W end, their upper sections linked to the gable by openwork parapets. Cylindrical arcade piers.

121 OUR LADY AND THE FIRST MARTYRS (R.C.), Heights Lane, Chellow Grange. The first church in England designed with a central altar (P. F. Anson, *Fashions in Church Furnishings*, 1960), 1935 by *J. H. Langtry-Langton* for Fr John O'Connor, the original of G. K. Chesterton's Father Brown. 'Not a very notable piece of building', wrote Eric Gill in 1936, but his own enthusiasm for central altars dates from this time (cf. Gorleston, Norfolk). Octagonal, in a Neo-Byzantine style, with a central lantern stage carried on a series of radiating semi-parabolic beams spanning the interior. – STATUE of St John Bosco by *Gill*.

FRIZINGHALL UNITED REFORMED CHURCH (Congregational), Aireville Road. 1890–1 by *Herbert Isitt*. Inexpert Gothic with a thin tower and spire.

BRADFORD UNIVERSITY SCHOOL OF MANAGEMENT, Emm Lane. 1874–7 by *Lockwood & Mawson*, built as the Airedale College, later the Yorkshire United Independent College, a training establishment for Congregationalist ministers. Set back from the road in sloping wooded grounds. C13 Gothic with Geometrical tracery, two-storeyed near-symmetrical composition with projecting gabled centre and r. cross-wing, former Master's house to l. Main hall in the wing with curious waggon-cum-hammerbeam roof. Behind it HEATON MOUNT, an ornate Italianate villa of 1864 by *J. T. Fairbank*. Symmetrical front, very spacious imperial staircase with naturalistic iron balustrade. Various C20 additions including the REFECTORY and the HEATON MOUNT EXTENSION, 1992 by the *John Brunton Partnership*, the former quite crisply elegant in glass and tubular steel, the latter quadrant-shaped in stone with heavy-handed sub-Postmodern detail.

The surrounding land, close to Lister Park (*see* Manningham, above), was developed as a high-class suburb from the early

1870s on. First came HEATON GROVE, on sloping ground N of Heaton Mount, off Keighley Road, a picturesque layout of semi-detached pairs in a vaguely chalet style, with spreading low-pitched roofs and deep eaves. Further up the hill to the W, in PARK DRIVE various villas of the 1880s in unexceptional Old English and Queen Anne styles mainly by *James Ledingham*, e.g. GABLEHURST and WOODWARD COURT; and one, No. 14A, of greater interest, almost certainly also by him (a reduced version of the same design in the next street up, Carlton Drive, definitely is) of *c.* 1896. Arts and Crafts Old English, with tall full-width gable broken by steps and Art Nouveau-inflected curves, unchamfered mullioned windows, big off-centre polygonal bay window crowned by ball finials, Voyseyesque battered buttress to the l. corner, and front doorway with elaborate Pennine-style lintel. W again in WILMER DRIVE two mildly Voyseyesque terraces, 1903, partly roughcast, altered.

Back at the foot of the slope, opposite Heaton Mount in KEIGHLEY ROAD and PARK GROVE, a development of generally smaller Old English villas, 1891–4 by *H. & E. Marten*, the best an asymmetrical semi-detached pair at the S junction of the two streets. Further E, off FRIZINGHALL ROAD, is FRIZING OLD HALL, the older part to the l. a three-bay block dated 1727, unusually up-to-date for its time in the Bradford area. Central doorway with lugged architrave surround, pretty leaf carving to the frieze, cornice continued as a stringcourse l. and r. Four-light mullioned windows with unchamfered mullions and surrounds, double-transomed central staircase window at the back. Similarly detailed slightly later extension to the r., with a large shell-hood to the front doorway, cornice on carved brackets to the back.

In the opposite direction, ½ m. NW of Heaton church at HEATON ROYDS, two C17 houses. The larger is ROYDS HALL, a piecemeal rebuilding of before and after 1671 for the Rhodes family, maltsters. Renovations late C19 and late C20. Near-symmetrical front with gabled cross-wings l. and r., both containing parlours. Also a gabled projection at the back, behind the housebody, containing the kitchen. Mullioned windows, that to the housebody of three-plus-three-plus-three round-headed lights, that to the chamber above of five. Lobby entry contrived within the l. cross-wing, close-studded partition in the r. Across the lane is HEATON ROYDS FARM, dated 1632 on the doorway in the E gable-end into the rear outshut. Mullioned windows of up to five lights, single-storey porch at the front. Passage cut through the W end of the house presumably when the later cottage was built against it, with reused four-centre-headed doorway. Segment-headed kitchen fireplace, C17 doors and much reused C17 panelling. Good single-aisled BARN, six bays. ½ m. W again in BINGLEY ROAD the former SHARP'S CARD FACTORY (now Hallmark Cards), 1936 by *Chippendale & Edmondson*. Very long four-storey range, ashlar-faced on a steel frame, with a rather absurd giant hexastile Ionic portico recessed into the centre.

p. 29

GIRLINGTON AND THORNTON ROAD

The W part of Manningham township, together with a little of the inner city. Mainly C19 residential, with the industrialized zone along Thornton Road to the S.

ST CHAD, Toller Lane. 1912–13 by *Nicol & Nicol* of Birmingham, a smaller stone-built version of their St Benedict, Bordesley Green (1909). Compact basilica in Byzantine-cum Romanesque style, with E apse and corresponding baptistry bay to the W. Arcades, with cylindrical piers, of red Staffordshire sandstone. Timber barrel roof. – Byzantine-style MOSAICS of Christ in Majesty in the main apse and the Virgin and Child in the NE chapel by *Powell & Sons*.

ST PHILIP, Washington Street. 1859–60 by *Mallinson & Healey*, the first and most modest of the Bradford Church Building Society churches. Cruciform, aisleless, with Dec details. Intersecting diagonal roof trusses at the crossing.

ST SAVIOUR, Ings Way, Fairweather Green. 1966 by *G. G. Pace*. Concrete frame, brick walling with small plain windows. Monopitch belfry at the E end, lower church hall adjoining to the W. Calm, functional interior, of asymmetrical cross-section varying throughout its length. – ORGAN CASE. A rectangular box of vertical slats.

OUR LADY OF LOURDES AND ST WILLIAM (R.C.), Ingleby Road. 1924 by *Charles Simpson*, son of Edward (*see* e.g. St Joseph, Little Horton, below). The tail-end of his father's style, much reduced and domesticated. Paired transepts.

ST PATRICK (R.C.), Sedgefield Terrace, Westgate. A picturesque group, just beyond the city centre. The church is by *George Goldie*, of *Weightman, Hadfield & Goldie*, 1852–3, conventional Dec of *c.* 1300 but with the big E window incorporating some rather fanciful Curvilinear tracery. Octagonal bell-turret on the S side now behind the PRESBYTERY added in 1866–7, a busy design with steep pavilion roof and first-floor oriel. – REREDOS of Caen stone. 1853, designed by *Goldie*. – STAINED GLASS. Lady Chapel E, 1853 by *Wailes*; E window, 1871 by *Hardman & Co.* (designer *John Hardman Powell*).

WHETLEY LANE BOARD SCHOOL, Whetley Lane. Excellent example of the 'domestic Gothic' manner which was used for several of the schools, 1873–4 by *T. H. & F. Healey*, with additional blocks of 1877 and 1885 by the same architects. Mullion-and-transom windows, and occasional foiled roundels (tower dem. *c.* 1950). Nearby, in Whetley Grove, RAND'S ALMSHOUSES, 1876 by *Andrews & Pepper*. Gothic, a short single-storey range with two-storey wings.

BRADFORD ROYAL INFIRMARY, Duckworth Lane. 1936 by *W. J. Morley & Son*, replacing the original premises in Westgate (1840–3 by *W. Rawstorne*, dem.). Parallel ward ranges of three and four storeys, many later additions. Across the road to the S is LADY ROYD, industrialist's house of 1865 by *Milnes & France* for Henry Illingworth of Whetley Mills (*see* below), now part of the Girls' Grammar School (main building, Squire

Lane, 1935–6 by *Eric Morley*). Slightly forbidding domestic Gothic with tower and spirelet over the entrance. Top-lit staircase hall evoking a medieval kitchen, with open timber roof and Burgesian chimneypiece. Library wing added 1878. Delightful entrance lodge, with cylindrical turret and archway across the drive. Just W of this DAISY BANK, now a hospital, the surprisingly modest house of Illingworth's brother Alfred, *c.* 1845 by *Andrews & Delaunay*. Routine pattern-book Tudor, altered and extended. NW of the infirmary, off Daisy Hill Lane, HILL TOP COTTAGES, housing for the elderly built *c.* 1905 by the Bradford Poor Law Guardians. One-storey rows on three sides of a spacious green, pebbledash with stone dressings. Gabled porches with wide arched entrances, mullioned windows.

OAKWOOD DYEWORKS, W end of City Road. 1858–61 by *Eli Milnes*. Striking Italianate entrance feature, a broad arch flanked by a belvedere tower with fancily louvred top stage. Altered three-storey range to r. Behind, little remains of what was one of Bradford's largest complexes of this type. Adjoining to the l. the contrastingly utilitarian BRICK LANE MILLS, *c.* 1869.

TRY MILLS, Thornton Road. 1865 by *J. Ogilvie*, spinning mill of compact plan beside the Bradford Beck. Storeyed ranges round three sides of a narrow yard. Street front with near-central arched entry, the part to the l. the warehouse, that to the r. the end of the spinning mill running at right angles. At the S end of this the engine house, where the power system was similar to that at Saltaire Mills, and squat octagonal chimney; then a further spinning range.

WHETLEY MILLS, Thornton Road. 1863 etc. by *Milnes & France* for Daniel Illingworth & Sons. The worsted spinning equivalent of Lumb Lane Mills (*see* Manningham, above), also with some similarities in layout. Wool warehouse along the street, five storeys on a rusticated basement, with taking-in doors on the yard side and timber floors on iron columns. Spinning mill across the yard, of similar size but a storey higher and of fireproof construction. In the yard between them the excellent chimney, octagonal on a square base, with bracketed cornice and scalloped rim. Attached to the W end of the mill the engine house and rope-drive tower of 1879, with tall round-headed windows and plaster decoration inside, the original smaller engine house standing to the S of this. W again the combing and other sheds mainly of 1871 onwards, to the N a reservoir and to the E, beside the entrance, the former foreman's house and behind it much altered warehousing for finished goods.

ALLERTON

ST PETER, Allerton Road. 1879 by *E. P. Peterson*. In the same manner as his St Mary Magdalene, Wood Street (*see*

Manningham, above) – plain E.E., tall and thin – but smaller and aisleless. Very odd flat w end, perversely asymmetrical, tapering steeply to the top stage of the pyramid-roofed turret.

WAR MEMORIAL, Ladyhill Park. 1922 by *Harold Brownsword*. Bronze sculptural group of a dying soldier supported by a female figure on one side, balanced by youth holding a laurel crown on the other.

RHODESWAY SCHOOL, Oaks Lane. By *Scherrer & Hicks*, completed 1960. Two and three storeys, curtain walling and blue engineering brick.

DEAN HOUSE, Allerton Lane (⅝ m. SW of the church). Triple-gabled front, the l. wing dated 1605, the housebody and r. wing 1620, doubtless replacing an earlier range. Mullioned windows to the former, mainly mullion-and-transom to the latter but the housebody window altered, formerly of six lights. Hearth passage detectable, blocked by a staircase. Other C17 houses are LOWER BAILEY FOLD, ¼ m. NW of Dean House, with transomed three-plus-three-light housebody window, and GRANGE FOLD, W of the school, a fragment with a few windows with round-headed lights.

EAST AND NORTH

BARKEREND, LAISTERDYKE AND THORNBURY

ST CLEMENT, Barkerend Road. 1892–4 by *E. P. Warren* of Westminster. A quiet building except for the fanciful NW bell-turret, octagonal with curious slate-faced louvres to the bell-openings, elaborate crenellations and, formerly, a spirelet. Small windows with modest Dec tracery. A generally quiet interior too, with moulded nave arcades and boarded wagon roofs, but its effect heightened by fine painted gesso DECORATION to the chancel roof and arcade spandrels by *Morris & Co.*, i.e. *Burne-Jones*, 1900–1. Rich dark colours, the arcade spandrels with large angels. – Also large PAINTINGS l. and r. of the altar by *W. M. Palin*, 1898. – REREDOS. Mosaic work by *Salviati* of Venice. – PULPIT. Free Neo-Jacobean, tapering oddly towards the top, on a low base of cusped miniature arches. – FONT. Of red stone, octagonal, also with miniature arches below the bowl. – STAINED GLASS. E window, chancel NE and S, by *Kempe*, 1900.

ST MARY, Pawson Street, Laisterdyke. 1861 by *Mallinson & Healey* for the Bradford Church Building Society. Workaday Dec with SW tower. Reordered interior.

ST MARY (R.C.), East Parade, close to the city centre. 1874–6 by *Edward Simpson* of Bradford, built to replace the first R.C. church in the town, of 1825. A big bulky mass in C13 French style, with a steeply pitched roof running unbroken over nave and chancel. Prominent clerestory with traceried windows and heavy buttresses, shallow windowless aisles, polygonal apse. Cylindrical arcade piers of polished Irish marble. – Elaborate

PULPIT by *B. Ricot* of Lille, *c.* 1880, timber with high-relief carved panels, a tall openwork spirelet canopy and double steps with traceried balustrade. – WALL PAINTINGS at spandrel level, by *Cracco*, *c.* 1920.

ST PETER (R.C.), Leeds Road. 1932–3 by *C. E. Fox* of Dewsbury. Brick, Lombardic-cum-Quattrocento style. Tall campanile with steep pyramidal cap, prominent in the neighbourhood.

THORNBURY CENTRE, Leeds Old Road, Thornbury. 1998–9 by *Allan Joyce Architects*. Multi-purpose complex providing an Anglican worship area which doubles as a conference hall – the building is on the site of the previous church, 1909, dem. 1991 – and meeting rooms, café, crèche and sports hall. Big curved copper roof on laminated timber beams, ashlar walls over a battered coursed stone plinth. Asymmetrical entrance front with recessed centre, leading to a full-height internal 'street', the spaces to each side unfussily utilitarian.

Former BATHS, Leeds Road. 1904–5 by *F. E. P. Edwards* (City Architect). Free Renaissance, mildly Art Nouveau (cf. Central Baths, City Centre Public Buildings, above).

BOARD SCHOOLS. A distinguished group. FEVERSHAM STREET (former), by *Lockwood & Mawson*, and BARKEREND, Hendford Drive, by *Andrews & Pepper*, are both amongst the earliest, of 1873–4, the former similar to Lilycroft School (*see* Manningham, above), the latter effective C13 'domestic' Gothic, a big T-shaped complex with some simplified plate tracery (cf. All Saints' School, Little Horton, below). Later are two by *C. H. Hargreaves*: the former HANSON HIGHER GRADE SCHOOL, Barkerend Road, 1897, a dominating four-storey block, broadly symmetrical, in Free Renaissance style; and LAPAGE STREET (now Moorfield Centre), 1903, mildly Art Nouveau Jacobean, with sinuous stringcourses on the gables and a prominent tower with ironwork cresting.

LEEDS ROAD HOSPITAL (Fever Hospital), Maudsley Street. 1872 by *Andrews & Pepper*. Plain low separate ward ranges, slightly more ornamented three-storey main block.

TRAM DEPOT (former), Leeds Road, Thornbury. 1900–2. An array of restrainedly shaped Renaissance gables. Offices to r. and workshops to rear 1915.

A few other items along BARKEREND ROAD, E from the inner ring road. On the N side a house with a five-bay ashlar front of *c.* 1800 but some C17 masonry behind. Then on the S side BARKEREND MILLS, in origin an important early steampowered spinning mill, founded *c.* 1815 by James Garnett, but now only a fragment. The principal remaining element is the mill of *c.* 1870, six storeys with fireproof construction, privy turrets at the W corners, stair-tower and truncated chimney at the NE. Power system of complex evolution, reflected in the late C19 projecting end of the engine house at the NW corner, with a big round-headed window, and the contemporary roperace bay, with characteristic sloping roof, against the N end. Then back on the N side, turning the corner with Hendford Drive, FOULIS COTTAGE, by *Barry Parker c.* 1900, an Arts and Crafts import which must always have seemed unlikely in this location. Coursed stone, with a timber-framed window band to the first floor. Pretty recessed entrance with miniature canted bay window adjoining, pretty polygonal oriel on the corner. Hipped roof. Further E again, in BYRON STREET, close to Hanson School (*see* above), BOLDSHAY HALL, a mid-C18 house with a smart five-bay front. Two storeys, pedimented doorway with Gibbs surround, quoins and eaves cornice.

UNDERCLIFFE AND BOLTON

Much inner-city clearance in Undercliffe; quarries and C20 suburbia in Bolton.

ST AUGUSTINE, Otley Road, Undercliffe. 1987 by *Ashfield Architects* of York, incorporating the unfinished NW tower and other parts of the previous church (1875–7 by *T. H. & F. Healey*, big, E.E.). Cheerful scheme with bright paintwork, blockwork walling matched to the colour of the retained masonry and exposed lightweight steel frame. Interior informally divided into a spacious foyer and the church proper with movable furnishings. – Adjoining to the E a small VICARAGE and a garden area with the crossing piers and lower courses of the E apse of the old building, and then the SCHOOL, 1872, enlarged 1911, again by *T. H. & F. Healey*. C13 Gothic with big simple wheel windows.

ST JAMES, Bolton Road. 1876–7 by *Andrews & Pepper*, looking across the valley to their Manningham Mills (*see* Manningham, above). A quite lavish commission, from James Atkinson Jowett of Bolton. C13 Anglo-French (cf. the same architects' Christ Church, Shipley, 1868–9). Tall NW tower and spire, its base forming the porch. Circular windows with plate tracery to the clerestory, a larger version of the same to the cross-gabled organ chamber. Three-bay nave arcades with short cylindrical piers and crocket capitals. In the spandrels angel corbels carrying colonnettes which support the roof-trusses, a rather unwieldy device. – Beautiful REREDOS PANEL of incised alabaster, representing the Last Supper, in the manner of *Clayton & Bell*. Set in an area of mosaic and tilework round the sanctuary. – STAINED GLASS. E window by *Shrigley & Hunt*, 1876. Pleasant muted colours.

UNDERCLIFFE CEMETERY, Undercliffe Lane. On a memorably elevated site overlooking the city. Laid out 1853–4 for the Bradford Cemetery Co. by the surveyor *William Gay*, previously registrar of Leicester cemetery. The two Gothic chapels, 1878 by *Lockwood & Mawson* (replacing the original pair by *Mallinson & Healey*), have been demolished, as have the other buildings. On the site of the Sexton's cottage at the Undercliffe Road entrance a small Italianate LODGE from Bowling Cemetery was re-erected in 1987. Of the MONUMENTS – a gamut of columns, obelisks, pedestals and pinnacles – the grandest are located along the broad spinal promenade which forms the core of Gay's scheme. Most conspicuous, closing its W end, is his big granite obelisk to Joseph Smith, land agent to the cemetery company, †1858. – Then on the l. Mary Mawson †1881, by her sons the architects *W. & R. Mawson* of whom William †1889 is also commemorated. Granite obelisk with incised Egyptian decoration (one of many in the cemetery), a portrait medallion of William and, bizarrely, a cross on the top. – On the r. William Pickard †1869 by *W. Ashton*, the tallest of the columns, of polished granite, surmounted by a figure of Hope. – Further, in a sunken central area on the l., Swithin Anderton †1860 by *I. Thornton*, an Albert Memorial type in local sandstone; and Alfred Illingworth †1907, an Egyptian mastaba in grey granite, with sphinxes guarding the entrance. – Further again, on the l. side of the E part of the promenade, the Behrens monument (Doris Behrens †1887) by *W. & R. Mawson* with carving by *Farmer & Brindley*, an ornate Corinthian aedicule with segmental pediment; and the Holden mausoleum (Jonathan Holden †1906), with a pediment to each side and a little dome on top. – N from here Miles Moulson †1856 by *John Throp* of Leeds, with a female figure leaning on an urn.

PEEL PARK, Bolton Road. Bradford's first public park, laid out *c.* 1853 on the former Bolton House estate, a pleasantly hilly site. Simple Italianate LODGES to S and NW. Beside the central Terrace a bronze STATUE of Sir Robert Peel, 1855 by *W. Behnes* (cf. Leeds, Headingly), which until 1957 stood in the city centre at the intersection of Leeds Road and Hall Ings. Also figures of Autumn and Spring, 1869 and 1877, by *W. Ashton*. To the E the terrace crosses an iron BRIDGE, made in 1857 by the *Bradford Railway Foundry*. Further N, near the lake, a DOORWAY from Bradford Hall, built 1705–7, which stood in Kirkgate, and a Baroque DRINKING FOUNTAIN, 1861. Overlooking the park on the N side, backing onto Lister Lane, is BOLTON HOUSE itself: early C19, modest, with five-bay front and a semicircular bow at one end. Also two Italianate villas of *c.* 1853, one with a belvedere tower.

Former BATHS, Otley Road, near the park S entrance. 1904–5 by *F. E. P. Edwards* (City Architect). Mildly Art Nouveau Free Renaissance (cf. Central Baths, City Centre Public Buildings, above).

CONDITIONING HOUSE (former), Cape Street, N of the city centre. 1900–2 by *F. Wild*, completed after his death in 1901 by the City Architect, *F. E. P. Edwards*. Built by the Bradford Corporation to provide laboratory facilities for checking the moisture content of textiles in order to determine their true length and weight. Large warehouse-like structure of four storeys and basement, with Free Renaissance details over the entrance and at the corner. Close by are MIDLAND MILLS, 1871–3 by *Andrews & Pepper* for Jeremiah Ambler & Sons. Integrated worsted mill much reduced in size. Main elements retained are two multi-storey ranges on either side of Cape Street, the S smartly finished with rock-faced basement and a pavilion-roofed corner tower with iron cresting and delightful emblematic weathervane. Also another block with ornamented turrets, and some north-light sheds.

SWAIN HOUSE PRIMARY SCHOOL, Radcliffe Avenue (½ m. N of St James's church). 1984 by the *City Architect's Department* (project architect *Ron Furniss*), one of the first of a group of near-identical schools built under the Bradford Schools Programme (cf. Manningham, above).

BOLTON OLD HALL, Cheltenham Road (⅜ m. WNW of Swain House School, at the edge of the C20 housing). Main range perhaps of 1627 (datestone now over a doorway in a garden wall), altered, with transomed housebody window of five lights; taller cross-wing to the l. remodelled *c.* 1700, the front end with three cross-windows to the first floor and an upright oval window under a semicircular hood in the gable above, all with broad and close early leading. Three-bay l. flank also with cross-windows, some of them altered, and at the back of the house another lighting the staircase. Inside, two posts remain of a timber-framed partition, or arcade, between the main range and its rear outshut. Housebody fireplace at the end of the room away from the entrance, re-set C17 panelling with enriched frieze, good early C18 staircase with turned balusters.

ECCLESHILL AND GREENGATES

ST LUKE, Harrogate Road, Eccleshill. 1846–8 by *Walker Rawstorne*. Looks at least ten years earlier. Minimally Dec windows. Belfry stage and spire of the w tower replaced in 1975 by an ugly concrete bell-frame. Short chancel added 1912. – STAINED GLASS. E window 1873 by *Heaton, Butler & Bayne*.

ST JOHN THE EVANGELIST, Harrogate Road, Greengates. 1892–3 by *Kendall & Bakes* of Idle. Meagre E.E., aisleless with thin low NW tower and spire.

ECCLESHILL METHODIST CHAPEL, now UKRAINIAN ORTHODOX, Stony Lane. 1854–5 by *James Simpson* of Leeds. Basic Italianate box. Traditional interior with apsidal-ended gallery and box pews, now divided by an iconostasis. ¼ m. N in Lands Lane, off Norman Lane, the previous METHODIST CHAPEL, built in 1775. Typical early Nonconformist scheme, with a pair of tall round-headed windows flanked by doorways each with a smaller window over. The pulpit was between the two tall windows with a gallery round the other three sides. Wesley preached here in 1776.

Former MECHANICS' INSTITUTE, Stone Hall Road, Eccleshill. 1868 by *S. Firth* of Eccleshill. Like another Nonconformist chapel, with pedimented front and two entrances. A focal point of the former village centre.

HAIGH HALL, ¼ m. SW of St John's church, off Haigh Hall Road. Little symmetrical block dated 1710. Single-storey porch with circular window over, restored mullioned windows l. and r.

GEORGE AND DRAGON INN, beside the Aire at Apperley Bridge. Twin-gabled block with mullioned windows, probably C17, and taller gabled wing to the l. dated 1704, much altered and extended mid C19 on. (A Latin inscription on an upstairs mantelpiece records, 'Not for the sake of making a show but as a work of necessity, Samuel Hemingway and Mary his wife enlarged this house, A.D. 1704. These things – food, drink, warmth, light, shelter – are life-sustaining: if you have them, remember to give thanks to God'.)

IDLE

HOLY TRINITY, Town Lane. 1828–30 by *John Oates*, a Commissioners' church. Lancet style, the W tower with clumsy pinnacles. Short chancel added 1864. Galleries on thin iron supports. – Beyond the churchyard to the SW its predecessor the former CHAPEL OF EASE (of Calverley), built in 1630. E window C17 Perp with panel tracery, the others smaller, straight-headed but also with round-arched lights. On the S side two doorways (one renewed in 1884) with ogee heads, early examples of the type in the C17 Pennines. The bellcote on the W gable has gone. Flat ceiling with a cove scooped out of it at the E end to accommodate the head of the window.

ST JOHN THE DIVINE, Idlethorp Way, Thorp Edge. 1960–3 by *Norman Outhwaite*. A focal point in the housing estate. Brick with a broad sweep of roof over deep eaves and low side walls. Small segment-headed window lights in various permutations, built up effectively on the big (ritual) W gable-end. Plain almost detached campanile. Impressive, severe interior with prominent latticework ORGAN CASE.

UNITED REFORMED CHURCH (Congregational), Westfield Lane. 1957 by *John Brunton & Partners*, obtrusively inserted between the wings of the U-shaped Italianate SUNDAY SCHOOL of 1867–8. The first chapel was built in 1717; the present one is the fourth.

IMMANUEL COLLEGE (Secondary School), Leeds Road. 1999–2001 by *Halliday Clark*. From the street a very bitty design with a plethora of different shapes and materials – render, composite panels and vertical cedar boarding, over a random rubble plinth. Built round a courtyard which is bisected by a glazed lattice-girder bridge spanning a sunken outdoor performance area. Two to four storeys.

THACKLEY PRIMARY SCHOOL, Town Lane and Leeds Road. 1883–4 by *Jowett Kendall* for the Idle School Board. Simplified domestic Gothic following the Bradford example.

IDLE MEDICAL CENTRE, Highfield Road. 1993–4 by *VjQ Architects* of Bradford. One of the city's most cheering modern buildings, the striking conceit of a broad three-storey cylinder of smooth reconstituted stone under a flat steel roof, and a two-storey rectangular block running off from it, the former containing the more public spaces and the latter the doctors' 126 consulting rooms. On the axis away from the block the top storey of the cylinder is cut back behind a glazed staircase feature, the breach spanned by a flying segment of the roof perimeter. The block is of stone to the ground floor, plywood cladding on a steel frame above. Mirror-image longitudinal monopitch roofs with a skylight between them.

The centre of Idle, steeply hilly, still retains a village character, mainly later C19 but with a few C17 houses surviving near the church. Immediately N of it THE GRANGE, dated 1632 at the back but apparently refronted in 1734 (date over doorway), the front of three bays, near-symmetrical but still with mullion-and-transom windows. Further W, in WESTFIELD LANE, one with five-light mullioned windows flanking the entrance; and SE off the HIGH STREET, facing onto WELL FOLD, one with a flattened-ogee-headed doorway at the front, transomed stair-case window at the back, and a range adjoining at right angles with a doorhead dated 1664. ⅜ m. NNE in LEEDS ROAD two pairs of semis, 1906, roughcast Arts and Crafts Old English (cf. Wilmer Drive, Heaton); and E of them in PARK ROAD, PARK HOUSE, 1752, five-bay block with rusticated quoins.

At THORP EDGE, ½ m. SE, eight-storey blocks of council flats, 1955.

SOUTH-WEST AND SOUTH

LITTLE HORTON AND UNIVERSITY

Variegated inner-city area, mainly C19–C20, but at Little Horton Green retaining an enclave of extraordinarily rustic character, with big gardens and open fields to N and S – and formerly also a notable group of C17 buildings in the local manner; but the two main examples, Horton Hall and Horton Old Hall, have been demolished.

Places of worship

ALL SAINTS, Little Horton Green. 1861–4, the *chef d'oeuvre* of *Mallinson & Healey*, completed after Healey's death in 1863 by his sons *T. H. & F. Healey*. The gift of Sir Francis Sharp Powell of Horton Hall. A big, lavish and impressive church very much in the manner of George Gilbert Scott. Ashlar. Commanding SE tower and spire with prominent lucarnes. Tall nave with transepts, aisles and N and S porches, polygonally apsed chancel. Tracery in the style of *c.* 1280–1300, the clerestory windows in the form of spheric triangles *à la* Westminster Abbey, those to the apse crowned by French-style gablets rising through the parapet. Richly moulded nave arcades with foliage capitals. – PULPIT. With fine iron and brass super-structure, by *Skidmore* of Coventry, on a low marble base. –

Good wrought-iron SCREEN to the organ chamber, also by him. – STAINED GLASS. An excellent scheme by *Clayton & Bell*, 1879, which complements the architecture most success-fully – apse, chancel N side (three windows) and S side (one), S transept S, N transept N and E. – SCHOOL. 1863, also by *Mallinson & Healey* for the same patron. C13 domestic Gothic and notably ambitious, foreshadowing the form of some of the Bradford Board Schools. T-shaped, with a tower (now without its spirelet) over one of the porches.

ST OSWALD, Christopher Street. 1890–1902 by *T. H. & F. Healey*, also the gift of Sir Francis Sharp Powell. NE tower with broach spire, triple-gabled cross-section (cf. St Barnabas Heaton). Dense somewhat fanciful Flamboyant tracery. No division between nave and chancel except inside just a thicker roof-truss than the others. – Some early C20 STAINED GLASS, including N aisle second from W by *Shrigley & Hunt*, 1912. – Good VICARAGE of 1904 opposite, with some mildly Art Nouveau details including a broad inviting porch.

ST JOSEPH (R.C.), Pakington Street. 1885–7 by *Edward Simpson*. A highly idiosyncratic version of E.E. Tall and generally quite plain, but with some very curious tracery details. Nave and chancel of equal height. Paired gabled transept elements, each with two big lancets and a vesica over. Windowless aisles, fussily gableted half-octagonal baptistry. Spacious interior, not unimpressive. Rather crude quatrefoil piers between the transept bays.

ANNESLEY METHODIST CHURCH, Little Horton Lane, now SERBIAN ORTHODOX. 1865–6 by *Andrews & Pepper*. Gothic, with a big traceried window in the gable-end and a quite elegant tower and spire flanking it. Gallery round three sides and two tiers of iron columns.

HORTON MORAVIAN CHURCH, Little Horton Lane. 1838. A neat little box in simple lancet style, with crowstepped gable-end. W gallery on thin iron supports.

LITTLE HORTON CONGREGATIONAL CHAPEL, Thornton Lane, now SHREE HINDU TEMPLE. 1874–5 by *T. H. & F. Healey*. Restrained Italianate with a pyramid-capped cam-panile. The Sunday School was on the ground floor and the chapel itself above.

MANNVILLE METHODIST NEW CONNECTION CHAPEL (former). *See* Bradford College, below.

RICHMOND-SHEARBRIDGE METHODIST CHAPEL, Shear-bridge Road, now ISLAMIC MISSION COLLEGE. 1906–7 by *Edgar Parkinson*. An Art Nouveau design, with little panels of stylized bas-relief foliage on either side of the entrance and good iron railings in front. Battered buttresses and squat turrets. Interior now subdivided. Plaster tunnel-vault with more foliage panels along the edges.

TRINITY BAPTIST CHAPEL, Little Horton Lane, now YMCA, 1856–7 by *Andrews & Delaunay*. Italianate, with giant pedi-ment. Three round-headed doorways in concave panelled reveals.

UNITARIAN CHAPEL, Russell Street. 1971 by *Kitson, Pyman & Partners* of Leeds, to replace the Chapel Lane Chapel (1867–8 by *Andrews & Pepper*) which was demolished in 1969 to make way for the new Magistrates' Court (*see* City Centre, Public Buildings, above). In a quiet backwater of the inner city. A quiet design too, of coursed stone with a pyramid roof over the worship area.

Public buildings

BRADFORD UNIVERSITY, Great Horton Road. Not one of the more memorable campuses architecturally. Developed from the Bradford Technical College (which, however, continued to have a separate existence, *see* Bradford College, below) as the Bradford Institute of Technology, established in 1957, and made a university in 1966. The first structure, the RICHMOND BUILDING, 1960–5 by the *City Architect's Department* adjoining the Technical College, is a shapeless thirteen-storey lump which rises to the occasion only in a literal sense. Behind it the WORKSHOP BLOCK with concrete barrel north-light roof. Then in 1964 the *Building Design Partnership* was appointed consultant architects and in 1966 a development plan was produced for the area immediately to the W, across Richmond Road, a problematic but potentially rewarding site with a steep-sided valley crossing it from SW to NE. BDP proposed a quite dense layout disposed round a variety of courtyards, with a central pedestrian spine running N–S across the valley and the buildings themselves of two generic types, academic and residential. In execution, however, the scheme was much reduced, the N half of the site beyond Longside Lane being developed for different purposes, and other modifications made which suggest a collective failure of confidence.

The landscaping, and individual buildings unless otherwise specified, are by *BDP*. At the E corner the HORTON BUILDING, 1966–7 by the *City Architect's Department* again. W of this the best work here, the CHESHAM BUILDING of 1966–70, the only part of BDP's original academic schema to be erected. Commendably crisp design in exposed aggregate with black timber window details on a reinforced-concrete frame, the main element starting as four storeys but with extra floors taking up the fall in the ground. Centre section crowned by a heavy projecting top hamper containing lecture theatres, a feature which would have been repeated at regular intervals if the system had been extended further. W again across the pedestrian spine are the first two residential blocks, UNIVERSITY HALL and BRADFORD HALL, 1970–1, three to six storeys, with a contrasting broken surface treatment of projecting window bays and contrastingly brick-built: in front of them the SPORTS HALL complex, 1973. But the switch to more brick for the rest of the academic buildings nullifies the contrast and represents a retreat into blandness.

The J. B. PRIESTLEY LIBRARY, 1974–5, is well sited at the core of the campus, straddling the valley with the pedestian walkway running along it halfway up, but is otherwise just a plain box with blind canted bays to the front;* beyond it the COMMUNAL BUILDING, 1975–6, mainly below walkway level, irregular with a light well in the middle and extensive use of chamfered corners. Finally the PEMBERTON and ASHFIELD BUILDINGS, 1990–1, a silly self-conscious affair with concave front and striped brickwork, dwarfed by the adjoining exposed stump of the Chesham Building at its tallest point; and the IPI BUILDING in Richmond Road, 2003 by *Rance Booth & Smith*, with angular glazed staircase compartment. In front of the Library a STATUE – 'Reunion' – of two kneeling figures, 1977 by *Josefina de Vasconcellos*.

The other residential blocks on the site are by *Wimpey Construction Ltd* (design & build), pebbledashed pauperized versions of BDP's. SHEARBRIDGE GREEN, 1977 at the SW corner, is disposed round an informal space above the valley, LONGSIDE and KIRKSTONE HALLS, 1984–91, along the N side, are more regular. The PHOENIX BUILDING, in the valley at the W end, is a C19 mill successfully reused. Further away, in Laisterbridge Lane, the REVIS BARBER and DENNIS BELLAMY HALLS, 1963–4 by the *City Architect's Department*, nine-storey slabs like municipal blocks of flats, and a hall of residence in *BDP*'s striped brickwork, 1993.

BRADFORD COLLEGE (former Technical College). A group of buildings in and about Great Horton Road. On the corner with Carlton Street the OLD BUILDING, 1880–2 by *Hope & Jardine*. Fine and fulsome Italianate. Central tower with tall octagonal lantern stage and domical top. To the r. six bays of giant Corinthian half-columns starting from ground level, but to the l. only pilasters and the windows also different. The reason is that the whole of the r. part is occupied by the main hall. Gallery with ornate front, two tiers of cast-iron columns, panelled ceiling. Many extensions: to the rear 1893 etc., to the l. 1930–3. Across the road the GROVE LIBRARY, built as the Mannville Methodist New Connection chapel, 1877 by *Hill & Swann*. Also Italianate, in a lighter mode. Two-storey front with half-height Corinthian portico and broken-based pediment. To the l. an addition of *c.* 1904 when the building became the College of Art. French accented with pavilion-roofed tower. Re-fitted as library 1988. In Carlton Street the LISTER BUILDING, 1909–11 by *R. G. Kirkby* (City Architect). Beaux-Arts classical with projecting centre of banded masonry framing columns *in antis*. Modern extensions at each end. Back in Great Horton Road two incursions by the *City Architect's Department*, the WESTBROOK BUILDING, 1964–5, a null slab, and the RANDALL WELL BUILDING, 1972–6, small-scale Brutalism.

---

*Garish entrance foyer added 1995.

ST ANDREW'S SCHOOL, Listerhills Road, now Interfaith Education Centre. 1857–8 by *Mallinson & Healey*. Gothic, a nicely Picturesque composition with tower and spirelet and good Dec tracery (St Andrew's church, 1853 by the same architects, dem. 1971).

ST LUKE'S HOSPITAL, Little Horton Lane. 1852 by *Lockwood & Mawson*. Built as the Workhouse, a quite elegant specimen in their simplified Italianate style (cf. Saltaire). Three storeys, with a little square belvedere over the centre and short cross-wings crowned by low octagonal lanterns. The detached two-storey entrance pavilion has been demolished. Other buildings *c.* 1860 to the rear, 1904 and 1905 to N and S, and 1989–93 by the *Percy Thomas Partnership*, the first phase of a big redevelopment plan.

Housing

From the city centre LITTLE HORTON LANE runs S into an area developed mainly in the 1840s and 1850s. Along Little Horton Lane itself a mixture of detached villas and short two- and three-storey terraces, the villas predominantly to a basic three-bay classical formula in ashlar with columned porches, e.g. No. 30, the first on the r., 1850 by *John Dixon*. But No. 54 has a wing to one side with pediment and big bold Serliana; and No. 68, the former St John's Rectory, 1852 by *Mallinson & Healey*, is appropriately Tudor Gothic, with steep gables and mullioned windows.* In the streets to l. and r. more modest two-storey terraces, the earliest and best in ANN PLACE (E) and EDMUND STREET (W), *c.* 1850, with a pattern of advancing and receding wall-planes. Also on the W side in SAWREY PLACE the MELBOURNE ALMSHOUSES, 1845, one storey in bad minimal Gothic, and in MELBOURNE PLACE more villas of the 1840s, including a semi-detached pair with obelisk gatepiers. Further E and SE, N and S of PARK ROAD, a zone of high-rise council flats – towers and Y-plan blocks – 1960–6.

Further SW is LITTLE HORTON GREEN. Horton Hall and Horton Old Hall stood side by side facing All Saints' church (*see* above). On the site of the former, HORTON HALL CLOSE, sheltered housing for the elderly, *c.* 1986 by the *Barton Willmore Partnership*, coursed stone, friendly broken composition. Surviving C17 houses are Nos. 4–9 – unpretentious, of hall range and cross-wing with mullioned windows of two to five lights – and then after some C19 cottages, LITTLE HORTON HALL, which is more ambitious. Double pile with two-gabled front and the entrance in the r. flank, directly into the house-body. Mullion-and-transom windows, of five lights to the parlour and chambers, of six and two to the housebody, the two-light at the chimney end. (The kitchen, behind the house-

---

*The church, in Manchester Road, 1838–9 by *R.H. Sharp*, dem. *c.* 1873; its successor, in Little Horton Lane, 1871–3 by *T.H. & F. Healey*, dem. 1970.

body, has a firehood.) Further on again, No. 41, a pleasantly detailed laithe house dated 1755, the house double-fronted, with mullioned windows but the mullions now unchamfered.

In the neighbourhood of the University there is less to see. CLAREMONT, to the s, across Great Horton Road, was one of the smartest addresses in mid-Victorian Bradford, laid out 1851 and built up *c.* 1853–61, by *Eli Milnes* amongst others, but now eroded by demolitions. Large semi-detached villa pairs, with Italianate details of varying literacy, and a variety of bay-window shapes. To the w, in PRESTON STREET, close to St Andrew's School, ST ANDREW'S VILLAS, superior back-to-backs, 1864 by *T. C. Hope* for the St Andrew's Building Club. Arranged in blocks of four, each block looking from the front like a pair of conventional semis. Minimal Gothic detail; gables, some crowstepped.

Textile mills

BRIGGELLA MILLS, Little Horton Lane, s of Little Horton Green. Integrated worsted mill, *c.* 1868–75 by *Thomas Barker* for J. Briggs & Co. Handsome warehouse range forming the street front, five storeys with ornamented former cart entrance in the centre; gabled boiler house, octagonal chimney and plain four-storey spinning mill behind; weaving shed with north-light sawtooth roof to N.

LEGRAMS MILL, Legrams Lane. 1871 by *Lockwood & Mawson* for George Hodgson. An ambitious scheme designed as an integrated mill but executed in a reduced form for spinning only. Big warehouse running along the street, in style reminiscent of the same architects' Saltaire Mills (q.v.). Ornate belvedere-capped privy towers at each corner, rusticated ground floor, taking-in doors at the rear, under a pediment, and a later series in the E end framed by pilasters. Fireproof construction to the ground floor only. North-light combing shed behind and then the spinning mill, of similar dimensions to the warehouse but completed only in 1903, with a rope-race bay of that date at the W end. Weaving sheds not built, truncated square chimney.

GREAT HORTON

Tight-knit mill-village centre on rising ground, surrounded by later development: a subsidiary focus at Lidget Green, downhill to the N.

Places of worship and public buildings

ST COLUMBA, Horton Grange Road. 1899–1902 by *T. H. & F. Healey*, the gift of Lady Powell of Horton Hall. Sub-

Pearsonian E.E., large and tall. Nave and chancel of equal height, lean-to (ritual) W porch, octagonal bell-turret on N side. Slightly chilly interior, the four W bays of the nave divided off up to impost level to form a parish room. Chancel N arcade openings divided into paired sub-arches with sculpture (by *Farmer & Brindley*) in the spandrels. – Good wrought-iron GRILLE to the organ chamber. – STAINED GLASS. A very effective set by *Kempe & Co.*, 1906–21, E window, NE chapel (four windows), N outer chapel (two), S chapel SE. Silver and blue the predominant tones. – S chapel SW by *A. K. Nicholson*, 1937.

82 ST JOHN THE EVANGELIST, Walshaw Street. 1871–4 by *T. H. & F. Healey*. A big lofty church of their usual coursed gritstone with ashlar dressings, in C13 Norman Gothic style. Strong clean outline. Very fine tall SE tower and spire (completed 1885), the tower unbuttressed and the spire with square Normandy-type corner pinnacles and one tier of big lucarnes. Semicircular apse, nave and chancel in one. New roof and W end partly rebuilt after a fire in 1956. Broad three-bay nave arcades on squat cylindrical piers with attached shafts. At the E end of the S aisle a pair of doorways under a single arch, with plate tracery in the spandrel above. – ¼ m. S in Southfield Lane is the church's predecessor, the former BELL CHAPEL of 1806. Plain rectangle with gabled ends, big Venetian window at the back.

ST WILFRID, St Wilfrid's Road, Lidget Green. 1905 by *Temple Moore*, and a major work of his. A big, quite simply detailed rectangle of pale stone, under a great expanse of red tile roof sweeping down over the aisles without a break. No break either between nave and chancel, free Dec windows with unobtrusively varied tracery patterns, tiny gabled bellcote at the NE corner. Light spacious interior of great beauty, just three main bays plus a narrower one at each end. Tall wave-moulded arcades, plastered wagon roof of pointed section with diaphragm ribs, transverse arches to the aisles. Relieving arches round the walls, and Temple Moore's mannerism of miniature wall passages at sill level housing the heating pipes. – Fine timber ALTAR FRONTAL, painted and gilded, a gift from the architect. – Across the road to the N the former SCHOOL, 1838 by *W. Andrews* of Bradford. Three bays, lancet style with engaging mask label stops.

GRANGE CONGREGATIONAL CHAPEL (former), Great Horton Road. 1892 by *T. C. Hope*. A revival of the Wesleyan octagon form. Jacobean ecclesiastical, the exposed sides with a gable and a species of traceried window. Also a tower in Scottish Baronial style, with little cylindrical bartizans and an (evidently truncated) octagonal top stage.

GREAT HORTON CONGREGATIONAL CHAPEL (former), off Great Horton Road. 1851–2 but still entirely in the Georgian tradition. Two-storey elevation with a central Venetian window to each floor and a pair of pedimented doorways. Interior subdivided but plain D-shaped gallery retained. Alongside is the former SUNDAY SCHOOL, 1868 by *Paull & Robinson*, a much

more assertive building, taller and standing forward to the
street. Gothic portal and above it a tower with stumpy spire.

GREAT HORTON METHODIST CHAPEL, Great Horton Road.
1814, 'renovated' and enlarged 1862 by *Samuel Jackson*.
The original building is barely discernible, the later work
consisting of both a handsome new front – a pedimented
Corinthian portico *in antis* between single flanking bays – and
an extension to the rear which more than doubles its length.
Interior comprehensively modernized, late C20.

TETLEY STREET BAPTIST CHAPEL, Horton Grange Road, now
JESUS CHRIST APOSTOLIC. 1903–4. A stunted steeple at a
busy crossroads.

SCHOLEMOOR CEMETERY, Necropolis Road, Lidget Green.
Opened 1860, Bradford's first municipal cemetery. Layout by
C. Gott, the Borough Surveyor, chapels (dem.), and the pleas-
ant Gothic REGISTRAR'S HOUSE beside the Necropolis Road
entrance, by *Eli Milnes*. In the Jewish burial ground a tiny
SYNAGOGUE with Star of David window in each gable-end.
CREMATORIUM, 1905 by the City Architect *F. E. P. Edwards*.
Arts and Crafts Perp with a tall tower.

BRANCH LIBRARY, Cross Lane. 1912–3 by *W. Williamson* (City
Architect). Prettily Art Nouveau Jacobean, crowned by a
timber flèche. Segmental barrel ceiling inside (cf. Manningham Branch Library, above).

GREAT HORTON BOARD SCHOOL, Cross Lane (now St
Oswald's Primary). 1884–6 by *Morley & Woodhouse*, one of two
which were the products of architectural competitions. Sumptuous Free Renaissance, built on the 'Prussian system', i.e.
with classrooms surrounding a central hall. The other is
GRANGE, Spencer Road, 1903 by *T. C. Hope*, in a quirky
version of the same style, with elaborate gables and eccentric
towers.

NUTTER ORPHANAGE (former), Cousen Road. 1888 by
T. C. Hope. Hard Jacobean with stiffly shaped gables and low
battlemented tower.

Perambulation: Housing and textile mills

The approach from the city centre is by GREAT HORTON ROAD.
Shortly before the junction with Cross Lane, set back on the
r., is CANNON MILL, 1855 by *Andrews & Delaunay* incorporating fragments of its predecessor, founded 1826. Spinning and
weaving by tenants in multiple occupation, on a 'room and
power' basis. Four-storey spinning mill with smart show front
in restrained classical style. Pedimented privy and staircase
turrets, pilaster-strips at the corners, engine house in three l.
bays distinguished by vermiculated rustication to the ground
floor and round-headed windows above. Fireproof construction on main floors. Altered weaving sheds with north-light
roofs behind, new engine house of 1880 further to l. Chimney,
and detached warehouse, at right angles to r., both demolished.

In front of the mill, a planned area of WORKERS' HOUSING (Union Road, Vine Street, Falcon Street, Hart Street, Lime Street), 1864–5 by *John Simpson* for G. G. Tetley, the mill's proprietor. Two-storey terraces stepping up the steep hillside, some with shared 'tunnels' through to the back yards, and pavilion-like corner shops at the main road end of each.

After the junction, on the l. is a sequence of the plain early C19 cottage terraces characteristic of the village centre; and on the r., round the former Congregational Chapel (*see* above), the BAKES STREET and HUNT YARD housing development, *c.* 1978 by *John Brunton & Partners*, terraces of reused coursed stone intimately disposed round yards with pedestrian access. In CROSS LANE itself, on the l. CROSS LANE MILLS, early spinning mill, begun 1821 for Eli Suddards. Basic three-storey ten-bay range with Venetian windows in the gable-ends. Beyond on the l. in COUSEN ROAD, an altered C17 house with doorway dated 1657; then in the maze of cottage-lined back streets to the r., Nos. 15–27 PERSEVERANCE LANE, an example of a type of early C19 workers' housing common in the S Bradford area, the row of single-storey 'low' houses. Originally a single room inside. Two-light windows with unchamfered mullions, tall chimneys.

Back via Southfield Lane to GREAT HORTON ROAD; and on the opposite side, in front of St John's church (*see* above), Nos. 634–636, dated 1697, a small double pile with central entrance, upright oval window over it, and mullioned windows originally all of six lights. Next to it the KINGS ARMS, with a Vanbrughian rusticated doorway dated 1739; then BROOKS-BANK HOUSE, 1746 but a notably *retardataire* design. The general idea of an C18 composition is present, in the broad symmetry of the scheme and the hipped roof with little modillions to the eaves. But the original doorhead – now inserted above the later C18 pedimented doorcase – is still of a traditional flat-arched shape, the windows are still mullioned and transomed, and although they appear at first to be symmetrically arranged those to the r. of the entrance are still emphasized housebody-wise by their size: they are of six lights, all the others of five. The r. side elevation is symmetrical too, with a big transomed staircase window flanked by smaller cross-windows, but the apparent block-like shape of the house is misleading. It is a half-H, with gabled wings to the rear. Then on the other side of the road again HARRIS COURT MILL, 1861 etc., a modest-sized spinning mill on a cramped site. Four-storey range with pyramid-roofed stair-turret towards the mill yard, rope-race bay against one end, and engine house at right angles. Truncated octagonal chimney, detached office building at the yard entrance.

Finally three OUTLIERS. The houses are HILL END HOUSE, ⅝ m. WSW in Windermere Road, 1714 and more what might be expected of its date than Brooksbank House, a five-bay block with quoins and former cross-windows; and WEST-FIELD, ¾ m. N at the junction of Horton Grange Road and

Legrams Lane (*see* Tetley Street Baptist Chapel, above), a domestic Gothic villa of 1873 by *Andrews & Pepper*. The mill is BANK TOP MILL, Beacon Road, high up ½ m. further WSW, 1860–6 by *Milnes & France* replacing a mill of 1817, but much altered and reduced. The main surviving feature is a pair of grand Italianate entrance gateways dated 1864.

CLAYTON

ST JOHN THE BAPTIST, Clayton Lane. 1849–50 by *Mallinson & Healey*. Dec with plain W tower. Nave clerestory of big trefoils. Interior much beautified 1914 etc. in marble and mosaic. – STAINED GLASS. A very motley collection including E window by *Barnett, c.* 1860; one in the N aisle by *Kempe*, 1898; W window 1918 by *Shrigley & Hunt*. – Former SCHOOL across the road to the S. 1859, also by *Mallinson & Healey*. Gothic, symmetrical.

Former THORNTON VIEW HOSPITAL, Thornton View Road, uphill ⅝ m. SSE, overlooking the village. Built as the North Bierley Union Workhouse, 1858 by *Lockwood & Mawson*, now a school. Ambitious scheme similar to the same architects' Bradford Workhouse (now St Luke's Hospital: *see* Little Horton, above) but a little more floridly detailed. Detached two-storey entrance range, long three-storey main building with gabled centre and two staircase turrets, and a further range beyond that. Tall octagonal chimney.

HIGHGATE MILL, Highgate Road, Clayton Heights (¾ m. S). Modest early C19 spinning mill preceded by a handsome Italianate rusticated archway of 1865 (cf. Bank Top Mill, Great Horton, above), set between two contemporary terraces of workers' housing. The mill is a plain three-storey block with an extension at one end dated 1861 and 1862. Square chimney.

BOWLING AND BIERLEY

Broad swathe of the inner and outer city, industrial and residential, without dominant focal points but containing the best early house within the built-up area of the city.

ST CHRISTOPHER, Holme Wood Road, Holme Wood. Housing estate church of 1967–8 (church hall 1961–2) by *Francis Johnson*. Brick.

ST JOHN, Wakefield Road, East Bowling. 1840–2 by *R. H. & S. Sharp* for the Bowling Iron Co. – hence the extensive use of cast iron. The Company's engineer, *Fred Stott*, assisted. Lancet style but quite solid-looking, with transepts, aisles, and W tower with spire. The interior is treated as a hall church and is vaulted in masonry throughout, the whole a rather enjoyable mixture of the structurally serious and the churchwardenly. The iron-work includes the colonnettes to the W doorway and the piers – with detached shafts – supporting the vault. Trefoil-headed blind arcading round the sanctuary, with a broader cusped ogee behind the altar. Gallery (altered) at the w end. – MONUMENT. William Field †1861, by *J. Edwards* of Bradford. Tablet with urn.

ST JOHN THE EVANGELIST, Rooley Lane, Bierley. 1766 by *Carr* for Richard Richardson of Bierley Hall as a private chapel. Enlarged and altered C19. A neat Palladian box in sandstone ashlar, pedimented at each end. On the w pediment a bell-turret with attached Tuscan colonettes, domical cap and obelisk spirelet. Below is a relieving arch containing a doorway with heavy Gibbs surround, fronted by an early C19 Tuscan porch moved to this position in 1879 from the middle of the s side. That has three more arches now all framing round-headed windows, and the e end a correspondingly overarched Venetian window. To the n a big transept in matching style added in 1821: more crudely detailed NE extension of 1830. Inside, a shallow w gallery with balustraded front, breaking forward over Doric columns. Deeper N gallery (now blocked off) occupying the transept, with similar balustrade and cast-iron supports. – PULPIT. C18, 'enriched with carving' in 1905. – Two large PAINTINGS, C18, formerly l. and r. of the altar, now in the transept. Before the chapel was built they were at Holy Trinity, Low Moor (*see* below). – STAINED GLASS. 1872 etc. by *G. J. Baguley*, an unfortunate intrusion. – MONUMENT. Anna Maria Clayton †1845, by *Waudby* of York. Wall tablet, still mid-C18 in character.

ST STEPHEN, St Stephen's Road, West Bowling. 1859–60 by *Mallinson & Healey* for the Bradford Church Building Society, transepts added and chancel extended 1886–7. An unexpected lurch into roguishness. C13 style with plate and bar tracery. No clerestory, but big gabled dormers instead. NW tower with helm cap. Polygonal apse with gablets over the windows. Interior dominated by the dark trussed rafter roof. – STAINED GLASS. Apse windows, and three in the s aisle, by *Powell Bros.* of Leeds, 1887–91, 1892 and 1904. – w window, a strange theatrical Christ in Glory, 1907 by *Jones & Willis*.

ST ANNE (R.C.) (former), Guy Street, Broomfields. 1890 by *Edward Simpson*. In the same vein as his St Joseph (*see* Little Horton, above) but smaller and starker, without the transepts. Octagonal bell-turret at the (ritual) e end, some odd tracery to the two big lancets at the other.

PROSPECT METHODIST CHAPEL, Usher Street, East Bowling, now GURU NANAK SIKH TEMPLE. 1871. In front the octagonal PROSPECT HALL of 1912, brick and stone with Baroque touches.

CITY TECHNOLOGY COLLEGE, Ripley Street, West Bowling, 1991 by the *John Brunton Partnership*. Eyecatching in blotchy brick with jagged monopitch roofs, centred on a 'mall' stepping up the slope of the site with CLASP system classroom blocks of one and two storeys to each side. A monument to its time. Nearby, NEWBY PRIMARY SCHOOL, Ryan Street, 1985 by the *City Architect's Department* (project architect *Ron*

Furniss), one of the near-identical group built under the Bradford Schools Programme (cf. Manningham, above).

DOUGLAS MILL, Bowling Old Lane, West Bowling. Spinning mill, mainly 1880–5 by *M. Brayshaw*, for Mitchell Bros. Partly demolished, the main surviving element the massive wool warehouse, a classic multi-storey block of five floors and twenty-four by seven bays, rehabilitated as offices 2004–5 by *Allen Tod Architects*. Staircase tower at the NW corner crowned by a pavilion roof with iron cresting; pediment-like gable-ends; and a pediment over the central three bays of the W flank, the middle one occupied by taking-in doors with rustic jambs and voussoirs. Two-storey lodge building to W: the plain older mill was behind this.

BOLLING HALL, Bowling Hall Road. Now a museum. From the Bolling family the property passed to the Tempests in 1497, then from the mid C17 onwards through a variety of ownerships. U-shaped, with the wings projecting to the N. The oldest part is the three-storey medieval tower at the SW corner, and on the site of the present hall range to the E of this would have been a timber-framed hall some members from which remain in the present building. Also probably medieval in origin is the W wing, behind the tower, but largely rebuilt perhaps in the early C16. The rest essentially of the C17, including a second tower at the SE corner to balance the medieval one, but with some notable early C18 alterations – of which more shortly – and the E wing remodelled 1779–80 by *John Carr* for Captain Charles Wood.

The medieval tower is of thin irregularly coursed stonework and has a garderobe turret at the SW corner but no other early details visible. The centrepiece of the S elevation is a spectacular hall window of five-plus-five lights with two transoms (stonework renewed); but Samuel Buck's view of *c.* 1720 shows two tiers of ordinary mullion-and-transom windows at this point. So both the window and the full-height great hall behind it must have been created after that – presumably for the early C18 owner Francis Lindley who died in 1734 – a remarkable case of architectural traditionalism. Symmetrically to each side of the window is a plain doorway with a cross-window over it, then higher up is the craziest assemblage of motifs, apparently introduced a few years later in the mid C18. Immediately above the hall window, indeed resting on it, is a semicircular one, above that a blind ogee and over the cross-windows smaller semicircles, also blind (the mullions are C20 insertions). To the l. of all this is a two-storey canted bay window of eight-by-two lights to each stage, which is shown in Buck's view; then next to the SW tower a narrow bay, perhaps corresponding to the cross-passage of the medieval house, with another cross-window and a semicircular and a circular window above. To the r. is a broad canted bay which is the end of Carr's remodelled E wing, and beyond that the SE tower with mullion-and-transom windows.

Further N, the outer flank of the W wing is of thin rough masonry like the medieval tower, the rebuilt fabric to N and E

of large squared blocks. Gable-end attic window probably early
C16, with three ogee-headed lights, but could it be reused? The
other windows C17, apparently all insertions. Rebuilt against
the outer flank a C17 doorway, flattened-ogee-headed. The E
wing has Carr's sash windows in the end, his staircase window
on the outer flank and mullion-and-transom windows on the
inner. The hall range has been doubled in depth by the addition of a second line of rooms along this side, still in the C17
but shortly after the main campaign. Mullion-and-transom
windows and a C19 Tudor-style doorway in the middle bay. It
replaced one with a segmental pediment.

The house is now entered through the base of the SW tower,
into the kitchen, in the W wing, with big inserted C17 fireplace.
The room above has an early C18 chimneypiece with a slightly
fanciful overmantel painting of the house from the N, and next
to this the first-floor room in the tower has richly moulded
ceiling beams and a garderobe in the turret. In the hall range
the first-floor room behind the C17 canted bay – the best in
the house – has a C17 timber chimneypiece with superimposed
orders and a charming mid-C17 plaster ceiling with strapwork-
like bands and between them branches with fruit, flowers and
perching birds (the ceiling frieze, and the portraits in the overmantel, are not original). In the room below simple early C18
panelling, and nearby some elements of timber framing, not
all *in situ*. Then the hall itself, finished in a plain C18 manner
with a modillion cornice and a gallery along the back wall only.
In the window an important body of armorial STAINED GLASS,
mainly early C16 of the Tempest phase, removed from the
house in the early C19 and returned in 1949. In the E wing are
Carr's drawing room, with an Adamesque ceiling, and behind
it the cantilevered main staircase with iron balustrade.

In the grounds N of the house one wall of a barn, presumably C17, which was otherwise demolished in 1928. The ogee-
headed doorway is probably mid-C18.

NEW HALL, Rooley Lane (the outer ring road). Now Golf Club.
1672, built by a younger son of the Richardson family of
Bierley Hall. H-plan with gabled wings, parlours at the front
of both and kitchen behind in the r. Two-storey porch half-
absorbed into the r. wing, with heavily moulded entrance, date
panel with scrolly decoration, and similar scrolls to the coping
of the parapet. Transomed windows, that to the hall of three-
plus-three-plus-three lights, the l. parlour's originally the same
but altered, the best chamber's of four-plus-four, others three-
plus-three. Continuous dripstones, the upper interrupted by a
few more scrolls at the r. end. Kitchen doorway on the r. flank
with elaborate ornamented doorhead. Chimneys lopped,
additions at back and to l. Interior altered. Segment-headed
fireplace at the low end of the hall.

YORKSHIRE BUILDING SOCIETY HEAD OFFICE, Rooley
Lane. Across the road from New Hall, with a wide view over
the city. 1990–2 by *Abbey Hanson Rowe*. Weightily symmetrical, a squat H in pale brick with ashlar dressings under a big

hipped roof. Three storeys, various semicircular bows. Glazed gabled centrepieces on both sides, opening onto a full-height 'atrium' with abstract mural sculpture in brick and green glass cullet by *Judith Bluck*. L-shaped four-storey additional block in the same manner, 1996–7.

PICTURE PALACE (former), Tong Street (Wakefield Road), Dudley Hill, 1912 by *Howorth & Howorth* of Cleckheaton. Red brick and white faience, with broken segmental pediment.

FROGDEN HOUSE, Shetcliffe Lane, Bierley (⅝ m. s of Bierley church), facing away from the road. 1625, with parlour cross-wing, no service end, and former entrance (now window) into the outshut behind the housebody. Over the doorway a cornice on brackets with shields above. Mullioned windows, that to the housebody of seven lights. (In the cross-wing a panelled partition with decorative frieze and built-in cupboard.)

BIERLEY HALL has been demolished.

WIBSEY, BANKFOOT AND BUTTERSHAW

The w part of the sprawling Bierley township, its focal point the former village centre of Wibsey, up on the rim of the city's bowl.

ST PAUL, St Paul's Avenue, Wibsey. 1838 by *Walker Rawstorne*, paid for by John Hardy of the Low Moor Iron Co. A thinner version of Holy Trinity, Low Moor (*see* below), lancet style with shallow transepts and w tower and spire.

ST MATTHEW, Carr Bottom Road, Bankfoot. 1848–9 by *Mallinson & Healey*, largely also at the expense of the Hardy family. Dec, quite modest, with a pretty bellcote on the w gable. Aisles but no clerestory. – STAINED GLASS. Includes E window by *Barnett*, 1851, and s aisle second from E by *Wailes & Strang*, 1900. – Across the road the former SCHOOL and SCHOOL HOUSE, now the Church Hall. 1853, simple Gothic also by *Mallinson & Healey*.

ST THERESA AND ST WINEFRIDE (R.C.), St Paul's Avenue. 1973 by *John H. Black*. Irregular pentagon in yellow brick. Crudely detailed.

RICHARD DUNN SPORTS CENTRE, Rooley Avenue, Bankfoot. 1974–7 by the *City Architect's Department* with *White, Young & Partners*, consultant structural engineers. Giant big top of double-skinned aluminium, with tensioned cable and lightweight girder supports. Conspicuous on the city's s skyline.

BUTTERSHAW HIGH SCHOOL, Reevy Road West. 1955 by the City Architect, *W. Clifford Brown*. Complex group of three- and four-storey blocks. Later extensions.

METHODIST SUNDAY SCHOOL (former), off Wibsey High Street (s side). *c.* 1854, plain low range still Georgian in character, with many-paned sash windows (the chapel dem.).

In CHAPEL FOLD, Wibsey, a track off the s end of St Enoch's Road, a c17 former open hall, with five-plus-five-light transomed window and big segment-headed fireplace at the

Bradford, Faxfleet Street Estate, living room.
Engraving, 1904

entrance end. Almost detached kitchen block set back to r. Also
in Wibsey an abundance of the single-storey 'low' houses (cf.
Great Horton, above), e.g. Nos. 39–51 REEVY ROAD.

FAXFLEET STREET ESTATE, off Carr Bottom Road. Early
council housing of 1902–4. Stone-built through terraces of two
storeys and attics, with narrow house frontages but the streets
quite wide. Sash windows altered.

BUTTERSHAW MILLS, Halifax Road. 1852 for Bottomley Bros.
Built as an integrated mill and a relatively early example of this
type of ordered, monumental design. Long four-storey spinning range with staircase tower at the sw corner, with Italianate
belvedere top and ornate weathervane. Big engine house
attached to the E end, with pedimented ends and tall round-
headed windows. Chimney, weaving shed and warehousing all
demolished.

LOW MOOR

Compact industrial zone developed following the foundation of
the Low Moor Ironworks in 1789.

HOLY TRINITY, Park House Road. In origin a chapel of ease
built by William Rookes of Royds Hall in 1606, largely rebuilt
1836–7 by *R. H. & S. Sharp*, with small w tower and spire and
shallow transepts. Chancel added 1883. The E window is still
that of 1606, Jacobean Perp with round-headed lights. The
work of 1836 is in a simple lancet style, reusing much of the
C17 stone. Curious sundial of 1713 set in the s wall. Internally
the transepts are treated as aisles, with crudely detailed three-
bay arcades. Galleries removed 1955. – MONUMENT. Wall

tablet to Mary Rookes †1793, and other members of the Rookes family, by *Fisher* of York. – Former SCHOOL, 100yds NW on Cleckheaton Road. 1814, erected by the Low Moor Iron Co. Pointed windows, altered.

ST MARK, Huddersfield Road. The original church 1855–7 by *Mallinson & Healey* for the Low Moor Iron Co., cruciform with a thin NE tower and spire. SE chapel and chancel extension 1892 by *T. H. & F. Healey*, wide aisles with double-pitched roofs 1912 also by them, producing a rather congested composition overall. C13 style with plate tracery. N and S sides of the crossing have sub-arches, with a vesica in the spandrel, added in 1912 (cf. St Columba, Great Horton, above). – STAINED GLASS. Includes chancel N and S by *Powell Bros.* of Leeds, 1892.

ROYDS HALL, Royds Hall Lane, in open country ⅝ m. W of St Mark's church. One of the best houses in the Bradford area, a classic example of a timber-framed structure probably of the mid C16 cased in stone during the C17. In this case there is a hall range of three-and-a-half bays, with open hall, and a three-bay service wing to the E: there was also a parlour wing to the W but that was rebuilt entirely. Long low irregular S front, with gables to the intermediate parts as well as to the cross-wings and the approximately central two-storey porch, and date-stones from 1640 to 1658. Also an additional gabled cross-wing to the r. of *c.* 1770. The porch (1640), marking the position of the C16 cross-passage, has an enriched four-centre-headed doorway and a four-light stepped window above. To the l. the vast hall window of four-plus-four-plus-four lights with a transom, occupying the whole width of the space; to the r. a much narrower bay (datestone 1651), with a most unusual double-stepped window of five lights to the upper floor, which represents the unique feature in the C16 house of an extra bay between the cross-passage and the service wing, its function unknown. Very long mullioned windows, of ten lights, to the first floor of the parlour wing (dates of 1656 and 1658) and ground floor of the former service wing, transomed window above the latter. Then the 1770 wing, fronted by a full-height canted bay with a little semicircular attic window at the top. At the back of the house a C17 range of rooms along the back of the hall range, with more gables and mullioned windows.

Interior much restored and embellished *c.* 1990, the hall in particular having been altered in the C18 and again, ruthlessly, *c.* 1920. Its two S wall-posts – free-standing because the C17 window is well S of the line of the C16 wall – are restorations, replacing 1920s steelwork, but the wall-plate and the two open trusses above remain, the latter with kingposts and curved braces to the ridge pole. N wall remodelled in the C17, with an inserted plank-and-muntin partition: close studding above it and to the W wall, towards the parlour wing. C17 chimney-breast occupying the place of the cross-passage but leaving space for a lobby entry at the front: previously there was a fire-hood backing onto the passage. In the W half-bay, where originally there was a dais canopy, a C17 gallery (restored) and staircase (reinstated from a different position), with vertically symmetrical balusters. The former service wing has similar roof trusses and wallframe, again with some close studding surviving at first-floor level, but has also been altered, a transverse partition removed and an imported C17 staircase and a new timber-framed partition installed. Imported panelling etc. in the parlour wing, restrained C18 detail in the 1770 range.

In front of the house a garden flanked by mid-C18 brick walls. At the SW corner a square one-bay SUMMERHOUSE with ashlar quoins, entablature and round-headed Gibbsian doorway. Extensive outbuildings. At the back a courtyard with an altered range to the W dated 1686 and an early C19 range to the N with reused doorway of 1663. W of the former a range with a datestone of 1669, again altered, which ends in a utilitarian late C18 COURTROOM on the upper floor, reached by external steps.

Of the IRONWORKS little remains apart from the boundary wall along New Works Road, the site intensively redeveloped for industry. At the junction of New Works Road and Huddersfield Road, the 30½-ton cast-iron FLYWHEEL from the former rolling mill is displayed. In PARK HOUSE ROAD beyond Holy Trinity church, PARK HOUSE, 1635, mullioned windows of four and six lights, and then UPPER PARK HOUSE, the windows with round-headed lights.

See also Esholt, Thornton, Tong, Wyke.

BRADLEY

The main village is Low Bradley. High Bradley is a small cluster of houses ½ m. N.

OLD HALL, Low Bradley. 1672. Tall double-pile block with near-symmetrical triple-gabled front. Attic windows in the gables of three stepped lights but with the centre light round-headed, making an approximation to a Serliana. Stepped hoodmoulds over. Central doorway with flattened-ogee head (cf. Fir Cottage, Addingham), ground-floor windows of three-plus-three lights to l., five lights to r. First-floor windows of three and four lights.

At FAR FOLD FARM, High Bradley, an aisled BARN, probably later C17, constructed using components from an earlier timber-framed building, perhaps of c. 1500. Three bays. King-post trusses, one with very broad curving principals. Chamfered and stopped tie-beams. Exterior much altered.

On the hillside ½ m. SSE of Low Bradley, a Neolithic LONG BARROW, surviving as a pile of gritstone boulders 200 ft (60 metres) long and 50 ft (15 metres) wide. Excavation in 1930 revealed a stone cist containing cremated and uncremated bones. Nearby to the SW a Bronze Age ROUND CAIRN c. 100 ft (30 metres) in diameter and 3 ft (1 metre) high.

BRAMHAM

ALL SAINTS. The church's setting at one end of a raised oval churchyard of unusual size suggests an important pre-Conquest site. Anglo-Saxon fabric is largely hidden in the nave walls and to this nave was added in the mid C12 the W tower, with small round-headed windows and two-light belfry openings (renewed in 1874) with dividing shaft, as at Aberford (q.v.). The top – battlements and a recessed spire – is Perp. N aisle late C12 and the S aisle and the chancel essentially C13, but the aisle fenestration, the S porch, the low tower window, the high-pitched roofs and the E window (replacing a Late Perp one) all date from *Perkin & Backhouse*'s restoration of 1853. They extended both aisles one bay E. Surviving lancets in the chancel and corbelled Perp battlements on the nave. On the N side a less scholarly, early Victorian vestry and organ chamber. Inside, the phasing is clearer. Three-bay late C12 N arcade. Tall, circular piers, plain, flat, moulded capitals. Unmoulded round arches. The S arcade is E.E., with tall octagonal piers and double-chamfered arches. Also E.E., the S doorway with two orders of colonnettes carrying stiff-leaf capitals and with dog-tooth decoration in the arch. The chancel lancets with trefoiled rere-arches. Perkin & Backhouse widened and raised the chancel arch and inserted the Norman-style tower arch. – ARCHITECTURAL FRAGMENT. Circular, with an interlaced design; possibly a crosshead. CII–CI2. – PANELLING. Traceried, Perp, rediscovered and reused in the C19 PULPIT and CLERGY STALLS. – Remarkable panelling on both sides of the chancel (after 1906) and SCREEN between chancel and S chapel (after 1911) by *Bromet & Thorman* of Tadcaster. A species of Gothic with pronounced Art Nouveau overtones; wildly asymmetrical panels of tracery separated by wide bands of plain wood (cf. Otley and Tadcaster). – S CHAPEL FURNISHINGS, including aisle screen, by *Sir Charles Nicholson*, 1920. – ROOD. By *Hicks & Charlewood* of Newcastle, 1935. – A number of Georgian WALL MONUMENTS, including those in the chancel by the *Taylors* of York to George Fox Lane, Lord Bingley, †1773, and his nephew James Fox, †1821.

The church lies at the foot of an escarpment, down which the limestone-built village descends to the old Great North Road. Two of the yeoman houses on the historic main street have evidence inside of early C17 timber frames and share three-cell, lobby-entry plans: the OLD MALT KILN on High Street has a rear outshut; HILLSIDE, on its continuation Town Hill, may have been a single storey. On the N side of the churchyard is the OLD HALL. With C18 fenestration, but an older H plan (subsequently altered and extended at the rear). 1681 is carved over the door, and 1640 was once carved above the hall fireplace. The break in the plinth suggests that the doorway was always in the centre. Another larger house is BRAMHAM LODGE on Aberford Road, of five bays, built before 1823.

BRAMHAM PARK

60   If ever house and gardens must be regarded as one ensemble, it
is here. Bramham is a grand and unusual c18 house, but its
gardens are grander and even more unusual. They are the least
altered and most remarkable survivals in England of planning on
a grand scale of a park in the French manner of Le Nôtre. There
must have been many more of this type in the early c18, but the
vigour of Brown and his followers swept them away and replaced
their canals by serpentine lakes and their avenues and long vistas
by winding drives and walks.

Bramham Park was created by *Robert Benson* (from 1713 the
first Lord Bingley), whose father – a self-made Yorkshire attorney
– had amassed considerable riches 'not without suspicion of great
frauds and oppression'. Work on both house and grounds appears
to have begun *c.* 1705. The house was probably designed by
Benson himself, who was well-known among his contemporaries
as an authority on architecture: he advised Lord Raby on the construction of Wentworth Castle (West Riding South) and the Duke
of Chandos at Cannons, and provided a scheme for remodelling
Ledston Hall (West Riding South) for Lady Betty Hastings. But
William Thornton – who worked at Wentworth and Ledston – also
appears to have been involved in some capacity: in 1711 he wrote
to Lady Hastings from Bramham. *Vitruvius Britannicus* gives 1710
as the date of completion, although the Earl of Mar found Benson
'pulling down the other half of his new house' in 1713, and plasterers and painters were still at work on the interior in 1728. In
1828 it was largely gutted by fire but little was done before its
sympathetic rehabilitation in 1906–14 by *Blow & Billerey*.

Built of golden sandstone ashlar, the house is a nobly restrained
design, horizontally rather than vertically accented. The
approach, however, is splendidly ceremonious, through an
outer GATEWAY, guarded by sphinxes, with monumental and
extravagant clustered Doric piers banded with vermiculated
rustication and surmounted by bears. Beyond this is the forecourt marked out by four obelisks. To the l. are the stables (*see*
below), and in front the house with the carriage drive sweeping up by two grand ramps to a rusticated platform in front of
the *piano nobile*. It is of one-and-a half storeys over a full basement, the façade eleven bays wide with an emphatic cornice

Bramham Park, entrance front.
Engraving after Colen Campbell, 1717

and balustraded parapet. In front of the first and second and the tenth and eleventh bays, themselves slightly brought forward, are projecting lower wings. From the side of these giant three-bay, vaulted Tuscan colonnades (with triglyph friezes) run out to otherwise detached three-bay pavilions, that on the l. housing the full-height kitchen, that on the r. originally the chapel. *Vitruvius Britannicus* shows these with parapets, but they have had hipped roofs since at least the early C19. The central doorway of the house is at the head of a short flight of balustraded steps, and has a heavy surround with triple key-stone and consoled cornice. The side elevations (screened from the entrance front by the colonnades) have full-height projections – a feature not shown in *Vitruvius Britannicus* but seemingly original. On the garden front the outer bays project only slightly but are as high as the façade. The big central doorway with Corinthian columns and a segmental pediment, and the curved double outer staircase with early C18-style wrought-iron work, are by *Blow & Billerey*.

The ENTRANCE HALL is a perfect 30-ft (9-metre) cube with giant pilasters, a rich cornice, niches and a rusticated fireplace. Although there is plenty of evidence of the fire in the fine ashlar, this is the most complete early C18 interior (though the ceiling is of 1990); other rooms at the s end of the house survived the blaze but were remodelled by *Blow & Billerey*. Although it is not always clear what is C18 and what is Edwardian, original joinery has an affinity with the work of *Thornton* and his Huguenot carvers at Beningbrough Hall (North Riding). In the former DINING ROOM (enlarged as a bedroom) is an overmantel with a slip of mirror glass beneath a painting like one in Beningbrough's drawing room; the stately Ionic pilasters also go round corners like those at the Saloon there. The adjoining SITTING ROOM (the Boudoir reduced) has an overdoor with a superbly carved basket of flowers, similar to others influenced by Berain and Marot at Beningborough and Wentworth Castle (West Riding South). S STAIRCASE with a chaste iron balustrade, probably part of refurbishment under-taken for James Fox in 1814. Otherwise, the interior is as remodelled by Blow & Billerey in early C18 fashion. They created a GALLERY along the garden front, where there had been a saloon and other rooms, and made a new dining room – now DRAWING ROOM – in the N side where an apartment had existed, the walls there lined with more Ionic pilasters.

The STABLES are later than the house and Palladian. Nine-bay centre with higher end pavilions. The middle part was erected *c.* 1724–7 and is attributed to *John Wood Sen.* of Bath, who also appears to have been Lord Bingley's surveyor for his house in Cavendish Square, London. It has a portico with four giant Tuscan columns, a pediment, and the usual clock turret with cupola. There is a wider interstice between the middle than between the outer columns of the portico, framing a pedimented and blocked doorway recessed in an arch. The pavilions are attributed to *Paine*, and were added *c.* 1760 by Benson's daughter Harriet and her husband George Fox Lane (2nd Lord Bingley from 1763). They have on the ground floor a rusticated and pedimented middle bay as if meant for entrances, and above them a large overarched Venetian window, with niches l. and r. and pediments on top without base (cf. Stockeld Park).

Development of the GROUNDS was in three phases. First, up to 1710, over 100 acres of pleasure grounds were laid out S and W of the house, characterized by intersecting *allées* flanked by high, clipped beech hedges and walks through beech plantations.* *George London*, the royal gardener, was paid £127 in 1709–10. Benson then added new rides, water features, and the NE avenue striding across the undulating parkland to the entrance forecourt. It appears that he was assisted during this phase by *John Wood Sen.*, whose plan of *c.* 1728 shows the changes. Finally, after Benson's death in 1731, garden buildings were introduced by his daughter Harriet and her husband George Fox Lane, some of which are described by Richard Pococke on his visit in 1750. A surprising feature of the layout is that beyond the garden (SW) front of the house the ground continues to rise quite steeply. Cut into this landscape, and perfectly scaled to the front, are the remains of a PARTERRE (since 1906 a Rose Garden) with retaining walls panelled with vermiculated rustication and articulated by rusticated pilaster strips. At its far end a shallow bow with a rustic cascade, formerly fed by a beast's-head spout (Wood's plan shows this as the termination of a thirty-step cascade). At the near corners of the parterre are exuberant piers (moved from the Obelisk Ponds, *see* below) with inward-turning volutes derived from Borromini and swan-neck pediment hats. The surrounding lawn was originally densely planted as a wilderness with serpentine walks in the manner of Kent, but none of this survives.

The principal axis of the layout has always been the BROAD WALK, running parallel with the garden front for over a mile, descending SE into the small valley which runs across the park and terminating on its other side at Black Fen plantation. At its NW end is a beech-sheltered TEMPLE, built by *Paine*, probably *c.* 1760 (converted to a chapel by *Blow & Billerey*). It has a pedimented centre, with lower canted flanks with niches, and a balustraded Ionic portico projecting from the front. Inside, the canted flanks are screened by scagliola columns. STATUES of Benson and his daughter by *Agostino Carlini*, 1771, were transferred from the old chapel in the N pavilion. Vaulted ceiling with good plaster decoration. Arched sanctuary recess. SW of this begins one of the tall and atmospheric beech-hedge *allées*, with an eyecatcher of a STATUE of a female classical figure on a pedestal with relief panels of martial and musical motifs.

---

*The layout of the gardens is shown in a plan, dated to no later than 1713. Most of the original beeches were felled after a gale in 1962 and the opportunity taken to systematically plant afresh so that the garden now closely resembles its C18 appearance.

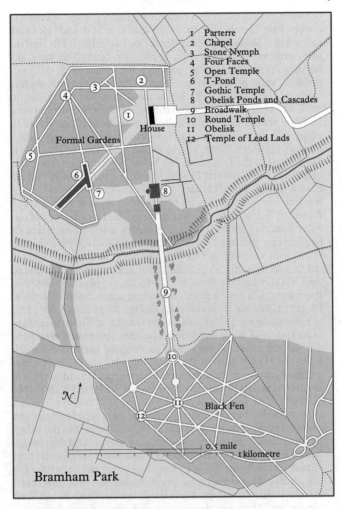

1 Parterre
2 Chapel
3 Stone Nymph
4 Four Faces
5 Open Temple
6 T-Pond
7 Gothic Temple
8 Obelisk Ponds and Cascades
9 Broadwalk
10 Round Temple
11 Obelisk
12 Temple of Lead Lads

House

Formal Gardens

N↑

Black Fen

0.5 mile
1 kilometre

Bramham Park

After a turn S, closely following but never revealing the edge of the park, the hedged walk reaches a second intersection, punctuated by a big URN on a pedestal, known as the 'Four Faces' after the masks of the Four Seasons. From here walks and avenues descend across the landscape in five directions creating vistas of varied length. Significantly, none has the mansion as its object. Instead the principal view is SE through the plantations towards open parkland. Bisecting this, the QUARTER MILE WALK which has at its head the OPEN TEMPLE, noted by Pococke in 1750. Its front has the familiar tripartite Venetian (or Palladio) motif, here employing the Tuscan order. S of the temple, at the edge of the plantation is a TERRACE WALK created along the garden's perimeter from the 1720s. At the SW corner it breaks out into a round (originally square) BASTION, overlooking the shallow valley on this side and with views SE towards the Round House at Black Fen (*see* below). The bastion also terminates a wide walk, apparently created as an afterthought in the 1720s, that provides the visitor with the first, indirect, view of the garden front of the house. This avenue includes the curious T POND, a canal that was being dug in 1728 and appears to have been the last of Wood's contributions. Its main arm lies along the walk but at its head is crossed at an oblique angle by a shorter canal on axis with the avenue leading back to the Four Faces. Visible at the other end of this axis is the Temple of the Lead Lads (*see* below) at the edge of the park. SE of here is a GOTHIC TEMPLE built in 1750. Closely derived from a plate in Batty Langley's *Gothic Architecture Improved*, this is a buttressed octagon with two-pointed arched windows and doors – filled with intersecting glazing – and a clerestory of circular windows set in spherical triangles. On top, ogee-shaped battlements pierced by trefoils. Inside, Gothick plaster panelling with shafting and foliate flourishes, and pretty Gothick stools and benches. A pyramid roof and vault were replaced with a water tank by *Blow & Billerey*. In the plantations NW of the temple is a pet cemetery including a quatrefoil column to Jet †1774, and NE from there the Gothic MUSEUM, built 1845.

Now along the Broad Walk to the OBELISK PONDS, an elaborate system of stone basins and cascades, apparently created in the second phase of work. The rectangular main pond is fed from the HALF-MOON POND to the SW – into which water emerges on the W side through a sea-serpent head – via two smaller basins. It is flanked on the line of the Broad Walk by two further ponds at lower level, that to the NW converted into a sunken garden but its counterpart to the SE in turn feeding more ornate basins, of decreasing size as they descend into the valley. Beyond these the water disappears underground but abandoned in the grass is the stonework of a lower stage, called the 'Great Cascade' on Wood's plan; then along the valley floor is the outline of a rectangular pond, which was the only water feature in the landscape by 1710. From here the Broad Walk climbs uphill to a now denuded avenue across the park to a HAHA surrounding the ROUND HOUSE, a circular Ionic temple seen by Pococke. A vaulted peristyle of sixteen unfluted columns around a shallow dome on a low drum (cf. Kent's Temple of the Ancient Virtues at Stowe or the Tuscan Rotunda at Duncombe Park, North Riding). The fine detail is now badly eroded. The temple is the focus of six rides, and the main vista behind it is continued further to the tall OBELISK, designed by *John Carr* and erected by Lord and Lady Bingley in memory of their only son Robert (†1768). It is of excellently worked ashlar and carries an urn but makes a very odd effect rising behind the rotunda in views along the Broad Walk. Did they perhaps intend to move the Round House? From the obelisk altogether ten rides fan out. S is the little Tuscan TEMPLE OF THE LEAD LADS, named after the lead statues that once crowned the pediment.

Adjoining Bramham Park are two lesser but also sizeable mansions:

BRAMHAM BIGGIN, ½ m. sw of the village. Formerly H-plan, gabled C17 house remodelled in 1755–6 by *James Paine*. Cramped three-bay centre with a Diocletian window to the second floor and projecting wings with Venetian windows on the ground floor. Mullioned windows at the rear where, following C19 alteration, the centre projects. Non-matching side elevations, with bay windows. (Two-storey entrance hall with cantilevered staircase and landing, with slim rod-and-vase balusters.)

BOWCLIFFE HALL, ½ m. s of the village. Begun by William Robinson, a Manchester cotton spinner, before his bankruptcy *c.* 1805, and completed by John Smyth (†1840). A five-bay main block with five-bay wings, terminated by quadrant screen walls. Centre with a three-bay open pediment into which rises the segmental pediment of a big tripartite window. Below that a Tuscan porch. Each of the wings has a niche containing a statue of a Rustic beneath an oculus; both wings were originally two-storey, the E wing heightened possibly in the mid C19 when the garden façade was extended to eight bays. Entrance hall screened by Ionic columns from the Imperial staircase, which returns to a landing with Corinthian columns.

In the grounds to the NW a tiny single-cell CHAPEL. The simple Perp windows with cusped lights, the door surround and doors made of original traceried Perp panelling may have been taken from Bramham church in the 1850s. C19 panelled roof. To the E a large kitchen with splendid arched chimneystacks, also detached stables, etc. and late C20 pastiche office blocks, and beyond those BOWCLIFFE FARMHOUSE, a C19 Tudor Gothic cube, symmetrical and embattled.

HANGAR. 1½ m. SE of the village in fields. The most significant relic of Bramham Moor airfield, operational 1915–19. Laminated timber frame with 80-ft (25-metre)-span Belfast trusses, triangular buttress and continuous clerestory glazing.

BRAMHOPE

CHAPEL. Erected in 1649 by Robert Dyneley of Bramhope Hall, 'an ardent and unswerving Puritan', and one of the most valuable *incunabula* of Low Church Protestant church-building in England. Its precise status was ambiguous, ostensibly a chapel of ease of Otley but in fact a proprietory chapel on Dyneley's estate. After the Restoration it continued to be served by nonconforming ministers until *c.* 1673, and thereafter was in established Anglican use until the new church (*see* below) was opened in 1881. Plain long low rectangle of coursed stone. Almost symmetrical s flank with two segment-headed doorways, straight-headed mullioned windows mainly of two and three lights, the heads of the lights arched. E window of five lights, and on the N side also a little one-light window at a higher level, lighting the pulpit. Walls and roof structure raised slightly, and W bellcote added, early C19. Plain kingpost trusses. – PULPIT. Against the N wall, a little E of centre. Two-decker, the pulpit proper mid-C17, octagonal, with an arched panel to the back-board and tester with corner pendants, the clerk's desk C18. – BOX PEWS, occupying almost all the rest of the space and mainly arranged to face the pulpit. Mostly C18 but some earlier or incorporating earlier panels. – FONT. Dated 1673. Small octagonal bowl on a fat cylindrical shaft with a square base. Octagonal plinth below. – MONUMENT. Esther Smith †1814 and her daughter Anne †1827, by *J. Gott*. Wall tablet with semi-reclining female figure and two urns.

ST GILES. 1881 by *Adams & Kelly*. Effective simple lancet style, with N aisle. Provision was made for one to the S. Parish hall on that side, 1977. – STAINED GLASS. Extensive series by *Heaton, Butler & Bayne*, 1881–1914, chancel, N aisle and nave S.

METHODIST CHAPEL. 1895–6 by *W. J. Morley*. Crude Dec, with spirelet. – STAINED GLASS. Another set by *Heaton, Butler & Bayne*, 1896–1931.

Bramhope Hall has been demolished. In HALL DRIVE a circular C18 GAZEBO commanding an extensive view N. Domed, two storeys, crudely restored.

BRAMHOPE TUNNEL. On the Leeds & Thirsk Railway, 1845–9 by *Thomas Grainger*, engineer. The N PORTAL is in woodland ½ m. NE of the church. Castellated, with a big cylindrical turret l. of the entrance, a smaller square one to the r., and square outer ones, smaller again, terminating the quadrant retaining walls.

BREARTON

3060

ST JOHN. 1836 by *J. P. Pritchett*, built as a chapel of ease of Knaresborough. Untouched little Gothic box, in magnesian limestone with grey gritstone dressings. Three-bay flanks with straight-headed windows of two cusped lights. Three-light E window with cusped intersecting tracery and mask-stops to the hoodmould, little octagonal chimney above. W bellcote and entrance. Altar flanked by two-decker pulpit to the r. and balancing sunken vestry enclosure, with tiny fireplace, to the l.

BROUGHTON

9050

No village. The church and the hall half a mile apart.

ALL SAINTS. Late Norman S doorway, with waterleaf capitals (the shafts missing), and plain blocked priest's doorway. Traces of a deeply splayed window l. of the latter. Short W tower with Dec bell-openings. Perp N aisle and chapel, under one low roof with the nave and chancel, and Perp fenestration, straight-headed with arched lights to N and S, the E window with crude tracery. Porch with reused timbers from the nave roof. Six-bay arcade with octagonal piers, the Norman chancel arch presumably dispensed with when the aisle was built. On the W face of the fifth pillar, obscured by a screen, an image niche (cf. Bracewell, Kirkby Malham). Also a shallow recess on the second pillar. Late medieval chancel roof, with cambered tie-beams. Nave roof C19. – SCREENS, to chapel. Straight-topped divisions with thin Flamboyant tracery to the heads. – FONT. Plain cylinder, possibly Norman, on octagonal base. – SCULPTURE. Two late medieval alabaster statues of the Virgin and Child, discovered in 1871, one (headless) with flowing draperies. – MONUMENTS. Some plain white marble tablets to members of the Tempest family.

BROUGHTON HALL. The long Picturesque ashlar façade, looking N across the Broughton Beck, appears to be wholly a product of the early-to-mid C19, an easy combination of the Grecian and the Italianate; but the Tempest family has been here since the C14 and the building history is a long and quite complicated one. Its starting point, represented by the nine-bay, two-and-a-half-storey core of the present building, is the 'lofty hall house' (Whitaker) said to have been built by the then Sir Stephen Tempest in 1597 and certainly complete by 1613. Tall but not particularly large, this evidently had a transverse great hall, running across the house from front to back, in the manner of Hardwick Hall, Derbyshire. What appears to be the upper half of this feature remains as the present entrance hall, the creation of which formed part of a mid-C18 remodelling in which the ground floor became a basement and canted-bay centrepieces were added to front and back, the former replacing the C16 porch. By the end of the C18 further remodelling had taken place and the house had acquired a service wing running out to the W and a chapel (R.C.) behind it.

The C19 alterations came in two main stages. The pair of monumental Grecian wings embracing the main block – that to the W merely a new front to part of the existing wing – are of 1809–11 by *William Atkinson*. The fronts are pedimented, of one bay, with attached Ionic columns *in antis* and Diocletian windows to the basement. Then in 1838–41 the rest of the N front was remodelled to match by *George Webster* of Kendal. Continuing Atkinson's order, he added the Ionic portico in front of the canted bay and refaced the rest of the block, with giant pilasters, more elaborate window surrounds and a top balustrade. The service wing and the chapel behind were similarly refaced and – the crucial touch – an Italianate clock tower was added at the W end of the wing, topped by a colonnaded octagonal cupola with acroteria fringing the dome. Finally, at the back, running out from the S canted bay, is a pretty conservatory of 1853–5 by *Andrews & Delaunay* of Bradford, erected in conjunction with improvements in the grounds (*see* below). Basilical with a dome over the bowed S end and fanciful cast-iron columns.

Of the interiors, the entrance hall has decoration of the mid C18, with scagiola columns screening the apsidal ends which occupy the canted bays, there is a C17 back staircase with fat turned balusters, and upstairs some altered C17 and early C18 panelling. But the other principal rooms (with much furniture by *Gillow* of Lancaster) are essentially of the *Atkinson* phase – the library and dining room in the main block and more ambitiously, preceded by a handsome vestibule with a somewhat Soanian saucer-dome, the red and white drawing rooms which occupy his E wing. Very restrained Regency manner, the former with an 'Egyptian'-style chimneypiece (1810), the latter with a shallow segmental vaulted ceiling – but the Ionic columns framing the doorway to the Red Drawing Room were added in 1836 and the white marble chimneypiece supplied by *Webster* in 1840. Also by *Webster*, it appears, is the interior remodelling of the chapel, Gothic with a plaster ribbed vault and family gallery. Stencilled decoration 1901.

In the GROUNDS the predominant effect is again of the mid C19, but with a few earlier features interspersed. The Broughton Beck was canalized *c.* 1790 and the STABLE BLOCK, W of the house, is of 1787, its front a simple Palladian scheme with pedimented centre and end bays, rusticated entrance and Diocletian windows. Wings embracing the courtyard behind. The EAST LODGE, ¾ m. ENE beside the main road, and the MIDDLE LODGE, between it and the house, are by *Webster*, 1839, the former cruciform with Ionic portico, the latter a more picturesque classical, with Serliana-fronted porch. The Italianate GAZEBO and associated terrace walls, on sloping ground E of the house, and the WEST LODGE, beyond the stables, are of 1855 by *Andrews & Delaunay*, as probably is the GAME LARDER between the stables and the house – the lodge spikily steep-roofed Tudor with variegated gables and ornate chimneys, in rusticated stonework with diagonal tooling, the larder in a similar style, rock-faced with steep gables, fancy bargeboards and central louvre-cum-flèche. But the *tapis vert* within the terrace walls, and the complex of PARTERRE, RETAINING WALL, STEPS and FOUNTAIN to the S of the house, in front of the conservatory, were designed 1855–6 by *W.A. Nesfield* (the *tapis vert* replanted 1900), who also advised on the laying-out of walks and the placing of statuary.

In the shrubbery S of the house a remarkably architectonic PRIVY dated 1819, circular with vermiculated eaves band and door surround. S again the former HOME FARM and SAWMILL complex, now offices, 1816. Utilitarian but quite extensive, the main building U-shaped, with separate cartsheds and Dutch barn to the S. In the former kitchen garden W of these, behind the stables, the UTOPIA PAVILION, elegantly understated award-winning design by *Hopkins Architects*, 2004–5. Central common room glazed to front and back, symmetrically flanked by timber-clad meeting rooms and service areas, all under a simple low-pitched roof with deep eaves.

BROUGHTON MILL, ¼ m. w of Broughton Hall. Former corn
   mill, now offices. Sundial dated 1823. Four storeys.
INGHEY BRIDGE, over the Aire, 1¼ m. ENE of Broughton Hall.
   1772–3, incorporating part of an earlier bridge, probably of the
   mid C17. Three segmental arches.

BROWSHOLME HALL   6040
Bowland Forest Low

Red sandstone house of the Parker family, an H-plan with rather
   short cross-wings, essentially of the C17 but altered on several
   later occasions, notably in the early C19 for Thomas Lister
   Parker. The precise dates of construction are not clear. Nothing
   of the pre-C17 house is identifiable, but a series of inventories
   from the 1590s to the 1630s indicates that little was changed
   during that period. The main reconstruction therefore was
   probably that of 1674, when the house is known to have been
   'beautified'. An attic window in the gable of the E wing,
   obscured by an early C19 clock, is of three lights with the centre
   one arched (cf. Bradley Old Hall, 1672), and the windows in
   the gabled dormers along the main range, removed in the mid
   C18, were of the same type. The exception is the off-centre
   frontispiece to the main range, of three superimposed orders
   of coupled columns, Doric, Ionic and Corinthian (not a particularly Yorkshire feature but cf. nearby Stonyhurst,
   Lancashire), which was probably added to the old house
   c. 1610 and then retained in the reconstruction – it is unrelated
   to both the masonry and the floor-levels behind. The orders
   are rather robustly handled and out of scale with each other,
   diminishing in height from bottom to top. To each side, continuous hoodmoulds to the ground and first floor but the
   windows Georgianized, those to the former in turn provided
   with mock-Jacobean mullions and transoms c. 1816. C17 mullioned windows, with separate hoodmoulds, to the second
   floor, cross-windows, of c. 1700, in the top stage of the frontispiece and on the W flank of the E wing. W wing rebuilt in
   1805 as two storeys instead of three, using the old materials
   but with the stonework rusticated, to accommodate a new
   drawing room by Wyatville, the front of the E wing rusticated
   to match presumably at the same time. To the W a single-storey
   extension, also rusticated, containing a picture gallery, added
   1807; and to the E a two-storey hipped-roofed block of c. 1711,
   containing the kitchen below and an apartment above. The
   back irregular, with a wing partly of the C17 and partly 1897 –
   a chapel was intended but not completed – with Gothic
   windows and an ornate porch.
      Long low hall which in the mid C18 occupied the whole of
   the ground floor of the main range, the W end divided off
   c. 1754 to form a dining room, later the library. This has

remarkable diagonally framed panelling of *c.* 1620 from Park-head, near Whalley (Lancashire), given to Thomas Lister Parker by James Taylor of Parkhead in 1809, and an Eliza-bethan overmantel from Hapton Tower near Blackburn, all restored in the C19. Behind the hall the main staircase, of C17 origin but reconstructed 1804, the staircase window with heraldic stained glass of various dates from C15 to C19; and above it the oak parlour, with fine enriched panelling of *c.* 1700. Another staircase in the E wing, of the 1711 phase, with turned and fluted balusters, fluted newels and enriched tread ends. The kitchen has segment-headed fireplaces with fluted key-stones, the apartment above panelling with fluted pilasters flanking the fireplace, and simple ceiling decoration. In the W wing, *Wyatville*'s drawing room is a restrained but very effec-tive design, with broad shallow segment-headed recesses to each side and mildly Jacobean-style doorcases (cf. Wollaton Hall, Nottingham). Italian chimneypiece in white marble. Ante-room behind it with much restored C17 overmantel.

SW of the hall the former STABLES, now a house, in origin mid-C18 but reconstructed in their present position in 1804. They had stood further E. Two storeys, five bays, with a broad central entrance framed by pilasters and entablature. Opposite, across the stableyard, a range of various dates, with an ornamented doorhead of the same type as at Stakes, Whitewell (q.v.). SOUTH LODGE, ¼ m. S, a charming antiquarian exercise of 1806. The lodge (enlarged later in the C19) with mullioned windows, hoodmoulds and cylindrical chimneys; and adjoin-ing it a segment-headed archway, probably C17, brought from Ingleton Hall, and a pedestrian arch crowned by a coat of arms and Jacobean-style strapwork. A small LAKE nearby, formed in 1805. WEST LODGE, beyond the stableyard. 1832, Tudor.

BROWSHOLME SPIRE, ¾ m. N, on a ridge with extensive views, an eyecatcher probably of the early C19. Stage-set two-dimensional battlemented turret of rough masonry, attached to a farmhouse.

BUCKDEN

9070

Large parish, and small village, at the head of Wharfedale, with numerous field barns along the valley bottom. The parish church is at Hubberholme (q.v.).

BUCKDEN HOUSE. Later C18 core built for the Heber family, much extended in the same style during the C19. Tripartite windows. Across the valley, in woodlands planted mid C19 by the Hon. Mrs Ramsden, a C19 DEER SHED, U-shaped and utilitarian.

MANOR HOUSE. Dated 1691 on a door lintel at the back and 1725 on a panel at the front. The former looks the more reli-able. Small double pile, with central entrance and four-light mullioned windows. Mullion-and-transom staircase window off-centre at the rear.

IVY COTTAGE. 1655 with large two-storey porch dated 1705 entered at the side. Doorway with moulded jambs and segmental pediment, first-floor window of three stepped lights to front.

Former SCHOOL. 1865 by *A. B. Higham* of Wakefield. Gothic. *See* also Hubberholme, Langstrothdale, Oughtershaw.

BURLEY-IN-WHARFEDALE

1040

Spreading dormitory village near Ilkley, but with a textile-manufacturing past. Long main street with the church at the E end.

ST MARY. 1841–3 by *Walker Rawstorne*, replacing a chapel of ease of Otley which had been rebuilt in the mid C17. Lancet style, rather clumsily detailed, with thin W tower and spire. Little flying buttresses between the spire and the tower pinnacles. Lower chancel added, and W gallery removed, 1870. – STAINED GLASS. Nave N (four windows) and SE by *Wailes*, 1862–70. Medallions and grisaille background. E window by *Ward & Hughes*, 1870. Nave SW by *Burlison & Grylls*, c. 1887. – MONUMENT. William Maude †1661. Painted oval panel, erected in 1781.

BURLEY HOUSE. S of the church at the start of the village. Handsome ashlar villa of 1783, for Thomas Maude. Five bays and two storeys with three-bay pedimented centre. Tuscan doorcase with pediment and attached columns. Overarched Venetian staircase window on the r. flank, canted bay on the l. Staircase with slender balusters, every third one twisted. Across the road BURLEY LODGE, a subsidiary part of the same architectural entity. Three broad bays, the centre with pediment and an overarched Serliana incorporating the doorway. To the l. an added three-bay wing with Gothick windows.

In the MAIN STREET W of the church the METHODIST CHAPEL, 1867–8 by *Lockwood & Mawson* but not in their usual manner. Muscular rock-faced Gothic, with plate-traceried rose window flanked by squat pyramid-roofed turrets. Interior, with cast-iron arcades, altered 2002. To the l. the previous chapel, 1816. Plain pedimented front with round-headed windows. Further W, the little naïve lancet-style UNITED REFORMED CHAPEL, 1839–40 by *J. P. Pritchett* for John Clapham; and then Clapham's house THE GRANGE, 1840 also by *Pritchett*, Tudor Gothic with near-symmetrical three-bay front. Between the two a glazed octagonal SUMMERHOUSE with miniature battlements. Across the street the LECTURE HALL, built in 1868 by the textile mill-owners, William Fison and the politician W. E. Forster, for recreational pursuits. Approximate Jacobean with prominent tower, shorn of its top stage. Back a little to the E of this IRON ROW runs N, a long cottage terrace of c. 1820 built for their workers by the previous owners of the mill. The mill itself, GREENHOLME MILL, is further N, beside the river. Established in 1792 for cotton spinning, rebuilt after 1850 by Fison and Forster as an integrated worsted mill. It was always primarily water-powered, with steam power only as a supplement. Big three- and four-storey ranges remain, other parts burnt down in 1966.

(EAST LODGE, Moor Lane. 1898 by Isitt, Adkin & Hill of Bradford. Low-key Free Renaissance in stone and render. Some Art Nouveau detail inside.) Good ENTRANCE LODGE, with battered buttresses and mullioned windows.

On BURLEY MOOR are numerous Bronze Age 'cup-and-ring' ROCK CARVINGS, a continuation of the concentration on Ilkley Moor (q.v.). Also two large burial cairns, ¼ m. W and ⅞ m. NW of Carr Bottom Reservoir, the GREAT SKIRTFUL OF STONES and the LITTLE SKIRTFUL OF STONES, the former c. 85 ft (c. 26 metres) in diameter and c. 5 ft (c. 1.5 metres) high. WNW of it are two STONE CIRCLES, the GRUBSTONES (¼ m.) and the TWELVE APOSTLES (⅞ m.), with irregularly spaced orthostats surrounded by a bank of earth and rubble, the latter 72 ft (22 metres) in diameter.

0060

BURNSALL

ST WILFRID. Broad ashlar-faced Perp W tower with three-light bell-openings, bearing a mason's mark also found on the W tower at Bolton Priory of 1520. Short nave with aisles embracing the tower, lower chancel with chapels, also all Perp apart from two windows of c. 1300 at the E end of the S chapel, and these may well be reused. Arcades with double-chamfered arches on short octagonal piers, three bays to nave, two to chancel. The church was 'repaired and butified' in 1612, an inscription in the S aisle records, at the cost of Sir William Craven, native of Appletreewick (q.v.) and Lord Mayor of London in 1611, and was heavily restored 1858–9 by John Varley of Skipton. His interventions included heightening and re-windowing the nave clerestory, much other refenestration, and new roofs, chancel arch and S porch – where some of the discarded door- and window heads are re-set under the benches (cf. Linton, Rylstone).

SCREENS, flanking the chancel. Part of Sir William Craven's 'butifying'. Extensively altered by Varley and partly re-restored in the 1890s. – PULPIT. C17, presumably also of Sir William Craven's time. Restored, and the baluster feet added, 1890s. – FONT. Norman, circular on a square base, with crude decoration on the base and the bowl. – SCULPTURE. A number of Anglo-Saxon pieces. Cross-head and shaft, with Scandinavian vertebral and ring-twist patterns, C10; cross-head with part of shaft attached, with rather clumsily designed interlace and meander forms and a substantial amount of original pigment,

C10; two shaft fragments with affronted beasts; large cross-head, C10–C11, perhaps belonging with a shaft fragment with an isolated interlace motif on each side; cross-neck fragment; small plain cross-head; two C10 hogback tombstones, one with its end-beasts and tegulated roof pattern well preserved, the other plain with minimalist end-beasts; and half of a third. – Alabaster panel of the Adoration of the Magi, with remains of colour. C15. – STAINED GLASS. E window 1915 by *Kempe & Co.*; S chapel E and N aisle NE by *Wailes, c.* 1858.

MONUMENTS. Robert Heye †1694. Small brass plate in a Baroque cartouche. – A group of C18 and early C19 wall tablets, including Thomas Waddilove of Thorpe, mason, †1802. The inscription surmounted by a bas-relief figure leaning on a sarcophagus. Erected by *John Waddilove*, 'son of the above. Statuary in London'. – In the churchyard, Henry Philip Dawson †1933 by *Eric Gill*. A blunt cross of silvery Portland stone. – Delightful LYCHGATE, with miniature kingpost roof trusses. C17 and again probably of Sir William Craven's time, when the churchyard was 'newly walled . . . gaites and all', but moved to its present position in 1882.

GRAMMAR SCHOOL, now primary school, S of the church. Founded 1602 by Sir William Craven (*see* above). Two-storeyed with asymmetrically placed gabled porch and mullioned windows. Of the longer section to the r. of the porch, the ground floor is the schoolroom and the space above, divided into a number of rooms by post-and-panel partitions with four-centre-headed doorways, was probably used as dormitories. The shorter part to the l., with a separate entrance, was the master's house.

COLTON HOUSE, opposite the church, facing away from the street. 1723. An interestingly hybrid design. Symmetrical front with a central two-storey porch, the windows of two and five lights with unchamfered mullions and architrave surrounds. The plan is a double pile with a lobby entry; but the surprising feature is the amount of accommodation, with two ground-floor front rooms to each side of the porch. Another doorway in the r. end elevation. Could this have been a double house (cf. Arnford Farmhouse, Hellifield), for two households, perhaps related?

BRIDGE, over the Wharfe. 1884, replacing one washed away by a flood. Five segmental arches, elegantly graduated, a dominant element in picturesque views of the village.

BURNT YATES

Clint

2060

ST ANDREW. 1883 by *George Mallinson*. Neo-Norman. Chunky W tower with octagonal belfry stage and squat spire. S aisle 1895.

SCHOOL. Founded 1760. The building of that date is a short range of two tall storeys, with three-light mullion-and-transom windows l. and r. of the doorway and three-light mullioned windows above them, the mullions and transoms all unchamfered. Raised bands at sill and lintel levels, quoins, and inscription above the doorway. To the l. an addition of 1763, of the same dimensions but accommodating three storeys, with similarly detailed windows. To the r., at right angles, a gabled schoolroom of 1849, basic Jacobean. Trustees' room of 1771–3 in the 1763 block, with panelled dado and original furniture.

ROSE COTTAGE, 1 m. E. Small timber-framed house probably of late medieval origin, cased in stone presumably in the C17. Common rafter roof, and a timber firehood which appears to be an insertion as the roof timbers are soot-blackened.

BURTON-IN-LONSDALE

The *caput* of a fee of the de Mowbray family in the Middle Ages, with a motte-and-bailey castle. Also the location of a market, the charter for which was granted to John de Mowbray in 1306; and the form of the village, a neat rectangle of streets on the slope above the river Greta, perhaps suggests an element of deliberate planning of the same period. In the C18 and C19 the village was the centre of a flourishing pottery industry but hardly any traces of this remain.

ALL SAINTS. 1868–70 by *Paley & Austin* replacing a chapel of ease, probably C17, of Thornton-in-Lonsdale. The gift of Thomas Thornton, nephew of the founder of Thornton's School (*see* below). An impressive and ambitious design, particularly effective when seen from the SE where the land falls away towards the river. E.E. style somewhat in the manner of J. L. Pearson, the windows a mixture of lancets and simple plate tracery. Tall S transeptal tower with slated broach spire and gabled chapel to E. Chancel taller than the nave, N aisle with double-pitched roof. Nave arcade with foliage capitals. Kingpost roof to nave, the chancel and the tower rib-vaulted. – STAINED GLASS. E window by *Hardman*, 1870; three S aisle windows by *Shrigley & Hunt*, 1909.

CASTLE. At the W end of the village. Well-preserved earthworks of the motte, an approximately square bailey W of it and a semi-circular one to the S. Probably mid-C12 in origin but with the motte heightened at a later date, probably early C14. Part of the stone revetment to its upper part remains.

THORNTON'S SCHOOL, now primary school, ¼ m. W, on the Lancaster road. 1851–3, built and endowed by Richard Thornton, a London entrepreneur and native of Burton. Rather stiff collegiate Gothic, with a two-storey central block under a broad gable – the master's and mistress's houses – and the single-storey boys' and girls' schoolroom ranges, also gabled, to l. and r. Twin porches, and a niche containing a bust of Thornton, on the centre block, panels inscribed 'Perseverance' and 'Industry' on the school ranges.

N of the church is a small green with a dignified house dated 1837 on the E side and one with a crenellated outbuilding to the W. E from here, in the HIGH STREET, the MANOR HOUSE, c. 1700, altered. Part two-and-a-half storeys, part three, with irregular fenestration including some former cross-windows. Later doorway with heavily rusticated surround and semicircular pediment, too small to fit, said to have been dated 1746. Further on the METHODIST CHAPEL, 1871 with gabled front, and HILLCROSS HOUSE, mid-C18, an odd little design with a central doorway above which the wall surface projects slightly. The doorway has a broken pediment on brackets surmounted, against the projection, by a tall concave-sided pedestal.

BRIDGE, over the Greta. Probably C18, repaired 1833. Three arches, semicircular cutwaters.

BURTON LEONARD

3060

ST LEONARD. 1877–8 by *C. Hodgson Fowler* (cf. Bishop Monkton). The medieval church had been replaced in 1782, probably by *William Belwood*. Magnesian limestone. Decent Dec, nave and chancel. A W tower had been proposed. – STAINED GLASS. Big showy E window by *Capronnier*, 1879.

E of the church a much altered C17 farmhouse. Stone, with some timber framing incorporated.

CALTON

9050

CALTON HALL. Modest early C19 block with a pair of canted bay windows, which incorporates traces of two more ambitious predecessors. Presumably from the 'very large old building' which was the home of the Parliamentary General John Lambert is a medieval pointed doorway at the corner of the E gable-end; and of the 'plain hall-like mansion' erected by his son there are traces internally of mullion-and-transom windows. C18 GATEPIERS with ball finials.

CALVERLEY

2030

Village on the S flank of Airedale between Leeds and Bradford, in open country with views across the wooded valley. Mainly C19, both terraces and villas, but with some significant reminders of its earlier history.

St Wilfrid. A quite large medieval church but very heavily restored in 1869–70 by *T. H. & F. Healey*, with the aisles and chancel entirely rebuilt – the latter at least quite faithfully, it appears. The big w tower less affected. Nave walls early Norman – see the blocked round-headed window visible inside above the s arcade. The lower stages of the tower are Dec, the w window with simple tracery; and so in principle is the chancel, with straight-headed N and s windows, and five-light E window with fanciful flowing tracery of mid-C14 type, East rather than West Riding in character. Aisles added probably in the C15 – the lancets in the rebuilt walls reused from an earlier rebuilding in 1844 – the arcades of four bays with octagonal piers, plain capitals, and double-chamfered arches. Perp also the top part of the tower, with corbelled-out battlemented parapet (cf. Guiseley etc.), and the (renewed) clerestory windows. Rebuilt s porch with ribbed tunnel-vault. Tall tower arch markedly off-centre. – COMMUNION TABLE early C17, C19 top. – FONT COVER. A very good Jacobean piece, octagonal with two tiers of openwork tracery and foliage, and a spirelet (cf. Skipton, Long Preston). – STAINED GLASS. E window of C14 and C15 fragments – figural, including a Crucifixion and a member of the Calverley family (*see* below), and heraldic – put together in 1870 by *Powell & Sons*. Re-restored 1992. – Chancel s middle by *Hardman*, 1870. – Chancel SE and SW, N aisle second, fourth and fifth from E, and s aisle SE and s middle, by *Clayton & Bell* 1870 and 1886–91. – MONUMENTS. Incised grave-slabs, Anglo-Saxon to C14, assembled in the tower in 1870. – A number of wall tablets, including Sir Walter Calverley †1749 and his wife Julia Blackett †1736, with lugged architrave surround and open pediment, erected in 1752. – In the vestry Sir Walter (Calverley) Blackett †1777. – In the churchyard more grave-slabs, C17–C18.

SW of the church Nos. 1 and 3 TOWN GATE, a handsome semi-detached pair of the mid C18, said to have been built by Sir Walter Calverley in 1737 as an estate office and pied-à-terre. Three storeys, three bays each, quoins, eaves cornice. Doorways side by side in adjacent bays, but there are signs that originally they were in the middle bay of each house. Across the road the former VICARAGE, 1886 by *T. H. & F. Healey*, Neo-Jacobean with a slight Pennine accent. Delightful detached gatehouse with round-headed archway under a gable.

CALVERLEY OLD HALL, further s in Woodhall Road. Important example of a medieval gentry residence, the seat of the Calverley family, subsequently of Esholt Hall (q.v.), until the mid C17. It has apparently always been a house of end-hall plan, the principal components a great hall of unusual size (26 ft (8 metres) wide) aligned N–S (actually NE–SW), a single cross-wing to the s of it (actual SW), accommodating a solar on the first floor and service rooms below, and a chapel attached corner-to-corner to the wing, projecting further E. The earliest in principle is the cross-wing, of c. 1300 and originally timber-framed, the exposed parts subsequently cased in stone: the hall and chapel, both of good-quality coursed stone from the outset, have been dated by dendrochronology to c. 1490, the hall replacing an earlier, narrower one, also of stone. Later elements are a small chamber block, probably of the mid C16, in the angle between the S wall of the cross-wing and the W wall of the chapel, again originally timber-framed and cased in stone later; and a C17 range W of that accommodating a dining room and kitchen. By the early C19 the house was divided into cottages, a coming-down-in-the-world reflected in both its cut-about state and its situation, hemmed in by C19 terraces etc. Extensive but incomplete restoration c. 1980 on for the Landmark Trust by *A. M. Mennim*.

The HALL, to the r. as seen from the road, is externally the most altered part, with an array of C17–C19 windows and doorways; but there are also the remains of a straight-headed C15 window of two cinquefoil-headed lights and the suggestive form of its big tall roof. At the back a massive chimney-breast, without its stack: N gable-end wall rebuilt in the C17. The interior is still partly subdivided but the excellent C15 roof structure is clearly visible: four trusses with arched braces rising from short hammerbeams, and a southernmost of different design, with a tie-beam – probably a spere-truss marking the position of the screen to the cross-passage. Carved brackets below the hammerbeams, brattishing to the wall-plate. The CHAPEL at the l. corner by contrast is readily recognizable, with a straight-headed E window of three trefoil-headed lights. Four-bay roof similar to the hall's on a smaller scale; and gallery over the W half, reached from the solar, with delicate traceried timber screen at the front, partly restored. The SOLAR wing has an eight-light C17 mullion-and-transom window to the first floor, and the tie-beams of a roof of c. 1400 resting on carved brackets, the existing roof reusing medieval components. The solar had a fireplace in the S wall.

30

Further W from the church, in Victoria Park, the WAR MEMORIAL, a bronze Victory by *L. F. Roslyn*, c. 1921 (cf. Wetherby). To one side the METHODIST CHAPEL, 1872, meagre Italianate. NW of the village, CALVERLEY WOOD, running down to the Aire, was in the 1850s the scene of an abortive attempt at a high-class villa development by the Thornhill estate (cf. Cragg Wood, Rawdon, on the opposite bank). Drives were laid out, and the Calverley Cutting created, running steeply straight up the slope to provide access to the village from Apperley Bridge; but only one villa of substance was built, the straightforwardly Italianate FERNCLIFFE (now Champion House), Clara Drive, c. 1855 by *Lockwood & Mawson*.

CALVERLEY BRIDGE, ⅛ m. E, over the Aire. 1776 by *John Gott*, who became West Riding Surveyor of Bridges the following year. Three-plus-one segmental arches. Plain but unwidened.

WOODHALL OLD HALL, Woodhall Lane, 1⅛ m. SSW. Double pile three rooms wide, dated 1707. Mullion-and-transom windows to the ground floor, six cross-windows to the first, and three vertical pairs of upright oval windows (cf. Hallas Old Hall, Cullingworth). Subdivided in 1839 with two new dated doorways matching the original. At the back two doorways with shaped lintels.

See also Farsley.

9040

CARLETON

Mill village across the Aire valley from Skipton.

ST MARY. 1858 by *F. H. Pownall* of London, replacing the medieval church. Vigorous C13 Gothic, rock-faced with stone slab roof. W tower with stair-turret. – FONT (former). Cylindrical, probably C13. – STAINED GLASS. E window and chancel S by *Clayton & Bell*, 1881 and 1889; W window 1901 by *Shrigley & Hunt*.

CARLETON MILL. In the centre of the village, and the dominant element in views from across the valley. 1861 for cotton spinning, now flats. Three storeys, with pavilion-roofed tower and tall octagonal chimney.

SPENCE'S COURT (formerly Spence's Hospital), further E. Almshouses founded 1693, modernized 1956 and 1974. Tight U-shaped plan, the open end of the narrow courtyard almost filled by incongruously large stately gatepiers, panelled and ball-capped, and wrought-iron gates. Round the courtyard a wooden gallery (renewed) on octagonal stone pillars. Most of the window openings on the outward-facing elevations inserted in 1974.

TRAPPES HALL, beside the beck. Substantial C17 house, square in plan. Full-width gables to N and S, a big dormer to E and W. Two mullion-and-transom windows on S side and one on N, others smaller and irregularly disposed. Spine wall incorporating chimney flues runs from N to S. Entry arrangements altered, but the original entrance appears to have been on the N side into a lobby against the N end of the spine. The NE room is the housebody, with a big arched fireplace flanked by round-headed doorways. Post-and-panel partition on the S side. Winding stair at the S end of the spine. The position of a fireplace (not visible) on the first floor suggests that the E half of the house at that level was occupied by a single large room lit by the mullion-and-transom window at its S end.

CARLETON BIGGIN, ¾ m. SE. Scant remains of a C16 lodge of the Cliffords (*see* Skipton), incorporated into a farmhouse of the mid C19. Plinth etc. of massive masonry to the W gable-end, re-set mullioned windows and datestone of 1571 in the wall above.

CARLTON

CARLTON HALL, East Carlton. C17 Pennine house of moderate size, a rectangular block with quasi-cross-wings at each end expressed only by gables front and back, and housebody in the middle of double-storey height (cf. Ryecroft, Tong, 1669). Big housebody window, of four-plus-four lights with a transom, the dripmould above the other ground-floor windows stepping up over it. The first-floor windows l. and r. are also transomed, of six lights, some of them renewed, those below mullioned only. Interior largely reconstructed *c.* 1900.

CASTLEY

CASTLEY HALL. Modest double pile of *c.* 1700 incorporating part of an earlier building. Five-bay s front with quoins and broken segmental pediment to the doorway, the cross-windows mainly altered. In the w gable-end another doorway, more cross-windows and two upright ovals. C17 mullioned windows to the basement at the rear.

WHARFEDALE VIADUCT. 1849, *Thomas Grainger* engineer, for the Leeds & Thirsk Railway. Twenty-one round-headed arches, on a bend.

CATTAL

BRIDGE, over the Nidd, a little upstream from the Roman crossing. *c.* 1800, three arches, pointed cutwaters.

(OLD THORNVILLE (alias Cattal Hall), ⅝ m. NE. Square red brick house, with six-bay s range containing an early C18 cantilevered staircase, and w range probably of the 1660s, with brick rustication, blocked bullseye windows (cf. Nun Monkton Priory and its outbuildings) and a Dutch gable.)

CAUTLEY
Sedbergh

ST MARK. 1845–7, a very early work of *William Butterfield.* Immensely serious little building with absolutely no quirks. Aisleless nave and chancel of local rubble, each with just a single two-light Dec window to each side. Bellcote with two ogee-headed openings, the only hint of extravagance. NW vestry added 1858–60. – FONT by Butterfield. Octagonal with running ornament round the bowl.

LOW HAYGARTH, 1⅜ m. N. 1728. Central two-storey porch, windows altered. Panelled partition between housebody and parlour, firehood, and staircase with turned balusters.

7070

CHAPEL-LE-DALE
Ingleton

High up the Greta valley between the truncated pyramid of Ingleborough and the long hog's-back of Whernside.

ST LEONARD. C17 origin, altered C18, restored 1869. Tiny low chapel less than 50 ft (c. 15 metres) long, the nave and chancel in one. Windows of two and three lights with arched heads on s side, probably C17, E window mainly C19. C18 pedimented bellcote on w gable, and round-headed doorway with keystone. C19 porch in similar style. – ALTAR RAIL, C17. – STAINED GLASS. Includes one s window by *Kempe*, 1898. – MONUMENT. 'To the memory of those who through accidents lost their lives, in constructing the railway works, between Settle, and Dent Head. This tablet was erected at the joint expense of their fellow workmen and the Midland Railway Company 1869 to 1876'.

106 RIBBLEHEAD VIADUCT, 2 m. NE. 1870–4 by the Midland Railway Company's chief engineer *John Sidney Crossley*. The epitome of the Settle–Carlisle line, a majestic twenty-four rock-faced arches aptly complementing the sternly magnificent scenery.

On limestone pavement ½ m. SE of the viaduct the slight remains of a VIKING FARMSTEAD, the main building 64 ft (19 metres) long with rubble walls 5 ft (1.5 metres) thick. Excavations in 1975–6 produced a number of coins of the mid C9, minted at York, and a small Scandinavian knife. Nearby to the w a mutilated Bronze Age ROUND BARROW, said to have been opened c. 1800 and to have contained a 'stone coffin and an entire human skeleton'.

7060

CLAPHAM

Very attractive Dales village, on both banks of the tree-girt Clapham Beck at the point where it debouches from a ravine in the Ingleborough massif.

ST JAMES. Perp w tower, embraced by the stumps of the medieval aisles. The rest 1814, a box-like hall church out of scale with the tower. Quoins, pointed windows with Gothic tracery inserted in 1899. Five-bay arcades with tall octagonal piers and single-chamfered arches. Flat aisle ceilings and coved nave ceiling immediately above them. Dado to the side walls made up from C17 pew-ends. – STAINED GLASS. E window 1898 by *Powell & Sons*.

INGLEBOROUGH HALL. *c.* 1814 by *William Atkinson* for James Farrer. Now an outdoor centre. S front of seven bays, the centre three forming a domed semicircular bow with giant Greek Doric columns attached. Three-bay entrance front to W, with columns *in antis* framing the centre, plain semicircular bow to E. Extensive service accommodation to N. Spacious D-shaped staircase hall with shallow domed ceiling, entered between Ionic columns of black fossil-bearing limestone. In the GROUNDS to the N, a TUNNEL for the old road – its portal, E of the church, with rock-faced voussoirs – and beyond this a LAKE, both of 1833.

In the village the OLD MANOR HOUSE, now Information Centre. Dated 1701 outside and in. Quite small but richly detailed. Central two-storey porch, with ornamented doorhead – a design of two stepped recesses with arched tops – and a stepped three-light window above, under a hoodmould with spiral stops. Big inglenook fireplace with joggle-jointed voussoirs and enriched keystone. Further S, the NEW INN, 1776, three storeys with tripartite windows, and the SCHOOL, 1864 by *E.G. Paley*, Gothic, given by the Farrer family.

CLAPDALE, 1 m. N. The 'great old castle . . . very large and strong' (Dodsworth), a seat of the Clapham family in the later Middle Ages, appears always to have been something much more modest than that, although perhaps semi-fortified. Roofless in the early C19 and much altered since. A single range with a pointed chamfered doorway at the rear end of a hallway, which may represent a medieval cross-passage. Garderobe turret at the NW corner. Only the thickness of the walls suggests that part of the building might have been carried up as a tower.

At NEWBY, 1¼ m. WNW, a spacious green and NEWBY HALL, also late medieval and much altered, L-shaped with C15 first-floor windows in each of the three gable-ends, all originally of two lights with trefoil heads. A C16 timber lintel with floral decoration re-set in the adjoining barn. In the C19 there were two arched doorways inside and an ornamented roof structure. Further N TOWN HEAD, 1720. Three-storey range with two-storey porch. Segment-headed doorway surmounted by a sort of baseless pediment and then by a hoodmould, windows with flat-faced mullions. Barn dated 1675.

LOWER HARDACRE, 2 m. WSW. Porch of two storeys and attic, entered at the side, dated 1664. Ornamented doorhead, and above it a one-light window with a trefoil head. Between the porch and the housebody are two doorways side by side, both with decorated lintels on the housebody side, one of which may have led to a staircase accommodated in the porch (cf. Kirkbeck, Bentham, and the Manor House, Halton Gill).

See also Keasden.

CLIFFORD

Limestone-built village with two churches. The Grimston brothers established a flax mill in 1831 and it was for their predominantly Irish workers that streets of new housing (e.g. Albion
Street) and the remarkable Roman Catholic church were built.

81   ST EDWARD KING AND CONFESSOR (R.C.). Built in 1845–8 by
J. A. Hansom, to a design obtained from a Scottish artist called
Ramsay; but the best feature, the proudly tall and mighty W
tower, was not completed until 1866–7 to revised designs by
George Goldie. The initiative to build this ambitious edifice was
Mrs Ralph Grimston's and Father Clifford's, the first priest.
Money was given by the Grimstons, Cliffords and Vavasours,
and small sums by the Pope, the Queen of France, the Grand
Duke of Parma, and the King of Sardinia. The style of the
church is Romanesque, but particularly in the case of Goldie's
tower more the Romanesque of W France than of England.
Open tall W porch under the tower, although the W door was
never open. Four storeys above, including a corner turret with
conical roof, and an upper stage with a pyramid roof. Nave
and chancel are one vessel, lower Lady Chapel at the E end.
Additions of 1998–9.

Seven-bay arcades with strong cylindrical piers, impressively
plain: only the third piers from the E, marking the sanctuary,
are decorated – one with scales, the other with a spiral moulding. Enclosing the raised sanctuary on three sides is a low,
arcaded stone screen (forming an ambulatory behind the high
altar). The screen originally continued into the third bay of the
arcade but was reduced during the otherwise sensitive reordering in 1990–1. Behind the screen are three stilted arch openings to the Lady Chapel; a rood, two vesicae and a wheel
window above. Apsidal niche in the Lady Chapel's E wall, with
intricately carved arch, containing a STATUE of the Virgin,
carved in 1844 by *Hoffmann*, a sculptor in Rome. He was a Jew
but tradition has it he changed faith over the work on this
statue. – STAINED GLASS. In the S chapel four windows by
Antoine Lusson (*Lusson & Bourdant*) of Paris and Mons, 1854;
also the N aisle NE, 1850. – S aisle SE by *Mayer & Co.* – N aisle,
first from W, made and given by *John & Francis Barnett* of York.

See
p. 761

ST LUKE, at the E end of the village. Built in 1840–2 by *J. B. &
W. Atkinson* at the instigation of George Lane Fox of Bramham
Park (q.v.), to counter the Catholicism of the new settlement.
Greek cross plan, the details E.E. Thin W tower. No aisles or
galleries. Arch-braced trusses springing from corbels, meeting
over the crossing like ribs.

Nearby on the roadside, a BAPTISMAL WELL within a
Gothic shelter designed in the 1840s by the *Rev. Lewthwaite*,
the first vicar of St Luke's. Lewthwaite also founded the former
CONVENT AND SCHOOL (now housing) opposite, built *c.* 1847
by *J. A. Hansom* for a community of Anglican sisters. Two
parts, a single-storey schoolroom to the r., with tall multiple

lancets with trefoil heads and a little projecting entrance tower. The convent (l.) is asymmetrical with a half-basement, bay windows with trefoil-headed lights and half-dormers. Lewthwaite converted to Rome in 1851 and the convent was expanded with an R.C. CHAPEL, 1880–1, and large extensions to the school in 1892 (mostly demolished).

ST JOHN'S CATHOLIC SCHOOL FOR THE DEAF, ½ m. N. A discordant front with the original, domestic building of 1875 at its centre and incorporating to its l. a chapel of 1888–9. At either end wings for boys and girls, begun in the early 1880s.

FLAX MILLS. The Grimstons' mill of 1831 has been demolished but two of their other buildings survive. In New Mill Lane is the former New Mill, brick-built of 1854, rebuilt after a fire in 1867 and horribly converted to flats, 1985. E across a beck is a smaller early C19 limestone-built mill of three storeys (Clifford Mill, also converted).

CLIFTON
Newall with Clifton

1040

Hamlet with a group of s-facing C17–C18 farmhouses, one behind the other at right angles to the lane. The OLD HALL is one. Part dated 1647, later cross-wing to l. with three-plus-three-light windows and a bullseye in the gable, under a cornice on brackets.

COLLINGHAM

3040

ST OSWALD. Small and upright. Perp W tower, unbuttressed. The church itself is older: much of the masonry of its nave and the W bay of the chancel is probably Anglo-Saxon, see the quoins of the nave's SE corner. Narrow chancel extended late C13 (trefoil-headed piscina inside), N aisle widened C14. C19 S porch and S buttresses. Inside, the N arcade with its tall circular piers may date from c. 1200 but the moulded capitals and pointed plaster arches are of the restoration of 1840–1, as are the odd arches spanning the nave and the lancets. – FUR-NISHINGS (pews, organ case, light fittings) by George Pace, 1962–6. – SCULPTURE. The most important feature of the church, substantial fragments of two Anglo-Saxon crosses and smaller fragments of others. The older is the so-called Apostles' Cross, with figures in niches up the four sides of the shaft, those on the front and back larger than those on the sides. The date is probably c. 800, and the figure under an arch carries on the tradition of the C8. The second, dated to the later C9, has a Runic inscription at the base and Scandinavian decoration of dragons and opposed beasts as well as interlace and one long scroll on the side. One of the smaller fragments is of a cross-head with interlace. – CRESSET STONE. Found in the vicarage garden in 1905. A large stone disk with eight hollows for tallow or oil lights. – ROYAL ARMS. 1706, with a spirited unicorn. – BRASS PLAQUE of c. 1739, on the chancel N wall. The extensive pastoral Instructions to Incumbents, as contained in the will of the devout patron, Lady Elizabeth Hastings of Ledston Hall (West Riding South). – C17 GRAVE-SLABS of the Beilby family. – STAINED GLASS. By *Ward & Hughes*, the E window (1880), N aisle first from E (1882) and tower W (1884). N aisle W, by *T. F. Curtis, Ward & Hughes*, 1902; beautifully executed. By the same firm the second and third windows from the E.

Built into a shed at the NW end of the churchyard is an ARCH of c. 1200, perhaps a former doorhead of the church. Semicircular with a roll moulding.

At LINTON, ½ m. N across the Wharfe, is a handsome C18 PAVILION in the garden of a house at the N end of Linton Lane. Originally at North Ferriby (East Riding), it is square with vermiculated quoins and voussoirs to arches on four sides. Ball finials at the corners of a pyramid roof surmounted by an urn.

ROMAN VILLA, Dalton Parlours, 1½ m. SW. Known since the C18 but first excavated in 1854–5, when a hypocaust and a villa were discovered. The site was occupied from 200 to 370 A.D. The villa was of the corridor type with wings and had an apsidal room with a C4 tesselated pavement with a very expressive Medusa head (now in the Yorkshire Museum). Further excavation on the same site in 1976–9 revealed not only the rest of the Roman complex, with a total of nine buildings including a bath house, but also the site of an extensive, palisaded IRON AGE ENCLOSURE with eight round-houses.

CONISTON COLD

ST PETER. 1841–6 by *George Webster* of Kendal for J. B. Garforth of Coniston Hall. Very similar to his church at Bardsea, Cumbria. Ashlar. E.E. style, with primitive plate tracery. W tower with octagonal belfry stage and spire, no chancel. Simple unaltered interior, with three-decker PULPIT. – Small Victorian ROYAL ARMS.

CONISTON HALL, 1841–9, also by *Webster* for J. B. Garforth, was demolished in 1970 apart from the Greek Doric entrance portico and a forecourt archway, which were retained as features on the drive to its successor. LODGE by *Webster*, two storeys with Greek Doric porch.

BRIDGE, over the river Aire. 1763 by *John Carr*, in his capacity as one of the Surveyors of Bridges for the West Riding.

Unornamented, of three arches, the central one semi-elliptical and the others segmental.

At BELL BUSK, 1 m. N, RAVEN FLATT FARMHOUSE. C17 with two-storey porch entered at the side.

CONISTONE

ST MARY. The two W bays of the arcade are Norman: plain unmoulded arches with hoodmoulds, square pier and responds with plain abaci. The other two bays Perp with the usual octagonal pier and double-chamfered arches. The rest of the nave and aisle rebuilt, and the chancel added, all à la Normande, by *Sharpe & Paley* 1846. – FONT. Plain square bowl, possibly Norman, on a restored stem and chamfered base.

A few C17 Dales farmhouses in the little village, including on the W side of the green TOPHAM'S, the lobby-entry type, dated 1630; RENSHAW COTTAGE, with a decorative plaster over-mantel dated 1697; and RENSHAW FARM, with a big two-storey porch of 1705 entered at the side. At the S end HEMPLANDS, much altered in the C19 but an account survives detailing its erection for Richard Wigglesworth in 1694–5. It cost *c*. £60. Porch bearing 1694 date.

BRIDGE, over the Wharfe. *c*. 1790–6 by the West Riding Bridges Surveyor *John Gott* and his son and successor *William Gott*, replacing one of the C17. Three arches.

See also Kilnsey.

CONONLEY

ST JOHN THE EVANGELIST. 1864 by *F. H. Pownall* (cf. Carleton), built as a chapel of ease of Kildwick. Unaisled rectangle in C13 Gothic, with much use of plate-traceried rose windows. – STAINED GLASS. E window 1895.

CONONLEY HALL. *c*. 1775 for the Swire family. Two-and-a-half storeys, with three-bay front and five-bay flank to l. Doorway with pediment on Tuscan half-columns. Spacious staircase the full height of the house, one room with Adam-style doorcases and entablature. Attached to the r. is part of the previous hall, with re-set datestone of 1683 and mullion-and-transom windows. Other C17 houses in the main street include PEAR TREE FARMHOUSE, with two three-light first-floor windows with flattened truncated-ogee heads.

In SKIPTON ROAD and MEADOW LANE an award-winning housing scheme, 1978–9 by *Wales, Wales & Rawson* for Craven District Council. Short two- and three-storey terraces in reclaimed stone informally arranged and carefully integrated with existing buildings on the site.

On the hillside ¾ m. SSW, well-preserved remains of CONON-LEY LEAD MINE, *c.* 1842 etc. for the Duke of Devonshire. The ENGINE HOUSE is roofless but stands to full height, a gabled rectangle very similar to the Cornish engine houses – the Devonshires' mineral agent J. C. Eddy was a Cornishman – with squat tapering CHIMNEY nearby. To the E is the mine-shaft PORTAL and beyond that, on the same alignment, the portal of the INCLINED PLANE, 1849, with rock-faced vous-soirs. N of this the probable MAGAZINE BUILDING, small and featureless, and to the S the RESERVOIR, approximately square.

COPGROVE

3060

No village. The church just outside the grounds of the hall.

ST MICHAEL. Very small, nave and lower chancel. One plain Norman window in the latter, unmoulded Norman chancel arch on imposts with crude zigzag; and internally in the nave N wall a late Norman arched recess of uncertain purpose, with nailhead ornament. Other chancel windows Dec and Perp, nave windows all from an extensive restoration of 1897–8 by *C. Hodgson Fowler.* Pedimented W bellcote probably early C19. – SCULPTURE. Incised panel, possibly pre-Christian, perhaps depicting a sacrifice. Re-set inside in the nave S wall. – Painted ROYAL ARMS of Charles II, the initials and the motto changed to those of Queen Anne. – STAINED GLASS. E window by *Hardman,* 1891.

COPGROVE HALL. *c.* 1820 by *Pritchett & Watson* for Thomas Duncombe. Two-storey block in fine gritstone ashlar. Entrance front (E) with single-storey Tuscan portico to the recessed three-bay centre, S of seven bays with segmental Tuscan porch, W with two segmental bows. Service courtyard to N, flanked by two short wings. Contemporary chimneypieces, doorcases etc. in the main rooms. Huge top-lit rectangular staircase hall in the middle of the house, with arcaded gallery round at first-floor level, partly remodelled *c.* 1920. STABLE BLOCK to the E, with rusticated quoins and gatepiers. Small LAKE and mid-C19 three-arched BRIDGE, to S.

COPT HEWICK

3070

HOLY INNOCENTS. 1876 by *Lewis & Broderick* of Ripon, one of a trio of modest brick-built structures erected by J. S. Hurst of Copt Hewick Hall. Plain lancets, polychrome bands. Semicir-cular apse to the chancel, timber flèche on the nave roof and projecting bell-frame in the apex of the W gable. – The other buildings, alongside, are the SCHOOL, 1887, and the CLOCK TOWER, 1893, a Toytown miniature Big Ben, both by Hurst's son *Arthur Hurst.*

BRIDGE, over the Ure, ⅞ m. SW. Probably C18. Six arches, widened on the upstream side.

COWGILL
Dent

ST JOHN. 1837–8 by *Edmund Sharpe* (cf. Howgill), the foundation stone laid by the geologist Adam Sedgwick. Lancet-style chapel, with unaisled nave and one-bay chancel. Slate-hung timber bellcote with stumpy spirelet. – MONUMENT. Anne Blackmore, daughter of Paul Nixson of Stone House Marble Works, †1888, and her parents. By *George Nelson.* Profile relief of a seated angel.

DEE SIDE HOUSE, 1⅝ m. SE. Now Youth Hostel. Early C19, with bargeboarded gables and Gothic-glazed casement windows. Farmhouses include HARBER GILL, ½ m. E, 1700. Porch with shaped door-lintel.

ARTEN GILL and DENT HEAD VIADUCTS on the Settle–Carlisle Line, 1⅜ m. ESE and 2⅛ m. SE. 1870–5, *J. S. Crossley* chief engineer. Eleven and ten arches, rock-faced limestone. Also DENT STATION, ⅝ m. ENE. *c.* 1876, by the Midland Railway Company's architect *J. H. Sanders,* his standard design for the line's smaller stations, single-storey with bargeboarded gables. 1150 ft (350 metres) above sea level, with a spectacular view down Dentdale.

COWLING

HOLY TRINITY. 1844–5 by *Chantrell,* a daughter church of Kildwick. Perp, quite large. W tower also serving as the porch, with doorway on the S side (cf. Lothersdale).

CARR HEAD HALL, ¾ m. NNE. Gentry house built probably in the 1750s for Richard Wainman. Various later alterations. Plain five-bay S front with pedimented Doric doorcase. E flank with canted bay added in C19. Early C20 columned entrance to N. Some good original interiors, the highlight a coved Baroque ceiling to the lobby above the entrance hall similar in style to the plasterwork of the 1730s by *Vassalli* and *Quadri* at Gisburne Park (q.v.) and Towneley Hall, Lancashire. An eagle in the centre and portrait medallions with busts in profile. In the rooms to each side pilasters flanking the chimneypieces, and enriched cornices and overmantels. Top-lit central staircase, cantilevered with wrought-iron balustrade, later C18 doorcases in the entrance hall.

C17 farmhouses in the parish include LONG CROFT, ½ m. N, with gabled cross-wing projecting at the rear and two-storey porch with jettied upper stage. Stepped windows, of five lights to the porch and three lights in the cross-wing gable. Lobby entry, big segment-headed fireplaces to both the housebody and the separate kitchen in the back part of the wing. Stone spiral staircase.

On the crest of Earl Crag, a gritstone outcrop E of the village, two EYECATCHERS, one at each end. To the W, WAINMAN'S PINNACLE, a sort of roughly built obelisk, in origin supposedly early C19, rebuilt 1898, for the Wainman family of Carr Head Hall. To the E LUND'S TOWER, a square rock-faced turret, 1887 for James Lund of Malsis Hall (*see* Glusburn).

⁴⁰⁵⁰

COWTHORPE
Tockwith

ST MICHAEL (Churches Conservation Trust). Built in 1456–8 by Sir Bryan Rouclyff, lawyer, Baron of the Exchequer, lord of the manor and patron of the living. The church mentioned in Domesday stood ½ m. SW, but in his petition Rouclyff described it as in a state of disrepair and difficult for villagers to reach. Nave, chancel and W tower – the feature of particular interest – which rises half inside and half outside the W wall. On the inside it is carried on corbels springing from the W wall, on the outside on two very massive side-spreading buttresses linked at their top by a deep arch with two chamfered transverse ribs above which the W wall of the tower rises flush. One thinks of a gatehouse, but instead of a door in the deep recess there is the large three-light W window. The bell-openings and most of the other windows are of two lights, straight-headed. C16 S porch. Scraped interior. The roof is of 1864, but reuses C15 principals. – Contemporary FONT. Square, with on each side a shield flanked by blank tracery, the shields with heraldry of the Rouclyffs and others. On a cruciform pedestal. –

²⁶ EASTER SEPULCHRE. A delightful and rare C15 survivor. It is of the movable type, like a chest with a gabled Dec canopy over. The chest has six blank panels, thickly cusped in the segmental arches. The canopy, carried on corner posts, has delicate pierced crestings, and the emblems of Rouclyff and of Burgh (from whom the manor was bequeathed to Sir Bryan). – COMMUNION RAIL. C17, with stubby balusters. – STAINED GLASS. Heraldic fragments, including the red lions' heads of the Rouclyffs. – MONUMENT. The grand but mutilated brass to Sir Bryan Rouclyff †1494 and his wife Joan Hammerton celebrates his role as 'fundator et constructor huius ecclesie',

as a lost inscription recorded. He and she – though that figure is lost too – hold a large model of the church. The surviving figure is 3 ft 3 in. (1 metre) long.

COWTHORPE HALL, NW of the church. Four-bay front of C17 brick, and a rear of C19 limestone ashlar, probably concealing an earlier building. (Lobby-entry plan, plaque inside with the shield of Rouclyff and Hammerton.)

CRACOE

CRACOE HOUSE. Early C18 double pile incorporating some C17 fabric at the rear. Five-bay front, with pedimented doorway and a band between the storeys ramped up at the ends (cf. St Helens, Eshton and Stone Gappe, Lothersdale), the windows with later sashes.

TOPPAN HOUSE. Dales farmhouse dated 1622, i.e. an early example.

SCHOOL. 1853. Effective simple Gothic.

CROSS ROADS WITH LEES
Haworth, Cross Roads and Stanbury

Agglomeration of industrial settlements across the valley from Haworth.

ST JAMES. 1909–10 by *J. B. Bailey & Son* of Keighley. Low-key Perp. The base of an intended, very squat, NW tower serves as a porch. The interior seems larger, with wide-arched nave arcades. – STAINED GLASS. E window in the manner of Clayton & Bell.

METHODIST CHAPEL. The former Sunday School, 1873. Attractive six-bay front with two-bay pedimented centre. The chapel proper, 1844, was demolished in 1966. On the other side of the road LEES FARM, a virtual pair to the Manor House at Stanbury of 1753 (q.v.). Symmetrical front with a combination of a doorway with pediment and pilasters, and windows with (unchamfered) mullions. Little round-headed window over the doorway.

LONGLANDS (Youth Hostel), ¼ m. WNW. 1884 by *W. & J. B. Bailey* for Edwin Merrall of Merrall Brothers, proprietors of Ebor Mill, Haworth (q.v.), in the valley just below the house. Jacobean style with gables, and some occasional quirky Free Renaissance details including a rather gross porte cochère. Staircase hall with elaborate arcaded upper stage and stained glass by *G. F. Malins*. Another Merrall house, Law House (dem.), was nearby.

VALE MILL, ½ m. NW in the narrow valley bottom. Integrated worsted mill of *c.* 1850–70 for Jonas Sugden formerly incorporating a water-powered cotton-spinning mill built by John Greenwood in 1792. The earliest part now is an L-shaped three-storey range dramatically spanning the road and the river which is presumably the warehouse building opened in 1852. Slightly later four-storey spinning mill to S, shed behind. Across the road a row of mill-workers' cottages with former schoolroom at one end, also built by Greenwood.

CULLINGWORTH

Mill village near Bingley.

ST JOHN. 1851–3 by *Perkin & Backhouse* of Leeds. Lancet style, cruciform, with tower and broach spire in the SW re-entrant and short polygonally apsed chancel. – STAINED GLASS. Chancel SE and S, and S transept S, by *Powell Bros* of Leeds, 1883 and 1889.

Some C17 houses W of the church. In the village centre the former METHODIST CHAPEL, 1824, the five-bay front with a sundial of 1832; the WAR MEMORIAL, 1924 by *J. B. Bailey & Son* of Keighley, a tall battered pedestal; and the entrance archway to CULLINGWORTH MILL, mid-C19, on the diagonal between the canted ends of two ranges set at right angles. To the NW, ELLAR CARR MILL, partly demolished and much altered, now housing. Founded late C18 for cotton spinning, converted to worsted *c.* 1830, redeveloped 1884 onwards. Remaining parts include a short three-storey range dated 1820 which contained a warehouse on the ground floor and workers' cottages above. Crenellated boundary wall with arched entrance, dated 1894.

HALLAS OLD HALL, ½ m. ESE. Double-pile block of *c.* 1700, three rooms wide with lobby entry (cf. Mytholme, Wilsden). Doorway with flattened ogee on the lintel, and an upright oval window in a rectangular frame (cf. East Riddlesden Hall, Keighley) above. Two bays of cross-windows to the l., four to the r. and then another doorway matching the first, giving independent access to the parlour.

HEWENDEN VIADUCT, ¾ m. SE. 1884, *John Fraser* engineer. On the Great Northern Railway's madcap high-level route from Bradford to Keighley via Denholme. Seventeen rock-faced arches, the tallest 120 ft (36 metres) high, on a sharp bend.

CATSTONES RING, ¾ m. N. Late prehistoric enclosed settlement site, approximately rectangular, the bank and ditch well defined on the E side. CASTLE STEAD RING, 1 m. WSW, is another, smaller and oval, the N half of the rampart surviving.

DACRE

The main settlement is Dacre Banks.

HOLY TRINITY. 1837. Lancet-style box with gawky W tower. Said to have been designed 'by a young lady of the neighbourhood' (*Gentleman's Magazine*).*

SUMMER BRIDGE, over the Nidd. Probably C17, widened and much rebuilt C19. Two arches.

ROYAL OAK INN. 1752. Altered three-bay front with some sub-Vanbrughian details.

LOW HALL, ⅝ m. S. C17 gentry house, a substantial block with a smart triple-gabled front. The datestone of 1635 looks imported, a lintel set above a doorway which is complete with its own Tudor-arched head. A date later in the century seems more likely, after the property had been acquired by the Lacon family in 1675. Mullion-and-transom windows to the ground and first floors under continuous dripmoulds, the lower on carved brackets. Also a little flattened-ogee-headed light to a first-floor closet, and a C20 copy below. In the gables two-light mullioned windows with round-headed lights and separate hoodmoulds. Carved finials to the gable verges. Interior largely reconstructed 1920.

Farmhouses include HAREWELL HALL, 1¼ m. NW, 1662, with gabled cross-wing.

DALLOWGILL

Laverton

ST PETER. 1846. Little E.E. chapel, nave and chancel.

FORTRESS DYKE CAMP, 1¼ m. NW. Approximately square enclosure, with earthen bank and ditch, covering nearly two acres on the open moor. Probably Iron Age or Romano-British.

DARLEY

Menwith with Darley

THE HOLME. At the E end of the suburban straggle of a village. Timber-framed house probably of *c.* 1500, cased in stone 1667. Thatched roof, mullioned windows, low full-length rear outshut. (The timber-framed building was of four bays, with an open hall, a chimney bay and service end to the E, and a storeyed parlour end to the W. Some panelling and doors of

---

*Pevsner noted a poster advertising the opening service, 'printed at Ripon in the attractive types of the day'.

1667.) Restored after a fire in 1983 which destroyed much of
the roof structure.

DARLEY MILL, at the w end. Picturesque grouping of a former
corn mill, water- and steam-powered, of *c.* 1800 onwards, and
the mill house, dated 1767. Main range of three storeys with
loading doors and a forebuilding with round-headed cart
entrances, two-storey engine house to the l. and the mill house
l. again. Behind the engine house the truncated chimney, and
at the back of the main building a breast-shot water wheel, of
timber with an iron rim. Some driving machinery inside. Now
a shop.

RAF MENWITH HILL, 1¼ m. SSE. The well-known assemblage
of white 'radomes' – fibreglass-covered geodesic globes – protecting equipment variously described as satellite tracking
dishes or listening devices. Constructed at several dates from
c. 1974 onwards. There are over a score in all, of different sizes,
amid the usual clutter of a military base.

0030

DENHOLME

Substantial C19 mill village high in the Pennines w of Bradford,
but all the mills have gone.

ST PAUL. On rising ground s of the village. 1843–6 by
R. D. Chantrell. E.E. style, quite large, with w tower and broach
spire. (Seven-bay nave arcades with quatrefoil piers, plaster
rib-vaults to nave and chancel, w gallery. – STAINED GLASS. E
window by *Wailes*, 1846.) Disused at the time of writing.

The main building in the centre is the former MECHANICS'
INSTITUTE, 1880. Simplest trecento Gothic with gabled front
end.

7080

DENT

Picturesque village of narrow cobbled streets and whitewashed
rubble-built cottages, in a dale where the settlement pattern is
otherwise one of scattered farmsteads.

ST ANDREW. Squat unbuttressed w tower of *c.* 1785, reusing
some of the materials from its predecessor, including the
straight-headed Perp belfry openings of two trefoil-headed
lights and the copings of the battlemented parapet. Blocked N
doorway, possibly Norman, re-set, with one slight chamfer and
a hoodmould. The rest appears Late Perp externally. Nave and
chancel in one, with aisles and chancel chapels. Clerestory
taken down *c.* 1785 and rebuilt in the major restoration by *Paley
& Austin*, 1889–90. Aisle and chapel windows all straight-

headed, most with uncusped round-headed lights, renewed E
window with a transom and five stepped round-headed lights
under a segmental hoodmould. Six-bay arcades in two parts of
three bays each, separated by a big octagonal pier which presumably marks the position of a former chancel arch. Cylindrical piers and double-chamfered arches to the W parts, the
piers at least probably early C13, the E all Perp with double-
chamfered arches on the usual octagonal piers. No tower arch.
– PULPIT. 1614, with lozenge ornament in the panels and a
bracketed desk bearing the date. Base and steps 1889. – PEWS.
In the aisles simple benches, probably early C18, with knobs
on the ends, facing into the nave. E and W of them, box pews
dated 1619, 1685, 1715 etc, rearranged 1889. – STAINED GLASS.
Four windows in the S aisle and S chapel by *Powell & Sons*,
1892 (two), 1897 and 1935. – E window by *Shrigley & Hunt*,
1912 – MONUMENTS include two early C18 Doric aedicules,
the inscriptions illegible.

At the NW corner of the churchyard the former GRAMMAR
SCHOOL, now a house. Founded 1604. Humble two-storey
range, probably early C18, with plain two-light windows. W
from the church the former NATIONAL SCHOOL, now village
hall, 1845. Tall two-light mullioned windows with hoodmoulds.
METHODIST CHAPEL, W again, 1834, and former CONGRE-
GATIONAL CHAPEL, further S, 1835, both with round-headed
windows. Interiors altered.

Outlying farmhouses include HIGH HOUSE, ¾ m. W, 1687, a
long range with mullioned windows of two and three lights and
single-light windows with rounded heads. Also HIGH HALL,
⅜ m. N, built 1625, rebuilt 1665, according to an inscription;
and BIGGERSIDE, ½ m. NNW, probably 1690: both altered,
with cylindrical chimneys.

GATE, 2¾ m. NW. 1888, incorporating part of an earlier farmhouse. Quirky combination of *cottage orné* and Old English.
Gothic porch, fancily bargeboarded gables, pointed sash
windows with glazing bars and hoodmoulds, canted bays with
battered bases and leaded casements, and cylindrical chimneys. Drawing room with inglenook. Low and rambling, part
of the house with the main rooms on the upper floor and a
basement below.

See also Cowgill.

DENTON   *1040*

ST HELEN. 1776 for Sir James Ibbetson of Denton Hall, presumably by *Carr* (*see* below), replacing a chapel of medieval
origin which stood closer to the hall. Hybrid Gothic-cum-
classical. Narrow three-bay rectangle with pointed windows,
including a sort of Venetian window at the E end. Engaged W
tower, the lower stage square with quatrefoil openings, the

upper an open octagonal belfry with battlements and pointed arches. C19 W porch. W gallery over the entrance vestibule, with three tall round-headed openings at the front. – FONT. Shallow octagonal bowl on an elegant splayed and fluted base. – STAINED GLASS. Centre light of the E window, 1700 by *Henry Gyles* of York, transferred from the previous chapel. King David playing his harp, with cherubs, musical scores and 'some not very consistent accompaniments of modern instruments' (Whitaker). An important example of English glass painting of the period. In the side light to the l. the arms of the Fairfax family, presumably contemporary. To the r. those of the Ibbetsons, 1776 by *William Peckitt* of York. – MONUMENTS. Sir James Ibbetson †1795, by *R. Cooke*. With female mourner and an urn from which issues a dying branch. – Lady Charlotte Ibbetson †1827, by *M. Taylor* of York. High-relief sarcophagus. – Sir Charles Ibbetson †1839, by *J. B. Leyland* of Halifax. A dying tree with its branches touching a tomb.

DENTON HALL. James Ibbetson, a Leeds clothier, bought the old seat of the Fairfaxes in 1735, and the present house was built for his grandson Sir James Ibbetson by *Carr* in 1772–8. Externally it presents a conventional Palladian scheme of rectangular main block and recessed service pavilions, chiefly notable for the quality of the sandstone ashlar and the satisfyingly crisp detail. The main block rather low, of two storeys over a submerged basement. Nine-bay S front, with pedimented three-bay centre treated as an engaged Ionic portico. The ground-floor windows and the front doorway also have pediments, segmental within the portico, triangular to each side. Central canted bays to the flanks, the back again with a pedimented centre but very plain, without even a doorway. The pavilions are of two lower storeys and three by four bays, with hipped roofs and columned cupolas, and are linked to the main block by short quadrant screens behind which are corridors at

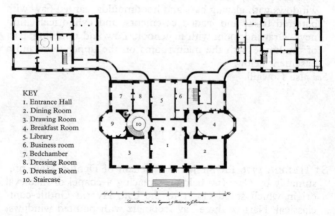

KEY
1. Entrance Hall
2. Dining Room
3. Drawing Room
4. Breakfast Room
5. Library
6. Business room
7. Bedchamber
8. Dressing Room
9. Dressing Room
10. Staircase

Denton Hall.
Ground-floor plan, before C20 alterations

basement level. They contained the kitchens to the E, and the wash-house and laundry, together with a dairy and a hot and cold bath, to the W. The main rooms have good-quality Adamesque plasterwork executed by *Thomas Rothwell* and some excellent chimneypieces, and were quite skilfully planned. Square entrance hall with a screen of four Ionic columns towards the back, flanked by balancing drawing and dining rooms. From the part of the hall behind the columns there is access to the r. to an apsidal-ended former breakfast room, extending into one of the canted bays; and to the l. to the staircase – circular, domed and top-lit, with a lively wrought-iron balustrade – beyond which is a large octagonal former dressing room extending into the other bay. Further back were the principal bedchamber, another dressing room, a library and a business room, but at this point the scheme is jarringly interrupted by a large Baronial-style billiards room made out of three of these spaces and a Jacobethan ballroom occupying the whole of the ground floor of the wash-house wing. In the latter a sumptuous C17 fireplace and overmantel brought from Coombe Abbey, Warwickshire. The surprising thing is that all this was done not in the 1870s but in the 1930s, the stock-in-trade of *White Allom & Co*.

Former STABLES by *Carr*, NW of the house. Fifteen-bay front, the centre and end parts of one storey, punctuated by the taller two-bay ends of a pair of wings projecting to the rear. Round-headed openings in a blind arcade. Also the EAST LODGES, ½ m. ESE. Octagonal, single-storeyed. Gatepiers and screen walls between them.

DRAUGHTON

0050

MANOR HOUSE. Dated 1659. Segment-headed housebody fireplace inserted later in C17, evidently replacing a timber firehood.

At CHELKER RESERVOIR, 1½ m. ESE, and at LOB WOOD, 2¼ m. E, beside the river Wharfe, respectively a CONTROL BUILDING and PUMPING STATION, 1978–80 by *Brian Clouston & Partners* for the Yorkshire Water Authority. Two buildings sensitively attuned to their surroundings, resembling traditional stone-built Pennine barns but in no sense pastiche. Careful massing and broken roof-lines.

DRIGHLINGTON

2020

ST PAUL. 1878–80 by *W. Swinden Barber* of Halifax, replacing a chapel of ease of Birstall built *c.* 1783. Perp, quite large and rather bleak, with a broad unbuttressed W tower. – FITTINGS. Scheme of *c.* 1928 by *Sir Charles Nicholson*, including main and chapel reredoses and screens to S aisle and tower. – MOSAIC decoration over the chancel arch, 1887. – STAINED GLASS. E window and five others by *Kempe*, 1878–1905; three more by *Kempe & Co.*, 1927–32.

BOARD SCHOOL (former), Whitehall Road. 1874–5 by *Lockwood & Mawson*. An unusual example, in the simplified Italianate style associated with their industrial buildings. One storey, with pyramid-roofed clock turret in the centre and gabled end-projections.

LUMB HALL, Back Lane. Handsome Pennine gentry house of the mid C17. Triple-gabled front with a wheel window to the upper floor of the porch (cf. East Riddlesden Hall, Keighley (*c.* 1648); also Barkisland Hall (1638) etc., West Riding South). Mullion-and-transom windows of six, eight and six lights (those to the first floor with the transom removed), and in the gables odd little trefoil-headed openings. The back also triple-gabled but with the centre slightly recessed, with a half-landing staircase window. Lobby entry, housebody with panelling and segment-headed fireplace, parlour similarly but more ornately finished, kitchen with a larger segment-headed fireplace back to back with the housebody's. Staircase opening off the house-body, with turned balusters. More arched fireplaces, panelling, and plaster decoration to the chambers.

DUNSFORTH

4060

ST MARY, Lower Dunsforth. 1860 by *Mallinson & Healey*. Conventional Dec. Nave, lower chancel, and SW tower-porch with broach spire. In the vestry a Norman doorway from the chapel previously on the site. One order of shafts with scalloped capitals, roll moulding and foliage pattern to the arch. Also another Norman capital. – STAINED GLASS in the chancel by *Wailes*.

Former SCHOOL HOUSE, 1861, to the E; former VICARAGE, 1866, to the W.

DUNSOP BRIDGE
Bowland Forest High

6050

ST HUBERT (R.C.), ⅜ m. W of the hamlet. 1864–5 by *E. W. Pugin*. Single unaisled vessel with semicircular apse. Lancet windows, bellcote on the W gable. N porch with half-hipped roof, the only touch of trickiness. – STOUP, just inside the door. Probably medieval, on a C19 marble shaft. – STAINED GLASS. E and W windows by *Capronnier*, 1865.

HAREDEN FARMHOUSE, ¾ m. w again. Dated 1690. Ornamented doorhead with three flattened ogees (cf. Stakes, Whitewell).

EARBY

9040

ALL SAINTS. 1909 by *Bromet & Thorman* of Tadcaster. Art Nouveau-inflected Gothic, with a very large tripartite E window with Flamboyant tracery. Nave and chancel of the same height. The N aisle and a proposed SW tower and W baptistry were not built. – FONT. From St John, Little Horton Lane, Bradford (1871–3 by *T. H. & F. Healey*, dem. 1965). Quatrefoil-shaped bowl with trefoil-headed arcading, on four stumpy columns with spiral decoration. – Abstract STAINED GLASS in the E window, 1975 by *A. Fisher & P. Archer.*

Former GRAMMAR SCHOOL, E of the church in industrial surroundings. Now a museum. In existence by 1658. Two storeys, with off-centre full-height porch. The longer part to the l., with windows of four-plus-four lights, was the school, the part to the r., with five-light windows, the master's house (cf. Burnsall). Interior gutted.

EAST ARDSLEY

3020

ST MICHAEL, Church Lane. 1880–1 by *W. Swinden Barber* of Halifax. Perp, quite large, with W tower (cf. Drighlington). Reused from the previous church is the Norman S doorway, with two orders of (renewed) colonettes and arch with two orders of zigzag and an innermost of curious raised saltires. – FONT. Dated 1663. Octagonal, with recessed panels. – PANELLING in the vestry, made from the box pews of the old church, one part dated 1634. – STAINED GLASS. Good series by *Heaton, Butler & Bayne*, c. 1881–98. – SW of the church the former VICARAGE, 1846. Neo-Jacobean with steep gables. In the grounds another memento of the old church, the re-erected head of a Perp window.

OLD HALL, Main Street. Pennine-style gentry house, dated 1622 on the W cross-wing and 1652 on the hall range, this and the E cross-wing doubtless replacing an earlier range.* The unusual feature is that the front of the hall range is symmetrical, with the two-storey gabled porch in the centre and so leading directly into the middle of the hall. Mullion-and-transom windows, near-continuous to both front and sides of the porch upper stage, of three lights to the hall range l. and r. of it, seven lights to the W cross-wing and five to the E – so

---

*Restored 1988 by *Darby, Miller & Brown* for the Yorkshire Buildings Preservation Trust.

the symmetry is not quite complete overall. Later C17 gabled block behind the hall range, probably for a kitchen – there are parlours at the front of both wings; lean-to addition of *c.* 1700, with cross-windows, against the flank of the E wing. Most of the interior detail also of this last period – the hall having lost a C17 plaster overmantel referred to in C19 descriptions: staircase with heavy turned balusters, E chamber with fielded panelling. E of the house a late C16 timber-framed BARN cased in stone probably in the C18. Three bays, kingpost trusses.

ARDSLEY MILLS, Bradford Road, ⅜ m. NW. Structurally advanced worsted spinning mill of 1912, for Thomas Ambler & Son of Bradford. Main building by *Mouchel & Partners* of London, using the Hennebique system of wide-spanning reinforced concrete construction for which they were UK agents: three by sixteen bays, two storeys and basement, with engine house attached at right angles halfway along the SE side – i.e. the 'double mill' form (cf. Knowle Mill, Keighley) – and water tower opposite against the other. The frame is fully exposed, infilled with large windows and a small amount of red brick. Flat roof behind Art Nouveau concrete parapet. The engine house has the same architectural vocabulary but wholly in brick; truncated cylindrical chimney. Detached two-storey OFFICE BLOCK to W, of brick with terracotta dressings in Art Nouveau Renaissance style; and beyond this brick-built terraces of workers' HOUSING.

BLACK GATES HOUSE, Bradford Road, ⅞ m. WNW. Mid-C18. Five-bay ashlar front. Pedimented doorcase with oddly elongated Tuscan half-columns, rusticated quoins. Diocletian windows in the gable-ends. (Cantilevered staircase with cast-iron balustrade and enriched ceiling.)

(HAIGH HALL, Batley Road, 1⅜ m. SW. C16 four-bay timber frame cased in stone in 1768. Kingpost trusses with cambered tie-beams. Doorway with blocked surround, reused C17 coat of arms of the Savile family. Extension to r. early C19.)

EAST KESWICK

ST MARY MAGDALENE. Daughter church of Harewood, 1856–7 by *Mallinson & Healey*. Dec style, aisleless, with pretty octagonal bellcote on the W gable (cf. Langcliffe). – STAINED GLASS. E window by *Powell Bros.* of Leeds, 1890; nave NE by *William Pape, c.* 1919.

EAST MORTON
Keighley

ST LUKE. 1849–51 by *Perkin & Backhouse* of Leeds. Lancet style, with Dec S aisle. – STAINED GLASS includes S aisle E, 1866 by *Heaton, Butler & Bayne.*

In MAIN ROAD a little double-pile house, 1669, with a stepped mullioned window in the l. gable-end. GREEN END FARM, further N in Green End Road, 1666, is similar, the ground-floor windows transomed: extensions to l. and r., the former joining the house to the barn, dated 1664, with big round-headed cart entrance under a gable. N again MORTON HALL, mid-C19 Grecian villa.

ELDROTH
Lawkland

CHAPEL. In existence by 1627, a chapel of ease of Clapham, extensively restored 1861. Tiny rectangular box. C17 Perp E window of three lights, plain two-light side windows mainly renewed. The other detail, including the outsize bellcote on the W gable, supported by a W buttress, all C19.

ELSLACK

ELSLACK HALL. Of medieval origin, much altered C16–C20. Short cross-wing to the W, a wing behind the E end demolished c. 1900 after a fire. C17 porch, with behind it a pointed chamfered doorway, and to the r. of it, lighting the central part of the house, a pair of lancets. In the E gable-end two six-light mullioned windows with arched lights, probably C16, one to each floor. Belonging to the house a large BARN c. 150 ft (46 metres) long, dated 1672, with Tudor-arched cart entrances.

BURWEN CASTLE. A pair of Roman forts, one within the other, on the line of the C1 road between Ribchester and Ilkley. The smaller and earlier one, of c. 70–80 A.D., was a square occupying the higher ground. The larger, of c. 210 A.D., is rectangular. Excavations in 1908–9 showed the former to have had a clay rampart on a stone base, the latter a rampart of stone, its line most distinct at the W end. Both are cut across towards the S side by a disused railway line.

EMBSAY

Spreading suburban village close to Skipton.

ST MARY. 1852–3 by *Thomas Shaw*. Run-of-the-mill Perp, with W tower. – STAINED GLASS. E window by *Capronnier*, 1870; nave S middle by *Kempe & Co.*, 1920; aisle middle by *Shrigley & Hunt*, c. 1927.

EMBSAY KIRK, N of the church, on the site of Embsay Priory (*see* Bolton Abbey). Villa of *c.* 1780 for William Baynes, a little old-fashioned for its date. Three storeys, with a canted bay in the centre and two bays to each side of it. Tall hipped roof. Inside, a delightful apsidal-ended staircase against the r. flank, and another staircase at the back, both with cantilevered stone steps.

MANOR HOUSE, Pasture Road. Dated 1636 inside. Two-storey porch bearing dates of 1652 and 1665, with round-headed entrance, jettied upper stage with six-light mullioned window and additional lights to the flanks, and stepped three-light window in the gable. Other mullioned windows of two to six lights. Lobby-entry plan. A little decorative plasterwork in the porch and housebody.

1040

ESHOLT
Bradford

Little estate village in a leafy oasis beside the river Aire. Esholt Hall is to the SE. The estate was bought by Bradford Corporation in 1906 in order to construct the Bradford Sewage Works (1906–13).

ST PAUL. 1840–2 by *Salvin*, for W. R. C. Stansfield of Esholt Hall. Small, lancet style, of nave with bellcote, and short chancel. – PULPIT. Incorporating small Flemish carved panels dated 1535, with high-relief figures in shell-headed niches.

OLD HALL. An enigmatic building on a moated site, the line of the moat still visible at the back. Two parts, the l. perhaps of *c.* 1600, much altered, with two mullioned windows with arched lights, the r. a taller projecting block with a gable across its whole width, probably mid-C17, with ordinary mullioned windows. Rear wing behind the l. part with some of the windows transomed. Inside some massive posts and beams in both parts but apparently integral with the masonry of the earlier phase. Also kingpost roof trusses in the C17 block.

Several cottage terraces, all late C18 to mid-C19 and entirely plain apart from one at the W end of the village, with two simple Venetian windows.

ESHOLT HALL. Built in 1706–10 for Sir Walter Calverley on the site of a Cistercian nunnery founded in the late C12: a window of two arched lights, presumably medieval, remains in the basement of the N range. The 'chief mason' was *Joseph Pape* of Farnley but the design, urbane and restrained, is not at all of local character. The house, of gritstone, is square, of seven by seven bays and two equal storeys, with a small inner courtyard (cf. Wallington Hall, Northumberland, built by Sir Walter Calverley's father-in-law in 1688). The main elevations are the S and E, the former with pedimented three-bay centre, the latter with the corresponding section slightly recessed. Quoins, modillions to eaves cornice and pediment, tall windows in slim architrave surrounds with plain raised panels above and below. s doorway with surround ramped up in the middle, under a segmental pediment on brackets, the E with more elaborate brackets flanking an enriched frieze. Above the first-floor window over it, an armorial panel. The w side has an off-centre entrance and porch, and canted bay over, all of 1832. Plain service wing of the same date to NW, mid-C19 conservatory (rebuilt) to NE, and between them to the N a laundry range with part of the MONUMENT to Elizabeth Pudsey, last Prioress of Esholt, †c. 1540, built into the wall. The interior of the house is disappointing, much altered C19–C20, with the courtyard built over at ground-floor level. Back staircase with twisted balusters.

w of the house the STABLES and coachhouse, with rainwater heads dated 1727 and 1730. Symmetrical range with pedimented archway in the middle. Flanking parts altered. To the s, built into the river bank, an early C18 GARDEN BUILDING. Heavy Vanbrughian doorway flanked by oculi. Three rooms within, one with a fireplace. Remains of a further part to the l. Said to be on the site of a medieval fulling mill. To the E, at the HOME FARM, a house dated 1691, derelict at the time of writing. Central lobby entry, the doorway with elaborate flattened-ogee head, mullioned windows of three and five lights. Continuous hoodmould above the ground-floor openings, with heavy carved stops. Also a C17 single-aisled barn and two stone-built Dutch barns, probably c. 1800. The approach to the house from the SE is along the line of a mile-long AVENUE planted by Sir Walter Calverley, now flanked by the sewage works.

ESHTON

ESHTON HALL. 1825–7 by *George Webster* of Kendal for Mathew Wilson. One of the earliest examples of the scholarly Jacobean Revival style which Webster pioneered (cf. Netherside Hall, Threshfield, and Underley Hall, Kirkby Lonsdale, Cumbria). Not huge but decidedly out to impress. Symmetrical main block of fine sandstone ashlar crowned by a parapet, the front with a centrepiece of superimposed pilaster orders and strapwork cresting. Big mullion-and-transom windows with sliding sashes, the sash-bars hidden behind the transoms. Contrasting service wing set back on the N side – lower, gabled and built of coursed limestone – with stepped lights to two of its windows. So the local Pennine style formed part of Webster's repertoire. At the junction of the main block and the wing an octagonal turret with ogee cupola – the one real concession to Picturesque values – added c. 1836. Quite sumptuous interior. Big central staircase hall with shallow octagonal dome and imperial staircase, interconnecting drawing room and library on the s side both with fitted bookcases and panelled ceilings. A number of the fine marble chimneypieces which were a speciality of the Webster firm.

HOME FARMHOUSE. C17, altered and extended C19. Two-storey porch originally entered at the side, with jettied upper stage and stepped three-light window.

ST HELENS, ½ m. NW. Early C18 double pile. Five-bay front, with segmental pediment to the doorway, rusticated quoins, and a stringcourse between the storeys ramped up at the ends (cf. Cracoe House and Stone Gappe, Lothersdale). Former cross-windows, now sashes, in architrave surrounds. The entrance leads directly into the housebody, with segment-headed fireplace. Dog-leg staircase with simple turned balusters.

FARFIELD HALL
Addingham

Handsome house of *c.* 1728 (rainwater head) for George Myers, gent. Not of local character, but nor stylistically can it be by Lord Burlington as stated by Whitaker – although the attribution is understandable given that the property adjoined Lord Burlington's estate of Bolton Abbey and Myers's father had been steward there. Double-pile block of two storeys to the front and flank, two-and-a-half at the back, the s front of seven bays with slightly projecting three-bay pedimented centrepiece framed by fluted giant Corinthian pilasters. Finely detailed entablature, the section of the frieze over the centrepiece with decoration derived from Chatsworth, and elaborate coat of arms in the pediment. Rusticated quoins, solid vermiculated parapet formerly crowned by big ornate urns, doorway with broken segmental pediment on brackets. E elevation of five bays with plain pedimented doorway, which leads into a transverse corridor. Several rooms with compartmented ceilings, including the SE parlour which also has panelling with pairs of fluted Ionic pilasters to each wall. Very good staircase, behind the former entrance hall, with three balusters to each tread, of different designs, one turned, one twisted, and one of two spiral strands (cf. Minster House, Ripon). Opening into the hall from there a round-headed doorway flanked by niches, forming a sort of Serliana. Could this be Lord Burlington's fingerprint?

Service wing to W incorporating fabric of the previous house, including some C17 roof trusses. Wing of *c.* 1920 continuing the E front to the N, along the line of the screen wall to the former service yard, containing a music room with Greek-key-ornamented chimneypiece and wall torchères. N of it a pair of very tall Doric gatepiers crowned by urns. S terrace and (largely lost) garden layout by *Thomas Mawson, c.* 1914.

FRIENDS' MEETING HOUSE (Historic Chapels Trust), N of the house beside the road. 1689, the site given by George Myers's grandfather. Tiny simple rectangle with mullioned windows. Elders' bench with raised central section fronted by a balustrade. In the graveyard, chest tombs of members of the Myers family, †1687–1737, a rarity amongst Quakers.

FARNHAM

St Oswald. An interesting church with an excellent Norman chancel, on a slightly larger scale than the rest. Three tall round-headed windows at the E end, similar trios to N and S, and w of these a doorway (the S renewed, the N blocked) with the windows' sill moulding curved up over it as a hoodmould. Also two smaller windows in the gable, and shallow clasping buttresses. At the SW corner, beyond the doorway, a C14 cusped lancet. Inside, the window embrasures form a continuous arcade articulated by shafts. Nave with aisles, the three E bays of the N arcade probably early C13, with cylindrical piers, simple moulded capitals and arches with one slight chamfer, their counterparts to the S of c. 1300, with octagonal piers and double-chamfered arches. The w bays on both sides, beyond a piece of plain wall, represent a lengthening of the nave, but again apparently in two phases, the S arch probably late C14, with foliage capitals, the N C15. Finally, c. 1500, the w tower was inserted into this additional bay but clear of the arcades, with its own N and S arches just in front of them. Only a belfry stage above the roof level, with straight-headed two-light openings, and tiny obelisk-like pinnacles probably from a repair campaign of 1759. Tudor-arched three-light w window. Decent restoration by *G. G. Scott*, 1854, his contributions including the roofs – that of the nave neatly contrived to follow the pitch of the chancel's at a just slightly lower level – most of the aisle windows, in Dec style, and the chancel arch. Reordering etc. 2001–2 by *R. G. Sims*. – Chamber ORGAN. 1820 by *Thomas Elliot* for the Rev. Thomas Collins, Rector 1819–69. – STAINED GLASS. In the chancel SW a small panel of fragments, late C14 or early C15, previously in the w window, re-set 1984. – Other chancel windows 1854 by *Wailes*. – S aisle E by *Morris & Co.* (*Burne-Jones*), 1875. St Cecilia, in rich dark colours.

Old Manor House. Dated 1667. Stone-built lobby-entry range with (renewed) mullioned windows, and a timber arcade, apparently coeval with the masonry, demarcating the rear outshut.

FARNHILL

Farnhill Hall. An important survival, the carcase of a house of the C14 – but extensively altered in the early C19 as to its roof-line, fenestration and interior planning. It was apparently not fortified although its most distinctive feature, a quartet of battlemented turrets marking the corners of the central section, and its position crowning a little knoll, might seem to suggest otherwise. Beyond the turrets are a chamber block to the w – raised from two to three storeys probably in the later c16 (datestone of 1560 in the garden) – and a corresponding kitchen block to the E, making a single three-unit range overall. Of the middle part about two-thirds was occupied by an open hall, the rest presumably by buttery and pantry with a chamber over. Above the N doorway – the present one a c19 replacement – is a gabled garret on big machicolations; to the r. of it are two hall windows, each of two tall trefoil-headed lights; and on the chamber block traces of another of the same type. (In one of the turrets a staircase from the first floor to the roof level.)

THE MULLIONS, in the village street, facing onto the canal. Early c18. Five-bay front with cross-windows, doorway with lugged surround. Stringcourse between the storeys ramped up at the ends (cf. Stone Gappe, Lothersdale).

FARNLEY

No village. Church and house ½ m. apart, on a gentle s-facing slope above the River Wharfe.

ALL SAINTS. Chapel of ease of Otley, in existence by the mid c13, largely rebuilt in 1851. Plain lancet style, nave and chancel in one, some early masonry remaining on the N side. W gallery and below it the squire's family PEW. – STAINED GLASS. In the E window, c17 armorial panels previously at Farnley Hall and before that at Hawksworth Hall (q.v.).

FARNLEY HALL. The seat of the Fawkes family, of two sharply contrasting parts: the c17 house, a rectangle of two storeys and attics originally facing s; and the new block added in front of it by *John Carr* in 1786–90 for Walter Hawksworth Fawkes, previously of Hawksworth Hall. His son, also Walter, was the friend and patron of Turner, whose famous series of water-colours of the house and grounds provides a detailed record of their appearance in the early c19.

The older part has been much altered, particularly in the 1870s when the E flank was turned into a new entrance front. To complicate matters, a number of architectural features had been brought from elsewhere by the younger Walter Fawkes, and some of these were moved again. The central porch of the new front, with round-headed entrance framed by free-standing columns, entablature and strapwork cresting, had been installed in a garden wall; and the (much renewed) canted bay window to the r. of it, with mullions and transoms and arched lights, had been where the porch is now. The former came originally from Menston Old Hall (q.v.), the latter from Lindley Hall (q.v.), a farmhouse on the estate; and a doorway dated 1624 in the wall to the r. of the house, with entablature and fluted columns, from Newall Old Hall at Otley. Wholly of the 1870s are the (false) gables – there had been gables originally but they had gone by Turner's time – and the larger bay window to the l. Other windows, which were de-Georgianized, have had that change reversed in the C20; and a big C19 kitchen wing on the N side has been demolished. Inside this part there are several sumptuous imported C17 overmantels, as well as some panelling which may always have been in the house. Two of them came from Hawksworth Hall in the younger Walter Fawkes's time – it has been suggested that he wished to create a suitable setting for his collection of Cromwellian memorabilia – but that in the drawing room, dated 1630, was bought at Newcastle in the late C19. It has reliefs of Adam and Eve, Abraham and Isaac, and Cain and Abel. On the panelling in this room paintings of birds, dogs, hunting scenes etc, *c.* 1821 by *George Walker*. Spacious staircase of *c.* 1700, with robust turned balusters.

Carr's front block, facing away S over the valley, was begun only months after Walter Hawksworth Fawkes had inherited. It is one of his most successful productions, the exterior extremely restrained, distinguished by its perfect proportions and beautifully precise gritstone ashlar. The front has a canted bay in the centre, the flanks an even five bays. Discreet guilloche band above the ground floor; Doric frieze and cornice, and balustraded parapet, above the first. The front doorway, in the canted bay, has a pedimented doorcase with Tuscan columns, and the windows of the W flank slim architrave surrounds. An oddity is that the other windows had the same surrounds but of wood and only added in the mid C19 – they are not shown in Turner's or other early C19 views, and they decayed and were removed in C20 – but the masonry linings in the window reveals suggest that stone surrounds were intended originally. The INTERIORS are exceptionally fine, repainted in the C20 in the colours shown in Turner's illustrations. Entrance hall-cum-saloon at right angles to the front, the inner as well as the outer end canted. Behind it the top-lit staircase hall. Cantilevered timber imperial staircase with slim balusters, preceded by screens of two unfluted columns to both floors, Ionic below, Corinthian above. Doorway at the halflanding into the first floor of the old house. To each side one two-bay and one three-bay room, one behind the other, in alternating order. On the E side the larger comes first, the dining room, with two attached Corinthian columns *in antis* at each end, exuberant Adam-style plasterwork, and *trompe l'oeil* reliefs – panels and medallions – painted by *Theodore de Bruyn* (cf. Basildon Park, Berkshire). Superb white marble chimneypiece by *John Fisher* of York. On the W side first the library, which has a ceiling derived from a plate in George Richardson's *Book of Ceilings* (1776), with an oval centre on flattened pendentives; then the drawing room, with a shallow segmental plaster tunnel-vault – dated 1790 – its decoration no more than broad, flat ornamented bands. Excellent chimneypieces again in both rooms. Even on the upper floor the planning and all the details are treated with the greatest care. Octagonal room over the entrance hall, reached from the staircase by a groin-vaulted lobby. Further groin-vaulted passages to l. and r. of the staircase.

In the garden behind the house, the so-called OLD DAIRY, a C17 gazebo brought from Newall Old Hall, square with a gable to each side, mullion-and-transom windows. NE of the house a set of C18 GATEPIERS with ball finials, probably from Hawksworth Hall; and beyond them beside the road the FARNLEY LODGE, C19, with mullioned windows and big hipped roof, incorporating a doorway dated 1672, with depressed ogee head. More C18 gatepiers beside it. Across the road THE SQUARE, a late C18 former model farm. U-shaped with a pyramid-roofed central pavilion with Venetian window to the ground floor, various round-headed openings above. The rest plain and altered. ½ m. ESE of the house the EAST LODGES, presumably part of the *Carr* phase, little pedimented boxes with railings and gatepiers between; and further on the C19 LEATHLEY LODGE, in the same style as the Farnley Lodge but octagonal.

FARSLEY
Calverley

2030

Mill village now forming part of the agglomeration linking Leeds and Bradford. The industrial continuation S, towards Pudsey (q.v.), is Stanningley.

ST JOHN, Town Street. 1842–3 by *W. Wallen* of Huddersfield. Lancet style. W tower (rebuilt 1895) with gawky square pinnacles, unaisled nave with W gallery, former organ chamber N of the chancel added 1875–6. Internal refurbishments 1892–3 etc. by *T. H. & F. Healey*. – Tiny portable FONT, a great rarity, dated 1667. Also the initials of the Rev. Elkanah Wales, minister of the Pudsey Chapel. Modern stand. – STAINED GLASS. Mostly by *Wailes*, 1867. – N of the church, across New Street, the former SCHOOL and schoolmaster's house, 1847–51 by *Perkin & Backhouse*. Thin Jacobean, the house with symmetrical front onto Town Street. To their E the Gothic Sunday School of 1887.

ST PAUL (former), off Richardshaw Lane, Stanningley. 1853–6 by *Perkin & Backhouse*. Cruciform, lancet style, with tower and broach spire in the NW re-entrant (cf. Cullingworth).

ST THOMAS, Stanningley Road (W end). 1839–41 by *H. Rogerson*. In the briefly fashionable Neo-Norman style, quite vigorously done. W tower with pyramid roof, nave and lower chancel. – STAINED GLASS. E windows and one nave S, 1869–70 by *F. Preedy*.

Chapels include the former CONGREGATIONAL, Bradford Road, 1855, a minor work of *Lockwood & Mawson*. E.E. In New Street WEST ROYD, a villa of 1866 by *Andrews & Pepper* with minimally French Gothic tower-porch.

CAPE MILLS, Coal Hill Lane. Woollen spinning from *c.* 1813, an integrated mill from *c.* 1864, much reduced. Surviving elements include a three-storey, eight-bay mill of *c.* 1830, with both an engine house incorporated in one end and a water-wheel pit adjoining; a twelve-bay extension of *c.* 1864, equally utilitarian; and an office range of 1891 by *C. S. Nelson* of Leeds. SUNNY BANK MILL, prominent at the foot of Town Street, was established in the 1830s, rebuilt 1912 etc.

FELLISCLIFFE
2050

WEST SYKE MANOR. Fragments of a timber frame of perhaps as early as the C14, encased in stone in the early C17. Mullioned windows of up to five lights, steeply pitched roof, thatched until *c.* 1970. (The timber house was probably of four bays, with an aisle to the rear. Much of the arcade plate, one post and part of another, and part of the front wall-plate remain. Indications of the early date include the uniform section of the posts throughout, notched lap-joints and evidence of double bracing. The roof was apparently of the 'lowland' common rafter type.)

COTE SYKE, ⅛ m. ENE. Dated 1702 on the simply ornamented doorhead at the r. end of front. Mullioned windows. Two further, more elaborate, ornamented doorheads, apparently slightly later, to the single-storey kitchen to the r. and barn to the l. Also another datestone, of 1735, with pious inscription. Torus-moulded parlour fireplace which could go with this date.

KETTLESING GRANGE, ⅛ m. WSW. 1731, also still with mullioned windows and the entrance at one end of the front, but the doorway Tudor-arched. Outbuilding to r. with raised cruck truss.

FERRENSBY
3060

LAKE VIEW FARMHOUSE. Facing the village pond. Elements of a timber-framed house of *c.* 1450 (dendrochronology), enclosed in C18 brick and a little rubble. Hall-and-cross-wing plan, but the wing (l.) apparently reduced in length at the front. Taller C18 block added to r. Part of the wallframe of the former open hall survives, with curved braces, and the remarkable smoke-blackened central truss, with tie-beam, collar, braces to both and a short kingpost above the latter. Floor on moulded beams, and fireplace flanked by lobby entry, inserted *c.* 1600.

FEWSTON

45 ST MICHAEL AND ST LAWRENCE. Squat w tower mainly Perp, the top stage *c.* 1800 with round-headed bell-openings and low battlemented parapet. The body of the church is a charming building of 1697. The s flank has cross-windows to the nave, shorter two-light windows to the lower chancel, all with lugged surrounds, pulvinated friezes and a continuous cornice over. But the e window is C17 Gothic, two-centre-headed, with Perp panel tracery and scrolly stops to the hoodmould. So the two styles continued to exist side by side. s porch with segment-headed doorway, the keystone bearing the date, and another doorway with keystone and lugged surround tucked in below one of the chancel windows. Heavy rusticated quoins. N aisle under the same roof as the nave, more simply detailed with plain two-light windows. Four-bay aisle arcade with stubby Tuscan columns. – FONT. *c.* 1697, octagonal, with carved oak cover. – ROYAL ARMS and CATECHISM BOARDS. Early C19, painted.

RESERVOIRS, in the valley below. Formed 1871–87 by the Leeds Corporation Water Works.

FLASBY

FLASBY HALL. Only a rebuilt rump remains of the picturesque Italianate villa, 1840 by *George Webster* of Kendal for Cooper Preston, itself a remodelling and extension of an earlier house. Quite vigorous simple detailing in fine ashlar, but the controlled asymmetry of the s front has been lost, as has the characteristic belvedere tower which stood at a pivotal position between the body of the house and the service range to the e. *See* also Winterburn.

FOLLIFOOT

ST JOSEPH AND ST JAMES. 1848. Small, in meagre lancet style. – REREDOS of alabaster, with high-relief carved panel.

At the top of the village street a tall early C19 ARCHWAY which was an entrance to Rudding Park (q.v.), the arch framed by Ionic pilasters and blocking course. Lower one-bay lodges attached to l. and r.

FOUNTAINS ABBEY
Lindrick with Studley Royal and Fountains

2060

'Oh what a beauty and perfection of ruin!!' Thus the Hon. John Byng, who throughout his diaries was so much readier to carp than to praise. By the time he wrote, this most picturesque of monastic ruins had already been acquired by William Aislabie of neighbouring Studley Royal (q.v.) and – with arrogant self-confidence and stupendous success – incorporated into his orna-mental grounds as their culminating feature, its lawned and landscaped setting his creation. But Fountains Abbey is of course much more than that. The best-preserved Cistercian monastery in Britain, it has a European importance among the surviving examples of the order's architecture: there is nowhere else in the country where the mind can so readily evoke an image of C12 monastic life, or the eye a picture of both the orderliness and vast extent, and the crispness and freshness, of Cistercian architec-ture in the wild North Country forests.

The origins and early history of Fountains are vividly recounted in the *Narratio de fundatione Fontanis monasterii,* a chronicle of *c.* 1207 compiled by a monk of the daughter house of Kirkstall from the memories of a colleague who had joined the Fountains community in 1135; and the meaning of some passages has been clarified by excavation, which has revealed traces of two churches preceding the present one, the first of timber and the second of stone. All three were built in rapid succession as the monastery developed from inauspicious beginnings towards its later status as the richest of English Cistercian foundations, with a whole family of daughter houses. The founding monks were a dissident reformist group from the Benedictine St Mary's Abbey in York, including the prior and the sacrist, who were perhaps influenced by the Cistercians newly arrived at Rievaulx. They sought the help of Archbishop Thurstan, who gave them shelter for a time and then, towards the end of 1132, assigned to them land in Skelldale as the site for a new monastery – 'a place remote from all the world, uninhabited, set with thorns . . . fit more, it seemed, for the dens of wild beasts than for the uses of mankind'. There, the chronicle relates, they spent the winter of 1132–3 living in caves and then in a hut they built below an elm tree; then early in 1133 they decided to seek adoption by the Cistercian order and sent a petition to Bernard of Clairvaux. In response he despatched a monk named Geoffrey d'Ainai to teach the monks the Cistercian way of life and to advise them on the erection of buildings – tasks in which he evidently specialized – and it was presumably under his guidance that the timber church and an adjoining domestic range were built. But the new monastery failed to attract patronage, and for another two years it still laboured under great difficulties, until in 1135 the wealthy Dean of York and two other canons of the cathedral retired to Fountains, bringing both respectability and some financial stability. The first stone church was begun *c.* 1136 and the first stone monastic buildings a few years later, *c.* 1140; and the first daughter house, at Haverholme in Lincolnshire, was established in 1137. In 1146, however, the abbey was sacked and burnt by followers of the new archbishop, William Fitzherbert, in an act of retaliation against the abbot, who was involved in moves to depose Fitzherbert and was the opposition candidate to replace him. But a complete rebuilding was not begun at once and for the time being the damaged buildings were repaired rather than replaced.

The third church was probably begun shortly after the election in 1150 of Abbot Richard of Clairvaux, a native of York who had been precentor at Clairvaux and abbot of Vauclair before coming to Fountains, and was certainly in progress by the time the restored Archbishop William visited in 1154. Work on the monastic buildings again started a few years later, probably in the 1160s, and on his death in 1170 Abbot Richard was buried in the new chapter house. Of his successor, Robert of Pipewell, who died in 1180, the chronicle records that 'he recommended work on the fabric of the church and erected sumptuous buildings'. So the work on the church was not continuous, but otherwise this statement is not easily interpreted. There are no references to building operations during the period 1180–1203, but it is clear from the architectural detail that the claustral buildings were not completed until *c.* 1200. The new E arm of the church was begun by Abbot John of York (1203–11) and completed by John of Kent (1220–47); but after that nothing of importance was done until *c.* 1500, when Abbot Darnton restored the church and then Abbot Huby built his great N tower. Dissolution took place in 1539. The site went first to Sir Richard Gresham, then in 1597 to Sir Stephen Proctor, who built Fountains Hall (*see* Environs, below) for himself close to the abbey gatehouse. The union with the Studley Royal estate took place in 1768: William Aislabie tidied up the ruins, removing trees and fallen debris, but his more controversial interventions – the piecing together of fragments of tracery, a parterre in the cloister and a 'heathen' statue in the presbytery – were removed during the C19.

Most of the buildings are of gritstone quarried from the cliff that forms the valley's N flank. In the works of the C13 contrasting detail was executed in Nidderdale marble, the fossiliferous limestone of the Yoredale series, polishable to dark grey or black, which outcropped on a grange of the abbey near Pateley Bridge; and in the late C15 and early C16 Abbots Darnton and Huby made widespread use of Magnesian limestone. Before the C14 all the roofs were of red tile or grey stone slab, but later many were lowered in pitch and covered with lead. The abbey has been the subject of extensive archaeological research. In 1790–1 the Ripon antiquary John Martin, inspired by reading Burton's *Monasticon*, excavated the chapter house in a successful search for the graves of the early abbots; and in 1840 his successor Richard Walbran began a twenty-year campaign of excavation, clearing the church, infirmary and abbot's house, and establishing a museum in the abbey's muniments room. Between 1873 and 1876 the standing ruins were recorded in great detail by William Burges's assistant Arthur Reeve – Burges was then engaged on the erection of St Mary Studley Royal – and in 1887–8 W.H. St John Hope carried out a series of excavations for the Yorkshire Archaeological Society, drawing heavily on Reeves's work and establishing for the first time the general layout of a Cistercian abbey. Throughout most of the C20 it was widely assumed that Fountains had little left to tell, until the excavations by Glyn Coppack in 1976–80 and 1984–8.

THE FIRST TWO CHURCHES

Excavation in 1979–80 revealed evidence of two TIMBER BUILD-INGS below the S transept of the present church, one aligned E–W and identifiable as a church, an unaisled rectangle of at least four bays, with N and S doors opposite each other; the other, to the S of it and aligned N–S, a domestic range probably of two storeys. Similar buildings are known to have existed at Clairvaux, Foigny and Meaux. A reference in the chronicle to carpenters at Fountains in 1134 may relate to these structures, and if so suggests that they were the work of skilled craftsmen, not the monks themselves.

Also established was part of the plan of the FIRST STONE CHURCH, and the rest can be deduced by analogy with other early Cistercian churches, e.g. at Waverley (*c.* 1128), Tintern (*c.* 1131) and Fountains's daughter house of Lysa in Norway (*c.* 1146). The church lay below the S transept, the crossing and part of the nave of its successor; and the parts found by excavation were the S transept and the S side of the crossing. The transept had two small E chapels with solid walls between them: deducible are a balancing N transept, square ends to the chapels and the presbytery, and an aisleless nave. The one unusual feature was that the inner chapels were slightly longer than the outer ones, perhaps a memory of the *echelon* form of the E end at St Mary's Abbey, York. The length of the nave can possibly be gauged from some slight irregularities in the E half of its replacement, which may have been built with the earlier nave still standing. In that case, the church was less than half the length of its successor; but it is noticeable that the first stone claustral buildings extended much further W, implying an intention, even then, to enlarge or rebuild it. Regarding the fire of 1146, the chronicle records graphically that all was burnt except the church and its adjoining 'offices', which were likened to 'a brand plucked from the burning'; and the accuracy of this account has been confirmed by excavation, which found that the S transept had been damaged but the rushes on the floor of the choir were not.

THE CHURCH OF c. 1150 ONWARDS

The C12 church, c. 300 ft (90 metres) long, consisted of a straight-ended two-bay presbytery, transepts each with three straight-ended E chapels separated by solid walls, an aisled nave of eleven bays, a W galilee porch, and a tower over the crossing. It therefore broadly conformed to the 'Bernardine' plan of the second church at Clairvaux, of 1135 onwards, but its immediate source was probably Abbot Ailred's church at Rievaulx, in the North Riding, begun in the 1140s. Fountains, however, is much the more ambitious and elaborate design, in which the forms of Cistercian architecture, with its antecedents in Burgundian Romanesque, are accompanied by occasional naturalized Anglo-Norman details. The church was built in at least three stages, the first accounting for the presbytery, crossing, transepts and probably the E five bays of the nave – i.e. the parts used by the monks – the last, of the 1170s, perhaps for no more than the tower and some other finishing touches. But the decision to make provision for a tower evidently belonged to the first phase as the crossing built then was of a proper tower-bearing type. The timing of the decision merits attention, as towers of any sort were originally forbidden under the Cistercian statutes – there was none at either Clairvaux or Rievaulx – but in 1157 it was decreed that 'stone towers with bells shall not be built'; so assuming it was a lantern, not a bell-tower, that at Fountains was permissible.

Of all this, the nave and the greater part of the transepts stand to their full height: the crossing tower has gone. To the visitor approaching from the NW, the EXTERIOR presents an impressively consistent scheme in beautifully precise masonry, with plain round-headed windows and broad, flat buttresses. No nook-shafts or suchlike enrichments. A partial exception to the prevailing austerity comes at the W end, with its doorway of six orders. Finely moulded arch similar to those of the entrances to the chapter house, completed by 1170 (*see* Monastic Buildings); worn scalloped capitals; and, originally, alternating attached and detached shafts (the detached ones missing). In front of the doorway was the galilee porch – a common Cistercian feature, e.g. Pontigny, c. 1150–60 – some fragments of which were re-erected in the 1850s: dainty small open arches with twin shafts and scalloped capitals, set on a high dado. Above is a vast W window inserted by Abbot

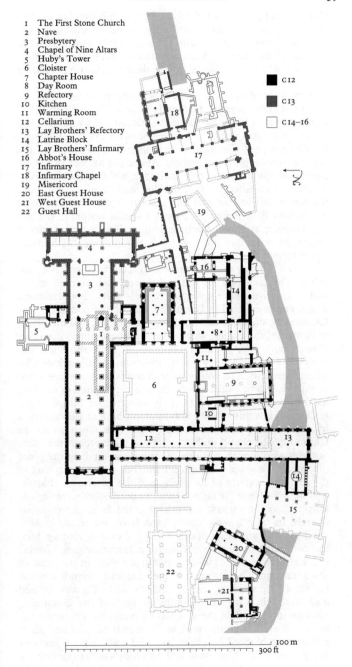

1   The First Stone Church
2   Nave
3   Presbytery
4   Chapel of Nine Altars
5   Huby's Tower
6   Cloister
7   Chapter House
8   Day Room
9   Refectory
10 Kitchen
11 Warming Room
12 Cellarium
13 Lay Brothers' Refectory
14 Latrine Block
15 Lay Brothers' Infirmary
16 Abbot's House
17 Infirmary
18 Infirmary Chapel
19 Misericord
20 East Guest House
21 West Guest House
22 Guest Hall

C12
C13
C14–16

Fountains Abbey.
Plan

Darnton in 1494 (date and rebus above), which replaced a trio of round-headed windows and a rose window, and to the l. a completely plain doorway into the N aisle, now blocked. In the N side of the aisle a wide segment-headed opening, now blocked, which was the barrow hole for delivering building materials.

Inspection of the INTERIOR is best begun further E. Of the C12 presbytery nothing further is known. The end wall has been excavated but is no longer visible. At the CROSSING the SE and NW piers stand to full height, with many-scalloped – i.e. Norman, not Cistercian – capitals still in position, but the other two have gone completely. Above the SE pier is a short shaft, perhaps an insertion of the 1170s, which it has been suggested was intended to carry the diagonal rib of a vault under the tower; but in that case the lantern function of the tower would have been negated. There is a similar feature in the late C12 crossing at Ripon Cathedral (q.v.). The E piers suffered under the weight of the tower – hence the big C14 buttress against the W face of the SE pier.

In the TRANSEPTS the general architectural system is established. The E chapels are entered through tall pointed arches and themselves have pointed tunnel-vaults, both features which had been used in Burgundy, the mother country of the Cistercians, since the early C12 (e.g. at Autun), and then both at Fontenay, the earliest well-preserved Burgundian Cistercian church, built 1139–47, and, it appears, at Rievaulx. Above the arches is a tall clerestory but no triforium, a hallmark of Cistercian austerity. The transepts themselves were never vaulted or intended to be vaulted, even though the method of vaulting used in the chapels is particularly effective for buttressing a high vault; but this was the arrangement both at Rievaulx and in a number of mid-C12 French Cistercian houses, such as Clermont. The chapel arches are of two plain orders, the outer one chamfered, with sections of stringcourse taking the place of capitals – a simple enough scheme but a slight softening of the extreme severity of Rievaulx; and the innermost chapels, now absorbed into the aisles of the C13 presbytery, were slightly longer than the others, a quirk repeated from the previous church. In their E walls the chapels have two round-headed windows with an oculus above them, and outside also a gablet: the oculi are another early Cistercian feature, e.g. at Noirlac and Le Thoronet (c. 1150–60), and also appear in the gable of the S transept. The central S chapel was later extended to the E, with a Perp window, and the arch to the l. of it was patched and remodelled by Abbot Huby as part of the continuing attempt to strengthen the SE crossing pier. The two remaining N chapels are less complete than those to the S, and both their arches were blocked by Huby. The end wall of the N transept is replaced by the high wide arch of Huby's tower (see below). Its counterpart to the S has a shallow central projection containing a staircase, and to the r. of this the evidence for the arrangement of the night stair from the monks' dormitory.

The original stair, from the dormitory built *c.* 1140, came down
to a tall doorway, now partly blocked, at ground level; but when
the E cloister range was rebuilt in the 1160s, with the dormitory at a higher level, a new doorway was made higher up in
the wall, leading to a staircase – at first of timber, later of stone
– which came down inside the transept against the W wall, as
at Bolton Priory (q.v.) and Fontenay. The W walls have two
tiers of round-headed windows, over high plain dados which
retain areas of C12 plaster and paint. The arches from the
transepts into the nave aisles were also round-headed – only
that in the N transept remains – an apparent anomaly which is
explained by the arrangements in the aisles themselves.

The monumental eleven-bay NAVE follows much the same
system in many respects: it was unvaulted, with a wagon roof
– see the wall arch against the W gable – has a two-storey elevation, with pointed arches to the arcades, and had transverse
pointed tunnel-vaults (that is, tunnel vaults running at right
angles to the length of the nave) in the aisles. But the scheme
is modified not only in the ways necessary to accommodate
continuous aisles rather than separate chapels – piers instead
of responds to the arcade, the aisle vaults resting on transverse
arches rather than solid walls – but in other ways as well. The
clerestory windows are slightly larger and the arcade slightly
taller; the arcade arches are more elaborate, double-chamfered
with a roll between and a hoodmould over; and the piers are
entirely Anglo-Norman in character, as if their design had been
left to the local masons: stout cylinders with two attached
shafts at the diagonals towards the aisle and many-scalloped
capitals. The transverse arches in the aisles, however, are plain
and semicircular – hence the form of the end arches from the
transepts. They rest on their own many-scalloped capitals at a
lower level of the piers than the main ones, and on the outer
walls on matching many-scalloped corbels. The arrangement
has something of the *ad hoc* about it but there are no signs of
change or change of mind. Cuts in the masonry where screens
etc. were attached indicate the functional divisions of the nave.
The monks' choir occupied the crossing and the two E bays,
the third was taken up by the pulpitum, which contained two
chapels flanking its central passage, and the fourth was the
retrochoir. The rest was the lay brothers' church, divided from
the retrochoir by the rood screen, against which its altar was
set. In the W wall are three round-headed arches with continuous mouldings, the middle one framing the W doorway, the
others originally containing benches. In the S aisle, towards its
W end, are three more doorways, of which the first (now
blocked) led into the lay brothers' cloister to the W of the W
claustral range (*see* Monastic Buildings), the second, now
leading into the range, was its predecessor, the previous range
having been narrower, and the third is the access to the lay
brothers' night stair. Further E, in the first bay from the E, is
another, leading into the monks' cloister, which is probably
earlier, reused from the first stone church.

The new E arm consisted of an aisled PRESBYTERY of five
bays, begun *c.* 1210 and completed *c.* 1220, and beyond that
an E transept, the CHAPEL OF NINE ALTARS – so called
because it accommodated nine chapels against the E wall –
added *c.* 1220–30. The presbytery was modelled on that at Jer-
vaulx Abbey, of *c.* 1200, and was probably by the same master,
who is thought also to have been responsible for the E.E. parts
of Beverley Minster. The only parallel to the transept is its
counterpart at Durham Cathedral, begun a little later in 1242
– but the late C12 chevet at Clairvaux also had nine chapels.
Of the presbytery only the aisle walls remain standing, with a
dado of trefoil-headed blind arcading – the Nidderdale marble
shafts, as elsewhere in the E arm, all robbed out – and above
that one tall lancet per bay, flanked by blind arches which are
awkwardly distorted to fit within the wall rib of the vault.
Outside, the windows are shafted, those on the N side originally

Fountains Abbey, Chapel of Nine Altars.
Engraving by J. & H. S. Storer, 1830

with gablets over. The arcade piers, of which the bases remain, were alternately octagonal and clustered. The Chapel of Nine Altars, however, stands virtually to full height, a design of great beauty. It is divided laterally into three parts by two-bay arcades continuing the line of those in the presbytery, each with a slender octagonal pier almost 50 ft (15 metres) high which originally had eight detached shafts of dark Nidderdale marble. Dado with trefoil-headed arcading as in the presbytery, and two tiers of lancet windows, again one per bay, the upper combined with a wall passage and both with flanking blind arches handled more elegantly than in the aisles. Full-height vaulting shafts between the bays, again robbed out. In the s wall, a doorway with a finely moulded semicircular head and three orders of colonettes on the outside, which gave access to a passage leading to the infirmary (*see* Monastic Buildings); and above it, cut into the lancet window, a large round-headed opening, probably for the abbot's pew. In the 1480s, under Abbot Darnton, the high vaults of both the transept and the presbytery were removed as unsafe, and the big E window – replacing a trio of lancets and an elaborate rose window, as at the W end – was inserted, together with new windows in the transept ends. On a repair above one of the s lancets a figure of St James of Compostella and a portrait corbel of Darnton wearing a mitre. Within the E dado a number of aumbries for the individual chapels, and in front of it some of the altar bases and floor piscinas: the chapels were separated by solid masonry partitions, replaced by timber screens in C15. Outside, along the E wall an impressive uniform row of tall buttresses, the centre two extended in Darnton's time.

Finally, attached to the N end of the C12 N transept is HUBY'S TOWER, big, sturdy and 160 ft (49 metres) high, given by Abbot Marmaduke Huby *c.* 1500 as a sign of his and his house's pride. By this date the Cistercian prohibition on bell-towers carried little weight, and a number of other northern monasteries built or began them, including Cistercian Furness, in Cumbria, and Augustinian Bolton Priory (q.v.). Five-light N window, three-light E and W windows. Three storeys above the roof-line, the first with four-centre-headed three-light windows, the next with large four-light bell-openings, and the topmost with much smaller straight-headed windows of three arched lights. Massive angle buttresses with niches, supporting diagonally set pinnacles, now truncated. Enriched battlements. Three bands of inscriptions, including the verse from the first Epistle to Timothy from which Huby took his motto, SOLI DEO HONOR ET GLORIA ('Honour and glory to God alone').

THE MONASTIC BUILDINGS

Fountains provides the best example in England, and beyond England, of the planning of a large Cistercian monastery, a form of layout which was developed from Benedictine use to accord with the Cistercians' special requirements, in particular the need to accommodate large numbers of lay brothers. The buildings lie to the S of the church, partly along and partly straddling the River Skell, the precise course of which was modified as necessary. The dimensions of the CLOISTER were set by the monastic buildings of *c.* 1140, parts of which survive in the present E and W ranges. The cloister walks themselves were rebuilt by Abbot John of Kent (1220–47). Nothing remains of them *in situ* but fragments of the arcades have been recovered: they were similar to the dado arcades in the presbytery and E transept, with pointed trefoil arches on coupled Nidderdale marble colonnettes.

The E RANGE starts at the N end with a passage-like space to the S of the S transept, entered through a plain round-headed archway, the W part of which was the LIBRARY, the E part the SACRISTY (the dividing wall has gone): the former has a plain tunnel-vault, the latter a heavy irregular ribbed vault with pointed transverse arches and an applied half-roll on the ribs. Traces of C12 painted decoration. To the l. of the entrance archway, in the W wall of the transept, is a matching recess which was the cloister book cupboard. Next is the CHAPTER HOUSE, which must have been completed by 1170 when Abbot Richard of Clairvaux was buried there; but the style is markedly different from that of the contemporary work in the church, apart from the W doorway, and closer to Gothic. Three splendid round-headed entrance arches, similar to the chapter house entrance at Fontenay (*c.* 1155), of five orders with waterleaf capitals (the colonnettes removed). The room itself was rib-vaulted, in six bays by three, with two rows of monolithic marble columns: vaulting corbels against the walls of simple foliage designs, round-headed windows. A foliage capital from one of the piers is in the site museum. S from the chapter house the side walls of the range, which extended well beyond the cloister almost as far as the river, are largely those of the 1140s building, heightened and remodelled. The earlier masonry can be most clearly recognized on the exterior elevation to the E, where its rough dressing and wide joints, and openings (mainly blocked) with only a slight chamfer, contrast sharply with the regular arrangement of windows and flat buttresses on the chapter house's S flank. The first room in this part is the PARLOUR of the 1160s, another narrow passage-like space, also rib-vaulted, with a sumptuous entrance matching those to the chapter house, a slightly plainer E door, of three orders with waterleaf capitals, and more traces of paintwork. The other was the monks' DAY ROOM, where manual work was undertaken within the confines of the cloister. It has a doorway also of three orders and was groin-vaulted, with plain corbels and a central row of short round piers. The whole of the first floor of the range, including the projection over the E part of the chapter house, was occupied by the MONKS' DORMITORY. Some round-headed windows, alternating with smaller straight-headed openings, remain on the E side.

The S RANGE appears to be largely of *c.* 1200. It starts with the DAY STAIR to the monks' dormitory, broad and formerly rib-vaulted, but the main part consists of the REFECTORY in the middle, oriented at right angles to the cloister walk in accordance with Cistercian practice, the kitchen to the W of it and the warming room to the E. The refectory doorway is again of five orders, with moulded capitals and another richly moulded semicircular head; and l. and r. of it is bold blind arcading with pointed as well as semicircular arches (cf. Ripon Cathedral, choir triforium, *c.* 1180), which contained the LAVATORIUM, the basins where the monks washed before meals. Other doorways plain. The refectory itself was another noble room. The walls of the N third, between the kitchen and warming room, are without detail; but the remainder is an unambiguously E.E. design, with tall shafted lancet windows, those in the end wall in two pairs with blocked remains of oculi above. The roof was carried on a five-bay arcade running down the middle. Dais at the S end. A wall passage below three of the lancets in the W wall, reached by a mural staircase, gave access to a corbelled-out refectory pulpit. The KITCHEN was rib-vaulted and had a double fireplace in the centre, pointed ventilation openings on the N side and a revolving door to the refectory. The WARMING ROOM – the only heated space within the cloister apart from the kitchen – is almost perfectly preserved, with its two vast fireplaces (one blocked), each over 16 ft (5 metres) wide, in the E wall. Vaulting in four oblong bays similar to that in the W range (*see* below), with a central pier of two half-octagons and two chamfered projections continued into the chamfered ribs without a capital. Above, reached from the monks' day stair, is the beautiful MUNIMENT ROOM. It has two groups of three stepped lancets facing towards the cloister and one, facing S, to the lobby off the staircase. Vaulting as in the warming room but with a cylindrical pier.

The W RANGE, 300 ft (90 metres) long with its S end spanning the river, contained on the first floor the huge LAY BROTHERS' DORMITORY, the largest of its kind. The range is the work of two main periods, the N half of *c.* 1160–80, the S part and the ground-floor vaulting throughout probably of *c.* 1200; but the N half of the E wall, alongside the cloister, is partly of the 1140s, refaced and heightened in the next phase with flat buttresses below and the windows of the dormitory above. The interior of the ground floor is one of the most impressive sights in English monastic architecture, a space of twenty-two bays, structurally uniform apart from the low tunnel-vault at the N end which carries the lay brothers' night stair, with a central row of polygonal piers running into the chamfered ribs of the vault without capitals. At the sides the ribs rise from half-octagonal wall-shafts against the 1140s E wall, from corbels elsewhere. The uninterrupted vista is, however, an anachronism, as the space was divided by partition walls – removed in the C18 – and served a variety of functions. The N two bays were the OUTER PARLOUR, the next six the CELLARIUM or storeroom, the next two the ENTRANCE

14

passage to the cloister, and the final twelve the lay brothers' REFECTORY. The long even W elevation is also impressive but again the effect is misleading as originally the lay brothers' cloister lay against the N half. This has on the ground floor round-headed double-chamfered windows, four double-chamfered doorways and polygonal buttresses, the S part larger double chamfered lancets and flat buttresses. Smaller plain windows, and shallower flat buttresses, above. At the junction of the two parts is a projecting block containing the lay brothers' DAY STAIRS, with the cellarer's office below; and at right angles at the S end of the range, built over the river, their LATRINE BLOCK. This evidently belongs to the 1160–80 phase, and so the full length of the range must have been intended even then. Attached to it to the W, and straddling the river, was the lay brothers' INFIRMARY, an aisled hall probably of c. 1200. N end wall with round-headed double-chamfered doorway and three similarly detailed windows above, but the sides had paired lancets and the arcades octagonal piers and pointed double-chamfered arches.

E of the E range was an extensive sequence of buildings which is much less well preserved, mostly with only a few courses of masonry standing. Attached to the S end of the range was the monks' LATRINE BLOCK, with drain to the river; and at right angles to that – the customary position – was the ABBOT'S HOUSE, with the abbot's accommodation on the first floor and a prison below. Further E was John of Kent's magnificent INFIRMARY of c. 1230, an aisled hall 180 ft (55 metres) long built across the river on four great tunnels. The doorway, at the NW corner, had five orders of colonettes, the cylindrical arcade piers – two re-erected in C19 – four banded shafts of Nidderdale marble each. Fragments have been recovered of paired lancet windows with an oculus over. Fireplaces at each end. Attached to the E side, rather than at one end as was usual, was *inter alia* the curiously insignificant INFIRMARY CHAPEL of the late C13; and to the W, also astride the river, in a position previously occupied by the infirmary latrine, lay the late C15 MISERICORD, a hall where on certain occasions meat could be eaten. It had a screens passage at its E end and a dais, with the abbot's table, at the W, connected by a passage to the abbot's lodging. The corresponding room at Clairvaux was called the *reffectoir gras*. The infirmary was linked to both the E cloister range and the Chapel of Nine Altars by a covered PASSAGE with a blind version of the trefoil-headed arcading of the cloister.

INNER AND OUTER COURTS

The Inner Court lay to the W of the church and the claustral buildings. For the lay brothers' infirmary, at its SE corner, *see*

Monastic Buildings, above. W of it is a handsome late C12
BRIDGE over the river, of three arches, ribbed underneath (the
parapets renewed after the Dissolution); and then the two
GUEST HOUSES, which were perhaps Robert of Pipewell's
'sumptuous buildings' of the 1170s. Each contained two lodgings of high status – a hall and a chamber – one to each floor.
The E guest house is the better-preserved. Round-headed
windows, those to the upper storey at the N end paired with a
big oculus over, which was blocked in the C14 when a chimney
flue was inserted. The ground floor was rib-vaulted, in six bays
with a central row of piers, some of the corbels with waterleaf
decoration, the ribs with a half-roll. The W guest house was
similar but smaller, the vaulted ground floor of four bays with
plain chamfered ribs. Footings of a C14 extension on the N side.
Immediately N of these was an aisled building of seven bays
(plan recorded by geophysical survey) which was probably the
GUEST HALL for poorer visitors built c. 1230 by John of Kent.
The base of one quatrefoil pier remains visible. At what was
the W extremity of the court are the fragmentary remains of
the C13 INNER GATEHOUSE, which had two gateway passages
at right angles to each other and a porter's lodge in the angle
between them. The E–W passage had a cross-wall halfway
along, with separate main and pedestrian gateways, and was
vaulted, as was the lodge.

The extensive Outer Court lay to the S of the river and was
the monastery's service area: only a small part of it falls within
the area open to the public. It was reached from the N–S
passage of the gatehouse by another BRIDGE, of the C13. W of
this is the ABBEY MILL, C12 in origin, extended and
re-windowed, with paired lancets, in the C13. It remained in
use until 1937. Re-roofed C17 and 1930s, N end rebuilt C18.
One C19 water wheel. SE of the mill the slight remains of a
complex which consisted of the WOOLHOUSE – an aisled barn
– and the bakehouse-cum-brewhouse.

ENVIRONS

FOUNTAINS HALL. Built by Sir Stephen Proctor, partly of stone   32
from the abbey ruins, probably by 1604 when he accommodated the infant Prince Charles and his retinue for a night.
Proctor was a thrusting Elizabethan industrialist, son of an
ironmaster, and a zealous Calvinist hunter of recusants – from
1606 Collector and Receiver of Fines on Penal Statutes – who
was hated and despised by his mainly Catholic gentry neighbours. The house has been persuasively attributed to *Robert
Smythson*. It has much in common, on a smaller scale, with
Smythson's Wollaton Hall – the corner towers and two-stage
recession to the centre, and the method of entrance to the great
hall – as well as the dramatic height and vertical accent, and

something of the jigsaw-puzzle-like ingenuity, more generally characteristic of his style. But some inconsistencies in the executed building suggest that he provided the designs only, not the supervision of the work.

The house stands low, backing against the steep side of the valley. Its core is a very compact half-H, with short gabled cross-wings projecting at the front only. Centre of two tall storeys, the hall below and the great chamber above, over a basement containing the kitchen, but with the hall fronted by a forebuilding with a central entrance (cf. Wollaton). Round-headed doorway flanked by coupled fluted Ionic columns carrying an entablature, with statuettes of martial figures in front of the columns and in niches above them. Mullion-and-transom windows of five lights to l. and r., with mullioned basement windows below them. On top of the forebuilding is a balustrade with five more martial statuettes, and then comes the spectacular fenestration of the great chamber, a virtual 'glass wall' with a tall semicircular double-transomed oriel of five lights in the centre and equally tall – but not quite matching – double-transomed five-light windows to l. and r. The cross-wings are of three storeys to the centre's two, plus an attic behind the restrainedly shaped gables. Broad three-storey bay windows – canted to the l., rectangular to the r. – with five lights and a single transom to each floor. Then the projecting corner towers (one wider than the other), straight-topped, with an extra storey equivalent to the cross-wing attics. Mullion-and-transom windows of three lights. Running across the whole front are entablatures similar to those at Hardwick Hall, but out of step with the actual floor levels behind. Two gabled stair-turrets at the back.

The particular ingenuity of the plan is focused on the internal arrangement of the centre and its forebuilding, which goes beyond even what was done at Wollaton and produces a delightful spatial surprise. The entrance is at a level intermediate between the basement and the hall, and opens onto the half-landing of a staircase, which to the r. runs up to the screens passage end of the hall and to the l. runs down to the kitchen. So a central entrance is combined both with the traditional, asymmetrical, arrangement of the hall and with the access between hall and services. Of the windows in the forebuilding, the top r. and the bottom l. light the staircase, the bottom r. the kitchen and the top l. the bay at the dais end of the hall; and there are two further small three-light windows in the wall between the hall and the staircase. Above the former screens passage – the screen has gone – is a pretty enclosed gallery, with a timber mullion-and-transom window overlooking the hall. The great chamber has a much worn and very ponderous stone fireplace with overmantel. Caryatids below, columns flanked by big obelisks above, framing a relief of the Judgment of Solomon, of very poor quality. Also a replica of a Jacobean ceiling, installed c. 1930. Stone spiral stair in the front l. tower, imported open-well staircase with turned balusters in

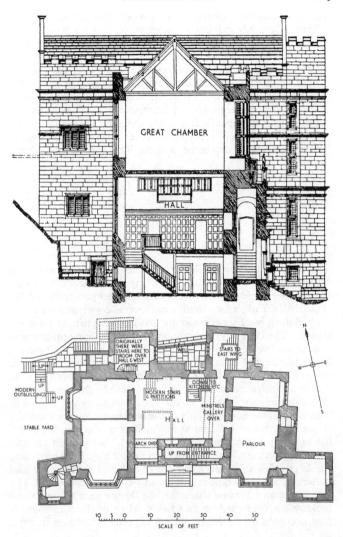

Fountains Hall.
Section and plan

the rear r. Some panelling and four-centre-headed fireplaces
in other rooms.

In front of the house a small walled garden with GATEPIERS,
probably early C17, with coupled colonettes. The plinth-like
blocks on top presumably from elsewhere.

PRECINCT WALL, along and E of Fountains Lane, S and SW of
the abbey. Extensive stretch of the early C13 wall which
enclosed the abbey outer court, much of it standing to full
height.

128   VISITOR CENTRE. 1987–92 by *Edward Cullinan* for the National Trust. Certainly making a statement on its own account and perhaps all a touch self-conscious, but how much preferable to any sort of pastiche or the bland vacuity of merely 'fitting in'. Quite large complex – of shop, café, exhibition space etc. – built round a square courtyard which is left open at one corner to frame a view of the top of the abbey tower, with different shapes and materials bluntly juxtaposed. Roofs a mixture of the steeply monopitched, in stone slab, and the gently curved in lead; elevations of vertically accented timber and glass above a base of rough dry-stone walling; light steel frame, largely visible.

2030

FULNECK
Pudsey

The Moravian Church (Renewed Unity of the Brethren) was established, or re-established, in Saxony in the early C18, tracing its origins to mid-C15 followers of the Bohemian reformer Jan Hus. By the early 1740s there were several congregations in the West Riding, but Fulneck was the first English purpose-built settlement. The land was bought in 1744 and a building programme was begun two years later, the community – previously based at Lightcliffe near Halifax – making use of existing buildings on the site in the meantime. By 1755 there were *c.* 200 members, by 1790 *c.* 400: a wide range of trades was represented – there was an aim of self-sufficiency – those of the textile industry predominant. The form of the planned part of the settlement is very simple, a single long terrace (cf. that at Fairfield near Manchester, established in the 1780s, centred on a square):* the earliest components were originally quite widely separated from each other and the later infills and extensions are of different dates, styles and materials, but the whole is still broadly symmetrical overall. The location retains its rural character, the Terrace on a s-facing slope looking out over gardens and fields. Most of the settlement is now occupied by the Moravian school, established here in 1753.

The earliest, and finest, component is the central CHAPEL block, or Congregation House, built in 1746–8 and consisting of the chapel itself in the middle on the first floor and domestic accommodation to l. and r. The architect is said to have been *Edward Graves* of Newark, who is otherwise unknown. The chapel has four tall round-headed windows and tightly between the inner two a broken-pedimented aedicule. The side parts are of two bays, demarcated by banded pilaster strips, and have two upper storeys equivalent to the height of the

---

*The architect Benjamin Henry Latrobe was born at Fulneck and as a young man, before emigrating to America, played a part in designing the Fairfield settlement.

chapel. Cornice and partly balustraded parapet above.* At the back the accommodation blocks project as short wings: between them a small pedimented block with cupola bellcote, added in 1779. The main fittings of the chapel interior are of 1750: the big PULPIT in the middle of the S wall; the GALLERY, on wooden Doric columns, round the other three sides; and the ORGAN by *Johann Snetzler* (case original, organ rebuilt 1929), originally in the E gallery and moved to the N in 1803, the gallery front altered to accommodate it. Benches in the body of the chapel 1889, replacing the box pews; ornamented cornice.

Next in 1749–52 came the two matching CHOIR HOUSES, communal accommodation for unmarried Sisters (E) and Brothers (W): the segregation of the sexes was a central principle of the layout. The houses are of brick – unusual this far W – large and rather bleak, of three-and-a-half storeys and seven bays, the middle three with a pediment containing a Venetian window. Both were extended on their outer flank in 1758 by the addition of workshop wings, but only the three-storey pavilion which terminated that on the Brothers' side survives, the rest replaced by C19 brick ranges for the school. Between the choir houses and the chapel block are plain stone-built three-storey ranges, that to the E the WIDOWS' HOUSE, opened in 1765, extended 1770–1807, the W the SCHOOL, of 1784–5. Behind the Terrace is THE STREET, an informal row of modest cottages where some of the married members of the community lived and worked. Also one building, No. 39, from the pre-Moravian period and used as the Congregation House until 1748. Five bays, quoins.

NESBIT HALL, ½ m. W. Dated 1761 on rainwater heads which also have the initials of Claud Nisbet, a Moravian financier. But he had only bought the property the previous year and died in 1761, so perhaps he just completed the house. Seven bays, the end pairs pedimented and framed by giant Tuscan pilasters, and at the back forming short wings. (Staircase with fine turned balusters.)

GARFORTH

4030

ST MARY, Church Lane. 1844–5 by *George Fowler Jones* of York, replacing a medieval church, mainly at the cost of the Gascoigne family of Parlington Hall, Aberford (q.v.). Lancet style,

---

*All this is hardly in keeping with the Moravian emphasis on simplicity, and the Elders later complained that the chapel should not have been built 'in so expensive and needlessly fine a manner' and that 'an unfaithful Architect did not follow their directions and by embellishing as he pleased caused them much grief and pain'; but in 1747 John Wesley had observed that 'The Germans suppose it will cost . . . about £3000, it will be well if it were not nearer ten. But that is no concern of the English Brethren; for they are told and patently believe that all the money will come from beyond the sea.'

cruciform, with a central tower and broach spire. Odd inward-sloping battlements at the spire base. Crossing interior quite effective, with many-shafted piers and moulded arches. Three-bay nave arcades with alternating round and octagonal piers in opposing rhythm. – STAINED GLASS. E lancets 'executed' – i.e., presumably, designed – by the *Gascoigne* sisters, *Mary* and *Elizabeth*, 1845. Chancel N and S, 1920 and 1930 by *Powell & Sons* (Whitefriars), not at their best; S transept E and S 1890 and 1897 by *Powell Bros.* of Leeds. – PARISH CENTRE, attached to the S transept, 1997 by *James Thorp & Partners*. Coursed stone, with a pitched slate roof supported by tubular steel 'trees' and purlins, the outer ones partly exposed at the gable-ends.

ST BENEDICT (R.C.), Aberford Road. 1997–8 by *Pascal J. Stienlet & Son*. Bitty, restless design in brick, hexagonal with a sharply pointed glazed gable. In front of this a vestibule between the low presbytery and church centre.

9050

GARGRAVE

Substantial village astride the river Aire W of Skipton. Pleasant sequence of stone-built houses facing the river.

ST ANDREW. Perp W tower of *c*. 1500. Diagonal buttresses, three-light belfry openings and W window, renewed battlements and crocketed pinnacles. The rest 1852 by *Rohde Hawkins*, also Perp. – SCULPTURE. Fragments of several Anglo-Saxon cross-heads and of a cross-shaft. The preponderance of pellet decoration suggests C10. – STAINED GLASS. E window by *Nixon & Ward*, 1852; chancel N and S (four), N aisle E, S aisle E, by *Capronnier*, 1854–65; aisle side windows by *Hardman*, *c*. 1855–70. – HEARSE SHED, in the churchyard. Early C19, with Gothic doorway.

BRIDGE, over the Aire. 1816–17 by *Thomas Anderton* of Gargrave. Three half-elliptical arches, of vigorously textured masonry.

PAGET HALL, Church Street. C17, in essence a single tall short range of two storeys and attic (cf. Newton Hall, Bank Newton). Handsome upper-cruck roof with collars and upper kingposts (cf. Friars Head, Winterburn). Later wing on S side. In SOUTH STREET, Nos. 17–18, C17 with three-storey porch; and in EAST STREET, Nos. 5–13, a two-storey cottage terrace of 1863 with the initials of Sir Mathew Wilson of Eshton Hall (q.v.). Gabled centrepiece forming a shop, all openings three-centre-headed.

ART DEPOT, off Eshton Road. Studio and workshop, 1998 by *Wales, Wales & Rawson*. High-tech single-storey frontage in glass, aluminium and steel, hidden away behind traditional stone walls.

GARGRAVE HOUSE, ¼ m. NW. House of *c*. 1800 comprehensively remodelled and enlarged 1913–17 by *J. B. Dunn* of Edinburgh for J. W. Coulthurst. Opulent Wrenaissance style in coursed stone with ample ashlar dressings, the entrance front asymmetrical with loggia-like porch, garden front with two segmental bows. Interiors equally plush.

The LEEDS AND LIVERPOOL CANAL passes by the village, the section from Leeds to this point in use by 1777, the onward summit section begun *c.* 1790. Of the latter phase the three-arched AQUEDUCT over the river and a number of LOCKS, by *Robert Whitworth*, engineer.

ROMAN VILLA, ½ m. SE. The most westerly of the group of villa sites centred on the Vale of York, surrounded by a double ditch part of which remains faintly visible. Partially excavated 1968–74. Pre-existing on the site were a pair of circular timber- and turf-built structures, one of which survived in use into the villa period. The earliest Romanized building was a house of the C2, 91 ft (28 metres) wide by 38 ft (12 metres) deep, with a front corridor and a central porch between slightly project-ing wings. It had a large central room *c.* 20 ft (6 metres) square with mosaic floor. There was also a bath-house, and a pair of smaller dwellings, probably of the early C3, again with mosaic floors. The main house went out of use in the late C3 or early C4 and was then demolished.

GARSDALE

ST JOHN THE BAPTIST. Chapel of ease of Dent, in existence by the mid C16, rebuilt 1860–1 by *Miles Thompson* of Kendal, former partner of George Webster. Lancet style, still entirely pre-Ecclesiological, with unaisled nave and short chancel. Engaging two-tier W bellcote. – STAINED GLASS. E window by *Kempe*, 1897.

SWARTH GILL, 1¼ m. WNW. Dated 1712. Three storeys, the top one perhaps added. Mullioned windows of three and four lights to the ground and first floors, blocked one-light windows to the second. Continuous hoodmoulds. (Panelled timber par-tition between the parlour and the former housebody, parlour fireplace with lintel on corbels.) ¼ m. further NW, BADGER DUBB, probably similar date but the front altered. Three storeys, cylindrical chimneys. Fielded panelling, some of it forming partitions, staircase with turned balusters.

DANDRYMIRE VIADUCT, Garsdale Head, 3½ m. ENE. On the Settle–Carlisle Line. 1871–5, *J. S. Crossley* chief engineer. Twelve rather low rock-faced arches.

GIGGLESWICK

Across the river Ribble from Settle, but retaining its separate village identity.

St Alkelda. Norman capitals reused as bases of two of the piers on the s side of the nave. Otherwise Perp throughout; but the unified effect belies a quite piecemeal building process. The earliest part is evidently the w tower, which is referred to – *novi campanilis* – in a document of 1449–50. Payments for the 'new chancel' were made between 1477 and 1485, and the rest appears to have followed after that. Extensively restored 1890–2 by *Paley & Austin*. The tower has two-light bell-openings still remembering Dec, battlements and a stair-turret at the se corner. Long nave and slightly lower chancel, aisles and chancel chapels, clerestory to the nave only, low s porch. Plain parapets to all parts. Straight-headed windows with cusped lights. s arcade of seven bays, n arcade of six. The usual octagonal piers and double-chamfered arches. No chancel arch. Roofs, and the e gable, all of 1890–2. – COMMUNION RAIL. 1676. The balusters still Jacobean in style, though more substantial. – PULPIT and READING DESK. 1680. Handsome, heavily panelled pieces, the pulpit bearing the emblems of the twelve tribes of Israel and the reading desk an inscription referring to them. Octagonal sounding-board. Formerly a three-decker, the clerk's desk removed *c.* 1890. – POOR BOX. 1684, inscribed 'Remember the Pore'. – ROYAL ARMS. 1716. Painted, crude, in a simple wooden frame. At the top the names and emblems of the tribes of Israel appear again, arranged round the sun. – Brass CANDELABRA in the nave, 1718. – CHARITY BOARD, early C19. – STAINED GLASS. Includes n aisle NE and next, and s aisle second from E, by *Hardman*, 1858–72; s chapel E and SW by *Powell & Sons*, 1900–1; E and W windows by *T. W. Camm* of Smethwick, 1891 and 1904. – MONUMENTS. Knight in armour, defaced, on the floor at E end of N aisle. Supposed to be Sir Richard Tempest †1488, who founded a chantry in this part of the church. – Two late medieval female figures, headless and otherwise badly damaged. Supposed to be Sybill Tempest †*c.* 1465 and Mabel Tempest †*c.* 1510, wives of Sir Richard. – Richard Frankland †1698. Baroque cartouche. – Dr George Birkbeck †1841, founder of Birkbeck College, the first English Mechanics' Institute. By *Leyland & Bromley* of Halifax and Leeds, with inscription composed by Birkbeck's friend Lord Brougham. Grecian tablet with profile portrait.

GIGGLESWICK SCHOOL. Founded *c.* 1507 by James Carr, a chantry priest. The school house, to the N of the church, was rebuilt in 1797 and again, by *E. G. Paley*, in 1851, but was demolished in 1960. Development after the 1850s was at the w end of the village, on a pleasant hillside site behind a plain three-bay house, Craven Bank, erected for the headmaster *c.* 1801. The buildings are rather grey and forbidding in accordance with Victorian ideals of scholastic architecture, but the green surroundings succeed in softening that severity: the architects were *Paley & Austin* (*Austin & Paley* after 1895). The long main range was built in two stages, the s half in 1868, the N in 1875. Three storeys in minimal Gothic style, with central tower and many gabled dormers. S of this are the class-room block and science block, 1886 and 1900 respectively, in an equally pared-down Jacobean, the latter with a loggia and low tower. N of it the former library building, 1923–6 by *Isaac Taylor*, with mullioned windows. In front, in addition to Craven Bank, two other earlier houses: the present headmaster's residence to the l., built *c.* 1840 as the vicarage, and to the r. the former usher's house, with mid-C19 Grecian front. Downhill from these again, across the road, the dining hall, 1998–9 by *John Squires*; and N of this, CATTERAL HALL, an early C18 house remodelled and extended in 1843 and much altered since. Low pyramid-roofed tower.

Away to the SW, in a magnificent position astride a rocky spur, is the SCHOOL CHAPEL, of 1897–1901 by *T. G. Jackson*. It was the gift of Walter Morrison of Malham Tarn House who was a member of the Board of Governors, and in his *Recollections* Jackson gives an account of the origins of the design: 'Mr. Walter Morrison called on me to ask whether I was disposed to try an architectural experiment . . . Morrison, who was much interested in the exploration of Palestine, wished to give a chapel to Giggleswick School in Yorkshire . . . Palestine suggested a dome, and the chapel was to have a dome. This delighted me. I had never built a dome (very few architects have) and I jumped at the offer . . . I had *carte blanche*, Morrison's only wish being that there should be nothing left for anyone else to do. I was determined to show that domes and Gothic architecture are not incompatible and, though I shocked all the purists, I am not dissatisfied with the result.' 89

Rockfaced red sandstone with bands of gritstone and limestone, and sandstone dressings. The dome of copper over terracotta. Latin cross plan, with very short transepts and E arm, and three-bay aisled nave. As Gothic it is decidedly un-purist quite apart from the dome. Restrained Elizabethan-style shaped gables to the terminations, domed octagonal turrets in the re-entrant angles, S doorway with Pennine-style ornamented lintel. W narthex with above it an Arts and Crafts Gothic rose window, big free Dec windows to E end and S transept, two giant blank arches to the N. The semicircular crossing arches with broad flat soffits have a Byzantine feel, nave arcades also with round arches, on cylindrical piers with naturalistic foliage capitals. Barrel roof with kingpost trusses. – PULPIT, PEWS, GALLERIES and ORGAN CASE of Argentinian cedar, executed to *Jackson*'s design by *Farmer and Brindley*. – LECTERN, of bronze, also designed by *Jackson*, executed by *Hart, Peard & Co.* – SCULPTURE. Bronze figures of Edward VI and Queen Victoria over the W door by *George Frampton*. – MOSAICS in the dome and pendentives executed by *Powell & Sons* to designs by *George Murray*. – SCRAFFITO decoration, to the crossing-arch soffits and elsewhere, executed by two of Jackson's Oxford pupils, *William Nicholls* and *Douglas Stewart*. – STAINED GLASS by *Burlison & Grylls*, the W window (the Creation) again designed by *Jackson* himself.

Near the chapel, also by *Jackson* in 1901 and paid for by Morrison, the Arts and Crafts-inspired GATEHOUSE, with Gothic archway, another Pennine-style doorhead and Lakeland cylindrical chimneys, and the CRICKET PAVILION, with open timber gables and ogee-domed clock turret.

In the village the best house is BECK HOUSE, at the w end of the main street, now also part of the school. Early C18 double pile. Seven-bay E front with projecting three-bay centre crowned by a heavy segmental pediment and above that by a low-pitched gable. Lower flanking sections with hipped lean-to roofs. In the pediment a window flanked by two oculi, lighting the attic. Another segmental pediment to the doorway, broken segmental pediments to the two windows l. and r. of it, triangular pediments to the first-floor windows above. Quoins. The rainwater heads dated 1787 relate to a change of ownership. Very tall staircase window at the back. s wing added 1926. Some early C18 fireplaces, including a massive one in the kitchen. Back staircase with turned balusters, main staircase renewed early C19. s of this, the former SETTLE UNION WORKHOUSE, now housing and a hospital. 1834 onwards, an irregular complex of two and three storeys. A similar distance SE, ARMISTEAD HOUSE, 1707. Three storeys, five bays, with an ornamented doorhead – duplicated on a second doorway in the C19 – of the type characteristic of the area. Probable former cross-windows, in crude surrounds. Two matching short wings at the rear.

p. 31

E from Beck House in the main street, the NATIONAL SCHOOL, built 1815, restored 1894. Round-headed windows. Then next to the church IVY FOLD, low and L-shaped, built by Anthony Lister, Vicar of Giggleswick 1641–86. Dates of 1652 inside, 1677 over the front doorway, 1669 over the doorway into the cross-wing, in all cases with Lister's initials. Lobby-entry plan with housebody fireplace flanked by two round-headed doorways. SE of the church the MARKET CROSS, probably C14 but only in its present position since 1840, then several more houses with ornamented doorheads, including No. 3 CHURCH STREET, 1689, and at the top of the hill SUTCLIFFE HOUSE, 1693, with a complicated stepped design.

p. 31

At STACKHOUSE, 1 m. N, some more houses of C17 origin, including CARRHOLME, with two-storey porch of 1669 entered at the side, and the OLD HALL, with a doorhead like that at Sutcliffe House dated 1695.

KINSEY CAVE, 1 m. NNW, above Giggleswick Scar. Excavations in 1925–32 revealed archaeological deposits of the Roman, Bronze Age and later Upper Palaeolithic periods.

GILDERSOME

ST PETER. 1989–92 by *Ashfield Architects*, replacing a church of 1873–5 by *Adams & Kelly*. Octagonal, of coursed stone. At the front a busy composition of foyer, meeting room etc., linking with the plain C19 school. – STAINED GLASS. The twelve apostles, in slots on the N side. By *Clare Morrisey*.

BAPTIST CHAPEL, Church Street. 1865 by *Simpson & Son* of Leeds. Pedimented Italianate front. Interior retaining apsidal-ended gallery on cast-iron columns but otherwise altered, with a false ceiling. Lower hall to l., 1887 by *J. R. Taylor*.

FRIENDS' MEETING HOUSE, Street Lane, approached through a C19 archway. Simple oblong of 1756–8, with C19 sash windows. Two rooms of unequal size with shuttered partition between them, the larger with panelled stand.

TURTON HALL, College Road. Mid-C18, tall ashlar block with five-bay front.

GISBURN

8040

A stone-built village of little more than a single main street, but a charter for a market was granted in 1260 and in the C18 it was generally described as a small town. The church is towards the E end and Gisburne Park, former seat of the Listers, Lords Ribblesdale (now a hospital) ½ m. to the N.

ST MARY. Short Norman W tower with tiny round-headed windows to N and S, Dec bell-openings and totally plain Norman tower arch. W door and window 1872. Aisled nave and long chancel with chapels, no clerestory. Trace of a C13 lancet window visible internally in the chancel N wall and re-set late C13 windows in the W ends of the aisles, of three stepped lancet lights under a two-centred arch. E window of five stepped lancets under a four-centred arch, i.e. Perp (cf. Kildwick, Bolton-by-Bowland). The aisles and chapels also mainly Perp, continuous and parapeted, the N with straight-headed windows with arched lights but the S a post-medieval rebuild above the plinth, with plain three-light mullioned windows. S porch with re-assembled round-headed outer doorway and pointed inner doorway with continuous mouldings. Two-bay Perp arcades to nave and chancel, with octagonal piers and double-chamfered arches. Double-chamfered chancel arch set on short, stout cylindrical piers, evidently a contrivance to accommodate the different widths of nave and chancel. – SCREENS. To the chancel and S chapel, and between the chancel and the chapels. Heavily restored. Single-light divisions with cusped arched lights. – STAINED GLASS. Fragmentary C15 figures in one S and one N chapel window. E window 1872, perhaps by *Hardman*. – MONUMENT. Sir John Assheton of Whalley †1697. Baroque aedicule.

On the N side of the main street CROMWELL HOUSE, dated 1635 in an inscription which records that it was built 'at the Costs and Charges of Thomas Lister £855 costed'. Three storeys, with off-centre full-height porch. Top-storey windows all of the stepped three-light type, the others C19. The puzzle is its original purpose, since at that time the Lister family seat was a large house only twenty years old SW of the village (dem. C18), and Thomas Lister bought the Low Hall, predecessor of Gisburne Park, in 1636. On the S side SNOW HILL HOUSE, a big C17 block of similar height, with irregularly placed mullioned windows. Where was the original doorway? Perhaps into one of the gable ends, onto which later buildings now abut. W of this KIRK HOUSE, early C18 three-bay front with pedimented doorway and windows with unchamfered mullions and transoms; and at the W end of the village a cottage dated 1705 which represents the previous stylistic stage, symmetrical but still with mullioned windows of traditional type. Also some C19 estate cottages bearing the Ribblesdale initial; and off the N side of the street, after a house with a smart late C18 ashlar front, a pair of delightful Gothick ENTRANCE LODGES to the grounds of Gisburne Park. These are of 1775–7 and evidently the joint design of the owner *Thomas Lister*, later first Lord Ribblesdale, and his surveyor *Mr Riley*. Fancifully pinnacled, with statuettes – delivered in 1779 – in the niches over the big arched windows.

GISBURNE PARK. The main part of the house was built 1728–36 (building accounts) for yet another Thomas Lister, and its principal feature is a wealth of fine Baroque plasterwork executed 1730–3 by *Quadri* and *Vassalli*. No architect is recorded but some sort of supervisory function was exercised by 'Mr Drake and Mr Townley' – the former presumably a member of the gentry family of that name from nearby Barnoldswick, the latter doubtless a connection of the Towneleys of Towneley Hall, Lancashire, where Vassalli and Quadri were employed at the same time. It consists of a front range facing S and short return wings running out at the back, formerly with a small inner courtyard between them. Externally it is very plain, rendered – an original feature – with ashlar dressings, the front of nine bays with the centre three slightly recessed. Flush quoins, simple cornice with bold modillions, rather narrow sash windows. The only hint of the richness within is the Baroque doorway, with Doric entablature curved upwards as a segmental arch. Behind all this it is probable that the old house, or part of it, was retained as service quarters: the 'new kitchen' built in 1727–8 adjoins to the W of where this would have been. At the N end of the E return wing there is now a square addition of 1789–90 for the future first Lord Ribblesdale, matching the previous work but a storey higher, and presumably of the same phase is a canted bay window next to it, forming the centre of the E flank. The rest of the back part rebuilt 1880 by *David & John Bryce*, which explains its slightly Scottish air, with dormer windows. Continuing the line of the S front to the W, in front of the former service courtyard, is a single-storey range also remodelled by the Bryces, then the pedimented S end of a simple C18 range on the W side of the yard, with a canted bay probably of the mid C19.

Inside, the plasterwork is encountered immediately, in the entrance hall, with a scheme of enriched wall panels and window reveals as well as ceiling, all quite delicately done, almost Rococo rather than Baroque. In the drawing room, to the r., a ceiling of similar character; but in the smaller room behind this in the E wing, where *Quadri*'s name and the date 1731 are stamped on the cornice, the treatment is more robust, the ceiling slightly coved and the wall decoration culminating in an overmantel with curved cornice like the front doorway. Fine contemporary marble chimneypiece. The climax is the staircase hall in the W wing, with particularly large and elab- 61 orate wall panels, some containing bas reliefs of putti playing musical instruments etc., others crowned by grotesque masks. Stone staircase with lyre-pattern iron balustrade, ceiling of *c.* 1880 with oval glazed dome. The room l. of the entrance hall has boldly detailed timber panelling; while the dining room of 1790, which occupies the addition at the NE corner, is circu-lar and of double-storey height, with an ornate domed ceiling. Inner courtyard roofed over to form a top-lit circulation space for the hospital, 1985–6 by *Sunderland Peacock & Associates*.

An elaborate formal design for the GROUNDS, by *P. Bourgignon*, 1735, is preserved. Part of a double avenue SW of the house survives. The buildings are mainly later. Immedi-ately N of the entrance lodges (*see* above) a pair of TUNNEL ENTRANCES to a short railway tunnel – in reality a covered cutting – beneath the drive. 1880, rock-faced and heavily castellated, with octagonal turrets. E of the house, in a wooded valley, the KEEPERS' COTTAGES, probably later C18, a pair of one-bay pedimented pavilions; but the nearby Temple, on a bluff overlooking the river Ribble, has gone. At the edge of the grounds ¼ m. W of the house, beside the river, MILL BRIDGE COTTAGE, of two dates, the earlier part *c.* 1730, with a Vanbrughian doorway and other detail similar to that on the house, the rest mid-C19 in Pennine style with mullioned windows. On the river bank nearby the ruins of the former DOG KENNELS, late C18, castellated with cyndrical turrets. In front of the cottage GISBURN BRIDGE, over the Ribble. C18, two arches.

STIRK HOUSE, 1 m. W. Now an hotel. C17. Front with two gables and two-and-a-half-storey gabled porch, the upper stage slightly jettied. Also a taller gabled turret to the l. C19 wing and much C20 enlargement.

GLASSHOUSES
Bishopside

1060

Small industrial settlement pleasantly situated in Nidderdale, centred on an earlier flax-spinning mill, created by the Metcalfe family *c.* 1855–75.

The MILL, in the valley bottom beside the river, originated in a water-powered corn mill converted to flax spinning in 1812 and bought by the Metcalfes in 1835. The existing building is of various dates from 1837 onwards, U-shaped, of two and three storeys – the middle range, rebuilt in the 1860s, with a gabled projecting centrepiece on the courtyard side crowned by a bell-cote. Internal construction with timber beams on plain iron columns. Large iron water wheel designed by *William Fairbairn* installed 1851, now at Quarry Bank Museum, Cheshire. Steam power added 1857, chimney dem. *c.* 1983. Big reservoir adjacent to the w.

The buildings of the settlement itself are mainly by *W. R. Corson* of Leeds (after 1861 *Corson & Aitken* of Manchester). Opposite the mill the former MILL MANAGER'S HOUSE (Fir Grove), 1869–70, gabled and half-hipped; beside it the SCHOOL, 1859–60, simplest Gothic; and behind them two plain terraces of workers' HOUSING, 1869 and 1873, punctuated by steep gables. Further up the hill, beyond the line of the railway, more housing, 1858 etc., and the METHODIST CHAPEL, 1866. Simple Gothic again, but with an apsidal-ended transept, short chancel taller than the nave, and a flèche (1875) over the 'crossing'. For George Metcalfe's own house, across the river beyond the reservoir, *see* Bewerley.

₈₀₅₀

GLEDSTONE HALL
Marton

Two successive houses, on different sites.

The old Gledstone Hall, which occupied an elevated ridge-top position WNW of West Marton, was begun *c.* 1770 by Richard Roundell (†1772) and completed by his brother, and is attributed to *John Carr* on stylistic grounds. It was demolished in 1928, but the adjacent STABLE BLOCK remains, now in part converted to a house and office. Nine-bay ashlar front which faced towards the house's flank, with pediments to the third and seventh bays and the entrance surmounted by an open colonnaded cupola on a high base. Memorable circular courtyard, of brick, with sixteen half-elliptical-headed arches opening into a groin-vaulted ambulatory. In the grounds the KENNELS HOUSE, also late C18 and perhaps by Carr, with three-bay loggia and Diocletian window over. Beside it a rectangular DOVECOTE, dated 1795.

The present hall, ⅜ m. NE, is by *Sir Edwin Lutyens* and was built in 1922–6 for the Lancashire industrialist Sir Amos Nelson, who had bought the estate in 1919. The site architect was *Richard Jaques*, of Burnley. Generally regarded as one of Lutyens's best late houses, it is of moderate size but formally classical in style – a *dix-huitième* chateau set down rather unexpectedly in the rolling Craven countryside – with walls of finely worked ashlar and a proud tall hipped roof of Cotswold stone slates. The entrance front has a big Ionic portico, slightly projecting end pavilions, and an elaborate *cour d'honneur* flanked by screen walls and closed to the N by wrought-iron gates made by the Marton blacksmith, beyond which is a pair of substantial square gate lodges with pyramidal roofs. But the main entrance drive to this point from the North Lodge (*see* below) was never completed. Behind the screen walls are service wings, the kitchen to the l., the garages – with a ballroom over – to the r. On the garden front the pedimented centre is less emphatic but the end pavilions project further, and in front of the intermediate parts, projecting just a little further again, are one-storey colonnades with balconies over. Carefully detailed windows with shutters. To l. and r. of the house a pair of pedimented garden loggias. Formal terraced garden, built up above the fall of the ground on great battered revetments and centred on a long rectangular basin aligned on the axis of the house and forecourt. The original planting scheme was devised by Lutyens's early patron *Gertrude Jekyll*, then in her eighties. Internally, the central axis is continued unbroken through a Doric vestibule and hall, but the vaulted transverse corridors are dog-legged in Lutyens's usual manner. Black-and-white marble paving in all these areas, and on the spacious staircase alternately black and white marble steps – handsome to look at but neck-breaking to walk on. The staircase balustrade has scrolls ingeniously forming an E.L. monogram. Other rooms simpler, with doors and one exquisite marble chimneypiece reused from the old house.

Two further LODGES by *Lutyens*. The NORTH LODGE, in Arts and Crafts vernacular style, with battered walls and chimneystacks and mullioned windows, the SOUTH LODGE, at the start of the drive to the old house, symmetrical with a pedimented doorway.

GLUSBURN

0040

Part of an agglomeration of settlements together with Sutton-in-Craven (q.v.) and Cross Hills, its core is a small model industrial village developed by worsted manufacturer John Cousen Horsfall and his architect *F. W. Petty* of Halifax from *c.* 1890 onwards alongside the existing mill.

The centrepiece is the GLUSBURN INSTITUTE, by *Petty*, built in several stages between 1892 and 1906. In its heyday the facilities included a library, a theatre and public baths. Fanciful mixed Renaissance style ranging from Jacobean to Baroque, the principal accent a squat tower crowned by an ashlar dome. Next to it a three-storeyed polygonal bay with exotic details. Plainer gables at the sides.

Of the MILL opposite, there remain the four-storey front range added *c.* 1900 and the octagonal chimney. E and W of the Institute are streets of plain terraced HOUSING, one dated 1902, and N of it a row of larger houses, in twos and threes, some with decorated gables, for the managers. W of the mill, the LODGE to Horsfall's own house (dem.), again in mixed Renaissance style.

OLD HALL, ¼ m. W. Incorrectly re-cut datestone probably ought to read 1687. Gabled front, mullioned windows of various sizes. Attached to the l. flank a square battlemented turret, C19. At ROYD HOUSE, ¾ m. N, a large five-bay aisled BARN, with re-set datestone of 1678. Also the remains of the C17 house, replaced by the present one in 1910, with big mullion-and-transom windows.

MALSIS HALL, ¾ m. W. Florid Italianate mansion of *c.* 1862 onwards by *Samuel Jackson* of Bradford for Keighley worsted manufacturer James Lund. Now a school. The near-symmetrical S-facing range with pedimented centre is the original house, the slightly taller E-facing entrance range, with central porte cochère, an addition of *c.* 1880. Also of the latter phase the belvedere tower and a service wing to the N. Some elaborate interiors, including the former dining and drawing rooms in the entrance range, with painted decoration. School CHAPEL, 1965–6 by *John Brunton & Partners* with STAINED GLASS by *John Piper*, 1967.

GOLDSBOROUGH

The slight hint of seigneurial orderliness is mainly due to Daniel Lascelles (*see* Plompton), who bought the estate in 1762. The approach to the village from the W is through rusticated gatepiers (by *Carr*, *c.* 1765). The church and hall are at the E end.

ST MARY. Re-set Norman S doorway, with one order of shafts, plain capitals, and zigzag and beakhead to the arch, the stonework much renewed. Otherwise mainly late E.E. and Dec – nave and chancel in one, aisles and N chapel, W tower – proceeding broadly from E to W. Restored by *G. G. Scott*, 1859. E window impressive and characteristic, of five stepped lancets under one arch, the end lights with a small circle over. Also single NE and SE lancets; then further W on the chancel S side two two-light Dec windows, with pointed trefoil heads to the lights and a trefoiled spheric triangle over, but the l. one longer than the other, with a transom. The S aisle has W and S windows of two trefoil-headed lights with a circle over, in the (renewed) former unfoiled, the latter quatrefoiled, but has apparently been extended a little to the E (*see* below), with Perp E window. N aisle and chapel largely rebuilt by *Scott*, with windows copied from the S aisle and added porch. Lower stages of the tower late C14 – see the head-stops to the one-light W window in the style of *c.* 1380; belfry stage of *c.* 1430 (heraldry), with paired two-light bell-openings, just about Perp, with a transom. Narrow tower arch with continuous moulding, the space within rib-vaulted. Dec s arcade of two bays, with octagonal pier, double-chamfered arches and capitals with knobbly foliage, and to the E of it a length of wall pierced by a Perp tomb-arch containing the tomb of Sir Richard de Goldsborough †1504 (*see* below) with a blocked window above. So this will date the E extension of the aisle. Later C14 N arcade of three bays with thin octagonal piers. Between the chancel and the N chapel a C13 arch with moulded responds, and then another tomb-arch, of the early C14 (*see* below). E.E.-style sedilia and piscina, a replica of the original, by *Scott*.

Wooden REREDOS, *c.* 1898 by *C. Hodgson Fowler*, carved by *Millburn* of York and painted by *Buckeridge & Floyce*. – PULPIT, FONT etc. by *Scott*, 1859, executed by *Farmer & Brindley*. – STAINED GLASS. s aisle E, dated 1696. The arms of the Hutton and Byerley families, with the motto 'Foyal and Loyal' in large letters. In the E window until 1859. – E window by *Capronnier*, 1859, 'toned down and improved' in 1898 by the provision of new backgrounds to the figures, by *A. O. Hemming*. – Chancel SE and NE and s aisle s by *Wailes*, 1859 – MONU-MENTS, an important series. – Under the chancel tomb-arch, well-carved effigy of a cross-legged knight, probably Richard de Goldsborough IV †1308, his feet on a lion and his head framed by its own little canopy, ogee with Dec foliage. The tomb-arch has big cusps and a crocketed gable over, enclosing a slim pointed trefoil. – Against the chancel s wall opposite, another cross-legged knight, similar to the first, probably Richard de Goldsborough V †*c.* 1333, on a low tomb-chest with blind arcading. – In the nave tomb-arch, Sir Richard de Golds-borough †1504 and his wife Elizabeth Vavasour. Tomb-chest without its effigies, the names of their children on the sides. Crocketed ogee hood to the arch, with heraldic stops. – Robert Byerley †1714, his wife Mary and their five children. By *Joseph Wilton*, erected in accordance with the will of Elizabeth Byerley, the last surviving of the children, †1766. Large pedi-mented astylar aedicule framing life-size figures of Faith and Charity wreathing an urn. On the uprights and lintel of the frame, medallions of those commemorated linked by swags and drops. Greek key to the frieze. The carving is excellent, the feeling gentle. – Daniel Lascelles †1784. White marble wall tablet in the shape of a sarcophagus.

GOLDSBOROUGH HALL. Tall rectangular house of brick with stone dressings, built *c.* 1625 by Sir Richard Hutton who had bought the estate in 1601, but extensively altered C18–C20. Three storeys, the top one partly in the roof, with three gables to the front (E) and sides, four to the back. At the front also a central two-storey porch with round-headed entrance flanked by paired fluted pilasters, two-storey half-octagonal bay windows l. and r., and above these three original six-light mullion-and-transom windows to the top floor. But the porch and bays were evidently reconstructed, and the windows between them similarly Georgianized, in a phase of *c.* 1740, with a crowning balustrade continued unbroken across both the projections and the intervening bays. Also of this phase are the two three-storey canted bays on the s side, again with balustrades, and probably some interventions at rooftop level, including a raising of the wall-head between and flanking the gables and the oculi within them. Part of one of the s bays was Jacobeanized in a modernization of 1922 by *Sydney Kitson*, between them is a regrettable conservatory of the mid C20, and at the same time most of the C18 windows were redone with fake sashes unworthy of the building. At the back are two huge staircase windows of four-plus-four lights, one above the other, the lower with two transoms, the upper (renewed) with three. To the N a mixture of more C17 mullion-and-transom windows and others of the mid C20.

Much of the INTERIOR was remodelled by *Carr*, 1764–5, the hall, to the l. of the entrance becoming a drawing room, the screens passage an entrance hall, the two rooms to the r. thrown together as a dining room, and the great chamber above the hall subdivided and lowered as dressing rooms. The main original feature is the staircase, behind the former hall, a dog-leg with quarter landings, rising the whole height of the house: big vertically symmetrical balusters and two pairs of plain stout continuous newel posts. *Ex situ* in the dining room a big Jacobean marble fireplace, with caryatids below, and bas-relief panels of Cain and Abel and Abraham and Isaac, framed by allegorical figures, above; and above the false ceilings of the dressing rooms the coved decorative plaster ceiling of the great chamber survives, much cut about. The main dressing room has some simple Adam-style decoration, the drawing room a marble chimneypiece. Elsewhere some Neo-Jacobean plaster-work, C19 and C20.

The house is approached through an archway (one of two) in a long two-storey range running along the village street to the N, which was built as STABLES probably *c.* 1730 and radically modified as housing *c.* 1980. The archways are in pyramid-roofed pavilions with an oculus to the first floor. Closing the w end of the street in formal fashion, round the corner from the gatepiers, is a former MODEL FARM, doubt-less of the 1760s for Daniel Lascelles and presumably by *Carr*. Farmhouse in the middle with canted-bay centre – one window nastily altered – and former farm building ranges l. and r. linked to the house by screen walls.

GRANTLEY

GRANTLEY HALL. In the narrow valley of the Skell close beside the river, which at this point is canalized, with a series of weirs. Mainly *c.* 1750 for Sir Fletcher Norton, later first Lord

Isaac Ware, design for 'a person of
distinction in the County of York'.
Engraving, 1756

Grantley: a statement that the house was 'enlarged and
improved about the year 1776' probably refers to the completion of the internal decoration, which was evidently a gradual
process. The long ashlar front, facing E, is a rather ill-digested
composition which seems to be related to Isaac Ware's 'design
for a person of distinction in the county of York' in his *Complete Body of Architecture*, 1756, but much garbled and inflated
in the execution. The centre is a canted bay of three storeys,
the ground and first floors conventionally Palladian but the tall
top stage finished with oculi and coupled Tuscan pilasters. l.
and r. of this is a narrow two-and-a-half-storey bay under a
half-pediment, and then two-storey six-bay flanking sections
with two-bay pedimented centres and giant angle pilasters. For
the most part this range is only one room and a corridor deep.
Plain S elevation, of three storeys the same height as the E
front's two, and eleven bays, the centre seven deeply recessed.
Doorcase with pediment on Tuscan columns. This part may
represent the earlier house, remodelled *c*. 1750, but no earlier
detail is visible. At the N end of the E front an additional single-
storey bay of *c*. 1900, and behind it, at the NW corner of the
house, the service wing of the same date.

Interior also considerably altered *c*. 1900. The entrance hall
had a three-bay arcade on each side, leading into an aisle, as
in Ware's plan, but the N aisle has been taken into the adjoining room and the arcade abolished. The neighbouring room to
the S has decoration of *c*. 1750 – pretty Rococo door surrounds
and chimneypiece, and a simple compartment ceiling – but
the room beyond was fitted up as a library *c*. 1900. The two
rooms to the N both have pleasant Adamesque ceilings and
chimneypieces, of *c*. 1776, but the second one, as well as the
first, has been enlarged, by the addition of the one-storey bay
at the N end of the range. In both, the extensions are marked
off by projecting attached columns. The oddest characteristic
is the absence of a proper main staircase: behind the entrance
hall there is just a mean little stair with plain stick balusters.

GRANTLEY OLD HALL, High Grantley. C17 double pile
of three storeys, with symmetrical elevations. Mullioned
windows, a number of those at the back stepped, of three
and four lights.

GRASSINGTON

The principal settlement of upper Wharfedale. A market existed
by the end of the C13 – it continued to be held into the C19 –
and some growth took place in the late C18 and early C19 with
the expansion of the lead-mining industry on Grassington Moor
by the Dukes of Devonshire. Attractive village street running
uphill off the main road, expanding into a little square and
nowhere pedantically straight.

GRASSINGTON OLD HALL, NW of the centre, off Wood Lane.
A remarkable survival, in origin of the later C13 probably for
the then Lord of the Manor, Robert de Plumpton. Two parallel ranges, one behind the other as the house is seen from the
road, and a porch attached to the r. corner of the front range;
but that cannot be the medieval arrangement. Early details,
probably not all *in situ*, are the doorway into the porch, on the
r. flank; two first-floor windows in the r. end of the front range,
of two lights with transoms and quatrefoiled plate-tracery
heads; a twin lancet window in the l. end of the back range;
and another doorway, leading into the back range from the
front. C17 mullioned windows to the r. end of the back range
and the staircase projection at the rear, perhaps related to the
purchase of the property in 1603 by the sitting tenant, George
Lister. Much restoration *c.* 1870, including all the roofs and all
the detail of the present entrance front.

In THE SQUARE the best building is GRASSINGTON HOUSE,
now an hotel. Mid-C18 for a Mr Brown, one of the promoters
of the Grassington to Pateley Bridge turnpike (1758). Six-bay
front with the l. half projecting forward as a wing. Two-and-a-
half storeys, rusticated quoins, architrave surrounds to the
windows, pedimented doorcase. Quite modest staircase with
turned balusters, but above it a decorative plaster ceiling with
shell motifs and central wreath. In the dining room a shell-
headed niche flanked by fluted pilasters and an overmantel
with guilloche ornament.

On the other side, CHURCH HOUSE, 1694, former farmhouse with enriched doorhead. At the top of Main Street,
where a number of roads meet, the TOWN HALL AND DEVON-
SHIRE INSTITUTE, plainest Jacobean, built 1855 as a Mechanics' Institute at the cost of the Duke of Devonshire, extended
1878, 1923 and in 1998 by *Brian Foxley Associates*. N in Chapel
Street the METHODIST CHAPEL, completed 1825. Gabled
front with round-headed windows, gallery with ramped box
pews round three sides of the interior. Further on TOWN-

HEAD, C17 farmhouse with a curious frieze of pebbles below the eaves, probably C19. s of the Town Hall, off Garrs Lane, the CONGREGATIONAL CHAPEL, 1811, with plain three-bay front. Gallery describing a semi-octagon, with balustraded backs to the pews, but obscured by internal alterations. SSE at the end of Low Lane, with splendid views across the valley, FAR SCAR, 1920 by *Sir Edward Maufe* for his brother Carl. Stone-built farmhouse style but not Yorkshire, with unchamfered mullioned windows. It appears that the house was intended to be larger with a symmetrical front.

Lower down again, N of the main road, the former NATIONAL SCHOOL, 1845 in simple Tudor style but altered and converted to housing. Also the BRIDGE, of four arches, over the Wharfe. *c.* 1603 replacing a timber one, repaired 1661, widened 1780 and the roadway raised 1824.

N of the village various Iron Age sites and Romano-British SETTLEMENTS, including that on LEA GREEN, 1¼ m. NNW, excavated in 1893. Small but well-defined enclosures of boulder walling. At YARNBURY, 1 m. NE on the edge of the Moor, the well-preserved earthwork of a small Late Neolithic or Early Bronze Age HENGE. Circular enclosure *c.* 70 ft (21 metres) in diameter, surrounded by a rock-cut ditch with external bank. Entrance causeway on the SE side.

Also extensive evidence of the LEAD MINING activity on the Moor. YARNBURY HOUSE was for a time the residence and office of the Duke of Devonshire's mining agent. Nearby a POWDER HOUSE, the COUNT HOUSE where lead was weighed, the former SMITHY (now a house) and a TUNNEL PORTAL dated 1828. Further on, the remains of the CUPOLA SMELT MILL, 1793, and an elaborate system of condensing FLUES running up the hillside to the CHIMNEY, restored in 1971. Also a six-mile-long leat, the DUKE'S WATER COURSE, various shafts, pits and dams.

GREAT MITTON

7030

Far-flung outpost of the old West Riding at the confluence of the Ribble and the Hodder, with Lancashire to the SE across the one and to the w across the other. No village to speak of.

ALL HALLOWS. Perp w tower, the successor to the 'belfry' referred to in 1438, with panel-traceried w window and rectangular SE stair-turret. Nave and chancel of *c.* 1300, see the Y-tracery of the two-light windows to each side and the tall five-light E window with intersected tracery. Slightly later lowside window on the s side of the chancel with a transom and trefoil-headed lights. s doorway under a hoodmould with headstops, moulded priest's doorway. Chancel arch with quadrant mouldings, early C14 sedilia with trefoiled heads. Nave roof with arch-braced collar-beams, short kingposts braced to the ridge, and cusped corner pieces between the purlins and the rafters. C19 beamed ceiling in the chancel. On the N side of the chancel is the Sherburne Chapel, added in 1594 by Sir Richard Sherburne of nearby Stonyhurst (Lancashire) as a family mausoleum, smartly ashlar-faced, with buttresses, parapet and traceried four-centre-headed four-light windows, all still entirely Perp. But the tablet bearing the date, over the W doorway, is framed by Tuscan half-columns and a cornice. Two-bay arcade towards the chancel, with double-chamfered arches and octagonal pier but square abaci above the moulded capitals with odd little pendants at the corners (cf. Standish, Lancashire).

ROOD SCREEN. Largely mid-C19, of cast iron and terracotta as well as timber, but incorporating from its predecessor an inscription referring to a C15 Abbot of Sawley, and the finely carved C15 dado panels. – SCREEN to the Sherburne Chapel. C15 dado, presumably from the previous chapel on the site, the superstructure c. 1594, with turned balusters but funny ogee heads to the lights, and iron cresting. – PULPIT. Early C18, incorporating some C17 carving. Lacking its base since the late C19. – PEWS. Retaining some C17 and C18 woodwork. Dates of 1628, 1715. – FONT. Plain, octagonal, presumably c. 1300. – FONT COVER. Dated 1593, a stumpy spirelet with carved panels. – W GALLERY. 1815, reconstructed 2000. Simple Gothic detail to the front. – CATECHISM BOARDS, flanking the E window. C19, with crocketed canopies. – STAINED GLASS. E window, nave NE and N middle, by *Alfred O. Hemming*, 1887, 1895 and 1901.

MONUMENTS in the Sherburne Chapel. Artistically what is most valuable at Great Mitton. – Sir Richard Sherburne †1594 and his wife Maud Bold †1588. Alabaster altar tomb with finely executed recumbent effigies, he in armour with his feet on a lion, she with a little dog playing with a tassle. The work of the Burton-on-Trent workshops. On the sides of the tomb-chest shields and standing figures of the children – sons on the S side, daughters on the N – framed by crudely detailed balusters. Nearby is a version of Sir Richard's effigy in stone, either a copy or a blueprint, formerly in the churchyard and badly defaced. – Richard Sherburne, son of the above, †1629 and his wife Catherine Stourton †1591. Wall monument with kneeling figures facing each other across a prayer-desk, framed by coupled Corinthian columns and entablature. Children, including baby twins in a cradle, below. – Richard Sherburne, son of the above, †1668; Richard Sherburne, *his* son, †1689 and his wife Isabel Ingleby †1693; and Richard Sherburne, *their* son, †1690. Three linked altar tombs with recumbent effigies – among the last in England before the C19 – forming a single composition. By *William Stanton*, commissioned by Isabel, i.e. c. 1690: they cost £253, paid in 1699. The figures are works of great beauty, the traditional postures elegantly reinterpreted. The men cross their legs like knights of the C14. – Richard Francis Sherburne, grandson of Richard and Isabel, †1702, aged nine. Also by *William Stanton*: payment of £160 in 1703. The little boy stands contemplating a skull and bones at his feet. Beautifully executed cherubs' heads above, aedicule framework with open segmental pediment. – Sir Nicholas Sherburne, father of the above, †1717 and his wife Catherine Charlton †1728. Baroque pedimented tablet. – Peregrine Widdrington †1743. With a three-dimensional urn against a circular recess.

In the churchyard, a C14 CROSS-HEAD, dug up *c.* 1800, on a late-C19 shaft. Circular, with a Crucifixion on each side and fine, if badly preserved, decoration.

GREAT MITTON HALL, beside the church. C17 range, evidently in origin the cross-wing of a larger house. On the SW flank the outline of a lower range running at right angles can be seen. In its place a porch with a reused C14 doorway with continuous mouldings. Impressive SE gable-end where the ground drops away, of two storeys and attic over a basement, with a pair of massive buttresses, a mullion-and-transom window of seven by two lights to the principal floor and long mullioned windows above. At the corner to the r. a gabled turret, probably for a staircase. Interior altered but retains a very fine nine-bay arched-brace roof, with collars and short kingposts, together with one big four-centre-headed fireplace and two four-centre-headed timber doorways which led into the lost range. Across the road an aisled BARN of similar date, of six bays with kingpost trusses, the masonry walls probably reconstructed; and the THREE FISHES INN, C19 with three medieval carved stones re-set above the doorway, one of them, with three fishes, a version of the arms of nearby Whalley Abbey (Lancashire).

EDISFORD BRIDGE, 1¾ m. NNE, over the Ribble. *c.* 1340, widened and partly rebuilt *c.* 1800. Four arches, the surviving medieval ones the first, third and fourth on the N side, which are slightly pointed and have longitudinal ribs to their soffits. The rebuilt second arch segmental and much wider. Just W of it EDISFORD BRIDGE HOUSE. *c.* 1800. Gabled front with Venetian window, ogee-headed windows with Gothick glazing bars.

LOWER HODDER BRIDGE, ¾ m. W. The old bridge, of 1562, is a picturesque ruin. Its three segmental arches, elegantly graded, remain but the superstructure has gone. The new bridge was built in 1826. Three half-elliptical arches. Rock-faced, with furrowed rustication to the parapet.

GREAT OUSEBURN

4060

ST MARY. Unbuttressed C12 W tower with belfry stage of the C13. Paired bell-openings to the latter with a chamfered shaft between them, and attractive pierced shutters rather than louvres: round-headed and pointed slits (S) and an inserted lancet (W) below. Round-headed double-chamfered tower arch on the plainest square imposts and jambs. Nave and aisles rebuilt *c.* 1820 as a block under a single roof, with the typical Y-tracery windows. Three-bay arcades, in origin of the early C13, with slim circular piers, simple moulded capitals and very sharply pointed double-chamfered arches, but extensively renewed in the rebuilding – all but the bases on the S side, the arches and some of the capitals on the N. Chancel Perp. S chapel and some restoration 1883 by *Paley & Austin*. – STAINED GLASS. E window 1866 by *Ward & Hughes*; chancel N 1884 by *Heaton, Butler & Bayne*; W (the best) 1885 by *Shrigley & Hunt*. – MONUMENTS. Two wall tablets with urns: Elizabeth Young †1779, by *Fisher* of York; and Sarah Horsfield †1780, by *W. Belwood*.

Village street of brick-built houses, a few incorporating remains of C17 timber framing (one dated 1637). The MANOR HOUSE, probably later C17, comprehensively restored and replanned *c.* 1995, retains a remarkable C17 plank door with applied geometrical decoration, a little bullseye window above, and an open-well staircase with stout turned balusters.

GREEN HAMMERTON

ST THOMAS. 1874–6 by *Sir G. G. Scott*, the daughter church of Whixley. Cruciform, with bellcote over the E end of the nave. The style is late C13. Coursed rock-faced walls. – STAINED GLASS includes E window, *c.* 1876 in the manner of *Clayton & Bell*.

The GREEN is a wide-verged cul-de-sac, with C18 brick cottages. Also one, now rendered, which has a C17 timber frame made up of reused earlier components; and opposite, the former CONGREGATIONAL CHAPEL, 1797 (now R.C.), with three-bay front of blind arches framing the windows.

GREENHOW
Bewerley

Scattered former lead-mining settlement 1300 ft (425 metres) up on the bleak moor. Mining took place in the area in Roman times: three lead pigs, stamped with the names of the Emperors Domitian and Trajan, have been found nearby, two of them also with the word BRIG, presumably short for Brigantes. Subsequent activity, from the Middle Ages to the C20, reached its peak in the late C18 and early C19.

ST MARY. 1857–8 by *W. R. Corson* of Leeds. An appropriately blunt design for its location, simplest Dec with a square-topped SW tower-porch with a similarly shaped stair-turret.

The remains of LEAD MINING activity are to the N of the village, including the fragmentary ruins of two SMELTING MILLS, Cockhill Mill, ½ m. NNE of the church, and Prosperous Mill, ¾ m. further, beside the Ashfold Side Beck, both probably late C18. Both had impressive ranges of segment-headed arches at the entrances to the ore hearths, with deep bevelled voussoirs, those at Cockhill on cast-iron columns. 1½ m. NE, the round-headed PORTAL of the Perseverance Level, dated 1825.

TOFT GATE LIMEKILN, beside the main road 1 m. E. c. 1860. Better-preserved remains of the tunnel-vaulted furnace and a flue, and the stump of the chimney.

GREWELTHORPE

ST JAMES. 1845–7 by *A. H. Cates* of York. Simplest Dec, with N aisle.

HACKFALL, NNE of the village. Pre-eminent example of a Sublime landscape pleasure ground of the mid C18, formed c. 1750 by William Aislabie of Studley Royal (q.v.). Now much overgrown and the surviving man-made features ruinous. The site is a steep concave wooded slope, rising 250 ft (80 metres) from a bend of the River Ure and bisected by the Grewelthorpe Beck, with a spectacular view from its higher reaches across the Vale of Mowbray to the North York Moors. The two main buildings are both perched on the abrupt rim of the slope, with oblique views of each other. They are MOWBRAY CASTLE, a Gothick tower, irregularly heptagonal in plan, to the SE; and the BANQUETING HOUSE at Mowbray Point to the NW (in course of restoration at the time of writing), a curious mixture of styles, the elevation away from the slope Gothick with a tufa-encrusted pediment, the other – which provided a 'surprise' view of the panorama – reminiscent of a Panini-esque *capriccio* on Roman ruins, with three tall apsidal recesses. Lower down, the RUSTIC TEMPLE, with canted-bay front, and overlooking the river FISHER'S HALL, dated 1750, a tufa-built Gothick octagon. Partly artificial cascades on the beck, winding paths.

ROMAN CAMP, ½ m. NNW of the village. Remains of a rectangular enclosure, with substantial earthwork bank and outer ditch on three sides, steep natural slope (and modern stone revetment) on the fourth.

GRINDLETON

ST AMBROSE. E of the village. 1805, replacing an earlier chapel, remodelled and slightly lengthened 1897–8 by *Austin & Paley*.

Of the 1805 phase are the thin gawky w tower, with crude battlements and semicircular openings, and three tall round-
headed windows on the s side with an attempt at Y-tracery.
Austin & Paley's windows by contrast approximate to C17
Pennine Gothic. Also theirs are the roofs and the rustic timber
arcade reminiscent of an aisled barn.

FRIENDS' MEETING HOUSE, 7/8 m. NE, across the River Ribble
from Sawley. 1777. Tripartite windows and central doorway,
cottage adjoining to l. under the same roof. Panelled elders'
bench at the s end, women's gallery over the N part, with top-
hung shutters. Nearby is BANK HALL, *c.* 1780, three storeys,
three bays. In the garden a naïve Gothic summerhouse and a
sundial made up of carved fragments from Sawley Abbey.

GUISELEY

Part of an agglomeration of settlements together with Yeadon and
Rawdon (qq.v.). The railway arrived in 1865.

ST OSWALD. A church of very great interest, although that is not
immediately apparent: intrusively restored 1866 by *Wilcock &*
Common, and doubled in size on the N side, with a new nave
and chancel, 1909–10 by *Sir Charles Nicholson*. Perp w tower
with diagonal buttresses, corbelled-out parapet with battlements (cf. Barwick-in-Elmet, Rothwell and Thorner) and
corner pinnacles. Excellent s transept, the date probably
c. 1260–75, against the w half of the chancel. Large s window,
of two-plus-two lights with bar tracery forming the usual three
foiled circles. E elevation with three even lancets. Chancel E
window Perp of five lights, with panel tracery. Cross-gables and
fenestration of the s aisle, lancets in the clerestory, and Neo-
Norman s porch, all inventions of 1866, when the s aisle and
much of the chancel were rebuilt, the w half of the latter raised
to the height of the nave; but the porch hints at what is to
come. Late Norman s doorway with two orders of colonnettes
and stylized foliage capitals. s arcade also Norman but cut
through a pre-existing wall, early Norman or Anglo-Saxon,
with three outsize quoins at the base of its E corner. The arcade
is of four bays, with quatrefoil piers and scalloped capitals. The
C13 archway between the chancel and the s transept has beautiful responds consisting of a detached central shaft surrounded by three smaller ones, also detached (cf. Dewsbury,
West Riding South). Moulded capitals, double-chamfered
arch. Similar archway on the N side of the chancel, where there
was a smaller transept or chapel. Arch from the transept to the
s aisle also C13, on single detached shafts. In the transept a
plain arched piscina. Nave N arcade Perp, with slim octagonal
piers and double-chamfered arches. Chancel arch 1866. N aisle
and chapel replaced by *Nicholson*'s addition, with its own N

aisle, its style taken from the Perp arcade but treated with the tactful freedom he is known for.

PULPIT. *c.* 1680. The top stage of a three-decker. Quite up-to-date, with raised-and-fielded panels. – PEW, in the transept. C17. Plain, with small knobs and the initials of Walter Calverley of Esholt Hall. Other Jacobean-style WOODWORK – screens, nave pews, font cover etc. – by *Nicholson*, 1910–30. – SCULPTURE. Anglo-Saxon cross-shaft, with a fragment of a cross-head set on top of it which is probably part of the same work. Probably C10. – STAINED GLASS. Three windows in the new chancel, tower window and S aisle SE, by *A. K. Nicholson*, brother of the architect, 1914 etc. S aisle middle and W window by *Powell & Sons*, 1910 and 1921. – MONUMENTS. A number of wall tablets, including Anna Wickham †1736, with pediment; Robert Stansfield †1772, by *Fisher* of York, with wreathed urn; Ann Rookes †1798, with bas-relief sarcophagus; Anna Maria Crompton †1819, daughter of the above, the same design signed *M. Taylor* of York. – In the CHURCHYARD numerous table tombs and a LAMPPOST, perhaps early C19, formed of three clustered Tuscan columns. Glazed lampholder on iron scrolls.

RECTORY (former), SE of the church. Fine gritstone house dated 1601, incorporating some timber-framed fabric which may be earlier. Restored 1907 by *Sir Charles Nicholson*. Near-symmetrical front with central two-storey porch and gables over the end bays. Over the doorway a Latin inscription expressing clerical sentiments. Mullioned-and-transomed ground-floor windows, of six and three lights to the r. of the porch, those to the l. larger and evidently altered in 1907. First-floor windows without transoms, apart from that on the porch, but with arched lights. Continuous dripmoulds to both storeys, open-work finials on the porch gable. 'Flying' chimneystack, largely detached from the gable, at the W end. Lean-to outshut and projecting wing at the back, both apparently additions. (Interior much altered 1907. Posts and one rail of a timber-framed wall between the main range and the outshut, with some close studding at the W end. Some stained glass by *A. K. Nicholson*. In the grounds the remains of a moat, and an outdoor stone bath.)

Former TRAMSHED, Otley Road. 1914 by *Sydney Kitson* for Leeds City Tramways. Long one-and-a-half-storey rock-faced façade, a public transport Palazzo del Tè, with heavy quoins and keystones, bosses and raised panels. Vehicle entrances in recessed end bays.

PARK GATE HOUSE, Park Road. Late C18 villa enlarged in later C19. Five-bay ashlar front facing away from the road, with three-bay pediment broken at the base by an ornamented semicircular relieving arch. Tripartite window below that, C19 Tuscan porch and l. and r. extensions. (Top-lit staircase.)

HOLLINS HILL FARMHOUSE, Hollins Hill, SW of the built-up area. Small double pile of 1720, with five-bay front and central lobby entry. Cross-windows all changed to sashes.

Segment-headed housebody fireplace, perhaps reused, and unusually another set at right angles to it, heating the kitchen behind the parlour. Dog-leg staircase with splat balusters rising from the housebody, plank and muntin partitions.
See also HAWKSWORTH HALL.

HALTON EAST

0050

HALTON HALL. Square C17 house with the main rooms arranged in an L-shape, the kitchen behind the parlour. Two main elevations facing S and E, reflecting this arrangement, both with a central doorway and two tiers of mullion-and-transom windows. Four-plus-four lights to the housebody, five lights on each elevation to the parlour, three-plus-three lights to the kitchen, and the same pattern repeated above. Fireplaces corbelled to housebody, segment-headed to kitchen.

HALTON GILL

8070

Tiny isolated hamlet at the top of Littondale, with a number of C17 houses.

ST JOHN (now a house). A chapel was in existence by 1577, rebuilt 1632 and again, apart from the N wall, in 1848 by *A. B. Higham* of Wakefield for the Dawson sisters of Settle. Low nave and chancel in Dec style. Attached to the W end, under the same roof, the former SCHOOL HOUSE dated 1626, the school founded by Henry Fawcett of Norwich, a native of Halton Gill, and his brother William. A small one-bay cottage, with a Gothic window provided by *Higham*. It also served as the curate's house.

MANOR HOUSE. Dated 1641, the datestone now re-set on the big two-storey porch of *c.* 1700. C19 Tudor-arched front doorway and renewal of mullioned windows. Lobby-entry plan, and the local peculiarity of the porch also containing the staircase (cf. Sawyers Garth, Litton). The stair is reached from the housebody and has turned balusters. Handsome stone fireplaces to housebody and parlour. (At WRATHMIRE FARM, C17 decorative plaster wall panel and arcaded frieze.)

HALTON WEST

8050

HALTON PLACE. Built 1770 as a secondary seat of the Yorke family of Bewerley in Nidderdale, by the London architect

John Crunden. An unusual design, a version of the Kentian tripartite formula previously used by James Paine at Stockeld
Park (q.v.), but scaled down and more simply detailed. Three-
bay, two-and-a-half-storey pedimented centrepiece, and broad
lower flanking bays each also pedimented. Tuscan porch *in
antis.* The house is built of rendered brick with ashlar dressings rather than of stone throughout. Some restrained Adam-
style plasterwork inside. Service wing to l., 1872.

BRIDGE, over the Ribble. Late C18, repaired *c.* 1850. Three
arches. ¼ m. SSE of Halton Place a substantial ROUND
BARROW, 15 ft (4.5 metres) high.

HAMPSTHWAITE

2050

ST THOMAS BECKET. Perp W tower with thin diagonal
buttresses, battlements and three-light bell-openings. Tower
arch of two continuous orders, the inner chamfered. The rest
rebuilt 1821 by *Thomas Driffield* of Knaresborough, and almost
entirely again in 1901–2 by *C. Hodgson Fowler,* supposedly following the form of the medieval church. Perp, with S aisle. The
N wall has rustic quoins, presumably retained *in situ* from the
1821 rebuilding. – PULPIT. C17, with diamond panelling, much
restored. – BOX PEW. Dated 1695, at the SW corner. The other
seating made up from the rest of the box pews, and other
woodwork, from the previous church. – FONT. Plain bowl, possibly Norman. – ROYAL ARMS. *c.* 1821, painted. – STAINED
GLASS. E window by *Shrigley & Hunt, c.* 1919. – MONUMENTS.
Small brass, mid-C14, with incomplete figure of a merchant.
Re-inscribed to Andrew Dixon †1570. – Some simple wall
tablets including The Rev. Timothy Metcalf Shann, Vicar
of Hampsthwaite, †1839 by *F. Webster* of Kendal. – Amy
Woodforde-Finden, popular composer, †1919. Executed by
George Wade, said to have been designed by an Italian named
Giudini. Recumbent effigy on a large box-like tomb-chest, all
in white marble. Little angels at the corners, curly draperies
and flowers on the sides, in very low relief, the effect a bit like
melting ice cream.

BRIDGE, over the Nidd. 1640, the roadway widened, with oversailing parapets supported on corbels, probably in the C19.
Three segmental arches.

HARDEN
Bingley

0030

ST SAVIOUR. 1891–2 by *T. H. & F. Healey.* Simple E.E., with N
aisle. Three-bay arcade with cylindrical piers. Nearby the

CONGREGATIONAL CHAPEL, 1865, the pedimented front with two tiers of round-headed windows, interior altered; and the plainer former METHODIST CHAPEL, 1853.

Several C17 houses on the fringes of the village.

WOODBANK, ⅜ m. E. 1635 for Stephen and Mary Ferrand. Compact U-shape with the wings at the back – the gap between them occupied by a later lean-to – and entrance in the r. flank. Basket-arched doorway with dripmould on carved brackets. Mullion-and-transom windows, of six lights to the parlour and parlour chamber, of eight and three to the housebody. Tenanted 1860–76 by the decorator John Aldam Heaton, who in 1861 installed three panels of very early stained glass by *Morris & Co.*, designed by *Rossetti* – Heaton's contact with the firm – their present whereabouts not known.

HARDEN HALL, ¼ m. S. Also a Ferrand house. Hall range and cross-wing with mullioned windows of up to six lights. Big gabled addition behind the service end, dated 1691, and another behind the housebody of *c.* 1700, with an upright oval window above a central doorway. (C17 staircase with turned balusters, panelling of the C17 and later.) Also two BARNS, one dated 1630.

IVY HOUSE, ⅜ m. SSW. 1676. Small double pile with gable-end entrance. Housebody has one window of three-plus-three lights, a two-light fire window, and a firehood.

HILL END, ⅜ m. WSW. Of two builds, the earlier part containing the housebody and service, the later, slightly taller, the entrance and parlour end. Nine-light windows to each floor in this part, and an early C18 doorway, with triglyph frieze and segmental pediment.

HAREWOOD

The territory of the Lascelles family since the mid C18 (Earls of Harewood from 1812), along the ridge of Harewood Bank s of the river Wharfe – T.D. Whitaker's 'fortunate place', with a church rich in fine monuments, an architecturally sophisticated castle and a neat model village, as well as a country house of the first rank set in a spacious park. That was the successor to Gawthorpe Hall, 1 m. SW of the castle and in the later Middle Ages the seat of the Gascoignes, the Gawthorpe and castle estates remaining separate until the mid C16; and the church is sited between the two residences. But the location of the village, further E at the park gates, is also its ancient one, not the product of C18 reorganizing: a charter for a market had been granted in 1209.

ALL SAINTS. On its own in the park NE of the house, within its tree-fringed churchyard. Perp, all of a piece, built *c.* 1410 for Elizabeth and Sybil Aldburgh, daughters and co-heiresses of Sir William Aldburgh, builder of the castle, replacing an earlier church on the same site. Short w tower embraced by the aisles, long nave and chancel of equal height, no clerestory. Uniform arched windows with panel tracery, mainly of three lights, the E and w of five. s porch repaired mid C18; E gable rebuilt, with battlements and Gothick quatrefoil, and battlements added to the aisle w ends, c. 1793. Restoration by *G. G. Scott*, 1862–3, including new roof, a single continuous span. Rather austere interior, the effect accentuated by Scott's removal of C18 wood-work. Four-bay nave arcades, the tall octagonal piers without capitals; single arches between the chancel and the side chapels, and beyond these on each side a tomb-arch. – PULPIT and FONT by *Scott*. Also the bowl of the OLD FONT, circular and heavily moulded, probably C13. – Outsize CLOCK on the tower, 1760 by *Hindley* of York, intended for the stables at Plompton (q.v.). – STAINED GLASS, mainly a false note, includes E window by *O'Connor*, 1855; s chapel E by *Capronnier*, 1866; s chapel SE by *W. Taylor* 'late of O'Connor', 1880; w window by *Kempe*, 1894.

MONUMENTS. The outstanding feature of the church is the series of six late medieval alabaster altar tombs with pairs of recumbent effigies – including the co-foundresses and their respective husbands – which form the largest concentration of alabaster monuments in any English parish church, evidently from a number of different workshops. Subject of a major conservation programme, 1979–81, during which they were returned, as closely as possible, to their original positions. – Sir William Gascoigne, Lord Chief Justice, †1419 and his first wife Elizabeth Mowbray. In the middle of the s chapel. He is shown in his judge's robes. Fine features. On the tomb-chest standing angels holding shields (cf. the monument to Sir Ralph Greene †1417 at Lowick, Northamptonshire, made by the workshop of *Thomas Prentys* and *Robert Sutton* at Chellaston, Derbyshire). No niches or canopies. The brass inscription fillet is a restoration. – Sir Richard Redman †1426 and his wife Elizabeth Aldburgh †1434. In the N tomb-arch. Well-carved effigies, he in plate armour identical to that of the Waterton effigy at Methley (q.v.). Tomb-chest with broad flat canopies and kneeling angels holding shields (also cf. the Waterton tomb). – Sir William Ryther †c. 1426 and his wife Sybil Aldburgh. In the s tomb-arch. The companion piece to the above, with very similar effigies but in poorer condition. The tomb-chest canopies narrower, alternating with shields, but the figures below them lost. – Sir William Gascoigne †c. 1465, grandson of the judge, and his wife Margaret Clarell. In the s aisle. He is in armour of the mid C15, with traces of the original colouring, she in the dress of a widow. Small figures of weepers, knights and ladies, in ogee-headed niches, on the parts of the tomb-chest sides which had survived the previous relocation of the monument to a corner of the s chapel. – Sir William Gascoigne, grandson of the above, †1487 and his wife Margaret Percy, w of his grandparents' and almost identical, he in armour and tabard, she again in widow's dress. The tomb-chest

figures include saints as well as the weepers, and at the E end,
with some original colouring, two angels holding a shield. –
Edward Redman †1510 and his wife Elizabeth Huddleston
†1529. In the N chapel. The latest and sculpturally the best,
attributed to the same hand as the monument to Sir John de
Strelley †1501 at Strelley, Nottinghamshire (q.v.). Crouched on
the lion at his feet the tiny figure of a bedesman. Tomb-chest
with niches containing saints, the subjects' three children, and
in the middle of each side angels holding a shield. – In contrast to these Sir Thomas Denison †1765, by *N. Hedges*. With
bust above a sarcophagus.

HAREWOOD CASTLE. ½ m. NE of the church, on a steep N-facing
slope, now surrounded by dense woodland. A compact fortified house rather than a true castle, for which licence to crenellate was granted in 1367: the manor of Harewood had passed
to Sir William Aldburgh *c.* 1364. Abandoned in the mid C17

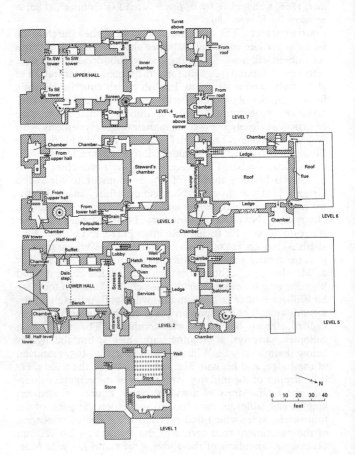

Harewood Castle.
Floor plans

but as a shell still standing almost to full height: an outer precinct wall has been lost. It is of the type of e.g. Langley Castle, Northumberland (*c.* 1350), essentially an elongated rectangle with projecting angle turrets at the s end and an entrance tower against the E side, intricately planned with many changes of level, exploiting the slope of the ground. The main part of the building was occupied by a lower hall at ground-floor level, with screens passage entered directly from the porch, and an upper hall or solar, of similar dimensions, above. The s towers contain five storeys of small chambers, linked to the halls by newel stairs; while at the N end there is a basement providing a guardroom and a barrel-vaulted storage room, the kitchen and service area on the level of the lower hall, a steward's chamber above that, and an inner chamber at the level of the upper hall. Over the porch were a portcullis chamber and then at upper-hall level a small chapel.

The stonework is of excellent quality, and much of the detail retains a surprising crispness. The windows are mainly straight-headed, quite large and divided only by mullions and transoms without any arching, almost C17 rather than C14 in appearance. But those to the chapel have a little tracery, the centre one flanked by the arms of Aldburgh and his patron Edward Balliol, the former puppet king of Scotland. In the porch the grooves for the portcullis remain. In the lower hall the most remarkable feature is the elaborate buffet recess at the w end p. 24 of the dais, with a richly cusped arch under a crocketed ogee hood, and a little window at the back. Also remains of a large fireplace in the s wall, stone benches along the sides and the sockets for the posts of the screen. In the kitchen two fire-places, an oven and a well recess. In the upper hall the position of upper and lower ends was evidently reversed, with the entrance and possibly a lobby, or at least a gallery, at the s end. There were two small fireplaces. Most of the chambers also have fireplaces, and garderobes.

HAREWOOD HOUSE

Henry Lascelles, a successful merchant and financier in the West India trade and director of the East India Company, who held the lucrative post of Collector of Customs in Barbados, bought the Harewood estates in 1739; but their transformation was due to his elder son Edwin, who inherited in 1753. The inception and development of the design of the house was an unsurprisingly complicated process. Lascelles's first projects were some improvements at Gawthorpe Hall itself in 1754–5, including a new porch, for which his architect was *John Carr*, and the new stable block nearby (*see* below), begun in 1755. But by then he was seeking plans for the new mansion 'from Every body in England' – the everybody including in due course the East India Company's Surveyor William Jones (architect of the Rotunda at

Harewood House, view of the north front before alteration.
Watercolour by Thomas Malton, 1788

Ranelagh Gardens), the young William Chambers (1756), and
possibly Matthew Brettingham and Capability Brown, as well as
Carr – and was seeking advice on them from the Earl of Leicester; then in 1758 he invited comments on Carr's scheme from
Robert Adam, who duly 'tickled it up' with some suggested modifications. The eventual outcome was a design by *Carr* with some
of Adam's suggestions incorporated into it by Carr himself, and
a scheme of interior decoration designed by *Adam* as a separate
commission some years later. The house was begun in 1759 and
completed structurally in 1764, the decoration begun in 1765 and
the house occupied in 1771, when Gawthorpe Hall was demolished. That, however, was not the end of the story for there followed in 1842–50 the drastic remodelling of the exterior, and
significant changes to the interior, by *Sir Charles Barry* for the
third Countess of Harewood. Further internal alterations during
the C20 have been minor in comparison.

The house stands on a s-facing slope, a little uphill from the site
of Gawthorpe Hall. It is built of gritstone ashlar quarried on
the estate. *Carr*'s design was for the most part an abbreviated
version of Campbell's third scheme for Wanstead, but its
impact was conditioned by the terrain, the house standing up
impressively to the s, above its rusticated basement, but slightly
less imposing on the N (entrance) side where the basement is
sunk in an area. Rectangular central block of one-and-a-half
storeys over the base, to the N of nine bays with an applied

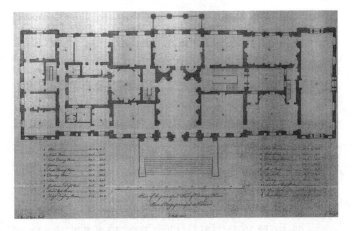

Harewood House.
Ground-floor plan, 1771

five-bay portico with pediment. Pediments also to the *piano nobile* windows, segmental within the portico, triangular without. To l. and r. are lower three-bay link sections with courtyards hidden behind them, and then wings running N–S, slightly taller again, their pavilion-like ends a single broad bay with an overarched Venetian window. On the s side the centre had a three-bay portico which was projecting instead of applied – the most significant of *Adam*'s suggestions. Aedicular windows on the links, coupled pilasters at the corners of the wings. Of *Barry*'s alterations, the first to be seen are the heavy balustraded parapet added to the main block, appearing to sit precariously on the slope of the roof, and the flat-roofed attic storeys added to the wings. Others on the N side are the elaborate coat of arms in the pediment, the giant pilasters flanking the portico, the abolition of columned recesses on the links and a similar reduction of detail on the wings; but the effect is essentially negative, a composition which is convincingly of neither the C18 nor the C19. On the s side the changes were more radical but more persuasive, imparting a characteristically early Victorian richness of texture and, with the new terrace in front (*see* below), something of the feel of a big *villa suburbana* of the Roman Campagna. The portico was done away with entirely, replaced by a perron and by giant pilasters along the whole length of the central block. Balconies to the Venetian windows in the wings, big coarse brackets above.

The INTERIOR was planned as two overlapping circuits, merging in the entrance hall and former saloon on the central axis and encircling the back courtyards to l. and r.,* the w

---

* One of *Adam*'s proposals in 1758 was to make the courtyards semicircular, with the curved sides towards the wings, and the suggestion was initially adopted for the w courtyard; but in 1762 the idea was abandoned and both courtyards made rectangular.

made up entirely of state rooms, the E partly more domestic. *Adam*'s decoration of the rooms was one of his largest schemes, executed by many of his usual contacts – the artists *Biagio Rebecca* and *Antonio Zucchi*, the carvers *William Collins* and *John Devall*, the plasterers *Joseph Rose Sen.* and *Jun.* – but it was perhaps never his most successful, for a number of reasons: the disjunction between planning and decoration, which evidently limited the scope for variety of shape and character in the rooms; the disjunction also between decoration and the design of furniture – one of the great C18 collections, commissioned separately, from *Thomas Chippendale*; and a degree of indecision regarding the function of some of the rooms, in a circuit which was in any case over-extended. For the modern visitor there is also the extent of later alteration: Adam's most distinctive interior at Harewood, an octagonal dressing room on the E side of the main block, was destroyed in the 1840s.

The ENTRANCE HALL (1766) presents a typical state of affairs. The formula of engaged Roman Doric columns alternating with niches was inherited from *Carr*'s blueprint. *Adam* introduced a degree of variety by changing the shape of the niches in the side walls; and his are the ornate lightly compartmented ceiling and the scheme of wall decoration, with rectangular and circular stucco reliefs by *Collins*. The side niches were then altered again, and one of the two chimneypieces removed, by *Barry*. The original colouring was probably all white: the present red marbling of the columns was suggested by a description of 1819. In the middle *Epstein*'s massive alabaster of a different Adam, 1938–9, installed in the 1960s. The least altered Adam interiors are the OLD LIBRARY to the l. of the hall and the MUSIC ROOM to the r., both designed in 1765, the former with a coved ceiling repainted *c.* 1990 in its original colours, recessed bookcases between Corinthian pilasters, and a grisaille overmantel and painted panels attributed to *Rebecca*; the latter with circular insets to the ceiling – Midas Judging a Musical Contest between Apollo and Pan, surrounded by Muses – also attributed to *Rebecca*, a wall scheme of large paintings of classical ruins by *Zucchi*, 1771, and an Axminster carpet echoing the ceiling design.* The former SALOON, beyond the hall – since the 1840s another LIBRARY – is again a mixture of Adam and Barry. Particularly fine deeply coved ceiling (designed 1767), twin marble chimneypieces executed by *Devall*, 1769, with pedimented overmantels of wood and stucco, attributed to *Collins*. But the apses flanking the entrance from the hall were converted by Barry into bookcases, losing their columnar screens in the process, and the end walls were deprived of their symmetry by the removal of false doors. Present colour scheme 1958.

The largest room, occupying the whole of the W wing, is the GALLERY (cf. Holkham Hall). Adam's penultimate design, of *c.* 1765, was for a sculpture gallery, with niches along the E wall

63

---

* But the *Reynolds* portrait over the chimneypiece, of Mrs Hale as Euphrosyne, did not come into the room until the C20.

– although Lascelles possessed no sculpture – but from the early C19 on it has served to accommodate parts of a growing picture collection. Altered by Barry, but restored in 1990 to more or less its state in the 1820s. Elaborate caryatid chimneypiece (1777), ceiling (designed 1769) of a type previously used at Lansdowne House, with inset paintings attributed to *Rebecca*; but the most prominent features are by *Chippendale* – the pier glasses and tables, and the spectacular window pelmets, carved to imitate fabric. Between the Gallery and the Music Room the DINING ROOM, entirely redone by Barry, with a heavily detailed coved ceiling. Mid-C18 chimneypiece imported *c.* 1990. Between the Saloon and the Gallery are two DRAWING ROOMS, where Adam's contribution was always limited. The first has a ceiling (designed 1768) based on an engraving of an ancient Roman example in Bartoli's *Antichi Sepolchri*, and another complementary Axminster carpet, but also a scheme of damask wall hangings – introduced in 1776, replicated in the 1990s – and extravagant wall and chimney glasses by *Chippendale*, striking a different note. The other, initially conceived of as a second dining room, has a 'French Chimney Piece' by *Thomas Atkinson*, 1785, and Adam's ceiling partly redecorated in 1852 by *Alfred Stevens*.

E of the Saloon are the former STATE DRESSING ROOM, now the SPANISH LIBRARY, and then the STATE BEDROOM, both designed in 1767. The former has another fine coved ceiling, similar to that in the Saloon at Nostell Priory (West Riding South), more of Barry's bookcases lining the walls and above them a zone of C17 Spanish embossed leather put up in the 1930s. In the latter a ceiling with similar motifs, but the bed alcove, framed by Ionic columns, was reduced in depth by Barry to make space for a corridor, so that *Chippendale*'s magnificent domed state bed, beautifully restored in 1999, is now only partly housed within it. The rest of the E circuit is made up mainly of bedrooms and dressing rooms. Next to the Old Library the former STUDY, *c.* 1766, now the China Room, with ceiling from Wood's *Palmyra*; and next to that PRINCESS MARY'S DRESSING ROOM, 1930 by *Sir Herbert Baker*, chichi Neo-Adam. Finally on the main floor, tucked away off the W side of the entrance hall, the STAIRCASE (not open to the public), originally by *Carr*, altered to imperial form by Barry. Iron balustrade of two different designs, that with a simple anthemion motif presumably Carr's, reused, the other Barry's own. Large painted panel of the house in its landscape by *Nicholas Dahl*, 1773, grisaille panels by *Zucchi*. Oval glazed dome. In the basement a columned SUB-HALL below the Saloon, and an impressive groin-vaulted KITCHEN below the Gallery.

Outside again, *Barry*'s S TERRACE, 1844–8, is on two levels, the narrow upper stage to which the perron descends, and the broad lower one with fountains and elaborate parterre (restored in 1994). Barry's travel journals suggest that the main influence on the design was the garden at Versailles. On the upper level two pairs of stone sphinxes by *Christopher Richardson* of Doncaster, *c.* 1770, which Barry moved from the N front. On the lower some big stone urns brought from Clumber Park, Nottinghamshire in 1937, and, replacing the central fountain, *Astrid Zydower*'s bronze Orpheus with a Leopard, *c.* 1982. The PARK beyond was the product of several phases and hands. *Capability Brown* was first consulted in 1758, but he did not actually work at Harewood until *c.* 1772–80, when his principal contribution was the formation of the LAKE to the S of the house; and in the meantime, works to the N including the creation of a Pleasure Ground on the crest of Harewood Bank (now reverted to woodland) had been carried out by *Thomas White*. Later, following advice from *Humphry Repton* to Edwin Lascelles's successor, the future first Earl, in 1800–2, the park was extended to the NE, towards the village (*see* below), with a new entrance aligned on its main street (the previous entrance on this side had been a little further NW, due E of the church); then in 1813 the Pleasure Ground was also extended E, by *James Webb*, said to have been a pupil of Brown, making use of old quarries as an approach to the castle (cf. Belsay, Northumberland), which was now exploited as a Picturesque eyetacher.

Of the numerous ancillary buildings the earliest is the STABLE BLOCK, downhill to the SW of the house, which was built in 1755–8. Its authorship is unclear. It was executed by *Carr*, but there is no direct evidence that he designed it and it is not in his style.* Quadrangle of one-and-a-half storeys, the principal front with a centrepiece derived from that of William Kent's Royal Mews at Charing Cross – pediment flanked by lower half-pediments, and engaged columns with frost-work blocking – and end bays with Diocletian windows and ramped parapet. Courtyard with colonnade of coupled Tuscan columns round three sides, evidently *Carr*'s addition to the design. ¼ m. W is STANK, an extensive complex of home farm etc. The centrepiece is a large quadrangle of farm buildings (now offices), 1795 by *Peter Atkinson Sen.* (and shown on an estate map of 1796). Simplified Palladian, one and two storeys, running up the hillside with oddly sloping masonry courses. To the r. a more informal group, fronted by the so-called GRANARY, perhaps the 'tower' referred to in the estate building accounts in the 1760s. Three storeys, with Venetian window on the S side and pyramid roof with lantern. To the l. the MENAGERIE, probably 1772–4 by *Carr*. Two-storey central block with pedimented three-bay centre, and detached L-shaped ranges l. and r., one and two storeys, running forward to pedimented pavilions.

Nearby, on the lake dam, a masonry CASCADE. In woodland S of the lake the rustic ROUGH BRIDGE and balustraded

---

*An engraving after a sketch by Carr's assistant William Lindley, on which the design is credited to Carr, cannot be taken as reliable evidence as it gives the date of the building as 1748.

NEW BRIDGE, the latter originally by *Carr*, *c.* 1769–71, rebuilt 1837–8, carrying the S drive over the picturesquely improved Stank Beck; and SE of them on the Leeds road the LOFT-HOUSE GATE – four pedimented gatepiers – 1771, also by *Carr*. On the rising ground hereabouts, close to the GREY STONE, a gritstone boulder with cup-and-ring markings, there was a temple by him, 1795; and 1¼ m. further S is another late C18 park entrance, the ALWOODLEY GATE, with lodges disguised as quadrant screens. But these low-key announcements were to be eclipsed by the new MAIN GATEWAY at the village, the design originally by *Repton*, reworked in execution *c.* 1803 apparently by *Carr* and the mason *John Muschamp Jun.* Big triumphal arch with attached Doric columns and heavy blocking course, and coffered vault to the passage. Spacious forecourt terminated by small cuboid pavilions with aedicular windows. NW from here, beneath Church Lane, a ROCK ARCH of rough boulders, constructed *c.* 1813 as part of the Pleasure Ground extension; and further W in the old Pleasure Ground a small domed ROTUNDA for admiring the view across the Wharfe to Almscliffe Crag, first built *c.* 1774 probably by *Carr*, reconstructed in the 1930s to a different design.

THE VILLAGE. Rebuilt very gradually and in quite piecemeal fashion, begun *c.* 1755 with designs evidently by *Carr*, but not completed until after 1800. The main element is THE AVENUE, the realigned old village street running E from opposite the park gateway; and the earliest and most ambitious part is a group on the N side based on Lord Burlington's design for a school and almshouses at Sevenoaks.* In the middle a house of seven bays with pedimented centre taller than the rest, and l. and r. one-and-a-half-storey ranges articulated by giant relieving arches with Diocletian windows in the heads. The l. of these was built as a ribbon factory, to provide employment in the locality, but the venture soon failed and by 1770 it was converted to cottages. The r. has triple-keystoned doorways. Further l. another large house, similar to the first; and to the r. a two-storey range with taller end pavilions again with blind arches, which was repeated opposite on the S side after 1800. Otherwise quite utilitarian two-storey cottage rows, which are continued on the E side of HARROGATE ROAD, running N–S between The Avenue and the park gateway. Here also, in the N part, the SCHOOL, *c.* 1768, with single-storey centre between taller cross-wings, C19 Gothic extension at the rear. Off the W side, N of the gateway, is THE SQUARE, misleadingly named, with two parallel cottage terraces and beyond them the former VICARAGE (now Moor House), *c.* 1800, five bays with open pediment and overarched Venetian window. Further N in Harrogate Road, flanking the entrance to Church Lane, a pair of pavilion-like two-bay houses with pedimental gables, also *c.* 1800.

69

*Published in Kent's *Designs of Inigo Jones*, 1727.

HAREWOOD BRIDGE, over the Wharfe, ¾ m. NW. Rebuilt 1729, doubled in width 1775 by *John Gott*. Four arches, the inner two on the older part very slightly pointed.

LOFTHOUSE FARMHOUSE, 1¼ m. SSE. Tall tripartite model farmhouse evidently intended as an eyecatcher.

At WIKE, 2 m. SSE, a former SCHOOL, founded 1739, much altered and extended C19–C20. Two large cross-windows to the schoolroom.

THE GRAMMAR SCHOOL AT LEEDS. *See* Alwoodley (Outer Leeds).

3050

HARROGATE

Harrogate as a town is a product of the second half of the C19, but as a spa its history is much longer, beginning *c.* 1571 when the similarity of the waters of the Tewit Well to those of Spa in the Ardennes was recognized by William Slingsby of Bilton Hall. In the 1590s Dr Timothy Bright called the spring the 'English Spaw', turning the place-name into a noun; and discovery of other mineral springs quickly followed. From at least the mid C17 on the locality did not lack custom but functioned as a 'rural' spa – Tobias Smollett's spa on 'a wild common' (1771). Facilities included many of the hotels which were to be an enduring feature of the town, and a group of handsome Neoclassical baths and pump rooms – the architectural climax of this phase – erected in the 1830s by rival proprietors, none of which has survived. One reason for the late onset of urbanization was the policy of the Duchy of Lancaster – the spa was located in the Duchy's Forest of Knaresborough – which was to discourage speculative development *à la* Cheltenham or Leamington. Another factor presumably was the peculiar topography of the place, with habitation, like the springs themselves, scattered over a wide area. By the later C18 two settlements had evolved, High Harrogate on its breezy plateau, alongside the turnpike road to Skipton and close to the St John's or 'Sweet' Well – a chalybeate spring like the Tewit Well – and Low Harrogate a mile to the W in the valley of the Coppice Beck, round the Old Sulphur Well or 'Stinking Spaw', prized for its purgative qualities. Directly between the two were enclosed fields; but indirectly they were linked by Harrogate's most distinctive landscape feature, the 200-plus acres of common known as the Stray – an irregular U-shape (its boundaries fixed under the Forest of Knaresborough Enclosure Award of 1778) with the two settlements at its extremities.

The key to the rapid development of the town of Harrogate, from *c.* 1860 onwards, was the creation of a commercial town centre, and new residential areas, on the land between High and Low Harrogate, in part behind existing buildings on its S and W fringes, facing onto the Stray. In 1859–62 the railway was extended through the middle of this area – previously it had

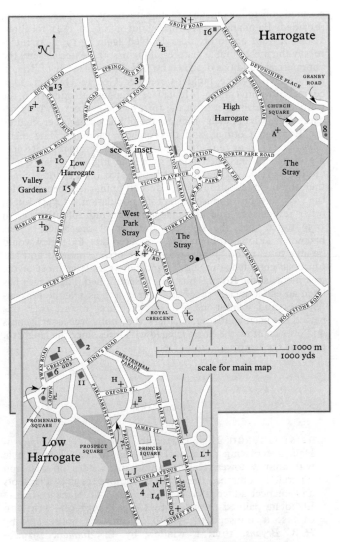

A	Christchurch	I	Municipal Buildings
B	St Luke (former)	2	Royal Hall
C	St Mark	3	Conference Centre
D	St Mary	4	Magistrates' Court
E	St Peter	5	Carnegie Library
F	St Wilfred	6	Mercer Art Gallery
G	St Robert	7	Royal Pump Room
H	Wesley Chapel	8	St John's Well
J	West Park United Reformed Church	9	Tewit Well
K	Trinity Methodist Church	10	(Magnesia Well Pump Room)
L	Baptist Church	11	Royal Baths
M	St Paul's United Reformed Church	12	Royal Bath Hospital (former)
N	Grove Road Methodist Chapel	13	Harrogate Ladies' College
		14	St Peter's Primary School
		15	Western Primary School
		16	Grove Road Primary School

reached only to the outskirts of the settlement – and a new station provided. Population rose from about 4,000 in 1841 to about 11,000 in 1881 and more than doubled again by 1901. Architecturally the most notable features of the first three decades are the commercial buildings designed by *J. H. Hirst*, formerly of Bristol, and erected by the builder-developer George Dawson, in a coarsely inventive Franco-Italianate strangely at odds with the town's genteel image: from the turn of the century and Harrogate's Edwardian heyday they are the public buildings erected by the Borough Council, and the Anglican churches. The many villas, detached or semi-detached, in the predominant gritstone, are in general less interesting, mainly in high Victorian quasi-Gothic or Italianate modes which persisted until *c.* 1900. Since then the town has also developed as an upmarket dormitory for the West Yorkshire conurbation (2001 population, 67,434), but in other respects its role has changed more radically. Pevsner in 1959 noted that 'the size and number of the hotels ... has become a serious problem' and wondered how long they would be able to carry on 'in an age of scarce private patients and less universal confidence in spas' – and ten years later most of the treatments at the Royal Baths were discontinued. The answer has been an economically successful reinvention as a venue for conferences and exhibitions. The architectural record over this period has been controversial, marked by both over-assertiveness and over-caution: the Stray, fringed with trees since the later C19, remains the town's greatest asset.

CHURCHES

CHRIST CHURCH, High Harrogate. 1830–1 by *John Oates* of Halifax, replacing a chapel of ease built in 1749. Lancet style with thin w tower. Gallery round three sides on cast-iron quatrefoil columns, the E parts removed 1923. Transepts and chancel added 1861–2 by *Lockwood & Mawson*. E.E. – Elaborate painted REREDOS by *Comper*, 1937–9. – STAINED GLASS. N transept N by *Wailes*, 1863; s transept s by *H. W. Bryans*, 1911; E window by *W. Aikman*, 1919. – MONUMENTS. Numerous early C19 wall tablets, many of them by *Fisher* of York.

ST LUKE, King's Road (now flats). 1895–7 by *T. H. & F. Healey* of Bradford, the fine tall NW tower and spire completed in 1902. Free late Dec, the five-light E window with dense Arts-and-Crafts-inspired tracery. Double transept on the s side.

ST MARK, Leeds Road. Weak Gothic w front in harsh yellow stone, completed in 1959 – a big w tower had been intended. The church itself is of 1898–1905 by *J. Oldrid Scott*, also C14 Dec, carefully detailed, with areas of chequerboard patterning in two types of stone. Tall clerestory, picturesque SE corner with the vestry and Lady Chapel building up to the chancel.

Opulent interior, the nave arcades with moulded arches dying into cylindrical piers, chancel s arcade with a tall concave-sided pier. W porch, parish room and imaginative internal reordering 1997–8 by *James Thorp* and *Brian Woodhams*. – REREDOS. By *Scott*, an alabaster relief. – STAINED GLASS. By *Powell & Sons*, the E window 1905, Lady Chapel 1909, aisles 1926 onwards.

ST MARY, Harlow Terrace. The parish church of Low Harrogate, 1915–16 by *Walter Tapper*: the previous church, 1822–5 by *Samuel Chapman* of Leeds, was in St Mary's Walk. Of Northamptonshire limestone. Cruciform with a pyramid-roofed central tower, aisles and chapels, low-key C14 style with flowing tracery. Arches dying into the the arcade piers, boarded roofs, gallery at the W end. – Contemporary FITTINGS, presumably by *Tapper*, include the painted REREDOS and the oak PULPIT, of West Country type. – STAINED GLASS. Mainly by *J. C. N. Bewsey*, including the E window, 1919. – MONUMENT. Surgeon-General R. C. Lofthouse of the Indian Medical Corps, †1907, the posthumous donor of the church. By *Tapper*. White marble effigy on a moulded slate tomb-chest with Renaissance ornament.

ST PETER, Prospect Square, the church of the town centre. 1870–6 by *J. H. Hirst*, the upper stages of the SW tower 1926 by *A. A. Gibson* of Harrogate. Busy rock-faced Geometrical with some French accents – apart from Gibson's tower, in a later Dec style. W galilee porch (now a shop), apsidal E end with seven lancets. Nave arcades with cylindrical piers, foliage caps and polychrome arches. Elaborate clerestory continued in front of the transepts, heavy arched-brace roof, and vaulted vestibule under the tower. – REREDOS, of painted panels, by *Bodley*, c. 1876, the wings added 1936. – Gilt iron CHANCEL SCREEN and gates, 1876, probably by *Hirst*. – SCULPTURE, including portrait roundels of bishops in the nave arcade spandrels, executed by *William Pashley*. – STAINED GLASS. Comprehensive scheme by *Burlison & Grylls*, executed over a period of over fifty years, the gently medievalizing style probably influenced by *Bodley*, who supervised the installation of the earlier pieces. E window and S transept 1876, W window 1885, N transept 1890. S chapel 1910, aisles 1921 etc.

ST WILFRID, Duchy Road. The biggest and by far the best of Harrogate's churches, the masterwork of *Temple Moore*. Built in several stages – the nave 1904–8, the crossing and chancel 1912–14, and the transept ends posthumously in 1926–8, supervised by his son-in-law *Leslie Moore*. Great church E.E style with lancet windows – a massive hunched block in pale Tadcaster limestone – wholly historicist in feeling but quietly inventive throughout in the handling of this traditional vocabulary. The first instance is the striking pointed W end, formed of four sides of a hexagon – a response, presumably, to the constrictions of the site. Transepts lower than the main vessel, the N terminating in a big tower-like porch-cum-organ-chamber – externally the most prominent feature – with deeply recessed doorway and blind windows, the S in an apse (the one French element in the design, cf. Noyon) with seven full-height lancets. Low square crossing tower (cf. nearby Ripon Cathedral) with pyramid roof, and square turrets flanking the straight E end. Calm dignified interior of restrained splendour, rib-vaulted throughout apart from the nave aisles (the vaults of wood in the nave, concrete with stone ribs elsewhere). Nave and chancel each of three bays, the latter slightly taller than the nave and of three storeys to the nave's two, with a fully developed gallery which is continued across the E end as a glazed triforium. Crossing virtually absorbed into the nave, with the clerestory continued above the transept arches. Transepts each with one wide and one narrow bay, the first with a sexpartite vault, the second a quadripartite. In the N a flight of steps like a monastic night stair to the organ loft. Moore's characteristic wall passages everywhere. At the E end, beyond the ambulatory, the Lady Chapel added 1935 by *Leslie Moore* to his own design but faithful to his father-in-law's style and intentions, the central space an elongated octagon demarcated by slender shafts. – A number of FITTINGS by *Moore*: the ROOD BEAM, *c.* 1914, and the PULPIT, 1916–17, both with painted decoration by *Head & Son*; SANCTUARY LAMPS, *c.* 1914, executed by *Hardman & Powell*; the SCREENS, 1919–20, executed by *Thompson & Co.*; and the FONT, of Verona marble. – Bas-relief PANELS, scenes from the life of Christ, by *Frances Darlington*, a local artist, *c.* 1914. – Other SCULPTURE by *Alfred Southwick*, *c.* 1935. – STAINED GLASS. By *Victor Milner*, 1911–37. Excellent work in a C13 style perfectly attuned to Moore's architecture. – SE of the church and linked to it by a three-bay loggia, the CHURCH HALL, 1934–5 by *Leslie Moore*. With a 'Lamella' roof, an ingenious form of timber construction invented in Germany in the 1920s.

ST ROBERT (R.C.), Robert Street. 1872–3 by *George Goldie*. Early French Gothic, rather stark, in brick with sparse stone dressings. Nave and chancel in one, with aisles. Low (ritual) SW tower with saddleback roof. – STAINED GLASS. Mainly *Lavers, Barraud & Westlake*, 1896–7.

WESLEY CHAPEL, Oxford Street. 1862 by *Lockwood & Mawson*, in their sound Italianate manner. Pedimented front with giant Corinthian half-columns and pilasters. Round-headed windows. Apsidal-ended gallery inside.

WEST PARK UNITED REFORMED CHURCH (formerly Congregational), West Park and Victoria Avenue. 1861–2, also by *Lockwood & Mawson* but spiky rock-faced Gothic. Ungainly SW tower and spire, the belfry stage octagonal. Quasi-hammerbeam roof with the hammers supported by thin cast-iron columns.

TRINITY METHODIST CHURCH, Trinity Road. 1877–80 by *Morley & Woodhouse* of Bradford. Gothic, also rock-faced, prominently situated with a quite stately front and tall (ritual) NW tower and spire (completed 1889), but the flanks rather meagre in comparison. Spacious well-appointed interior with gallery round three sides. – STAINED GLASS. Includes N transept window, 1919 by *Clayton & Bell*, well past their prime.

BAPTIST CHURCH, Victoria Avenue. 1882–3 by *William Peachey* of Darlington. The counterpart to the West Park church at the other end of the street, with a very similar tower and spire.

ST PAUL'S UNITED REFORMED CHURCH (formerly Presbyterian), Victoria Avenue. 1883–5 by *Newcombe & Knowles* of Newcastle upon Tyne. Free Perp, a more interesting design with a clerestory contrived within the roof like a continuous dormer. (Ritual) NW tower with octagonal belfry stage.

GROVE ROAD METHODIST CHAPEL, Grove Road. 1896–7 by *W. J. Morley*. Ornate approximate Quattrocento, with a two-bay pediment and a big arched porch. Sunday School adjoining to l.

See also Outer Harrogate.

PUBLIC BUILDINGS

The main concentration, amounting almost to a civic zone, is in Low Harrogate, with the Municipal Buildings and the Royal Baths diagonally opposite each other across Crescent Gardens, the Royal Hall to the E and the Conference Centre beyond it, and the Royal Pump Room, Art Gallery and Valley Gardens a little to the w.

MUNICIPAL BUILDINGS, Crescent Gardens. 1931 by *L. H. Clarke*, the deputy Borough Engineer. On the site of the New Victoria Baths, of 1871. Long discreetly classical range with a pedimented centre, rather too well-mannered perhaps in relation to its Victorian and Edwardian neighbours.

ROYAL HALL, Ripon Road. 1902–3 by *Robert Beale* and *Frank Matcham*. The little-known Beale won the competition for which Matcham was the adjudicator, and the council then appointed them both. Multi-purpose auditorium of a type associated with German and Belgian spas – hence its original name, the 'Kursaal'. Cheerfully louche mixed Renaissance style, with funny short columns between the upper-floor windows and several fancifully shaped lanterns and cupolas. Lavishly decorated interior with coved and coffered ceiling, boxes backing onto a tunnel-vaulted ambulatory, and gallery above. Now hemmed in by utilitarian exhibition halls – originally there were gardens. Adjoining to the r., at the corner with King's Road, was the town's most distinguished spa building, with a Greek Doric hexastyle portico, the Spa Rooms, 1835 by *John Clark* (dem. 1939, the portico columns re-erected at Harlow Carr Gardens, 1½ m. SW). On the site is HALL M, 1999–2000 by the *Parr Partnership*, fronted by a revisionist rendering of the portico with the pediment and roof of glass; but the effect is quite spoilt by an ugly glass staircase tower to one side, just a little higher than the rest of the building.

[124] **CONFERENCE CENTRE**, King's Road. 1976–82 by *Morgan Bentley Ferguson Cale & Partners*. Impressive if costly, a tall steel-roofed cylinder, glazed below and faced in cream ceramic panels above, with six perimeter towers of hot red brick. The comprehensively equipped 2,000-seat auditorium occupies the top of the building. Below it the foyers, with virtuoso spiral access ramps in smooth concrete. To the r., also part of the complex, the MOAT HOUSE HOTEL, an eleven-storey brick and glass slab in three canted sections.

MAGISTRATES' COURT, Victoria Avenue. 1988–9 by *North Yorkshire County Council Property Services* (Director *A. E. Twiggs*). Near-symmetrical in smooth stone blocks, with hipped roof and basket-arched openings.

CARNEGIE LIBRARY, Victoria Avenue. All that was built of a much larger scheme for a Town Hall, 1904–6 by *H. T. Hare*, in heavy Beaux-Arts classical style. This is the l. range, with a front end of one-and-a-half bays. In the main bay two giant Ionic columns *in antis* framing an aedicular window with blocked columns. In the other the entrance, with blocked architrave surround, and lunette over. The r. flank is still no more than an unsightly blank of pebbledash.

MERCER ART GALLERY, Swan Road. 1874 by *Arthur Hiscoe*, built as an Assembly Room. Single-storey restrained Italianate, with round-headed windows and pedimented centre bay, but steep French pavilion roofs over the end bays.

[99] **ROYAL PUMP ROOM**, Crown Place, over the Old Sulphur Well which had been discovered in the early C17. 1842 by *I. T. Shutt*, son of the proprietor of the Old Swan Hotel, for the Harrogate Improvement Commissioners, a body which had been established the previous year. It replaced a structure of 1807–8 by *Thomas Chippendale* of Otley which was then re-erected over the Tewit Well (*see* below). Domed octagon with shallow pedimented projections on the cardinal sides. The detail is debased Grecian, the dome ogee with iron cresting. Iron and glass annex 1912–13 by *L. H. Clarke*. Now a museum.

ST JOHN'S WELL, on the Stray, at High Harrogate, discovered in 1631. Pump room also of 1842 by *Shutt* for the Commissioners, a much smaller octagon – a mere kiosk – even less correctly detailed, with an openwork parapet and no dome. It replaced a structure of 1786.

TEWIT WELL, also on the Stray, not far from the SW corner. The cover brought from the Old Sulphur Well in 1842 is an open domed rotunda with twelve Tuscan columns.

MAGNESIA WELL PUMP ROOM, Valley Gardens. Now a refreshment kiosk. 1895. Iron-framed octagon with a bronze dome. Further W, hidden in trees, the OLD PUMP ROOM, 1858 by *J. Stead*. Square, very small, Gothic with gabled front. The GARDENS themselves were laid out *c.* 1880 onwards. Along the N side the SUN PAVILION and COLONNADE, 1933 by *L. H. Clarke*. Another octagon, with a low glazed dome. Long pergola extending to the E, with brick piers and Tuscan columns, punctuated by two smaller pavilions.

ROYAL BATHS, Crescent Road. On the site of the Montpellier Baths, of 1834. 1894–7 by *F. T. Baggalay & F. Bristowe* of London, now mainly converted to bars etc. Long, rather bitty classical façade of one main storey over a basement, with much use of pedimented aedicular windows. Central dome and immediately behind it two closely set towers. The most memorable parts are the central concourse below the dome, redolent of Roman-bath forms with coupled free-standing Corinthian columns carrying the entablature; and the still functioning TURKISH BATHS, a steamy warren of horseshoe arches and glazed brickwork. At the back the former Lounge Hall, 1938–9 by *L. H. Clarke*, incorporating the elaborate entrance and steps of the Winter Gardens previously on the site. Interior altered.

Former ROYAL BATH HOSPITAL, Cornwall Road. Founded 1826, rebuilt 1888–9 by *Worthington & Elgood* of Manchester, now flats. Diluted Loire chateau style. The asymmetrically placed tower has lost its upper stages.

SWIMMING BATHS, Jennyfield Drive. 1999 by *Shepherd Building Services* (design and build). With wave-shaped anodized aluminium roof on girder supports.

HARROGATE LADIES' COLLEGE, Clarence Drive. 1902–4. Institutional Old English, with tall brick tower-porch and big half-timbered gables. Chapel, 1923, built from the stone of the old St Mary's church (*see* Churches, above).

ST PETER'S PRIMARY SCHOOL, Belford Road. Built as the Cottage Hospital, 1882–3 by *John Adams* of Harrogate. Stylistically unstable, plain Jacobean with a Gothic main doorway, two others with Vanbrughian triple keystones, and a French pavilion roof on the central tower.

WESTERN PRIMARY SCHOOL, Cold Bath Road, and GROVE ROAD PRIMARY SCHOOL, Grove Road. By *T. E. Marshall* of Harrogate for the Harrogate School Board, 1895–7 and 1896–7 respectively. Both compact symmetrical blocks in a gritstone version of the London Board School Queen Anne manner, the latter a tall three storeys with prominent steep-roofed stair-turrets flanking the entrance.

PERAMBULATIONS

1. Low Harrogate

After the public buildings, the main themes are the hotels and the occasional pockets of early C19 development. A starting point is the extreme NW corner of the Stray, where it dips down from the main plateau into a leafy informal square. On the W side, at the foot of Cold Bath Road, the WHITE HART HOTEL, rebuilt in 1846, one of Harrogate's best buildings and the first hotel in the town of a wholly urban character, which set a new standard of ambition. But there is nothing gaudy or showy about it – on the contrary it is reticent to the point of severity. Completely even three-storey ashlar front of eleven bays with round-headed ground-floor windows. Entrance off-centre in bay eight, with coupled Ionic columns and a white hart on the entablature. A little way up COLD BATH ROAD to the s, a few modest early C19 houses, one pair with the shallow segmental bows which are a recurring motif of early Harrogate. At right angles to the White Hart on the N side of the square, the CROWN HOTEL, a much bigger and more extrovert affair. Three-bay centre section a rebuilding of 1847 – the hotel was in existence by 1740 – with giant Tuscan pilasters to the first and second floors. Wings l. and r. added 1870 by *J. H. Hirst* for George Dawson, of the same height and width as the centre but more exuberantly Italianate, the w flank with a big pilastered semicircular bow facing the Royal Pump Room. On the E flank further extension and remodelling of 1899 by *W. J. Morley*, in a yet more florid mixed Renaissance style with a tower crowned by a cylindrical lantern. To the r., at the NE corner of the square, the WHITE COTTAGE, a little octagonal kiosk of *c.* 1822 which was the ticket office to the Montpellier Pump Room (1822, rebuilt 1870 by *Hirst*, dem. 1954) and the Montpellier Baths (*see* Royal Baths, above).

Now past the E flank of the Crown Hotel and l. into CRESCENT ROAD. Turning the corner and continuing w a three-storey shop terrace by *Hirst* for George Dawson, a good example of their developments. The first part, of 1874–5, has almost the effect of a giant round-headed glazed arcade, the ground- and first-floor windows segment-headed between banded piers. Some odd incised decoration to the second floor, urns on the cornice. The part at the far end, 1884–6, continuing l. again into CROWN PLACE, behind the Royal Pump Room, and joining up with the w flank of the hotel, has shop windows with Cockerellesque shouldered heads, but with big keystones in the lintels. Intermediate section *c.* 1890. At its w end Crescent Road opens into an attractive hilly space between the Royal Pump Room and the Valley Gardens (*see* Public Buildings, above). On the E side, N from Crescent Road, a plain block of of *c.* 1827 etc.; on the N – PROMENADE SQUARE – a pretty cottagey row; and at the top NW corner a three-storey pair with segmental bows, which was built by 1815. Beyond this in CORNWALL ROAD, overlooking the Valley Gardens, the former GRAND HOTEL (now flats), 1899–1903 by *Whitehead & Smetham* of Harrogate. Tall but picturesquely grouped, with half-octagonal bays carried up to a series of ogee domes. Mixed Renaissance detail. The name, metropolitan and international, is also significant: no more White Harts and Crowns.

Back and N from Promenade Square, along SWAN ROAD, with on the l. a terrace of three-bay houses of *c.* 1845, still Late Georgian in character with heavy Grecian doorcases. Then the OLD SWAN HOTEL, established *c.* 1700, rebuilt *c.* 1820, comprehensively remodelled and extended 1878. Large but plain, with mansard roof. Swan Road joins RIPON ROAD opposite

the towering bulk of the HOTEL MAJESTIC, the apogee of   117
Harrogate's hotel building. 1898–1900 by *G. D. Martin* for
Frederick Hotels. Of red brick, symmetrical, with Flemish
gables and a copper dome over the centre of the s front. Interior appropriately sumptuous: the idea was 'to suggest a noble-
man's family mansion of the Georgian period'. Behind the
hotel in SPRINGFIELD AVENUE a group of mildly Arts-and-
Crafts-influenced semis of *c.* 1903, some of them by *A. A.
Gibson* of Harrogate. A little gritstone mixed with tile-hanging,
mock half-timbering and casement windows. Now back down
Ripon Road to the s and opposite the Royal Hall (*see* Public
Buildings, above) the HOTEL ST GEORGE, established *c.* 1778,
rebuilt 1850, enlarged 1901, an Italianate jumble. Straight
ahead, running uphill again, is PARLIAMENT STREET, the
start of the main shopping area of the town. On the l. corner,
with King's Road, a plain three-storey block of the 1840s, then
further up on the same side the WESTMINSTER ARCADE,
1898. Crude Gothic façade with a crazy tower, crowned by bartizans and spire, projecting in the middle. Two-storey interior,
the upper level served by a gallery. At the top of the street, the
Stray opens out again to the r., Prospect Square to the l.

2. The town centre

PROSPECT SQUARE, planned *c.* 1865, makes an agreeable introduction to the town centre, open to the Stray on the w side.
In the centre the WAR MEMORIAL, 1923 by *Prestwich & Sons*
of Leigh, Lancashire, a stout obelisk with bas-relief panels on
the base by *Gilbert Ledward*. The N and E sides of the square
are formed by convex crescents, designed by *J. H. Hirst* and
built by George Dawson, with *Hirst*'s St Peter's church (*see*
Churches, above) at the NE corner between them – a striking
piece of townscape. CAMBRIDGE CRESCENT, to the N,   p. 316
1867–8, represents the essence of Hirst's and Dawson's *risqué*
Franco-Italianate. Three storeys, plus attics with dormers.
Round-headed windows in coarse flat surrounds, on the
second floor in pairs and recessed within shouldered outer
arches. Banded pilaster strips and much incised decoration.
PROSPECT CRESCENT, to the E, is later, 1873–80, and slightly
more respectable, with giant Corinthian pilasters to the first
and second floors, but also a plethora of canted bays and
prominent pavilion roofs, with iron cresting, over the centre
and ends.

From here a brief foray can be made into some more of the
shopping streets, first NE, to the E end of OXFORD STREET
and the GRAND THEATRE AND OPERA HOUSE, an overblown
name for a theatre of modest size and appearance. 1898–1900
by *Frank Tugwell* of London. Plain brick exterior with an octagonal turret at the apex of the narrow triangular site, attractive
intimate auditorium with the usual repertoire of ornament. In
the foyer a mildly Art Nouveau bas-relief frieze by *Frances*

Harrogate, Cambridge Crescent.
Engraving by Rock & Co., 1872

Darlington, depicting the history of drama. Opposite to the N, across CHELTENHAM PARADE, the former EMPIRE THEATRE, built 1872 as a Primitive Methodist chapel, now shops. Round-headed first-floor windows, and a segmental pediment to the centre of the Mount Parade front. Next S up Beulah Street to the absurd VICTORIA SHOPPING CENTRE, 1991–2 by *Cullearn & Phillips* of Manchester, an inept pastiche of Palladio's basilica with DIY statues on the parapet. Beyond, in STATION SQUARE, the VICTORIA MONUMENT, 1887, celebrating her Jubilee, a miniature Albert Memorial with standing statue of the Queen by *Webber*; then at the S end, turning the corner into Station Parade, the former STATION HOTEL, 1873 onwards by *Arthur Hiscoe* in his Franco-Italian manner. Opposite, across STATION PARADE, the COPTHALL TOWER, 1964–5 by *Taylor, Bown & Miller*, an unlovely slab, with railway station below. Back along JAMES STREET, with two more developments designed by *Hirst*. On the l., along from the Station Hotel, a terrace built in the 1860s by Richard Ellis, a leading figure in the Victoria Park Company (*see* below), of brick rather than stone but with the usual over-sized detail; then on the r. a block with two pediments and shouldered-arched windows to the second floor, built by Dawson in 1870.

Now S along PROSPECT PLACE and its continuation WEST PARK, facing onto the Stray, starting with the former PROSPECT HOTEL, rebuilt 1859, much enlarged 1870 by *Perkin & Backhouse* of Leeds, with a fancy tower the effect of which is negated by a further storey added in 1936–7. Then after some altered residential terraces of the mid C19, and the W end of Victoria Avenue, a handsome early C19 terrace, of

three storeys with Doric and Ionic doorcases and porches and
the usual segmental bow windows. Some more scattered examples of the same mode further s again. Next, to VICTORIA
AVENUE, laid out in 1860, the spacious centrepiece of the Victoria Park Company's residential development. The first buildings to be erected, in 1861–2, were the two at the w end, the
West Park United Reformed Church (*see* Churches, above) to
the N, and the BELVIDERE a large villa by *Perkin & Backhouse*,
to the s. Meagre Jacobethan with a Tudor-Gothic porte
cochère. The rest of the area was built up only gradually, into
the 1880s. Many of the villas remain. The second on the l.,
VANDERBILT COURT, was George Dawson's final home,
c. 1880 apparently by *Hirst*, but tame compared to his terraces
and crescents, in a tentatively Flemish style. After it the entry
into PRINCES SQUARE, 1867 onwards by *H. E. Bown* of
Harrogate, the w side a bizarre Italo-French mixture. Then off
to the s, in BELFORD ROAD opposite St Peter's School (*see*
Public Buildings, above), the ROGERS ALMSHOUSES, 1868 by
Andrews & Pepper of Bradford, rock-faced domestic Gothic
round three sides of a square, with a pyramid-roofed clock
tower in the middle; and tucked away beyond them ALBERT
TERRACE, an attractive earlier row, *c.* 1850, still Georgian in
character. In the SE quarter of the layout two curving streets,
East Park Road and South Park Road, relieve the predominant
formality: at its E end Victoria Avenue joins a slightly earlier
street, Queen Parade, running SE to the Stray. N of the NE
sector, at the start of EAST PARADE, the ODEON CINEMA,
1936 by *Harry Weedon*. Brown brick and cream faience, asymmetrical with curved entrance on the corner and projecting
slab tower. Interior subdivided. From there Station Avenue
and North Park Road lead to High Harrogate.

3. *High Harrogate*

The area round the wide NE end of the Stray. In the middle of
the open space, E of Christ Church (*see* Churches, above),
CHURCH SQUARE, an outward-facing island block. Some
early C19 cottages at the s and E corners and on the NE side
MANSFIELD HOUSE, built 1788 as a theatre. Seven bays with
a steep pediment over the centre three and a doorway with
Tuscan columns. On the w side of the space are PARK PARADE
and its N continuation REGENT PARADE. At the s end the
former QUEEN HOTEL, now Cedar Court Hotel, on the site
of Harrogate's first inn, the Queen's Head, opened in 1687.
Rebuilt 1855 etc., a long three-storey range with pedimented
three-bay centre: the r. part, with ballroom, enlarged 1861.
Then comes PARK PLACE, a thirteen-storey block of flats,
1961 by *Morris de Metz*; but after that a quite lengthy sequence
of generally modest houses mainly of the early and mid C19,
including Nos. 18–19, an urban-looking ashlar pair, of three
storeys with Regency-style iron balconies to the first floor;

No. 20, similar, 'newly erected' in 1796; No. 23, the former
Parsonage, mid-C18 altered, with its gable-end towards the
street; and No. 31 (Register Office), c. 1830, seven bays, the
end ones recessed, porch with Doric columns. Further on, the
sequence takes in the start of WESTMORLAND STREET,
running W, with plain ashlar-faced, two-storey terraces (now
with C20 shopfronts) mainly built in 1842; then at the N end
of Regent Parade is a late C18 pair with shallow bowed shop
windows. On the NE flank, in DEVONSHIRE PLACE, the rather
denatured remains of the former COUNTY HOTEL, the last of
several different names, rebuilt early C19 as a simple rustic
range with a gabled three-storey centre, the r. wing demolished
c. 1900. Further SE, in GRANBY ROAD, the more easily recognized former GRANBY HOTEL (now a retirement home),
described in 1871 as 'of gigantic proportions'. Successor to an
inn established by 1700, rebuilt by 1821, but much remodelled
and extended since, particularly in 1899. Rendered, quite
plain, with a central canted bay. Beyond it a mutilated mid-
C19 Grecian villa and a semi-detached pair in similar style.

   Also two outliers to be noted. Facing Christ Church across
the Stray from the SE, WEDDERBURN HOUSE, 1786 for
Alexander Wedderburn, the future Lord Chancellor, as his
Harrogate pied-à-terre. Five-bay front in gritstone ashlar, with
projecting pedimented three-bay centre. The first and fifth bays
with niches containing statues, and recessed panels over, to the
ground floor, the second and fourth with blind arches framing
the windows. Later porch. To the N, in SKIPTON ROAD,
GROVE HOUSE, now a convalescent home. Plain block of three
storeys and five bays built c. 1745–54 as yet another inn, remodelled and extended as a private house c. 1890–1900 by *T. Butler
Wilson* of Leeds in a variety of styles. Crenellated parapet,
porch and off-centre tower; two-storey flanking wings, also
crenellated and evidently designed to suggest they are parts of
the original building altered at a later date; and back parts Old
English, with gables and half-timbering. Some lavish but
undistinguished interiors including a big staircase hall, vaguely
Jacobean.

4. The West End Park area

Start at the roundabout at the S end of WEST PARK, the meeting
point of the two parts of the Stray and a busy road junction.
On the corner, PRINCE OF WALES MANSIONS, another plain-
faced former hotel, rebuilt 1860–1, later heightened and
enlarged. E of this, in YORK PLACE, one group of early C19
houses with segmental bows and Tuscan doorcases, but altered
in the later C19. Across the junction to the SW is the suburb of
WEST END PARK, laid out from 1867 'upon a most comprehensive and elegant plan' apparently by *H. E. Bown*. At the
centre a long narrow figure with semicircular ends, called the
Oval, with houses facing outward onto a surrounding strip of

green and access roads at the diagonals. The N and E edges of the estate were built up by 1871, the E side of the Oval and the NW corner by 1878, but development of the rest was not completed until the mid C20. The best of the villas are two near-matching examples at the NE corner, in TRINITY ROAD, flanking the Trinity Methodist Church (*see* Churches, above), exuberantly Italianate with outsize semicircular bows and octagonal tower-porches, one capped by a dome. Also some terraces, and near the SE corner in LEEDS ROAD the ROYAL CRESCENT, with little pavilion roofs to the end units.

Finally E along the S edge of the Stray, past the Tewit Well (*see* Public Buildings, above), to CAVENDISH AVENUE and THE GABLES, an excellent Arts and Crafts house of 1903–5 by *Parker & Unwin*. Low-key gently asymmetrical exterior in unpainted roughcast, with gables and plain mullioned windows, the only hint of display a bigger double-transomed window of five-plus-three-plus-five lights wrapped round the SE corner. This lights the double-height living room, with a gallery on two sides, one part curving forward above the fireplace, the other with the staircase rising behind it. A number of fireplaces with dark tiled surrounds and copper hoods.

114

OUTER HARROGATE

1. North: Bilton

ST JOHN, Crab Lane. 1851–7 by *G. G. Scott*. Ornate E.E., quite large, with strong W tower designed to carry a spire. Nave arcades with clustered piers and both stiff-leaf and naturalistic foliage. – STAINED GLASS. E windows by *Crace*, 1857. Groups of figures in medallions. Chancel N by *Ward & Hughes*, chancel S by *C. E. Clutterbuck*, also 1857.

ST JOSEPH (R.C.), Skipton Road. 1924–5 by *W. H. H. Marten* of Bradford, extended 2001–2. Crenellated E end, gabled dormers at the sides. The church, with timber arcades, is on the first floor. – STAINED GLASS. N transept window by *Kathleen Quigley*.

Former SCHOOL (now a house), Bachelor Gardens, ³⁄₈ m. N of St John's church. 1793. Five bays, two storeys, with inscription over the doorway.

2. East: Starbeck

ST ANDREW, High Street. 1909–10 by *Austin & Paley*. Free Perp, the W end with canted corners, bellcote on the N side. – STAINED GLASS. E window by *Shrigley & Hunt*, 1931, still C19 in style; W window 1963 by *P. H. Warren Wilson*.

STARBECK HALL, High Street, W of the level crossing. Built 1810 as the Harrogate Workhouse. Three-storey block with a surprising shaped gable, crowned by an urn finial, over the centre three bays of the front. Doorcase with cornice on brackets, probably reused.

Former STARBECK SPA, Spa Street. Group of buildings of c. 1823–30 in Tudor Gothic style: a four-centre-headed archway; beyond it the well-head, an octagonal panelled pier; and the bath house – only the front wall now remaining – with the attendant's house to the l. The spring was discovered in the early C17.

Nos. 197 and 199 HOOKSTONE CHASE, ½ m. SSE of the church. Pair of simple semi-detached cottages, 1902–3 by *Parker & Unwin*. Brick with small-paned casement windows, gables and dormers. A forerunner of countless suburban semis of the interwar years.

BILTON HALL, Bilton Lane, ⅞ m. NNE of the church. Now a nursing home. Compact brick-built house of the C17 – the successor to William Slingsby's residence – remodelled and enlarged in 1853. W elevation with narrow gabled projections at each end and a rebuilt patch, of similar dimensions, in the middle: presumably there was an entrance and a porch here. Mullion-and-transom windows of various sizes, irregularly arranged, to the ground and first floors, small mullioned windows to the second. C19 extension in simple Jacobean style, with entrance to the S. Further additions 1978.

3. South: Oatlands and Crimple

119 WHITE LODGE, Hookstone Road. Accomplished modernistic house of c. 1935, by *Col. R. B. Armistead* for himself. White rendered walls and flat roof, the main (S) front balanced without being rigidly symmetrical, with occasional curves to soften the prevailing rectangularity. Fitted furniture by *Betty Joel*, some of which remains.

THE INSPIRE, Hornbeam Park. Office building as millennial folly, a steep mirror-glazed pyramid. 2002–4 by *P & HS Architects*.

CRIMPLE VIADUCT. 1848 by *J. C. Birkinshaw* engineer, for the York & North Midland Railway (i.e. George Hudson). Thirty-one arches in rock-faced gritstone, with a maximum height of over 110 ft (34 metres).

4. West: Harlow Hill and Oakdale

ALL SAINTS (Harlow Hill Cemetery Chapel), Otley Road. 1870–1 by *I. T. Shutt*, built as a chapel of ease of St Mary, Low Harrogate. Ignorant Gothic, with plate-traceried windows and a cylindrical turret.

HARLOW HILL TOWER, Otley Road. Built in 1829 as a viewing point. Totally plain square tower, 90 ft (27 metres) high, the top altered. Next to it a cylindrical gritstone WATER TOWER, c. 1902.

CENTRAL HOUSE, Otley Road. *c.* 1980 by *Gillinson Barnett & Partners*. Smoothly finished office block of quadrangular form. Three storeys.

HARLOW CARR GARDENS, Cragg Lane. *See* Public Buildings (Royal Hall), above.

WEST HILL, Kent Road, ½ m. W of St Wilfrid's church. Inter-war modernistic house, white-painted with a flat roof, probably by *Col. R. B. Armistead* (*see* White Lodge, above).

See also Pannal.

HARTLINGTON

0060

HARTLINGTON HALL. 1894 by *George Corson* for Henry Philip Dawson. Restrained Pennine-style Neo-Jacobean. Elaborate staircase rising from the main hall.

WATER MILL, now flats. Late C18, originally a corn mill, later converted to cotton- and flax-spinning. Three storeys, seven bays. Restored cast-iron water wheel.

HARTWITH

2060

ST JUDE. Founded 1751 as a chapel of ease of Kirkby Malzeard. Rebuilt 1830, a little lancet-style box. One-bay chancel, porch and bellcote added 1875.

No village, but a number of noteworthy outlying houses.

DOUGILL HALL, ¾ m. W. 1722 for John Dougill (date and initials on the doorway lintel). Double-pile block of two-and-a-half storeys with a handsome five-bay front, a good example of the local manner of the early C18. Cross-windows with architrave surrounds, cornices and pulvinated friezes, to the ground and first floors; similarly detailed two-light mullioned windows to the attic; doorway with lugged and shouldered architrave. Eaves cornice and parapet, projecting forward slightly over the centre bay and the ends. At the back, chamfered mullioned windows, a big cross-window to the staircase, and a formerly detached block of 1696, perhaps built as a kitchen. (Good interior detail: panelling with fluted pilasters and a round-headed corner cupboard in the front parlour, decorative plasterwork to the ceiling beam in the rear parlour, staircase with turned balusters.) N of it CLOUGH HOUSE, 1654, with ornamented doorhead.

MANOR HOUSE FARM, 1 m. SW. Probably *c.* 1670, with a striking shallow two-storey porch of 1696. Lugged architrave surround to the doorway, and above it a wheel window of six lights (cf. East Riddlesden Hall, Keighley and the Manor House, Threshfield). Mullioned windows of three-plus-three lights to the parlour, housebody and kitchen. Lobby-entry plan. Enriched panelled partition dated 1680 between the housebody and the parlour, housebody fireplace with an architrave similar to that round the porch entrance, kitchen fireplace with stopped and chamfered bressumer. Narrow rear outshut with a dairy behind the parlour. In an outbuilding a re-set doorhead of 1670, possibly removed from the house when the porch was added.

HARDCASTLE GARTH, 1 m. SE. Pair of houses forming an L-shape, dated 1666 and 1703, built by members of the Hardcastle family. Tudor-arched doorways, mullioned windows. There may have been a third house in the group, now lost – see the datestone of 1736, with Hardcastle initials, re-set in a neighbouring farm building.

BRIMHAM LODGE, 1 m. NE, on the site of a park lodge of the abbots of Fountains. 1661 for Thomas Braithwaite, gent., of Ambleside, Cumbria, an impressive house of unusual form – a long tall range of two storeys and attic, with no cross-wings or porch at the front but a rear wing behind the hall. Mullioned windows of up to six lights, including an attic window in the E gable-end of four lights, stepped. Front doorway with a flattened-ogee head, and a little ogee-headed window above it. Inside, the ground floor of the main range consists of a hall, a parlour to the r., another little parlour to the l. and the kitchen beyond that. Several moulded four-centre-headed fireplaces, and a quantity of C17 panelling and panelled partitions. Staircase, in the rear wing, with turned balusters. Upper cruck roof trusses. Nearby, at BRIMHAM HALL, an C18 farmhouse on the site of a grange of Fountains Abbey, the motto of Abbot Huby (d. 1526), SOLI DEO HONOR ET GLORIA ('Honour and glory to God alone'), and other fragments of Gothic script, built into a barn.

BRIMHAM HOUSE, 2 m. NNW, amid the fantastic gritstone formations of Brimham Rocks. Built 1792 by Lord Grantley as a residence for the caretaker of the rocks. Five-bay front with round-headed windows and curious banded stonework.

BRAISTY WOODS, 1⅝ m. NW. Mid-C18 main range with Tuscan doorcase. One room with round-headed cupboards framed by pilasters, l. and r. of the fireplace. C17 cross-wing to l., with painted plasterwork inside incorporating a rose and a thistle, perhaps a reference to the Act of Union, 1706.

HAWKSWORTH HALL
Guiseley

Long, irregular façade of several dates, in essence C17 but extensively Georgianized. The l. part is a half-H-plan house of shortly before 1611, the date on the ceiling of the great chamber, over the hall. Two-storey former porch beside the l. wing, with mullion-and-transom window of five arched lights

to the upper stage and crocketed finial on the gable. Other windows mainly C18: the l. wing fronted by a two-storey canted bay by *Carr*, *c.* 1774, with a new dining room by him behind it; the r. wing, approximately in the middle of the present house, converted into an entrance hall, with pedimented doorway, perhaps as part of the same phase of work. The r. part of the house is a range added in 1664, with gables at the far end roughly balancing the former porch and the l. wing. It contained a kitchen and additional parlours. Windows again early and later C18, some Jacobeanized in the C19. (The great chamber ceiling – which details of the roof structure above suggest is either an integral feature or at least intended from the outset – is a segmental barrel-vault with ribs forming a pattern of squares and diamonds, strapwork pendant in the middle and coats of arms flanked by allegorical figures (Prudence, Justice, Temperance and Fortitude) in the tympana. Panelling and Tudor-arched fireplace below, and more C17 panelling in the E range. *Carr*'s dining room retains a columnar screen and restrained decoration. Also some chimneypieces in his style, C18 staircase with slender balusters.)
A few other C17 houses W of the hall, two said to incorporate remains of earlier timber framing.

HAWORTH

Classic Pennine village, much expanded during the C19, now rather choked by the Brontë tourist industry. Narrow main street slanting up the hillside, the church at the top and the mills in the valley bottom.

ST MICHAEL. 1879–80 by *T. H. & F. Healey* in dull Perp style, apart from the W tower of the old church – a chapel of ease of Bradford – retained rather awkwardly at the SW corner. The chapel was built in 1655 and the tower is presumably in essence of that date, but heightened above the belfry stage, and much refaced, *c.* 1870. Y-tracery bell-openings, big three-light arched window lower down on the S side. The rest of the building had C17 Perp windows, a central quasi-Perp arcade (cf. St John, Leeds), and S wall rebuilt in 1755. Its demolition was widely condemned at the time. – COMMUNION TABLE, C17, and brass CANDELABRA, 1759, both in the S chapel. – STAINED GLASS. E window, chancel N and S, and S aisle third and fourth from E, by *Clayton & Bell*, 1881–5; W window by *Capronnier*, 1882; S chapel E, S aisle first and second from E, and tower window, by *Powell Bros.* of Leeds, 1881–3. – MONUMENT. Grace Greenwood †1822. With drooping tree. – In the churchyard the FONT from the old church, 1742. Square baluster inscribed with the date, the name of the incumbent, W. Grimshaw, and biblical text.

HALL GREEN BAPTIST CHAPEL, in a prominent position at the crossroads at the bottom of the Main Street. 1824–5. Plain five-bay pedimented front with two tiers of round-headed windows. Gallery forming an elongated half-octagon. Rear extension, housing the organ, added 1840. Pulpit 1900. The WEST LANE BAPTIST CHAPEL at the top of the village, 1844, has a similar, smoother front, interior altered.

PRIMARY SCHOOL (former Hartington Middle School), Rawdon Road. 1982 by *Bradford City Council Architect's Department* (project architect *J. K. Tyler*). Quite large complex in reused stone with wide sweeping low-pitched roofs, unfussily detailed. Nearby, in Butt Lane, the former BOARD SCHOOL, 1896, also quite large, in minimal Queen Anne style.

The PARSONAGE (Brontë Museum) is just beyond the church-yard to the w. Built 1778–9. Five-bay front with quoins and pedimented Tuscan doorcase. Plain one-bay extension to r. 1878 by *Milnes & France* of Bradford for the Rev. Patrick Brontë's successor, the Rev. John Wade. A museum since 1928. To the N of the churchyard the former NATIONAL SCHOOL, 1832, with pointed windows. Tudor-style gabled addition of *c.* 1850 to l. In the MAIN STREET mainly plain modest C19 buildings. In a narrow gap the GATES into the churchyard, 1824, the piers rus-ticated with ogee caps (cf. Ponden Hall, Stanbury), the corner of the church behind its best contribution to the villagescape. At the top, where the street divides, the former YORKSHIRE PENNY BANK, now information centre, with miniature pavil-ion roof. Beyond, in WEST LANE opposite the chapel, a small HOUSING scheme of 1967 by the Keighley Borough Architect *B. A. Waddington*, coursed stone two-storey terraces stepping up the slope; and nearby in NORTH STREET, No. 26, C17, L-shaped with Tudor-arched doorway at the end of the hall range away from the cross-wing, and mullioned windows with round-headed lights. Back in the Main Street and near the bottom, the former HAWORTH CO-OPERATIVE STORE, 1896 – three storeys, simple Italianate – and beyond this, at the crossroads, another C17 house, the OLD HALL. Mullion-and-transom windows of up to eight lights, two-storey porch with moulded three-centre-headed entry, the mullioned window above con-tinued onto the flanks. Gabled rear outshut.

Further down again in the valley bottom, an interesting group centred on BRIDGE HOUSE, mid-C18, five bays with quoins and Ionic pedimented doorcase. The adjoining BRIDGEHOUSE MILL originated in a water-powered cotton-spinning mill built *c.* 1790 and converted to worsted in the early C19. Mid-C19 four-storey front range to the r. of the house, in two parts, the first incorporating an impressive earlier archway with banded pilasters and keystone mask – a pedi-mented centre bay with Venetian window sits above it. Set back to the l. of the house a former BARN-cum-stable-block, with a pediment containing a Diocletian window over the cart entrance and odd round-headed two-light windows to one side. The original mill was behind this.

A little to the N is the RAILWAY STATION, 1867, enlarged *c.* 1890 (*see* Oakworth); and ¼ m. further, along the valley, EBOR MILL, one of the best examples locally. Integrated worsted mill built in several stages from *c.* 1850 onwards for Merrall Brothers, incorporating an earlier water-powered spinning mill of *c.* 1819. The dominant element is the new spinning mill of 1887 by *W. & J. B. Bailey* of Keighley, of six storeys and eighteen bays, with an earlier engine house absorbed into the N end, staircase tower at the S, and fireproof construction to the ground floor. The 1819 building is on the S side of the mill yard, of three storeys and originally seven bays with a wheel chamber at its E end, later extended to E and W. On the N side is the warehouse, two storeys with segment-headed windows and gabled central loading bay, and behind it the weaving shed, with north-light roof. On the W the boiler house, with beyond it to the N the tall chimney, of shortly before 1887, octagonal with a bracketed cap. S of the mill a row of workers' cottages and the mill dam, and back further S, at the road junction, EBOR HOUSE, 1829, the residence of the builder of the original mill. A modest three bays, later extended l. and r.

see p. 761

See also Cross Roads with Lees, Stanbury.

HAZLEWOOD CASTLE
Stutton with Hazlewood

4030

The home of the Vavasour family from the mid C13 until 1908. Sir William Vavasour was granted a licence to crenellate in 1290, but the house was remodelled *c.* 1770 for Sir Walter Vavasour so that it now appears from the S as a low, thickset castellated Georgian mansion of two storeys over a high basement, with a five-bay centre between two projecting two-bay wings. Doorway with Doric columns and pediment. The terrace in front is by *Sydney Kitson*, who in 1909–10 reduced the house and made alterations for E. O. Simpson, a Leeds solicitor; the casement windows are also of this date, replacing C18 sashes. The medieval house is represented by the middle five bays (hall) and W wing (solar). They are built over undercrofts, still barrel-vaulted under the wing. Attached to the wing's W side is a crookedly set tower, possibly C15, of two bays; a second tower of late C15/early C16 date, projects from the rear (NW) corner of the main block.* The E wing and the adjoining service range appear to be early C17 (arms of Sir Thomas Vavasour †1632 inside and kitchen fireplaces of that date). Set back to the E of this is the large late C13 chapel (*see* below). The rear of the house was remodelled in 1960–7 with a crenellated tower containing the entrance. In the late C18, however, this elevation

---

* It has been suggested that this may be the earliest part of the house – a pele tower which survived the sacking of the castle during the Barons' War in the 1260s.

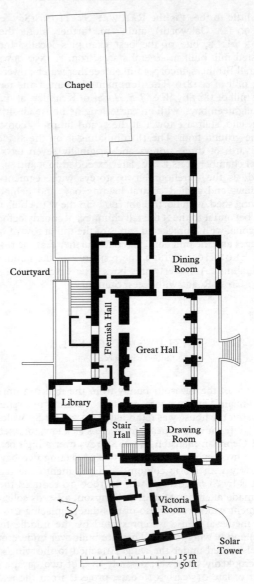

Hazlewood Castle.
Plan

had been overlaid by a gaunt, three-storey addition that continued as a wing along the W side of the N courtyard (re-laid
as a formal water garden after 1960). Demolished *c.* 1910, only
its arcaded ground floor survives, partly incorporated into a

Neo-Georgian N wing. Abutting this is a genuine C18 pavilion.

The GREAT HALL (50 by 28 ft; 15 by 8.5 metres) as remodelled c. 1770 is divided into five by three bays with arcades of attached Roman Doric columns with entablature blocks carrying the coved vaults of a lightly enriched ceiling. The most advanced feature is the omission of an architrave and frieze in each of the bays, remarkable for its date (cf. George Dance Jun.'s All Hallows, London Wall, London, of 1765–7). The arch-heads have medallions painted with the Vavasour arms, except on the S side where they are glazed. Excellent Doric marble fireplace. The doors seem earlier. On the N side, a medieval window revealed in 1910; two shouldered lights with a shouldered lintel under a depressed rere-arch. Restored mullions and window seat. Traces have been discovered of other windows and newel stairs in the NE and NW corners.

E of the hall, the DINING ROOM, also with fine c. 1770 Neoclassical decoration; the buffet and fireplace are probably by *Kitson* (cf. Gledhow Manor, Leeds, p. 521). W of the hall Sir Walter created a DRAWING ROOM, now with Adamesque decoration of 1910, and STAIR HALL, its cantilevered staircase with simple iron balusters. E of this a domed circular antechamber with quadrant niches. Several rooms have fittings introduced by Donald Hart after 1960. In the W wing the VICTORIA ROOM has a Gothic ceiling and heavily carved oak doors from *Waterhouse*'s Eaton Hall, Cheshire (dem. 1961), and embossed metallic wallpaper from the Great Exhibition. Hart built the odd Gothic fireplace with massive pyramidal hood on dwarf columns. The LIBRARY, in the solar tower, has a medieval beamed ceiling but also imported Solomonic columns and an Early Renaissance fireplace. The FLEMISH HALL, behind the Great Hall, has intricate panelling, including a balcony front, dated 1673–83, allegedly from a Carmelite church in Ghent. Round-arched panels between pilasters, with relief scenes from the Bible and Carmelite history. The elaborate fireplace is from Heath Old Hall (West Riding South, c. 1585; dem.). Superimposed pairs of columns and a large, dynamic relief in the overmantel of the Death of Jezebel. The entrance from the N courtyard has doors from Eaton Hall.

The CHAPEL (R.C.), detached to the E, remains almost complete in its medieval form externally. Licences to support a chaplain were issued in 1286 and 1299 and William Vavasour (†1313) gave instructions for his burial in 'the new chapel'. It has windows with renewed Y-tracery, a blocked E window, a double bellcote over the W gable, and a S doorway with two continuous chamfers. The excellent door is C15, with blank tracery all over. Interior remodelled in the C18, with coved ceiling, modillion cornice and a balustraded family pew at the W end (at that time connected to the demolished N wing). Splendid stone REREDOS with paired Corinthian columns, an open and broken segmental pediment, and pedestals carved with the Instruments of the Passion. PAINTING by *Adam Kossowski*, 1975. – ALTAR and

TABERNACLE, Spanish, gilt. The ornately pierced frontal, bearing the symbols of the Passion, screens a reliquary. – AUMBRY. C15. A panel carved with a bishop, a merchant, the Virgin and Child, and St Margaret of Antioch. – Also C15, the carved stone POOR BOX with English inscription, a pair of bearded heads and an iron door. – Several MONUMENTS, especially two cross-legged Knights, one under an elaborate crocketed ogee gable with tracery, the other under a simpler ogee arch with high pinnacle. Possibly Sir William Vavasour †1313 and his son Walter †1315. – Sir Thomas Vavasour †1632 and wife, with two large frontal kneeling figures against an arcade. Children in relief beneath. The kneeling figures, however, may be Sir Thomas's father Ralph and his wife, as such a monument was described in the C17. – Sir Walter Vavasour †1713. Semi-reclining figure. His wife kneeling at his feet, also two children and a putto at the head-end. The figures do not seem quite correctly placed, and the architecture is damaged.

Outside, late medieval CROSS with a tapering octagonal shaft, moulded cornice and the remains of a foliate cross-head.

Former STABLES. Shown on a plan of 1768. On the N side of the courtyard. Of eight bays and two storeys, the centre projecting slightly under a pedimented gable. NE of the courtyard is an octagonal late C18 Gothick FOLLY, possibly a summer-house. Trefoil-headed ground-floor windows (now blocked), oculi above, and castellated parapet.

HEALAUGH

7   ST JOHN. On a little rise at the end of the village. A Norman church of three phases: nave, chancel and narrow w tower of c. 1150, N aisle of c. 1175 and priest's door a little later again. The pyramid-roofed top stage of the tower is of c. 1860 when the church was restored: small round-headed s window below. Decorated corbel tables to nave and chancel. Sumptuous s
8   doorway, one of the finest in the West Riding. Two orders of colonnettes, the capitals with tangled foliage trails issuing from human and animal masks, and tiny beasts amongst them. Four orders of arches, the outermost – almost a hoodmould – with a Christ in Judgement at the apex flanked by zigzag; and the next with a group of seated and kneeling figures who are probably the patrons of the church, a local land-holder named Bertram Haget and his wife, and members of their family or household. Outwards from these are inverted figures plunging into Hell, and then a series of masks. Third order with beakheads, the innermost a roll moulding.[*] E of the doorway

* Precedents for some of the details have been located in SW France, and the agent of transmission may have been a monk named Gilbert from Marmoutier near Tours – parent house of Holy Trinity Priory, York – who had established a hermitage on Haget's land at Healaugh in 1140.

a mass dial. Then the priest's doorway, with one order of colonettes, waterleaf capitals, and an arch moulding with a keeled roll. One lancet to the N aisle, other windows Perp, and Perp also the N chapel.

Plain tower arch. Chancel arch with one order of colonettes and then thick semicircular responds which are truncated a little above floor level: so a low stone screen must be assumed, to account for this. Capitals similar to those of the S doorway but with the foliage now orderly rather than tangled. Trellis, and more trails, scrolls and small animals, to the shafts and responds. Heavy arch with two chamfers and a thick soffit roll. The later Norman N arcade is of three bays, with quatrefoil piers, big (re-cut) waterleaf capitals, and arches like the chancel arch. Single very broad arch between the chancel and the chapel, inserted to accommodate a squire's pew, now moved. Perp sedilia. – PULPIT. C19 concoction with Jacobean bits, reputedly chair backs. – SOUTH DOOR. With tracery, probably C15. – STAINED GLASS. N aisle W by *Kempe*, 1900. – MONUMENT. Thomas Lord Wharton †1568 and his two wives. Alabaster altar tomb with recumbent effigies, he in full armour. On the long sides of the chest, shields flanked by their children. Twisted balusters between the groups.

OLD HALL, S of the churchyard. Attractive house of the later C17, a three-and-a-half-bay hall range and a N cross-wing, made (nearly) symmetrical by the addition of the S wing *c.* 1860 for the squarson, the Rev. E. H. Brooksbank. Brick, two storeys, quoins, C19 hipped roof. Typical late C17 window surrounds but differing slightly between the two genuine C17 parts: does this signify a difference of date or of status? S again the OLD VICARAGE, contemporary with the enlargement of the Hall and for the most part echoing its style. Cross-wing gable with pierced scrolly bargeboards.

HEALAUGH PRIORY, 1¼ m. SW. A priory of the Augustinian Canons established in 1218 as a successor to Gilbert's hermitage, and acquired after the Dissolution by Thomas Lord Wharton who, it appears, converted the monastic buildings into a large house which was itemized in his probate inventory of 1568.[*] Visible on the site now, amongst the modern farm buildings, are three detached ranges within an enclosure bounded on three sides by a substantially intact MOAT. The two running parallel to each other – the E now a farmhouse called Healaugh Priory, the W now a barn – are evidently the reused parts of the E and W claustral ranges; and it has been suggested that Wharton linked these together with a new range, now lost, across their N ends to create a house of half-H plan. The church will have been a little further to the N.

The E RANGE is the more complete. If the normal Augustinian plan was followed this would have accommodated the dormitory, and the chapter house would have been immediately to the N. Magnesian limestone, two storeys. Crenellated

---

[*] *See* J. A. Ashbee, University of York MA thesis, 1993.

five-bay W elevation with quite regularly arranged late Perp windows of two and three lights, similar fenestration in the S gable-end, and four corbelled-out chimney-breasts at first-floor level on the E side (the stacks gone) – these details all of Wharton's time, one of the windows cutting through a shouldered doorway. The chimneys suggest that the first floor was made into a series of chambers. (Interior much altered but retaining two four-centre-headed fireplaces.) The W RANGE, which was presumably the prior's lodging and guest hall, has been greatly reduced in length. Medieval W wall of limestone with altered C16 windows, the others of brick, probably C19; but behind the latter are elements of a timber-framed structure of the C16 – posts and wall-plate – and the roof has C16 kingpost trusses with moulded tie-beams. So there was a substantial post-Dissolution rebuilding here. (Two inserted fireplaces at the N end.)

The third building, a farmhouse called HEALAUGH MANOR WEST, further W again, is essentially of the mid C19 but reusing earlier materials. Eccentric three-bay front with symmetrically arranged windows of the C16 type already encountered, and over the entrance one of two trefoil-headed lights, possibly medieval. Also a false corbel table of unrelated fragments, and assorted curios including a cat with a shield.

HEBDEN

ST PETER. Built 1840–1 as a chapel of ease of Linton, from the 'rough designs' of the 'energetic and much beloved' curate, the *Rev. John Pearson Fearon*. Lancet style. W tower with corner finials, unaisled nave and short plaster-vaulted chancel.

BRIDGE, over Hebden Beck. 1827 by *Bernard Hartley*, the West Riding Surveyor of Bridges. One arch, rock-faced masonry.

At No. 7 BROOK STREET a little C17 decorative plasterwork – a frieze and part of an overmantel.

HELLIFIELD

A railway village predominantly, the point at which the line running N from Blackburn, completed in 1879, joins the Leeds to Carlisle line. Earlier buildings are mainly away from the nucleus.

ST AIDAN. 1905–6 by *Connon & Chorley* of Leeds. Free Late Gothic. Broad, low and aisleless with sturdy N tower. Solid arched-brace roof trusses. A successful design of its kind. – STAINED GLASS. E window by *Mayer*, W by *A. K. Nicholson*, both 1909.

RAILWAY STATION. 1880 by the Midland Railway Co.'s architect *C. Trubshaw*. An 'island' station, reached from the station
yard by a subway. Extensive glazed canopies on the usual ornamented cast-iron pillars completely surround the narrow
central building.

HELLIFIELD PEEL, ½ m. S. Restored from a ruinous state
2004–6 by *Brewster Bye Architects* of Leeds (project architect
Francis Shaw). The medieval tower house was the product of
two distinct phases. The earlier, probably of the C14, provided
a three-storey solar tower, attached to an aisled hall of uncertain date: see the roof-line of the hall on the E flank of the tower,
the two narrow ogee-headed windows in the NE staircase turret,
and the ogee-headed piscina of the former chapel on the second
floor. In the second, to which a licence to crenellate granted in
1440 may relate, the hall was evidently done away with and the
tower enlarged to form a tower house proper, with the addition
of two projecting turrets on the W flank. In the C17 and C18 the
building was further extended to the W, and re-windowed: the
battlemented parapet is in part a convincing C18 copy but
apparently otherwise of the C16. C19 and C20 additions to E and
W have been demolished. At the entrance to the drive, at HEL-
LIFIELD GREEN, a mid-C19 Grecian villa.

ARNFORD FARMHOUSE, 1¼ m. W. A very remarkable building,
probably of *c.* 1700. It was built as two houses which are virtually identical mirror images of each other – that is, a semi-
detached pair. Perhaps they were built for two brothers, or by
the landowner for the tenants of two adjacent farms. Single
long range two rooms deep. Each house has a central entrance,
two bays to each side of it with cross-windows to the ground
and first floors, and a slightly off-centre dormer gable with a
two-light window oddly surmounted by a single round-headed
light. The pointed tympana over the doorways are probably a
C19 embellishment. More cross-windows to the gable-ends,
two-light mullioned windows at the back. Inside, each has a
housebody and heated parlour at the front: segment-headed
housebody fireplace in the W house. The original staircases, in
the back range of rooms, have been removed.

HETTON

NORTON VIEW. Modest C17 farmhouse, with early C18
additions advertised by cross-windows and other openings in
architrave surrounds: an extension at the E end providing, *inter
alia*, a kitchen and a stable, and a gabled rear outshut towards
the street incorporating a dairy and a porch. Behind the latter
the original lobby entry.

ROCK FARM. Small double pile, dated 1758. Unchamfered mullioned windows at the front and cross-window to the staircase.
The chamfered mullioned windows doubtless reused.

HORSFORTH

Village grown into a big suburban area contiguous with W Leeds, the expansion partly from the 1870s on (tram 1872), mainly C20. Long main street retaining a little of its earlier character.

ST MARGARET. 1877–83 by *Pearson*. Prominently situated in what was then open country W of the village, successor to a chapel of 1758 at the S end of Town Street (dem. 1885). Large, serious building of squared gritstone in the architect's trademark E.E. style. Five-bay nave with low aisles and high clerestory, two-bay chancel very slightly lower. Tall SE tower with broach spire, completed in 1901 to a changed design by *J. B. Fraser* of Leeds: Pearson had intended the spire to be pyramidal. N side of varied outline, with a transept to the chancel and cross-gabled two-bay Lady Chapel against the aisle. Lancet windows in discreetly inventive permutations: five of even height at the W end, various stepped groups under relieving arches. At the E end three two-light windows with Y-tracery also under a relieving arch. Interior depending mainly on its height for effect, with spatial incident confined to the junction of the N aisle and the Lady Chapel where four arches rise from a single pier. Nave arcades with cylindrical piers, arched-brace roof. – REREDOS. 1911 by *F. L. Pearson*, the architect's son. Stone, elaborately architectural, with high-relief carving. Also by him that to the Lady Chapel, 1916, a contrasting bas-relief in painted and gilded gesso. – STAINED GLASS. Includes E and W windows by *Hardman*, 1905 and 1929; Lady Chapel NE and NW, 1934 by *Powell & Sons*.

ST JAMES, off Low Lane. 1847–8 by *C. W. Burleigh* of Leeds. Formulaic Dec, with W bellcote and aisles with double-pitched roofs, the S added 1904. – STAINED GLASS. E window 1922 by *W. Pape*.

GROVE METHODIST CHAPEL, off Town Street. 1867. Rock-faced Gothic. Big tower-like porch at the (ritual) NW corner, an elongated octagon with steep hipped roof. Facing onto the entrance yard the MANSE, 1772, five bays with cornice on brackets over the doorway.

LIBRARY, Town Street. 1881, built as the Mechanics' Institution. Two tall storeys, three bays, in stone-built Queen Anne style, the centre bay with a porch below and an odd pedimented oriel above. Extensions, to the l. 1975 by *Broadbent Thompson & Partners*, at the back 2006 by *Leeds City Council Architectural Design Services*.

Little else within the village needs singling out. Off the S end of Town Street, in Drury Lane, UPPER BANK HOUSE, c. 1838. Ashlar, five bays with Ionic porch. Off Troy Road, ½ m. NE of the Library, TROY HILL, C17 double pile with (altered) near-symmetrical three-bay front. Mullion-and-transom windows.

TRINITY AND ALL SAINTS COLLEGE, Brownberrie Lane, ¾ m.
NNW of the Library. 1965–8 by *Weightman & Bullen*, as an R.C.
teacher training college, now a College of Higher Education.
Four-storey central teaching block, rectangular with inner
courtyard; hexagonal chapel attached to one corner, with
central spirelet; and a constellation of accommodation pavilions to E and W (cf. the same architects' former R.C. training
college at Childwall, Liverpool, now Liverpool Hope University). Materials are brick and concrete. In the CHAPEL, bronze
and fibreglass SCULPTURE by *Charles I'Anson* and *J. Garcia-
Maria*, 1970–1, and Primitivist STAINED GLASS designed by
G. Faczynski, 1979–80. The main later addition is the LIBRARY
(Andrew Kean Learning Centre), 2001–3 by *DLA Architecture*,
mannered in beige brick.

PORTAL (S) of the Bramhope Railway Tunnel (*see* Bramhope),
1½ m. N. 1845–9 by *Thomas Grainger*. Bold design of a parabolic arch with rusticated voussoirs, and entablature over.

HORSFORTH MILL, Low Lane, ⅞ m. ESE (S of the Leeds ring
road). Worsted spinning mill of *c.* 1903 (now offices), the main
survivor of the former concentration of mills along the beck at
Woodside. Four storeys, and a hip-roofed tower at one corner.
Later brick block against the front.

NEWLAY BRIDGE, over the Aire, ⅞ m. S. 1819, made by *Aydon
& Elwell* of the Shelf Iron Works near Bradford, for John
Pollard of Newlay House, Bramley. Cast-iron, a single low seg-
mental arch. Railings with pierced Gothick standards. At the
N end a TOLL HOUSE, with two crude Venetian windows.

NEWLAITHES MANOR, Newlaithes Road, ⅞ m. SSW. Irregular
front of no obvious antiquity, the centre part rendered, the r.
end projecting. The latter is evidently the earliest element, a
timber-framed parlour wing possibly of the late C16, cased in
stone later. The central part is of hybrid construction, probably early C17, the walls of stone but with a substantial timber
arcade demarcating the rear outshut (cf. East End, Norwood).
Mullioned windows and Tudor-arched doorway at the back.
Some *ex situ* C16 and C17 panelling including a little linenfold.*

LOW HALL, Low Hall Road, 1⅛ m. WSW. C17 complex, much
altered and added to. Front (E) with mullion-and-transom
windows, including a canted bay with an entrance cut into it,
and blocked C17 doorway with flattened-ogee head. At the
back a formerly detached three-storey block at right angles,
with mullioned windows and a two-storey rear outshut
(remnant of a timber arcade inside). Also an aisled barn,
originally perhaps of five bays, now of four: kingpost trusses.

---

*Nearby Newlaithes Hall, by *Robert Lugar* before 1828, an early example of Tudor
Revival, was dem. in 1964.

HORTON-IN-CRAVEN

CONGREGATIONAL CHAPEL. 1816. Plain four-bay front with round-headed doorways in the first and last bays. In the back wall two tall pointed windows flanking the pulpit. Interior with gallery round three sides, describing a half-octagon, with ramped box pews and panelled front. Below it a large box pew for the choir. Pulpit replaced by a big raised rostrum in the late C19. Adjoining to the s is the previous chapel, of 1717, converted into a manse.

HORTON HOUSE. Early C18 block. Front now of three bays but a view of *c.* 1720 shows a five-bay arrangement, with what were probably cross-windows. Doorway with moulded surround, rustic quoins. Unchamfered mullions and transoms at the back. Gatepiers with ball finials.

HORTON HALL, ¼ m. NW. C17 farmhouse with slightly later off-centre two-storey porch, the jettied upper stage with a stepped three-light window. Porch ceiling joists with deeply cut roll mouldings.

HORTON-IN-RIBBLESDALE

Scattered upland village at the foot of Penyghent, much affected by quarrying.

ST OSWALD. Perp w tower. Nave and chancel in one, with aisles. Straight-headed windows, some with cusped, some with uncusped lights. But the s doorway and the arcades are Norman, the doorway with zigzag decoration on the face of the inner arch, the arcades a decidedly rough and outlandish scheme, inconsistent from N to S. On the N side the first two piers are cylindrical but the second two are octagonal, with very primitive chamfered capitals; and the fourth arch is chamfered but the first three are not. To the s there are three cylindrical piers and one octagonal, and four arches with a very slight chamfer. The fifth arch on both sides is a later replacement, with double chamfers, but the E responds seem to be Norman. Is there a confused memory of schemes with alternating cylindrical and octagonal piers, e.g. Pittington, Co. Durham? In the aisles, corbels for aisle roofs at a slightly lower level than the present continuous roof-span. Conservative restoration, 1879 by *T. H. & F. Healey.* – FONT. Norman, tubshaped, with herringbone decoration, on a square base. – STAINED GLASS. A few small medieval fragments in the w window.

BRACKENBOTTOM FARMHOUSE, ½ m. E. Small early C18 block with its back to the lane. One room with a finely detailed C18 fitted cupboard with scrolled pediment and simple decorative plasterwork (cf. No. 10 Victoria Street, Settle).

At SELSIDE, 2¾ m. NW, THE SHAWS, a similar block, later extended, with smart ashlar porch dated 1738. Pediment and Ionic pilasters. Front of the house of coursed stone with unchamfered mullions, apparently renewed in the late C19.

LODGE HALL, 4 m. NNW. 1687 for Christopher Weatherhead, a Quaker, who later also built Knight Stainforth Hall, Stainforth. A remarkably ambitious house for its remote location, 900 ft (280 metres) above sea level, and an eccentric one in some respects, related to The Folly at Settle (q.v.). Tall and compact, of two storeys and attic, it consists of a very short hall range facing E, a single cross-wing to the r., and an outshut containing the staircase in the angle between them at the back. But the wing is not gabled at the front and so the effect is simply of a façade in two parts, the r. slightly projecting. At one time there were traces of foundations to the l. of the hall range, but not in a form which suggested a corresponding S cross-wing. The hall range has a central doorway surmounted by a heavy arched canopy on moulded corbels and flanked by curious carvings of halberds (cf. New Hall, Rathmell). Simply decorated doorhead. To l. and r. of the doorway are symmetrically disposed cross-windows to the ground and first floors; high up above it a stepped three-light window lighting the attic; and close to the l. corner of the range at first-floor and attic levels small vesica-shaped windows with their own little hoodmoulds. But particularly odd, a near-repeat from The Folly, is the treatment of the l. corner of the cross-wing, next to the hall, which has windows to each floor wrapped round it, with a single transomed light facing E and S, and hoodmoulds continued from the r. windows of the hall range. To the r. again a three-light transomed window to each floor. Inside, the front doorway leads into the centre of the hall, in the up-to-date – or at least, non-traditional – way. (The staircase beyond is of stone, rising round a square core. In the parlour, at the front of the cross-wing, a fireplace with a lintel like one of the doorheads of the locality, with a truncated-ogee motif. Kitchen behind, with big arched fireplace.)

HOWGILL
Sedbergh

HOLY TRINITY. 1838, by *Edmund Sharpe* (cf. Cowgill). Humble upland chapel in simple lancet style. Narrow unaisled nave and one-bay chancel, both with low-pitched roofs. Unaltered interior with W gallery over the entrance vestibule, plain pews and pulpit, and partitioned enclosure for the font.

CROOK OF LUNE BRIDGE, 1⅛ m. NW. Possibly C16, repaired 1702, 1758 and 1817. Two arches of rough construction, the voussoirs of slate.

HUBBERHOLME
Buckden

St Michael. The church nearest the head of Wharfedale, a simple upland building of rough limestone rubble and markedly squat proportions, standing beside the river. In origin a chapel of ease of Arncliffe, it is first mentioned during the lifetime of William de Percy (†1245) in the Percy Chartulary, but most of the present structure seems to be much later than that. Restored 'with the greatest care' 1863 by *Ewan Christian*.

Short unbuttressed w tower, evidently post-Reformation, with small plain rectangular belfry openings; but a more precise dating may be possible (*see* below). Nave and chancel in one, aisles under the same roof, with plain parapet. The windows mainly Perp and straight-headed – some with cusped lights, some uncusped, and some oddly bereft of their lintels – but extensively rearranged by *Christian*. Two at the E end his own inventions. s porch, with segment-headed doorway, dated 1696. Round-headed inner doorway also probably C17. But the plain round-headed tower arch is apparently Norman, inexpertly reused. Where did it come from? If there was previously a chancel arch which was later removed (cf. Broughton) it could perhaps have been that. Perp N arcade of three-plus-one bays – the caesura where the chancel arch would have been – with very short octagonal piers and depressed two-centred double-chamfered arches, the E arch excessively wide for its height. Four-bay s arcade again probably post-Reformation and presumably coeval with the putative abolition of a chancel arch. Round arches without any dressing or moulding (cf. Grasmere, Cumbria, *c*. 1562, and Hawkshead, Cumbria, 1578 and 1633), on octagonal piers without proper capitals: the arches would have looked less outlandish before the wall plaster was removed in 1863. Plain stout roof by *Christian*.

rood screen and loft. Rare survivals, the screen dated 1558 and signed as the 'opus' of *William Jake*, carpenter, the loft the only example in the West Riding. Restored 1863. But there are complications. The two elements do not go together; the loft is back-to-front, the more elaborate side – with finely pierced tracery panels and remains of colouring – facing E instead of w; and both are slightly too wide for the church's central vessel, ending in mid air under the arches to each side rather than against the arcade piers and spandrels. The screen also bears – if *Christian*'s restoration is faithful – a badge of the Percy family, but their association with Hubberholme had come to an end some twenty years before 1558. A possible interpretation is that the screen was a pre-existing parclose screen – there had been a Percy family chantry in the church – the loft came from elsewhere, and that William Jake's 'opus' was the installation of both in their present position. So this, the removal of the chancel arch and the building of the tower, and the provision of the s aisle and arcade – a precondition for the erection of screen and loft – would all go together, a very rare case of Marian ecclesiology.

FONT. Polygonal, probably Perp in spite of two very elementary heads; but the rounded stem may be earlier – STAINED GLASS. N chapel E by *Clayton & Bell*, 1867; s chapel E by *Powell Bros.* of Leeds, 1883; N aisle second from w by *Ballantine* of Edinburgh, 1907, and NW by *Morris & Co.*, 1918; s aisle second from w by *Kempe & Co.*, 1920. – MONUMENT. Charles Ramsden †1856 by *Walsh* of Leeds. Tablet with urn.

HUNSINGORE

4050

ST JOHN. 1867–8 by *Kirk & Parry* of Sleaford, Lincolnshire, at the cost of Joseph Dent of Ribston Hall (q.v.): the Dents were a Lincolnshire family. Rock-faced Dec, SW tower with Lincolnshire-style broach spire, polygonal apse. Its 'venerable' predecessor had been restored in the C18. – (ROYAL ARMS of Charles II, painted on an oval board. – STAINED GLASS. Chancel and baptistery windows by *Ward & Hughes*, 1871 and 1874; s aisle by *Hardman*, 1872 and 1877; w window by *Mayer*, 1876. – In the vestry N two C17 oval panels, one heraldic, the other, dated 1615, with the cipher of the Goodricke family (*see* Ribston Hall).)

WATER MILL, at the s end of the village, now a house. Dated 1809. Coursed stone, two storeys, with oculus in the front gable. Other windows altered. (Undershot wheel and some other fittings remain.)

ILKLEY

1040

The town stands in the stately valley of lower Wharfedale, on the s side of the river below the gritstone crags of Ilkley Moor. The site of the Roman fort of Olicana, at the intersection of the roads from Manchester to Aldborough and from Tadcaster to Ribchester, by the beginning of C19 it was a village of some 400 inhabitants which functioned in a small way as a 'bathing place'. The supposed curative properties of the waters from a spring on the moor – attributed impartially to bathing or drinking – had been noted over a century earlier and the first bath constructed *c.* 1700; but the popularity of the spa was greatly stimulated by the advent of 'scientific' treatment and the building of hydropathic establishments. The first, the 'Ben Rhydding', was built in 1843–4 and a number of others quickly followed, notably the palatial Wells House of 1854–6. The fashion for hydropathy, however, proved to be quite short-lived and the more potent cause of Ilkley's rapid growth during the second half of the C19 was its development as a dormitory town for the wealthy middle classes of Bradford and Leeds. The crucial factors were the arrival of the railway in 1865 and a series of land sales by the Middleton family, squires of Ilkley, from 1867 onwards: the population rose from 811 in 1851 to 7,455 in 1901. From the old village centre round the parish church, the town expanded first s up the hillside to the open moor, then in other directions. Architecturally, the results range from angular High Victorian Gothic in dark gritstone to the whitewashed Modern idiom of the interwar period. Lutyens in 1911 was predictably scornful: 'The . . . villas have a window from this, a door from that, etc – a pot pourri of Yorkeological details. The result is futile and absolutely unconvincing!' But the revived Pennine style is actually much less common than might be expected, and more noticeable is the popularity of materials and styles – mock half-timbering, red tile roofs and tile-hung gables – adopted from the South of England. Today the town maintains its dormitory role. The centre has suffered only a small number of insensitive developments and retains its Victorian and Edwardian character largely intact.

CHURCHES

ALL SAINTS. Short Perp w tower with diagonal buttresses, the body of the church radically enlarged in 1860–1. The nave, with aisles and low clerestory, was lengthened by a bay to the E, its s aisle rebuilt and a new chancel erected, lower than the nave like its predecessor. Perp windows remain in the N aisle and s clerestory, straight-headed with uncusped arched lights. Nave arcades, now of four bays, with octagonal piers and double-chamfered arches, one capital on the N side with crude horizontal and vertical reeding. The puzzle is the s doorway, on C19 footings but otherwise apparently C13, with dogtooth ornament. But there are no imposts and the mouldings seem too large-scale for their position. N clerestory windows 1880, N chapel etc. 1927. – FONT. Plain block with chamfered corners. The COVER C17, with a finial of miniature obelisks and inverted consoles. – PEW, at the w end of the N aisle. 1633. Superstructure with big vertically symmetrical balusters. – SCULPTURE. Two Roman altars, formerly built into the tower, one bearing a bas-relief figure, the other a relief of a sacrificial pitcher. – Three Anglo-Saxon cross-shafts, together with a cross-head on the tallest which does not belong to it but is of similar date. The shortest, probably of the mid-to-late C9, has a demi-figure holding a book and beasts in panels two of which have similarities to one on a coin of the Northumbrian King Eadbert (737–58). The next has panels of paired contorted beasts, simple vine scrolls and possibly traces of two human figures: date late C8 to early C9. The tallest, of the

Ilkley, All Saints, Anglo-Saxon cross-shaft.
Drawing, 1915

mid-to-late C9, is one of the most important Anglian crosses of its date in the North. On the front a figure of Christ enthroned, above three panels of beasts – a confronted pair (cf. Otley) and two single, contorted – on the back the symbols of the four Evangelists as draped demi-figures in panels, and on the sides tight vine scrolls. – STAINED GLASS. E window by *Warrington*, 1861, a striking large-scale Crucifixion. Chancel s, two by *Clayton & Bell*, 1861 and 1867. Chancel N, s aisle E and w, by *Wailes*, 1856, 1864, 1878. w window by *Ward & Hughes*, 1871. N aisle NE by *Morris & Co.*, 1922. – MONUMENTS. Large finely executed effigy of a cross-legged knight. Probably Sir Peter Middleton †1336, otherwise his uncle Sir Adam †1315. – A number of crude brasses, mainly inscriptions only. Mostly C17.

ST MARGARET, Queen's Road. 1878–9 by *Norman Shaw*. A big church, broadly Perp, but quite low-key in some respects. The main exception is the exterior of the chancel, aisleless but as tall as the nave, and thanks to the fall of the ground rising high above a basement, with blind arches and much blank masonry. The w end by contrast seems emphatically horizontal, burrowing into the hillside. Long nave with aisles and clerestory, short full-height transepts E of the chancel arch, very broad E and w windows of many lights. Whimsically detailed bellcote over the chancel arch (initially a tower was proposed in this position but the idea was abandoned at an early stage because of fears about the stability of the ground). Octagonal boilerroom chimneystacks, and an odd stepped window, on the s transept E side. Airy spacious interior with very wide chancel arch. – A number of FITTINGS by *Shaw* and his associates but in general not specially memorable. FONT, 1879, perhaps by *E. S. Prior*, who was clerk of works, under a CANOPY of 1911 by *Shaw*, *H. S. Chorley* and *T. G. Davidson*. PULPIT, 1881 by *Shaw*. CHANCEL SCREEN, 1898–9 by *Shaw* and *Percy Ginham*. – The REREDOS is later, 1925 by *J. H. Gibbons*, and ironically perhaps the most successful item. Elaborate scheme of folding panels in carved and painted wood. – STAINED GLASS. Mostly by *Powell & Sons*, 1897–1919. Dense, intricate designs. – Two windows in the E bay of the s aisle, by *Morris & Co.*, the larger 1894, the smaller 1902, a design by *Burne-Jones*.

ST JOHN, Bolling Road, Ben Rhydding. 1905–12 by *Connon & Chorley* of Leeds. Suburban Perp with prominent NW tower.

SACRED HEART (R.C.), Stockeld Road. Core of 1878–9 by *Edward Simpson*, major enlargement 1979 by *P. H. Langtry-Langton*, with aisle-like lateral extensions, Gothic w portal and extra windows in the apse. – Abstract STAINED GLASS, c. 1979 by *John Hardman Studios*.

METHODIST AND UNITED REFORMED CHURCH (formerly Congregational), The Grove. 1868–9 by *J. P. Pritchett Jun.* Spikily Dec, with tall NE (ritual SW) tower and spire. Interior altered.

FRIENDS' MEETING HOUSE, Queen's Road. 1869. Rather coarsely detailed. Shouldered openings and a rose window.

BAPTIST CHAPEL, Kings Road. 1902 by *Garside & Pennington*.
  Built as the Sunday School. The front Gothic, the sides with
  gabled lunettes.

BEN RHYDDING METHODIST CHURCH, Wheatley Lane. 1909,
  also by *Garside & Pennington*. Interesting free Perp design, with
  some affinities to Shaw's All Saints, Leek. Tremendously squat
  (ritual) w tower with battered clasping buttresses and pyramid
  roof, half embraced by the aisles, which inside is effectively
  absorbed into the nave, with the full-width tower arch springing from the nave arcades.

CHRISTIAN SCIENCE CHURCH, Wells Road. 1939 by *F. L.
  Charlton* of Leeds. Low block with diagonally set entrance at
  the corner.

CEMETERY, Ashlands Road. Two CHAPELS, 1876–8 by *John
  Shaw*. Hamfisted Gothic, with spirelets. The MONUMENTS
  include that to Elizabeth Catherine Fletcher †1904 by *Eric Gill*.
  Sandstone cross with raised lettering.

PUBLIC BUILDINGS

TOWN HALL, Station Road. 1906–8 by *William Bakewell* of
  Leeds. An attractive composition in a mixed Northern Renaissance style. Recessed centre with tall hipped roof crowned by
  a clock turret. Continuous band of fenestration to the first floor
  with an oriel over the entrance, flanking turrets with ogee caps.
  Forward-standing blocks to l. and r. containing the public
  library and a public hall, with big round-headed mullion-and-
  transom windows, their upper halves above eaves level and
  forming gabled lunettes. Roundels and bas-relief figures to
  each side.

MANOR HOUSE (Museum), Castle Hill. Medieval origin, possibly C14, largely rebuilt *c.* 1600 etc. Hall-and-cross-wings plan,
  with cross-passage, single-storey hall with lateral fireplace, and
  a gabled two-storey projecting window bay at the high end of
  the hall. The earliest parts are the two-centre-headed front
  doorway and a little of the masonry round it, the corresponding back doorway at the other end of the cross-passage, and a
  section of the wall between the passage and the service wing,
  with two shouldered-arched doorways. On the front r. of the
  entrance, the hall, both storeys of the window bay, and the
  upper floor of the parlour cross-wing have mullion-and-
  transom windows with round-headed lights, and the ground
  floor of the wing a mullioned window also with arched lights.
  The anomaly is the small mullioned window with plain lights
  to the chamber over the hall, but a possible explanation is that
  this is the lower half of another mullion-and-transom window,
  the upper half of which perhaps rose into another gable since
  removed – the wall-head at this point shows some signs of
  disturbance. The front of the service wing, to the l., has plain

mullioned windows, probably later C17, inserted. Chamfered and stopped ceiling beams to hall and parlour, screen to the cross-passage a restoration of *c.* 1961 – when the Museum function was instituted – using the original mortices. Garderobe closet in the parlour chamber. The hall range and parlour cross-wing both have handsome kingpost roofs, rather steeply pitched, with curved braces to the ridges, both of which incorporate some medieval timbers; but they have evidently been reconstructed and sit rather uncomfortably on the present wall-heads.

WHITE WELLS. The bath house on the moor above the town. The present building is mainly of *c.* 1791, although perhaps incorporating some earlier masonry; and given its place in the town's history is a surprisingly humble affair, a plain white-washed range in four sections of alternating heights. The two lower parts contain the baths and were originally unroofed, the roofs added in the C19; and the two-storey block between them housed changing rooms etc. The baths are elliptical, *c.* 8 ft (2.5 metres) long, with steps at one end: one is visible, the other hidden by a modern floor. The E end of the range was added in 1829, and contained stables below and a waiting room above. The former CHARITY BATH for less well-off customers, a short distance W, was also built in 1829, again with an unroofed bath behind screen walls and a two-storey changing block.

SWIMMING POOL, Denton Road, Middleton. 1935 by *A. Skinner*, the District Council's Surveyor. Circular with a tiered fountain in the middle.

GRAMMAR SCHOOL, Cowpasture Road. 1892–3 by *C. H. Hargreaves*. Rather bleak, with central pyramid-roofed tower and mullion-and-transom windows.

ALL SAINTS NATIONAL SCHOOL (former), Leeds Road. 1871–2 by *T. H. & F. Healey*. Similar to some of their Bradford schools. Simple C13 Gothic, with plate-traceried wheel windows and a pyramid-roofed tower next to the master's house. The new ALL SAINTS PRIMARY SCHOOL is in Skipton Road. 2002 by *Bradford City Council Design and Construction Services* (job architect *Fiona Kelly*). White-rendered walls – a refreshing change from the gritstone norm – and monopitch roofs.

ASHLANDS PRIMARY SCHOOL, Leeds Road. 1953 by *Hubert Bennett*, West Riding County Architect. Long, low and very attractively grouped. Snecked stone walls, flat roofs and some vertical timber boarding.

[107] RAILWAY STATION, Station Road. 1865 by the Midland Railway Company's architect *J. H. Sanders*. Low symmetrical Neo-Palladian forebuilding, with a big Serliana in the central pavilion. The train shed behind converted into shop units 1989 by *William Gower & Partners*.

BRIDGES over the Wharfe. The OLD BRIDGE is of *c.* 1674–6, replacing one destroyed by a flood in 1673, the parapets rebuilt. Three arches, elegant, but very steep and narrow. The NEW

Bridge, 1904–6 by *James Fraser* of Leeds, and its approach roads, were built in connection with the residential development of Middleton, across the river to the N. Single segmental arch of iron girders, springing from castellated abutments.

PERAMBULATIONS

1. The town

The parish church stands on the S half of the site of the Roman Fort, probably first established during the governorship of Julius Agricola (78–84 AD), which covered an area of over three acres. Excavations in 1919–21 showed that originally it had a clay rampart on a stone foundation and gateways of timber, and that it was reconstructed probably in the late C2 with a rampart of stone. Its N perimeter is partly represented by a heavily modified earthwork, with a short stretch of the C2 masonry visible at the NW corner, behind the Manor House. When it ceased to be garrisoned is not known.

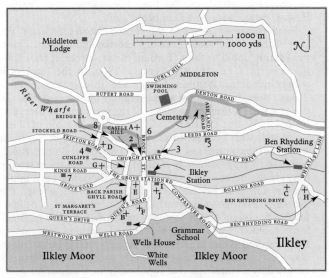

A	All Saints	1	Town Hall
B	St Margaret	2	Manor House (Museum)
C	St John	3	Former All Saints Primary School
D	Sacred Heart (R.C.)	4	All Saints Primary School
E	Methodist and United Reformed	5	Ashlands Primary School
	Church	6	New Bridge
F	Friends Meeting House	7	Heathcote
G	Baptist Chapel	8	Ilkley Bridge
H	Ben Rhydding Methodist Church		
J	Christian Science Church		

W and NW of the church are a few survivals of the pre-C19 village. The most important is the MANOR HOUSE (*see* Public Buildings, above). To the W in CHURCH STREET, the ALBERT INN, 1709, small double pile with central lobby entry (cf. Addingham Moorside). An upright oval window above the doorway but the others still mullioned, with hoodmoulds. Then on the other side THE BOX TREE, similar date and dimensions, with steeply pedimented doorway, the front otherwise much altered; and further on, in SKIPTON ROAD, the OLD GRAMMAR SCHOOL, 1637 (now a shop), just a little single-storey block with central doorway and two four-light mullioned windows. Off to the N, in BRIDGE LANE, CASTLE HOUSE, mid-C18, three widely spaced bays, two-and-a-half storeys. Doorway with pediment and Gibbs surround, the central keystone and the pediment tympanum both vermiculated; the window above also with Gibbs surround, other windows of two lights with a broad unchamfered mullion. In amongst these, in Skipton Road the former LISTER'S ARMS HOTEL, 1825, the first of Ilkley's C19 hotels, two-and-a-half storeys, one-plus-three-plus-one bays; and in Church Street the N end of THE ARCADE, 1895, with tall basket-arched entrance and steep pyramid-roofed tower. Round the corner in CUNLIFFE ROAD, the MASONIC HALL and CONSTITUTIONAL CLUB, *c.* 1900, an engaging hybrid, mixing Free Renaissance and Pennine Revival details with a half-timbered gable.

From the crossroads E of the church BROOK STREET, the core of the commercial centre of Victorian and modern Ilkley, runs gently uphill to the S. Turning the SE corner of the crossroads is the CRESCENT HOTEL, *c.* 1860, in the form of a convex quadrant. Restrained Italianate, three storeys, with a Tuscan portico set against a recessed bay on the diagonal. On the SE corner a simpler quadrant of shops, of similar date, and further up BARCLAYS BANK, 1888 by *J. & E. Critchley* of Ilkley, Loire-style with a corner turret. At the top the other two main streets of the commercial centre, The Grove and Station Road, run r. and l. Approximately straight on, climbing more steeply towards the moor, is WELLS ROAD. In the lower part, opposite the Christian Science Church (*see* Churches, above), the former METHODIST ASSEMBLY HALL, now flats, a delightful Art Nouveau design of 1903–4 by *Adkin & Hill* of Bradford. Gabled front with big arched window combining Perp-inspired panel tracery and larger rectangular lights in classically moulded frames. Tower to one side formerly crowned by an umbrella-like cupola. On the l. side of the more open upper part of the road WEST VIEW, a terrace including some houses of the 1830s which formed the nucleus of the residential development of the area. Behind it the former VICARAGE, 1848, plain gabled Tudor, and ILKLEY HALL, a three-bay villa of *c.* 1825, much extended. At the top, next to the moor, with spectacular views over the valley, WELLS HOUSE, the former hydro, now apartments. 1854–6 by

Cuthbert Brodrick, and a fine example of his vigorous but controlled monumental Italianate, a palazzo-like square block with broad festively crested angle towers. Three storeys, the ground floor with vermiculated rustication. Grounds laid out by *Joshua Major*, 1856, but now largely occupied by pretentious housing, *c*. 2000.

From the upper part of Wells Road a diversion can be made E, across to COWPASTURE ROAD and, opposite the Grammar School, the CRAIGLANDS HOTEL, another former hydro. Main part 1859, rather institutional, of three storeys and seven bays with a one-bay pedimented centre. Extension to the l. of the 1860s with a semicircular bow, further extension probably of the 1880s in a perfunctory Scottish Baronial, with crowstepped gables and diminutive corner turrets. More rewarding is the area to the W, below and beyond Wells House, which was developed with villas and terraces from *c*. 1870 onwards. In QUEEN'S ROAD, after the Friends' Meeting House (*see* Churches, above), DEACONESS COURT, 1869 by *T. C. Hope* of Bradford, which established the standard formula of the villas of the 1870s and 1880s: spiky domestic Gothic with towers over the porches.* Further up, just beyond *Norman Shaw*'s St Margaret's Church (*see* Churches, above) on the other side of the road, is ST JOHN'S, also by *Shaw*, 1878–9. Brutally converted to flats *c*. 1955. Stone-built Old English, a single range canted part-way along (cf. Merrist Wood, Surrey, etc.). Striking sheer E end with prominent clustered chimney and quasi-Pennine-style (blocked) doorway. Big rectangular bay window at NE corner. Additionally hereabouts, opposite the church, a group of Bronze Age CARVED STONES moved from the moor (*see* Ilkley Moor, below) in 1890–2. Then in QUEEN'S DRIVE two contrasting houses again by the stylistically versatile *T. C. Hope*, ARDEN LEA, 1881, asymmetrical Italianate, altered, and a semi-detached pair, ARDEN CROFT and BRIARWOOD, 1897, southern Old English with big half-timbered gables, tile-hanging and tile roofs. Further up again, in WESTWOOD DRIVE, is WESTWOOD LODGE, 1875 by *George Smith* of Bradford, a particularly good example of the standard type, the porch tower of four storeys and crowned by a truncated pyramid roof.

Back down via St Margaret's Terrace and, in BACK PARISH GHYLL ROAD, the former ILKLEY HOSPITAL, now sheltered housing. 1862 by *Perkin & Backhouse* of Leeds, Scottish Baronial with crowstepped gables. This faces towards THE GROVE, with at the w end the MEMORIAL GARDEN and the WAR MEMORIAL, 1922 by *J. J. Joass*. Panelled Portland stone cenotaph crowned by an urn, and a short distance behind it a small loggia in the same material. A pair of later shelters in differently coloured artificial stone rather spoils the effect.

---

* Built as a school: enlarged 1874.

116

Beyond is another leafy residential area, of *c.* 1900. In KING'S
ROAD, about halfway along, is *Lutyens*'s HEATHCOTE, 1906–7
for J. T. Hemingway, a Bradford wool merchant. The house
marks the change in Lutyens's style from Arts and Crafts
vernacular to Edwardian imperialist classical, and its salient
characteristic, inside as well as out, is its unrelenting monumentality. As a result it seems more like a town hall than a
private dwelling, and it is ironically appropriate that it is now
used as prestige offices. Lutyens's motive in adopting this
approach seems to have been no more elevated than a desire
to lord it over an environment which he despised: the site was
'in an ultra suburban locality over which villas of a dreadful
kind and many colours wantonly distribute themselves . . . The
material was York stone – a stone without a soul to call its own,
as sober as a teetotaller . . . I wanted something persisting and
dominating . . . to stratify the diarrhoetic conditions produced
by the promiscuous villadom . . .' He was, he wrote, 'scolded
for not being Yorkshire in Yorkshire': what the client, who 'had

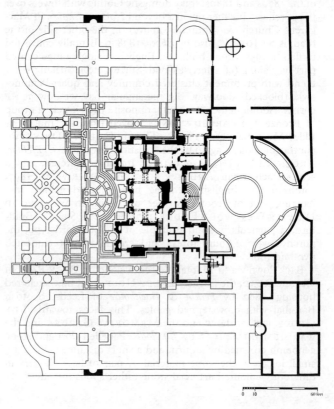

Ilkley, Heathcote.
Plan of house and garden

the judgment to value the policy of the free hand', thought of it is not recorded.

There are some familiar virtues, however: the close and effective relationship between house and garden – the latter done in collaboration with *Gertrude Jekyll* – the inventive detailing of the paved areas in the garden and forecourt, with slates and tiles set on edge, and the tight planning of the interior in a building which is not as large as it looks. The design sources include Sanmichele – Lutyens's own name for the house – and the French *grand siècle* (rather than Palladio, or any permutation of English Palladianism); the building materials gritstone and carboniferous sandstone, and red pantiles for the roofs. Screen wall to the street, with entrance gatepiers set in a semicircular recess which is then answered by the circular pattern of the forecourt paving. Rigorously symmetrical, the house consists of a tall three-storey central block under a steep hipped roof; two-storey cross-wings, also with hipped roofs, projecting to both N and S; and yet lower outer pavilions flanking the N ends of these. The entrance front (N) is relatively restrained, with blind rusticated arches to the ground floor and Gallic segment-headed windows above. The garden front, however, has 'too much architecture chasing too little wall space' (Gradidge). Sanmichelean Doric order to the ground floor, busy multiple recessions to the centre. Prominent paired chimneystacks with bulgy rustication, copied from Shaw's Bryanston. Elaborate S terrace, aligned on gabled arbours beyond the formal gardens to E and W, and beyond it at a lower level a big levelled lawn flanked by informal planting. Inside, as in the earlier vernacular houses, a through central axis is avoided, the front door leading into a vaulted entrance vestibule running to the r. The main hall is centrally placed on the S side, tripartite with coupled green marble columns. The two are linked by a circular lobby, opening into one corner of the hall, which also gives access to the staircase against the W flank, a rather absurdly grand scheme in the Wren manner, with black marble stairs, Tijouesque wrought-iron balustrade, and columns and pilasters to the upper stage. Dining room with outsize marble fireplace – a classical inglenook – in the SE corner of the house, drawing room in the SW, domed billiard room in the NW pavilion and kitchen in the NE. Lutyens also designed the original furniture for the house.

Further W again two examples of the type of house which Lutyens condemned. In VICTORIA AVENUE between King's Road and Grove Road, THE BRIERY, 1897 by *Isitt, Adkin & Hill*. Charming Arts and Crafts Old English with occasional Pennine Revival details. Coursed gritstone and white render, slate-hung gables and red tile roof. Big mullion-and-transom staircase window with flattened truncated ogees on the lintels, porch (altered) with Pennine-style lintel, elaborate inglenook chimney-breast on the N side. Front garden wall with Art Nouveau gateway, octagonal gazebo with fancy weather-vane. Now a convent, with unsympathetic mid-C20 additions.

Beyond this, in GROVE ROAD, is HIGH GREEN, 1907 by
Walter Brierley of York, an altogether more sober affair, simple
Pennine-style without idiosyncrasies. Mullion-and-transom
windows and plain gables.

2. Ben Rhydding

The former hamlet of Wheatley, E of the town centre, its modern
name taken from the hydro established here in 1844 (dem.
1955). The main survival of the pre-Victorian settlement is
WHEATLEY HALL, by the station. C17 Pennine farmhouse of
two builds, the later part to the l. Mullion-and-transom
windows to the ground floor, mullioned windows above. Position of the doorway altered. Chamfered straight-headed doorways inside. 1 m. SSE, on the hillside beyond the built-up area,
HIGH STEAD, 1596, altered. Hybrid construction, the external walls of stone but much structural timber inside. Mullioned
windows of three and four lights, two with ornamented stops
to the hoodmoulds. Diagonally set chimneystacks. Between the
two, about halfway up BEN RHYDDING DRIVE, is PLOVER-
FIELD, 1880s, one of the earliest villas in this part of the town,
a vast black-and-white pile with tile-hung gables and tile roof.
Perhaps by *Edward Dodgshun* of Leeds, who in 1896 provided
a matching gatehouse (the archway now filled in) with Teu-
tonic turret, and a coachhouse. A little further up, FIVE OAKS,
1929–30 by *J. C. Procter* of Leeds. Modernistic, almost Art
Deco, with white-rendered walls and a flat roof, but symmetrical. The gently curved S balcony and occasional circular
windows suggest a nautical reference. Some detail lost, both
outside and in, but fireplaces remain. Further w, in BEN
RHYDDING ROAD, WHEATLEY LAWN, 1898 by *Empsall &
Clarkson* of Bradford, sub-Shavian stone-built Old English,
including a canted end copied from Shaw's St John's (*see*
above). Lower down, off Valley Drive, VALLEY LODGE,
award-winning housing scheme of 1976–7 by the *York University Design Unit* (project architect *John McNeill*) for the Green-
down Housing Association. Two cleanly detailed brick-built
two-storey terraces forming a V-shape, deftly inserted into an
existing garden layout.

3. Middleton

Across the River Wharfe to the N. Residential development from
1900 onwards but including some important earlier survivals.

MYDDLETON LODGE. High up on the hillside, with a superb
view S across the valley to Ilkley Moor. *c*. 1600 for the Middleton family, squires of Ilkley. As the name 'lodge' implies, it
was not the family's principal seat – that was at Stockeld Park
near Wetherby (q.v.) – and it has the experimental character

and compact shape generally associated with the term at that
time. There are some C19 additions and alterations but its form
remains clear: a square double-pile block which is probably the
earliest fully fledged example of the type in this part of
the country. Four storeys, the bottom one a semi-basement,
the top partly in the roof. Quite simple detailing, with symmetrically arranged mullion-and-transom windows, the one
flourish a canted first-floor oriel window to the centre of the
front, above the entrance. Two gables to front and back, one
to the side – the spine wall between the two ranges of rooms
being discontinued at the top-storey level. Chimneystacks at
the angles, serving a consistent system of diagonally set corner
fireplaces. Slightly later stair-turret against the W flank, with a
tier of rooms behind it slightly later again. Front doorway
remodelled in the mid C19, in a grotto style with bulgy rustication. Attached to the NW corner of the house a chapel built
in 1825. Pointed windows with timber tracery. Service wing to
the NE, 1848, porch on the E flank 1906. Inside, the main
feature is the staircase, of the 'cage' type with continuous
moulded newel posts throughout its height, and fat vertically
symmetrical balusters. The fireplaces are plain, chamfered and
Tudor-arched. Gallery on quatrefoil columns in the chapel.
Just SE of the house an C18 GAZEBO, plain and square externally but inside circular with shell-headed niches and a little
fireplace on the diagonals.

LOW HALL, Rupert Road. Another house of the Middletons,
down in the valley and now part of the upmarket suburbia.
Two storeys, long and low. Late medieval origin, radically
reconstructed probably early C17, much altered and extended
C18–C20. At the front a fragment of a tall trefoil-headed
window, possibly C14, which may have lit the high end of the
hall, and next to it a two-storey C17 porch with reused doorway.
So in the early C17 reconstruction the positions of the high and
low ends appear to have been reversed. Traces of medieval
wall-plates inside, and other medieval timbers reused in early
C18 roof trusses. Big segment-headed housebody fireplace of
c. 1700, flanked by straight-headed doorways; post-and-panel
partition to the porch chamber with flattened-ogee-headed
doorway.

From the C20 two contrasting examples suffice. First STONE-
DENE, also in Rupert Road. 1914 by *Edward Maufe* for his
cousin Philip Maufe, E wing added by the same architect in
1919. Vernacular revival in stone and render, characterized by
long strips of mullioned windows with unchamfered frames
and mullions. Pennine lintel to the front doorway but otherwise not of particularly local character. Second THE WHITE
HOUSE, a little further E in Curly Hill, another of *J. C. Procter*'s
modernistic designs, also of 1929–30, this time asymmetrical.
Sympathetically extended 1993 by *David Bamford*. Finally, up
the hill again to the NE, beyond the built-up area, RED
GABLES. Single-storey cottage retaining four cruck trusses,
probably C16 in origin. Thatched until C20.

ILKLEY MOOR

Ilkley Moor and its SE continuation Burley Moor, have the biggest concentration of BRONZE AGE ROCK CARVINGS in the country. Their principal motif is the 'cup and ring' – a small hollow encircled by one or more annular grooves – while occasionally there are grooves forming other patterns. Examples are the BARMISHAW STONE, ⅜ m. WSW of White Wells (*see* Public Buildings, above), the BADGER STONE, ¼ m. S of that, and the HANGINGSTONE QUARRY ROCK, a large flat slab ⅝ m. E of White Wells. Further S and SE are groups, including PANCAKE ROCK, a prominent slab crowning an outcrop, associated with settlement enclosures and burial cairns.

The SWASTIKA STONE, 1½ m. W of White Wells, has carving of a different type, with a number of 'cups' enclosed by a groove describing a curvilinear version of a swastika. It is much later than the others, probably of either the Iron Age or even the Dark Ages. Similar figures have been located in Italy and Sweden.

INGLETON

ST MARY. Perp W tower. The rest 1886–7 by *Cornelius Sherlock* of Liverpool. Dec style, in hammer-dressed limestone with gritstone ashlar dressings. – FONT. Norman, and one of the best in the West Riding. Cylindrical bowl with intersected arcading framing biblical figures – including the Virgin and Child with the Three Magi – and the Tree of Life. Base *c.* 1858. – STAINED GLASS. includes S aisle E by *Powell & Sons*, 1903.

A well-known beauty spot on account of its setting, at the foot of Ingleborough, and its gorges and waterfalls, but its architectural attractions are limited. The principal feature is the handsome VIADUCT which carried the 'little' North-Western line over the River Greta. 1859–60, *J. E. Errington* engineer. Rock-faced limestone, eleven arches. TWISTLETON MANOR HOUSE, ½ m. N, is a small double pile with a steeply pedimented porch dated 1717. At COLD COTES, 2 m. SE, BRACKENBURY FARMHOUSE, 1696, has a doorhead with three cusped recesses.

INGLEBOROUGH HILL-FORT. The highest hill-fort in England, occupying the sloping 15-acre plateau which forms the summit of the mountain, 2370 ft (720 metres) above sea level. Rampart of highly unusual construction, consisting of gritstone rubble contained within boxes composed of upright slabs and drystone walling, much damaged during the C20. Position of the original entrances uncertain. Within the fort twenty hut circles are visible, mainly towards the E side; but it is very unlikely that the site was permanently occupied, and either a seasonal occupation as part of a transhumance cycle, or a ritual use, are suggested. Date uncertain, probably Iron Age.

YARLSBER CAMP, 1 m. ESE. Iron Age earthwork enclosure
   covering 1½ acres.
See also Chapel-le-Dale.

JOHN OF GAUNT'S CASTLE
Haverah Park

2050

Well-preserved earthwork, and fragmentary masonry remains, of
   a royal hunting lodge: a roughly square moated enclosure on
   a steep-sided spur, containing a square platform on which the
   foundations of a tower, and some stonework of a gatehouse,
   survive. In origin probably of the late C12 when Haverah Park,
   a royal deerpark, was created; but the moat was formed, and
   repairs carried out, in 1333. Acquired by John of Gaunt in
   1372. Cut into the SE corner of the earthen bank beyond the
   moat are a tunnel-vaulted storeroom of post-medieval date and
   the remains of another.

KEARBY

3040

SPRING CLOSE FARM. Plain stone-built range incorporating
   some remains of a timber-framed house, possibly of as early as
   c. 1300 (evidence of passing braces). Originally aisled, at least
   four bays. Two-storey former porch on S side, probably C17,
   but no detail of that period visible.

KEASDEN
Clapham

7060

ST MATTHEW. 1873 by *G. T. Redmayne* of Manchester. Isolated
   upland chapel with a superb view of Ingleborough, built at the
   cost of James Farrer of Ingleborough Hall. Simplest rock-faced
   Gothic with nave and chancel in one.
MIDDLE BIRKS, 1¼ m. SE. Two-storey porch dated 1697, the
   doorway, with decorated lintel, flanked by single-light windows
   with shouldered-arch heads, all under a stepped hoodmould
   of complex profile. Stepped three-light window above. The
   upper stage inside has two tiers of bolection-moulded plaster
   frames and a decorative frieze. A possible date of 1633 on the
   body of the house.

KEIGHLEY

To T. D. Whitaker in 1805 Keighley presented 'the smoke of man-ufactories and . . . the din of recent population'. Four years earlier in 1801 the population was 5,745. But as a town it was not of recent origin: in 1695 it contained 100 houses, and there had been a market since the early C14. Although there had long been a domestic woollen and worsted industry dispersed throughout the parish, the town's subsequent industrial profile was complex. The first, water-powered, factories were for cotton rather than worsted spinning – including the first cotton mill in Yorkshire, Low Mill, completed in 1780 for the Lancastrian partnership of Clayton and Walshman – but in the early C19 there was a general reversion to worsted manufacture; and other industries were textile-related engineering and paper making. The population rose to 11,176 in 1831, 21,859 in 1861 and 36,176 in 1891: the 2001 figure, for a rather larger area, is 46,989.

The town stands near the confluence of the rivers Worth and Aire, with the steep valley sides rising all around. Its fabric now is mainly of the late C19 onwards. The main street is North Street, running N–S, which was laid out in 1786 as part of a realignment of the Keighley to Kendal turnpike (opened in 1753), and was widened in the 1890s to create a pleasantly spacious central area not without some townscape quality. The original spine of the town was further S, running at right angles, with Low Street to the E and High Street to the W; but apart from the curve of Church Street, S again, there is little to remind one of the pre-Victorian past, and mid-C20 clearances virtually eliminated the High Street as a recognizable entity altogether. Another dramatic change, as in other mill towns, has been the felling of the forest of mill chimneys, which extended right into the centre: a selec-tion of the surviving mills, all in more peripheral locations, is given below. The suburbs and outskirts also have some other items of interest, including a number of C19 industrialists' houses and in particular Keighley's best building, the C17 East Riddles-den Hall.

PLACES OF WORSHIP

ST ANDREW, Church Street. 1846–8 by *R. D. Chantrell*, on the site of the medieval church and of its successor, built in 1805. Commendably solid-looking, in the Perp style. Big W tower, long six-bay nave with aisles and clerestory, and lower chancel. Tall arcades with octagonal piers, deep W gallery. W doorway 1900. Churchyard with old trees on the S side but opened up to the street by demolitions on the N. – FONT. 1661. Octagonal bowl with simple ornament. Discarded 1848, reinstated 1934 with a new base and the elaborate timber canopy of its C19 replacement. – BENEFACTION BOARD. 1713. – STAINED

GLASS. Chancel NW, by *Morris & Co.*, 1881. Four figures on a quarry ground. E window by *Shrigley & Hunt.* – MONUMENTS. Four medieval grave-slabs, one evidently of Gilbert Kighley †c. 1380, with identifying inscription, now illegible. The others have crosses, and one a pair of pincers. – John Greenwood †1807. Perp-style canopied altar tomb, erected 1848.

ALL SAINTS, Highfield Lane. 1907 by *J. B. Bailey & Son* of Keighley. Perp, with transepts, but unfinished: only one bay of the nave was built. Three more and a tower were intended. On a steeply sloping site, the E end facing down the hill.

ST JOHN, Ingrow. 1841–3 by *Walker Rawstorne* of Bradford. Neo-Norman, quite large, with a tall strong W tower, broad unaisled nave and short tunnel-vaulted chancel with apse. Long narrow windows like round-headed lancets. Matching vestry, forming a basement quasi-ambulatory, added 1884. – STAINED GLASS. Several good windows by *Clayton & Bell*, 1882–1904. Nave NE 1892 by *Powell Bros.* of Leeds.

ST ANNE (R.C.), North Street. By *Pugin*, 1838–40, but altered and much enlarged 1906–7 by *Edward Simpson* of Bradford. The original building (illustrated in Pugin's *Present State*) was very plain and modest, an unaisled nave and short lower chancel with the simple lancet windows popular among less exacting architects. In the 1907 alterations the church was reoriented, the chancel becoming a narthex with an entrance below the E window, a S aisle was added to the nave and a new chancel provided to the W, preceded by a crossing with short double transepts (cf. St Joseph, Bradford). Eclectic Late Gothic, the E doorway with trumeau, tympanum and

Keighley, St Anne.
Engraving after A. W. N. Pugin, 1843

crenellations on the hoodmould. – STAINED GLASS. E window
by *Willement*, 1841. – On the S side the PRESBYTERY, 1838,
presumably by *Pugin*, with lancets and gables, later extended.
On the N the SCHOOL, 1859, enlarged 1902 etc. Three storeys,
with mullion-and-transom windows.

ST JOSEPH (R.C.), Queen's Road. 1934 by *Godfrey L. Clarke*.
Chunky Neo-Norman, a surprisingly effective design. Cruciform with squat central tower, apsidal (ritual) E end with
ambulatory. Light spacious interior.

TEMPLE STREET METHODIST CHAPEL, Temple Row, now
TEMPLE STREET MOSQUE. 1845–6 by *James Simpson* of
Leeds, the third chapel on the site. Dignified classical block,
the front of four bays with a pair of single-storey porches with
coupled Tuscan columns, and corresponding coupled pilasters
framing the windows above. Interior altered. Two stained-glass
windows by *Morris & Co.*, 1921, are now in Cliffe Castle
Museum (*see* Public Buildings, below). Former SUNDAY
SCHOOL, 1905, adjoining.

SWEDENBORGIAN CHURCH, Devonshire Street, now CHRIST
THE KING (R.C.). 1891. Meagre Gothic with SW spirelet.

Former BAPTIST CHAPEL. *See* The Town, below.

CEMETERY, Skipton Road. 1857. On sloping ground, with trees
and winding paths. One of the pair of humble Gothic CHAPELS
remains. Many C19 MONUMENTS including the Butterfield
Mausoleum (*see* Cliffe Castle, below), *c.* 1875, a small Gothic
bizarrerie with an outsize pinnacle on top.

See also Outer Keighley.

PUBLIC BUILDINGS

TOWN HALL, Bow Street. 1900–1 by *John Haggas* and *J. B.
Bailey & Son*. Four storeys, with a narrow gabled front in Free
Renaissance style. Art Nouveau bas-relief panels executed by
A. F. Smith. The lower part to the r., dull Jacobean, is the former
POST OFFICE, 1891 by *Sir Henry Tanner*. Panelled council
chamber with mildly Art Nouveau details.

Former SCHOOL BOARD OFFICES, Lawkholme Crescent. 1893
by *James Ledingham* of Bradford. A neat little building on a
corner site, also Free Renaissance but more creatively done
than the Town Hall. Sparrowe's Mansion window turning the
corner.

COUNTY COURT, North Street. *c.* 1847. One storey, five bays,
the centre three recessed, with segment-headed windows and
banded pilasters.

POLICE STATION. *See* The Town, below.

PUBLIC LIBRARY, North Street. 1902–4 by *McEwan & Swan* of
Birmingham, competition winners. Another Free Renaissance
design, low and informally grouped, but very trickily detailed.
Steep pedimental gables, two of them broken with little

obelisks in the breach, odd diamond-shaped first-floor windows with curvaceous strapwork surrounds, and a squat cupola. At the side tall thin gabled semi-dormers, done as cross-windows. Aisled first-floor reading room with segmental arches on Ionic columns, and segmental barrel roof.

CLIFFE CASTLE (Museum), Skipton Road. C19 mansion of complicated building history, in an elevated position on the NW edge of the town, but severely mutilated in 1956–9 when converted to its present use. Its starting point, represented by the l. two-thirds of the E (garden) front, was a house of c. 1830 by *George Webster* called Cliffe Hall, built for Christopher Netherwood, a Keighley lawyer. It was in Webster's usual Jacobean style, symmetrical with shaped gables. This was remodelled and greatly enlarged in 1875–8 by *George Smith* of Bradford for textile manufacturer H. I. Butterfield, the additions including no fewer than three tall battlemented towers, one over the new (S) entrance, preceded by a porte cochère, and another to the N; and further extensions, including a Crystal-Palace-style winter garden and a Gothic music room, were made in 1880–2 by *W. Bailey* of Keighley. In the 1950s the N tower was demolished, the front one reduced in height, and the gabled top storey of the house itself was removed. The winter garden had gone already: plain extension of 1971 on its site. Some opulent Second Empire reception rooms of the 1870s along the garden front, with painted ceilings by *Leroux*, but the staircase hall is Gothic, with poor-quality stained glass by *Powell Bros.* of Leeds in the big traceried window. Octagonal exhibition hall, top-lit and galleried, 1956–9 by *Sir Albert Richardson*, on the site of the kitchens. Well-wooded grounds sloping down to the road. At the SE corner a Gothic entrance archway, presumably by *Smith*; and towards the NW another tower, which was attached to outbuildings now largely demolished.

KEIGHLEY COLLEGE, Cavendish Street and North Street. The original Technical College building is of 1954–7 by *Hubert Bennett*, then West Riding County Architect. Utilitarian modern range of five storeys, faced in stone and glass. The block to the l., on the corner site, has a front range of 1964–8 by *John Poulson*, echoing Bennett's design, but the rest is part of the former Mechanics' Institute, 1868–70 by *Lockwood & Mawson* with N addition of 1886 etc. The Institute had been badly damaged by fire in 1962 but previously was the dominant building of the town centre, Gothic with a pavilion-roofed tower. Tall gable-end facing onto North Street.

OAKBANK SCHOOL, Oakworth Road. 1961–4 by *Scherrer & Hicks* of Manchester. Quadrangular, curtain-walled, of three storeys. Oakbank itself, an industrialist's Italianate mansion of 1872, was retained as part of the scheme. S extension 1979.

RAILWAY STATION, Bradford Road. The railway reached Keighley, from Leeds and Bradford, in 1847. The present station is of 1883–5, probably by the Midland Railway Company architect *Charles Trubshaw*, its forebuilding and forecourt straddling the track, in effect forming a sideways extension of the road bridge. Single-storey Free Renaissance façade of thirteen bays, with shallow canopy. Top-lit booking hall. *See* also Outer Keighley s.

BUS STATION, Lawkholme Crescent. Passenger concourse 2001–2 by *Watson & Batty* of Guiseley. An exceedingly mannered design with jagged roof-line, the walls mainly of glass with some fun and games in masonry at each end.

THE TOWN

Only a very brief perambulation is possible, in an area virtually confined to the length of North Street. Just beyond its s end, in HIGH STREET, on the s side a tall narrow pedimented façade of *c.* 1900 in Art Nouveau classical style, with stumpy attached Doric columns to the first floor, bas-relief carved panels flanking the windows of the second, and an oculus with elaborately contorted surround in the pediment. The building behind is older, built as the Liberal Club in 1876. Further w on the N side an altered five-bay house of the early CI9, with pedimented three-bay centre. In NORTH STREET itself, the s part is the most densely built up and still markedly homogeneous, three-storeyed ashlar developments mainly of the 1890s in various mixed classical styles, e.g. RUSSELL CHAMBERS, 1893, and NATWEST BANK, formerly Bradford District Bank, 1892. Beyond, on the w side, first a pair of smart Italianate blocks, of two storeys and four bays, one now BARCLAYS BANK, the other the POLICE STATION, which were built shortly before the street was widened, with front gardens. Then after the Library, the former TEMPERANCE HALL, now a pub, 1895–6 by *W. & J. B. Bailey*, in 'what is termed in the phraseology of the craft "free classic"' (*Keighley News*) – i.e. debased Italianate – with a broad cupola over the corner. Behind the Library in HIGHFIELD LANE the front building of the former BATHS, 1867–76 by *Lockwood & Mawson*, now housing, Gothic like the Mechanics' Institute (*see* Keighley College, above); and opposite behind the Temperance Hall the former BAPTIST CHAPEL, 1865, in a mongrel round-arched style. Meanwhile on the E side North Street opens out first into BOW STREET and then into Town Hall Square. On the s side of the former, behind the bus station, the utilitarian AIREDALE SHOPPING CENTRE, product of a central area redevelopment plan, 1968 by *J. Seymour Harris & Partners*, refurbished 1986 by the same architects, with glazed roofs over the walks. TOWN HALL SQUARE, at the junction with Cavendish Street, was laid out after the Town Hall was built, leaving the plain back of the building exposed to view. In the middle the WAR MEMORIAL, 1924, a truncated obelisk with bronze figures – 'Peace Victory' on top, servicemen to each side – by *H. C. Fehr*. Further N again

beyond Keighley College, the PICTURE HOUSE, 1913, white
faience with pedimental gable. Then Skipton Road, with villas
and residential terraces.

Other items worth singling out are more scattered. In EAST
PARADE, the E continuation of Low Street, the ROYAL
ARCADE and CROWN BUILDINGS, 1899. Three-storey front,
cheerfully impure Italianate, and plain glass-roofed arcade
within. In SOUTH STREET, s from the High Street, first
MANTRA HOUSE, built as an engineering works, 1931, in a
massive simplified-classical style. Eight bays, two storeys, with
hugely squat giant pilasters, broad segment-headed windows
between them, and a deep parapet rising in the middle into a
wide primitive pediment. ¼ m. further, diagonally opposite
Knowle Mill (see Textile Mills, below) but unconnected with
it, KNOWLE HOUSE, early C19 ashlar villa for John Greenwood, cotton and worsted spinner, with a semicircular bow
towards the road. To the SW, ¼ m. along OAKWORTH ROAD
past high-rise blocks of council flats of 1959–60, the former
WORKHOUSE, 1858, now housing, simplest gabled Gothic. NE
of the centre, off HARD INGS ROAD in Victoria Park, EAST-
WOOD HOUSE, 1819 for worsted spinner William Sugden. The
town's museum from 1899 to 1959, now the embarrassed
appendage of a leisure centre. Five-bay pedimented centre with
Doric columned porch, but the single flanking bays have a different, Soanian, character, with panelled pilaster strips, chunky
antefixae on the blocking course and big tripartite windows.
And uphill to the NW of North Street, at the beginning of
WOODVILLE ROAD in the town's best residential area,
LAUREL MOUNT, 1885 by W.H. & A. Sugden of Keighley for
Ira Ickringill, another worsted spinner. Carefully detailed
Queen Anne, not large but complete with garden terrace and
loggia. The select residential zone then continues further NW
into Utley (see Outer Keighley NW).

TEXTILE MILLS

AIREWORTH MILLS, Aireworth Road (NE). An early example,
founded 1787 for cotton spinning, rebuilt 1808 and converted
to worsted spinning 1813. Power-loom weaving introduced
1835, and steam power added either at the same time or shortly
afterwards. Long plain three-storey range, largely gutted, with
wheel chamber at the E end, fronted by a segment-headed
entry. Engine and boiler houses of c. 1850 to the w, with truncated octagonal chimney beyond and late C19 replacement
engine house in brick in front. At the back of the range a semicircular stair-turret of the mid C19, with crude battlements.
Later addition to E, mid- and late C19 warehouses and sheds
N and S. Large millpond to s subsequently built over.

BECKS MILL, Becks Road (SW). 1907 for Robert Clough & Co. of Grove Mills (*see* Outer Keighley S) to provide extra capacity for worsted spinning, and probably the first electric-powered textile mill in Yorkshire. Six-storey block with staircase tower on the E side. Fireproof construction with hollow brick floors on steel beams and cast-iron columns. Sawtooth roof with iron trusses.

DALTON MILLS, Dalton Lane (E). Keighley's grandest, *c.* 1866–77 by *W. Sugden* of Leek for J. & J. Craven, in approximately Italianate style with round- and segment-headed windows, numerous steeply pyramid-roofed turrets and a unique ornate chimney. Worsted, mainly spinning, with three separate multistorey mills and their appendages which were occupied partly by tenants. The earliest, in operation by 1870, is Tower Mill near the NE corner of the site, five storeys and nine by seven bays. Attached shed to E with north-light sawtooth roof, apparently also used for spinning; and at its S end the engine house, with big round-headed windows, and boiler house. Beyond them is the chimney, encased in a square tower which originally terminated in a steep pavilion roof crowned by a viewing platform, above which the chimney itself, with an openwork top, rose a little higher; but the tower was subsequently continued up to the full height. The other two mills are long parallel three-storey ranges, running E–W and linked at the W end by another range, perhaps a warehouse: Genappe Mill to the N, thirty-eight bays, begun 1868, and New Mill to the S, thirty-three bays, begun 1869. Both were powered by a second steam engine, said to have been the largest in the world at the time, in an engine house, larger and grander than the first, attached to the NE corner of New Mill. Its boiler house, between it and the chimney, has been demolished. Between Genappe Mill and Tower Mill, its archway facing the new engine house, is the ornate entrance-cum-office building dated 1872, with knobbly rustication and fancy bell-turret. (The mills are all of non-fireproof construction, with timber floors on cast-iron columns, the columns on the top floor of New Mill in pairs linked by elaborate pierced iron panels.)

GROVE MILLS, Ingrow. *See* Outer Keighley S.

KNOWLE MILL, South Street. Early C20 worsted spinning mill by *J. B. Bailey & Son* in the form of a single long four-storey range which was built in two stages, the l. seventeen bays in 1906–8, the r. nineteen in 1926. Rope race for power transmission between the two parts; engine house, boiler house and slightly truncated square brick chimney at the back. Plain elevations, timber beams on cast-iron columns.

LOW MILL, Gresley Road (E). Not much to see. The original mill of 1780, a four-storey range of sixteen bays with an external water wheel at the S end, has been demolished; and all that remains of the early buildings is a plainer ten-bay extension of it to the S of *c.* 1800 incorporating a wheel chamber, originally of two storeys, later raised to three. The mill had machinery made under the direction of Richard

Arkwright and a Newcomen-type steam engine for pumping water from the tailrace back into the dam. Converted to worsted spinning mid C19.

TURKEY MILL, Goose Eye. *See* Outer Keighley W.

OUTER KEIGHLEY

1. North-east: Riddlesden

ST MARY, Banks Lane. 1847–8. Lancet style, small, with short chancel.

EAST RIDDLESDEN HALL (National Trust). A sudden oasis off the Bradford Road, the house and its attendant buildings grouped round a pond. This is one of the best-known of C17 Pennine houses, mainly built *c.* 1648 by James Murgatroyd, a clothier of Warley near Halifax (West Riding South), who had bought the property in 1638; but its plan is a curious one, of complex evolution, in which the functions of some of the rooms are not quite clear. All that can be deduced regarding its predecessor is that its service end was to the NW. The principal part of the present building is to the SE: a rectangular block, slightly deeper than it is wide, with two-storey porches linked by a through passage along its NW flank. The elevations to NE and SW are virtual mirror images. The porches have battlements and crocketed pinnacles, round-headed doorways framed by entablature and fluted columns, and to the first floor a wheel window of eight lights, with straight spokes and cusped heads towards the circumference. That links the house to a group in Murgatroyd's home locality, e.g. Barkisland Hall (1638), Wood Lane Hall, Sowerby (1649), and Kershaw House, Luddenden (1650), the last also built by him. Next to the porch on both floors a mullion-and-transom window of twelve lights, divided into four sets of three, and then one of three-plus-three lights to each floor. Two gables, the first with a stepped window of three-plus-three lights below, two-plus-two above, the second with an ordinary transomed window of three lights. Plinth with scrolly decoration. On the NE side the second tier of windows has some of the lights blocked, and probably did so from the outset as an earlier outbuilding stands close to the front of the house at this point (*see* below). The SE flank of the block has three gables, again with three-light transomed windows, and three-plus-three-light windows below.

Inside, the biggest room, with a big segment-headed fireplace in the spine wall, is next to the passage on the NE side of the block. It seems to be the room described as a 'kichen' in an inventory of 1662, but that must be an error and it is more likely to have been a hall or housebody: all the other rooms in the block are reached through it and the furniture listed, including chairs with cushions, does not suggest a

38

p. 360

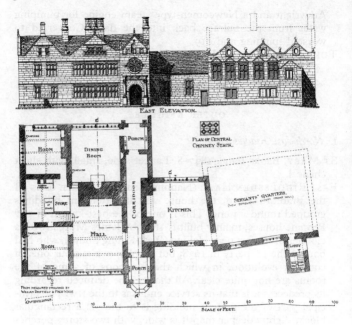

Keighley, East Riddlesden Hall.
Plan and north-east elevation, 1913

service use. The room behind it, facing SW – presumably the
'Dineing Parlour' – and the room beyond it to the SE – probably Murgatroyd's 'owne Parlour' – both have decorative
plaster ceilings with thin ribs forming geometrical patterns,
little pendants at some of the intersections and further enrichment in the panels, the rib-pattern in the latter's derived from
a design in Serlio.* Also panelling, and in the dining parlour a
stone fireplace with pendant semicircles on the lintel and
carved timber overmantel (with date of 1648). The position of
the original staircase is not known but it was probably more
or less that of its C18 replacement – with slender turned balusters – behind the E parlour. Of the first-floor rooms, that over
the dining parlour has a similar fireplace and overmantel, and
panelling, and even the little room over the NE porch is similarly equipped. Fireplaces also in some of the attic rooms.

NW of this block is a much smaller element, evidently of
similar date, which probably replaces the hall of the previous
house. It is of one storey only – just a single room – with two
cross-windows on the NE side, presumably an alteration, and
a transom window of three-times-three lights to the SW; but
the interior arrangements show that it was not completed.

* Dr Claire Gapper's observation.

Backing against the through passage of the SE block is another
big arched fireplace, framed by crude columns and entablature; but above it is a second, smaller one. So an upper storey
was intended but not built; and no ceiling was provided, the
space instead being left open to the roof. In any case the function of the room in the new house seems to have been uncertain – it is apparently that described in the 1662 inventory as
the 'hall body', but it was only sparsely furnished. In the room
now is a staircase, with elaborate newel posts and square
tapered balusters, from Guilsborough Grammar School,
Northamptonshire (1668), installed by the National Trust in
1973. NW again is a wing built in 1692 by Murgatroyd's grandson Edmund Starkie (date and initials formerly over the
entrance), of which only the front wall and front porch remain.
It must have replaced the service end of the old house, as the
inventory lists, *inter alia*, the 'old kichen' and 'old buttery'
apparently in this position. The details are characteristic of the
end of the C17 in the area: three uniform gables with ball finials
and upright oval windows in oblong panels, tall closely set first-
floor cross-windows under steep triangular pediments, but
mullioned windows to the subsidiary floor below. Presumably
the upper floor consisted of guest lodgings with independent
access through the porch, and the ground floor of service
accommodation; but as the latter was probably too low for a
kitchen a possibility would be that the rebuilt 'hall' was down-
graded to serve that function.

The OUTBUILDING range, at an acute angle to the NE front, is
dated 1642. It has four small doorways with simply ornamented lintels, widely set small two-light windows to the upper
floor, and a crenellated parapet with masks and the motto VIVE
LE ROY. Fireplace with flattened-ogee head, fragments of decorative plaster frieze. N of it a fine C17 aisled BARN, 120 by 40
ft (40 by 13 metres), with two round-arched gabled cart
entrances to each side, and trefoil-headed mistal doorways.
Eight bays, with the arcade posts on high padstones. Sturdy
kingpost roof trusses with curved braces to the ridge. At right
angles is a second barn, also aisled but more plainly detailed.
In a garden wall behind the Starkie wing, a series of NICHES
with elaborately shaped heads, which have been variously
interpreted as bee boles or falcons' mews.

WEST RIDDLESDEN HALL, Scott Lane. The earliest part
appears to be the short back wing, which is dated 1687 inside.
four-plus-four-light ground-floor window, C19 Pennine-style
porch with wheel window. The main range, butting against this
at right angles, appears to be just slightly later, with a handsome S front which can be compared with the 1692 work at
East Riddlesden Hall. Here again there are three uniform
gables with upright oval windows in rectangular panels, and
ball finials. Central doorway with broad torus-moulded surround and a cross-window over it. But the rest of the windows,
although symmetrically arranged, are still mullioned and transomed, of four-plus-four lights, and unrelated to the gables.

At the back very long mullioned windows, C18–C19 extensions of earlier ones, which suggest use as a weaving shop.

Nos. 7–13 BANKS LANE. Small double pile of the type with a regular five-bay front, former cross-windows, and central doorway, dated 1700. The doorway has an architrave surround: two blocked upright oval windows in the w gable end. The AIREDALE HEIFER, further E in Bradford Road, is another example, much altered internally.

2. East: Marley

MARLEY HALL. Isolated on a little knoll overlooking the railway. Built 1627 for John Savile and formerly larger than it is now, with a double-gabled block at the w end. What remains is the hall range, of one storey and attic, and a cross-wing to the E. Transomed hall window of six lights, gable with a two-light window above, single-storey porch. (The hall has a decorative plaster ceiling and a segment-headed fireplace.) In front of the porch an archway crowned by a gable containing the Savile arms. Garden wall with moulded coping l. and r.

3. South: Ingrow

ST JOHN. *See* Places of Worship, above.

WESLEY PLACE SUNDAY SCHOOL, Halifax Road. 1862, rather brutally converted to housing 1988. Restrained Italianate, with two pedimental gables. The chapel, rebuilt 1867–8, was demolished in 1954. Next to it a thirteen-storey block of council flats, 1964.

RAILWAY STATION. On the Keighley & Worth Valley line. An enthusiasts' re-creation, the little Italianate station building formerly at Foulridge, Lancashire, re-erected 1988–9. Station gates from Keighley Goods Yard.

Of GROVE MILLS, beside the River Worth, the integrated worsted mill built 1864–77 by Robert Clough & Co., only the stump of one five-storey range remains;* but between it and Halifax Road are four streets of workers' HOUSING built by the firm, *c.* 1890 by *David Weatherhead* of Keighley. The terraces are 'through-by-lights', an improved version of back-to-backs. Broad pedimental gables across the terrace ends. Further up the hillside to the E, two unremarkable Clough family houses, WOODWORTH, *c.* 1865, plain Italianate, and in woods along Hainworth Wood Road RED HOLT, 1889 by *Mawson & Hudson* of Bradford, modest Old English.

---

*The original cotton-spinning mill had been founded in 1797 and a new steam-powered worsted mill built in 1836.

4. West: Braithwaite, Laycock and Goose Eye

ST MATTHEW, Braithwaite, now SWEDENBORGIAN. 1854. Modest lancet style, quasi-cruciform, the transepts just gabled projections.

Some C17 houses at Braithwaite and Laycock: dates of 1648, 1666 etc. At Goose Eye, a tiny industrial hamlet down in the narrow valley beyond Laycock, TURKEY MILL, a water-powered cotton mill founded 1797, enlarged and converted to paper making in the early C19, and steam power added. Partly demolished, the remainder now housing. Main range apparently of 1822 and later, three storeys. A shorter one at right angles, with a round-headed wheel arch, is presumably part of the original building. Stump of octagonal chimney.

5. North-west: Utley

MANOR FARMHOUSE, off Greenhead Lane. 1677. Double pile p. 29 with through passage. Housebody fireplace at the end opposite the passage, parlours to l. and r. Mullioned windows. The most favoured C19 residential area, with views over Airedale, was further up the hillside, e.g. HAWKSTONE, Shann Lane, 1865 for textile manufacturer B. F. Marriner. Gothic, of modest size but with a prominent tower.

WHINBURN LODGE, Hollins Lane. The best of Keighley's industrialists' houses, in Arts and Crafts Old English style, built in two stages for textile machinery maker Sir Prince Smith. Excellent quality craftsmanship throughout. The original house is of 1897 by *James Ledingham*, quite compact, of three storeys with gables. It was extended in 1912–13 by *Simpson & Ayrton* of London, with a massive tower at one end and a baronial hall running out at right angles to the front, with a tall canted bay at its end and a canted porch in the corner. Big inglenook, gallery, and arched-brace roof inside the hall; heavy dog-leg staircase with massive square newels and turned balusters; plaster ceilings in other rooms evidently made from casts of C17 originals. Elaborate garden of 1912–13, possibly by *Thomas Mawson*, with terraces, pergola and water features, neglected at the time of writing.

See also East Morton, Oakworth.

KELBROOK

9040

ST MARY. 1838–9. A daughter church of Thornton-in-Craven, the gift of Miss Frances Currer of Eshton Hall. Lancet-style box with narrow w tower. Chancel, transepts and porch added later C19. – W GALLERY on thin cast-iron supports.

MIDDLE HAGUE FARMHOUSE, ½ m. SSW. Small rectangular block with two-storey porch dated 1678 attached to the E gable-end. Simply ornamented doorhead.

KETTLEWELL

Dales village running down both banks of the Cam Gill Beck to its confluence with the Wharfe.

ST MARY. W tower remaining from the church of 1820 by *Thomas Anderton* of Gargrave, which replaced the medieval one. Round-headed and pointed windows, with Gothick glazing bars, pointed bell-openings. The body of the church rebuilt again 1883–5 by *T. H. & F. Healey* in mechanical Perp style. – FONT. C13, circular with small corner ornaments, two of them in stiff-leaf. – MONUMENT. William Briscoe †1851 by *E. Pearce* of London. Still Neoclassical, a bas-relief sarcophagus surmounted by a shrouded urn.

Overlooking the churchyard the MANOR HOUSE, mid-C18. Five-bay front with panel flanked by scrolls over the doorway. Round-headed staircase window to rear.

FOLD FARM, E of the church. What appears to be a C17 stone farmhouse much altered in the C19 conceals an elaborate arched-brace roof to a former open hall, probably of the early C16, together with the principal posts of the timber-framed walls. Three trusses (two bays) remain, rising from enriched corbels on the posts: short kingposts on the collars, longitudinal braces to the ridge decorated with flowers, cusped wind-braces from the trusses to the purlins (cf. Horbury Hall, West Riding South). C17 newel staircase in a stair-turret at the rear.

OLD HALL, opposite across the beck. C17 house of hearth-passage plan. Five-light mullion-and-transom window to the parlour, the same and a fire-window to the housebody.

Some more C17 houses at STARBOTTON, 2 m. NNW, including HILLTOP HOUSE, with a rear kitchen block, perhaps originally detached, of 1670. Altered front.

SCARGILL HOUSE, ⅞ m. S. Plain 1920s Neo-Georgian incorporating an earlier farmhouse, converted to a Christian holiday and conference centre 1959. Additions made by *G. G. Pace & R. G. Sims* from 1961. First and most ambitious the CHAPEL dominating the complex, a simple rectangle with tall steeply pitched roof, glazed gable-ends and low side walls of limestone rubble. Impressive plain timber roof trusses. Altar to one side. Others are the CONFERENCE LOUNGE, polygonal with a central clerestory, and a series of pavilion-like RESIDENTIAL BLOCKS round small courtyards.

TOR DYKE, 2 m. NNE, across the head of Scale Park. Well-preserved ditch and rampart, c. 1¼ m. long, guarding access from Upper Wharfedale into Coverdale (North Riding). Date uncertain, either Iron Age or Dark Age.

KILDWICK

On the steep N flank of Airedale, overlooking a sprawl of modern commercial development on the valley bottom. The village is

joined Siamese-twin-wise to Farnhill (q.v.), to the w, with the
church, towards the bottom of the slope, and Kildwick Hall, at
the top, in one parish, and most of the village street, at an intermediate level, in the other. It is also divided on the other axis by
the Leeds and Liverpool Canal, the street passing under this
obliquely, through a tunnel. A grange of Bolton Priory in the
Middle Ages.

St Andrew. The so-called 'lang kirk' of Craven at 145 ft (48
    metres) is one of the longest in the West Riding. Perp w tower,
    of gritstone blocks, broad and crenellated with a stair-turret at
    the se corner. Nave of six bays and chancel of four, without
    structural division between them; aisles and chancel chapels.
    The nave falls into two parts, the first four bays Dec and the
    other two Perp; and it appears that the latter represent the area
    of a former chancel, the present chancel being added in a
    second Perp phase. A further peculiarity, doubtless due to the
    sloping site, is that the cross-section of the church is asym-
    metrical, with a low clerestory on the s side only. To the n the
    aisle roof is at a higher level, continuous with that of the nave.
    The Dec bays of the nave arcades, with quatrefoil piers and
    double-chamfered arches, are probably no later than c. 1300
    (cf. Skipton);* but the aisle windows alongside, with reticu-
    lated tracery, are some decades later (also cf. Skipton). Those
    on the n side are straight-headed but to the s the heads are
    truncated – the windows here presumably reused after a
    widening of the aisle which brought the eaves down to a lower
    level. The Perp arcade piers are octagonal, the windows,
    including the clerestory, mainly straight-headed apart from
    that at the e end, of seven lancet lights under a three-centred
    arch (cf. Gisburn, Bolton-by-Bowland). Kingpost roof, with
    arched-brace subsidiary trusses in the nave and ornamented
    wind-braces between the rafters and purlins. w window and
    doorway renewed c. 1868, s porch 1873. Restoration 1901–3 by
    Austin & Paley.
    SCREENS, flanking the chancel and at the w end of the s
    chapel. Perp, simple, that on the n side heavily restored. C17
    dates on dados refer to seating in the chancel. – PEWS. Eltoft
    family pew in the n chapel, inscribed 1633 EE, with enriched
    panels and balustraded superstructure. Other simple reused
    pieces in the n chapel and chancel, dated 1624, 1716 etc. –
    Brass eagle LECTERN, 1875 by *Hardman.* – FONT. Octagonal,
    Perp, with Instruments of the Passion. Base and cover 1868. –
    SCULPTURE. Fragments of Anglo-Saxon crosses. One cross-
    head and five different shafts are represented. Two of the shafts
    have figures, the other three close interlace. Nothing seems
    earlier than C10. – COPE. Made of material from a Chinese
    Imperial garment, removed from the Imperial Palace at Beijing
    in 1947. – ROYAL ARMS, painted. Signed and dated *G. Fether,*
    1727. – STAINED GLASS. Includes n aisle third from w, 1873

---

*The sw pier has as its base an inverted Norman capital from the previous
building.

by *O'Connor & Taylor*, with startling blue sky; and s aisle fourth
from w by *Powell Bros.* of Leeds, *c.* 1884. – MONUMENTS. Sir
Robert de Styveton (or Steeton) †1307. Large early C14 effigy
of a cross-legged knight, on a tomb-chest of 1854. – Henry
Currer †1723. Pedimented tablet flanked by putti. – Henry
Currer †1756. Large, with sarcophagus surmounted by a putto
holding a medallion, in front of a crowning obelisk. – Various
tablets including Thomas Garforth †1811 and Caroline Wray
†1817, both by *C. Fisher* of York.

At the s and w entrances to the churchyard rusticated
GATEPIERS, probably early C19, with wrought-iron gates and
overthrows. Within it, a HEARSE SHED, *c.* 1825.

BRIDGE, over the Aire. Built 1305–13 at the cost of the Bolton
Priory Canons. Four arches, two segmental and two pointed,
with chamfered longitudinal ribs to the undersides. Triangular
cutwaters. Widened on the e side 1780.

KILDWICK HALL. A memorable group, of house and ancilliary
buildings. The main part of the former is probably of the 1650s:
see the arms of Currer and Haworth over the entrance – i.e.
Hugh Currer (inherited 1653) and his wife Ann Haworth
(†1656) – and a rainwater head dated 1663 reused on the Justice
Room (*see* below). Three storeys, the top one partly in the roof.
Compact half-H plan, with full-height porch against the r.
cross-wing. Gables to the wings, porch and the front
of the hall range. Mullion-and-transom windows to the ground
and first floors, three-light mullioned windows with truncated-
ogee heads (cf. Friars Head, Winterburn) to the top storey of
the hall range and porch. On the w flank staggered two-light
windows lighting the staircase. At the back a two-storey kitchen
block dated 1673 inside, originally detached but now linked to
the main building by a range running along the back of the
latter, the w part of which is probably of the early C18, the e
part 1858. The hall is entered directly from the porch and has
its fireplace – moulded and segment-headed – at the opposite
end. Moulded ceiling beams and panelling, some *ex situ*. The
staircase is beyond, in the rear part of the w wing, of stone with
C17 plasterwork to the landing ceilings. One first-floor room in
the e wing has C17 panelling, inlaid overmantel with blind
arcading, and decorative plasterwork to the frieze and ceiling
beam soffit. C17 stone fireplaces in some other upper rooms.

In front of the house is a garden wall crowned by urns, and
remarkably grand early C18 GATEPIERS, rusticated and fronted
by pilasters, and crowned by half-pediments which in turn are
surmounted by lions. A further set of gatepiers opposite across
the road, to the lower garden. At the w end of the wall, at right
angles to the house, is the so-called JUSTICE ROOM, a smart
design of *c.* 1700 so presumably built for Henry Currer (†1723)
who was an active Justice of the Peace; but there is no firm evidence of its having been used for this purpose. Two storeys –
the lower was a coachhouse – and two by three bays. Tall cross-
windows, pedimented ends, rusticated quoins to the first floor,
angle pilasters below. The original entrance was at the N end
– the external steps up to the first floor on the garden side were

probably added in C19. At the far E end of the wall a small C17
GARDEN PAVILION. Square, with a gable to each side. Hoodmould stops similar to those on the kitchen block of the house.
Coved ceiling with enriched frieze. W of the house a BARN, now
housing, dated 1671.

GRANGE HALL, ½ m. E of Kildwick Hall. C17 house in part possibly of 1614–20. L-shaped, with a kitchen wing behind the hall
and a staircase compartment in the angle. At the front a one-
storey porch crowned by a stone balustrade, and two gables,
one with a stepped three-light attic window and the other
incongruously surmounted by a later chimney. In one of the
first-floor rooms a segmentally coved ceiling with geometrical
patterns of moulded ribs (cf. Hawksworth Hall) and vine-scroll
decoration to one of the tympana. C17 panelling and two overmantels to the ground floor, staircase with vertically
symmetrical balusters.

At the top of PRIEST BANK, between the two halls, a C17 house
extensively restored 1899. The front gable with a three-light
window under a truncated-ogee hoodmould similar to those at
Kildwick Hall probably belongs to the restoration phase.

KILLINGHALL

Suburban village close to Harrogate.

ST THOMAS. Daughter church of Ripley, 1879–80 by *W. Swinden
Barber* of Halifax. Ordinary Dec, not small, with aisles and
clerestory. – STAINED GLASS. Two windows in the N aisle and
one in the S by *Kempe & Co.*, 1918 and 1926. Two in the S aisle
by *Powell Bros.* of Leeds, *c.* 1891.

BRIDGE, over the Nidd. Probably *c.* 1600, doubled in width probably C18. Two arches, the old parts longitudinally ribbed.

KENNEL HALL. C17, altered. Deep rectangular gritstone block
but not a true double pile. The l. half contains the former
housebody (the position of the front door has been changed)
with a cellar behind it, but the r. half on the ground floor seems
originally to have been a single big room the full depth of the
house. C19 M-section roof reusing earlier timbers.

HOLLINS HALL FARM, 1 m. WSW. Lobby-entry farmhouse with
mullioned windows and off-centre two-storey porch, dated as
late as 1732. A second doorway, matching that in the porch, to
the l. of it. Heightened and re-roofed C19.

KILNSEY
Conistone with Kilnsey

KILNSEY OLD HALL. 1648 for Christopher Wade (date and
initials on the doorway lintel), probably on the site of a grange

of Fountains Abbey. Used as a farm building from *c.* 1800, restored to domestic use 1999–2001. A tall compact L-shape, its planning related to the steeply sloping site. The principal rooms – the hall and a parlour – are on the first floor, but the entrance, at the r. end of the (NE) front, and the cross-passage behind it, are a half-storey lower, at what at that point is ground level, and the ground floor of the rear wing, behind the cross-passage, is also at this level. Above the entrance is another, re-set, doorway, reached by external steps of the agricultural phase, and to the l. is a cart entrance of *c.* 1800. Hall window of three-plus-three lights, smaller mullioned windows to the second floor. The smartest elevation is the SE gable-end, looking out over the valley. Parlour window again of three-plus-three lights, four-light window to the chamber above, and carved finials to the kneelers of the gable. Inside, most remarkably, given the building's history, the hall and the parlour both retain substantial fragments of decorative plaster friezes. C17 fireplaces in several rooms, including two in the rear wing. One question that remains is, where was the kitchen? The obvious answer would be on the ground floor, below the hall or the parlour, but there is no sign of a fireplace there. The alternative would be a detached kitchen to the rear (cf. Kildwick Hall), since lost.

E of the house, the remains of an elaborate detached GATE-HOUSE, probably later C17 (see the fragment of an upright oval window). What survives is a small rectangular building with a mullioned window of three round-headed lights (cf. The Folly, Settle, *c.* 1675): the stringcourse above the window at its right-hand end continues into the springing of what would have been the arch over the gate.

CHAPEL HOUSE, ¾ m. s. Front block of 1783 for John Tennant. Three-by-three bays with tripartite windows and pedimented doorcase, staircase with turned balusters. Earlier parts probably C17, C20 additions at the rear. On limestone terraces ¾ m. s again, a Romano-British SETTLEMENT site, with hut circles and complex field system.

KIPPAX

Large mainly C20 village in former mining country, crowning an escarpment N of the River Aire. In the C12 apparently the *caput* of part of the fee of the Lacy family, with a ringwork castle.

ST MARY. Within the area of the former castle bailey. Substantial Norman church of *c.* 1100, characterized by extensive use of herringbone masonry. W tower, spacious aisleless nave, and chancel: on the nave N side three original windows, high up, and traces of a doorway. Priest's doorway (chancel s) probably late C12, round-headed without but pointed within; to the r. a C13 window of two lancets; E window and the present N

and s doorways *c.* 1300, the former of four lights with intersecting tracery. Other medieval windows on the s side with
plain mullions, presumably post-Reformation, instead of
proper tracery; and two in Geometrical style evidently from
the restoration of 1875–6 by *H. R. Gough*. Tower belfry stage
Perp (bequest for the tower fabric 1430), restored 1893 by
G. Fowler Jones & Son. Wide Perp chancel arch on corbels, nave
roof rebuilt 1950 reusing some C15 timbers, chancel roof
1875–6. – Remarkable C13 PISCINA in the chancel SE corner,
of two arches at right angles, meeting on a short shaft. Two
bowls in the w-facing arch, one in the N-facing. – FONT. Dated
1663. Octagonal, chalice-shaped, with names of the churchwardens and friezes of small raised semicircles. Contemporary
COVER with carved panels and fretwork crown. – SCULPTURE.
Two fragments of an Anglo-Saxon cross-shaft. On the front a
standing figure, the hands outstretched above two objects with
spear-shaped heads. Two beasts in the panel below, stylized
scroll above. C10. – STAINED GLASS includes E window and
chancel SE by *Heaton, Butler & Bayne*, 1886 and 1890; nave s
third from E by *Hardman*, 1884. – MONUMENTS. Four near-
identical pedimented wall tablets to members of the Bland
family of Kippax Park, two erected in 1735 by Sir John Bland
to his ancestors Sir Thomas †1657 and Sir Francis †1663; Sir
John †1742 (erected 1756); and Sir Hungerford †1756. –
William Medhurst †1747. Tablet with broken pediment, an urn
in the breach.

CASTLE. The earthen ringwork is preserved, NW of the church.
Internal diameter of *c.* 80 ft (25 metres). The short length of
masonry walling is post-medieval.

ROYAL OAK INN, formerly Kippax House. Near the central road
junction. Mid-C18 box, the N (street) front of six bays, the s of
five. Quoins, hipped roof. Interior much altered but retaining
a little Rococo ceiling decoration.

KIPPAX PARK, s of the village, remodelled and extended in
Gothick style *c.* 1750 by *Daniel Garrett*, was demolished in the
mid 1950s. Two mementos are the C18 rusticated gatepiers in
the High Street, and a pretty Gothic lodge with canted outer
bays, probably early C19, 1¼ m. SSE on the Castleford road.

KIRKBY MALHAM 8060

ST MICHAEL. Handsome Pennine church, Perp throughout,
sensitively restored 1879–80 by *Paley & Austin* largely at the
cost of Walter Morrison of Malham Tarn House (*see* Malham
Moor). Squared gritstone. W tower with three-light bell-
openings and rather low battlements, escutcheons of four local
families on the SW buttress and that of Fountains Abbey on
the SE, and on the s flank the letters, apparently, EMR – for
'Erexit Maria Regina'? (i.e. 'Mary Queen [of Heaven] built it').

Nave and chancel without structural division, aisles embracing the tower and similarly continuous with the chancel chapels. Crenellated parapet to the first two-and-a-half bays of the nave, the rest plain (cf. Skipton), straight-headed windows with arched lights to aisles and clerestory, E window renewed in the restoration. Squat battlemented porch with ribbed tunnel-vault. Arcades of six bays with octagonal piers and double-chamfered arches. Some headstops to the hoodmoulds. Niches for images on the W faces of the three W piers on each side and a seventh on the S face of the SW pier (cf. Bracewell, Broughton), all rather crudely executed. Low-pitched roof with tie-beams and very short kingposts.

PANELLING in the sanctuary (Walter Morrison Memorial). 1923 by *Guy Dawber*. – COMMUNION RAIL. C17, with vertically symmetrical balusters. – SCREENS, to the S chapel and tower arches. 1883. Jacobean-style. – BOX PEWS. An extensive series. The best, with balustraded superstructures, in the N chapel, one inscribed James Ward 1631. The remainder cut down and otherwise altered in the C19 restoration but retaining handsome ramped-up backs at the W ends of each block. In the N aisle dates from 1677 to 1724 and initials of occupants. – FONT. Probably C12, primitive, cylindrical, on a C19 base. – STAINED GLASS. S aisle W, sanctuary N and S, small panels, C16 German, the last dated 1589. – W window 1880 by *Hardman*. N aisle, four by *A. K. Nicholson*, c. 1920. – MONUMENT. John Lambert of Calton †1701, 'son and heir of Major-General John Lambert . . . being the last heir male in whom that ancient family of ye Lamberts in a line from William the Conqueror (and related to him by marriage) is now extinct.' Baroque cartouche. – HEARSE SHED, in the churchyard, against the N chapel. 1847.

VICARAGE. Immediately W of the church, but the Vicarage only since the C19. Dated 1622, much restored and enlarged 1866. Three storeys in elevation (although internally the upper two have been thrown into one) with a three-storey porch. Stepped three-light window in the porch gable, mullion-and-transom windows to the hall and parlour, of six and five lights respectively.

SCHOOL, ½ m. NNE. 1872–4, also at the cost of Walter Morrison, who is said to have designed the 'general plan and architecture'. Long Westmorland slate roof, mullion-and-transom windows.

HANLITH HALL, ½ m. E. Largely rebuilt, in Pennine Revival style, 1892 and 1912. Previously of early C19 appearance, with a C17 doorway.

KIRKBY MALZEARD

ST ANDREW. Heavily restored 1878–80 by *A. W. Blomfield* and again, after a fire in 1908, by *J. Oldrid Scott*. Perp W tower with decorative frieze round the plinth, three-light w window and bell-openings, diagonal buttresses, crenellated parapet. Perp also the s porch with sharply pointed double-chamfered entrance, and the two-storey NE vestry with one-light straight-headed windows and rectangular stair-turret. So, largely, was the chancel, with big Tudor-arched windows, and a matching phase of refenestration elsewhere; but the Perp-style tracery is all *Blomfield*'s. The remainder is in principle earlier. Of the Norman church there remain the masonry of the nave s wall, the s jamb of the chancel arch, with a single (renewed) shaft and plain cushion cap, and the quite sumptuous s doorway. Two orders of shafts with scalloped capitals, arch of three orders with zigzag and billet decoration. Of the C13 are the N aisle and chapel,* with an arcade continuous to nave and chancel – the chancel arch rising from one of the piers – originally of eight bays but with the w arch blocked when the tower was built, encroaching on the w end of the nave. Cylindrical piers, renewed 1908, with capitals of *Scott*'s own design, and double-chamfered arches. One lancet window at the w end of the aisle, and two taller ones, now blocked by the vestry, at the E end of the chapel. Also C13 the re-set piscina in the chancel, but the much renewed sedilia next to it is Dec, with gablets and ogee arches. – CHARITY BOARDS, mid-C19. – STAINED GLASS. In the vestry, fragments from the C15, including parts of figures. – Nave SE by *Heaton, Butler & Bayne*, chancel s third from w, by *Ward & Hughes*, E window attributed to *Percy Bacon*, all after 1908. – BRASS. William and Francis (*sic*) Mann †1594 and 1604. Two small kneeling figures.

Stone-built village with a long main street – a market charter was granted to John de Mowbray in 1307 – but very little else to single out. At the E end, beyond MOWBRAY HOUSE, C18 with mid-C19 Italianate refronting, the just perceptible earthwork of the CASTLE, one of the C12 fortresses of Roger de Mowbray.

KIRKBY OVERBLOW

ALL SAINTS. Much repaired and rebuilt during the incumbency of the Rev. Dr Charles Cooper, 1774–1804, some of the details recorded on a board inside the church. The w tower, apparently Perp, is said to have been 'rebuilt' in 1781, but 'restored' would probably be a better word. The parapet, with battlements, is recognizable as being of this period, but the w and s windows evidently received further attention in 1910. The nave and its appurtenances appear to have been largely rebuilt in a 'repair' of 1778–80, apart from the N wall, with a plain Norman N doorway, blocked and truncated, and the walls of the early

---

*The aisle N wall rebuilt by *Blomfield*.

CI4 N transept, with trefoil-headed W window and two-light Dec E window; but the S side was further 'raised and beautified' in 1802. S aisle of the same width and height as the nave itself, with twinned pointed windows, battlements matching those on the tower, good Gothic buttresses and characteristic textured masonry. S porch also of 1802, with open pediment and pointed doorway. Lean-to roof to the transept balancing that on the aisle, and three-light transept N window with intersected tracery, presumably a restoration. Four-bay arcade with cylindrical piers, plain octagonal capitals and hollow-chamfered semicircular arches. Also some interventions of 1870–2 by *G. E. Street*, including the chancel arch and two Dec windows on the N side. Lower chancel 'restored and decorated' by Dr Cooper in 1799, again with the battlements and textured stonework, but the windows renewed in 1892 after a fire. – STAINED GLASS. N transept N by *Kempe*, 1893. E window 1910, in the manner of Kempe. – MONUMENTS. Dorothy Cooper (wife of the Rector) †1793. By *Coade* of Lambeth, that is with decorative elements of *Coade* stone. Above the inscription a small high-relief sarcophagus bearing a medallion of a mourning woman. – William Lister Fenton Scott †1842. By *Noble*, of London. With profile portrait.

Small stone-built village. E of the church RECTORY COTTAGE, early CI8, five bays, with heavy alternately raised quoins, similarly treated surrounds to the doorway and a panel above it, and a band between the storeys ramped up at the ends (cf. Leathley Hall etc.).

LOW HALL, ¼ m. NE. An attractive group, with some complications of nomenclature as a result of its history. The original house, now Old Low Hall, was a timber-framed structure probably of the CI6, cased in stone in the CI7, U-shaped and facing S; but only the W range remains. Its front, to the E, has five-light mullioned windows to both floors and a moulded four-centre-headed doorway. Two massive chimney-breasts at the back, much rebuilt. Of the timber frame there remain the principal horizontals and verticals of a four-bay structure up to the present eaves level, including a number of dragon beams, but nothing of the roof, perhaps suggesting that the CI6 house was a storey higher than the stone version. Also a very large segment-headed fireplace, some plain CI7 panelling, and on the first floor a little decorative plasterwork, much restored, in two of the window reveals.

The E range would have been approximately where the front garden wall, with gatepiers crowned by obelisks, is now. Beyond is a forecourt, with on the S side a much grander pair of gatepiers, tall and rusticated, of *c.* 1700; and on the E, facing the old hall, the former stable range also of that date, which is the present Low Hall. Two storeys, with hipped roof, eaves cornice, and cross-windows linked vertically by apron-like raised panels. C20 porch, and a former cart entrance converted into a three-light window. Inside is an elaborate heraldic overmantel brought from the old hall.

KIRKBY HOUSE, ¼ m. W, with the ground falling away steeply at the front. 1931 by *John C. Procter* of Leeds, in the Modern style of France and Germany (cf. Five Oaks and the White House, Ilkley). White-rendered walls of brick, flat roof, and long horizontal lines. Balanced asymmetry with some discreet curves.

ROUGEMONT CASTLE, 2½ m. SW, beside the River Wharfe. Earthworks of a D-shaped enclosure – a ringwork – and of a large outer bailey, also roughly D-shaped, to the N and W, all now in thick woodland. Probably C12, the predecessor of Harewood Castle on the other side of the river.

KIRK DEIGHTON

3050

A street of limestone cottages and houses, with the church on a small rise at its head.

ALL SAINTS. Handsome Perp W tower with diagonal buttresses, tall two-light belfry openings with ogee heads, W window, battlemented parapet and recessed spire. Nave clerestory also Perp, s aisle Dec, with straight-head windows, both these parts also battlemented. s porch with broad, moulded round arch (much renewed) and a stepped gable and a nice roof inside. But the N aisle was originally Norman (*see* below), widened probably *c.* 1300 – see the doorway and windows. Chancel heavily restored 1849 with an unorthodox E window. The C15(?) N vestry incorporates the re-set (and renewed) C14 E window of the N chapel. Inside the Norman N arcade remains, of three bays, with massive quatrefoil piers, simple capitals and round arches of two broad square orders. The Dec s arcade has octagonal piers and double-chamfered arches. Tower arch with continuous triple chamfer; the tower has a quadripartite vault with roll and fillet mouldings. Medieval roofs to the nave (panels and tie-beams) and s aisle. Chancel arch of 1849 with unscholarly Neo-Norman details (apparently derived from an architectural fragment inset above the E arch of the s arcade). Further restoration 1874 by *Perkin & Backhouse*. – Minton TILES of 1874 around the sanctuary. – STAINED GLASS. By *Ward & Hughes*, the tower window (1875), E window (1881) and s aisle E (1889). Chancel s, first from E, by *M., A. & W. H. O'Connor*, 1872; second from E, 1858 by *Barnett* of York, crisply coloured. – MONUMENTS. C12–C13 carved stones incised with crosses. – the Rev. Richard Burton †1656. Alabaster. Oval frame and frontal figure kneeling in prayer.

KIRK DEIGHTON HALL, by the E end of the church. The vicarage until the late C19. Five-bay early C18 front, given a third storey *c.* 1790, a Tuscan porch about twenty years later, and a library extension, r., *c.* 1870.

INGMANTHORPE HALL, Sandbeck Lane, 1 m. E. Now flats. Early C19, of beautiful honey-coloured ashlar. Three storeys (the upper storey perhaps later), five bays, with the middle three of the entrance front breaking forward and the centre bowed. Outsized Neo-Renaissance porte cochère, perhaps of 1880, the date of the large single-storey addition to the l. (for ballroom, smoking room and billiard room) with pilastered façade. Entrance hall with hooded Gothic fireplace; inner hall with big cantilevered stone staircase. Former STABLES to the rear extended in pastiche style for housing.

4050

KIRK HAMMERTON

5   ST JOHN. A whole Saxon church, of w tower, short nave and lower chancel, now forming the s third of a church otherwise of 1890–1 by *C. Hodgson Fowler*. The Saxon masonry is of large roughly squared gritstone blocks, the side-alternate quoins of cyclopean size. Dating is uncertain. The tower has much in common with the late Saxon 'Lincolnshire' type – tall slender proportions, and a belfry stage marked off by a stringcourse three-quarters of the way up, with round-headed twin openings on mid-wall shafts and throughstone imposts. Taylor & Taylor, however, date the rest of the building to an earlier phase, possibly as early as the C8, but it has since been suggested that the evidence for two separate phases is inconclusive. The tower also has a tall narrow w doorway with parabolic arch, and unmatching shafts and capitals presumably reused from elsewhere in the church. s doorway framed by a band of stripwork at the usual distance from the actual opening, partly renewed by *Fowler* in a generally restrained restoration carried out at the same time as the enlargement; and to the E of it the remains of a second doorway, blocked and cut into by a Dec window – two lights, straight-headed – its function unexplained. Remains of stripwork round its internal, rather than external, face perhaps suggest that it led into a *porticus* (cf. Ledsham, West Riding South), but there are no other signs of one. In the chancel s side one small blocked Saxon window, flanked by a tall round-headed Norman window to the l. and a much smaller E.E. lancet to the r. E window Perp. Tall plain tower arch, the imposts evidently cut back in the early C19. Blocked opening above. Chancel arch of two orders, with imposts simply of two blocks, one above the other, the upper projecting; the r. jamb cut back in 1834, the whole of the l. side renewed in 1891. Small E.E. piscina. A N aisle was added *c.* 1200, its arcade of two bays with cylindrical pier, octagonal capitals and double-chamfered arches: that remains, but the aisle itself made way for the nave of the new church, in conventional Dec style. Roofs to the old also 1891.

REREDOS in the old chancel. Made of Dutch carved panels of *c.* 1600, installed in 1891. – COMMUNION RAIL. C17, with chunky balusters. – ROYAL ARMS of George III, painted. –

Painted DECORATION. 1895–8 by *George Ostrehan*. Extensive scheme, of saints, emblems, foliage patterns, diaper-work etc. throughout both chancels and on the spandrels of the N arcade. – STAINED GLASS. E window by *Kempe*, 1894; old chancel SE and E, 1900 and 1906 by *C. E. Tute*.

KIRK HAMMERTON HALL, S of the church with its back to the road. Generously windowed three-bay front range of *c.* 1820, four-bay wing at right angles, facing E, of *c.* 1740. Further additions of 1880.

SKIP BRIDGE, 1m. E, over the Nidd. Early C19. Three arches, segmental cutwaters.

KNARESBOROUGH

3050

The town is picturesquely situated above the steep-sided defile where the River Nidd cuts through the Magnesian Limestone belt, a scene dominated in the Middle Ages by a royal castle and since the mid C19 by a castellated railway viaduct. The medieval settlement consisted of three parts: the borough centred on its market place at the gates of the castle, which was evidently established by the mid C12 (market first mentioned in 1206); the ecclesiastical Manor of Beechill downhill to the NW, centred on the parish church; and beyond that the hamlet of Bond End leading to the High Bridge over the river. From the C17 to the early C19 the town was an important centre for linen manufacture, but little other industry developed and expansion virtually came to a halt between the mid C19 and the mid C20 (population was 4,006 in 1821, 5,942 in 1931, 14,000 in 1991). There is some pleasant unpretentious Georgian townscape, variously of limestone, gritstone and brick; and behind the façades some remains of C16 and C17 timber framing. A local curiosity is a number of buildings painted in a black-and-white chequer pattern, a practice apparently started in the C19 to identify establishments offering facilities for tourists.

CHURCHES

ST JOHN. A large and rewarding church built of Magnesian limestone, set in a spacious tree-lined churchyard. Central tower embraced by the aisles but showing on its flanks the roof-line of former transepts, the fabric of which the aisle E bays in part incorporate. The lower stages of the tower are of *c.* 1200, with shallow clasping buttresses and a stair-turret at the NW corner. Belfry stage apparently C14, with two-light bell-openings, the pretty lead spike probably early C16. The nave and aisles are Perp, the latter a regular five bays with buttresses and plain parapet, and doorways in both W bays, the S preceded by a porch with attractive C18 ironwork in the head of the entrance arch. On the W front two worn niches flanking the W doorway; but the doorway itself belongs to the extensive restoration of 1871–2 by *Ewan Christian* – as do all the window tracery, the W gable, with another window, the steeply pitched nave roof behind it and the squat nave clerestory, the formation of which required the raising of the nave walls. Of the E parts, the N and E walls of the chancel are essentially Norman: see the blocked round-headed windows in the E wall, cut into by the present E window – of *c.* 1330–50, with (renewed) reticulated tracery* – and the fragments of a stringcourse with crude zigzag decoration. The visible part of the S wall evidently rebuilt by Christian. S chapel mid-C14, with another reticulated E window (but *see* below); N chapel late C13, with two windows of Geometrical tracery including quatrefoiled circles; NE vestry probably C16. Nave arcades of four bays with very tall octagonal piers and double-chamfered arches. Impressive also the crossing of *c.* 1200, with sharply pointed triple-chamfered arches on tripartite responds, the middle shaft keeled, and a much slenderer shaft with stylized leaf capital in each corner between the responds. The stair-turret has slit windows in the W side, now facing along the N aisle: so the pre-Perp nave was aisleless. The S chapel has more good-quality detail of the mid C14 – crocketed and ogee-headed tomb-recess, sedilia and piscina, and a statue niche with three-dimensional ogee canopy l. of the altar. But the arch into the chapel from the former transept, although much renewed, is quite sumptuous E.E, with multiple clustered shafts and nailhead and dogtooth decoration. So there must have been a chapel here before the present one. Arches between the S and N chapels and the chancel double- and triple-chamfered respectively. Roofs all C19.

REREDOS of Caen stone. 1872 by *Forsyth*. – COMMUNION RAILS in the crossing made from C17 balustrading, 1977. – FONT. Perp, octagonal, with concave sides. Handsome cover of *c.* 1700, with foliage scrolls, suspended from an elaborate wrought-iron bracket. – POOR BOX (now in the vestry). Dated 1600, with the names of two churchwardens. On a decorated pillar. – ROYAL ARMS, dated 1700. – PAINTINGS of Moses and Aaron, C18, in the chancel. – STAINED GLASS. E window by *R. B. Edmundson*, 1861, garish; S aisle second from E, N aisle second from E, and S chapel E, by *O'Connor*, 1868, 1873, 1875; chancel SW and S aisle W by *Morris & Co.*, 1872–3, the figures mainly designed by *Ford Madox Brown*, with others by *Morris, Burne-Jones* and *Peter Paul Marshall*; W window by *Clayton & Bell*, 1872. – MONUMENTS to the Slingsby family, in the N chapel. – Francis Slingsby †1600 and his wife Mary Percy †1598. By *Thomas Browne*, 1601. Recumbent stone effigies, oddly attenuated, on a tomb-chest with panelled pilasters. – Sir Henry Slingsby, eldest son of the above, †1634. By *William*

---

*The church was reconsecrated in 1343: the town had been burnt by Scots in 1318.

Wright of Charing Cross. Upright alabaster figure wrapped in a shroud (cf. Nicholas Stone's monument to John Donne, 1631, in St Paul's Cathedral), within an aedicule of black Corinthian columns and baseless pediment. The symbolism – a reference to resurrection at the Last Judgement – would have been clearer before a painted inscription, VENITE AD JUDICIU[M] was lost, and the angel over the pediment lost its trumpet. – Sir William Slingsby, Sir Henry's brother, †1638, perhaps also by *Wright* (Adam White). A second but contrasting upright figure, set in a simple round-headed niche. He wears a broad-rimmed hat and stands cross-legged – a classically derived pose previously unknown in English funerary sculpture – with his left hand against his cheek, his elbow on the hilt of his sword, and his right hand resting on a cartouche bearing the Slingsby arms. The mood is one of gently melancholic contemplation. – Lady Dorothy †1673, marble cartouche. – Sir Charles †1869. Recumbent effigy by *Boehm*. – At the edge of the churchyard E of the church a HEARSE SHED, *c.* 1800.

HOLY TRINITY. 1854–6 by *Joseph Fawcett* of Knaresborough. The big NW tower with broach spire is a prominent landmark, but the church is tucked away behind the houses along Briggate and approached through a gabled Gothic archway. Gritstone. Geometrical style with some tricky details, particularly the trios of lancets to the clerestory. (Nave arcades with cylindrical piers. – STAINED GLASS includes E window and chancel S by *Hardman*, 1863–74; S aisle E by *Ward & Hughes*, 1867; tower by *O'Connor*, 1866; N aisle NE by *Harry Stammers*, 1953.)

ST MARY (R.C.), Bond End. A very early post-Emancipation example, 1831 by *John Child* of Leeds (and later of Knaresborough). It looks, doubtless intentionally, almost more like a house than a chapel – two storeys and five bays in coursed gritstone, with slightly projecting pedimented three-bay centre. Porch with canted corners, and above it a niche with statue. Former sash windows replaced by casements and the lower tier reduced in height. Interior also altered. Three-bay presbytery attached to l.

UNITED REFORMED CHURCH, Gracious Street. 1864 by *J. P. Pritchett Jun.* Gothic, with horribly thin turret and spirelet.

Former PRIMITIVE METHODIST CHAPEL. *See* Perambulation, below.

CHAPEL OF OUR LADY OF THE CRAG. *See* Outer Knaresborough.

KNARESBOROUGH CASTLE

Crowning the highest and steepest part of the bluff above the river. There are records of building work in 1129–30, 1207 and *c.* 1300–12, the second including the excavation, or enlarging, of the dry ditch on the town side and the last accounting for most of the surviving fabric. The castle was taken by Parliamentary forces in 1644, and largely demolished *c.* 1648. The site, and what was left in the way of ruins, became a public park in 1897.

There were two wards, the outer to the E towards the town, the inner to the W on the cliff top. Of the ditch, the central, NE, segment has been filled in but the rest remains; but of the curtain wall circuit very little can now be seen apart from the semicircular fronts of the two towers of the main E gatehouse, built for Edward I *c.* 1300. The arch between them fell *c.* 1847. The most important of the surviving elements is a substantial part of the KING'S TOWER, on the N side of the inner ward at its junction with the outer, perhaps on the site of an earlier keep. Built for Edward II in 1307–12 by the London master mason *Hugh of Titchmarsh*, it was a residential tower providing for luxurious comfort as well as security (cf. Marten's Tower at Chepstow Castle, Gwent (1286–93) and the E tower at Helmsley, North Riding as remodelled *c.* 1300), and a design of great sophistication, executed in excellent quality stonework. Geometrically complex shape, essentially a rectangle with the N face treated as a huge canted bay, making an irregular hexagon overall, but apparently framed by an equilateral triangle defined by three cylindrical turrets, in the centre of the N elevation and at the SE and SW corners, the SW only surviving. Three storeys and cellar. The principal room was on the first floor, reached by a vaulted staircase (lost) rising from a porch attached to the SE corner of the tower, of which a little fabric, including the springings of the vault, remains. At the head of the stair was an ante-room, with a window overlooking the inner ward, and then two sets of doors and a portcullis. The chamber itself has a dais at the far (W) end, with remains of a fireplace to the r., a broad blind arch against the end wall and a large pointed window to the l., again facing over the inner ward, now without its tracery but retaining its hoodmould and ballflower ornament. On the top floor, reached by a spiral staircase, there was a second room of similar size, probably a bedchamber, and a chapel, but of this little masonry is preserved.

The main room of the ground floor and the cellar below it are both based on an octagon and are both rib-vaulted, with a central pillar, octagonal to the ground floor, cylindrical to the cellar. The ribs are hollow-chamfered and die into the pillars and walls without capitals: in the cellar they are arranged in four groups of three, on the ground floor they divide into tierceron pairs. It has been suggested that the ground-floor room, which can be entered both directly from the inner ward and by a spiral stair from the floor above, may have been the wardrobe, for the storage of valuables. Additional rib-vaulted bays on the S side, towards the entrance; fireplace; mural chambers opening off, that to the NW a garderobe; and a further one, L-shaped, in the SW corner, accessible only from outside. In the room now some architectural fragments from St Robert's Priory (*see* Outer Knaresborough, below). The cellar is reached by (later) steps from the ward, with medieval graffiti on the retaining walls.

The other structure to survive is the former COURT HOUSE of the Honour of Knaresborough (now a museum), a low two-storey range on the E side of the inner ward. The ground floor is probably C14, with arched doorway and a shouldered fireplace inside, the upper of c. 1600, with mullioned windows and Tudor-arched doorway. Roof-level raised, and the matching SW end bay added, c. 1830. At the other end a small prison block of 1786, built on the footings of a medieval chapel. Surprisingly large round-headed windows at the sides, altered in the C20, front window C19. The courtroom, on the first floor of the court house, is probably in essence of c. 1600. Two enclosures defined by rough dado-height partitions, and at one end an elevated bench with panelled back.

PUBLIC BUILDINGS

TOWN HALL, Market Place. 1862 by *John Child* (*see* St Mary, above), on the site of the medieval Tolbooth. Straightforwardly Italianate, five bays and two tall storeys, the upper with big windows and cast-iron balcony, the lower rusticated with segment-headed arches, mostly glazed.

OLD GRAMMAR SCHOOL, on the E side of the churchyard. Founded 1616, rebuilt 1741. Plain rendered range, two storeys, six bays. Now a house. Nearby on the S side the former CHARITY SCHOOL, 1868, with half-hipped gables and a little Gothic detail.

Former NATIONAL SCHOOLS, Castle Yard. On one side the boys' school, dated 1814 on a scrolled tablet above the eaves at one end. A plain single-storeyed ashlar rectangle, two by five bays with hipped roof. Opposite on the other side the girls' and infants', 1837, similar but two-storeyed, the upper floor perhaps added c. 1850. Attached to the latter the former DISPENSARY, 1853, like a three-bay house with pedimented projecting centre and a pedimented porch with triglyph frieze; and opposite this, next to the boys' school, the site of the Sessions House of 1837–8 by *Bernard Hartley Jun.*, now occupied by the lumpish late C20 Police Station.

HENSHAWS ARTS & CRAFTS CENTRE, Bond End. 1999 by *Jane Darbyshire & David Kendall Architects* and *Jackson & Calvert*, for Henshaws Society for Blind People. Workshops for visually impaired young people learning craft skills, combined with a public space. The building occupies the walled former kitchen garden of Conyngham Hall (*see* Perambulation, below), with an eyecatching entrance feature – an open brick rotunda – at one corner, but the rest more persuasively low-key, one- and two-storey ranges in a mix of yellow brick and timber boarding, with curved steel roofs, forming two courtyards.

2 VIADUCT. 1851 by *Thomas Grainger*, engineer, for the East & West Yorkshire Junction Railway. It was a second attempt, the first, begun in 1847, having collapsed the following year when nearly complete. Four arches, 80 feet (24 metres) high, with rounded cutwaters continued up as turret-like buttresses. Pevsner called it 'one of the most notable railway crimes in England', but Speight's assessment of 1894 – 'in admirable keeping with the style of the ancient castle and town' – has been more widely endorsed. Between it and the utilitarian station (1890), the line crosses the foot of Kirkgate on a level crossing, and the sudden appearance of the trains between the houses is one of the curiosities of the town. Beyond the station a tunnel under the High Street.

HIGH BRIDGE, over the Nidd. Medieval origin, repaired in 1773, and widened in 1828–9 and *c.* 1920. Two arches, the old parts slightly pointed, with chamfered ribs. Further downstream LOW BRIDGE, rebuilt 1779, also two arches.

PERAMBULATION

The starting point is the MARKET PLACE, small and intimate, an irregular L-shape as a result of an encroaching block at the W corner including the Town Hall (*see* Public Buildings, above) but originally extending much further SW, as far as the castle. Some simple fabric of the C18, mainly of brick, but also several instances of concealed timber framing, their presence usually advertised by gables and the use of render. On the SE side the OLD ROYAL OAK, refronted C20 but together with No. 7 to the l. evidently in essence the four-bay 'faire mansion house' described as 'lately newbuilt' in 1611. (C17 panelling, fireplace etc. in the chamber above the former hall.) At the E corner Nos. 2–4, with some heavily moulded beams, probably early C17, to the ground floor; and along the NE side a sequence of three, each with two gables obscured to varying degrees by refacing. No. 12, 'newly built' in 1625, has a blocked timber mullioned attic window on the r. flank, a kitchen fireplace in the basement, and collared trusses. No. 16 – the 'Oldest Chemists Shop in England' – is probably C16 and formed the r. end of a house of five bays. C18 projecting shop windows on C20 supports. Extensive C19 shop fittings etc. now mostly obscured or dismantled.

From the N corner out into the HIGH STREET. Opposite, an exceptionally charming late C18 shopfront, with segmental fanlight tops to the two bow windows and columns and brackets framing the doorway. Nearby also two contrasting C19 banks: a little to the r. NATWEST, the former Knaresborough & Claro Banking Co., an ashlar palazzo of 1858, and on the corner with the Market Place entry BARCLAYS, the former Bradford Old Bank of 1881, tall gabled free Renaissance, of

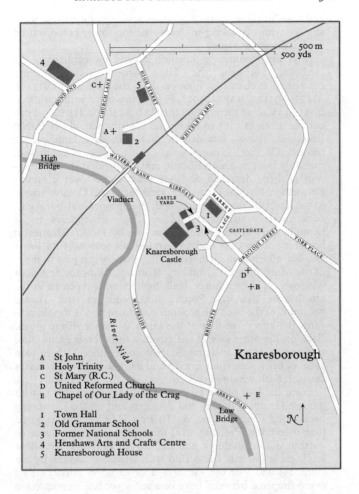

4   BOND END   c+   CHURCH LANE   5   HIGH STREET   WHITELEY YARD

500 m
500 yds

A+   2

High
Bridge

WATERBAG BANK   KIRKGATE

Viaduct   CASTLE YARD   MARKET   I   PLACE

3   CASTLEGATE   GRACIOUS STREET   YORK PLACE

Knaresborough
Castle

D+
+B

WATERSIDE

River Nidd   BRIGGATE   Knaresborough

ABBEY ROAD   + E

Low
Bridge

N

A   St John
B   Holy Trinity
C   St Mary (R.C.)
D   United Reformed Church
E   Chapel of Our Lady of the Crag

1   Town Hall
2   Old Grammar School
3   Former National Schools
4   Henshaws Arts and Crafts Centre
5   Knaresborough House

brick with stone dressings. Otherwise the town-centre section
of the street has not much to show, the SE part rather cut about
– but another pair of bowed shop windows at No. 14 – the first
stretch downhill to the NW with some more heavily disguised
remains of timber framing. On the r. the BOROUGH BAILIFF
and Nos. 72–78, both with much altered C18 fronts: in the
former, elements of a C16 cross-wing and cross-passage, a
handsome late C17 staircase with turned balusters beyond the
passage and some *ex situ* C17 panelling; in the latter, parts of
the buildings recorded as under construction in 1611. On the
l. Nos. 85–87, low and rendered, with close-studded former
back wall and cambered tie-beams. Then through an archway
on the r., in WHITELEY YARD, a former flax-dressing shop

and warehouse built in 1825 (now housing). Gritstone, three storeys, with two taking-in doors, the top storey perhaps used for handloom weaving.

After this, continuing downhill beyond the confines of the medieval borough, the High Street becomes more residential in character. First on the r. the former PRIMITIVE METHODIST CHAPEL, 1901, Free Renaissance with mutilated front and altered turret; then the OLD SCHOOL HOUSE, a C18 cottage given in 1765 to house the Charity School (*see* Public Buildings, above), founded in that year, as a large plaque records. On the l. Nos. 99–103, *c.* 1700, brick, re-windowed, probably built as a single house and subdivided shortly afterwards; then, detached and set back in its own grounds, KNARESBOROUGH HOUSE, *c.* 1768 for James Collins, lawyer to the Lascelles family (Harewood, Plompton, Goldsborough), conventionally attributed to *Carr*. The date appears in the heraldic glass in the staircase window, by *Peckitt*. Magnesian limestone. Five bays and two-and-a-half storeys, with lower two-bay attachments – mostly a single storey but part to the r. of two, disturbing the symmetry. Balusters below the first-floor windows (cf. Leventhorpe Hall, Swillington), repeated in the attachment parapets. Porch with pediment and Tuscan columns. At the back the grounds run down beside the churchyard, the effect like that of the big house on a village green. Back on the other side of the street, a little lower again, Nos. 104–106, *c.* 1700, an attractive pair (now offices), three bays each, of brick with stone quoins and a bracketed wooden eaves cornice. Sash windows C18.

From the foot of the High Street BOND END runs l., with modest Georgian houses and cottages, and on the l., running back along Church Lane, ST JOHN'S HOUSE, with exposed timber framing. Probably C16, three bays with a rear aisle or outshut. Close studding and big curved braces at first-floor level, gable towards Bond End with kingpost (hidden by the chimney) and V-struts. Ground floor cased in gritstone. Big stone fireplace between bays one and two, late C17 staircase perhaps repositioned. Then set back on the r. side, the DOWER HOUSE HOTEL, once a property of the Slingsbys. Oddly shaped front, apparently mid-C18, of brick with stone quoins and keystones, with two storeys of seven bays but a blind attic of only five, with sloping ends, which screens three parallel roofs; and the presence of an earlier building is confirmed by elements of timber framing visible inside. Mid-C18 staircase, with turned balusters. Extensive late C20 additions at the rear. At the end, beside the High Bridge (*see* Public Buildings, above) the entrance to the spacious riverside grounds of CONYNGHAM HALL (now offices). Gritstone. Entrance front probably of shortly after 1905 when the estate was bought by C. E. Charlesworth (armorial glass in the back stairs windows), with full-height four-column Ionic portico, the pediment excessively steep, and two bays l. and r. with pedimented ground-floor windows. Behind this only a little remains of the house of *c.* 1760, rather more of the additions to it, including two canted bays on the l. flank and presumably the one on the r., evidently carried out for the Countess of Conyngham who bought the property in 1796. Top-lit staircase hall apparently of the *c.* 1905 phase inserted into the older part of the building, with columned first-floor gallery; but the former dining room to the r. has a good-quality Adam-style decorative scheme of *c.* 1800, with plasterwork to walls and ceiling, and fitted buffets in the niches flanking the entrance. On some of the doors upstairs, painted decoration of the same period. Attached to the w corner of the house the modest late C18 STABLES, quadrangular with pedimented trefoil-headed entrance on the NE side.

The return to the town centre starts with the first part of WATERSIDE, which follows the river bank through the defile with picturesque views of the houses perched on the slope. Up on the l. TENTER LODGE, 1780 with early C19 castellated additions, then on the r., in the shadow of the viaduct, the so-called OLD MANOR HOUSE, identifiable by its chequerboard paintwork. Small, L-plan and much altered, but retaining inside extensive multiple-phase timber framing, an overmantel dated 1661 and other C17 panelling. From here CASTLE MILL can be seen in the distance below the castle bluff, a complex with a complicated history now extensively restored and rebuilt as housing. Established in 1770 as a paper mill, apparently incorporating a water wheel erected in 1764 to pump water to the town, developed for cotton spinning in 1791, flax spinning from *c.* 1811, and linen weaving – as the town's biggest textile mill – from *c.* 1849. A three-storey brick and stone block on the river bank, with a millrace, can probably be identified as the paper mill. Stone-built two-storey eleven-bay flax-spinning mill, and an engine house and chimney of *c.* 1847, adjoining.

Now back a little from the Manor House and up WATERBAG BANK, cobbled and very steep, with on the r. MANOR COTTAGE, thatched and whitewashed. Remains of a C16–C17 timber frame inside, with an outshut towards the street and a lobby entry. The ascent continues past the corner of the churchyard and over the level crossing into KIRKGATE. On the r. No. 25 (Working Men's Club), a rather battered mid-C18 house of five bays and two-and-a-half storeys with quoins and pedimented doorcase; then set back at right angles in a cul-de-sac CASTLE CLIFFE, also mid-C18, with Gibbs surrounds to the ground-floor windows and doorway and an upright oval window in the gable-end. These and their neighbours overlook the defile at the back. Further up, a three-storey C18 warehouse, brick and stone, altered in the C19; and at the top on the r. corner Nos. 1–5, in origin probably C16, described in 1611 as a 'hospital for six poor folk'. Rendered, apparently timber-framed, moulded beams and kingpost trusses visible inside. To the r., in CASTLEGATE, the tower-like CASTLE VAULTS, mid-C18, three-and-a-half storeys but only one bay wide, with a canted bay window to the upper floors and three pilasters below it. To the l. the Market Place again.

Finally, a little E from the Market Place, forming the SE continuation of the High Street, is YORK PLACE, which has some of the stateliest later C18 houses in Knaresborough. They include in particular NEWTON HOUSE on the l. side – limestone, three bays, with two shallow segmental bow windows, a central Diocletian window and a not quite full-width pediment – and then set back and detached on the r., FYSCHE HALL (now a Freemasons' lodge), before 1776, five bays with pediment over the centre three and added Tuscan porch. Later C19 extension to the r. Also, before Fysche Hall THE OLD TANNERY, formerly a linen mill, now flats – limestone, four storeys – and beyond it, set further back, ROSE COTTAGE, incorporating a one-bay fragment of a brick house dated 1685. Blocked doorway with broken segmental pediment, quoins, moulded stringcourse.

OUTER KNARESBOROUGH

A loose sequence of curiosities along ABBEY ROAD, which runs along the l. bank of the Nidd downstream from Low Bridge (*see* Public Buildings, above), the first part at the foot of a limestone cliff. First FORT MONTAGUE, an extraordinary rock dwelling partly cut into the vertical cliff face, partly on the cliff top above, constructed between 1770 and 1791 by a linen weaver called *Thomas Hill* and his son for their own use. Four superimposed rooms connected by a rock-cut staircase, with battlemented parapet, and a separate building on the cliff top, also battlemented, originally with Gothick windows. Cut into the base of the cliff just beyond the fort is the CHAPEL OF OUR LADY OF THE CRAG, an oratory made by *John Mason*, tenant of the adjacent town quarry, in 1407–8, evidently on his own initiative as a pious act. The external features are a small two-light Perp window, altered to a mullion and a transom, and an arched doorway, but to the r. of these is an over-life-size relief of a knight in armour, his intended identity unknown, probably added sometime between 1695 and 1739 (and renewed in the C19). The interior is minute (12 by 8 ft (3.5 by 2.5 metres)), but has a vault of eight ribs with a boss in the centre, colonnettes against the walls, altar with cusped blank arches, a canopied niche above it, and a piscina, all carved from the rock. The crude masks on one side are presumably post-medieval, like the knight. The chapel had no connection with the hermit Robert of Knaresborough (†1218), or with the pilgrimage cult which developed after his death – but confusion on that point had arisen by the C18: the association was confined to the other two items. His hermitage, ST ROBERT'S CAVE, is 1 m. further downstream, in a low outcrop between the river and the road just before Grimbald Bridge. On the ledge in front of the cave the excavated remains of a living area and a chapel (said to have been built for the hermit at the cost of his brother Walter Flower, Mayor of York). In the latter his putative first grave. Halfway back again is the site of ST ROBERT'S PRIORY, a house of Trinitarian friars founded in his honour *c.* 1252, where his body is said to have been re-interred. There are no standing remains but some architectural fragments are set into an outbuilding at a nearby house called The Priory.

LANGCLIFFE   8060

Dales village near Settle centred on a roughly square green.

ST JOHN THE EVANGELIST on the E side. 1851 by *Mallinson & Healey*, a daughter church of Giggleswick. Simplest Dec, unaisled, with a charming octagonal bellcote on the (ritual) W gable (cf. St Matthew Bankfoot, Bradford). Arched-brace roof. – STAINED GLASS. E window and nave NW apparently by *Warrington*, 1851; chancel SE and SW by *Lavers, Barraud & Westlake*, 1869.

At the SE corner, the former METHODIST CHAPEL, 1903, with odd flattened Palladian window and domed bellcote. Sunday School of 1851 attached. At the NW corner some C17 houses including MANOR FARMHOUSE, 1678, its original front, with an ornamented doorhead, facing away from the green. Segment-headed housebody fireplace flanked by doorways, painted decoration on the housebody ceiling beams, and a remarkable roof structure with ornamented pendant king blocks.*

LANGCLIFFE HALL. A house with a number of unexpected features, C17 in origin but extensively refurbished in the 1860s. The C17 building is of three storeys and an outward-facing L-shape, the longer front to the S and the shorter to the W; and running W from the N end of the latter is a so-called stable range of the early C18. The S front was completely refaced in the 1860s, with a central porch and bay windows. Most of the detail of the W front is also of the 1860s, apart from the doorway in the middle, the cross-windows flanking it and a mullion-and-transom window further to the l. The doorway has an ornamented lintel with two three-quarter-round recesses, and moulding on the jambs similar to that to the front doorway of The Folly at Settle; and as at The Folly there is also a surround of very curious design. To each side is a roll moulding and then a sort of architrave, and the line of the latter is continued above in an approximately semicircular pediment or gablet; but at impost level it is interrupted by strange wing-like features, like the reversed halves of a Mannerist broken

---

*Timber block at the apex of a roof truss, supporting the ridge (cf. kingpost).

pediment, which cut into the surrounds of the cross-windows. But how much of this is of a piece? Incongruous urns have been added, crowning the 'wings' and the gablet, and the tympanum of the gablet has been disturbed and an alien datestone of 1602 introduced: perhaps the 'wings' are later insertions also. A further puzzle is that the surround seems too elaborate for a secondary entrance, yet the form of the C17 house suggests that its main front was to the s, not the w: at the back, in the angle between the two ranges, is a staircase turret which opens out of the s range. But an early C18 view shows that by that date, at any rate, there was no entrance in the s front and there was one where the present doorway is. The stable range, of five-plus-one bays, is also a surprisingly smart design, with cross-windows in architrave surrounds and central to the five-bay section another striking doorway, with blocked architrave surround and Michelangelesque guttae to each side. In a garden wall is a doorway dated 1712 which seems to form part of the same phase of work: it may even have come from the range, perhaps from the fifth bay where there is a C19 cart entrance. Also in the garden wall a re-set doorhead dated 1660. The interior detail of the house is largely C19. Early C17 Flemish heraldic glass re-set in the staircase window.

LANGCLIFFE MILL. By the river, ½ m. w. Cotton-spinning mill, water-powered, on the site of a corn mill. Built 1783–4 for Clayton and Walshman – who in 1780 had completed the first cotton mill in Yorkshire, Low Mill at Keighley – and extended c. 1830, when supplementary steam power was introduced. Long five-storey range, the w half, with blocked millrace entry, being the earlier part. Truncated mill chimney of brick. Now a paper mill. Manager's house, LANGCLIFFE PLACE – 1784, altered – to NE, millpond to N. ½ m. s, LANGCLIFFE SHED, an associated weaving mill reusing the same water supply, established c. 1840 and later also converted to steam power. One-storey shed with sawtooth roof. Square rock-faced chimney.

HOFFMAN LIME KILN, ¾ m. N. 1872–3. For industrial-scale lime production, working on the principle of continuous operation with the fires moving round an annular firing chamber. Hippodrome-shaped structure of limestone rubble, over 300 ft (90 metres) long, the chamber stage with battered sides and a series of low round-headed entrances, giving onto a ledge which carried a tramway bringing the limestone from the quarry behind. The upper stage, from which coal was fed into the chamber and where a chimney for the exhaust flues stood, has largely disappeared. The chamber is semicircular in cross-section, an impressively Piranesian space in its unfunctionally unencumbered state.

VICTORIA CAVE, 1 m. E, in the limestone scar above the village. First excavated 1838. Finds have included flint tools and a decorated lance point of reindeer antler, of the later Upper Palaeolithic – the earliest evidence of humans in the area – a Mesolithic bone harpoon, and bronze and bone artefacts of the CI to C4 A.D. Also animal bones ranging back to an Upper Pleistocene interglacial era. The smaller JUBILEE CAVE, nearby to the N, has produced material of the Late Paleolithic, Mesolithic, Iron Age and Roman periods.

LANGSTROTHDALE

Buckden

YOCKENTHWAITE HALL. Later C18 farmhouse, grander than average for the neighbourhood. Three-plus-one bays.

On the N bank of the river ⅜ m. WNW, a Bronze Age STONE CIRCLE, c. 25 ft (7.5 metres) in diameter, which may be the kerb of an otherwise denuded burial cairn. Twenty-four closely set boulders: gaps to the SE and NE may have accommodated others.

At DEEPDALE, ½ m. further WNW, a house with a two-storey porch dated 1693. Ornamented doorhead of round and pointed blind arches.

COWSIDE, ⅝ m. WNW again. 1707, with similarities to the Manor House at Buckden (q.v.). Central entry, mullioned windows of four to six lights. Unusual arrangment to the rear, approximating to a double pile, with two gabled service wings flanking an outshut containing the staircase (but cf. Town Head, Austwick).

LAWKLAND

LAWKLAND HALL. Highly picturesque house of several dates, mainly C17, built by a cadet branch of the Ingleby family of Ripley Castle who acquired the estate c. 1572: bought in 1914 by a Bradford industrialist, J.N. Ambler, and extensively but sensitively modernized for him during the 1920s. Hall range and cross-wings, the parlour (W) wing of three storeys, the rest of two apart from a tall staircase turret, crowned by a belvedere, in the angle between the hall and the parlour wing on the S side. The house faces N, where the front of the hall range is dated 1679: three bays with cross-windows, central doorway with decorated lintel, a central gabled dormer – and a pair of little oculi, probably insertions, to the r. But the rest of the range in essence is probably earlier, and it seems likely that its original front was to the S. On that side, at the junction of the hall and the service end there is a two-storey gabled projection, and it is probable that this was built as an entrance porch: it is difficult to account for it otherwise, and the relationship between it and the hall fireplace produces a textbook lobby-entry arrangement. The service end originally projected to the N only, but attached to this S projection is a further service range running S which presumably also formed part of the 1679 alterations. The oldest part of the house appears to be the parlour wing, on the evidence of a priest's hole in a chimney-breast at second-floor level – the Inglebys were Roman Catholics until the later C18 – which if genuine would mean that the wing could not be later than *c.* 1625. It retains a few C17 mullion-and-transom windows: others, here and on the service end and the S side of the hall range, are of the 1920s. Inside, the predominant impression is also of that period. Rearranged – and possibly imported – early C18 staircase, and some C16–C17 panelling amongst the C20 woodwork. But one first-floor room in the parlour wing has early C18 panelling apparently *in situ.* In the stair-turret a stone spiral staircase and a number of nicely detailed Tudor-arched doorways, but at least one of these has either been moved or is a copy. The pyramid roof of the turret is dated 1758.

ARMITSTEAD FARMHOUSE, 1m. SE. Early C19 front. Three bays with pedimented centre, and pedimented Serliana-like entrance (cf. the Police Station, Settle). Tripartite windows.

See also Eldroth.

LEATHLEY

Scatter of gritstone buildings in Lower Wharfedale.

ST OSWALD. On an abrupt low ridge, perhaps a pre-Christian burial site. Early Norman W tower, tall and unbuttressed, movingly primeval-looking. Plain round-headed bell-openings, one to each face, tiny slit windows to the intermediate stages, tall narrow W doorway. Early Norman also the chancel arch, heavy and unmoulded, the imposts with a slight nick between the vertical face of the abacus and the chamfer below; and the details of the nave W wall suggest the nave was yet slightly earlier than the tower. There is no tower arch, only a plain doorway (its present threshold, oddly, *c.* 2 ft (0.6 metres) above the nave floor level) and above it a W window, splayed on the nave side and useless if the tower was already in place. The body of the church externally of brief but varied outline, all Perp in appearance but much restored in 1869 by *J.B. Fraser* of Leeds. Very short nave with aisles under the same roof, slightly lower chancel with chapels similarly roofed. The E part of the S aisle, with cross-gable, is wholly of the C19 but the gable repeats a C17 feature. Other aisle and chapel windows straight-headed with arched lights, some of them renewed, C19 Perp E window. Two-bay Perp nave arcades, broad and low, with octagonal piers, double-chamfered arches and the capitals decorated with the Tudor rose, the Percy crescent and fetterlock, and other motifs, widely spaced. Broad single arches between the chancel and chapels. Crude C14 piscina. Roofs all

1869. – DOOR, in the doorway between nave and tower. C12, with remarkable decorative ironwork, wild and abundant – bars, scrolls, hinges and one human figure. Probably the original external door as the face is more weathered than the rear. – STAINED GLASS. E window by *Clayton & Bell*, 1874. – MONUMENTS. A few wall tablets, including Ellen Hopton †1664, with broken pediment and heraldic cartouche, and Robert Hitch of Leathley Hall, †1723.

ALMSHOUSES, E of the church. Founded 1769 by Ann Hitch. Handsome row, with one-and-a-half-storey central pavilion – originally a schoolroom, it appears – and single-storey wings. Big semicircular window over the schoolroom doorway,

LEATHLEY HALL, ¼ m. further E. A part only of the 'large and convenient edifice' which was 'improved' by Robert Hitch shortly before 1718. This was evidently his new E wing. Nine-bay front with quoins, very elongated windows and a string-course between the storeys ramped up at each end (cf. Stone Gappe, Lothersdale, 1725). But the projecting gabled three-bay centre, and the staircase hall behind it, are C20. To the SE is his STABLE BLOCK, with the same quoins and ramped string course, and a hipped roof. A few altered cross-windows remaining to the ground floor, two-light mullioned windows above.

Former METHODIST CHAPEL, NE of the almshouses. 1826. Little hipped-roofed box with sash windows. Ramped pews. Beyond it THE COTTAGE, early C17 house of hybrid construction, the outer walls of stone but enclosing a three-bay timber arcade, substantially intact, between the body of the house and the rear outshut (cf. East End, Norwood).

LEATHLEY MILL, ½ m. N of the church. Probably mid-C18, altered C19. Plain two-storey range with lean-to wheelhouse. Undershot water wheel of iron and wood, driving gear and four sets of stones. Long leat to N.

LEEDS

2030

BY SUSAN WRATHMELL, JOHN MINNIS
AND RICHARD POLLARD

INTRODUCTION*

'Leeds is a town of commercial traditions dating back to the C15,' wrote Pevsner in 1959; it is also the largest city in Yorkshire, its boundaries extending far beyond the built-up area into the rural West Riding. Its centre lies on the gently sloping N bank of the Aire, whose valley cuts through the Millstone Grit of the Pennines and from Leeds passes SE through the Yorkshire coal measures, whose seams of sandstone and clay provided the bricks for the burgeoning town of the C17 and C18 and later fired its industrial strength. The country is hilly, but not mountainous. The height rises from 70 ft at Knostrop in the SE to Cookridge in the NW. For the purpose of this guide the boundaries of the City are those of the urban area before 1974 (population 501,080 in 1971). Description of the city centre is restricted to both banks of the Aire and streets to the N, roughly circumscribed by the Inner Ring Road. The inner areas of Leeds which were formerly part of the C19 township (The Bank, Burmantofts, Sheepscar and Woodhouse) are then described, followed by an account of the outer urban areas, many of which were already part of the extensive Leeds parish in the medieval period.

Leeds may have been the site of *Cambodunum*, a stronghold of the Brigantes tribe, mentioned in the *Antonine Itinerary*. There was a fording point here across the Aire, the site of which has been found close to Leeds Bridge, and this must have ensured its importance from an early date. Finds of Roman material and the line of a road running E of the river crossing suggest a *mansio* for travellers, while on Quarry Hill, at the E edge of the city centre, earthworks are mentioned in the C18 and C19; possibly remains of a 'fort by the river-bend'. Leeds was also probably a major early Anglo-Saxon settlement. Bede in 730 mentions 'the region known as Loidis', from which the city's name derives, and a monastery of Abbot Thrythwulf. Firmer proof of Leeds as a religious centre by the C9 and C10 is provided by the fragments of at least six crosses with Scandinavian-influenced decoration.

The manor of Leeds, gifted to Ilbert de Lacy after the Conquest, extended from Woodhouse Moor in the NW to Knostrop in the SE. The small village was centred on the church (dedicated to St Peter and on the site of present parish church) with a single street, now Kirkgate, extending uphill to the W. ½ m. upriver was the manorial mill and standing on a slight eminence above this the manor house and its park. The other major landowners were the monks of Kirkstall whose possessions extended across a vast tract from the abbey to the village of Adel in the N.

The transformation from village to town came in 1207, following the foundation of the Borough of Leeds by the Lord of the Manor, Maurice de Payne. A wide street, Briggate, was set out running uphill from the river crossing. It was broad enough for a large market, in operation by 1258, and on each side thirty ½-acre plots were provided for burgesses, establishing the street

*The introduction to Leeds has been prepared for this volume by Charles O'Brien.

pattern which is still clearly discerned in the many narrow yards off Briggate. They paid fixed rents to the manor for a house plot and an allotment (toft) at Burmantofts, E of the town beyond the Sheepscar Beck; income was to come from trade or a craft, fostering business in the town. Of foremost importance was the trade in broad cloths prepared and made in the fulling mills and workshops of the town and the surrounding villages. The market for cloth was held on the bridge and from the late C16 this became the source of considerable prosperity. By 1615 the thriving town had a Moot Hall and from 1636, if not earlier, the new church of St John built at the N end of Briggate beyond the head row. Its benefactor was John Harrison, woollen merchant, who also provided almshouses and schools. The ambition of his fellow merchants to become a self-governing body in control of the cloth trade was realized by the creation of a Corporation in 1626 (the manor was broken up shortly after), whose members could inspect cloth produced in Leeds and exclude merchants from outside the town. The growth of exports of broad cloth to the Continent led them eventually to fund the construction of the Aire & Calder Navigation, begun in 1699, to carry large cargo boats to Hull.

For the C18 we are better provided with surviving evidence of buildings in Leeds. John Cossins's *New and Exact Plan of the Town of Leeds*, published 1725, details the elevations of several of the newly built brick merchants' houses, the church of Holy Trinity on Boar Lane, and the town's first White Cloth Hall on Kirkgate, built in 1710–11 as a rival to the covered cloth hall at Wakefield. The Bucks' prospect of 1745 gives further details, showing that the buildings of the town had also spread S of the bridge, but the

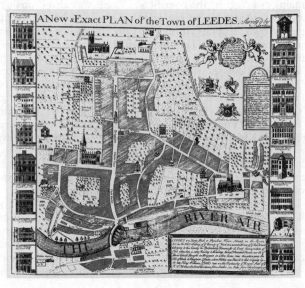

Leeds.
Map by John Cossins, 1725

centre still scarcely extended beyond the medieval streets of Briggate, Kirkgate, Boar Lane and Head Row. Land to the w of Boar
Lane at this time remained unexploited. This was the former park
of the manor house, where plots were first released in 1757 by
the Wilson family for construction of the large Coloured (or
Mixed) Cloth Hall (now the site of the Post Office on City
Square) followed by the Infirmary, which stood behind it. By the
end of the 1790s, the Park Estate, the first example of Georgian
town planning in Leeds, had been laid out to the w of the Infirmary with brick terraces in Park Row, Park Square, Park Place,
South Parade etc. Development of a similar character then continued E of Park Row (Albion Street, Commercial Street etc.)
and N of the Head Row. Further N, still in isolation at this time,
was a small number of quite ambitious mansions at Little
Woodhouse.

Alongside the changing character of the town there emerged
diverse industries along the river, its tributaries, and the Leeds
and Liverpool Canal (opened in 1777, bringing access to colonial markets). Armley Mills was an early example of a large-scale
woollen mill but the way towards the factory system, with all
processes for cloth production under one roof, was led by the
enterprising Benjamin Gott, who in 1791 began his mighty,
steam-powered Bean Ing (or Park) Mills in Leeds. Nothing else   p. 50
on this scale was attempted in the woollen industry but a com-
parably ambitious enterprise for flax milling was begun at
Holbeck, s of the Aire, in 1794. Flax milling became the speciality of Leeds until the collapse of the industry in the mid C19, and
several of Marshall's former employees, e.g. Hives & Atkinson,
soon spread out to build their own (less showy) factories in the
boom years after 1820 (there were thirty-seven flax mills by 1855).
Also during this period there emerged at Sheepscar and
Buslingthorpe large-scale enterprises for tanning, one of the
major employers in early C19 Leeds. Supplying the mills with
machine parts were new engineering works and foundries, most
famously Matthew Murray's 'Round Foundry', also at Holbeck,
which in 1812 pioneered the first commercially successful steam
locomotive and rack and pinion railway to haul coal into Leeds
from the Middleton Colliery, s of the town.

The wealth generated during these years was increasingly
invested in improvements to the town: in this period alone were
built a new Court House, Corn Exchange, Philosophical Hall,
Market buildings and Commercial Rooms – all in a severe
Grecian style and all since demolished. The most important survivor of this period, but of an entirely different character, is the
Gothic parish church as rebuilt in 1838–41 by *R. D. Chantrell*, the
most prolific of the early C19 architects in Leeds. In the outer
townships too are some remarkably well-executed and large
houses in Greek Revival style, the best of these are the mansion
in Roundhay Park, *c*. 1815, Armley House, built for Gott by
Smirke c. 1816, and Gledhow Grove designed by *John Clark* for
John Hives, flax spinner, in 1835. Trade to and from Leeds along
the river and canal increased and a further stimulus was provided

by the railways. The first stations were outside the town: E at
Marsh Lane (the Leeds & Selby Railway of 1834), and at Hunslet
(the North Midland Railway line to Derby and London, 1840)
but in 1846 the Leeds & Bradford Railway opened Wellington
Station on Wellington Street; the Leeds & Thirsk Railway's
Central Station followed on an adjoining site in 1849. Each was
further developed for the Midland Railway and Great Northern
Railway and a huge complex of goods depots filled a vast area
along the river by the end of the C19.

In the streets close to these stations emerged impressive storage
and display warehouses, and new premises for the associated
businesses of banking and insurance which by the later years of
the C19 had made Park Lane into a thoroughfare of increasingly
handsome character. Of the Victorian Age the most familiar
building is of course the Town Hall by *Cuthbert Brodrick*, 1852–8,
the first of his trio of major buildings for the city which was completed by the Corn Exchange (1860–2), and Mechanics' Institute
(1865–8). The 1850s, 60s and 70s also delivered up other new
institutions, the Infirmary by *George Gilbert Scott*, 1863–9 (not the
first but the most important and influential instance of the
secular Gothic Revival in Leeds and with a pavilion plan highly
progressive for its date) and the Yorkshire College at Woodhouse,
whose buildings by *Waterhouse* from 1877 formed the nucleus of
the University. At the fringes of the town appeared the prison
(Armley) and workhouse (Burmantofts), both by *Perkin & Backhouse*. They were one of a burgeoning number of local firms who
secured much of the available work in Leeds after 1860, also
including *George Corson* – who worked across the private and
public sphere in a variety of styles – and *Thomas Ambler* whose
commercial work for the clothing magnate John Barran is even
more eclectic, including the wholesale rebuilding of Boar Lane –
one of the enhancements of the town centre set in place from the
late 1860s – and, later, the unforgettable clothing factory in Park
Square. The benefits of street improvements were partly
devalued, however, by the construction of the railway viaduct
from Richmond Hill on the E side of the city to Leeds Station,
cutting through much of the S half of the town in 1869 and iso-
lating the parish church. The final act of the C19 was Leeds's elevation to city status, celebrated by the creation of City Square at
the junction of Park Lane and Boar Lane, leading one observer
to note that 'the centre of Leeds has been practically re-carved
and polished'. This boast was made, tellingly, in a guide for shop-
pers, for whom later C19 Leeds catered handsomely with a series
of arcades and covered markets. Much of what makes these, and
many other buildings of the period, attractive is the use of the
glazed tiles and architectural terracotta which was produced from
the 1870s at the Burmantofts works of the Leeds Fireclay Co.

Suburban development spread steadily N from Woodhouse
into Headingley, Chapel Allerton, Potternewton, Gledhow and
Roundhay as estates were sold off for building streets of terraces
and semi-detached houses. These were of every class, the best at
Weetwood, Headingley and Roundhay where the park was

opened to the public in 1872. Development was often protracted, however, only accelerating in the last decades of the C19 and early years of the C20 as the electric trams made a suburban home a realistic possibility. Local architects were much engaged in these activities and in the later period it is the work of *Bedford & Kitson* that stands out, not only in the more handsome villas but also in commercial and public buildings in the new suburbs; both members of the firm were active in building and altering homes for their extended families – Kitson was the son of the locomotive engineer Sir James Kitson and was related to the Denison, Beckett and Tetley families, the elite of Victorian and Edwardian Leeds. At the other end of the social scale, the sale of Lord Cardigan's estates in the 1860s–80s* – from Kirkstall to Burley and Hyde Park – was the cue for development of large districts of working-class back-to-backs; the same were to be seen spreading over Harehills, SE of Potternewton, Burmantofts and the industrial townships of Armley, Hunslet, Holbeck and Wortley. The cause of the housing reformers made little progress in Leeds. In these places new landmarks were formed by mission churches – both Anglican and Roman Catholic – and the Board Schools, sixty-one in total, designed in Gothic and Italianate styles by the Board's architects.

By 1901 Leeds was the fourth largest city in England, with a population of 429,000. This massive increase in a century (from just 53,000 in 1801) was partly added to by Irish immigrants, mostly employed in the flax trade, many of whom settled on The Bank at the E edge of the city in the mid C19 and, later, by Jews from Eastern Europe who made their home in the Leylands, on the NE edge of the centre, and found work in the mass production of clothing. Pioneered in Leeds by John Barran in the 1850s this eventually joined engineering and printing as one of the city's principal industries, reaching its greatest strength during the First World War with the manufacture of uniforms and, afterwards, when Montague Burton's empire began to supply its ready-made suits from its central factory at Burmantofts.

Outlying villages of the West Riding were gradually drawn into the city's boundaries in the early C20, notably during and after the construction of the Outer Ring Road, begun in 1926, which prompted further speculative development along its route and the arterial roads towards the city centre. From 1934 the Corporation finally began to address seriously the need for slum clearances and the building of municipal housing (although back-to-backs were still being erected in this decade by private developers). Most of this was in the form of low-density cottage estates at the edges of the city, e.g. Gipton, but the showpiece was the scheme of flats built for over 3,000 people at Quarry Hill in 1935–41 (dem. 1976). This unusually ambitious venture was carried out in conjunction with the major redevelopment by *Sir Reginald Blomfield* of the Headrow as a grand boulevard across

---

*These estates mostly comprised the former lands of the monks of Kirkstall, which were acquired shortly after the Dissolution by the Savile family and inherited by the Earls of Cardigan in the early C19.

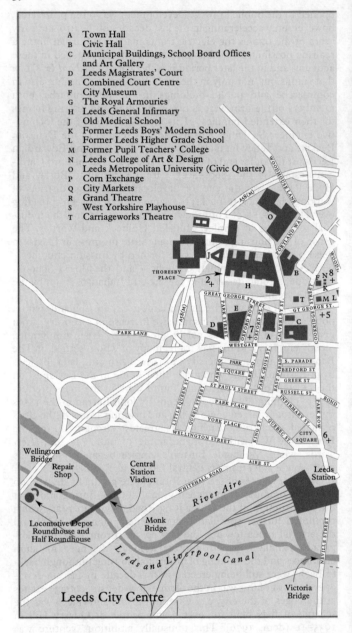

A   Town Hall
B   Civic Hall
C   Municipal Buildings, School Board Offices and Art Gallery
D   Leeds Magistrates' Court
E   Combined Court Centre
F   City Museum
G   The Royal Armouries
H   Leeds General Infirmary
J   Old Medical School
K   Former Leeds Boys' Modern School
L   Former Leeds Higher Grade School
M   Former Pupil Teachers' College
N   Leeds College of Art & Design
O   Leeds Metropolitan University (Civic Quarter)
P   Corn Exchange
Q   City Markets
R   Grand Theatre
S   West Yorkshire Playhouse
T   Carriageworks Theatre

Leeds City Centre

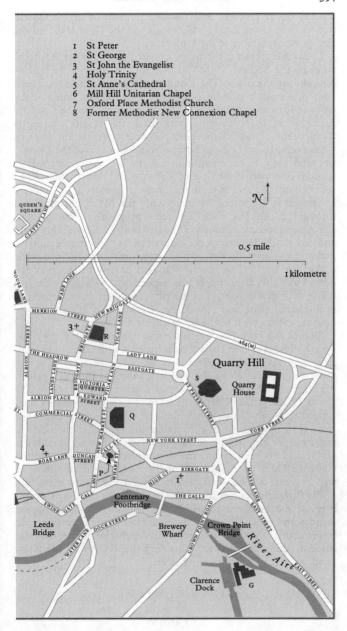

1 St Peter
2 St George
3 St John the Evangelist
4 Holy Trinity
5 St Anne's Cathedral
6 Mill Hill Unitarian Chapel
7 Oxford Place Methodist Church
8 Former Methodist New Connexion Chapel

the city centre and was only one of a number of large-scale initiatives in interwar Leeds, which included the Civic Hall and the first great expansion of the University.

Leeds was spared the damage wreaked among other industrial cities by the Second World War but not the appetite for replanning during the peace. The Council's Development Plan, issued 1951–5, set out a grandiose scheme for rebuilding much of the city's civic centre under *R. A. H. Livett*, appointed as the first City Architect in 1946. Progress was fitful, the results frequently disappointing. Instead the best post-war contribution remains *Chamberlin, Powell & Bon*'s adventurous extension of the University after 1963. In anticipation of this the University successfully secured the partial sinking of the planned Inner Ring Road (opened in 1964 and in truth an inner city motorway); elsewhere its impact is a disaster. More recently the M621 has ploughed through s Leeds. Far more destructive proposals for comprehensive redevelopment of much of the city centre followed after 1968 and did much damage in the pursuit of 'vertical segregation' of pedestrians and traffic before plans were quietly abandoned at the end of the 1970s. The general standard of new buildings of the period was also dispiritingly low, especially the visually offensive office slabs that dominate in the city centre. Extensive clearance of industrial areas and rebuilding of slums also left a legacy of housing estates both in the inner city and suburbs.

Against this backdrop a defence was mounted of the city's historic buildings and in the 1980s coincided with efforts to regenerate and revive areas affected by industrial decline in s and central Leeds and along the Kirkstall Valley, as the city's principal employers became the financial and service industries. The Leeds Development Corporation (1988–95) was primarily concerned with the disused sites along the Aire and the canal but since then the process of conversion and reuse has extended to other former industrial areas, e.g. the former Round Foundry at Holbeck. Less certain was the masterplan for the area around Clarence Dock on the s bank of the Aire, where the intention was to create a residential district around the tourist attraction of the Royal Armouries Museum. In the 1990s the City Council oversaw the excellent refurbishment of the Briggate shopping arcades and other buildings. Since 2000 a more worrying trend has emerged of scheme after scheme of high-rise offices, flats and student residences that are changing the skyline of Leeds for good but not perhaps for the better.

CITY CENTRE

CHURCHES

Anglican

80 ST PETER,[*] Kirkgate. 1837–41 by *R. D. Chantrell* for Dr Walter Farquhar Hook, vicar from 1837 until 1859. Internally,

---

[*] This entry has been contributed by Christopher Webster.

probably the country's most important church of its date, and largely unaltered. The cruciform plan, with an outer N aisle to the nave and chancel, follows the footprint of its medieval predecessor. Chantrell's main innovation was to move the tower from the crossing to the N transept, thus opening up the internal vista from nave to altar and, at the same time, giving the tower greater prominence when seen from the town centre. Chantrell's chosen style of 'the transition from Decorated to Perpendicular' is seen to effect in the tower's elaborate openwork battlements and pinnacles, so too in the W window's tracery with a rich ogee hoodmould. The entrance is in the middle of the N side, under the tower. The chancel and nave are of equal length, four bays to the E, four bays to the W. They both have clerestories and tall aisles, and the chancel has a shallow apse. The outer N aisle, no higher than a cloister to allow light to pass over it and into the clerestory of the inner N aisle, has straight-headed reticulated windows, while the S side, in some ways more elegant, has tall, slender Early Perpstyle windows spanning ground and gallery levels. The choir vestry is of 1901 by *C. R. Chorley*, the Wesley Room over the vestry by *Denis Mason Jones*, 1974.

Inside, the principles of formal classical planning that Chantrell acquired while a pupil of Soane are evident. One enters at the base of the tower into a lofty, carefully contrived symmetrical space of almost Fonthillian proportions, with glazed doors l. and r. to the outer N aisles. Ahead on the N–S axis is the massive, sombre organ case, by *Chantrell*, occupying the whole of the S transept. Hook appointed as his organist S. S. Wesley – probably the foremost church musician of his day – and inaugurated daily choral services with his choir placed in the chancel; notable innovations for a church of this date.

p. 400

At the crossing the full E and W vistas open up to reveal the majestic interior, as well as the dichotomy of the design. The raised E end is dignified, with generous space in the sanctuary and in front of the altar for the new ideas of Victorian ritualism – claimed by Addleshaw and Ettchells to be 'the first great instance of Catholic feeling in an Anglican church'. The W end, however, with its pews and galleries focused on the huge pulpit, is still very much in the 'preaching box' tradition, a tradition despised by forward thinkers from the mid 1840s. Crossing and transepts are lierne-vaulted (in plaster), the apse is fan-vaulted (also in plaster). The nave and chancel ceilings have almost flat panels separated by substantial transverse beams embellished with arcaded decoration on their sides, actually the lower part of the largely concealed roof trusses. Piers of four shafts with fillets on two sides and thinner diagonal shafts to the nave and finely moulded arches, all essentially Dec. The unusual panelling of the walls between the arches and the clerestory may have been influenced by similar features at Bruges Cathedral where Chantrell was working concurrently. Galleries extend around three sides of the nave. They are supported on cast-iron columns and slightly detached from the stone piers, to show, as Chantrell put it, 'they are merely furniture'. Richly Dec fronts, possibly papier mâché but painted in imitation of wood (some other apparently wooden decoration e.g. on pew-ends, is cast iron). The galleries continue into the first two bays of the chancel. Here their fronts appear to provide the choir stalls with canopies, although this effect was unintended, for in Chantrell's early scheme the chancel was to be have been filled only with further pews and galleries extending to the E wall. Restoration and imaginative colour scheme by *Martin Stancliffe*, 1989. Lady Chapel (outer N chancel aisle), 1922. City of Leeds Room (outer N nave aisle) 1975, by *Denis Mason Jones*, modified in 2000 by Stancliffe. The large vestry has its original fittings and strongroom, still redolent of the church as power-house of Victorian Anglicanism.

FURNISHINGS. Chancel: REREDOS, marble, designed by *G. E. Street* with mosaics from cartoons by *Clayton & Bell*, executed by *Earp* and *Rust*. Unveiled 1888. – Apse MOSAICS by *Salviati* of Venice, 1876. Statues of the four Evangelists, each side of the E window, by *Messrs Dennis Lee & Walsh*, 1861. – Pair of free-standing, delicate wooden SEDILIA, designed by *C. E. Kempe*, 1891. – Early C10 stone CROSS, in the Anglo-Scandinavian style, including a panel depicting Weland the Smith in his flying machine. This is the best-preserved of fragments of at least six crosses discovered during the rebuilding in 1838 (others are in the City Museum). – PULPIT, 1841, carved by *Fentiman*. – FONT, designed by *Butterfield*, erected 1883. Old FONT, by the S door, octagonal, C15, with

Leeds, St Peter, interior looking west.
Lithograph by Shaw and Groom, *c.* 1841

later ogee-shaped, crocketed wooden cover. – N transept: etched glass SCREEN, Jacob's Ladder by *Sally Scott*, 1998. Early C18 statue of St Peter, in wood, over the inside of N door. – Brass LECTERN by *Leaver* of Maidenhead, *c.* 1870. – Lady Chapel: ROYAL ARMS over entrance from tower, C18, altered 1801; REREDOS, by *F. C. Eden*, with references to the style of his master, Comper, dedicated 1922. City of Leeds Room: former Civic Pew front, 1660, with coat of arms and Jacobean strapwork decoration.

STAINED GLASS. The following is a selection of the major windows. N chancel aisle, E window: mainly C16 Flemish glass collected by John Summers and assembled by *Thomas Wilmhirst*, 1841. Apse: 1846, by *Wilmhirst*. S wall of S chancel aisle 1862, designed by *E. M. Barry*, made by *Wailes*. S aisle: St Peter window, made by *Wright* of Leeds, designed by *Schwanfelder*, 1811, but still in the C18 tradition. W window, upper part: 1841, by *David Evans* of Shrewsbury, after a design by *Chantrell*, showing the coats of arms of the patrons. W window, lower part: 1856, by *Evans*. W end of N nave aisle: 1863, by *Heaton, Butler & Bayne*. City of Leeds Room: 'Penny Window', 1841, one of several windows in Geometric glass by *John Bower*. Other good mid-Victorian glass by *O'Connor* (Lady Chapel, 1853, 1861 and 1866), *Warrington* (S chapel, 1858), *Wailes* (N chapel, 1860) and *Capronnier* (N aisle W, 1875).

MONUMENTS. A large number, the important monuments are in chronological order as follows: S chancel aisle: effigy of knight, cross-legged, *c.* 1330, damaged. Close by, brass of Sir John Langton, †1459 and his wife; brass to Thomas Clarell, a former vicar of Leeds, †1469, with chalice but no effigy; table tomb to Thomas Hardwick, †1577, with fine fresco panel depicting Hardwick and his family. Lady Chapel: John Thoresby, †1679, tablet with bust by *Andrew Carpenter*; Captains Walker and Beckett, †1809, by *J. Flaxman*, 1811, with relief of Victory, mourning, under a palm tree; Thomas Lloyd, †1828, by *Joseph Gott*, frontal bust on a base with an inscription flanked by two Leeds Volunteers; Roger Holt Leigh, †1831, by *R. Westmacott Jun.*, relief showing Leigh seated on a Greek chair, with books on a table. S chancel aisle: Ralph Thoresby, the Leeds antiquary, †1725, inscription under a crocketed gable and between pinnacles, 1841, designed by *Chantrell* 'to exhibit a model of what a Gothic monument ought to be'. S of the altar: William Beckett, †1863, portrait on a high base on which stands an angel and two children, representing Charity, by *Baron Marochetti*. N of the altar: Dean W. F. Hook, †1875 (buried in Chichester); designed by *G. G. Scott*, executed by *Walsh* of Leeds with figures by *Keyworth Jun.* of Hull. Recumbent effigy on a tomb-chest with arched open sides. Naturalistic foliage in the spandrels. This shrine-like motif seems to be derived from the shrines of St Cantelupe at Hereford and St Frideswide at Oxford, two cathedrals restored by Scott in 1842 etc. and 1870 etc. There are many other good monuments from the late C17–C19, especially under the tower and in the City of Leeds Room.*

From 1869 the railway cut the church off from the centre of Leeds so effectively that to Pevsner in 1959 it seemed 'to stand at a half-commercial, half-derelict dead end'. Today the surroundings have been revitalized and the churchyard, principally s of the church, is an attractive and quiet corner. Paved with gravestones, all apparently late C18 or early C19. At the NE corner, facing the street, is the WAR MEMORIAL (Leeds Rifles) of 1921 by *Lutyens*, one of his slender War Crosses, incorporating a shelf at its base.

ST GEORGE, Great George Street. 1836–8 by *John Clark*. Large, with tall lancets and a w tower; the pinnacles and a tall spire are a restoration, without finesse, of 2006 (original removed 1962). E apse and vestry by *Henry Walker*, 1898–1900. Long Room (N side), 1974. Wide aiseless nave, originally with galleries on three sides: the area below the w gallery screened off in 1962, the N and S galleries removed in 1989–91 when the pews were replaced with tiered seating by *James Thorp & Partners*. Queenpost roof supported on deep brackets and moulded corbels. – Altarpiece PAINTING by *C. W. Cope*, 1841, commissioned by John Atkinson, mill-owner, '. . . He ever liveth to make intercession for them'. – STAINED GLASS. Chancel apse, two groups: SS Matthew, George and Mark, and SS Luke, Philip and John, by *William Pape*, 1938. Nave N wall, upper part, Suffer Little Children by *Powell Bros.*; E wall, two medallions of the Crucifixion and Resurrection, 1861. These echo the S nave window, the Baptism of Christ and The Sower, a memorial to Christopher Beckett (†1855). A cleverly integrated central panel of 1990 (inserted when the gallery was removed) depicts new growth. At the base of the tower a glazed panel commemorates the Rev. Don Robins (1900–48), who converted the CRYPT as a shelter for the unemployed (refurbished 1999 by *Mark Tabert*). Near the w entrance, the Crypt Chapel, 2003 – bare stone walls with a glowing brick vault above and, like icons on patches of old plaster, portraits of staff and clients by *Steve Simpson* on the theme of the Last Supper.

CHURCH CENTRE and housing, NW, 2005–6 by *AXIS Architecture*.

ST JOHN THE EVANGELIST,** New Briggate. Founded by John Harrison, wool merchant and philanthropist. Consecrated in 1634 and virtually intact in spite of changes in the C19. Plans for its demolition in 1865 were averted by the actions of the youthful *Richard Norman Shaw* who argued for its restoration, which he undertook in 1866–8. Shaw later spoke of his 'dismal failures', labouring under constant pressure and penny-pinching by the trustees, and from 1884 was re-engaged to supervise a period of 'reparation' by Canon John Scott, a

---

* The monument to Michael Sadler, noted by Pevsner in 1959, is now in St George's Fields, *see* p. 470.

** This entry has been contributed by Janet Douglas.

Leeds, St John, exterior.
Engraving, 1715

cousin of Sir (George) Gilbert Scott.* *George Gilbert Scott Jun.* was involved in a second restoration, 1885–8, and further work was continued up to 1903 by his pupil *Temple Moore*.

The exterior remains true to the traditions of late medieval West Yorkshire church building – square mullioned windows, strong buttresses and battlements – and is outwardly largely Perp. Rectangular plan, lacking a well-defined chancel, w tower, nave, s aisle and s porch. Built of fine-grained local sandstone; Shaw's restorations are distinguished by coarse-grained sandstone peppered with quartz pebbles. The embattled tower is of three stages but only the base with a single window in each face is original. Its plain upper stages with small belfry windows were taken down in 1810 and replaced in 1838 by *John Clark*. Large three-light bell-openings with odd tracery and ogee hoodmoulds; twelve-foiled circular surrounds beneath them. Angle buttresses and tall corner pinnacles. The nave and aisle have straight-headed windows with cusped lights, but with odd little arch-heads above the middle of each window. At the E end, twin gable-ends. Some windows have odd Flamboyant tracery, more Dec than Perp, probably by Norman Shaw. He added the N vestry and the C17 pastiche S porch and gates.

Internally the most remarkable feature is that the church is of two naves rather than a nave and s aisle, divided by a central arcade and separated from the E end by a carved oak screen

51

---

*Scott had supported Shaw's case for retaining the church.

across the breadth of the church. Originally the church was orientated N–S with pews facing the pulpit on the N wall (reorientated in 1807). The arches of the central arcade, with two sunk-quadrant mouldings typical of the C14, are supported by stone piers, octagonal at the W end but then changing to a more complex moulded form with recessed quadrants in the diagonals and classical capitals with acanthus leaves and ball ornaments. The twin roof of the nave is of a basic truss construction and the lack of coordination between the arcade and the trusses is evidence of the piecemeal approach of C17 provincial builders. Suspended from the great oak ties are curious drop pendants, but even more curious are the carved corbels: most are angels with musical instruments, but in the corners are strange hermaphrodite figures. The pretty plaster panels of the ceiling (originally painted) contain strapwork and flowing naturalistic mouldings with various motifs: owls (the symbol of Leeds), Pan-like horn blowers, and peacocks with serpents in their beaks. Later wooden battens securing the panels ran straight across the central medallions, some of which were originally lion heads. Above the screen, semicircular wooden arches are infilled with strapwork spandrels.

The arrangements of the chancel and chapel are wholly Victorian. Shaw was largely responsible for the present chancel. Separating it from the Harrison Chapel is an oak gate added by *Moore* in 1890.

FURNISHINGS. The glorious carved C17 woodwork is by *Francis Gunby*, predominantly domestic in character. Sumptuous oak SCREEN (cf. Wakefield Cathedral, West Riding South) with solid panelled dado and an arcade of tapering pillars with Ionic capitals and delicate filigree arches, over which runs a richly carved frieze of hearts, rosettes, tulips, vine leaves and animal grotesques. Human and lion heads support the projecting parts of the cornice. Set within elaborate crestings are ROYAL ARMS, which were removed in 1866–8, although the crestings were reintroduced in 1890–1 to enclose religious symbols designed by *Temple Moore* (now on W wall). The arms, reinstated in the 1970s, are curiosities. Over the N screen, James I who died in 1625, nine years before the church's consecration. The S screen bears the arms of Charles I as Prince of Wales. Can the church have been constructed and furnished well before 1634? – PULPIT with tester (strikingly similar to the pulpit in the chapel at Temple Newsam House, where Gunby worked for Sir Arthur Ingram): equally sumptuous, also dismantled 1866–8 but reconstructed in the 1880s using original fragments skilfully blended with new work. The base comprises four tiers of panelling with pilasters, strapwork and carved heads; the eagles (the symbol of St John) to the sides of the back-board are original. – LECTERN. 1880s. Assembled from parts of the old reading desk. – PEWS retain original bench ends with urn-shaped finials and strapwork panels. – FONT, by *Shaw*, a well-detailed octagonal bowl carved by one of his favourite craftsmen, *James Forsyth*. It originally stood beneath the tester taken from the C17 pulpit; the ensemble was adorned with elaborate metalwork (whereabouts unknown). – Chancel: C17 COMMUNION TABLE with bulbous legs ending with Ionic capitals and a strapwork frieze with carved heads with cavalier-type moustaches. Although the chancel always held benches for communicants, the table's original position is uncertain, and it appears to have been in the s chapel in 1787. – REREDOS, a composite piece: gold *Salviati* mosaics commissioned by *Shaw*, but in a setting by *Temple Moore*, reusing two angel corbels removed when the organ was rebuilt in 1885. Carved central panel, bought locally by Canon Scott, probably the door of a tabernacle. Probably Continental. ALTAR RAIL and ORGAN CASE (dated 1871) by *Shaw*; the choir stalls were introduced as part of his 'reparation'. Harrison Chapel: panelled by *Temple Moore* with the pew doors removed in the 1860s.

PAINTING: W wall. Portrait of John Harrison, given to the church by his nephew, the Rev. Henry Robinson. In 1860, it was moved to the council chamber of the new Town Hall and later placed in the Art Gallery. It was finally restored to St John's in 1923.

STAINED GLASS: mostly undistinguished, dating from 1868–1902. Clockwise from the porch: four small windows by *C. E. Tute*, 1897 and 1902. W wall: Scenes from the Life of John the Baptist by *Lavers, Barraud & Westlake*, 1869; tower window by *Hardman & Co.*, 1901; two small windows by *Victor Milner* who often worked for Temple Moore. N wall: fourth window by *Tute*, 1894, has particularly charming owls in the lower lights. E window: by *Ward & Hughes*, 1870. Harrison Chapel: memorial E window to John Harrison (†1656), by *Burlison & Grylls*, 1885, including scenes (some fanciful) from Harrison's life. Nave, s wall: mostly by *Lavers, Barraud & Westlake*, except for third window (Christ with the Woman of Samaria) by *C. E. Kempe*.

MONUMENTS. John Harrison †1656. A large tablet without any figures. Classical forms without frills. It bears the inscription written on the original by Dr Lake, Vicar of Leeds 1660–3. Moved to its present position in the 1860s with a setting designed by Shaw. The remaining monuments are largely of local interest, commemorating the lives of Leeds woollen merchants and incumbents of the church.

CHURCHYARD: paved with gravestones. Wall and arched E gateway are by *Shaw*. At the SW corner stands the Parish Hall and caretaker's house built in 1815 as a charity school on the site of the chapel attached to Harrison's almshouses.

HOLY TRINITY, Boar Lane. 1722–7 by *William Etty* of York, almost exactly contemporary with Gibbs's St Martin-in-the-Fields, London, whose influence is very obvious in the details. Fleeces stamped onto the lead drainpipe fixings are a small reminder of the source of the wealth of the merchants by whom the church was built. Ralph Thoresby, merchant, diarist and local historian, was among those who met the cost. The s side

of the church faces Boar Lane. It has doorways with Gibbs surrounds in the first and last bays, and five bays of windows with
alternating open triangular and segmental pediments, carved
without fuss. Square gallery windows above in plain surrounds.
Dividing the bays, giant Doric pilasters support a triglyph
frieze, cornice and blocking course surmounted by flaming
urns. Apse with Venetian window. The w (entrance) façade has
a tower with a balustraded clock stage, as designed by Etty.
A timber spire was added to this (shown on Cossins's map of
1725) but it blew down in 1839 and was replaced by
R. D. Chantrell with a graceful tower that rises in diminishing
stages to 180 ft (55 metres), the top stage with concave sides.
High and light interior with splendid giant Corinthian columns
supporting a shallow tunnel-vault. Greek-key pattern on the
soffits and modillion cornice. Excellent plasterwork in the apse
with putti in the spandrels of the E window and fruiting
garlands. Narrow side aisles, originally with galleries – these
were removed during restoration by *Thomas Winn*, 1883–4,
along with box pews, choir stalls and flooring. The pedestals
of the columns were lowered to the height of the new pews.

– PULPIT with inlaid side panels and tester with star inlay.
– REREDOS carved with swags and gilded pelican. Lady Chapel
(N aisle): a PAINTING of the Annunciation in Pre-Raphaelite
style. – STAINED GLASS: E window by *William Wailes*, 1848; the
Ascension with the Evangelists in the side windows. S aisle, SE
by *Michael O'Connor*, 1866, with lustrous colours; SW, the
Good Shepherd, 1903. S clerestory (Raising of Lazarus), signed
by *Powell Bros.*, 1895. – MONUMENTS. A few from St Paul, Park
Square (dem. 1905). N aisle, W end, Anne Sheepshanks 'of
simple and domestic habits' †1821; Greek Revival with urn and
palm tree. Henry Robinson, †1736, local benefactor and
founder of the church. Palladian marble aedicule supported by
putti and garlands with Latin inscription. To its l., a plaque
carved with drapery lists his acts of charity 'To procure the
Bounty of Q. Anne' for twenty-one vicarages, chapels and
churches. His nephew James Scott (†1782), first minister of
Holy Trinity, is commemorated in the S aisle, 'Regretted by the
wife, and lamented by the good'. – CHURCH HALL, N, 1982–3.
Gritstone.

Roman Catholic

ST ANNE'S CATHEDRAL, Cookridge Street. Arts and Crafts
Gothic by *J. H. Eastwood*, assisted by *S. K. Greenslade* of Exeter,
1901–4, succeeding 'Old St Anne' (*John Child*, 1838; dem.
1904). An awkward site onto which is squeezed an aisled nave
and chancel under a single roof, shallow transepts with E
chapels, chapter house, presbytery and a large basement. Walls
of large blocks of Weldon stone, carved details in buff-coloured
Ketton limestone. Compact and impressive W front, a tripartite composition of tall gable flanked by bulky chamfered but

tresses terminating in Gothic turrets with freely carved panels and squat truncated finials; lower side aisles. Deeply recessed w entrance carved with symbols of the Passion on the arch moulding and canopied niches in the reveals. A large Calvary dominates, set on a stepped and moulded stone parapet. Three-stage N tower rising almost directly from the street. Square buttresses, battered lower stage, high plain middle stage, and upper belfry with pairs of traceried and louvred windows, modest pyramid roof (an early design shows it taller). The tower was originally intended for the entrance front but was moved to its less imposing position after threats of litigation over loss of light to the warehouses opposite. Elongated clerestory windows with sinuous tracery, in wide segmental arches. Plain square buttresses project above the moulded parapet. The transept gables have paired windows and an elaborate carving round a louvred panel. The E end stands higher but the roof-line is continuous, with more tall windows lighting the choir gallery. Neat octagonal CHAPTER HOUSE, evocative of medieval precedent, with single-light windows and a pointed roof finished with stumpy lead finial.

The INTERIOR has been reordered on several occasions, mostly to the detriment of the early C20 work, before successful enhancement in 2005–6 by *Buttress Fuller Alsop Williams*. It is almost square on plan, with a nave of four bays, the short transepts entered from the wider E bay. Arcade piers have heavy roll or chamfered mouldings carried up to canopied statue niches, features that continue on the face of the chancel arch. Attractive detail of Dec and Art Nouveau forms. Four-bay chancel raised higher than the nave in response to the sloping site but deeper, narrower and loftier; a dramatic effect. The steps, of 2005–6, curve outwards as a setting for the altar and incorporate ambos, sympathetically detailed. Enclosing the sanctuary, an arcaded ambulatory beneath a choir gallery, a late change to Eastwood's plans. On the S side, the Lady Chapel. Three bays with a shallow two-bay S aisle, the panelled capitals of the arcade piers in free Art Nouveau Gothic.

FURNISHINGS. Many of the lavish fittings were lost to mid-C20 reorderings. – Perp REREDOS by *Greenslade*, 1901, made by *Flint Bros.* of Clapham. Similar to Pearson's work at Truro and Hove. Eight saints associated with the cathedral and the early Yorkshire Church flank a low-relief carving of the Coronation of Our Lady. Ornate canopy with elaborate frieze of fruits. As a backdrop, MOSAICS by *Cesare Formilli*, 1928, replacing his encaustic paintings (to *Eastwood's* design) on the same subjects (St Francis, the Ascension, St Patrick, and the Assumption). – Sandstone ALTAR, the CANONS' STALLS and CATHEDRA (the latter incorporated with elements of Eastwood's original) of 2005–6 by *Richard Williams* of BFAW. – ORGAN. *Norman & Beard*, 1904. – (The PULPIT, made by *J. F. Bentley c.* 1895 during his enhancement of the old church, has been removed. Traceried alabaster side panels and 'Feed my sheep' in opus sectile.) – FONT, nave W end.

Stone, octagonal, with angels supporting. Probably mid-C19, from 'Old St Anne'. – LANTERNS, to nave and transept: a fine Neo-Gothic set.

Lady Chapel: – Outstanding REREDOS from 'Old St Anne' by *A. W. N. Pugin*, 1842, made by *George Myers*. Dec. Under nodding ogee canopies, S S Anne and Wilfrid flank the Virgin and six smaller figures, all richly painted in red, blue and gold. The ALTAR is from St Mary's Chapel, Lady Lane (1794), encased and enriched by Pugin with large panels of quatrefoil tracery. – PEWS, designed by *Canon Thomas Shine*, made 1915 by *Arthur Walker*, a local cabinetmaker. – MURAL PAINTINGS, in the arch spandrels of the Lady Chapel, of 1915 or 1937. Not good. – STATUE above the entrance of Our Lady Immaculate, by *Boulton* of Cheltenham, 1933. – Shrine of Our Lady of Perpetual Succour (S transept). A tall Dec piece with an open lantern. By Eastwood, carved by *H. H. Martyn & Co.* of Cheltenham, 1913; incorporating an earlier icon. – Chapel of the Sacred Heart (N transept). By *Greenslade*, 1903, the stone REREDOS carved by *Nathaniel Hitch* (statue by *Formilli*, 1922); marble ALTAR with carving of the Last Supper, a vein of brown marble linking the head of St John with Christ's heart. – Chapel of St Joseph, 1904, timber and gilt REREDOS by *Eastwood*; ALTAR with St Joseph on his deathbed carved by *H. H. Martyn & Co.* – War Memorial Chapel (N aisle E): fittings by *Formilli*, 1920, including modest memorial plaques with laurel wreath surrounds. – Pietà Chapel: Pieta by *R. L. Boulton & Sons* of Cheltenham, 1913, after Michelangelo; dark green marble walls by *Leeds Marble Works*; cross by *Arthur Walker*, 1924. – Former baptistery: sickly marble walls, 1926 by Formilli. Good wrought-iron GATES of 1963 by *Weightman & Bullen*: doves and droplets below a copper band representing flowing water. – Shrine of the Diocesan Martyrs (S aisle): large iconographic PAINTING by *Richard Lomas*, 1988, above the shrine of St Urban, by *Greenslade*: brown marble, metal casket with crowns and olive wreaths. – STAINED GLASS: E window, by *Eastwood*, 1912, with his sun-ray motif; his other designs were not completed. S transept: scenes from the life of Christ, bought privately by Canon Shine in 1920. Unknown provenance. Delicate patterned glass was installed by *Kayll & Reed*, 1931. It matches their work in the N transept: the Crucifixion (1927) and Resurrection (1929). Symbolic emblems in the Pietà Chapel and the baptistery, 1927.

CATHEDRAL HOUSE (presbytery and offices), Great George Street, also by *Eastwood*, occupies almost a quarter of the total site. Domestic Free Style in stone and cream, sand-faced Suffolk brick with Ketton stone dressings. Three storeys and seven bays, with central deep porch and mullion-and-transom window frames, one in a canted bay. Uphill, also now cathedral offices, a former Masonic Hall by *J. M. Bottomley*, over-restored in 1991. Red and yellow brick with a broad front under a pedimented gable, topped by a bell-turret. –

CATHEDRAL HALL by *Damond Lock Grabowski & Partners* (*DLG Architects*), completed 2003, a sympathetic Arts and Crafts design.

Nonconformist

MILL HILL UNITARIAN CHAPEL, City Square. Built 1847–8 by *Bowman & Crowther* of Manchester, replacing an earlier chapel of 1674, where Joseph Priestley was minister in the late C18. 'No longer essentially different from buildings for the Established Church', noted Pevsner. Perp, with a chancel, its design indebted to Chantrell's St Peter (*see* above) but without a tower. Crocketed pinnacles and larger lantern finials have been removed, except on the S front. Poor S porch, of *c.* 1960 when the nave was partitioned. Inside, clustered columns support the arch-braced nave roof. Angels carved in wood and stone. Shallow N chancel, embellished from the later C19, when the small congregation was led by Sir James Kitson, later first Lord Airedale (†1911). – REREDOS with mosaics (Christ and the Prophets) by *Salviati*, *c.* 1884; the raised green marble flooring is of 1924, with inset memorial to the influential minister Charles Hargrove (†1918). – Tall elaborate Caen stone PULPIT. – Numbered PEWS with ornate crocketed finials and doors. – STAINED GLASS: W side. In the W entrance, an obscured N window signed by *Warrington* of London, 1860. Also by him, undated, the NW window with scenes from the life of Christ. E wall, obscured by the S gallery stairs, a fine early *Morris & Co.* window in memory of Ann Kitson (†1865): pelican in her piety and figures of Ruth, Martha and Mary Magdalen designed by *Morris*; Dorcas by *Ford Madox Brown*. Martha and Mary again in the next, by *Powell Bros.*, then two by *Clayton & Bell c.* 1880. Chancel: Lord Airedale (James Kitson) memorial window by *A. K. Nicholson*, 1912, with figures of Ralph Thoresby, Joseph Priestley and Kitson. Several MEMORIALS survive from the C17 chapel.

OXFORD PLACE METHODIST CHAPEL, Oxford Place, immediately W of the Town Hall. The simple Oxford Row façade with round-headed windows is *James Simpson*'s original chapel of 1835, which was remodelled in 1896–1903 by *G. F. Danby & W. H. Thorp* and turned to face the Town Hall. Baroque taste with gusto. Local red pressed brick with stripy Morley Moor sandstone dressings, a symmetrical two-storey façade with Ionic columns and obelisk finials. Gabled and pedimented centre with domed cupolas over the outer bays. Linking this to the contemporary, and matching, Oxford Chambers is a mighty tower, with a balustraded top stage and tall, stone cupola.

Former METHODIST NEW CONNEXION CHAPEL, Rossington Street and Woodhouse Lane. Now a pub. By *William Hill*, 1857–8. Pedimented. Brick with richly carved stonework. Schoolrooms and an institute in the basement, all substantially funded by the popular Alderman Henry Marsden, whose statue stands on Woodhouse Moor (*see* p. 471).

PUBLIC BUILDINGS

1. Civic, administrative, etc.

95 TOWN HALL, Headrow.* 1852–8 by *Cuthbert Brodrick*. Leeds can be proud of its Town Hall, one of the most convincing buildings of its date in the country, and of the classical buildings of its date no doubt the most successful. Leeds was not the first of the major industrial towns to express its increasing wealth and importance in terms of monumental masonry. Birmingham and Liverpool had led the way, but in 1851 a group of prominent citizens founded the Leeds Improvement Society in the belief that 'if a noble municipal palace that might fairly vie with some of the best Town Halls of the continent were to be erected in the middle of their hitherto squalid and unbeautiful town, it would become a practical admonition to the populace of the value of beauty and art, and in course of time men would learn to live up to it'. In the same year a site was bought on the w side of town for £9,500 from John Blayds, a wealthy merchant and landowner. In 1852 it was decided to hold an open architectural competition, of which Sir Charles Barry was appointed assessor.

Of the sixteen designs submitted, that of Cuthbert Brodrick, a virtually unknown young man from Hull, was selected. He had been trained in the office of Henry Francis Lockwood and after completing his pupillage had travelled in Europe for two years, making a serious study of historic and contemporary buildings. Brodrick's success at Leeds seemed to have repeated the pattern of the competition for St George's Hall, Liverpool, which had been won by twenty-five-year-old Harvey Lonsdale Elmes in 1839. Both were young men when their designs were selected, and it was commented that 'previously quite unknown talent has suddenly burst into notice'.

The Instructions to Architects, which was sent to all the contestants, revealed the innovatory nature of the proposed building. It was to contain under one roof a hall capable of holding 8,000 people standing and with an orchestra and balcony, refreshment rooms and kitchens, servants' hall, changing rooms for musicians, a mayoral suite, a Council Chamber, accommodation for the council officers, four courtrooms and accommodation for the police. In this it exceeded Birmingham Town Hall (Joseph Hansom & Edward Welch; begun 1832), in which the auditorium *was* the Roman temple with little space in the podium for other accommodation; even Elmes's St George's Hall contains only two courtrooms in addition to the great central hall and a small concert hall. By contrast, Leeds

---

*This entry has been contributed by Derek Linstrum.

wanted a municipal palace. The Instructions required 'a neat and commodious exterior' but made no reference to the architectural style that was to be adopted. Probably it was not thought necessary. Comparable buildings, such as St George's Hall, Liverpool, the Fitzwilliam Museum, Cambridge (G. Basevi and C. R. Cockerell, begun 1836) and the Royal Exchange, London (Sir W. Tite 1841–4) had been built in a classical style from which there was no reason to depart. Nor was there any reference to the materials but once again it would have been expected that stone would be used, especially as the West Yorkshire towns were close to many quarries that could offer a variety of different types.

The meagre sum provided – £35,000 – was derided in the professional journals. Maybe that is why only sixteen entries were received, compared with Birmingham's seventy; but Brodrick took the requirement seriously and suggested a rational plan in which the basilican hall was central and each of the four corners was to be expressed as a projecting pavilion containing a courtroom and adjacent accommodation. With great ingenuity Brodrick placed the Council Chamber at the S end of the Hall above the entrance hall. It was to be semicircular in plan, maybe deriving from Jacques Gondoin's École de Chirurgie (1769–74), one of the most famous late C18 buildings in Paris, and 'capable of forming part of the Hall; by merely opening the folding doors, this will give additional space for at least 300 spectators sitting'. This relatively simple, straightforward arrangement was altered by the decision to provide more accommodation by doubling the number of rooms on the E and W sides, giving the building its more solid quadrangular appearance which almost fills the site, and the decision to build a tower which required replanning of the S rooms.

The main contract, in the sum of £41,835 was signed on 25 July 1853. It specifically excluded the construction of a tower recommended by Sir Charles Barry. In 1854, however, the Council instructed Brodrick to make provision in the foundations for a tower.* The money, £5,500, was only provided in 1856 and as work progressed there was a willingness to allow further embellishments: these subtly changed the character of what had begun as a design in the French Neoclassical style to one in which, wrote Pevsner, 'the Baroque is nearer'.

EXTERIOR. The Town Hall is bounded on the N by Great George Street, on the E by Calverley Street, and on the W by Oxford Place. The monumental flight of steps leading to the S FRONT is an impressive prelude to the great ten-column Corinthian colonnade. This is reminiscent of French Neoclassical buildings, many of which Brodrick had probably seen on his European tour, such as the Paris Bourse (A.-T. Brongniart,

---

*Although Brodrick produced an engraved perspective in 1853 including a tall colonnaded structure consisting of an octagonal base surmounted by an elongated rotunda and a classical spire.

1808–25), the Grand Théâtre, Bordeaux (V. Louis, 1773–80), the theatre in Nantes (M. Crucy, 1784–8) and the Palais de Justice, Lyons (L.-P. Baltard, 1835–47). There are pavilions to l. and r. with Corinthian columns between coupled pilasters and arched windows in two storeys. This pattern is repeated with variations on the E and W elevations. The central part of the N façade, with smooth ashlar and rounded corners, also displays a French Neoclassical character. The entrance steps are flanked by the access to the former police station (l.) and cells (r.), an alteration by Brodrick in 1864–7 in an appropriate rusticated Newgate style and guarded by four Portland stone lions carved by *W. D. Keyworth*. *John Thomas*'s carved allegory around the S entrance, probably suggested by the richness of decoration on the New Louvre in Paris (H.-M. Lefuel, begun in 1852) illustrates Leeds 'in its commercial and industrial character, fostering and encouraging the Arts and Sciences'.

Above the S colonnade is the proud TOWER, 225 ft (68.6 metres) high, with a detached square colonnade of six columns to each side and a big, tall, rather elongated square lead-covered dome with concave sides crowned by a cupola. If there was a precedent it was the tower of Thomas Archer's early C18 St Philip's church, Birmingham. Embellishments added as work progressed include the monumental vases on the balustraded parapets, like those at Chatsworth and Castle Howard, and the utilitarian ventilation shafts which were turned into elaborately carved ornaments reminiscent of Roman stelae. Stylized rosettes were added to the sculpture on the tower – a detail that was almost a signature of Brodrick's work.

INTERIOR. In the competition design the colonnade on the S front was intended to be matched internally by a three-bay-wide vestibule and a staircase leading to an upper Council Chamber; but the work required in anticipation of the erection of the tower caused a major revision of this part of the building which resulted in the higher, square and domed VESTIBULE with apses on the E and W sides. The floor was laid with *Minton* encaustic tiles in an elaborate geometric pattern; this was re-laid by the same firm in 2002 during restoration by *John Thorp*, the Civic Architect. In the centre was placed an 8 ft 6 in. (2.6 metre)-high Carrara marble statue of Queen Victoria carved by *Matthew Noble*, above which the four pendentives of the dome are painted with a tribute from the four corners of the world. The statue now occupies the E apse, moved here after the Prince Consort's death in 1861, when the vestibule acquired the character of a mausoleum. In the opposite apse, a statue of the Prince, also by Noble, 1865. Both stand on polished granite pedestals: the same funereal material was used in 1874 by *Alfred Morant*, the Borough Engineer, to face the dado of the vestibule. He also added the more colourful decorative tiles in the corridors and staircases.

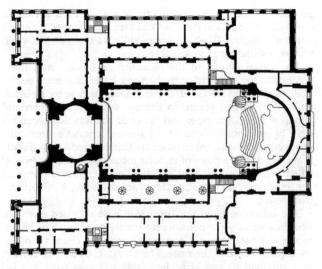

Leeds, Town Hall.
Plan

The design of the VICTORIA HALL is influenced by Liverpool's St George's Hall and indirectly by the Baths of Caracalla, its basilican form expressed by coupled Corinthian columns and pilasters separating the bays. Probably the use of this architectural feature reflects Brodrick's visit to Genoa where he saw and drew the staircase in the Palazzo dell'Università (1623). The pinioned owls in the capitals appear to be a Brodrick invention and alternate with rams' heads, both symbols drawn from the arms of the borough.* Tributes to the Golden Fleece reappear in the carvings by *John Thomas* in keystones over the lunette windows above the entablature. From these hung ten cut-glass chandeliers: three have survived and now hang in the Civic Hall (*see* below). The present Art Deco light fittings were installed in the 1930s. The windows were originally glazed with coloured glass made by *Edmundson & Son* of Manchester. The balcony across the s end of the hall was added by *W.H. Thorp* in 1890 while the four side boxes were added by *John Thorp* in 2000. Their design is based on an unsigned drawing attributed to Brodrick.

The richness of Victorian decoration is seen at its most opulent here, in which every possible surface and moulding is gilded or painted. The present scheme (dating from 1978–9) is based on a proposal made in 1894 by *John Dibblee Crace* and published in *The Art of Colour Decoration* (1912). High dark green podium, *rosso antico* columns and pilasters with bronze-gilt capitals and ornamented entablature, from which springs the blue- and ivory-panelled vault. One unusual feature,

---

*The owls derive from the coat of arms of Sir John Savile, first elected Alderman of Leeds in 1626.

probably unique, is the painted frieze with Latin and English mottoes, among them HONESTY IS THE BEST POLICY; LABOR OMNIA VINCIT ('Work conquers all'); WEAVE TRUTH WITH TRUST; IN UNION IS STRENGTH.

The visual climax to the sequence of spaces from the s colonnade to the N end of the Victoria Hall is the great organ, built by *Gray & Davidson*, the architectural case by *Brodrick*. One of the largest organs in Europe, with four manuals and pedals, it had 6,500 pipes and the swell box was the largest yet built by an English firm. At the summit against a deep blue apse powdered with golden stars are the civic arms, and slightly lower are flanking pairs of circular towers of pipes, on each of which stands a gilded angelic figure; lower still, at the original console level, four Baroque terms are sounding a celebratory trumpeting.

The other rooms in the Town Hall have survived less well. Brodrick was also responsible for the decoration of the court-rooms and the Council Chamber, varying the character of the rooms according to their use. The CIVIL COURT (NE corner; now subdivided) was lit by large side windows with coupled Corinthian pilasters and an elegant serpentine-fronted cast-iron public gallery. Its character was almost C18, while the austere top-lit BOROUGH COURT (SW) with its grained, solid divisions and single Corinthian pilasters, represents the severity of the law and the solemnity of the justice meted out here. The CRIMINAL COURT (NW) was partly destroyed by fire in 1991 and has not been reinstated. The original COUNCIL CHAMBER (now the Albert Room, E of the vestibule) still retains much of a richly decorated palazzo-like room, top-lit through a pattern of little painted glass domes. Here the coupled pilasters are fluted and the capitals include an owl looking outwards on each side.

118 CIVIC HALL, Millennium Square. 1931–3 by *E. Vincent Harris*. The concept is broadly Palladian, of Portland stone under a roof of green Cumbrian slates, with a symmetrical front and pedimented Corinthian portico flanked by Wren-style towers. Pevsner's assessment was one of qualified approval: 'As ambitious as the Town Hall but not quite as self-confident . . . 1933 could no longer use the classical or Baroque idiom with anything like the robust conviction of the Victorians. England in its official architecture clung to the mood of grandeur, but the bottom had fallen out of it. Yet the towers by their very thinness and duplication impress from a distance, and the oddities of detail – oddities imitated from Lutyens – are at least more acceptable than the deadly correctness of others of the incorrigible classicists of 1930.'

The Civic Hall stands on a steep slope making it a forceful landmark. Its site is triangular, broadening as it climbs the hill so that the long rear wings are splayed. s portico of four giant Corinthian columns under a heavy attic with a carved coat of arms by *John Hodge* just contained by the pediment. Three pairs of elaborate wrought-iron gates by *Wippell* screen the entrance doors; pedimented Gibbs surrounds to the windows of the ground floor and enormous sash windows light the Banqueting Hall above. Monumental flanking towers topped by niched, pedimented pavilions and tall, tapering spires like that of St Vedast, Cheapside, straightened and stiffened. Perched at the top are comical gilded owl finials by *Hodge*. At the base of the towers, over side entrances, are four busy cherubs by *Hermon Cawthra*, originally intended for a balustraded s terrace. Projecting stiffly at the sides are massive carved and gilded brackets in late C17 style, holding clocks. The E and W wings are of unequal length and the longer W wing is angled at the N end to enclose the N courtyard (only four storeys on the inner sides). Sober carving by *Frank Tory & Sons* of Sheffield. Within the courtyard, councillors' entrance under a large owl in a cheerful floral wreath, probably by Hodge. The Council Chamber rises behind, its parapet with ramped walls, between two service towers.

Richly coloured INTERIOR, but dignified and sombre. Long (90 ft (27.5 metres)), low T-plan ENTRANCE HALL, with twenty-six vivid green scagliola columns by *Bellman, Ivey & Carter*. The grand staircase, with treads of alternating black and white marble, a motif derived from Lutyens (cf. Gledstone Hall, q.v.), is lit by the atmospheric glow from four stained-glass windows with Yorkist heraldry by *George Kruger Gray*, a frequent collaborator with Harris. First floor RECEPTION HALL, under three saucer domes on deep pendentives separated by barrel-vaults, a variation on Harris's design for Sheffield City Hall and, as there, painted by *Gray*. Chandeliers made for the Town Hall by *Osler* of Manchester to *Brodrick*'s design. The BANQUETING HALL is Early Georgian style: oak panelling, fluted Corinthian pilasters, Kent-style doorpieces and mighty gilt wood candelabra. A gallery at each end and the Lord Mayor's and Lady Mayoress's parlours, also panelled, in English walnut, made by *John P. White & Sons*. Marble fireplaces; rose-tinted mirror in the Lady Mayoress's room. Amphitheatre-style COUNCIL CHAMBER, sunk in three tiers below entrance level, lit by a high clerestory. Galleries and wall linings of English walnut, the upper parts of the walls faced in hollow artificial stone panels by the *May Acoustic Co.*

Former MUNICIPAL BUILDINGS (former School Board Offices, Central Library and Art Gallery), Calverley Street and Victoria Square. Won in competition in 1876 by *George Corson*; built 1878–84 to house the Corporation's offices, Public Library and School Board.

The competition design illustrated in *The Builder* was for a single composition along Calverley Street but as built is divided into two by Alexander Street. Franco-Italianate style, much of the detail paying homage to the Town Hall, opposite. The SCHOOL BOARD OFFICES building (now Leeds Metropolitan University; refurbished by *Carey Jones Architects*, 1994) is tall, deeper than it is wide and of five bays with a projecting centre rising to an octagonal attic pavilion. Round-arched windows divided by fluted Corinthian columns and enriched with balusters and carving in the spandrels. The attic storey, with pairs of narrow windows, contained examination rooms. The outer entrance arch has niches containing figures of schoolchildren. Central tunnel-vaulted corridor, its walls lined with fluted pilasters, and at the rear a hidden treasure: cantilevered double-helix staircase in a square top-lit well. Stout stone columns with stiff-leaf capitals are linked by scrolled, iron balustrades and the walls lined with glazed white tiles, some patterned in blue and brown. On the top floor, a central top-lit hall (since subdivided) had galleries for one hundred pupils.

The façade of the former Municipal Offices and Library (now CENTRAL LIBRARY) is symmetrical, similarly detailed but of three storeys and on a grander scale with the central and outer bays breaking forward slightly, their paired corner pilasters carried up to chunky finials at the corners of tall pyramidal roofs. Coupled columns and pilasters in superimposed orders. Fine iron entrance gates by *Mr Jones* of Manchester, and railings with pairs of crowned owl finials. Short entrance vestibule with Doric marble columns supporting a vaulted, coffered ceiling. An elaborately carved alabaster screen by *Farmer & Brindley* separates this from the top-lit full-height INNER HALL, in Renaissance style with round-arched openings at each level, some filled by stained glass, with elaborately figured capitals. The screen to the Lending Library (former Pay Office) is by *J. W. Appleyard*, with stone roundel over, depicting medieval citizens queuing to pay their taxes, overlooked by Leeds's protective owl. N and S are staircases (N to the former offices; S to the upper floors of library), both with remarkable ensembles of carved animals and grotesques clinging to the handrails in the exotic style of William Burges. On the first floor, the former Lending Library (now Art Library) has vaults carried on arches clad in delicate pale terracotta tiles; above is the former Reference Library (now Local Studies), double-height, galleried, lit by a clerestory (cast-iron roof structure by *Dawson & Nunneley*, 1881). Segmental- and round-arched terracotta-lined openings for the books. The mirrored end walls are probably part of the 1901–10 refurbishment, when new shelving was put in by the City Engineer, *W. T. Lancaster*.

Throughout the interior are enrichments of carved stone, coloured glass, *Doulton*'s terracotta and mosaic and tiles by *Smith & Co.* of Coalville, *Minton, Hollins & Co.* and *Maw & Co.* This is used to most spectacular effect in the former READING ROOM (restored 2006–7 as the Tiled Hall of the Art Gallery) on the ground floor's S front, which is 80 ft (24.5 metres) by 40 ft (12 metres) wide, with pairs of polished granite columns and capitals of Harehills stone carved into delicate foliage, all different. Between the columns, transverse iron girders support segmental vaults made beautiful by multicoloured patterns of glazed hexagonal bricks by the *Farnley Iron Co.* Decorative gold bosses conceal air vents. Pale pink terracotta portrait medallions of great writers by *Benjamin Creswick*.

In 1886–8 the reading room became the entrance to the new ART GALLERY, which adjoins to the E. This is by *W. H. Thorp* (Corson's proposals were rejected) and is largely obscured on its S front by the angular addition of 1980–2 for the HENRY MOORE SCULPTURE GALLERY by *John Thorp* with *Neville Conder* of *Casson & Conder* as consultant architect. Windowless but for horizontal slots in the walls; a C19 window is reused as the gallery's S entrance. Outside, Moore's *Reclining Woman 80* (1980–2), one of the last of his monumental works on this theme. The 1880s building has an impressive Imperial staircase with giant columns of Hopton Wood stone. STATUE: Queen Anne, by *Andrew Carpenter*, 1712, taken from the 1710 Moot Hall in Briggate.

A bridge links the gallery to the HENRY MOORE INSTITUTE of 1989–93 by *Jeremy Dixon & Edward Jones*, with *BDP*. They converted warehouses on Cookridge Street (*see* Perambulation 3) and dramatically refaced the gable-end to Victoria Square in highly polished dark green, almost black, igneous rock with a crenellated parapet and fissure-like entrance passage. The top-lit main exhibition space was created by infilling an existing courtyard.

In front of the Art Gallery and Institute is VICTORIA SQUARE, created in 1936–7 by *J. C. Procter*, after demolition of a row of houses in Centenary Street (the line of which is suggested by the sunken path on the square's N side). Procter intended to rebuild the Municipal Buildings as its backdrop (*see The Builder*, 1939). The WAR MEMORIAL of 1922, by *H. C. Fehr*, was previously in City Square. Carrara marble plinth flanked by beautiful bronze statues of St George and the Dragon and Peace releasing a dove. Fehr's figure of Victory was removed in 1967; the present winged figure with bowed head is by *Ian Judd* and *Andy Elton*, 1992.

LEEDS MAGISTRATES' COURT, Westgate. By *R. Cornfield* of the *Leeds Design Consultancy*, 1994. Curved front, highly coloured in pale buff brick with long flanks in red and blue. Central entrance with squat pedimented porch, columns *in antis*, coat of arms. At the flanks, projecting gabled pavilions step up and back. Successful interior with a dramatic curved cantilevered staircase. High up are *Coade* stone plaques from Thomas Taylor's Park Row Court House (1811–13; dem. 1901). Luminous, narrow central atrium with plain columns, the terrazzo flooring carried up to form the bases, and sparkling gold-flecked walls. Similarly well-lit separate circulation areas for magistrates, prisoners and the public. Five levels of public areas furnished in a different wood at each level, progressively lighter in tone from ground floor to top.

COMBINED COURT CENTRE, Oxford Row/Westgate. By *S. Spielrein* of the *Property Services Agency*, 1977–80. Deferential to its C19 neighbours; it is kept low, just four storeys high with a defiant battered plinth and sheer walls of hard red brick and vertical openings. Oxford Row entrance remodelled in 2000 when a giant stone cube carved with the royal arms was re-set on a high plinth.

Former GENERAL POST OFFICE, City Square. *See* Perambulation 2a.

2. *Libraries, galleries, museums*

CENTRAL LIBRARY. *See* Municipal Buildings, above.

CITY MUSEUM, Cookridge Street.* Formerly the Mechanics' Institute. Won in competition in 1860 by *Cuthbert Brodrick*, shortly after winning the design for the Corn Exchange (*see* below). Built 1865–8. It succeeded the first Mechanics' Institute established in Park Row in 1825. Adapted as the City Museum 2005–8 by *Austin-Smith: Lord*.

The exterior is heavy and serious, another of Brodrick's essays on the character of local stone, which was confined to the S and W façades (the N and E sides were not exposed at the time it was built). This facing is treated as a repetitive pattern of a single window set within an arch filled with a shell tympanum and a roundel, in reality a small circular window, in each of the interstices. It was, perhaps, a memory of Alberti's church of San Francesco, Rimini (1450) although it also refers to the published designs of J.-N.-L. Durand (1760–1834). Placed dramatically in the centre of the W façade is a very Parisian concept of a frontispiece, partly outside and partly inside the high recessed doorway or loggia. The latter has giant-order pilasters, above which is a sculptured tympanum similar in style and execution to contemporary decoration of the Paris Opéra and the New Louvre.

Brodrick's plan was for a circular lecture room at the centre of a rectangular shell containing library and reading room, a casts room, studios for painting, carving and modelling; engineering and plumbing workshops, classrooms, dining rooms and a large room for moral instruction. The entrance is to a landing with staircases up and down. Ahead is one of the entrances into the former lecture room, which has a balcony with cast-iron balustrade. Here is another memory of Parisian architecture: the Cirque d'Hiver (J.-I. Hittorff; 1851–2), with windows immediately below 'an iron roof of somewhat novel construction'. The construction of the circular floor was also innovative, its weight supported by cast-iron columns below – a ring of sixteen surrounding a central column. Ionic columns in the lecture room, library and reading room and for the staircase entrance.

LEEDS ART GALLERY and HENRY MOORE INSTITUTE. *See* Municipal Buildings, above.

THE ROYAL ARMOURIES, Clarence Dock. 1995–6 by *Derek Walker Associates*, designed to house the collections previously

---

*This entry has been contributed by Derek Linstrum.

displayed at the Tower of London. Fortress-like, of four nearly
windowless storeys of banded gunmetal-coloured brick, and a
tall glazed octagonal staircase tower hung with a display of
weaponry inside. Entrance on the s side, leading into a central
top-lit street with double-height galleries on each side opening
to exhibition spaces. Alongside the river, a TILT YARD and
WORKSHOPS.

3. Hospital and medical buildings

LEEDS GENERAL INFIRMARY, Great George Street. By *George
Gilbert Scott*, 1863–9, succeeding John Carr's infirmary of
1768–71. William Beckett, member of the Infirmary Building
Committee, had employed Scott to design his bank premises
in Park Row in 1862 and here provided Scott with an opportunity to realize aspects of his unexecuted Gothic design for
the Foreign Office (1859). One of the first hospitals in England
to adopt the pavilion plan of ward blocks pioneered at Lari-
boisière Hospital, Paris, which Scott had visited with Dr Chadwick, the Infirmary's chief physician. At its core is a central
(originally covered) courtyard aligned E–W and surrounded on
four sides by corridors that on the N and s sides serve the ward
blocks. These are set at right angles (three on the N, two on
the s) and terminate in splayed turrets containing water closets.
Open-ended courts lay between each wing (now infilled). The
façade towards Great George Street was symmetrical before
the matching wing to the r. was added by *George Corson* in
1891–2. Three storeys high, with a lively roof-line of steep
slopes and pinnacles. Highly decorated in red brick with
Bramley Fall stone dressings, richly patterned Venetian Gothic
windows and red granite pillars. Scott took advantage of the
sloping site on this side, placing the outer two-storey wards
over offices, so that they are level with the wards at the rear,
with arcaded single-storey links between the wings. A central
three-bay porte cochère with corner pillars of Derbyshire limestone, similar to that at Scott's Midland Hotel, St Pancras
(won in competition in 1865–6 while the Infirmary was under
construction). The two small sandstone draped urns flanking
the entrance steps were brought from Carr's Infirmary.

ENTRANCE HALL, with small, French Gothic fireplace, continuing into a corridor whose roof trusses are supported on
corbels sprouting medicinal plants carved by *Brindley*. Tripartite screen at the N end with a Romanesque arch between
pointed openings, with polished granite columns. STAIRCASE
HALL, with an Imperial cast-iron and stone stair, the return
flights cantilevered and lit at first floor by tall three-light lancets
with patterned glass by *O'Connor* of London, 1868. On the
stairs a memorial to Lord Moynihan, 1938 by *Lutyens*, with a
tondo holding a bust by *Sir William Reid Dick*. A three-bay
Gothic arcade opens into the corridor along the s side of the
central courtyard (its glazed roof was removed in 1911). s of

the staircase landing was the lantern-roofed operating theatre. E of the courtyard garden is the small CHAPEL of St Luke, opened 1869. Three-light canted E window, stained glass of 1868 and 1880 given by Sir Andrew and Lady Fairbairn and John Deakin Heaton, honorary physician 1850–80. W organ gallery and 'Lamb of God' rose window with angel figures playing instruments. Carved oak pulpit (dedicated to the memory of William Gott †1863) and panelled reredos of 1926–9 which once incorporated small oak figures of Florence Nightingale and St Luke. *Corson*'s grand OUTPATIENTS' BUILDING of 1891–2 continues the E–W axis of Scott's plan.

Of the numerous additions the following should be mentioned: on Great George Street, E of Scott's and Corson's matching buildings, the red brick KING EDWARD MEMORIAL WING of 1913 by *Sidney Kitson*, classical with detached columns to the façade, then the BROTHERTON WING facing Calverley Street. Planned in 1926, opened 1940, by *Kitson, Parish, Ledgard & Pyman* in collaboration with *Stanley Hall & Easton & Robertson*. Dignified, with a uniform Portland stone frontage entirely in sympathy with Vincent Harris's Civic Hall (*see* above) opposite. Streamlined sun balconies at the S end. The style is continued in Kitson's 1937 extension, with rounded corner stair-tower, to the NURSES' HOME to the N of the Brotherton Wing. The earlier parts of the home, behind this to the W, are of 1915–17 (red brick, also by Kitson) and 1897 by *W. H. & R. W. Thorp*, in Free Renaissance style. W of the Nurses' Home, with an entrance off Clarendon Way is the JUBILEE WING by *Llewelyn Davies Weeks*, 1993–9. L-plan, seven storeys, red brick and white metal cladding with louvred sun-shades. Landscaping by *Tess Jaray* and five spiky metal sculptures by *Tom Lomax*. The wing joins the C19 infirmary with buildings to the W erected as part of a planned 1960s development of the hospital and medical school (*see* below) as a single unit linked with the University campus (*see* p. 474). These include the dramatic GENERATING STATION of 1974, concrete and steel frames clad in grey brick with a pair of fluted concrete chimneys, and to its E the six-storey WORSLEY BUILDING AND LEEDS DENTAL INSTITUTE by *Building Design Partnership* (Preston Group), 1979. This has a double courtyard plan and a bridge to the University campus to the N (*see* p. 476), with which it shares its tough aesthetic of vertical window slots separated by full-height piers. Against its dull opacity a fine contrast is made by the transparency of the LEEDS INSTITUTE OF GENETICS, HEALTH AND THERAPEUTICS (LIGHT), 2004 by *Fairhursts Design Group*. To the S, bridging the ring road, is the mundane CLARENDON WING of *c.* 1980.

OLD MEDICAL SCHOOL, Thoresby Place. Founded 1831, the present building erected 1894 by *W. H. Thorp*, for 400 students of the Yorkshire College, with which the Medical School amalgamated in 1884 (*see* Leeds University, p. 471). Collegiate Tudor Gothic, of three storeys, with a battlemented entrance tower with ogee-domed stair-turret and a domed lantern. Red brick and Morley Moor sandstone with terracotta dressings; carving by *J. W. Appleyard*. Hexagonal arcaded entrance hall, paved in lovely glowing pink mosaic with bands of flowers; the walls lined with mellow green Burmantofts faience moulded into naturalistic patterns and coats of arms of the Royal Colleges of Physicians and Surgeons and the Victoria University. The Latin inscription is taken from Matthew 10:8, 'Heal the sick . . .' Vaulting shafts of faience support the ribs of the oak roof. Off the hall, a wide staircase with ornate iron balustrade. Originally three ranges around a court, the W side infilled by *J. C. Procter* in 1930, still in a Tudor style. This faces the ALGERNON FIRTH INSTITUTE OF PATHOLOGY, also by *Procter*, 1933, in Art Deco style with raised centre. Sombre brown brick, expressively used in the window recesses. Stepped roof-line with the concrete frame exposed and glazed to light laboratories.

4. *Educational Institutions*

Former LEEDS BOYS' MODERN SCHOOL, Rossington Street. 1888, probably by *William Landless*, the School Board's Clerk of Works. Nine bays, two storeys with basement and attics, brick with stone classical detailing including the date in the entrance pediment and distinctive terracotta panels.

Former LEEDS GRAMMAR SCHOOL. *See* UNIVERSITY BUSINESS SCHOOL.

Former LEEDS HIGHER GRADE SCHOOL, Woodhouse Lane/Rossington Street. Now council offices. 1889 by *Birchall & Kelly*. Domineering classical, brick with giant stone Ionic pilasters supporting an entablature and a weighty attic added *c.* 1890 by *William Landless* to increase accommodation to 2,500 pupils. In two tiers, the upper part enclosing a roof playground. Rooms were provided for blind, deaf and dumb children, and there was a caretaker's flat and gym in the deep basement. Converted 1994–5 by *Leeds Design Consultancy*.

Former PUPIL TEACHERS' COLLEGE, Rossington Street. For the Leeds School Board, 1900 by *W. S. Braithwaite* (now offices). In an eclectic Queen Anne style, four storeys, the principal (E) façade with square open turrets, Diocletian windows and oval plaques. Inside, a beautiful balconied central hall, tiled and top-lit, formerly surrounded by over thirty teaching rooms for 600 students.

LEEDS COLLEGE OF ART AND DESIGN, Vernon Street. By *Bedford & Kitson*, 1901–3. Three storeys and a basement, of hot red brick banded in stone; the style is Baroque but in a surprisingly functional manner. Steel-framed, the finely detailed lintels exposed over the studio windows. W entrance in a showier Gibbsian surround. Large mosaic panel above with two relaxed muses, 'Art' and 'Design', and three laurel wreaths set against a brilliant gold background. Designed by *Gerald*

Moira, made by *Rust & Co*. The basement and first-floor studios have a novel arrangement for maximizing light by setting back the floors from the façade. Glazed hipped roof.

(PARK LANE COLLEGE. Seven-storey teaching block by *Allen Tod Architecture*, 2005, with one façade of photovoltaic cells.)

LEEDS METROPOLITAN UNIVERSITY (CIVIC QUARTER), Calverley Street and Woodhouse Lane. Commissioned in 1951 to amalgamate on one site the city's Colleges of Technology, Art, Commerce and Housecraft (renamed Leeds Central Colleges). Built 1955–69. By *Yorke, Rosenberg & Mardall*. Refounded as Leeds Polytechnic in 1970, and Leeds Metropolitan University, 1992.

YRM's original scheme for a single campus with shared Assembly Hall, Students' Union and Library was altered during construction. The first part to be completed in 1955, a three-storey range to Portland Way, was demolished in 2007.* The ten-storey Teaching Block of 1958 survives, originally curtain-walled but re-clad with dark glazing in 2000 by the *Bowman Riley Partnership*. YRM's original scheme proposed extension of this slab to three times its present length but a design for three towers was substituted in 1966–9. The overall height remained the same, but the result is undermined by its lack of unity. Each of the towers (Buildings D, F and H) have tight grids of grey pre-cast aggregate cladding. They group around a low podium containing the refectory.

The NE corner of the campus to Woodhouse Lane was substantially altered and re-clad in 1999–2000 by the *Bowman Riley Partnership* to create the livelier LESLIE SILVER BUILDING, which incorporates the main entrance and library. Five storeys in yellow brick and aluminium cladding with a curved glass entrance screen flanked by high brick stair-towers. In the entrance lobby: 'One Hundred Books' by *Stephen Hurrel*, 2002. Ten paired glass shelves support sheets of blue glass etched with the author and title of a book selected by staff. Inside, the lobby opens into a light reception area, the Library is glazed in alongside a corridor to the Calverley Street entrance.

THE ROSE BOWL, across Portland Way behind the Civic Hall, is by *Sheppard Robson* (begun 2007). It will provide teaching rooms and offices in a U-plan around an elevated cylinder containing the lecture theatres.

BROADCASTING PLACE, Woodhouse Lane, is a major expansion of the LMU's Civic Quarter across the Inner Ring Road. The core, Old Broadcasting House, is a 2006 conversion of the former FRIENDS' MEETING HOUSE by *Edward Birchall*, 1866–8. Classical. Arcaded porch with Tuscan columns, five-bay front with modillion cornice and large pediment. In 2008 this is being surrounded by new buildings, including a twenty-three storey residential tower, with sharply angular plans and cladding of weathered steel. By *Feilden Clegg Bradley Studios*.

---

*In 2008 a masterplan for replacement of the original buildings is being prepared by *Broadway Malyan*.

BRUNSWICK BUILDING, E of Woodhouse Lane, was planned in 1969 when Patrick Nuttgens was the Director of the Colleges. Executed 1973–9 by *D. M. Wrightson* and *Christopher Kaye* working for *E. W. Stanley* of Leeds City Council. Empty in 2008 and awaiting probable demolition, it was a grand but compromised scheme of three linked four-storey blocks built on one of the city's highest points, and canted around a stepped courtyard in the form of an amphitheatre (originally designed to be covered by a glass roof). The composition is monumental with buff tile-clad walls pierced by vertical and horizontal openings; the inner faces of the buildings are glazed, the outer walls to the busy roads left impressively blank and boldly sculptural. The planned Engineering Block on the E side of the courtyard was never built, its steel connecting rods left exposed. Nearby, under construction in 2008, OPAL 3, a twenty-seven storey tower for student accommodation by *Morrison Design*, is already intruding visually as far away as Briggate.

LEEDS UNIVERSITY. *See* Inner Leeds: Woodhouse.

5. Transport: railway, canal and bridges

LEEDS STATION, New Station Street/City Square/Prince's Square. An amalgamation of two formerly separate stations – Wellington Station (1846, dem.) and New Station (1869 by *Thomas Prosser* for the North Eastern Railway and London & North Western Railway) – which were joined together as City Station in 1938. Of that date the brick-faced CONCOURSE by *W. H. Hamlyn*, chief architect of the London, Midland & Scottish Railway, which is integrated with the company's Queens Hotel and offices on City Square (*see* Perambulation 2a). Art Deco interior of top-lit coffered ceiling with pendant lights (restored 1999 by *Carey Jones Architects*). New Station was rebuilt in 1967, contemporary with the ugly office slab rising above it – City House by *John Poulson*. Train shed remodelled in 2001–3, by *Mackellar Architecture* to a scheme by *EGS Design Architects* of Manchester: High Tech, with monopitch roofs carried on tree-like trusses.

The station's substructure is known as the DARK ARCHES, a groin-vaulted tunnel and service roadway created beneath New Station in 1869. *T. E. Harrison* was the consulting engineer, its construction supervised by *Robert Hodgson*. Several vaults at the W end were rebuilt with blue engineering brick, *c.* 1900–4 after a fire. As it crosses the Aire at its W end sublime views open upstream through tall arches faced with giant blocks of rock-faced gritstone; those lining the river bed are visible when the water is low. W of the river, the vaults have been imaginatively refurbished as shop units associated with Granary wharf.*

---

*The river's turbulence is caused by a sharp turn S at the ancient weir or 'High Dam' (visible from Princes Square, *see* p. 452) where, in the medieval period, water was diverted E as a stream powering the manorial corn mill. The gritstone voussoirs of the 1846 viaduct for Wellington Station are just visible in the distance.

RAILWAY BUILDINGS: W of Leeds Station along the Aire and Leeds and Liverpool Canal is a group of buildings associated with the Leeds & Thirsk Railway, the site of whose depot is occupied by the Aireside Centre (1983 by *D. Y. Davies Associates*), S of Wellington Street. In its midst is preserved a 32-ft (7-metre)-high WAGON HOIST TOWER of snecked dressed gritstone with rusticated ashlar dressings. Erected 1846, probably by *Thomas Grainger*, to move wagons off his CENTRAL STATION VIADUCT, which is mostly demolished except for a 984-ft (300-metre) fragment spanning the river and canal to the SW. Gritstone ashlar blocks with rusticated voussoirs and keystones, one segmental arch over the Aire, another over the canal and about thirty more branching to the S. Parapet with vase-shaped balusters. S of the canal by Wellington Road are the remains of the L&TR's LOCOMOTIVE DEPOT, comprising a ROUND-HOUSE, HALF ROUND-HOUSE and REPAIR SHOP of 1849–53 by *Grainger* with *John Bourne*, the L&TR's resident engineer. The Round-house is actually a twenty-sided polygon for twenty locomotives, with arched openings to each bay and an internal arcade of similar form. Single storey of pressed brick and cast-iron construction. Pitched slate roof, the centre originally open above the turntable. Main entrance on the E side, a tall elliptical arch with incised radiating voussoirs and a pediment above the cornice. The REPAIR SHOP is an impressively long single-storey brick range with stone dressings and tall round-arched windows separated by brick pilasters. Between these two, the HALF ROUND-HOUSE (transformed into commercial premises by *Jaques Associates*, 1998). Tall segmental arch openings, brick pilasters and brick piers to support a travelling crane inside.

LEEDS AND LIVERPOOL CANAL. The canal was begun in 1770; its terminus at Leeds opened 1777. Close to the canal's junction with the Aire at GRANARY WHARF is a former WARE-HOUSE of *c.* 1776, engineer *Robert Owen*, converted to offices in 1994–5 by *BDP*. Four storeys, gritstone, truly Pennine vernacular – massive walls, a stone roof, small windows with flat-faced mullions and tiers of loading doors. Inside later C19 fire-proof construction of cast-iron columns and brick arches, contemporary with a low extension built over a dock. The BASIN was enlarged 1818–20, and in 1845–6 the wide Canal Dock was provided with a link (now curtailed) beneath the railway arches to the river for access to mills upstream. Of this date a BRIDGE and modest, single-storey and basement former CANAL OFFICE to the W. Wide panelled entrance, sash windows with margin lights and panelled boardroom inside. Brick LOCK-KEEPER'S HOUSE added after 1847.

BRIDGES. – CROWN POINT BRIDGE. *See* Perambulation 7. – LEEDS BRIDGE. *See* Perambulation 1. – MONK BRIDGE, carrying Whitehall Road across the canal and river, is by *Thomas Hewson*, engineer, 1886. It replaced an unusual suspension bridge of 1827 by *George Leather Jun.* The main span is 108 ft (33 metres), of lattice-girder construction with massive gritstone abutments. – VICTORIA BRIDGE, Neville Street. *See* Perambulation 7. – WELLINGTON BRIDGE. *See* Perambulation 6.

6. Markets and exchanges

CORN EXCHANGE,* Call Lane. 1860–2 by *Cuthbert Brodrick*;   94
converted to a shopping centre in 1989–90 by *Alsop & Lyall*.
A building of national, maybe international importance, described by Pevsner as 'remarkably independent and functional . . . Reserved for members originally and not in the least inviting'. Many regard this as Brodrick's finest work, possessing an unusual unity of external and internal elements as well as a repertoire of his idiosyncratic stonework details. The building is 190 ft (58 metres) long, 136 ft (41.5 metres) wide and 86 ft (26 metres) high from the basement to the top of its great dome. There were few precedents for a free-standing building of oval plan-form but the obvious source is the domed Halle au Blé (by Nicolas Le Camus de Mézières; 1763–7) which Brodrick had seen on his first visit to Paris in 1844.

The exterior is faced entirely with meticulously cut diamond-pointed rusticated local stone, probably Northern Italian in inspiration, out of which are punched two rows of identical semicircular-headed windows. At first-floor level there is a continuous guilloche band (probably of little millstones) which binds the building together, as does the upper frieze of garlands and ox skulls. At the upper level between each pair of windows Brodrick placed one of his characteristic rosettes or paterae which were becoming his lithic signature; they are also incorporated in the idiosyncratic pediment over a side door, and another version appears in metal ventilator gratings placed at regular intervals in the patterned masonry. The use of curves throughout is continued in two projecting ears, one being the semicircular hexastyle Tuscan portico at the SW corner and the other a partly enclosed matching bay containing the staircase to the upper floor of offices. The whole sits on a rusticated base and the subsidiary entrances are marked by massive scrolls that seem to have been hewn out of the living rock. Everything is precisely conceived and executed.

Inside, the large airy hall is surrounded by two storeys of doorways in arched surrounds, apparently following the pattern of the Halle au Blé where the central court was encircled by a vaulted arcade. The upper storey has a cast-iron gallery and Brodrick originally devised this arrangement to separate the offices from the buying and selling on the main floor and storage in the basement. The walls were of coloured brickwork (now overpainted) possibly buff or light red with darker bricks used to emphasize the doorways. A large

---

*This entry has been contributed by Derek Linstrum.

circular opening was cut into the floor of the hall in 1989–90 to connect it with the basement; new ironwork and staircases copy Brodrick's original designs. From a heavy moulded entablature spring the ribs of the great DOME, constructed from a mixture of wrought iron, cast iron and timber which form a lightweight criss-cross pattern that presages C20 space frames. It is clearly inspired by the dome erected over the Halle au Blé in 1808–13 (by F.-J. Bélanger), which used a system of cast-iron ribs tied with wrought-iron rings. In the centre of the dome is an elliptical oculus as was envisaged from the beginning; the glazed panel on the N side was added and is the only asymmetrical element in the building. At each end of the dome the longitudinal ribs are drawn together in the apotheosis of the curve behind a large cast-iron lunette; one bears the Leeds civic arms and the other a clock and symbols of the building's purpose. The cost of the ironwork was £8,050 (approximately two-thirds that of the masonry); it was fabricated locally by *Butler & Co.* of Kirkstall Forge.

CITY MARKETS, Kirkgate and Vicar Lane. 1904 by *John & Joseph Leeming*, replacing a glass and iron market hall erected in 1857 for fruit and vegetable traders. An extravagant display in Flemish style, with Art Nouveau detailing, from draped well-fed putti by *Thewlis & Co.* supporting the entablature between shops on the ground floor, to the elaborate chimneys, balustrades, domes and steeple of the skyline. The street frontage comprised eighteen shops, an hotel, restaurant, billiard hall, and coffee and club rooms. Refurbished 1992 by *Povall Worthington*. Inside the restored market hall the atmosphere is rich and airy. The massive steel and cast-iron structure, by *J. Bagshaw & Sons* of Batley, has a total of 28 clustered Corinthian columns supporting a glazed clerestory, lantern roofs and central octagon carried on lightweight trusses. Fierce dragons support the gallery, reached via spiral stone stairs at the corner entrances. These have moulded inner arches of Burmantofts faience and walls lined with glazed bricks. At the E side are the brick rows originally added to the earlier market hall in 1875 for fruit and vegetable shops: still in use but altered.

7. Theatres

CITY VARIETIES MUSIC HALL, Swan Street. 1865 by *George Smith* for local developer and entrepreneur, Charles Thornton. Plain façade, but its long, narrow auditorium is a remarkable and atmospheric survival. Cast-iron columns with foliage capitals support two tiers of bow-fronted balconies (the upper tier slightly modified in the 1880s) with plaster enrichments of swags, medallions and female busts. The shallow stage projects under a three-centred proscenium arch surmounted by the royal arms.

GRAND THEATRE, New Briggate. 1877–8 by *George Corson*, assisted by *J. R. Watson*. Eclectic brick and stone façade in a

Leeds, Grand Theatre.
Engraving, 1878

hybrid of Romanesque and Gothic, including round arches to
the main entrance with rose window above and gable tourelles.
Six bays to the r. for shops, originally set into Gothic arches
but now with 1930s sunburst glazing. At the s end is an
entrance to the separate Assembly Room under a squat tower
with pyramid roof. Little-altered interior: original ticket
offices, steep main staircase and a labyrinth of passages for different classes of patron leading to the magnificently decorated

auditorium. This has opulent red and green painted *carton-pierre* decoration glowing with gilding. Clustered Gothic shafts and boxes, flanked by draped figures, frame the proscenium; the saucer-domed richly encrusted ceiling is carried on four pendentives of fan-vault form. Three tiers of balconies, their plaster fronts deeply undercut into elaborate foliated scrolls and bosses. Major refurbishment in 2006–8 by *BDP* has revealed tiles (by *Whetstone* of Coalville) in the public spaces and restored the Assembly Room to Corson's original design (hidden by Baroque decoration after conversion to a cinema in the early C20) with its vaulted ceiling.

WEST YORKSHIRE PLAYHOUSE, St Peter's Street. 1985–90 by the *Appleton Partnership*. Buff and brown banded brickwork, blue window frames, long low slate roof and distinctive diaper-patterned flytower, a well-scaled if awkward example of the later C20 'Leeds Look'. The interior is more appealing, containing the amphitheatre-style 750-seat Quarry Theatre and the more intimate 350-seat gallery-style Courtyard Theatre. Exposed structural girders and services in the restaurant – a raised area with fine views over the Eastgate approach.

CARRIAGEWORKS THEATRE, Millennium Square. 2005–6 by *Panter Hudspith Architects* as a new home for the Civic Theatre, previously in the Mechanics' Institute (now City Museum, *see* above). Brick sides and white stone facing in deference to the City Hall opposite.

PERAMBULATIONS

1. The Old Town

The perambulation begins on LEEDS BRIDGE, as rebuilt in 1871–3 by *T. Dyne Steel*, engineer (*W.H. Barlow*, consulting engineer). Rusticated ashlar abutments support a single graceful segmental arch of cast-iron ribs, made by *John Butler* of Stanningley, embellished with flowing vine scrolls. Cast-iron balustrade, delicately effected in perforated and interlinked rings with embossed flower heads beneath a heavy rail. BRIGGATE lies straight ahead to the N. Laid out from 1207, it became the town's main thoroughfare and later the centre of its cloth trade. The lower end of the street is separated from the part uphill by the railway viaduct of 1869. The narrow medieval burgage plots were bought up in the early C18 for the building of larger houses, of which Nos. 3–5 (w side) is a survival. Seven bays, the central three projecting with quoins and dentil cornice. Later subdivided, with shopfronts, now poorly treated. C18 and early C19 warehouses and cottages lie behind in BLAYD'S YARD, with a long three-storey workshop in Heaton's Yard (now Court), alongside the railway arches. Another major early C18 survival lies opposite, beyond the viaduct. – QUEEN'S COURT, an elegant brick cloth merchant's house and business premises. Eight bays between stone quoins, the central two bays breaking forward slightly, over a narrow-arched passage to the yard behind. Three-storey wings in a U-plan to the rear housed cloth-finishing and packaging workshops and warehouses. By the mid C19 the yard was lined with 'blind-back' slum cottages and workshops. At the back of the yard a narrow alleyway leads to Call Lane, which follows the line of a medieval lane at the back of the original burgage plots. For the rest of Briggate, *see* below.

The perambulation now proceeds W along SWINEGATE, the medieval route from the river to the manor house. Dominating the corner is the GOLDEN LION HOTEL. Italianate of 1879 by *Thomas Ambler*, for the clothing manufacturer John Barran, built on the site of his first ready-made clothing workshop. A couple of minor commercial buildings lie beyond, Nos. 14–16 – shops and offices by *George Corson*, 1870, with a corner tower on corbel rounds, and No. 18 with a narrow Dutch gable and corner entrance. Swinegate's S side has the large MALMAISON HOTEL, originally the headquarters of Leeds City Tramways. Dated 1915 (is it by *Sydney Kitson* who designed the Corporation tram depots at Beckett Street and Guiseley?). Free Edwardian Baroque, very red brick and terracotta. Until *c.* 1900 much of this area was packed with mills along the river (*see* Perambulation 7). PROSPECT HOUSE to the W was built *c.* 1900 for Charles Walker, Mill Furnishers, with ornate pedimented gables. Between here and the railway is the large cleared site of the city's C19 tram depot, still largely undeveloped in 2008. N of the railway viaducts, on the site of the castle and later manor house, is THE SCARBROUGH facing BISHOPGATE STREET. Nice early C20 pub frontage of glazed terracotta Ionic columns, moulded swags and lettered parapet. Tucked in close to the viaduct at the corner with MILL HILL, the PRINCE OF WALES pub with an elaborate carved brick crest; then Nos. 9–10, a three-storey merchant's house and workshop of the first half of the C18. Six-bay façade of dark brick with gauged brick headers, divided in the late C19 into two shops with chambers over. Next door, Nos. 7–8 is a much larger early C19 workshop and warehouse, of four storeys with a top-lit attic, the taking-in doors reduced to windows with bracketed lintels in the later C19. Nos. 4–6 is a refronting *c.* 1870 of a mid-C18 merchant's house of three storeys with a central archway to the rear yard, flanked by two sets of paired windows.

BOAR LANE, the medieval route between the manor house and Briggate, was widened in 1869–76, following the building of New Station (*see* Leeds Station, Public Buildings). Construction of large commercial buildings on both sides of the street was promoted by John Barran, clothing manufacturer and property speculator, who was Mayor in 1870–1. The tall façades of varied and eclectic styles, topped by a delightful skyline of moulded parapets, dormers, statuary and spiky turrets, are attributed to *Thomas Ambler*. The N side was mostly demolished after 1968 under plans to build a series of linked shopping precincts and arcades with elevated pedestrian walkways crossing Boar Lane. A remnant of this ill-fated scheme is the unlovely LEEDS SHOPPING PLAZA by *John Brunton & Partners* of Bradford, 1974–8. E of Albion Street, Nos. 58–63 are Italianate four-storey warehouses with shops, completed 1875, but the major landmark is Holy Trinity church, the sole C18 survivor (*see* Churches). On its W side, Trinity Street rises sharply uphill N into the dreary Trinity Arcade, completed in 1974. This was originally intended to connect with a walkway over Boar Lane (due for redevelopment in 2008 as a series of covered precincts by *EMBT* and *Stanley Bragg Partnership*).

Almost the entire S side of Boar Lane has been retained. It begins at the W end with a pre-Ambler, business-like 1830s warehouse range in brick with stone dressings. Its neighbour is a late C20 facsimile. The grand sweep of Thomas Ambler's frontages begins with THE GRIFFIN HOTEL, *c.* 1872, red brick Gothic with finely carved stone details, cast-iron cresting, oriel windows, pinnacles and gargoyles. Its corner has a pavilion roof and clock (with letters rather than numerals) well-placed to encourage travellers to the station. On the opposite corner of Mill Hill, the former Saracen's Head is Italianate with elaborate corner pediment. Its panelled pilaster strips with carved capitals repeat across the classical frontages of VICTORIA BUILDINGS (Nos. 24–28), which continues into New Station Street, a carriage road made in 1873. High up on the corner, a bust of Queen Victoria in a pedimented niche; the parapet was originally crowned with urns. E of New Station Street is a thin sliver of brick Neo-Jacobean with stone window surrounds, panelled gables, and clinging stone beasts, before a substantial four-storey Italianate palazzo (formerly Leeds Mercantile Bank) with thickly rope-moulded doorway, moulded arches and fine carved panels of foliage and birds (including the Leeds owl) rising to a deep, bracketed eaves cornice, made top-heavy by paired dormer windows under segmental arches. It is cleverly integrated on its E side with the mirror-glazed façade of THE BOURSE, offices of 1993 by *Sir Basil Spence Partnership*, which is built across a former side street. Then Nos. 19–21, another palazzo in solidly sculpted gritstone ashlar, lightened by oriel windows above the side entrance. Built as the Leeds Corporation Gas Offices but converted after 1884 by *C. S. Nelson* of Leeds into an hotel, restaurant and *bodega* (wine merchant) with a rear extension. Rustication and recessed plain panels to the renewed shopfronts, motifs carried through the restrained brick and stone corner block attached to the l.

Nos. 15 and 16 Boar Lane were built as five narrow properties, each treated differently but creating a symmetrical composition of eclectic style. Ornament is kept to the central three bays with Italianate round arches to the first and second floors beneath a pierced stone parapet but with quirky decorative fish-scale-slated tourelles above the splayed outer corners. Rear rebuilt in 1992–3 by *Chapman Taylor & Partners*, who also planned TREVELYAN SQUARE on the land behind and designed the six-storey offices on the square's s side. Successfully evocative of Leeds's Late Victorian architecture, with contrasting brick bands, tiered bays and vast gable windows. In the centre of the square are gardens and the popular 'Talbot Fountain', protected by hounds with fleur-de-lys ears, salvaged from Castle Carr, near Halifax (dem. from 1962). Ambler's sequence along Boar Lane continues with two narrow ornate four-storey façades, both Gothic, the first of brick with stone detailing and gargoyles on the gabled finials, the second of stone with elaborate ogee tracery based on Ruskin's illustrations of the Ca' d'Oro in Venice. Finally, to the corner with Briggate, Ambler's *tour de force* for Barran, who reserved this prime site for his shop, with chambers and the Trevelyan Temperance Hotel above. Of brick and stone, in Italianate Second Empire style with dormers and mansards peppering the roofline of its thirteen-bay façade. Two tall entrances surmounted by carved pediments with cornucopia and carved heads.

DUNCAN STREET continues the line of Boar Lane E of Briggate and terminates at Brodrick's stout Corn Exchange (*see* Public Buildings, p. 425). The N side was rebuilt *c.* 1900. Three elaborate Baroque Revival blocks with a touch of Art Nouveau decoration, and two narrow gabled brick frontages in a more modest Jacobean. On the corner, shops and offices by *Percy Robinson* for Messrs Hepworth, gents' outfitters, *c.* 1904. Four storeys faced in Burmantofts terracotta modelled with high-relief ornament – swags, scrolls and female figures – by their chief modeller, *E. Caldwell Spruce*. Ornate gabled attic storey with corner turret. Nos. 5–9 also by *Robinson*: No. 7 has a pedimented gable with obelisk finial and square turrets to the outer bays, the parapets rebuilt in 1992. *H. A. Chapman & J. W. Thackray* designed Duncan Chambers, the paired shops and offices at the E end in 1905, their names impressed at each end of the building. Faience-clad with distinctive semicircular attic windows to the third floor and another domed corner tower. Round the end of Duncan Street in NEW MARKET STREET, BACKAWELL HOUSE (Nos. 22–24) of *c.* 1880 is attributed to *Smith & Tweedale*. Four storeys, strongly characterful with two high moulded brick arches, infilled with tiers of canted bay windows. Duncan Street's s side is mostly by *Ambler*: a long classical seven-bay range built 1882 as offices and warehouse for William Tunstall. Symmetrical with a central carriage arch, pilastered shopfronts and a fine carving of the town's coat of arms. Access to the warehouse was at the rear, through the archway to HIRST'S YARD. This also has two-storey brick workshops complete with hoist, loading door and bollards, providing a good impression of its early C19 character. The Neo-Tudor former Whip Inn is also by *Ambler*.

The w end of Hirst's Yard leads to BRIGGATE and the fascinating TIME BALL BUILDINGS, two C17 houses, barely identifiable behind elaborate stucco decoration applied in 1876 by John Dyson, jeweller and watchmaker. It takes its name from the captivating mechanism attached to the large Gothic clock of 1910 above the entrance. A second clock has a figure of Father Time carved by *J. W. Appleyard*. The shopfront's shutters were raised by a mechanism in the basement. Full-height display window under a dome. Interior converted but retaining most of its ornate Late Victorian fittings, including chandeliers bought at the 1890 Paris Exhibition, galleries and rear workshop. On the E side of Briggate, Queen's Court has already been seen, but through a narrow opening is LAMBERT'S YARD, with the remains of a late C16 or early C17 timber-framed, three-storey building with jettied upper storeys beneath a gable. Possibly the former cross-wing of a larger hall house. Then REGENT HOUSE (Nos. 160–161), a 1980s fibreglass replica of the rusticated classical façade of the 1834 Royal Buildings and Hotel. Only the carving of the royal arms above the entrance is original.

N into the main part of Briggate, now pedestrianized, the street's character changes as C20 commercial buildings dominate on both sides. On the E side bleakly functional blocks flank the ebullient former Post Office Exchange, 1907 by *Percy Robinson*, in brick and terracotta with Renaissance columns, wreaths and swags. On the W side, N of Boar Lane: BURTON'S shop and arcade, steel frame and pre-cast concrete with white tile cladding of 1963 by *T. H. French*; deeply recessed window bays in the upper floors. Then a Leeds institution: MARKS & SPENCER, who began with a stall at Kirkgate Market in 1884. The present building, begun in 1939 (completed post-war) was built (by *Norman Jones & Rigby* of Southport) to the modular system devised for M&S by their consultant architect, *Robert Lutyens*. Unusual stripped classical black granite façade, the only example besides Lutyens's own store in London's Oxford Street. Next Nos. 50–51, the premises of Thornton & Co., India Rubber Manufacturers, by *Sydney Kitson* in two phases, both identical, 1909 (l.) and 1910 (r.), with classical fluted columns *in antis*. Of steel frame and reinforced concrete clad in matt-faced white 'Marmo' faience from Burmantofts. A narrow passage N of this building leads to the cramped TURK'S HEAD YARD and WHITELOCK'S pub. There was an inn here *c.* 1716, the likely date for the present two-storey ranges of pub, brewhouse and five former cottages. The three cottages at the far end are of three storeys, a single room to each floor and sliding sash windows at the top. The pub renamed and rebuilt in 1886, the date of its richly decorated interior of stained glass, marble counters, engraved mirrors, brasswork and faience work, probably from Burmantofts. For the N end of Briggate *see* Perambulation 3.

KIRKGATE, E of Briggate, was the village street between the parish church and the open fields, established before Briggate was set out in 1207. The town's first Cloth Hall was built on its S side in 1711 and became the focus of its expanding trading area. The street starts badly with the monotonous former Littlewood's (s corner) of 1971, giving the impression that Kirkgate is an uninteresting side street, belying its historical importance. Opposite, *Chorley, Gribbon & Foggitt*'s DEBENHAM'S, of 1936, has attractive zigzag bronze fenestration. Further on, beyond Fish Street, interest is confined to the upper floors, in particular the former Golden Cock Inn, an Art Deco refronting in white 'Marmo' faience, with fluted half-columns, blue tiles and the inn sign set high up. Opposite, CENTRAL BUILDINGS by *Thomas W. Cutler*, 1901, shops and offices built on the site of the Central Market, Duncan Street (1824–7 by *Francis Goodwin*, with handsome Neo-Grecian frontage, dem. 1893). Bold Queen Anne Revival in brick with brown faience giant rusticated pilasters between the shopfronts surmounted by brackets with obelisk finials. Fine wrought-iron gates to the inner yard. From a level stretch at the top of Kirkgate, Chantrell's careful siting of the parish church tower (*see* Churches) can be appreciated in the view SE downhill, since 1869 bisected by the railway viaduct. Closer to, the eye is irresistibly drawn to the ornate City Markets (*see* Public Buildings).

Kirkgate E of Vicar Lane has a varied mix. On the SW side, the former London & Midland Bank, 1892 by *William Bakewell*. Tall, confident, two-storey Italianate stone front with paired Corinthian pilasters and deep-set Florentine tracery to the upper windows. Fine carving by *J. W. Appleyard* includes King Midas. Kirkgate was widened c. 1870 and its NE side largely rebuilt. The substantial former Yorkshire Penny Bank, by *Smith & Tweedale*, 1899, squats on the corner with New York Street. Brick with terracotta to ground floor, banded upper floor, short columns and three lead domes. On NEW YORK STREET, Nos. 1–19, c. 1885 by *W. B. Perkin* for Charles Burrow, a shoe dealer, with a cocoa house, bank and shops below workshops and offices. Modest Italianate, enhanced by moulded stringcourses and some terracotta. Further E, a second Temperance establishment; *Thomas Ambler*'s St James's Hall and Westminster Buildings of 1877. Tall windows with traceried heads lit an upper-floor lecture room and club rooms; plain sash windows to dormitories for 'strangers and working men' on the third floor. Extended in 1884 by *Ambler* and *William Thorp* for W. J. Armitage, the owner of the Farnley Iron Co. Polychromatic Gothic with a neat crocketed gable above the entrance to Westminster Buildings.

The SW side of Kirkgate was untouched by road widening and still has plain brick shops and houses of the mid C19 with narrow frontages. Behind the boarded-up frontage of Nos. 98–101 is an important survival: the first WHITE CLOTH HALL, built in 1711 as a covered market for undyed cloth. Originally a U-plan open to the street, its yard was infilled with housing in the early C19 by James Boyne. Plans of 1997 for refurbishment by *John Lyall Architects* remain unrealized. Beyond the railway viaduct is Leeds Parish Church of St Peter (*see* Churches), crudely cut off from the town by the line, which ploughed through the N part of its extended churchyard. Gravestones litter the embankment. Tucked into the railway arches is a row of four large blue steel pods with hinged fronts, like giant handbags, for a BAR AND NIGHTCLUB by *Union North Architects*, 2001: a clever scheme, but the siting is unfortunate. W of the church some early C19 buildings on HIGH COURT LANE, then the long flank of the OLD BREWERY, in polychrome brick, dated 1868. It stands at the junction with THE CALLS along the backs of the riverside warehouses, for which *see* Perambulation 7.

CROWN STREET, to the W, was the route uphill from the river to the town's third White Cloth Hall. Built in 1775–6, attributed to *William Johnson*, but partly demolished by the railway viaduct *c.* 1869 (in compensation for which the NER erected a new Cloth Hall in King Street, *see* Hotel Metropole, Perambulation 6). Part of the entrance range survives. Single-storeyed with blank arcading and an entrance with a tunnel-vaulted passage behind. Round cupola on a square base; it housed the bell from the previous White Cloth Hall of 1756. Behind, single-storey wings originally enclosed a large court-yard, now partly infilled with a restaurant and offices by *John Lyall Architects*, 1991–2. The N wing, now separated by Assembly Street, has an arcaded lower storey and an upper storey added in 1777 for assembly rooms. (Reception room and large ballroom with original plaster decoration and fine Palladian windows.) Refurbished by *David Readman, c.* 1990. Finally, CLOTH HALL STREET which has an outstanding five-storey apartment building by *Allford Hall Monaghan Morris*, 2003–5, describing a gentle arc along the S side of the street in response to the grand ellipse of the Corn Exchange opposite (*see* Public Buildings). Vibrant exterior clad in a mosaic of glazing, coloured ceramic panels and brickwork.

2. City Square to Albion Place

The perambulation has been divided into two parts but can be followed consecutively. It covers the W part of the city centre, first developed during the later C18 and early C19 when land was made available for building outside the medieval core. The first part is indicative of the major rebuilding in this area as it became the centre of the Late Victorian city.

2a. City Square to Park Square

CITY SQUARE, laid out in 1893–1903 to mark Leeds's elevation to City status, was the idea of the industrialist and Lord Mayor, T. Walter Harding, and designed by *William Bakewell*, architect of Harding's Tower Works (*see* Holbeck, p. 556). At the apex of the square, facing E along Boar Lane, a massive bronze equestrian STATUE of the Black Prince by *Thomas Brock*, one of several works in the square intended by Harding to provide a showcase for British sculpture. High granite pedestal with bronze low reliefs of battles on land and at sea and an elaborate carved band with the names of great men of the C14. Forming an arc around the square's perimeter is a marble balustrade, which originally encircled the statue, given its present form during a successful rearrangement of the square in 2002 by *John Thorp*, Civic Architect. Raised on pedestals are eight nymphs, Morn and Even by *Alfred Drury*, holding lamps. On the square's N side, life-size statues represent local industrial, social, religious and scientific endeavour: James Watt and John Harrison by *H. C. Fehr*; Dr Hook, vicar of Leeds, by *F. W. Pomeroy*; and Joseph Priestley by *Drury* (the last two donated by Harding).

The backdrop to the square is the imposing former GENERAL POST OFFICE, built on the site of the 1757 Coloured Cloth Hall. 1896 by *Henry Tanner*. Northern Renaissance style with a lively roof-line of gables, chimneys and central turret; good sculpture including four statues by *W. S. Frith* above the entrances representing forms of communication, and figures of Art and Science. Converted by *Garnett Netherwood Architects*, 2005–6, to a restaurant (in the columned great hall) and hotel. Then, moving anti-clockwise around the square, between Wellington Street and Quebec Street, the former MAJESTIC CINEMA (now Majestyk nightclub), dated 1921, by *Pascal J. Stienlet*, faced in white 'Marmo' terracotta from Burmantofts. Moulded decorative swags and panels depicting musical instruments. Inside, a Greek-style frieze and coffered dome within the former auditorium. Dominant on the square's S side, the rather dull, stripped classical façade of THE QUEENS HOTEL of 1937 by *W. H. Hamlyn*, architect to the London, Midland & Scottish Railway, replacing their earlier hotel. Ten storeys faced in white Portland stone, with brown brick sides and rear. Pedimented attic pavilions and a porte cochère carried on massive drum columns with the companies' heraldic shields. Gorgeous Art Deco interior by *W. Curtis Green*, consultant architect. Principal hall, bars, function rooms, and even some of the bedrooms, in an expensively jazzy taste with original fittings. w of the hotel, a separate smaller block for the LM&SR's OFFICES, with an angled front to Aire Street, contains the entrance to the contemporary station concourse (*see* Public Buildings) and originally included a cinema (now nightclub). Then, on the corner with Boar Lane and Mill Hill the impressive copper-domed rotunda of the stolid granite Yorkshire District Bank (now a bar), by *W. W. Gwyther*, 1899. Ten giant Corinthian attached columns and parapet embellished with statues and urns. Panels carved by *J. Thewlis*. On the opposite corner, the PARK PLAZA HOTEL, a re-cladding in 2003 of *Kitson, Pyman & Partners'* Exchange House office tower of 1965. The Mill Hill Unitarian Chapel (*see* Churches), E side, is the square's only survival from before 1893.

Its schools, which lay to the N, were replaced by No. I PARK ROW of 1996–7 by *Fletcher Joseph Architects*, a laboured homage to the late C19 buildings in Park Row; bands of red granite and an octagonal corner dome. Rather better is the Postmodern No. I CITY SQUARE of 1996–8 by *Dominic Boyes* of *Abbey Hanson Rowe*. Twelve storeys of offices with a solid black granite base blending into upper storeys of white stone. Rounded S façade bisected by a marble-faced atrium with wall-climber lifts and a tensile sun shade. Striking bronze Egyptian-style detail to the windows and a SCULPTURE of birds in flight by *Lorne McKean*.

INFIRMARY STREET, behind the Post Office, was laid out after 1805 as 'West Street' and was originally open on its N side as far as South Parade. On the site of the Infirmary itself (by John Carr, 1768–71; dem. 1893) is the former Yorkshire Penny Bank by *Perkin & Bulmer*, 1893–4, exuberant Baronial Gothic with five arcaded windows to the banking hall and an emphatic corner staircase tower topped with gargoyles and slated spire. Good carved decoration on both façades; the elaborate wrought-iron gates and railings are by *George Wragge* of Manchester; exquisitely detailed lamps over the entrances. Inside, original panelled rooms and marble fireplaces, stained-glass windows by *Powell Bros.* of Leeds; marble and mosaic work by *Pattison & Sons* of Manchester. Bulmer added an extra bay for offices and dining room in 1904.

The buildings of KING STREET are mostly Late Victorian and Edwardian, e.g. GOODBARD HOUSE (Allied Irish Bank) built as the 'Hotel de Ville' hotel, restaurant and offices in 1905. Edwardian Baroque, with an attic storey of the 1980s. Across King Street, on the S corner of St Paul's Street, an imposing example of the new building methods and materials of 1910: ATLAS HOUSE, five-storey insurance offices by *Perkin & Bulmer* in Renaissance style. Built using the Kahn system of concrete framing and faced in dazzling white 'Marmo' terracotta. Confidently composed display of Renaissance trim with wide curving pilastered corner and ornate sculpture by *Thewlis & Co.* including Atlas struggling beneath the weight of the globe. Next on this side, at the entrance to Park Place, the rather overbearing former BANK OF ENGLAND, 1969–71 by *K. Appleby* of *Building Design Partnership* (Manchester).* An inverted ziggurat, its form perhaps influenced by Kallmann, McKinnell & Knowles's Boston City Hall (1962–8), with each floor projecting out over the one below and strongly vertical window sections. Grey Cornish granite and bronze cladding. The finesse of the design is compromised by a shot-blasted concrete deck, designed to receive an anticipated elevated walkway. For buildings to the S *see* Perambulation 6.

Now W into PARK PLACE, our introduction to the late C18 Park Estate. Only the N side was built up at first, providing

*The bank is on the site of *Brodrick*'s celebrated warehouse of 1862 (*The Builder*, 1862), dem. 1967.

views s to the Aire. Two almost-symmetrical groups (a central three-storey pedimented house flanked by slightly lower neighbours) flank Central Street, each of local red brick with stone detailing. Pedimented doorcases, twelve-pane sashes and some original area railings with acorn finials. Nos. 5, 6 and 7, by *William Lindley* of Doncaster, were begun in 1777 for the banker John Arthington, who lived at No. 6. It has stone architraves to the centre windows and an oculus in the pediment, but lost its ground floor in the mid 1960s when plate glass was inserted. Nos. 5 and 7 were completed by Arthington's widow; their top floors have also been rebuilt, breaking the line of the sill band. The rest of Park Place's N side was built 1788–94 to designs by *William Hargrave*. At the w end Nos. 17–19, a highly impressive Adamesque composition with a dignified pedimented centre and giant Ionic pilasters dividing it into 3 + 5 + 3 bays. The arcaded ground floor and doorcases have been carefully restored. No. 16 strikes a different chord: its wide round-arched entrance and ground floor are entirely covered in relief-patterned tiles, apparently to a modest design by *F. Mosley* (listed in *J. C. Edwards of Ruabon*'s catalogue of 1900). The s side was built up with commercial buildings from the mid C19; they are of the type also seen in the streets to the s attracted by the presence of the railway stations and goods depots on Wellington Street. Best is Nos. 42–46, Gothic Revival offices and warehousing by *George Corson*, 1870.

ST PAUL'S STREET lies parallel to the N between Park Place and Park Square. Its character is predominantly late C19, dominated on the N side by the Hispano-Moorish style ST PAUL'S HOUSE of 1878 by *Thomas Ambler*, which also faces the square. Formerly a factory and warehouse designed for John Barran, pioneer of mass-produced clothing. 164 ft (50 metres) long, richly coloured in red and pink brick with *Doulton*'s terracotta. Ground-floor and mezzanine windows tied together by a giant segment-headed arch, first- and second-floor windows tied together by a giant trabeated frame. Then a small third floor with Moorish arches. Only the façade survived conversion to offices by *Booth Shaw & Partners* in 1975–6. The 'truly Mohammedan cresting', as Pevsner described it, with pretty pierced parapet and cinquefoil openings, is a reinstatement of the original, along with the five corner minaretlets, copied in fibreglass. The original tiled SE corner entrance with cusped arch and paired columns has been made into a window, with a new entrance on Park Square. Reduced to fit this are original ornate wrought-iron gates with ribbon-like scrolls and flowers by *Francis Skidmore*.

PARK SQUARE was laid out in 1788 with St Paul's church at its SE corner (1791–3 by *Thomas* or *William Johnson*, dem. 1905). Building around the square was by several hands and without consistency of scale and elevation. It began on the E side c. 1790, where the most prominent house is No. 8, built for William Wilson, either by *William Hargrave* (cf. Park Place) or *William Lawrance*. Its centre projects very slightly

104

and is pedimented, and the entrance has a carefully restored wooden doorcase with rusticated jambs and elaborate fluted columns supporting the open pediment. Pretty stucco ornamental festoon above the door. No. 9 was the vicarage to St Paul's, its terracotta façade added in 1908 following the demolition of the church. The next three houses were built by *Lawrance*. Lovely wood and plaster doorcases: fluted Corinthian columns at No. 10 (where Lawrance lived) and plaster lion and wreath at No. 11. The N side of the square was in progress from 1793; of this date the grandest house (No. 41, in the centre), five bays wide, with Tuscan columns at the entrance and a pediment with oval window. It was built for Thomas Bolland, attorney and clerk. To its r, No. 42, also pedimented, by *John Cordingley*, of two storeys with panelled door and fanlight under an open pediment supported by three-quarter Tuscan columns. (Column-on-vase balusters to the staircase), and to the l. Nos. 39–40 by *Thomas Johnson*, a three-storey, three-bay mirror-pair; with stone console brackets to the entrance entablatures. Nos. 43 and 45 are by *Hargrave*, but probably built after 1800, the changing styles indicated by plain stone door surrounds, tripartite sash windows and inside a staircase with column newels and plain rail. Nos. 36–38, built after 1815, have fine stone detailing: stone parapet panels carved with festoons of drapery and flanking scrolls. On the w side of the Square, Nos. 24–31, a row of modest three-storey houses built by *John Cordingley c.* 1793–1806, with a varied show of doorcases and area railings with leaf, bud and spearhead finials. The fine interior of No. 26 has panelling, a fireplace with fluted Ionic columns, turned staircase balusters and Adam-style plasterwork. Tuscan three-quarter stone columns outside No. 27. Behind No. 30 (No. 9 Somers Street) is a unique survival of the workshops and warehouses built behind most cloth merchants' houses in the late c18. Three storeys and five windows long, the top row has side-sliding sashes typical of the date. Cloth bought at the Cloth Halls was brought to these workshops to be checked, pressed and packaged for despatch.

2b. Park Row to Albion Place

PARK ROW, the medieval N–S route between Park Lane (now The Headrow, *see* p. 449) and the manor house, was developed as the main thoroughfare of the late c18 Park Estate development, but of the buildings of that period there is no trace. These were replaced by the Victorian banks and offices celebrated by Atkinson Grimshaw in 1882. In 1896 *The Builder* described it as 'the Pall-Mall of Leeds' and such is the street's continued commercial importance that all the buildings in Grimshaw's painting have been replaced and several others noted by Pevsner in 1959 have also gone. Nevertheless, one may still experience the full flavour of commercial Leeds in Park Row alone.

From the s end, the flavour is C20, beginning with the 1990s corner blocks at City Square (*see* Perambulation 2a). No. 1 City Square occupies the site of *Thomas Taylor*'s Court House and prison (1811–13; later the Post Office, dem. 1901). Next, a Neo-Georgian block by the *Office of Works*, 1938–9, and then a palazzo-style former York City & County Bank, by *Smith & Tweedale*, 1892. Pedimented corner entrance with monolithic Peterhead granite columns; vermiculated rustication to ground floor, arcaded windows in the upper floor between attached pairs of Corinthian columns. The carved detail is by *J. W. Appleyard*. Opposite, LLOYDS BANK of 1972–7, by *Abbey Hanson Rowe*, is an impressive seven-storey tower over shops and car park, clad in brown Finnish granite. The high-level entrance on the podium was part of the infamous late 1960s scheme for elevated walkways. Sculpture of the bank's horse emblem in steel rods by *Peter Tysoe*. N, with its entrance on Bond Street, is NATWEST, *c.* 1965: stripped classical, of grey granite with dressings of ebony diorite and seven storeys of Portland stone offices. This is the unworthy replacement of *George Gilbert Scott*'s celebrated two-storey Gothic Beckett's Bank of 1863–7; the first major Victorian casualty in the rebuilding of Park Row after 1960. Across the street, the unavoidably prominent HSBC (formerly Midland Bank) of 1966–9 by *Whinney, Son & Austen Hall*, built on the site of the Philosophical Hall (1819–22 by *R. D. Chantrell*). It housed the city's museum and was one of Leeds's few wartime losses. Tucked behind in BOND COURT is the surprising survival of a handsome early C19 house (Nos. 11–14), cement-rendered and lined to imitate ashlar, with continuous sill bands. Later C19 upper floor, the ground floor restored to look like a pair. N of here on Park Row, the streetscape improves with GREEK STREET CHAMBERS (Nos. 31–32, now a pub) of 1898 by *Alfred Waterhouse* for Williams, Brown & Co.'s Bank. Heavily striped in pink and grey granite at ground floor, red brick and Burmantofts buff faience above. Peterhead granite columns at the entrance and characteristic Waterhouse pavilion roofs at the corner bays.

Across Greek Street, the former BANK OF LIVERPOOL & MARTIN'S BANK of 1922–3 (now a pub). Portland Stone, rusticated and carved; plinth of rock-finished pale grey granite. Quoins extend the full height of the building, with vermiculated rustication. Then the former SCOTTISH UNION & NATIONAL INSURANCE CO. offices of 1909 by *Perkin & Bulmer* in a lavish Baroque style. Four storeys and an attic with emphatic cornice and corner dome. The structure is a reinforced-concrete frame, probably the earliest in the city, clad in Burmantofts glazed white 'Marmo' terracotta. Excellent sculpture by *Thewlis & Co.* including allegorical figures and crouching caryatids carrying the balconies.

Opposite, on the site of George Corson's Sun Fire Offices, Nos. 15–16 of 1995, by *Carey Jones Architects*, a seven-storey planar glass frontage set between granite flanks – a rare and refreshing appearance of the High-Tech school in Leeds.

Its neighbour (No. 18) is a small visual treat, built as the West Riding Union Bank in Free Baroque style in 1900 by *Oliver & Dodgshun* who also had their offices here. Four storeys, with fluted Corinthian pilasters rising to a heavy cornice. Ground floor of rich red Swedish granite carved with strapwork, and above this a full-width sculpted sandstone frieze signed by *Joseph Thewlis*, representing the bank's trading interests. Minerva sits on an Art Nouveau throne flanked by figures representing shipping interests in Africa and American railroad investment. Over the entrances 'Trade' and 'Commerce' are personified by female figures (representing Peace and Justice, Purity and Plenty), supporting coats of arms. Next, *Alfred Waterhouse*'s striking Northern Renaissance former PRUDENTIAL ASSURANCE BUILDING of 1890–4. Granite below, stripes of red brick and Burmantofts buff terracotta above, not popular with his clients who preferred their usual red. In the mid 1960s the roof was stripped above eaves level, including its gable dormers and corner spire, restored in 1989–90 by *Abbey Hanson Rowe*, who retained the façade for new offices, with good fresh terracotta work by *Shaw* of Darwen. Its neighbour is ST ANDREWS CHAMBERS of 1869 by *George Corson* for the Scottish Widows' Fund. Porch supported by four monolithic Peterhead granite pillars resting on blue-grey Aberdeen granite; Yorkshire sandstones carved with Scottish emblems on the first floor, revealed after recent cleaning. The E side concludes with an elaborate Flemish-style building by *E. J. Dodgshun*, 1894, for Peacock & Son, warehousemen. The corresponding corner of Park Row is taken by the former BRANCH BANK OF ENGLAND (now offices and a pub) by *P. C. Hardwick*, 1862–4. Fine-grained Halifax sandstone on a base of massive Millstone Grit blocks. Symmetrical façades on three sides of three storeys beneath a balustraded parapet with urns. Pedimented and segmental windows between channelled pilasters. The entrance on South Parade has reveals of Peterhead granite, one of the earliest uses in the town.

SOUTH PARADE has on its s side the post-war FRIENDS PROVIDENT BUILDING, five storeys of clean white Portland stone, with an impressive entrance portal of columns *in antis* in a massive moulded surround with a carved plaque; stripped classical above. No. 12, of *c.* 1900, are substantial offices in ashlar with banded rustication. Columns support a segmental broken pediment above the entrance, and a wide hollow-chamfered window has a female mask on the keystone. Later upper storey. Towards the w end on the N side, the former Legal and General Assurance Office, *c.* 1930–1, stripped classical by *Braithwaite & Jackman*, three storeys of Portland stone above a black granite base.

EAST PARADE was laid out between 1779 and 1788 but is now entirely of the C19 and C20. At the N end between Headrow and South Parade, *William Bakewell*'s Pearl Assurance Co. offices of 1911 (*see* Perambulation 4). Bakewell was forced to compensate for the loss of light to HEPPER HOUSE,

opposite, by enlarging its windows. The rest is of 1863 by
George Corson for John Hepper, auctioneer. Venetian Gothic,
an early example of the style in Leeds, in sandstone and Peterhead granite; Moorish terracotta tiles in the entrance lobby.
Two salerooms, both with coved ceilings and plain fire surrounds, are supported below on paired cast-iron columns. In
the first-floor front office a marble fireplace. Preserved in the
basement are the wall and window sills of an C18 house.
Pevsner noted other 'wealthy Georgian brick houses' in Park
Row in 1959, now demolished; downhill is a 1980s rebuilding
in facsimile. Beyond, EAST PARADE CHAMBERS, Free Renais-
sance-style offices of 1899, in yellow faience with a shaped
gable, slim buttresses and projecting timber oriels to the first
floor. Next door, Italianate offices for the County Fire and
Provident Life Association, *c.* 1870, with a statue of Britannia
and lion above the heavy modillion cornice. On the NW corner
with St Paul's Street, No. 1 (Zurich) of 1992–4 by *William
Gower & Partners* is Postmodern, but in the stripy C19 style of
Waterhouse with small square windows and gables.

Now back to Park Row along GREEK STREET, which was
being developed in 1817 by Joseph Green of Bradford. The sole
survivor is No. 7, a five-bay house, now restaurant and offices.
Rendered brickwork and quoins with a central doorway with
Ionic half-columns supporting a deep frieze and pediment.
Between here and Russell Street is an innovative car park
(an 'Auto-Silopark system') by *Maurice Sanders Associates*,
1968–70, for Leeds Corporation. Thirteen floors and two basements, of pre-cast concrete with vertical aluminium bars on
each façade. Cars are left at the entrance to be elevated and
'pigeon-holed'.

Now E along BOND STREET into the main shopping area,
passing between the Leeds Shopping Plaza, clad in reflecting
panels and local sandstone, on the r. and on the l. the big, ugly
podium of WEST RIDING HOUSE of 1970 by *Trevor Spence &
Partners*, a sixteen-storey slab with horizontal bands of glazing.
ALBION STREET, running N–S in a steep incline between Boar
Lane and The Headrow, was developed in the 1790s by *Thomas
Johnson*. Plots were offered for sale in 1792, intended for
superior residences, not shops.

COMMERCIAL STREET runs E of Albion Street with early
to mid-C19 survivals at the W end. First, on the N corner, an
impressive Venetian palazzo of 1852–5 by *W. Bruce Gingell* of
Bristol, for the Leeds & Yorkshire Assurance Co. This was one
of the first purpose-built offices in the town, leading the way
for the grand architecture seen in Park Row. Heavily vermiculated plinth with paired giant Corinthian three-quarter
columns and entablature decorated with festoons and masks,
all sumptuously carved. Next, Nos. 21–23, a mid-C19 shop and
offices, ashlar, three storeys and classical, with wide three-light
windows. The only major Georgian public building in the city
centre is the refined Neo-Grecian LEEDS LIBRARY. Founded
in Kirkgate in 1768, now the oldest 'proprietary' subscription

library in Britain. The part facing the street is of 1808 by *Thomas Johnson*, of five bays and two-and-a-half storeys with a rusticated ground floor containing shops under wide segment-headed arches; giant unfluted pilasters above. The original entrance in the l. bay was moved to the centre in 1880–1 by *Thomas Ambler*, who created the present tiled hall and staircase. Johnson's first-floor reading room is at the front: E gallery with slender spiral staircase of 1821 (ironwork by *T. Nelson*); N and W galleries of 1836 by *R. D. Chantrell*; the W staircase a replica. Parallel at the rear, Ambler's 'New Room' of 1881, with steel gallery of 1900 by *H. S. Chorley* with *George Corson*; scrolled ironwork by *James Allan & Son*. The early C19 scale continues opposite, where the corner building (Monsoon) appears to be *Thomas Taylor*'s Union Bank of 1812–13. Three storeys and five bays, with later parapet and urns.

Further E, No. 31, on a narrow plot, rendered, four storeys with giant Doric corner pilasters; a furniture warehouse by 1831. Then plaster and stone refacings of *c.* 1925: the Halifax Bank with a shallow pediment and, on the corner, the elaborately swagged Trinity House. Opposite, a contrasting small three-storey shop (No. 14) of 1868 by *George Corson*, in his eclectic Gothic style with stepped gables. The ground floor originally had showy arched windows. Then eccentric striped red and white terracotta for the Leeds Goldsmiths' Company on the corner to Lands Lane, by *Thomas Winn*, 1901. Three storeys and attic, alive with dormers, pinnacles and a bold cylindrical turret. Inside is an elaborate balustered staircase lit by stained glass with abstract flower motifs. The E end of Commercial Street was extended to Briggate 1806. Of *c.* 1900 the corner buildings with Lands Lane (N) and Trinity Street (S), including 'Record Chambers' (S side) built for the Irish Linen Co. with curved plate-glass display windows on the upper floor. But this junction ('Central Square') has been the centre of too much attention, with improvements of 1991–2 by *Faulkner Browns* introducing a mess of street furniture, lamps, steel poles and wires overhead.

ALBION PLACE, parallel to the N, was extended to Briggate in 1903 and now provides one of the most attractive views in Leeds, eastwards across Briggate towards the City Markets. Sadly, the view W is overwhelmed by West Riding House (*see* above). On the S side, from the W end, the former YMCA by *W. H. Thorp*, 1908. Grand Baroque with swagged urns over the segmental-pedimented porch and a Venetian stair window to first floor. Next, the former County and High Courts of 1870, by the County Court Surveyor *T. C. Sorby*, built in two sections, of red brick with stone dressings. On the l., the two-and three-storey former County Court, the façade divided 1 + 3 + 1 + 3 + 1 with Doric columns supporting an entablature to the entrances in the centre and the ends; on its r. the High Court of three storeys and three bays with a rusticated ashlar ground floor and heavy cornices. Heavy square-section area railings with strapwork panels to front. From 1878 LEEDS

LAW SOCIETY have had their offices at No. 1 Albion Place (N side), built as house and consulting rooms in 1795 by *Thomas Johnson* for the surgeon William Hey who owned most of the land on Commercial and Bond Streets. Nine bays with five-bay pediment. Buff sandstone plinth and warm red brick above. Stone steps rise to an impressive entrance with Tuscan columns *in antis* and keyed arch over the fanlight. To the E is the LEEDS CLUB, founded in 1849 for the town's flourishing professional classes. The very grand Italianate building is a remodelling of 1863, supervised by *Thomas Ambler*, of two earlier houses erected for William Hey. Three storeys and seven windows wide, with moulded round arches to the ground floor. Porch with paired Ionic columns. Equally grand inside – original fine classical plaster decoration, big marble fireplaces, panelled doors, fluted Composite columns. On the ground floor a reception lounge and dining room; a wide staircase with ornate cast-iron balusters rises to a room lined with composite pilasters, ornate frieze and coved ceiling. In the basement a much-admired cloakroom (marble sinks and stall dividers etc.). Later C19 Italianate office block next door, No. 4, brick, Doric columns supporting a grand balustraded balcony over the porch. At the corner with Lands Lane is the former CHURCH INSTITUTE. Polychrome gabled Gothic, in the style of *c.* 1300 but of 1866–8 by *Adams & Kelly*. It contained a lecture hall for 800, a library with 10,000 volumes and walls painted with frescoes of the saints. Converted to shops and offices by *Hadfield Cawkwell Davidson & Partners* in 1980 and given projecting Gothic display windows.

3. *Briggate and Vicar Lane: arcades and markets*

BRIGGATE, the wide market street of the medieval town, is still a thriving shopping area, successfully pedestrianized in 2006. The medieval street pattern of long, narrow burgage plots with yards behind the frontages was easily adapted for a series of covered shopping arcades from the 1870s onwards, the first of which is THORNTON'S ARCADE (W side, N end) of 1877–8 by *George Smith* for Charles Thornton (*see* also Perambulation 5). Mixed Gothic Renaissance façade of brick and painted stone, with a high arch and pavilion roof. Restored in 1992–4, the interior is long and narrow (242 ft by 15 ft; 74 by 4.5 metres), with a glazed roof carried on cast-iron pierced Gothic cross-arches rising from slender shafts with foliate capitals and brackets with dragons. The shopfronts, with rooms above, form a tripartite Gothic composition of arcade, triforium and clerestory. Charming animated clock at the W end with figures from Walter Scott's Ivanhoe: Robin Hood, Friar Tuck, Richard Coeur de Lion, and Gurth the Swineherd. Designed by *J. W. Appleyard* and made by *Potts & Sons* of Leeds.

Downhill and parallel to Thornton's Arcade is the QUEEN'S ARCADE of 1889 by *Edward Clark* of London, erected behind four- and three-storey frontages of the C18 and C19 and altered in 1896 when two shops s of the entrance were rebuilt and the arcade entrance widened. It is announced by a fine bracket clock (the main front faces Lands Lane to the W – a classical painted brick and sandstone façade of three storeys). The interior, restored 1994, is rather garishly painted. Pilasters with ornate capitals separate the ground-floor shops; white glazed bricks line the walls above, reflecting light from the glass roof, which is supported by cast-iron trusses. Unlike Thornton's this has a novel two-storey galleried arrangement. On the upper floor of the N side was the Queen's Arcade Hotel, with office, bar, two billiard rooms and a smoke room. The upper floor on the s side was designed as a separate 'street' of small shops opening off the gallery, each with a kitchen and bedroom above the level of the arcade roof.

The walk now continues along Briggate. Between the two arcades, No. 76 was Marks & Spencer's new shop by 1909; the curious rendered Art Deco façade is of 1926. Other points of interest on this side are ANGEL INN YARD where the late C18 Angel Inn overlooks a small square. Three storeys with attics, walls of hand-made red-brown bricks. Altered by *Thomas Winn*, 1904. Further down at the corner with Albion Place is a five-storey Edwardian Baroque shop by *Percy Robinson*, 1903, for Eveleigh Bishop, 'stationer, printer, fancy goods importer, jeweller and silversmith'. Clad in Burmantofts faience, and ornamented with green stone columns, pedimented dormers and obelisk finials above the ramped parapet. Across Albion Place a much-altered corner shop for Charles Kirkness by *Thomas Ambler & Son*, 1902. The PACK HORSE INN is in the yard of that name just below; its brick gabled end bay has part of a C16 or early C17 timber frame inside, preserved in a refurbishment in 1987.

The highlight of Briggate is VICTORIA QUARTER on the E side. This spectacular development of 1898–1904 by *Frank Matcham* for the Leeds Estates Company swept away the slums around the old meat market ('Shambles'), between Briggate and Vicar Lane. Three blocks are divided across two streets – Queen Victoria Street and King Edward Street – and incorporate the entrance to Bay Horse Yard at the N end. The whole architecture is one and the same design. Each part is of three storeys and an attic, unified by flamboyant façades of warm pink and buff terracotta elaborated in a free Baroque style with swags, strapwork and scrolls, Dutch gables, domes and corner turrets. The main attraction is the COUNTY ARCADE within the N block; one of the most beautiful interiors in the city, expertly restored by *Derek Latham & Co.* in 1988–90. T-plan, 394 ft (120 metres) long, and glowing with decoration in marble, mosaic and Burmantofts faience. Separating the (mostly restored) mahogany shopfronts, with their curved glass display cases, are columns and pilasters of Siena marble which carry balustraded balconies and stone ball finials. Above, the arched cast-iron roof has, at intervals, three glazed domes raised on pendentives of richly coloured and gilded mosaics. The central dome, over the crossing, depicts figures representing Leeds's industries. Below is a fine circular mosaic floor by *Joanna Veevers* of 1988–90. Also of this date the glazed roof over Queen Victoria Street, carried on a free-standing steel frame, with bright stained glass by *Brian Clarke*, abstractly patterned like woven fabric. The roof projects over Briggate with no attempt to integrate and is in poor contrast to the sensitive insertion into the block to the s of the glass façade of the HARVEY NICHOLS store of 1997 by *Brooker Flynn Architects* (this originally contained *Matcham*'s Empire Palace Theatre, thoughtlessly destroyed in 1962). The third block of the original scheme lies along King Edward Street, with the former County Café and King Edward Restaurant (now shops). The latter, on the corner with Fish Street, retains gold mosaics of fish, game and wine. For the s end of Briggate *see* Perambulation 1.

The Victoria Quarter presents an equally impressive E front to VICAR LANE, facing other grand four-storey commercial buildings of *c.* 1900 (for the City Markets to the s, *see* Public Buildings). First, Nos. 50–56, on the corner with Ludgate Hill, by *G. F. Bowman*, with an elaborate terracotta façade restored after a fire in 1993. Paired columns flank the former corner entrance to the Bradford Bank. Turret with lead dome and finial flanked by dormers with stepped gables at the top. Three-light segmental-arched furniture showroom windows to first floor. Next, Nos. 58–62, a non-matching pair of shops, offices and Temperance hotel by *W. H. Thorp*. Brick, stone dressings and terracotta panels, modest Renaissance style with pediments and pinnacles on the skyline. Wray's Buildings extend along Sidney Street. Jacobean style, its original entrance and paired round-headed windows in moulded arches with a name plaque and relief of figures with flowers. Ornate Dutch gables and four massive clustered chimneys of moulded brick. Then Coronation Buildings, by *D. Dodgson*, 1902, clad in red terracotta, distinctive hexagonal banded pilasters rising to truncated pinnacles above the cornice. Finally Nos. 76–88 on the corner to Eastgate by *G. F. Bowman*. Distinctive red brick with thin bands of buff terracotta, first-floor display windows with voussoirs; canted corner bay to Eastgate surmounted by a small turret and dome.

4. The Town Hall and Civic Quarter

The perambulation begins at the Town Hall. Brodrick set his building at the N end of its site, leaving a wide, open space facing what was then Park Lane. The street was remodelled in the 1930s as THE HEADROW (for which *see* Perambulation 5), when the square in front of the Town Hall was levelled and extended E to form a civic space in front of the Municipal Buildings and Art Gallery (*see* Public Buildings). The range opposite begins at the corner of Park Row with the muscular backside of the late classical former Bank of England (*see* Perambulation 2b). After some later C20 rebuilding there follows ATHENAEUM HOUSE, four storeys of restrained Tudor Gothic by *William Bakewell c.* 1890. Tall robed figures in canopied niches represent the Arts; its free Gothic neighbour, the former PEARL LIFE ASSURANCE CO. (est. 1864), is also by *Bakewell,* dated 1911. Gleaming Portland stone, one of the first uses in the city. Continuing W up to Park Cross Street, the flamboyant former Jubilee Hotel and Chambers of 1904 by *Thomas Winn,* with a corner tower and scrolled pediments in bright red brick and terracotta. Terminating the view W from the Jubilee Hotel along WESTGATE is WESTGATE POINT, by *David Lyons & Associates,* 1987, typifying the 'Leeds Look' of the period. Six and eight storeys in red and yellow brick with a cranked plan, deep eaves and stepped stair windows but weak for its landmark site. Visible across the submerged Ring Road is ONE PARK LANE, a slick glass office block, completed 2003 by *Carey Jones Architects.* N of Westgate Point is the MAGISTRATES' COURT (*see* Public Buildings) and to its E the COMBINED COURT CENTRE.

In OXFORD PLACE, between the Town Hall and the Methodist church (*see* Churches), BRITANNIA BUILDINGS is probably contemporary with the development of this area *c.* 1866. Three-storey brick offices in delightful Gothic Revival style with ornate stone arched entrance, slender columns with foliate capitals and quatrefoils. Perhaps by *Charles Fowler* who was practising here in 1867. Of a similar date Nos. 35–41 GREAT GEORGE STREET, elaborate Gothic Revival shops and offices with a turreted corner at Oxford Row. The style suggests *Ambler.* The N side of Great George Street is dominated by Scott's General Infirmary and its associated buildings, including the Old Medical School set uphill to the W (*see* Public Buildings). To its NW lay the Mount Pleasant estate of Christopher Beckett who provided land for the building of St George's church (*see* Churches). On the S side, opposite the church, the bulky former CENTAUR CLOTHING FACTORY, 1889 by *E. J. Dodgshun.* Six storeys of red brick, eclectic style, with a rounded corner crowned by a conoid roof and Dutch gables to the attic. Elaborate corner entrance with fluted columns and wrought ironwork. E of this, the S side is lined with modest houses, shops and offices of the mid C19. On the N side facing the back of the Town Hall, Nos. 24–28, a group of 1865 beginning with the VICTORIA HOTEL. Seven bays, symmetrical, Italianate Gothic marble columns with foliate capitals to the first floor and entrance; the interior panelling, tiles and etched glass, probably dating from Tetley's purchase in 1916, are not all original. No. 26 is by *George Corson* for Edmund and Joseph Wormald, photographers. Its single-bay wide front is elaborated with an arcaded entrance with cusped heads, moulded stone cornices and sill bands and canted first-floor oriel. Italianate brick corbelling and a truncated pyramid roof with gabled dormer and fleur-de-lys finials. Next the two-storey ashlar former MASONIC HALL by *Perkin & Sons* (now a pub). An odd assemblage of Gothic motifs: gabled entrance to the r. and cusped arch windows with shafts to the first floor; masonic emblems are carved in quatrefoil panels between the windows. Corbelled cornice with trefoil openings in the parapet and a wide stepped gable decorated with the six-pointed star and crocketed finials.

Great George Street's N side now opens to MILLENNIUM SQUARE. Created in 1999–2000 by the Civic Architect, *John Thorp* from the dull wedge-shaped gardens laid out in 1933 as a setting for the Civic Hall. He closed Portland Crescent to extend the square E to Cookridge Street for a view of Brodrick's Mechanics' Institute (City Museum, *see* Public Buildings). The S part is the Mandela Garden, re-created in 2001 with formal planting, a busy pool and Both Hands, a bronze by *Kenneth Armitage* evoking the spirit of reconciliation. In the square's NE corner a striking grenade-shaped structure, 'Off-kilter', by *Richard Wilson*, 2000, abuts the long and extensively glazed frontage of a five-storey bar and apartment complex by *West & Machell*, 2000–1.

On the S side of the square, the Carriageworks Theatre (*see* Public Buildings) of 2005–6 interwoven with the large commercial and industrial group along GREAT GEORGE STREET. This includes the former West Riding Carriage Works of 1848, built for J. F. Clark, whose house adjoins the handsome office frontage of rusticated ashlar and brick. Rear courtyard surrounded by former workshops. Adjacent is a distinguished Italianate corner warehouse (No. 39 Cookridge Street). Brick and stone with large segmental and round-arched windows and a fancy corner entrance, with Doric columns *in antis*. Probably built *c.* 1866 for Roodhouse & Sons, cabinet manufacturers, but extended behind *c.* 1900 by Chorley & Pickersgill for their printworks, now known as the ELECTRIC PRESS BUILDING. Large tapering square chimneyshaft with white lettering. Immediately across Cookridge Street, the LEONARDO BUILDING (No. 4), contained the printworks' offices. Red brick, four storeys in an eclectic Italianate style with a higher, splayed corner tower displaying a rich mix of motifs. Rear extension by *John Thorp*, Civic Architect, 1998.

Facing St Anne's Cathedral (*see* Churches), Nos. 23–35 COOKRIDGE STREET, offices and warehouses built 1840–7 for William Smith, woollen cloth merchant of Roundhay Hall, Gledhow. Possibly by *James Simpson*. Three storeys turning the corner with Great George Street with a bowed and recessed entrance. Wide cart entrance and courtyard plan, well-proportioned façade, ashlar ground floor, and red brick above. Shopfronts of 1899 by *Ambler*. Nos. 19–21 of similar date; although purpose-built as offices and warehouses, the design derives from C18 private houses (e.g. Nos. 17–19 Park Place). Seven bays, brick with ashlar dressings, giant pilasters supporting a paired modillion cornice. Continued in a similar style as Nos. 11–17, now mostly the Henry Moore Institute (*see* Public Buildings). Sensitive restoration by *Michael Devenish* of *CoDA Conservation*, 1994. N along Cookridge Street is Brodrick's mighty Mechanics' Institute of 1865–8 (*see* Public Buildings, City Museum). It now looks onto Millennium Square but originally faced Brodrick's Moorish-style Oriental Baths of 1866 (refronted in the ubiquitous Gothic style in 1882 and demolished 1969). Still surviving uphill, Nos. 49–51, a pair of shops with original fronts of 1864, also by *Brodrick*. In a strange angular Gothic: arcaded first-floor windows with low cusped wrought-iron balconies; paired sashes on the second floor set into blind Gothic arches and twin straight gables with triangular lights. Dwarfing these the church-like spiky Gothic front of the former COLISEUM THEATRE by *William Bakewell*, 1885. Tripartite façade of pale Morley sandstone, with gabled outer bays and a central portal beneath a rose window and round-headed plate-traceried windows on either side. Atop the central gable is a figure of Britannia. Functional brick flanks. Much altered interior, which once seated 3,000 for circuses and other spectacles. E of Cookridge Street are several major educational establishments (for which *see* Public Buildings).

To the N, just within the Ring Road but brutally cut off by the busy Woodhouse Lane, is QUEEN SQUARE, a modest Georgian oasis of red brick houses built up on the W side of Claypit Lane by developers *John* and *George Bischoff*, 1806–22. The houses are on three sides, the earliest on the NW of three storeys. Nos. 1–3 are pedimented with three-quarter Tuscan columns flanking the doorways and a blind elliptical window in the pediment. Original railings to Nos. 3–4 with cup-and-cover finials. The rest are smaller, many with stone wedge lintels and fanlights. As at Park Square, the rows were built with access to warehouses and workshops at the rear. No. 8 (NE side) preserves the *c.* 1900 shopfront of Kayll & Reed, stained-glass-makers and signwriters, with gilded lettering on the fascia. The houses on the SW have doorways with wooden reeded pilasters. Late C19 gas lampposts with fluted shafts and a small central garden. Much of the square has been restored for Leeds Metropolitan University. Behind Nos. 1–6 (entrance in Queen Square Court), the SCHOOL OF THE BUILT ENVIRONMENT by *Allen Tod Architecture*, 2005, displays a set of STAINED GLASS by *Geoffrey Fuller Webb*, mostly from 1906–7, depicting the history of the public works contractors, S. Pearson and Son. Originally installed in The Whitehall Club, London, but given by Weetwood Pearson, Lord Cowdray, in 1979 for the Brunswick Building (*see* Public Buildings). In CLAYPIT LANE stands Joseph Hepworth's former clothing factory (now Ventura) of 1891 by *H. A. Cheers*, and its ten-storey headquarters of 1973 by *K. Peers* of the *P-E Consulting Group*. Marble-faced podium and curtain-walled slab with reflective bronze windows. These are now dominated by the massive PLAZA student flats by *Carey Jones Architects*, begun in 2007, with a thirty-seven storey tower.

5. The Headrow to Quarry Hill: a circular tour

THE HEADROW was the major civic initiative of interwar Leeds, creating a grand 80-ft (25-metre)-wide boulevard across the N half of the city centre, clearing the narrow medieval Lower Head Row and Upper Head Row E and W of Briggate. *Sir Reginald Blomfield* was engaged to devise the grand ranges of offices, shops and department stores planned for the street. These were begun in 1927 but their final execution delayed until after the Second World War. The street begins E of Cookridge Street with Blomfield's PERMANENT HOUSE AND HEADROW BUILDINGS of 1929–31, a long classical range of brick and Portland stone stepping up the steep slope in five stages. 'Tame and dull', said Pevsner, 'but the scale is an asset.' Towards the W end is a tall arch surmounted by columns *in antis*; a feature derived directly from The Quadrant, Regent Street, London. This now forms the entrance to THE LIGHT, a two-level retail development by *DLG Architects*, 1999–2002 with a bright and airy interior. Permanent House has a seamless N extension along Cookridge Street by *G. W. Atkinson*, 1955.

The Headrow's S side, where existing frontages went unaltered, is more mixed. Opposite Permanent House, from the corner with Park Row, ST ANDREW HOUSE, by *Gillinson Barnett & Partners*, a rebuild of 1977, which retains a late C19 façade to Park Row (*see* Perambulation 2b) but fails to connect visually. Uphill, the former Green Dragon Hotel of *c.* 1900 has finely carved buff sandstone dressings, including muscular Atlantes. Then, at the corner with Albion Street, five-storey offices for the Leeds & Holbeck, now Leeds Building Society, 1930, by *Chorley, Gribbon & Foggitt*. Sand-faced brick and Portland stone, harmonizing with the Blomfield buildings but without the flamboyance.

E of Albion Street The Headrow slopes downhill. On the N side is the former HEADROW HOUSE planned for by Blomfield and following his style but built 1951–5 by *Arthur S. Ash* of London as a ten-storey tower on a reduced site. It overlooks Dortmund Square, laid out in 1980, which has the bland ST JOHN'S CENTRE shopping mall by *Gillinson Partnership*, 1985. Then follows the former Lewis's Department Store (now BROADGATE, converted in 2008 by *Fairhursts Design Group*), designed in 1931 by *Blomfield* as a continuous seven-storey range but only completed up to the second floor in 1932, the rest added in the 1950s by *Atkinson & Shaw*, omitting much of the original classical detail. Extra floors have been added during conversion and a glass wall created at the rear overlooking St John's churchyard.

Opposite, THORNTON'S BUILDINGS of 1873, a development of shops, offices and top-lit workshops for Charles Thornton, a local entrepreneur (*see* Thornton's Arcade, p. 443). Italianate, brick with sandstone details. Three storeys and a deep cornice, paired and triple-arched windows with pilasters. Large carved stone gables over the corner and entrance to its chambers on the nine-bay Headrow frontage. To its s, off Lands Lane, is SWAN STREET, where Thornton had founded the City Varieties Music Hall (*see* Public Buildings).

At the same time as the grand rebuilding of the N side of The Headrow, surviving older frontages along the s side were refronted and improved. At the corner with Briggate is a remarkable survival of a block of four Late Georgian shops, shown in an 1828 engraving. Three storeys and eight bays. The four shallow rusticated arches of the ground-floor shops have gone but the fenestration, roof-line and chimneys survive. Cement stucco rustication and pedimented N gable added 1928–30 by *William Whitehead & Percy Robinson*. Next, Nos. 15– 39, early C19 houses and shops refaced in 'Marmo' faience with pediments, pilasters and urns by *William Whitehead*, 1929. Then the Three Legs pub, of *c.* 1900 with a treacle-brown glazed faience and buff terracotta front for Tetley's brewery. The entrance to Rockley Hall Yard is a refronting of 1929 by *William Pearson*, classical with a shallow pedimented blocking course. Rockley Hall and its estate belonged to the wool merchant John Harrison in the early C17; some of the hall's roof timbers are thought to survive in a C19 brick rear wing.

E of New Briggate, a large block executed to Blomfield's design by *George H. Shipley & G. W. Atkinson*, 1929–30. It contained the Paramount Cinema, with an interior designed by the cinema and theatre specialist *Frank T. Verity* (now destroyed). At the corner with Vicar Lane, LLOYD'S BANK. Its façade is of 1930–2 by *Blomfield* – giant Doric pilasters, badge, and fine classical detailing – but the interior fitted out by *Kitson, Parish, Ledgard & Pyman* whose offices were in the chambers above. It is matched on the opposite corners of this crossing by later designs for Martin's Bank (NE) and Barclays (SW) of 1938.

From here EASTGATE continues The Headrow scheme downhill, the buildings mostly executed post-war, including the former SHELL BP HOUSE (N side) of 1953 by *Cotton, Ballard & Blow*. Then a plainer pre-war range of four storeys stepping downhill, by *Blomfield* with detailing by *G. W. Atkinson*. The street frontages terminate on each side with E-facing blocks: on the N side is the former Kingston Unity Friendly Society, by Blomfield with additional work attributed to *Kirk & Tomlinson*, 1930, on the s a similar design for the Yorkshire Hussar. At the end of Eastgate is a picturesque former petrol station by *Blomfield*, 1932, set on a traffic island. Tiny arcaded hexagon with tent-like copper roof and torch finial. Now centrepiece of the MILLENNIUM FOUNTAIN by *John Thorp*, Civic Architect, 2000. STATUE of the Leeds airman Arthur Aaron V.C. (†1943), by *Graham Ibbeson*, 2001. A sentimental figure group shows Aaron with the future generation. In 2007 outline permission was granted for a major retail and residential development centred on Eastgate (masterplan: *Terry Farrell & Partners*; architects *Heatherwick Studio, John McAslan & Partners,* the *Jerde Partnership* and *Benoy*), which promises partial rebuilding of its s side and reconstruction of a large area to the N.

On QUARRY HILL, the visual focus at the end of Eastgate, a striking counterpoint to the formal boulevard was originally made by the 'Chinese Wall' of the Quarry Hill Flats (1935–41 by *R. A. H. Livett*, director of the Corporation's Housing Dept. dem. 1977). Now dominant on the skyline is the forbidding QUARRY HOUSE, a 'design and build' scheme of 1993 by *Building Design Partnership*. Overbearing façades in red brick and sandstone on a granite plinth, with a dark glazed curtain wall lighting the central galleried atrium, flanked by wings behind portcullis-like grids of glazing. On the E side, away from the city, a central drum-like tower with finial. Two inner court-yards, imaginatively landscaped by *Susan Tebby*. On the hill's sw corner is the West Yorkshire Playhouse (*see* Public Buildings) and behind this the BBC offices, by *DLA Architecture*, 2002–4, with a generous curved front. This is linked with the COLLEGE OF MUSIC, a contrasting block in buff brick with curved roof by *Allen Tod Architecture*, 1997, with next to it a thirteen-storey teaching and accommodation block of 2005, a dark brick base and dominating glass-panelled tower. Permission has been granted for several large-scale developments, the first of these a fifteen-storey residential tower by *Brewster Bye Architects*, squeezed between the Playhouse and the BBC.

The walk returns w along LADY LANE, parallel with The Headrow, for buildings between The Headrow and the Inner Ring Road. Lady Lane was the medieval route NE out of town before the creation of Eastgate. A sole relic of the mid C19 is TEMPLAR HOUSE, a former Methodist chapel, 1840 by *James Simpson*. (It stands on the site of St Mary, the first Roman Catholic chapel of 1794.) Classical, two storeys, in red brick with stone detailing and paired entrances in architraves. Round-arched windows. Much abused and neglected after it was converted into a warehouse but due for restoration under the plans for Eastgate's redevelopment (*see* above). Lady Lane joins VICAR LANE, at the N end of which is *William Hill*'s impressive Italianate former Chest Clinic of 1865, which served the Leylands district to the N (*see* p. 465). S is the GRAND ARCADE by *Smith & Tweedale*, 1897; in an eccentric Renaissance style using Burmantofts faience and blue and yellow tiles at the entrances. Two parallel arcades ran between Vicar Lane and New Briggate, with a cross-passage opening onto Merrion Street, whose plain brick façade has a round arch under a gable and three paired shopfronts with odd inverted consoles as mullions to the upper-floor windows. Inside, what little attention has been given to the interior in the later C20 has not brought out its charms. Glazed roof supported by timber arches and rows of shops with some original Ionic pilasters. There is no gallery here, only small bay windows, canted bays or deeply recessed with more curious mullions. At the E end an animated clock by *Potts* of Leeds: armoured knights guard castle doors, which open to release exotic costumed figures.

s of Grand Arcade's entrance on NEW BRIGGATE is the Grand Theatre (*see* Public Buildings). This extension of Briggate was made in the C17, contemporary with the building of St John's church (*see* Churches) whose principal benefactor, John Harrison, also established a small group of almshouses (dem.). However, N of the church in a short cul de sac (formerly St John's Place) is an unexpected survival of a house built in 1720 for the merchant Matthew Wilson and the only one remaining of those shown on Cossins's map of Leeds in 1725. The proportions survive, with a central entrance, sash windows and end stacks, but the red brick walls were given a heavy render imitating rock-faced ashlar after 1860.

MERRION STREET to the N, laid out in 1830, was widened at the same time as The Headrow, *c.* 1930. At the corner, shops and offices in the Blomfield style. Continuing W, immediately on the l. are shops and ST JOHN'S HOUSE, 1930 (now a pub) by *G. W. Atkinson*, Architect to the Receiver of Wade's Charity (founded 1530), whose buildings had been cleared for The Headrow. Tudor revival, timber framing and brick, two storeys with attics, five irregular bays with external chimneystacks, and striking S front of jettied gables overlooking the churchyard. The Charity's boardroom and offices were on the ground floor; on the first floor was Atkinson's drawing office. The rest of Merrion Street is unmemorable but too large to ignore is the massive MERRION SHOPPING CENTRE, occupying the entire site between Wade and Woodhouse Lanes, of 1962–4 by *Gillinson, Barnett & Allen*. A novel scheme for its date, integrating a nightclub, dance hall and cinema with a pedestrian shopping precinct. This was originally open (but soon enclosed) with shops on two levels connected by stairs and 'a moving pavement'. Fourteen-storey slab of offices and multi-storey car park, clad in dreary grey and white mosaic tiles. Challenging it at the corner of Albion Street and Great George Street is K2 THE CUBE, *Abbey Holford Rowe*'s sleek 2002 conversion and recladding of Dudley House (1972) into twenty storeys of apartments, with offices and retail in six-storey additions clad in glass and terracotta; corner balconies and distinctive fin-like roof.

6. *Wellington Street and neighbourhood*

The perambulation can begin at the W entrance to Leeds Station (*see* p. 423) in PRINCES SQUARE, which has as its backdrop PRINCES EXCHANGE, a highly successful design by *Carey Jones Architects*, 1999, on a triangular site. Sharp, prow-like front with repetitive horizontal fins and glazed envelope extending over an open ground floor. Behind, a view opens up along the N bank of the Aire* lined with late C20 and early C21

---

*Here was the site of the medieval High Dam, built to divert water from the Aire into a channel powering the manorial corn mill. The river itself turns sharply S here through the 'Dark Arches' (*see* p. 423).

blocks of offices and flats on former industrial lands, including No. 1 WHITEHALL ROAD by *Abbey Hanson Rowe*, 1997, five storeys, clinical in white and green cladding, and apartments of 2004 by *Aedeas AHR*; up to fifteen storeys, brick cladding, aluminium and glass, with porthole windows and stepped roof-line. Furthest W, WHITEHALL QUAYS, flats by *Carey Jones Architects*, 2004–5.

WELLINGTON STREET, to the N, was mostly laid out in 1817 although the E end is of *c.* 1809; represented on the N side by a small row of former houses. The street's principal interest is the Victorian display warehouses, the finest group in the city, where mill-owners dealt directly with their buyers. Nos. 17 and 19 (S side) by *George Corson*, 1859, are characteristic. No. 17 (Churchill House) was built for Thomas Pawson, a woollen manufacturer who owned Stonebridge Mills, Wortley; the second has John Sykes & Son's initials over the door. Rusticated basement storeys and Venetian Gothic detailing to prominent central entrances; they originally extended further E. Next to these an impressive six-storey brick-clad former clothing factory and warehouse (Nos. 21–3) with full-height glazing (altered) to each floor, of 1900 for R. B. Brown & Sons, wholesale clothiers. Built 'in the American system' i.e. steel-framed with open floors, fire-proof walls, and a water tank on the roof for the sprinkler system. W at the corner with Thirsk Row, the former Great Northern Hotel (now flats) of 1869 by *M. E. Hadfield & Son* of Sheffield. The top three floors were destroyed in the 'Great Fire of Leeds' in 1906, and crudely remodelled in the late C20 but lively sculpture by *Theodore Phyffers* survives. The GNR's terminus at Central Station was just to the E, its site now occupied by flats of 2004–5 by *Carey Jones Architects* (a re-cladding of the Brutalist mail sorting office which succeeded the station). To its W covering the area S to the river was a huge goods depot serving the various railway companies. For the railway buildings here *see* p. 424.

The best C19 survivals are along Wellington Street's N side between King Street and Queen Street. KINGS HOUSE, at the corner with King Street, was built in two phases: the first part was one of *George Corson*'s earliest major warehouses, 1861. Italian Gothic, the ground floor of rusticated ashlar masonry, and fine red brick with bands of blue; tower to King Street. Matching extension of 1870 (Blemann House). Then No. 56, Gothic Revival of 1873 by *Henry Walker*: four bays of ashlar, the porch to the r. carried up as a canted bay with turret and gargoyles. Gable filled with plate tracery and more stone beasts. Built for the hide and leather manufacturer George Morrell whose tannery was in Armley. Rooms for clerks and offices on the first floor, with basement and upper-floor stores for leather. No. 60 was occupied by Walter Stead, cloth manufacturer, who built WATERLOO HOUSE (No. 58), 1868 by *Edward Birchall*. Extravagantly decorated façade of seven bays and five storeys ornamented with stone banding and eccentric Gothic mouldings; pink granite columns support a

heavy entrance porch. Polychrome brickwork is used with
abandon. Then two early developments: a short row of plain
earlier C19 shops and houses with tiny attic windows followed
by a plain *c.* 1840 wool warehouse (No. 42) with its principal
front to Britannia Street. W of here, to the corner with Queen
Street is APSLEY HOUSE, a large former drapery and haber-
dashery warehouse of 1903 for Crowe & Company by *Corson*
and *W. Evan Jones* with *Perkin & Bulmer*, associate architects.
A traditional composition with ornate entrance, raised ground
floor and elaborate railings but with a steel frame clad in pink
terracotta and red brick. Arched office windows and three
storeys of large upper-floor windows, with slightly canted bays
with ornamented panels between.

Now N along Queen Street and into YORK PLACE, which
was laid out as Cobourg Place by 1821. The earliest buildings
are merchants houses of *c.* 1830, e.g. No. 21 (S side), a wide
five-bay house of some distinction with heavy pilastered doorcase and, E of Britannia Street, a matching pair (Nos. 11 and
12) of three-storey red brick houses over basements. They were
in use as woollen warehouses by 1886 and by that time other
purpose-built warehouses and offices had encroached, e.g. on
the N side No. 30, and the much larger and ornamental Nos.
37–41 (by *George Corson*), both Gothic Revival of *c.* 1870 with
the motif familiar from Wellington Street of gabled hoods over
the entrances with trefoil arches and corbelled brackets. But
the most impressive is Aintree House (Nos. 1–2, S side) by
Stephen Smith, *c.* 1870 for G. R. Portway & Co., woollen manufacturers. 'The best of the functional warehouses' (Pevsner).
It has arched ground-floor windows and three upper storeys
all linked by slender giant arcading. Heavy rustication to the
basement piers and deep, bracketed eaves cornice. Smith was
articled to William Hill and both were strongly influenced by
Cuthbert Brodrick's confident style.

Facing down York Place on KING STREET is the HOTEL
METROPOLE, by *Chorley, Connon & Chorley*, 1897–9, in an
undisciplined French Loire taste. Red terracotta, with writhing
sculptural detail to a three-storey bowed centre with columns
and canted oriels on giant, elongated consoles. The stone
cupola is from the (fourth) White Cloth Hall of 1868, formerly
on this site. Inside, giant columns and a cantilevered, bronze-
panelled staircase evoke the extravagance of Late Victorian
Leeds. Just to the N in QUEBEC STREET, running down to
City Square, is the former Leeds & County Liberal Club (now
QUEBECS HOTEL) by *Chorley & Connon*, 1890, in vivid red
Ruabon terracotta. Eccentric Free Renaissance with Art
Nouveau motifs. Splendid interior, including a sweeping
staircase with lions supporting wrought-iron lamps on the
balustrade and a stair window with stained-glass badges of
Yorkshire towns by *Powell Bros.* Opposite, the bulky but impres-
sive CLOTH HALL COURT of 1980–3 by *T. P. Bennett & Son*.
Stone-clad, with C18 sympathies: shallow cambered arches to

the ground floor. For the buildings on City Square *see* Perambulation 2a.

There is one other building of significance in this area: the YORKSHIRE POST NEWSPAPERS headquarters, on the approach to Wellington Bridge. 1968–70 by the *John Madin Design Group* of Birmingham. Mostly built in reinforced concrete with exposed Dorset shingle aggregate finish. The public entrance is an octagonal double-height foyer with top-lit library in the storey above. Opening from this is the advertising hall; once a streamlined, airy space now compromised by internal alterations. Rising above this section on the E side a tall slab for offices, overlooking a roof garden. At the rear, extending to the riverbank, is the Press Hall, 108 ft (33 metres) long and 34 ft (10.4 metres) high, of steel-frame construction designed for later expansion. This is the site of Benjamin Gott's celebrated Bean Ing (or Park) Mills, the earliest proper textile factory in Leeds, begun in 1791. By 1830 it housed powered spinning and weaving, offices and a large warehouse. 'The elegant WELLINGTON BRIDGE, spanning the Aire, was designed for Gott by *John Rennie* in 1817, but has been partially obscured by later widening. SE of the bridge is CITY ISLAND, flats by *Brewster Bye Architects*, 2005. Three curved blocks with stepped roof-lines. For the railway buildings to the S and E *see* p. 424.

7. The riverside: Victoria Bridge to Clarence Dock

NEVILLE STREET, running S of Leeds Station, was laid out in 1829 with a footbridge across the Aire to Holbeck. This was rebuilt as VICTORIA BRIDGE in 1837–9 by *George Leather Jun.* of Bradford. Graceful rusticated elliptical arch with Greek motifs. Its immediate surroundings are now overshadowed by several early C21 high-rise developments. These have also encroached upon Granary Wharf (*see* p. 424) at the entrance to the Leeds and Liverpool Canal, upstream of the bridge, as part of a mixed-use scheme by *Carey Jones Architects* with *CZWG* and *Allies & Morrison* (under construction in 2008). Most intrusive is BRIDGEWATER PLACE of 2004–7 by *Aedeas Architects*, intended as a landmark at the S end of the bridge but of a scale determined to overpower everything else. Pale reconstituted stone, with a monumental residential tower rising to thirty-two storeys, the tallest in the city, and an eight-storey atrium linking this to a lower range for offices.

Now E along the river's S bank, past the ASDA offices, one of the first commercial developments on the post-industrial riverside, built in 1988 by *John Brunton Partnership*: long and low three storeys, in brick with Postmodern details. On the opposite bank, late C20 warehouse-style offices and VICTORIA MILLS (dated 1836), rising to five storeys over the water. Continuing up to Leeds Bridge on the N bank, a sequence of late

C20 offices and flats e.g. SOVEREIGN HOUSE, late 1990s, and THE QUAYS, of 2004–5 by *Carey Jones Architects*. On the S bank are a few older survivors, including a warehouse, with their backs to the river and principal elevations to WATER LANE: here too is the OLD RED LION, which retains its early C19 character and nice plaster sign above the door.

The rebuilding of Leeds Bridge in 1873 saw clearance of most of the buildings on its southern approach (BRIDGE END) and rebuilding in the varied styles of the date, e.g. LEEDS BRIDGE HOUSE, S at the junction with Hunslet Road, of *c.* 1875, a five-storey flat-iron-shaped landmark, with Romanesque detailing, a corbelled top storey and much use of ornamental brickwork. On Hunslet Road's E side, at the corner with Dock Street is THE ADELPHI pub; flamboyant Jaco-bethan by *Thomas Winn* for Tetley's, 1897. Polished red granite ground floor, red brick and ashlar detailing above; palatial inte-rior with tiled floors, mahogany and etched glass doors, tiling, overmantels and original furnishings.

Buildings associated with the Aire & Calder Navigation occupy both banks of the river E of Leeds Bridge. Visible on the N bank are the tall rusticated arches of the NAVIGATION WAREHOUSE of 1827; its upper storeys rebuilt following a fire in the mid 1960s. Its predecessor gave its name to Warehouse Hill to the E, now an open wharf but formerly a narrow stretch of moorings cut off from the riverbank by a mill race (now cul-verted). Cossins's map (1725) shows it packed with buildings and part was known as 'Low Holland'. For the other buildings to the E *see* below. The Navigation Co.'s former offices are on the S bank at the corner with DOCK STREET; built 1906. Behind stood their wharf, now partly occupied by flats of 2003–4 by *Carey Jones Architects*, who also converted early C19 warehouses overlooking the river. Opposite, a few buildings contemporary with the Navigation's early years, including a row of small three-storey mid-C18 merchant houses and ware-houses. At the W end No. 16, rendered brick with long and short stone quoins to the entrance bay, stone plinth and key blocks, the r. bay rebuilt. Between Dock Street and the river is VICTORIA QUAYS, low-rise housing of 1985–8 by *Downes Illingworth & Partners*, one of the first schemes of its kind along the river and partly incorporating former Navigation Co. ware-housing. The centrepiece is the narrow basin of the Aire & Calder Dock of 1818 (*Thomas Wood*, engineer) and the stately red brick former FLYBOAT WAREHOUSE built on its N side *c.* 1825. This has central gables on two sides and extends beyond the edge of the dock with a low segmental arched entrance at water level (partly blocked). Bridging the dock basin is a reused roof truss, salvaged from a shed that origi-nally spanned the W end of the dock. Along the S side, housing converted from a mid-C19 former WAREHOUSE with four gables of unequal size with pronounced eaves on the rear ele-vation to Dock Street. Also on this side, hefty bracketed stone loading platforms. Facing this, DOCK STREET WORKSHOPS

(Nos. 30–38), a nice early C19 brick terrace with round-arched doorways and entries, and sash windows. Restored in 1986. To the E is BREWERY WHARF, a major residential development by *DLA Architecture* on land formerly occupied by part of TETLEY'S BREWERY, which lies to the S (founded 1822; it had buildings of 1864–72 by *George Corson*, now replaced, and many additions by *Bedford & Kitson*). It incorporates a three-storey glazed rotunda (now a restaurant), designed as the brewery's exhibition centre in 1993 by *Carey Jones Architects*. Crossing the river here is the CENTENARY FOOTBRIDGE, a cable-stayed design of 1992–3 by *Ove Arup & Partners* for the Leeds Development Corporation. The view E and W along the N bank is of converted riverside warehouses. The DESIGN INNOVATION CENTRE (E of the bridge) is by *Allen Tod Architects*, 1988, with steel and glass bays projecting over the river. W of the bridge the former Fletland Corn Mill, three parallel ranges with gables, the l. and r. bays *c.* 1800, originally flanking an open wharf, the centre range infill of after 1866 with projecting loading bay. On the street side, the buildings are nicely irregular around a courtyard and the industrial character has been preserved during conversion to an hotel (42 The Calls) in 1991 by *David Clarke Associates*. Upstream, a large early C19 warehouse of seven storeys to the river, six behind, straddles an ancient mill goit. Converted to offices and flats by *Allen Tod Architects*, 1994–5. Next a three-storey former grain store, C18, with a canted façade. Converted by H. G. Atkinson, Builders' Merchant *c.* 1898; on the rendered street front bold lettering.

Along the backs of these warehouses runs THE CALLS, a narrow cobbled road which, like Dock Street, carries a memory of the C19 riverside. A silver ball FOUNTAIN commemorates the Leeds Development Corporation's work here, 1988–95. E along the street on the N side is a view to the parish church (*see* Churches). The S side is continuously built up and concludes with THE CHANDLERS, formerly the premises of William Turton, corn chandler, rebuilt in 1876. Four storeys, red brick Italianate, with trios of round-arched windows in the upper floors, a large arch to the corner pedestrian entrance and a keystone with a horse's head above the entrance to the yard. The remarkable feature here is the lofty cylindrical look-out tower with cast-iron cresting at the top; a useful vantage point on the river. Partly converted to housing in 1987 by *Denison Peters Ltd.* (new build of three and four storeys, with mono-pitch roofs, informally grouped towards the riverside walk); further development along The Calls in 2008.

CROWN POINT BRIDGE is the most attractive of the bridges across the Aire in the city centre. Built 1840–2, designed by *George Leather Jun.* of Bradford, with big stone abutments and a low segmental arch spanning the river, its latticework spandrels formed of cast-iron Gothic cusped tracery, made at the Park Iron Works, Sheffield. Ornate traceried balustrade of interweaving mouchettes. Widened and reconstructed 1994

(*James McArthur*, engineer). Just s of the bridge, marooned on the busy approach road, is the unexpected survival of CHAD-WICK LODGE, a smart villa built between 1779 and 1790 by John Chadwick whose dyeworks were on the river. Neat Millstone Grit façade, almost square in plan, with pediment to front and back; the show (s) front is five bays and of ashlar, the three-bay rear has a tall staircase window with interlaced tracery.

Downstream from Crown Point Bridge is Leeds Dam, a weir first documented in 1636. To bypass this the Navigation created a cut with locks; both cut and weir are now as rebuilt *c.* 1835 by *George Leather Jun.*, who had just completed the Navigation's canal between the Aire at Knottingley and their docks at Goole (West Riding South). The increase in traffic must have encouraged their decision to build the large 'New' or CLARENCE DOCK on the s bank of the river in 1840–3. This is a rectangular basin (about 325 ft by 163 ft; 100 by 50 metres) with stone quay walls; extended in the later C19 with two narrower basins at the NW corner and s end. In the 1980s the Leeds Development Corporation hoped to encourage redevelopment of the dock's environs by launching a competition for a masterplan (won by *Browne Smith Baker*) and securing the Royal Armouries (*see* Public Buildings) as a tourist attraction. Most of what one sees, however, is of 2002–8; a mixed-use development of flats and offices by *Carey Jones Architects*, quite varied in character with the signature accent a nineteen-storey tower of curved profile, with walls of white reconstituted stone contrasting with lower elements in dark engineering brick.

A footbridge (2007) leads back to the N bank and Fearne's Island, a strip of land which was separated from the river bank by a mill goit, above Leeds Dam, and the Timble Beck. FEARN ISLAND MILLS has two plain C19 brick buildings (a dye house and engine house), converted to flats by *Cartwright Pickard*, 2006. To its E are the former BANK MILLS, an impressive complex built for Hives & Atkinson, former partners in Marshall's Mills (Holbeck). They acquired the site in 1823 and eventually developed one of the largest flax mills in Leeds. The surviving parts, facing the river, date from *c.* 1831–3, apparently by *John Clark*. The w group (now Roberts Wharf, converted 2006–7 by *DLA Architecure*), was 'B' Mill; six storeys to the river and twenty-one bays long, plainly handled in red brick with continuous stringcourses. At the sw corner a big, tapered chimneystack and rising from the E end a mighty circular turret, containing the staircase, hoist and water tank. Inside, fireproof construction of cast-iron columns and jack arches. Extended E ('D' Mill) in 1856, this section four storeys only but projecting forward to the river's edge. Rounded corners and dentilled cornice. At the rear a tall, five-storey wing built 1888 after the buildings had been converted for papermaking and printing by Roberts Mart & Co. E is the former 'C' Mill (now Rose Wharf), two six-storey blocks comprising the mill (sixteen bays with arched windows at ground floor and also a tapered chimney at the NW corner; cruciform cast-iron columns inside) and the narrower tow warehouse. Converted as offices by and for *Carey Jones Architects* in 1997, with glazed staircases between the two blocks and at the W end. A separate four-storey range to the W was the yarn warehouse, apparently built in 1824 when it stood alongside 'A' Mill (dem.).

N of Bank Mills on the other side of EAST STREET, and partially obscured by new flats by *Design Group 3 Architects,* are the former EAST STREET MILLS built up after 1825 by Moses Atkinson, flax spinner. The earliest block is the long range along the E side of the yard, which incorporates the chimney towards its S end. (Cruciform cast-iron columns inside.) A mid-C19 N range forms an L-plan, terminating in a cross-wing. For buildings to the N *see* Inner Leeds, The Bank (below). W of this group a residential block – FLAX PLACE – by *Carey Jones Architects.*

INNER LEEDS

THE BANK
(Richmond Hill)

The Bank rises steeply to the E of the city centre and is encircled by the busy roads of Marsh Lane, York Road and East Street by the river. Urbanization accelerated after 1800. From this time mills lined the river and in 1834 the Leeds & Selby Railway cut their line through the hill to their terminus at Marsh Lane (largely superseded after the NER extended the line to connect with Leeds Station in 1869). The area became home to many Irish Catholics, especially in the aftermath of the potato famine. Their numbers reached almost 15,000 in 1861, over 12 per cent of the population of Leeds (and 50 per cent in The Bank). Tightly packed housing, including some of the worst slums in Leeds, once covered the hill but this was almost entirely cleared in the C20, leaving only the large Victorian mission churches as a reminder. The C21 landscape is a patchwork of post-war housing, open space, semi-derelict industrial land, devastating road schemes, and along the bank of the Aire, converted textile mills, for which *see* above.

ST HILDA, Cross Green Lane. 1876–82 by *J. T. Micklethwaite.* A daughter church of St Saviour (*see* below) and built in accordance with the same High Anglican principles with an austere, powerful, brick exterior and beautiful interior. High nave and chancel under one roof, double bellcote. Thin stair-turret on the N side at the junction of nave and chancel with a romantic conical spirelet. Lancets, paired in the clerestory, and simple Geometrical tracery. The interior – made wonderfully light by the elevated setting, clear glass and white walls – has octagonal piers and double-chamfered arches and a segmental and closely panelled roof intended to be decorated with striking gilded sun-rays. The painted wooden FURNISHINGS in Late Perp style by *W. H. Wood* of Newcastle were not installed until the C20 and display the continued vitality of the Gothic tradition: – REREDOS with six panels painted by *Percy C. Bacon*, an elaborate frame of 1927 and a canopy arching forward over the high altar. – Handsome FONT of Frosterley marble, the bowl octagonal on a fine base under a 25-ft (7.6-metre)-high painted CANOPY of 1936–8 by *C. Wood*, the sculpture by *Alfred Southwick*. – Octagonal PULPIT of 1882, given a sounding board and decorated in 1917. – Magnificent ROOD SCREEN of 1922–3, based on *Micklethwaite*'s original proposals but modified by *W. H. Wood*, with seven statues by *Southwick* in canopied niches and bas-relief panels of the Incarnation and Resurrection added in 1924 by *J. T. Ogelby* of Newcastle. – ROOD of 1904 by *Micklethwaite*, on a separate beam, with Oberammergau figures embellished and painted in 1912. – STATUES of St Hilda above the main door by *George Hodgson Fowler*, 1903 and, holding a model of the church, by *Southwick*, 1938. – STAINED GLASS by *Burlison & Grylls*: E window inserted in stages 1891–1902, S window of Lady Chapel 1905. – Attached CLERGY HOUSE by *Micklethwaite*.

ST SAVIOUR, Ellerby Road. The most important Victorian church in Leeds, and the beginning of Anglo-Catholicism in England. Built 1842–5 by *John Macduff Derick* for Dr E. B. Pusey, one of the founders of the Oxford Movement. Pusey as 'Mr Z' paid for the whole church and insisted on it bearing the words 'Ye who enter this Holy place, pray for the Sinner who built it' incised in the floor inside the W doorway. It was to be a monument of renewed Anglican faith in a district with a population described by Sabine Baring-Gould as of 'gross profligacy combined perhaps with attendance at socialistic meetings'. St Saviour's encompassed much of the turbulent history of the Church of England in the mid C19: as the prototype Oxford Movement church at which most of its leaders preached; as the first post-Reformation parish in which the daily mass was restored; and as one of the first to be opened without pew rents. Within six years its clergy had twice defected to Rome.

The most serious architecture is as splendid as its history has been stormy, both scholarly and emotionally potent. Prominently sited high above the River Aire with a tall flight of steps leading to its W end, it is tall, not long, with small clerestory, transepts, N porch and crossing tower of 1937 by *Leslie Moore* following Derick's design. Derick originally envisaged a rich and splendid spire modelled on that of St Mary, Oxford and pinnacles along the eaves of the roof. Tracery in the style of *c.* 1300. Five-light E, W and transept-end windows. Tall three-light windows in the chancel, two lights in the aisles. Carved corbel heads were added to the doorways in 1866 by

Street, among them Dr Hook at the N transept door. Inside the W door are Dr Pusey and Charles Marriott, vicar of St Mary, Oxford.

The interior has undergone three major refurbishments. The first in 1866–7 by *Street* who raised the altar, replaced the original pulpit and had *Clayton & Bell* decorate the roofs and paint frescoes on the chancel walls. The second was by *Bodley* in 1888–90, who built the Pusey Memorial Chapel and carried out the stencilling on the nave roof. The third, in 1963 by *George Pace* obliterated the Victorian painted decoration and painted the interior white (now, happily, stripped). It is of lofty proportions, especially in the aisleless chancel and at the crossing. Windows fill almost all the wall surfaces. Tall octagonal piers with no mouldings, double chamfered arches. – REREDOS by *Bodley*, part of the 1890 scheme but not installed until 1902, tripartite, richly carved in deep relief, the statuary added 1902–12. – HIGH ALTAR, mensa of grey marble with oak legs, part of the original furnishings, with retable containing a central TABERNACLE by *Bodley*. – FONT by *Street*, 1871, circular with four leaf-shaped panels, inlaid with white marble, the cover of 1885 by *J. T. Micklethwaite*, decorated and gilded in 1923 by *Frances Darlington*. – PULPIT (of 1899), ROOD and CHANCEL SCREEN (both of 1890) also by *Bodley*, the central part of the screen now in the N porch. – Painted REREDOS in the Pusey Chapel by *Frances Darlington*, 1922, forms the First World War memorial. – STATUES in wall-mounted niches by *Thomas Garner*. Oak cupboards by Bodley contain Dr Pusey's robes. STATUE of Our Lady by *Temple Moore*, painted and gilded, on the site of the original pulpit. – STAINED GLASS. An important scheme that cost 17 per cent of the total for the church. Windows in the nave, clerestory and chancel executed by *Michael O'Connor* to Pusey's directions and worked out by him with Benjamin Webb of the Cambridge Camden Society. The E window, the Ascension, is also believed to be by *O'Connor*. The glass is of great merit, in the style of the C13, and of glowing colours, predominantly blue and green – Pevsner saw nothing yet of what he viewed as Victorian insipidity. N and S transept and W windows by *A. W. N. Pugin*; the latter originally depicted angels catching the blood of Christ in chalices and had to be altered before the bishop would consecrate the church. Several windows by *Morris & Co.*, with green again the dominant colour. The N aisle N window of 1868 is by *Morris* himself. Single figures of saints and amongst them, to one's surprise, Fra Angelico – a sign of the respect of the Pre-Raphaelites for the most Christian of Pre-Raphaelite painters. N aisle fourth window by *Morris* and *Burne-Jones*, 1870. In the porch, 1878 by *Burne-Jones*. In the S aisle, fifth window by *Ford Madox Brown* 1872, fourth window 1872 by *G. J. Baguley*. – Pusey Chapel windows all of 1890 by *Powell Bros*.

Adjacent to the church, a large contemporary Gothic CLERGY HOUSE, its eaves punctuated with gabled half-dormers.

s, on East Street, St Saviour's School (now business premises). Built 1839–40 for Dr Hook, before the Pusey mission. Unconvincing Tudorbethan range, stone-built, of two storeys and eleven bays, with little octagonal domed turrets at the corners and in the centre.

Mount St Mary (R.C., former), off Ellerby Road* in a very prominent position facing the city. Financed as a mission by the French Order of the Oblates of Mary Immaculate, no doubt as a challenge to St Saviour. First phase 1853–7 (nave and aisles), the design by *Joseph Hansom* but later handed over to *W. Wardell*. Chancel and transepts added by *E. W. Pugin*, 1866. A NW steeple was never built but the exterior is nevertheless massive – 188 ft (57 metres) long, 60 ft (18 metres) wide and 83 ft (25 metres) high. Geometrical tracery, W front with eight-light window and a narthex rather than a porch. Cross-gabled aisles and transepts with rose windows. Very tall circular piers have four detached shafts with shaft-rings. Polygonal apse with three thin tall two-light windows. Lady Chapel and five other altars. – STAINED GLASS. In the apse (boarded up) by *J. H. Powell*.**

The PRESBYTERY was built in two phases, the first part to *Wardell*'s design. The adjacent St Mary's Convent of 1861 is by *M. E. Hadfield* and has a low tower with a spire placed almost inconsequentially at one end. A COLLEGE was added in 1901. Built around a courtyard with the college on the NW side. All are in a simple Gothic style, the convent walls buttressed.

LIBRARY AND BATHS (former), York Road. 1903 by *H. A. Chapman*. Just the street range survives. Free C17 revival style, with a narrow tower, l., with ogee timber turret and in the centre the two big gables of the library, with Venetian and mullioned-and-transomed windows. Entrance under the r. gable, with stone panels inscribed with the names of writers.

Saxton Gardens, N of Richmond Street. Flats of 1955–8. The scheme was prepared pre-war, following slum clearance, by *R. A. H. Livett*. Seven long slabs in parallel, *Zeilenbau* style, of five to ten storeys high, rising in height as they climb the hill. Reinforced concrete frames with buff and dark brown brick cladding. Pairs of flats on each floor share a lift and, as at Quarry Hill, were originally equipped with a Garchey system for disposing of rubbish into an incinerator. Refurbished in 2004, with some striking use of colour to express the balconies and service shafts. The two largest blocks have been re-clad and remodelled as flats for sale, 2007–8 by *Union North Architects* for Urban Splash, with landscaping, including garden allotments, by *Austin Smith: Lord*.

East Street Mills and Bank Mills. *See* p. 459–9.

---

*The church closed in 1989. In 2008 permission has been granted for the demolition and replacement of the nave and aisles as part of a residential scheme.
**A TABERNACLE by *Pugin* and ALTAR RAILS by *Hardman* are now in store. Other fittings have been stolen, including the carved oak ALTAR by *Benedict Labre*.

BURMANTOFTS

Immediately E of the city centre and N of York Road, and formerly the location of the medieval town's allotments, or tofts. There was little building until the early C19. The industrial school and workhouse were erected in the 1840s and 1850s, close to the city's largest cemetery. Back-to-backs were soon intermingled with factories along the Sheepscar Beck and the area also had collieries, including that established by William Wilcock and John Lassey in 1842, in which a seam of fireclay was discovered. After that the firm turned to brickmaking and the manufacture of sanitaryware, becoming nationally famous after 1879 when Wilcock & Co., under the management of James Holroyd, began to design and produce slabs of decorative architectural faience and terracotta. The works of the Leeds Fireclay Co. – as the concern became in 1889 – closed in 1957. The site was cleared for council housing, part of the comprehensive mixed-density redevelopment of the area.

ST AGNES, Stoney Rock Lane. 1886–7 by *Kelly & Birchall*. Nave and chancel in one with aisles continued unbroken to form a vestry. Of coursed rock-faced stone. Between nave and chancel on the S side, a slender turret with an octagonal top, which Pevsner thought 'silly'. Five-light E window with Geometrical tracery. – REREDOS. 1891. Three canopied niches, in Burmantofts faience (now painted white). – STAINED GLASS. The richly coloured E window and those in the N aisle by *Charles E. Steel*, 1930–3. – By *Powell Bros.*, the S aisle W, 1889, S aisle and N aisle W of 1903. – Four-light W window with figures by *Wailes* of 1867 from the E window of St Stephen, Burmantofts (closed 1939). – WALL TABLET in a faience surround to James Holroyd †1890, 'the founder of the Burmantofts Faience Works', erected by his workforce.

ST PATRICK (R.C., former), Burmantofts Street by York Road. 1889–91 by *John Kelly*. Now theatre store. Powerful red brick exterior, with gables to each of the five nave bays, a blind apse and a rounded NW baptistery. A number of the chapel ALTARS have alabaster REREDOSES. – Fine apse WALL PAINTING with Christ Crucified. – Large, compactly planned SCHOOL and PRESBYTERY at the E end.

W of St Peter is the site of ST MARY, Mabgate (1825 by *Thomas Taylor*, dem. 1979; diocesan offices of 1981 on the site of the nave). To its E, on St Mary's Lane, is the two-storey former SUNDAY SCHOOL of 1830. Thin Georgian lancets and buttresses give way to more robust modelling and archaeological Gothic detailing in the caretaker's house, attached N, built in the 1860s.

BECKETT STREET CEMETERY. Opened 1845, the first and largest of the three cemeteries established by the Leeds Corporation. Equally divided between Anglicans and Nonconformists; there are over 180,000 burials. The chapels have been demolished. Twin Tudor-style LODGES of 1880 by *W. S. Braithwaite*. – MONUMENTS. The most intriguing, off Anglican Walk to the r., is that to Sarah Kidney (†1895), wife of the 'oldest steeplejack in England' which was in the form of a factory chimney 8 ft (2.5 metres) high, sadly vandalized in 2004. – Christopher Burn (†1849), r. of Dissenters' Walk, a ship's master, has a fine carving of a Humber keel in its pediment. Many 'guinea graves' with shared headstones inscribed on both sides.

ST JAMES' UNIVERSITY HOSPITAL, Beckett Street, opposite the cemetery. Developed around two mid-Victorian Poor Law institutions. First on this site, the former Moral and Industrial Training School (now SOUTHSIDE BUILDING) of 1846–8, built for the Leeds Guardians. Three storeys, Neo-Jacobean, with canted bays at the ends and centre, emphasized by slender octagonal turrets which terminate in ogee domes. To its N, the impressive former workhouse (now THACKRAY MEDICAL MUSEUM), of 1858–62 by *Perkin & Backhouse*. With shaped gables, square bay windows, a pierced parapet, and a projecting centre with a handsome tower that has corner turrets capped by ogee-shaped roofs. To its S, the cruciform CHAPEL, an eclectic Romanesque and Lombardic Gothic mix in red brick, with blue and white polychromy. Inside, capitals carved with flowers, birds and animals, the broad chancel arch with chevrons. STAINED GLASS. E windows by *Celtic Studios*, 1952. Set back behind, is the former 'Idiotic Ward' of the workhouse infirmary, built 1862–3.

Most of the infirmary buildings were replaced in the C20, especially by boxy yellow brick buildings in the 1970s. The CLINICAL SCIENCES BUILDING, 1979 by *Building Design Partnership*, is more distinguished. The latest addition is the massive ONCOLOGY WING, 2007 by *Anshen Dyer*, at the S end of the site. E-plan, with three broad, eight-storey towers, each with a podium, and the perimeter of the upper storeys supported by angled struts and wrapped in seamed copper cladding.

YORK ROAD LIBRARY AND BATHS (former). *See* THE BANK.

HOPE FOUNDRY, Mabgate/Hope Road. A brass and iron foundry from *c.* 1820. Grand Greek Revival three-storey entrance range of *c.* 1831–50, partly preserved. Brick with ashlar dressings. Mighty battered portal with big dentils and cast-iron lion masks to the capitals of broad tapered pilasters. Adjoining offices of 1910 (Hope House), Wrenaissance style.

HUDSON ROAD MILLS. The vast factory (now a distribution centre) of Montague Burton Ltd., designed by its Chief Architect, *Harry Wilson*, 1922–34. It incorporated an existing mill. The entrance front is long and single-storey, with strips of windows within cement surrounds. Red brick with blue brick diapering lending an Art Deco touch. Faience panels, like the shops, proclaim 'Montague Burton – The Tailor of Taste'. Single-storey range to the l. in similar vein with an entrance flanked by four square attached columns with jazzy capitals. The SW front, containing the offices, is three-storey, also red brick with raised attics over the entrances. By 1939 Burton's employed 10,500 workers; the canteen could accommodate 8,000 at a single sitting. – WAR MEMORIAL: bronze plaque of 1948 by *Nathaniel Martin*, flanked by two fluted columns topped by urns.

THE LEYLANDS, SHEEPSCAR and BUSLINGTHORPE

The NE corner of inner Leeds is a chain of working-class industrial districts – the Leylands, Sheepscar and then Buslingthorpe – which developed along the Sheepscar and Meanwood Becks. The Leylands in the C19 and early C20 had a large Jewish population, many of whom were employed in the clothing industry. To the N the valley was the centre of the Leeds tanning industry.

NORTH STREET runs from the inner ring road through the heart of the Leylands and Sheepscar. On the E side, CRISPIN HOUSE, the former Heatons' Clothing Factory of 1914–16. Five storeys and seventeen bays of steel-framed fire-proof construction clad in red brick with white 'Marmo' detailing and distinctive corner dome. Converted to apartments with a rooftop extension. Opposite, CENTENARY HOUSE by *Bedford & Kitson*, 1904, built as a public dispensary for the Leeds Society for Deaf and Blind People. Neo-Wren with Gibbs detailing. Five storeys, a bowed corner, and good carving e.g. a large putti supporting an oriel window over the main entrance and a woman holding a book in the tympanum above the outpatients' entrance on the S side. Continuing N the former SMITHFIELD HOTEL (E side), a symmetrical Italianate range of the mid C19 with a raised centre and clock turret; it was absorbed into the Smithfield Ironworks of Thomas Green & Sons, which stood behind. All along the W side of the street here the extensive LOVELL PARK ESTATE, with a mixture of low-rise housing and high-rise point blocks of 1967. N at the corner with Benson Street, E side, THE EAGLE TAVERN, built in 1826 by *James Bussey*, stonemason, and opened as a pub by his son after the passing of the 1830 Beer Act. Nearby, prominent on an acute corner site, is a former London, City & Midland Bank, *c.* 1880s by *William Bakewell*, a vigorous and eclectic design sprouting a curious corner turret. This area is now a dehumanizing traffic gyratory. N at the corner with Roundhay Road is the mildly *Moderne* former SHEEPSCAR BRANCH LIBRARY (West Yorkshire Archive Service) of 1938.

⅜ m. N along SHEEPSCAR STREET, the former SHEEPSCAR TANNERY. Established in the 1840s. Two impressive buildings to the street, both 1850s, form a forty-four-bay façade of five storeys. The S part has a louvred top storey for drying skins; other floors were probably used for warehousing and finishing. Adjacent to the N, set back, is the BUSLINGTHORPE TANNERY, with a good survival of buildings from the second half of the C19, and beyond that on Buslingthorpe Lane, the smaller HILL TOP TANNERY. Both of these sites began in the early C19 as dyeworks.

NW, at the junction with MEANWOOD ROAD, are the former CARR MILLS, founded in 1810 by Abraham Rhodes. Converted into housing in 2004–7 with large new buildings E and N. Three early ranges survive: a modest entrance block, and two five-storey wings of the 1820s, set at an acute angle with each other. The S wing made early use of parabolic cast-iron beams and joists in its fireproof construction. Further up Meanwood Road, where E of the beck the valley is still green, is the former BAPTIST SCHOOL, a striking and powerful composition of 1881 by *Smith & Tweedale*, like a temple. Terracotta and red brick, much of it carved. Front with a steep pediment gable with richly moulded tympanum, and prominent chimney behind. N of this SUGARWELL COURT, the former CLIFF TANNERY of 1866. Massive L-shaped range to the fore, of twenty-four (S) and twenty-three bays (W), each of rusticated sandstone with ashlar dressings and two storeys articulated by pilasters. An added storey, probably *c.* 1900, has large arched windows. (Inside, cast-iron columns supporting timber cross-beams. DCMS.) The ground floors were open to a covered tan yard behind; this and a third, E, range are demolished. Converted to housing 1993, with new stone-clad blocks.

(SEVENTH DAY ADVENTIST CHURCH, Meanwood Road. The former Clowes Primitive Methodist Chapel of 1893–4 by *Ambler & Bowman*. Galleried interior.)

WOODHOUSE
including Little Woodhouse and Leeds University

At the NW edge of the city centre, Woodhouse was once part of the estates of Kirkstall Abbey, with the Lord of the manor's waste on higher ground to the N. Ancient rights of pasture were protected there, and Woodhouse Moor for centuries was a place for market, fairs and assembly. Mr Kendall, a merchant, built a house here in about 1588, and in the early C18 Ralph Thoresby wrote that Little Woodhouse was 'one of the pleasantest hamlets'. Seven villas were built in this area between 1740 and 1790 and there was much infilling thereafter with development creeping N from the town along Woodhouse Lane, especially after 1815 and requiring new churches for the area. By that time Woodhouse was home to merchants, industrialists, clergy and physicians. The emergence of Headingley to the N as a respectable new suburb made Clarendon Road (laid out 1839) a popular residential area; meanwhile the spread of industry up the Meanwood Valley consigned the area E of Woodhouse Lane proper to back-to-back terracing. Finally in 1877, a site W of the lane was purchased for the Yorkshire College, which as it grew into the University of Leeds caused a profound change in the character of Woodhouse. Since the mid C20 it has entirely dominated the suburb.

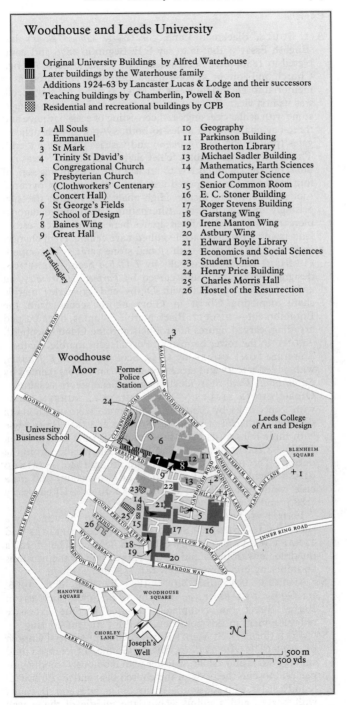

Woodhouse and Leeds University

■ Original University Buildings by Alfred Waterhouse
▦ Later buildings by the Waterhouse family
▦ Additions 1924–63 by Lancaster Lucas & Lodge and their successors
▦ Teaching buildings by Chamberlin, Powell & Bon
▦ Residential and recreational buildings by CPB

1 All Souls
2 Emmanuel
3 St Mark
4 Trinity St David's
   Congregational Church
5 Presbyterian Church
   (Clothworkers' Centenary
   Concert Hall)
6 St George's Fields
7 School of Design
8 Baines Wing
9 Great Hall

10 Geography
11 Parkinson Building
12 Brotherton Library
13 Michael Sadler Building
14 Mathematics, Earth Sciences
    and Computer Science
15 Senior Common Room
16 E. C. Stoner Building
17 Roger Stevens Building
18 Garstang Wing
19 Irene Manton Wing
20 Astbury Wing
21 Edward Boyle Library
22 Economics and Social Sciences
23 Student Union
24 Henry Price Building
25 Charles Morris Hall
26 Hostel of the Resurrection

Churches

ALL SOULS, Blackman Lane. *Sir George Gilbert Scott*'s last
'English Essay' – that is to say E.E. Begun in 1876 and completed in 1880, after Scott's death, by *J. Oldrid Scott*. A High
Church mission in a poor neighbourhood, conceived as a
memorial to Dean Hook (*see* St Peter, p. 398); his son, Cecil,
was its first vicar. Built on an impressive scale in coursed gritstone with ashlar dressings and consisting of a six-bay nave and
three-bay chancel with aisles to both, SW porch with delicate
gates (presumably by *Skidmore*) and vestries under the E end.
The central tower – Scott's 'chief element of dignity' – was not
built, but the executed NW tower is a fine work by his son, of
four stages of superimposed arcading with a stumpy pyramid
roof and baptistery inside. High-quality carving in the surprisingly intimate interior. Alternating round and octagonal
piers and double-chamfered arches beneath triplet clerestory
lancets and a painted barrel-vaulted nave ceiling. High chancel
arch, the chancel itself with ribbed stone vault. – The superb
FURNISHINGS are principally by *J. Oldrid Scott*. – REREDOS,
designed with *Kempe* and carved by *Farmer & Brindley*, an
elaborate arcaded piece with Derby and Frosterley marble
shafts depicting Christ in Glory above scenes from the
Entombment. – PULPIT. Black marble columns, open cusped
arcading, carved figures of prophets and the Good Shepherd.
– FONT, in the tower baptistery. Fossiliferous marble, shafts. –
Towering FONT COVER by G.G. Scott's pupil *R. J. Johnson*,
with gilded tracery and crocketed finials, and doors painted by
Susan Emily Ford, 1891, illustrating the benefactors as saints. –
Ornate CHOIR STALLS. – Dwarf CHANCEL SCREEN, stone
with iron GATES by *Skidmore*. – Elaborate oak ORGAN CASE
designed with *Hill* of London, 1892. – LECTERN. Brass eagle
with three lions at its base, in memory of Anna Felicia Hook
†1880. – CHAIRS were provided for the congregation from the
outset. – The ROOD was the last major fitting: 1940. – STAINED
GLASS. Richly coloured E window (a Crucifixion) and nave
aisle windows by *Clayton & Bell*, 1880–1910. – Choir vestry
(1880) and W window (1881) by *Kempe*.

Former VICARAGE (now flats), attached to the vestry by a
short cloister, SUNDAY SCHOOL (for 1,500), OFFICES and
TENANT HALL, all of 1885–6 by *R. J. Johnson*. They form a
quadrangle with the E end of the church and in the centre is
an imposing preaching CROSS, 18 ft (5.5 metres) high.

ST ANDREW, Cavendish Street. 1844 by *Scott*, dem. 1966.
Its Gothic VICARAGE, *c.* 1860 by *G. E. Street*, survives on
Burley Street but completely dwarfed by the extensive
redevelopment in this neighbourhood for student housing.

ST MARK (former), St Mark's Road. A Commissioners' Church
of 1823–6 by *Atkinson & Sharp*. Gothic, of coursed and
squared stone and ashlar. W tower with fabulously spindly pinnacles; those to the body of the church dismantled. Built with
N and S aisles, with substantial quatrefoil arcades and rib-vaults
with bosses, and a pulpit against the middle of the N wall

(*Chantrell* added galleries in 1833 and 1837). In 1873 *Adams & Kelly* created a chancel in the two E bays, and made the windows and tower Perp. – STAINED GLASS. E window by *Wailes*, 1853. – N aisle with two windows by *Clayton & Bell*, 1874 and 1896, two by *R. B. Edmundson*, one by *Whall*, 1918, and the E window by *O'Connor*, 1856. – All the work in the S aisle is of 1970 by *Kayll*.

Some eccentric Victorian MONUMENTS in the wooded churchyard. Two are in memory of occupants of Bagbie Lodge: Richard Driver †1859, with a curious arched stone canopy springing from squat square marble shafts at the four corners; and Thomas Whiteley †1879 (and his wife), a most peculiar Gothic fantasia. On a base stands a hefty traceried canopy with quatrefoil columns at the corners, from within which an octagonal pillar rises through the gable roof to expand into a square finial, niched on each face. – S, William Alexander, †1862, Grand Master of the Independent Order of Odd Fellows, and family, by *J. Leach*, Becket Street. An inscribed pedestal with medallion and oversailing and bowed cornice which once carried a group of grieving family and mourners. – Also, N, a pedestal supporting an Ionic column with square urn finial erected to George Johnston Crowther †1861, described as 'useful without being conspicuous', and Robert Mawer, †1854, and his wife, 22 yds SW of the tower, with complex circular base supporting two almost human-size angels draped over a square column. The angels and an urn now decapitated.

EMMANUEL CHURCH (former), Woodhouse Lane/Cavendish Road. 1876–80 by *Adams & Kelly*. Handsome large cruciform E.E. body of rock-faced ashlar with a smooth and massive crossing steeple added *c.* 1920. Remodelled in 2004 by *Halliday Clark* to provide seminar rooms and accommodation for the University's Chaplaincy. Behind it the EMMANUEL INSTITUTE, the former Chaplaincy, internally remodelled by the University Estates Department with a first-floor workshop theatre.

TRINITY ST DAVID'S CONGREGATIONAL CHURCH (former), Woodhouse Lane. 1899–1901 by *G. F. Danby*. Perp with N steeple. Subdivided in 2004 when it (and its extensive attached hall and Sunday School) were adapted to nightclub and café-bar. – STAINED GLASS in the chancel by *Atkinson*.

PRESBYTERIAN CHURCH (former), Cavendish Road, in the centre of the campus. Now UNIVERSITY CLOTHWORKERS' CENTENARY CONCERT HALL. 1870 by *J. B. Fraser*, converted 1974–5. Red brick, essentially Italianate with round-arched windows but with a projecting centre under a tower with an elaborate stone cupola. Nice Italianate plasterwork to the main hall. Restored in 2004 by *Harrogate Design*, when the basement was converted to practice rooms. – SCHOOL OF MUSIC behind, by *Harrogate Design*, 2003.

BLENHEIM BAPTIST CHURCH (former), Woodhouse Lane. *c.* 1858 by *William Hill*. Nave and aisles under one roof and a large traceried five-light W window; lancet windows in brick panels, NW spire with lucarnes.

FRIENDS' MEETING HOUSE (former), Woodhouse Lane. *See* p. 422.

Public Buildings

POLICE STATION, FIRE STATION AND LIBRARY (former), Woodhouse Lane and Clarendon Road. Dated 1901, in the extravagant free Italianate style of *W. H. Thorp*, with landmark lead-domed clock tower. Pickaxes and hoses are carved on the keystone of the traceried central window.

LEEDS GRAMMAR SCHOOL (former), Moorland Road. Now UNIVERSITY BUSINESS SCHOOL. By *E. M. Barry* (brother of the headmaster), 1858–9. Decorated Gothic to a long, cruciform plan, with gabled flanks and a spirelet over the 'crossing'. At the corner with Clarendon Road, a CHAPEL, also by Barry, in matching style. Large additions to the W are by *Austin & Paley* from 1904–5. Adapted in 1995 by *Carey Jones Architects*, who added the INNOVATION CENTRE fronting Clarendon Road, 2001, and a glazed arcade along the S side of the school.

QUARRY MOUNT SCHOOL, Cross Quarry Street. 1885 by *Richard Adams*, a good example of his mature work: red-brick free Gothic with gables, mullioned-and-transomed windows and much brick decoration. A narrow clock tower separates the infants and girls (l.) from boys (r.).

LEEDS COLLEGE OF ART AND DESIGN, Blenheim Walk. 1981–5 by *M. Thurmott*, City Architect (project architect, *R. Shepley*). Eclectic Postmodern, an early example of what became known as the 'Leeds Look'. Banded brickwork in bold colours extends to paving and flanking walls; L-plan on a corner site, four storeys, bold entrance and staircase tower with bullseye glazing. Long bands of windows light the top-floor studios, under deep eaves. Extended *c.* 2006 by *Alan Holmes* of *Leeds Design*.

ST GEORGE'S FIELDS, between University Road and Clarendon Road, surrounded on all sides by buildings of the university. Formerly Leeds General Cemetery, opened 1835. The design was won in competition by *John Clark*. Central CHAPEL in the form of an Ionic temple, with a shallow portico to the W front. The E end has sash windows between square piers. GATEHOUSE, N, also Greek Revival, with giant Doric columns *in antis* on the exterior and flanked by projecting lodges within, with battered pilasters and urns. MONUMENTS: by the chapel, a STATUE of Michael Sadler (linen merchant and supporter of the Ten Hours Bill) by *Patric Park* of London, 1837; originally at Leeds parish church. Next to the gatehouse, a fine C19 MONUMENT to heroic Leeds firemen, their gallantry recorded on an obelisk shielded by a firemen's hat with a carving of a fire engine. The cemetery was acquired by the University in 1965 and largely cleared of gravestones, many of which were used to form the mounds in the resulting greensward. The 'guinea graves' have been reused as paving.

WOODHOUSE MOOR. The only public open space in Leeds until the later C19 and the site of the city's public and political meetings. Acquired in 1855 by the Corporation who had already established their waterworks on the moor's E side (the reservoir, on Clarendon Road, now covered over). LODGE on Woodhouse Lane, a Picturesque single-storey cottage. Several STATUES. The best, close to the lodge, is the stately memorial to Queen Victoria by *George Frampton*, 1903, moved here in 1937 from in front of the Town Hall. Portland stone base and bronze figures, the Queen in coronation robes flanked by 'Peace' and originally 'Industry'. Coats of arms, and radiant sun carved on the back. Across Woodhouse Lane to the E, Henry Marsden, 1878, by *John Throp* of Leeds. Carrara marble whiskered figure in mayoral robes, its high plinth carved with reliefs of 'Benevolence' (missing), 'Education' and 'Industry' (represented by the stone-crushing machine developed by Marsden after emigrating to the United States in 1848). On the moor's S corner, the Duke of Wellington in bronze by *Marochetti*, 1854. He also stood outside the Town Hall until 1937. For the statue of Sir Robert Peel, *see* Headingley.

LEEDS UNIVERSITY*

Of all Britain's universities, Leeds has grown most rapidly since 1945, and by 2007 had 30,500 students. Its origins were modest, however, and it had only 1,750 full-time students in 1939. It began as the Yorkshire College of Science in 1874, inspired by Owens College in Manchester, and first took rented premises in Cookridge Street. Medical students took classes from 1875 and College and Medical School (*see* p. 420) amalgamated in 1884. In 1887 it joined Manchester and Liverpool as the smallest element of the Victoria University, an association that lasted until 1904 when Leeds perforce assumed independent university status.

The university buildings have overlain Woodhouse in three main phases of building, which are described in chronological order. In 1877 Yorkshire College appointed as its architect *Alfred Waterhouse* on the strength of his work for Owens College, Manchester, completed in 1874. His work at Leeds is humble in comparison. Fund-raising yielded only £20,000 of a hoped-for £60,000, and building was made possible only by the munificence of the Clothworkers' Company of London, anxious to improve the scientific basis of their industry after the Paris International Exhibition of 1867. His descendants continued his work but were succeeded in 1926 by *Lanchester, Lucas & Lodge* following a limited competition for a master-plan to bring belated civic dignity to the institution (a move to

*This entry has been contributed by Elain Harwood.

Weetwood had previously been considered). Building, mainly to the N and E, continued into the 1950s. Finally *Chamberlin, Powell & Bon* completed a major phase of building to the S during the 1960s. The phases are distinctive for their very different sizes, scales and especially materials: red brick giving way to Portland stone and then to concrete. Pevsner complained of Waterhouse's dryness and considered that Lanchester, Lucas & Lodge's classical revival style 'achieves nothing'; now we are more sympathetic to their rich materials and grand spaces, particularly of Waterhouse's Great Hall and the interwar work that gives the university its greatest landmark. Chamberlin, Powell and Bon's work has an industrial monumentality and genuine flexibility that withstands accretions, while creating the precinct's one grand space. They created a central axis leading to a central lecture theatre complex and formal square; had a second square intended to the E been realized the jagged end of the Economics and Social Science Building would have been resolved but too many good buildings would have been lost. All these architects were initially welcomed enthusiastically by the University, but in the course of their subsequent long building campaigns this was replaced by a mistrust that Leeds was not getting its due, and a search for a clean and uncontested break. Most recently the University has preferred to work with local architects, producing decent if unexceptional buildings.

UNIVERSITY ROAD originated as the drive to BEECH GROVE HOUSE (now the Leeds Social Sciences Institute), one of a number of suburban houses to survive within the campus (*see* also Perambulation). Built 1799 for Abram Rhodes, cloth merchant, originally with workshops and associated buildings. Symmetrical with a central bow; Neo-Norman porch and plate-glass sash windows probably added *c.* 1840 for John Ogden March, ironfounder. The Waterhouse buildings are grouped E and W of Clothworkers' Court on the N side of University Road. To the W end the SCHOOL OF DESIGN is of two phases, incorporating the original Clothworkers (Textiles) Building (now Wool Division) of 1879–80. This has a near-blind red brick façade with Spinkwell Quarry stone arcading concealing top-lit weaving sheds behind; a two-storey part at right angles originally for a lecture theatre and first-floor museum (no longer so used). W extension, dated 1911, by *Paul Waterhouse* for the Spinning Department, in matching style but with a freer Gothic tower.

In 1880 Sir Edward Baines, Chairman of the College Council, donated £3,000 towards the long, three-storey BAINES WING, at the E end of University Road. Built 1881–5 (dated 1883), with regular gables and a stubby tower topped by one of Waterhouse's steep pyramid roofs. His proposed clock tower to the E was unrealized: instead *Paul Waterhouse* extended the wing in 1908 and in 1912 added the link, in Arts and Crafts style, between the Baines Wing and his father's GREAT HALL of 1890–4. This is banded in stone and with a large Perp traceried window flanked by towers having tall pyramidal roofs and bartizans. Inside, a particularly handsome staircase supported on paired columns and lined with green Burmantofts tiles (an effect Waterhouse later repeated at University College Hospital, London) leads to a well-lit hall used for lectures and examinations. It has a S gallery, columns with floral capitals and 'YC' monogrammed in the cornice. A library and refectory were originally set on the floors below. It is joined to the earliest buildings by a two-storey range forming the backdrop of CLOTHWORKERS COURT. W of these buildings, the former Agriculture Building (now GEOGRAPHY) was funded by the Board of Agriculture following a donation by Walter Morrison (*see* Malham Moor) in 1913, but not built until 1923–7 by *Michael Waterhouse*.

In 1926 *Lanchester, Lucas & Lodge* proposed an imposing clock tower on the curve of WOODHOUSE LANE, although building did not begin until the following decade. The PARKINSON BUILDING, initiated in 1936 but not formally opened until 1951, was conceived in the masterplan as an arts and administration block. After Frank Parkinson offered £200,000 for its construction this was revised to incorporate a council chamber, committee rooms and offices. Monumental E front with a recessed Ionic portico up wide steps. The clock tower, faced in Portland stone, in four stages with a low-pitched pyramid roof, is in *Thomas Lodge*'s distinctive Greek Revival style (the university's relations with *H. V. Lanchester* had quickly soured) and this spare aesthetic continues inside to the grand ENTRANCE HALL, a lofty double-height space running through the long axis with austere stripped classical columns defining aisles on each side. Light fittings by *Troughton & Young*, 1947–8. Behind the Parkinson Building, and without any street presence, is the BROTHERTON LIBRARY of 1935–6, for which Sir Edward Brotherton, the chemical manufacturer, had offered up to £100,000 and his private book collection of 80,000 volumes. Circular reading room 160 ft (48.8 metres) in diameter, with a gallery and Swedish green marble columns supporting a concrete dome. Oak panelling and fittings, with carvings of the University and Brotherton's arms, and symbols representing Arts and Science in the plasterwork of the dome, make for resplendent, cool grandeur.

Lodge conceived the design of the utilitarian sequence of post-war buildings to the S of University Road, adjacent to the STUDENTS' UNION (*J. C. Procter*, 1939), mostly in red brick and stone: UNIVERSITY HOUSE (refectory and senior common room) of 1955, and facing, MAN MADE FIBRES of 1954–6, with SCULPTURE on that theme at roof level by *Mitzi Cunliffe*. Lodge's assistant *Allan Johnson* served as executive architect for these and also completed the MICHAEL SADLER BUILDING FOR ARTS, S of the Parkinson Building. In its entrance hall the outstanding but highly unusual WAR MEMORIAL of 1923 by *Eric Gill*. The subject, Our Lord driving the Moneychangers out of the Temple, and the depiction of figures in modern dress were hugely controversial with local dignitaries and the press. Gill intended it as a personal attack on modern commerce, seeing the Christ figure as a form of self-portrait backed by the hound of St Dominic (Gill had joined the Dominican order in 1921). Glass by *Mark Angus*, 1989. Johnson continued the line of science and engineering buildings up Woodhouse Lane, with extensions to Chemistry and Physics, and the Houldsworth School in 1958 and 1964, Civil Engineering in 1960, Mechanical Engineering in 1961 (with a powerful fibreglass relief designed by Johnson and made by *Alec Dearnby* over its entrance), and Electrical and Electronic Engineering in 1963.

The University used Lodge's forthcoming retirement, announced in 1956, to rethink its strategy for the teaching precinct, seeking advice from *Leslie Martin* and *J. M. Richards*, the latter then a visiting lecturer here. A limited competition by interview resulted in the appointment of *Chamberlin, Powell & Bon (CPB)* in 1959, preferred to Denys Lasdun. Peter (Joe) Chamberlin was the partner in charge and principal designer save where noted. Their work extends s down the steep slope to the Inner Ring Road, which was sunk on the firm's recommendations so that the University retained its link with the Infirmary, Medical School and the city centre. The changes in level informed the circulation pattern of the new work. CPB's detailed report, published in 1960 and revised in 1963, was based on interviews with staff and flow charts of student movements through the precinct and offered a model throughout the 1960s for subsequent studies of university campuses, old and new. The architects recalculated projected student numbers, estimating in the 1960 plan that they needed to build for 7,000 by 1970, a figure subsequently raised to 10,000 as a result of the Robbins Report, and looked closely at the relationship between departments as well as their individual needs. From this evolved the PLAN of a central block of communal lecture theatres and the disposition around it of the other departments, designed to be used more flexibly. The buildings are used far more intensively today. Chamberlin originally acceded that other architects be brought in to design buildings according to his masterplan, and indeed suggested BDP for the Medical School, but he quickly sought for CPB to design the whole scheme, a cause of argument with the University authorities.

The BUILDINGS are based on a modular tartan grid based on the unit of the Forticrete concrete cladding blocks, which allowed subdivision for partitioning at 20-in. (50-cm.) intervals. A system of internal block partitions allowed the occasional flexibility required as departments changed or lecturers moved on. Clustered beams and columns at 40-ft (12-metre) intervals incorporated space between them for services. The other flexible element was what Powell called 'the joker in the pack' – small teaching units or flats on the top floor of the blocks into which larger departments could expand over time, as has happened. Finally, CPB devised colour-coded internal walkways between the buildings at three levels across and down the hillside, of which only the uppermost, the red route, survives.

The main buildings, painted in 1996–7, are grouped around CHANCELLORS COURT, likened by CPB in their 1960 report to the great Oxbridge quadrangles. It was re-landscaped in 1995 with sculptural interventions by *Lorna Green*: Meet, Sit and Talk of 1995 and Conservation of 1999. Considered twee by purists when first created, the landscaping is maturing well a decade later and has made the square a popular meeting place. A broad flight of steps leads impressively s to N to a climax of the long, level terraces of the Waterhouse buildings. CPB's first perspectives repeat the shell domes they had used at New Hall, Cambridge, also designed in 1960. The form eventually adopted emerged only around 1963, its service-led approach to construction comparable with Louis Kahn's Richards Medical Research Laboratories at the University of Philadelphia. First came MATHEMATICS, EARTH SCIENCES and COMPUTER SCIENCE, completed in 1966. At right angles, the former SENIOR COMMON ROOM of 1964–7, denoted by its external staircases and originally with a suite of lounges and bars on its principal, second floor; the main bar at the s end with large windows on three sides still has a sunken dance floor. Across the main axis is the E. C. STONER BUILDING (Physics), much the longest of the spine ranges – at sixteen irregular bays long and with steps to an unrealized building intended as part of the abandoned 'green route'; its elegance shows the hand of Geoffry Powell. The centrepiece of Chancellors Court is the ROGER STEVENS BUILDING, 1968–70, with sixteen small raked lecture theatres set in four banks of four, with nine larger theatres placed at right angles over a glazed ground-floor café and basement television studio. All are expressed externally. Inside, the raked theatres are set directly off staircases with doors off every step so latecomers can sneak on to the ends of the benches. It was a prototype for the planning of CPB's Barbican Theatre, London. The concrete beams which form the steps and benches form part of the structure of the floor, and the ceiling of the lecture theatre below. The café benches are also by CPB. Refurbishment by *Braithwaite & Jackman*, 1998. On the E side of the exterior a craggy rough bronze SCULPTURE of 1970 by *William Chattaway*, originally commissioned by the Midland Bank with the title Spirit of Free Enterprise but salvaged and renamed Hermes by the University when the bank was sold in 1983.

To the s, towards Clarendon Way, are the spine blocks of GARSTANG and IRENE MANTON for biophysics and biological sciences, completed in 1969–70. Irene Manton was extended by *Ellwood Hooson* for biology, and linked to Garstang in 1995–7 by a research building (ASTBURY) that repeats the fenestration pattern of the old but uses metal cladding; it was extended again in 2000 to accommodate microbiology. Links were also provided to the Worsley Building, s of Clarendon Way (*see* p. 420). N is the EDWARD BOYLE LIBRARY, completed by CPB in 1975 and extended by *Jackson & Calvert* in 1994 by infilling the space deliberately left for this purpose, part of which was occupied by columns supporting a suspended sculpture by *Quentin Bell* (now in the Baines Wing courtyard). The plan is an open well surrounded by reading cubicles, stepped towards the windows. Jackson and Calvert's suspended structure and demands for computer clusters prompted a more enclosed solution for the addition. The final block, for ECONOMICS AND SOCIAL SCIENCE, was handed over in 1978 but its N and NE elevations remain incomplete. It was intended to link into a second court, CONVOCATION COURT, which was never built. CPB also extended the pre-war STUDENTS' UNION with a partly submerged structure down the side of the hill that ends in a glazed pyramid over a debating chamber (popular in university briefs of the early 1960s but now the Raven Theatre). This was extended again in 2001 by *Farrell & Clark*. Also by CPB was the original sports complex at the s end of the precinct, remodelled and extended by *Jones, Stocks & Partners*, 1986. For twenty years Leeds Playhouse occupied the adjacent building, by *William Horton-Evans*, now a CONFERENCE CENTRE, remodelled in 2003 by *Farrell & Clark*.

The University long had a policy of building HALLS OF RESIDENCE on cheaper land away from its central precinct. *CPB* looked into the cost of providing buses and duplicating facilities, and recommended building high-density student flats within the precinct. These included the 'joker' flats, and two new blocks. The HENRY PRICE RESIDENCES is a 'flying freehold' across the wall of St George's Fields on Clarendon Road (*see* above). Built to *Christoph Bon*'s designs in 1963–4, it was followed by CHARLES MORRIS HALL in Mount Preston Street – also by Bon – in 1964–6, originally linked to the 'red route' across the precinct, and with two tall blocks originally for men and a lower range for women containing dining and common room facilities. Accrington brick was used for the purely residential blocks, to contrast with the concrete of the teaching buildings and in homage to the red brick terraces they replaced.

Former HOSTEL OF THE RESURRECTION (a.k.a. the Priory of St Wilfred), Springfield Mount. Established by the Community of the Resurrection (Mirfield, West Riding South) as a residence for students reading theology at Leeds. By *Temple Moore*, built 1907–10 and 1927–8 (under *Leslie Moore*'s supervision). A noble façade, the style collegiate Tudor in red-brown brick with stone quoins, a turreted four-storey gatehouse and traceried windows. Inside, chapel, refectory and meeting rooms, with panelling, fireplaces and a fine staircase, and to the rear a cloister-like rear courtyard garden.

UNIVERSITY CLOTHWORKERS' CENTENARY CONCERT HALL and SCHOOL OF MUSIC. *See* PRESBYTERIAN CHURCH, above.

Perambulation

On the E side of WOODHOUSE LANE, slightly S of University Road, is BLENHEIM TERRACE, erected in phases from 1824 to 1839 for T. E. Upton, a local solicitor and building speculator. It is an unusually long row of over twenty brick houses of different sizes but all of three storeys and basement (now in other uses) set behind long, narrow front gardens with tall stone gatepiers. E of this along Blackman Lane is BLENHEIM SQUARE, begun in 1822 as Finsbury Square. The E side was built by 1831 with three-bay houses of three storeys plus basements. The N side followed a few decades later, but the others were never built; the Anglican mission church of All Souls and the back-to-backs to the W are emblematic of the failure of the suburb as industry spread up the valley of the Meanwood Beck (*see* p. 465).

W of the campus is LITTLE WOODHOUSE. A tour begins near the S end of Clarendon Road with WOODHOUSE SQUARE, planned from 1825 for John Atkinson of Little Woodhouse Hall (*see* below) but built up only from 1840 and without any consistency. Of that date WAVERLEY HOUSE (W side) by *John Clark*. Built as two houses with one entrance on the S front. Solid, six bays, three storeys over a basement and shallow pediment. On the square's S side, Nos. 2–9 of 1845–6 by *Richard William Moore*, just after he had completed his pupillage with R. D. Chantrell. Two storeys; Nos. 6–7 are taller, intended as the centre of a symmetrical design, but the W end was not completed. An attractive group, somewhat weighed down by the flamboyant Early Victorian dressings. The square's E side is much later, e.g. Nos. 12 and 14 by *George Corson*, 1868 and 1869, the former with tourelles to the S gable and a round corner tower. Built for George Herbert Rayner, an importer of valonia (acorn cups for tanning and dyeing). In the gardens, levelled up in 1941, a bronze STATUE of Sir Peter Fairbairn, engineer and Mayor at the time of the Town Hall opening. By *Matthew Noble*, 1868. He faces the town, his left hand resting on a column covered with symbolic cloth, cog wheel and chain of office, a scroll in his right hand.

N of the square, at right angles, are terraced houses ('The Claremonts') of after 1894, built over the gardens of CLAREMONT, a smart S-facing house of two storeys with a pediment, 'new built' in 1772 for the Quaker merchant John Elam but altered after 1856 with porch and bay windows by *George Corson* for Dr John Deakin Heaton, physician and co-founder of the Yorkshire College. Inside, a fine C18 cantilevered stone staircase and good *Minton* floor tiles. Some fittings from demolished houses (imported since 1968 by the Yorkshire Archaeological Society), including a 1740 doorcase from Scarcroft Grange and white marble fireplaces from Osmondthorpe Hall, the carving thought to be by *Flaxman*. The library furniture is of 1925–6 by *Kitson, Parish & Ledgard* (from the Society's previous premises in Park Lane).

To the w, on the N side of Hanover Square, is DENISON HALL. Built 1786 for John Wilkinson Denison, one of Leeds's wealthiest merchants, who acquired Claremont in that year and divided its estate. The design is by *William Lindley* of Doncaster, and follows the Adamish style of his master John Carr. Three-storey, five-bay centre flanked by bowed two-storey wings. Giant Ionic pilasters to the centre three bays and a pediment with swags and urns. Modest pedimented E entrance, with Doric columns and delicate carved swags. Typical Neoclassical entrance vestibule screened by columns *in antis*. Central oval staircase hall with a dramatic cantilevered staircase, its wrought-iron balustrade of S-scrolls and ribbon-like motifs by *John Rogers*; similar to Carr's stair at Norton Place, Lincolnshire. Adam-style plasterwork in the dome above and in the former music room above the entrance. At the w end of the house a cantilevered stone staircase with plain square-section balusters, probably inserted *c.* 1824–6 when the house was divided in two by George Rawson, stuff merchant. He also speculated at this time in the development of HANOVER SQUARE, for which designs were provided by *Pritchett & Watson*; the private garden was promoted as 'Hanover Square Park', laid out by *Joshua Major*. No. 11 (NE corner) was designed as two houses, built 1826–30, probably for John Clapham (*see* The Grange, Burley-in-Wharfedale), who planned further developments here. Late Georgian style, red brick, six windows wide and three storeys high over stone cellars, the area protected by railings. Of the same period, also Nos. 37–40 (SW corner); Nos. 37 and 38 have an attractive wide entrance framed by paired Tuscan columns supporting a heavy entablature. The rest of the plots were filled a generation later with less prestigious terraced houses. On the w side, the terrace has rear extensions for workshops added *c.* 1889 for the use of travelling drapers trading with surrounding villages. On the S side a Sunday School built *c.* 1900 and just outside the square a chapel.

Now back to CLAREMONT ROAD. On its E side, diagonally opposite Claremont, is LITTLE WOODHOUSE HALL, built for Christopher Thompson, gentleman, and described in 1741 as a 'new house empty'. Long, plain three-storey S façade, with later C18 shallow two-storey canted bays; on the E front an entrance range with Doric porch, added *c.* 1840 by *John Clark*. Remarkable interiors of 1847 by *William Reid Corson* and *Edward la Trobe Bateman*, designed with advice from *Owen Jones* – the circular staircase hall with bright mosaic around an eight-pointed star. Staircase with a cast-iron balustrade of scrolls and flowers under a glass dome with interlacing ribs.*

---

*Six lunettes painted for the house by *John Everett Millais* are now in the City Art Gallery.

A little N, off HYDE TERRACE, is SPRINGFIELD HOUSE, built in 1792 for Thomas Livesey, a cloth dresser. Once a gracious two-storey brick house with central pediment and pedimented doorcase.

Now for CLARENDON ROAD, N of Little Woodhouse Hall, mostly built up with a mixture of villas and terraces after 1839. The styles are mid-to-later Victorian eclectic. CLARENDON HOUSE (No. 20, E side) built 1853–7 for William Braithwaite, surgeon, is solid Italianate, of two storeys with a neat oriel window over the entrance and ornate chimneys. Nos. 22 and 24 by *Isaac Dixon*, 1859, are simpler but share a central portico whose columns have capitals lavishly carved with eagles and grapes. Also, SOUTHFIELD HOUSE (No. 40, W side) built 1867–70 for James Reffitt, dyer. It has an ornate tower, a scrolled gable and a stone roundel carved with plants. The grandest house, however, is FAIRBAIRN HOUSE (W side), of 1840–1, a handsome Neoclassical mansion by *John Clark* for Peter Fairbairn, engineer, set back behind a shallow curved driveway guarded by pairs of pedimented stone gatepiers with side panels ornamented like riveted steel plates. It is of two storeys and seven bays, on an ashlar plinth, with giant Corinthian pilasters, a small pedimented doorway and an attic storey behind a heavy balustraded blocking course. Greek ornament inside and a screen of fluted columns to the fine Imperial staircase with scrolled iron balustrade. Some of the heavy plasterwork was probably added in 1858 when Queen Victoria and Prince Albert stayed here for the opening of the Town Hall. Secondary oval newel stair with Egyptian lotus balusters to the basement (fire-proof construction of cast-iron beams and segmental brick arches). Later converted into a clergy training school, with red brick pilastered N extension. Tall chapel on the S side, by *Temple Moore*, 1896. Blocked round gable window; three-light tracery. Inside, ribbed barrel-vaulted ceiling.

BELLE VUE HOUSE, Belle Vue Road/Kendal Bank. Small, pedimented red brick mansion of 1792, built for Michael Wainhouse, cloth merchant. Five bays, two storeys over basement Venetian stair window to rear. Wainhouse had workshops and a warehouse at the end of its curving drive from Park Lane. The grounds were built up with back-to-back houses in the 1860s, and now by late 1970s housing. The extensive view is now being obscured by the gargantuan student flats being erected in this area.

HARRISON'S ALMSHOUSES, Raglan Road. By *John Clark*, c. 1840, and possibly with late C19 additions. Two-storey, brick, Tudor style. Central crenellated entrance tower with oriel. Wings to the rear.

JOSEPH'S WELL, Chorley Lane, S of Woodhouse Square. A vast former clothing factory built 1888–1904 for Sir John Barran, employing over 2,000 workers. Four and five storeys in brick and terracotta, typically freely styled for its date. Ornate warehouse (E) wing, the main entrance under a deep segmental arch and the ground floor rusticated, with much use of heavy

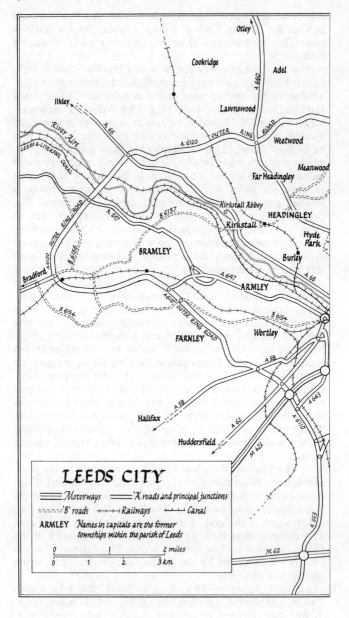

LEEDS CITY

Motorways ——— 'A' roads and principal junctions ———

'B' roads - - - - Railways +++++ Canal —+—

ARMLEY *Names in capitals are the former townships within the parish of Leeds*

0   1   2 miles
0   1   2   3 km

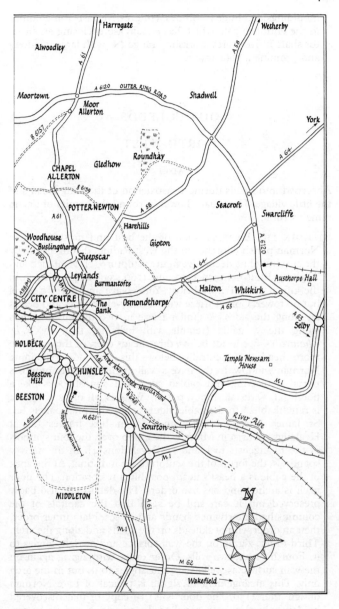

mouldings and huge keystones. (Impressive cast-iron columns in the entrance hall, which has a staircase enclosing an elevator shaft.) Five-storey workshop range (N) with large windows and prominent stair-tower.

OUTER LEEDS

NORTH-WEST

ADEL

Absorbed into Leeds during construction of the Ring Road s of the little village. The N part, however, round the hamlet of Eccup remains rural.

ST JOHN THE BAPTIST. One of the best and most complete Norman parish churches in the West Riding, distinguished by the survival of its decorative figure sculpture (cf. Healaugh and Wighill). Built between 1150 and 1160, replacing a church in the gift of Holy Trinity Priory, York. Nave and lower chancel but no tower. Corbel-frieze with seventy-eight faces and beasts all along the sides. A similar frieze in two diminishing tiers along the w gable (rebuilt with bellcote, 1839 by *R. D. Chantrell*) – five heads below, three heads over. At the apex one more head. Set centrally below this, the one remaining Norman window. In the nave s wall memorably sumptuous s portal, projecting and gabled so that it almost looks like a porch (cf. Kirkstall Abbey, p. 505). What is left of its sculpture is remarkable.* In the gable, figures carved on flat panels (cf. St James Boroughbridge) and set in box frames (as at Healaugh). Christ in Majesty, the Lamb over, the four symbols of the Evangelists to l. and r. (Revelations 4). In the narrow spandrels, the forms of the sculpture are indistinct. At the apex of the gable is a beast's head, possibly a restoration. The door itself is arched and has five orders. The details are also badly preserved but it can still be seen that the capitals of the columns had intertwined bands and leaves. Plain inner order, then an order with beakheads up the shafts and along the arch. Third order, zigzag on the wall surface and at right angles to it. Fourth order, two rolls. Outer order with zigzag again on the wall surface as well as at right angles to it, but in the arch only. This arrangement of zigzag is typical of Late Norman design after 1150. The door is a C19 copy of that discovered hidden behind an C18 panelled door in 1843 and its bronze door ring a replica of the original (stolen in 2002), probably made in York *c.* 1200, with a monster's head, probably a lion, clasping the ring and a man's head protruding from its mouth. Also in the s wall a straight-headed two-light Dec window set

_____

*The portal was protected by a rough shelter until shortly after the details of its sculpture were recorded by Whitaker in 1816. The present shelter is of 1982.

Leeds, St John Adel, south doorway.
Lithograph, *c.* 1842

low in the chancel and two straight-headed Late Perp windows
in the nave, and a small unmoulded priest's doorway. The three
small lancets in the E wall are part of the sympathetic restoration in 1878–9 by *G. E. Street*; he re-set the Late Perp E window
in his vestry, raised the nave roof and renewed windows in the
W wall; the small windows in the N and S walls, placed high up
above a stringcourse, are largely his too.

The nave is of wide, comfortable proportions, with a splendid chancel arch. Semicircular responds, two orders of shafts
to the W, none to the E, though the carving of just two
beakheads at the springing of the arch on the S side proves that
at least one E order was projected. This detail appears to prove
that the sculptural detail was done *in situ*. The capitals are of
special interest. The responds have on the N side the Baptism
of Christ, on the S side the Crucifixion. For the Baptism, notice
the familiar motif of the mount of water round Christ's legs,
and the angel flying horizontally and holding a chrisom

(medieval christening robe). The Devil (as a dragon) is trying to drink the water while John the Baptist and the ghost of King David, holding a branch of the Jesse Tree, stand on the bank. The Crucifixion has Joseph of Arimathaea supporting the arm of Christ while Nicodemus pulls the last nail from his feet. The middle capitals on both sides have dragon-like beasts, the outer capitals on the N side a centaur with bow, on the S side a horseman with lance. Arches with dogtooth, beakhead, a chain of box frames, and zigzag (on, and at right angles to, the wall). Beakheads carved with a variety of grotesques, principally devils, many of whom delight in devouring children.

Chancel roof rebuilt in 1844 by *Chantrell*. Street introduced the choir and clergy stalls and re-floored the nave. – Plain stone ALTAR from St Edward, Holbeck (*Bodley*, 1903–4; dem.). – FONT. Simple octagonal bowl, possibly the original, recovered from the churchyard in 1858. – FONT COVER, 1921 by *Sydney Kitson*, octagonal, carved with panels of the sacraments. – PULPIT and CHANCEL SCREEN, by *Temple Moore* 1890s, both altered. – Three PAINTINGS by *Van der Bank*, 1748: Crucifixion and Ascension and, much smaller, Gethsemane. – STAINED GLASS. Chancel: E windows of 1887; central S window and N window opposite, by *Harry Harvey*, of 1971; SW window by *Henry Gyles* of York to his friend Thomas Kirke †1706. – In the vestry the former E window, removed in 1879, has heraldic glass with prominent royal arms by the same, 1681. – Nave: SE, by *F. C. Eden* 1933; next, Tubal-Cain instructs an apprentice next to a furnace and anvil in memory of R. W. Eddison, engineer, †1900; SW, 1955 by *Harry Stammers*, pretty frieze with birds, rabbits, etc. on a foliage background. – MONUMENTS. Two in the churchyard, both of 1884: Suzannah Audus Hirst by *A. Welsh*, a young winged figure carrying a garland; and Elizabeth and William Hill (the architect) by *Hodgson*, a cross in a Norman arch, flanked by angels. Near the entrance to the churchyard FRAGMENTS including a possibly Roman stone coffin.

E of the church, the former RECTORY. A polite pedimented front range, *c.* 1770, but the L-plan rear part is dated 1652, of coursed stone encasing an earlier timber frame. Further alterations *c.* 1819 and 1858 (porch). Circular painted ceiling above the staircase. Late C18 ICE HOUSE, N, and handsome little Georgian STABLES (now the Parish Hall), with tall, pediment centre and oval pitching eyes. A little further E, YORK GATE, a Pennine Revival house with an outstanding garden, created 1951–94 by Frederick Spencer and his son, Robin Spencer, as a series of compartments divided by yew and beech hedges.

BODINGTON HALL OF RESIDENCE (UNIVERSITY OF LEEDS), Otley Road. 1959–63 by *Jones & Stocks*. A cluster of eight blocks, rising across a gentle slope, mainly of four storeys, some linked, gathered round a central Community Block.

Engulfed by much C20 suburban housing S of the village are some substantial Victorian and later villas (cf. Weetwood to the S). Colonization was begun by Edwin Eddison (1806–67), a

Quaker lawyer and first Town Clerk of Leeds. At the s end of
LONG CAUSEWAY in SMITHY MILLS LANE is ADEL LODGE,
the home of J. E. Eddison (a son). Jacobean style with stepped
gables. In the same style is OAK LEA, built for William Croys-
dale, the dyestuff manufacturer, in the 1870s, with shaped
gables, twisted chimneystacks and dramatic porch with banded
columns, shields, plentiful strapwork. Lodges, stables and carriage house (now housing). N, set well back at the junction with
Dunstarn Lane, is a Gothic mansion of 1877 designed by
William Hill for himself. In ST HELEN'S LANE, W, is ATHILL
COURT (s side), a substantial Neo-Wren-cum-Neo-Georgian,
house of *c.* 1921, a touch Mannerist, for a clothing manufacturer, Mr May. On the N side ST HELEN'S COTTAGE is a C17
survivor, two bays, with low mullioned windows (extended
c. 1980). On the corner with ST HELEN'S LANE, FOURS
CROFT, *Moderne* Domestic Revival, hipped roof, shaped
Deco-ish door surround. By contrast, on the opposite corner,
ADEL LANE, to the W, WHITE LODGE (No. 116) of 1935 by
J. C. Procter is pure Modernism: white rendered, flat roofs, two
wings at right angles, an entrance tower introducing curves.
Further s, now surrounded by housing off Adel Lane, is ADEL
GRANGE (nursing home). 1864–6 by *Waterhouse* for Robert
Lawson Ford, a solicitor. Symmetrical garden front – with two
gables, and large mullioned-and-transomed bay windows with
pierced quatrefoil parapets – combined with an asymmetric
entrance elevation – dominated by a large staircase window
with stained glass, a Gothic arched porch, and massive chimneystack.

ADEL MILL FARM, Eccup Lane, 3/8 m. N of the church. An
extensive complex, part mill part model farm (now housing).
Developed from 1848 by Edwin Eddison. Several cottages and
the farmhouse in two parts, the l. half C18 vernacular, the taller
r. half Victorian.

'ROMAN CAMP'. An earthwork enclosure, square and covering
two acres, lies 100 yds s of the Ilkley–Doncaster Roman road.
Presumed to have been a fort, although there is no evidence
of occupation. Thoresby described the discovery and destruction of the remains of 'a Roman town, which by the ruins
seems to have been very considerable', and 'the foundations of
houses, many of which were three or four courses high . . .'
Excavations in 1933 and 1938 produced evidence of occupation in the surrounding area, and Roman artefacts including
pottery, broaches and stone coffins have been discovered,
(some now in Leeds City Museum).

BURLEY

The first village w of Leeds on the Kirkstall road, within Headingley township. Following the sale of the Cardigan estate in the
1860s, much of the area was built over with back-to-back
housing, continuous with Hyde Park (*see* below) to the N. Later

suburban housing to the W Kirkstall Road is the boundary between the housing and the industrialized strip along the bank of the River Aire.

ALL HALLOWS. *See* Hyde Park, p. 501.

ST MARGARET. *See* Hyde Park, p. 501.

ST MATTHIAS, St Matthias Street. 1853–4 by *Perkin & Backhouse*, paid for by John Smith of Burley House. Geometrical tracery. The tall S broach spire, funded by William Beckett, is the best part of a good muscular High Victorian design. Gabled N aisle and W porch added 1886. Coursed and squared gritstone and ashlar. (Chancel roof with arched braces, and boarded panels painted with shields and gilded. – REREDOS. Painted stone arcade with angels and quatrefoils, Caen stone panels with vines and branches, alabaster chancel wall erected 1893. – PULPIT by *J.L. Pearson*, 1892. An excellent piece in alabaster on a marble base, carved with Old Testament preachers. – FONT, octagonal, Caen stone. – TOWER SCREEN. – STAINED GLASS. Fine eight-light E window of Saints by *Francis Barnett* of Edinburgh. N transept by *Mayer & Co.*, 1885 – MEMORIAL, S transept, to Anne Catherine Jane Smith, †1854. By *Spence* of Rome. Relief of female figure and angel in a Gothic frame with crocketed pinnacles.)

BURLEY WESLEYAN METHODIST CHURCH, Cardigan Lane. 1897–8 by *G.F. Danby*. Coursed rock-faced gritstone, ashlar details. Dec style, with corner steeple. Alongside, the former SUNDAY SCHOOL (now hall) of 1904–5 by *Danby & Simpson* with ungainly octagonal corner turrets.

PERAMBULATION. A few scattered early buildings remain e.g. No. 64 CARDIGAN LANE (opposite the Wesleyan Methodist Church). Late C18 with a S front of four uneven bays; converted to a chapel in the C19, see the bowed section at the rear. On Kirkstall Road, at the corner with Greenhow Road, THE CARDIGAN ARMS of 1893 with lively gables (inside, original woodwork and glazed partitions). A red-brick brewhouse and stables enclose a rear yard. ½ m. further W is an early C19 building (now housing) with small open pediment and arched openings, possibly built as the stables for Wanstead House, one of the suburban villas shown on Fowler's map of 1834. Opposite, across the road, BURLEY MILLS (converted for offices, 2000). Built for worsted processing in 1799 by *James Graham* for Wormald, Gott & Wormald. Altered 1822, again after a fire in 1918. Plain three-storey range, fifteen bays long, straddling the mill goit. Behind, a later engine house, formerly separate but now with a glazed link for the entrance, crossed by steel bridges. This is nothing original, but it is quite well done. Also an early weaving and spinning range and a dryhouse.

COOKRIDGE AND LAWNSWOOD

Opened up for suburban development by the construction of the Ring Road; it was absorbed into the city in 1926. Public and private housing estates followed, including Ireland Wood (from 1948), Moseley Wood (1957), and Holt Park (1973), with its brutal district centre.

ST PAUL, Reynel Drive, Ireland Wood. 1965, by *Geoffrey Davy* of *Kitson, Parish, Ledgard & Pyman* (cf. St David, Beeston and St James & St Cyprian, Harehills). A brick octagon with bold and tall tiled roof rising to a central louvred belfry. Long slit windows. A narthex also serves the adjoining church hall of 1951 by the same firm, previously used for worship. ALTAR against the E wall, with tubular steel CROSS in front of the seven-light E window. Abstract STAINED GLASS.

LAWNSWOOD CEMETERY, Otley Road. Opened in 1875 by the Headingley-cum-Burley Burial Board to cater for the expanding suburbs of Headingley and Far Headingley (qq.v). The layout and most of the buildings were designed by *George Corson* (he died 1910 and is buried here), assisted by *William Gay*, the designer of Undercliffe Cemetery, Bradford. The plan has a curving drive describing a gentle arc around a large clump of trees which screen the chapels and crematorium. Monuments line a mixture of straight and curving paths with trees and shrubs raised on platforms forming verdant islands.

Tudor-style LODGE, modified in 1907. The CEMETERY CHAPELS occupy a roughly central position, and are linked at right angles by an open colonnade of three arches with short columns of polished granite. The style is a muscular Gothic, lightened by a romantic octagonal turret with louvred belfry and a tiled spire. STAINED GLASS of 1893 in a side window and in the apsed chancel of the Anglican chapel. Attached S is the CREMATORIUM of 1905 by *W. S. Braithwaite* in matching Gothic style, the first in Britain to use a gas cremator. It has a tall square tower with an octagonal belfry disguising the flue. SW of this, the refined Neo-Georgian COLUMBARIUM by *Col. A. E. Kirk* (*Kirk & Tomlinson*), 1933, its setting more formal than the earlier parts of the cemetery. Its tall CHAPEL has a portico, continued as long L-shaped colonnaded wings. Inside, marble-clad walls with vertical brick bands raised across the vault. Recessed top-lit bays have shelves for the deposited ashes.

MONUMENTS. – Arthur Currer Briggs, †1906, of Henry Briggs & Son, colliery owners. By *William Hamo Thornycroft*, a bronze relief of a sower watched by an angel set in a pedimented slab. – Ethel Preston, †1911, an extraordinary monument with a life-size statue wearing elegant Edwardian dress standing under a Corinthian porch with balustrade above, reputedly that of her home, The Grange, Beeston (dem.). It has a working door left slightly ajar. – Charles Henry Johnson, †1912 with an Art Nouveau surround; – Sam Wilson, †1918, worsted coating manufacturer and benefactor of the Leeds City Art Gallery. A spectacular memorial by *E. Caldwell Spruce*, chief modeller for the Leeds Fireclay Co., reflecting Wilson's interest in Symbolist painting, displaying in its brooding intensity the influence of G. F. Watts. Black marble inset with a relief of a skull and snakes representing Death, with kneeling bronze figures of Faith and Benevolence flanking splayed plinths and surmounted by a tall bronze angel, holding a torch aloft.

COOKRIDGE HOSPITAL, Hospital Lane, Ireland Wood. 1868–9 by *Norman Shaw* – by him the W parts of the imposing W block, a typical pavilion plan, in picturesque Home Counties tradition. E wing in same style, added 1893. E is the former Ida Hospital by *Chorley & Connon*, 1887–8, in Shaw's style. Single-storey, half-butterfly plan – an early use – designed for a mixture of small and large wards opening onto sun verandas. Its non-identical twin opened alongside in 1905, named after its financier Robert Arthington. Many later additions.

LODGE, by *Norman Shaw*. Large timber brackets support a deep jettied upper floor with oriel and projecting gable. Perhaps his too is the gabled stone POST BOX.

COOKRIDGE HALL (Country Club), Cookridge Lane. Engulfed in additions for its present use as a health club. The main range, facing S, is of 1754–5 for Charles Sheffield who acquired the house in 1722. The architect, according to accounts, was a *Mr Stox*. Two storeys and five bays, the central three bays break forward slightly and are pedimented. A Venetian window within an overarch reaches up into the broken pediment. The rear pile retains C17 fabric at basement level (see windows and door), with a kitchen above, built 1748. Rear wing, making an L-plan, extended progressively in the C18 and early C19.

Richard Wormald, a Leeds woollen merchant, bought the estate in 1820. He built the surviving COACHHOUSE and STABLE, W of the house, and ICE HOUSE, E.

Three former FARMS are of interest: HIGH FARM, Farrar Lane. Enveloped by housing and converted into a pub in 1977 by the *Millard Design Partnership*. Three-bay farmhouse rebuilt *c.* 1725, extended to the rear *c.* 1816. Inside re-set door lintel carved with 1(6)38. Barn, stables and outbuildings were adapted as part of the pub complex. The barn with C17 or earlier timber-frame, clad in stone and N aisle added possibly *c.* 1725. Three trusses with wall posts, kingposts and raked struts; building extended W with further trusses, and E in C19 brick. CRAG HOUSE FARM, off Smithy Lane. Three-unit C17 FARMHOUSE with mullioned windows (that lighting the house-body of six lights with king mullion) across the ground floor under a continuous dripmould stepped over doorway with flattened Tudor arch. The first floor raised and altered. To the W a timber-framed BARN, encased in stone in the C17. Five bays with truncated S aisle. Kingposts, raked struts, principal rafters and straight braces. At nearby MOSELEY FARM, the former BARN also has a S aisle (a timber felling date of 1659 is given) and kingpost roof, with braces from tie-beam to principal rafters and trenched purlins.

STONE HUT CIRCLE SETTLEMENT, Iveson Wood. The visible remains include two substantial hut circles between 40ft and

45ft diameter. The rubble walls of the hut circles survive to a
width of 10ft and a height of 2ft.

FAR HEADINGLEY

Far Headingley was part of the holdings of Kirkstall Abbey and
the site of one of its granges. The monastic estate was sold after
the Dissolution to the Foxcroft family (*see* also Weetwood) and
later acquired by the Wades, who created a country estate around
their house. The village was separated from Headingley to the S
by Headingley Moor and had its own chapel, on the site of the
present church. With the enclosure of the moor in 1829 cottages
spread N until eventually there was a mix of terraces and larger
villas.

ST CHAD, Otley Road. A big church with a tall nave, aisles and
very handsome W tower of three stages with Dec windows,
clock and three belfry openings. The slender, finely proportioned spire has diaper-patterned bands. Built in 1868, paid for
by the Becketts of Kirkstall Grange who offered the land with
£10,000. Designed by *Edmund Beckett Denison* (later Lord
Grimthorpe, now usually remembered for his drastic restoration of St Alban's Cathedral in 1879) but largely executed by
W. H. Crossland. The chancel, continuing the line of the nave
roof unbroken, is of 1909–11 by *J. Harold Gibbons*, in the tough
unmoulded style of his master Temple Moore. It replaced a
polygonal apse of French Gothic inspiration and incorporates
a Lady Chapel (N) and organ chamber (S). E wall divided into
two panels by a pilaster, the window set high between buttresses. Rich interior, immensely long, the nave, choir and
chancel each distinguished by differing roof treatments – the
nave with exposed trusses, the ribs in the choir continued as
shafts and the chancel with thin decorative ribs – yet preserving the essential unity. Arcades of circular columns support
narrow arches with lush carving, the bossy Dec-style foliage
on the capitals inspired by Selby Abbey choir and the Percy
Shrine at Beverley. Narrow aisles with moulded stone trusses.
A tall arch with four orders leads to the tower baptistery with
mosaic paving of 1896. The clerestory windows have Gothick
glazing bars.
   The originality of Gibbons's detailing is striking. A favourite
motif is the shouldered arch, used in the wall passage that runs
at high level below the E window behind the reredos and in the
curious pierced piers (each adorned with a small carved lizard)
that divide the Lady Chapel from the nave. The Lady Chapel,
with a vaulted stone ceiling above the sanctuary and internal
arcading to the small N windows, is lined with plain painted
panelling and displays an innovative handling of Gothic forms.
Extremely tall circular piers on the S side of the choir aisle. –
Magnificent wooden REREDOS by *Gibbons*, executed by
Boulton & Sons, perhaps even surpassing that of Temple Moore

at St Michael, Headingley. Heavily gilded with a blue background, it depicts incidents from the Book of Revelation. At its centre, God in Majesty with adoring figures at His feet in deep relief, set within an ogee-shaped frame with an exquisite traceried canopy. Four panels below with the symbols of the Evangelists. On the outermost parts, the leaves of the vine mingled with grotesque figures. – PULPIT. Timber, octagonal with carving of St Chad holding a model of a church. – CHOIR STALLS with much carved foliage. – FONT. Sandstone with short clustered columns, the bowl carved with flowers. – Three MOSAICS from the former reredos of 1887 by a *Signor Capello*, re-erected at the NE end of the choir aisle, depict the Crucifixion on a plain gold background. – STAINED GLASS. E window (The Redemption of Creation) in Arts and Crafts style of 1922 by *Margaret Rope* provides a glorious counterpoint to the reredos below. Of five lights with Adam and Eve in the centre, a variety of animals both domestic and exotic, and a deep blue expressing chaos at its base. – More excellent glass in the chancel and the chancel clerestory, including figures of saints by *Hardman* of 1871–7, taken from the old chancel. – In the S aisle from the E: one by *Hardman & Co.*, 1886, two windows of 1900 and 1908 by *Kayll & Co.*, one by *Clayton & Bell* of 1882. S and N aisle W windows by *Powell & Sons* 1904. By the same firm, the S aisle fifth from E and the N chapel N window, both 1917.

ST OSWALD, Highbury Mount. A small brick mission church of 1889–90 by *Smith & Tweedale*, extended W by two bays and with a N aisle in 1900.

Former HOLLIN LANE SCHOOL. 1839–40, Neo-Tudor style, extended in 1872.

COTTAGE ROAD CINEMA. The former Headingley Picture House, converted from a motor garage in 1912. Refronted in the 1930s. Wood-panelled interior.

WATERWORKS, Otley Road. Filtration beds were excavated E of Otley Road from 1837 by the Leeds Waterworks Co. W of the road in Church Wood Avenue is the quirky Gothic former METER HOUSE, built *c.* 1905 when further beds were created (now built over).

In OTLEY ROAD, ST CHAD'S GARDENS (Nos. 114–120, E side) is a group of four Dutch-gabled brick and faience villas of 1885, built to display the products of Wilcock & Co.'s Burmantofts pottery, whose proprietor James Holroyd lived in Headingley. Corner brackets with dragons and griffins and moulded stringcourses, probably the work of *Maurice B. Adams*. ¼ m. E off Moor Road is CASTLE GROVE, a plain three-bay house of 1831–4, much embellished *c.* 1870 (a porch, bay windows and rear wings) and 1896 by *T. Butler Wilson* who added wings, an Italianate tower and a great copper dome over the staircase. Inside, this is coffered with coloured glass in the top light; circular windows with elaborate plaster cornucopias and masks. Double-height saloon with gallery on Ionic piers, a coffered ceiling and big fireplace in C17 style. The room l. of the entrance has a heavy plaster ceiling with terms and a massive timber chimneypiece, that to the r. is in early C18 style. Another ornate ceiling in the panelled and screened billiard room.

SPENFIELD, Otley Road, E side, ½ m. N of St Chad. Built 1875–7 by *George Corson* for James Walter Oxley, banker, whose father lived nearby at Weetwood. Concealed within a severe, vaguely Gothic, exterior is one of the most opulent and best-preserved expressions of Victorian *haut bourgeois* taste in the North. A grand, top-lit and galleried staircase hall runs from front to back, with Byzantine-style arcades (cf. Corson's Central Library, p. 418) and a stained-glass window depicting birds, domestic and sporting scenes in a C17 style. The dining room (r.) has a mirrored buffet and intensely compartmentalized ceiling painted with fruits on a gold ground. The drawing room (l.), redecorated by Corson and *George Armitage* in 1888, is an outstanding expression of Aesthetic Movement taste – luxuriant foliate frieze, peacock-coloured stained glass and peacock tail overmantel, and marquetry wall panelling incorporating *Morris & Co.* fabric and shelves and cabinets for Oxley's collection of European and Oriental *objets d'art* (much of which proved to be fake after he bequeathed it to the City). N of the entrance front a big billiard room, added 1890, reached from a columned and rib-vaulted gallery intended for a collection of sculpture and antiquities.

Beckett Park (Leeds Metropolitan University)
West of St Chad

An extensive residential campus, developed in the grounds of KIRKSTALL GRANGE, which survives at the SW entrance off St Chad's Drive. The present house is that rebuilt in 1752 by *James Paine* for Walter Wade; in the C19 it became the home of the Beckett family. An early example of the 'villa with wings' although the r. wing has been demolished. The source appears to be a design by Colen Campbell in *Vitruvius Britannicus* (vol. III, plate 29), itself based on Palladio's Villa Pisani, Montagnana. Main block of three bays with a giant dentilled pediment across the entire width. Centre bay slightly recessed with a semicircular arch breaking the base of the pediment. First-floor windows have pediments and splayed surrounds. The surviving wing echoes this composition on a smaller scale. Bay windows added *c.* 1890 by *Chorley & Connon* who also enclosed the porch. Top-lit main stair in the centre of the building, the staircase hall octagonal (cf. the central saloon at Chiswick House). Stairs and first-floor gallery with bow-fronted iron balustrades. Some original plasterwork here, elsewhere late C19 Rococo-style ceilings.

The Becketts sold part of their estate to Leeds Corporation for its Training College, begun in 1911. The buildings of the

CAMPUS are by *G. W. Atkinson*. Impressively formal layout with the main building (James Graham Hall) facing a rectangular green. Lifeless 350-ft (107-metre) frontage with central part raised and brought forward with a pediment above four Corinthian columns *in antis*. Segmental pediments to the raised end pavilions. Paired pilasters on the upper floors. It was planned with a central hall flanked by two quadrangles. E and W of the green are Neo-Georgian residential blocks, each of three storeys with wings at the rear. Cavendish House is a later addition of 1915 by *Sydney Kitson*.

The E part of the park was sold off for suburban housing, but the W part became a public park. Here in Queen's Wood is the VICTORIA ARCH, probably of 1766 but altered in 1858 to commemorate Queen Victoria's opening of the Town Hall. Possibly built as an eyecatcher, it has four giant Ionic columns supporting a pediment. The frieze of glazed tiles is later. A tiny picturesque Tudor LODGE of *c.* 1830 marks the entrance to the park from the Otley Road at St Chad's Drive.

HEADINGLEY

Part of the estate of Kirkstall Abbey, which was bought up by the Savile family after the Dissolution. In the C17 it had huddles of cottages and Headingley Hall, but more houses were built on the S-facing slopes of Headingley Hill after the opening of the Otley–Leeds Turnpike in 1754 (now Headingley Lane). 'In no village in the parish are the effects of the prosperity of Leeds more visible than in Headingley, Chapeltown only excepted,' wrote the Leeds historian Edward Parsons in 1834. Suburban development accelerated soon after this until the area between Headingley Lane and Woodhouse Ridge was filled with villas, many of them of considerable architectural distinction. Exclusivity was preserved by tightly drawn restrictive covenants, making Headingley the prime residential area of Leeds. Smart development also took place to the W along Cardigan Road but by the late C19 a social division had grown up S of Headingley Lane below which grand houses would not sell. In their place came modest but respectable terraced housing, including some back-to-backs. Superior development continued instead northwards, extending towards Far Headingley (q.v.). The expansion of the Leeds universities at the end of the C20 has led to the building of student residences and the conversion of much housing to student digs but this has not affected the appeal of the narrow, thickly wooded roads between Headingley Lane and the Ridge, which still look much as they did in the paintings of Atkinson Grimshaw from the 1870s.

Churches

ST MICHAEL AND ALL ANGELS, Headingley Lane. 1884–6 by *J. L. Pearson*, assisted by *C. R. Chorley*. Built on the site of the

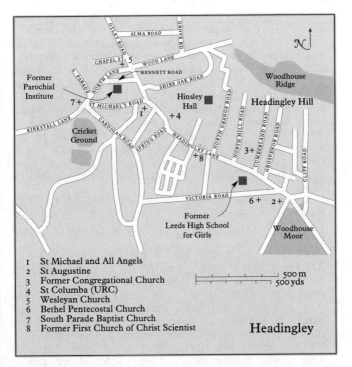

Headingley

1 St Michael and All Angels
2 St Augustine
3 Former Congregational Church
4 St Columba (URC)
5 Wesleyan Church
6 Bethel Pentecostal Church
7 South Parade Baptist Church
8 Former First Church of Christ Scientist

chapel of ease of 1626 (rebuilt by *Chantrell*, 1837). A typically proud and prosperous church for the suburb, in the C13 Gothic perfected by Pearson at Truro. Of cruciform plan, with nave and chancel of equal length, transepts and a thin 200-ft (61-metre) w tower, embraced by the aisles, and broach spire with tall octagonal pinnacles at the angles (completed in 1890, its design reminiscent of the twin towers of Pearson's original scheme for Truro). Large clerestorey, single lancets to the chancel and pairs to the nave. Two rows of triple lancets at the E end. The N porch (added 1890) has five carved figures by *Thomas Earp* of Christ flanked by SS Peter and Paul (l.) and Daniel and Isaiah (r.).

Spacious interior of dramatic height. Nave of three bays with plain circular piers to the arcades that have attached wall-shafts carrying the pointed transverse arches which support the flat timber roof, a device later employed by Pearson at St John, Redhill, Surrey, and All Saints, Hove, Sussex. These handsome but sober arches also frame the crossing and chancel. – Painted ALTAR by *Hardman & Co.*, 1891. The extravagant gilded and carved wooden REREDOS is of 1905 by *Temple Moore*. Christ in Glory flanked by St George and St Michael and eighteen figures influential in the history of the Church in the North of England, set in canopied niches. CHANCEL SCREEN of 1891–2 by *Pearson*. – TRIPTYCH in the Lady Chapel by *Pearson*, added in 1897. – FONT, octagonal, alabaster, carved with panels of biblical scenes. – PULPIT, alabaster and marble, richly carved with figures in arcaded niches, on short granite columns. – LECTERN by *Pearson*. – ORGAN CASE of 1890 by Pearson also. – SCULPTURE of Virgin and Child in the Lady Chapel and SCREEN enclosing the children's corner by *Robert Thompson*. – STAINED GLASS. – Some N and S aisle windows were reused from the previous church. – E and W windows of 1886 by *J.H. Powell* for *John Hardman & Co.*, and three more by this combination in the Lady Chapel, of 1887–8. – N aisle, first to third from E by *Wailes (& Strang)*, 1866–89. S aisle fourth from E, 1886 by *T.W. Camm* for *Winfield & Co.* – Porch windows by *Hardman*, 1890.

Next to the church, on the corner of St Michael's Lane, the former Headingley NATIONAL SCHOOL of 1834, in the usual Gothic with a pretty bellcote, extended by *Chorley & Connon* in 1889 and 1893.

ST AUGUSTINE, Hyde Park Terrace. A big church of 1870–1 by *J.B. Fraser* with a 186-ft (57-metre) tall SE tower and spire, pierced pinnacles on the angles of the octagonal top stage, completed in 1878. Dec style with Geometrical tracery. It has N and S chapels in the position of transepts but these are roofed parallel to the nave to allow the clerestory lancets to run through from the chancel to the W end. Well-preserved interior. Five-bay arcades with label stops of carved heads of apostles with shields bearing their emblems. Polished red granite columns, excellent carving of leaves of hawthorn, ivy, etc. on the capitals. Impressive clustered columns at the junction of the transepts and the chancel arch responds, the latter of polished granite. Tall chancel arch on short black marble shafts, angel capitals. Trussed spur roofs, that in the chancel boarded with bosses. – REREDOS. 1882, probably by *Fraser*, of pink veined marble, mosaic of the Last Supper in the centre, canopies above and flanked by panels with biblical passages. – ALTAR of cedar, richly decorated, arcaded with grouped ebony shafts. – PULPIT executed by *Charles Mawer*, in Caen stone, square with two marble shafts on dark serpentine and Irish green marble bases. Three circular mosaics on a gold background with richly diapered spandrels by *Simpson*. – FONT, carved with angels holding crosses, texts, etc., also by *Mawer*. – Early C20 Arts and Crafts electric LIGHT FITTINGS, brass orbs from which extend pendants with leaf-form decoration on square plaques. – STAINED GLASS. Five-light E window, the Doctrine of the Atonement, by *Kempe*, 1883. – Two windows in the S transept of 1900 by *Powell Bros.*, two in the N transept by *Kayll & Co.*, 1909.

HEADINGLEY HILL CONGREGATIONAL CHURCH (former), Headingley Lane and Cumberland Road. 1864–6 by *Cuthbert Brodrick*, his only church. Superficially conventional with a SW tower but with characteristically original detail. Elevated for impact above a basement with six prominent gabled bays on the N and S sides, each with a tall two-light window within a pointed head and buttresses topped by a crouching beast. The W front has a double-pointed-arch doorway under a gable enriched with carved rosettes. The capitals, on red sandstone colonettes, are described by Derek Linstrum as 'a sort of Gothic Corinthian'. Topping the tower is a spire of obelisk form, pierced with the architect's favourite rosette motifs. Converted to offices in 1981, now once more in use as a church.

ST COLUMBA UNITED REFORMED CHURCH, Headingley Lane. 1964–6 by *W. & J. A. Tocher*. A striking composition, on sloping ground, of church and hall joined on the S side by a curving, almost continuously glazed link (containing meeting rooms), cantilevered above car parking on canted concrete piers. The brickwork of the E end comes to a sharp prow, a point echoed in the deep overhangs of the multi-gabled roof. Slender W tower rising from a broad porch. Clerestory-lit interior with a flexible layout. Some FITTINGS and PLAQUES from *Brodrick*'s Headingley Hill Congregational Church (*see* above). – STAINED GLASS in the E window from Cavendish Road Presbyterian Church (1878 by *J. B. Fraser*).

WESLEYAN CHURCH, Otley Road. 1844–5, probably by *James Simpson*. The first Methodist chapel in Leeds built in the Gothic style. Transepts, side galleries and an apse of 1862. – A SUNDAY SCHOOL, opened in 1857, was rebuilt in Chapel Street in 1908–9.

BETHEL PENTECOSTAL CHURCH, Victoria Road. Former Free Methodist Chapel. 1885–6 by *W. S. Braithwaite*. A Gothic insertion into a classical terrace. Tall gable with a large W window with Geometrical tracery flanked by smaller two-light windows. Thin tower with a narrow pediment, and spirelet with conical top. Clerestory with timber quatrefoil openings. Internally, iron columns and galleries on three sides with a curving front. Sunday School and classrooms below.

SOUTH PARADE BAPTIST CHURCH. The Sunday Schools, on the corner of South Parade and Water Grove, were built first, by *Percy Robinson*, 1909. Late Gothic style with a low tower intended to link to the church. This followed in 1925–7, designed by *Jones & Stocks*, in a freer Gothic, with transepts. Ribbed plaster ceiling, E end with oak wainscotting and rostrum, this on marble piers. Reordered in 1999 by *Robert West*, including a glazed S narthex.

FIRST CHURCH OF CHRIST SCIENTIST (former), Headingley Lane, 1912 by *William Peel Schofield*. The school to the r. was constructed first, the church followed in 1932. A low Portland stone block sparsely decorated with Egyptian pilasters. The porch projects slightly and is surmounted by an urn.

Public Buildings

DEVONSHIRE HALL (University of Leeds) and LEEDS GIRLS'
HIGH SCHOOL (former). *See* Perambulation b.

HINSLEY HALL (Conference Centre), off Headingley Lane.
1867 by *Wilson & Willcox* of Bath as Wesley College. Gothic.
Low, a little starved, and symmetrical, with a middle tower
with a large and prominent conical roof. Geometric tracery in
the ground-floor windows, on the upper floor steeply gabled
windows rising into the roof. Enlarged behind in 1902 by
Danby & Simpson with a tutor's house and CHAPEL in Perp
style. Refurbished 1998–9 by *Abbey Holford Rowe* who added a
top-lit octagonal chapel with ashlar walls.

HEADINGLEY HOME FOR GIRLS (former), Cliff Road. 1873 by
W. H. Thorp, with additions of 1876. Symmetrical brick front
with projecting wings at each end, porches with pointed arches,
and blue diapering.

PAROCHIAL INSTITUTE (former), Bennett Road. 1883–4 by
George Corson. Heavy and ornate porch which has short
columns with naturalistic foliage and a dramatic sculpted panel
of St George defeating the dragon on the front, royal arms to
the side. Asymmetrical twin gable façade, the smaller to the l.
projecting forward with a quatrefoil window, the larger with a
big five-light traceried window. The hall has a tunnel-vault with
decorative wrought-iron trusses.

HEADINGLEY CRICKET GROUND, North Lane. Established
1888. Headquarters of the Yorkshire Cricket Club since 1903.
Construction of a new pavilion by *Alsop Architects* was due to
commence in 2009. – The SIR LEONARD HUTTON
MEMORIAL GATES by *Chrysalis Arts Ltd.*, 2001, depict scenes
from his life.

Perambulations

a. The centre of Headingley

The principal ornament of the centre of Headingley is St Michael
(*see* above) at the N end of HEADINGLEY LANE. Opposite, in the
middle of the road junction, is the WAR MEMORIAL by *Sydney
Kitson*, 1922. Further N on the E side the former YORKSHIRE
BANK of *c.* 1932 by *Chorley, Gribbon & Foggitt*, classical in red
brick and Portland stone, and the HSBC BANK, 1913–14 by
Kitson, ashlar-fronted with pilasters and a secondary order of
attached Doric columns. E along SHIRE OAK ROAD is HEAD-
INGLEY HALL, erected *c.* 1795, although the house was in existence by 1649 when John Killingbeck, Mayor of Leeds, set his
initials in an archway. Enlarged in the 1830s and again in the
1880s when a billiard room and a two-storey bay window were
added. Otherwise a plain exterior with coped gables and kneelers. Shire Oak Road was laid out with half-acre plots in 1885–6
by *George Corson*, with the intention that purchasers would put
up houses to his design. Development was slow and several of
the houses are by other hands, including Neo-Georgian SHIRE

OAK DENE (Nos. 4–6, s side), by *F. W. Bedford*, 1894, an urbane pair designed to look like one large house with a central doorway and two-storey bay windows. Next is an hotel, formerly Bellamona and Ravenstone, of the mid 1880s by *Corson* with applied half-timbering and corner turrets. The most impressive house is ARNCLIFFE also by *Bedford*, designed for his brother, 1892–4. An early example of the butterfly plan, with a central hall flanked by a dining room and a drawing room, the stairs behind the hall and a service wing to the rear. Its style is broadly C17 Flemish with mullioned-and-transomed windows and a little strapwork decoration. The interior retains its fireplaces and panelling and has plasterwork by *George Bankart*, including one ceiling loosely based on the Plantin House, Antwerp. A charming summerhouse with conical roof and Venetian window survives from the former Dutch garden.

REDHILL (No. 33, N side) was built 1900–1 by *Bedford & Kitson* for Joseph Nicholson, with additions by *Kitson* of 1911 for Edward Audus Hirst. Tile-hung and half-timbered, a particularly successful rendering of Shaw's Old English style. Nicely balanced garden front with two tiled gables and a much larger projecting half-timbered one. Inside, an Art Nouveau chimneypiece and stained glass by *George Walton*.

In WOOD LANE to the N several large houses, including ST IVES (s side), Gothic of 1869 by *Corson*, and on GROVE ROAD, turning N, ASHFIELD, a tall 1860s Italianate house, possibly by *Brodrick*, with large eaves brackets and a semicircular window; the porch, with its paired square columns joined by a central band, exhibits his characteristic tough detailing.

On the corner of Grove Road with ALMA ROAD, WHEAT-FIELD LODGE is an 1880s Italianate house with unusual additions of 1892 by *T. Butler Wilson*, including a bow window and two towers that bulge out from the retaining wall to Alma Road. Ionic screen in the principal ground-floor room, first-floor screen of coupled Tuscan marble columns. Wilson's impressive stables have rusticated banding, modillion eaves and semicircular fan-lights above each window. Further w along Alma Road, set back on the N side, is MOORFIELD COURT of 1855–6, built for William Joy, a chemical manufacturer. Large Gothic mansion with an octagonal three-storey tower with octagonal corner turrets, and a spire above the entrance bay. The decoration is sumptuous. Inside, the hall with cusped arches on polished granite columns, panelled rooms with pendant ceilings and a vaulted octagonal chapel. No. 9 of *c.* 1860 is broadly classical, its façade with four wide pilasters, the windows round-headed and paired under seg-mental mouldings. The oversized detailing suggests the hand of *Brodrick:* he was the architect of OAKFIELD (No. 7, now Bro-drick Court), an idiosyncratic Neo-Grecian design of 1859, three bays wide topped by a pediment with a circular window extend-ing the full length of the façade with exaggeratedly overhanging eaves on large coupled brackets.

OTLEY ROAD is the continuation N of Headingley Lane. s is the repellent ARNDALE CENTRE (1965) but on the w side is the

Wesleyan Church (*see* above) surrounded by an interesting group of mid-C19 workers' housing. The semi-detached Neo-Tudor ALMA COTTAGES are *c.* 1860s and have some grand outside privies, in blocks of two with crenellated parapets. Then Nos. 1–9 CHAPEL TERRACE and Nos. 1–8 CHAPEL SQUARE, two stone terraces of *c.* 1850 back-to-backs linked at right angles. These retain Georgian proportions. More through terraces in similar style nearby. On NORTH LANE stands the Neo-Jacobean former PUMPING STATION of 1860 (extended 1866 and 1879; now a pub), with behind it in Bennett Road the former Parochial Institute (*see* above). Further on the former LOUNGE CINEMA, built in 1916 by *C.C. Chadwick* & *William Watson*, has a long street façade with much faience, extended N *c.* 2000 with a sweeping parabolic glass front. S, in ST MICHAEL'S ROAD, two elegant small 1830s houses (Nos. 76 and 78) with Neoclassical porches and margin lights (cf. Harrogate Road, Chapel Allerton).

The area SE of the Cricket Ground (*see* Public Buildings) along CARDIGAN ROAD was the site of the short-lived LEEDS ZOOLOGICAL AND BOTANICAL GARDENS, which opened in 1840 but failed by 1848. The gardens, designed by *William Billington*, a Wakefield engineer, and *Edward Davies*, landscape gardener, were surrounded by a high stone wall, part of which survives near the junction with Chapel Lane. By 1893 high-quality mansions covered the Botanical Gardens Estate, beginning in 1868 with MANOR COURT (No. 43 Cardigan Road, originally Clareville) by *Corson*, a heavy design with round-headed dormers, much brick cogging, and stumpy columns to the porch. On the W side CARDIGAN HOUSE (No. 84), 1870 by *Edward Birchall*, is larger with a corner turret resting on a massive shaft and quatrefoils in the staircase window. By contrast, Nos. 49–51 (originally The Old Gardens, now flats and much extended) by *F.W. Bedford* of 1893 is in the tile-hung Old English style. Designed to look like a single house and completely asymmetrical with a large end chimney and two big gables that are slightly jettied. Next on the E side is the former BEAR PIT of the zoo, constructed of large rusticated blocks with two circular castellated viewing turrets. The circular pit had a gateway in the form of a Serlian arch and cages in the basement, reputedly for eagles. Then two more striking mansions of 1894, almost identical and both with tall central towers: SANDHOLME HOUSE (No. 114) and LEEFIELD HOUSE (No. 116) by *Daniel Dodgson* who had carried out much work for their owners, the speculative builders Benjamin and William Walmsley.

Return to the centre of Headingley along SPRING ROAD. On the r., by the junction with Headingley Lane, is SPRING BANK of *c.* 1857 by *John Fox* for Robert Ellershaw. Large with shaped gables of C17 type. Enlarged in 1877–8 by *C.R. Chorley* for Sir James Kitson (cf. Elmete Hall, Roundhay) and, after Kitson had moved to Gledhow Hall (*see* below), by *William Thorp* who added the l. half of the garden front in 1885–6. Across Headingley Lane the United Reformed Church (*see* above) and then, hidden down a long drive and announced by a Gothic lodge of 1866, HEADINGLEY CASTLE of 1843–6, the largest of *John Child*'s Tudor-

Gothic houses. Now flats. Symmetrical with a three-storey tower whose octagonal corner buttresses transmute into panelled turrets on the upper storey. Battlemented throughout. Central porte cochère, an oriel window above. An octagonal rib-vaulted entrance hall with a big central pendant and niches sets the tone for the restrained Gothic detailing of the interior. It leads to a lantern-lit staircase hall rising the full height of the house. Fire-proofed basement of brick vaults sprung from cast-iron I-beams.

b. Headingley Hill

A perambulation can begin at St Augustine, s of which, at the edge of Woodhouse Moor, is a bronze STATUE of Sir Robert Peel by *William Behnes*, 1852, originally erected outside the Court House (dem.) in Park Row. NE of the church on HEADINGLEY LANE, s side, is ROSE COURT, a fine five-bay house of c. 1842 by *John Clark*. Its central bay is brought forward with a broad tetrastyle portico with a pediment on Tuscan columns. The s (garden) elevation has its entrance recessed behind four Tuscan columns *in antis*. Equally elegant interior with a tiled circular staircase hall (cf. Clark's Little Woodhouse Hall, p. 478) with attached Corinthian columns and pilasters and a vaulted ceiling. The octagonal ground-floor central room also has a vault, and niches. Music room l. with excellent plaster decoration to the paired composite order pilasters, a frieze of putti with lyres and a coved and panelled ceiling; another good frieze in the r. room. The house was later occupied by the Leeds Girls' High School (now at Alwoodley), and behind is the impressive Neo-Georgian former SCHOOL BUILDINGS of 1905–6 by *Connon & Chorley* Planned around a central two-storey hall with galleries giving access to classrooms.

Across Headingley Lane is Headingley Hill, developed with a series of dead-end roads that are lined with C19 villas, set well back and partly hidden by the mature planting. The following is a selection from e to w. In GROSVENOR ROAD is GROSVENOR HOUSE, elegant Neoclassical of c. 1840, three bays with pilasters at the corners of the ground floor and a porch with fluted columns and anthemion capitals. Greek key decoration below the first-floor windows. At the top is HILLY RIDGE HOUSE of 1839, classical and plain. Between Grosvenor Road and Cumberland Road is HEADINGLEY TERRACE, a group of five three-bay houses of the 1840s, the end and centre houses brought forward and gabled. CUMBERLAND ROAD begins with Brodrick's Con-gregational church (*see* above) and next to it, ASHWOOD VILLAS, a planned development of semi-detached and terraced villas, c. 1870 and mainly Gothic. Then, further up on the e side, two contrasting villas (ELMFIELD and SPRING HILL), the first debased and asymmetrical classical, the second Gothic, but both of 1846 by *Thomas Shaw* – a graphic illustration of his eclecti-cism. Facing is DEVONSHIRE HALL (Leeds University), created from Regent Villas, two pairs of mid-C19 semi-detached houses.

The w pair (now Old Hall) have a fine interior, possibly by *John Child*. Behind is the former gatehouse which has a large rounded arch topped by a pierced parapet and a pair of single-storey wings whose eaves cornice extends to form imposts to the central arch. The houses are now incorporated within a formal arrangement of 1928 by *J.C. Procter & F.L. Charlton*, with a tall central hall and three-storey residential wings extending around a courtyard, rendered above a stone ground floor. The hall has a two-storey oriel that rises above a balustraded parapet to form a crenellated clock tower. The wings have an arcaded ground floor with four-centred arches. Just beyond, CUMBERLAND PRIORY, a small and pretty Gothic house of *c.* 1841, probably by *John Child* for himself. Projecting central gabled bay with an oriel.

Two of the finest villas on Headingley Hill are best seen from NORTH HILL ROAD to the w. First, ASHWOOD (No. 48 Headingley Lane, now Hilton Court), of *c.* 1836 for Joseph Austin, probably by *John Child*, classical in form, but with traceried windows, some in large canted bays, dripmoulds and tall grouped octagonal chimneys. Next door, HEADINGLEY HILL HOUSE, of similar date, a symmetrical Greek villa with two projecting bays flanking an Ionic porch and a balustraded balcony above. It closely resembles a design in Francis Goodwin's *Domestic Architecture* (1833–4). North Hill Road itself showcases the two principal phases of Headingley Hill's development. Some building took place in the 1830s e.g. HOLMFIELD (W side), a rambling Tudor villa of 1835 with an oriel and timber porch with cusped lights. The best houses followed the purchase of land in 1897 by Norris Hepworth, the clothing manufacturer. Nos. 3–5 are probably by *Bedford & Kitson*, tile-hung with big half-timbered projecting gabled bays in the Shaw style. *Bedford & Kitson* also designed LINCOMBE (No. 7) for H. M. Hepworth in 1898–9. The house is clearly influenced by Voysey in the use of roughcast surfaces, windows with leaded lights and ashlar mullions, iron eaves brackets and dormers in the hipped roof. But it is boxy, lacking the low, rooted look of the best of Voysey's work. Interior with simple timber fire surrounds with tiled inserts and much white timber panelling. Divided into flats in 2001 with a highly sympathetic rebuilding of the coachhouse by *David Cook* of *C.R.L. Architects*. Another *Bedford & Kitson* house is HIGHGARTH (No. 9), a simpler roughcast Arts and Crafts essay of 1901–2 with plain timber mullions. No. 17, an early C19 picturesque Tudor villa, is twin gabled and has an embattled parapet.

At the top of North Hill Road turn l. past numerous blocks of student accommodation in James Baillie Park to join NORTH GRANGE MOUNT. What catches the eye is the NORTH HILL HOUSE (E side), a strikingly original Neo-Gothic design built for William Walker in 1846, now in a bad way. Symmetrical, its predominant motif is the pair of very broad five-light full-height bay windows with Perp tracery over each light, the ground floor given a double dose with heavily cusped quatrefoil top lights. The windows are tall, the lower ones extending almost to the ground.

115

Equally extravagant is the entrance, slightly projecting with a four-centred arch below a panel of contorted tracery, flanked by pilasters which rise to become pinnacles. A castellated parapet completes the composition. Inside, the hall and one of the main ground-floor rooms have friezes of pointed arch arcading. A panelled billiard room was added by *S.E. Smith* in 1881. The rest of the street was developed *c.* 1910 by Robert Wood with semi-detached houses but at the top of the hill is a block of mansion flats, GRANGE COURT by *Joseph J. Wood*, 1911–12, the first of its kind in Leeds and unusual for the suburbs. Symmetrical with projecting wings, four storeys to the front and five to the rear, where the site slopes downhill. Red brick, with rendered top floor and quoins; floors of Hennebique concrete. Principal entrance in ashlar inscribed RW and PARUM SUFFICIT ('A little is enough'). Balconies run across the façade on elegant curved brackets, above the windows jolly plaster decoration of birds and fruit. Most flats have two or three bedrooms, the basement had communal dining and recreation rooms together with caretaker's and maid's flats. A further block of 1923 in slightly simplified style to the E.

Finally down NORTH GRANGE ROAD which has more early C19 Neoclassical villas and on the w side, LYNDHURST (No. 13) of 1887 by *Chorley & Connon*, with an irregular half-timbered front, moulded brick window surrounds, and angled porch. Back on HEADINGLEY LANE (s side) are BUCKINGHAM VILLAS, a particularly large and ornate Gothic pair of 1870 by *S.E. Smith*, and w of Buckingham Road, BUCKINGHAM HOUSE, substantial and elegant Neo-Grecian villa of *c.* 1840, and the former FIRST CHURCH OF CHRIST SCIENTIST (*see* above).

HYDE PARK

The area, w of Woodhouse Moor, historically part of the Cardigan estate (cf. Burley) and much built over from the 1860s with churches, schools and back-to-back houses, e.g. the toast rack of nine tight E–W streets built by 1881 either side of Thornville Road, known collectively as THE HAROLDS. They have the standard blocks of eight dictated by the 1866 Leeds Improvement Act.

ALL HALLOWS, Regent Terrace. 1970 by *Peter Brown* of *Castelow & Partners*. A fire destroyed the previous church (1886 by *Kelly & Birchall*). Stone-faced, with an irregular plan, recently extended. Sparse interior. LIGHT FITTINGS and STAINED GLASS by *Frank Roper*. The old VICARAGE of 1903–4 by *Bedford & Kitson* remains, in use as a night shelter.

ST AUGUSTINE. *See* Headingley.

ST MARGARET, Cardigan Road. Designed 1901, by *Temple Moore*, built 1907–9 in a reduced form and completed at the w end by *George Pace*, 1963–4. Conceived intellectually with a southern sibling, All Saints, Tooting Graveney, London. An austerely imposing mission church in a poor neighbourhood, even without the vast W tower originally envisaged. Transitional style with lancets. Nave and chancel in one, the aisles with four cross-gables and a clerestory, all in hard red brick with some stone dressing. Pace's façade is starker still, with a brutal porch, rising to two storeys at the sides and a cluster of tall narrow square-headed windows with concrete mullions and transoms. Magnificent, wholly convincing interior stripped of the frivolous, with soaring brick and timber rib-vaults rendered in imitation of creamy stone. The broad nave has massive circular stone piers and double aisles with transverse tunnel vaults springing from slender quatrefoils piers. Beneath the aisle lancets a plain round-arched arcade set into the aisle walls. No chancel division, tiered lancets in the E wall. – STAINED GLASS. E lancet (the Crucifixion) by *Victor Milner*, 1913.

OUR LADY OF LOURDES (R.C.), Cardigan Road. Large and unprepossessing Jesuit church, developed from a brick hall of 1926 by *J. Armstrong* (completed in 1930 by *Edward Simpson & Son*). Venetian window at the front. Reordered in 1959 by *Derek Walker* of *Walker & Biggin* by reconstructing the E end. Nave and sanctuary are in one, with a barrel-vaulted ceiling and N and S of the sanctuary striking steel SCREENS projecting from the walls, with STAINED GLASS by *Roy Lewis*. They are set over a Lady Chapel (S) and doors to the presbytery (N). Also, low-relief modelling of angelic faces by *Jill Messenger* of Leeds. – BALDACHINO, a metal grid with many small lights.

HYDE PARK METHODIST MISSION, Hyde Park Road. 1976 by *James Thorp* of *Brooks Thorp Partners,* succeeding four C19 Methodist churches.* Brown brick exposed outside and in. The cubic worship space, with chamfered corners, is lit by a projecting feature with fins between the glazing. This is just the tallest element within a multi-purpose complex.

LEEDS GRAND MOSQUE, Woodsley Road. The former church of the Sacred Heart (R.C.), 1963–5 by *Derek Walker* (converted 1994). Brutalist. The glazed baptistery has been flanked by additions for its present use, a curved roof added to the sanctuary and the interior divided.

MAKKAH MASJID MOSQUE, Brudenell Road. 2003, the design by *Priest Woodward Associates* modified by *Atba Al-Samarraie* of *Archi-Structure*. Cream brick with bright red and blue polychromy. Two corner towers with minarets, a third minaret, taller and slimmer, at the E end; here also an open green dome. To Thornville Road a portico with glazed blue trim and four barley-sugar columns of cut brick. Prayer halls on each of three floors, with space for 3,000.

---

*They were: BELLE VUE PRIMITIVE METHODIST CHAPEL, 1872 By *Joseph Wright*, CARDIGAN ROAD PRIMITIVE METHODIST CHAPEL, 1894–5 by *T. & C. B. Howdill*, VENTNOR STREET METHODIST NEW CONNEXION, 1872–3 by *William Hill*, and WOODHOUSE MOOR WESLEYAN METHODIST CHAPEL, 1874–5 by *C. O. Ellison* and *G. F. Danby*.

SHREE HINDU MANDIR, Alexandra Road. By *Rajesh Sompura*, completed in 2001, and built by Indian craftsmen. It incorporates parts of a C19 stone building (probably a stable). On the N side an intricate carved mandapa (porch) with a sikhara (spire), and buttresses terminating in traditional chattri (small domed towers). Inside, against the W wall a riot of colour in the marble shrines.

ROYAL PARK PRIMARY SCHOOL, Queens Road. Board School by *William Landless*, 1892, and on the big scale adopted by that date. Symmetrical, red brick with pilasters, with a central hall flanked N and S by two-storey ranges each with big balustraded porches for the boys' and girls' entrances. Monstrous gateposts with rock-faced rustication provide an element of the sublime.

HYDE PARK PICTURE HOUSE, Brudenell Road. 1914 by *Thomas Winn & Sons*. Remarkably well preserved. Good corner site with a two-storey canted façade under a Dutch gable with ball finials, mostly brick with dressings of white Burmantofts 'Marmo' faience and open lower storey with attractive lettering in a frieze supported by free Ionic columns. Many original fittings and an auditorium still lit by gas 'modesty' lighting. The screen (concealed behind its modern successor) is painted onto the wall with a surround of gilded cherubs and swags. Art Deco panels at the rear of the balcony are later additions.

KIRKSTALL

There is no evidence for a medieval village at Kirkstall, only for the great Cistercian abbey, established in 1152, in the wooded Aire valley 3 m. upstream from Leeds. After the Dissolution, the extensive abbey lands at Kirkstall passed from Thomas Cranmer to Robert Savile of Howley, and in 1671 largely to the Brudenell family, later Earls of Cardigan, who remained the principal landowner until the late C19. However, the architect of its transformation was the other major landowner, Sir James Graham (1753–1825), M.P. for Carlisle. He not only modernized existing mills (including Abbey Mills) and built new ones, spending considerable sums improving the goit that ran from the Abbey Dam, but also erected houses for clothiers. Other employers included the Butlers and Beecrofts at Kirkstall Forge (*see* below). Communications were central to growth: two important ancient roads met at Kirkstall on their way to Leeds, those to Otley and to Bradford (across Kirkstall Bridge), and they were joined in the 1820 by a new turnpike to Guiseley (now the A65). The opening of the Leeds and Liverpool Canal and, in the 1840s, railway lines to Bradford and Thirsk were followed from the 1870s by trams to Leeds, horse-drawn at first, electric from 1897. Combined with the sale of the Cardigan estate in the 1890s, these finally transformed Kirkstall into a suburb, a process completed by the Corporation and the private builder in the C20.

KIRKSTALL ABBEY*

12   The Abbey was founded in 1147 at Barnoldswick in Craven by Cistercian monks and lay brothers from Fountains. Finding the place and its people inhospitable, in 1152 they obtained through the influence of their patron, the great magnate Henry de Lacy, an alternative secluded site in the Aire valley which they called Kirkstall. Their first dwellings here would have been of timber but these were soon replaced by the surviving buildings, constructed from local Bramley Fall gritstone and paid for by de Lacy. According to a late medieval account of the Abbey's foundation, the church and all the main buildings round the cloister were erected before the death of the first abbot, Alexander, in 1182. On the evidence of the structural sequence, it has been argued that the church itself had been completed by de Lacy's death in 1177. This campaign is an important exemplar of the Late Norman Transitional style. Later building campaigns were few in number and limited in scope. Some are assigned to the early C13, including the E part of the chapter house, the infirmary hall and the abbot's lodging. From the late C15 and early C16 date new kitchens, a reconstruction of the refectory and a new belfry on the church crossing. At its Dissolution in 1539 the community comprised an abbot and thirty monks. From that date the buildings and precinct were used for farming. The main losses have been the infirmary buildings to the SE and a whole series of ancillary buildings – barn, corn mill, malthouse, bakehouse, guesthouse – W of the abbey church. To safeguard the ruins from suburban growth, Colonel John North acquired the site from the Cardigan estate and gave it to the City Corporation. The fabric was repaired by *J. T. Micklethwaite* in 1890–5 and the precinct laid out as a public park. Further excavations were conducted between 1950 and 1964 of mainly the buildings S of the cloister and in the infirmary, and from 1979 to 1986 of the principal guesthouse. In 2006 *Purcell Miller Tritton* undertook further repairs to the fabric and created a new visitors' centre from the lay brothers' reredorter.

The only surviving medieval building N of the A65 is the C12 INNER GATEHOUSE, now incorporated in the ABBEY HOUSE MUSEUM. It was converted into a farmhouse after 1539 and much extended, notably in the 1830s when John Butler of Kirkstall Forge (*see* below) set about 'beautifying' the house, and in the early 1890s when Colonel T. Walter Harding introduced the Jacobethan-style interiors. The gateway itself is three bays deep and rib-vaulted. The arches to the N and S are round-headed and wide. Between the S and the middle bay is a division into a pointed arch for pedestrians and a wider round arch for horses and carts. Between this and the N bay is a wide pointed arch. The ribs have a tripartite roll moulding. There were evidently buildings on each side of the passage, as well as

---

*The account of Kirkstall Abbey is by Stuart Wrathmell, with additional information by Richard Pollard.

rooms above it. At the sw corner is a spiral staircase rebuilt in the C19.

Of all the Cistercian abbeys of England, Kirkstall is among those whose remaining buildings stand up highest. It requires little imagination to place roofs on the church and the monastic buildings around the cloister.

The ABBEY CHURCH is arranged according to the typical Cistercian plan: nave and aisles, transepts with, along their E sides, three straight-ended chapels each and a farther-projecting straight-ended presbytery. Like the church at Fountains, begun soon after 1150, the transept chapels are covered with pointed tunnel vaults, derived from the Romanesque architecture of Burgundy, but the chancel and aisles have pointed rib-vaulting, in which John Bilson* saw the native influence of Durham where such vaulting had been created as early as c. 1095.

The EXTERIOR of the church is for its date comparatively plain: broad flat buttresses and round-arched windows, their hood-moulds connected by a stringcourse. The nave and aisles are divided by the buttresses into eight bays. The presbytery is similarly divided into three bays, though the rib-vaulting inside is in two, and this has caused some scholars to argue that the rib-vaulting was a late innovation, once work was well advanced. The transept gables contain vesica windows. On the s transept gable (but not the N) the buttresses are linked by semicircular arches to form arcading, a feature repeated in the W and S cloister ranges. The few later openings include two aisle windows (in the third bay from the crossing on each side), transept chapel windows and the vast Perp E window of the presbytery. This replaced a large circular window with complex interlacing tracery and four flanking oculi, set above three tall round-headed windows. Perp tracery was also inserted in other C12 openings. The only additions to the C12 fabric are the square Perp gable turrets with tiers of paired blank miniature arches and pyramid roofs, and more obviously the partially preserved belfry stage of the TOWER, added by Abbot Marshall between 1509 and 1528 (that is, when Fountains also received its great N tower), with one large window on each side. The stage below has clear evidence of windows and of grooves for the original high-pitched roofs, showing that the C12 tower would have projected only a little above roof level, presumably in partial acknowledgement of the prohibition of stone bell-towers enacted by the Order's General Chapter in 1157. The additional weight of Marshall's belfry led to the collapse of the NW corner of the tower in 1779.

The most elaborate elevation is the W FRONT, with its pair of larger windows (with traces of later tracery and moulded arches of two orders carried originally by detached shafts) and an impressive PORTAL crowned by a gable, whose sides stand on wall-shafts. In the gable and above the portal proper are

*J. Bilson and W. H. St John Hope, *Architectural Description of Kirkstall Abbey*, 1907.

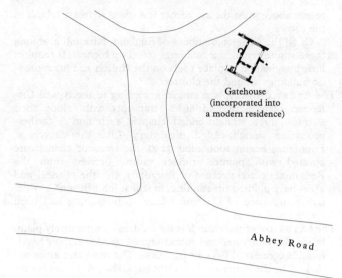

Gatehouse
(incorporated into
a modern residence)

Abbey Road

Great Chamber
with Solar over

Guest Hall

Pantry

Buttery

Stable

Yard

Cellar

Guest House

Outer
Court

Foundations of Bake House

Cellarer's Range
and
Laybrothers' Range

Reredorter of
Lay Brothers over

|————————————————————| 100 m
|————————————————————| 300 ft

Kirkstall Abbey.
Plan

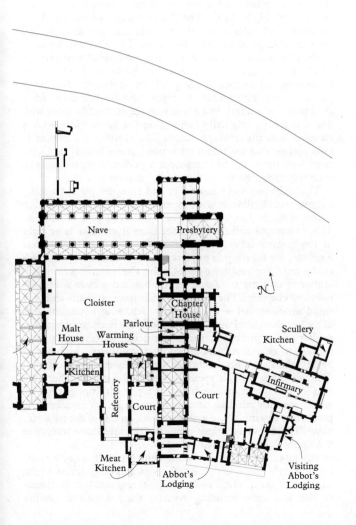

four intersecting blank arches. The portal is round-arched and
has five orders, whose capitals are many-scalloped, the arch
orders moulded except for the middle one which has zigzag at
right angles to the wall plane. Further important detail can be
found on a second, smaller but no less ornate doorway near
the W end of the N aisle wall, which has an opening framed by
a very large crenellation motif. Within that, the capitals of the
three orders are as before, the middle with zigzag likewise. The
doorway seems, from excavated foundations and from the scars
of walls to each side, to have provided access to the church
from a long, narrow porch or passage projecting N.

The INTERIOR is described from E to W. As at Fountains, all the
constructive arches are pointed, while all the minor ones (e.g.
for windows and doorways) are round. In the presbytery the
transverse arches and cross-ribs have a broad rectangular
section with big half-rolls. The N wall is bare but the S wall has
round-arched recesses for the piscina, sedilia and credence,
with mouldings of extreme simplicity. The SEDILIA niche is
flanked by shafts, and these have the many-scalloped capitals
which go on appearing throughout Kirkstall. Each of the
tunnel-vaulted chapels leading off the transepts also has a
piscina. The S transept has the night stairs leading down from
the monk's dormitory and a wall passage on the first floor with
heavy columns originally connecting the same place with a
chamber over the transept chapels. The crossing has extremely
lofty arches; that towards the E is much more heavily moulded
than the others. In the N transept a perfectly plain doorway,
probably giving access to the monks' cemetery.

The eight-bay NAVE has heavy and complex piers, basically
circular with shallow convex members and between them slim
shafts or fillets, but the details vary from one pair to another.
The E responds and the first three pairs from the E have eight
of the convex lobes with four shafts and four angle fillets
between, the fourth pair of piers has angle fillets only, the fifth
shafts only, the rest have lobes only. The capitals are many-
scalloped and the moulding of the pointed arches is of half-
rolls and chamfers. The clerestory walls have no shafts and only
small windows, below a nave roof which, as at Fountains, was
of timber. Also like Fountains, the aisles are in contrast vaulted,
similar to the presbytery vaults but here the rectangular projection is chamfered. The ribs and transverse arches rest
against the aisle walls on corbels with many-scalloped capitals.
Though these capitals recur throughout Kirkstall, there are
also in the church other interesting types with upright leaves,
and some with interlace ornament, which is also found on the
presbytery piscina, along with knotwork on one of the nave pier
bases. These may be minor echoes of the interlaced tracery in
the original presbytery rose window.

CONVENTUAL BUILDINGS: S of the church's W doorway was the
lay brother's range, with a small doorway giving access to the
CLOISTER garth. The cloister alleys have gone, but fragments
of the limestone arcading remain, their waterleaf capitals

proving that the arcades were built at the end of the initial construction phase, *c.* 1180. The arrangement of rooms around the cloister followed the Cistercian standard and is very similar to Fountains. At the E end of the N SIDE is the monks' doorway into the church, round-headed and of three orders with scalloped capitals. On the E SIDE, S of the transept, there is the arch of the book cupboard, then the library and vestry. After that follows the CHAPTER HOUSE. This is clearly the work of two periods, its W part of the later C12, its E part of the C13. The W part has one of the Cistercians' elaborate façades with, unusually, a pair of large entrance arches flanked by smaller pairs. All the arches are round, the capitals scalloped as usual. Inside, the W part is square with one central circular pier surrounded by eight detached shafts, and four rib-vaulted bays, in which the profile of some of the ribs are keeled. The E part is *c.* 1230 and has more elegant rib-mouldings that spring from very small corbels. In the E wall are two groups of three stepped lancets (restored with round heads), in the N and S walls pairs of pointed lancets. The walls of the rebuilt part are faced with a number of stone coffins, presumably disturbed during the works. Next is the PARLOUR, of the same period as the W part of the chapter house, then the original stairs to the monks' dormitory that ran over the whole of this range. Beyond is a passage that gave access to the infirmary and abbot's lodging (*see* below), and beyond that the MONKS' DAY ROOM of five bays, its unribbed groin-vault (collapsed 1824) once supported on scalloped corbels and a central row of circular pillars. Beyond this is the main drain above which stood the monks' reredorter, attached to the S end of their dormitory.

In the S CLOISTER RANGE the E doorway is C13 and marks a modified entrance to the dorter stairs. It was cut into the corner of the WARMING HOUSE which has a large C15 fireplace in the W wall. Between the entrances to the warming house and the refectory to the W are the pointed trefoiled arches of a wall-mounted C13 LAVATORIUM, its hand-washing basins formerly furnished with a piped water supply. This lavatorium replaced an earlier, free-standing one in this corner of the cloisters. The REFECTORY was originally placed in the Benedictine tradition parallel with the S walk of the cloister, but was later reoriented at right angles, the preferred Cistercian position. This enabled enlargement of the KITCHENS to the W; consequently the original refectory entrance, close to that of the kitchens, was blocked. Further changes were made in the later C15 to cater for the by then greater toleration among Cistercians of meat-eating. The refectory was divided horizontally to provide a meat refectory on the ground floor, served by a new meat kitchen at its SE corner, while the old kitchen continued to serve the non-meat refectory on the first floor. Each dining hall had its own entrance from the cloister alley – the two doorways just W of the lavatorium, one a rebuilt C12 opening with a C15 hoodmould.

As in other Cistercian abbeys, the facilities provided for the Kirkstall monks on the E and S sides of the cloister were to some extent replicated for the lay brothers in a series of buildings to the W and SW. The principal element within this group was the W RANGE, now forming the W side of the cloister, from which it was originally cut off by a wall that bounded a wide lane running along the E side of the building. The scar of the wall (removed in C15) can be seen in the S wall of the church, E of the simple doorway that gave the lay brothers access to the nave. The S and W walls of the range are largely absent. Its ground floor of eleven bays was vaulted from end to end, the vaults supported by scalloped corbels in the walls and by a central row of columns (only one base of a pier is *in situ*). The N part contained the stores for the cellarer, while the five bays at the S end formed the LAY BROTHERS' REFECTORY. Above was their DORMITORY, access from it to the church being provided by external steps descending into the lane. The doorway itself was evidently reached by steps within, and has a low arch with joggled voussoirs.

Attached to the SW corner of the dormitory was the LAY BROTHERS' REREDORTER, largely intact but converted to a barn, standing obliquely to the W range but squarely over the main drain. A VISITORS' CENTRE since the 1980s, in 2006 it was reworked by *Purcell Miller Tritton*, with a timber-framed lean-to on the N side inspired by a pentice. The original large archways into the reredorter's ground floor, two to each side, are now blocked and on the N partly destroyed by an C18 cart entrance. The roof has kingpost trusses of the 1750s. Above the stringcourse, narrow openings lit the first-floor latrines themselves, accessed from the dormitory. The lay brothers' infirmary would have been somewhere nearby, perhaps represented by wall foundations excavated just S of the reredorter in the 1960s.

The cloister lane originally continued beyond the S end of the W range, with the kitchens that provided for both lay brothers and monks on its E side. In the late C12 it was spanned by two archways that continued the line of the S range. Clearly not part of the original plan, these left the ground floor open but allowed the adjacent buildings to be linked at first-floor level. The arches were later walled up and the ground floor between them seems to have become a malthouse in the C15, with ovens in its E and W walls and a large stone vat attached to the S wall. Along the S side of the malthouse, kitchen and refectory were yards which contained ancillary buildings whose foundations have been revealed in excavations. To the E is the C15 MEAT KITCHEN, attached to the SE corner of the refectory and on the E adjoining the monks' reredorter. Now very ruined, it contains fireplaces and ovens. Near its SW corner, a circular-plan building, probably a dovecote. S of the monks' reredorter a fishpond, originally perhaps one of a series, survived into the C18.

On the E side of the monks' reredorter stands the ABBOT'S LODGING, a three-storey, self-contained house, built *c.* 1230 and one of the earliest known examples of such residences. Its function is suggested by its location. Abbots were supposed to 'lie in the dorter', but before the end of the C12 they were starting to build separate living quarters (e.g. at Rievaulx and Fountains). The attachment of the house to the monks' reredorter, technically part of the dorter, may have made the new accommodation appear less in breach of the rule than it would otherwise have done. Its principal chamber was, effectively, a first-floor hall, set over a basement and reached by an external flight of steps from the yard on the N side, which led into a lobby lit by square-headed lights. The hall itself was originally lit by two large windows on each side, formed by pairs of lancet lights enclosed externally by a round-headed arch. The solar above the hall, of a similar size and reached by a wooden continuation of the spacious main staircase, was lit by similar windows to those in the hall, one in the S wall surviving complete. An oriel window also in the S wall seems to have lit the top of the main staircase. Fireplaces were inserted into the N wall of both hall and solar in the C15, one above the other. To the E is another oblong building, earlier than the abbot's lodging but also of the C13 and later connected to it. Little survives except parts of its gable walls. Scars in these walls indicate that the two rooms of the ground floor were covered by quadripartite vaulting. Above, the E gable wall contains the jambs of a lancet window. There is a pointed-oval window in the W gable. The building is thought to have contained a kitchen and cellar on the ground floor and a chapel above, originally serving the infirmary but later the abbot's lodging and the visiting abbot's lodging as well.

The INFIRMARY buildings survive only a few courses high. The principal element is a C13 aisled hall of five bays, later developed into a series of private cubicles, some with fireplaces. Built at the same time, running S from the infirmary hall to the chapel and kitchen block, is a building which may have served as the visiting abbot's lodging. In the C15 it was furnished with a large, first-floor oriel window in its E wall, the base of which remains. N of the infirmary hall are the foundations of C15 kitchens and scullery. Excavation has revealed an earlier aisled hall, running N–S beneath these foundations and constructed with timber posts. It was probably the original infirmary hall, used during the late C12 and early C13.

The GUESTHOUSE, W of the abbey church. Foundations uncovered in 1893, along with other ancillary buildings. Used by patrons and other lords and their households. This was a typical aisled hall of the C13, with a two-storey solar block (with surviving latrines) at one end and services, kitchens and bakehouse at the other. On the W side, beyond the main drain, a subsidiary hall was converted in the later Middle Ages to stables and smithy. There would have been other lodgings for wayfarers, probably close to the outer gatehouse in the northern boundary of the precinct.

Churches and Public Buildings

ST STEPHEN, Morris Lane. A thousand-seater preaching box, with lancets and w steeple, by *R. D. Chantrell*, 1828–9. The land was donated by the 7th Earl of Cardigan. Transepts, crossing and larger chancel of 1860 by *Perkin & Bulmer*. The E window was moved to the s transept, the galleries removed and the plaster ceiling replaced by an open roof. In 1893–4 *Henry Walker* added a porch and extended the chancel, incorporating the Oastler Vault beneath with arched openings to the churchyard on the N and s sides. – FURNISHINGS. Choir stalls, pulpit and prayer desk, 1860. – STAINED GLASS. N aisle. First window by *Michael O'Connor*, 1868. Two windows by *Wailes*, in the N aisle, presented 1864 (Resurrection, Good Samaritan and Christ with the Children); and s aisle, 1870.

   SCHOOL. Opened in 1822. Schoolmaster's house to the side. Extended 1865–6 and 1890.

ST MARY, Hawkswood Avenue. 1932–5 by *W. D. Caröe*, his final church, paid for by H. M. Butler of Kirkstall Forge to serve the new housing estate of Hawksworth Wood. Though modest, it illustrates the spatial dexterity, the depth of historical under-standing, the mastery of all detail and the insistence on fine craftsmanship that mark out Caröe as one of the Late Gothic masters. Most unusually for the West Riding it is faced in knapped flint, which at the E and W ends is elaborated as flush-work panels. There is a clear delineation between the lower courses put down by local contractors, and the finer stuff added by Norfolk men brought in to finish the job properly. Central buttress at both E and W ends, at the angles, but not the sides. N and s porches. Nave, chancel and sanctuary dimin-ishing in width, but not roof-line, with an ashlar bellcote at the s junction of nave and chancel. Narrow passage aisles, no cap-itals to the arcades. Exquisite FURNISHINGS, as one expects of Caröe, including screens, stalls, pulpit and font. Mixed Renaissance and Gothic motifs. Reordered in 1972 by *Alban Caröe* with some skill, moving the altar W and the font from the NW baptistery to the W wall.

ZION UNITED METHODIST CHURCH, Victoria Road. Italianate design seating 600 by *Crabtree* of Shipley, erected 1866–7.

FIRST WORLD WAR MEMORIAL, Bridge Road. Tall Portland stone cross by *Basil Butler*.

BEECROFT STREET SCHOOL (former). 1882 by *Richard Adams*. Classical and stone-built, rather than his usual red brick Gothic. An arcade provided shelter to the playground.

KIRKSTALL BRIDGE, ⅜ m. s of the abbey, crossing the Aire. Cast-iron bridge of 1912, at least the fourth on site.

HOUSING. PEEL SQUARE, off Commercial Road s of Kirkstall Bridge, is a rare surviving example of court housing, built in the mid C19. – MORRIS LANE, with fine views of the Abbey and the Aire valley, has respectable villas on the E side, includ-ing the Gothic CROOKED ACRES, of *c.* 1881. On the W side, by contrast, are streets of back-to-backs, including on

NORMAN MOUNT, VIEW and ROW examples of 1932–7 which were amongst the last to be built in Leeds. MONKSWOOD, Vesper Road, is a close of houses of 1972 by the *Brooks Thorp Partnership* for a group of friends and colleagues, who formed a Housing Society to create a place for their families to grow up in together. It was conceived as pavilions set amidst a garden – there were to be no boundaries between plots. The shells, of concrete block, were finished individually, but all external changes must be approved by the Society.

ABBEY MILLS, ¼ m. SE of the Abbey off Abbey Road. A goit was first constructed by the monks in the C12 but the present buildings postdate a fire of 1799. They include a lodge, cottages, an early C19 four-storey drying house (with the characteristic small windows). Beyond is the three-storey mill itself, constructed in 1822–34, partly of masonry recovered from the fire.

KIRKSTALL FORGE, W of the Abbey off Abbey Road operated from the late C16 to 2002. Established by John Savile as a wrought iron bloomery by exploiting one of the medieval Abbey goits, the surviving structures of the Lower Forge date from after its purchase by the Beecroft and Butler families in 1778–9, when it was reordered to manufacture hand tools. The impressive but roofless HAMMER SHOP, with round arches, still houses its original iron water wheel and tilt hammer, as well as later plant. Some date from the C19 move into axle and line shafting production. Flanking the gates, COTTAGES, STABLES etc. Near the junction of the drive and Abbey Road a charming obelisk MILESTONE with rusticated banding, erected in 1829 and claiming equidistance between London and Edinburgh. The extensive site is scheduled for mixed-use redevelopment.

MEANWOOD

Meanwood straddles the valley of the Meanwood Beck, whose principal industry was tanning. At Meanwood Hall lived the Denisons and, later, the Becketts, who provided a new church, schools and an institute. Suburbia arrived with the electric tram (in 1901) and engulfed the large mansions to S and E, though to the N the valley is preserved as a public park.

HOLY TRINITY, Church Lane. 1848–9 by *William Railton*, architect to the Church Commissioners. Lancet windows. Thinly detailed but impressively massed, with a steep nave roof and tall broach spire atop a three-stage crossing tower. Four-light W window of 1876–7 by *J. M. Teale* of Doncaster, who added the S aisle and lengthened the S transept. Chancel lengthened by *Edward Birchall*, 1882, with S organ loft (now vestry). Octagonal nave piers, carved bosses to corbels, open trusses. Nave crossing arch of four orders springing from low clustered piers. Organ loft created in the S crossing in 1973. Beneath it, the former HIGH ALTAR, with a low REREDOS given in 1921, with figurative painted panels. – FONT. Stone, octagonal, carved with well-detailed blank arcade. – STAINED GLASS. Six windows by *Frederick Preedy*, 1864–85, including the E window and transepts, S aisle and W window. – A fine pair of S aisle windows in Art Nouveau style to Marian and Walter Rowley by *J. W. Knowles*, 1924.

SE is the Becketts' imposing MAUSOLEUM. 1850s, perhaps by *Railton*. E.E. in detail but almost Hindu or Bhuddist in character. Square, with massively chamfered plinths and a pyramidal stone roof busy with lucarnes, gables and gabled niches containing carved flower heads and Beckett coat of arms, rising to a peculiar finial. Bold LYCHGATE, mid-C19. Four steep gables almost reaching the ground, and arches with giant cusps.

PERAMBULATION. Start at the S end of GREEN ROAD, at the messy suburban centre, with the *Moderne* BECKETT'S ARMS pub, built 1939. Canted plan and a few jazzy details. On the opposite corner of Bridge Road, the METHODIST CHURCH. A conventional work of 1881 by *William Hill*, extended in 1886. Now along Green Road until it is crossed by CHURCH LANE. On this, r., the simple former WESLEYAN CHAPEL, by *Samuel Prince*, 1811. Altered 1883. Round-headed windows in plain surrounds, entrance in the centre of the long side.

MEANWOOD INSTITUTE was built *c.* 1840 for William Beckett and extended in 1885. Brick with an ashlar front and mullioned windows. It makes an attractive group with the cottages of TANNERY SQUARE, erected 1834–7, and to their l. six former back-to-backs of the 1850s (both well renovated in 1975). Beyond them the FIRST WORLD WAR MEMORIAL by *A. R. Powys*, Secretary of the S.P.A.B., *c.* 1920 – a weatherboarded shelter covering a gritstone memorial – and MEANWOOD SCHOOL (and schoolmaster's house) provided by the Becketts in 1840. Additions of 1872 by *Adams & Kelly*, and of 1890 and 1912. Largely single-storey, Gothic, with pointed traceried windows. In 1994–5 it was partially rebuilt behind retained façades and expanded very successfully by *Brett Gaunt* as a cluster of buildings around two intimate courtyards. The road, by now really a lane, then breaks out into the open of the Meanwood Beck valley, arriving at HUSTLER'S ROW, a terrace of twenty cottages erected in 1848–9 by John Hustler for workers in his adjacent quarry.

MEANWOOD TANNERY (former), Church Lane, W of Green Road. Converted to flats in 1998. Large (twenty-one by twenty-seven bays), L-shaped complex of 1857, for Samuel Smith. Stone-built, three storeys, with a big cart entrance; the upper storeys were for drying skins and formerly had louvred wooden panels where now there are windows. The iron-roofed tanning yard was demolished in 1998. Other more modest buildings, also converted to housing, are early C19 and were originally part of a paper mill operating here from 1785 until a fire *c.* 1852. Former millpond to the W; the site has been used for milling since the C13.

CARR MANOR, Stonegate Road. 1881, the first major work of [113]
E. S. Prior, for Dr Thomas Albutt. In the style of a C17 Pennine
manor house. On the site of Carr House. s front of five gables,
those on the r. set back from the projecting centre, the two on
the l. seamless additions of 1899–1900 by *Bedford & Kitson* for
Col. F. W. Tannett-Walker. An arcade of three curious segmental arches connect this later w end with a N range, forming
the entrance to a rear courtyard. The interior has much panelling, elaborate fireplaces and moulded plaster ceilings in C17
style. STABLES by *Prior* with coved eaves to timber and roughcast panels, a dovecote in the gable and a re-set datestone of
1796. COTTAGES also by Prior to match. In the grounds, a circular classical ARBOUR with fluted Ionic columns, topped by
an open wrought-iron dome, probably by *Bedford & Kitson*.

MEANWOOD HALL, off Woodlea Park. Built *c.* 1762 for Thomas
Denison, with N wing of 1814 for Joseph Lees. The main block
was remodelled by *John Clark* for Christopher Beckett *c.* 1834
in a manner presaging the heavier classical decoration of the
1840s and 1850s. Ground floor of channelled rustication,
balconies and ornate hoods with scrolled brackets to the first-
floor windows, an eaves cornice with deep brackets and a heavy
balustrade. Projecting centre with a porch of four Ionic fluted
columns. At the ends, full-height bows. Very original treatment
of the chimneys which comprise four stacks linked at the top
by a dentilled cornice, terminating in Soanian hoods. Grand
entrance hall lit by a clerestory with a cantilevered divided
staircase and a coffered ceiling. The house became part of a
mental hospital in 1919 and, following its closure, is now surrounded by housing set within its former park.

MEANWOOD TOWERS, Towers Way, set incongruously in a
housing estate. Now flats. A High Victorian Gothic fantasy of
1867 by *E. W. Pugin* for Thomas Kennedy, a partner in Fair-
bairns, textile engineers. It has remarkably tall ornamental
chimneystacks (now cut down), oriels, gargoyles and gables.
Cusped traceried windows and a heavy first-floor loggia above
one of the many bay windows. In 1873 Pugin was bankrupt
and *Norman Shaw* carried out interior decoration, also rebuilding the top of the tower in a half-timbered, gabled manner,
since truncated. Many fittings retained including a timber and
painted glass screen in the hall, doors, panelling, medieval-style
fireplaces, a black marble staircase and stained glass. There is
no trace of the building put up in the grounds to house the
Schulze organ now at St Bartholomew, Armley (*see* p. 563).
LODGE on Stonegate Road.

MEANWOOD VALLEY URBAN FARM, Sugar Well Road, off
Meanwood Road. The core is a laboratory (office) and herbal
distillery (café) built in the 1870s by John Clapham, a botanical chemist, who erected the adjoining Oakdale House in 1885.
The most interesting building is the EPICENTRE, of 1998–9
by *OSA*, based on Walter Segal's 'Self Build' environmental
housing. Done with some élan, particularly in the exposed
forked frames of locally grown larch which rake out through

the s front to support a monopitch turf roof. Passive heating and cooling determines planning: whilst the partially buried N and s sides have few openings, the double-height s façade is completely glazed and fronts a 'greenspace' from which warmed air is ventilated (in summer) or circulated (in winter). Other technologies include lightweight, adjustable timber walling, recycled newspaper insulation, compost toilets and reed-bed drainage system.

REVOLUTION WELL, Stonegate Road. A gritstone well-house erected by Joseph Oates of Carr House (*see* Carr Manor) in 1788 to commemorate the Glorious Revolution.

WEETWOOD

Weetwood has a complete sequence of grand, stone Victorian villas in spacious wooded grounds along both sides of Weetwood Lane, which winds uphill between Far Headingley and the Ring Road. Development was sparked by the sale of 280 acres in 1858 by the Englefield family. In spite of changing use and new buildings in the neighbourhood, nowhere is the flavour of the affluent suburban world of Leeds's bankers, industrialists and merchants better preserved.

The houses start N of Weetwood Mill Lane with THE HOLLIES, a rather dull Gothic house built by *W.H. Thorp* in 1864 for William George Brown, whose father, a Bradford stuff merchant, had acquired 93 acres in 1858. The grounds, which incorporated quarry workings, were given to the city in 1920 and are a part of Meanwood Park. On the w side of Weetwood Lane, a pair of fanciful and freely Gothic houses of *c.* 1873–5 by *John Simpson* with busy precipitous roof-lines including 'steeples' over the central entrances: WEETWOOD MANOR (built for Frederick Baines, editor of the *Leeds Mercury*) and BARDON HILL, which was altered *c.* 1902 by *Thomas Winn* for Joseph Pickersgill, millionaire racehorse owner and bookie. He reconstructed the COACHHOUSE AND STABLES and built a handsome new LODGE, both in a Vernacular Revival style.

Adjoining to the N, the grounds of BARDON GRANGE (University of Leeds halls of residence), built for William Brown and attributed (including the coachhouse, stables and lodge) to *Cuthbert Brodrick, c.* 1861; cf. No. 9, Alma Road, Headingley). Roll-moulded architraves throughout. W of Bardon Grange is OXLEY HALL, formerly Weetwood Villa, built for Henry Oxley, banker, in 1861–4 by *John Simpson*. Altered by *W.H. Thorp*, probably in the late 1880s, and further extended by *Perkin & Bulmer*. A tall Jacobean-style composition with another lively roofscape, and cantilevered staircase. Remodelled in 1926–8 with a big new wing, w, by *J.C. Procter & F.L. Charlton* as halls of residence for female students. LODGE by *Simpson*. Extensive halls of the 1990s encroach on both houses.

At this point the interest shifts E of Weetwood Lane, where the houses overlook the Meanwood Beck. First, QUARRY DENE, Jacobethan-style of 1881–6 by *W.H. Thorp* with the entrance in a turret crowned by an ogee dome. Altered and service wing added by *Sydney Kitson* for his brother Edward Christian, 1905–6. Vernacular Revival stable, 1881–3. The house is set on a platform amidst quarry workings, making dramatic rock gardens all around which once formed part of the grounds of The Hollies. Next to the N is OXLEY CROFT, dated 1898, designed by *F. W. Bedford* as a speculative venture for George William Brown, its first tenant being Joseph Wicksteed, engineer. Vernacular Revival with some fine Arts and Crafts interiors, including a panelled hall with inglenook. Amidst C20 housing N of this is MOORLANDS SCHOOL (formerly Foxhill), one of *George Corson*'s earliest commissions; built 1861–2 for Francis Tetley. It combines Romanesque and Gothic features and originally had a huge tower (lowered by *Kitson* as part of extensive remodelling in 1913–15 for his father-in-law, C. F. Tetley). Finally, overlooking Adel to the N, WEETWOOD GROVE (now flats) in Foxhill Court, an idiosyncratic Gothic house of 1861 by *Thomas Ambler* for T. W. Stansfield, a Bradford wool merchant. Overly busy S façade: columned porch with gargoyle, three stepped gables, a large crenellated canted bay, a rose window and lancets. 1880s rear wing, partly refaced with half-timbering, with angled entrance at timber cladding and angled entrance at the join, and a turret.

Off Weetwood Lane's W side, and set close to the Ring Road, is WEETWOOD HALL (hotel and conference centre). Built for Daniel Foxcroft in 1625. The doorcase, with thin Ionic columns, has the date but apart from this feature, and some mullioned windows at the rear, the house looks Georgian – it is of three storeys, seven bays across the front and three to the side, with sash windows, a hipped roof and ashlar walls. The plan is double pile; if this is original it is early for Yorkshire. Three good early C17 plaster ceilings, some restored or C19, with pomegranate trails, birds, flowers etc. The fragment of frieze in the small parlour r. of the entrance illustrates dogs hunting a stag. The Jacobean-style N wing is by *W.H. Thorp*, 1887, for Alfred Cooke, the printer (*see* Hunslet). Of the same build the adjoining W door and bay window. E, small Georgian STABLES with primitive Venetian window above twin carriage arches. They form a court with former HALLS OF RESIDENCE built for Leeds University, 1925–7, a cruciform range with embattled tower over the 'crossing', and the extensive additions of the 1990s for the conference centre, which continue W of the house. LODGES on Otley Road and Weetwood Lane by *Thorp*.

BODINGTON HALLS OF RESIDENCE. *See* Adel.

NORTH AND NORTH-EAST

ALWOODLEY

A township in Harewood parish until 1928, now the northern-most suburb of the city, continuous with Moor Allerton and Moortown to the s.

St Paul the Apostle (R.C.), King Lane. Small, of brick. 1995–6, by *Jos Townend* of *Edwin Trotter Associates*. Centrally planned, the altar lit by a glazed fin projecting from the roof. – HALL. The earlier, gabled church by *R. A. Ronchetti*, 1952–3.

The Grammar School at Leeds, Harrogate Road. An extensive complex, on the edge of the green belt, of 1997 by *JSPB* for the Grammar School previously at Woodhouse (*see* above) and extended in 2008 to accommodate Leeds Girls' High School (formerly in Headingley, q.v.). Mainly of two storeys, the planning – around a series of partially open courts – is generous and successful but the stone-clad and gabled architecture bland.

Alwoodley Golf Club, Wigton Lane. Opened in 1907, the course was the first designed by *Dr Alister MacKenzie*, a founder member, who later laid out the famous course at Augusta National, Georgia. Handsome CLUBHOUSE of 1994–5 by *Charles Morris*, large but of cottagey Arts and Crafts inspiration: a sweeping plan with dominant pitched roofs extending over a veranda along the course side, broken by a bowed bay and terminating in round pavilions.

Two good examples of Modernism amidst the suburban sprawl. INGLEDEW COURT, e of Harrogate Road, is an unexpected seven-storey slab by *Derek Walker*, completed 1970, the rigour of its eighteen-bay s elevation diluted by glazed balconies. In Alwoodley Lane, GOULD HOUSE (No. 189), is a single-storey house of 1967 by *David Walker, John Attenborough & Bryn Jones*. Clear and opaque glass skin, raised on a brick plinth with external stairs, and a circular lift that emerges in the living room. Flexibly planned interior, with pivoting walls. Brick-clad service chambers.

CHAPEL ALLERTON

Recorded as Alretun in Domesday. The first chapel appears to have been established by the mid C13 and was several times rebuilt. A small community had grown up by the end of the C17 and the village was acclaimed by Edward Parsons in 1834 as 'by far the most beautiful and respectable in the Parish of Leeds'. Following the enclosure of Chapeltown Moor s of Stainbeck Lane in 1809, a great variety of houses was built, but the centre remained largely undeveloped until the arrival of the electric tram in the early C20. By that time the church had been rebuilt on a new site. Then large houses went up around Allerton Park, and the remaining fields were built over in the 1930s.

St Matthew, Wood Lane. A late work by *G.F. Bodley*, 1897–9, 90
succeeding the old parish church (*see* Perambulation). Its most
striking feature is the bold and sturdy detached sw porch
tower, which is linked to the nave by a low passage. The tall
chancel and nave are under one roof but without a clerestory,
the aisles lean-to. Refined Perp elevations with simple mouldings and narrow buttresses. Three-light windows except for the
e window. Spacious, austere and undeniably sombre interior.
Six-bay nave with slender quatrefoil piers of c14 type with
plain moulded capitals. Timber tunnel-vaulted ceiling, ribbed
and panelled in the chancel. Stone corbels and timber brackets to the aisle ceilings, painted with badges and chevrons. –
Timber REREDOS of Christ in Glory, the Annunciation and
Saints, under traceried canopies. – CHANCEL SCREEN, the one
note of richness, gilded and traceried, carrying an organ loft
and ORGAN CASE. – FONT. Dated 1637, from the old church.
A small polygonal bowl with inscription and very elementary
ornament on the underside. – STAINED GLASS in the chancel,
s chapel and second window in the N aisle by *Burlison & Grylls*.
– E window of 1900 by *Bodley*. – s aisle, 1915–22, by *Clayton
& Bell*. – s and N aisles w windows, 1923, by *Shrigley & Hunt*.
– Porch, 1948, by *Maile & Son*.

PUBLIC LIBRARY, Harrogate Road and Town Street. 1904 by
W.H. Thorp, done with gusto. The building also contained the
police station and fire station. Free Renaissance, with shaped
gables, obelisk pinnacles etc. Jolly oval windows in swirling
cartouche surrounds in the gables and a tall chimney to the
library.

FORMER PARISH HALL. THE ALCUIN SCHOOL, Woodland
Lane. 1912 by *Sydney Kitson*. A suave design in red brick with
buttresses topped by urns at each end and much use of circular windows in lower wings.

CHAPEL ALLERTON PRIMARY SCHOOL, Harrogate Road/
Methley Drive. 1878 by *Richard Adams*. Single storey, red brick
with twin gables flanking a long centre. Cusped tracery in the
upper lights of the mullioned-and-transomed windows, the
upper parts of the gables divided into panels with brick-
nogging.

WESLEYAN SUNDAY SCHOOL (former), Town Street. Erected
1794, converted to a school in 1878. Two storeys of coursed
stone, the central part of the front projecting slightly with a
pediment. Tall round-headed windows and a pedimented
doorway with attached Doric columns.

Perambulation

The historic centre is the junction of Harrogate Road, Stainbeck
Lane and Town Street. To the w, set back on the N side of
Stainbeck Lane, is the oldest house in the area, Clough House,
now THE MUSTARD POT pub. Early c18, brick, of five bays,
similar in style to the merchants' houses then being erected in
central Leeds and, as there, with a former workshop range l.,

possibly used for cloth-finishing. Inside, a stone fire surround with a shouldered architrave and the coat of arms of the Henson family. Further w on the N side, ALLERTON HALL, also C18 but sprawling, with a handsome bow-fronted three-storey wing and a stable block behind, the latter incorporated into the house in 1898. Extensive late C19 additions to the w with a jettied and coved half-timbered gable, followed by the long N wing of 1898–1901 by *Temple Moore* in a convincing Queen Anne style with modillion eaves and some circular windows.

In HENCONNER LANE to the s, two pedimented late C18 houses: NEWTON VILLA, ashlar with a Diocletian window, and the handsome ROSE MOUNT of *c.* 1780, red brick with a wide five-bay front and a Doric porch. Off Henconner Lane is POTTERNEWTON GARDENS by *Yorkshire Development Group*, 1973, an infill estate in an area of terraced houses. It retains the existing street pattern but has a mix of two-storey houses, flats and patio houses, each with private gardens and open entrance courts. Carried out in white brick, and well detailed and landscaped.

Now back to HARROGATE ROAD, where N of Stainbeck Lane on the w side is the former YORKSHIRE BANK COMPUTER CENTRE of 1968 by *Braithwaite & Jackman*, a crisp sculptural composition of ribbed *in-situ* concrete and brown brick with an oversailing upper storey (re-clad in dark glass) and shallow strip windows. On this side N of Wood Lane is WESTFIELD TERRACE, very large three-storey houses of *c.* 1870 with canted bays, set back from the road on a private driveway with large round gateposts, quite unlike anything else as far out in the suburbs as this. Opposite, and in scale a great contrast, Nos. 150–170, a handsome ashlar early C19 terrace, two-storey with console brackets and corniced hoods over the doors. Continuing on similar lines back to the centre are Nos. 198–218 and Nos. 226–230, a long row, mostly double-fronted, not a formal terrace but individual houses very alike. No. 208 has an ornate Edwardian rendered façade.

Back at the centre off to the E runs TOWN STREET, with on its N side the former Wesleyan Sunday School (*see* above) and N of that the HAWTHORNS, a series of streets of small terraced cottages from *c.* 1900 with applied half-timbering, tile-hanging and gabled dormers. The excellent TOWN STREET HOUSING of *c.* 1970 by *E.W. Stanley*, City Architect (assisted by *D.M. Wrightson*) retains the curve of the original road as a pedestrian path with small squares leading off it. The grey brick houses have monopitched roofs and simple elevations. A varied building line and extensive planting add charm. To the E of the Town Street housing off Gledhow Lane is an area of smart suburbia centred on ALLERTON PARK, which forms a loop N of Gledhow Lane. It was laid out with large houses by *Bedford & Kitson* at the beginning of the C20. There has been some interesting redevelopment since, e.g. Nos. 2 and 2a, striking houses by *Bauman Lyons Architects* of 1995 and 1998. The first is of conventional brick construction, its dominant motif a clerestory running the length of the house. Full-height entrance hall in the centre. Its neighbour has a timber frame, rendered externally, and two wings, extensively glazed on the principal s-facing elevations, which meet at an oblique angle. Roofs are monopitched with deep eaves. Double-height living space in the shorter l. wing, split-level bedrooms with balconies and service areas r. Then WEBTON COURT, a fine Domestic Revival house of 1902–3 by *Bedford & Kitson* for W. J. Cousins. Nicely balanced garden front, almost symmetrical, with close studding above a stone ground floor, other elevations tile-hung. Recessed entrance set in a screen with Art Nouveau stained glass. Interior with restrained plasterwork of flowing foliage designs to the ribs of the drawing room ceiling, an arched inglenook and well-crafted fittings. Cottage and stable in similar style but altered. Nos. 11a–c are a trio of self-build eco-houses of 1993–6 by *Jonathan Lindh*, three-storey, timber-framed with roofs partly sedum-clad, a prominent timber balcony and steps. A reed bed treats waste water.

Now s to GLEDHOW LANE. CHAPEL ALLERTON HALL, at first sight a rather shapeless red brick house of the 1860s, was the home of Sir John Barran, the clothing manufacturer. It incorporates work of *c.* 1830 at the rear. C18 STABLES, unsympathetically converted. The highlight of Chapel Allerton, best seen from Allerton Park, is GLEDHOW MANOR (Nos. 350–352 Gledhow Lane, built as Red House) of 1903 by *Bedford & Kitson*. A large and ambitious Neo-Georgian mansion, now flats, built for Commander Bernal Bagshawe, proprietor of the Kirkstall Forge. U-shaped front, in red brick with stone dressings. The wings have two-storey canted bay windows; between these is a single storey outer hall fronted by a broad semicircular portico with paired Ionic columns. The house is planned around its square top-lit central hall and at first floor is a gallery approached through fluted Ionic columns *in antis*, built to exhibit Bagshawe's collection of C18 prints. Fine woodwork, original tiling and light fittings. Stained glass in the vestibule and staircase, probably by *George Walton*. The service quarters are in a NE wing. Impressive STABLES (also converted to houses), off Allerton Park. More Arts and Crafts in character: the upper floor roughcast, broad sliding sash windows and a big carriage arch with a deeply moulded cornice on one side and tile voussoirs on the other.

Finally, down CHURCH LANE to THE ELMS, a house built in several phases, the earliest of *c.* 1730, cottage-like and now rendered, extended at right angles *c.* 1750 by five bays in brick with a pedimented doorcase, itself enlarged with a taller wing, the front canted, in the early C19. Return to the centre through the GRAVEYARD of the old parish church (dem. 1935). It was possibly of C17 origin but completely rebuilt in 1737 and again in the C19. – Table tomb of John Hives †1843. In the form of a Roman altar. Scrolled ends to the top slab, below a dentilled cornice and Doric frieze with triglyphs with paterae.

GLEDHOW

A district in the E part of Chapel Allerton township (*see* above), along the steep-sided valley of the Gledhow Beck, whose hilly and picturesque topography caused it to be known as 'Little Switzerland' in the C19. It was largely untouched by suburban development until the 1900s.

GLEDHOW HALL, Gledhow Lane. Constructed soon after 1766 for Jeremiah Dixon. Attributed to *John Carr*. Two storeys, ashlar, with a hipped roof behind a balustraded parapet. The w front has a central door with a Gibbs surround and pediment between a pair of two-storey canted bays. A third broad bay on the s front. Rear extensions and alterations of *c.* 1885–90

Leeds, Gledhow Hall, bathroom.
Engraving, *c.* 1890

by *Chorley & Connon* for Sir James Kitson, later Lord Airedale, providing two projecting bays and an entrance with two pairs of decorated Ionic columns *in antis* forming a loggia, and a corner entrance porch with Tuscan columns. A service block to the l. The remarkable bathroom, tiled entirely in Burmantofts faience, is of this period but most of the interior is of the remodelling in 1911–12 by *Sydney Kitson* for Lord Airedale and his heir. The inner and outer halls are in the manner of Carr, on whom Kitson was an authority.

LODGE, mid-C19, with additions by *Chorley & Connon*. Gritstone STABLES with a cupola, and an early C20 MOTOR HOUSE, a cast-iron frame and glazed roof in the stableyard. Coursed rubble FOOTBRIDGE dated 1768 built across Gledhow Lane to Home Farm.

ROUNDHAY HALL, Jackson Avenue. A private hospital since 1989. Formerly Allerton Hall, built 1841–2 by *Samuel Sharp* for William Smith, stuff merchant. A finely proportioned Grecian mansion with a giant four-column Corinthian portico, the pediment with acroteria. Very broad corner pilasters. The s front has a bowed central ground-floor bay with Corinthian pilasters and a tripartite window over. Much originality in the treatment of the chimneys which are paired with cylindrical moulded shafts. Splendid oval entrance hall with a mosaic floor and a handsome T-plan staircase under a coved dome. Wall niches with casts of Canova's Venus and The Shepherd Boy by *Bertel Thorvaldsen*, added by Sir Edward (later Lord) Brotherton of Wakefield, who lived here from 1916 to 1930. Vaulted landing on the first floor leading to rooms with elegant Neoclassical plaster decoration. LODGE, in Thorn Lane, with bowed centre, and projecting roof supported on square columns.

HILLSIDE, Gledhow Lane. A pair of C19 cottages altered and extended in 1901–3 by *Sydney Kitson* for his own occupation. He added the columned loggia for views down the Gledhow Valley.

GIPTON SPA, Gledhow Valley Road, at the s end of the wooded valley. Small gabled bath house, reputedly of 1671 but probably rebuilt *c.* 1800, with an open-air plunge bath adjoining with a platform on three sides.

J. S. Brocklesby was commissioned in 1914 to design an estate of smart houses set in a well-wooded landscape, SE of Gledhow Hall, along GLEDHOW WOOD ROAD. Only six houses were built before war intervened; one pair (Nos. 37–39) is semi-detached, the others detached including Stone House (No. 3 Coppice Way) with a crowstepped gable, and The Cairn (No. 47) with a mansard roof. All are in the local stone and have dormers and pantiled roofs, a style later employed by Brocklesby at Merton, South London. To the N, GLEDHOW LODGE (No. 55) mid-C19, three bays, stone with a curious timber-framed and rendered extension of 1906 by *Sydney Kitson* (now The Croft) to provide staff quarters for Gledhow Hall.

For houses w of Gledhow Valley Road, including Gledhow Manor, *see* Chapel Allerton and Potternewton.

MOOR ALLERTON AND MOORTOWN

The N part of Chapel Allerton township. Since the development of the Ring Road in the 1920s encouraged large scale suburban house building it has been nearly continuous with Alwoodley (*see* above).

ST JOHN THE EVANGELIST, Harrogate Road. 1853 by *Joseph Thompson*, enlarged in 1889 with transepts, N vestry, organ chamber and lengthened chancel. A small church with thin lancets and buttresses and a W broach steeple with quatrefoil lights. Wide arches to transepts and chancel, scissor-brace roofs. – Timber-framed LYCHGATE, dated 1913. – WAR MEMORIAL, S. Portland stone cross by *Herbert Ambler*, 1921. Former SCHOOL, 1855, N of the church.

ST STEPHEN, King Lane. A conventional hall church of 1954; an early work by *Geoffrey Davy* of *Kitson, Parish, Ledgard & Pyman*.

IMMACULATE HEART OF MARY (R.C.), Harrogate Road. 1956 by *R. A. Ronchetti*. Quite effective massing in a simplified Byzantine style. Apsidal E end, crossing at the W end with tall transepts and a slim octagonal tower flanked by substantial buttresses.

UNITED HEBREW CONGREGATION SYNAGOGUE, Shadwell Lane. 1985–6 by *P. H. Langtry-Langton*. It succeeded the Great Synagogue, Belgrave Street (1861, for the oldest congregation in the city, dem.) and New Synagogue, Chapeltown Road (1928–32, now the Northern School of Contemporary Dance, *see* p. 528). A flamboyant fusion of classical and Byzantine motifs, with a complex plan of three courtyards, a large hall separated from the shul by a movable partition, a small shul and meeting rooms. Ladies sit behind high partly glazed SCREENS on four sides of the shul, instead of having a separate gallery. Stained glass, and other artefacts, have been reused. – BIMAH, incorporating parts of that of the New Synagogue. – PULPIT, 1898, from the Great Synagogue. – ARK. Neoclassical surround with paired Composite columns and a broken pediment. Its doors, with Neo-Egyptian details, probably come from the New Synagogue. – STAINED GLASS. Mostly of 1902–22 from the Great Synagogue. The glass from the New Synagogue is quite different with jazzy motifs, especially good on the N side of the Shul (Passover, Pentecost and Sukkot) of 1929–30 by *David Hillman*.

Outside, SCULPTURE Shalom by *Naomi Blake*, 1987, to the victims of the Holocaust.

BETH HAMEDRASH HAGADOL SYNAGOGUE, Street Lane. 1969 by *G. Alan Burnett*. The synagogue's sixth building since 1874. Very large, seating 950. Concrete-framed with grey brick cladding, the hexagonal shape of the main shul clearly expressed. Central lantern. Impressive interior, the deep roof beams forming in a Star of David, the centre open to form the glazed lantern. – Central BIMAH, its corners splayed to repeat the shape of the hall. – ARK with lettering representing the Ten Commandments.

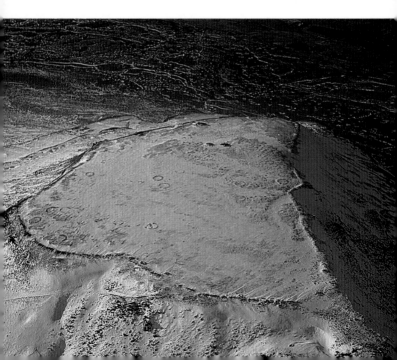

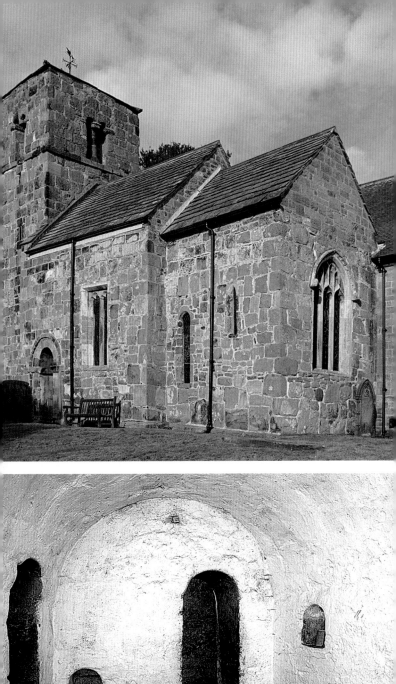

11. Fountains Abbey, church and monastic buildings from the w,
    c. 1150–1200, tower c. 1500 (p. 255)
12. Leeds, Kirkstall Abbey, church and chapter house range from the sw,
    c. 1152–80 (p. 504)

13. Fountains Abbey, nave and s aisle interior, *c.* 1150–60 (p. 261)
14. Fountains Abbey, ground floor of the w claustral range, vaulting,
    c. 1200 (p. 265)

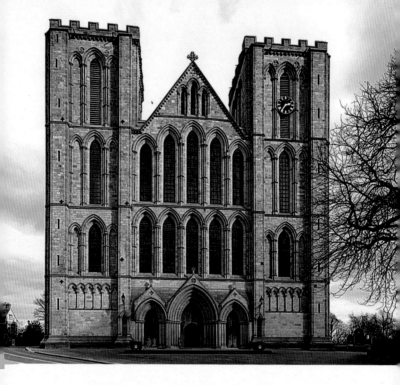

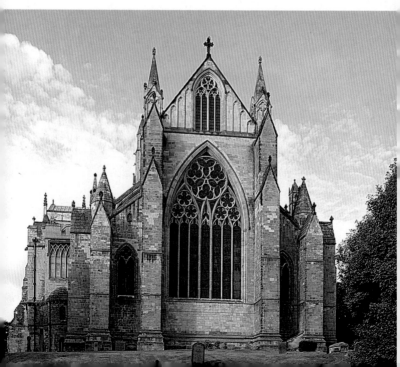

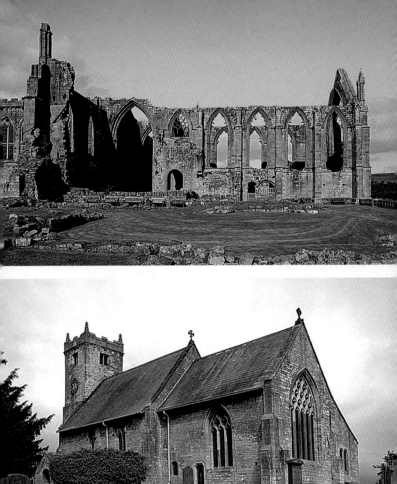

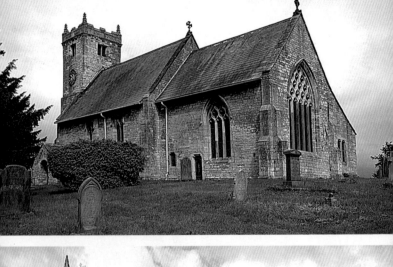

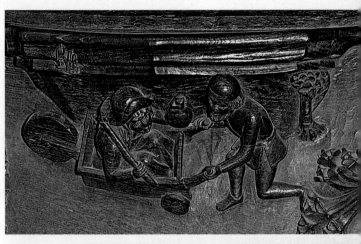

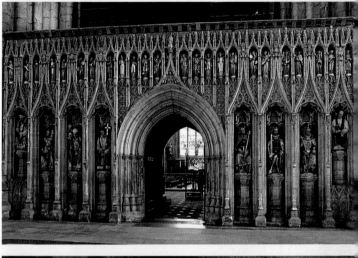

55. Bolton Abbey, Old Rectory
   (formerly Boyle School),
   1700 (p. 136)

56. Ripon, St Agnes House,
   fireplace and overmantel,
   c. 1693 (p. 666)

57. Ripley Castle, tower, 1555, remainder by William Belwood, 1783–6
    (p. 634)
58. Clapham, Ingleborough Hall, by William Atkinson, *c.* 1814 (p. 227)
59. Leeds, Woodhouse, Denison Hall, by William Lindley, 1786 (p. 478)
60. Bramham Park, garden front and Broad Walk, *c.* 1705–10 (p. 206)

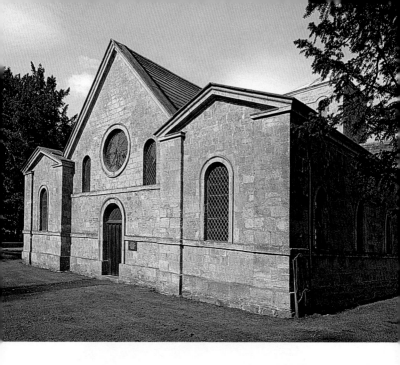

76. Ripon Cathedral,
    monument to
    William Weddell
    †1792, with bust
    by Nollekens,
    1795 (p. 662)
77. Little Ouseburn,
    Thompson
    Mausoleum,
    attributed to
    Roger Morris,
    1743 (p. 575)
78. Bradford
    Cathedral,
    monument to
    Abraham Balme
    †1796, by
    Flaxman,
    c. 1810 (p. 152)
79. Goldsborough,
    St Mary,
    monument to
    Robert Byerley
    †1714, his wife
    Mary and their
    five children, by
    Joseph Wilton,
    c. 1770 (p. 283)

INSTRUCT THE IGNORANT

80. Leeds, St Peter, by R.D. Chantrell, 1837–41 (p. 398)
81. Clifford, St Edward, 1845–8, tower completed by George Goldie, 1866–7 (p. 228)

82. Bradford, Great Horton, St John, by T.H. & F. Healey, 1871–4 (p. 194)
83. Leeds, Armley, St Bartholomew, by Walker & Athron, 1872–8 (p. 562)

84. Bolton Priory,
    stained glass,
    nave s side,
    designed by
    A.W.N. Pugin,
    1850–2, executed
    by J.G. Crace,
    1853 (p. 136)

85. Skelton, Christ
    the Consoler,
    by William Burges,
    1871–6, interior
    (p. 701)

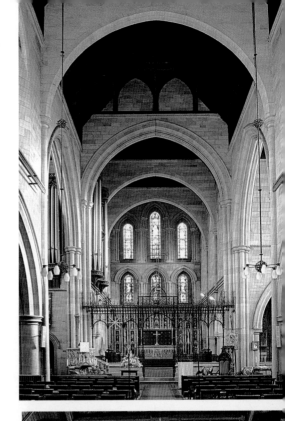

86. Leeds, Headingley,
    St Michael,
    by J.L. Pearson,
    1884–6, interior
    (p. 493)

87. Leeds, Potternewton,
    St Aidan, by
    R.J. Johnson &
    A. Crawford Hick,
    1891–4, interior,
    mosaics by
    Sir Frank Brangwyn,
    1916 (p. 526)

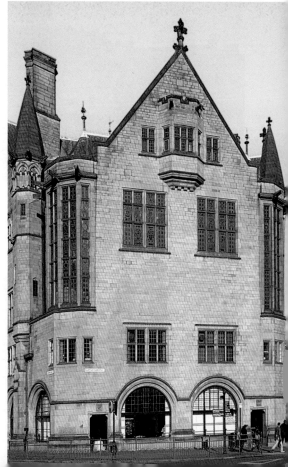

98. Bolton-by-Bowland, school, by Paley & Austin, 1874 (p. 140)
99. Harrogate, Royal Pump Room, by I.T. Shutt, 1842 (p. 312)
100. Leeds, Armley Library, by Percy Robinson, 1901 (p. 564)
101. Leeds University, Great Hall, by Alfred Waterhouse, 1890–4,
     staircase (p. 473)

110. Leeds, Little
Woodhouse Hall,
staircase hall,
by W.R. Corson
and E. la Trobe
Bateman, 1847
(p. 478)

111. Bingley, Harden
Grange, stained
glass, by Morris
& Co., 1862,
now at Cliffe
Castle Museum,
Keighley (p. 129)

112. Allerton
Mauleverer,
Allerton Park, by
George Martin,
1848–51, central
hall (p. 99)

118. Leeds, Civic Hall, by E. Vincent Harris, 1931–3 (p. 414)
119. Harrogate, White Lodge, by Col. R.B. Armistead, c. 1935 (p. 320)

120. Leeds, Gipton, Epiphany, by N.F. Cachemaille-Day, 1936–8, interior
     (p. 539)
121. Bradford, Heaton, Our Lady and the First Martyrs, by J.H. Langtry-
     Langton, 1935, interior (p. 178)

127. Bingley relief road, footbridge, by Ove Arup & Partners and Amec Civil Engineering Ltd., 2001–3 (p. 124)

128. Fountains Abbey, Visitor Centre, by Edward Cullinan, 1987–92 (p. 270)

MOOR ALLERTON HALL, s off Lidgett Lane. A modest C18 house (now flats) of three bays, with taller early C19 wings projecting with bowed fronts, a balustraded parapet across the centre, and central Tuscan porch. Right return of three bays the centre slightly projecting. All stuccoed.

MOORTOWN GOLF CLUB, Harrogate Lane. Course laid out 1909 by *Dr Alister MacKenzie* (cf. Alwoodley Golf Club).

AQUEDUCT, 1½ m. W of St John. Part of the Leeds Water Works Co.'s Eccup Reservoir scheme, opened 1843. Designed by *Henry Abraham* and executed by *George Leather & Son*. Seven semi-elliptical arches sweep 34 ft (10.5 metres) above the Adel Beck.

POTTERNEWTON

Including Chapeltown and Harehills

Late in the C18 the township of Potternewton, set on the high ground N of Leeds, became favoured as a place for the well-to-do to build mansions. But its present character is the result of unrelated C19 development s of Harehills Lane, begun when the estates were parcelled off for building suburban housing. From the 1820s this crept N up Chapeltown Road, beginning in 1826 with the development of Earl Cowper's estate for 'New Leeds', although only a few houses were built and the remainder of the area was eventually filled in the late C19 by large terraced houses. The Newton Park Estate, w of Chapeltown Road, developed from the 1870s, and emulated Headingley in the quality of its houses and layout of broad tree-lined streets. A gap remained between this and New Leeds until the Harehills Grove Estate was laid out from 1886 with a grid of good-quality semi-detached and terraced houses.

Harehills, the SE area of the township, was also developed in the late C19 but as an artisan district, divided from the smarter houses and streets of Potternewton by Roundhay Road, with small terraced houses and back-to-backs..

After 1918 Potternewton's large houses became home to immigrant communities, beginning with Jews moving from The Leylands (*see* p. 465) to the s part of the area, now commonly known as Chapeltown, and since 1945 to West Indians, Asians and refugees from the Balkans and the Middle East. This is reflected in changing uses for many buildings, especially the former churches.

Places of Worship

ST AIDAN, Roundhay Road, Harehills. Built at the request of Dr Jayne, vicar of Leeds, to serve the new working-class district. A massive basilica, externally gaunt but with a rich interior. Built 1891–4 by *R. J. Johnson & A. Crawford Hick* of Newcastle (won in competition in 1889). The Romanesque style is a

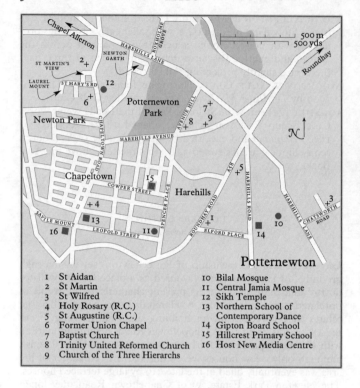

1 St Aidan
2 St Martin
3 St Wilfred
4 Holy Rosary (R.C.)
5 St Augustine (R.C.)
6 Former Union Chapel
7 Baptist Church
8 Trinity United Reformed Church
9 Church of the Three Hierarchs
10 Bilal Mosque
11 Central Jamia Mosque
12 Sikh Temple
13 Northern School of Contemporary Dance
14 Gipton Board School
15 Hillcrest Primary School
16 Host New Media Centre

scholarly hybrid, drawing equally on Italian, German and French sources (Johnson had produced a series of lithographs of French Romanesque architecture in 1885). Some of the external decoration, notably the corbel table, is based on that of Lund Cathedral, Sweden. Of red brick, the curved apse flanked by a small sw tower and the lower part of an unbuilt nw tower which would have been 200 ft (61 metres) tall. Paired windows in both aisles and clerestory, the walls articulated by pilasters. Apsed w baptistery. Inside, a broad nave and narrow aisles with long arcades of plain round arches on circular columns with richly carved capitals in Byzantine style. Completed in 1902, each is different. Splendid ceiled ROOF with tie-beams and crown-posts supporting a tunnel-vault.

Sumptuous FURNISHINGS AND DECORATION. The set piece is the pictorial scheme for the apse and chancel, although this was not begun until 1910, commissioned from *Sir Frank Brangwyn* and paid for by Robert H. Kitson, nephew of the vicar.* It was originally to have been in tempera but eventually executed by *Rust & Co.* in MOSAICS (thought less susceptible to the city's pollution). Around the apse scenes from the life of St Aidan are set in a poetic landscape under an agitated sky. Slender trees with long bare trunks – a motif beloved

---

*Brangwyn had designed a dining room for Kitson's Sicilian villa with furniture and painted frieze.

of Arts and Crafts artists and designers. The figures mostly in white, but some accented in vehement scarlet. The chancel and nave are separated by CANCELLI on which a procession of white-robed neophytes moves up the chancel steps towards the opening in the centre, eager to be baptized by St Aidan. – Massive FONT, 1896, of onyx with Irish green marble columns, and wrought-iron FONT COVER by *Sydney Kitson*, made in 1914 by *Silas Paul* of Leeds School of Art. – PULPIT, 1895, of Caen stone on marble columns with an almost Moorish arcade, designed by *Crawford Hick*, with modelling, sculptured panels and carving by *John Roddis* of Birmingham. – ALTAR RAILS, alabaster with brass infill, 1895, those in the SE chapel of 1909 by *Kitson*. – CHOIR STALLS. C17 classical style, and in similar style the carved SCREEN across the apsed SE chapel, the PANELLING in the W apse, carved and with biblical scenes depicting children, and the ORGAN CASE. – ROOD, carved by a *Ralph Hedley* of Newcastle in 1898; kneeling angels to l. and r. – Painted STATIONS OF THE CROSS of 1950 and STATUE of the Redeemer in the N aisle by *Josef Heu*. – STAINED GLASS mainly by *Percy Bacon & Bros.*: SE chapel, two windows of 1906–7, S aisle, W window, 1893, and baptistery, 1895.

N of the church are the HALL and SCHOOLROOM built to a design by *Chorley & Connon* who had earlier produced a design for the church.

ST CYPRIAN AND ST JAMES, Coldcotes Avenue, Harehills. 1958–9 by *Geoffrey Davy* of *Kitson, Parish, Ledgard & Pyman*. The first of his suburban churches to show an interest in progressive planning and with his typical taste for decorative exposed brick, inside and out, e.g. the pineapple-like effect of sawtooth bond of the E wall. The canted W end contains the organ from St James, York Street (dem.) above the choir stalls (intended to remove the traditional division between priest and congregation). The nave walls taper towards the E end, intensifying the focus on the altar. Varnished deal-boarded ceiling and tall slit windows filled with Belgian 'antique' GLASS, some coloured in abstract patterns. Small rectangular windows punched into the W wall, also with coloured glass, in the manner of Le Corbusier.

ST MARTIN, Chapeltown Road. Built for the Newton Park Estate in 1879–81 by *Adams & Kelly*. Dec style, of Potternewton stone. Its intended W steeple, commenced in 1898, was truncated a little above the nave roof giving the W end an unfinished look. Heavy buttresses to the tower, nave and chancel, the latter topped with finials. Six-bay clerestory with four-light windows, E window with Geometrical tracery. The plain exterior scarcely prepares one for the riches inside. Six-bay nave with double-chamfered arches on tall quatrefoil piers, the capitals carved with foliage by *Thewlis & Co.* not completed until 1901. The roof trusses continue as shafts with capitals and brackets, alternately decorated with foliage and heads. Splendid and well-preserved WALL PAINTINGS of 1913 by *Hemming & Co.* cover the whole of the chancel walls and the chancel arch. Paintings on a Te Deum theme are set in canopied panels divided by chevrons. Above them, angels, who include both black and oriental figures, carrying scrolls. – Carved and gilded REREDOS. It replaced the original stone piece between 1898 and 1905. Nativity in the centre, two further paintings each side in traceried panels and a highly naturalistic style. The lower side panels, each with paintings of four northern saints, were added by 1913. – Ornate CHOIR STALLS with poppyheads, metal gates, and brackets carved with angels. – PULPIT, of Caen stone, by *J. Throp*. A demi-angel supporting the desk, and with cusped openings set in ogee arches on four short columns; enlarged 1898. – Encaustic TILES. – STAINED GLASS. A fine set by *Kempe*: the seven-light E window of 1890; N aisle, a war memorial window, 1921, with roundels depicting the Calvary against a realistic and moving depiction of the shattered trees and mud of the Western Front and soldiers receiving field communion; S aisle of 1903 and 1909; W window of 1898. S chapel S window by *William Pape*, 1956. N aisle w window of 1894 by *C. E. Tute*. Porch window, *Charles Powell*, 1893.

In St Martin's View, the CHURCH INSTITUTE, a large and ornate Perp-style hall of 1902 by *Percy Robinson*.

ST WILFRID, Chatsworth Road, Harehills. Built 1932 to a design of 1913 by *Sydney Kitson*, modified by *James Parish*. Austere red brick exterior with Dec tracery, intersecting in the E and W windows, and a continuous roof over nave and chancel broken by three dormers above the aisles on each side. SW porch and the base of a projected SE tower. Six-bay nave, arcades with octagonal piers and double-chamfered arches. Substantial oak trusses and moulded tie-beams. The w three bays were partitioned *c*. 1988.

HOLY ROSARY CHURCH (R.C.), Chapeltown Road. 1936–7 by *Marten & Burnett*. Sparing simplified Romanesque style.

ST AUGUSTINE (R.C.), Harehills Road, Harehills. 1936 by *Gribbon, Foggitt & Brown*. Red brick in an austere stripped-down modernism that externally has echoes of Cachemaille-Day's St Saviour's, Eltham and contemporary Scandinavian work. Slit-like paired windows and V-shaped buttresses powerfully articulate the nave walls and give a strong vertical emphasis. Internally, the roof beams and piers of reinforced concrete are the dominant features. The church was reordered in 1960 by *Derek Walker* who brought the altar forward. BALDACCHINO by *Walker* and MOSAIC of the Risen Christ on the chancel E wall by *Roy Lewis*.

UNION CHAPEL (former), Chapeltown Road. 1887 by *Archibald Neill* for shared use by Baptists and Congregationalists. Bizarre front with a prominent semi-octagonal porch, heavily buttressed with an open balustrade and crocketed pinnacles, projecting from a gabled octagonal lantern, to which it is linked by flying buttresses. Behind perches a low tower flanked by gabled transepts. Short, broad nave and centrally planned interior.

BAPTIST CHURCH, Harehills Lane. Red brick, Italian Romanesque. 1928 by *Herbert J. Manchip* with big corbels and a rose window in the W front. Three-bay nave with broad rounded arches and domed E baptistery as the focal point.
SCHOOL, behind by *Cubitt & Manchip*, 1906–7.

TRINITY UNITED REFORMED CHURCH, Avenue Hill and Harehills Avenue. Formerly Presbyterian. 1906 by *W. H. Beevers*, paired lancets and buttresses with a chunky SW tower on a good corner site.

GREEK ORTHODOX CHURCH OF THE THREE HIERARCHS, Harehills Avenue. Originally Primitive Methodist. 1902 by *W. Hugill Dinsley* of Chorley, Lancs. Broad-fronted and including a NW tower with a short spire and three windows below a relieving arch, the central of two lights. A school, lit by a continuously glazed clerestory, is behind the church.

UNITED HEBREW CONGREGATION SYNAGOGUE. *See* NORTHERN SCHOOL OF CONTEMPORARY DANCE, below.

BILAL MOSQUE, Harehills Lane. Opened 1999; design by *Atba Al-Samarraie* of *Archi-Structure*. The largest mosque in Leeds and prominent in views from the city centre. Buff-coloured blockwork, the walls topped with shaped gablets. At each corner of the principal front tall octagonal minarets. Central porch with a tall arched opening and smaller minarets. Low onion dome.

CENTRAL JAMIA MOSQUE, Spencer Place. 1997–2000 by *Finn & Downes Associates*. Steel-frame clad in polychrome brick. Large central dome and minarets, round staircase towers at the angles of the building. Three floors, the lower forming a basement, the top floor a gallery below the dome. At the rear is the former CHADSSIDISHE SHUL SYNAGOGUE: a brick box of 1935.

SIKH TEMPLE, Chapeltown Road. 1998–2000 by *Singh & Partners*. The largest Sikh temple in Leeds, for the oldest congregation. Quite boxy, in yellow brick, with a projecting porch, octagonal turrets with onion domes and a larger central dome.

Public Buildings

NORTHERN SCHOOL OF CONTEMPORARY DANCE, Chapeltown Road. The former United Hebrew Congregation Synagogue of 1929–32 by *J. Stanley Wright*, very successfully adapted by *Allen Tod Architects*, 1995–8. Neo-Byzantine with a massive central dome, its curve pierced by triplets of round-arched windows, a lower dome at the E end and small domes above stair-towers either side of the W entrance with its Neo-Egyptian stone portico. Octagonal former prayer hall (now auditorium) with women's gallery on octagonal stone piers. Marble ARK and a Star of David at the apex of the roof from which a bronze pendant light is suspended. STAINED GLASS with Star of David motif. Large, but not overbearing, brick and glass extensions for studios with a library and offices in the basement.

The School also incorporates a three-bay villa of 1835 with a plain Doric porch with attached columns, a rare survival of 'New Leeds' (*see* Perambulation c, below).

GIPTON BOARD SCHOOL (former), Harehills Road. Imposing but lively Renaissance Revival block of 1897 by *W. S. Braithwaite*. Three storeys, of red brick and stone dressings and lots of glass, with projecting circulation towers with elaborate carved doorways, very tall staircase windows and pyramid roofs. Varied shaped gables. Now offices and enterprise centre.

HILLCREST PRIMARY SCHOOL, Cowper Street. The last and grandest of the Leeds Board Schools. 1906 by *Philip Robson*, and in the Queen Anne style introduced to school architecture by his father E. R. Robson in the 1870s, but incorporating free Baroque domed corner turrets and giant pilasters. Big shaped gable to the central hall, balanced effectively by two lower gables flanking it on the Cowper Street elevation. Entrance with Ionic columns. The arcaded basement provided a covered play area.

HOST NEW MEDIA CENTRE, Savile Mount. Former Jewish Institute and Jubilee Hall, 1934 by *G. Alan Burnett*, converted 2000–1 by *Bauman Lyons Architects* for studios and workspaces. Brick, of three storeys and basement, the key motif narrow oriels on the upper floors. New entrance, on the site of a demolished extension, set at an angle with modish horizontal timber boarding, brightly coloured render and exposed steel. Inside, a full-height staircase hall lit by one of the oriels.

Perambulations

a. Harehills Lane and the Harehills Grove estate

The significant buildings of Potternewton are scattered over the suburb so a continuous perambulation is not possible, but might begin with HAREHILLS LANE which runs from the N end of Chapeltown Road SE across the slope of the hill. On the N side is Potternewton's grandest surviving C19 house: GLEDHOW GROVE, of 1835–40 by *John Clark* for John Hives, partner in Hives & Atkinson, flax spinners of Bank Mills, East Street (p. 458). A stately Greek Revival mansion: eleven bays wide, two storeys, stone-built with a broad eaves cornice, deep entablature and corner pilasters. Giant Ionic portico of two attached columns *in antis*. Inside, a spacious staircase covered by a shallow tunnel-vault, Ionic columns to the ground floor, Corinthian to the first. The stables, NW, have a clock tower as the centrepiece in the form of an Egyptian pylon, its front in ashlar, the rest in coursed rubble. Gateposts are topped with Soanian caps and the chimneys have stacks like Ionic columns, a feature shared with the LODGE on Harehills Lane.

E of Gledhow Grove on the hill in ROXHOLME GROVE is GLEDHOW MOUNT, also early C19, with principal front facing S to the city. It is almost square and severe with a Doric porch,

pilastered quoins and stone bands the only decoration.
Between both houses, and in the area generally, there has been
much C20 development, most of it of little value. Much the
most interesting is the housing in NEWTON GARTH, S of Harehills Lane off the E side of Newton Road, of 1969 by *Derek
Walker Associates*. Two rows of terraced houses overlooking a
communal garden, from which they were originally separated
by private gardens. The houses, two storeys in the N row, three
to the S with the fall in the ground, are built of blockwork,
austere and flat-roofed. They have S-facing roof terraces and
are built above garages opening to the roads behind, a concept
developed by Walker at Milton Keynes in the late 1970s. Also
of interest is the appropriately named CORBIE STEPS (No. 89
Harehills Lane), a quaint amalgam of Arts and Crafts and
Scots Baronial by *J. S. Brocklesby*, 1914, with a projecting
crowstepped central gable, mullioned windows and a corner
entrance.

S of Harehills Lane is POTTERNEWTON PARK, created in
1906 after Leeds Corporation purchased the early C19 mansion
of Harehills Grove (now POTTERNEWTON MANSION) and its
grounds for public use. The house was built *c.* 1817 for James
Brown, a wool merchant, in elegant and refined Grecian, the
height of fashionable taste. Seven-bay S front, two-storeyed
with the roof hidden behind a balustraded parapet. The centre
has a curved Ionic porch with a tripartite window over. Circular top light to the staircase and fine iron balusters.

The grounds descend S to HAREHILLS AVENUE. This was
the tree-lined introduction to the Harehills Grove Estate, laid
out to the S from 1886, by John Brown of Harehills Grove, with
a grid of substantial good-quality semi-detached and terraced
houses. They do not require individual mention but at the W
end of Harehills Avenue, set back behind long gardens on
the N side, is NEWTON GROVE, a handsome 1850s terrace of
broadly Italianate three-storey houses by several hands and
variously treated. In the centre is a detached villa with a
pediment above all three bays, reminiscent of *Brodrick*'s Oakfield, Headingley (*see* p. 497), but without his powerfully
outsized detailing.

b. West of Chapeltown Road: Newton Park Estate

The Newton Park Estate was laid out by the Lupton family of
Newton Hall (now dem.). Its LODGE (of 1856) and gateposts
survive on Chapeltown Road by St Martin's church, which
was built for the new estate (*see* Places of Worship). Francis
and Darnton Lupton first engaged *George Corson* to draw up
plans for developing their estate at the beginning of the 1870s
but building was only begun in 1879 to plans by *Chorley &
Connon* (who also designed most of the houses). The principal street is ST MARY'S ROAD, a gated street S of St Martin's

off Chapeltown Road. On the r., Nos. 1–10, a terrace of 1894 by *Smith & Tweedale*, the houses with similar plans but varied façades whose attractive detailing includes half-timbered gables, paired windows with deep sashes, and shell-like porches. ELTONHURST and OAKFIELD of 1885 are semi-detached houses by *Chorley & Connon* in Domestic Revival style with the full gamut of fish-scale tiling, applied half-timbering, decorated plaster coving below big gables, their roofs continued as catslides to ground-floor level. Their largest house on the estate is the twin-gabled ROCKLAND of 1886 for Francis Lupton. The most attractive is PENRAEVON of 1881 in Laurel Mount. Again Domestic Revival but in stone, with a half-timbered gable above an oriel window, leaded lights and a pretty timber porch.

The estate was given a highly original SHOPPING PARADE at Nos. 168–176 CHAPELTOWN ROAD in 1890 by *Archibald Neill*. Less wild than his nearby Union Chapel (*see* Places of Worship) but still bizarrely detailed, the first floor of the central pair of shops set back behind large arches, while banded attached columns between each shop transmute above capitals to form tapering buttresses rising above the eaves. Two splendid carved lions perch above the shopfronts at each end. Coursed stone and mullions throughout.

c. *South-East of Chapeltown Road: 'New Leeds'*

Chapeltown Road formed the w boundary of the ill-fated suburb of NEW LEEDS, intended as a grand rival to Bath or Edinburgh New Town. 55 acres (now bounded by Spencer Place (E), Cowper Street (N), Leopold Street (S) and Chapeltown Road (W)) were sold by Earl Cowper to its developers in 1826, but they were bankrupt by 1829 and the Earl bought the land back. Only a few houses were built: three survive in SPENCER PLACE. NEWTON HOUSE, No. 54, restored 2003, is the most handsome. Fine ashlar façade of five bays, the central three brought forward slightly and the ground-floor windows set in arched recesses either side of a Doric porch, corner pilasters and a parapet. SPENCER HOUSE, No. 52, is rendered with a bow-fronted bay in the centre. No. 50 is slightly fussy, the combination of a tripartite window below a pediment, ground-floor bow windows and a big porch too much for its modest size. Beyond is the Central Jamia Mosque (*see* Places of Worship).

ROUND HOUSE, Potternewton Mount. Late C18 tower windmill, converted into a house in the C20 with tiers of windows on three sides.

ROUNDHAY

Despite regrettable losses and tactless redevelopment, Roundhay is one of the best suburbs of industrial England, laid out around one of its great municipal parks. This occupies roughly one third of the medieval deerpark of the de Lacy family, later Crown property which was mostly sold in 1803 to Samuel Elam and Thomas Nicholson, Leeds-born Quaker businessmen. They divided the estate N and S of Wetherby Road (turnpiked in 1811), Nicholson creating an elegant country seat to the N within a picturesque landscape of wooded belts, follies and lakes, and Elam taking the land to the S as an investment, realized after his bankruptcy and death in 1811 by the development of grand classical villas. In 1871 the Nicholson estate was bought at auction for £139,000 by Sir John Barran, the Lord Mayor, and his colleagues for use as a public park, and sold to the Corporation. Its development was to be funded by the sale of surplus land for smart villas – as at Regent's Park and elsewhere. Plans for both were drawn up by *George Corson* in 1873 but little was achieved at first, largely discouraged by the absence of transport to and from the city centre for trippers and commuters alike. It was the arrival of the electric tram in the 1890s that made a success of park and suburb. Roundhay was taken into Leeds in 1912.

Churches and Public Buildings

ST JOHN, Wetherby Road, just E of the entrance to Roundhay Park. 1824–6 by *Thomas Taylor*. Built at the expense of Stephen Nicholson, son of John. A small and weak design of lancets and buttresses, with a narrow, aisleless cruciform plan and broached crossing steeple. Chancel extended 1885, and vestry added. Thin arch-braced trusses rising from equally thin engaged, full-height shafts, and canted board ceiling. W GALLERY with Gothic frontal by *Sydney Kitson*, 1905. – REREDOS. Wooden pentatych, gilded frame and five painted scenes. (*Opus sectile* dado PANELLING along the E wall, a First World War memorial, with saints in niches.) – PULPIT. Victorian and rich. – STAINED GLASS. Chancel E, three windows by *Ward & Hughes*, 1869; in the S transept, three by *O'Connor*, 1871. Nave S by *Heaton, Butler & Bayne*, 1889 and 1901. – A number of WALL PLAQUES, some Late Georgian with funeral urns.

The church is the centrepiece of a pious Gothic group donated by the Nicholsons: SCHOOL and ALMSHOUSES of 1833 combined in a long, low, single-storey range; behind them the PARSONAGE with matching cusped bargeboards and slender octagonal chimneystacks with castellated caps, the vertical accents now absent from the other building.

St Edmund, Lidgett Park Road. An ambitious building by *W. Carby Hall*, architect of many houses in the suburb. Begun 1907 but completed in stages: 1910 (nave); 1925 (SE memorial chapel) and 1935 (chancel). There is the base of an intended s tower. In the broad nave, a powerful rhythm is created by transverse arches which run down into strong lozenge-shaped arcade piers, with timber cross-vaulting between. High passage aisles with their own arches between each bay. Ill-proportioned clerestory with small windows. Reordered in 2001 by relocating the altar to a platform under the crossing, and removing the choir stalls. Impressive FURNISHINGS, e.g. FONT and PULPIT of alabaster by *Jones & Willis* of Birmingham, the former with bronze panels and a steeple-like buttressed cover. Copious quantities of STAINED GLASS, including a five-light E window by *Charles E. Moore* of 1949–50, a four-light w window by *Victor Milner* of 1912 and several works of the 1920s–40s by *Powell & Sons*.

The substantial C16 vernacular revival style CHURCH HALL, E, served as the church from 1900.

Lidgett Park Methodist Church, North Park Avenue, opposite St Edmund. 1926 by *Arthur Brocklehurst & Co.* of Manchester. Free Late Perp idiom with vestigial stylized tracery. Slender (liturgical) SW tower and canted w porch. Impressive hammerbeam nave roof. Good-quality PEWS, PULPIT and octagonal FONT (reordered 2001). – STAINED GLASS. E window by *W. F. Clokey & Co.* of Belfast, 1945 (possibly also the s side of the nave). Richly coloured in the Arts and Crafts manner with densely treated subjects. – To the s, the SCHOOLS, HALL and CLASSROOMS of 1903–6 by *W. H. Beevers*.

St Andrew United Reformed Church, Shaftesbury Avenue. 1907–8 by *W. H. Beevers*. Confident freely handled Perp in rock-faced gritstone, with a prominent but slim SW tower to capitalize on the corner site. Five-bay nave, aisleless and wide apsidal chancel. Reordered in 2005. – Good STAINED GLASS by *A. L. Moore* (N transept and two, two-light chancel windows of 1920). – E window by *Kayll & Reed*, 1907. – Parish rooms etc. of 1938. N is the MEMORIAL HALL, the previous church begun in 1901 by the Leeds Congregational Council as part of a programme to establish churches in the new suburbs.

Roundhay School Technology College, Old Park Road. The former Roundhay High School for Boys by *Fred Broadbent*, 1924. A large, symmetrical complex, extended *c.* 2004. Mainly brick, classical with Wrenaissance emphases (cf. West Leeds Boys High School, Armley).

Roundhay Park. Opened in 1872. The largest public park in Leeds (373 acres). At its centre, raised on a slight eminence, is the Nicholsons' MANSION (empty in 2009). The house was occupied by 1816, and is very probably by *Thomas Taylor*, who designed the Union Bank in Leeds for Thomas Nicholson in

1812–13.* Seven-bay s front of two storeys with an impressive portico of four giant Ionic columns carrying a pediment. Doric angle pilasters, repeated on the E and W fronts where they flank shallow bow windows. Large conservatory on the W side. Elegant Imperial staircase with iron balustrade set in a semi-oval hall under a big oval lantern. The STABLES, W, were complete by 1821. Nine-bay W front, the central three projecting, emphasized by a pediment. Nice cupola above a clock tower. N of these, PARK COTTAGES, in coursed squared gritstone and of eleven bays divided by pilasters, the basement arcaded.

From the s entrance on Wetherby Road (LODGES of 1811, classical), Nicholson created a drive through the parkland along the W side of the WATERLOO LAKE: 'a miniature Windermere' of 33 acres, completed in 1815. At its s end was a waterfall, popularly known as 'Lovers Leap', since destroyed. On the W side, a BOATHOUSE of 1902. The lake is fed at its N end by a series of CASCADES and two waterfalls, crossed by a rustic BRIDGE, which flow through The Ravine, a deep wooded valley, from the smaller Upper Lake. Eyecatchers were placed picturesquely within this landscape, including the SHAM CASTLE at the N end of the main lake within a wooded setting. Reputedly designed by *George Nettleton*, it has circular crenellated towers and a Gothic traceried window over a pointed archway. By the Upper Lake stood a rustic Gothic Hermitage with boathouse underneath (since destroyed).

W of PRINCE'S AVENUE (laid out N–S through the park according to Corson's plan of 1873) are the former kitchen gardens, with hothouses and vineries, partly reused after 1872 with the addition of a glass conservatory. Coronation House (now Tropical World), added in 1911 for tropical plants, has been rebuilt beyond recognition. Adjacent to the s, CANAL GARDENS, with a central rectangular canal, rustic bridges and a tall enclosing wall. Of Corson's scheme for landscaping the Park in 1873 little was carried out. SE of the mansion, however, is the ROTUNDA, a classical domed drinking fountain with unfluted columns and Corinthian entablature. Presented in 1882 by Barran, at a personal cost of £3,000. The design is by his favourite architect, *Thomas Ambler*. At the NE corner of the park is part of the original boundary ditch of the deerpark. In 2008 the Park was nearing the end of major refurbishment and restoration (architectural work by *Purcell Miller Tritton*).

Perambulations

The suburb is divided into two by the park and a continuous perambulation is not possible. Description begins with the area s of the Park, then W.

---

* Although *John Clark* has been credited with the design, he was not active in Leeds until 1824.

In the centre of Roundhay, at the junction of Wetherby Road, Princes Drive and Roundhay Road, is the OAKWOOD CLOCK TOWER, an esoterically Baroque structure surmounted by dome and tiny cupola. Originally designed for *J. & J. Leeming*'s City Markets (1904, *see* p. 426) but placed here in 1912, the date of the awkward tiled shelter spreading around its base. Buildings here are mainly from the boom years after 1891, including on Roundhay Road a Jacobean-style shopping parade by *W. Carby Hall*, at the N end of which is the eyecatching OAKWOOD FISH BAR, a dazzling Art Deco façade of *c.* 1938–40 in Vitrolite and stainless steel with a giant porthole window.

Now for the area to the S, where development began in the 1820s on the Elam holding. OAKWOOD LANE climbs SE from the Roundhay Road into an area of extensive C20 suburbia built in the grounds of the early villas. First, on the r., is OAKWOOD HOUSE, a superior classical villa, built for Robert Hudson, woollen merchant, whose family occupied several of the early houses. Quite plain, like most, but for full-height bay windows. Later extended. On the E side, beyond Springwood Road, is the former lodge to SPRINGWOOD HOUSE, which stands to the E. Built 1826 for Stephen Nicholson. Simplest Grecian with a pediment overall. Cantilevered stair inside.

Further S in OAKWOOD GRANGE LANE is BEDFORD HOUSE, stuccoed with canted bays, then 250yds N on the same side of the lane is another substantial house, OAKWOOD HALL, whose pleasant grounds serve as a reminder of those lost elsewhere. S front of seven bays under a balustraded parapet, the outer bays again canted. The lane now becomes a narrow path and another 250yds on, facing OAKWOOD GREEN, is a fine house (now Eller Close). Elegant seven bay range with Greek Doric portico, built in the 1820s by William Ledgard, woollen manufacturer. Its rear is an earlier Georgian house, with canted bay in the centre. Boxy Late Victorian Domestic Revival style coachhouse and stables.

E of NORTH LANE, North Hill – a villa of the 1820s by *Thomas Taylor* for Stephen Nicholson – has gone, but to the SE on this road is NORTH GROVE (W side) and, opposite, a larger mansion, THE GROVE, which was built in 1839 for Joshua Burton, wool stapler. Both have segmental bays. In the other direction, North Lane runs down to WETHERBY ROAD, lined with mature trees and middling late C19 houses set back. This marked the boundary between the Elam and Nicholson holdings.

The bigger houses begun on Nicholson's land after in 1873 can be seen along PARK AVENUE, sweeping NE of the clock tower and open on one side to the park. Its width oozes wealth, but there are now more gates and lodges than villas. The earliest houses are impressively sized, though their number has been thinned and the quality diluted by alteration, demolition and development. The largest and earliest of the houses in WEST AVENUE is *W. H. Thorp*'s huge WOODLANDS, built for Charles Barran in the early 1880s. Opposite on PARK

AVENUE beyond the junction with West Avenue, HATWOOD (No. 8) was designed for himself by *George Hatton c.* 1900. To the E PARKSTONE and GREYSTONE, then where PARK AVENUE curves round behind these houses is an Old English-style LODGE (timber vernacular, good plasterwork) to Wood-bourne (dem.), a grand house by *Smith & Tweedale* also of the 1880s. PARKMONT, 1883 by *Ambler* for John Barran Jun., is Old English too, but cut from a plainer cloth and now so swollen by extensions as to be almost unrecognizable.

OLD PARK ROAD runs along the W side of the Park. To its W is the area largely completed according to Corson's plan of 1873. Here plots were gradually released with strict covenants intended to attract 'quality'; houses were to be generally of stone, have plots of at least ⅓ acre, and to sell for an agreed minimum price. The tree-lined streets were built up by 1901, and in their maturity are now magnificently verdant. The solid detached and semi-detached houses are of a more modest scale than those on Park Road, and built in a mixture of stone and roughcast or in a debased Old English style. *W. H. Beevers* designed many of them, and lived in Shaftesbury Avenue (*see* St Andrew). Slightly N is the Lidgett Park estate, developed by J. W. Archer. His architect was *W. Carby Hall* (*see* St Edmund).

ELMETE LANE. Running up the E side of the park between fields and paddocks is a fragment of the estate that was never suburbanized. BEECHWOOD, E of the Lane, is a five-bay early C19 house with a Tuscan porch, a canted bay on its E side and a substantial rear service wing. More interesting and impressive is ELMETE HALL, on the W side further up the hill. Built *c.* 1815 but comprehensively rebuilt and extended in 1865 by *Dobson & Chorley* as a grandiose classical villa for Sir James Kitson. It was not done cheaply, but nor was it composed lucidly. Entrance front, W, with the centre projecting as almost a complete octagon; this formerly rose two storeys higher to make a tower. Narrow oriel over the door. Asymmetrical S front, its r. half set back with a pyramid roof over its E corner to make a tower. At the centre of the house is a domed drum containing the staircase. (Cantilevered stone stair inside with scrolling iron balustrade under a vault filled with a coloured, petal-pattern skylight.) Converted into offices, 2006, with a Modernist box entirely filling the former service yard on the N side joining the office wing to the stables.

¾ m. N is COBBLE HALL FARM. The farmhouse, probably C18, was remodelled by the Nicholsons to form a picturesque castellated Gothick eyecatcher in views W across their park.

ROUNDHAY HALL. *See* Gledhow.

SHADWELL

Formerly a township in Thorner (q.v.) but absorbed into the City of Leeds in 1912. It is in two parts: the village itself, still detached, and suburban development along Shadwell Lane, now merged with Alwoodley and Moor Allerton (*see* above) on the outer edge of the city.

St Paul, Main Street. By *R. D. Chantrell*, consecrated 1842 as a chapel of ease to Thorner. Neo-Norman, of just four bays, with a w bellcote and e apse. Queenpost roof, w gallery on four wooden columns, with organ. Wooden reredos by *Martin Travers*, 1920s, with low reliefs of St Peter and St Paul (simplified and repainted by *Frank Lisle*, 1967–8). Wooden baldachino with dove suspended from the chancel ceiling. The chief interest is the stained glass, installed in 1849 by the Tractarian curate, Frederick Hathaway. Apse windows in the style of Pugin, the centre one signed by *O'Connor*. The nave windows are a kaleidoscopic collection of fragments from at least three sources of different ages, perhaps arranged by *Bower* of Hunslet.

Library, Main Street. Former Wesleyan chapel, early C19, like a plain, three-bay house.

Leeds Industrial School (former), Shadwell Lane. Dated 1879, probably by *Richard Adams*, Leeds School Board architect. Coursed gritstone. Two storeys and twenty bays long, with pedimented centre and pedimented end pavilions.

Red Hall, Red Hall Lane, ¾ m s on the w side of Wetherby Road. Now offices, at the edge of the Leeds municipal nurseries. Red brick with a nine-bay front of two storeys, apparently comprising an C18 centre of five bays (the house belonged to the Ibbetsons 1710–61) with early C19 two-bay additions. The three centre bays project slightly under a pediment. Pedimented doorway and large semicircular window above with fan glazing, set in an overarch. This window and those either side light a double-height hall with carved doorcases, modillion cornice and ceiling rose. Large (C19?) fireplace with heavy console brackets and carved device of the Ibbetsons. Fine mid-C18 staircase with column-on-vase balusters and carved string; service stair with the same. At the rear, two gables, possibly C17. Beyond, a stable and service yard.

dovecote, 150 yds nw, C18. Square, of coursed gritstone, with pyramid roof and cupola (crudely restored).

Shadwell Grange, s of Shadwell Lane. A complex of suburban villa, farmhouse, cottage, and farm buildings. The farm buildings, *c.* 1810, form a large formal U-plan, open to the s. Attached sw is the house, built in the 1820s for Stephen Nicholson of Roundhay Park. It has five-bay façades w and s (with central full-height bay). Altered and extended for Henry Barran, son of Sir John Barran, by *Bedford & Kitson* in 1903, including the parapet and pediment on the s façade, and enriched entrance on the w. Pretty lodge of the same date.

EAST

CROSSGATES AND MANSTON

Suburban development started in the late C19 around the railway station but the greatest period of expansion was in the 1930s and building continued post 1945.

St James the Great, Church Road, Manston. 1911–14 by *Chorley & Connon*. It replaced a church of 1846–7 by *Perkin & Backhouse*. Dec. style. Only three bays of the nave, the chancel, lady chapel and s aisle were built, the latter with windows breaking through the eaves forming three gables. Chunky buttresses. The nave was extended to the w in 1939.

Crossgates Wesleyan Methodist Church, Austhorpe Road. The original chapel is of 1882, replaced in 1892 by a larger building alongside and subsequently used as the schools. Both by *G. F. Danby*, in a complementary red brick Gothic, the earlier building with a rose window, the later with slim corner turrets.

Arndale Centre, Station Road, Crossgates. 1967, the first Arndale centre to be opened and one of the first covered shopping malls in England. Single level shops along broad L-shaped malls with natural lighting through a clerestory. Refurbished with new atria but the basic form remains unaltered.

GIPTON

Historically part of the Potternewton township (*see* above), but now one of the bleakest C20 Corporation housing estates, begun in 1934.

Epiphany, Foundry Lane. 1936–8 by *N. F. Cachemaille-Day*, 120 built as part of the same gift which funded St Wilfrid, Halton (*see* below). 'A building of remarkable originality, and internally . . . an exceptionally happy blend of the C20 idiom with just sufficient Gothic allusion to make it acceptable to the Church of England worshipper' (Pevsner). Brick, with a reinforced concrete frame. The e end is the most impressive feature, composed of sweeping curves and stepped up like that of a French Romanesque church: low semicircle of the Lady Chapel, higher semicircle of the ambulatory, yet higher pitched roof. An intended 100-ft (31-metre) bell-tower over the sw porch was not built and a flèche surmounted by an illuminated star over the altar was substituted (removed 1976). The interior, now painted white, has 60-ft (18.5-metre)-high circular concrete piers supporting flat ceilings, those of the aisles slightly lower than the nave. Transepts two bays deep. The chancel is barely distinguishable from the nave with an apse of the same height and an ambulatory around. The sanctuary is slightly raised on a circular plinth with simple curved altar rails and seats built in, anticipating the late C20 move towards nave altars. Service rooms curve outside the sides of the ambulatory and are separated from it by more, equally tall, circular piers and half-high screen walls. The Lady Chapel is theatrically raised by sixteen steps behind the altar with access from the ambulatory and thus visible from the nave, an arrangement developed from St Nicholas, Burnage, Manchester. The windows are very slim, narrow and straight-headed, and they are very close to each other all along the sides and end. The choir galleries are most unusually behind the altar, facing the nave on the same level as the Lady Chapel. STAINED GLASS by *Christopher Webb* in the Lady Chapel depicting the Epiphany stars with blue the dominant colour: 'Expressionist, not to say jazzy', thought Pevsner.

ST NICHOLAS (R.C.), Oakwood Lane. The first overtly Modernist Roman Catholic church in Leeds, opened 1961. By *Weightman & Bullen*, with a tall, slender pierced campanile over a baptistery (now office) separated from the church by a narthex. The folded roof of the square nave, generously glazed with closely spaced mullions, rakes up to a blocky tower over the sanctuary, recalling St Paul, Glenrothes, Fife, by Gillespie, Kidd & Coia (1957). The tower provided concealed light to the altar, which was originally against the E wall. – FONT (now in the N aisle) and PULPIT of marble. Interior originally painted gold and white, to match the MOSAIC on the E wall and complement the abstract STAINED GLASS dalle-de-verre in the side chapels off the S aisle by *Pierre Fourmaintreaux* of *Whitefriars Studio*.

HALTON

An interwar suburb, continuous with Whitkirk.

ST WILFRID, Selby Road. 1937–9 by *A. Randall Wells*. His last building, a fascinating work marking the ultimate development of his individualistic strand of Arts and Crafts architecture. The cost was met by the Sunderland shipbuilder Sir John Priestman, who had funded St Andrew's, Roker, Sunderland (Co. Durham), where Randall Wells was E.S. Prior's site architect.

The church is faced in narrow courses with coping of upright stone slabs as on the top of dry-stone walls. It has a cruciform plan, the nave with low passage aisles, and the windows all above them. The massing is bold and planar, with flush glazing and blocky transepts and chancel contrasted with an apsidal E end and, over the low crossing tower, the sharp and spiky form of the stocky wooden spire with many little gables around its octagonal timber substructure. The architecture is essentially ahistoric, but with allusions to the Gothic, such as the windows, which derive from groups of stepped E.E. lancets, though the insertion of one large horizontal rectangle into each group is odd. Light floods the white-painted interior, with its simple unmoulded arches and the steep, folded vaulting like an upturned ship. Reordering was completed in 1987: chapel screens in the transepts were removed, and the altar brought forward on a platform w of the choir. Behind this, like a reredos, a fabric screen woven by *Evelyn Ross*. The apse is now a Lady Chapel. – WOODWORK. Designed by *Randall Wells* as a contrast to the coolness of the interior. Delightfully lively turned balusters very closely set for screens, pulpit, communion rail, etc. – FONT. From Barton, North Riding. Lined with a large C18 silver punch bowl. – SCULPTURE. Statue of St Wilfrid by *Eric Gill* or his studio, s transept, c. 1939. Also in the s transept the best of a programme of works by local sculptor *Irene Payne*, this depicting Jesus offering the church to his mother. Of c. 1951, in the manner of Barbara Hepworth. By contrast Our Lady (1947) in the N transept is stiff. Also a series of reliefs of 1947 mounted in the nave, titled Mysteries of the Rosary, which convey a real sense of mystery.

HALTON PRIMARY SCHOOL, Selby Road and School Lane. A remnant of the C19 village. Built in 1842 on site of an earlier Grammar School. Single storey, gables and mullioned windows. Post-war school to the N.

OSMONDTHORPE

ST PHILIP, Osmondthorpe Lane. 1932–3 by *F. L. Charlton*; the first suburban church completed under Bishop Burroughs' Church Forward Movement (cf. St Cross, Middleton). Early Christian style with, inside, great reinforced-concrete round arches rhythmically spanning the nave (cf. Charlton's St Cross, Middleton). Charlton-designed FITTINGS, all in chunky oak characteristic of the maker, *Robert Thompson*. FONT and PULPIT with jazzy zigzags.

CORPUS CHRISTI (R.C.), Neville Road. 1962 by *Reynolds & Scott* for the Order of the Oblates of Mary Immaculate (cf. Mount St Mary, p. 462). Remarkably large and recherché basilican-plan church in a Romanesque/Early Christian style with 90-ft (28-metre)-high sw bell-tower. Brick, except the stone-faced centre of the w front. Broad w portico of Tuscan columns. Huge, broad, barrel-vaulted nave with six transepts and passage aisles, whose three-bay arcades are echoed in the clerestory lights cut from the curving vault. w organ gallery over a narthex. Chapels flanking the shallow chancel. Extensive use of marbles – quite an expense – for wall surfaces and the FITTINGS. Minimal reordering. STAINED GLASS by *Earley Studios* of Dublin. The w window is a copy of Murillo's Assumption of Our Lady. This is flanked by a Baroque ORGAN CASE.

SEACROFT AND SWARCLIFFE

Seacroft is a settlement of ancient foundation on the eastern outskirts of Leeds, originally in the parish of Whitkirk (q.v.). From
1937 it was subsumed in the city's largest council estate. The early
stages follow the typical pre-war cottage layout but much of the
housing built on both sides of York Road (A64) and across the
Ring Road into Swarcliffe was erected after the Second World
War. Thirteen multi-storey blocks, 5,539 houses, 1,760 flats and
maisonettes were built by 1968: the tower blocks still dominate
the skyline of E Leeds.

ST JAMES, York Road and The Green. 1844–5 by *Thomas Hellyer*
of Ryde, Isle of Wight. Built on the initiative of the Vicar of
Whitkirk, and John Wilson of Seacroft Grange. It cost £3,174.
Lancet windows. N transept and two-bay aisle with, at the W
end, a tower with broach spire. In 1932 S nave fenestration
altered, to accommodate a new two-light window with quatrefoil. Five-bay nave with chancel arch flanked by paired
niches; that on the r. had the Lord's Prayer inscribed on slate,
now painted over. Aisle arcade with round piers and double-
chamfered arches, the two W bays now screened off. –
REREDOS of Caen stone by the architect. – FONT, 1878. With
a massive octagonal bowl of alabaster, and columns at the
angles of the multi-stone stem. Executed by a *Mr Lomas*, successor to *Hall & Co.* of Derby. – STAINED GLASS. Three-light
E window of 1845. – Chancel N, two lancets of 1868, and nave
S, a two-light lancet of 1869, both by *Hardman*.

ASCENSION, Foundry Mill Street. 1961. Remarkably conservative for its date with paired round-headed windows in an Early
Christian manner and cruciform plan with the sanctuary under
the tower – surmounted by a curious gazebo-like lantern – and
a chapel in the eastern arm. Plain interior.

ST LUKE, Stanks Lane North, Swarcliffe. By *M. J. Farmer*,
opened 1963. Steeply pitched slated roof canted at the W end
with the entire gable-end glazed. Full-height nave windows.

ST RICHARD, Ramshead Hill, Seacroft. 1955–6 by *Jones &
Stocks*. Church and hall under a single roof, separated by a
movable partition. On a sharply falling site, with a tall gabled
E wall that has a cross extending almost its full height and a
SE tower over the porch.

OUR LADY OF GOOD COUNSEL (R.C.), Kentmere Avenue.
1958–60 by *Arthur Farebrother & Partners*. Large, Early
Christian style with a NW campanile. Tall paired, round-headed
windows and pantiled roofs.

ST GREGORY THE GREAT (R.C.), Swarcliffe Drive, Swarcliffe.
1969–70 by *L. A. G. Pritchard Son & Partners*. Octagonal plan
under a hyperbolic paraboloid roof. Cutting into the octagon,
a triangular baptistery and chapel, also triangular and top-lit.
Both have terrazzo tile facings. A glazed narthex opens into the
square nave. – STAINED GLASS by *J. Faczynski*, notably 60 ft
(18.5 metres) long by 10 ft (3 metres) tall window above the

sanctuary. – STATIONS OF THE CROSS by the same artist, painted in black line on coloured glass and set in an abstract composition. – Ceramic RELIEFS by *A. Kossowski* for shrines to St Gregory and Our Lady. A substantial sacristy is linked by a glazed corridor to the presbytery.

SEACROFT HOSPITAL, York Road. An infectious diseases hospital of 1900–4 by *E. T. Hall*. Brick, with a prominent and sturdy tapering tower on the centre line of a well-preserved symmetrical layout, with detached single-storey wards linked by walkways under iron awnings.

The centre of Seacroft is the spacious former village GREEN, with the church of St James on the S side, a row of cottages and houses on the N side, and at the NE corner SEACROFT GRANGE (disused in 2008). A Jacobethan-style rebuilding of 1834–7 by *Matthew Habershon* for John Wilson, in ashlar, and with prominent gables, chimneys etc. The superb late C17 staircase brought from Austhorpe Hall (*see* p. 549) has been taken into store. The COACH HOUSE is vernacular, apart from the four-pointed arches.

TEMPLE NEWSAM HOUSE*

First recorded in the Domesday Book in 1086 (as Neuhusum or 'at the new houses'), the manor of Newsam became a property of the Knights Templar in 1155** but after their suppression eventually passed to the Darcy family. Thomas Darcy – a courtier, mercenary and later crony of Thomas Wolsey – built the first house on the present site *c.* 1488–1521. It had a courtyard plan, entered through a gatehouse in the N range, but after it was bought in 1622 by Sir Arthur Ingram, a London merchant, the E range, containing lodgings, was demolished, probably after a fire in 1636, and the gatehouse taken down, creating the house essentially as one finds it today. Sir Arthur also erected a retaining wall with gates between the N and S wings but these were taken down in 1719 and replaced with a lower wall, also since removed.

In its style the house is still purely Jacobean, of the type of Hatfield, Blickling and Bramshill, but much of the C16 W range remains visible: diaper-patterned brickwork and symmetrical arrangements of large polygonal and small rectangular bay windows. Sandstone dressings to the E face change to limestone with Gothic panelling. These would originally have looked much more Perp for the transoms are later, possibly C17, insertions. Excavations suggest that there were stair-towers at the inner angles of the wings, and that the W face of

---

34

*This entry has been contributed by Anthony Wells-Cole.
**The Templars' preceptory (including a hall, chamber, chapel and kitchen in 1311) is thought to have stood at Temple Thorpe Farm.

the W range had three central bays flanked by polygonal stair-cases or privy towers – blocked doorways survive inside. In the centre of the courtyard face of the N wing is a moulded stone doorway, truncated when the courtyard was raised in the C18. The S front was completely asymmetrical, the kitchens at the E end with pantries etc. in an extension at the SE corner. Ingram added the large canted bay windows to the inner and outer elevations and unified the skyline with a stone balustrade. On the courtyard side this is in the form of a loyal inscription, set up in 1628 (and renewed with the present iron letters – cast by *Wigglesworth & Eyres & Co.* at Seacroft – in 1788). At the E end of the N wing are basement windows with arched lights, for Sir Arthur's chapel. Originally square-headed, the arches are a contrivance. The original mullioned-and-transomed windows were altered to sashes with stone architraves in a piecemeal campaign between *c.* 1719 and 1745 – piecemeal because Rich, 5th Viscount Irwin, speculated reck-lessly in the South Sea Company and lost a fortune in 1720. However, they were restored to their previous form in the 1890s during works for Emily Meynell Ingram (the scars where their architraves were hacked off can still be seen) and she remodelled the N front, which had been given a pedimented Palladian frontispiece in the earlier C18: the present façade is in sandstone. The porch in the S wing with round-arched entrance flanked by coupled Ionic columns must be Sir Arthur's, but the panel and bust are of *c.* 1670–80 and the lime-stone cladding above and faux quoins belong to the remodel-ling of this elevation after 1788 by *William Johnson* of Leeds for Frances, widow of the 9th Viscount. His façade is asym-metrical and ill-coordinated: limestone dressings, lintels with roundels and fluting, mullions with Gothick panels. The cupola over the W wing is his too.

The house and park were sold to Leeds Corporation in 1922 by Lord Halifax but the sale did not include the contents, and the historic decoration of virtually every INTERIOR was oblit-erated for use as the City's Art Gallery during the Second World War. Many of the rooms have been restored since 1983, mostly reflecting changes made in the C18 and C19.

On the ground floor of the S wing is the GREAT HALL of the Tudor and Jacobean house, formerly entered via a screens passage but altered in the later C18 by *Johnson*, who made it the centrepiece of five new reception rooms. Panelling and ceiling with plaster ribs and cartouches in the 'Old English' style were added in the 1820s, during changes made for Isabella, Marchioness of Hertford (†1834). STAINED GLASS in the bay window is C16–C18 and was removed from the chapel (*see* below). At the E end, on the site of the buttery or pantry, is MR WOOD'S LIBRARY, of 1912 by *Ralph Freeman-Smith* of *Lenygon's*, a mostly convincing essay in the Early Georgian style. Next, the BLUE DRAWING ROOM, as remodelled (from the late C18 Best Dining Room) in 1827–9, with imported

Régence door architraves and hand-painted Chinese wallpaper (given by the Prince of Wales in 1806) embellished with birds cut from Audubon's *Birds of America*. W of the Great Hall is the TERRACE ROOM, another Regency interior, hung with Brussels tapestries. It was adapted from the ante-room created by Wyatt in *c.* 1777 for his new staircase (*see* below). Beyond it, the DINING ROOM (originally the Parlour) retains its 1630s plaster ceiling and frieze by *Francis Gunby* (cf. St John, Briggate), as well as much of its panelling. The room was remodelled in 1889–91 by *C. E. Kempe*. The chimneypiece and overmantel are adapted from those in the hall at Hardwick, Derbyshire. The cellars of this wing (not open to the public) contain evidence of Darcy's early C16 house in the form of four-centred arches, an oak door frame and probably a buttery hatch guarding the kitchen.

The LITTLE GALLERY (also by Kempe, 1889–91, with moulded plaster frieze) connects the Dining Room to Kempe's OAK STAIRCASE, since 1894 the link between the S and W wings. To create a staircase here passages and rooms at three levels were shortened and even then it failed to link the floors to the two-storey S wing and the three-storey W wing. It continues the 'Old English' theme of the Great Hall and Dining Room and is very grand and archaeological. Plasterwork, perhaps by *Battiscombe & Harris*: the ceiling of West Country pattern, frieze aping Speke or Burton Agnes, soffits of stairflights and landings inspired by the gallery ceiling at Hatfield. Joinery and carving by *Norman & Burt* of Burgess Hill, Sussex: the oak newel posts have carved decoration by *William Court*, some copied from the staircase from Slaugham Place, Sussex (now in Lewes Town Hall); the newel figures with heraldic shields were added in 1897. (The stair replaced Wyatt's top-lit staircase of *c.* 1777 and evidence of his chaste Neoclassical plasterwork and lantern survives behind the Victorian decoration.)

The FIRST FLOOR of the W WING continues the grand processional route that began in the Great Hall and culminates in the Picture Gallery in the N wing (*see* below). The GALLERY PASSAGE, now with panelling and plasterwork by Kempe, was created in 1745 to link the S and N wings. C18 plasterwork concealed behind the panelling masks clustered shafts of the Tudor chamber which spanned the centre of this wing (carved oak lintels of the matching transverse chamber on the ground floor are visible in the Stone Passage and Still Room, *see* below). The passage terminates at the N WING, which on this floor was occupied by Sir Arthur Ingram's Gallery (finished *c.* 1635) before it was reconstructed in 1738–46 as (from E to W) the Library, Picture Gallery and Crimson Bedroom. This was the major achievement of Henry, 7th Viscount Irwin, and *Daniel Garrett* was almost certainly the architect throughout. The LIBRARY has a giant order derived from Palladio and lively proto-Rococo plasterwork of 1743 by *Thomas Perritt*. It was converted into a chapel by *G. F. Bodley* in 1877: only the organ by *Wordsworth & Maskell* of Leeds remains. The PICTURE GALLERY also has a Perritt ceiling with portrait medallions of George I, George II and other members of the royal family. *Richard Fisher* of York was the carver who decorated the joinery. Two fireplaces by *Robert Doe* of London after designs by *William Kent* published in 1735 have overmantel paintings by *Antonio Joli*. Original furniture by *James Pascall* and Grand Tour paintings by *Antonio Marini*. Hidden are blocked windows and fragments of the elaborate moulded plasterwork of Sir Arthur's Gallery, and patches of genuine stuccowork – one marbled with traces of gilt leather-mâché – from the early Tudor rooms that Sir Arthur destroyed in creating his Gallery.

The rooms on the outside of the W wing are also mostly mid-C18 in character. For example the GOTHICK ROOM has a chimneypiece, virtuoso overmantel frame and Rococo plasterwork all of 1759 (the remarkable contemporary Gothic Revival 'stucco paper' was reprinted in 1993). However, behind the Boudoir is an C18 servant's 'Dark Room' formed from a larger C16 interior: its brick fire-arch and oak-ribbed plaster ceiling survive. The STONE STAIRCASE linking the W and N wings is perhaps of *c.* 1788; it was given the elegant wrought-iron balustrade of Wyatt's staircase in 1894. In the S WING where there are now a series of late C18 rooms was the 'Greate Chambr' (of the 1565 inventory), over the present Great Hall and Blue Drawing Room. Its entrance from the stairs is marked by a moulded stone jamb hidden behind later work. The chamber was divided in the mid C18 and again by *Johnson* to create the SOUTH PASSAGE, with little Gothick brackets under the cornice. Of the adjoining rooms, at the E end is the PRINCE'S ROOM with a chimneypiece and doorcases rescued from Methley Hall (q.v.) in the 1950s; at the W end, the DARNLEY ROOM of *c.* 1897 by Kempe, panelled and fitted with plasterwork reproducing C17 originals elsewhere in the house. Much Jacobean plasterwork survives behind later decoration, including a complete ceiling beneath the floor of the Grey Room next door.

The SECOND FLOOR of the W wing contained in the C16 important rooms including, perhaps, the chapel, but all were much altered in the C18. One room has Late Gothic/Early Renaissance panelling of 1542 brought from Bretton Hall, near Barnsley, in 1947: built-in cupboard with portraits of Sir Thomas Wentworth and his two wives; more carvings on the bed. Other rooms here had their C18 architectural features removed in the 1940s, in an attempt to recapture their early Tudor character. A shallow niche has been revealed in one room together with a blocked fireplace and several blocked doors, one leading to what may have been a stair-turret. Several more C16 fire-arches survive elsewhere, behind later decoration.

Most of the GROUND FLOOR and BASEMENT of the W and N wings are not open to the public. In the basement of the N wing is the former SERVANTS' HALL of *c.* 1718–19, and at the E end the C17 CHAPEL converted *c.* 1788 into the kitchen and now partly restored with some of its original decoration and FURNISHINGS, including *John Carleton*'s painting of The Supper at Emmaus and his series of eighteen Old Testament figures (painted in 1636–7). – Carved oak PULPIT of 1636, by *Thomas Ventris Jun.*, a small-panelled example of contemporary Leeds type (cf. St John's, Briggate). – REREDOS by *Bodley*, 1877. The ground floor contains the Stone Passage and Steward's Room, created *c.* 1719, and North Hall panelled by Kempe in 1897. Towards the E end one room, now at mezzanine level, has the best surviving length of moulded plaster frieze of the 1630s. In the centre of the W wing, the Still Room has been restored along with its china 'presses' dating from 1740.

NE of the house are the STABLES. They were built in the 1740s, probably designed by *Daniel Garrett*, and extended by *Capability Brown* in the 1760s. Brick with stone dressings. Pretty cupola over W range with single-handed clock and weathervane in the form of a cock, the Ingram crest. The small two-room structure attached to the SW corner was built – perhaps by *William Johnson* – from the late C18 onwards as a DAIRY and appears to incorporate lengths of the 'out walls' created by *William Etty c.* 1726–7. To the N is the FARM. The GREAT BARN is the oldest building, built in 1694 (despite its incorrectly restored datestone). C18 dovecote, farmhouse and ancillary buildings, of brick and vernacular in character.

GARDENS AND PARK. SW of the house is the MOUNT, only survivor of the Tudor park and gardens. The S GARDEN dates from the 1970s but has a fountain cast by *Andrew Handyside & Co.* of Derby *c.* 1875 which was the centrepiece of the Italianate garden laid out by Emily Meynell Ingram.

The PARK that Leeds bought in 1922 consisted of 917 acres. Its spatial and visual structure today is still recognizably that of *Capability Brown* in the 1760s. He retained the C17 AVENUES to W and N, together with the EAST AVENUE, laid out by *William Etty* of York between 1710 and 1715 with bridges, cascades and fish ponds. The Gothick E lodges by *Carr* were demolished in 1946. Approaching on foot along this avenue the house rises up, vanishes, then reappears, closer and more impressive each time. Most visitors, however, approach from the NW, or the N, between LODGES built 1742, perhaps to designs by *Sir Andrew Fountaine*. The SPHINX GATES, NE of the house, are *Brown*'s, copying Lord Burlington's at Chiswick: rusticated stone piers topped by lead sphinxes, gates cast by *Robert Johnson* in 1768. (Flanking walls of modern brick and incongruous cast-iron railings, N of the gates, rescued from Board Schools in Leeds in the 1970s.) Remains of Brown's HA-HA survive nearby and beyond the ponds is his little pedimented prostyle TEMPLE with columns of clustered shafts. The ha-ha beyond the bowling green W of the house was introduced after 1904. Open-cast coal mining during and after the Second World War defaced most of the S of the estate and the historic tranquillity has been destroyed by the motorway crossing the Aire Valley. This should be screened by landscaping and tree planting.

In the park, forming the E boundary of Avenue Wood, is a section of GRIM'S DITCH, a defensive earthwork running N–S for about 2½ m. It stands up to 52ft wide with the bank 2ft high and the ditch 2ft deep. Like the Aberford Dykes, it has been associated with the Anglo-Saxon kingdom of Elmet but has now been dated to 790–400 B.C.

WHITKIRK

Formerly in the township of Temple Newsam, now engulfed by suburban development.

ST MARY, Selby Road, by Colton Road. Perp, except for the extension to the chancel of 1900–1 by *Bodley*. A sturdy building, W tower of the type like Rothwell and Barwick, but with a spike (cf. Knaresborough). Short nave with clerestory, aisles with three-light windows and parapets projecting on heavy corbels, some carved as grotesque masks (cf. Bramham), and a S porch with closely placed transverse single-chamfered ribs. Four-bay arcades with short octagonal piers, double-chamfered arches. Roofs largely of 1855–6, but nave and S aisle retain medieval bosses. One-bay N chapel, the S chapel, founded as a chantry *c.* 1448, of two, with a smaller third under which stands the Scargill monument (*see below*). Door to the former rood stair, N aisle. Reordered by *Peter Hill* in 1980 with new stone ALTARS for the S chapel and the chancel, now brought forward on a raised floor. Bodley's former S parclose SCREEN repositioned across the rear of the chancel to create a sacristy behind. Choir stalls removed, and C19 CHOIR STALLS from Harewood church placed at the rear of the nave. – Plain C10–C11 FONT, reintroduced. – STAINED GLASS. Tower window, 1855 by *Willement*, from the N chapel. – Four windows by *Michael O'Connor*, 1856: chancel E, N aisle, 2nd and 4th from E and S aisle 3rd from E. – S aisle 4th from E by *Burlison & Grylls*, 1862. By the same firm the chancel windows of 1901. – Two windows in the S aisles with Ingram arms by *Powell & Sons*, 1901, and S chapel E window of the same date by *Alfred Beer*. – MONUMENTS. Sir Robert Scargill †1531–2 and his wife †1546–7, no doubt erected after her death. Two recumbent alabaster effigies. Tomb-chest with a few mourners standing rather lonely each against a horizontal rectangular cusped panel. The panels are separated by spiral-twisted colonnettes. The lettering is still black-letter. – The 2nd Viscount Irwin of Temple Newsam (†1688) and his wife (†1746) and daughter (†1688), erected 1697. Completed by *John van Nost,* but very probably begun by *Edward Pearce* who made designs. A tomb-chest with tall 'reredos' background with pilasters and segmental pediment. The sides of the chest were removed in the 1960s, and the lowered effigies have an injurious effect on the proportions of the monument. Semi-reclining effigy of the young Viscount in meticulously rendered dress and with wig.

To his l. his wife seated in a mournful attitude, to his r. their only daughter who died at the age of two. She sits in her little shirt and contemplates a skull. – John Smeaton, the celebrated engineer, †1792. Tablet with, on top of it, a portrait of the Eddystone lighthouse. By *Robert Cooke*. Smeaton was born in the parish and is buried beneath the chancel. – Viscount Irwin, by *Nollekens*, 1810. Amply draped woman standing and bending over an urn. Grey convex-sided obelisk at the back. – Lord William Gordon, by *Henry Westmacott*, 1824. Small standing figure of Lord William as a Gordon Highlander.

AUSTHORPE HALL, Austhorpe Lane, ½ m. NE of the church at the edge of the built-up area. Handsome brick-built house dated 1694, a two-storey rectangle of seven by three bays, with hipped stone slab roof, stone dressings, wooden eaves cornice and wooden one-bay pediment. Quoins to both the angles and the centre bay; cross-windows, with lugged surrounds and wooden mullions and transoms, linked vertically by raised panels; doorway with pulvinated frieze and broken pediment. A number of rooms with good-quality panelling, and one with a simple compartmented ceiling. The main staircase, to the rear of the central hall, is a mid-C19 replacement, the original moved to Seacroft Grange (q.v.): back stairs alongside with bulbous balusters. Stone-built single-storey kitchen block at the rear, perhaps part of an earlier house.

THORPE PARK BUSINESS PARK, ¾ m. E of the church, by the M1 junction. INNOVATE GREEN OFFICE, by *Rio Architects*, 2005–7. Two blocks, of two and three storeys, joined by a full-height atrium. The design uses the building's thermal mass and heavy insulation for temperature control, and maximum penetration of natural light through the plan etc. to minimize carbon emissions.

SOUTH AND SOUTH-EAST

BEESTON

Listed in Domesday as a township of Leeds parish. The manor was held in two moieties by the C15; one was Cad Beeston, now more often called Beeston Hill (*see* below). For centuries Beeston was a mining district, and later also a rhubarb cultivating area. Suburban development did not begin in earnest until the start of the C20. Since the war, the historic centre along Town Street with its cottages and passageways has been almost entirely redeveloped in dismal fashion.

ST MARY, Town Street. On the site of a chapel of ease. By *C. H. Thornton*, 1877 (chancel) and 1885–6 (nave and aisles) in E.E. style with steep roof and undersized SW tower with octagonal belfry and spirelet. Re-set Perp window at the E end of the S aisle (C16 heraldic glass in the tracery) and three, three-light mullioned windows. – FONT. C17, chamfered shaft, strapwork decoration to the bowl. – PULPIT. Given 1886: octagonal, arcaded panels. – ALTAR, REREDOS, SANCTUARY PANELLING and CHANCEL SCREEN, Gothic, 1920 by *Bridgeman & Sons*. – W GALLERY. *c.* 1876, refaced in 1932 when a new ORGAN was installed. – ARCHITECTURAL FRAGMENTS. In the vestry. C12; crudely arranged as an arch over a doorway, with varied chevron and zig-zag pattern voussoirs and bits of stringcourse springing from cushion capitals. – STAINED GLASS. The oldest and best Victorian glass is the E window of *c.* 1878, by *Thomas Baillie (Baillie & Mayer)*, the rest by *Powell Bros*, 1894–5, and *Kayll & Co.*, 1905. – MEMORIALS. From the old church. BRASS. Elizabeth Hodgson †1648, with coat of arms and long Latin inscription (second, smaller, brass to a woman of the same name †1669 and her husband †1649). – John Jackson of Cottingley Hall †1695, surmounted by a coat of arms.

ST DAVID, Waincliffe Drive/Dewsbury Road. 1960–1 by *Geoffrey Davy* of *Kitson, Parish, Ledgard & Pyman* (cf. St Cyprian & St James, Harehills, and St Paul, Cookridge). Modest scale, with brick walls (painted white inside) but with a striking distorted rectangular plan under a diagonally aligned hyperbolic paraboloid roof, which is raised at the SE corner over a full-height window inset with a stone cross. On the N side a stepped row of tall slit windows. Inside, the S wall curves around to embrace the PULPIT, concealing the light from the SE window, and both corners of the N wall are curved too. The FONT originally stood in the NW corner under a circular skylight.

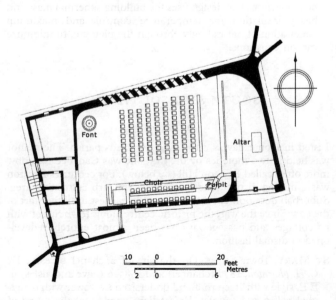

Leeds, Beeston, St David.
Plan

BEESTON METHODIST CHURCH, Town Street (now closed). 1865–6, almost certainly by *William Hill*, with a substantial hall beneath the chapel. Organ chamber, 1896, and later vestry. BOX PEWS, ROSTRUM and CHOIR STALLS with ORGAN behind (gallery now concealed). – STAINED GLASS. In the E wall, a First World War memorial by *William Pape*.

CITY EVANGELICAL CHURCH, Cemetery Road. Former Baptist church by *Walter Hobson & Co.*, 1901. Pilasters, round-headed first-floor windows and raised pediment over the centre. Full basement with large hall. Galleried interior. – SUNDAY SCHOOL of 1875 behind, facing Malvern Street, with large hall at right angles.

STANK HALL, E of Dewsbury Road, 1 m. S of Town Street, opposite the entrance to the White Rose Shopping Centre. Remains of a house built by the Beeston family, who created a hunting park here in the later C15. Two storeys and two bays wide, originally timber-framed but later encased in gritstone and later brick. In the N wall (C17) is a chimneystack widened to incorporate a corbelled latrine. (Inside are three pairs of principal posts, bressumer and wall-plate with short straight braces, a cross-wall close-studded on the first floor, kingpost trusses, ridge with longitudinal brace). To the N across the path is an aisled BARN, of seven bays with a kingpost roof; its frame, partly exposed on both sides. The W side has a felling date of 1448–90 but the S cross-wing is C17 with scroll-stopped mullioned windows and a blocked ogee-arched doorway in the centre of the upper floor. S of the house, and originally attached to it, is NEW HALL, built by Christopher Hodgson (†1642), attorney to the Council of the North. Gritstone, of three storeys, with a gabled two-bay W façade and central stack.

BEESTON HILL

Historically part of Holbeck township (*see* below) but rent from the rest of the area by the M621. The crown of Beeston Hill is a remarkably well-preserved Late Victorian and Edwardian working-class suburb.

HOLY SPIRIT, Tempest Road. 1903–6 by *Prothero & Phillot* of Cheltenham. A grand but incomplete church. Nave and chancel, under one roof, and N and S aisles, but the base only of a NE tower. Perp fenestration: to the aisles with flattened two-pointed arches, at the E end a very impressive seven-light window. The church is bigger than it appears, for the nave and aisles are dramatically sunk below a platform at the W end and the chancel at the other. Five-bay arcades, continued to the E wall; pointed barrel-vault with ROOD beam over the chancel steps. – C17-style oak FURNISHINGS (installed 1950) from the Priory of St Wilfrid, Little Woodhouse (i.e. probably by *Temple Moore*). – REREDOS with coved canopy, delightful SEDILIA, again canopied, PANELLING opposite, an inlaid LECTERN and at the W end STALLS attached to a screened porch or pew. This shelters the stone FONT, octagonal with good traceried panels. – The splendid High Gothic wooden PULPIT on a quatrefoil was donated in 1972. – Also, CHOIR STALLS with muscular pierced fronts. – STAINED GLASS. Middle three lights of the E window by *G.E.R. Smith*, 1946.

ST LUKE, Malvern Road. 1871–2 by *Richard Adams*. Nave, chancel and aisles, with only a small W bellcote. Later vestry across the heavily buttressed W end. Arcades have quatrefoil piers and double-chamfered arches with stern carved visages of Evangelists and prophets between, sporting magnificent beards. Reordered in the mid-1980s with altar platform: CHANCEL SCREEN now forms a W vestibule, PULPIT re-set incongruously in the S aisle wall. – FONT, with clustered grey marble columns and octagonal bowl.

TRINITY METHODIST CHURCH (former), Tempest Road. 1907 by *W. S. Braithwaite*. An ambitious chapel, one of the last to be undertaken for the Methodist New Connexion, with a prominent corner tower, the lower stage square, the upper octagonal with a spire. Now flats.

HOLBECK CEMETERY, Fairfax Road. Opened 1857. Layout by *Joshua Major*. Gothic LODGE (with replacement pantile roof) and fine cast-iron Gothic GATES with traceried panels and fleur-de-lys finials. W of the lodge a towering MEMORIAL to Henry Marsden, †1876, engineer and Mayor of Leeds. High plinth with inscribed panels and corner angels under curious bell-shaped canopies, then a stepped base to an almost full-size female figure kneeling before a low desk.

POLICE STATION, FIRE STATION AND PUBLIC LIBRARY (former), Dewsbury Road/Hunslet Hall Road. By *Bedford & Kitson*, 1901–3. Free Baroque, two strongly horizontal storeys, ashlar below and red brick with ashlar bands above. (Interior with stained glass, apparently by *George Walton*.)

BEESTON HILL BOARD SCHOOL (former), Beeston Road. 1880 by *Richard Adams;* rear wing added before 1908. Symmetrical, freely classical, front of fifteen bays and two storeys, the ends projecting slightly as pavilions, the centre as a three-storey frontispiece with superimposed pilasters and a pedimented attic. To its l. a ground-floor arcade, originally open, designed as a covered playground. Converted to community use in 2008 by *Brewster Bye Architects*.

BEWERLEY COMMUNITY SCHOOL, Hunslet Hall Road. 2006 by *Architectural Design Services* of Leeds City Council. Two former primary schools amalgamated with a children's care centre. Single-storey, the plan inspired by the Fibonacci spiral, coiling out from a circular central hall to form a serrated perimeter.

THE MANOR HOUSE, Temple Crescent. Extensively restored in 1985; now offices. To the street an early C19 house, but attached at right angles to its rear is a two-bay hall, dated by dendrochronology to 1420. This was part of the manor house of Cad Beeston erected by the de Rome family. Close-studded walls with big curved braces (exposed above a high, later, stone sill), modern. Timber mullioned windows (reusing the original mortices and peg holes) and doors at the W end in the presumed position of the screens passage. The eaves have been raised, probably in the C17 to accommodate an inserted floor. Inside, a fine crown-post roof of the type found in early C15 York: braced cambered tie-beams and crown-posts, with downward-curving braces, carrying a braced collar-purlin. On the site of (or incorporating parts of) the service range, a wing (formerly cottages) of stone and brick with early C19 fenestration.

HOLBECK

Partly on the flood plain S of the River Aire, and originally part of Hunslet (*see* below); it became a separate township in the early C19. In 1834 Parsons described Holbeck as one of the most crowded, most filthy and unhealthy villages in the country; by the end of the century it was a dense suburb of back-to-back streets and mills and foundries utilizing the canalized and culverted Hol Beck, the Leeds and Liverpool Canal and the Aire. The housing was some of the worst in the city and clearance had already begun by 1900. It continued through the C20 in association with new housing schemes, such as the staggered row of five identical T-plan, ten-storey towers erected behind St Matthew's from 1959. Remarkably, Holbeck, which once boasted numerous churches and chapels, is now without a single working religious building. Several initiatives have been launched to regenerate the area, partly through improvements to its built environment, notably in the reuse of former industrial buildings as part of the creaction of Holbeck Urban Village.

ST MATTHEW (former), St Matthew's Street. Now a community centre. A Commissioner's church of 1829–32 by *R. D. Chantrell*, replacing a chapel of ease. Designed to seat 1,200. Lancets, geometric E window, un-archaeological pinnacles. These also on the broached W steeple added in 1860 by *William Hill*. – STAINED GLASS, in the chancel, by *R. B. Edmundson*, Manchester.* CHURCHYARD. An iron OBELISK erected in memory of Matthew Murray of the Round Foundry, †1827, and his wife Mary, †1836, who are buried in a vault below. Presumably cast in his foundry (*see* below).

ST EDWARD, Brown Lane. *Bodley*'s church of 1904 has gone, and only the VICARAGE – a very modest work – still stands.

PROSPECT UNITED METHODIST CHAPEL (former), Domestic Street. *Thomas Ambler*, 1880–1. Plain brick except for a grand,

---

*A window attributed to *Thomas Wright* of Leeds is preserved at the Stained Glass Museum at Ely Cathedral.

if ill-resolved, Baroque Revival front in ashlar. The centre has
a giant Corinthian portico of two columns and two pilasters,
bowed outward in a semicircle, and containing a single-storey
circular and domed vestibule. Pilastered corner projections,
balustraded parapet and a plain pedimented gable set back
above the portico. Galleried interior. (Above an inserted ceiling
a coved ceiling of rich plasterwork with decorative pendant
'trumpet' vents.) Behind the chapel an integrated hall set at
right angles.

HOLBECK CEMETERY. *See* Beeston Hill.

HOLBECK PUBLIC LIBRARY (former), Nineveh Road and Marshall Street. Now offices. Typically exuberant Free Style of
1901 by *William Bakewell* in red brick and terracotta with some
Art Nouveau detail.

LEEDS UNITED FOOTBALL CLUB, Elland Road. Looming over
its dismal immediate surroundings, the EAST STAND (capacity 17,000) is a landmark of s Leeds. By *Hadfield Cawkwell
Davidson & Partners*, 1993, when it was proclaimed as the
largest cantilevered stand in the world. Football was first
played at the ground in 1898.

MARSHALL'S MILLS, Marshall Street. John Marshall was after
Benjamin Gott the most important Leeds industrialist in the
first half of the C19. In 1791 he founded flax mills N of Hol
Beck, close to the canal. The earliest survival, however, is the
FLAX WAREHOUSE (now offices), at the N end of Marshall
Street, of 1806–8. Plain red brick, with segmental-arched openings and a slate roof, stone window sills and blocks to
strengthen the walling and support the floors. Original stone
stair inside, part of fire-proofing measures which included cruciform cast-iron columns (made at Murray's foundry, *see*
below), iron floor beams and brick arches. Next s is the massive
U-plan brick FLAX MILL. Five-storey N wing of 1817 distinguished by oculi and lunette windows and integral chimney in
the roadside gable. Parallel s range of 1827 and a linking range
to road of 1830, with distinctive inverted header arches below
the lower windows and stone sill bands, both by *John Clark*.

Lastly, one of the architectural splendours of the Industrial
Revolution, the remarkable Egyptian Revival TEMPLE MILLS,
1838–43, designed by local engineer *James Combe* and *Joseph
Bonomi Jun.*, an Egyptologist and second curator of the Soane
Museum. Set back facing the street is the two-storey OFFICE
BLOCK of 1840–3, its design based on the Temple of Antaeopo-
lis and the Temple of Horus at Edfu. Battered walls and
concave entablature frame six beautiful lotus columns rising
between screen walls one third of their height, with tall upper-
floor sash windows comfortably recessed behind. The coarse
gritstone is well suited to the bold carving of snake motifs,
hieroglyphs and winged solar discs. To the l. is the vast SHEN
of 1838–40, its exterior derived from the 'Typhonium' at
Dendera, with attached lotus columns along the battered walls.
A single-storey block over a basement, which contained the
power transmission and ventilation systems; engine house on

Leeds, Temple Mills.
Engraving, 1843

the N side. The shed is about two acres in area, and unique for
its date because it was intended for preparation, spinning,
twisting thread and weaving cloth on a single floor. Hollow
cast-iron columns (acting as drainpipes for the roof) in imitation of bundled lotus stalks support shallow groined brick
vaults pierced by sixty-five circular openings (with conical
roof-lights) – an ingenious design in the spirit of Soane. It was
inspired by the weaving shed at Deanston Spinning Mill, Stir-
lingshire, of 1830–1, where the roof, as here, was insulated with
turf (reputedly grazed by sheep). There is also a tiny pylon-
form gate LODGE, but sadly the obelisk-chimney referred to by
Pevsner has gone. Close by, glimpsed from Union Place, is the
two-storey former MILL SCHOOL of *c.* 1830, rendered brick
with a hipped roof; Marshall was a stern but paternalistic
Liberal and advocated educational reform.

MIDLAND JUNCTION FOUNDRY, Silver Street. Established
1793 by Joshua Wordsworth to make machinery for the linen
textile industry. Three-storey workshops and a small beam
engine house of brick (with characteristic stone strengtheners
and round privy windows) flank a narrow cobbled yard
bridged by a range with cast-iron open-sided walkway and
loading deck. The foundry stood on the W edge of Marshall's
vast reservoirs, which were crossed in 1869 by the London &
North Western Railway's VIADUCT.

ROUND FOUNDRY MEDIA CENTRE, Water Lane, between
David and Marshall Streets. Late C18 to mid-C19 domestic and
industrial buildings associated with Matthew Murray's
Round Foundry, refurbished and converted by *Building Design*

Partnership in 2001–4 (masterplan by *Regan Miller Associates*) as the first stage of Holbeck Urban Village. Murray, a mechanic born in Newcastle upon Tyne, developed a flax-spinning machine for John Marshall in the 1780s, and as a partner in Fenton, Murray & Wood developed here from 1795 one of the first integrated engineering works, making structural ironwork, machines, tools and steam engines. Murray died in 1826, the firm in 1844.

The Round Foundry itself burnt down in 1873; its site on Foundry Street is marked by a circular inscription cast in steel enclosing a pavement of tumbled stone setts. But many other buildings survive, beginning on David Street w, with No. 97, a foundry of the 1850s with seven bays of tall round-arched windows like a chapel. A bronze plaque erected in 1929 records Murray's achievements. Next, the wide three-storey gable-end of Murray's GREEN SAND FOUNDRY of *c.* 1796. Windows are later insertions, the original building being windowless to keep the innovative mould-making process secret from competitors. Then, a row of early c19 two-storey offices and storerooms with built-up entry far r., abutting the original DRY SAND FOUNDRY (where casting was done), on the corner with Foundry Street. Natural light was evidently important here. One tall narrow arched window to the street (a two-storey addition conceals other features) and more to Foundry Street, along with a wide archway. Inside a high, airy open space, thin brick walls on slight stone foundations buttressed internally. On the E side to the yard, an entrance of some pretension – attached stone Tuscan columns support a round brick arch flanked by blind arcades. On its S side, the now rendered three-storey FITTING-UP SHOP of 1795–1802 has loading doors and an inserted cartway.

On the w side of Foundry Street a white-painted single-storey Italianate corner OFFICE built 1870 for Jonas Brown & Sons, joiners, their monogram over the corner entrance. Behind are JOINERS' WORKSHOPS and storage rooms of 1797 and later, extensively rebuilt 1860–77 and again in 2001–2. Behind, in Saw Mill Yard, the N and S ranges of joiners' workshops, with arcaded ground floor, have been successfully converted. New APARTMENTS, steel-framed, with glazed and aluminium panels and cedar boards, blend well with the important survivals but the blocks of flats between Saw Mill Yard and Marshall Street are bulky and poorly finished. At the S end of the site, Smith, Beacock & Tannett's VICTORIA FOUNDRY of 1863–82, converted by replicating its distinctive three-gabled NE façade – each a different phase – and retaining the iron structural frame.

TEMPLE MILLS, Marshall Street. *See* Marshall's Mills, above.

TOWER WORKS, Globe Road. One of the principal industrial monuments S of the canal, its distinctive skyline familiar to train passengers arriving from the w. Founded by T. R. Harding to manufacture steel pins for carding and combing machines for the textile industry. The earliest part is the range to Globe

Road, by *Thomas Shaw*, 1864–6. Thirteen bays of polychrome brickwork with fine ashlar entrance with paired pilasters and a giant keystone. Sheds behind this have been demolished but still preserved is the slender and ornate brick chimney, with a belfry stage, deep cornice and tall octagonal crown, its design derived from the (much taller) C13 Torre dei Lamberti, in Verona. Extensions W of 1899 by *William Bakewell*, for T. Walter Harding, Lord Mayor of Leeds (*see* also City Square, p. 434), included the splendid four-stage 'Big Tower', inspired by Giotto's campanile for the Duomo in Florence, of polychrome brick and moulded terracotta embellished with gilded Burmantofts tiles on the 'belfry' stage and a cast-iron crown and pinnacle. It incorporated a filter system to retrieve steel dust. The ENGINE HOUSE has a rare tiled interior with blind arcading decorated with ten plaster portrait medallions, designed by *Alfred Drury*, of industrial pioneers, including Arkwright (spinning), Cartwright (combing) and Lister (owner of Manningham Mills, Bradford), as well as the Hardings, father and son. The third tower, at the NE corner of the works, dates from rebuilding in the 1920s; it is squat and plain Italianate in the manner of the defensive C13 towers of San Gimignano but with brick panels below the parapet. Closed since 1979; replanning of the works as a mixed development is planned by *Bauman Lyons Architects* in 2009.

HUNSLET

Hunslet, mentioned in Domesday, included the territory of what in the C19 became the township of Holbeck (*see* above). By the late C19 it was synonymous with manufacturing – textiles, printing and especially heavy engineering, including the manufacture of railway locomotives. Little of this remains, but Hunslet remains an industrial area. Its commercial and retail centre was redeveloped after the war and in 2009 much of the area, like Beeston Hill and Holbeck to the W, is scheduled for regeneration.

ST MARY, Church Street. 1975 by *Peter Hill* of *Hill Mawson Partnership*, faced in red sandstone from the previous church (1862–4 by *Perkin & Backhouse*) and retaining its tall E.E. steeple. This has corner buttresses battered towards the base and a broach spire with lucarnes. The new church is austere, even defensive, a round-cornered box with a clearly expressed tripartite plan of centrally planned worship space separated from four meeting rooms by a glazed narthex. Some slit windows and a shallow clerestory band. The sanctuary is dominated by an extraordinary canopy like a flower head descending from the ceiling and terminated by a cast aluminium SCULPTURE, The Apostles and the People, by *Frank Roper*. Roper also carried out the STAINED GLASS.

SALEM CONGREGATIONAL CHAPEL (former), Hunslet Road and Salem Place. Opened in 1791. Of squared gritstone, the original round-headed windows visible on the N and S sides. The chapel was originally supported by an influential congregation of business and professional families but from the late C19 was reorganized to serve the predominantly working-class district, and extended in 1901 with a new elliptical entrance (W) front and parapet with carved wreath. The result is more like an early C20 picture house than a chapel. Ancillary buildings to the N.

HUNSLET BAPTIST TABERNACLE, Low Road, S of Stafford Street. Built 1835–7, altered and enlarged *c.* 1880. Simple brick box – almost square – with two tiers of round-headed windows and a rendered façade, with twin doors, enriched by bands and dentilled eaves.

GURDWARA GURUNANAK NISHKAM SEWAK JATHA, Lady Pit Lane and Greenmount Lane. Opened 1987. The former Rington's tea factory of 1936. Steel-framed and brick-clad, of three storeys and penthouse, with large windows, an enriched cornice and handsome entrances with fanlights.

HUNSLET CEMETERY, Middleton Road. Opened 1845. Tudorbethan style LODGES with slender octagonal stacks, Gothic gate piers. Across the main axis, the two CHAPELS in a single – reasonably accurate – Neo-Norman building.

SCOTT ALMSHOUSES, Middleton Road, N of the cemetery. Inscribed with the date, 1896, the name of the architect, *John E. Leak*, and benefactor, John Scott, who left £10,000 in his will. Ten dwellings arranged around a little court in three blocks. Clunky freely Jacobean style, with bay windows and paired porches divided by a Tuscan column forming a continuous ground-floor projection to each block. The focus of the court is a marble bust of Scott on a pilastered plinth.

There are a few other interesting buildings hidden away in Hunslet. Among the streets of C19 terraces between Dewsbury Road, Tunstall Road and the motorway is a rare C18 survivor: BURTON HOUSE, Burton Avenue. Brick box with a five-bay façade and open pediments to both the middle three bays and the doorcase. Isolated amidst industry, expressways and car parks just S of Tetley's Brewery in HUNSLET ROAD (Nos. 37 and 39) and SHEAF STREET (Nos. 16 and 18) are two rare examples of pre-1866 back-to-back houses, probably built *c.* 1850–66 (now derelict). In Sheaf Street they possibly contain cellar dwellings, the most censured of all C19 slum housing. The Hunslet Road houses have pilastered doorcases. Across the N end facing Crown Point Road is a pair of (altered) houses meeting in a shallow V, with unusual L-shaped blind-backed plans, each having façades on two streets.

THE GARDEN GATE PUB, Whitfield Way. Startling two-tone ceramic façade of 1903, probably from Burmantofts, in Free Renaissance style. Brown glazed faience below, biscuit terracotta above. Extravagant interiors, with abundant decorative tiling, mosaic floors, moulded plasterwork, etched glass, mahogany doors, fireplaces and partitions, mirrored overmantels and pendant light fittings. Best is the 'Vaults' with a tremendous, bowed ceramic counter; a hatch in the glazed spine corridor serves the Smoke Room, the Tap Room and saloon. The pub was supplied by a small tower brewery behind, now demolished.

Industrial Buildings

ANGEL WINGS, Hunslet Road and the Hunslet Distributor. A simple but sympathetic amalgamation and conversion of a chapel and various industrial buildings, all C19, given a touch of Las Vegas in the shape of a glazed Postmodern portico facing Hunslet Lane, incorporating the angelic sculpture.

BRAIME'S PRESSED STEEL (former), Hunslet Road and Ingham Street. Built 1911–13 on the site of an earlier foundry. The firm were leading specialists in this industry. Stepped façade of red brick with many round-arched windows, including an office suite unusual in quality and decorative detail for surviving engineering works of the period. Behind, and to the side, a sequence of large steel-framed ranges of different dates. (Well-preserved office interiors, with panelling, a billiard room, etc., and windows overlooking the workshops.)

COOKE'S PRINTERS (former), Hunslet Road and Leathley Road. A printing works of 1881 (rebuilt after fire in 1894), by *Thomas Ambler* for Alf Cooke Ltd., a leading firm in one of Leeds's major industries. The principal thirty-bay elevation has a conventional form – brick and stone dressings, hipped roof – but unconventional detailing: the ground floor has alternating segmental-headed windows and projecting bays with gabled canopies over small semicircular-headed windows; the first floor is arcaded with elliptical arches and pilasters; the second has two-light round-headed windows with slender columns between. This façade finishes at a canted corner bay, with a pilastered and pedimented entrance, carried up to a domed clock tower dating from the post-fire rebuilding. (Behind the façade is an iron frame with three tiers of columns making two storeys of galleries around a long central area under a lightweight roof.)

LOCOMOTIVE WORKS. In JACK LANE are fragments of the principal works. First, the former BOYNE ENGINE WORKS (of Manning, Wardle & Co., founded 1858), with a simple, brick, two-storey block of OFFICES of seven symmetrical bays, possibly of two builds. Cast-iron GATEPIERS with pedimented caps and raised strapwork. E are the former offices of the HUNSLET ENGINE COMPANY (established 1864, closed 1995), probably *c.* 1880.

HUNSLET MILL, Goodman Street (between Atkinson Street and the Aire). The last and, individually, the largest of the great early C19 flax-spinning mills in Leeds. Erected 1838–40 for John Wilkinson, probably to designs by *William Fairbairn*. Forming a tremendous gaunt cliff of brick on the river bank is the (long-derelict) seven-storey MILL, of twenty-five by three bays. Attached to its s end, facing Goodman Street, an OFFICE AND WAREHOUSE range. Raised from two to three storeys *c.* 1842 when it was refronted, probably by *John Clark.* Almost in the centre, a slightly projecting entrance with carriage arch flanked by doorways set in banded rusticated masonry with voussoirs. Both ranges have a staircase tower at the rear and are of fireproof construction: brick jack arches, stone flags and cast-iron columns and beams, the latter of Fairbairn's elliptical type. Other buildings have been demolished.

Adjoining the site to the w are the former VICTORIA MILLS, also built for flax milling, for W. B. Holdsworth. At right angles to Goodman Street the mill range of *c.* 1835–8: six storeys and fourteen by three bays, with engine house and chimney at the N end. Two smaller ranges to the w at right angles and w of them on Atkinson Street a three-storey entrance range of sixteen bays built *c.* 1865 for Tiltley & Co. The carriage arch has mighty voussoirs of vermiculated rustication.

TETLEY'S BREWERY. *See* p. 457.

MIDDLETON

A township in the parish of Rothwell (q.v.) high above the Aire valley. The boundary with Leeds parish is still marked by a medieval BANK AND DITCH in Beeston Park Wood, ½ m. NW of St Mary. From 1706 the manor was owned by the Brandling family of Northumberland, who developed the Middleton collieries, mined since at least the C15. In 1758 Charles Brandling built the first waggonway in the area, connecting his pits to staithes on the Aire; it was the first railway to be authorized by Act of Parliament. This was adapted in 1812 as a rack railway by *John Blenkinsop,* and ran the first commercially successful steam locomotive in the world, designed by Matthew Murray of the Round Foundry (*see* Holbeck). Though the last pit closed in 1968, part of the MIDDLETON RAILWAY is still operated from the station on Moor Road.

The remnants of the pre-1900 village lie on and off Town Street either side of St Mary. On its N side, the PARK of Middleton Hall (a pedimented Georgian house, dem. 1962 after a fire) became a public park in 1920, the same year as the start of the Middleton estate, the first of two vast low-density Corporation-built cottage estates with circuses and avenues; BELLE ISLE followed from 1937, but was completed long after the war with quite different housing. There is precious little to relieve the low-rise monotony apart from the views over the City and the E, and the ambitious, freely Wrenaissance MIDDLETON ARMS, on Middleton Circus.

ST MARY, Town Street. By *Chantrell,* consecrated 1846. Quite an academic E.E. exercise with separately roofed chancel and aisles, multiple lancets E (three stepped) and W (five equal), and a SW tower S of the S aisle. It lost its spire to subsidence in 1939. – STAINED GLASS. Good windows by *Wailes,* 1848, at either end: the E on the theme of Christ, the W the Evangelists and their Gospels. Other windows by him in the chancel, 1849–52.

St Cross, Middleton Park Avenue. 1933–4 by *F. L. Charlton* for the Middleton estate (cf. St Philip, Osmondthorpe, also built under the Church Forward Movement). Brick-faced and concrete framed, Early Christian style with a campanile. Five-bay arcades with broad rounded arches on cruciform piers; pointed Gothic arches spanning the nave. W bays partitioned, and dreadful suspended ceiling along the centre of the nave, both 1982. – HIGH ALTAR, CREDENCE TABLE and LECTERN by *Charlton*; made by *Robert Thompson*, who also did the aisle SCREENS. – PULPIT from St John, Adel (*see* above), and perhaps therefore by *Street*, with a Norman-style frieze of intersecting blind arcading. – C19 octagonal FONT, from Ainderby Steeple, North. Riding. – CRUCIFIX, made in Oberammergau. From Christ Church, Meadow Lane, Hunslet (1823–5 by *Chantrell*, dem. 1975).

St John and St Barnabas, Low Grange View, Belle Isle. 1938–9 by *Gribbon, Foggitt & Brown* for the politician-cleric, the Rev. Charles Jenkinson, and superseding the churches at Holbeck, of which he had been vicar, after the slums were cleared and their inhabitants rehoused at Belle Isle. Plain, boxy, buttressed and brick. Blank gabled W end with a large brick cross, a short NW turret and SW entrance. Big, broad, aisleless interior with flat ceiling, the chancel only slightly narrower than the nave. Organ at the W end. Crypt refurbished 2002 as a family centre, with a fussy unharmonious entrance at the SW corner. – ALTAR by *Frances Stephens*, 1961. Many fittings from the demolished churches of St John the Evangelist (1850, *G. G. Scott*) and St Barnabas (1854–5, *J. T. Fairbank*): PULPIT, LECTERN, COMMUNION BENCHES and Lady Chapel ALTAR are from St John, the FONT from St Barnabas. – STATUES in niches flanking the chancel, N, Bishop Azariah (the first Indian Bishop) and S, St George and the Dragon. – STAINED GLASS. Figures, mostly by *Powell Bros* (from St Barnabas) and *Wailes* (from St John), re-set in clear glass in almost all windows (including the vicar's garage).

The church is the centrepiece of a large T-shaped complex of ancillary buildings.

Methodist Church, Hopewell View. 1896 by *Howdill & Howdill*. Brick, Free Renaissance style with a little NW tower. Barrel-vaulted interior, its fittings largely unaltered. – Large HALL of 1886 attached behind.

STOURTON

Thwaite Mills (Museum), Thwaite Lane. Water-powered former oil-seed and corn mill, on a narrow strip of land between the River Aire and the Aire & Calder Navigation, now hidden away behind an industrial estate. 1823–5 by *Hewes &*

Wren, millwrights and engineers of Manchester, for the Aire & Calder Navigation Co. Brick, nine bays and two-and-a-half storeys, straddling the mill race, with a later engine house and cylindrical chimney to the N and a four-bay extension to the S. Two breast-shot water wheels inside, together with associated drives and other machinery. Also the mill manager's house detached to the SW, a formal three bays with corner pilaster strips and ashlar doorcase. Warehouse, workshop, stables etc., early and mid-C19, to E.

WEST

ARMLEY

Rising steeply W of Leeds and forming a ridge along the S side of the Aire valley, Armley was a small cloth-making village in the C17 with its own chapel of ease. From 1777 the Leeds and Liverpool Canal encouraged cloth mills and from the mid C19 the railways through the Aire valley and to Bradford brought heavy engineering. Large numbers of back-to-back houses were built, with churches and other institutions following in their wake. The population trebled from 9,200 in 1871 to 27,500 in 1901.

CHURCHES AND PUBLIC BUILDINGS

CHRIST CHURCH, Armley Ridge Road. 1869–72 by *Adams & Kelly,* in well-executed but slightly mechanical E.E. Tall W tower. Reordered by *Kitson & Partners,* 1983; the two W bays now form a narthex. – REREDOS. Arcaded with cusps and crocketed pinnacles, filling the width of the chancel. – STAINED GLASS. By *Clayton & Bell,* the E window 1884, chancel S 1885 and W 1890. N aisle, fourth window by *E. Pickett & Son,* 1948, the seventh by *Harry Stammers,* 1951. S aisle, seventh and eighth windows by *Charles E. Steel,* 1950.

CHURCH HALL. 1905–6 by *Beckwith & Webster,* with a medallion 'Little Children Come Unto Me' dated 1860 inserted in the gable. Behind the church in Theaker Lane, the SCHOOL of 1871, single-storey Gothic, U-shaped with a central entrance and additions of 1895 by *Smith & Tweedale,* and of 1992 to the rear.

83   ST BARTHOLOMEW, Wesley Road. One of Leeds's finest Victorian churches. 1872–8 by *Walker & Athron,* their sole large-scale work and a prominent and slightly forbidding presence on the skyline, built of Horsforth sandstone. Tall and cruciform, in E.E. style with lancet windows and lofty crossing tower (completed to a modified design in 1903–4), conforming in every way to the Tractarian ideal. The influence of Street's St Philip and St James, Oxford (1860–6), Burges's St Finn Bar, Cork (1863) and, especially, Teulon's St Stephen's, Hampstead (1869), are evident in the massing of the E end,

where transepts and polygonal apse are kept close to the tower. The awkward detailing of the tower (which is larger than the crossing and has to be supported on small retaining arches between the nave and transepts), the undersized spirelets and a certain thinness apparent in the aisle elevations may be criticized, but the magnificent scale of the building overcomes any lingering doubts. Choir vestry, 1896. Gabled and arched LYCHGATE, 1888.

The interior, faced with Ancaster limestone, is 73 ft (22 metres) high but seems, if anything, taller because of the spacious clerestory. The six-bay nave has quatrefoil piers clasped in the centre and plain capitals, and a roof with tie-bar trusses on attached columns with large part-gilded angels holding shields. Crossing, short chancel and apse, all rib-vaulted. – REREDOS, 1877 by *Thomas Earp*, large and architectural, the lower part of alabaster carved with the Adoration of the Magi, the upper of Caen stone, arcaded, with painted tiles by *Powell Bros.* depicting the Crucifixion. – FONT. Octagonal and arcaded with rich red and black marbles. – PULPIT, 1884 by *Adams & Kelly*, of alabaster and grey marble, with a small sculpture of St Bartholomew copied from that by Peter Vischer (*c.* 1460–1529) at the shrine of St Sebald, Nuremberg. – CHOIR STALLS, carved by *Earp* to the design of *Walker & Athron*. – Grand ORGAN CASE by *Walker & Athron*, 1879, almost entirely filling the N transept above a rib-vaulted arcade to the N chapel. Gothic in detail but Baroque in inspiration, with panels based on Morris wallpaper designs, and carved angels crowning it. The organ was built by *J. F. Schulze*, originally for a summer-house in the grounds of Meanwood Towers (*see* p. 515). – MOSAIC PANELS by *Powell & Sons*. E end: seven panels under the E window, 1879, partly obscured by the reredos. Below these, tiled figures Praise and Prayer and SS Luke, John and Bartholomew, executed 1925–34. W end: *opus sectile* work of 1884, the Baptism of Christ, mainly British saints except, r., Bishop Selwyn and Dean Hook, the latter seemingly an afterthought. The scheme was intended to continue above the arcading in the nave. – STAINED GLASS. In the apse and S transept, of 1878–80 and the W windows of 1881, all by *Clayton & Bell*. Those in the nave by *Powell Bros.* of 1882–3. An understated and delicate scheme with no single colour predominant. – MONUMENTS. Benjamin Gott Jun. (†1814, while in Greece on the Grand Tour) by *Joseph Gott*, a distant relation. A weeping figure in antique dress with a funerary urn and a standing figure of Faith representing the triumph of Christian Piety over Grief. – Benjamin Gott Sen. †1839 also by *Gott*. Comfortably semi-reclining figure on a mattress rolled up at the top. He is realistically depicted, wearing a woollen cloth jacket of the highest quality to signify his role in the development of the textile industry.

St Bartholomew replaced the C17 Armley Chapel (enlarged 1825 and 1834–5 by *Chantrell*). Its foundations survive as a burial enclosure for the Gott family.

PRIMITIVE METHODIST CHAPEL (former), Armley Road. 1905 by *Howdill & Howdill*, making skilful use of its corner site. Red brick and terracotta in a Free Renaissance style with a Venetian window flanked by prominent twin ventilation towers. Inside, cast-iron Ionic columns.

UNITED METHODIST FREE CHURCH (former), Hall Road. 1898–1900 by *Walter Hanstock & Son*. Red brick, Wrenaissance but with Florentine windows in the nave. Two stocky W towers and oversized rounded broken pediment.

CEMETERY, Green Hill Road. Opened 1887. Chapel and lodge by *J. P. Pritchett*.

100 ARMLEY LIBRARY, Stocks Hill. 1901 by *Percy Robinson*. Flemish Renaissance with two big shaped gables and plenty of ashlar channelled rustication to contrast with the brickwork. On the corner a low clock tower, topped by a louvred cupola, seems out of scale with the curved entrance loggia that wraps around its base. Interior with a top-lit barrel-vaulted ceiling, mosaic floors and a handsome glazed screen with Art Nouveau glass.

TEMPERANCE HALL AND MECHANICS' INSTITUTE (former), Wesley Road. 1866–7, built by the Armley Temperance Society. Chapel-like.

ARMLEY BOARD SCHOOL (now Tower Court). 1878 by *Richard Adams*. A grand thirteen-bay composition in an elaborate but decidedly wayward Italianate. The front is articulated by projecting end bays with pediments and a central clock tower.

STANNINGLEY ROAD BOARD SCHOOL (now Armley Park Court). 1900 by *W. S. Braithwaite*. Elegant and competently handled Neo-Jacobean. Elaborate gables and two projecting domed ventilation towers to the symmetrical façade (cf. Leeds Pupil Teachers' College, p. 421).

WEST LEEDS BOYS' HIGH SCHOOL, Town Street/Whingate. (Now Old School Lofts.) 1906–7, by *William Broadbent*, in up-to-date free Baroque. Twenty-six-bay frontage with a raised centre and two three-storey wings, each with a cupola. Big windows, attached columns and rusticated pilasters. Two ornate projecting porches with paired Ionic columns and segmental open pediments.

ARMLEY LEISURE CENTRE, Carr Crofts. Monumental Neo-Georgian swimming baths of 1929–30 by the *City Architect*.

ST MARY'S HOSPITAL, Green Hill Road. Built as the Bramley Union Workhouse, 1871–2, by *C. S. & A. J. Nelson*. It was intended for 220 inhabitants. Brick with scanty Gothic detail, the long low main range set well back and symmetrical about a small central tower. A single-storey block along the N drive housed receiving wards and offices, at the rear the first infirmary (N) faces a replacement of 1895 (S).

ARMLEY PRISON, Stanningley Road. Built as Leeds's borough gaol in 1843–7, the competition for which had been won by *Hurst & Moffat* of Doncaster. Negotiations broke down and *Perkin & Backhouse* took over the design, although they may have produced a new plan to accommodate more prisoners. Of the castellated type favoured in the mid C19, with a mighty gatehouse with splayed and battered towers and corbelled crenellated parapets flanking a large round-arched doorway. Its grimness is emphasized by the tooled ashlar facings and rock-faced dark gritstone of the walls which have corner turrets. Armley Prison, like Reading, is one of the earliest to follow the model radial plan of Pentonville (Joshua Jebb, 1840–2), with four three-storey wings radiating from a central hall in the form of a half-cartwheel. It accommodated 291 prisoners on the separate system, i.e. individual cells and exercise yards. Women and children were originally held in two of the radial wings, which had cells on one side of the corridor only. These were doubled up 1856 and in the 1870s. All the cell blocks were extended in the 1880s.

ARMLEY PARK, Stanningley Road. Opened 1893. Jubilee FOUNTAIN, 1897, paid for by William Gott of Armley House. Fluted pilasters, a reeded stem and gadrooned bowl. FIRST WORLD WAR MEMORIAL. An unusual Gothic wayside cross.

Perambulation

The historic backbone of Armley is TOWN STREET and its E extension STOCKS HILL. Just off this in CRAB LANE, the MALT SHOVEL, C18 with mullioned windows. On the corner with Stocks Hill the HSBC BANK (formerly London City & Midland) of 1909 by *Sydney Kitson*, faced in white faience, part of a good early C20 group at this junction, including the exuberant Armley Library (*see* above), and YORKSHIRE BANK, 1936 by *C. Medley*, in a *Moderne* style. From here Town Street has groups of small C19 shops and cottages.

Upper Armley begins after the scruffy remnant of ARMLEY MOOR, enclosed in the 1790s. On the S side of Town Street are remnants of the township's mixed agrarian and industrial past: No. 1 ROSCOE TERRACE just off the street, a late C17 (farm?)house with quoins and mullioned windows, altered in the C18, and beyond Wortley Road, WEAVERS COURT, a row of late C18 three-storey weavers' houses. A communal loom room occupied the third storey with large paired windows. Archway to cottages at the rear. Opposite, The Barleycorn, early C19, with a lively front added in 1898. Then, two small mills face each other across the street. SHAW MILLS has a mid-C19 three-storey brick range with Dutch-gabled ends and broad segmental windows, to which a lower block at right angles is linked by a house, possibly the owner's. WESTFIELD MILLS. Early C19 four-storey, hipped roof range with paired windows, divided by stone mullions, now incorporated into a *c.* 2007 apartment development. The streets N and S of Town Street here are tightly packed with rows of late C19 back-to-back and blind-back houses. In EDINBURGH GROVE and EDINBURGH TERRACE are two parallel terraces of blind-backs of the 1890s with a mere six-inch gap between them demarking unrelated development on different parcels of land. Off Hill Top Road, THE TOWERS, a group of *c.* 1870 villas with thin, spiky towers and impressive carved lions on the gateposts that provide evidence of substantial wealth in C19 Armley. In Tower Lane to the E, some C17 vernacular survivals.

WALKER'S ALMSHOUSES, Church Road. Erected 1883. Gothic, two-storeyed, the central pair of houses brought forward and given a large gable.

ARMLEY HOUSE, Gott's Park. The Armley Estate was the property of Thomas Woolrich, a Leeds merchant who in *c.* 1781 built a villa here, facing E down the Aire valley. It had a big canted bay and low pavilion wings, in the style of Carr. Benjamin Gott, owner of Armley Mills (*see* below), purchased the property in 1803 and turned to *Humphry Repton* for advice on remodelling house and grounds as his principal residence (Gott previously lived close to the Bean Ing Mills in Leeds). Replanting of the grounds began at once but the house's present Grecian appearance is due to *Robert Smirke, c.* 1817. This was his first domestic work in this style and it was quickly influential in Leeds.

The main E front has a grand tetrastyle temple portico, in Smirke's favoured Ionic order from the Temple on the Ilissus, into which projects the canted bay of the earlier house, an unusual combination. Steps up to the portico give it an elevated position. This central block is flanked by low wings, curving to the W, which formerly linked to plain two-storey pavilions (dem. in the 1950s). The interior was innovative, Gott displaying the same interest in fire-proof construction as he had at Armley Mills, with cast-iron beams supporting vaulted masonry floors, a cast-iron service stair and cast-iron panelled

Leeds, Armley House.
Engraving, 1821

doors. Some of this may still be seen; a faux timber panelled door leads to the basement while the cast-iron ribs of the roof to the wings are also exposed internally.

Repton's LANDSCAPING created a setting in which Gott's mills and house would be seen together by travellers along the Kirkstall Road. From the house, the mills became the focus of the view E towards Leeds, while an opening in a plantation provided a suitably picturesque vignette of Kirkstall Abbey to the W. In spite of much later building these views are still framed by a screen of trees in front of the house.

Industrial Buildings

ARMLEY MILLS (Leeds Industrial Museum), W of Canal Road between the Leeds and Liverpool Canal and the River Aire. Woollen mills, first developed in 1788 by Colonel Thomas Lloyd from an existing fulling mill and corn mill. Acquired in 1804 by Benjamin Gott, who rebuilt the MAIN RANGE in 1805 after a fire destroyed the fulling mill of 1788. It is L-shaped with a long four-storey N–S wing straddling the mill race (the mill was powered by two water wheels, whose gearing enabled them to outperform steam engines until *c.* 1840); the E wing incorporates the former corn mill (rebuilt in 1797 and converted to textile production *c.* 1810), built into the slope of the canal embankment. Regular façades of coursed stone, punctuated by small windows. BEAM ENGINE HOUSE added *c.* 1854 with an imposing tapering chimneystack on a panelled pedestal. Inside, brick jack-arches, cylindrical cast-iron columns and T-section cast-iron beams, one of the first examples of fire-proof construction in England and the earliest surviving in Yorkshire (*see* also Marshall's Mills, p. 554). Fulling stocks originally extended down the centre of the ground floor, with scribbling and carding machines on the second and third floors and mechanics' workshops at the top. The lower floor of the former corn mill has cruciform cast-iron columns but the top floor retains a small portion of the original sheet-iron nailed to the underside of joists for fire-proofing in 1807.

N of the mill, a long low CLOTH-DRYING HOUSE of the 1820s with curvaceous cast-iron roof trusses, the W end formerly housing a gas plant (the main range had been gas-lit from 1809, with apparatus by *Boulton & Watt*). On the canal embankment to the N, a semi-detached pair of MILL MANAGERS' HOUSES, here by 1793. Quite plain with mullioned windows but with tall round-arched stair windows to the rear. Lower wings resemble Pennine weavers' cottages, with first-floor loom shops attached on each side. Adjacent, a mid-C19 nine-bay warehouse.

LUTAS LEATHLEY & CO. DRESS WAREHOUSE (former), Stanningley Road. 1891, by *James Fawcett*. A good example of a small cloth warehouse with ground floor retail premises. Four-storey, fire-proof structure of concrete floors and steel beams, with red brick walls decorated with incised stone bands at lintel level.

SCOTCH FOUNDRY WAREHOUSE (former), Canal Road, high above the valley. By *Walter A. Hobson*, 1897, for Mathieson, Wilson & Co., ironfounders (founded 1888). Red brick, most ornate, with extensive iron cresting along the parapets. Hobson almost certainly designed the OFFICES of the company's CARLTON WORKS of 1898, s of the railway, enriched by cut brick panels and banding, nicely carved timber mullions between large paired windows, a Flemish gable and a corner turret. Cast-iron firegrates were made here.

SHAW MILLS and WESTFIELD MILLS. *See* Perambulations.

WINKER GREEN MILLS, Stanningley Road. An early example of an integrated cloth factory, developed by William Eyres & Sons from 1824 around a mill of *c.* 1803. Four-storey s range of 1825–32, probably for hand spinning and handloom weaving; the two E bays are later. Paired windows and taking-in doors. The original mill was mostly destroyed by fire in 1833; on its site a large (nineteen-bay) four-storey brick and stone range (partly fireproofed on the ground floor, which contained the willey machines). Its E extension is of 1836 (incorporating the engine house of the earlier mill, and with a new engine house on the s elevation). Later buildings include a (shortened) warehouse of *c.* 1840 and single-storey weaving sheds.

VIADUCT, crossing the canal and Aire s of Armley Mills. 1849 by *Thomas Grainger*, for the Leeds & Thirsk Railway. Twenty-one arches with segmental heads and powerful buttresses.

BRAMLEY

Bramley, w of the Aire, had a chapel of ease to Leeds church from the C12. The steep wooded bank of the river opposite Kirkstall Forge (*see* p. 513), called Bramley Falls, is studded with abandoned quarry workings which produced a hardy gritstone. Inevitably textiles were also an important industry, and some mill buildings survive near Stanningley Road. The centre, around Town Street, was devastated by comprehensive redevelopment in the 1960s and 70s, which swept away tightly bound terraces, ginnels and cottages and replaced them with a landscape of low-rise housing, a slab-block district centre and bleak acres of grass and tarmac. To the SE on the Stanningley Road is Wyther, one of the city's interwar cottage estates, and s of the A647 at Swinnow Moor is one of its post-war mixed-height developments, with four tower blocks, houses, flats and maisonettes begun in 1951.

ST PETER, Hough Lane. Dec of 1861 by *Perkin & Backhouse*, replacing the C18 chapel of St Margaret, but brutally reduced in the 1970s, except for the NW steeple. – Gothic SCREEN re-set in the N arcade. – STAINED GLASS. Two windows by *Morris & Co.*, 1875, with foliage and medallions, one in the N aisle;

medallions from the other (from the N transept) re-set in the chancel. E, overlooking Town Street, is the Gothic cupola of the old chapel, with pinnacle set peculiarly on top.

VENERABLE BEDE (R.C.), Stanningley Road. The church for Wyther, of 1938 by *Gribbon, Foggitt & Brown* (cf. St Augustine R.C., Harehills (Potternewton) and St John and St Barnabas, Belle Isle (Middleton)). Square with a short, broad w tower. Using bold massive forms and much uninterrupted brickwork with minimal decoration, showing the influence of Verlade and Cachemaille-Day. Broadly spaced, straight-headed windows nave windows, though the full undercroft has continuous glazing. Whitewashed interior with stark unmoulded Gothic arches rising in a continuous curve from the floor to the apex.

BRAMLEY BOARD SCHOOL (former), Hough Lane. Single-storey. 1877 by *Richard Adams* in gritstone rather than his usual brick; extended 1900.

BRAMLEY PUBLIC BATHS, Broad Lane. 1904 by *J. Lane Fox* for the Corporation. Eclectic C17 style. Entrance hall with delight-ful timber ticket booth with Art Nouveau stained glass. The pool has a gallery and inserted stained glass in the large gable window of a stylized lake scene.

PERAMBULATION. SE of St Peter, in LOWER TOWN STREET, marooned amidst later C20 housing, is a small timber-framed house (No. 112) later largely encased in coursed rubble. Gable-end to the road, a corner chimney, outshut and exposed beside this a post and angle brace rising to the wall-plate. Beneath St Peter's a pavement raised on an C18 retaining wall with village pump and trough in rusticated arches. Better survival rates on the w side of UPPER TOWN STREET. The former MANOR HOUSE (No. 259) is C18 but neither large nor accomplished, and altered. The entrance is a Doric portico *in antis* – a C19 intervention? Beyond the prominent former SALEM BAPTIST SUNDAY SCHOOL is a group starting with the N side of MOORFIELDS, a three-storey mid-C19 terrace, each house with a single bay of paired mullioned windows. Then, set at right angles to the road, a more sophisticated C18 house (No. 331) – of three bays plus a later one – with modillion eaves brackets and a segmental pediment over the door. Its rear forms one side of the entrance to HALEY'S YARD, with an early-to-mid-C19 range of workshops and warehousing running back along the other side. Lastly BROAD LANE, where there is a high, gabled former BOARD SCHOOL and, beyond, the baths (*see* above).

In HOUGHLEY LANE, Wyther, Nos. 1 and 2 CHEADLE COTTAGES. Built as one house – finials dated 1663 are now garden ornaments. A single range, with a stringcourse rising over the doorway's large lintel and mullioned windows, those to the first floor originally four lights each; those on the ground up to five. Back-to-back hearths once heated kitchen and parlour. The main doorway (No. 1) opened into the former;

the latter (No. 2) has a wide C17 fireplace with chamfered voussoirs. Good C17 plasterwork in an upper room of No. 1 including a frieze with mythological figures – and kingpost trusses with curved side braces. Nearby, THE COTTAGE, built as a farmhouse in 1646 by Richard Ellison. It had a two-unit lobby-entry plan. Central chamfered door-surround of quoins and flat-arched lintel carved with date and initials. One six-light chamfered mullioned window l.; a five-light window to the r. is now at the first floor of the l. gable, inserted when the roof was raised in the mid C19. Later in the century a new wing with canted bays was added r. at right angles.

KIRKSTALL BREWERY (student residences), Broad Lane, beside the Leeds and Liverpool Canal. Converted from c. 1994 by *Bowman Riley* for Leeds Metropolitan University. Established 1833. The group stacking up Broad Lane from the canal bridge is dominated by the TOWER BREWERY, built after 1872. Blank arcades, balustraded parapet and brick chimney; next to it the former covered entrance, and then on the corner with the canal the OFFICES. Attached porch with a modillion cornice. N along the canal-side a twin-gabled three-storey block from the earliest phase, then a nine-bay range one storey higher and much altered, and finally a regular four-storey twenty-bay fermenting and racking range built by Benjamin Dawson and Co. in 1867, with small round-arched windows on four floors. Loading doorways (blocked) below.

Lining the canal bank opposite and rising up the valley on the yard side are student halls, the nearest in neo-industrial vernacular with quarry-faced stone facing, the further ones in brick. Amidst these is COOPER HOUSE, built by Henry Cooper who leased land from Sir James Graham in 1793 and erected maltings (cleared for the brewery in the C19).

FARNLEY

A small village on a hill above the Aire valley on the w edge of Leeds, with a chapel of ease to Leeds church since the Middle Ages. Largely suburbanized after the Ring Road was constructed, but still with some rural character.

ST MICHAEL AND ALL ANGELS, Lawns Lane. Amidst mature beeches on the edge of Farnley Park. 1885 by *Chorley & Connon*. Nave, aisle and chancel and mainly lancets; s tower unbuilt. Slender octagonal nave piers; high and wide chancel arch. The chief benefactor was A. H. Pawson of Lawns House and the *Farnley Iron Co.*, New Farnley, which produced the wall band of moulded terracotta tiles with raised floral scroll design. By the s porch is the cupola from the previous church

by *John Carr, c.* 1761. – FONT. By *Burstall & Taylor* of Leeds,
1875. Clustered columns supporting round bowl, and projecting saints' heads. – REREDOS; 1906. Caen stone arched niches
with alabaster columns, containing *opus sectile* scenes of the
Sermon on the Mount, St Michael and St Gabriel. Raised on
a new platform, 1914. – Octagonal PULPIT, with cusped open
panels, and poppyhead CHOIR STALLS by local craftsman
Henry Clayton. – TRACERY FRAGMENTS, from the medieval
chapel, discovered in the walls of Carr's church during demolition. – STAINED GLASS. E window of 1885 by *Heaton, Butler
& Bayne.* Last Supper, Crucifixion and the Ascension. – MON-
UMENTS, from the old chapel, several to the Armitage family
of Farnley Hall. – FIRST WORLD WAR MEMORIAL. *Kayll &
Reed,* 1921, *opus sectile.*

In the churchyard a good collection of LEDGER STONES
from the C17–C19, the earlier ones in the manner of Morley
(q.v.), with naive skulls etc.

FARNLEY HILL METHODIST CHURCH AND SUNDAY
SCHOOL, Stonebridge Lane (now closed). A pleasantly
jumbled composition on the hillside. Regular chapel façade of
1796–7: two storeys, five bays with domestic sashes, quoins.
Porches of 1873 replacing the former central entrance. Pyramid
roof, formerly with pediment over the slightly projecting
middle bays and a cupola. Attached r. the Sunday School,
dated 1828, of two bays, one projecting to the pavement (since
extension in 1921), with steep steps up to a first-floor entrance.
Venetian windows, some reused. Well-preserved interior with
horseshoe GALLERY of 1828 and double-decker PULPIT; organ
loft created 1866–7.

WAR MEMORIAL, Lawns Lane. *c.* 1920. Portland stone pylon
carved poorly with low-relief figures.

Much of the older village was swept away by C20 suburbaniza-
tion, but survivors include LAWNS HOUSE, Chapel Lane,
opposite the church. Now offices. Early C19 five-bay ashlar
mansion with pediment and Ionic porch. On the r. elevation a
porch with re-set pediment and inscription: 'P /WA 1764', possibly for the Pawson family. Also WHEATFIELD HOUSE in
Cross Lane (now flats), C18 and polite, with quoins, eaves
cornice, and a Tuscan doorcase supporting an open segmental pediment.

FARNLEY HALL (Leeds City Council offices), Hall Lane, ¼ m.
N of St Michael. The principal S range was built *c.* 1806 for
Edward Armitage, wool merchant, whose father bought the
manor from the Danby family in 1799. Ashlar, of seven bays,
the central one wider and projecting a little, and embellished
with tetrastyle Doric porch, tripartite window and pediment.
Only one room deep. The E wing is longer, lower and coarser.
It is essentially C18 but may in part be a remnant of the house
of Sir Thomas Danby, built in 1586 and largely demolished in
1756 (doorways and windows in the cellar and C17 panelling
in a first-floor room). Reset over an archway is a decayed stone

panel with the arms of Sir Thomas and an illegible inscription which gave the date of building. Behind the house, STABLES, probably C17, rebuilt *c.* 1806. Also, W, a C17 BARN, its timber frame encased in red brick *c.* 1806. Kingpost trusses with angled struts.

The GROUNDS, acquired by the city in 1944 and opened to the public, have a layout principally dating from the early C19, but there had been a deerpark from the middle ages. In the NW corner against a long wall is a GAZEBO of *c.* 1806, a square two-storey building with a pyramid roof.

NEW FARNLEY, 1 m. SW of the old village, was founded in 1844 for employees of the Farnley Iron Co. It absorbed a vernacular row on the N side of LOW MOOR SIDE (WELLHOLME COTTAGE is reputed to be cruck-built). At the corner of Lawns Lane and Forge Row are ALMSHOUSES of 1896 by *Troup*, low and thinly C17 in style. 1 m. further SW is the little cluster of UPPER MOOR SIDE. INGS HALL FARM BARN has an early C17 timber frame, with later gritstone walls. (Single-aisled timber-frame with curved braces to kingpost trusses, two tiers of purlins, the latter trenched into the backs of the principal rafters. DCMS).

STONEBRIDGE MILLS. *See* WORTLEY

WORTLEY

Wortley appears in Domesday as Riston(e). Now, Upper and Lower Wortley are mainly C20 suburban development, but there were mills here and in the C19 and C20 Upper Wortley was a major manufacturing centre for fire-bricks and sanitary ware. New Wortley was an industrial suburb on the S bank of the Leeds and Liverpool Canal; for the railway buildings in this area *see* p. 424.

ST JOHN THE EVANGELIST, Dixon Lane. 1898 by *W. Swinden Barber*. Superseding the Bell Chapel of 1787 (which stood to the N until 1921). Large, gaunt and stone-faced with Swinden Barber's characteristically flat elevations punctured by Perp windows. W tower never erected; the rendered W elevation with bellcote was created in 1956–7, originally with intersecting tracery in the intended tower arch, in 2002 replaced by a rose window. – STAINED GLASS. Good five-light E window, *Kayll & Co.*, 1899; the other five windows by the same firm, 1901.

WORTLEY WESLEYAN METHODIST CHAPEL (former), Greenside Road. 1846–7, a typical box with pedimented gable over two tiers of round-headed windows. Sunday School extended 1899; big mullioned-and-transomed windows under cross-gables.

GURU NANAK SIKH GURDAWARA, Tong Road, New Wortley. The former Mount Pisgah United Methodist Free Church of 1877. Handsome Italianate.

LOWER WORTLEY UNITED FREE METHODIST CHURCH, Branch Road. 1884–5 by *T. Howdill*. Italianate.

Former SCHOOLS. Three designs by *Richard Adams* for the Leeds School Board, all red brick Gothic. UPPER WORTLEY, Ashley Road and LOWER WORTLEY, Lower Wortley Road, are of 1876 with muscular High Gothic detail. Both were single-storey, planned around a central hall, but Lower Wortley was expanded *c.* 1885 with additions of two and three storeys; its buttressed rear extension had an arcaded covered playground. NEW WORTLEY, Kildare Terrace, opened 1884, is two-storey, its mullioned-and-transomed windows with round-headed upper lights. Two hipped-roofed blocks (for boys and girls) separated by a single-bay fillet (for infants). At either end are gabled entrance and staircase towers.

CLIFF HOUSE, Fawcett Lane, Lower Wortley. A good early 1840s villa built for Joseph Cliff, manufacturer of fire-bricks, pipes and sanitary ware. Two-storey ashlar façades with wide corner pilasters, a distinctive wide cornice, and a low-pitched hipped roof. Five-bay s front, three-bay sides, the W with bow window, the E with porch. The house is elevated above the valley of the Wortley Beck; at the entrance is a two-storey LODGE with canted bay. Inner and outer GATEPIERS with flattened pyramid caps connected by quadrant walls to another pair of larger piers with vermiculated rustication.

HIGHFIELD HOUSE, Lynwood View, Lower Wortley. Grandly composed, small early C19 house (now divided). The street side is the rear: a three-bay centre with round-arched stair window and lower single-bay wings projecting; the middle bay of the ashlar s façade projects slightly and has a door with Tuscan columns supporting a pediment.

CASTLETON MILL, Castleton Close, New Wortley. Built for flax spinning in 1836–8 by *Matthew Murray*, for William Hargrave, and powered originally by a *Fenton, Murray & Wood* beam engine. Four storeys, fireproof construction, with a distinguished semicircular stair-turret at the E end.

STONEBRIDGE MILLS, Stonebridge Lane. Established before 1805 on the Wortley Beck as a steam-powered woollen scribbling and fulling mill. It was operating as an integrated woollen factory by 1819. Surviving buildings include: the original nine-bay, three-storey mill (timber floors and cast-iron columns) with attached engine house; a multi-phase early C19 workshop range with large windows to the upper storey for the hand spinners; cottages and post-1850 mills and sheds.

LINDLEY

2040

LINDLEY HALL. Main range probably of C16 origin. Mullioned windows with arched lights to the ground floor, irregularly spaced cross-windows above. Cross-wing to r. rebuilt 1852: previously a bay window had been moved to Farnley Hall (q.v.).

RESERVOIR, in the valley below. Completed 1876 by the Leeds Corporation Water Works.

9060   LINTON

ST MICHAEL. Away from the village, beside the River Wharfe. A delightful little church with its short square C17 bell-turret, corbelled out and finished with a pyramid roof. W window Dec with flowing tracery, N aisle W window with Y-tracery (its counterpart to the S a copy or renewal of the early C19), those to the aisle flanks straight-headed, with some unusual tracery details to the N and ogee-headed lights to the S. The restoration of 1861 by *John Varley* of Skipton provided all the others – to the nave clerestory, chancel chapels and E end – and the porch, with cusped former window heads re-set under the benches (cf. Burnsall, Rylstone). The interior reveals a much earlier building. The two E bays of the N nave arcade are Late Norman, with a short circular pier on a waterholding base (cf. the W crossing piers at Bolton Abbey) and round arches with only a slight chamfer. The chancel arch also has the same plain Norman imposts and the same chamfer but the arch is pointed. But embedded in the wall N of the chancel arch, facing into the N aisle, is a second circular pier, matching the first. So the intention must have been to continue the arcade further E, without a chancel arch (cf. Long Marston), but in execution a more conventional form was adopted. The two W bays of the arcade, after a piece of plain wall, are C14 or later, with an octagonal pier and pointed, double-chamfered arches. The S nave arcade is similar but the piers are taller. The two chapels appear Perp. In the N aisle a tomb-recess with heavy ogee head, in the S aisle two with cusped two-centred heads. Roofs of 1861, to the chancel a flat ceiling with re-set carved bosses. – FONT. A plain cylinder, probably Norman. – Large ROYAL ARMS of George III, painted on boards. – CHARITY BOARD, C18. – STAINED GLASS. E window 1887 by *Powell Bros.* of Leeds; S chapel E and SE by *Ballantine* of Edinburgh, 1890 and 1897.

The village green is also delightful, with a C17 PACKHORSE BRIDGE, and a clapper bridge, crossing the Linton Beck. At one end FOUNTAIN'S HOSPITAL, almshouses founded under the will of Richard Fountain, 1721. Surprisingly grand and impressive façade, the style showing a close knowledge of the work of Vanbrugh: the architect is not known but the possible candidates are *William Etty* or *William Wakefield*. Dominant one-bay centrepiece, taller than the rest, end bays projecting forward as wings, and two-bay intermediate sections. The centre has giant Doric angle pilasters with big urns over, and a square cupola flanked by volutes. Round-headed doorway recessed in a zone of banded rustication – virtually identical to that in the NE wing at Castle Howard – and above it a blind

Venetian window with the centre light treated as a niche. The wings have pediments and heavy blocked quoins, the openings in the intermediate parts similarly detailed surrounds with triple keystones. At the back the building does not extend as one might expect: behind the centrepiece is a chapel, with another Venetian window at its far end.

At the other end of the green LINTON HALL, a C17 lobby-entry farmhouse with a two-storey porch and adjoining three-storey cross-wing both of *c.* 1700. The porch has a doorway with semi-circular pediment and architrave surround, a cross-window above, also with architrave, and a curvy gable. Same windows to the wing, most of them Georgianized. Its gable shows signs of C19 alteration: perhaps there was a curvy one here also. Other C17 houses are TROUTBECK/BECKSIDE (originally one), 1642, and WHITE ABBEY. LINTON HOUSE has a plain seven-bay C18 front with a pedimented doorcase.

LITTLE OUSEBURN

HOLY TRINITY. Tall unbuttressed Norman W tower of variegated stonework, with paired round-headed bell-openings on an octagonal dividing shaft. Perp battlements and corner pinnacles enclosing a little saddleback roof. Short nave with C14 aisles, the windows straight-headed with ogee-arched lights. Chancel of equal length, with two Norman slit windows on the N side, two pairs of C13 lancets and a plain round-headed priest's door on the S. Good early C14 E window, of five lights with cusped intersecting tracery (cf. Whixley), but the design at the apex altered to Perp panel tracery presumably in the C15. Other changes came with an extensive restoration of 1875 by *Paley & Austin*: the chancel heightened, with the priest's doorway and the l. set of lancets transposed and the E window re-set at a higher level, and the N aisle largely rebuilt. Two-bay nave arcades with octagonal piers and sharply pointed double-chamfered arches, oddly stilted. Chancel arch probably of the same phase. Tower arch with plain jambs and hollow-chamfered imposts but the semicircular head a further alteration of 1875. – CHOIR STALLS. Mainly C19 but incorporating C16 poppyhead pew-ends. – STAINED GLASS. E window by *Charles E. Steel*, 1928.

In the churchyard the THOMPSON MAUSOLEUM, erected in 1743 by Henry Thompson of Kirby Hall (†1760) SIBI ET SUIS ('for him and his'). Excellent design with some particularly interesting details, a pseudo-peripteral rotunda of the Roman Doric order with a plain low drum and shallow lead dome. The attached columns are without bases. More unorthodox are their number – thirteen – although the internal perimeter of the building is of eight bays – and an unevenness in the inter-columniation, the bay containing the entrance being slightly wider than the rest; while the inscription above the doorway occupies a fishtailed panel – a *tabula ansata* – a form with sepulchral associations in Antiquity of which this is one of the earliest examples in England. The architect is not known but a possible candidate would be *Roger Morris*: he may have been responsible for two other mid-C18 examples of the baseless Roman Doric, the Temple of Piety at Studley Royal (q.v.) and Mereworth church, Kent, and he was later co-architect of Kirby Hall (*see* below).

MOAT HALL. Rendered triple-pile block with a complex building history, heavily restored *c.* 2000 – the timber cross-windows of the five-bay front are of that phase. (The oldest part is the middle range, which was evidently the parlour cross-wing of a substantial timber-framed house of the late C15. Part of the close-studded W wall survives, together with two lateral partition walls, the closed kingpost trusses above them, with A-struts from the tie-beam to the kingpost and braces to the ridge pole, and one very handsome moulded ceiling beam with a tracery pattern to the soffit. Between the two partitions an open-well staircase of *c.* 1700, with stout turned balusters. Front range (E) probably of C16 origin, evidently replacing the medieval hall, and remodelled *c.* 1700. Much altered C16 roof trusses. Plain back range C19.)

BRIDGE, over the Ouse Gill Beck. Probably mid-C18. Brick with stone dressings, three arches.

KIRBY HALL, ⅜ m. ESE. The house built *c.* 1747–52 for Stephen Thompson, son of Henry (*see* above), during the latter's lifetime, was demolished *c.* 1920. It was designed by *Roger Morris* and *Lord Burlington* to a plan by the owner and executed by *John Carr*, who also provided 'inside finishings'. What remains are the front wall of the basement storey, a plain two-and-a-half-storey service wing added in 1857–60, and various subsidiary buildings. The STABLE BLOCK beside the wing, mid-C18, is probably by *Carr*, brick with open-pedimented entrance bay crowned by an octagonal attic stage (cf. Plompton) and flanked by blind arcading. ¼ m. NW, on the road to Aldwark Bridge, the OLD LODGE, probably *c.* 1814 by *Robert Lugar*, a little ashlar cube with oversailing pyramid roof and minute pedimented porch. Two-storey C20 extension at the back. ⅜ m. WSW, opposite the end of the village street, the NEW LODGE, mid-C19, cruciform with Tuscan portico, the associated gates and gatepiers dated 1874. Near this KIRBY HALL FARM, C18 model-farmhouse-cum-eyecatcher, the tall projecting centre bay with two-storey relieving arch. The GROUNDS were landscaped by *J.B. Papworth*, 1833: a silted-up lake is discernible.

LITTLETHORPE

ST MICHAEL. 1878, virtually a pair to Holy Innocents, Copt Hewick (q.v.) and so presumably also by *Lewis & Broderick* of

Ripon. Brick, occasionally polychrome, with lancet windows. Cantilevered timber bell-frame in the apex of the w gable, lead-covered flèche on the nave roof. – STAINED GLASS. E window and nave s middle by *Ward & Hughes*, 1878 and 1880; w window and nave NW by *Kempe*, 1893 and 1906.

(HOLLIN HALL, 1⅜ m. SSW, off the Ripon–Harrogate road. Brick house of *c.* 1700 altered and enlarged 1810–13 by *Charles Watson*. The core is a two-storey range with a nine-bay front facing E, the centre bay and the end pairs slightly projecting (cf. Newby Hall), the former under a pediment with a bulls-eye window, the latter with stone quoins. Parapet, porch with Tuscan columns and some alterations to the windows all of 1810–13. At the back, two gables. s flank of six bays, the l. part an addition by *Watson*, converting the range into an L-shape. Extensive service and outbuilding ranges, also mainly of that phase, to N and NW, forming a courtyard. Some good carved timber chimneypieces and a little panelling inside. – Early C19 STABLES to N, of limestone.)

LITTON

SAWYERS GARTH. C17 lobby-entry farmhouse, with extension to the r. dated 1709 and porch dated 1714. One of two houses in Littondale with the peculiarity of the staircase being located within the porch, alongside the entrance passage (cf. the Manor House, Halton Gill). The stair has turned balusters and is reached from the housebody. Exterior much altered C19.

LOFTHOUSE

CHRIST CHURCH. Odd-looking product of a lancet-style church of 1840 by *Perkin & Backhouse*, a much taller chancel of 1889, and a remodelling of 1991 by *James Thorp*. Three short stages stepping up from w to E.

Two yeoman houses nearby, only superficially similar. N of the church PYEMONT HOUSE, mid-C17, brick-built but with a timber arcade structure inside demarcating the rear outshut. Unmatched cross-wings E and W. Arms incorporating three miners' picks formerly visible over the porch entrance, one C17 window on the E flank with mullions and transoms of rendered brick. Parlours in both wings, with a little decorative plaster. Nos. 176–180 LEEDS ROAD, ⅛ m. s, has elements of an early C17 timber frame, mainly cased in brick of the C18 and C19 but still exposed on the front gable of the cross-wing, a king-post truss with multiple V-struts. Similar trusses etc. inside, and a staircase with splat balusters. Stone rusticated quoins on the cross-wing flank, facing the road. (Also CARLTON HALL,

Queen Street, Carlton, ¾ m. N, rendered, with remains of timber framing, and a ceiling boss with the arms and initials of Elizabeth I, in the main (N–S) range.)

THORPE HALL, Thorpe on the Hill, 1¼ m. WNW. In poor repair. Dated 1735 on rainwater heads. Brick with stone dressings, two-and-a-half storeys with five-bay fronts to E and S, both with pedimented doorcases. Part of the S front reduced in height as a result of a lowering of the roof level over the back of the house. Fine interior decoration largely lost. Fragments of timber framing in the service wing.

LONG MARSTON

5050

ALL SAINTS. Late Norman church with nave and chancel in one and N aisle. Simple, unbuttressed Perp W tower. S doorway with three orders of colonnettes and waterleaf and leaf capitals. In the arch mouldings keeled rolls. Also Late Norman a nave window, a chancel N window (now into the vestry, added c. 1400), a blocked priest's door, and the large N arcade. This has three bays with heavy circular piers carrying the plainest moulded capitals and round arches with two slight chamfers. Three doorways with shouldered lintels: one now from the chancel to the vestry, and one in the opposite wall and another in the N aisle, both blocked. Restored by *Scott* in 1869: his are the E window with flowing tracery, the N transept, and the open wagon roof with braced crown-post truss between nave and chancel. – MONUMENTS, now in the tower. James Thwaites †1602. Originally in the N chapel. An unusual design. No effigies or busts, at least now, but two arches and three tapering pilasters with lion masks, an entablature and a strapwork top. – Henry Calverley †1740. Little obelisk with busts at its three corners, he at the apex, his wife and daughter at its foot. – STAINED GLASS. E window by *Hardman*, 1869.

LONG MARSTON HALL, Tockwith Road. The estate was acquired from the Thwaites in the 1670s by Sir Henry Thompson (†1683), a wine merchant and Lord Mayor of York. Either he or his son Edward built a brick U-plan house (sketched by Buck). A fire in the C18 destroyed its centre, and the S wing was then cut down as a separate farmhouse (now The Old Granary) but the N wing survives, with two tall storeys, quoins, a replacement pantile roof, and C18 windows. Nicely preserved open-well staircase with thick turned balusters. Set back to the N is a plain brick range, also two tall storeys, whose first-floor rooms are lined with C17 panelling. There is evidence that this was the Thwaites' house, remodelled as service accommodation, although the brickwork of the two parts matches closely. Attached beyond, a small C18 wine warehouse with big vaulted cellar and barrel ramp.

In Church Road, LONG MARSTON MANOR was the rectory. Long, mid-C18 front of eight bays. THE OLD THATCH has outer walls of brick and cobble concealing a small double-aisled, lobby-entry house. Possibly C16. Nearby the OLD POST OFFICE and LODORE HOUSE were built as a five-bay brick farmhouse in the early C18. Central entrance but still a lobby entry.

LONG PRESTON

Ribblesdale village disposed round a series of variously shaped greens. In 1896 the houses were described as 'mostly . . . comparatively modern'.

ST MARY. Dec w tower, nave and aisles; chancel and chapels rebuilt 1867–8 by *T.H. & F. Healey*. No clerestory. Windows simple but consistent, of two lights. Tower is of curious form, only apparent inside the church. The lower stages are rectangular in plan, the longer axis N–S, but the belfry is square and jettied out on the E side below the nave roof, on four big corbels linked by miniature arches. The lower parts are also largely of solid masonry, with a small rib-vaulted space at each level, the lower connected to the nave by a low doorway. Nave arcades of four bays with octagonal piers, typical C14 capitals and double-chamfered arches. Nave roof with kingposts and slightly cambered tie-beams. Aisle roofs with cusped windbraces. – PULPIT. Later C17, on a bulbous base. – FONT. Probably Norman. Plain, circular, with tall tapering bowl. The FONT COVER is dated 1726 but still Jacobean in character. Hexagonal, two tiers, the upper with simple openwork foliage, and stumpy crocketed spire. – CHARITY BOARD. Early C19. – STAINED GLASS. Ten windows by *Capronnier*, dates from 1858 to 1887. – SUNDIAL SHAFT in the churchyard, dated 1667. Octagonal on a rectangular base.
ALMSHOUSES at the S end of the village. Founded 1613, rebuilt 1859. Utilitarian single-storey range with taller central former chapel. N of the churchyard the former SCHOOL, 1819, humble, with two round-headed windows with Gothic glazing bars. At CROMWELL HOUSE, towards the N end of the village, a re-set doorway dated 1685 with spiral decoration to the lintel (cf. Constitution Hill, Settle).

LOTHERSDALE

Small scattered village in a narrow valley, the outlying houses up on the valley sides.

CHRIST CHURCH. 1837–8 by *Chantrell*, built as a chapel of ease
of Carleton. Perp. w tower-cum-porch, with entrance on the S
side (cf. Cowling), and wide unaisled nave. Chancel added
1884. Interior still with BOX PEWS. – STAINED GLASS. E
window, by *Burlison & Grylls*, 1884.

Former FRIENDS' MEETING HOUSE. 1799. Three large sash
windows to the meeting room, two-storey part to the r. which
accommodated the entrance lobby and a cottage.

DALE END MILL. Former worsted mill, water- and steam-
powered, mainly *c.* 1860 but on the site of a corn mill converted to cotton spinning *c.* 1792. In a wheelhouse next to the
weaving shed, a water wheel installed in 1861 which at 45 ft
(nearly 14 metres) in diameter was probably the largest in Yorkshire. Breast-shot, of mixed cast-iron and timber construction.
Three-storey central range running N–S and a detached square
chimney.

STONE GAPPE, ⅜ m. E. 1725 for William Bawden, remodelled
probably *c.* 1800 for William Sidgwick of Skipton who bought
the estate in 1796. Extensively restored by *Wales, Wales &
Rawson*, 1992–4. The date and Bawden's initials appear on one
of the chimneys, which have the local peculiarity of being decorated with shallow blind arcading (cf. School Street, Steeton).
Three storeys, the S front with a canted bay in the centre and
two bays to each side (cf. Embsay Kirk). The bay is an addition of the *c.* 1800 phase, but the stringcourses between the
storeys, ramped up at the ends (cf. St Helens, Eshton), the
quoins, the heavy eaves cornice, and the rest of the window
openings on the front – originally they were cross-windows –
are all of 1725. But was the roof originally hipped, as now, or
gabled at the ends? Canted porch of *c.* 1800 against the E flank,
remodelled 1998. Apsidal-ended staircase with cantilevered
stone steps and cast-iron balusters also of *c.* 1800. The original of Charlotte Brontë's Gateshead Hall in *Jane Eyre*.

WOODHEAD, ⅜ m. SSW. 1673. Two-storey porch entered at the
side, the upper stage slightly jettied. Over the doorway a large
panel bearing a devotional verse.

THE KNOTT, ¾ m. WNW. Another two-storey porch with jettied
upper stage, dated 1695, but most exotically detailed. Upper
window of three stepped lights with the centre light round-
headed, under a stepped hoodmould (cf. Old Hall, Bradley),
and flanked by bulbous balusters enriched with rings of cable
moulding (cf. Winewall Farm, Trawden, Lancashire). Ornamented lintel to the doorway below. The porch originally stood
at the r. end of the front but was moved in 1895.

4030   LOTHERTON

No village. In 1968 the hall, with its contents, was bequeathed
by Sir Alvary Gascoigne to Leeds City Council, which maintains
it as a country house museum.

CHAPEL. Late Norman, built as a chapel of ease of Sherburn-in-Elmet, nave and lower chancel of rough rubble. Restored 1917 by *John Bilson*. Plain unchamfered s doorway, but that on the N side much more elaborate, with leaf capitals (the shafts missing) and keeled mouldings. So the medieval settlement was probably to the N. One tiny Norman window on the s side of the nave, another (widened) at the E end and a third in the chancel N wall. On the s side also two post-medieval windows, mullioned. w wall rebuilt C17 or C18 a little to the E of its original position, but the gabled bellcote on it perhaps in origin medieval, reconstructed. Plain low chancel 'arch' with a flat lintel replacing the C12 arched head, widened a little in 1917. Kingpost roof truss in the chancel probably C15. Nave floor lowered 1917 apart from a section at the w end. – PULPIT and DESK. C17, originally forming a two-decker, rearranged in 1917 with the desk to the r. of the chancel arch and the pulpit, with tester, to the l. – WALL PAINTING in the chancel, uncovered in 1917. Lines imitating the joints of dressed stone, framing flowers and shields. – Other items commissioned or imported in the C20 by the Gascoigne family. ROOD by *Sir Ninian Comper*, 1920. – FONT. Plaster copy, the original probably Italian C15, with barley-sugar stem. – Carved wood REREDOS mounted on the nave N wall, late C17, N Italian or s German. – Oak CHEST, serving as the altar, C17 German, with reliefs of biblical subjects.

LOTHERTON HALL. Immediately E of the chapel, the entrance front at right angles to it. Ironically, given Sir Alvary Gascoigne's public spiritedness, the house is almost entirely devoid of architectural merit – the product of piecemeal late C19 and early C20 expansion for Col. F.R.T. Gascoigne from a modest core of *c.* 1810, unified only negatively by grey roughcast and brown stone dressings. Its value lies rather in its contents. The core is represented on the s (garden) front by a two-storey segmental bow and the two bays to the r. of it. Range running E from this 1893–6 by *J. Osborne Smith* of London, extended 1924; w wing at right angles, with porte cochère on the w side, 1903 by the Lotherton agent, *T.H. Prater*. In the entrance-cum-staircase hall a handsome late C17 stone chimneypiece with heraldic overmantel, from Huddleston Hall (West Riding South), restored 1903, and spreading Neo-Jacobean-cum-Wrenaissance staircase. In the boudoir, behind the segmental bow, a primitivist Greek Doric columnar screen still *in situ* from the early C19, and late C18 chimneypiece brought from Parlington Hall, Aberford (q.v.), the Gascoignes' previous seat. Formal GARDEN of *c.* 1903 by *Mrs Gascoigne* and *William Goldring*, with a SUMMERHOUSE, originally a porch (1896), displaced by the w wing. NE of it a PORTE COCHÈRE from Parlington Hall, with pediment and coupled Doric columns.

w of the chapel the OLD HOUSE, C17, L-shaped. Stone with a little concealed timber framing, some mullioned windows. Staircase of *c.* 1700 with turned balusters, kingpost roof trusses. Plain early C20 stables etc. adjoining.

LOW SNOWDEN
Askwith

LOW HALL. C17 lobby-entry farmhouse with slightly later two-storey porch, the upper stage jettied. Housebody fireplace with joggled voussoirs. Nearby a smaller house misleadingly renamed the MANOR HOUSE, originally timber-framed and cased in stone in 1683 (date on the door lintel). The roof raised slightly *c.* 1900 – previously it was thatched. A number of wall-posts remain, and a huge cambered bressumer beam to the fireplace. At the back a sunken vaulted dairy with pitched roof (restored).

SHAW HALL, ¾ m. NW. Long C17 range of two builds. The original house is the E two-thirds, with mullion-and-transom windows. Its entrance was presumably in the W gable-end. The present entrance is into the W extension, preceded by a gabled porch dated 1687 which partly masks the joint between the two parts. In the angle to the r. of this a low quarter-round projection, perhaps the remains of a stair-turret. Fireplace with enriched brackets in the W room. Gatepiers with pyramid caps.

On the moor SW of Low Hall several Bronze Age 'cup-and-ring' ROCK CARVINGS (cf. Ilkley Moor).

MALHAM

Celebrated for its situation close to Malham Cove, a dramatic limestone cliff, from the foot of which issues the beck which runs through the village, crossed *inter alia* by an C18 CLAPPER BRIDGE.

C17 houses include HILL TOP FARMHOUSE, W of the bridge, a notably early example, dated 1617. Extended to the l. in the C18. Two-storey porch with pigeon loft and indications that it may once have incorporated a staircase (cf. The Manor House, Halton Gill and Sawyers Garth, Litton). Another rectangular staircase projection at the back. Mullioned windows. On the chimney-breast of the parlour chamber a faded ochre painting of a figure in C17 dress. HILL TOP HOUSE, a sleekly ashlar-faced Grecian villa of *c.* 1830, is an unexpected neighbour.

OLD GRAMMAR SCHOOL, E of the bridge. Founded 1717. Small, with two tall round-headed windows, and a reused C17 date-stone. Now a house.

BUCK INN. Rebuilt *c.* 1870 for Walter Morrison of Malham Tarn House (Malham Moor), possibly to his own design. Approximate C17 Pennine style, including a stepped mullioned window, and Westmorland slate roof (cf. Kirkby Malham School). Asymmetrical composition. The mosaic floor given by Ruskin has disappeared.

On the slopes N of the village an abundance of medieval strip LYNCHETS, and then in the vicinity of Malham Cove a wealth of prehistoric remains, particularly Iron Age SETTLEMENT sites, with hut circles in small enclosures and wider field systems. One is on the hillside ¼ m. E of the Cove, its field system to the NE. Also many Bronze Age burial CAIRNS, e.g. that crowning a slight eminence on the limestone plateau, 1½ m. NNE of the village.

ROMAN CAMP, ½ m. E of the cairn, crossed by Mastiles Lane. Probably late C1. Large, a rectangle of 20 acres, with slight but generally well-defined earthen rampart and intermittent outer ditch. Traces of entrances to E, N and S.

MALHAM MOOR   *8060*

Area of austerely beautiful limestone upland N of Malham Cove, centred on Malham Tarn.

MALHAM TARN HOUSE. 'Shooting box' built 1777–80 to the design of the owner, *Thomas Lister*, later first Lord Ribblesdale (*see* Gisburn). Enlarged C19, particularly *c.* 1870 for Walter Morrison, whose millionaire father had bought the estate in 1852. Lister's house has a restrained two-storey S front in fine sandstone ashlar overlooking the tarn – the level of which was raised in 1791 – with a canted-bay centrepiece and single flanking bays, now preceded by a C19 veranda. Morrison's addition, of the same material but just slightly taller, is a range set against the E flank, with an asymmetrically placed Italianate tower-cum-entrance porch – the belvedere top stages removed in 1963 – and a shallow segmental bay window to the S end. Service wing, stable block etc. of *c.* 1850 at the rear, of coursed limestone. Interiors, including a top-lit staircase with wrought-iron balustrade, all C19 and presumably for the most part redone after a fire in 1873. Two BOATHOUSES on the tarn, the W of *c.* 1800 and primitively crenellated, the E mid-C19 with round-headed openings.

At WATERHOUSES, ½ m. W, the former HOME FARM, SCHOOL HOUSE and ESTATE COTTAGES, 1872–4 for Walter Morrison and perhaps designed by him (cf. Kirkby Malham School). Simple quasi-Pennine style, with Westmorland slate roofs.

A few modest C17 farmhouses on the Moor, including DARN-BROOK HOUSE, 2 m. N. Datestone 1664, re-roofed C19, small mullioned windows.

SMELT MILL CHIMNEY, 1 m. SW. Probably late C18. Stumpy, *c.* 15 ft (5 metres) high, in two tapering cylindrical stages of rough coursed rubble. The flue and footings of the mill itself are also discernible. The mill was first built in the early C18 to serve the lead-mining industry on the Moor, but was subsequently modified to process the zinc ore which was discovered in the locality in 1788.

MARKENFIELD HALL

Excellent example of a fortified house – 'to the outward show fair and stately', as a C16 description puts it – for which a licence to crenellate was granted in 1310. The builder, John de Markenfield, a pluralist cleric and royal servant, became Chancellor of the Exchequer in the same year. It was evidently begun a little earlier than that, *c.* 1290 – see the window details etc. – but the licence can doubtless be taken at face value, as referring to the crenellation as a finishing touch. Various alterations of the C15 to C17, before downgrading to a farmhouse – the Markenfields forfeited the property in 1569 following participation in the Rising of the North – and repairs in C18. Some tactful restoration *c.* 1851–68 by the Ripon antiquary *Richard Walbran* for the third Lord Grantley.

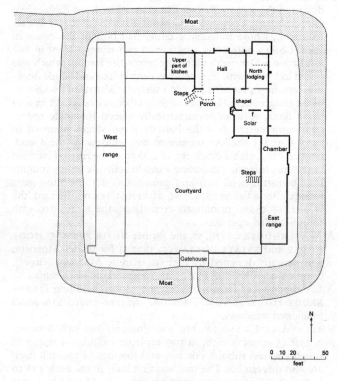

Markenfield Hall.
Plan

The site is moated, with the buildings disposed round a rectangular courtyard: L-shaped hall block at the NE corner – the principal element, taller than the rest – former lodgings range along the rest of the E side, former kitchen block W of the hall on the N side, a range of outbuildings to the W, and a gatehouse flanked by screen walls to the S. The main rooms of the HALL BLOCK are all on the upper floor, above an undercroft which was originally vaulted throughout: the E–W range contains the hall to the W and a lodging to the E, the S wing the chapel and the probable solar beyond it to the S.* The crenellated parapet, originally with a wall-walk behind, is all of a piece. The hall is of three bays, and originally had a central hearth and a screens passage at the W end. It was reached by an external staircase, to a porch of which the roof-line can still be seen. To the l. a narrow C19 window, of the *Walbran* restoration. To the r., two tall transomed windows, each of two trefoil-headed lights with an unencircled quatrefoil above; but the second of these has evidently been shifted slightly to the l. *c.* 1310 to make space for the present W wall of the chapel and for a doorway into the chapel from the hall. Prior to that, the chapel wall was probably *c.* 8 ft (2.5 metres) further E – see the pattern of the vaulting in the chapel undercroft – and there would have been no internal access at first-floor level between the hall and the rest of the building, as there is no doorway at the E end of the hall. At its W end, largely obscured by the C17 roof of the kitchen block, is a blocked segment-headed window, of two lights with Geometrical tracery.

After the chapel, the courtyard side of the S wing has an octagonal staircase turret with candlesnuffer spirelet. Then the solar end, with a two-centre-headed ground-floor doorway – and a number of square two-light mullioned windows, some C19 restorations, which formed part of a C16 modernization when an additional floor was inserted into the solar and the N lodging. On the E side, facing onto the moat, is the handsome chapel window, of three trefoil-headed lights, the middle one higher than the others, and three encircled quatrefoils in the head: so the defences were designed more to impress than to withstand a serious attack. Also more of the C16 mullioned windows, and further r. a lancet. On the N elevation a lean-to garderobe projection serving the N lodging, another lancet, and then two more of the two-light hall windows, flanking a big chimney-breast – the latter an insertion probably of the mid C14, replacing the hall central hearth. The window now in the W bay was previously where the chimney-breast is, and the W bay then contained a doorway at the N end of the screens passage, which gave access to the service wing via a covered staircase – see again the line of the roof, cut into by the window.

*It has been argued that the block incorporates some yet earlier fabric, of before de Markenfield's time.

Inside, the undercroft vaulting survives only in the area below the N lodging and, fragmentarily, in that below the chapel, but the wall arches and corbels remain throughout. Heavy single-chamfered ribs. In the hall undercroft a big segment-headed fireplace, perhaps that of the hall itself moved to its present position probably in the C16: in the hall a replica, 2004. An incongruous staircase of *c.* 1900 goes up into the middle of the hall: previously, since the C16, there had been a staircase at the NE corner. Hall roof probably C18. The chapel has on the S side a fine ogee-headed piscina bearing the Markenfield arms, a blocked doorway to the solar, with moulded hood, and two later doorways, one beside the piscina formed from a squint. The wall between the chapel and the N lodging was originally timber-framed, later rebuilt in stone and subsequently (1981) with brick voussoirs to the blind arches. The solar, the N lodging and the room below the former, in the undercroft, all have segment-headed medieval fireplaces.

The KITCHEN block replaced a timber-framed service range. It is datable by the heraldry to *c.* 1410, but was re-windowed as well as re-roofed in the C17. Huge segment-headed fireplace, chimney with fanciful crenellated top, apparently part of *Walbran*'s restoration. The LODGING range on the E side of the courtyard is evidently of de Markenfield's time – see e.g. the three small lancet windows, one on the W side, two on the E – but it has been altered much more extensively than the hall block. According to the description of 1570 it also had battlements and a vaulted undercroft, but nothing remains of these or even of a parapet. Two C15 doorways on the courtyard side, with moulded surrounds and heraldic hoodmould stops – presumably part of a reorganization of the lodgings – were originally at first-floor level, brought down to the ground floor by *Walbran*. It has been suggested that the original entrance to the courtyard was through this range – there are traces of a large arched opening between the two doorways – but the entrance was in its present position by 1570, before the existing GATEHOUSE itself was built. This is of the early C17 (dendrochronology), with small two-light mullioned windows and gables with finials. The range on the W side of the courtyard was described in 1570 as 'stables, brewhouses and offices' and much of it now appears to be post-medieval, with a series of round-headed doorways; but two lost medieval windows in the S gable-end, shown in an early C19 view, and part of a chimney-breast near the SW corner, perhaps suggest the presence of further lodgings.

S of the moat are two blocks of FARM BUILDINGS, flanking the route to the gatehouse, the outer range of each block a C17 barn or service range, with occasional mullioned windows, the rest essentially a scheme of 1853, in sympathetic C17 style, perhaps by *Walbran*. Further away, much of the circuit of the medieval PARK PALE can be traced, with a ditch and a (largely rebuilt) drystone wall.

MARKINGTON

St Michael. 1843–4 by *A.H. Cates* of York, built on the initiative of the Wilberforce family of Markington Hall. Simplest Dec. Nave and lower chancel, bellcote rebuilt 1968. Narrow sharply pointed chancel arch and pulpit reached by a doorway from the vestry (cf. South Stainley). – stained glass. E window by *Wailes*, 1870; nave NE by *O'Connor*, 1871. Chancel SE, nave SW and W window, designed by *C.E. Tute*, architect son of the vicar, 1888, 1890, 1899.

Markington Hall. Probably C17 in essence, much altered C18–C20. Hall and cross-wings, in a mixture of Magnesian limestone and gritstone. Central doorway with a stringcourse stepped up over it, mullioned windows to the ground floor l. and r., and to the r. wing. Segment-headed fireplace to the hall. E of the house an aisled barn, probably in origin late C15. The structure of that date had a main vessel of three wide bays with a common rafter roof, and the aisles continued round the ends. Bays one and three have been subdivided, with additional aisle posts, principal rafters inserted, and the end aisles absorbed into the main vessel, with the roof extended to form gables at each end. The walls were presumably timber-framed but have been rebuilt in rubble. Across the stream to the N, Low Mill, an early C19 corn mill. Three storeys. Breast-shot water wheel housed in the middle of the building.

How Hill Tower, 1½ m. NNW, crowning an abrupt hillock. Eyecatcher erected 1722 by John Aislabie of Studley Royal, on the site of a chapel built or rebuilt by Abbot Huby of Fountains (†1526). Square tower with round-headed openings in heavy raised surrounds and pyramid roof, incorporating re-set stonework bearing Huby's ubiquitous motto. Barn-like attachments probably later C18.

MARTON

Two small settlements, East and West, a mile apart.

St Peter, at East Marton. Broad, short Norman W tower with tiny round-headed openings, and some fragments of Norman decorative stonework built into the N wall of the nave. The outside walls of the body of the church ('cancellos hosce sacratos Deo') rebuilt 1769 by the Rector, the Rev. John Heber. Odd mixture of styles, presumably an attempt at some fidelity to the medieval structure. Classical porch with pediment, but the entry is very slightly pointed, the inner door more so and the windows all of three arched lights. Nave and chancel in one, and S aisle. Four-bay arcade, with double-chamfered arches on octagonal piers, presumably Perp but perhaps heightened. Tower arch with moulded hood on sculpted stops. Flat ceiling with modillion cornice. – BOX PEWS. The Lord of the Manor's pew in the S aisle and a smaller one for the Rector's family on the N side. – FONT. Norman, plain cylinder. – SCULPTURE. Fragment of a Romanesque cross-shaft found near Tadcaster. One figure, perhaps St Michael, in confrontation with a dragon, and possibly another enmeshed in the coils of a serpent which extends round all four surfaces of the shaft. – CATECHISM BOARDS. C19, with pointed heads. – HATCHMENTS. Five, for members of the Roundell family of Gledstone Hall. C19. – STAINED GLASS. Two windows on the N side and one on the S by *W. Taylor*, successor to the *O'Connor* firm, *c*. 1875 and 1882. Striking figural groups.

DOUBLE-ARCHED BRIDGE, carrying the main road over the Leeds and Liverpool Canal. *c*. 1790 by the canal engineer *Robert Whitworth*. In effect two ordinary single-arched canal bridges, one on top of the other, to gain the height needed for the road.

CRICKLE HALL, ½ m. E. C17. Tall, short range with a symmetrical front. Three-storey gabled porch, a single bay of small three-light mullioned windows to each side of it, larger mullioned windows to the gable-ends. Big central chimneystack.

At West Marton, BALE HOUSE, small early C18 double pile. Five-bay front with cross-windows in architrave surrounds, and rusticated quoins. Of MARTON HALL, the home of the Heber family, only a fragment and an attached outbuilding range remain, mainly C19 with some earlier elements. 1 m. N, INGTHORPE GRANGE, with three-storey porch dated 1672. Another inscription on the porch, in a panel the shape of a truncated triangle, may be *ex situ*. Three gables side by side, with stepped three-light windows. Ground-floor windows extended downwards in the C19, when the floor level was lowered, the house doubled in depth and the S flank remodelled as an entrance front. Big segment-headed fireplace in the housebody, C19 plaster ribbed vaults in the S porch and staircase hall.

See also Gledstone Hall.

MARTON CUM GRAFTON

Effectively a single rather scattered village with two centres.

CHRIST CHURCH, Marton. 1875 by the London architect *John Ladds*, but incorporating a quantity of material salvaged from the previous church, which stood a little to the S. Nave, chancel and prominent W bellcote, in chunky C13 style with Geometrical tracery. The reused items include an elaborate Norman doorway, much restored, on the S side of the chancel, leading into the vestry. Three orders of shafts, the outermost decorated with spirals, the inner with zigzag (l.) and trellis (r.), decorated capitals, and more zigzag and a rope moulding to the arch.

Others are the plain head of the N doorway, also Norman –
with a tympanum formed of what appears to be part of a grave-
slab, with a crude cross in a roundel – the N and S lancets of
the chancel, and a straight-headed two-light Dec window to
the vestry. – Painted ROYAL ARMS of Queen Anne, with the
initials GR added. – STAINED GLASS. E window 1914 by
A.O. Hemming. – MONUMENT. The Rev. J.R. Lunn, instigator
of the rebuilding, †1899. C14-style brass, with effigy in an ogee-
headed tabernacle.

MENSTON

1040

ST JOHN. 1870–1 by *Price & Linklater* of Manchester. Small, in
E.E. style. N aisle added 1886. – STAINED GLASS. E windows
1876 by *J.W. Knowles*; w 1897 by *Powell Bros.* of Leeds.
OLD HALL (alias Fairfax Hall), w of the church. *Ex situ* datestone of 1653. L-shaped but formerly larger, with another
cross-wing, making it a half-H,* and much restored *c.* 1910. At
the front end of the remaining wing a two-storey canted bay
window with mullions and transoms.
MENSTON GRANGE, w again. Long one-and-a-half-pile range
with slightly off-centre two-storey porch dated 1672. Mullioned windows, one with the lights arched.
HIGH ROYDS MENTAL HOSPITAL (former). 1884–8 by the
West Riding County Surveyor *J. Vickers Edwards.* Vast barrack-
like rock-faced complex, originally served by its own railway
branch line, with a plethora of pyramid-roofed water towers
with sparse Gothic detail. Early example of the *echelon* plan,
with the ward blocks stepping back symmetrically to each side
of a central administration building – male patients to the l.,
female to the r. – and linked by a system of corridors. Recreation hall and service blocks – laundry, kitchen, stores, workshops – behind. The intention was to maximize the amount of
daylight reaching the wards and to separate the different types
of patient. The ward blocks are of two storeys, the administration block of three, its tower taller than the others, formerly
with a gabled timber superstructure. Conversion to housing is
proposed.

METHLEY

3020

A sense of incompleteness is palpable. There is an important
church with an outstanding series of monuments, but Methley
Hall 1 m. w, the great house of the Waterton and Savile families,

*A porch was moved to Farnley Hall (q.v.) in the early C19.

Methley, St Oswald, monument to Sir Robert Waterton †1425
and his wife Cecily Fleming.
Lithograph after J.W. Hugall, 1842

was demolished in 1963.★ Nor is there a real village of Methley,
only the former colliery settlement of Mickletown, across the
railway to the NE, and some scattered houses elsewhere.

ST OSWALD. Much restored and rebuilt in several phases, the
first of 1874 by *H.R. Gough*, the second of 1900–1 by *Prothero*

★ The great hall screen and gallery, of the early C17, are in store in the care of Leeds
City Council.

& Phillott of Cheltenham. The lower stage of the nave N wall
is C13, with the jamb of a lancet window exposed inside, but
standing on earlier footings. Dec refenestration – three
windows with reticulated tracery – and Dec S aisle, with similar
windows. Perp are the W tower (restored 1900–1) with
corbelled-out parapet and big pinnacles (and a spire from the
C18 until 1937); the S porch, with stone slab roof carried on
chamfered-arched ribs; and the nave clerestory stage. But the
clerestory windows were Gothicked in 1874 – previously they
were plainly mullioned – and the renewal of the parapets presumably also belongs to that phase. Perp also the S chapel
(refaced 1938), continuing the S aisle without a break, which
is probably datable to *c.* 1484 (chantry foundation) but if
so appears to have replaced an earlier chapel (*see* below).
Segment-headed four-light windows with panel tracery. Dec S
nave arcade of three bays with octagonal piers and double-
chamfered arches, chancel arch also double-chamfered, on
head corbels. Good (restored) nave roof with tracery above the
tie-beams, resting on brackets supported by angel corbels. Panelled ceiling to the S aisle and chapel, with painted decoration
redone in 1954. Of the chancel only the lower stage of the S
wall, between it and the S chapel, and the big reused grotesque
corbels supporting the roof are pre-C20. In the wall one full-
sized arch; and then a tomb-arch containing the tomb of Sir
Robert Waterton †1425, who provided for the building of a
chapel – hence the presumed existence of a predecessor to the
present one. N wall of 1900–1 with a two-bay arcade; sanctuary bay and E end, and N vestry-cum-organ chamber beyond
the arcade, 1925–6 by *Chorley & Gribbon* of Leeds.
    SCREENS. Between the aisle and the chapel: Perp, with
delicate tracery, restored. Chancel N side: two tiers of closely
set Tuscan colonettes, perhaps recycled from a late C17 altar
rail. – PULPIT. 1708. A tube-like octagon. – LECTERN.
A spectacular C19 made-up piece, consisting of an elaborate
hexagonal stand in Continental Late Gothic style incorporating three genuine early C16 carved figurines of German workmanship, and a huge eagle made by *Robert Ellis & Co.* of New
York and exhibited in Philadelphia in 1867.* It was given to
the church in 1869. – FONT COVER. Made in accordance with
the will of Richard Webster of Methley, painter, †1585. Octagonal with two tiers of openwork panels and a spire. Plain font
re-assembled 1901. – SCULPTURE. Weathered panel of a seated
and crowned St Oswald. To the r. of the chancel arch, formerly
over the S doorway. Probably C14, to judge by the canopy. –
C17 funerary HELMETS and GAUNTLETS in the S chapel. – In
the tower a CATECHISM BOARD, probably from a scheme of
adornment of the chancel carried out in 1708. – STAINED
GLASS. In the chapel E window, well-preserved C15 glass
assembled in 1874 from all the chapel windows and the old
chancel E window. Eight saints and eight small angels, and

---

* See C. Tracy, *Continental Church Furniture in England* (2001).

fragments at the bottom of the lights. – E window by *A.K. Nicholson*, 1926 (glass from the previous E window, 1874 by *Charles Gibbs*, in the vestry E); nave NE and N middle by *Wailes*, 1856; w window by *Willement*, 1874.

MONUMENTS. Two defaced stone effigies of the C14, since 1901 in separate recesses in the nave N and S aisle walls but originally part of the same monument. According to a C17 account the subjects were two brothers, a priest and a lawyer, who built part of the church, presumably the S aisle. – The others mainly in the S chapel. Sir Robert Waterton †1425 and his wife Cecily Fleming. Alabaster tomb-chest with recumbent effigies, exceptionally finely carved and probably the work of alabaster carvers based at York. He is in armour identical to that of the contemporary Redman and Ryther effigies at Harewood (q.v.). Striking individual face, large head-dresses to both figures. At his feet a lion (valour), at hers little dogs (fidelity). On the chest sides St Paul (NW), the Trinity (S centre) and kneeling angels holding shields. The round-headed tomb arch is similarly elaborate, cusped and sub-cusped, with vaulted soffit and lion-mask stops to the hoodmould. – Lionel, Lord Welles †1461 and his wife Cecily Waterton (daughter of the above), the counterpart, opposite against the chapel S wall, but probably originally in the centre. Also alabaster, but evidently from one of the Midlands workshops: Lord Welles's features are widely replicated elsewhere (e.g. Robert, Lord Hungerford †1459 at Salisbury Cathedral and Richard Neville, Earl of Salisbury, †1460 at Burghfield, Berks). On the side panels of the tomb-chest which survived the relocation standing angels holding shields.

p. 590

Sir John Savile †1607, his son Sir Henry †1632 and the latter's second wife Elizabeth Wentworth. Moved from the chapel to the S aisle in 1948. Massive tall tomb-chest of black and white marble with three recumbent effigies, attributed by Adam White to the London sculptor *William Wright*. Also shown are two children of Lady Savile who died young (both with skulls), a son kneeling at her feet and an infant daughter on the l. side of the chest. Otherwise on the chest sides Ionic columns and coats of arms. – Charles Savile †1741. By *Scheemakers*. Semi-reclining figure in martial Roman dress, with his mourning wife (†1759) seated at his feet. The effigy was evidently intended to be seen from an angle, otherwise appearing excessively foreshortened. A large pedimented backplate was removed in 1901. – John Savile, first Earl of Mexborough, †1778. By *Wilton*, 1780. Elegant semi-reclining figure in his peerage robes, pointing heavenwards. – Sarah, Dowager Countess of Mexborough, †1821. By *Westmacott*, but not one of his best. Tablet with two heavily draped allegorical figures, Hope and Religion, flanking the inscription. Relief of the Raising of Lazarus below. – Two tablets, Elizabeth, Countess of Mexborough, †1821 and Henry Savile †1828, both with a female figure leaning on an urn, by *R. Blore* of London. – John Savile, second Earl of Mexborough, †1830. Pedimented aedicule with free-standing columns, oddly C17 in style, by *Fisher* of York. – In the churchyard, SW of the tower, a grave-slab probably of *c.* 1300, with sloping top and ornamented cross-head.

CHURCH SIDE HOUSE, NW of the church. Short stone-built range of the later C17 – the rainwater head of 1642 does not belong – with symmetrical front characterized by two big gabled dormers. Some mullioned windows remaining. SE of the church the former SCHOOL, 1847, enlarged 1859, Gothic; and beyond it the former RECTORY, 1842 by *Salvin* (who had worked at the hall), picturesque Jacobean-cum-Gothic. The latter's predecessor, the OLD RECTORY, is ¾ m NE, at Lower Mickletown. *c.* 1700 for the Rev. Gilbert Atkinson, rector 1685–1709, a brick double pile with hipped roof and five-bay front, the middle bay slightly projecting. Sash windows, evidently replacing casements (staircase with stout turned balusters). So the contrast with Church Side House is instructive. ⅞ m. further SE, off Green Lane, DUNFORD HOUSE, 'lately built' in 1759. Five bays, two-and-a-half storeys, with Venetian window over the entrance and a Diocletian window above that (Good interior fittings). In the other direction, ¾ m. WNW of the church, S of the main road, a single-storey row of former ALMSHOUSES, C17, with Tudor-arched doorways and tiny two-light windows (renewed). Another row was demolished in the 1920s.

CLUMPCLIFFE. Interesting group on rising ground a little NW of the site of Methley Hall, 1⅜ m. W of the church. The HOUSE, probably of before 1618, is a long S-facing stone-built range with mullion-and-transom windows of up to eight lights, an added two-storey porch off-centre at the front (with its entrance blocked) and another against the E gable-end. Garderobe turret at the NW corner and next to it on the rear wall a big chimney-breast of brick. To the NE an aisled BARN, cased in brick, built of timber felled in 1588–9. Five bays, king-post trusses. N of the house is a remarkable, but now derelict, GAZEBO complex, built by Sir John Savile of Methley Hall *c.* 1708 (rainwater heads). Three detached buildings forming the N, E, and W sides of a courtyard, of brick with stone dressings. The gazebo itself had a single-storey five-bay front range under a hipped roof with dormer windows but behind this a taller section, now collapsed, crowned by a balustrade and cupola.* The flanking units are repeats of the front part, and are said to have been stables.

MICKLEY
Azerley

ST JOHN. 1841 by *John Harper*, for the Dalton family of Sleningford Grange, North Stainley. Built of cobbles. Lancet style,

---

* Shown in Samuel Buck's drawing of *c.* 1720. He also shows the S side of the courtyard closed by railings and an elaborate gate, and describes the complex as a 'Dogg Kenel'.

with one-bay chancel and w bellcote. The gabled VICARAGE next door is larger.

Former METHODIST CHAPEL. Little early C19 box with two round-headed sash windows.

NEWFIELD, 1¼ m. SE. Neo-Palladian villa by *Erith & Terry*, 1979–81.

AZERLEY TOWER, 1⅞ m. SSE. 1839. Thin battered square tower rising from a single-storey Gothic cottage. Said to have been built as a gamekeeper's house and look-out.

0070

MIDDLESMOOR
Stonebeck Up

Tight upland hamlet high on a steep hillside near the head of Nidderdale, with magnificent views over the valley.

ST CHAD. 1865–6 by *W.H. Crossland*, replacing a chapel of ease of Kirby Malzeard consecrated 1484. Dull conventional Dec, w tower, nave with N aisle, and chancel. – SCULPTURE. Anglo-Saxon cross, crudely ornamented, the head with two cross-bars. Probably C10.* – STAINED GLASS. E and W windows by *Atkinson Bros.* of Newcastle upon Tyne, 1896 and 1908; nave SE by *Shrigley & Hunt*, 1919.

Farmhouses further up the dale include LOW WOODALE, 2 m. NNW, 1687, with central lobby entry, six-light mullioned windows to housebody and parlour, and rear staircase-cum-service wing. At THROPE HOUSE, ¾ m. NE, 1741, a Venetian window to the staircase and an ornate kitchen fireplace. Altered front with quoins.

ANGRAM and SCAR HOUSE RESERVOIRS, 3 m. WNW and 2¼ m. NW, at the head of the dale, 1904–19 and 1921–36 respectively for the Bradford Corporation Water Works. The engineers were *James Watson* for Angram, and *Lewis Mitchell* and *William Newlands* for Scar House. A heroic undertaking which involved the construction of a light railway up the dale from Pateley Bridge, 1904–8, for the transport of workmen and materials. Tall masonry dams, with an architectural vocabulary of turrets and crenellations – extraordinarily passé by 1936 – repeated from the earlier Gouthwaite Reservoir at Ramsgill (q.v.).

8040

MIDDOP

MIDDOP HALL. Ancestral home of the Lister family, later of Gisburn (q.v.) and elsewhere. Probably C16, now a single range

---

* Collingwood's supposed inscription, deciphered as 'The Cross of St Ceadda', is now interpreted as a group of purely decorative motifs.

but originally larger. Mullioned windows with round-headed lights. In a C19 farm building attached to the front at right angles, some barely discernible architectural fragments, perhaps from the 'north wing' referred to by Whitaker in 1805.

MOOR MONKTON

ALL SAINTS, ½ m. S of the village, perhaps at the site of an earlier settlement. A Norman church of nave and lower chancel. – One C12 window in the nave, one in the chancel, and also a priest's door (single-chamfered) and the S doorway. This has one order of shafts, and a single waterleaf capital. The porch is of the restoration of 1878–9 by *James Fowler* of Louth, who also remodelled the C18 W tower and probably invented many of the simple chamfered lancets and Norman-style E window. Chancel and tower arches both small with restored, unmoulded arches on plain imposts. – FONT with gadrooned bowl. – SCULPTURE. In the porch, a small headless relief of a draped figure. What is its date? – MONUMENTS. In the porch wall, a slab less than 2 ft (0.6 metres) long with a sunk quatrefoil near the top and a sunk half-quatrefoil at the bottom, in which a praying figure appears, head and bust, and feet. Early C14 (cf. Gilling East, North Riding, and Staunton-in-the-Vale, Nottinghamshire). In the tower an anonymous C18 memorial to an infant, on its deathbed framed by drapes. Above, cherubs supporting a shield.

RED HOUSE, 1½ m. E of the village by the Ouse. Remains of the house begun in 1607 by Sir Henry Slingsby (†1634)* and continued by his son, Sir Henry Jun., refaced in Tudor Gothic style in 1860. Sir Thomas Slingsby (†1835) had demolished the rest by *c.* 1821. There are few visibly C17 features – what looks to be a small barrel-vaulted long gallery in the roof and some mullioned-and-transomed windows at the rear – but the extent of the original house can be ascertained from the width of the formal garden laid out within walls on the SW side. The remarkable CHAPEL, probably finished *c.* 1621, was left freestanding by the demolitions. A brick-built rectangle, it has two tiers of windows on the S side, the upper with arched and cusped heads to the lights. E window fully and correctly Perp but oddly off-centre because a room is incorporated along the N side of the building. The W wall was rebuilt by Sir Thomas: round-headed doorway and a moralising inscription in carved brick re-set from the house. Intimate interior with contemporary timber FITTINGS, including PANELLING, a SCREEN with two tiers of balusters of square section supporting a W GALLERY occupying half the building, PEWS with carved Gothic ends (reused), an elaborately carved PULPIT made in 1621, and a bowed COMMUNION RAIL of apparently late C17

---

* His monument, by *William Wright*, is at St John, Knaresborough.

date with generously moulded balusters, at the foot overgrown with leaves. The STAIRCASE to the gallery and upper room is from the house, made in 1637 by *John Gowland*, turned balusters and newel posts supporting heraldic beasts described by Sir Henry Jun. as 'a crest . . . of my especial friends & of my brother-in-Laws'. One is the 'blackamore cast in led' by *Andreas Kearne*, the German associate of Nicholas Stone. It once held candlesticks. – WALL PAINTING across the N wall of Moses and Aaron with the Decalogue between, done after 1836. – In the E window C17 PAINTED GLASS, a mixture of sacred fragments (the four saint's heads and cherubs appear to be all that survive of twelve apostles painted by *Richard Butler* in 1622) and heraldic devices, including Prince of Wales feathers, attributed to *Barnard Dinninghoff* (cf. his glass at Gilling Castle, North Riding) transferred from the 'Star Chamber' when the house was reduced.

Outside the E front is the almost unrecognizable remains of a stone STATUE by *Kearne* of Sir Henry Jun.'s champion horse. It was set up originally on the MOATED PLATFORM, NW of the house, site of the 'Rede House' for which licence to crenellate was granted in 1392.

2020

MORLEY

Mill town up on a ridge SW of Leeds. As an urban entity it is the product of the later C19: population was 2,108 in 1801, 4,821 in 1851, 9,607 in 1871, 18,725 in 1891, 21,623 in 1901. Architecturally it is identified by its extraordinarily ambitious Town Hall, with a proud tower visible from afar: the contrast with the small size and generally unaspiring character of the rest of the town centre could not be greater.

ST PAUL, South Queen Street. 1893–5 by *G. Fellowes Prynne*. Long and broad, with no break externally between nave and chancel, but at the E end the chancel of the previous church (1875–7 by *W.H. Parkinson* of Leeds) retained as a much lower sanctuary. C13 Gothic, with low aisles, clerestory of small quatrefoils, and N and S chapels of contrasting form. A big W tower was intended. Choir altered internally *c.* 1935, with trilobe-section vault mediating the change in scale between the sanctuary and the main vessel.

ST PETER, Victoria Road. 1829–30 by *R.D. Chantrell*. A Commissioners' church (cost £2,968). Lancet style. W tower with broach spire, aisleless body. Chancel added, and N and S galleries removed, 1884–5 by *Hanstock & Sheard* of Batley. – At the corner of the churchyard the former SCHOOL, 1832, Tudor Gothic, altered.

ST ANDREW, Bruntcliffe Road. 1889–91. E.E., with unfinished SW tower.

St Mary's-in-the-Wood United Reformed Church, Troy Road. The town's historic ecclesiastical site, the C19 church replacing a former chapel of ease of Batley, of medieval origin, which in this Nonconformist stronghold had been continuously in the possession of the Congregationalists since the late C17. It is by *Lockwood & Mawson*, 1876–8, crude Dec with prominent SW tower and spire. Cast-iron columns supporting the roof, gallery round three sides. – Large ROYAL ARMS of Charles II, dated 1664, painted on boards, from the old chapel. – In the churchyard the SCATCHERD MAUSOLEUM, late C17 (first memorial 1688), an ashlar cube of markedly hybrid style, with angle pilasters, Gothic doorway, and a truncated-ogee-headed relieving arch framing the latter. – Also an outstanding collection of GRAVE-SLABS from the mid C17 to mid C18, with elaborate low-relief carving: scrolled borders, arched frames with keystones and capitals, trumpeting angels, hearts, skeletons etc. – The former SUNDAY SCHOOL, of 1900, now church hall, is further S, in Commercial Street. Large and surprisingly grand, with showy Neo-Baroque façade. Seven bays, the centre three with segmental pediment. Banded rustication to the ground floor, engaged Composite columns to the first.

CENTRAL METHODIST CHAPEL, Wesley Street. 1860–1 by *James Simpson* of Leeds. Straightforwardly Italianate with four-bay pedimented front. Paired entrances with Tuscan half-columns, round- and segment-headed windows. In the pediment an oculus with ornate frame. Spacious and well-preserved interior, with apsidal-ended gallery, BOX PEWS at both levels, mahogany PULPIT, and ORGAN CASE of 1863. Attached to the rear the METHODIST HALL, *c.* 1970 by *Brooks Thorp Partners*.

92

PRIMITIVE METHODIST CHAPEL (former), Fountain Street. 1885–6 by *T.A. Buttery* of Morley. Ashlar front of five bays, the middle three an engaged Corinthian portico; but the Italianate detail now a little mixed chronologically. Former SUNDAY SCHOOL to the r., 1878. Opposite, the former TEMPERANCE HALL, 1895, cheerful Free Renaissance.

TOWN HALL, Queen Street. 1892–5 by competition winner *G.A. Fox* of Dewsbury. The cost was £41,227. Handsome but unoriginal, a descendant of Leeds Town Hall, and more particularly almost a repeat of Leeds's earlier progeny, the town hall at Bolton, Lancashire (1866–73) – the architect of which, William Hill, was a Leeds man: a square block articulated by a giant Composite order, of free-standing columns at the front, pilasters at the sides, with a domed clock tower over the entrance. The form of the front is entirely that of Bolton rather than Leeds, with the columns coming forward in the centre as a hexastile pedimented portico, preceded by steps, and anta-like solid windowless end bays. So too are the banded rustication of the basement and the detailed treatment of the tower, with an arched opening between coupled pilasters below the complicated clock stage; while the programme of the SCULPTURE in the pediment – Justice supported by Industry,

Commerce, Science and the Arts – is not hugely dissimilar. Sides with the centre recessed (cf. Leeds) and the pilasters confined to the projecting parts (l.), the front one only (r.). Back plainer again. Interiors quite sumptuous but a little dull. Stone-lined spine corridor with iron-balustraded staircase rising along one side, and STAINED GLASS by *E.S. Watkin* illustrating another mixed bag of attributes. The municipal state-rooms – council chamber, mayor's parlour, committee room and banqueting suite – are along the front, and at the back are a galleried public hall and a courtroom.

PUBLIC LIBRARY, Commercial Street. 1905–6. Routine Edwardian classical, but memorable on account of the tiled decoration of the entrance vestibule, designed by *G.M. Forsyth* and executed by *R.R. Tomlinson*, with a deep frieze of portraits of and quotations from English literary figures in a linear Art Nouveau style.

BOARD SCHOOLS include PEEL STREET (now Joseph Priestley College), 1880, domestic Gothic with a long symmetrical frontage; and VICTORIA ROAD, 1898–9 by *T.A. Buttery & I.B. Birds*, Free Renaissance, on the 'Prussian' system (classrooms round a central hall).

The centre is virtually confined to a single street, QUEEN STREET, and the only sequence of a thoroughly urban character is opposite the Town Hall and broadly contemporary with it: first the former CO-OPERATIVE CENTRAL STORES, opened in 1899 (now Barclays Bank), Free Renaissance with corner cupola, then two purpose-built banks – HSBC, slightly more classical, with cross-windows, and NATWEST, odd quasi-Gothic. Also on the other side, r. of the Town Hall, LLOYDS BANK, 1891, Italianate. Behind the Town Hall there were mills until 1962. Further S some uninspired later C20 replacements, mainly on the same small scale as the earlier buildings. Further N, where the street dips steeply downhill, is SCATCHERD PARK, opened 1911, enlarged 1939 over the site of the mid-C18 Morley House. At the head of steps here the WAR MEMORIAL, 1927, a bronze Britannia by *W.H. Gilbert* (cast by *H.H. Martyn & Co.*) on a battered granite plinth. N again, on Dawson Hill, MORLEY HALL, with a doorway at the side dated 1683 but otherwise all of C19 appearance. Two storeys, variegated.

CRANK MILLS, Station Road. Carding and fulling mill of *c.* 1792, claimed to be the first steam-powered woollen mill in West Yorkshire. Three storeys, seven bays, with later three-bay extension to the l., stepping up the hill, mid-C19 lean-to engine house to the r. The crank and flywheel of the original engine were outside, against the r. gable wall – hence the name.

A group of mills of the late C19 and early C20 survives at Tingley Common, ⅞ m. SSE of the centre – mainly of brick, as was usual in Morley by that time – including OAK MILLS, Texas Street, an integrated woollen mill of 1906, perhaps by

T.A. Buttery. Main building of three storeys and seventeen bays with stair and water tower at the s corner – half of a planned double mill – originally used for weaving and carding as well as spinning; detached engine and boiler house to the SE, with square chimney; weaving shed behind them eventually built in 1929; office and warehouse range along the street.

Of HOWLEY HALL, 1½ m. SSW, the prodigy house built *c.* 1590 by the courtier Sir John Savile and demolished in the early C18, there remain some low masonry courses near the clubhouse of the Howley Hall Golf Club. Also earthwork traces of the extensive gardens.

NETHER POPPLETON

5050

St EVERILDA. Beside a track at the end of the village. An interesting small church, once a little larger. Wide unmoulded Norman chancel arch on simple chamfered imposts; then almost halfway along the N and S walls of the chancel are similar blocked arches, just a little higher, and further E on the s side another, much lower. Did these lead into transept-like side chapels? In the taller s arch a two-light Dec window, and above the lower arch a plain straight-headed one, perhaps C17. Straight-headed Dec E window of three trefoil-headed lights. Nave restored, and a N aisle and W bell-turret removed, in 1842. Dec one-light SW window and straight-headed three-light SE window, all other openings C19. C19 bellcote over the chancel arch. – Simple PULPIT, *c.* 1700. – Unpretentious nave GALLERY, to the N and W sides, and painted ROYAL ARMS, all doubtless of 1842 (the arms dated). – STAINED GLASS. In the E window, early and late C14 fragments including a Coronation of the Virgin. Some more tiny fragments in the nave SE. – MONUMENTS. Sir Thomas Hutton †1620. Large kneeling figure in profile, in a round-headed niche framed by panelled pilasters and entablature. – Anne Hutton †1651. Smaller praying demi-figure, crudely framed, turned slightly to face towards the altar. – Richard Hutton and two wives. Mid-C17. Three small figures, he in the centre kneeling frontally, the wives l. and r., standing and turned slightly inward, one carrying a baby, the other with a child in front. In an aedicule with free-standing Tuscan columns and broken pediment. – LYCHGATE by *G. G. Pace*, 1949.

Beside the churchyard a single-aisled BARN, probably *c.* 1600, much altered and reduced, and heavily restored 1998–2000. Brick walling C18, three bays at the W end lost to fire in 1928. Four collar- and tie-beam roof trusses, but only two of the original posts. Some C18 brick houses in the village street. (Poppleton Hall was demolished *c.* 1960 but a circular SUMMER-HOUSE remains, overlooking the river Ouse, dated 1795.)

NEWBY HALL

'The finest house I saw in Yorkshire' (Celia Fiennes, 1697). It was also one of the most up-to-date, a big flat-roofed three-storey block, of red brick with stone dressings, built *c.* 1685–93 for the Newcastle coal magnate Sir Edward Blackett who had bought the estate in 1677. As to authorship, the latest research suggests that Daniel Defoe's ascription of the design to none other than *Sir Christopher Wren* should not be dismissed out of hand,* although *John Etty* of York was also involved in some capacity. In 1748 the estate was sold again, to Richard Elcock Weddell, son of a York tradesman, who the previous year had inherited a fortune from his bachelor uncle Thomas Weddell which was 'to be laid out in the purchase of lands'; and under his son the virtuoso William Weddell, who inherited in 1762, the house became finer still. Weddell began his improvements immediately after he returned home from his Grand Tour to Italy of 1764–5, during which he had assembled a notable collection of Antique sculpture. The inside of the house was transformed and two wings were built running out from the E front, one containing the Sculpture Gallery, the other the kitchen. The interiors were mainly by *Robert Adam*, the exterior works first by *John Carr* and later by *William Belwood* of York, who started here as Adam's local executant architect. Also consulted briefly were Sir William Chambers and perhaps *James Stuart*. On Weddell's death in 1792 Newby passed to his cousin, Thomas Robinson third Lord Grantham, later Earl de Grey, amateur architect and first President of the Institute of British Architects; and subsequently it went to the Vyners and then the Comptons. Some further changes were made during the C19 but the main architectural undertaking on the estate was *Burges*'s new church at Skelton (q.v.).

The house is now approached from the E, but the original entrance was to the W – the change was evidently made *c.* 1757 by *Carr* for Richard Weddell – and the C17 design is better

p. 37

preserved on that side. Nine bays, the centre one and the end pairs projecting slightly, with quoins, the centre also with a segmental pediment above the first floor. Former doorway with coupled Corinthian columns, richly ornamented entablature and another segmental pediment, its centre recessed. Windows sashed from the outset, with lugged architrave surrounds; stringcourses between the storeys. Balustraded parapet, originally interrupted over the centre bay by a third pediment, this time triangular. A big cupola over the centre of the house has also been removed, and the roof rebuilt with low-pitched hips. Later block to the l., the ground floor a dining room added in 1808 by *Lord Grantham* assisted by *John Shaw*, the obtrusive upper stage a billiard room of 1892–4 by *Walker &*

---

* *Georgian Group Journal*, 2008. A small payment was made in 1694 to 'the Servants of Sir Christopher Wren'.

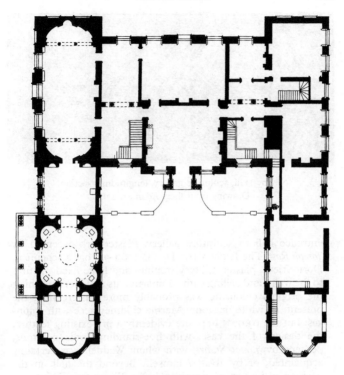

Newby Hall.
Plan

Strong of Liverpool. The s end of the house, of five bays, also
has the emphasized centre bay with segmental pediment above
the first floor, and a former doorway with another segmental
pediment, on enriched brackets. To the r. is the sculpture
gallery – which like its counterpart the kitchen wing takes the
place of a C17 service pavilion. As built by *Carr*, 1765, both had
a one-and-a-half-storey, three-bay centre and single-storey
two-bay flanking sections, the balustraded attic stages of the
latter and the compensating tall parapets to the centres, decorated with swags, being added by *Belwood* in 1784. Also *Carr*'s
the single-storey balustraded Tuscan portico to the centre of
the gallery s front (his design for the gallery interior, commented on by Chambers, was superseded by *Adam*'s). The elevations facing onto the E forecourt are plainer, without
entrances: the E ends have canted bays. On the body of the
house here the slightly projecting three-bay centrepiece is
Carr's, c. 1757, the porch, with coupled Ionic columns and
ornamented blocking course, *Belwood*'s, c. 1777.

Adam's interiors, a wonderfully successful combination of
sophisticated learning and elegance and a comfortably human
scale, were designed to form an anti-clockwise sequence from

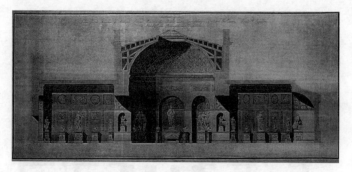

Newby Hall, sculpture gallery, longitudinal section.
Drawing by Robert Adam, *c.* 1767

entrance hall to sculpture gallery. Plasterwork executed by
Joseph Rose. The ENTRANCE HALL, 1769–72, has a scheme of
Doric frieze, plaster military trophies and large fixed pictures
to the walls, and ceiling with compartments and more trophies:
the original colouring was probably more austere than the
present, all white or stone. Marble chimneypiece with sphinxes; but the ORGAN opposite evidently a pre-existing feature,
the design of the case, with free-standing Ionic columns,
perhaps by *James Stuart*, with whom Weddell was certainly
acquainted, or by *Weddell* himself. Beyond the hall, in the
position of its C17 predecessor, is the TAPESTRY DRAWING
ROOM, so-called from the *Gobelins* tapestries which were the
starting point for the whole. Weddell probably visited the Gobelins factory either on a visit to Paris in 1763 or on his way
home from Italy in 1765. The tapestries were of a new design
intended specifically for the English market, featuring large
medallions of the Elements executed by *Neilson* from paintings
by *Boucher.* Weddell's was the second set to be woven – the first
was for Lord Coventry's Croome Court, Worcestershire – and
was despatched in stages between 1767 and 1769. Ceiling
designed 1769, with inset paintings by *Zucchi*, the ground
repainted in unhistorically subdued colours to accord with the
fading of the tapestries; marble chimneypiece, 1774, on the
spine wall where the C17 interconnecting doorway was. Axminster carpet complementary to the ceiling, designed 1775 by
Adam; important furniture attributed to *Chippendale*. S of the
Tapestry Room, between it and Weddell's Dining Room, was
a small apsed ante-room, decorated in the Etruscan style,
unfortunately abolished in 1807 and the space thrown in with
the Staircase Hall to the E. The STAIRCASE itself, of timber,
cantilevered, in three flights, is a survivor from the pre-Weddell
house but embellished with the rest of the space *c.* 1771. Delicate iron balustrade of honeysuckle pattern (cf. Osterley),
Ionic columnar screen in green marble to the ground floor,
arcaded first-floor screen echoing Chambers's at Gower

House, Whitehall (design exhibited at the Royal Academy in 1770).

s again, along all the s flank of the C17 house, is the former Dining Room, 1767–9, converted into a LIBRARY in 1807 by the third Lord Grantham. Apsidal ends screened by fluted Corinthian columns (cf. Syon), ornate plaster wall panels, frieze and ceiling; painted overdoors, overmantel and ceiling inset – a *Triumph of Bacchus* – by *Zucchi*; marble chimneypiece with Bacchic terms (cf. a chimneypiece by Piranesi published in the *Diversi Manieri* of 1769). The original colour scheme was tentatively 'Etruscan' – a very early example of the taste applied to a domestic interior – and in 1783 *Adam* designed a suite of painted Etruscan-style furniture for the room. Some pieces remain elsewhere in the house. At the E end it opens into the SCULPTURE GALLERY, 1766–72, the two together forming one of Adam's most effective essays in picturesque planning. A persuasively Roman sequence of three spaces, a central domed rotunda flanked by flat-ceilinged squares, its immediate model was evidently George Dance's design for 'A public gallery for statues, pictures, etc.', produced in Rome in 1762 – when James Adam was in the city – and awarded the Gold Medal of the Accademia de Parma in 1763. Big niches, suitable for statues, on the diagonals of the rotunda, smaller ones to the square spaces and the linking sections, larger apse at the far end, in the canted bay. Elaborate plaster decoration – criticized as excessive by another collector, Charles Towneley, in 1779 – to walls, ceilings and niche-heads, including pilasterstrips of grotesques and bas-relief panels (Bacchus and Ariadne). Coffering – and a glazed oculus – to the dome. The marble floor proposed by Adam was not executed. Most of Weddell's collection remains.

On the N side of the house were smaller-scale private rooms, including Weddell's Library, now the DRAWING ROOM and much altered. Of *Adam*'s scheme of 1769 there remains the ceiling: his bookcases were replaced by *Belwood* in 1789, and all but one of the replacements have gone also. At the head of the stairs a circular DRESSING ROOM, part of a 'State Lodging Apartment' of *c.* 1775, otherwise altered, with grotesque panels and ceiling medallions painted by *Mrs Weddell*. Beyond the Drawing Room is *Lord Grantham*'s DINING ROOM of 1808, with segment-headed rectangular recesses at each end, their soffits coffered, and a frieze copied from a design by Grantham's father for Baldersby Park. The BILLIARD ROOM above, 1892–4 by *Walker & Strong*, and the staircase to it, are in a joltingly alien, if perfectly amiable, Neo-Jacobean.

Of the formal layout of the GROUNDS shown in Kip's view of 1707, probably by *London & Wise*, traces remain of the diagonal lime avenues converging on the W front. The minimalist Brownian landscaping is by *Thomas White*, *c.* 1766. But the immediate surroundings of the house were partly remodelled in the 1870s by *Burges* for Lady Mary Vyner. By him are the elaborate forecourt GATEPIERS and gates aligned on the E

entrance, the (altered) balustrading s of the house which
enclosed a parterre, and the pedimented terminal feature of
the terrace beyond, now absorbed into the fine garden running
down to the River Ure, created 1921 on by Major Edward
Compton. On the E side of this two timber and glass PAVIL-
IONS, one of 1981 by *Patrick Minns*, a geometrical *jeu d'esprit*
of intersecting equilateral triangles, the other a simplified
hexagonal version done locally in 2004. In the park E from the
gates a C17 equestrian STATUE of Charles II which has a complicated history. It was the gift to the City of London, *c.* 1672,
of the city goldsmith Sir Robert Vyner, but it appears that only
the figure and the pedestal were carved for that occasion,
perhaps by *Jasper Latham*, and that the horse was 'bought at
Rome'. Set up in the Stocks Market in the City, in 1737 it was
moved to an inn-yard to make way for the building of the
Mansion House. In 1779 it was moved to the Vyners' seat at
Gautby in Lincolnshire, and then to Newby in 1883.

N of the house, the handsome STABLES (now offices), by
Belwood, 1777. Large quadrangle, the front (E) and the s side
of fine ashlar, with pedimented centres and end bays crowned
by crouching lions on panelled blocking courses. Tall arched
openings framing Diocletian windows above glazed columnar
screens in the end bays on the s side (cf. the original façade of
the York Assembly Rooms), flanking arches blind below the
Diocletian windows at the front. Rusticated entrance archway,
cupola over. N and W sides, and courtyard elevations, of brick
with stone dressings. In the courtyard an ornate watering
trough. Beyond the stables the former ORANGERY, 1790,
apparently by *Weddell* himself, with segmental bowed centre
and exotically detailed pilaster strips, the windows reduced in
size in the C19. Finally the SKELTON LODGES, 1 m. E, again
by *Belwood*, 1777. Extraordinarily elongated complex, over
300 ft (90 metres) long, facing towards the Boroughbridge
road. Gatepiers with vermiculated rustication, the inner pair
crowned by cinerary urns copied from one in Weddell's collection, flanked first by cubic pyramid-roofed inner lodges and
then by low, chunky outer ones and tall end piers, all linked
together by straight screen walls.

NEWTON

Former FRIENDS' MEETING HOUSE. At the top of the village.
1767. With two-storey cottage to l. under the same roof. Plain
doorways and plain two-light windows to both. Meeting room
altered but retains gallery.

At the bottom of the village NEWTON HALL, later C18. Five bays
with pedimented doorway. At right angles across the road the
former stables, now the PARKER'S ARMS HOTEL, a more
striking composition. Also five bays, with tripartite windows to

ground and first floor in bays one and five, round-headed doorways with matching windows over in bays two and four, and a
tripartite window with a Venetian window over in the middle.
Further up SALISBURY HALL (formerly Newton Old Hall).
c. 1700, with four cross-windows to the first floor, mullioned
windows below – one, oddly, with an upper tier of lights added.
Doorway with simple ornamented lintel. Staircase with turned
balusters and ball finials on the newels. E of this the former
NATIONAL SCHOOL and school house, 1842, plain Jacobean
with a pointy gablet.

FOULSCALES, ¾ m. SSW. Probably early C17, altered. Single
range with early C18 outshut along part of the N side. Mullioned and one-light windows, all unusually small. On the W
gable-end a corbelled-out first-floor garderobe projection,
a curious survival of medieval practice. In the housebody an
C18 fireplace with the lintel on plain brackets and signs of a
firehood.

KNOWLMERE, 1¼ m. WSW. Routine mid-C19 Neo-Jacobean
mansion, beautifully situated.

NEWTON KYME

4040

Church and house form a pretty picture at the edge of extensive
parkland.

ST ANDREW. One little window in the chancel S wall, and a collection of reused responds and imposts supporting the arch
between N chapel and chancel, and the W respond of the aisle
arcade look late Saxon. The extension of the chancel is E.E.:
see the S lancet in a round-arched reveal and the SEDILIA, the
priest's doorway with a pointed-trefoiled head, and a PISCINA
with shouldered surrounds. The octagonal pier of the arcade
must be *c.* 1300 and supports single-chamfered round arches;
the low arch between chapel and chancel is round-arched too,
and double-chamfered. Of the same period, the nave S doorway
and aisle and chapel N windows (Y-tracery). Mid-C14 E
windows with reticulated tracery. Multiple phase tower,
with two-centred arch and Perp battlements. Restored by
W. Swinden Barber, 1893–4 (roofs and vestry). – FONT. Simple
Norman tub. – SCULPTURE. At the porch entrance, carved and
scratched-in figures and symbols, some medieval, e.g. the arms
of the Talbois family, others perhaps C18. In the squint, a rough
sculpted head, inscribed John Fx (Fairfax) 1613; brought from
Pateley Bridge in 1939. – STAINED GLASS. E window (1853),
nave SW (1860) and N chapel (1875) all by *Wailes.* Some
heraldic glass in the N aisle. – MONUMENTS. A very good collection of tablets in the N chapel including an unusual painted
wooden memorial to Katherine Fairfax †1695. – Admiral
Robert Fairfax †1725. Splendid relief of a man o'war running
before the wind. – Frances Fairfax †1725, Baroque cartouche.

– In the chancel, William Fairfax †1762. A scroll unrolled horizontally. – In the nave, Matthew Smith †1797, signed by *William Stead* of York. – In the churchyard, s of the church, two medieval grave-slabs. – Headstone to Frank Norman by *Ernest George Gillick*, 1917. Exquisitely and subtly modelled, with angels in prayer – s of that, an ogee arch, early c20, perhaps copying a detail from the castle ruins (*see* below).

NEWTON KYME HALL, next to the church. Built by Admiral Fairfax after 1695 as a hip-roofed mansion of seven narrow bays on the s front – now overlaid by a Tuscan colonnade to the ground floor and a pretty cast-iron veranda above, and flanked by early c19 wings with canted bay windows. Eight-bay e front, with an attached panel carved with the arms of Elizabeth I. Rambling c18 w (kitchen) wing. Typical late c17 staircase hall with well-carved joinery. Neoclassical interiors in each of the wings: the drawing room has a screen of Ionic columns; the dining room canted ends and niches and delicate plasterwork including husk drops and friezes featuring urns (possibly Edwardian?).

In the gardens – separated from the park by a HA-HA – a fragment of the CASTLE, or manor house, thought to have been founded by the de Kyme family in the c13, and fortified in the following century by the Talbois. No more than a wall remains with a single-chamfered lancet window high up. A lower wall has a shapeless doorway, possibly rebuilt as a part of c19 garden design, and other fragments are incorporated into a rock garden.

w of the hall, the OLD RECTORY, 1771 by *William Marshall*, mason. Five-bay façade and ball finials on the parapet. THE DOWER HOUSE is perhaps *c.* 1700–10 but has an earlier refenestrated cross-wing with an external stack. Later rear additions.

(TOULSTON HALL FARM, ¾ m. SE. A platform marks the site of the Tudor Toulston Hall. Remnants of a c16 formal garden.)

ROMAN FORTS. ½ m. NW by the Wharfe, close to the ford on the Roman road to Aldborough. The earliest fort, of earth and timber, is overlaid by its successor of A.D. 290, a raised platform covering about 10 acres. It remained in continuous occupation until the c4. Within the vicinity have been found evidence of Roman CAMPS, an Iron Age ENCLOSURE, Bronze Age BARROWS and a Neolithic HENGE MONUMENT.

NIDD

Small church and large mansion, both of gritstone, close together at the edge of the park.

ST PAUL AND ST MARGARET. 1866–8 by *T. H. & F. Healey* for Miss Elizabeth Rawson of Nidd Hall, replacing a medieval church. c13 style with w tower. N aisle added 1908. – STAINED GLASS includes e window 1867 by *W. Holland*; nave SE *c.* 1867 by *Barnett*; aisle NW and chancel SW 1889 and 1890 by *Hardman*; aisle NE and second from E by *Kempe*, 1892 and 1901, the first particularly good.

NIDD HALL, now an hotel. Plainest classical, of several phases. Starting point is the house built *c.* 1830 for Benjamin Rawson of Bradford which forms the SE corner of the present, a balustraded two-and-a-half-storey block which had a five-bay entrance front facing S and a longer E elevation with a canted bay in the centre. New entrance range facing W, of three much broader bays, added by 1855, its flank adding a further three bays to the S front matching the original. Porte cochère (W) and major enlargement to the N 1890–3 for the future 14th Viscount Mountgarret, the extended E front again matching the 1830s work, with another full-height canted bay towards its N end and a two-storey bow slightly off-centre in between. Octagonal two-storey entrance hall in the W range and rectangular staircase hall behind it, both with C19 Neo-Georgian decoration – the staircase with an arrangement of columnar screens evidently based on those at Newby Hall (q.v.). N of the house the STABLES, *c.* 1893, with pyramid-roofed tower.

SOUTH LODGE, ⅝ m. S, on the Ripley–Knaresborough Road. *c.* 1890 but in a convincing early C19 Neoclassical style. One storey, with half-octagonal projection fronted by an Ionic colonnade. To the W the former RAILWAY HOTEL, *c.* 1849, also entirely classical. Three-bay front towards the road, with Tuscan porch and lunette window over; r. flank, which faced onto the railway (part of the former Leeds & Thirsk: now gone), also of three bays, treated as a giant engaged Tuscan portico. To the E various interventions of the 14th Viscount Mountgarret including the hot red brick ALMSHOUSES, 1900.

NIDD VIADUCT, I m. S again. 1849, *Thomas Grainger* engineer. Seven arches.

NORTH DEIGHTON

3050

OLD HALL, Spofforth Lane. C17 origins behind an attractive eight-bay S front with early or mid-C18 sash windows. The rear has mullioned windows, the back stairs some splat balusters. Blind Diocletian window in the W end. E of the house, a range of the late C16 or early C17 with mullioned windows and five Tudor-arched doorways along the W side (some C19 or C20). Square DOVECOTE, perhaps C18. E of the Old Hall is a green with a nice row of early C19 COTTAGES to the S, a nearly symmetrical group in dressed stone. The two-storey ones have wide eaves and central chimneys. They have a formal relationship (now obscured by trees) with THE MANOR, a restrained early C19 villa built by the Ingilbys of Ripley Castle (q.v.).

MOTTE AND BAILEY. Howe Hill, ¼ m. E. The motte survives to a height of almost 66 ft (20 metres) surrounded by a bailey bank. Possibly the site of the manorial complex of the Percys, Lords of the Manor before the Ingilbys.

BOWL BARROW (Green Howe), ¼ m. SW. 60 ft (18 metres) in diameter and 8 ft (2.5 metres) high. Probably Late Neolithic or Early Bronze Age. Excavations in 1938–42 revealed evidence of six interments including a child.

NORTH STAINLEY

ST MARY. Little single cell of 1840, with a chancel of equal length added 1891 by *R. J. Withers*. Y-tracery and lancets to the nave, simple Dec windows to chancel. S door with foliage carving by *Charles Summerfield*, 1904. – REREDOS of mosaic, *c.* 1891. – STAINED GLASS. E window *c.* 1860, in the manner of Clayton & Bell. Nave SE by *Barnett* of York, 1869. Nave NE by *Lavers, Barraud & Westlake*, 1873.

SCHOOL. 1871, given by the Staveley family. Charming Gothic miniature with shouldered-arched doorway and windows.

NORTH STAINLEY HALL. The seat of the Staveleys. Brick-fronted double-pile box of five close-set bays and two-and-a-half storeys (the other elevations of rendered cobble). The carcase perhaps of 1715 (date over the doorway), but most of the stone dressings and most of the internal finishing evidently later, probably after 1735 when the then Miles Staveley came of age. Restored and judiciously tweaked 1984–8 by *Robert Aagaard*. Quoins, doorcase with pediment on blocked Tuscan columns, lugged and shouldered window architraves which cut across rubbed brick window heads, eaves cornice – superimposed on an earlier stringcourse – and low parapet. To the r. a C19 screen wall fronting the service yard, and then a pyramid-roofed pavilion by Aagaard; at the back the stump of the previous house, with steeply pitched roof, and later additions. Inside, the l. front room has high-quality decoration of *c.* 1750 – lugged and shouldered wall panels with swan-neck pediments, broken-pedimented doorcase, and Rococo ornament to the chimneypiece and beamed ceiling. One upstairs room with simpler bolection-moulded panelling, presumably of the 1715 phase, staircase with gadrooned balusters.

Village largely late C20.

SLENINGFORD PARK, ¾ m. NW. The stone-built counterpart to North Stainley Hall, *c.* 1730 for Sir John Wray of Fillingham, Lincolnshire. Five bays and two-and-a-half storeys, pedimented doorcase with blocked pilasters and quintuple keystone. Later three-bay wings, two storeys to r., one to l. Entrance hall with pedimented overmantel, big plain C19 staircase, modillioned cornice to the original staircase compartment, now subdivided, and simple bolection-moulded panelling to other upstairs rooms. Palladian STABLE BLOCK, with Diocletian windows, *c.* 1760.

OLD SLENINGFORD HALL, 1⅜ m. w. *c.* 1810. Garden front of ashlar, five bays with pedimented three-bay centre. Lower two-bay wings. The entrance front less formal, rendered, with a Tuscan porch. Contemporary STABLE BLOCK, with two pyramid-roofed towers, and GROUNDS, with tufa-lined terraces and walks.

SLENINGFORD MILL, 1 m. NNW. Probably *c.* 1773. Two-storey cobble-built range, with gabled wheelhouse at the back. Undershot iron water wheel, driving machinery and millstones.

MIDDLE PARKS FARM, 1½ m. SE. Late medieval in origin, in the Archbishop of York's Ripon Park, perhaps a lodge. L-shaped, the front gable-end of the cross-wing of C16 ashlar and brick with a mullioned window of three round-headed lights, the rest with C18–C19 brick and stone casing a timber frame of which a number of the posts survive. Also surviving are the smoke-blackened common rafter roofs. In the cross-wing a C17 decorative plaster ceiling with ribs and pendants, and a fireplace with pilasters and escutcheons to the overmantel.

At SUTTON GRANGE, 1⅞ m. s, the site of a grange of Fountains Abbey, an aisled barn of medieval origin, evidently rebuilt shortly after the Dissolution, with walls of rubble instead of timber. Five bays, queen-strut trusses. Now a house.

ROMAN VILLA, ⅞ m. SSE. Discovered in 1866 and excavated sporadically over a number of years, revealing a complex of several phases. In origin early C2, but soon destroyed and then rebuilt, surrounded by a substantial earthen double rampart forming a rectangular enclosure. It was subsequently destroyed and rebuilt a second time, but whether it was then destroyed again or merely abandoned is unclear. In its final form the complex included a detached bath house and another detached building with two heated rooms and a mosaic floor.

NORWOOD

2050

A loose scatter of farmhouses overlooking the Washburn valley.

SCOW HALL. Timber-framed house probably of the C16, cased in stone in C17, apparently in more than one phase. Extensively restored *c.* 2000. Long low range with a triangular-headed doorway and crenellated cresting to one of the chimneystacks. The C16 building was of at least four bays, probably, as now, with a hearth passage. Two of the trusses remain substantially complete, with kingposts, diagonal struts parallel to the rafters, and studded partitions at first-floor level. Also much of the wall-plates, and part of the studding of the rear wall. Inserted masonry chimney-breast in the smoke bay. Nearby SCOW COTTAGE, 1619. Housebody fireplace with timber bressumer, the jambs replaced in stone and dated 1668, as is a first-floor fireplace.

EAST END, 1½ m. NE. Three-storey porch dated 1625. Hybrid construction, mainly of stone but with a three-bay timber arcade, largely intact, towards the rear outshut. Housebody window of three-plus-three lights. 'Flying' chimneystack at the E end, detached from the gable: that at the W end, where a later range of building abuts, was apparently of the same type. Both serve big three-centre-headed fireplaces. Vaulted sunken dairy behind the outshut.

DOB PARK BRIDGE, 1 m. S. Packhorse bridge over the Washburn. In existence in the C16, rebuilt 1738. One high segmental arch.

BANK SLACK, 1¼ m. NNE. Bank-and-ditch linear earthwork, 1¼ m. long, following a serpentine course along a S-facing slope, its function presumably obstructive. Probably Dark Age.

NUN MONKTON

Huge cul-de-sac village green with scattered brick houses and a tall maypole, in the wide flat land bordering the river Ouse. The church and the hall lie beyond the far end, at the end of an avenue terminating in a splendid weeping beech.

ST MARY. A priory for Benedictine nuns was founded by William de Arches c. 1150. All that survives is the aisleless nave of the church; but that is a fragment of the highest value. A curiosity is that it appears to have been built not bay-by-bay westwards but over the whole ground-plan in at least two phases, over a period from c. 1175 to c. 1240. The E parts of the church were

Nun Monkton, St Mary, interior looking west.
Lithograph by W. Bevan, 1842

demolished after the Dissolution and the present E end, together with the adjoining bays of the side walls and a general restoration, are of 1873 by *J. W. Walton* of Durham.

The evolution of the design can be seen most clearly in the W front. Excellent Late Norman W doorway, with five orders of colonnettes (some renewed), double chevron to three of the arch orders and a keeled moulding to the other two. The capitals of the colonnettes deserve close study. They are as it were just pre-stiff-leaf: that is, they have foliage details which are reminiscent of stiff-leaf but the carving is all still close to a solid square core. The doorway stands within a shallow gabled projection, and here the style definitely changes, with pellet decoration to the gable, a trefoil-headed niche in the tympanum, and miniature shafts l. and r. with waterleaf capitals. To each side of the portal is a pair of round-headed niches also in this manner – the outer one of each pair on a clasping corner buttress – with nook-shafts carrying more waterleaf capitals. In one of the niches a sadly weathered statue, the proportions and surviving details of which Pevsner likened to those of the sculpture on the W front of Wells Cathedral, of *c.* 1230–40. In that case it would be an addition here, but would go with the upper parts of the building. Above the doorway are three very tall and widely spaced stepped lancets, with banded shafts, dogtooth to the jambs and nailhead to the hoodmoulds. Then a steeply pitched gable interrupted in the middle by a low square bell-turret with shouldered openings and (rebuilt) pyramid roof. The sides, of five medieval bays and two more of 1873, have lancet windows to the upper stage, and flat buttresses. To the S also two Norman doorways – the first triple-chamfered, the other plain – and a third further E reconstructed in 1873 from a jamb then surviving, with the same vocabulary of ornament as the W portal.

The outstanding feature, a fine example of classic E.E., is to be found inside, where above the plain lower stage the side walls have an elaborate triforium-like wall passage developed from the corresponding middle stage of the late C12 nave at Ripon (q.v.). Alternating wide and narrow bays defined by slender wall-shafts, the wide ones containing the rere-arches of the windows, the narrow ones shorter but very narrow paired openings onto the passage and above them a trefoil-headed niche, all enriched with banded shafts with moulded capitals, and more nailhead and dogtooth. Also most effective is the substructure to the turret at the W end, of two massive square piers, plain apart from chamfered corners, linked by an arch at the very top and to the W wall by similar arches, slightly lower. Roof of 1873: there had been a pretty plaster rib-vault of *c.* 1800. – STAINED GLASS. E windows by *Morris & Co.*, 1873. Scenes from the life of the Virgin (designed by *Burne-Jones*) and various angels (by *Morris*), set against a background of dense foliage: 'the finest stained glass in the West Riding' (Pevsner, 1959). – Also *inter alia* the W windows, 1911 by *Powell & Sons*. – MONUMENTS. Two medieval grave-slabs, carved with ornate crosses. – Nathaniel Paylor †1748. Marble tablet with urn (in the vestry).

36 THE PRIORY. The confusing name of the big house, immediately s of the church on the site of the conventual buildings. An important work of the mid C17, probably of the 1660s – and at any rate before the hearth tax of 1672 – for George Paylor, who had acquired the estate in 1650. Of brick and essentially a two-storey double pile with a hipped roof, its special feature is a giant order of pilasters (cf. e.g. Lees Court, Kent, c. 1652, and – the nearest local parallel – Cowick Hall, West Riding South (remodelled mid-C18)), which is applied not only to the seven-bay (s) front but also to the flanks, of four slightly wider bays, and to the back (where the end pairs of bays project slightly as short wings). A peculiarity is that the end pilasters on each elevation are inset slightly from the corners – which have flush stone quoins – and this links the design directly to one in Serlio's Book VII.* Others are the Mannerist impurity of a single stone blocking course on each, and the relationship between the pilasters and the oversailing eaves, which are carried on pairs of brackets resting directly on the capitals (cf. Cowick). Former cross-windows, now sashed, the ground-floor ones with an intermittent stone band between them – another Mannerist detail – and moulded brick cornices over. Ashlar doorcase with swan-neck pediment, evidently one of the changes made in 1929 by *Col. R. B. Armistead*: the columned porch which it replaced was reinstated on the w flank. Hip-roofed dormers, prominent cross-shaped chimneys. In the end of the NE wing a blocked bullseye.

42 Interior altered in the early and mid C18 as well as in 1929, when a new entrance hall was made on the w side, so that the original dispositions are not quite clear. The main C17 survival is the staircase, in the back part of the house but slightly to one side, a position which perhaps hints at something of the traditional high-end/low-end arrangement. The staircase itself is of curious form, a dog-leg with part of the string and handrail of each flight describing a downward curve like an elongated ramp – in order to accommodate very shallow quarter landings. Stout bulbous balusters, panelled newel posts carrying carved figurines. The two large central rooms at the front were presumably the hall or housebody below and a great chamber above, but both have lost their C17 character: in the latter a good mid-C18 marble chimneypiece. The SE ground-floor room has panelling of the early C18, with enriched frieze and overmantel.

At one corner of the garden, close to the river, a handsome early C18 SUMMERHOUSE, square with pedimented entrance bay, detailing all in brick – raised quoins, rusticated jambs – and ogee lead roof. Also in the garden a number of charming

* *Country Life*, 6 November 1980.

mid-C18 lead STATUES – rustic dancers, deities etc. – possibly attributable to *Andrew Carpenter*; and a curious pyramid-shaped naïve carving of rural scenes, probably C19. Just NW of the church are the former OFFICES. Two parallel blocks, one homely C18 but the other mid-C17 and all of rusticated brick-work (cf. Archbishop Frewen's work at Bishopthorpe Palace, West Riding South, 1662). Also rusticated flat-arch voussoirs to the ground-floor windows. Hipped roof.

OAKENSHAW
Cleckheaton

1020

ST ANDREW. 1888–9 by *Milnes & France*, not their usual line of work. Slightly quirky E.E. style. NW tower-porch with octagonal top stage and short spire. W window of three two-light elements with bar tracery and a vesica over the middle one. Other windows mainly groups of simple lancets. Long nave with S aisle – the intended N counterpart not executed – and lower chancel. – STAINED GLASS. E windows by *Kempe*, 1902. W windows 1910 by *Heaton, Butler & Bayne*.

CROSS, at the crossroads W of the church. Apparently late C18, an eccentric beautification by the Richardson family of Bierley Hall (dem.). Tall Gothick pillar with four attached colonnettes, on a stepped circular base, surmounted by a cube bearing a sundial and a bell-shaped cap.

OAKWORTH
Keighley

0030

Long spreading Pennine village close to the town, on the N side of the Worth valley.

CHRIST CHURCH. 1845–6 by *W. Wallen* of Huddersfield. Still in the lancet style but quite substantial, with blunt W tower.

ST JOHN, Newsholme, ⅞ m. NW. Formed in 1844 out of part of a C17 farmhouse. The house is an irregular double pile dated 1670, with the entrance in the E gable-end. Mullioned windows with round-headed lights, ornamented doorhead. The chapel occupies the W half of the upper floor, its roof level raised and its windows correspondingly lengthened, with transoms added. The interior is roughly square, with two-bay timber arcades.

SLACK LANE BAPTIST CHAPEL, ½ m. NW, on the way to New-sholme. Now flats. 1879–80 by *J. Judson* of Keighley. Urban-looking Italianate design with pedimented ashlar front. The original chapel, 1821, is a little to the N. Totally plain, also altered inside.

RAILWAY STATION, at the bottom of Station Road, ⅝ m. SE. On the Keighley & Worth Valley line. 1867, perhaps by the Midland Railway Co.'s architect *J. H. Sanders*, with extension of *c.* 1910. A little Italianate dolls' house (like all the line's stations) preserved as a period piece.

OAKWORTH HALL, E of the church, on the corner with Providence Lane. Modest house dated 1702, still with mullioned windows. Opposed front and back doorways both with ornamented lintels, the former with two semicircles cut out of it (cf. the Manor House, Oldfield, below), the latter with three recessed semicircles and spiral decoration.

OAKWORTH HOUSE a little further E, a florid Franco-Italian mansion of *c.* 1870 by *George Smith* of Bradford for woolcombing magnate Sir Isaac Holden, was burnt down in 1909 and all that remains is the porte cochère. The grounds, with elaborate front wall and gatepiers, became a public park in 1925. LOWER PROVIDENCE MILL, Providence Lane, 1874–5 etc. for worsted spinning, was demolished in 1984 apart from the prominent cylindrical chimney.

LAVEROCK HALL, 1 m. WSW. Just-about gentry house of 1641 for Henry and Mary Pighills (re-cut date and initials on the front). Compact hall-and-cross-wings plan, the wings projecting slightly at the front only, the hall deeper than it is long, formerly with a through passage. Three gables to front and back, mullioned windows of up to eight round-headed lights.

Some more C17 houses, again modest, ½ m. further on at OLD-FIELD.

MANOR HOUSE. With two-storey porch partly absorbed into a later gable-end, the doorway with two semicircles cut out of the lintel (cf. Oakworth Hall, above), the slightly oversailing upper stage with an oval window. The date 1669 on the lintel seems surprisingly early. The part to the l., with mullioned windows, is dated 1673.

OLDFIELD HOUSE, Small double pile with re-set datestone of 1677, extended to each side *c.* 1820. Mullioned first-floor windows of six and nine lights, ground-floor openings all altered probably in the mid C18 when a pedimented central doorway was provided – the original doorway was to the r. More mullioned windows at the back, of four lights. In the parlour (l.) a C17 wall painting of a greyhound.

OTLEY

Stone-built market town on the s bank of the Wharfe below the gritstone escarpment of the Chevin. It was the centre of an important estate of the Archbishops of York from the C10 or earlier, and possibly also the site of a monastery or major minster established even before that. Part of the site of the Archbishops' manor house, on the river bank W of the bridge, has been exca-

vated, revealing traces of a chapel range of several phases from
the C11 to the C13 – some footings are left exposed in a little park
– and in the early C13 Archbishop de Grey established the market
(Royal Charter 1248) and perhaps founded a borough. But in the
later Middle Ages Otley's significance as an archiepiscopal seat
seems to have declined, and the parish church apart there are
now few signs of great age. During the C19, with a range of industries established – tanning, paper making and printing machinery manufacture as well as textiles – the population rose steadily,
from 2,600 in 1811 to 4,626 in 1851 and 9,230 in 1901; and the
predominant impression is of a town of that period, with a smattering of generally modest buildings of the previous century. C20
incursions in the centre are no more than might be expected.

CHURCHES

ALL SAINTS. Curiously proportioned, as a result partly of
restorations in 1851 and 1867, partly of its enigmatic early
history. Norman chancel, low with (restored) long round-
headed windows to N and S, the big E window Perp; and re-set
late Norman N doorway, with one order of colonnettes carrying waterleaf capitals. But it has been surmised that the nave,
which is remarkably long and wide as well as much taller than
the chancel, might in origin be earlier – the quoins still visible
at the NW corner are quite different from the chancel's – and
therefore possibly of pre-Conquest date. If so it would be the
largest surviving Anglo-Saxon structure in the North of
England, but if it was a monastery church or a minster that
would be an explanation. The next stage was apparently the
addition of the transepts, perhaps C13 although with tall Perp
three-light end windows; then the W tower, early C14, short and
unbuttressed, with low battlements, a spike and two-light bell-
openings with cusped Y-tracery. W window inserted 1884.
Aisles Perp, S porch C18, with open pediment. Nave clerestory
windows, gable over the chancel arch, with a similar window,
and nave roof, replacing one of flatter pitch, all 1851. Arcades
of four-plus-one bays, with octagonal piers and double-chamfered arches, inaccurately restored in 1867. Cambered tie-
beam roof trusses to the chancel.

REREDOS. 1912 by *Bromet & Thorman* of Tadcaster. Ornate
free Arts and Crafts Gothic. High-relief figures and delicate
filigree panels. – COMMUNION RAIL. Late C17 or early C18.
Good solid work with strong balusters. – PULPIT. C18, the cut-
down top stage of a three-decker. Square, with fluted curved
corners. – PANELLING in the vestry, made up from parts of
old pews, one with the date 1582. – SCULPTURE. Extensive
collection of Anglo-Saxon fragments, the most important of
them parts of two fine early cross-shafts which have been cited
as further evidence for the existence of a monastic house.

The first, of the mid or late C8, of which there are three pieces, has a tier of boldly cut demi-figures holding books, probably Evangelists, in round-headed arches, and originally below them a monk kneeling at the feet of an angel. On the back and sides bold foliage scrolls, one framing busts of angels, another inhabited by birds and beasts. Parallels with the Ruthwell and Bewcastle crosses have been drawn, and sources in Antiquity and the Near East suggested. Of the other, probably early C9, a single piece remains, the front and back each with a splendid high-relief rampant griffin – 'the most dramatic beasts in Anglo-Saxon sculpture' (Cramp). Interlace on one side, and stylized griffins tail-to-tail on the other, but much more shallowly and inexpertly carved. Also parts of a third cross-shaft, with crude interlace, C10, and of grave-slabs, one with typical late Viking incised ornament in the Ringerike style, C11.

STAINED GLASS. E window 1852 by *St Helens Glass Co*. Large figures in shrill colours. S transept and N aisle 1862 by *Clayton & Bell*; N transept 1869 by *Ward & Hughes*; S aisle first from E by *O'Connor*, second from E by *Hardman*, both also 1869. – MONUMENTS. Lindley and Palmes families. Brass plate with heraldic family tree, dated 1593. The crude stone surround with steep pediment looks mid C17. – John Dyneley †1610. Altar tomb set into the wall, the recess above flanked by fat balusters. – William Vavasour †1618. Coarse strapwork display

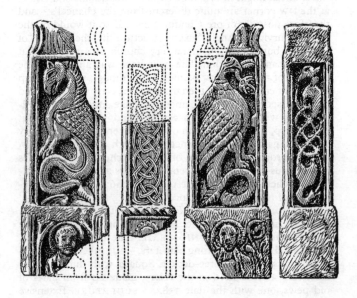

Otley, All Saints, Anglo-Saxon sculpture.
Drawing, 1915

crowned by a pediment, incorporating a small relief of a shrouded corpse – Thomas, Lord Fairfax †1640 and his wife Helen Aske †1620. Altar tomb with recumbent effigies. The sides of the tomb-chest rather crudely detailed, with coats of arms and panelled pilasters. Ornate panel with inscription on the wall above. – Edmund Barker †1695 and Dorothy Barker †1705. Little Baroque tablets. – Several wall monuments of the Fawkes family of Farnley Hall, including Thomas †1707, with putti and draperies; Francis †1747, signed by *John Carr*, with lugged architrave surround and open pediment; Ayscough †1771, with profile portrait medallion; Francis †1786 and Walter †1792, both by *Fisher* of York, the former with portrait medallion and high-relief sarcophagus. – Walter Fawkes †1825. Elaborate Neo-Dec wall recess.

N of the churchyard, across Church Lane, the monument to the workmen killed during the construction of the Bramhope railway tunnel, 1845–9, a miniaturized variation on the castellated N portal of the tunnel (q.v.). Nearby the former VICARAGE, built 1673 and restored in 1713 according to an inscription on the N side but altered out of recognition on the S.

OUR LADY AND ALL SAINTS (R.C.), Bridge Street. 1850–1 by *C.F. Hansom* (cf. Sicklinghall). Simplest Dec, long unaisled nave and chancel, and octagonal SW turret.

UNITED REFORMED CHURCH (Congregational), Bridge Street. 1897–9 by *T.H. & F. Healey*. Like one of their Anglican churches. Gothic, in the style of *c.* 1300–50. Nave with aisles and clerestory and full-height double transepts, separate two-bay chancel, and octagonal NW turret with traceried lantern stage and spirelet. But the nave rather broad and the aisles low. Shallow W gallery. – STAINED GLASS. E window 1919 by *Heaton, Butler & Bayne*. – Attached to the E the former SUNDAY SCHOOL, 1881–2 also by *T.H. & F. Healey*.

METHODIST CHAPEL, Boroughgate. 1874 by *Edward Taylor* of York. Very large, in restrained Italianate style. Pedimented ashlar façade with recessed flanking bays under Palladian half-pediments, the centre with three round-headed entrances below, round-headed windows above. Rock-faced flanks with blocking course and small pediment over the centre. Slightly raked floor with box pews arranged auditorium-wise, apsidal-ended gallery, also box-pewed, on cast-iron columns with foliage capitals. Big rostrum, detailed to match the gallery front. Some alterations 1972–3. – To the r. the WESLEY HALL, 1903–5 by *Danby & Simpson* of Leeds, rather worldly Free Renaissance, with another pediment. – Further W, set back on the other side of the street, the previous METHODIST CHAPEL, 1826, now housing. Four-bay front with the flanking bays, containing doorways, slightly recessed but the angles beyond coming forward again, like broad pilaster-strips. Round-headed windows, hipped roof.

CEMETERY, Pool Road. *c.* 1870. Two Gothic CHAPELS, with an archway crowned by a broach spire between them.

PUBLIC BUILDINGS

CIVIC CENTRE, Cross Green. Built as the Mechanics' Institute, 1869–71 by *Charles Fowler* of Leeds. Grand North Italian palazzo. Five bays and two storeys, the upper a tall *piano nobile* with long round-headed windows forming a near-continuous arcade. Banded piers framing the centre bay and at the corners. Doric porch with coupled columns to the ground floor, bracketed frieze and balustraded parapet above. Rear extension for the Art and Science School, 1895 by *Alfred Marshall* of Otley in uncertain mongrel style.

Former COURT HOUSE, Courthouse Lane. Now Arts Centre. 1875 by *Bernard Hartley*, the third of the West Riding Bridge Surveyors of that name. Perfunctory Jacobean. Cell block at right angles to w.

OLD GRAMMAR SCHOOL. *See* The Town, below.

Former BOARD SCHOOL, Cattle Market Street. 1879. Inferior Gothic, with flèche.

WHARFEDALE GENERAL HOSPITAL, Newall Carr Road, N of the river. The original parts 1873 by *C. S. & A. J. Nelson*, built as the Wharfedale Union Workhouse. One-storey gabled fore-building in simple Gothic, main range behind at right angles, two storeys with pavilion-roofed central tower. To the w the infirmary block, 1905–7, with pyramid-roofed corner projections. New hospital in front of this, 2003 by *Taylor Young*, a bland three-storeyed square.

BRIDGE, over the Wharfe. Late C17, replacing the medieval bridge which had been 'overturned' by the flood of 1673. Widened on the upstream side 1776 and again, with a concrete cantilever, in 1957. Seven segmental arches, the C17 parts with chamfered ribs.

THE TOWN

The plan of the town is pleasingly intricate, centred on a crossroads the routes N and S from which are dog-legged, and with a number of more or less irregular spaces which are perhaps the residue of a large single borough market area which has been filled up by building. But little needs singling out beyond a small innermost core. The SE quarter of the crossroads is occupied by the MARKET PLACE, but with a small island block at its NW corner towards the intersection itself. On the S side the BLACK BULL and No. 38 are still just recognizably C17, with formerly mullioned windows. On the N, beyond the island block, Nos. 16 and 18, mid-C18, with a pediment across its whole width (cf. Newall Hall, below). Within the pediment a Diocletian window, its sill awkwardly interrupting the base. Three first-floor windows, the middle one with cornice and pulvinated frieze, modern shopfront below. On the w side of the square the JUBILEE CLOCK, 1888 by *Alfred Marshall*, a square masonry digit crowned by the clock faces and fancy iron cresting, and next to it the BUTTER CROSS, a plain C19 shelter. Beyond the clock, facing it across KIRKGATE, the OLD HALL, a handsome house of *c.* 1700 again marred by the shopfronts. Five bays, three storeys. Former cross-windows to the first floor, with lugged surrounds and alternating triangular and segmental pediments, cross-windows still surviving to the second. At this level the middle bay is a canted oriel, the small slightly projecting round-headed window below it evidently a later interpolation.

N of this a couple of Late Victorian commercial buildings with Art Nouveau touches, one dated 1899; then turning the SW corner of the crossroads the BLACK HORSE HOTEL, rebuilt 1901, jolly Anglo-Dutch Renaissance with big gabled dormers. Its counterpart on the NW corner, facing E onto MANOR SQUARE, is the former ROYAL WHITE HORSE HOTEL, rebuilt 1865. Long three-storey front with round-headed Italianate windows and projecting porch. The square, funnel-shaped, is the first part of the dog-legged route running N. Prominent at its N end is the OLD GRAMMAR SCHOOL, founded 1611 but the present building erected in 1840, a quite convincing essay in C17 Pennine style in part reusing old materials. Three-gabled block of two tall storeys. In the middle a full-height canted bay window with mullions and transoms, to l. and r. doorways with more mullion-and-transom windows over. To the r. an archway from Caley Hall, Pool (dem.), re-erected mid C20. Plain interior with cast-iron columns, remodelled 2003–4 by the *David R. Bamford Partnership*. Half behind this, near the site of its medieval predecessor, the MANOR HOUSE, an ashlar-fronted box of 1792. Five bays, two-and-a-half storeys. C19 Tuscan porch and wing to l. Diocletian windows to the attic at the back, and more of the same on the single-storey former STABLES nearby.

Beyond this, an intermittent mainly C18 sequence runs E from the Market Place on the N side of BOROUGHGATE, the components including another house of five bays and two-and-a-half storeys, with Tuscan doorcase; a short three-storey row; then after the former Methodist Chapel (*see* Churches, above) an altered house with Vanbrughian doorway and a Diocletian attic window; and the WHITE SWAN, with small plain Venetian windows and an extension to the r. of 1901 ending in a gateway with a painted panel of the swan over the arch. The sequence ends at the Civic Centre (*see* Public Buildings, above) in CROSS GREEN, a triangular space perhaps marking the E end of the medieval borough. Another plain C18 house on the s side. W from the crossroads in WESTGATE the former WESTGATE ARCADE, 1893, cheerful Neo-Jacobean front with gabled dormer, the arcade itself altered; and further s in KIRKGATE a plain mid-C19 commercial building with pedimented one-bay centre. Round the corner from there in BONDGATE two more C18 items: a long low house starting the s side, dated

1753 on a concave-sided panel linking the doorway and the window above; and then on the N side the BOWLING GREEN HOTEL, 1755, built as Assembly Rooms, five bays with plain Venetian window over the entrance.

Also a few items on the outskirts. N of the river, off the E side of BILLAMS HILL, now hemmed in by modern suburbia, NEWALL HALL, a small mid-C18 country house with a giant pediment across the whole width of the five-bay front in the manner of Paine's Kirkstall Grange, Leeds, 1752 (p. 491). In the pediment a trio of windows, the middle one round-headed: below it a gap in the pediment base partly occupied by the pediment over the central first-floor window. C19 bay windows and columned porch to the ground floor. Entrance hall, staircase and landing all quite small-scale, with chunky pedimented doorcases and plaster details. ⅜ m. W, off Weston Lane, ASHFIELD HOUSE, ashlar villa of c. 1830 with mid-C19 additions. Finally at the W end of the town itself, in ILKLEY ROAD, the OTLEY MILL former worsted-spinning complex, early C19 onwards, much reduced. Two- and three-storey ranges, engine house, truncated chimney.

8080

OUGHTERSHAW
Buckden

OUGHTERSHAW SCHOOL. Small three-bay rectangle intended to serve as both school and chapel, built in 1857 by Charles Woodd of Oughtershaw Hall in memory of his first wife. It was probably designed by *Ruskin* who was a friend of Woodd's. The family archives contain letters from him about the school, and the details of the design suggest his hand – the masonry of contrasting limestone and gritstone bands, the entrance at the E end elaborately Romanesque and the deep-set windows part Norman, part Venetian in style.

OUGHTERSHAW HALL. Simple Neo-Jacobean, built for Woodd in 1850 and extended for him in 1863 by *Ewan Christian* (*see* Hubberholme). Woodd also reclaimed tracts of the adjoining moorland in accordance with the principles of Ruskin and the Guild of St George.

3020

OULTON

Agglomerated with Rothwell (q.v.). Church and hall in parkland at the S end, then some hints of an old settlement, then N again a big C20 suburb including Woodlesford.

75　ST JOHN. 1827–9 by *Thomas Rickman* (*Rickman & Hutchinson*) for John Blayds III of Oulton Hall in accordance with the will

of his father: the Blaydses were Leeds bankers. It is one of
Rickman's most successful church designs – 'one of the most
chaste and elegant churches of pointed architecture to be met
with in the Kingdom' according to Thomas Allen in 1831, his
choice of epithets entirely apt. E.E. style with lancet windows.
Fine bold w tower with a slender spire, linked to the corner
pinnacles by little flyers. Nave with aisles and clerestory, fully
developed chancel with polygonal apse, hexagonal s vestry like
a miniature chapter house. Harmonious, dignified interior,
vaulted throughout (in brick), but lighter than would have been
intended, with much of the stonework painted and much clear
glazing (*see* below). w gallery for the organ canted forward on
a little arcade. In the chancel, rich arcading to the apse, in the
Geometrical style; and on the n side the MONUMENT to John
Blayds II (formerly Calverley) †1827, the posthumous founder
of the church, a cusped and gabled tomb-recess containing an
inscription. – Other integral fittings are the PULPIT and
READING DESK, both of stone with built-in book-rests; and the
PEWS and DADO, with tracery ornament of cast-iron. –
STAINED GLASS. Of the thirty-five windows designed by
Rickman, which were described in 1829 as displaying 'much
skill in the architect' (*Leeds Mercury*), only a few remain in
place, the rest removed in 1966.

ALL SAINTS (former), Church Street, Woodlesford. 1870 by
Perkin & Backhouse. Geometrical style with SE tower, the spire
demolished.

OULTON HALL, restored from advanced dereliction in the 1990s
as an hotel. Ashlar mansion in restrained classical style, mainly
of 1851–4 by *Perkin & Backhouse*. The modest C18 house had
been remodelled and extended *c*. 1822 by *Robert Smirke* but
badly damaged by fire in 1850. A further enlargement was
made in 1888–91 by *Chorley & Connon*. The most instructive
part is the E elevation. The plain five-bay centre remembers the
front of the old house, and the lower stages of the slightly projecting wider bays l. and r., with tripartite windows under low
segmental relieving arches, echo Smirke's single-storey pavilion additions. The entrance range, to the N, is Chorley &
Connon's addition, with Smirke's tripartite windows repeated
in the side bays and a porch with coupled Ionic columns in
the centre. Behind this is a reconstruction of Perkin & Backhouse's big top-lit central hall. The vast and obtrusive hotel
wing to the w, replacing the service wing and stables, is the
downside of the restoration. The PARK had been created by
Repton c. 1809, and retains much of its character in spite of
conversion to a golf course. The present drive, from the N, and
the formal garden to the s were laid out by *W.A. Nesfield*,
1851–2.

In the area just N and E of the church a few timber-framed
houses, C16 and C17, more or less altered. At the foot of LEEDS
ROAD the former NOOK INN, small, on a curious T-shaped
plan, perhaps non-domestic. On the gable of the wing projecting at the centre of the front the date 10 April 1611 and the

name Edrus Tailor: the short main range may be earlier. Close
studding with passing braces to the first floor, later masonry
walls below. Gables with tie-beams and kingposts, that to the
front wing with V-struts, the others with A-struts. Similar
trusses within the main range. To the SE Nos. 9–13 FARRER
LANE: three-bay range, probably C16, with slightly later extensions to the rear, with twin gables, and to the l. bay at the front,
with a chimneystack against its E flank, all cased in a mixture
of brick and stone in the C17 apart from some of the gables.
Stonework details include a blocked Tudor-arched doorway
and another Tudor-arched doorhead beside it. Part of the
close-studded framing of the front wall exposed inside. Also N
of this the MANOR HOUSE, Calverley Road: near it the former
SCHOOL, 1860, enlarged 1877, Jacobean style with dinky
porch-cum-bellcote. C17 stone building is represented by
OULTON FARMHOUSE, Wakefield Road, ½ m. S.

EASHALD MANSION, Woodlesford, backing onto Aberford
Road. Grecian villa of c. 1843 by W. Wallen,* its garden built
over. Three by four bays, with giant pilaster-strips and a porch
with Ionic columns.

OXENHOPE

Mill village winding up the hillside high above the Worth valley.

ST MARY. At the top. 1849 by *Ignatius Bonomi & J. A. Cory*. A
remarkable essay in the Early Norman style, authentically
severe and massive looking, without any revivalist frills. Exaggeratedly sturdy squat W tower, nave and lower chancel and N
aisle all with small plain windows, arcade with short cylindrical piers. Also a two-bay arcade into the tower. Unfortunately
the deplorably flimsy roof trusses rather spoil the effect. –
STAINED GLASS. E window by *Morris & Co.*, 1912. Insipid.

RAILWAY STATION. At the bottom. 1867 etc., similar to
Oakworth (q.v.).

In the middle of LOWER TOWN, the mid-C19 main range (now
housing) and chimney of BRIDGE MILL. N of them in YATE
LANE, No. 15, mid-C18, five bays with a doorcase of Ionic
pilasters and segmental pediment, and to the r. part of the
earlier house, with mullioned windows. Further up the lane
YATE HOUSE, also mid-C18 but a real case of architectural
retrospection. Doorway with pediment on Tuscan pilasters, and
a round-headed window above it (cf. Manor House, Stanbury,
1753); but the house is only one room deep, the doorway is off-
centre and the other windows, asymmetrically arranged, are
mullioned and transomed, of four and three-plus-three lights,
with the components** all chamfered in the traditional way.

---

*Information from Christopher Webster.
** Some of these are evidently reused, but not all of them.

MOULD GREAVE, ¾ m. NW of Lower Town, off Lee Lane. Farm-house entirely in the C17 manner but dated 1742. Can that be right? In the light of Yate House perhaps it could. Mullioned windows of four to nine lights, moulded segment-headed doorway, two ornamented hoodmould stops. Parlours l. and r. of the housebody (cf. Manor Farm, Utley, Keighley): originally there was a hearth passage. Central rear outshut, subsequently expanded.

Outlying former worsted mills include SYKES MILL, ½ m. ESE, beside the (later) Leeming Reservoir. c. 1847. Three-storey range with engine house at W end, boiler house beyond, and cylindrical chimney. Now flats.

PANNAL
Harrogate

3050

A suburban village rather than a suburb.

ST ROBERT. Perp W tower. Chancel Dec, the E window with reticulated tracery, S doorway with ogee head. Nave of 1772, with quoins and a blocked N doorway with heavily rusticated surround, the windows Gothicized presumably in a refurbish-ment of 1882–4 when the chancel floor level was raised – see the head of the sedilia. Extensive C20 additions on S side. – FONT. Probably c. 1772. Oval, of polished grey limestone, with carved wooden cover.

PARLINGTON HALL *see* ABERFORD

PATELEY BRIDGE
Bishopside

1060

The chief settlement of Nidderdale, at an important river crossing point. A charter for a weekly market was granted to the Archbishop of York in 1319, turnpikes were established in the 1750s, and the railway from Harrogate arrived in 1862.

ST CUTHBERT. 1825–7 by *Woodhead & Hurst* of Doncaster, replacing the old church up the steep hill to the E of the village. Lancet style, with W tower flanked by N and S porches, broad unaisled five-bay nave and narrower one-bay chancel. Windows with intersecting tracery, of three lights apart from the E window which has four. – Painted ROYAL ARMS of George III, dated 1788. – STAINED GLASS. E window signed 'F. Comere & J. Capronnier, Glass-painters, Drawers and Inventors, Brussels 1893 Belgium'. Still mid-C19 in style.

St Mary (old church). A chapel of ease of Ripon in existence by the early C14. Small aisled rectangle – roofless, and lacking its arcades, since the C19 – with an unbuttressed w tower dated 1691. A few small single-chamfered windows with pointed lights, single and in pairs, probably medieval. E window, with odd Gothicizing details probably C18, others C17.

St Cuthbert's Primary School, w of the church. Built as a Board School, 1875 by *Corson & Aitken* of Manchester (*see* Glasshouses: George Metcalfe of Glasshouses Mill was Chairman of the School Board). Mullion-and-transom windows. Fanciful tower with gargoyles, miniature bartizans and a stumpy spire.

Bridge, over the Nidd. Three arches. In part probably C17.

The High Street is picturesquely steep and narrow but little needs singling out and there are some unfortunate gaps. On the N side the Talbot Hotel, C18, three-bay front crowned by two gables, with angle quoins, ball finials and a Tuscan doorcase; and further up No. 41, turning a corner, with early C19 windows curved round it.

See also Glasshouses, Wilsill.

PAYTHORNE

8050

Methodist Chapel. 1830. Tiny three-bay box, with raked box pews occupying the r. half.

Bridge, over the Ribble, ¼ m. s. Probably C17, widened and partly rebuilt C19. Four arches, the old parts longitudinally ribbed.

Park House, 1¾ m. sw. One of several C17 farmhouses in the neighbourhood with an off-centre two-storey porch the upper stage of which has a stepped mullioned window – here of four lights rather than the usual three. Wide three-centre-headed doorway. Nine-light window – three sets of three – to the l., big segment-headed fireplace in the room to the r., central rear outshut for the staircase. Two arched-brace roof trusses with collars and short kingposts.

PLOMPTON

3050

Daniel Lascelles, younger brother of Edwin, of Harewood, bought the estate in the mid 1750s, formed the well-known pleasure grounds and erected a number of estate buildings. A large mansion was also begun, *c.* 1761, but the project was abandoned the following year when Lascelles bought nearby Goldsborough Hall as his main residence. His architect was *John Carr*.

The pleasure grounds, at PLOMPTON ROCKS, came first, begun in 1755. An important example of the wilder woodland type, they occupy a shallow valley with a series of abrupt gritstone outcrops along one side, which were made the more dramatic by the creation of a LAKE drowning their lower levels. There are two structures by *Carr*, 1755–6, his DAM, much overgrown, a powerful, almost Vanbrughian, design with a pair of heavily rusticated buttresses carrying huge vermiculated ball finials; and a small BOATHOUSE squeezed into a cleft in the rocks, with segmental tunnel vault of cyclopean masonry.

The main estate building, NE of the rocks, is an elaborate quadrangular STABLE BLOCK, *c.* 1757–8, which incorporates as its S range the 'Little Hall' apparently intended by Lascelles as his single man's occasional residence and evidently part of the scheme from the outset.* Front facing S, with pedimented centre. In it an arched recess with Gibbs surround, framing a Serliana-type doorway to the ground floor and a window with a balcony above. Niches l. and r. of the doorway, single flanking bays, and then screen walls with ball machicolation up to the ends of the E and W ranges. Of the rest of the complex, now also housing, the W range contains the main entrance, a tall rusticated arch crowned by an open pediment and a prominent octagonal tower. Three bays of blind arcading l. and r.

Behind the stables to the N the FARMHOUSE, tripartite with hipped roofs and more blind arches, and extensive former model farm buildings. Another model farm, PLOMPTON HIGH GRANGE, 1760, is to the SE. Perfunctorily Gothic, partly demolished. To the S, by the entrance to the pleasure grounds, a pair of plain one-storey LODGES, and nearby at PLOMPTON SQUARE a cottage to the Palladian formula of a pedimented centre and half-pediments to each side.

POOL

2040

ST WILFRID. 1838–40 by *Chantrell*, replacing a chapel perhaps of C17 origin. Little lancet-style box with miniature W tower and broach spire. Paired windows at the sides. It cost £308. Re-pewed etc. 1880, apse added 1891 by *T. H. & F. Healey.* – STAINED GLASS. Three windows in the apse by *Morris & Co.*, 1866, re-set from the three lancets of the original E end. Figures in small square panels set against a patterned ground. – Nave S, first and second from E, 1873 by *Heaton, Butler & Bayne.*
BRIDGE, over the Wharfe. After 1793, doubled in width on the W side mid C20. Seven segmental arches.
POOL HALL, facing away from the street. C18, of several phases. Venetian windows in the gables.

---

* Cf. the *Beauties of England and Wales*, which implies that the 'elegant little lodge' was only conceived of after the abandonment of the mansion house scheme.

2030

PUDSEY

The main component in the industrial and residential agglomeration linking Leeds and Bradford, and itself the product of an unplanned coalescence of textile-producing hamlets and cottage clusters 'like seeds scattered unawares' over the hilltop. The settlement which in the late C19 developed into a town centre of sorts – cut about in the mid C20 – was Lowtown, to the E. The parish church is further W, at Chapeltown, amongst C20 suburban infill.

St Lawrence, Church Lane. 1821–4 by *Thomas Taylor*, successor to a chapel of ease of Calverley which had been rebuilt *c.* 1770 (dem. 1879). A Commissioners' church, and a big and unusually lavish one (cost: £13,475). Good W tower with battlements and crocketed pinnacles, five-bay body with aisles and clerestory, also battlemented, but just an insignificant half-bay altar housing at the E end. Windows with intersected tracery (Y-tracery in the clerestory). The weakness is the clumsy square tops of the buttresses. Impressively tall interior with octagonal piers to the arcades, N, S and W galleries, refronted in 1924, and a pretty ceiling like a ribbed vault with a flat zone along the middle. Reordered 2002. – ROYAL ARMS of George IV, attached to the original reredos, since 1874 in the W gallery. – STAINED GLASS includes two windows in the N aisle by *A. Ballantine* of Edinburgh, 1908 and 1910. Good deep colours. – NE, in Church Lane, the former VICARAGE, 1831 by *John Child* of Leeds. Three-bay front with simple Gothick detail, and matching bay to r. added 1870. Alterations and further additions l. and r. C20.

Trinity Methodist Chapel (former), Wesley Square, Lowtown. 1898–9 by *W.H. Dinsley* of Chorley, replacing a chapel of 1816. At the head of steps continuing the upward slope of the little cul-de-sac square, the best townscape in Pudsey. Grandly Italianate façade of five bays, the centre three a pedimented Corinthian portico *in antis*, the l. one crowned by a complicated ogee-capped bell-turret. Interior subdivided, but retaining its panelled ceiling.

Cemetery, Cemetery Road. 1875. Formal layout by *W. Gay* (cf. Undercliffe, Bradford), centred on a pair of Gothic CHAPELS, by *F.B. Payton* of Bradford, linked by a tall archway-tower with broach spire, a prominent feature in the neighbourhood.

Town Hall, Lowtown. Built as the Mechanics' Institute, 1879–80 by *Hope & Jardine* of Bradford, competition winners. Large and tall, on a triangular site at the town's main crossroads. Domestic Gothic with close-set gabled semi-dormers and a corner tower marred by a weak replacement top stage.

Pudsey Grangefield School, Richardshaw Lane. 1910 by *Jowett Kendall* of Bradford, built as the Pudsey and District Secondary and Technical School. Long symmetrical front in Jacobean-cum-Queen-Anne style, with two glazed cupolas. Later buildings to rear.

A few other items in the town. At the LOWTOWN crossroads, across from the Town Hall, the NATWEST BANK, *c.* 1890.

Cheerful Loire style with an oriel. Further E, just beyond Wesley Square (*see* above), BOOTH'S YARD, a fold development with C17 and C18 cottages lining the narrow alley. In CHAPELTOWN, just w of the church No. 3, a solitary modest C17 house; then on the other side of the road, on the site of the chapel of ease (*see* above), the WAR MEMORIAL, 1922, a tall cenotaph by *Brierley & Rutherford* surmounted by a bronze soldier by *Henry Poole*. Further SW, in GREENSIDE, Nos. 42 and 44 (facing onto Greenside Grove), dated 1713, also very modest, incorporating remains of earlier timber framing. Mullioned windows still.

TYERSAL HALL, Tyersal Lane, 1¼ m. WSW. Porch dated 1691. Flat front without gables, short wings at the back with an outshut between them. Mullioned windows. Centre part opened up internally in the mid C19 to create a fake medieval aisled hall. Further alterations late C20.

See also Fulneck.

RAMSGILL
Stonebeck Down

1070

ST MARY. 1842, the gift of the Yorke family of Bewerley. Little lancet box with a narrow w tower. – STAINED GLASS. E, NE and SE windows by *Powell Bros.* of Leeds, 1890 and 1895. – At the corner of the churchyard, the remains of the CHAPEL of a grange of Byland Abbey. Gable-end with three short lancets.

BOUTHWAITE GRANGE, ⅜ m. NE. 1673, extended and refronted 1720, with central doorway and regularly disposed two-light mullioned windows. Segment-headed housebody fireplace, and some panelled partitions, of the earlier phase; other fireplaces, bolection-moulded panelling in the housebody, and staircase with turned balusters, all of the later.

S of the hamlet GOUTHWAITE RESERVOIR, 1893–1901 for the Bradford Corporation Water Works. *James Watson*, engineer. On the dam a pair of octagonal battlemented pavilions with circular turrets attached, and a roadway carried on half-elliptical arches. To one side a big lodge in Scottish Baronial style. On the w bank of the reservoir GOUTHWAITE HALL and GOUTHWAITE FARM, built 1900 in part from the materials of the C17 Gouthwaite Hall, the site of which was flooded. Gables and mullioned windows.

RATHMELL
8050

HOLY TRINITY. 1842, a daughter church of Giggleswick. Lancet-style box with thin w tower. Chancel added 1883 by *T. H. & F. Healey*, also with lancets. – STAINED GLASS.

A number of windows by *Capronnier*, *c*. 1870–90. Two at the W end, flanking the tower arch, by *Powell Bros.* of Leeds, *c*. 1878 and *c*. 1893.

COLLEGE FOLD, NW of the church. The first English academy for training Nonconformist ministers was established here in 1670 by the Rev. Richard Frankland, a native of Rathmell. Two-storey range at right angles to the road, now cottages. Several three-light stepped windows, and one larger window to the ground floor, formerly of four lights. At the back a re-set lintel dated 1686.

CAPPLESIDE, ½ m. SW. Plain early C19 three-bay front range, but behind it is a much altered early C18 block, with cross-windows and a blocked doorway with architrave surround. A doorhead dated 1721, re-set in a barn, may have come from this. Further C19 wing beyond. Early C18 staircase with panelled newels and turned balusters. Arts and Crafts Pennine-style farm building of 1890, designed by the owner *John Geldard*.

Several late C17 farmhouses in the parish, including LITTLE-BANK, 1½ m. NNW, a small double pile with two-storey porch dated 1693. The latter has an off-centre entrance with orna-mented lintel and a stepped three-light window to the upper floor, the lights round-headed. Housebody window of five lights, also arched, one cross-window at the back. C19 front range at right angles. In the main first-floor room an C18 door-case with pilasters and entablature, staircase with turned balusters. On the hillside behind, LUMB FARM, 1702, with doorhead like that at Sutcliffe House, Giggleswick (q.v.), and an elaborate inglenook fireplace. Segmental arch with decorated keystone, and one end resting on a stout column beyond which a narrower arch gives access to the rest of the house. At the other end is a chimney corner with bench, lit by a fire window. At NEW HALL, ¼ m. S of Littlebank, a door-head out of the normal run, re-set in what is now an out-building. Seven-lobed arch flanked by carvings of halberd heads (cf. Lodge Hall, Horton-in-Ribblesdale), and in the tympanum an incised demi-figure of an angel. Dated 1679 according to Ambler, but the inscription is no longer legible.

2030

RAWDON

Diffuse suburbanized settlement on the N flank of Airedale which divides into three parts.

RAWDON VILLAGE

ST PETER. In origin a chapel of ease of Guiseley established in the mid C17. Squat unbuttressed W tower dated 1706: the rest, and the top stage of the tower, rebuilt 1864 by *A. Crawford* of Leeds. Dec, with short chancel and cross-gabled s aisle, but some of the old masonry apparently reused on the N side. – STAINED GLASS includes E window by *Wailes*, 1864, s aisle E by *Morris & Co.*, 1867. – w of the church the former SCHOOL, 1710. Two storeys with rusticated quoins, windows altered.

PRIMARY SCHOOL, Town Street. 1955 by *Hubert Bennett*, West Riding County Architect. Two storeys with monopitch roof. Curtain walling and snecked stone.

RAWDON HALL, ½ m. WSW of the church, s of the main road. Early C17 house of the Rawdon family, with date of 1625 and the initials of Francis Rawdon on the big projecting parlour wing and those of his father on the porch of the hall range. The latter part has a transomed hall window of seven lights, four-light window above it with the lights ogee-headed, and a hearth passage. Window of two round-headed lights to the upper stage of the porch. The wing is L-shaped and partly of three storeys, with the fall of the ground. Mullioned windows of four to six lights. (C17 panelling and two carved timber overmantels inside.)

BENTON PARK AND LITTLE LONDON

W and NW of the village, mainly C19–C20, running into Yeadon (q.v.).

FRIENDS' MEETING HOUSE, Quakers Lane. 1697. Enlarged and re-fitted 1826, re-windowed 1840. Plain low rectangle with off-centre doorway. Interior divided into two unequal parts by a partition with sliding shutters. In the larger room a dado-height central barrier between the men's and women's seating, at right angles to the elders' bench across the far end.

TRINITY CHURCH (Baptist, Methodist, United Reformed), New Road Side, beside the roundabout. The former Benton Park Congregational Chapel, 1846 by *John Clark* at the cost of Henry Forbes and Robert Milligan (*see* Cragg Wood, below). Gawky lancet style, the gabled front with blind arcading over the entrance. Gallery round three sides, on iron supports. – To the l. the SUNDAY SCHOOL, 1868, still in the same outdated mode.

BENTON PARK SCHOOL, Harrogate Road. 1960 by *Sir John Burnet Tait Durrant & Partners*. Two and four storeys, reinforced concrete frame with glass and brick infill.

LITTLEMOOR BOARD SCHOOL, Harrogate Road and Batter Lane. 1879. Accomplished domestic Gothic, with pyramid-roofed tower and at the back a little loggia with octagonal colonnettes.

MICKLEFIELD HOUSE (now Council Offices), New Road Side. Allegedly of 1662, 'restored' – or rather rebuilt – in 1847 in eccentric Gothic manner. Extended W in the same spirit in 1872.

LANE HEAD HOUSE, Apperley Lane. Early C18 relative of Esholt
Hall (q.v.). S front of five bays with rusticated quoins and tall
windows in architrave surrounds. Top floor, with pilaster-strips
at the angles, evidently added mid C18. Further alterations C19
and C20.

CRAGG WOOD

A band of woodland interspersed with gritstone outcrops, on the
side of the valley SW of the village, which was in part developed
in the mid C19 as a romantic sylvan suburb for the commercial
elite of Bradford. The begetters of the scheme were the stuff merchant Robert Milligan, Bradford's first mayor, and then after his
death in 1862 his brother-in-law and erstwhile business partner
Nathaniel Briggs. Serpentine roads were laid out mainly running
along the slope E from Apperley Lane, and little stone-lined paths
running down it. The building plots in theory were to be of not
less than seven acres, and in addition to the houses a small group
of public buildings, now all converted to residential use, was
erected. But the layout was never completed and few of the
houses are of much architectural ambition: perhaps the most
interesting was Milligan's own, Acacia, 1847 by *John Clark*, and
that has been demolished.

Near the W extremity of the layout, off Apperley Lane and Acacia
Park Crescent, is SUMMER HILL, *c.* 1850, the house of another
Milligan business partner, Henry Forbes. Simple Picturesque
Neo-Jacobean with fancy bargeboards and octagonal chimneystacks. In fields downhill SE of this the utilitarian agricultural complex of ACACIA FARM, 1847 by *Clark*, the main
element now surviving of Robert Milligan's establishment. N
of Summer Hill CRAGG WOOD DRIVE starts at the former
NORTH LODGE to Acacia, one storey with Tudor-arched
windows, and descends past Nathaniel Briggs's totally unremarkable CLIFFE HOUSE, *c.* 1860. From there a diversion can
be made to the topmost of the roads, CLIFFE DRIVE, and
to BUCKSTONE HALL, 1884 by *W. & R. Mawson* for Herbert
Dewhirst (whose wife was Milligan's great-niece). Rock-faced,
with tower. Meanwhile, at the junction of Cragg Wood Drive
and WOODLANDS DRIVE are CRAGG ROYD (now Carlton)
and CRAGG MOUNT, both 1865 by *Lockwood & Mawson*
for Nathaniel Briggs. Gabled domestic Gothic, the former,
which was occupied by Briggs's son, with a pyramid-roofed
tower-porch, the latter more modest, an ordinary suburban
villa.

E from here, along Woodlands Drive, is the group of former
public buildings. First the church of OUR LADY OF GOOD
COUNSEL AND ST JOSEPH (R.C.), a late-comer of 1907–9,
by *Edward Simpson*. Quirky Gothic, with small rectangular S
windows set in vesica-shaped panels, and polygonal apse. Then

the RAWDON BAPTIST COLLEGE, now Larchwood, built for training ministers. 1858–9 by *J. H. Paull* of Cardiff, the site sold by Milligan at half-price. Long S-facing range in severe Jacobean style with simply shaped gables, the centre part of three storeys under a big hipped roof, the rest of two. Thirdly the WOODLANDS CONVALESCENT HOME, 1877 by *Andrews & Pepper* for the dyeing magnate Sir Henry Ripley, Milligan's son-in-law and successor at Acacia. Similar style but in brick. Quadrangular, two storeys and attic. Further on at the end of the road, at the E edge of the layout, WOODLEIGH HALL, the grandest of the surviving houses. 1869 by *Lockwood & Mawson* for textile manufacturer Moses Bottomley, but virtually a repeat of *Andrews & Delaunay*'s Moor Park, Beckwithshaw (q.v.) – profuse Jacobethan with a debased Italianate tower centrally placed over the entrance. Conservatory to r., loggia to l., huge top-lit staircase hall, panelled and painted ceilings. *See* also Woodhouse Grove School.

RIBSTON HALL
Great Ribston with Walshford

3050

The long, low brick house in a loop of the River Nidd is the work of two main periods. It was built *c.* 1674 (datestone) for Sir Henry Goodricke – soldier, diplomat, politician and a man of 'great reading and travell', whose family had bought the estate in 1542 – then extensively remodelled in the 1770s for his great-grandson, almost certainly by *John Carr*. An earlier phase is represented by the chapel attached to the SE flank of the house, built in 1444 as part of a Preceptory of the Knights Hospitaller (previously of the Templars) but much restored in the mid C19 for Joseph Dent, who had bought the property in turn in 1836.

The particular characteristic of Goodricke's house, to judge from views by Kip and others, was its markedly French flavour: a two-storeyed half-H with the wings projecting on the entrance (NE) side, with separate steeply pitched hipped roofs to the centre and wings and the entrance front preceded by a *cour d'honneur* flanked by lower office ranges. Little of this remains, the forecourt buildings gone, the C18 roof low-pitched with deep bracketed eaves, and the entrance front redone in the plainest manner, with the wings apparently reduced in length and a pedimented Tuscan doorcase the only enrichment. Less altered is the SW front, facing the river – a uniform fifteen bays, with quoins, doorway with broken segmental pediment and Corinthian columns, and panels between the ground- and first-floor windows framed by curious pilaster strips (cf. Le Muet's *Art of Fair Building*, English edition 1670). A further feature, lost in the C18 landscaping of the park, was an extraordinary series of terrace-ramparts to the S and W of the house, constructed in 1688, perhaps reflecting a current French taste for Vauban-inspired 'military' gardens, but perhaps – given that Goodricke was at that moment instrumental in securing York for William of Orange and may have anticipated civil strife ahead – of genuinely defensive purpose.

(Inside, the centrepiece is the splendid SALOON, of c. 1775, carved out of the middle five bays on the SW side. Elaborate coved ceiling broadly in the Adam style but designed without that master's skill in composition – see e.g. the big half-paterae in the central flat coupled rather uneasily with semicircular motifs of a different design in the cove. Also trophies, of musical instruments etc., identical to those in *Carr*'s great room at Thirsk Hall, North Riding, 1771–4. Wall scheme of large paintings, copies after Guercino, Reni and Volterra executed in Rome in the 1770s; fine marble chimneypieces, with bas-relief tablets; main doorcase with pediment and Corinthian columns. The present colour scheme 1846 by the London decorator *Charles Moxon*. Also of the 1770s phase the former dining room, with Ionic columnar screen. From the earlier period are an elaborate overmantel with rather stiffly carved garlands and game birds, and another with a painted allegory of Fame.)

The CHAPEL, a straightforward rectangle, was 'repaired and embellished' by Sir Henry Goodricke in 1700 as well as by Joseph Dent c. 1850. Two chamfered C15 doorways remain, one re-set, one blocked, with hoodmoulds on headstops. Perp E and W windows, and reticulated S window, all from the second restoration. – (FONT, with spiral-fluted bowl, and PANELLING round the sanctuary, excellently carved with religious symbols etc., both doubtless of 1700, the latter again markedly French in style (a similarity to Hardouin Mansart's stalls in Nôtre Dame, Paris, has been noted) and probably the work of Huguenot craftsmen. – SCULPTURE. Several small pieces, including a C15 English alabaster panel. – STAINED GLASS. E window after Reynolds's at New College, Oxford, probably early C19; W window by *Willement*, 1852. – MONUMENTS. Tablet to C17 members of the Goodricke family, dated 1652; another to Sir Henry Goodricke †1705. – Two brass matrices, l. and r. of the altar.)

N of the house the STABLES, attributed to *Carr*, c. 1775. Brick, quadrangular, of four separate ranges, the front one of nine bays with three-bay pedimented centre, timber cupola and round-headed windows in relieving arches (cf. the stables at Escrick Park, East Riding). With them will go the two pairs of LODGES, pedimented ashlar boxes with some banded rustication, one pair SE of the house but on the W bank of the river, after the three-arched BRIDGE built – or rather presumably rebuilt – in 1855, the other 1¼ m. E beside the old Great North Road, flanking gatepiers surmounted by lions and sphinxes.

See also Walshford.

RIMINGTON

CONGREGATIONAL CHAPEL, Martin Top. 1817. Four round-headed windows, the centre two slightly raised, to flank the pulpit, two plain doorways, and a sundial in the centre. Attached manse to r., 1836. Interior re-fitted later in the C19, with raked pews facing the front.

RIPLEY

The model village and the big house beside it – misleadingly called the castle – form a harmonious composition of great charm, all in fine gritstone, and are largely the work of two successive generations of the Ingilby family: Sir John Ingilby (†1815) at the castle and his son Sir William Amcotts Ingilby (†1854) who rebuilt the village. But the Ingilbys have been at Ripley since the early C14, obtaining a charter for a market in 1357, and in the rebuilding the earlier topography of the site was retained. The main street opens out about a third of the way along into a triangular marketplace, running W past the church on the S side to the castle gate on the other.

ALL SAINTS. Said to have been rebuilt on its present site *c.* 1400 after the previous church, further S, had collapsed or become unstable. Narrow W tower of at least two phases, the lower half normal Perp, with diagonal buttresses and (renewed) three-light W window, the unbuttressed upper part, with small two-light openings, and the clumsy oblong SE stair-turret, mainly or wholly of 1567 (date on the turret). Also of this phase is the nave clerestory. Nave with aisles, chancel with chapels, the S transeptal with a two-storey sacristy or priest's lodging adjoining to the E, its lower storey coeval with the transept, the upper added. Window tracery all renewed in the extensive restoration of 1862 by *J. B. & W. Atkinson* of York, confusingly in an inappropriate Middle Pointed. Nave arcades of five bays, the N with cylindrical piers which are presumably reused C13 material from the old church, the S the standard local Perp. But the capitals are all of plaster, 1862. Between both arcades and the E end of the nave is a lower and narrower segment-headed arch for a monument. In the chancel, a squint from the sacristy, and a handsome piscina and credence with cusped ogee-headed arches. Roofs all 1862, the chancel with painted DECORATION, 1890. – SCREEN between the S aisle and the S chapel. With heavy ogee-headed entrance flanked by narrower ogee-headed lights, perhaps reused from the old church. – BENEFACTION BOARDS, early C19. – STAINED GLASS. Extensive scheme of 1862: E window by *Ward & Hughes*; sanctuary N by *Clayton & Bell*; sanctuary S by *Wailes*; N chapel E, S chapel, and S aisle second and third from E, by *Warrington*; S aisle SE and fourth from E by *Ballantine*. – W window by *Powell & Sons*, 1904.

MONUMENTS. Recumbent effigies and tomb-chest of a knight and lady, under the S tomb-arch, brought from the previous church, probably Sir Thomas Ingilby II †1381 and his wife Katherine Mauleverer. He is in armour, with his head on the Ingilby boar's-head crest. On the sides of the chest standing weepers under ogee canopies, and between them panels with shields. Fine dainty workmanship, very similar to the tomb of John Lord Neville †1388 and his wife at Durham Cathedral. – Richard Kendal, Rector of Ripley, †1421. Small brass with a chalice. – Sir William Ingilby †1617. Recumbent effigy on a tomb-chest. Back-plate with coat of arms, a cartouche containing a fulsome epitaph – and a deflating postscript, in place by 1623: 'No pompe or pride, let God be honoured'. – Elizabeth Ingilby †1679, aged twelve, and her sisters Katherine †1701 and Mary †1743. Marble tomb-chest without effigies, erected at Mary's instigation and evidently after her death, as the inscription is all of a piece. – Sir John Ingilby †1741. Marble sarcophagus, badly eroded. – Wall tablets including Sir William Amcotts Ingilby †1854 by *Skelton* of York, with primitivist pediment. – In the churchyard the base of a PENITENTIAL CROSS, with eight recesses for – very uncomfortable – kneeling.

RIPLEY CASTLE. The earliest part is the gatehouse, which is datable by the heraldry to *c.* 1450: it stands on the S side of the spacious courtyard, with the house itself half l. behind. Next, dated 1555 in an inscription, is the tower which forms the house's projecting SW corner. The remainder is of 1783 onwards for Sir John Ingilby by *William Belwood* of York: the house of 1783–6, replacing the medieval building against which the tower abutted, and the L-shaped coachhouse and stable range, attached to the NE corner of the house and enclosing the courtyard to the N and E, which was begun in 1786 but not completed until 1812, long after Belwood's death. Ingilby explained his approach in a letter of 1784:

> 'When we began upon my old mansion it was in such wretched condition that we were obliged to do a great deal more at it than was at first intended. I was determined upon preserving as much as possible of the old place and by that means have spoiled my plan in the opinion of some people, but notwithstanding the inconveniences of our Ancestor's buildings I prefer them to modern structures; any man who has money can build a House, but few can shew the same house his family has lived in so many years as the Ingilbys have done at Ripley.'

The GATEHOUSE has an arched main entrance and to the l. of it an elaborate three-centre-headed pedestrian entry, with the Ingilby badge on the arch and shields on the spandrels. Straight-headed window of three cinquefoil-headed lights above, and crenellated parapet. Lower sections to l. and r., with battlements added by *Belwood* in 1788–90 – previously they had pitched roofs. Groin-vaulted gateway passage, and very wide segment-headed inner archway, presumably another alteration of 1788–90. Also an inscription over the porter's lodge door, 'Parlez au Suisse', added by the much-travelled Sir William Amcotts Ingilby who is said to have employed a Swiss gate-keeper and referred to the house as the 'Schloss'. The TOWER is of three storeys, with diagonal buttresses, battlements and taller stair-turret at the SW corner. Rectangular oriel window to the top floor on the E side, C19 mullion-and-transom windows to the ground floor, restored mullioned windows above to the W.

Belwood's buildings are in a minimal Gothic style – battlements, bluntly pointed windows, label mouldings, and on the stable range squat towers with arrowslits. On the house itself the Gothic detail is generally more sparse but the elevations are not rigorously symmetrical. S front with a tower-like pavilion at the SE corner, roughly balancing the old tower to the l., and a delightful quadrant-shaped porch with five Gothic arches in the angle with the latter; W elevation with a big Venetian staircase window, and N with a central semicircular bow and projecting kitchen wing to the l. But the elegant INTERIOR is all classically detailed and formally planned. Entrance hall with beyond it, through an opening flanked by Doric columns *in antis*, an elliptical 'tribune' or inner hall, domed and top-lit, with a gallery at first-floor level; and beyond that, occupying the semicircular bow on the N front, a circular drawing room. To the r. are the dining room and morning room, with a service corridor concealed between them; to the l. the apsidal-ended staircase and the main drawing room, the former with elaborate heraldic glass in the Venetian window, by *William Peckitt* of York, 1785, the latter with a fine decorative plaster ceiling by *Francis & Thomas Wolstenholme*. In the tower, the ground-floor room is a C19 library, the first floor was two rooms, thrown into one in C19, both with Tudor-arched fireplaces and good early C17 plaster ceilings. Thick vine scrolls to the beams, panels containing coats of arms etc. Top room with the dated inscription and a probable priest's hole off.

NE of the house a walled garden, with an ORANGERY, probably *c.* 1818. Round-headed openings between fluted Ionic pilasters, canted corners. To l. and r. smaller pavilions in the same style. Further N, at the end of a walk aligned on the back of the orangery, a temple-front GAZEBO, probably also *c.* 1818. In the park NW of the house, two serpentine LAKES, formed in 1844 supposedly using a plan of the late C18. Between them a three-arched BRIDGE above a weir. Further W, a DEER SHED, 1852.

THE VILLAGE. Rebuilt by Sir William Amcotts Ingilby *c.* 1820–35, a mixture of cottage terraces and larger individual houses. The predominant type is a three-bay house in a style very similar to Belwood's at the castle, with hipped roof and pointed sash windows under label mouldings, and in some cases a doorway based on the pedestrian arch of the castle gatehouse. Others are more emphatically Tudor-Gothic, with gables and mullioned windows with arched lights; but it seems unlikely that the differences mark a chronological progression. In the Market Place the MARKET CROSS, probably C17, with stopped and chamfered shaft topped by a sundial. Off the N part of the main street the SCHOOL, founded 1702, rebuilt 1830, with mullioned windows; and further on, on the E side, the last and stateliest addition, the TOWN HALL of 1854, completed by Sir William Amcotts Ingilby's widow. He called it the 'Hotel de Ville'. Fanciful collegiate Gothic, the front with crowstepped gable and elaborate canted bay window.

NEWTON HALL, ¾ m. NNE. Lodge of the Vavasours of Weston Hall (q.v.) remodelled in the mid C19 as a square farmhouse. Tall front doorway with coats of arms of the Vavasours and Ingilbys. To one side a small stone building, probably early C17, incorporating remains of earlier timber framing. Big arched fireplace at the W end, its stack detached from the gable (cf. East End, Norwood). In its masonry form it may have served as a detached kitchen.

RIPON

The town is situated close to the confluence of the rivers Ure and Skell, its centre on a plateau above the N bank of the latter with the cathedral adjacent to the E. Although long referred to as a 'city', it remains a market-town size (2001 population 15,922). Good distant views of the cathedral include that from the NE, on the road to Sharow, middle-distance and closer ones, looking up from river level, those from Skellbank (W), and from the Bondgate Green and St Agnesgate areas (S and SE).

THE CATHEDRAL

BY CHRISTOPHER WILSON

INTRODUCTION

Before its elevation to cathedral rank in 1836 this was a collegiate church, the Minster of SS Peter and Wilfrid. Around 660 Alhfrith, a son of King Oswiu of Northumbria, founded at Ripon a monastery which was Irish-influenced in its observance and probably stood on the w side of St Marygate. A year or two later this community withdrew and the site was made over to Wilfrid, who introduced a version of the Benedictine rule and transferred the monastery to the present site overlooking the River Skell. The move will have been intended to emphasize the break with the original foundation, for Wilfrid was one of the key figures in the reorientation of the Northumbrian Church towards Rome and away from 'Celtic' monasticism. In 664 Wilfrid became Bishop of Northumbria, and some time in the early-to-mid 670s he built the church at Ripon whose crypt still survives (see St Wilfrid's Church, below). From 681 to 686, during a period when he was banished from Northumbria, the Minster served as a cathedral. Around 875 the Danes sacked the monastery, after which it became a foundation of secular clergy. In 948 Ripon was burnt during King Eadred's punitive expedition to Northumbria, and the buildings remained in ruins until they were restored by St Oswald, Archbishop of York (971–92). From the late C10 to the late C12 the architectural history of Ripon is a blank, but it is probable that there was some late C11 or early C12 rebuilding of the church, for Ripon, like its fellow collegiate minsters at Beverley and Southwell, was by then functioning as a kind of sub-cathedral within the huge York diocese and had an archiepiscopal residence immediately adjacent to the church. The Minster also served an 86-square-mile parish which remained unsubdivided even after the introduction of the fully fledged parish system in the C11 and C12.

A rebuilding 'de novo' was ordered by Roger of Pont l'Evêque, Archbishop of York, shortly before his death in 1181. We learn this from a deed in which Roger gives £1,000 in old money, i.e. coinage pre-dating the currency reform of late 1180. Ripon will never have received Roger's money, as Henry II declared him intestate, confiscated his treasure and the revenues of the see, and revoked all grants made during his last illness. The choir and N transept begun by Roger is the outstanding surviving work of northern England's prolific, long-lasting and remarkably homogeneous Early Gothic tradition, although its significance has undoubtedly been enhanced by the disappearance of most of the main level of the choir of York Minster, which Roger had been building from no later than 1160. Like the York choir, Ripon is a strange amalgam of ideas drawn from the most innovatory and most conservative strands of mid-C12 French architecture: Early

Gothic and the simplified version of Burgundian Romanesque disseminated by the Cistercians. Such an intermingling would have been unthinkable in the heartland of French Gothic, the Ile-de-France, but it had taken place by the early 1150s farther north, in Picardy. The outstanding example in that region was the now mostly ruined Premonstratensian abbey church at Dommartin near Amiens, begun in 1153 and dedicated in 1163. By the early 1160s this hybrid style was spreading rapidly among northern English Cistercian monasteries such as Roche near Sheffield, Furness in Cumbria and Kirkstead in Lincolnshire. Despite being unorthodox in Ile-de-France terms, Roger's work at Ripon is, alongside the post-1174 rebuilding of the E arm of Canterbury Cathedral, the most heavily French-influenced English building of the last quarter of the C12. Had it survived complete and been finished in accordance with the original intentions, Ripon's first phase would probably now be reputed one of the outstanding works of Early Gothic architecture anywhere. Even after the original concept had been compromised by the omission of the high vault, the interior elevations were to be hugely influential in northern England (cf. Byland Abbey and Old Malton Priory, North Riding, and Tynemouth Priory, Northumberland).

The late C12 church at Ripon proclaimed the foundation's allegiance to York even in its ground plan, which reproduced that of York Minster as it then existed, including its singular aisleless late C11 nave. Archbishop Roger's successor Geoffrey Plantagenet (1191–1212), who resided much at Ripon, supported the continuation of the rebuilding, but the two-towered W front in the E.E. style was probably started c. 1233 when Archbishop Walter de Grey issued an indulgence in favour of the Minster's fabric. Although definitely not planned in the late C12, this façade will have reinforced the resemblance to York Minster, where either Roger or Geoffrey had added a W front with two towers to the aisleless C11 nave. It is likely that the W towers were also intended to compensate for the removal of the upper storey of the crossing tower some time in the early C13, an emergency measure made necessary by the unstable and sandy subsoil below the cathedral. The total length of Ripon Minster by the early C13 was c. 289 ft (89 metres), significantly shorter than the churches of its two peer institutions, Beverley Minster (c. 350 ft; 108 metres) and Southwell Minster (332 ft; 102 metres).

An approximate start date for the C13 remodelling of the E end of the C12 choir is given by an indulgence of 1284, the first of a series extending into the early C14. Like the late C13 parts of York Minster, the design is influenced exceptionally strongly by French Rayonnant, and it is probable that the architect at both sites was the same man, namely *Simon*. The reconstruction of the E choir bays was followed by the building of a new Lady Chapel S of the choir c. 1300, the reglazing of the whole church 1290–1330,[*] the provision in the mid C14 of a new High Altar

---

[*] C18 and early C19 views show virtually every C12 and early C13 window in the church subdivided by two-light tracery of the period 1290–1330.

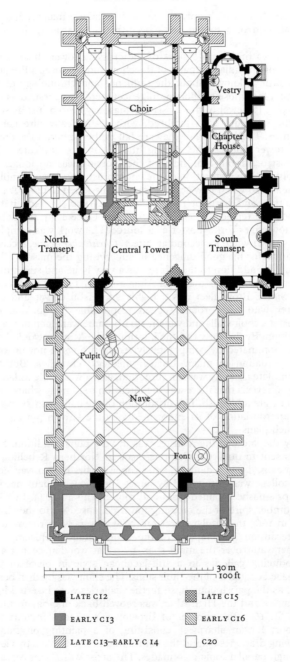

Ripon Cathedral.
Plan

screen (from which only the en suite sedilia remains), and the installation of a timber vault over the choir around the same time.

In 1450 the E and S sides of the crossing tower sheared off, wrecking the adjacent parts of the choir and S transept. Remarkably little is known about the sequence and chronology of the repairs, for whose support indulgences were being issued as late as 1482. Renewal of the crossing's masonry ceased just as soon as the structure was stabilized, with aesthetically dire consequences. The building of the very tall timber spire on the crossing tower some time during the later C15 indicates that reconstructing all four sides of the crossing was no longer an ambition. The restoration of the choir must have been complete or nearly so when new stalls were commissioned *c.* 1489. A new pulpitum and transept roofs followed *c.* 1500. In 1503 it was decided to replace the aisleless C12 nave. Once again the design acknowledges York Minster as a source. The work was complete by 1520–21 when its second architect, *Christopher Scune,* received a bonus 'for his good diligence in supervising the masons'. The last major addition to the fabric was a very large and sumptuous wooden reredos for the High Altar made in 1522–3 by *William Brownfleet.* Brownfleet was a highly successful carver and carpenter who had probably been responsible for making the Minster's choir stalls and who in 1511 became wakeman or mayor of Ripon. By the early C16 the interior of the Minster would have been dominated by comparatively recent fittings, a not uncommon situation in major English medieval churches. But the incomplete crossing was not forgotten, and a will made as late as 1545–6 reveals that there was the intention to remedy what is still today a great blemish. The dissolution of the college in 1547 and the appropriation of its endowments by the Crown put an end to such plans.

By the late C16 the Minster was in very poor condition. Soldiers sent to quell the Catholic-inspired Northern Rebellion of 1569 caused much damage, and proper repairs had to wait until the college was re-founded by James I in 1604. Parliamentarian troops smashed stained glass and monuments in 1643. In 1660 the timber spire of the crossing tower collapsed on to the choir, and in 1664 the similar spires on the W towers were removed as a precaution. The repairs to the choir entailed replacing the timber vault over the main span by a flat wooden ceiling and introducing galleries in a still-Jacobean style in place of the damaged canopies of the choir stalls. The choir was by then being used as the parish church, so further galleries were inserted into the aisles and the High Altar was moved back one bay to the E wall. In 1663 the remains of Brownfleet's reredos became the support for an altarpiece consisting of a painting on canvas showing draperies behind the communion table flanked by views through parallel Ionic colonnades. The artist was *Robert Streeter,* Charles II's Sergeant Painter, best known for his ceiling in the Sheldonian Theatre, Oxford. Presumably he was recruited by the dean, Christopher Wren's friend John Wilkins. Between 1664 and

1674 the York glass-painter *Henry Gyles* made armorial glass for several windows, more than for any other church.*

In 1829–31 *Edward Blore* re-Gothicized the choir by installing a plaster vault and remodelling the late C13 E wall arcading as a Perp-style altarpiece. At the same time the early C16 roof was replaced by a featureless flat wooden ceiling. After the establishment of the see of Ripon in 1836, the Church Commissioners employed *William Railton* to repair the W front and to install anachronistic Romanesque-style rib-vaults of plaster and papier mâché over the transepts. In 1859 *George Gilbert Scott* was consulted about a comprehensive programme of restoration and in 1862 he began work. The choir was reopened in 1869, the nave in 1872. The result was one of Scott's least controversial cathedral restorations, with neither the major structural editing nor the noisy new fittings that characterize much of his work in this field. His priorities were threefold: removing the gimcrack and historically uninformed additions to the medieval fabric made by his earlier C19 predecessors and replacing them with convincing re-creations carried out in appropriate materials; purging the E and W fronts and the choir stalls of later and stylistically disparate alterations; and re-creating the pre-1500 exterior by restoring spires to all three towers and raising the main roofs of nave and choir to their original steep pitch. In the last he was least successful, as he was allowed only to re-create the high roof of the choir. Scott also returned the building to a structurally secure state by underpinning the W towers and inserting steel lattice beams into the N and W sides of the crossing tower.

ST WILFRID'S CHURCH

St Wilfrid's biographer Stephen tells us that in 669 his subject returned from a period of voluntary exile in Mercia and Kent, accompanied by masons and artisans of almost every kind. Wilfrid's first priority was the restoration of the cathedral at York, and he is known to have built the monastic church at Hexham in 671–3, so it is likely that his church at Ripon belonged to the mid-670s. Stephen says that it was constructed of dressed stone with divers columns and *porticus*. The latter were probably side aisles rather than the box-like annexes commonly found in pre-Conquest churches, for Wilfrid's ardent admiration of Rome's Christian traditions will surely have led him to commission a church of basilican format. We can be confident that the CRYPT which lies below the crossing of the C12 church belongs to St Wilfrid's time because it is very similar to the slightly larger crypt at Hexham singled out for mention by Stephen. Access is by two sloping passages, that

6

---

* Most of Gyles's glass was destroyed in the late C18 and C19. The last surviving part of Streeter's altarpiece was thrown away only in the mid-1960s. The only visual records of the Minster in its late C17 state seem to be the drawings made *c.* 1816–18 by John Buckler (British Library, Additional MS 36395).

on the N side connected to a vestibule W of the main chamber
and emerging E of the crypt, that on the S side connected to
the main chamber and leading W. The tunnel-vaulted main
chamber is just 11 ft 6 in. (3.5 metres) long and 7 ft 8 in. (2.4
metres) wide. Five round-headed lamp niches, one in the N
wall later made to connect with the N passage to form a hole
known as 'St Wilfrid's Needle'. In the E wall a large round-
headed niche (for relics?) and below that traces of an altar
demolished in 1568. The narrow W vestibule is aligned N–S and
covered by a half-tunnel-vault springing from the W wall.
The vaults over the main chamber and the vestibule are constructed by the unusual and ingenious method of resting slabs
on transverse ribs which are broader at the intrados than at
the extrados. Much reused Roman masonry (*see* below,
FURNISHINGS, choir N aisle), and some original plaster of
Roman pinkness. The floor was of *opus signinum*. This information about internal finishes is the only good consequence of
the decision taken in 1974 to install a treasury, for whose fittings chases were cut into the masonry. After much controversy
the treasury was moved out in the 1980s.

How did the crypt relate to the rest of Wilfrid's church? In
1930 two thick pre-Conquest walls were found just below the
pavement of the crossing. They were aligned E–W and flanked
the lateral walls of the crypt's main chamber. On their internal
faces towards the W were the lowest parts of two engaged
columns, which probably marked the entrance to the sanctuary
(*see* below, FURNISHINGS, S choir annexe). Whether Wilfridian
or (more probably) late C10, these walls tend to confirm that
the High Altar stood directly above the crypt. Wilfrid must have
been familiar with Gregory the Great's reordering of the sanctuary of St Peter's basilica, which placed the High Altar immediately over the supposed tomb of the apostle. The aim was to
separate liturgical observance from pilgrim traffic but also to
associate Christ's sacrifice as commemorated in the Mass with
the sacrifice of the martyr Peter. Although the annular crypt
at St Peter's is quite unlike Ripon architecturally, the functional
affinity is clear since there can be no doubt that Ripon's main
chamber contained relics. Pilgrims probably entered the N
passage outside the E end of the church, passed through the
vestibule into the main room, leaving by the S passage which,
even if it emerged within the church, would have been well
clear of the sanctuary.

EXTERIOR

The overall shortness of the cathedral and its lack of a lofty
central tower (consequences of the unreliable terrain) combine
with the loss of the three spires in the 1660s to create a decidedly hunched silhouette, one that would have satisfied no
medieval generation. The exterior remains essentially as Scott left
it in the 1870s despite large campaigns of masonry repair during

the second half of the C20. The late C12 and early C13 work is built of warm light brown sandstone said to be from a quarry at Hackfall 9 m. up the River Ure; the later phases mainly use Magnesian limestone.

Choir

The choir has six aisled bays. The three E bays were mostly replaced from *c.* 1284 and have abnormally massive buttressing – evidence that their late C12 predecessors had been slipping down the steep incline to the E. The 'cross-sectional' E front is of a kind used very widely in northern England from the late C13 to the mid C14 for both E and W fronts. Its centrepiece is a tall and elegantly detailed seven-light Rayonnant window with a big circle enclosing alternating trefoils and trilobes. Below this are two three-light units with the three 'piled up' circles beloved of late C13 English architects and a single central light enclosing an impaled trefoil. A playful touch is the way the apex of the central light punctures the large circle so as to be able to impale the lowest trilobe there. Nearly all the elements of the tracery can be seen in the contemporary chapter house at York Minster, and it is likely that the architect was *Simon,* who has been credited with all the late C13 work at York Minster. The E aisle windows have a quadrilobe over two lights. The abnormal narrowness of the aisles perpetuates a feature of the C12 choir. On the corners of the aisles low octagonal stair-turrets with polygonal pinnacles of E.E. type, on the corners of the main vessel square Rayonnant pinnacles with blind tracery. The E gable is *Scott*'s invention but the lower Perp gable it replaced also had blind tracery lights flanking a relatively narrow window. *Blore* removed from between the main buttresses an annexe (a C15 or early C16 sacristy?) which impinged on the bottom of the E window.

On the N side of the choir the two easternmost aisle windows are like those in the E walls of the aisles. The three late C12 W bays retain original shallow pilaster-like buttresses on a high plain plinth, the top of which corresponds to the floor level inside. Inserted early C14 windows of two lights with simple flowing tracery and parapet of the same date. The original windows (preserved only on the S side and visible from within the S choir annexe, *see* below) were round-headed openings with nook-shafts. The four-light clerestory windows of the three E bays are a simplified version of the E window. In conformity to English practice, the flying buttresses here are not continued on to the E wall. The late C12 clerestory windows resemble the original aisle windows in having nook-shafts but differ in being flanked by blind lancets. The wall plane of the clerestory and gallery stands well forward of that of the C13 bays (*see* below, interior). The gallery roof was removed in the 1660s to convert the gallery openings into windows. It is a pity that Scott was not able to reinstate this roof and its

s counterpart and thereby restore the choir's external contours
and original lighting. On the s side of the choir the easternmost clerestory window contains ogee forms that are clearly
due to later alteration. The w clerestory bays and the tracery
of the westernmost C13 clerestory window belong to the repairs
which followed the partial collapse of the crossing tower in
1450.

South choir annex

Most of the s choir aisle is concealed by a three-storey annexe
consisting of two late C12 levels surmounted by an early C14
Lady Chapel. The steeply sloping ground allows the bottom
level to be below the pavement of the choir, whose building it
must postdate because from inside one can see the remains of
the fully finished buttressing and plinth of the s aisle. The
plinth at the w end of the annex courses with the s transept
plinth and must have been built together with it. The irregular rhythm of the windows at this level is due to a wall
dividing the interior space into two. Both C12 levels end in an
apse with shaft-buttresses. The semi-octagonal projection from
the SE corner (partly obscured by later buttressing) contained
a garderobe. The middle storey was kept low to avoid inter-
fering with the s aisle windows. Large circular windows in the
w bays, a rectangular window in the easternmost bay. Original
corbel table. The decision to build the Lady Chapel on top of
the C12 annex – a unique position – must be due to the lack
of level and stable ground E of the choir. Its large rectangular
windows have varied numbers of lights but a consistent intersecting pattern. The very short verticals at the apexes of the
arches do not affect the glazed openings and therefore just miss
qualifying as proto-Perp. Straight-headed windows were a
fashion in the York area *c.* 1300–10 (cf. e.g. chancels at Acaster
Malbis, West Riding South and Skipwith, East Riding). The E
window is set in a shallow projection which appears to grow
out of the half-domed apse roof. Battlements with long
merlons and cruciform arrow loops. Buttresses on only the E
part of the annexe.

Transepts

The transepts are externally the best-preserved parts of the C12
church. The overall effect is severe. Apart from the E clerestory
of the N transept, which is treated as in the choir, shafts and
mouldings are restricted to the lower windows of the E aisles
and main fronts. The latter have two tiers of three evenly sized
windows with much blank wall in between and portals set in
shallow projections close to the w corners. The N portal has an
unmoulded trefoiled opening and three arch orders. On its E
jamb are crocket capitals, on its w jamb 'palmette' capitals akin

to some at Byland. The removal from the s portal of a classical (late C17?) porch in the 1830s probably explains the unconvincing form of the arch in the outermost of the four orders,
but the unusual paired jamb shafts are authenticated by the
survival of their original capitals. Each transept has an E aisle
but no W aisle. The N wall of the N transept E aisle is set back
from the main part of the N front, a Cistercian feature not
repeated on the s transept. Tall thin turrets on the high corners
of the N transept with (later?) conical tops.* Simple early C14
two-light tracery inserted into most of the lower windows. The
early C16 re-roofing necessitated gables lower in pitch than
their predecessors – see the roof-lines on the crossing tower –
and the addition of much plain masonry above the original
corbel tables of the E and W walls. The s transept is more
heavily buttressed than the N transept on account of the
sloping ground here. Its E clerestory belongs to a different
phase of the post-1450 rebuilding from the adjacent s choir
clerestory. The jumble of hacked-about masonry below the
SE corner of the crossing tower includes parts of the C12
clerestories and middle storeys of both transept and choir,
proof that the SE pier of the crossing did not collapse in 1450.

Crossing tower

Ripon's central tower is low, irregular in plan and heterogeneous
in fabric. The late C12 N and W sides have each a pair of round-
headed, nook-shafted windows set close to the corners. Their
heads were originally level with the ridges of the main roofs.
The corbel table, very similar to those on the early C13 W
towers, was installed when the C12 bell-stage was taken off. A
clue to the original height is the strange feature of rings set at
different intervals on the nook-shafts to the buttresses on the
N face. If these intervals continued upwards the levels of the
rings would have coincided for the first time about 56 ft (17
metres) above the main wall-heads. The two N corners are not
right-angled (*see* below, Interior). The post-1450 s and E sides
are each treated as two bays with short two-light Perp windows
centred in each bay. The renewal of only two sides after 1450
indicates that the clergy's main priority was the completion of
the tall octagonal timber spire, the dominant feature of the
Ripon skyline until its collapse in 1660.

Nave

The Perp rebuilding consists of five aisled bays and the clerestory
of the short easternmost bay of the late C12 aisleless nave. The
s side was begun *c.* 1503 and completed before the N side was

---

*Built into a buttress at the NW corner of the N transept are two pieces of pre-
Conquest carved interlace.

begun in 1512, a sequence which enabled *Christopher Scune*, the second architect, to introduce numerous minor changes. The s aisle walls have unusual three-stage buttresses whose very bold projection was no doubt a response to the shelving ground. The form of the gablets is based on those on the crossing tower. Their systematic use in preference to set-offs and the diagonally turned pinnacles (incomplete here) recur on the tower built at Fountains by Abbot Huby (1494–1526). Scune's N aisle buttresses have only two stages. Three-light aisle windows (two-light in the E bay) with quite richly moulded surrounds, smaller on the N side than on the s. A close parallel for the tracery is in the E window of the chapel of Snape Castle (North Riding), some 10 m. N of Ripon (before 1451). Unbuttressed clerestory with the beginnings of diagonally set pinnacles and provision for downpipes (an up-to-date feature).

West front

15 This is the West Riding's outstanding example of the austerely elegant and disciplined strand of E.E. The two w towers as well as the central section consist of four levels whose heights are more nearly equal than in most E.E. facades, and the general effect of evenness and consistency is enhanced by the almost uniform width of the lancets that are the dominant element of the design. Apart from the portals, which are given a modicum of recession, the relief is even and fairly shallow. There is dogtooth or nailhead on all windows and stringcourses and stiffleaf on the capitals of the lower central windows, but no sign of the ornamental profuseness characteristic of the Lincoln-influenced strand of E.E. The buttresses rise sheer and without interruption from set-offs (cf. Beverley Minster, East Riding). The niches hollowing out the lowest parts of the inner buttresses are the only hint here of the quirkiness that characterizes so much E.E. Symmetry is disturbed only by some variations of detail in the top storeys of the towers. In the central section a gentle upward motion is generated by the gradation of the three portals, by the stepped arrangement of the five upper lancets, and by the placing of the string between the upper and lower lancets higher than the strings on the towers. A far more powerful counter to the rather static impression created by the approximately square proportions of the whole will have been the original C13 timber spires that rose directly from the corbel tables of the towers (cf. Sutton St Mary, Lincolnshire). The C15 spires that survived until 1664 stood well behind the crenellated parapets, but there is no reason to suppose that they were higher than their C13 predecessors. Ripon's towers originally projected laterally from the aisleless late C12 nave to form a façade almost twice as wide as the nave itself. The immediate source of this arrangement was undoubtedly the now-destroyed late C12 w front of York Minster, but there were earlier English w façades with towers projecting

laterally from conventional aisled naves at St Botolph's Priory, Colchester (*c.* 1150) and St Paul's Cathedral, London (*c.* 1170). *Scott* removed later (Perp?) masonry infilling between the gables of the w portals as well as two-light tracery that had been inserted into the lancets *c.* 1300. The justifications he offers in his *Recollections* are that the tracery was badly decayed and that to have replicated it would have been to miss the opportunity to retrieve the original perfection of the design. From a present-day perspective these are no doubt dangerous arguments, but it is hard not to see their force in this particular case. The only non-E.E. elements allowed to remain by Scott are the C15 crenellations on the towers (renewed in the late C18) and the medieval-looking nail-studded DOORS, the central one with the date 1673.

<h2 style="text-align:center">INTERIOR</h2>

Choir

The main elevation of the EARLY GOTHIC CHOIR survives only 17 in the three w bays on the N side. Visualizing their original appearance entails mentally subtracting several later alterations: the early C13 blocking of the main arcade in the westernmost bay, the absorption of the entire w edge of the same bay into the thick C15 E crossing arch, the glazing of the middle storey in the 1660s and the addition of a wooden high vault in the mid C14 (now a near-replica by *Scott*). The main arcade occupies more than half the total height of the elevation and has acutely pointed arches on remarkably slender supports. The intervals between the piers are extremely wide in relation to the girth of the piers, as in the arcades of most French Early Gothic cathedrals.* The original effect of openness is impaired by the high choir stalls but can still be appreciated in the altered E bays. The combination of very shallow arcade arches with bulky high vault responds, together with the strange idea of setting those elements on piers whose abaci have to be supplemented by corbels, also derives from French Early Gothic cathedrals (e.g. Noyon and Laon). The even odder idea of equipping the roll mouldings on the main vessel side of the arcade arches with bases identical to those under the responds to the high vault has many parallels in late C12 West French Gothic, including prominent examples on the wall arcades in the choir of Poitiers Cathedral (begun 1162). Most or even all of Ripon's French Gothic borrowings might have been anticipated in Archbishop Roger's choir at York. Certainly paralleled there were the rather complex mouldings of the main part of the arcade arches (small rolls alternating with arrises).

*For Ripon's French sources *see* C. Wilson in *Cistercian Art and Architecture in the British Isles*, ed. Norton and Park (1986), 86–116. For the structural sequences and chronology *see* S. Harrison and P. Barker in *Journal of the British Archaeological Association*, CLII (1999), 49–78.

The clustered piers formed of eight shafts (those in the cardinal directions slightly bigger than the others) are the most
important borrowing from Cistercian architecture, although
they too were almost certainly present at York. The type
originated in mid-C12 chapter houses in the Cistercian order's
Burgundian homeland (Fontenay, Pontigny). The Cistercians
are not known to have used it in churches but by about 1150
that had begun to happen in Picardy, in churches built for
other orders (Benedictine nuns' church at Bertaucourt-les-
Dames and Premonstratensian canons' church at Dommartin). By the 1160s the northern English Cistercians were
frequently using it in their churches. The stepped formation of
the main arcade capitals and bases maintains continuity with
Romanesque 'frontality' (cf. Pontigny) and contrasts oddly
with the irregular half-octagonal plan of the aisle responds
which approach Gothic 'diagonality' (cf. Fontenay). The severe
'chalice' capitals also show Pontigny's influence, but the circular sub-bases derive from Cistercian-inspired clustered piers
in Picardy (e.g. Bertaucourt-les-Dames).

The middle storey is comparatively low and consists of fairly
narrow round-arched openings flanked by single pointed blind
arches. The openings enclose pointed sub-arches under small
single quatrefoils. This was a unique design at the time, so how
was it conceived of by the designer? One possibility is that it
was simply a compressed version of the high galleries which
were a standard component of great church architecture in
both English Romanesque and French Early Gothic. It is more
likely that the openings were made narrow in order to echo the
middle storey of the three narrow bays which made up the
original E wall of the main vessel of the choir (*see* below).
Except for the vault responds, all shafts are lathe-turned monoliths, a more economical technique than coursed shafts.

The much greater thickness of the two upper storeys compared to the exceptionally thin main arcades means that their
outer parts overhang the aisle vaults, although of course there
is no sign of that in the vaults themselves. As in the French
Early Gothic cathedrals, the purpose of this asymmetrical
loading or 'false bearing' is to allow slender and open main
arcades to be combined with upper walls massive enough to
resist the outward thrusts from a masonry high vault. When
the two lower storeys were being built the intention was to
cover the main span with a stone vault – see the bulky vault
responds, the capitals set just below the base of the clerestory,
and the inclusion of the right number of shafts needed to
receive the transverse, diagonal and wall ribs of quadripartite
vaulting. The decision to abandon this vault might well have
been due to the loss of Archbishop Roger's £1,000 bequest in
1181. By the time the clerestory was in hand there was certainly no intention to install a vault, for where its springings
would have been there are blind arches (now concealed by
Scott's timber vault). The wall passage and triple openings,
standard in the clerestories of English great churches from the

late C11, were probably retained from the original scheme. Distinctly non-standard are the curious tripartite arches enclosing the clerestory openings, apparently *ad hoc* inventions intended to lend a purposeful air to the outer shafts of the high vault responds. The substitution of a horizontal boarded timber ceiling for the masonry vault would account for the anomalous semicircular form of the E crossing arch.* A pointed arch would have risen well above the top of the clerestory and a high vault of the same pitch would have had steeply sloping lateral ridges (cf. the vault over the so-called chapter house at Trondheim Cathedral in Norway, probably by the same architect as the main level of the York choir). A further singularity of the abandoned high vault which can be recovered is the division of its easternmost compartment into three cells to accommodate the clerestory of the three-bay E wall. This arrangement was echoed in the end walls of the transepts (*see* below) and it can also be seen in the E choir wall at Tynemouth Priory, a building whose lateral elevations copied closely those of Ripon's choir.

The late C12 aisle elevations are simply treated. The windows lack nook-shafts and the three-shaft coursed responds are corbelled out above a completely plain dado. The capitals have rather basic waterleaf. The quadripartite vaulting in the W bays of the N aisle is original. Its consistently pointed ribs are a French Gothic trait – cf. English Romanesque vaults with pointed arches and ribs, where the diagonal ribs are still semicircular (e.g. Kirkstall Abbey (q.v.) and Durham Cathedral). The unsightly plaster-less state of the webs has the merit of revealing that they are built with the courses parallel to the ridges, the standard French Gothic technique but one very rarely used in C12 and C13 England. The transverse ribs have large roll mouldings flanked by hollow chamfers, the diagonal ribs triple rolls. The S aisle wall is slightly thicker than the N wall, an indication that right from the start there was anxiety about building close to unstable and sloping ground. In the early C13, when the E crossing piers began to sink, the westernmost vault compartments in both aisles were reinforced by means of T-shaped configurations of chamfered arches, but only the N aisle still retains this feature.

How did Roger's choir end towards the E? The overall form of the central vessel as it exists today – six bays rising to full height and ending in a flat E wall – is almost certainly due to the remodelling of the E bays in the late C13. In 1864, when Scott's restoration of the choir was under way, the local antiquary J. R. Walbran claimed that he had recently seen evidence that the late C12 choir had five full-height bays and a rectangular E ambulatory linking the side aisles. Unfortunately, Walbran did not record the details of his findings, but it is likely that when the choir pavement was taken up traces had been

---

*The E crossing arch was demolished in the C15 but can be assumed to have resembled the surviving semicircular N and W arches.

revealed of an E arcade running between the easternmost
free-standing piers. Walbran's evidence was doubtless made
available to Scott, who in 1874 published a plan showing an
ambulatory separated from the main vessel by a three-bay E
arcade. Byland Abbey, whose main elevations follow Ripon's
very closely, has an E end of just this kind, although there the
E 'ambulatory' was divided by wooden screens into a series of
chapels. The E responds to the main arcades at Ripon are partly
late C12 and if they are *in situ* remains of Roger's choir they
would be a stumbling-block to the Walbran–Scott reconstruction. It is far more likely that they were assembled in the late
C13 from recycled components of piers from the demolished E
arcade, for they are the only parts of the E wall whose masonry
is not C13 and their formation as exact halves of the free-
standing piers would have been extremely unusual in the
late C12.*

The architect of the LATE C13 RECONSTRUCTION OF THE
E END (probably *Simon, see* above) was clearly anxious to
ensure that his work did not share the fate of the original E
bays. A concern to maximize the solidity of the walls accounts
for the the relative narrowness and straight-sided jambs of all
windows, and the omission from the E walls of the aisles and
main vessel of the kind of continuous passage found in the terminal walls of other major Yorkshire churches (e.g. Selby
Abbey and York Minster). The wall arcading consists of single
blind tracery lights enclosing trefoil-impaling arches.** Its lean
profiling and continuous mouldings are characteristic of
advanced late C13 Rayonnant in NW Europe as a whole. The
main elevations of the E bays follow the general disposition of
the late C12 bays, although the individual elements are almost
all drawn from the contemporary repertory. The clerestory's
inner layer of tracery echoes the actual window tracery (cf. the
Angel Choir at Lincoln). The middle storey consists of round-
headed openings flanked by blind trefoil-impaling lancets.
Their tracery consists of three lights and two circles, a relatively rare combination. As in the aisle wall arcade and the
clerestory, the heads and jambs of all arches are moulded continuously. The only fundamental change is the abandoning of
false bearing in favour of centring the walls above the arcade
arches. This entailed moving the main wall plane forward, and,
as has already been noted, recessing the exterior wall plane of
the upper storeys. In the third bay on the N the extra order
added to the front of the arcade arch collides with the adjacent C12 vault responds in a quite amazingly cackhanded way,
one highlighted rather than disguised by the crudely carved
little heads inserted at the junction. The new vault responds

---

* Harrison and Barker suggest that the C13 arch mouldings in the S arcades are evidence there were not enough C12 voussoirs of the right curvature available to be
recycled, as would indeed have been the case if the main vessel was terminated by
an E wall with an arcade consisting of three narrow bays.
** The arcading on the E wall of the main vessel was heavily restored by *Scott* in
undoing *Blore*'s remodelling of it as an altarpiece.

are thin and corbelled out from the main arcade spandrels. Heads on the corbels and foliage on the capitals.

The intention in the late C13 was to build a masonry high vault. This is clear from the presence of stone springers and the flying buttresses already noted, but the eventual substitution in the C14 of a timber vault (cf. York chapter house in the 1290s) may reflect worries about overloading. The vault was destroyed in 1660 but traces of a wall rib above the E window show it was semicircular, a form determined by the C12 E crossing arch. *Blore*'s early C19 plaster vault, like Scott's timber successor, was made steeply pointed to take account of the very tall E crossing arch as rebuilt in the C15. Scott's vault incorporates vigorously carved C14 BOSSES salvaged when the vault was destroyed. The subjects include the Creation of Adam, God speaking to Eve, the Expulsion from Paradise, the Annunciation and the Head of Christ (Vernicle). The cylindrical shape of the heads and the contrast between the tightly clad upper bodies and the voluminous draperies below indicate a date of *c*. 1350. Of the large bosses only that with the Crucifixion is certainly Victorian.

The three W bays of the main vessel on the S side and the upper storeys of the next bay were rebuilt after the crossing tower collapsed in 1450. The main arcades as well as the upper storeys are now capital-less and continuously moulded (except for the E side of the easternmost pier, which receives a late C13 arch). Perp panelling on the spandrels of the arcades. In the W bay the panelling extends downwards over the solid masonry buttressing the rebuilt tower. The need to include a high middle storey must have irked the C15 architect even more than his late C13 predecessor, yet he dutifully echoes the latter's work while using the Perp idiom of his own time. The clerestory here has no inner screen of tracery.

South choir annex

The lowest of the annex's three levels contains two rooms, the W one entered via a stair contrived in the thickness of the S transept E wall. In both rooms square-section piers and vaults with semicircular transverse ribs and segmental diagonal ribs, the latter slightly chamfered. Unsightly reinforcement of the transverse ribs of the S compartments in the W room (by *Sir Albert Richardson* in the 1950s?). Cinquepartite vault over the apse in the E room. There would have been an altar here in the C12, for altars were a normal feature of medieval sacristies. Originally the middle level was meant to be entered from the S choir aisle through two doors. That in the third bay from the E (now blocked and only partly surviving) was to have led into a further sacristy, that in the fifth bay into the chapter house. In a change of plan the chapter house was allotted the whole of the middle level. The two-and-a-half double bays of vaulting remaining from an original four have slightly chamfered

ribs and steeply sloping lateral ridges next to the walls. The
slender columns, which do not sit directly above the piers in
the lowest level, have circular abaci and 'waterholding' bases
indicating a date close to 1200. Some time in the late medieval
period the E part of this room was walled off and its vault
replaced by a timber ceiling. In 1956 Richardson renewed the
ceiling and cut a wide round arch through the partition wall.
The single room occupying the whole of the top level (built
c. 1300 as a Lady Chapel and used as a library from the early
C17) has plain wall surfaces relieved only by a simple PISCINA
and an IMAGE BRACKET carved as a crouching, grimacing
layman. The N wall is the well-preserved exterior masonry of
the C12 and C13 S choir aisle wall. The W bays are topped by
a C15 moulded cornice with two gargoyle-like grotesques. Early
C19 drawings record a richly decorated early C17 ceiling.
Scott's Perp-style ceiling has cusping with nicely varied carving
in the corners of its panels, perhaps salvage from the destroyed
nave roof of c. 1520.

Crossing

The crossing at Ripon is one of the most disconcerting sights in
any English cathedral. Mostly that is due to the incompleteness of the rebuilding following the fall of the E and S sides of
the tower in 1450, but one does not have to stand under the
tower for very long to realize that its plan is far from being a
regular square. The fault lies with the late C12 NW pier, which
is set well to the N of where it ought to be. The displacement,
surely too great to be an error of setting out,* was presumably
due to the wish to make the unaisled nave wider than the
central vessel of the choir. But why was the widening not
achieved by planting the W crossing piers equidistantly from
the main E–W axis so that both N and S sides of the crossing
swung outwards by an equal amount? This would have given
the nave the exceptional span of 44 ft (13.5 metres), the same
as York Minster's late C11 nave. After the NW pier was begun
it must have been decided to make the interval between it and
the SW pier hardly more than that separating the E crossing
piers, thereby creating the present lopsided plan.

The NW pier is the only C12 crossing pier not engulfed by
the masonry of the much more massive supports installed after
1450. It has a large circular base (cf. the choir piers) and each
of its responds has three shafts, the central of which front
boldly projecting dosserets. The flanking shaft on the crossing
side narrows near the top and carries a short shaft with a diagonally turned capital which can have had no other function
than to receive a diagonal vault-rib. Traces of a similar arrangement remain in the SW corner. It is surprising to find provision

---

* But bad setting out is also evident in the transepts and nave, the latter's main E–W
axis being both misaligned and at an angle relative to that of the choir.

for a vault so low down in the crossing and at a point in time when vaults over the main spans of the choir and transepts had been given up. Once again, the Cistercians provide a precedent, for the mid-C12 church at Fountains seems to have had a rib-vault immediately above the crossing arches. This was carried on short shafts that also look like an afterthought, and there too the coverings of the main vessels of the nave and the transepts were of timber. The rib-vault planned or actually built over the Ripon crossing must have been of timber, for the thrusts exerted by a masonry vault would have endangered the thin and hollowed-out walls of the tower (*see* below). A curious low E extension of *c.* 1190 to the NW pier has a single monolithic shaft. It now carries a statue but its original function is unclear.

The two crossing arches that spring from the NW pier are semicircular, but the springing of the W arch is well below that of the N one. The aim must have been to avoid the inherent structural weakness in the kind of segmental arch which the wide span of the nave would have necessitated had the springings all been set at one level. The N crossing arch has three orders symmetrically disposed but the W arch has an asymmetrical distribution of orders, most of them on its W side. Perhaps there was a desire to treat its W face like the chancel arch of a parish church. The W face certainly resembled a chancel arch to the extent of framing the great rood (see the rebates and corbels for the rood beam). The C12 crossing arches are thin by any standards, especially in relation to the walls of the tower, which overhang internally above continuous rows of corbels. Above that are pairs of closely spaced lancets combined with a wall passage. The next level has trios of large round-headed arches (mostly windows) and a further passage. These arches have been reinforced quite soon after their construction by inserting narrower openings flanked by tall and very narrow pointed arches. Before long there was a second strengthening which entailed blocking the flanking arches except for their tops. From the outset the structure of the tower must have been vulnerable on account of being so hollowed out by passages, and it is not surprising that the C15 E and S walls lack passages and are much thicker. The architectural qualities of the C15 crossing design are only fully apparent in the SE angle, where the five-shaft responds meet and a further shaft is included under a shaft ascending into the corner of the lantern. The responds have conventionally Perp bases, but their continuously undulating horizontal section is closer to early C13 than to Perp norms. The same is true of the deep hollows and roll mouldings on the notably steep arches.

Transepts

Discussion starts with the N TRANSEPT, where the C12 work is earlier and better-preserved than in the S transept. The main

difference between its E elevation and the original choir elevations is that the high vault responds start at floor level. That
arrangement is made possible by the greater bulk of the piers,
which in turn is due to the fact that their E faces originally
joined on to substantial walls dividing the aisle into two chapels
and separating the S chapel from the N choir aisle. From within
the aisle it is possible to see the traces of the dividing wall carefully removed from under the purposely wide-soffited transverse arch and from the back of the pier. Transept chapels
treated as spatially distinct compartments are a Cistercian
feature (cf. e.g. Fountains). The vaults differ from those in the
choir aisles in having simple roll-moulded ridge ribs. Ridge ribs
only became normal late in the E.E. period but they occur in
a handful of French Early Gothic buildings (e.g. Airaines and
Lucheux near Amiens). The wall separating the S chapel from
the N choir aisle was no doubt retained on account of its prox-
imity to the E piers of the crossing tower, which were already
sinking in the early C13. That process, which caused severe distortion in the southernmost arch of the main arcade, seems to
have been arrested, for the much smaller C13 entrance contemporary with its blocking shows no distortion.

The main vessel of the N transept was to have resembled the
choir in being covered by a stone vault, but the responds on
the E and W walls have three rather than five shafts, an indication that the wall ribs planned in the choir were to have been
omitted here. The decision not to vault must have been taken
by the time that the NE corner had risen to the top of the
gallery, for the shaft there lacks a capital corresponding to
those on the three-shaft responds. The clerestory differs from
the choir's in having single shafts instead of blind arches above
the intended vault responds. The N wall of the main vessel has
high-set windows at main arcade level, pairs of pointed arches
at gallery level and triple clerestory units enclosed in round
arches rather than the tripartite arches that the E wall continues
from the choir. Starting in the NE corner, the mouldings of
arches and jambs in the clerestory become simpler, a change
betokening economy. The upper two levels of the N wall are
linked by corbelled-out monolithic shafts that rise to the C12
ceiling level. As was noted above, the lower and earlier parts
of these shafts must have been introduced in order to echo the
now lost E wall of the C12 choir. The W wall combines elements
of the N and E elevations and is disrupted by an early C16 arch
opening into the N nave aisle. Early C16 timber ceiling (restored
by *Scott*) with cusped panels and tie-beams supported on
robustly carved figures above shields.

Part of the evidence that the C12 work in the S TRANSEPT
is later than in the N transept is its greater distance from Cistercian tradition. The E aisle is a true aisle without solid walls
separating the chapels, as can be seen by the full-length triple
vault responds incorporating monolithic shafts. The wall
between the N chapel and the S choir aisle, part of the early
C13 stabilization of the E crossing arch, is pierced by a C15 door

leading to a now removed loft over part of the W end of the S choir aisle. The E wall of the central vessel was totally rebuilt in the later C15 by an architect who was clearly not the designer of the post-1450 parts of the choir. The main outlines of the C12 design were followed, but the detailing is by turns ponderous (main arcade) and desiccated (cuspless Y-traceried gallery openings). C15 also the door into the S choir aisle and the three image niches above it. The C12 S and W walls closely resemble their counterparts in the N transept, the only important changes being in the wall-shafts on the W wall, which are thinner and lack capitals for a high vault. Timber ceiling similar to that in the N transept. The inserted early C16 arch leading into the S nave aisle is higher and therefore even more disruptive than its N counterpart. In 1996 *Neil McFadyen* enclosed the lower half of the E aisle to provide space for various utilities. This entailed disencumbering the former N chapel of a straight stone stair by *Scott* leading to the top level of the S choir annexe. Access is now via an open spiral stair of timber projecting far too far into the main vessel. The finish and the sub-late-C17 details would not look out of place in a swanky late C20 'Neo-Geo' house.

Nave

The five-bay aisled nave, which succeeded the aisleless C12 nave   21
c. 1503–21, is the most important rebuilding project undertaken at any major northern English church in the early C16. That there was a change of architect during construction is effectively proved by the switch from the crabbed profile of the bases of the W piers of the S arcade to the more orthodox Perp bases of the E piers, which also appear throughout the N arcade. *Christopher Scune* is first mentioned as being in charge in 1514, but he probably took over some time before, and it must have been he who revised the S arcade bases and introduced further revisions of detail when the N side was begun in 1512.*

The most remarkable thing about the nave's design is that it straddles the divide between great church and parish church architecture, two normally quite distinct genres. The tallness of the clerestory and the thickness of the high walls – enough to allow wall passages in the clerestory – are the only features of the main vessel which obviously belong to the great church tradition, being borrowings from the region's most important Perp exemplar, the late C14 E arm of York Minster. But there are also details drawn from the earlier Perp work at Ripon: the hollows framed by fillets on the diagonal faces of the piers (cf.

---

*Scune is one of the north of England's few documented examples of a late medieval architectural pluralist. In 1505–15 he was in charge of the spire on the W tower at Louth in Lincolnshire and by 1515 he was master mason to Durham Cathedral Priory.

the E side of the easternmost C15 choir pier), the thin corbelled-out wall-shafts (cf. the choir again), and the elaborately sub-divided mouldings of the arcade arches (cf. the crossing arches). This heavy reliance on Ripon and York indicates that the anonymous first architect was a local man. But his debts to great church design cannot disguise the fundamental affinity of his scheme with parish church architecture, a relationship which explains the two-storey format, the ceiled and virtually flat tie-beam roof (destroyed in 1830), and the shape of the piers, an enriched version of the four-shaft-and-four-hollow formation routinely used in Perp parish churches in most of E and S England. Was the compromise between the great church and parish church formats an acknowledgement of the parochial functions of the nave, or was it merely a consequence of the huge preponderance of parish churches in the output of the Perp period? The parish church aspect of the nave is now less obvious than originally, thanks to *Scott*'s decision to install a fictive tunnel vault of timber modelled on the C14 wooden vaulting over York Minster's transepts. Presumably Scott was deliberately setting out to make the nave look more cathedral-like than it had been originally. The early C16 roof concealed the upper parts of the second tier of lancets in the W wall but Scott's vault fits neatly round their heads without rising higher than the outer roof of 1830, which had to be kept in place above it. Its unrelieved brownness has a lowering effect in more senses than one.

In the main vessel Scune's only significant alteration to the design inherited from his predecessor was the introduction of casement mouldings into the arches of the N arcade. On the westernmost free-standing pier are shields carved with the arms of Ripon and the important local gentry family of Pigot of Clotherholme, the latter also on the post-1450 choir bays and the pulpitum. In the N aisle, where direct comparison with the first architect's design is less easy to make, Scune panelled the window reveals and substituted responds of concave-sided polygonal section for the much more conventional triple shafts used in the S aisle. The quadripartite vaults over both aisles (executed by Scott but fulfilling original intentions as indicated by springers and wall ribs) are probably another debt to the York choir. The fact that they are contemporary with the sump-tuous fan-vaults in Bath Abbey, Henry VII's Chapel at West-minster Abbey and King's College Chapel, Cambridge, highlights the original nave designer's isolation from the main centres of architectural innovation in Early Tudor England. A concern for economy is evident from the unaltered state of the parts of the E faces of the C13 towers that appear at the W ends of the aisles.

Substantial fragments of late C12 work survive at the E and W extremities of the nave. It is immediately clear from these that the original nave was aisleless and had three-level eleva-tions: a high and absolutely plain dado, a much higher middle zone and a clerestory. No doubt the easternmost parts of the

Ripon Cathedral.
Reconstruction of the interior elevation of the C12 nave

two lower levels were kept in place in the early C16 in order to buttress the crossing. The middle zone here has single units consisting of paired arches under a quatrefoil and an enclosing arch. There are also the beginnings of the next unit to the w. The triple shafts dividing these units above the dado are treated exactly like those on the end walls of the transepts, i.e. they are corbelled out and the outer ones are allocated to the enclosing arches. On the N side, a little way above the capitals of the enclosing arches, the central half-shaft jerks forward very oddly, the aim being, presumably, to switch to a more boldly projecting shaft.

At the w end of the nave the evidence consists of one long bay pierced by (later) arches into the w towers and to the E of that a short bay whose middle zone is very like that surviving at the E end of the nave. The long bay has a clerestory which is a simplified version of the clerestories in the E parts of the church, but the top level of the short bay has only an arcaded passage without windows. Scott demonstrated that the parts of the C12 nave demolished in the early C16 must have comprised four long and three short bays. His close examination of the extreme westernmost limits of the N and S walls revealed that a further short bay at the W end had been removed when the E.E. W front was built. Stuart Harrison and Paul Barker have shown that the arches opening into the W towers were cut through in the early C13 and that the unlit short bays corresponded to exceptionally long buttresses. Remains of two of these can be seen externally between the E sides of the towers and the early C16 clerestory. Scars visible internally at the E ends of the aisles show where the masonry of the easternmost buttresses was plucked away in the early C16. Scott assumed that the four blind lancets in the truncated middle storey of the long W bay were repeated in all the other long bays, but Harrison and Barker have convincingly demonstrated that originally there were large round-arched windows where the central pairs of blind lancets are. These windows are not visible from within the W towers because the C12 masonry above the inserted arches is concealed by C13 blind arcading echoing the elevations of the other walls.

The alternation between generously lit long bays and unlit short bays must have been very striking. Was its purpose to enliven a prosaic space or was it a way of including an abnormal amount of buttressing in order to cope with the unstable subsoil? It may have been both, for medieval design was frequently a matter of aestheticizing choices made on other than aesthetic grounds. As has been noted already, the basic concept of the Ripon nave derived from York Minster's late C11 nave, but there is no possibility that the Ripon architect based the detail of his elevations on York, where the buttresses were of normal size. The passages through the E.E. W wall are set slightly higher than those in the two late C12 upper storeys of the nave, and the wall-heads of the latter had to be raised because the outermost of the upper W lancets rise considerably above them. Vertical slots in this added masonry show that the early C13 nave roof was of the trussed-rafter type. A blocked door originally intended to open westwards from the lower passage in the W crossing wall makes it very likely that the late C12 scheme envisaged a tie-beam roof with a flat boarded ceiling.

FURNISHINGS, STAINED GLASS AND MONUMENTS

Crypt

ALABASTER PANEL of the Resurrection from a C15 retable. Another panel from the same altarpiece is in an E chapel of the N transept. The polychromy has been extensively renewed. In 1567 a servant of the Minster was in trouble for concealing six of the church's alabaster retables to protect them from destruction by the authorities.

Choir

HIGH ALTAR by *Comper*, 1922. A very characteristic ensemble, the iconography of its large standing figures (Christ the Redeemer, SS Michael and George) indicative of its function as a war memorial. Figures of the cathedral's patrons SS Peter and Wilfrid on brackets either side of the E window, an ecclesiologically informed feature. – SEDILIA and PISCINA, *c.* 1345–50, moved to the easternmost bay from the next bay W by *Scott*. The upper parts of the sedilia canopies had been destroyed and therefore Scott re-created the finials on the nodding ogees and most of the straight-sided gablets. The exuberant foliage of Scott's carvers is rather at odds with the original work, which has moved away from full-blown Late Dec lusciousness as exemplified by the Percy Tomb (*c.* 1340) at Beverley. Crisp, almost metallic fleurons stud the canopy supports. Still wholly Dec in spirit are the grotesque figures lurking behind the cusp terminations of the nodding ogees. Their heads are carved in the round but their bodies are reliefs forming part of the soffits. Below the seats quatrefoils framing varied and expressive heads in low relief (cf. borders and frames in early and mid-C14 English embroideries and East Anglian manuscripts). At the E corner is a support higher than the others, an indication that the sedilia and piscina were originally merely adjuncts to a contemporary High Altar reredos.

CHOIR STALLS. Dated 1489 on a misericord and 1494 on the easternmost desk end on the S side. Often ascribed to the Ripon-based carver *William Brownfleet* together with the later stalls at Manchester Cathedral and Beverley Minster. The fall of the central tower's spire in 1660 ruined the eight easternmost canopies on each side, although some parts were reused on the fronts of the galleries which took their place. The making good done under *Scott* is extremely skilful, though the opening out of the backs of many of the lateral stalls spoils the sense of enclosure. The canopies belong to a very long-lived northern English tradition inaugurated *c.* 1370 at Lincoln Cathedral. The closest parallels were with the York Minster stalls of *c.* 1420 (burnt in 1829). The lower stage consists of three-sided canopies, from each face of which project smaller two-sided canopies. The upper stage is made up of niches (now empty) formed of openwork tracery and connected by extensions of this openwork to pinnacles rising from the lower stage. The canopy of the return stall N of the W entrance is richer than the others. The canopy-work on the E-facing wings, in a much livelier and less traditional idiom, has almost exact counterparts at Manchester. The execution is somewhat rougher than at Manchester and Beverley, where there is no recurrence of the erratic placing of the pendants on the lower stage of the canopies or of the untidy junctions between lateral and return stalls due to the off-centre door of the previous pulpitum. Above the door is timber blind tracery and above that a richly decorated oriel-like projection with, at its centre, the singular

feature of a wooden hand that can be moved up and down to
beat time. Most of the bench ends are poppy-heads but that
dated 1494 has an elephant and castle. There are thirty-two
original MISERICORDS, some of which show the influence of
very recently issued Continental prints. A prime example is
the man wheeling a woman in a three-wheeled barrow, an
adaptation of a print by 'Master bxg' who was active in the
Frankfurt region from the 1470s. Also of particular interest are:
(S side, E to W) Samson carrying the gates of Gaza; Jonah
emerging from the whale; pelican, fox and goose; pigs dancing
and making music; mermaid; (N side, E to W) Green Man; fox
caught by hounds; fox preaching from a pulpit.

PARCLOSE SCREENS in the main arcades, of surprisingly
varied formats. Basically late C15 or early C16 but extensively
restored by *Scott*. – COMMUNION RAIL and LECTERN, brass
and doubtless by *Scott*. – STAINED GLASS. E window. Central
figure of Christ by *Wailes*. 1854, other figures, scenes and background renewed by *A. O. Hemming*. 1896.

Choir North Aisle

ROMAN FRAGMENT, a block with bands of abstract geometrical
decoration, found in 1964 reused as a step in the N passage of
the crypt. – Fragmentary ANGLO-SCANDINAVIAN CROSS-
HEAD, found in 1974. It shows Sigurd sucking his thumb over
the dead dragon Fafnir. – FONT, probably late C12, circular
with trefoiled arcade on eight thick shafts. – STAINED GLASS.
E window by *Wailes*, 1865. N windows, from E: *Heaton, Butler
& Bayne* (two), 1871 and 1870; *O'Connor*. 1868; *H. M. Barnett*
of Newcastle, 1870; *Comper*, 1926.

Choir South aisle

DOOR to the chapter house. The woodwork and the elaborate
C-hinges and scrolls on the l. are C19, but the simpler Cs on
the r. are tentatively dated by Jane Geddes to the C14. –
SCREEN. 1970 by *Leslie Durbin*. Wrought-iron, tinselly silver
squiggles. – STAINED GLASS. E window by *Wailes*. 1865. –
MONUMENT. Moysis Fowler, first dean of Ripon †1608. Very
bad stiffly reclining figure in barbarously detailed aedicule.
Vandalized by Roundheads in 1643.

South choir annex

Inverted and made to support the altar in the apse of the lowest
storey, the lowest part of a COLUMN (diameter 3 ft 6 in.; 1.1
metres) removed in 1930 from a wall of the pre-Conquest
church found in the crossing. Possibly Wilfridian but more
probably late C10 (*see* St Wilfrid's church, above). – ARMOIRE,

also in the lowest storey, early C15. – STAINED GLASS in E window of former Lady Chapel, from the E choir window. Fifteen shields, mostly by *William Peckitt*. 1791, but some earlier. In the adjacent s windows miscellaneous fragments, the most remarkable in the small easternmost window: C15 animal quarries and small pieces of *Henry Gyles*'s w nave window of 1664. – MONUMENT. Anthony Higgin, second Dean †1624. Frontal demi-figure, decapitated by Roundheads in 1643, in gabled frame. In the mid C19 it was moved from a position further E on the same wall and turned into a kind of overmantel by the insertion of a fireplace below it.

Crossing

PULPITUM. A country cousin to York Minster's immensely grand mid-C15 choir screen, with a similar contrast between deeply moulded and ogee-topped entrance and side sections containing image niches. Eight niches (six larger and two smaller), the spaces between their gablets and pinnacles filled by an upper tier of small niches. The rather wayward tracery motifs at this level are not the only Dec hankerings. The one feature clearly of *c.* 1500 or soon afterwards is the tracery at the backs of the main niches. This is designed to appear behind the heads of standing images, as whoever decided to introduce seated figures in 1947 failed to grasp. The original occupants' iconography is unknown. The shields on the plinths suggest that individual images were paid for by different donors. The only original figure sculpture remaining is the seated God the Father under the ogee over the entrance. The w face of the pulpitum is correctly centred, unlike the doorway in the E face. Original traceried wooden DOORS in the w doorway. The passage through the pulpitum is covered by a tunnel vault with many closely spaced transverse ribs, a dainty version of a type usually encountered in military architecture. – ORGAN CASE, 1878 by *Scott*, relatively plain and, according to his *Recollections*, 'too big, I fear, as usual'. – STATUE of James I, on the E extension of the NW crossing pier. A thoroughly naïve piece made in 1603 for the southernmost niche of the York pulpitum. Brought to Ripon in 1811 and put up here *c.* 1850.

24

North transept

PULPIT, stone, hexagonal in plan, closely panelled, presumably early C16 and obviously incomplete and *ex situ*. The original nave pulpit? – STAINED GLASS. E wall of E aisle, from N: *Ward & Hughes*, 1872; *Harry Harvey*, 1977. Lower windows of N wall, from E: *Ward & Hughes*, 1875; *Wailes*, 1858; partly by *Henry Gyles*, 1664 and partly by *H. M. Barnett*, 1858. – ALABASTER PANELS. In E aisle, Coronation of the Virgin (N chapel), from the same C15 altarpiece as the panel in the crypt,

and St Wilfrid with his 'burning iron' (s chapel). – MONU-
MENTS. In E aisle, Sir Thomas Markenfield of Markenfield
Hall and wife, c. 1390, freestone effigies on tomb-chest with
shields. Sir Thomas's paling-shaped livery collar enclosing a
hart is doubtless a variant of Richard II's famous White Hart
badge.* – Against N wall of main vessel, Sir Thomas Markenfield †1487 and wife, damaged alabaster effigies on high tomb-
chest with shields in panels of unusual form. – Many C18–C19
wall tablets including John Lister †1788, with profile portrait
medallion, and three by *M. Taylor* of York – Anne Blackett
†1805, Mabel Kilvington †1809, Peter Snowden †1825 – all
with half-draped urn (*see* also s nave aisle and sw tower).

South transept

WALL PAINTINGS. In the E aisle (and within the rooms installed
there in 1996) early C14 Adoration of the Shepherds (N wall of
N chapel) and red false masonry and a horizontal band of intersecting circles, possibly c. 1200 (s chapel). All in poor condition and in urgent need of conservation. – STAINED GLASS.
Lower windows of s wall, by *Wailes*, 1856. – ROYAL ARMS in
their 1604–88 form, on the w wall, an exuberantly painted (late
C17?) panel. – MONUMENTS. Sir John Mallorie of Studley
Royal †1655 and his son William Mallorie †1666. In the E aisle
and, like others there, moved up in 1996 to make way for the
rooms below. Wall monument with gadrooned sarcophagus
and concave-sided pediment, erected 1678. – John Aislabie of
Studley Royal †1742 and other members of the Aislabie family.
Also in the E aisle. Large panel framed by consoles and an
entablature with fluted frieze. – William Weddell of Newby
Hall, connoisseur and collector of Antique sculpture, †1792.
On the s wall of the central vessel. The cathedral's outstanding monument, a half-rotunda based fairly closely on the Choragic Monument of Lysicrates as illustrated in the first volume
of Stuart and Revett's *Antiquities of Athens* (1762). Within it an
excellent marble bust by *Nollekens*, dated 1795 – a second
version of one at Newby, of c. 1789 – standing on a copy of an
Antique pedestal, also at Newby, which Weddell had bought
from Piranesi.

Nave

COMMUNION RAIL, now defining a nave sanctuary. Not homogeneous but presumably at least partly from the post-1660 re-
fitting of the choir. Vertically symmetrical balusters, projecting
centre linked to the rest by concave sections. – PULPIT, 1913,
by *Henry Wilson*, easily the finest post-medieval fitting in the

* The s window of the same king's remodelling of Westminster Hall had a label
stop carved with a very similar design (see plaster cast in Soane Museum).

cathedral. Perfectly exemplifying the combination, found in all Wilson's church furniture from the early 1890s onwards, of stripped-down Byzantinizing architecture with floridly organic Arts and Crafts sculptural forms. Bowl of polylobed plan on thickly clustered pale green marble columns, its compact outlines little disturbed by the bronze and silver decoration, which includes bracketed-out statues of Anglo-Saxon saints. In the staircase no period references at all. Wilson's sounding-board disappeared in the interwar period. Its successor is by *Sir Albert Richardson*, 1960. – STAINED GLASS. W window, parable of the Wise and Foolish Virgins, by *Burlison & Grylls*, 1886, replacing a non-figural window of 1870 by *Hardman*. – MONUMENTS. Hugh Ripley, first Mayor of Ripon †1637. Near the NE corner. Erected by the Corporation in 1730 in place of the C17 monument, which had been defaced in 1643. Executed by *Daniel Harvey* of York. Oddly proportioned frontally kneeling figure, presumably a copy of the C17 original, in a Corinthian aedicule. – Wall tablets include Marmaduke Hodgson †1834 by *J. King* of York, Grecian with sarcophagus and primitive pediment; and John Hodgson †1847, a repeat of the same design, by *Walsh & Lee* of Leeds.

Nave North aisle

Elaborate Tudor Perp-style CANOPY on W wall, formerly over the archbishop's stall in the choir, by *Archer* of Oxford, 1812. – Quatrefoiled Perp stone PLINTH reputedly from the base of St Wilfrid's shrine at the E end of the N choir aisle. – STAINED GLASS, from E: *Comper*, 1921, its rich colouring and bold design not what one associates with Comper's glass; excellent heraldic window by *Thomas Willement*, 1840, given by Baron Grantley of Markenfield; armorial glass by *Henry Gyles*, only that in the centre light of 1664 and *in situ*; *Burlison & Grylls*, 1885; *Ward & Hughes* (two), 1875 and 1874. MONUMENTS. William Norton †1721. Corinthian aedicule with free-standing columns and broken segmental pediment framing a round-headed panel. – Anna Hutchinson †1730. Baroque cartouche.

Nave South aisle

FONT, early C16, of black Tournai 'marble'. Octagonal, concave-sided and with shields and lozenges on bowl and base, the execution decidedly rough. – STAINED GLASS, from E: *Heaton, Butler & Bayne* (two), 1860 and 1858; *Clayton & Bell*, 1872; *Hardman* (two), 1858; fourteen roundels made up in 1724 from glass of *c.* 1300 (the present arrangement of the late 1950s). The faces of St Andrew and several kneeling donors darkened by corrosion but the excellent quality of their painting still recognizable. In the bottom row the arms of Edward Prince of Wales (1284–1307). – MONUMENTS. On a low early C16 table tomb, the remains of a Flemish incised grave slab of *c.* 1360–70. The charming if enigmatic scene of a kneeling figure and a lion in a grove was at the feet of the lost effigy. – Hellen Bayne †1695, good Baroque cartouche. – Wall tablets including Jane Squires †1736, with portrait medallion; Grace Staines †1771 by *Fisher* of York; Samuel Coates †1809 by *M. Taylor.*

West towers

STAINED GLASS (NW tower). N window by *Ward & Hughes.* 1875. – MONUMENT (SW tower). Sir Edward Blackett of Newby Hall †1718, one of the few known works of *John Hancock.* Very large, with pompous bewigged semi-reclining figure flanked by standing figures of his two wives. Tall segment-headed architectural backplate with pilasters and two putti. Banished here in the mid-1970s from the E aisle of the N transept. – Two tablets by *M. Taylor,* Christopher Oxley †1803 and Margaret Oxley †1819, the former with urn.

THE PRECINCT

The main buildings of the medieval precinct were the church-yard wall, with gates to W and E; the Palace of the Archbishops of York, to the NW; the prebendal houses of the seven canons; the communal residence of the Vicars Choral, known as the Bedern; and the Ladykirk (Chapel of St Mary) a little to the NE. Very little of any of this survives, but some of the successor buildings contribute to a continuing sense of the precinct as a visual as well as an historical entity.

Running along the cathedral N side is MINSTER ROAD. At the W end, behind a high garden wall, the OLD COURTHOUSE, probably an outlying remnant of the Archbishops' Palace (*see* also Perambulation 1, below), said to have been used as the Canons' Courthouse, and in the C18–C19 used as a gaol. Now a private house. Two-storey stone-built range, perhaps C14 in origin, with a narrower extension at the S end, the upper stage of the latter rebuilt in flimsy timber framing probably in the C17. Blocked ground-floor lancet window on the E side of the main building, blocked late medieval doorway on the extension. All other openings C19, including the pointed doorway at first-floor level reached by external steps, which is evidently in the position of the original entrance as it leads into a cross-passage. The putative courtroom occupies the whole of the first floor N of the passage, with a common rafter roof over it which could be C14. C17 roof over the rest of the range. Two C19 cells, with iron-plated ceilings and studded doors, on the ground floor. Further E, after the C19 COURT HOUSE (*see* Public

Buildings, below), the OLD DEANERY (now hotel), stone-built H-plan house of 1625, much altered mainly in 1799 and 1859. At the front all the openings are of the latter date, the royal arms of the former. At the back the space between the wings filled by a rendered block which may be the 'brick building towards the garden' added 1715 by *Heneage Dering*, Dean of Ripon and amateur architect, but remodelled presumably in 1799. Sturdy late C17 open-well staircase in the E wing, with big turned balusters and square newels carrying ball finials. The building occupies the site of the 'new' Bedern erected in the early C15 – the early C14 old Bedern is traditionally supposed to have been sited SW of the cathedral, on Bedern Bank – and in front of it is a length of medieval boundary WALL, with high plinth and steep moulded coping, which presumably separated the Bedern from the churchyard. Round the corner in ST MARYGATE is a similar stretch, ABBOT HUBY'S WALL, which was the churchyard wall of the Ladykirk, rebuilt by Abbot Huby of Fountains *c.* 1502. Four of the prebendal houses were also in this locality.

On sloping ground S of the cathedral W front, off the E side of BEDERN BANK, is MINSTER HOUSE, the grandest house in Ripon, now the Deanery but originally unconnected with the church, built in the early C18 by the Oxley family. Brick with stone dressings. W front with projecting centre which looks as if it should be of three bays, with a sort of laterally expanded Serliana incorporating the entrance – the piers between the openings excessively broad – but just a single window above. Two-bay flanking sections, and alternately raised ashlar quoins. S front of seven bays with slim architrave surrounds to the windows and broken pediment to the doorway. Very fine spacious staircase, with three delicate balusters per tread, one turned, one twisted and one a spiral of two strands (cf. Farfield Hall). Archway flanked by half-columns leading off the landing, modillioned cornice, moulded plaster ceiling. Panelling in all the main rooms, some with fluted pilasters flanking fireplaces, enriched cornices etc. Pedimented doorcases in the entrance hall. In front of the house a later C18 COACH HOUSE with pyramid-roofed end bays, Diocletian windows.

Between Minster House and the cathedral a path leads E through the churchyard and then S downhill to HIGH ST AGNESGATE, with a good sequence of houses, all but one on the S side with the river Skell beyond, one at least of which is certainly the descendant of a medieval prebendal house. This is the THORPE PREBEND HOUSE (Heritage Centre) at the W end, a half-H facing away from the street towards the river and the New Bridge (*see* Perambulation 2, below). Unimpressive rendered exterior but in origin timber-framed, the framing partly encased, more generally replaced, in brick from *c.* 1700 onwards. The earliest part is the E wing, probably mid-C16 when the prebend was held by Marmaduke Bradley, previously last Abbot of Fountains. Much of the four-bay frame, of plain light close studding, and the common rafter roof remain. The roofs of the rest probably early C17, this part having presumably replaced the medieval building. Curious staircase with rather coarse triple spiral balusters, perhaps an invention of 1914, when the house was 'restored' and converted into a museum, reflecting local examples. Next E the ruins of ST ANNE'S HOSPITAL, a medieval almshouse, apparently C14. The building resembled a two-cell church, the 'nave' forming the accommodation for the inmates, the 'chancel' the chapel. The former has gone almost completely: of the latter the walls remain, including the double-chamfered 'chancel' arch. Two-light E window with minimal Dec tracery, straight-headed two-light Perp s window, little cusped piscina. Behind it the new ALMSHOUSES, of 1869. Single-storey block with heavy Gothic detail.

Opposite is the OLD HALL, with narrow red brick front range dated 1738, set at right angles to the street and largely hidden by the garden wall. (Staircase hall with excellent mid-C18 plaster decoration (cf. Bishopton Lodge, Outer Ripon, below). Large Judgement of Paris on the main ceiling, owl of Minerva framed by swags over the window, Cupid on the ceiling under the landing. Staircase with slender balusters, panelling.) Earlier wing at the back. E again two houses of early C18 origin with their fronts towards the river; then the best of the group, ST AGNES HOUSE. Largely c. 1693 (painted date inside), of brick now rendered, but retaining four earlier raised-cruck roof trusses in the main range – see the steep pitch outside – and engagingly remodelled at the front in the mid C18. Five unequal bays, with stone dressings. Vanbrughian doorway, and fenestration (apart from the two l. windows, brutally altered) all of little circular oculi with heavy keyblocks. Of the 1690s the big chimney-breast at the W end, with steep miniature pediments, triangular and segmental, on the set-offs; the rear wing with flattened Dutch gable; and the comprehensive good-quality interior fittings. Handsome staircase rising from the housebody, with turned balusters and enriched inverted brackets at the foot, which are repeated at the entrance to the main first-floor room. Much bolection-moulded panelling, and several corner fireplaces, that in the hall with enriched overmantel, that in the room adjoining echoed by a corner cupboard, and two on the first floor with painted overmantels, landscapes in the Dutch style. Back stair with splat balusters.

56

THE CITY

The pre-Conquest settlement evidently lay to the E of the present centre, N of the cathedral in the area of St Marygate and Stonebridgegate, with a parish church of All Hallows – hence

Allhallowgate – which appears to have been abandoned by the C13; and excavation has shown that a wooded knoll, Ailey Hill, a little further E again, was an Anglo-Saxon cemetery of the C8–C10. The shift W appears to be linked with the growth of the town in the C12, which was encouraged by the archbishops of York: royal recognition of the right to hold a weekly market was secured by Archbishop Thurstan in the 1130s, and the town was first mentioned as a borough in 1194. The 'archbishop's market place', apparently at the W end of Allhallowgate, in the area of the present Old Market Place, was in existence by the beginning

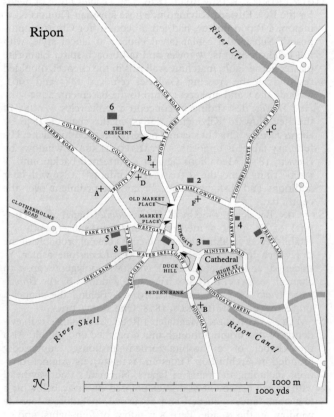

A	Holy Trinity	I	Town Hall
B	St John	2	County Council Offices
C	St Mary Magdalen	3	Court House
D	St Wilfred	4	House of Correction
E	Methodist Chapel (former)	5	Spa Baths
F	Primitive Methodist Chapel	6	College of Ripon and York St John (former)
		7	Cathedral Primary School
		8	Cottage Hospital

of the C13; and the present Market Place itself, S of this, was probably formed in the later C13. By the mid C16 the town's textile industry was in decay, but it was later known for the manufacture of spurs and saddles. In 1773 the Ripon Canal was opened, linking the town to the River Ure 2½ m. downstream. Its streets now present a quite mundane image of modest brick-built elevations mainly of the early and mid C19, behind which fragments of plain timber framing of the C16–C17 are occasionally preserved.*

CHURCHES

HOLY TRINITY, Kirkby Road. 1826–7 by *Thomas Taylor* of Leeds for the Rev. Edward Kilvington, whose kinsman Thomas Kilvington, a Ripon doctor, had left a bequest 'for Christian purposes'. Substantial ashlar-faced church in lancet style, with full-height transepts, W tower and tall broach spire. Elaborate plaster lierne vault, matching wall ribs in the chancel, moulded responds at the crossing. Galleries removed 1883 and 1902. Outside the E end an access ramp to the basement, 2002–3 by *Paul Hewitt*, descending in concentric semicircles. – BUST of the Rev. Edward Kilvington, †1835, in the chancel, 1836 by *Angus Fletcher*. On a hexagonal pedestal, in a Gothic niche. His funerary tablet is opposite. – STAINED GLASS. E windows by *Barnett*, 1873. Medallions against a patterned background. – NE in Trinity Lane, the SCHOOL (now infants'), 1836 with later additions and disfigurements. Primitivist pediment over the centre bay.

ST JOHN, Bondgate. 1869 by *W. H. Crossland*. Chapel of the Hospital of St John, a medieval foundation subsequently re-established as an almshouse, replacing a chapel probably of the C14 which had been enlarged in 1812. Limestone ashlar, Y-traceried and straight-headed windows, polygonal apse to chancel. – STAINED GLASS. Two apse windows by the *Bromsgrove Guild* (*A. J. Davies*), after 1915. – Behind the chapel a single row of ALMSHOUSES, 1878. One storey, brick.

ST MARY MAGDALEN, Magdalen's Road. Little single cell, evidently of C12 origin although much patched and rebuilt. Also the chapel of a hospital-turned-almshouse, supposedly founded by Archbishop Thurstan (1114–39), its original functions including the relief of lepers. Norman S doorway-head with zigzag ornament and later pointed doorway below it; a few small lancets, cusped and uncusped, including a lowside window on the N side; Perp E window, of four lights, and of the same period the low-pitched roof-line and the plain parapet. Big buttress at the W end, bellcote above. Restorations 1917 and 1989. – Cusped piscina and a number of medieval FURNISHINGS inside. Plain stone ALTAR; a simple mosaic

---

* Celia Fiennes in 1697 oddly described Ripon as 'mostly built of Stone', evidently misinterpreting the plaster cladding of the timber frames.

PAVEMENT in front of it; two pairs of BENCH ENDS, attached to modern benches; and the SCREEN, sturdy Perp with close-set mullions and a little tracery, heavily restored. – S of the chapel a short row of ALMSHOUSES, 1892, one storey in simple stone-built Tudor Gothic. Across the road another row, brick, *c.* 1878, and the NEW CHAPEL, 1868 again by *W. H. Crossland*, now a house. One cell, Dec and Perp.

ST WILFRID (R.C.), Coltsgate Hill. 1860–2 by *J. A. Hansom*. Theatrical design in attenuated early French Gothic, with plate tracery. The outstanding feature is the very tall, tower-like chancel, rising above the nave, apsidal-ended and developing into an elongated octagon at eaves level, with exceptionally long windows, very steep roof of patterned slates with an iron cresting, and a tricky little w-facing lucarne. The nave is not low either, of five bays with narrow aisles and a clerestory of quatrefoils and sexfoils. Arcades with cylindrical piers, foliage capitals and unchamfered arches, the chancel melodramatically lighter. – Big spiky REREDOS by *Edward Pugin*. – STAINED GLASS mainly of wretched quality but including a little by *Barnett* of Newcastle. – Contemporary former PRESBYTERY, also by *Hansom*, attached to the S side, busily picturesque with a semicircular staircase projection under another pointy roof.

Former METHODIST CHAPEL, Coltsgate Hill. 1861, probably by *James Simpson* of Leeds. Sound Italianate in brick with stone dressings. Four-bay pedimented front with paired entrances framed by Tuscan half-columns, round- and segment-headed windows, carved enrichment in the pediment.

PRIMITIVE METHODIST CHAPEL, Allhallowgate. 1880–1 by *G. Race* of Weardale. Brick, vile.

CEMETERY, Kirkby Road. 1894. One CHAPEL, Perp, with turret.

PUBLIC BUILDINGS

TOWN HALL, Market Place. On the S side, in the middle of the continuous run of buildings. 1799–1801 by *James Wyatt*. Built primarily as Assembly Rooms, at the cost of Mrs Elizabeth Allanson of Studley Royal, but with some space set aside for Corporation use. Stuccoed five-bay front with pedimented three-bay centre, its upper stage an engaged Ionic portico. Rustication and round-headed windows to the ground floor. In the frieze the Corporation motto, 'Except ye Lord keep ye Cittie, ye wakeman waketh in vain', added in 1886 (the building was eventually acquired by the Corporation in 1897). Principal room across the whole width of the front on the first floor, with very restrained decoration, musicians' gallery over the entrance, chimneypieces at each end.

COUNTY COUNCIL OFFICES, Allhallowgate. The former Ripon Union Workhouse, 1854 by *Perkin & Backhouse* of Leeds. Brick with stone dressings, simple Neo-Jacobean with shaped gables. Detached gatehouse range in front.

COURT HOUSE, Minster Road. 1830. Built for the Quarter Sessions, later used as a Magistrates' Court, now a museum. Single-storey ashlar block with hipped roof. Four round-headed windows with Gothick glazing bars, and between the first and second the doorway with pediment and Tuscan columns. Little-altered interior with justices' bench in a shallow recess, justices' and jury rooms.

Former HOUSE OF CORRECTION, St Marygate. Front part 1686 etc., now a private house (Dean's Croft); cell block behind added 1816 by the third *Lord Grantham* (*see* Newby Hall), now a museum. The original building is a three-storey range of rendered brick and stone set at right angles to the street, of appropriately institutional appearance with six bays of uniform two-light windows, but it appears that the two r. bays and the top storey are early additions. Walled front garden with early C19 royal arms over the entrance. Cell block of brick with a hipped roof, two storeys, the interior brick-vaulted throughout with the cells opening off spine corridors.

SPA BATHS, Park Street. 1904–5 by *S. Stead*. The product of an attempt to emulate the facilities of neighbouring Harrogate, exploiting the waters from a nearby sulphur spring. Floridly detailed façade in red brick and orange terracotta, with prominent porte cochère, the style 'an oriental rendering of the Renaissance, suggestive of luxury, opulence and refinement' (G. Parker, 1913). Similarly ornate terracotta-lined Pump Room, water tower behind. Utilitarian swimming pool added 1936. In the SPA GARDENS, laid out *c.* 1904 by the Corporation gardener *J. T. Simpson*, a bandstand and a bronze STATUE of the first Marquess of Ripon, 1912 by *F. Derwent Wood*.

Former COLLEGE OF RIPON AND YORK ST JOHN, College Road. 1860–2 by *J. B. & W. Atkinson* of York. Built as the Diocesan Training College for Schoolmistresses, now flats. Restrained domestic Italianate in brick with stone dressings, with oversailing hipped roofs. Three-storey, seven-bay central block, and two-storey wings running at right angles. Former CHAPEL attached to the r., 1897–8 by *J. Oldrid Scott*, Gothic; C20 additions to l.

GRAMMAR SCHOOL, Clotherholme Road. Main building 1888–9 by *George Corson* of Leeds. In shiny Leeds red brick, with mullion-and-transom windows and pyramid-roofed clock tower. Adjoining is an earlier block, 1827, like a big early C19 villa. Deep bracketed eaves and a curious Greek Doric temple-front porch in rationalist mode, with the triglyphs of the frieze continued back as stone ceiling joists and empty gaps, instead of metopes, between them.

CATHEDRAL PRIMARY SCHOOL, Priest Lane. 2000–1 by *Allcock & Grieves*. Main part crescent-shaped, of varied height. Brick walls with battered stone-faced buttresses, zinc roof.

COTTAGE HOSPITAL, Firby Lane. 1850, built as the Ripon Dispensary. Modest Italianate, brick with stone dressings, with pedimented centre. Wings added 1888 etc.

CANAL BASIN. *See* Perambulation 2, below.

NORTH BRIDGE, over the Ure. Medieval origin but much rebuilt since: it was 'in great decay and ruinous' in 1608. Twice widened on the upstream side, the second time in 1880–1. Eight arches, some slightly pointed, others semicircular or segmental. For bridges over the Skell *see* Perambulations, below.

PERAMBULATIONS

1. The Market Place

An approximate rectangle. In the middle is the OBELISK, over 80 ft (24 metres) high, designed by *Nicholas Hawksmoor*, an authority on 'Obelisk Language', first built in 1702 (by *William Etty* and *William Cowling*), then rebuilt, as a misleadingly worded inscription records, in 1781. The original, one of the earliest examples in Britain of an obelisk of monumental size, was largely paid for by John Aislabie of Studley Royal, M.P. for Ripon and the town's Mayor in 1702, the rebuilding by his son William who had been M.P. for the town for sixty years. It appears to have been based on the Vatican obelisk as re-erected by Domenico Fontana in 1586. Very tall multi-stage base, weathervane with Borough emblems on top.

Overall, however, the Market Place is disappointing (Defoe had described it as 'the finest and most beautiful square that is to be seen of its kind in England'), the effectiveness of simple C18–C19 façades very easily eroded by only a small number of indifferent mid-C20 interpolations. At the N end Nos. 17–18, late C17 brick, apparently built as two houses of unequal size with a passage between them. Hipped roof with eaves cornice, part of a moulded band between the storeys on the r. flank. Altered front originally of eight bays, the first-floor window openings remaining, two of them blocked, the others with C19 sashes etc. Two short gabled wings at the back, the gables tumbled. (In the larger house (No. 17) a staircase with sturdy turned balusters, square newels and ball finials (cf. the Old Deanery, above), and upstairs a diamond-shaped ceiling panel with a relief of a pelican). At the NW corner of the square is the ghost of a C17 timber-framed house with jettied twin-gabled front, the r. gable rebuilt a storey higher in the C19 and the whole now covered with absurd flimsy mock half-timbering.

At the SW corner the so-called WAKEMAN'S HOUSE, which is the parlour wing of a timber-framed hall-and-cross-wings building probably of the C16, the rest of which, to the rear, was demolished in 1917. It was apparently the home of Hugh Ripley, last 'wakeman' and first Mayor of Ripon (†1637: for his monument *see* Cathedral, above). Street front originally jettied but much altered – the full-width gable, projecting windows and central doorway all secondary features – and destructively over-restored. The structure itself is of two bays, with a side access passage at the E end (and the W end unhistorically exposed by further demolition), close-studded with curved wind-braces, and king-strut roof trusses with diagonal studding. Staircase with splat balusters of eccentric design. Further E on the S side, next to the Town Hall (*see* Public Buildings, above), a four-bay house formerly dated 1739, built by the Chambers family, relatives of the architect (who attended Ripon Grammar School); and then near the SE corner one of *c.* 1800, two bays, with pedimental gable framing a Diocletian window.

2. South-East of the Market Place: Kirkgate and Bondgate Green

From the SE corner of the square KIRKGATE runs towards the cathedral, picturesquely narrow and winding with the townscape *coup* of the cathedral W front at the far end, but with only a little of individual note. Down to the r. in DUCK HILL the former TEMPERANCE HALL, 1859, pedimented front of brick with stone dressings; then Nos. 7–9 Kirkgate, refronted mid-C19 with continuous ornamented shopfront below, six pedimented windows above, but further back retaining a C16 common rafter roof running parallel to the street and evidence of cross-wings to l. and r. Nos. 10–11 next door, contrastingly tall, had a jettied twin-gabled front (shown in Turner's view of the street in 1797) the roof-line from which remains behind the present plain early C19 elevation; and further elements of timber framing remain behind similar fronts at Nos. 12–13 and No. 19. Meanwhile on the N side of the street is a timber-framed late-medieval GATEHOUSE which presumably was that of the Archbishops' Palace (*see* Precinct, above). Two bays, the E with the entrance, the W now encased in later building to front and back. Above the entrance two big curved braces from the bressumer to the posts l. and r., and infill of stone chips. Two fine crown-post roof trusses, with cambered tie-beams, and curved braces from the tie-beams to the heads of the posts and longitudinally from their bases to the collar-purlin.

From the E end of Kirkgate BEDERN BANK descends to the s. For Minster House *see* Precinct, above. On the W side BEDERN COURT (housing), 1987 by *McNeil Beechey*, self-consciously tweaked and gabled and unworthy of its situation. The previous buildings had been demolished for a road-widening scheme which was then abandoned. Beyond the roundabout at the bottom two bridges cross the Skell. To the s, after a pleasant early C19 cottage group, BONDGATE BRIDGE, 1892, the third on the site, lattice-girder single span. To the SE NEW BRIDGE, 1809–12, three arches of vigorously tooled and rusticated masonry. Beyond the latter is BONDGATE GREEN, part of the Boroughbridge road. On the S side first an C18 cottage row and then the terminal basin and wharf of the RIPON CANAL, 1770–3 by *John Smeaton* and *William Jessop*. Rusticated GATEPIERS to the wharf dated 1829, very modest two-storey WAREHOUSE probably *c.* 1773. Warehouse-kitsch

HOUSING, 2000 by *Clive Wren*, on the N side of the basin, a couple of early C19 houses on the S.

3. Other directions from the Market Place

From the SW corner SKELLGATE also descends S, with more simple C18–C19 cottage rows. On the E side No. 17, lower with the remains of a C17 timber frame behind the render. At the junction with Water Skellgate the former PUBLIC ROOMS, 1834, rendered, very plain, five bays with long sash windows to the upper floor; and next to it the former MASONIC HALL, 1902, red brick Queen Anne style. At the end of the street, BORRAGE BRIDGE over the Skell, rebuilt 1765, widened C19, of three small arches, and prominent beside it the former VARNISH AND ENAMEL WORKS, 1925. Shiny red brick block with hipped roof, two storeys and attic, with gables framing big Diocletian windows.

W from the same corner of the Market Place, in WESTGATE, just one dignified early C19 house, three bays and three storeys with Tuscan doorcase, and a few hints of rendered timber framing; but on the N side of its continuation PARK STREET – the road to Studley Royal – a variegated group of substantial houses, C18 and C19. Behind one, with C19 canted bay windows, a pair of early C18 GAZEBOS, two storeys with stone quoins, coved eaves and pyramidal roofs crowned by ball finials. Between them a curious raised terrace, perhaps added later, with balustrade at the front, four rusticated arches below, and a back wall formed of four niches in rusticated surrounds, between lower linking sections. The next house, C18, has a Venetian window and vermiculated keystones.

A little N from here, in KIRKBY ROAD beyond Holy Trinity church (*see* Churches, above), CONEY GARTH, an early C19 villa of yellow brick, with half-elliptical Tuscan porch, oversailing hipped roof, and iron veranda. And NE from there, via COLTSGATE HILL, with a particularly attractive run of early C19 cottages opposite St Wilfrid's church (*see* above), NORTH STREET can be reached, part of the spine of the town N of the Market Place. Mainly modest early-to-mid C19: on the E side Nos. 20–21, with small-paned shopfront. Further N off the W side, in an area of genteel mid-C19 expansion, THE CRESCENT, a group of Italianate detached villas and semi-detached pairs forming a loose quadrant fronted by trees, the earlier ones (Nos. 1–5 and No. 12), of *c.* 1850, quite restrained, the later (two three-storey pairs and a villa adjoining) going florid. Then at the junction of North Street and Palace Road the VICTORIA CLOCK TOWER, an effective townscape punctuation mark, 1898 by *George Corson*. Ashlar, profuse Tudor Gothic with octagonal buttresses and a crown of eight ogee ribs. Statue of Queen Victoria in a canopied niche, by *Milburn* of York. On the way back to the Market Place, in the OLD MARKET PLACE, an insignificant triangle, the BLACK BULL HOTEL, with remains of a C16–C17 timber frame behind the early and mid-C19 front.

OUTER RIPON

BISHOPTON LODGE, ¾ m. W of the Market Place at Bishopton, a pleasant S-facing cluster. Built *c.* 1750 by William Aislabie of Studley Royal as the steward's house. Brick with stucco dressings. Pyramid-roofed three-bay block linked to lower pedimented one-bay pavilions by carriage archways. Quoins on the main block, Diocletian windows in the pediments. 1920s canted bay window l. of the front door. Good Rococo ornamental plaster ceiling in the staircase hall, with a putto holding a laurel sprig. *Cortese* was working at Studley Royal at the time.

Former EPISCOPAL PALACE, 1 m. NW of the Victoria Tower, off the Masham road. Now in multiple occupation. 1838–41 by *William Railton*, with chapel added by him 1846–7. The house Tudor Gothic, a rectangular block with central courtyard. Principal elevations to S and E, gently asymmetrical, the E (entrance) front with two-storey porch, the service accommodation at the NW corner. Imperial staircase with traceried balustrade, other interiors mainly altered. The CHAPEL is attached to the E front by a lower corridor. Perp, with canted apse. (Interior divided but retains three STAINED GLASS windows in the apse by *Wailes*, 1850–2.)

ROECLIFFE

3060

ST MARY. Daughter church of Aldborough, 1843–4 by *R. H. Sharp* for Andrew Lawson of Aldborough Manor (q.v.). A tiny single cell in a scholarly, if idiosyncratic, Neo-Norman style. The most remarkable feature is the stone tunnel vault over the whole of the interior, unornamented apart from the proscenium-like 'chancel' arch just before the E end; but by the 1870s it was showing signs of failure and the big external buttresses were added. Further stabilization 1986 for the Redundant Churches Fund (now Churches Conservation Trust). – Also a highly eclectic assemblage of FITTINGS. Two-decker PULPIT, made out of a C17 pulpit from Holy Trinity, Hull, with geometric panels. – BOX PEW opposite, incorporating three low-relief panels of architectural subjects, one dated 1619. – Other PEWS, also raised above the floor level, running along the N, S and W walls in college chapel fashion. – FONT. Mid-C19 drum in 'Saxon' style. – Linenfold PANELLING round the sanctuary, probably C16, said to have come from Nun Monkton Priory. – Marble PAVING to the sanctuary and steps. From York

Minster, salvaged after the fire of 1829. – DOOR into the Vestry. Perp (restored), with tracery panels, also removed from York Minster after the 1829 fire. – In the vestry more PANELLING, C16 and C17, with Biblical scenes, and mid-C19 FIREPLACE, with incised faces on the arch. – STAINED GLASS. E window 1847 by *Barnett* of York. Virgin and Child, after Pinturicchio. W window 1909. – MONUMENTS to the Lawson family in an enclosure in the churchyard, including an Anglo-Saxon cross to A. S. Lawson †1914.

Former VICARAGE, W of the church. 1856, brick, in a less definable round-arched style.

SCHOOL, on an island site bisecting the green. 1874 for Isabell Lawson as a memorial to her husband, larger than usual for a small village. Dark brick with stone dressings. Gabled Gothic front, broadly symmetrical, with a polygonal turret in the middle, its timber bellcote stage and spirelet rebuilt in 1984 to a simplified design. School house to the r.

ROTHWELL

3020

Greatly overgrown village in former colliery country. There was a medieval manor house W of the church.

HOLY TRINITY, Church Street. Perp W tower of the mid C15 (bequest 1460) and virtually identical to those at Barwick-in-Elmet, Thorner and Whitkirk (Leeds) (qq.v.), with diagonal buttresses, corbelled-out parapet and crocketed corner pinnacles. Restored in 1877 and 1900. The rest – also Perp-looking, quite large – almost entirely rebuilt in more than one phase during the C19, the medieval survivals confined to the S doorway, with its studded door, and the handsome nave ceiling of *c.* 1500, with many carved bosses. Chancel 1825–6 by *Atkinson & Sharp* of York (who also widened the nave N aisle, removing the medieval arcade) but Gothicized in 1849–50, the N chapel presumably being added at the same time. Nave N arcade, aisle and clerestory rebuilt again 1873 by *C. R. Chorley* of Leeds, evidently copying the then still surviving S side; the S side itself rebuilt 1892 by *T. H. & W. E. Richardson* of Leeds. – REREDOS. Designed by *A. W. Blomfield* and executed by *Powell & Sons*, 1888. Caen stone with mosaic panels – Carved PEWS, 1858. – FONT. Dated 1662, and also carrying the initials of king, vicar and churchwardens. Octagonal. The cover is a replica of the C17 one, made in 1907, incorporating surviving parts of the original on the S side. Openwork pedestal and spirelet. – SCULPTURE. Various Norman fragments, including two with beasts etc. in arched panels, one with some pre-Conquest motifs, the other with curious baluster-like divisions between the panels. – STAINED GLASS. Two windows in the N aisle with heraldic glass of *c.* 1826 by *John Bower* of Rothwell from the previous N aisle, reinstated after 1873. – E window by

Hardman, 1883; W by *Wailes*; chancel S, N chapel NW, N aisle
NE by *Ward & Hughes*, 1867–81; S aisle SE by *Shrigley & Hunt*,
1903. – MONUMENTS. Late C17 and early C18 tablets in the
chancel, including Francis Legh †1715, a swagged roundel. –
Mary Anne Faviell †1841, by *J. Towne*, London, 1842. Excellent quality wall monument with seated mourning husband
and praying little daughter, in high relief.

COUNCIL OFFICES, Marsh Street. 1895 by *T. H. & W. E.
Richardson*. Domestic Gothic, two storeys, with symmetrical
gabled front and a little timber clock turret with spirelet.

Former PARISH POORHOUSE, Springfield Street. 1772. Later a
debtors' prison, now residential. Brick, much altered, the
original narrow window openings superseded. Front with
centre part projecting under a pedimental gable.

Village centre cut about. Further E HAZELWOOD COTTAGES,
Oulton Lane, lowly timber-framed house, late C16 or early C17,
cased in rendered stone. One-and-a-half storeys, the housebody perhaps originally open to the roof.

RUDDING PARK
Follifoot

Begun 1807 for the Hon. William Gordon, the architect
unknown. There had been a previous house, and proposals for
improving the grounds had been made by *Repton* in 1790.
Repairs and unspecified other works *c.* 1834 by *R. D. Chantrell*
for Sir Joseph Radcliffe, who bought the property in 1824. Now
an hotel, with further alterations and additions *c.* 1990–2 by
Bolton & Crosby. The house is an essay in refined restraint, a
two-storey rectangle of the finest gritstone ashlar, with a
former office wing at right angles at the back. Single-storey
Tuscan portico with four widely spaced columns, flanked by a
pair of shallow segmental bows. Another of these in the middle
of each of the flanks, and a fifth at the back in line with the l.
front bow – a perhaps slightly excessive number overall. Fine
top-lit staircase hall in the centre of the house, behind the
entrance hall, the two linked by a wide doorway flanked by a
pair of round-headed openings which may be one of *Chantrell*'s
contributions. Imperial staircase, laterally extended with the
cantilevered upper flights running against the rear wall before
returning. Simple iron handrail, circular glazed dome. Reception rooms, including a library, on the S side of the house, with
restrained ceiling decoration and marble chimneypieces, the
corresponding rooms on the N side thrown into one in the hotel
conversion. The office wing also much altered, absorbing part
of the former stable block, with clock turret, behind. New hotel
wing beyond, very approximately in the style of the house.

Alongside the house, in violent contrast, is the CHAPEL
(R.C.), 1877–9 by *A. E. Purdie*. It is the size of a parish church

and extraordinarily lavish, in spiky rock-faced Gothic. Nave and chancel of equal height with a bellcote at the junction, aisles and side chapels. Geometrical tracery. A tall NW tower and spire were also intended but only the base was built, serving as a porch. Octagonal memorial chapel at the E end added 1907, also by *Purdie*. Arcades of five-plus-one bays with cylindrical piers of polished Aberdeen granite and big naturalistic foliage capitals, wall-shafts of the same granite on angel corbels. Very elaborate stone reredos. – STAINED GLASS. E window *c*. 1879, in the manner of Heaton, Butler & Bayne. S chapel E by *Morris & Co.*, 1918.

In the garden a large URN from the Crystal Palace, brought here in the 1950s.

RUFFORTH

ALL SAINTS. 1894–5 by *Demaine & Brierley* of York. Paid for by Sarah Middlewood in memory of her husband.* Nave and chancel and sturdy S tower with recessed spire. Perp-style tracery tinged with Art Nouveau. Re-set in the S porch and as the entrance to the vestry are two plain Norman doorways from the previous church. Nave with barrel ceiling. S aisle with the old E and W windows re-set: the three-light Perp E window has a C16(?) STAINED GLASS armorial shield. – ALTAR and REREDOS, 1898. Painted, the altar with little statues of saints in niches, the reredos with figurative scenes. – FONT. A beautiful octagonal piece in dark green marble with scalloped bowl and thin shafts attached to the stem. – MONUMENT. Large wall plaque of 1836 by *Skelton* of York to members of the Thompson family, surmounted by urns and dove.

RYLSTONE

ST PETER. 1852–3 by *E. G. Paley*, of *Sharpe & Paley* of Lancaster, replacing a church of medieval origin much remodelled in 1820. Mixed Perp and Dec style, with W tower and low short chancel. Medieval window heads re-set under the porch benches. – ROYAL ARMS. Painted, C18. – STAINED GLASS. E window by *Hardman*, W window by *Wailes*, 1871, S aisle SW by *Capronnier*, 1881.

Miniature Dales village round a pond. On the S side RYLSTONE HOUSE, early C19 with a smart three-bay ashlar front. Behind this KENNELS, with two-storey porch dated 1705 formerly

---

* They lived at the Manor House, which was remodelled as the vicarage as part of the same gift.

entered at the side, one of a trio of small C17 farmhouses here with the entrance at the l. end of the front. NE of the church, the earthwork of an ornamental WATER GARDEN, probably C16, which was attached to the lost manor house of the Norton family.

FOX HOUSE BARN, ½ m. W. 1711. Built as a Friends' Meeting House, now a dwelling. Mullioned windows. Walled former burial ground in front.

NORTON TOWER, on rising ground 1 m. SSE. Fragmentary ruins of a rectangular tower, built by the Nortons in the mid C16 evidently in connection with a dispute over hunting rights. Slighted after the Rising of the North, 1569.

SCALE HOUSE, 1¼ m. S. Double pile of c. 1700 with Italianate additions of 1866 by *Edward Birchall* of Leeds – three corner towers and a new porticoed entrance front between two of them, on the W side. The 1700 house has a five-bay front facing S, with cross-windows in architrave surrounds (the original pedimented doorway replaced by one to match in the C19) and eaves cornice with curious projections above each bay, growing from the first-floor window keystones. At the back a tall central porch, with an apron-like raised panel linking the doorway and the cross-window above, and a bullseye window in the gable. Three-bay lean-to service range against the E flank. Inside, the NE room of the main block has a big segment-headed kitchen fireplace flanked by an integral doorway leading to a staircase, with fat turned balusters, in the lean-to range beyond. Inserted main staircase said to have been brought from 'a Belgian Castle'.

1030

SALTAIRE
Shipley

Saltaire was the creation of the Bradford industrialist Sir Titus Salt (1803–76), the town's biggest employer by the mid C19, who had made a fortune from the manufacture of worsted from alpaca and mohair. His decision to move his whole business out of Bradford to a new site in the open countryside of Airedale, and to build a model village for his workforce, was taken in 1850. The new mill would facilitate more efficient working practices – in Bradford Salt's operation was spread over several different mills – and benefit from superior transport links and water supply; while as well as being provided with better housing and healthier, more attractive surroundings than in the polluted, overcrowded town, and with facilities for their intellectual and spiritual welfare, his employees would also be subject to a degree of social control ('No pawnshops, no pubs,' commented Pevsner in 1959: modern Saltaire is altogether more relaxed). The idea can be traced back to Robert Owen's New Lanark (1800), and concern about the living conditions of the working classes had

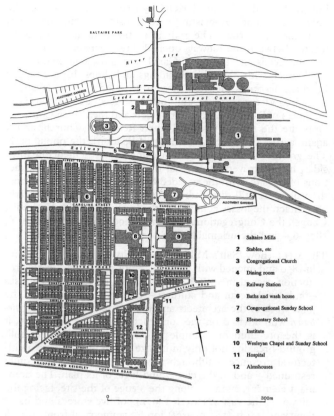

Saltaire.
Plan.

1 Saltaire Mills
2 Stables, etc
3 Congregational Church
4 Dining room
5 Railway Station
6 Baths and wash house
7 Congregational Sunday School
8 Elementary School
9 Institute
10 Wesleyan Chapel and Sunday School
11 Hospital
12 Almshouses

0   300m

quickened during the 1840s with the foundation of bodies such
as the Society for Improving the Condition of the Labouring
Classes (1844): in Yorkshire Salt's initiative was narrowly anticipated by that of Col. Edward Akroyd at Copley near Halifax
(West Riding South) of 1849 – a much smaller development –
but it has been suggested that its immediate inspiration was the
idealized account of a model industrial village in Disraeli's *Sybil*
(1845). What was exceptional about Saltaire was its size – by the
time it was completed, in 1871, there were 824 houses and a population of 4,300 – and the comprehensiveness of its amenities:
'Nothing is done by halves at Saltaire' (W. Cudworth, 1876).

The architects for the whole scheme were the Bradford firm
of *Lockwood & Mawson*, and the style almost throughout is their
characteristic Italianate (cf. the more 'self-conscious' (Linstrum)
Old English of Copley), at effectively varied levels of elaboration
according to the status of the individual buildings. The village
forms a compact grid on gently sloping ground running down-

hill (N) from the Bradford–Keighley road, its regularity broken
only by a second pre-existing road crossing the site diagonally
from the SW corner. The mill is at the bottom, strategically
located between the railway, opened three years earlier in 1847,
and the Leeds and Liverpool Canal, and is reached by the principal street, with the public buildings and shops disposed along
it, which descends the slope close to the E edge of the layout (it
is called Victoria Road: the other streets are named after
members of Salt's family, the architects and the Prince Consort).
Opposite the mill (W) is the United Reformed Church, and N
again, across the river (so actually in Baildon), the public park.
The growth of Shipley, now enclosing the settlement on three
sides, has destroyed its original rural character, but the attractions of the site, with the wooded hillside of Shipley Glen across
the valley, are still discernible. The whole also remains remarkably intact, the losses confined to the wash-house, the Methodist
Chapel, the Congregational Sunday School – an afterthought of
1875–6 – and the original bridge over the river to the park.

The MILL (now 'Salt's Mill'), of necessity was built first, begun
in 1850 and opened with great celebrations in 1853. Textile production ceased in 1986 but a successful package of new uses
– industrial, retail and cultural – has been put in place. The
joint work of the architects and the engineer *Sir William Fairbairn* who advised on the construction and the machinery, it
is the pre-eminent example of an integrated worsted mill,
ground-breaking not only in its size but in its emphatic architectural presence – although in general the detailing is quite
restrained – and in the clarity and logic of its plan. The dominant element, running along the S edge of the site, facing the
railway, is the vast SPINNING MILL, of five storeys and basement and 545 ft (165 metres) long. Symmetrical front, with a
pair of internal engine houses flanking the central entrance
arches and flanked in turn by a pair of belvedere-capped
turrets. Fireproof construction with tunnel vaults of hollow

Saltaire Mills, south elevation.
Watercolour, *c.* 1853

brick on cast-iron beams and simply decorated iron columns, lightweight iron roof trusses. Power transmission was originally by upright shafts, later replaced by rope drives. At right angles behind the centre is the WAREHOUSE, its N end with taking-in doors over the canal and broad pedimented projections to l. and r. Same height as the spinning mill but with floors and roof trusses of timber. E and W of the warehouse are north-light sheds, the W for combing and other preparatory processes, the E for weaving; and W of the former, facing onto Victoria Road and forming the mill's polite front, the office range. Two storeys, twenty-one bays, with projecting ends and an ornate pedimented bellcote over the centre. At the SE corner of the site is the square tapering chimney (the original boiler house demolished), unfortunately shorn of its bracketed top in 1971. Additional sheds further E, c. 1880 onwards.

To the N, between the canal and the river on the site of a water-powered mill, is the NEW MILL (now offices), built in 1865–8 to provide an additional spinning mill and a dyeworks. Two four-storey ranges at right angles, and an elaborate tower-chimney based on the campanile of Sta Maria Gloriosa dei Frari at Venice (cf. Tower Works, Leeds), complete with 'belfry' stage and octagonal crown.

Aligned on the centre of the office range is the splendid UNITED REFORMED CHURCH (former Congregational), 1856–9, one of the most sumptuous of all Nonconformist churches. Grand semicircular portico with six Corinthian columns; and above it a circular tower with engaged columns, iron grilles to the bell-openings and a ribbed dome – i.e. a Victorian Baroque descendant of the Choragic Monument of Lysicrates.* Six-bay flanks with giant pilasters, segmental apse. Aisleless interior with more engaged columns and a coffered segmental tunnel vault with penetrations. Small gallery – the Salt 'family pew' – over the entrance. – Ornate PEWS with scrolled ends. – Vast ORGAN, filling the apse, 1880 etc. replacing a smaller one. – Two huge GASOLIERS, ormulu and glass, by *Hausburg* of Liverpool. – In the circular vestibule a BUST of Sir Titus Salt by *Thomas Milnes*, 1856, presented by his employees. On the base two alpacas. – Attached to the S side of the church the SALT MAUSOLEUM, c. 1870. Square, domed, with Quattrocento ornament. Inside, the MONUMENT to Sir Titus Salt †1876 by *J. Adams-Acton*. Large angel in a pedimented frame. – Flanking the approach from Victoria Road two further buildings connected with the mill, the former DINING ROOM to the S – 1853, seven bays with pilasters – and the STABLES to the N.

The HOUSING, all S of the railway, was built in stages between 1853 and 1868, broadly proceeding from N to S. It is not quite uniform, both because of differences intended to correspond to the various grades in the mill workforce – although in practice the pattern of habitation was not so rigidly hierarchical –

*The passing resemblance of tower and portico to those of St Mary, Banbury (1790–1822) is probably coincidental.

and because of slight changes in design between the earlier and later phases. The standard component is the two-storey through terrace – the earlier ones, completed by 1857, running up the slope, the later mainly at right angles to it – with each house having a parlour, kitchen, two or three bedrooms, and a back yard containing a privy which could be cleared from a service lane at least 7 ft (2 metres) wide (cf. the back-to-back terraces of Copley). Larger houses, in GEORGE STREET, WILLIAM HENRY STREET and elsewhere, intended for over-lookers, also had front gardens, a scullery and a cellar, while in ALBERT ROAD on the W edge of the village are well-appointed semis, built in the last phase, intended for senior executives. The smallest houses of the earlier phases are devoid of architectural enrichment, but otherwise the articulating motifs of the simplified Italianate style include round-headed doors and ground-floor windows, hip-roofed end pavilions on the earlier terraces (carried up an extra storey on the over-lookers' rows, where they were intended as boarding houses) and gabled pavilions on the commonest later type – the effect at its best reminiscent of a Palladian model village of the C18.

Of the public buildings in VICTORIA ROAD the most ambitious is the INSTITUTE, 1869–72, very much in the Victorian Town Hall manner. Two-storey, eleven-bay front, central tower with steep truncated-pyramid roof, ornate Baroque portal with figures of Art and Science by *Milnes*. In the main hall a coved ceiling and a gallery on fluted cast-iron columns. Opposite is the former SCHOOL, 1867–8, one-storey, rock-faced, with three gabled elements and colonnades between them. Both buildings are set back from the street with the corners of their forecourts marked by *Milnes*'s four LIONS, said to have been intended for Nelson's Column in Trafalgar Square. Further S the ALMSHOUSES and HOSPITAL, 1867–8, a rectangular quadran-gle with one range on the E side of the street, three to the W. Slightly different style, busy rock-faced Trecento, mainly single-storeyed with two-storey gabled pavilions. The hospital, at the NE corner, was originally one of these, but in 1925 was extended S into the E range and heightened to three storeys. Finally the PARK, laid out 1870–1 by *William Gay*. Axial E–W terrace, winding paths to N, sports area to S. Semicircular PAVILION backing against the terrace, and behind it a bronze STATUE of Sir Titus Salt, 1903 by *F. Derwent Wood*, on a tall plinth with bas-reliefs of alpaca and angora. Picturesque Italianate E LODGE by *Lockwood & Mawson*, ornamental SHELTERS.

SALTERFORTH

ANCHOR INN. *c.* 1800, beside the Leeds and Liverpool Canal. Pedimented doorway with outsize quintuple keystone, i.e. a style of the earlier C18.

WOOD END FARMHOUSE, ¾ m. SSW. Two-storey lean-to porch dated 1686 at the l. end of the front, with the name DAVID BROWN inscribed in large letters on the door lintel.

SAWLEY

1½ m. W of Fountains Abbey

2060

ST MICHAEL. 1878–9 by *Edward Birchall* of Leeds. The previous chapel was repaired in 1769. Basic Dec. – STAINED GLASS. E window, and chancel SE and SW, by *Taylor & O'Connor*, 1879–80; nave NE and W window by *Clayton & Bell*, 1909 and 1911.

HOG HALL, ½ m. ENE. Hall range probably C16, low, much altered, with a mullioned window of three round-headed lights. C17 cross-wing, the windows of up to five lights.

ROUGH HOUSE, 1 m E. Late C18 rustic gazebo, presumably for William Aislabie as an outlier of the Studley Royal estate. Three pointed arches. Rough gable-ends with verges like incompetent crowsteps. Now a dwelling.

(SAWLEY HALL, ¾ m. SE. Late C18. Seven bays and two-and-a-half storeys, with quoins and blocking course. Centre bay framed by Adamesque giant pilasters. Doorcase with pediment and Doric columns. Staircase with slender column balusters, dining room with columnar screen and enriched buffet recess. Outbuildings include a C19 GIN GANG.)

LACON HALL, ½ m. S. Low range four rooms long, formerly with a porch dated 1655. Mullioned windows. (Parts of an earlier timber-framed building – some posts, braces and lengths of wall-plate – incorporated inside.)

BUTTERTON BRIDGE, 1 m. SW. Probably C14, on the line of a track from Fountains Abbey to the abbey's estates in Nidderdale and Craven. One pointed arch, with parallel chamfered ribs. In a field between it and Lacon Hall the remains of the medieval LACON CROSS, which probably marked the route.

SAWLEY

2 m. S of Bolton-by-Bowland

7040

SAWLEY ABBEY. A Cistercian house beside the River Ribble, founded in 1148 from Newminster in Northumberland – which was a daughter house of Fountains – under the patronage of William de Percy. It was always a poor foundation, plagued by harvest failures on its wet and infertile lands. The upstanding remains are neither extensive nor particularly evocative, largely confined to parts of the nave and transepts of the church, but excavation of the rest has given a reasonably clear idea of the establishment.

The church was of two main periods, the first beginning
c. 1150, the second of the C14. The C12 building was of the
usual early Cistercian type, consisting of an unaisled straight-
ended chancel, transepts each with three straight-ended
chapels separated by solid walls, and an unaisled nave –
although in this case only the two eastern bays of the nave were
built in the first phase, stopping *c.* 1160, the remainder following later in the C12. In the C14 a long narrow chapel was
built along the N side of the nave; but shortly afterwards the
nave itself was shortened once again, to three bays – the demolished part, the lay brothers' choir, apparently no longer being
required – and a new presbytery – aisled, straight-ended, of
four bays – was added to the E. The monks' stalls were now
accommodated in the old chancel and a new pulpitum built
across the the E side of the crossing. Little detail from all this
survives. Between the entrances to the transept chapels are
semi-octagonal wall-shafts which presumably continued up the
full height of the elevation and divided it into distinct bays, as
in some mid-C12 French Cistercian houses such as Ourscamp.
In the S transept the night stair to the former dormitory can
also still be seen. In the presbytery the piers were of the type
with four semicircular shafts and four concave quadrants;
opinions differ as to whether or not the E walls of the inner
transept chapels were removed to open into the aisles.

The conventual buildings were mainly of the later C12 and
early C13, and arranged in the orthodox Cistercian manner
except that the cloister was rectangular, longer from N to S
than E to W. Along its E side were the slype, the (rather narrow)
chapter house and probably the sacristy, then further S in the
same range were the monks' parlour and the day stair, and
above all of this would have been the monks' dormitory. The
chapter house doorway had three orders of shafts to the cloister and three to the interior. At right angles to this range,
running out to the E, was the latrine block, the drain of which
is clearly discernible. On the S side of the cloister was the
refectory, oriented at right angles to the cloister walk in the
Cistercian way, with the warming house to the E of it and the
kitchen to the W. The W range will have been the lay brothers'
quarters, but in the later Middle Ages it was evidently converted into a lodging for the abbot; and a further range at right
angles to the W, now a much altered cottage, is probably also
of pre-Reformation origin, as an addition to this. Fragments
of timber framing inside, including a blocked doorway with
a flattened-ogee head. A block of masonry at the NW corner
of the W range, with a fireplace and a bread oven, may be of
post-Dissolution date when the site was granted to Sir Arthur
Darcy.

N of the abbey, the road was until the mid C20 spanned by two
ARCHES, which had been extensively repaired *c.* 1848 when the
ruins were investigated by the antiquary Richard Walbran,
incorporating carved stones from the site, but were evidently
in origin parts of an abbey gatehouse. One of them was re-

erected beside the road in 1962. Beyond is the BRIDGE over
the Ribble, probably late C18, widened. Three arches.

s of the abbey, SOUTHPORT HOUSE, with an elaborate ornamented doorhead similar to one at Bolton-by-Bowland, dated
as late as 1720. GREENHEAD FARMHOUSE, ½ m. ESE, has a
two-storey porch dated 1711 with another ornamented doorhead of similar design, a three-light first-floor window with
the middle light arched (cf. Alder House, Bolton-by-
Bowland), and the upper stage jettied at the level of the
window sill. SAWLEY GRANGE FARMHOUSE, 1 m. ENE,
incorporates slight remains of an aisled barn, presumably of
an abbey grange.

SCARCROFT

3040

Suburban scatter along the Leeds–Wetherby road. Three villas of
the early-to-mid C19, each with twin lodges at the drive
entrance.

SCARCROFT LODGE. c. 1830, ashlar. Five-by-five bays, the front
with columned Tuscan porch *in antis*, r. flank with central bow
window. Later C19 additions to l. and rear, including an Italianate tower; C20 extensions beyond. To the N a big aggregate-
faced office block of the 1970s by *Abbey Hanson Rowe* for the
Yorkshire Electricity Board. Three storeys, the top one oversailing on tall pilotis. The lodges, by the main road (E side),
have corner pilasters and wide-eaved pyramid roofs.

HIGH GABLES, ⅜ m. N, also E of the main road. 1830 by *J. &
T. Uttley*, a geometrical conceit in Neo-Jacobean style, of rendered brick with stone dressings. Symmetrical front with three
gables, but the flanking ones angled outwards at 45 degrees.
The returns then meet at right angles at the back of the house,
so that the plan overall is an irregular pentagon. A little octagonal entrance hall inside. The lodges, no longer quite matching, have shaped gables. Grounds built over.

OAKLANDS MANOR, ½ m. ENE of Scarcroft Lodge, s of Thorner
Lane. c. 1844, classical again. Three-bay front with giant
pilasters, a pediment over the centre and columned porch; r.
flank with single-storey segmental bows. The lodges also
pilastered, with mansard roofs.

SCOTTON

3050

St THOMAS. 1888–9 by *C. Hodgson Fowler*, built as a chapel of
ease of Farnham. Dec-to-Perp, small. Nave and chancel of
equal height with bellcote between. – STAINED GLASS. E
window, 1996 by *Anne Sotheran*.

OLD HALL. C17 stone-built H-plan house incorporating remains of its timber-framed predecessor, probably of the late C15. The rebuilding was done in two phases, the earlier (E) in rough rubble, the later (W) more architectonic in ashlar, both parts much altered since. Some mullioned windows, that to the housebody restored. Beside it against the W wing, and also part of the later phase, the porch, with catslide roof continued from the wing and round-headed entrance in the flank rather than at the front. On the flank of the E (parlour) wing a length of C15 wall-plate is visible, marking the position of the main survivals of the early structure inside – a number of wall-posts and two bays (three trusses) of a crown-post roof, with collar-purlin, two side purlins, and extensive use of curved windbraces (cf. No. 31 North Street, York). The footprint of the open housebody also discernible: to judge by its unusual depth it was probably aisled on the N side, and a longitudinal beam a few feet in from the N front may mark the position of the arcade plate. Other features include three curious timber-

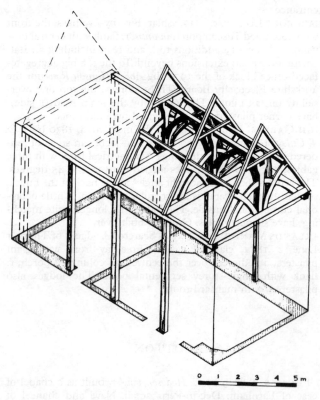

Scotton Old Hall, parlour cross-wing.
Isometric diagram, 1984

framed doorways (one of them altered), two between the housebody and the parlour wing and one into the entrance lobby, with crude wavy lintels below arched heads and the tympanum bisected by a thin stud. – Large C17 single-aisled BARN nearby.

OLD MANOR HOUSE (alias PERCY HOUSE), on the N side of the churchyard. From the street appears entirely C20, of stone, but inside retains elements of timber framing, probably C16 – three pairs of wall-posts, a close-studded partition, windbraces – and a plaster ceiling with badges of the Percy and Fawkes families. The Fawkes connection dates from the late C16 (Edith Fawkes, mother of Guy), and previously the property had belonged to the Percys.

SCRIVEN

3050

Now a suburb of Knaresborough (q.v.), but retaining a pretty village green.

HOME FARM, on the S side. Good example of a Vale of York timber-framed house of *c.* 1500, three-and-a-half bays with rear (S) outshut, and hipped common rafter roof. Close studding exposed at the E end, preserved more extensively within. Alterations of *c.* 1600 including reconstruction of the lower parts of the walls in gritstone, with mullioned windows; the upper level at the front cased in brick early C18. The half-bay (second from E) appears to have been the fire-bay of the open hall – although the roof is smoke-blackened throughout its length: it is now occupied by a big stone fireplace of *c.* 1600, with integral stone bench and timber bressumer (and C18 brick chimney above), and the lobby entry in front of this. Also of this phase are the delightful wall paintings in the front parlour (E bay), with birds and plants in arches; the chamber inserted over the hall; and probably the plank-and-muntin partition between the hall and the service rooms in the W bay. C18 fireplace in the parlour inserted late C20. MAY TREE HOUSE, opposite, is a very similar case apart from the absence of a rear outshut – the frame dated to *c.* 1520 (dendrochronology), front rebuilt all in brick – (and a third common rafter roof, C16, survives at PARK CORNER, just beyond the SE corner of the Green). At ROUNDELLS MANOR, on the E side, some reused C16 carved stonework.

SCRIVEN PARK, W of the Green, the seat of the Slingsbys remodelled *c.* 1728–30 perhaps by *William Wakefield*, was demolished in 1954. Remaining are the former STABLES – the present Scriven Hall – built in 1682 (building contract), a two-storey limestone range with hipped roof, the front (W) a slightly irregular seven bays with arched entrance under a broken segmental pediment, and mullioned windows, mostly C20 renewals and insertions. Also the GATEPIERS onto Ripley Road

31

39

(Knaresborough), ⅜ m. s, of the 1728 phase, with bulgy banded rustication, the inner ones surmounted by a quartet of scrolls carrying a swagged vase, the outer with ball finials; and ¼ m. NW of the Green the KENNELS, now a house, late C18 with Gothick windows.

SEDBERGH

Little stone-built town, more Cumbrian than Yorkshire in character, very attractively situated at the foot of the Howgill Fells. In essence it consists of little more than a single long main street together with the buildings and playing fields of Sedbergh School, expansively disposed all along the s side of the town on a ledge above the valley bottom.

ST ANDREW. Church with some archaeological complexities. Nave and chancel with aisles and chancel chapels, clerestory to the nave only, the chancel slightly lower, w tower narrower than the nave. The exterior appears predominantly Perp, of rough shaly rubble and plainly detailed. Windows mainly straight-headed with uncusped round-arched lights, two on the s side and the N aisle w with the lights cusped. E window of five stepped round-headed lights under a segmental hood-mould (cf. Dent). The only obvious oddity is the unbuttressed corbelled-out bell-stage of the tower, but cf. Beetham, Cumbria. Straight-headed three-light bell openings, again uncusped. Parapets to the aisles and chapels, from the restoration of 1886 by *Paley & Austin*. The interior also superficially unified, with no chancel arch (cf. Giggleswick), and arcades of circular piers and mainly round arches with a single slight chamfer (the E arches on both sides very slightly pointed). But the N arcade is of eight bays and the s of six and markedly lower, and both are heavily restored. The w wall of the nave is evidently Norman: see the traces of two round-headed windows above the head of the later, sharply pointed, tower arch, and outside the shallow buttress at the NW corner. So too probably are the w wall of the N aisle, with the remains of another round-headed window visible internally, and the N doorway, round-headed with a hollow chamfer and a hood-mould. So the first two bays of the N arcade will be Norman also, up to a big square pier which doubtless indicates a break in the building campaign. But the w respond of the s arcade is tripartite with a keeled middle member, i.e. of *c.* 1200, and so the whole of this arcade is presumably in principle of that date. Did the rest of the N arcade pre- or postdate it? The fifth arch on the s side is double-chamfered and is evidently a replacement. On the N side are the remains of an earlier clerestory, below the present one. Finally, the s aisle w window has cusped Y-tracery, i.e. of *c.* 1300, the s doorway may be of the same date, and the tower is of two different builds, with a clear change in the masonry halfway up. – SOUNDING BOARD. C18, with inlay. The PULPIT itself, together with the pews and choir stalls, was supplied by *Waring & Gillow* as part of the 1886 restoration. – POOR BOX. Dated 1633. – STAINED GLASS. E window by *Victor Milner*, 1893. Striking large-scale Call of St Andrew. – S aisle middle and N aisle NW by *Kempe*, 1897. – MONUMENTS. Sir John Otway †1693. Baroque cartouche. – Dr John Dawson †1820, by *Robert William Sievier*. Bust in a round-headed niche.

CONGREGATIONAL CHAPEL, Main Street. 1878 by *Stephen Shaw* of Kendal. Crude four-centre-headed windows.

SEDBERGH SCHOOL. Founded *c.* 1525 by Roger Lupton, Provost of Eton. The OLD SCHOOL, SE of the church, now the school library, was built in 1716. Narrow seven-bay range, not at all local in style, with two tiers of quite large round-headed windows on both sides, the lower ones taller than the upper, with (renewed) mullions and transoms and broad moulded surrounds. Big round-headed doorway in the W end, framed by pilasters, Doric entablature and segmental pediment, smaller re-set C17 doorway in the E. Quoins. Interior remodelled 1957–8 by *Sir Albert Richardson* as a single space with a gallery at the upper level, all in South American timber.

The other buildings are mainly to the S and SW of this, beyond the cricket pitch. Most belong to the period 1878–1907 and are by *Paley & Austin* (*Austin & Paley* after 1895). In the group to the S is the school CHAPEL, 1895–7, a fine large building of grey and red sandstone. Free Perp, cruciform with a flèche over the crossing. Seven-bay nave with low narrow aisles and a tall clerestory of straight-headed two-light transomed windows, wider full-height W aisle to the N transept (the S without), unaisled chancel with a very large E window. Nave arcades with hollow-chamfered segmental arches dying into the short octagonal piers, tall two-bay arcade to the N transept, similarly detailed. No chancel arch. – REREDOS, of alabaster, 1898. – STAINED GLASS. Mostly by *Kempe*, 1898–1912, an impressive sequence. – N aisle W, and two small windows in the porch, by *Shrigley & Hunt*, 1927 etc. Nearby are *Paley & Austin*'s school houses. The earliest is SCHOOL HOUSE, further S, 1878. Simple Jacobean, gently asymmetrical, with a low tower. SEDGWICK HOUSE, to the SW, 1879, is similar in plan but much more up to date stylistically, a sandstone version of the collegiate Queen Anne of Basil Champneys, with sash windows, hipped roofs, shaped gables and a shell-hood over the housemaster's door. HART HOUSE, to the W, 1890, is a more utilitarian version of the same formula, in local shale. Between this and the chapel various buildings including the former GYMNASIUM, now the music rehearsal centre, 1885, and the SPORTS HALL and QUEEN'S HALL, 1989 and 1993 by the *Armstrong, Douglas & Ferguson Partnership*. A short distance to the NW are the old CLASSROOM BLOCK, 1879 and 1889, simple Jacobean again, and beyond it POWELL HALL, 1904–6, the school's assembly hall, Perp with a broad open timber roof. In front of the class-room block to the s, at a lower level, the impressive WAR MEMORIAL CLOISTER, 1924 by *Sir Hubert Worthington*, a classical arcaded loggia set into the slope of the ground, with a beautiful view s across the valley.

In the town, the mid-point of the main street, backing onto the churchyard, is occupied by the MARKET HALL and READING ROOM of 1858 (a market was granted in 1251), the gift of the then headmaster of the school, the Rev. J.H. Evans. Two storeys, the lower with shouldered-arched openings, now glazed, the upper with a stepped mullioned window in a vaguely local c17 style. A little to the w is EVANS HOUSE, mid-c18, renamed after the same headmaster (it had been acquired by the school in 1784). Quite plain externally, of five bays and three storeys with a matching c19 three-bay addition to the l. Quoins, central doorway with a pediment on attached Ionic columns. Staircase with three turned balusters per tread. A little to the E is another mid-c18 town house, MARSHALL HOUSE, also three storeys, with segmental pediment to the doorway. Fireplace with fluted keystone, reused panelling with a date of 1687, and staircase incorporating a lead *pissoir* at one of the half-landings. Behind Marshall House in RAILTON YARD, reached from Back Lane, a row of cottages of *c.* 1800, one of them with a (restored) timber-built external spinning gallery, the only surviving example of a feature once common in the Sedbergh area. Further E, at the edge of the town along the continuation of the main street, THORNS HALL, probably c17, enlarged and altered c19. Gabled two-storey porch with round-headed doorway, and behind and above it a gabled dormer with two-light mullioned window. Extensive c17 and c18 panelling inside, including a panelled partition between housebody and parlour. Staircase with fat turned balusters. High up the steep hillside behind to the N, CASTLEHAW TOWER, a well-preserved motte-and-bailey earthwork, pre-sumably c12, the motte elliptical, the sloping bailey to the w. Behind this CASTLEHAW FARMHOUSE, 1701, with mullioned windows, some renewed.

SE of the main street, the OLD VICARAGE. Probably c17 origin, with cylindrical chimneys. To the s, on the road to Dent, beyond the school, the former WORKHOUSE, now housing, 1853–4 but still early c19 in character. Five-bay front with gabled centre. Then MILLTHROP BRIDGE over the River Rawthey, probably c17. Very narrow, two arches.

OUTER SEDBERGH

ST GREGORY, 1½ m. w. Mission chapel and schoolroom built *c.* 1860 by the Upton family of Ingmire Hall, remodelled as a single space *c.* 1907. Unpretentious little building with plain square-headed windows and a rectangular hipped-roofed lantern along the ridge of the roof. – STAINED GLASS. Seven windows of *c.* 1907. Charming Arts and Crafts-inspired rural scenes.

FRIENDS' MEETING HOUSE, Brigflatts, 1¼ m. WSW. Famous early example, dated 1675 and externally resembling a yeoman farmhouse of the period. Two-storey porch and three-light mullioned windows – a pair one above another to the l. of the porch, two at an intermediate level to the r. of it, and another pair one above the other to the far r. Elders' bench along the S wall inside, below the intermediate-level windows. Galleries round the other three sides – those to the N and E added 1714 – reached by a staircase in line with the entrance, also added then. Balustraded fronts, on sturdy wooden posts. In 1749 the W gallery, which is deeper than the others, was converted into a women's chamber, with a shuttered partition along the front. This and the space below converted into a caretaker's cottage in 1900.

46–7

INGMIRE HALL, 1¼ m. W. Castle-style house of 1838 incorporating some earlier fabric, largely destroyed by fire in 1928. Surviving elements include a big square tower with a cylindrical corner turret, a gabled range, partly earlier, which appears to have become a service wing, and a much altered stable block.

HIGH OAKS, 2 m. WSW. 1706. Two-and-a-half storeys, short front range and broad gabled rear wing. Single-storey porch bearing the date, ground- and first-floor windows formerly mullioned, three small one-light windows to the second floor. (Interior features include a panelled partition between the entrance hall – taken out of the housebody – and the parlour; full-height staircase with turned balusters and ball finials on the newel posts; and a spice cupboard in the housebody, also dated 1706.) THE HILL, nearby, 1712, is similar in form.

LINCOLNS INN BRIDGE, 1⅝ m. W, over the Lune. Probably C17, repaired 1780 etc. Two arches of slightly different profiles, rough plain construction.

LUNE VIADUCT, 1¾ m. WNW. On the former 'little' North-Western line. 1859–60, *J. E. Errington* engineer. Six red sandstone masonry arches, and a wide segmental central span of cast iron, springing from battered piers with ornamental parapets.

STONE HALL, 1 m. ENE. Three-storey central porch formerly dated 1692. Plan-form otherwise similar to High Oaks. Cylindrical chimneys, windows altered. Big housebody fireplace with lintel on corbels, staircase with splat balusters, upper cruck roof trusses. Nearby HOLLIN HILL, 1712. A sort of double pile, but with all the internal walls – the longitudinal spine as well as those within each range – formed of panelled timber partitions rather than of masonry. Mid-C18 fireplace with corbelled lintel in the housebody, the earlier

smokehood above still surviving. Staircase with turned balusters. Cylindrical chimneys, big c18 barn attached to r.
FARFIELD MILL, 1¼ m. E. Former water-powered woollen-
spinning mill. 1836, burnt out and rebuilt 1909. Nine bays,
three storeys.
See also Cautley and Howgill.

SETTLE

The market town of Ribblesdale – the market charter granted in
1249 – memorably situated at the foot of a limestone outcrop,
Castleberg, on the E side of the river. In the c17 and c18 it was
known for its tanning industry, and by 1800 cotton spinning had
been established, at first by a process of adapting riverside corn
mills. The main route through the town is essentially a product
of the Keighley–Kendal turnpike, which came into being in 1753;
and in comparison with that the impact on the centre of the
Settle–Carlisle railway, completed in 1876, was quite limited.
There is one large and remarkably ambitious house of the c17,
The Folly, and a number of the late c17 ornamented doorheads
of which there is a particular concentration in the Settle area;
and otherwise a pleasant but unpretentious stone-built townscape of predominantly pre-railway vintage, up to the mid c19.
Its most characteristic part is the intricate network of steep and
narrow lanes forming upper Settle, immediately below Castleberg and giving directly onto open countryside: later c19 and c20
expansion is largely confined to the w, beyond the railway, and
the s.

HOLY ASCENSION, Church Street. 1836–8 by *Thomas Rickman*,
but not one of his best (the old church is across the river at
Giggleswick (q.v.)). In the usual lancet style, the only individual feature the low sw tower-porch with taller polygonal corner
turret capped by a spirelet. Broad aisleless body with thin
timber roof trusses. – STAINED GLASS. Includes E window by
O'Connor, 1848; N side fourth from w by *Morris & Co.*, 1913.
FRIENDS' MEETING HOUSE, Kirkgate. Dated 1678 on the
simply ornamented doorhead. Two tiers of windows in chamfered surrounds. Typical utilitarian interior with elders' bench
at the s end and women's gallery, screened by shutters, over
the N half.
ZION CONGREGATIONAL CHAPEL, Castleberg Lane. 1816.
Plain three-bay front with round-headed openings. Apsidal-
ended gallery inside.
ST JOHN'S METHODIST CHAPEL, Church Street. 1892–3 by
J. Wills of Derby. Gothic, with spirelet.
TOWN HALL, Market Place. 1832–3 by *George Webster* of Kendal.
Built as 'public rooms' including an assembly or lecture room
together with a market hall, newsroom, library and savings
bank. Detached rectangular block in Jacobean style, with

symmetrical but slightly varied triple-gabled elevations, the middle gables on the long sides shaped. Mullion-and-transom windows, some of them with the central light stepped up in local C17 fashion.

RAILWAY STATION, Station Road. 1876 for the Midland Railway by the company's architect *J. H. Sanders*. The best-preserved of the Settle–Carlisle line stations. Sanders's standard design for the largest stations on the line, single-storeyed with ornamental bargeboards. To the N the STATIONMASTER'S HOUSE and WATER TANK building, to the S the timber SIGNAL BOX.

The centre of Settle is the MARKET PLACE, which is where the town's pre-turnpike spine and the turnpike route intersect, the latter consisting of Duke Street – previously Duck Street – to the S and, from 1804, Church Street to the NW, the former running through upper Settle and along High Street, from the SE, and then along Kirkgate – referring to the church at Giggleswick – to the W. The dominant element is the Town Hall (*see* above), occupying the S side. In the middle the FOUNTAIN, a tapered Tuscan column, probably C18 and said to be the shaft of the old market cross, set on a plinth of 1870, with vermiculated masonry, incorporating a drinking trough. On the W side the NAKED MAN CAFE, with a crude relief of a – fully clothed – male figure dated 1663 and a simple doorhead. To the E is the SHAMBLES, a very curious building, evidently built as a sort of market hall but with a row of cottages above. The lower part is fronted by a loggia of six round-headed arches, but this seems to have been built simply to support the balcony access to the cottages. At the back of the loggia is a second row of six arches, now serving as shopfronts, but the space in front of them is taken up by an area lighting the cellar. The structure is said to be of C17 origin, but the arches look to be C18 at the earliest. The cottages were rebuilt in 1898. Beyond, at the SE corner, on the l. two C19 bank buildings, HSBC, 1870, of brick – a great rarity here – with pedimented centrepiece, and LLOYDS TSB, 1865, single-storey rock-faced Quattrocento. On the r., in CHEAPSIDE, behind the Town Hall, an interestingly variegated group. First a C17 cottage with stepped three-light windows; then a grandly architectural former warehouse of *c.* 1800; then three (altered) C18 houses, two with rainwater heads dated 1777 but the first of them evidently earlier than that, with a shell-hood sitting rather awkwardly above the architrave surround to the doorway. The warehouse is of three storeys and three bays, with a full-width pediment containing a bullseye window, central round-headed entrance and matching taking-in doors above it. The crane for lifting goods still remains.

From the same corner the High Street, short and insignificant, leads to THE FOLLY, built in the 1670s for a lawyer and landowner named Richard Preston. The date, variously recorded as 1675 or 1679, and Preston's initials were on the lintel of the front doorway but have long ago eroded away. It is called The Folly not without reason, for its details are exotic

p. 694

Settle, The Folly.
Engraving, 1878

and extravagant – or at least, rather indiscriminately eclectic. Three storeys, with short gabled cross-wings, that to the r. (parlour) end projecting at the front only. The central range has to the ground floor the front doorway on the l. and the wide hall window filling most of the rest of the space. The doorway has a fantastic surround with extraordinary column-like flanking elements, gadrooned rather than fluted, narrowing into necks near their tops, and terminating in a series of mouldings which have a distant resemblance to the astragal and echinus of a Doric shaft and capital. It has been suggested that their source, freely interpreted, was the designs for balusters in Vredeman de Vries's *Architectura* (1581). Lintel with explicitly Gothic details – a pair of pointed arches – above which is a stepped moulding and a polygonal finial. The hall window is of five-plus-four lights, transomed, and the lights have arched heads – at this date probably a conscious neo-medievalism. But the window is then continued further without a break, so that it not only extends across the whole width of the parlour wing – in six-plus-five lights – but also continues round both corners onto the flanks. The l. (service) wing has a different design, with an asymmetrically placed window of five-plus-four lights which continues round the corner to the r., and to the l. a kitchen doorway with a lintel similar to that of the main door.

This 'glass wall' technique in which the corners are supported on the window posts only (cf. e.g. Astley Hall, Chorley, Lancashire, *c.* 1660) is continued on the first floor, but perhaps the most disconcerting aspect is that there is more window,

35

p. 31

and less solid wall, at the bottom of the building than further up. Above the hall there are six-light transomed windows to the first and second floors; but both wings at first-floor level have windows carried round the corners, in the form of a cross-window facing in each direction, and in the middle the type of three-light transomed window which incorporates a Serliana, created by raising the transom of the central light to form an arch. The whole of this composition was probably derived from one of Serlio's designs for Venetian palazzi in his *Book of Architecture*. The top storey is more conventional, with two cross-windows to each wing; but the capricious nature of the design is emphasized by the use, on those sections of the corners which are not occupied by windows, of robust rusticated quoins.

Inside, there is a lobby entry to the hall, which has a big segment-headed fireplace with joggle-jointed voussoirs and a moulding similar to that round the front door, flanked by round-headed doorways, one leading to the lobby and the other (formerly) to the kitchen. Moulded ceiling beams, a little C17 panelling at the high end, and two C17 doors. Opening off it to the rear, and housed in a separately roofed turret, is the spacious main staircase – dog-legged, with barley-sugar balusters (a quite early instance) – which rises the full height of the house. Another big segment-headed fireplace in the kitchen, two smaller C17 fireplaces on the first floor. The top two storeys of the turret, above the staircase, were presumably intended as a belvedere, and the upper of these looks as if it may be an addition.

Beyond The Folly in VICTORIA STREET, No. 10, on the l., has an ornamented doorhead of 1664, the exterior otherwise largely C19 in appearance. One room with high-quality C18 detail – enriched panelling, a cupboard with *trompe l'oeil* painted shell-head, and simple decorative plaster ceiling (cf. Brackenbottom Farmhouse, Horton-in-Ribblesdale). Further up the former NATIONAL SCHOOL, 1856, Gothic and gabled; then on the r. in COMMERCIAL STREET the former PRIMITIVE METHODIST CHAPEL, 1841, domestic-looking with basement and central door.

Back to the Market Place, and up to the NE in CONSTITUTION HILL a house with a doorhead dated 1694, with two lobes bearing spiral decoration (cf. Cromwell House, Long Preston). Later semicircular canopy over. Set back at the SW corner, MILNTHORPE'S, early C19 with handsome original shopfront. W from here, in KIRKGATE, some modest townscape and in an alley on the l. a cottage with a doorhead similar to that at No. 10 Victoria Street and also dated 1664. Then opposite the Friends' Meeting House (*see* above), the VICTORIA HALL, 1853 by E. G. *Paley*, with vigorously textured Italianate front under a broad gable; and beyond the railway bridge MARSHFIELD HOUSE, *c.* 1790 for John Parker, heir to Browsholme Hall (q.v.). Seven bays, the end ones slightly recessed. Octagonal entrance hall, and staircase with turned balusters. s from the same corner of the Market Place, in DUKE STREET, on the l. another ornamented doorhead, dated 1671, re-set in the GOLDEN LION HOTEL, and intermittently some dignified Late Georgian town houses. They include ASH-FIELD HOUSE, *c.* 1830 for the banker William Birkbeck (brother of the educationalist George Birkbeck), five bays and two-and-a-half storeys with semicircular porch on four Tuscan columns; and another of the same date opposite – now the POLICE STATION – five bays, ashlar, with pedimented Serliana incorporating the entrance. Further on, round a bend in the road, THE TERRACE, *c.* 1840, three houses of three bays each with the middle one breaking forward slightly, handsomely done in Grecian style. Primitive pediments over the doorways and the central bay, astylar pilaster strips at the angles.

On the outskirts of the town, ¼ m. further s, the FALCON MANOR HOTEL, formerly INGFIELD, 1841 by *George Webster* for the Rev. H. J. Swale, first vicar of Settle. Jacobean-style like the Town Hall but now just slightly asymmetrical. Top-lit imperial staircase. ½ m. further again ANLEY HOUSE, *c.* 1818 for John Birkbeck, cousin and partner of William. Restrained ashlar block of three broad bays, with Greek Doric tetrastyle entrance porch. Service wing to N with mid-C19 pyramid-roofed tower. D-shaped staircase, again top-lit. In the opposite direction, ¼ m. NW of the church, the BRIDGE over the Ribble. Probably C17, widened 1783. Two segmental arches, the undersides of the original parts longitudinally ribbed. s of this, beside the river, KING'S MILL, built for cotton spinning *c.* 1830. Four storeys, thirteen bays. Floors on cast-iron columns.

SHAROW

ST JOHN. 1824–5 by *George Knowles* of Lucan House, Sharow, 'an able and successful civil engineer' (*see* his monument, below). Built as a chapel of ease of Ripon. Perp-style, ashlar-faced. Tall w tower, remarkably serious, with angle buttresses and battlements. Very wide three-bay body, also battlemented, with big three-light traceried windows, and a flat timber ceiling with beams and carved bosses. Two-bay chancel added 1873–4 with the original E window re-set. – STAINED GLASS. E window 1853, an important work by *George Hedgeland*. Theatrical rendering of Biblical scenes, two of them after Raphael. – Nave N centre *c.* 1860 by *Barnett*; SE *c.* 1860 in the manner of *Wailes*; s centre 1862 by *O'Connor*. Tower (w) 1886 by *Kempe*. – Nave NE and chancel s by *Heaton, Butler & Bayne*, 1903 and 1935 respectively, the latter charmingly *retardataire*. – Nave NW 1939 by *Morris & Co*. Better than most of their late work, with

arresting dark colours. – MONUMENTS. George Knowles
†1856, by *Thomas Milnes*. Wall tablet with semicircular relief of
a broken bridge below the inscription. – In the churchyard
Charles Piazzi Smyth, astronomer and Egyptologist, †1900 and
his wife Jessie †1896. Pyramid *c.* 5ft (1.5 metres) high, with a
cross on top. – SCHOOL, 1857, brick with stone dressings. Mullioned windows with fancy glazing.

SHAROW HALL. Plain rendered house of *c.* 1800 with later additions. Handsome timber imperial staircase from Wiganthorpe
Hall, North Riding (by *Carr*, 1777–8, dem. 1955).

SHIPLEY

1030

Former mill town situated at the confluence of the Aire and the
Bradford Beck, developed from village origins particularly during
the second half of the C19. The Leeds and Liverpool Canal
arrived in 1774, the railway in 1846. Population was *c.* 1,400 in
1801, 3,272 in 1851, *c.* 15,500 in 1876. Now an appendage of
Bradford, effectively eviscerated by road widening from the 1930s
onwards and an ineffably dreary central area redevelopment
scheme of 1955–62. The W parts of the town now almost encircle the model industrial village of Saltaire, originally built in open
country, which is described separately.

ST PAUL, Kirkgate. 1823–6 by *John Oates*. A Commissioners'
church: cost £7,961. W tower with battlements and big crocketed pinnacles. Broad five-bay nave and short lower chancel,
also battlemented. Former porches flanking the tower, long
transomed windows with cusped intersecting tracery. Two galleries in the nave, but also tall arcades in front of them, with
strong octagonal piers. Plaster ribbed vault in the chancel. –
PULPIT. 1876. On an extraordinarily tall carved stone base.
Part of a major reordering which also included the extension
of the chancel W into the nave, with prominent organ case
adjoining, and the removal of a W gallery. – STAINED GLASS.
E window by *Barnett*, 1858–60. Two windows in the N aisle by
Clayton & Bell, 1869. Three in the S aisle by *Powell Bros.* of
Leeds, 1875 and 1888, and one by *Heaton, Butler & Bayne*,
1894. – VICARAGE, E of the church. *c.* 1909 by *T.H. & F.
Healey*. Mildly Old English. – Further E, opposite the Town
Hall, the former CHURCH SCHOOL, 1858 by *Samuel Jackson*
of Bradford. Gothic, with master's house to l. Front block
added in 1886.

CHRIST CHURCH, Windhill. 1868–9 by *Andrews & Pepper*. Tall
and stark, in early French Gothic (cf. the same architects' St
James, Bradford, 1876–7). Big plate-traceried rose window at
the W end, nave clerestory of cinquefoiled roundels, smoothly
semicircular apse to the chancel. A NE tower and spire were

intended. Four-bay nave arcades with cylindrical piers and crocket capitals.

St Peter, Moorhead Lane. 1909 by *T. H. & F. Healey*. Well-mannered free Perp at the smart w end of the town. Quite large, with a big unbuttressed w tower and the Healeys' trademark double transepts. Elaborate traceried roof trusses.

Wesleyan Reformed Church (now Christian Life), Manor Lane. 1863 by *J. Crabtree & Sons* of Shipley. Low three-bay ashlar front with pedimented centre and Doric doorcase.

Salvation Army Citadel, Rhodes Place. 1892. Stage-set-like castellated front.

Town Hall, Kirkgate. 1931–2 by *Anderton & Bailey*. Unexciting C17 domestic classical, French accented. Three storeys and basement, thirteen bays, with a mansard roof over the projecting centre.

Central Board School (Wycliffe Primary), Saltaire Road. 1876 by *Jackson & Longley*. Large, symmetrical, with two storey central pavilion, in simplified Italianate style.

Woodend Board School (former), Windhill. 1885 by *Sam Wright* of Windhill. Also ambitious, in the Bradford manner. L-shaped with a tall pavilion-roofed clock tower. Mullion-and-transom windows, gables.

Tramshed (now bar), Bingley Road. 1904. Two low-pitched gables over the entrances. Diocletian windows on the flank towards the road.

The redevelopment scheme focused on the creation of a new Market Square, with on its n side the Market Hall, 1960–2 by *Shingler Risden Associates*, with boxy clock tower. To the sw a further phase, some improvement on the first, 1982–4 by *John Brunton & Partners*, incorporating a Public Library together with a health centre, sheltered housing and a supermarket. Low, with pitched slate roofs. To the e, in Otley Road, the badly mauled Low Hall (Conservative Club), only survivor of four houses of gentry or near-gentry status which formerly stood in the town centre; l. wing C17, recessed three-bay centre and r. wing *c.* 1700, with cross-windows. The centre had a balustraded parapet.

Further n, between the canal and the river, Victoria Works, former worsted mill, 1873 etc. by *Jackson & Longley*. Two handsome Italianate front ranges of five storeys with fireproof construction, and an excellent octagonal chimney with prominent bracketed top. Further back a four-storey warehouse range, other buildings demolished. Nearby Crown House (Government Offices), 1970 by the *Robinson Partnership*. Two elongated hexagons, the smaller of five storeys, the larger of two, with horizontal bands of glazing. Dining and social area at the back, with a roof of steep lead-covered pyramids.

New Close Farm, off Glen View Road, ⅞ m. wsw of St Peter's church. Late C17, altered. Beside it an aisled barn, probably C17, restored. Seven bays, kingpost trusses.

See also Saltaire.

SICKLINGHALL

ST PETER. 1881 by *W.H. Parkinson* of Leeds. Small single cell with polygonal apse. Trefoil-headed lancets.

ST MARY IMMACULATE (R.C.). 1849–54 by *C.F. Hansom*, brother of Joseph Aloysius, for the Middleton family of Stockeld Park (q.v.). Dec, nave and chancel. N transept added *c.* 1865. W gallery on two cast-iron columns. Former monastic buildings adjoining to S. Gothic dormers.

WOOD HALL, 1 m. SSE. *c.* 1800 by *Carr*, for William Fenton Scott, a Leeds banker. Now an hotel. Two storeys, with a segmental bow in the centre, fronted on the ground floor by a segmental portico with Tuscan columns, and three bays to each side. Tuscan pilasters behind the portico and Ionic pilasters above. Entrance hall at right angles to the front, with canted ends (cf. Farnley Hall), the doorway at the inner end with niches l. and r. and an open roundel over. Cantilevered return staircase beyond, with a delicate wrought-iron balustrade, other main rooms redone 1910 by *Connon & Chorley* of Leeds in C18 style. Rather overbearing hotel wing to r., *c.* 1990.

SILSDEN

Minor Airedale mill town, rapidly expanding as a dormitory settlement.

ST JAMES. 1815, built as a chapel of ease of Kildwick, replacing a chapel of 1712. A preliminary design, dated 1814, attached to the Faculty, is by *J. Holgate*. Three-bay box with W tower. Thoroughly modernized 1876, with Dec windows and a one-bay chancel. Tower heightened, and needle spire added, 1896. W gallery from the 1815 phase, on Tuscan columns. Some reordering by *G. Pace*, 1968. – STAINED GLASS includes SW window by *Kempe & Co.*, 1925.

OUR LADY OF MOUNT CARMEL (R.C.). Built as the Wesleyan Methodist church, 1869–70. Cruciform, with big Dec W window and thin octagonal SW turret and spirelet.

TOWN HALL. 1883 by *J.B. Bailey* and *W.H. Sugden*, of Keighley. Built as the Mechanics' Institute. Robust Neo-Wren manner, with giant segmental pediment breaking forward at each end on columns supported by consoles. Big Serliana in the middle, rising into the pediment.

WATERLOO MILL, Howden Road. Former worsted mill, beside the Leeds and Liverpool Canal. Main building *c.* 1870, four storeys and seventeen bays. New engine house added in 1916, still housing the steam engine which was installed at that time. Massive rock-faced voussoirs to the openings. Octagonal chimney on square base with bracketed cornice.

ECOLOGY BUILDING SOCIETY HEADQUARTERS, Belton Road, s of the canal. 2003 by *Hodson Architects*. Low modest block designed to embody the Society's principles of sustainability and low energy use. Pitched roof, on trusses of recycled scrap timber, planted with low-growing vegetation to replace the insect habitat of the building's footprint. Elevations faced partly with dry-stone walling of reused stone, partly with timber boarding. Rainwater runoff stored to flush the lavatories. Circular meeting room of load-bearing straw bales, lime-plastered, added in 2005.

BRIDGE, over the Aire. 1804 by *Bernard Hartley*, the West Riding Surveyor of Bridges, doubled in width mid C20. Three segmental arches.

In BRADLEY ROAD, N of the church, OLD HALL, 1682. Double-pile block with triple-gabled front. Mullion-and-transom windows, formerly of eight lights to the housebody, of six to l. and r., and of six and four lights above. Next to it an aisled BARN, C17, five bays, and then two three-bay houses dated 1787 and 1793. In NORTH STREET, a house of 1696 with decorated hoodmould stops.

Outlying C17 houses include HOLDEN GATE, 2 m. SE, with reused datestone of 1619 and an unusually handsome single-aisled BARN dated 1641. Round-headed and chamfered cart entry set in a gabled porch. Five bays, with a mixture of king-post and queenpost trusses. In the C17 part of LANE HOUSE, 1¼ m. NW, a panel of painted decoration dated 1689 incorporating a pelican in its piety and a (repainted) devotional text.

On RIVOCK EDGE, a gritstone outcrop ½ m. ENE of Holden Gate, a group of Bronze Age 'cup-and-ring' ROCK CARVINGS, outliers of the concentration on Ilkley Moor (q.v.).

SKELTON

p. 54 CHRIST THE CONSOLER. Within the grounds of Newby Hall (q.v.), and approached from the end of the village street along a yew avenue. 1871–6 by *William Burges* for Lady Mary Vyner, as a memorial to her youngest son who had been murdered by Greek bandits in 1870. It is reported to have cost *c*. £25,000, and is the sister church of the similarly opulent St Mary Studley Royal (q.v.), built for Lady Vyner's son-in-law and daughter the Marquess and Marchioness of Ripon. C13 English Gothic with occasional French imports, delivered *fortissimo* with Burges's usual inventiveness. Picturesque composition of nave with aisles and clerestory, much lower chancel, and tower and spire over what would otherwise be the E bay of the N aisle, the spire with big Norman Gothic pyramidal corner pinnacles sprouting from its base. Outsize rose window at the w end, with muscular Geometrical tracery and some of the extensive

SCULPTURE – here the Four Ages of Man – executed by *Thomas Nicholls*. Excessively squat E window of five lights, similarly detailed, with his Christ the Consoler over. Lancets in pairs to the aisles, trios to the clerestory, close-set windows of two lights with cusped plate tracery, encrusted with dogtooth, to the chancel sides. Porch entrance and S doorway both with elaborately lobed arches and stiff-leaf capitals. Good Shepherd in the porch gable.

The nave interior is markedly tall and narrow, in four bays. Arcades with quatrefoil piers, heavily moulded arches decorated with dogtooth, and very prominent Purbeck-type shafts in front of the piers, rising to big carved corbels supporting the roof tie-beams. More shafts to the clerestory, waggon roof with kingpost trusses, remarkable half-trilobe roofs in the aisles. Chancel arch with multiple shafts of different colours and carved angels on the soffit, and filling the high space above it the climax, *Nicholls*'s Ascension, with the witnesses squeezed into a miniature four-bay arcade. Then the chancel, low and rib-vaulted, with more coloured shafting, Lincoln-style double tracery to the windows, and marble-lined dado.

The foremost of *Burges*'s FURNISHINGS is the ORGAN CASE, where the E bay of the N nave arcade would have been, an integral part of the architecture jutting forward from the organ chamber in the tower. Tracery and simple painted decoration. Below it the console balcony projecting on an elephantine corbel. Others are the REREDOS, 1874, of alabaster with recessed medallions, carved by *James Redfern*; the CHOIR STALLS, with misericords and carved bench ends; and the FONT, of Tennessee marble on a cluster of marble colonnettes, with a tall tabernacle-like COVER executed by *Walden*, 1874. – STAINED GLASS. An uncommonly excellent scheme throughout, executed by *Saunders & Co.* from sketches by *H. W. Lonsdale* and cartoons by *Fred Weekes*. Small panels with the figures in bright clear colours, the subjects related to the theme of consolation. – MONUMENT. In the churchyard at the E end of the church. Robert Vyner †1915 and his wife Eleanor Shafto †1913. Many-tiered polygon like an Eleanor cross.

SE of the churchyard CHURCH COTTAGE, presumably by *Burges*, c. 1873. One storey, with big chimney and veranda lintel on heavy brackets. In the village street ST HELEN'S CHAPEL, 1811, the predecessor to Burges's church. Tiny rectangle with three-light Gothic windows to E and W.

SKELTON LODGES. *See* Newby Hall.

SKIPTON

What remains in the memory about Skipton is a composition of High Street, church and castle: the High Street opening broad

p. 705 and funnel-wise at the top to the church in its tree-lined church-yard; and the castle behind, first built in Norman times by Robert de Romille and his successors and the property of the Cliffords from the early C14. By then there was a market and a small woollen industry, and it is probable that the High Street was laid out deliberately as a market area. Further industrial development, a mixture of both wool and cotton, followed the completion in 1777* of the Leeds to Skipton section of the Leeds and Liverpool Canal – the first textile mill was erected in 1785 – and even more the arrival of the railway in 1847. The population was 2,305 in 1801, 4,842 in 1831, 6,078 in 1871, 12,974 in 1911. The growth was at first accommodated in tightly packed 'yards' on the narrow burgage plots along the High Street, and the town in general took on a predominantly C19 appearance – mainly of modest architectural quality but cohesively gritstone-built. Less can be said for the changes of the mid C20 when much of the Georgian Newmarket Street and many of the yards were demolished; but there has been some improvement since.

CHURCHES

20 HOLY TRINITY. Mainly Perp in appearance but with substantial Dec elements. Repairs by Lady Anne Clifford in 1655 following damage in the Civil War. Documentary dates are 1304–7 for the Dec chancel and c. 1483 for its successor. Perp W tower, tall, strong and simple, in part occupying the place of the W bay of the Dec nave. Four-light belfry openings, five-light W window and thin diagonal buttresses. It was 'built up again . . . and leaded over' by Lady Anne Clifford, but how much is her rebuilding? Certainly the crocketed corner pinnacles, one of which bears her name and the date 1655, and presumably the crenellated parapets; but perhaps no more than that. Nave and chancel in one with clerestories, aisles and chancel chapels, the parapets to the first four bays of the nave and aisle on the S side crenellated, the rest plain (the S chapel with finials renewed in the C19). The side windows straight-headed, mostly Perp with cusped arched lights; but two in each of the aisles, with reticulated tracery, are of c. 1350 (cf. Kildwick), as is the arched window re-set at the E end of the N chapel, also reticulated with mouchette and dagger infillings to the mesh. The E window of the S chapel is a clumsy simplified version probably done in 1653. Big Perp two-centred main E window corresponding to 22 that in the tower. Inside, the quatrefoil piers to the three W bays of the seven-bay arcades are probably no later than c. 1300 (again, cf. Kildwick). The other piers are octagonal and all the arches double-chamfered. Perp tower arch and half-octagonal W responds. Early C14 sedilia in the S aisle, but presumably re-

*The section from W of Bingley to Skipton had been completed first, in 1773.

set from the previous chancel. Four seats with pointed trefoiled arches. In the N aisle a small opening perhaps leading originally to an anchorite's cell. Nave and chancel roof of *c.* 1500, low-pitched with moulded tie-beams, big decorated bosses below the kingposts, and smaller bosses on the subsidiary rafters. The cusped braces supporting the tie-beams, their corbels and the enriched cornices the main element in a tactful restoration of 1854 by *John A. Cory.* s porch 1866 by *John Lowe* of Manchester. N transept and NW vestry 1908 by *Austin & Paley.*

REREDOS of Caen stone. 1874 by *G. G. Scott.* – ROOD SCREEN. Formerly dated 1533. Round-headed four-light divisions with Perp tracery, the main posts with the Rod of Life. Small angel figures front and back not in their original positions. The rood loft removed in 1802. Simple Gothic screens to N and S of 1919 and 1928 respectively. – FONT COVER. A very fine Jacobean piece, octagonal and of two tiers with a crocketed spirelet. The lower tier has openwork tracery decoration, the upper openwork foliage. – WALL PAINTING towards the W end of the S aisle. Fragment of a figure of Death, probably C17. – ROYAL ARMS. Dated 1798 and signed 'Smith pinxt.', for *George Smith*, a local painter. Illusionistic Gothick frame. – CHARITY BOARD. 1847, in the form of a Gothic doorway. – STAINED GLASS. In one of the S aisle windows two diamonds bearing the initials A P (Anne Pembroke) for Lady Anne Clifford. – Five windows by *Capronnier*, E 1859, S chapel E 1870, N chapel E 1872, S chapel second from E 1873, S aisle second from E 1899, garish and *retardataire*. – N chapel N and S chapel SE by *Powell Bros.* of Leeds, 1892 and 1902. S aisle SE by *Kempe*, 1903, signed with his wheatsheaf. W window by *Shrigley & Hunt*, 1921.

MONUMENTS. Henry Clifford, first Earl of Cumberland, †1542, and Margaret Percy, his second wife, N side of the chancel. Purbeck marble tomb-chest with cusped quatrefoil panels containing shields, heavily restored 1867. On the black marble top brass effigies, C19 replicas of the originals, *c.* 3 ft (1 metre) long. – Henry Clifford, second Earl, †1570, and Anne Dacre, his second wife, †1581. Brasses, also mainly C19 replicas, on a vertical stone slab standing at the E end of the first Earl's monument. Kneeling figures of the Earl, his Countess, two sons and three daughters. – Francis Clifford †1589, aged five. Miniature tomb-chest, still with quatrefoils, W of the first Earl's. – George Clifford, third Earl, †1605. S side of the chancel. Tomb-chest with many shields. No effigy on the black marble top. Erected by his daughter, Lady Anne Clifford, 1654. – Also a number of wall tablets, late C18 to mid-C19, including John Birtwhistle †1786, with bas-relief trophy and half-shrouded urn; Oglethorpe Wainman †1800, by *Webster* of Kendal, and Margaret Chippindale †1817, by *Fairey* of Kendal, both variations on the same theme; John Baynes †1820, also by *Webster* but Gothic, in the form of a mural tomb-recess; William Alcock †1819, a high-relief sarcophagus by *W. Pistell*, London, and Jane Brown †1829, the same; Lt. Alexander

Birtwhistle †1855, and Capt. William Birtwhistle †1856, both by *D. A. Bowd* of Cheltenham, with naval and military emblems respectively.

CHRIST CHURCH, Keighley Road. 1837–9 by *R. D. Chantrell*. In the E.E. style with Geometrical tracery, the detail a bit mechanical but the outline satisfyingly bold and solid. W tower, nave with aisles and clerestory, full-length chancel raised over a basement. Plaster rib-vaulted interior, re-fitted 1906–7 by *Bromet & Thorman* of Tadcaster. Painted DECORATION in the chancel by *Sir Charles Nicholson*, 1925. Parish room 1982 by *Wales, Wales & Rawson*.

ST STEPHEN (R.C.), off Gargrave Road. 1836–8 by *Richard Lane* of Manchester, paid for by the Tempest family of Broughton Hall. An aisleless rectangle in the lancet style but not the Commissioners' manner, rather a later and more precise E.E. Extended by two matching bays at the (ritual) E end, and a porch added at the W, 1853 by *Andrews & Delaunay*. – REREDOS, of Caen stone, 1853. Said at the time to have been 'carved from the designs of the late lamented Mr. Pugin' but probably by his son *E. W. Pugin*, to whose spikily attenuated manner it conforms. – STAINED GLASS. Mainly by *Hardman*, 1853 etc., but the (ritual) SW and W windows by *Capronnier*, 1856 and 1857. – MONUMENTS. Several brasses to C19 members of the Tempest family, including Elizabeth Tempest †1845, designed by *Pugin* senior and executed by *Hardman*.

At the foot of the avenue leading up to the church, the SCHOOL-cum-PRESBYTERY, 1854 by *Andrews & Delaunay*. Two storeys in a handsome collegiate Gothic, gabled and dormered. Also by the same architects ST MONICA'S CONVENT, 1861, attached to the church at right angles. Similar but plainer and much extended at the rear.

FRIENDS' MEETING HOUSE, The Ginnel, off Newmarket Street. 1693. Very humble little building with a plain rendered front, the windows altered. Elders' bench across one end inside, partition with top-hung shutters inserted 1761.

METHODIST AND UNITED REFORMED CHURCH (formerly Congregational), Newmarket Street. 1914–15 by *James Totty* of Rotherham, the third on the site. Meagre Art Nouveau Gothic. Next to it the former SUNDAY SCHOOL, 1890 by *T. H. & F. Healey*, plainer but of similar size.

Former WESLEYAN METHODIST CHAPEL, Water Street. Now County Council Offices. 1864–5. Italianate, with engaged temple-front centrepiece. Behind it the big SCHOOL, 1890; and 150 yards N, in Chapel Hill, its predecessor the former METHODIST CHAPEL of 1811. Elegant three-bay ashlar front with pediment and round-headed windows with Gothic glazing bars.

Former PRIMITIVE METHODIST CHAPEL, Coach Street. 1835, with more round-headed windows but much degraded.

CEMETERY, Carleton Road. Laid out 1873 by *John Varley*. A pair of matching CHAPELS, with stumpy broach spires.

The site is strongly fortified to the N, where there is an almost
vertical drop to the Eller Beck. Of the de Romilles' building
nothing remains. The earliest surviving element is the inner gatehouse, which was probably built for William de Fors I Count of
Aumâle to whom the property had passed in 1190; and the rest
of the inner bailey defences – a compact D-shaped circuit with
massive close-set round towers – followed probably in the time
of his son William II (†1241). Having later passed to the Crown
the castle was granted to Robert de Clifford in 1310, and it was
probably he who built the outer gatehouse and curtain wall. Subsequent works were of a palatially domestic rather than a military character. They were the improvements of c. 1500 for Henry
Lord Clifford, the 'Shepherd Lord', mainly within the inner
bailey; the addition of a range outside it to the E in 1536–7 for
his son the first Earl of Cumberland; and the remodelling of the
outer gatehouse as an ornamental showpiece, c. 1629 for Henry
Clifford, the future fifth Earl, during the lifetime of his father.
The castle was besieged in the Civil War, slighted in 1648 and
then restored by Lady Anne Clifford in 1657–9. But the extent
of the damage, and of her work, can be exaggerated. It remained
the property of her descendants, the Earls of Thanet and Lords
Hothfield, into the C20 and remains fully roofed, although only
part of it (the E range, not open to the public) is furnished and
inhabited.

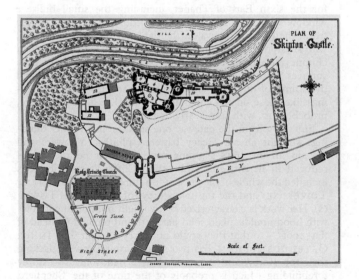

Skipton Castle and environs.
Plan, 1878

The entrance from the town into the outer bailey is by the
OUTER GATEHOUSE, with its powerful fat round corner
towers to front and back. The fabric of these remains predominantly of the early C14, but the whole of the taller central
section appears to be of *c.* 1629. The four-centred head of the
entrance archway does not fit with the jambs below, and the
Clifford arms above it were formerly accompanied by Henry
Clifford's initials and the 1629 date. His initials and those of
his wife also appear on a downpipe at the back. Doubtless also
of this time are the cross-windows, mainly Georgianized,
inserted in the towers and flanks; and more particularly the
handsome openwork parapet to the central section, with
the Clifford motto 'Desormais' ('Henceforth') (cf. Temple
Newsam House, after 1622) and a quotation adapted from
Horace in praise of 'George' running round below it – a reference to the celebrated third Earl of Cumberland who was
Henry Clifford's uncle. The parapet has frequently been attributed to Lady Anne Clifford, but it is intimately linked with
further elements in Henry Clifford's remodelling. The most
remarkable is the allegorical shell-work GROTTO inside on the
r., which is one of the earliest in the country (cf. the grotto at
Woburn Abbey made for his cousin the fourth Earl of Bedford
c. 1630): Clifford was known for his 'skill in architecture' and
there is a contemporary reference to his 'curious newe structures' at Skipton. The link between grotto and parapet is provided by a shell-work frieze in the room above the archway,
which also incorporates both the 'Desormais' motto in large
letters similar to those in the parapet and Clifford's initials.
Further alterations to the gatehouse were made in the late C17
for the sixth Earl of Thanet, including the small bullseye
window with four keyblocks above the coat of arms at the
front, the blind windows on the flanks of the central section,
with keystones and segmental pediments, and a torus-moulded
chimneypiece inside. Of the outer bailey CURTAIN WALL little
survives. To the r. a later garden wall running along its line and
the stump of one C14 semicircular tower with plinth mouldings like those on the gatehouse. To the l. a domestic range,
probably C17, with some early C19 details.

Emerging from the gateway one sees the main inner buildings straight ahead. Heavy battered plinths to towers and
curtain. In the 1648 slighting much of their perimeter was
reduced in height, and Lady Anne Clifford's contributions
included the whole of the present top storey of the MUNIMENT
TOWER (SE) and the top two storeys of the WATCH TOWER
(S). Her work is characterized by two-light mullioned windows
with hoodmoulds, plain solid parapets and pitched (instead of
flat) roofs – so that they could not carry cannon. The INNER
GATEHOUSE to the l. has two smaller round towers, lacking
their top storey, and is preceded by a handsome two-storey
forebuilding which is probably of the time of the 'Shepherd
Lord', *c.* 1500. Mullioned windows with arched lights, including a canted oriel with a recessed panel designed for a coat of

27

40
see
p. 761

28

arms but now occupied by Lady Anne Clifford's commemorative inscription. Below it a richly moulded Tudor-arched doorway with little animal carvings in the spandrels. Within the gatehouse entrance passage a portcullis groove and then a succession of two segmental arches on semi-octagonal responds, the first with inserted C13 moulded capitals. On the inner face a taller segment-headed archway of two unmoulded orders.

The INNER BAILEY or CONDUIT COURT is small, irregular and extremely picturesque, with a yew tree in the centre growing out of the early C16 conduit basin. Its present appearance, with the same repertoire of detail as the forebuilding, is doubtless largely due to the 'Shepherd Lord'. Over a doorway on the S side the arms of his mother and his wife combined, rainwater heads of Lady Anne Clifford's time. The N range, running along the cliff edge, is presumably in essence of the C13 although much altered since, and contains the GREAT HALL on the upper floor, reached by an external staircase. Segment-headed entrance with a late C17 blind oval over. Moulded Tudor-arched doorway at the dais end, two at the service end under thin ogee hoodmoulds with fleur-de-lys finials, all probably c. 1500. Plain C17 segment-headed fireplace. W of it the KITCHEN with two big fireplaces, one incorporating ovens, and a simple C17 arched-brace roof. The E side of the court is formed by the APARTMENT RANGE added by the Shepherd Lord. Symmetrical façade with a pair of two-storey canted bays and a central doorway surmounted by another heraldic panel, containing the Clifford arms. The first-floor rooms have moulded Tudor-arched fireplaces: those below were in the C19 converted into a kitchen etc. serving the East Range. Inside the Watch and Muniment towers the joint

Skipton Castle, Inner Bailey.
Engraving by R. and E. Taylor, 1878

between the C13 masonry and Lady Anne Clifford's thinner walling above can be seen clearly. The Watch Tower and the s turret of the Gatehouse have fireplaces set in front of arrowslit embrasures. Beneath the Gatehouse entrance passage a space now vaulted but in origin probably a drawbridge pit.

Steps now need to be retraced to see the EAST RANGE of 1536–7, facing s onto the E part of the outer bailey. It was built in preparation for the marriage of the first Earl of Cumberland's son to Eleanor Brandon, the king's niece, and contained a long gallery – a notably early example – on the upper floor. The main accents are a pair of half-octagonal bay windows, and at the far end a big polygonal tower incorporating some masonry from its C15 predecessor. The bay windows retain their original openings to the ground floor, with uncusped arched lights, but to the first floor have a form with panel tracery in the heads, restored in 1970. At that level also some plain cross-windows of the sixth Earl of Thanet's time (rainwater head dated 1686). In the tower one earlier window with cusped ogee-headed lights. The interior much altered, the long gallery divided up in the C18; but some enriched C16 panelling has been reused. In the w part of the outer bailey is the early C14 former CHAPEL, with the remains of Geometrical tracery – a pattern of three encircled quatrefoils – in the windows, and a shouldered-arched doorway at an upper level on the s side which probably gave onto the wall-walk of the outer bailey curtain. On the N side the former sacristy, possibly two-storeyed, with two squints into the chapel, and inside the s wall the remains of sedilia and piscina with trefoiled heads. Behind the chapel the STABLES, mainly C19 in appearance but retaining some medieval and C17 details, and next to this the COACHHOUSE, c. 1800 with Gothic doorway framed in banded masonry.

PUBLIC BUILDINGS

TOWN HALL, High Street. 1861–2 by *John Denison Jee* of Liverpool. Restrained Neo-Palladian in fine ashlar, seven bays with a two-storey pedimented portico. Assembly room at the back heightened and redecorated in their Italianate manner by *Lockwood & Mawson*, 1878.

Former COUNTY COURT, Otley Street. 1847. Modest but dignified, a single storey with segment-headed windows and battered plinth.

MAGISTRATES' COURT, Otley Street. 1971–3 by *West Riding County Architect's Department* (County Architect *K. C. Evans*). Single-storeyed in coursed stone with a complicated arrangement of lead-covered pitched roofs.

PUBLIC LIBRARY, High Street, opposite the Town Hall. A Carnegie Trust foundation, 1910 by *Broughton & Hartley*. Mixed Renaissance, three storeys, tall and townish.

OLD GRAMMAR SCHOOL, Shortbank Road, E of the town centre. Founded 1548 and originally housed in a former chapel of the Knights Hospitallers. The main building, with two-storey porch, may in part represent this, but much rebuilt C17 and the detail mainly C19. New schoolroom at right angles to r. (now an electricity substation), 1841 probably by *R. D. Chantrell*. Plain Jacobean style with a stepped three-light window in the gable-end. Former headmaster's house, late C18, now the CROSS KEYS HOTEL, adjoining to l. Doorway with splayed surround, tripartite windows to each side and Venetian windows above.

GRAMMAR SCHOOL, Gargrave Road. Successor to the old school, 1875 by *Paley & Austin*. Sound and serious Jacobean, with one touch of fantasy in the tall chimneystack at the back with its campanile-style top stage. Additional buildings 1933 etc.

AIREVILLE SCHOOL, off Gargrave Road, on the W edge of the town. Built as a house, Aireville Hall, 1836 for Henry Alcock, one of the partners in the Craven Bank, perhaps by *George Webster*. Also Jacobean style, gently asymmetrical with gables, prominent chimneystacks and a big single-storey porch on the entrance front. Picturesque gabled LODGE by the Gargrave Road entrance, school buildings 1963 etc.

Former RAIKESWOOD HOSPITAL, Gargrave Road. The third in a sequence of public buildings with St Stephen's School (*see* St Stephen's Church, above) and the Grammar School. Built as a workhouse, 1839–40 by *Webster*, now housing. A stripped-down version of a classical country house. Three-storey main block with pedimented centre, and long lower flanking wings.

HEALTH CENTRE, High Street, N of the Town Hall. 1963, infill by *West Riding County Architect's Department* (County Architect *A. W. Glover*). _{dem.}

RAILWAY STATION, Broughton Road. 1875. One-storey dim Jacobean, with later extension.

PERAMBULATION

Centred on the HIGH STREET, starting at the N end by the early C18 GATEPIERS to the churchyard and the tall Beaux-Arts WAR MEMORIAL of 1921, in Portland stone with bronze sculpture by *John Cassidy*. The E side begins with No. 3, later C18 with a pair of canted bay windows and a pedimented doorcase with clustered Gothick half-columns. Beyond it to the NE, THE BAILEY has just the castle outer wall on one side – a pleasant leafy approach to the town centre – but off it on the r. is the OVERDALE COURT housing scheme, 1981 by the *Pearce Bottomley Partnership* for the Harewood Housing Society. Intimately grouped blocks in coursed stone with concrete dressings and pitched roofs. The corresponding street to the NW is MILL BRIDGE, with on the r. LIMESTONE HOUSE, distinguished by its building material, early C19 with the ground-floor windows in segment-headed recesses. Then the bridge itself over the Eller Beck and the SPRINGS CANAL, a feeder to the Leeds and Liverpool, where they emerge from the picturesque wooded gorge behind the castle. On the r. here HIGH CORN MILL, a nondescript jumble of C19–C20 building but the site of a mill since medieval times. Behind it at a higher level the former Methodist Chapel (*see* Churches, above) is visible.

Moving s down the HIGH STREET itself, on the w side, first the BLACK HORSE HOTEL, much altered 1818 and later but retaining a datestone of 1676; then in front of the Library (*see* Public Buildings, above) the STATUE of Sir Mathew Wilson, first M.P. for the Skipton division, 1888 by *A. Bruce Joy*; then No. 38, C18 with giant pilasters framing the two upper storeys. On the E side, beyond the Town Hall (*see* Public Buildings, above), the RED LION HOTEL, where a plain C19 front hides the ghost of a late medieval timber-framed hall house to which a storeyed front range was added probably in the C17. Inside, a fragment of the front wall of the medieval housebody and next to it an inserted C17 stone fireplace and chimney-breast, backing onto the cross-passage. On the other side of the passage there was formerly a trio of ogee-headed timber doorways leading into the service end. Then No. 35 with two C18 tripartite windows to the first floor linked by a blind round-headed arch to make a species of super-Serliana. After that OTLEY STREET runs E. On the N side terraces of the 1840s and 1850s, still Georgian in character. On the s the entrance to the CRAVEN COURT shopping arcade, 1987, egregious mock-Victorian nonsense.

In the lower part of the street an island block intervenes, with Sheep Street behind it to the w. On the E side a group of Victorian commercial buildings, first BARCLAYS BANK, built as the Craven Bank in 1849. Giant Ionic pilasters above a banded ground floor but asymmetrical, of four-plus-two bays, and evidently lacking another section to the l. Then the HSBC, a more florid Italianate of 1888, and HIGH STREET HOUSE, 1895 with an iron-crested pavilion roof over the centre. In the island block the OLD TOWN HALL or TOL-BOOTH, of 1789. Blocked round-headed arcading below, and to the first floor pilasters with odd fluted capitals, quoins, and a frieze with fluting and paterae. On the Sheep Street side, external steps to the pedimented first-floor doorway, which has a similarly detailed frieze. The w side of SHEEP STREET has plain late C18–early C19 frontages, above the shopfronts, but No. 6 retains another Gothick pedimented doorcase. Through an archway here are CRAVEN TERRACE, the best of the surviving 'yards', *c.* 1850 and again still Georgian in character, and VICTORIA SQUARE, 1986 by *Wales, Wales & Rawson*. Low-key stone-built Neo-vernacular with occasional Tuscan touches.

From the s end of the High Street three streets diverge. E is NEWMARKET STREET, with on the r. the DEVONSHIRE HOTEL, the best C18 building in the town, erected in 1728–30 for *Lord Burlington* (*see* Bolton Abbey) and presumably after a design by him. Five-bay front with a three-bay pedimented centre, under a low-pitched pyramidal roof. These, and the neat square plan, all hint at a Palladian inspiration – the roof form recently used by Lord Herbert at Marble Hill – but the proportions, with two equal main storeys below the attic, are rather unPalladian and some of the detailing is rather coarse, with rusticated quoins and plain raised window surrounds. Later two-storey wing to r., interior much altered. The original purpose of the house is not clear. After Lord Burlington's death it was let as tenements and it had become an hotel by 1790. Opposite is a little early C19 formal terrace, rather cut about, with a five-storey office block (1973) looming incongruously behind – the one serious infringement of the scale of the town centre; and then an early C19 house with a handsome ashlar front. Entrance with Ionic columns *in antis*, segmental relieving arches over this and the ground-floor windows.

s is KEIGHLEY ROAD, with just the CRAVEN HALL, 1897, built as the Liberal Club. Tall and prominent in Free Renaissance style, with Sparrowe's Mansion windows. Not much either now in SWADFORD STREET to the w, apart from the COCK AND BOTTLE INN. C17 front with mullioned attic windows with arched middle lights but otherwise remodelled in the C19. After this on the r., in COACH STREET, a group of CANAL WAREHOUSES, now converted to shops etc., forms a little square; and then Swadford Street is continued by BROUGHTON ROAD, which leads to the town's two best industrial buildings, beside the Leeds and Liverpool Canal. First, off to the r., VICTORIA MILL, 1847, built as a corn mill, converted into flats 1990. Big rectangular block of ten-by-seven bays, with twin gables and two sets of taking-in doors to front and back. Octagonal chimney. Then BELLE VUE MILLS, founded 1829 by John Dewhurst as a steam-powered factory first used for worsted spinning and weaving, rebuilt 1831 as a cotton-spinning mill, and the present complex built in stages mainly between 1852 and 1870 by *Wren & Hopkinson* of Manchester. Series of fireproof multi-storey ranges with the usual spare Italianate detail, iron-crested water tower on the main block (1870). Dyehouse of *c.* 1900, in the s side of the road, and tall chimney, 1901–2 by *Stott & Sons* of Manchester – of brick, unusually for the area – both demolished. see p. 761

SLAIDBURN

7050

Very attractive compact village in the wooded Hodder valley, its streets forming a T-shape with the church at the foot of the upright, to the s.

St Andrew. All Perp apart from one two-light Dec window on the s side. w tower with angle buttresses with many set-offs, and rectangular NE stair turret. w doorway and window, and above these two canopied image niches one above the other. Nave and chancel in one, with clerestory, aisles and chancel chapels, all rendered. Straight-headed windows with arched and cusped lights. N doorway probably C18, E wall rebuilt 1866. Arcades of octagonal piers and double-chamfered arches, of five bays to N and six bays to s. Roof with arch-braced collars and cusped wind-braces between the rafters and the purlins. – CHANCEL SCREEN. A specially fine mid-C17 piece, similar to the screens at St John, Leeds (q.v.), and Wakefield Cathedral (West Riding South), of 1634–5. Tapering square uprights and openwork spandrels and frieze, but no obelisks or strapwork superstructure. – PARCLOSE SCREENS. Of two styles. Those flanking the chancel are straightforwardly Perp with a little thin panel tracery, but one at the entrance to the s chapel has incipient Renaissance decoration to the top rail. – PULPIT. Uncommonly handsome C18 three-decker, with raised and fielded panels to all three stages, stair with slim turned balusters, and sounding-board with carved entablature. – PEWS. Big C18 box pews immediately E and W of the chancel screen – i.e., an undisturbed Georgian arrangement – and in the N and s aisles nearby. Others throughout the rest of the church, some with slightly enriched ends, dated 1616, 1676, 1749 etc. – FONT COVER. Stumpy hexagonal spirelet. Probably late C16 (cf. Great Mitton). – ROYAL ARMS, painted, 1738. – Brass CANDELABRA in the nave, C18. – STAINED GLASS. E window, a large Adoration of the Magi, 1869. – MONUMENTS. A uniform set of early C19 tablets to members of the Wigglesworth family, one signed *Walsh & Dunbar* of Leeds. – Another to members of the Wilkinson family, Gothic by *F. Webster* of Kendal.

GRAMMAR SCHOOL, N of the church. Now primary school. Founded 1717 by John Brennand, gent. A handsome building, orderly and substantial. Symmetrical two-storey front of seven bays, with cross-windows in flattish architrave surrounds, doorway with open segmental pediment on fluted Doric pilasters, and rusticated quoins. Interior gutted *c.* 1880 and now a single large space. Short one-storey wing at the back.

In the village little needs to be singled out. It is of unusually uniform character, largely consisting of sash-windowed early C19 cottages facing onto cobbled frontages. At the junction of the streets the HARK TO BOUNTY INN, mainly early C19 in appearance but incorporating some C17 fabric, including three Tudor-arched doorways in the r. part of the front. Large first-floor room, used for meetings of the court of the Forest of Bowland after the Moot Hall was demolished *c.* 1870, with a panelled partition at one end tenoned into a tie-beam. Opposite, WATERLOO BUILDINGS, 1843, simple Jacobean with mullioned windows under hoodmoulds and sharply pointed gablets. At another junction further E the WAR MEMORIAL, unveiled 1923. Octagonal pier crowned by a cast figure of a soldier, a repeat of that at Clitheroe (Lancashire) by *L. F. Roslyn*. Opposite this the former GIRLS' SCHOOL, Gothic, 1873, on the site of the Moot Hall.

TOWNHEAD. The big house of Slaidburn, N of the village, built by the Wigglesworth family. A double-pile block of two-and-a-half storeys with a five-bay front facing S, apparently of the mid C18 but not quite what it seems. A sketch of 'Townhead . . . from the South' of *c.* 1720 shows a larger building, then probably quite new – and unusually up-to-date for the area – of two storeys with a five-bay centre and short hipped-roofed cross-wings. Could the present house be a reduction of this, shorn of the cross-wings but with the top storey added? That could explain some odd disjunctions between exterior and interior, but the position is further confused by alterations of the mid C19 in imitation mid-C18 style.

The exterior is quite plain. Heavy moulded eaves cornice to S and E, bracketed eaves to N and W. Quoins. S doorway with pilasters supporting a Doric entablature and pediment, but unexpectedly leading into the staircase compartment, under the half-landing, not the entrance hall. E flank, facing down the drive, of five narrower bays, also with a central doorway; but this is a fake, backing onto the spine wall of the house. (It appears to have been moved from elsewhere, and to have replaced an equally functionless window, doubtless in the mid C19 when the windows flanking it were also altered.) The actual entrance is in the unprepossessing N front, through a C19 porch with a pastiche of a late C17 shell-hood. C19 service wing with battlemented parapet to the W. The main feature is the staircase hall, with an elaborate Palladian decorative scheme of enriched wall panels, pedimented doorcases, bold bracketed cornices and compartmented ceiling, but unPalladian in its proportions, a confined space rising the full height of the house. The staircase, up to the first floor only, is slightly altered, with a C19 balustrade. Fittings of similar character in several other rooms, evidently a mixture of the real thing and quite skilful pastiche.

ELLERBECK, ¾ m. WNW. 1694. Two storeys and attic, with big full-height porch-cum-wing at the front. Off-centre doorway with ornamented lintel, mullioned windows.

HAMMERTON HALL, 1 m. NNE. Impressive symmetrical E-plan house, probably built in the early C17 for the Breres family. Gabled ashlar porch of three storeys – the rest of two storeys and attic – with a moulded Tudor-arched doorway, and jettied first floor with a mullion-and-transom window (largely blocked) running continuously round all three sides. To the top stage, and to the gables of the cross-wings, three-light windows with truncated-ogee heads (cf. Friars Head, Winterburn). Other front windows all originally of six lights, some altered. The interior has been subdivided and the original arrangements are not all clear. In the l. wing, a massive kitchen-type segment-headed fireplace – so that was presumably the service end – and on the l. of the axis of the front door a timber-framed partition with a (blocked) flattened-ogee-headed doorway. Also a stone spiral staircase in the service wing, a Tudor-arched stone doorway and some *ex situ* C17 panelling. Roof trusses with collars carrying short king-posts and curved wind-braces.

HARROP HALL, 1⅝ m. ESE. Main range C17, with altered mullioned windows. Doorway dated 1719, with ornamented lintel very similar to one of 1716 at Bolton-by-Bowland (q.v.); and to the r. a cross-wing presumably also of 1719, with cross-windows and banded pilaster strips at the corners. Staircase in line with the front door and lit by a cross-window at the back, with turned balusters and moulded newels crowned by ball finials. Gatepiers with ball finials.

SOUTH STAINLEY

ST WILFRID. 1845 by *A. H. Cates* of York, replacing a chapel of medieval origin. E.E., in Magnesian limestone. Nave and chancel. Charming octagonal bellcote on the w gable, with shouldered-arched openings on the diagonals, corbelled out from a w buttress. Tall very sharply pointed chancel arch. Pulpit reached from the vestry by a doorway set diagonally in the corner behind it. (cf. Markington). – ARCHITECTURAL FRAGMENT in the churchyard. A Gothic capital, now serving as a sundial, presumably from the old chapel.

MANOR FARM. The lower part is a small timber-framed house, of two bays with a rear aisle, probably C16, cased in gritstone in the C17. The posts, wall-plate, arcade-plate, tie-beams and common rafter roof all remain. At one end a later fireplace with bressumer beam and firehood, outside the timber frame itself and now within the mid-C19 E block. Behind that a semi-subterranean vaulted dairy.

CAYTON HALL, ½ m. w. Pretty front range of c. 1770 for John Messenger, of Magnesian limestone with gritstone dressings. Three bays, with Venetian windows to the ground floor and pedimented Tuscan doorcase. Earlier gritstone back range at right angles, altered C18 and C19. Tall service stair window at the far end. One front room with decoration of c. 1770, spacious staircase with Venetian window. In the back range an upstairs room with wall painting of drapery which was probably the backdrop to an altar – the Messengers were Roman Catholics. Behind the house the STABLES, a rough rustic building part dated 1726 and part 1750, with a room with similar painted decoration. ¾ m. w again the site of the DESERTED VILLAGE of High Cayton.

SPOFFORTH

Long rather suburbanized village near the E extremity of the grit-stone belt, the *caput* of the Percy family estates in the C12 and C13. A charter for a market was granted to William de Percy in 1224.

ALL SAINTS. Quite large, with a tall Perp w tower. Diagonal but-tresses, and a very tall tower arch with three hollow chamfers. The body of the church – nave with aisles and clerestory, lower unaisled chancel – is externally all Neo-Norman, rebuilt 1854–5 by *J. W. Hugall* of Cheltenham (previously there were some Dec windows in the aisles, and the clerestory and chancel were Perp). But inside the genuine late Norman or Transitional nave arcades and chancel arch survive, as does the head of the s doorway, with a roll moulding and beakhead ornament. The arcades are of five bays, and give an impression of having been built from w to E. Cylindrical piers on the s side – apart from one octagonal Perp replacement – quatrefoil on the N; the capitals flat, with late C12 decoration, including waterleaf, on the s side only. Arches of two orders (many of them rebuilt) and entirely plain apart from the w two on the N side, both with a roll mould-ing on the soffit, one with single chevron ornament, the other with double. The w responds are hidden by the organ, but their counterparts to the E are tripartite with the middle shaft keeled. Chancel arch with similar responds and waterleaf capitals, and the arch itself slightly pointed, with two hollow chamfers deco-rated with pellets. – SCULPTURE. Fragment of an Anglo-Saxon cross-shaft with close interlace decoration. C10. – MONU-MENTS. Damaged effigy of a cross-legged knight, in a (restored) cusped recess in the chancel N wall, said to be Sir Robert de Plumpton III †1323. – A group of wall tablets to members of the Middleton family of Stockeld Park, including John Middleton †1700. Finely carved cartouche in white marble.

OLD RECTORY, w of the church. From the front the house looks wholly Georgian, of two-plus-three-plus-two not quite uniform bays; but at the back of the l. part is a blocked two-light first-floor window of *c.* 1300 with a quatrefoil in plate tracery in the head (cf. Markenfield Hall), and the entrance to the grounds is a rebuilt medieval two-centred archway which was uncovered in a stable in 1928. A fine C18 staircase inside, with ornate balusters and fluted newels.

MASSEY GARTH/CHANTRY HOUSE, s of the church. Of plain early C19 appearance, but the central of the three short paral-lel ranges which form the r. part is again much earlier, a small building of *c.* 1200. In its front wall a round-headed doorway with two bell capitals remaining on the l. side (the shafts below missing), and opposite in the rear wall another simpler doorway.

SPOFFORTH CASTLE. Ruin of an important and architecturally distinguished fortified house rather than a castle, the residence of the Percy family. Licence to crenellate was granted to Henry de Percy in 1308: before that the house was presumably unfortified. The existing building is essentially a single range of two storeys, 140 ft (42.5 metres) long and 60 ft (18 metres) wide, and was the body of the house, with the great hall and other principal rooms on the upper floor; but it is built against a W-facing rock outcrop, so that on the E side there is direct access into the upper level, and on that side there was doubtless a courtyard with ancillary buildings. Three main periods are identifiable. The undercroft of the great hall, which occupied the S two-thirds of the range, is of the early C13; then in the early C14 the block containing the solar was added to the N, the hall undercroft vaulted and the hall itself probably rebuilt, at least in part; and in the C15 the hall was rebuilt again.

The regular two-storey W elevation is the most impressive, and particularly the solar block at the N end. Polygonal stair-turret with a spirelet at the NW corner, and to the upper floor remains of extremely fine two-light windows with Geometrical tracery. Below are a doorway and a one-light window with a pointed-trefoiled head, both later alterations. The solar itself was on the N side of the block, with a smaller room, perhaps originally a chapel, between it and the hall, and a subsidiary chamber, with a garderobe, in a rectangular projection at the NE corner. The ground-floor rooms were vaulted: that below the solar has a fireplace with a pointed arch and a window with a similarly shaped rere-arch beside it. The hall undercroft has small straight-headed windows, four in the W wall and one at each end – that to N now facing into the solar block – and N and S doorways. The C14 ribbed vault was supported on a row of octagonal piers dividing the space into two aisles, and on corbels on the walls and the outcrop. The entrance to the hall from the courtyard was in the second of the four bays on the E side. The plain later doorway next to it in the first bay probably led to the buttery and kitchen. The tracery of the large hall windows is also best seen on the E side. They were of two lights, with cusped heads.

MANOR HOUSE, opposite the castle. Modest lobby-entry double pile of c. 1700. Five-bay front with quoins. Presumably there were cross-windows – the present ones are C20. Two-light mullioned window in the S gable-end, pantile roof. (C18 staircase with turned balusters of two different designs.)

See also Stockeld Park.

STAINBURN

ST MARY. Small Norman church, built as a chapel of ease of Kirkby Overblow, alone on a quiet hillside. Nave and lower chancel, with a C17 bellcote at their junction. Small slit-like windows, one at the W end, two on the S side of the nave, one on the chancel N side. S doorway with plain tympanum, chancel arch of two unchamfered orders with the plainest of imposts. Perp E window in rebuilt E end, S porch probably also C15. Various windows of the C17, including one with an odd triangular head, and at the SW corner a cross-window which once lit a W gallery. Limited restoration, including a new roof to the chancel, 1894 by *C. Hodgson Fowler*. – FONT. Norman, cylindrical with intersected arcading and ornament including two crude heads in the spandrels. Cover probably C17. – PEWS. Mainly with plain ends with a roll moulding on the top, probably C16. Three with turned finials, C17.

STAINFORTH

ST PETER. 1839–41 by *Edmund Sharpe* of Lancaster. A daughter church of Giggleswick, built on the initiative of the Dawson sisters of Settle and of Hornby Castle, Lancashire (where Sharpe & Paley worked a few years later). Simple Perp. W tower with stepped battlements, wide unaisled nave and narrower one-bay chancel. – STAINED GLASS includes E window, 1842, and nave SE, 1873 by *Powell & Sons*.

Noteworthy doorheads include those at KERN KNOTTS and RISTON HOUSE, both 1684 and near the small triangular green on the other side of the beck – the latter (re-set) with pointed recesses (cf. The Folly, Settle) – and at BURNSIDE FARM, 1697, recalling C17 designs for decorative panelling. STAINFORTH HOUSE, opposite the church, has a late C19 billiards room, top-lit by an elaborate lantern. p. 31

TAITLANDS, ³/₈ m. S, now Youth Hostel. *c.* 1840, a smaller Ionic version of Anley House, Settle (q.v.). Three-bay entrance front with columned porch backing onto a slightly projecting central bay with banded masonry. Panelled angle pilasters. Short service wing to N.

KNIGHT STAINFORTH HALL, ½ m. W. *c.* 1700 for Christopher Weatherhead, previously builder of Lodge Hall, Horton-in-Ribblesdale (q.v.). A sundial over the front doorway, dated 1724, provides a *terminus ante quem*. The house has none of the eccentricity of Weatherhead's earlier project. L-shaped, the main range with a continuous rear outshut, and two-and-a-half storeys. Symmetrical seven-bay front with cross-windows, low two-light mullioned windows to the attic except in bays three and five. W flank with two gables and several one-light transomed windows. Re-set arched doorways on return of rear wing and in cellar. The front doorway leads into the centre of the hall. Torus-moulded fireplace in one first-floor room.

PACKHORSE BRIDGE, over the River Ribble between the village and Knight Stainforth. Probably *c.* 1700. Single span, entirely plain.

STANBURY

Haworth, Cross Roads and Stanbury

A narrow street along a ridge.

ST GABRIEL. Chapel of ease built in 1848 at the instigation of the Rev. Patrick Brontë, a tiny Tudor-style box. – PULPIT. The top stage of the three-decker pulpit discarded at the rebuilding of Haworth church (q.v.), installed here in 1910.

At the W end of the village the former SCHOOL, 1805, one storey with (restored) Venetian windows. At the E end the MANOR HOUSE, 1753, a modest farmhouse nicely illustrating regional mores. The façade is symmetrical, with a pilastered and pedimented doorcase, and a round-headed panel above it containing the datestone; but the windows are mullioned, of four lights with unchamfered mullions, like the windows of contemporary weavers' cottages (cf. Lees Farm, Cross Roads with Lees).

LOWER LAITHE RESERVOIR, S of the village. 1914–25 for Keighley Corporation, *M. Ratcliffe Barnett*, engineer. E of the dam, the SLADEN VALLEY TREATMENT WORKS, 1992 by the *Robinson Partnership* for Yorkshire Water. Remembering stone-built farm buildings but not pastiche.

PONDEN MILL, ⅝ m. W. Early cotton-spinning mill on the River Worth, 1791–2 for Robert Heaton of Ponden Hall. Repaired after a fire in 1795, converted to worsted spinning and steam power added *c.* 1850. Three storeys and nine bays, with staircase and counting house in the W bay and attached wheelhouse (altered) to the E. Later engine houses beyond that and short cylindrical chimney behind.

PONDEN HALL, ½ m. further W, in a fine position overlooking another reservoir (1872–6). Hearth-passage house of two main periods, the housebody and the parlour end C17, with mullion-and-transom windows to the ground floor, the passage and the service end rebuilt – according to an otherwise confusing inscription which also refers to another building – in 1801. Pedimented doorcase with Tuscan pilasters, round-headed inscription panel above (cf. Stanbury Manor House) and more mullioned windows but now with the mullions unchamfered. Tudor-arched fireplace in the room over the parlour. Front garden wall punctuated by piers with ogee finials.

STAVELEY

ALL SAINTS. Built 1864 under the supervision of *John Lowe* of Manchester. But the design had been made *c.* 1840: hence its pre-Ecclesiological character – W tower with broach spire, broad nave, short chancel, lancet windows. It replaced a church of 1831 by *Peter Atkinson*, which in turn had replaced the ancient one. – SCULPTURE. Anglo-Saxon cross-shaft with a stylized scroll on the front, and very faint on the r. side two small figures, the upper blowing a horn, the lower, bearded and helmeted, holding a spear. Above the first a bird, beside the other a large dog (or wolf?). Probably C10. – STAINED GLASS. E window by *Capronnier*, 1875; several in the nave by *R. B. Edmundson* and *Ward & Hughes*, 1864.

STAVELEY MILL, ¼ m. w. Probably early C19, built as a water-powered flax mill, later a corn mill. Three storeys, six bays, the ground floor of stone, the upper two of brick. Now housing.

STEETON

ST STEPHEN. 1880–1 by *T. H. & F. Healey*. C13 Gothic, unaisled, with tall unbuttressed SE tower and broach spire. – PAINTED DECORATION to the roof, designed by the architects and executed by *J. Hindle* of Steeton, 1884. – STAINED GLASS. E window by *Powell Bros.* of Leeds, 1881, in memory of the Rev. Herbert Todd, Vicar of Kildwick (†1880), on whose initiative the church was built, and containing a portrait of him. – W window by *Clayton & Bell*, 1913. – S of the church, the SUNDAY SCHOOL, 1896, presumably also by *T. H. & F. Healey*. Gothic, one storey.

AIREDALE GENERAL HOSPITAL. 1966–71 by *Booth, Hancock, Johnson & Partners* (project architects *R. K. Maxfield* and *N. Bentham*) for Leeds Regional Hospital Board. No-nonsense value-for-money 650-bed hospital on the 'best buy' low-rise principle. One and two storeys. Pre-cast concrete wall panels, and concrete slab floors and roofs. Spinal corridor plan, with the wards and departments opening off to each side, the wards cross-shaped and facing onto a mixture of closed and open courtyards. Much subsequent expansion, as provided for in the brief, including a new OPERATING THEATRE BLOCK on the S side, 1995–6 by the *Richard Eaves Partnership*, in a starkly contrasted manner, brick-built with pitched roof.

STEETON MANOR (formerly CURRERWOOD). Delectable Arts and Crafts Pennine-style house up on the hillside above the hospital, 1895 by *W. H. Sugden* of Keighley for worsted manufacturer Sir Swire Smith. Tall and gabled, with battlemented two-storey porch and massive projecting chimney-breast. (Elaborate plaster ceilings.)

In the village, Nos. 44 and 46 SCHOOL STREET, 1710. Small double pile with off-centre lobby entry. Former cross-windows, in one bay to the l. of the doorway and two to the r. Architrave surrounds, quoins. Chimney decorated with shallow blind arcading (cf. Micklethwaite Grange, Bingley, and Stone Gappe, Lothersdale, etc.). Remarkable wide roof truss with octagonal stop-chamfered kingpost and six chamfered curved struts. The chimney design is repeated at a house in the HIGH STREET nearby, also dated 1710.

VICTORIA TOWER. Prominent on the valley side SE of the village. 1887, built by H.I. Butterfield of Cliffe Castle, Keighley (q.v.), to commemorate Queen Victoria's Jubilee. Square, 70 ft (21 metres) high, with battered ground-floor stage and heavy crenellated top hamper.

3040

STOCKELD PARK
Spofforth with Stockeld

By *James Paine*, 1758–63 for William Middleton, and one of his finest works, its quality still evident in spite of C19 alterations and additions. Of an eminently original and dramatic appearance – the distillation of what Robert Adam called 'movement' – but its sources, as a creative reworking of the idea of the Palladian villa, all belong to an established Anglo-Palladian repertoire. The original entrance front is to the S, away from the present approach. Striking triple-pedimented outline derived in particular from the wings at Holkham Hall, with a three-bay centre of two-and-a-half storeys and lower flanking sections of a single broad bay. The ground floor, containing the main rooms, is rusticated. The side parts have canted bay windows at this level; and above them great deep relieving arches rising through the open bases of the pediments, a juxtaposition developed from the flanking sections of Lord Burlington's original front at the York Assembly Rooms. The back was plainer but taller, as a result of the fall of the ground, with an exposed basement, rockily rusticated. Gibbs surrounds

Stockeld Park, south front.
Engraving after James Paine, 1767

to the windows of the main floor above. Paine's design included a pair of flanking service pavilions on this side, linked to the house by basement-level corridors, but Middleton died in 1763 and his successors merely retained the offices of the previous house, on the E flank, instead. That remained the state of affairs until the alterations of 1892–6, by *T. H. & F. Healey* for R. J. Foster, proprietor of the Black Dyke Mills at Queensbury. A new service wing was built on the E side, replacing the old one, and a new entrance, with a portico, made to the N. The architectural vocabulary is more or less Paine's but the spirit of the composition decidedly is not, both wing and portico rather too presumptuous.

Inside, the main feature is the spectacular staircase hall in   62
the middle of the house, apsidal-ended with the cantilevered staircase rising vertiginously right to the attic, its plain bow-fronted iron balustrade creating a rippling motion throughout the whole height of the space. Oval glazed dome but little other decoration. In the apses pairs of big niches each containing two doorways, with curved doors. Dining room in the SE corner also apsidal-ended, with marble chimneypiece, but the rooms on the W and N sides altered in the 1890s. The original chapel (R.C.), which was two-storeyed, taking in the basement, was floored over to form a library in the upper half, with the columnar screen of its gallery retained. Adjoining drawing room with Adam-style ceiling by *Waring & Gillow*, new entrance hall, behind the N portico, formed from two smaller rooms.

In the garden W of the house a small SUMMERHOUSE, presumably by *Paine*, a miniature of the Palladian church-front formula with a pediment flanked by lower half-pediments. The present (Anglican) CHAPEL, 1895 by *T. H. & F. Healey*, is NE of the house, cut into an earlier C19 range of outbuildings. Pedimented one-bay front with engaged columns and pilasters. Transepts added 1907–9 by *Detmar Blow*. – STAINED GLASS by *Victor Milner*, 1909. – 1 m. E, beside the road, the WETHERBY LODGE, C18, a pair of pyramid-roofed pavilions linked by an arch. Vermiculated quoins.

STOCKS
Easington

The hamlet was destroyed by the formation of the Stocks Reservoir in 1925–6.

ST JAMES. 1851–2, dismantled 1925 and rebuilt in a much reduced form on higher ground above the level of the reservoir in 1938. E.E. style with steeply pitched roof but no more than a little three-bay box. The original had a chancel and aisles.

A few isolated farmhouses of interest.

HIGHER STONY BANK, 1 m. SSE, on the road to Slaidburn. Exotically detailed specimen of *c.* 1700. Central two-storey porch with an ornamented lintel to the doorway, under a hood-mould with decorated stops, jettied upper stage with an ogee-headed window, and a lean-to roof. Mullion-and-transom ground-floor windows to each side, with some of the lights arched and again with fancy stops to the hoodmoulds, and an ornamented upright oval window to the first floor. Continuous outshut at the rear, barn adjoining to l., probably added later.

STEPHEN PARK, ⅝ m. ENE. Small double pile with gabled two-storey porch dated 1700. Simple ornamented doorhead.

HIGH HALSTEAD, 2⅜ m. N. 1687. Small house with exotic decoration to what is now the front gable-end, but which was probably the off-centre porch of a larger building, the rest of which, to the l., has been replaced by another house. Doorway (now a window) with ornamented lintel similar to that of The Folly at Settle (q.v.), and above it a stringcourse with gadrooned ornament and crude little masks. On the r. flank a segment-headed one-light window to the ground floor and one with a shouldered head above.

STUDLEY ROGER

2070

Cluster of houses at the East Gate to Studley Royal.

LAURENCE HOUSE/DOWNING HOUSE (originally one). *c.* 1800, brick. The broad end bays pedimented, with lunettes in the pediments, canted bay windows below. Pedimented doorcase to the three-bay centre section.

PLUMPTON HALL, ¼ m. S. C17, altered, of stone. L-shaped, with Tudor-arched doorway under an ornamented lintel in the E–W range, stepped three-light windows in the gable-ends of the N–S range, the lights round-headed. (Late C18 staircase with turned balusters.)

STUDLEY ROYAL

2060

Lindrick with Studley Royal and Fountains

At Studley Royal two sharply contrasted entities are juxtaposed: the famous ornamental grounds created by John Aislabie in the early C18 and further developed by his son William, and prominent within them the church of the 1870s, built for the first Marquess and Marchioness of Ripon. Studley Royal House, also mainly C18, was gutted by fire in 1946 and subsequently demolished. Aislabie senior (†1742), M.P. for Ripon from 1695, had pursued a political career which had brought him various lucrative positions and culminated in his appointment as Chancellor of the Exchequer in 1718; but he then became implicated in the scandal of the South Sea Bubble, and in 1721 he was expelled from Parliament and retired to his estates. Work on the grounds – and possibly also the reconstruction of the house – had already been started by then, and continued until *c.* 1735; but it was William Aislabie who in 1768 added to the layout the long-coveted ruins of Fountains Abbey (q.v.). The future Marquess of Ripon succeeded to the estate in 1859.

ST MARY. Memorably located at the head of the main avenue 88 in the park. 1871–8 by *William Burges*, and in Pevsner's estimation his 'ecclesiastical masterpiece'. It is said to have cost £50,000. The style is characteristically eclectic – C13 English Gothic, earlier French Gothic, and a smattering of medieval Italian details – and the result characteristically individual. But the configuration is formal and orthodox, an obvious response to the formality of the site: for Studley's sister church at Skelton (q.v.), built for the Marchioness's mother, Burges adopted a more picturesque, irregular form. W tower with spire rising from an octagonal belfry stage framed by octagonal spirelets. Bell-openings with gablets running up onto the spire, two tiers of lucarnes. W window of four lights incorporating a rose and Geometrical tracery, tremendously squat trefoil-headed W doorway, under a lean-to porch carried on a segmental arch. Nave with aisles and clerestory. Simple paired cinquefoil-headed lancets of *c.* 1300. At the chancel the pitch goes up. Paired two-light windows with Geometrical tracery and Gallic crocketed gablets. Then the E end, the climax of the design facing down the avenue. Big four-light window similar to that at the W end, with typically overscaled mouldings, and perched precariously above it a trio of gableted tabernacles containing SCULPTURE* – all here executed by *Thomas Nicholls* – their finials rising above the line of the main gable. 'Crazy' was Pevsner's epithet: but everything is precisely calculated as to its visual impact.

The interior is even more effective, a dream of E.E. glory. Nave arcades of four bays, the piers cylindrical with four Purbeck-type shafts as at Salisbury and the arches with dog-tooth decoration, but all quite restrained. Clerestory low with trefoil-headed rere-arches. Three-lobe roof, as at e.g. San Zeno, Verona. The chancel again more elaborate, and in part later stylistically, subdivided into a choir, with pointed wagon roof, and the astonishing centralized sanctuary, with a Gothic dome – derived, Professor Crook suggests, from the sacristy at Padua Cathedral. Double tracery to the windows, from the Angel Choir at Lincoln, and much use of marble wall-shafts, now of varied and progressively brighter colours – green, red and orange as well as black. On the S side a winged lion of

---

*A Crucifixion and groups of saints. N.B. also, in the S porch gable, the Annunciation.

Judah supporting a shaft, another Italianate feature, providing a projecting support for the inner zone of tracery above the sedilia recess. Walls below the windows lined with alabaster. Also painted and gilded DECORATION to the roof – blessed spirits, angels etc. – executed by *Fred Weekes* and *Campbell Smith & Co.*, and MOSAIC FLOORING – Jerusalem and the Garden of Eden – all illustrating the theme of Paradise Regained.

Of the FITTINGS by *Burges* the most prominent is the ORGAN CASE in the N nave arcade, dramatically top-heavy, with a little trefoil-section domelet – a Burges fingerprint, from Messina Cathedral – above the console. Probably some painted decoration was intended (cf. Skelton). Others are the CHOIR STALLS, with carved bench-ends and misericords; the FONT, 1874–5, of purple Tennessee marble, with high-relief panels in gilded bronze of the Ages of Man, executed by *Nicholls*; and the VESTRY DOOR, 1876, Burges's own gift to the church, with a brass relief of the Virgin and Child. – STAINED GLASS. An integrated scheme of excellent quality, the type of designs of which William Morris would have approved, executed by *Saunders & Co.* from sketches by *H. W. Lonsdale* and cartoons by *Weekes*. In the aisles a single tier of figures, in the chancel two – scenes from the Book of Revelation – complemented by further painted decoration on the window reveals. – MONUMENT. First Marquess and Marchioness of Ripon †1909 and 1907. White marble effigies on a tomb-chest of verde antico and cipollino. Arcaded screen of the same materials. Very precious.

Beside the avenue E of the church a picturesque estate COTTAGE – or rather a substantial house – also by *Burges*, 1873. Gables, dormers, mullion-and-transom windows and a big canted bay, partly timber-framed.

The GROUNDS fall into two clearly defined parts. To the S, some distance from the site of the house and always independent of it, lie the pleasure grounds proper, a composition of woodland, water and diverse strategically sited garden buildings which makes superbly effective use of its site – the 'Genius of the Place', as Pope put it – along the narrow, winding and steep-sided valley of the Skell downstream from the abbey. To the N is the spacious deerpark, centred on the mile-long lime avenue running uphill from E to W and aligned to the E on the towers of Ripon Cathedral two miles away. The house was towards its N boundary. The authorship of Aislabie's works presents some problems. His gardener was *William Fisher*, but he appears to have been an executant rather than a designer. It has been suggested that parts of the layout may reflect the influence of John James's translation of Dezallier d'Argenville's *Theory and Practice of Gardening* (1712), but there is no evidence that James was actually consulted. As to buildings, shortly before his death in 1729 *Colen Campbell* provided designs for the stables, with *Roger Morris* acting as his assistant, and it is possible that Morris continued to be employed into the 1730s; but prior to that only the names of the masons – *John Simpson, Robert Doe* and *Thomas Buck* – are recorded.

The best approach is from Studley Roger by the EAST GATE at the foot of the avenue, a handsome structure probably of *c.* 1730 with openings forming a squat Serliana. Much vermiculated rustication, ball finials on top. Single-storey lodges to l. and r., enlarged 1840. At the w end of the avenue beyond the church (*see* above) is the previous eyecatcher, a diagonally set OBELISK erected in 1804, which in turn replaced a pyramid put up by William Aislabie in 1742 in memory of his father. Apart from these elements the formality of the deerpark has been rather eroded in the later C18 and early C19. Over to the N, next to the site of the house, the former STABLES, which were themselves converted into a house after the 1946 fire. Built 1729–30, a monumental quadrangular design based on the C17 stables at Wilton which *Campbell* had illustrated in *Vitruvius Britannicus*. Seven-bay open arcade to the E front, with blocking to the piers, corner pavilions with similarly blocked quoins. *Campbell*'s principal modifications to the blueprint were the raising of the pavilions into low pyramid-roofed Palladian towers, the pedimented windows below these and the pedimented doorway on the s side: two of *Morris*'s drawings for the arcade he pronounced 'very ugly'. In 1755–6 the w elevation was rebuilt, with blind Diocletian windows, and part of the range behind made into a chapel (now the drawing room), a double cube with Rococo plasterwork by *Cortese* to the coved ceiling. Also a fine mid-C18 chimneypiece and plasterwork above it, brought from the old house in 1946. To the E the block faces down a second avenue, now fragmentary, aligned on Ripon Cathedral. To the NE, in a little dip, the ROUGH BRIDGE, probably later C18, which carried the drive from the house to the East Gate. Two arches of very rough masonry. NW of it the modest early C18 LINDRICK GATES.

s of the main avenue a small LAKE, approximately semicircular, at a point where the Skell valley opens out a little, marks the approach to the pleasure grounds. At its outflow, to the NE, a pair of SPHINXES, installed *c.* 1727. At its head, to the s, is the CASCADE, begun in 1719, beyond which, within the pleasure grounds, is the CANAL, a formalized stretch of the river which was 'just finished' in 1725. Flanking the cascade are a pair of rusticated piers crowned by balls and a pair of Palladian FISHING PAVILIONS, with pyramid roofs and Venetian windows, added in 1727. To the r. the former STEWARDS' HOUSE, of *c.* 1860, and then the fine wrought-iron pleasure-ground GATES of *c.* 1730, flanked by quadrant walls. Within, up on the w side of the valley is the BANQUETING HOUSE, probably the 'greenhouse' built *c.* 1727–30 and almost certainly by *Campbell*, given its similarity to his Ebberston Lodge (North Riding) and his known involvement at Studley. Three bays, with icicle-rusticated pilasters, and round-headed openings with mask keystones. Balustraded parapet crowned by urns, flanks also rusticated. Interior equally elaborate, with apses at

each end, excellent chimneypiece with swan-neck pedimented
overmantel, flanked by doorways in round-headed recesses,
and coved ceiling. Virtuoso undercut wood carving to the overmantel and flanking the apses, by *Richard Fisher* of York,
enriched plaster roundels over the doors, and high-quality
plasterwork to the ceiling and the apse semi-domes. The lawn
in front originally sunken and geometrical, later made more
naturalistic.

67   On the E side of the canal the valley is widened to form a
semicircular tree-backed 'theatre' – Pope's 'Genius of the Place'
again, 'That . . . scoops in circling Theatres the Vale' – occupied
by the circular MOON POND and two CRESCENT PONDS.
Hereabouts various lead STATUES, including Neptune in the
middle of the Moon Pond, probably supplied by *Andrew Carpenter*, *c.* 1730; and overlooking the Moon Pond the TEMPLE
OF PIETY, probably of the 1730s and perhaps by *Morris*. Hexastyle Roman Doric temple front with baseless columns. Morris
may have been responsible for two other mid-C18 examples of
this unusual version of the order, the Thompson Mausoleum
at Little Ouseburn (q.v.) and Mereworth church, Kent. The
source in this case was evidently a drawing by Palladio of the
Temple of Piety at Rome, which shows the central intercolum-
niation as wider than the others, as it is here. In the room
behind a plaster bas-relief roundel by *Cortese*, 1749. s from here,
at the head of the canal, another cascade and the RUSTIC
BRIDGE, in reality a culvert portal for a short stretch of the
river which runs underground, akin to Kent's for the cascade
at Rousham with three low arches in rough masonry. Nearby,
the so-called QUEBEC MONUMENT, a pier crowned by an urn,
and a stone STATUE of Hercules and Antaeus, both probably
c. 1730; and a little further on, at the limit of the estate until
1768, the HALF MOON POND, which served as a reservoir for
the water features of the pleasure grounds. Back again, and
from near the Temple of Piety a path leads up through the
woods on the E side of the valley – and a grotto-like TUNNEL
– to the OCTAGON TOWER perched above the lake, a building
of two different dates and styles: the Palladian lower stage, with
round-headed windows, probably of the mid 1730s, the Gothic
porch and upper parts, with pinnacles and pointed quatrefoils,
added *c.* 1742–3 for William Aislabie. From here a serpentine
high-level walk leads s, first to the TEMPLE OF FAME, a small
open rotunda of 1781 (a similar rotunda had previously stood
near to the Banqueting House), and then to the magnificent
SURPRISE VIEW, over the Half Moon Pond to the E end of
Fountains Abbey. The viewpoint is occupied – and made to
work as a surprise – by a little timber Gothic shelter, ANN
BOLEYN's SEAT, originally late C18 but reconstructed many
times since. When the view is reversed the seat, painted dark,
is virtually invisible, as it should be. From the seat the walk continued towards the abbey, over the rustic GALAND BRIDGE.

Finally, back in the deerpark, in the valley downstream from
the outflow at the NE end of the lake, the picturesque SEVEN

BRIDGES WALK, created by William Aislabie in the 1740s with a series of rustic one-arched bridges over the winding river, each accompanied by a paved ford for carriages. It led to a Chinese house 'now building' in 1745, and is overlooked from the top of a rocky outcrop by the DEVIL'S CHIMNEY, a small square block of heavy masonry said to have been based on the supposed monument of the Horatii and the Curiatii at Ariccia. Away to the s from here the ruinous MACKERSHAW GATE, similar to the East Gate. Lodges with Venetian windows.

SUTTON-IN-CRAVEN

Tightly-knit Pennine village centre on the s flank of Airedale. Much C19 and C20 expansion to E and N.

ST THOMAS. 1868–9 by *W. H. Crossland*. A daughter church of Kildwick, the bequest of Thomas Bairstow, a Sutton mill-owner. Broadly Dec, with w tower. Straight-headed two-light clerestory windows arranged in pairs, rose window with Flamboyant tracery to the organ chamber. – STAINED GLASS includes E window, 1870 by *Clayton & Bell*, w window 1878.

A few modest C17 and C18 houses in the old village, including one in WEST LANE dated 1639 inside. At the N end the dominant bulk of GREENROYD MILL, mid-C19 for worsted spinning. Three- and four-storey ranges at right angles, boiler house and cylindrical chimney. Beyond the s end was SUTTON HALL, built 1893–4 for the mill's proprietor, J. W. Hartley, by *Samuel Jackson* of Bradford, but all that remains is the sumptuous Neo-Jacobean entrance gateway with its attached flanking lodges. The gateway is battlemented, with octagonal turrets to each side, the lodges two-storeyed, with gables, dormers and bay windows.

SWILLINGTON

ST MARY. Perp w tower, refaced in gritstone ashlar 1884 by *C. R. Chorley* of Leeds, and low body of the church in pale Magnesian limestone: the gritstone has blackened, accentuating the contrast. The tower is of the local type with corbelled-out parapet (cf. Barwick-in-Elmet, Rothwell, etc.), but with some of the detail modified in the refacing. Of the rest, the nave walls are probably Norman: see the blocked window cut into by the N arcade. The aisles and chancel are Dec, a consistent scheme with buttresses and windows of two and three lights – extensively renewed in a restoration of *c.* 1860 – the larger ones with flowing tracery. Perp s porch with stone roof on chamfered transverse arches (cf. Methley); small two-light clerestory windows, plainly mullioned (also cf. Methley), possibly post-Reformation. Restored five-bay Dec arcades with octagonal piers and double-chamfered arches, restored ogee-arched Perp sedilia, and trefoil-headed piscina. Chancel roof 1902, utilitarian metal nave roof 1952. – ROYAL ARMS of George I, dated 1723 (repainted 1764). – STAINED GLASS. E window and s aisle E by *T. F. Curtis* of *Ward & Hughes*, 1901 and 1918. – MONUMENTS. In the s aisle an ogee-headed tomb-recess, and within it a glass case containing the remains of an oak effigy. Near it a medieval grave-slab, with cross. – William Dyneley †1607. Large limestone slab with long inscription in old-fashioned black-letter script. – Several C18 wall tablets, mainly to members of the Lowther family of Swillington House (*see* below), including the Rev. Richard †1702, an aedicule with putti on top, skulls and hourglass below; Sir William †1729 and his wife Amabell †1734, two matching Baroque cartouches; Amabell †1762, oval, with putto; and Sir William †1788, by *Fisher* of York, with urn. Also Harpham Green †1771, an unusual design with a scroll unrolled against the side of a Gothic tomb-chest and held in place by two books and an urn; and Susanna Lloyd †1797, by *Taylor* of York, also with urn.

SCHOOL, beside the churchyard. 1865, Gothic. Village mainly C20.

SWILLINGTON HOUSE, ¾ m. SSW, remodelled by *Henry Flitcroft c.* 1738 and enlarged 1803–4, was damaged by mining subsidence and demolished *c.* 1950. The mid-C19 STABLES survive, two ranges at right angles, one with a cupola, both with giant pilasters and segment-headed relieving arches between them. Also two LODGES along the main road, the N probably early C19, a one-and-a-half-storey hexagon with lower canted wings, the s mid-C19 Grecian with antae and pilasters.

LEVENTHORPE HALL, 1 m. WSW. 1774 by *Carr*: an inscription gives both date and architect. Two storeys, the front with a canted bay in the centre which embraced a circular entrance hall, and two bays l. and r.; the back with two canted bays and flat two-bay centre. Balustrading below the first-floor windows. Flanking service wings demolished, interior stripped. Former STABLES, dated 1856, with clock turret crowned by a cupola.

SWINDEN

SWINDEN HALL. Re-cut date 1657 over the front doorway. Chronologically it seems convincing. Three storeys. Short front range and a rear wing at right angles which has been extended to one side probably in the C19. Symmetrical front with full-height central gabled porch and a single bay of windows to each side, of three-plus-three lights to the ground floor, five to the first and three, stepped, to the second. Big chimney-breasts to the gable-ends. The rear wing extension links the house to a lower range with an ornamented door lintel. Interior much altered. In the rear wing, a big fireplace with moulded surround on the ground floor and a decorative plaster overmantel panel on the first.

SWINSTY HALL

1050

Timble

Important and impressive house mainly, it appears, of the early C17. It divides into two parts, very clearly differentiated, a tall main block to the r. and a much lower element, including the service accommodation, set back to the l. The former was probably built in the 1620s for Henry Robinson of Old Laund, Lancashire, who had acquired the property in 1590: his initials and the date 1627 appear in the glazing of two of the front windows. Two storeys and attic, with a projecting parlour wing to the r., over a basement accommodated by the fall of the ground, and a full-height porch to the l. There is no evidence that it was ever the intention to continue the same design further to the l. to make a more symmetrical composition with the porch in the centre. Three-centre-headed porch doorway, richly moulded, mullion-and-transom window above continued without a break onto the porch sides, three-light stepped window to the top storey. Hall window of three-plus-four-plus-three lights, with transom, occupying all the available space, and another of the same design to the great chamber above. More mullion-and-transom windows, and another stepped window, to the parlour end. Pyramid-capped finials to the gables. At the back, a broad gabled projection housing *inter alia* the staircase, with staggered two-light windows. The hall, entered directly from the porch, has a big segment-headed fireplace on the back wall, panelling dated 1639 moved from the floor above, and at the high end steps and a little raised platform, with vertically symmetrical balusters, giving access to the parlour. More C17 panelling in that room. Staircase of stone rising round a rectangular core. Very fine roofs to the hall range and the parlour wing, of three and two bays respectively, with arch-braced collar-beams carrying short kingposts, and two tiers of cusped wind-braces. But the attic floors at their present levels, only just below the bases of the trusses, are certainly also a part of the original design (cf. Great Mitton Hall).

The lower part is L-shaped, with one range running out at the back. This latter is the kitchen block and was originally detached – at its s end, in what is now the wall between the two ranges, is a window, facing s. It is presumably of much the same date as the main building or slightly later (cf. Kildwick Hall). At the NE corner is a two-storey porch with another stepped window to the upper floor. Very large kitchen fireplace, with oven. The front range, running E–W, is of *c.* 1700 – see the oculus under a cornice on the rear elevation – but it replaces a range on the same orientation set a little further forward, the roof-line of which is preserved on the adjoining W flank of the main building. This was presumably a part of the previous house on the site, which documentary evidence indicates had been built *c.* 1575.

RESERVOIR. *See* Fewston.

4040

TADCASTER

Tadcaster is a brewing town, and even if the 'unmistakable sweet and sickly smell' no longer 'seems to pervade it at all times of year, day and night', its townscape is dominated by the competing enterprises of John and Samuel Smith. But its earlier importance was as a crossing on the Wharfe for roads to York and as a quarrying centre – 'Calcaria', a place where limestone was extracted, was the name of a Roman settlement here. A castle was built in the late C11, the charter for a market was first granted in 1270 and it was a river port too, from where its celebrated creamy limestone was exported in the Middle Ages.* By the end of the C17 the town was a major coaching stop on the London–York road, with numerous inns along the main street. Brewing on a large scale began in the C19, exploiting the local lime-rich spring waters for making light bitter: three of the town's four breweries still operate.

ST MARY, Kirkgate. Mainly Perp, its medieval character maintained in spite of drastic reconstruction in 1875–7 when *Edward Birchall* of Leeds took down all but the big W tower and re-erected it on a 5-ft (1.5-metre)-high plinth, to safeguard it from floods. The tower has paired two-light transomed bell-openings, an image niche to the S side, battlements and pinnacles. The diagonal buttresses also end in pinnacles, and these stand detached from the body of the tower and a little lower than the others – a refinement unusual in the North. S aisle, S porch and clerestory also with pinnacles, and the clerestory embattled. The windows are straight-headed, except for the E and W, those to the S chapel a little more elaborate than the others, with some minimal panel tracery. The simpler N aisle and chapel were widened in 1897–8 by *Bromet & Thorman*; the aisle W window is theirs.

The interior reveals an earlier history. The corners of the nave are Norman, and a Norman arch with decorated capitals and an order of point-to-point zigzag is re-erected in the W wall of the S aisle (some other Norman fragments and a fragment

---

* The most famous quarry was at Thevesdale 1½ m. SW (now Jackdaw Crag Quarry) which supplied stone for York Minster.

of an Anglo-Saxon CROSS). Nave arcades of three bays, the N of *c.* 1300 with cylindrical piers, moulded capitals and double-chamfered arches, the S C14, with octagonal piers. Chancel and chapels all Perp, with two-bay arcades, the S with small fleurons on the responds, the capitals of the octagonal pier and the E arch, the N with arches dying into the imposts. – FONT. C15, simple. – Remarkable FITTINGS by *Bromet & Thorman* in their distinctive Art Nouveau Gothic (cf. Bramham). The carvers were *Ralph Hedley* of Newcastle upon Tyne, and later his sons. E wall PANELLING, 1906; W ORGAN SCREEN, of an almost Chinese delicacy, 1907; PULPIT, 1912; SCREENS to S chapel, 1915. – STAINED GLASS. In the S aisle W window some C15 fragments, including a roundel of St Catherine trampling the Emperor and a C16 roundel of foreign workmanship. – E window by *Morris & Co.*, 1877, fifteen fine large figures against a foliage background, and many small ones above. Two panels of angels with censers, in the top tier, designed by *Morris*, the rest by *Burne-Jones*. – N aisle NW by *Adam & Small* of Glasgow, 1879, in the Walter Crane style. N aisle, three windows by *W.H. Constable* of Cambridge, 1879. S chapel SE by *Powell & Sons*, 1887, entirely in imitation of the Flemish style of *c.* 1520.

METHODIST CHURCH, High Street. 1828. Local limestone ashlar. Centre block of two tall storeys between slightly projecting and slightly lower three-storey, two-bay wings, like houses. Entrance with radial fanlight. Interior radically remodelled in 1981.

TADCASTER GRAMMAR SCHOOL, Toulston Lane, 1½ m. w. Founded in the town in 1557 by Bishop Oglethorpe. The present campus was created in the grounds of TOULSTON LODGE, a mid-C19 house extensively remodelled in 1890 for the brewer, H.H. Riley-Smith. The school buildings, of 1957–60 by *A. W. Glover*, West Riding County Architect, form a quadrangle open on its N side. Brick and timber-clad blocks of mixed heights, the three-storey elements for the Lower School (E, with gymnasiums attached), Upper School and Sixth Form (S). The W range contains the hall, canteen, etc. Additions to the SW for new Library etc., 2001–6 by *North Yorkshire County Council Architects*.

TADCASTER COMMUNITY SWIMMING POOL, Westgate. Completed 1994, by the *Goddard Manton Partnership*. The entrance, gym and offices are housed in a C19 barn, which projects into the new part containing two pools under a sweeping double-curved roof supported by steel 'trees'.

PERAMBULATION

The BRIDGE over the Wharfe is a good-looking, early C18 structure of seven arches, widened *c.* 1791 to designs probably by *Carr*. The Roman crossing is believed to have been upstream, near the site of the late C11 CASTLE, of which the motte, the inner bailey and N part of the outer bailey are still visible above the W bank. The outer ditch to the N (16 ft (5 metres) deep) is filled; the S part of the bailey is built over, and the E part of the motte cut into. The castle was re-fortified in 1642; after its destruction the site was laid out as pleasure grounds in the C18. ¼ m. N is the handsome railway VIADUCT built in 1847–8, probably by *J. C. Birkinshaw*, to carry George Hudson's unrealized York–Leeds line. Stone, eleven arches, including two wider than the rest spanning the river. On the E side of the river, off Spring Court, a castellated house facing the river.

BRIDGE STREET running up from the W side of the river has a pleasantly Georgian character. Many buildings are of three storeys in warm orangey brick, although where Bridge Street becomes HIGH STREET is THE ANGEL AND WHITE HORSE (S side) with a limestone front. This is C18 but the structure dates at least back to the C16 (when it was known as the Red Hart): see the timber framing and blocked ogee-headed doorway in the carriage arch. To the r. is a good Georgian frontage (originally The White Horse, now offices of the Old Brewery, *see* below) in brick with full-height canted bays and a four-column Tuscan porch. Inside, an open-well staircase with turned balusters. One room has an elaborate C19 cornice and plaster ceiling adorned with musical instruments, etc. To its r. the mid-C19 TOWN HALL, three bays, pedimented and quite unprepossessing. Behind, with buildings along both sides of New Street, is Samuel Smith's OLD BREWERY, established in 1758 by Backhouse & Hartley but reconstructed in 1886, after the Smiths' business had been divided. Many C20 additions.

KIRKGATE, running N off High Street towards the church, has the most important houses. Nos. 16–18 is a handsome, if much restored, ashlar house of four bays with bold modillion cornice, called the Duke of Somerset's House. The sixth Duke held the manor from 1682 until 1714. The building looks post 1700, and if indeed it is his, it was probably built for his agent. Opposite is THE ARK (Tadcaster Town Council Offices), a much restored later C15 timber-framed hall with solar cross-wing (r.). The wing was extended further out in the late C16 and has a jettied gable supported by carved corbels, traditionally Noah and his wife. A corresponding wing was demolished before restoration in 1959–67, when numerous later additions were removed. Close-studded hall frame almost entirely rebuilt but using some old timbers. It seems to be a hybrid of styles of construction uncommon in this area: not only downward curving braces in the wall between hall and wing, of the type found in the W of the West Riding, but also roof trusses with very short king posts typical of the uplands. Vicarage Lane, alongside, leads to a second medieval house of interest, the OLD VICARAGE: a limestone-built hall and solar cross-wing (r.) – roof timbers dated to *c.* 1474. Thoroughly restored *c.* 2004, exposing roof trusses in the

gables of the wing. Many mullioned windows and a tall reconstructed four-light hall window with cusped heads and
transom.The solar appears to have been conventional, of two
storeys with an external stack, but formerly at least a bay
longer. The principal range consisted formerly of a two-and-a-
half-bay hall, a screens passage, then a service room (with
chamber over) and a staircase. An axial corridor led to the
kitchen in the end bay. Hall and kitchen were open to the roof
until the C18. Unusually complete and varied roof trusses:
those at either end of the hall have short kingposts, the truss
between them was once set on wall-posts rising from corbels
and has an arch-braced collar, while at the lower end – between
the two-storey bay and the kitchen – is one of (curved) strut-
ted purlin form.

Up to the end of Kirkgate two good brick houses on the w
side (Nos. 47 and 49), both earlier C18 and of three storeys
with quoins; the nearer of five bays with pedimented doorcase.
Then the street bends l. and becomes WESTGATE. Here is the
old SUNDAY SCHOOL of 1788, one of the earliest in the
country. Single-storey, rendered. Twin doors in the middle,
with a Venetian window either side (probably of 1908 when the
school was enlarged), and then further doorways in little side
wings. C19 hipped, arch-braced roof. Beyond is the broad junction with Chapel Street, one of the possible sites of the
medieval market, with at its centre the WAR MEMORIAL, a
slender Celtic cross, 1921. Here the S side of the street is left
open to a green sward round the back of the Old Vicarage with
a memorable backdrop of the two breweries looming above the
High Street. The dominant building is JOHN SMITH'S TAD-
CASTER BREWERY, completed in 1883 by *Scamell & Colyer for*
£150,000, and a splendid example of a large-scale Victorian
tower brewery, built of quarry-faced stone, with much frilly
ironwork. The original buildings are at the corner of High
Street and CENTRE LANE, with four-storey warehouse and
three storey offices to the l., brewing tower to the r. with prominent oriel, then a long two-storey fermenting house. Above all
rises the octagonal chimney with its iron-braced shaft. Opposite, on the N side of LEEDS ROAD, the MANOR FARM YOUTH
CENTRE, a late C15 aisled barn. Five bays survive inside a later
stone case.

THORNER

3040

Pleasant mainly stone-built village street with the church at the
end.

ST PETER. Perp w tower with diagonal buttresses, corbelled-
out parapet and crocketed pinnacles (cf. Barwick-in-Elmet,

Rothwell, Whitkirk (Leeds)). Also a little C15 masonry in the aisle walls and the piers of the three-bay nave arcades. The rest 1855 by *Mallinson & Healey*, the castellated capitals of the arcades their invention. Reordered 2005. – STAINED GLASS. Includes E window by *Hardman*, 1876; S chapel S (two) and N aisle first and second from E by *Powell Bros.* of Leeds, 1878–92. – In the churchyard the WAR MEMORIAL, a tall cross by *Sydney Kitson*, 1920.

METHODIST CHAPEL, Carr Lane. 1877–8 by *G.F. Danby* of Leeds. Now flats. Dec style, with spirelet.

BARN, Carr Lane. Late medieval, aisled, of seven bays. Curved braces from the posts to the arcade plates and tie-beams. Cased in stone probably C18, converted to housing and heavily restored 2005. In the MAIN STREET, No. 30 also retains some elements of timber framing, probably late C16, behind the stonework.

FIELDHEAD, 1¼ m. SSW. Feebly Neo-Jacobean villa of *c.* 1840, with symmetrical gabled front. Some imported C17 and C18 panelling inside.

THORNTHWAITE

ST SAVIOUR. 1810, a rebuilding of a chapel of ease of Hampsthwaite founded in 1402. Little single cell in open country, with pointed Y-tracery windows at the sides and E end. W porch and bellcote *c.* 1893.

PADSIDE HALL, 1½ m. WNW. Substantial house of the C16–C17, much reduced and otherwise altered, the building history of which is unclear. It was briefly the property of Sir William Ingilby of Ripley Castle (†1579) and then sold to the Wigglesworth family. The house was U-shaped, with the courtyard closed on the S side by a screen wall; but the W (parlour) wing is ruinous and a turret at the NE corner of the building was demolished in 1893. Tudor-arched doorway in the screen wall, mullioned windows of two to five lights. The oldest surviving part appears to be the front wall of the hall range, the projecting parts of the cross-wings butting against it; but an inventory of 1579 seems to accord with a hall and cross-wings plan. So the hall and the turret were probably of Sir William's time or earlier, the wings rebuilt, and the courtyard wall added, in the early C17 by the Wigglesworths.

In the hall, a massive fireplace bressumer across the parlour end, supported by a free-standing column, and two stopped and chamfered doorways into the service end. Two moulded chimneypieces of *c.* 1700 in that part. The former kitchen, in the S part of the wing, was for a period used as a barn and has a C19 cart entrance towards the courtyard. Segment-headed kitchen fireplace set in a big chimney-breast against the outer flank. Restoration and further alterations *c.* 1980.

THORNTON

Bradford

Pennine village w of the city, an important freestone quarrying centre in the C19. The turnpike road (Thornton Road), opened in 1826, runs parallel to the village street, to the s.

St James, Thornton Road. 1870–2 by *T. H. & F. Healey*, successor to a chapel of ease of Bradford perhaps of C16 origin (*see* below). E.E. style, with clean uncluttered outline (cf. St John, Great Horton, Bradford). Plate-traceried rose windows to w end and clerestory, lancets elsewhere. Tall unbuttressed se tower with plain broach spire, nave and chancel of equal height. Interior spacious but lopsided, with an aisle on the s side only – the option of adding one to the n was not taken up. – Font. 1679, one of several items from the chapel. Small octagonal bowl with Latin inscription, on an octagonal shaft with square base. Still entirely in the medieval tradition. – Pillar, dated 1687. In the porch. *c.* 3 ft (1 metre) high, chamfered with a square top. The most feasible suggestion as to its function is that it carried a sundial. – Stained glass. e window by *Morris & Co.*, 1872, lacking the freshness of their earliest work. s aisle middle, 1897 by *Mayer & Co.* of Munich. – Monuments. Wall tablets, including John Hirst †1789 by *Stead* of York.

The remains of the Old Chapel itself are in the churchyard across the road to the s. It was rebuilt in 1612 – an inscription states 'built' but there is documentary evidence of its earlier existence – largely rebuilt again in 1756 and further 'beautified' in 1818 during the incumbency of the Rev. Patrick Brontë. Surviving are the C17 e gable-end wall, with the inscription and a Jacobean Perp window, and the reassembled belfry stage of the w turret added in 1818, octagonal with battlements and plain pointed arches.

Kipping Chapel (Congregational), Market Street. 1843, replacing a chapel of 1769. Three-bay front with debased Grecian detail. Interior altered.

Viaduct, w of the village. 1878, *J. Fraser* engineer, on the (former) Bradford–Denholme–Keighley line. Twenty arches.

Prospect Mill, Thornton Road. Former worsted mill, *c.* 1848 onwards for Joshua Craven & Son, four parallel ranges on steeply sloping ground. At the top, along the road, a warehouse dated 1855. Three storeys, fourteen bays, and smartly detailed with rusticated ground floor and bracketed cornice. The other ranges are plainer: another warehouse, 1849, three storeys, originally two; then the mill proper, built shortly before that date, four storeys and attic, originally of eleven bays with Venetian windows in the gable-ends, extended to the e *c.* 1860; and at the bottom a second mill, *c.* 1860, three storeys with privy and staircase turrets at the corners. All are traditionally constructed with timber floors on cast-iron columns. The two mills are linked at their w ends by a late C19 engine house with round-headed windows: the chimney was to the W of the 1849 warehouse. The firm engaged in weaving as well as spinning, but there were no weaving sheds, so either the traditional system of putting-out to handloom weavers was maintained or there must have been power looms installed in unconventional locations within the complex. Attached to the E of the 1855 warehouse is a pair of houses built by Joshua Craven in 1831 (date and initials), from which the business was evidently run in its pre-factory phase. E again, at right angles, a row of mid-C19 workers' cottages; and beyond that ASHFIELD HOUSE, the later Craven family residence, a conventional Italianate villa of c. 1860.

Numerous early C19 workers' housing developments in the village, some of them dated, including CLOGGERS ROW, 1806, at the E end of Market Street and SOUTH SQUARE on Thornton Road, 1832, a little cul-de-sac with stone nameplate. S of the churchyard is THORNTON HALL, in origin C17 or earlier, much reduced in size and the remainder modernized, in 1886. What remains is the S range of a house which evidently faced E. C17, three storeys with regular three-bay S flank, the windows (partly renewed) of six lights with transoms to the ground and first floors, of five lights without transom to the second. Stringcourses between the storeys. Same forms to the E gable-end; then a short two-storey E range, with the entrance, built or rebuilt in 1886. Pennine Revival details here and on the coach house.

Also three outlying houses, mainly C17, which deserve notice.

First LEVENTHORPE HALL, in Thornton Road, ¾ m. E, towards Bradford. Late C17 double pile also much altered in the C19 – reduced in height and partly rebuilt – but reusing old materials. Derelict at time of writing. Five-bay front facing E, with central doorway and cross-windows (some of them blocked) to the ground and first floors. Traces of second-floor windows in what are now the E gables of the C19 roof. The form of the C17 roof is not known but it is unlikely to have been the same as its successor's, with an E–W valley which is obstructed by two original chimney-breasts, in line in the centre of each range. N side with four-light transomed windows, including a middle one at intermediate height lighting the staircase. S and W sides largely rebuilt in the C19, the former with reused transomed windows and both with single-storey porches of recycled material. Altered lobby entry, segment-headed fireplace in the SE room. N of the house a BARN, mainly C18, with hip-roofed porch.

Secondly UPPER HEADLEY, Headley Lane, ⅝ m. SW of the church, preceded by a high garden wall with a round-headed archway, dated 1669, set in a little recess with stone seats l. and r. The oldest part of the house – early for a stone-built Pennine yeoman house – appears to be the parlour cross-wing to the l., with the date 1589 on one of the gable kneelers (on the other the name W. Midgley). Plain mullioned windows at the front, but in the r. return two big upright ovals of c. 1690 (cf. West Scholes House, below). The hall range butts against this, doubtless replacing an earlier range, of timber framing: re-cut date of 1604 on the porch, but that is an addition (see the blocked window behind) and probably the datestone was transferred when it was built. Mullion-and-transom windows, that to the housebody of eight lights; and an inserted cross-window, perhaps coeval with the porch (and the ovals). But the most remarkable feature, an extraordinary survival, is the early ornamental leaded glazing. Subdivided lozenges in the centre of the lights, and above them round-headed panes with further subdivision in the spandrels, like Jacobean Perp panel tracery. Internal arrangements suggest a hearth passage, later dispensed with. Firehood to the housebody, some C17 panelling and other ornamental woodwork, probably reused.

Thirdly WEST SCHOLES HOUSE, Brewery Lane, ½ m. s again. Dated 1694. Big upright oval window (blocked) over the entrance and another on the return of the projecting parlour end to the l., just as at Upper Headley (except that the projection is not gabled). Transomed housebody window of seven lights.

The WALLS OF JERICHO, 1⅛ m. NW of the church, built of, and to retain, quarry waste – turning the lane between them into a gloomy canyon – have been demolished.

THORNTON-IN-CRAVEN

9040

ST MARY. Outside the village. Battlemented Perp w tower, dated 1510 on the s side. The body of the church markedly low and short in comparison, under one roof, with aisles narrowly embracing the tower. A worn inscription over the E window implies a mid-C15 date. Straight-headed windows, mostly with plain arched lights, but one window on the N side has them cusped and ogee-headed. E window renewed C19. No division between nave and chancel. Four-bay arcades with double-chamfered arches on low octagonal piers. Crudely executed face on the NW pier. Double-chamfered tower arch on semi-octagonal responds. – SCREENS. N and s of the choir. Heavily restored. Simple straight-headed openings with thin Flamboyant tracery. – PEWS. Remade from C17 pews. Two knobs on each end. – ROYAL ARMS. 1816. Painted, on an oval panel. – STAINED GLASS. E window by *Kempe*, 1898. – MONUMENTS. The Rev. Henry Richardson, Rector of Thornton, †1778, and his son the Rev. Henry Richardson Currer †1784. Two identical works, l. and r. of the altar, by *J. Devaere*. Tablet surmounted by a winged putto shrouding an urn. – WELLHOUSE, in the churchyard. Erected over the 'ancient and health-giving spring' by the Rev. Henry Richardson in 1764. Octagonal, with a monolithic circular cover like a teapot lid.

ALMSHOUSES, near the church. 1815. One-storeyed, very modest, but with a pediment over the centre three bays.

In the village centre some C18 houses including THE GRANGE, the former Rectory built by the Rev. Henry Richardson in 1754. Five bays, with quoins and chunky pedimented doorcase – 'a model of simplicity and elegance on a small scale' (Whitaker), but altered in the C19 with canted bay windows l. and r. Also THE COTTAGE, 1923 by *Richard Jaques* of Burnley, who at the time was Lutyens's site architect at Gledstone Hall (q.v.). Striking façade in roughcast with ashlar dressings. Starkly splayed and pointed doorway, to the r. a big canted bay rising above the eaves, with mullion-and-transom window lighting the staircase, and to the l. a semicircular bow window with the central light of the window above it a corresponding miniature bow. Tightly planned interior with inglenook to the drawing room.

THORNTON-IN-LONSDALE

6070

ST OSWALD. Perp w tower, with modern pyramid roof. The body of the church rebuilt 1869–70 by *Paley & Austin* and then largely rebuilt by them again, to the same design, in 1934–5 after a fire. Retained in the first rebuilding, and replicated in the second, was a three-bay Norman N arcade. Cylindrical piers with attached half-shafts at the diagonals, fluted capitals, one arch slightly chamfered, the second with a roll moulding and the third with zigzag. The rest of the building in a mechanical Dec style.

HALSTEADS, S of the church. C17 Pennine farmhouse modernized and extended as a gentry residence in the early C19. Simple Tudor Gothic windows. Incongruous Doric porch added mid C20. (Roof trusses with carved king-blocks.) An ornamented doorhead dated 1670 re-set in an outbuilding may relate to the C17 house. Derelict at time of writing.

MASONGILL HOUSE, 1¾ m. NW. Modest C18 block. Rendered three-bay front with central dormer crowned by a pediment-like gable. A pair of single-storey ashlar pavilions to l. and r., with open pediments and angle pilasters, added in mid C19.

APRON FULL OF STONES, 3½ m. NNE, beside the Kingsdale Beck. Bronze Age burial cairn of gritstone boulders, excavated in 1972.

THORP ARCH

4040

Retaining an estate village air in spite of late C20 expansion, with a number of semi-detached cottages of the mid and late C19 around the small green and up the main street.

ALL SAINTS. ¼ m. E of the village. Substantially remodelled by
G. E. *Street*, 1871–2, with lancets and geometric tracery. The S
doorway – which has been moved at least twice – is Norman.
It has one order of (replacement) colonnettes with decorated
scalloped capitals, and beakheads in the arch. Part of a tympanum with chequer-board decoration is built into the porch
wall. Perp W tower; and also medieval some masonry in the
nave S wall and parts of the chancel, including restored tomb
recess and PISCINA. – REREDOS. Alabaster, with seven-bay
shafted arcade, pinnacles. – FURNISHINGS. A fine set by *Robert
Thompson*, 1938. – SCULPTURE in the S porch: fragments of an
Anglo-Saxon CROSS with thin loose knotwork; a stone with
faces on two adjoining sides, medieval; and a headless figure
of very crude workmanship. – STAINED GLASS. Chancel S by
Wailes, 1850. – N of the tower are two old FONTS: a tub and an
octagonal one on a slender shaft; probably that given in 1759.

THORP ARCH HALL. ¼ m. W of the village. 1749–56 for William
Gossip, one of the earliest works of *John Carr* (now subdivided). Nothing grand: five bays and two storeys, with lower
pyramid-roofed three-bay wings housing the offices and
stables. Pedimented doorcase (the sills of the ground-floor
windows have been lowered). Transverse inner hall with a staircase at each end rising to a first-floor 'gallery'. There were two
dining rooms. Plasterwork by *Thomas Perritt* and some good
joinery e.g. the drawing room chimneypiece – to which a Greek
key frieze was added because Gossip thought it too low. Rustic
Gothick S LODGE.

BRIDGE. *See* Boston Spa.

RAILWAY STATION (former), Church Causeway, 1½ m. NE. 1847
by *G. T. Andrews* for the York & North Midland Railway. Very
handsome Gothic. Separate GOODS SHED with a large timber
canopy (cf. Wetherby).

MANOR MILL, Bridge Foot. Now housing. The earliest surviving part, dated 1681, is at right angles to the river and was
erected to mill rape seed. Two wheel pits, and the remains of
mullioned windows and depressed four-centred arched doorways. Altered and raised (see scars in gables), possibly in
1765–6. A flying walkway connects to a long range to the E.
This is of three parts: a four-storey kiln house, and two phases
of cottages and storage, eventually all of three storeys.

ROYAL ORDNANCE FILLING FACTORY (former), 1 m. NE. Built
in 1940–2 and closed in 1958, most of the site now Thorp Arch
Trading Estate. It had a grid-plan layout covering 620 acres,
its own internal railway system and at its height employed
18,000 workers. About a third of the original structures survive
in other use, many still protected by concrete blast walls and
earth bunds. They were erected to standardized plans using
standardized materials and components e.g single-skin brick
walls and steel window frames. Flat concrete slab roofs were
used over magazines and lightweight steel roof trusses over
working areas (because they were less likely to collapse in the
event of explosion). Three of five 'butterfly buildings' survive,

which consist of a small building for melting TNT, between parallel ranges for filling rockets and grenades.

BRITISH LIBRARY DOCUMENT SUPPLY CENTRE, on the N section of the former ROF site. Established in 1961, and housed partly in former ROF buildings and partly in a massive purpose-built DOCUMENT STORE by *IDC Ltd.* for the *Property Services Agency.* Erected in two identical parts (1972–5 and 1980) each of four principal storeys (eight floors within) with large service towers attached: from the top down the storeys recede so that the concrete frame becomes entirely independent. First and second floors fully glazed, the others concealed by pre-cast cladding (originally unpainted) with slit windows composed in syncopated rhythms. Inside 70 miles of shelving.

THORPE

0060

MANOR HOUSE. Handsome mid-C18 five-bay front, of rendered rubble with gritstone dressings – pedimented Doric doorcase, architrave surrounds to the windows, quoins and bold eaves cornice. This belongs to an added front range, which turned the house into a double pile. The older back part has chamfered cross-windows. A big C19 farm building opposite, and to one side a C17 barn with massive corbels to the projecting cart entrance.

THORPE UNDERWOOD HALL

4050

1902–3 by *Walter Brierley* for F.W. Slingsby. Now a school. Opulent Neo-Jacobean in brick with stone dressings, with many large mullion-and-transom windows. Entrance front (N) symmetrical in mass, with central two-storey porch and projecting gabled end bays, but not in fenestration. (Interiors equally sumptuous, with massive carved stone fireplaces, panelling etc.) Within the grounds N of the house, partly visible over the perimeter wall, MONKS HOUSE, C17, all brick. Lobby-entry front range facing W, with central cluster of diagonally set chimneystacks and shaped gables to each end. Another simpler shaped gable to the back part. Mullioned windows with the brick surrounds and mullions now rendered.

THRESHFIELD

9060

A village of two parts, the old centre round a little green and a suburban area on the way to Grassington along Station Road, where the railway line from Skipton (1902) terminated.

Threshfield, Netherside Hall.
Engraving by R. and E. Taylor, 1878

St Margaret Clitherow (R.C.), Station Road. One of the many small-scale offspring of the Metropolitan Cathedral at Liverpool, 1972–3 by *P. H. Langtry Langton*. Limestone rubble walls. Approximately square in plan, with lead-clad flying buttresses at the corners which are continued upwards along the angles of the pyramid roof. Triangular-profile roof-light over the altar. Pleasantly low-key interior. – SCULPTURE by *John Ashworth*. – Abstract STAINED GLASS by *Jane Duff*.

GRAMMAR SCHOOL, now primary school, ⅜ m. SE, near the river. Founded 1674 by the Rev. Matthew Hewitt. Two-storey gabled porch at the l. end of the front with stepped upper three-light window. The other windows mullioned.

UPPER WHARFEDALE SCHOOL, Station Road. 1953 by *Hubert Bennett*, West Riding County Architect. Informally planned with low-pitched roofs, brick and stone. Additions 2006 etc.

Two contrasting C17 houses in the old village. MANOR HOUSE. Compact double-pile block with an impressive three-storey porch. First floor with four-light mullion-and-transom window and additional lights to the sides, second floor with a wheel window of six lights divided by an inner concentric circle (cf. Manor House Farm, Hartwith, Nidderdale), gable with small semicircular recess. The rest of the house drastically remodelled in the C19, reduced in height and completely re-windowed; but the outline of mullion-and-transom windows flanking the porch can still be made out – as can the internal arrangement, with a lobby entry and the kitchen behind the housebody, both with segment-headed fireplaces. Round the corner PARK GRANGE, 1680. Lobby-entry range with the front of gritstone ashlar. Moulded three-centre-headed doorway, mullioned windows of three-plus-three lights to the housebody and the chamber over, of four and five lights elsewhere.

Winding staircase in a projection at the rear, good moulded fireplaces to the housebody and the former kitchen end.

p. 741   NETHERSIDE HALL, 1 m. NNW, beautifully framed by trees. 1820–2, almost certainly an early work of *George Webster* of Kendal. The house is very much in his scholarly Jacobean Revival style and the client was Alexander Nowell, for whom he designed Underley Hall, Kirkby Lonsdale (Cumbria) a few years later. It is a remarkably early example of the idiom by any hand; but the plan is essentially that of a later C18 classical villa, with a rigidly symmetrical main block and a lower service wing to one side (cf. Eshton Hall). Loggia-like three-bay porch but the rest of the detail – mullion-and-transom windows, low-pitched gables, prominent chimneystacks – quite simple. Inside, a big top-lit central hall with a first-floor gallery, and balancing main and service stairs off it. Some plasterwork and woodwork. Now a school.

Prehistoric SETTLEMENT sites in the parish, with hut circles and associated field systems, include one ½ m. S of Netherside Hall. On higher ground 2¼ m. WNW of this, the mutilated remains of a Bronze Age STONE CIRCLE – three upright stones on a turf-covered mound.

4050   TOCKWITH

EPIPHANY. 1866 by *Mallinson & Healey*, the daughter church of Bilton-in-Ainsty. Large, aisleless and cruciform, in the Geometrical style, with a cylindrical bell-turret, and a good deal of unfinished sculpture outside. – STAINED GLASS, of 1866. E window and S transept window by *Hardman* and W windows by *Wailes*.

At the centre of the village, with its gable-end to the street, is the THATCHED COTTAGE. C17 brick walls encase a three-bay, single-aisled timber frame of probably C16 date. Next to it is PIPE HALL, the unusual survival of a Late Georgian muniment room but destructively converted into a house in the 1990s – windows were inserted where originally it was nearly windowless, and the unusual plan and good staircase are lost.

2030   TONG
                                  Bradford

Church and big house in a green lung between Bradford and Leeds.

ST JAMES. 1727 for Sir George Tempest, second baronet, who had also built the hall. The mason was *John Nelson* of Birstall. It replaced a small mainly Norman church on the same site, a chapel of ease of Birstall, and a certain amount of material was recycled in the rebuilding. w tower, three-bay nave and two-bay chancel, all of sandstone ashlar, the tower with plain pilaster strips to the middle and top stages and a reused two-light Perp w window, the nave and chancel with simply detailed round-headed windows. N aisle of rougher, recycled stone with straight-headed two-light windows, probably C16, the lights round-headed. Also reused is the tower arch – Norman, with scalloped capitals – presumably the original chancel arch, suitably heightened; but the three-bay nave arcade, with Tuscan columns, is evidently all of the C18, in spite of the traditional double-chamfering to the arches. Gothic E window of c. 1882. – Exceptionally complete C18 FURNISHINGS, the ideal of the Georgian country church: COMMUNION RAIL; three-decker PULPIT at the SE corner of the nave, with tester dated 1727; BOX PEWS throughout, including two in the chancel, larger and taller than the rest, the N the Tempest family pew, with a little fireplace in the corner behind the chancel arch, the s presumably for the parson's family; FONT, with scalloped bowl on a stout cylindrical shaft; and w GALLERY, 1731, on plain timber posts. Also some pieces of C17 woodwork in the N aisle, presumably parts of pews; a panelled DADO in the sanctuary; C19 Gothic CATECHISM BOARDS flanking the E window; and several HATCHMENTS of the Tempest family. – STAINED GLASS. E window 1882 by *Lavers, Barraud & Westlake*, the one irreconcilably alien element.

TONG HALL. In wooded grounds behind the church. 1702–4, by the lawyer-architect *Theophilus Shelton* of Heath, near Wakefield, according to a lost inscription, with alterations of 1773–4 by *John Platt* of Rotherham. Now offices. An exceptional house for the area in several respects, the most obvious its building material, which is brick (with stone dressings) – the most substantial use of it this far towards the Pennines in the C18. Vertically accented block with a pedimented three-bay centre slightly taller than the marginally projecting two-bay flanking sections. Originally the latter were of two storeys, the former of two-and-a-half, but in 1773 the whole was heightened by one storey and in the process the drama of the composition was dissipated: while the form of the central attic was broadly replicated, the bold main cornice and the high parapets to the flanking parts were lost. As to other detail, there are quoins, window frames with cornices, and aprons below them. In the basement, which is wholly of stone, the windows are of traditional mullioned type: the others were evidently sashed from the outset, although the existing sashes are probably all of 1773. Of that date also the present front doorway, with cornice on brackets; but above it is the original Baroque achievement of the Tempest arms, and re-set in the fanlight a special rarity, a SUNDIAL of STAINED GLASS almost certainly by *Henry Gyles*, with the sun and the four seasons (cf. Nunappleton Hall, West Riding South). N front similar but with two-storey canted bays of 1773 to the flanking sections. Mid-C20 lift tower against the E side, the sorest of thumbs.

p. 40

The interior was equally up-to-date and more lavish. In the entrance hall a sumptuously carved timber overmantel in the manner of Le Pautre and Marot, with two stags, floral decoration and a grotesque mask, beneath an open segmental pediment. Archway to the staircase behind, of elmwood with sprouting-up leaves at the base of each baluster, rearranged *c.* 1902 when the staircase compartment was reduced in size. To the l. of the entrance hall a room with bold bolection-moulded elm panelling and inlaid overmantel, and behind it one with similar panelling but carefully copied into the 1773 bay. To the r. two rooms with Adam-style decoration of the later phase. More original panelling, and an overmantel with enriched surround, in the room above the entrance hall. Back-stairs with turned balusters, brick-vaulted basement.

W of the house the former STABLES, a quadrangle partly coeval with it and partly of 1811. Again mainly of brick with stone dressings, including on the earlier parts mullioned windows like those in the house basement. The same formula was also applied, presumably at the same time, to a house on the E side of the churchyard: an earlier, C17 wing is of stone.

37 RYECROFT, 1⅛ m. W, on the edge of the Bradford built-up area. Dated 1669, and most unusual as a C17 yeoman house built from scratch with a housebody of double-storey height. Single range with a rear outshut along two-thirds of its length. House-body window of four-plus-four lights with a transom and the dripmould between the storeys stepping up over it (cf. Carlton Hall, Carlton). Kitchen, parlour and chamber windows all mullioned only. Lobby entry against the flank of the house-body fire-hood, the latter with bressumer supported on two corbelled posts. Gallery with turned balusters against the back and the parlour end walls, staircase inserted mid C20. Post-and-muntin partition towards the parlour.

7050

TOSSIDE
Gisburn Forest

A handful of buildings at an upland crossroads.

ST BARTHOLOMEW. Chapel of ease in existence by 1650, rebuilt in the later C18. Nave and chancel in one, with round-headed windows to the sides and Venetian window to the E end. Little square bellcote, with broach spirelet, and gabled S porch with round-headed entrance, probably *c.* 1843, when repairs were carried out. – PULPIT. An irregular hexagon incorporating some C17 woodwork. – FONT. 1619. Plain, octagonal, with a long inscription.

CONGREGATIONAL CHAPEL, ¼ m. SW. 1812–13. Three-bay front with two tiers of windows, the manse adjoining to the r., of two bays, under the same roof. Little-altered interior, with

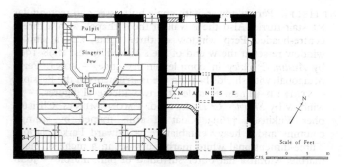

Tosside, Congregational Chapel.
Plan

gallery round three sides describing an elongated semi-octagon, and a large raised singers' enclosure in the middle, in front of the late C19 rostrum pulpit. Turned wooden columns supporting the gallery, panelled box pews above and below.

CRACOE HILL, ⅞ m. s. Farmhouse with curly ornamented door-head dated 1691.

UPPER POPPLETON

5050

Suburban village close to York, with a pleasant green. The railway arrived in 1848.

ALL SAINTS. 1891 by *C. Hodgson Fowler*. Nave, chancel, and a w bell-turret with spirelet, supported by three stepped arches inside the church – a striking effect. Dec details. Reused from the medieval church (chapel of ease of St Mary Bishophill Junior, York) are the plain Norman head of the s doorway and a straight-headed window, of two ogee-headed lights, on the N side. Parish room attached to N, and internal reordering etc., 1960–5 by *G. G. Pace*. – PAINTING. Large Flemish Late Mannerist Adoration of the Magi, a copy of one by *Maerten de Vos*, 1599, for Notre Dame de la Chaussée, Valenciennes, now in the Musée des Beaux-Arts there. Bought by the church in 1946.

WADDINGTON

7040

Across the river Ribble from Clitheroe (Lancashire). A beck runs alongside the village street.

St Helen. Perp w tower, with angle buttresses and rectangular NE stair-turret. Also the E wall of the S chapel, with a three-centre-headed Perp window of three lights, and a similar window re-set at the w end of the s aisle. The rest 1898–1901 by *Austin & Paley* in complementary style. – FONT. Perp, octagonal, with shields bearing the Instruments of the Passion. – STAINED GLASS. N aisle NE, two medieval figures. – W window by *Shrigley & Hunt*, 1900. – MONUMENTS. Christopher Wilkinson †1693. Coat of arms framed by stumpy columns and a heavy entablature. – Edward Parker †1794. Three-dimensional white marble urn set in a niche of black marble, within a flat outer surround of pink marble. – John Parker †1797. Similar but with both niche and surround of black marble.

METHODIST CHAPEL, in the village centre. Gothic, with tower. Dates of 1889 and 1907.

WADDINGTON HOSPITAL. Almshouses founded 1701. The modest pedimented gateway is not that shown in an early C18 view and is probably later C18. The buildings behind rebuilt in the late C19, one storey with timbered porches, forming three sides of a quadrangle. In the middle of the far side a detached Gothic chapel.

WADDINGTON HALL. Set back from the main street, opposite the church. Pre-Reformation in origin, much altered C17 etc., largely rebuilt 1900 and further interfered with since. Two storeys, half-H plan. One cross-window of *c.* 1700 remains, to the front of the r. wing. To the street a garden gateway and two sets of rather gross gatepiers, of 1900.

WADDOW HALL, ¾ m. SSE. Plain five-bay house of *c.* 1800, much enlarged and altered. Matching four-bay extension to l., top hamper added after 1927. Some earlier masonry at the back. D-shaped staircase.

LANE SIDE, ½ m. ENE, on the road to West Bradford. 1752. Three-bay front with Vanbrughian doorway and above it a large ornamented plaque bearing the date.

WALSHFORD
Great Ribston with Walshford

A few houses on the old Great North Road at the E entrance to the park of Ribston Hall (q.v.).

BRIDGE INN. Sprawling complex of the mid C20 on, of which the core is a small Georgian farmhouse and its outbuildings. In the dining room (former stables) fine Rococo plasterwork of *c.* 1750 – ceiling and enriched wall panels – from Halnaby Hall, North Riding (dem. 1952). Some pedimented window surrounds outside, probably from the same source.

WALTON

4040

St Peter. Narrow w tower with Norman tower arch on the simplest imposts, reused if the lower part of the tower is not
Norman refaced. Top Perp, corbelled out (with contemporary
bell-frame). Nave and chancel all of *c.* 1340–50. Tall straight-   19
headed two-light windows in the nave, the lights ogee-headed.
Chancel windows arched and reticulated, the E a very handsome example of five lights. Characteristic doorways with
shouldered heads, and a lowside window on the s side with the
same. Porch c18.
    Tall chancel arch, the arch and responds double-chamfered.
Elaborate recess in the chancel N wall, with sevenfold cusping,
crocketed ogee gable and tall, pencil-thin pinnacles. Roofs etc.
by *W.M. Fawcett* of Cambridge, 1890–1. – PULPIT of *c.* 1890
incorporating some c17 panelling. – MONUMENTS. In the
recess, a badly preserved effigy of a Knight, late c14. – Nicolas
Fairfax †1702/3 (*sic*). Wall tablet with cherubs and skulls to the
frame and elaborately mounted arms above.
Old Vicarage. se of the church. Coursed limestone L-shape
dated 1684, incorporating elements of earlier timber-framing
inside. Doorway with Pennine-type flattened-ogee head (cf.
Old Hall, Bradley, 1672), mullioned windows. Alterations and
additions.
deerpark, Hall Park Road ⅔ m. NE. A detached park of the
medieval manor of Thorp Arch (q.v.). Hall Park Farm stands
on the site of the lodge. Enclosing embankment preserved in
many places.

WEETON

2040

St Barnabas. 1851–2 by *G. G. Scott* for the third Earl of Harewood. Quite lavish but oddly proportioned. Quasi-cruciform
plan with rather squat central tower and tall spire, unaisled
nave and chancel, and low lean-to aisles at the crossing rather
than proper transepts. The tower has a clerestory stage above
the aisles, of little E.E. lancets set in an arcade, then cusped
lancet bell-openings, two per side, and a prominent se stair-
turret; the spire a single tier of oversize lucarnes. Nave and
chancel windows with Geometrical tracery. The interior is
more successful, the crossing clerestory acting as a lantern at
the centre of the church. Two-bay N and s arcades into the
aisles, and bigger E and W crossing arches, all with elaborate
E.E. mouldings. – REREDOS and sanctuary floor, of *Minton*
tiles. – Tall openwork FONT COVER of oak (cf. Bradford,
Skipton etc.), carved by *Rattee* of Cambridge. – METALWORK.
Candelabra in the crossing, wall lamps in the nave, standard
lamps in the sanctuary, all excellent workmanship in brass. –
STAINED GLASS. Chancel windows and nave sw by *Wailes*,

1855; w window also by *Wailes*, 1875. – Former VICARAGE, beside the churchyard. *c.* 1855. Domestic Gothic, large, with many gables.

OLD HALL. Round-headed doorway of *c.* 1700 flanked by big pilasters. (The house itself presumably earlier, with some remains of timber structure inside.)

WEST BRADFORD

7040

ST CATHERINE. Little Gothic box of 1898–9, built as a chapel of ease of Waddington. – STAINED GLASS. E window by *Morris & Co.*, 1899, the design by *Burne-Jones*.

PILLINGS. 1722, with mullion-and-transom windows and off-centre pedimented doorway.

EAVES HALL, ⅜ m. NW. 1922 by *Hitchon & Pickup* of Burnley. Formally Neo-Wren, in red brick with Portland stone dressings. Dark panelling inside. Now an hotel.

WEST END
Thruscross

1050

The hamlet disappeared beneath the Thruscross Reservoir in 1966.

HUDSON'S HOUSE, 1½ m. WNW of the reservoir dam. An inscription records that 'Stephen Hudson Built This House 1765'. Rustic Palladian. Three bays, with Venetian windows to the ground and first floors.

ROCKING HALL, 2¾ m. W of the dam, 1,300 ft (395 metres) up on the moor. Shooting box of the Dukes of Devonshire (*see* Bolton Abbey), probably also of the 1760s, a remarkably architectonic miniature. Quasi-Palladian scheme of a gabled centre section with a blind arch framing a doorway, and lower flanking bays under half-gables. Simple massive detail. Blocked masonry to the centre part below impost level, blocked and rock-faced quoins and arch voussoirs above, and a big crude mask on the keystone.

WESTON

1040

The church and the hall lie at the end of a narrow winding lane running gently downhill between tall park walls.

ALL SAINTS. Small and rustic, the w end picturesquely irregular with cyclopic asymmetrically placed buttresses and C17 bellcote. C17 also the s porch, dated 1686, the doorway with a heavy lugged surround and a keystone. One small Norman window high up on the s side of the nave, and beside it an arched Perp window of three lights and a straight-headed window of two. Plain Norman chancel arch, probably altered in 1819 when the church was 'repaired and amended'. Low steeply-roofed Perp N aisle with straight-headed windows, the lights round-arched. Two-bay arcade with double-chamfered arches and raised decorative motifs on the capitals, one of the arches blocked. N chapel probably post-Reformation, with a round-headed double-chamfered archway to the chancel, the responds with ornamented capitals. Chancel and chapel windows mainly C19. – PULPIT. A fine big C18 three-decker, with seven-sided sounding board. – BOX PEWS throughout the church, including a big musicians' pew opposite the pulpit, complete with music stand. Plain, largely renewed in 1840. – ROYAL ARMS of Queen Anne, carved. – CATECHISM BOARDS. 1723, restored in 1819. – STAINED GLASS. Some medieval fragments in the nave middle s window. – In the E window and chancel N, armorial panels of c. 1600, attributed to *Barnard Dinninghoff*. Possibly the heraldic glass which was previously in the windows of the Banqueting House at the hall (q.v.). – Chancel SE and SW, and chapel N, by *Burckhardt Brothers* of Munich, 1871 and 1882. Aisle N by *Ward & Hughes*, 1910. – MONUMENTS. Sir William Stopham (?) †1317. Ridged tomb-chest with a shield and a cross-hilted sword. – William Vavasour †1587. Tomb-chest in a coarsely detailed ogee-arched wall recess. – John Blencow †1630. Tablet flanked by volutes.

WESTON HALL. In essence the house built for Sir Mauger Vavasour c. 1600 (date of 1602 inside), but much altered and presenting a rather confused appearance. It seems to have consisted of a main range facing E, with the ends raised up an extra storey as corner pavilions, and return wings behind each end at the back (a view of c. 1720 supplies some of the missing details). The parlour end was evidently to the N. Later changes included a partial reorientation in the mid C18, with a new entrance range facing W.

Of the Elizabethan house the parts remaining in a relatively untouched state are the NE pavilion and the NW wing behind it. The former is fronted by a spectacular three-storey canted bay window rising from a rectangular base and crowned by a little gable. The windows are mullioned and transomed, each of two-plus-six-plus-two lights, and there is a smaller mullioned window below to the basement. The N flank of the wing is similarly smart, with another full-height canted bay window, cross windows l. and r. and a balustraded parapet over. Further s, the middle part of the E front is of early C19 appearance, with big mullioned windows crowned by cornices and the curious feature of two round-headed doorways side-by-side, forming a garden entrance; but the windows seem to replicate what was there previously, shown in a view of 1793. Then the SE pavilion, which has been reduced to the same height as the centre but is broader than its counterpart, of three narrow bays. The first is a rectangular projection which appears to represent the Elizabethan entrance porch, then a big chimney-breast, and finally a bay with another mullion-and-transom window. Over these bays some reused balustrading. Big buttress at the SE corner. Of the SW wing there is nothing to be seen, but a truncated stump of it may have been absorbed into the S half of the mid-C18 entrance range – a utilitarian six bays, two storeys and basement, backing onto the main building – which also extends N into the previous space between the wings. N of it, filling in more of the space, is an early C18 kitchen block.

Inside, three rooms at the parlour end have panelling of c. 1600, one also some plaster ceiling decoration and the best a fireplace with an elaborate fluted frieze to the lintel and arcaded timber overmantel. Also a C17 staircase with turned and splat balusters. S from here, behind the twin doorways in the E front, is an early C19 staircase hall; and then what were presumably the Elizabethan great hall and great chamber are discernible, one above the other, the latter now an early C19 drawing room with Adam-style ceiling. An arched doorway on the W side of the hall, hidden in a cupboard, is perhaps a survivor from a previous house.

E of the house, where in the early C18 there was a walled garden, a very lavish and sophisticated BANQUETING HOUSE, also c. 1600 for Sir Mauger Vavasour. Three storeys, square, with a canted bay at the front, its ground floor containing a doorway. Mullion-and-transom windows, roundels and panels containing heraldic devices, parapet crowned by open merlons and strapwork and at the front corners by little chimneys. At the back a staircase turret carried up an extra storey as a belvedere, with all-round transomed fenestration. Tudor-arched corner fireplaces in the first- and second-floor rooms. Between the house and the church a five-bay aisled BARN, probably C16 in origin but the present stone walling later. Kingpost trusses with curved principal rafters, and a full complement of wind-braces. N of the house an ICE HOUSE, dated 1838.

DOB PARK LODGE, 2¼ m. NNE, overlooking the Washburn valley. Ruined fragment of a standing or occasional lodge of the Vavasours, probably mid-C17. It was of three storeys, roughly square with a number of rectangular projections. Surviving part of W front has regularly placed cross windows, the bottom tier with cornices on brackets.

WETHERBY

On the N bank of the Wharfe, at the point where it is crossed by the Great North Road (by-passed since 1959). A bridge was erected c. 1233, a market charter was granted in 1240 and excavations in 1922 w of Scott Lane revealed what was interpreted as evidence of a castle, in existence by the end of the C13. The manor passed to the Cavendish family and by 1824, when the sixth Duke of Devonshire sold, they owned all but two plots in the town.

ST JAMES. 1839–41 by *J. B. & W. Atkinson*, successor to a chapel of ease (of Spofforth) in the Market Place. Chancel extended *c.* 1876 by the same architects. A version of E.E. (cf. St Luke, Clifford) with w tower (pinnacles of 1939; originals taller). E end with five stepped shafted lancets, the side windows groups of stepped lancets under a round arch, with a more scholarly wheel window over the s porch. Big, broad barn inside. Tower arch remodelled in 1888 by *Chorley & Connon*. – ROYAL ARMS, 1776, from the old chapel. – STAINED GLASS. E window, 1878. w window 1889 by *Powell Bros*.

ST JOSEPH (R.C.), Westgate. 1984–6 by *Vincente Stienlet* of *Pascal J. Stienlet & Son*, cleverly inserted between the former church (now hall, l.) of 1880–1 by *Edward Simpson* and presbytery (r.). Slate-roofed porch sweeping up to a glazed gable in the centre. Spacious interior, under a tent-like roof pierced by irregular openings. Gable window with STAINED GLASS by *Gerard Lawson*. SCULPTURE by *Fenwick Lawson*.

TOWN HALL. *See* Perambulation below.

WORKHOUSE (former), Linton Road. By *J. B. & W. Atkinson*, opened 1863. A small provincial example, the main building divided symmetrically between the sexes.

RAILWAY GOODS SHED (former), N of York Road. A handsome building of 1847 by *G. T. Andrews* for George Hudson's York & North Midland Railway (cf. Thorp Arch).

PERAMBULATION

The old BRIDGE was widened on its w side in 1769–73 and on the E side in 1826 by *Bernard Hartley & Son*. Six arches, segmental and round. On the parapet, the WAR MEMORIAL, with a bronze figure of Victory by *L. F. Roslyn*, 1922 (cf. Calverley). Upstream of the bridge the adjoining sites of the town mill and a brewery have been redeveloped but the town centre still consists mostly of C18 and C19 limestone buildings. Its two parallel main streets meet at the bridge end: the old Great North Road (High Street and North Street, partly widened 1929) and MARKET PLACE. This has the TOWN HALL at its N end, built in 1845 by *J. B. & W. Atkinson* on the island site formerly occupied by the town's chapel of ease. Latest classical. Assembly room on the first floor with a coved ceiling. The intimate streetscape around the Town Hall is the most attractive in the town and includes to the s the SHAMBLES (later covered market), erected as part of improvements by the Devonshire estate between 1811 and 1824. Simple eleven-bay arcade; the more architectural façade facing the Town Hall was erected in 1911. Laid out as part of the same early C19 scheme were

CROSS STREET and VICTORIA STREET, its continuation E of
High Street, which was developed with a uniform terrace of
twenty-five cottages along the S side. On its N side Brunswick
Yard had stabling for post horses. Next to this on the corner
with HIGH STREET is the former Devonshire Arms, one of the
town's numerous coaching inns (thirteen by 1824). On High
Street's E side, the C18 ANGEL INN, with pedimented doorcase, boasted stabling for over 100 horses. The SWAN AND
TALBOT on NORTH STREET is in its details early C18 – see
the Doric aedicule to the door with a frieze of vermiculation
and triglyphs – but in the form of its roofs and wing – seen
more clearly from the rear – it could be substantially earlier.

The larger houses are W of the town centre. Among those
on WESTGATE one has a late C18 BATH HOUSE, of two storeys
to the river. Victorian FORD BANK has a carefully balanced
Modernist extension by *OMI Architects*, completed in 2003,
with gardens descending to a timber deck projecting from the
riverbank.

WETHERBY GRANGE, *c.* 1784 by *James Wyatt* for Beilby Thompson, was demolished in 1962. It stood by the Wharfe ⅞ m. SE
of the bridge. Two LODGES, probably later, survive after a
fashion, one a shell beside the roundabout S of the bridge, the
other in the middle of a road junction below the A1, 1¼ m.
further SSE. Similar designs, both with a balustraded parapet
and a semicircular porch on two Doric columns. Also the
former STABLES, 1793, between the bridge and the first roundabout, incorporated into a C21 housing development. Two-
storey, tripartite range with a pediment.

WHITEWELL
Bowland Forest Low

ST MICHAEL. Chapel of ease of Whalley (Lancashire) in existence by the mid C16. Rebuilt 1817. Tall straight-headed two-
light windows with transoms and Perp tracery, tiny square
bellcote with segment-headed openings and pyramid cap. One
similar window and the bellcote are shown in a view of the
chapel before rebuilding. Shallow one-bay chancel added 1896.
– W GALLERY, 1825, on thin iron columns. Simple Gothic decoration to the front. – ROYAL ARMS, painted, *c.* 1817. –
STAINED GLASS. E window. Big Adoration of the Magi, *c.* 1896.
Beside the chapel the WHITEWELL HOTEL, the oldest part 1836
in a quite persuasive C17 Pennine style.

STAKES, 2⅛ m. SSW. Probably later C17. T-shaped house, the
upright as wide as it is long with the peculiarity of a central
doorway on both sides (one now a window). Was there, or was
there intended to be, another cross-wing, making an H? Both
doorways have an ornamented lintel with a design formed of
three flattened ogees; and above the N one is a rhyming motto:

NUNC MEA/MOX HUIUS/SED POSTEA/NESCIO CUIUS/NEMO SIBI NATUS ('Now it is mine, next it will be his, thereafter I know not whose. Nobody is born for himself alone') (cf. Barkisland Hall, West Riding South, 1638). The S doorway is flanked by cross-windows, the N elevation altered. The interior of the upright is subdivided by a timber partition on both floors, with part of it occupied by the staircase – panelled newels and vertically symmetrical balusters – but this shows signs of having been moved. On the cross-wing there are mullion-and-transom windows of five-by-two lights to both floors at the gable-ends, and more transomed windows on the W flank. Big arched fireplace inside. At LOWER LEES, ⅝ m. NE, a similar doorhead dated 1678. Another is at Hareden Farmhouse, Dunsop Bridge (q.v.), 1690.

WHIXLEY

ASCENSION. One C12 window in the N wall of the chancel. The rest is essentially of *c.* 1300–10, and a rarity for a village church in being so extensively in one style. Some restoration by *G. G. Scott*, 1862. W tower with SW stair-turret and a large five-light W window, with cusped intersecting tracery broken at the apex by a star-like cinquefoil in a circle. Perp belfry stage with renewed parapet and a pyramid roof. Aisles embracing the tower, chancel slightly lower than the nave, with ornate buttresses and pinnacles, and three-light windows in deep reveals again with intersecting tracery – uncusped to the aisles, extensively renewed to the chancel. Stylistically harmonious S porch by *Scott*. E window like the W but with a sexfoil instead of a cinquefoil. Spacious elegant interior. Three-bay nave arcades, with quatrefoil piers, finely moulded capitals, arches with a chamfer and an ovolo, and hoodmoulds on headstops. Similar details to the three tower arches and the chancel arch. Good crown-post roof to the nave, apparently all of 1862 apart from the tie-beams. Dec piscina in the S aisle. – FONT. Medieval, large and plain. – STAINED GLASS. Includes E window, 1897 by *Powell & Sons*, and chancel NE, 1896 by *Clayton & Bell*. – MONUMENT. Christopher Tancred, founder of Tancred's Hospital (*see* Whixley Hall, below), †1754. A huge plain mid-C19 marble sarcophagus, moved from the former chapel at Whixley Hall in 1905.

Former METHODIST CHAPEL. 1808. Rendered brick. Gable-end to street, with fancy bargeboards; pattern of round-headed windows at the back indicating position of lost pulpit and galleries.

WHIXLEY HALL. Handsome brick-built house, erected in more than one phase during the second half of the C17. Some internal remodelling *c.* 1718 by *William Etty*, extensive restoration and alterations 1907 by *Walter Brierley*. Half-H plan with the wings to the rear (N), two storeys. Late C17 S front of seven bays, the end pairs slightly projecting, with a hipped roof on deep bracketed eaves. Timber cross-windows, restored by *Brierley*, each vertical pair linked by a raised panel, and Carolean-style ashlar doorcase also by him. The w flank, with a (re-set) datestone of 1680, is in the same manner, a regular eight bays; but the E wing is earlier, with a datestone of 1654, also probably re-set, a stone mullion-and-transom window in the N end, and traces of others, including a very large staircase window on the irregular E flank, together with more cross-windows, one at least Brierley's interpolation. The N ends of both wings are gabled, the E with tumbled brickwork. Inside, *Etty* created a two-storey entrance hall with giant pilasters – the effect must have been similar to that of the hall at Bramham Park (q.v.), if on a more domestic scale – but it was reduced to a single storey and otherwise remodelled in 1907. Behind it a monumental staircase with very big balusters and broad handrail, which presumably belongs to the same phase; and the same may also apply to fittings in the w wing – an exceedingly fine overmantel with brilliantly carved garlands in the style of Grinling Gibbons in the front ground-floor room, and panelling and doorcases in a sequence of rooms on the first floor. In the E wing a mid-C17 staircase, with ornate vertically symmetrical balusters and angularly carved newel posts.

The history of the house is curious. The seat of the Tancred family, under the will of Christopher Tancred (†1754) it became an almshouse – Tancred's Hospital – for twelve 'decayed gentlemen', and remained in this use until *c.* 1880.

THE OLD COTTAGE, High Street. Fragmentary timber frame, probably C16, cased in C18 brick. Three bays, and end and rear aisles. Lobby entry.

WIGGLESWORTH

WIGGLESWORTH HALL. Complex of several buildings and dates. The most straightforward is a modest two-storey double-pile house of *c.* 1700–20. Five-bay front with cross-windows, mullioned windows at the back including a pair at the half-landings of the dog-leg staircase. Detached to the r. of this, running at right angles, is a range of C17 appearance, with mullioned windows, and at its S end an archway which appears to be the remains of a C17 porch, the S part of the building having been demolished. Its core, however, is earlier, part of a medieval range running E–W which originally extended further to the E: there are three crown-post roof trusses, numbered 3, 4, 5. E again is a smaller range, largely C20, which incorporates a pointed medieval doorway. The very large aisled BARN to the S was burnt out in 1959. Many tiers of vents to the gable-end.

WIGHILL

ALL SAINTS. On a slight rise at the S end of the village. A Norman church of nave and N aisle under one roof, and a lower chancel, with a short C15 W tower. Assorted square-headed, mainly Perp windows. What gives architectural importance to the church, however, is the S doorway of *c*. 1150, one of the most sumptuous and one of the best-preserved (in part thanks to the C18 porch) amongst the group of Norman doorways in village churches near York (cf. Healaugh and Adel). Two orders of colonnettes and an inner order on paired shafts. The outer capitals with crisply carved scenes of the Deposition and Salome dancing, related to the locally popular parable of the Wise and Foolish Virgins. The other capitals with foliage, both in the form of scrolls and as upright acanthus-like leaves. The label with chevron, and the outer order arch with beakhead. But the second-order arch has seventeen figures or scenes, arranged, it seems, without any principle: an eagle, bearded and crowned heads (the twenty-four Elders), a fox and hen, a man and an animal fighting, a winged demon confronting a griffin, monster heads, and so on. At the apex, four odd voussoirs – one unfinished, two reused, and one actually a corbel. Late C12 N arcade of four bays, with short, broad quatrefoil piers, the four lobes keeled. Round arches with two slight chamfers. Ogee-headed SEDILIA, restored PISCINA and remains of an aumbry. Chancel arch cut back, chancel re-roofed, arched-brace nave roof much restored, and N chapel made into a vestry, all by *W.H. Brierley*, 1912–13. – Plenty of interest in the furnishings. – COMMUNION RAIL and PULPIT, both C17, the latter with blind arcading. – Low CHANCEL SCREEN, like another communion rail, installed by *Brierley* incorporating late C17 balusters. – PEWS. Plain shape with plain, rather crude poppyheads. Late medieval. – DADO PANELLING made up from the C17 and C18 box pews. – SCULPTURE. Fragment of a cross-shaft with interlace embedded in nave S wall, earlier C10. – STAINED GLASS. Fragments of the C15 in the head of a chancel S window, and in the N aisle. Here also C18 fragments. – MONUMENTS. C14 recess on the S side of the chancel, said to have contained figures of a knight in armour and his wife with a marginal inscription. – Robert Stapleton †1634. Recumbent armour-clad effigy of alabaster, well carved, at his feet an excellent Saracen's head (the family crest). Big tomb-chest with black Ionic colonnettes and six kneeling children, enclosed by thick iron railings. Moved from the N chapel to the N aisle by Brierley. – Henry Stapleton †1779. Big tablet with urn by *Fisher* of York.

Near the church BROOK HALL, built *c*. 1835, possibly by *J. B. & W. Atkinson*, with additions of 1894 by *W. H. Brierley* (now mostly dem.) and 1938 (N service wing) by *Col. R. B. Armistead*. But until the C20 only Main Street, some way to the N, was built up. At its W end is MANOR FARMHOUSE, on the site of Wighill Hall, seat of the Stapleton family (dem. C18) and incorporating from it a splendid doorway of *c.* 1600: Tudor arch with armorial bearing over, framed by fluted Corinthian columns with strapwork decoration to the bases and an entablature surmounted by two armorial cartouches. Wighill Park, successor to Wighill Hall, 1 m. N on a rise in the park, was in turn largely demolished in the 1950s, but the STABLES, with cupola, remain.

0030 # WILSDEN

Long Pennine mill village straggling up a hill. The church, by *Oates*, 1823–5, has been demolished.

BOARD SCHOOL (Wilsden Primary), Tweedy Street. 1876 by *E. P. Peterson* of Bradford, altered. Gables and minimal Gothic detail. In the Main Street SPRING MILL HOUSE, late C18, with two Venetian windows to each floor and the MILL immediately adjoining, built 1832–4 for worsted spinning but largely rebuilt after 1905.

MYTHOLME, ¾ m. N. *c.* 1700, a virtual mirror image of Hallas Old Hall, Cullingworth (q.v.) – the porch, with a reused datestone of 1685, is apparently C20. Four bays of cross-windows to the l., two to the r. Parlour-end chimney with blind arcading (cf. Micklethwaite Grange, Bingley). Nearby, in Sandy Banks, a former SCHOOL, endowed 1680. One storey, mullioned windows with arched lights. Extended C20.

1060 # WILSILL
Bishopside

ST MICHAEL. Chapel of ease of Pateley Bridge, 1905–6 by *Bland & Bown* of Harrogate. Pedestrian Neo-Norman, nave and chancel.

Some C17 farmhouses, and KILN HOUSE, ⅜ m. E, possibly C16 in origin, with two cruck trusses. One storey and attic, porch with moulded doorways, mullioned windows. Lobby entry and behind it the housebody fireplace with stopped and chamfered bressumer. Two more cruck trusses at FELLBECK OLD HALL, ¾ m. NE, otherwise rebuilt 1685, perhaps originally with a cross-passage. Heavily restored *c.* 1985.

2070 # WINKSLEY

ST CUTHBERT AND ST OSWALD. 1914–17 by *Connon & Chorley* of Leeds, the gift of Lady Furness of Grantley Hall in memory of her husband. An accomplished and lavish design in free Perp, with a strong w tower. Straight-headed w window of three lights, the niche above it, and various inscriptions in the walls of the tower all apparently reused, with some renewal, from the chapel rebuilt in 1502–4 by Abbot Huby of Fountains, via its successor, built in 1822. The inscriptions include Huby's motto, SOLI DEO HONOR ET GLORIA ('Honour and glory to God alone'), and inside, his initials. Broad three-bay nave with Albi-like full-height recesses to each side rather than aisles, with transverse pointed tunnel vaults and little linking arches through the internal buttresses. Chancel of the same height, gabled organ chamber to N, timber rib-vault to the space under the tower, which serves as a narthex. – REREDOS, PULPIT and FONT, of veined marble, executed by *Farmer & Brindley*. – STAINED GLASS. w window, and middle N and s nave windows by *Heaton, Butler & Bayne*. E window by *Charles E. Steel* of Leeds.

GATE BRIDGE MILL, 1 m. NW. Probably early C19. Two storeys, with lean-to wheelhouse at the back. Machinery complete: breast-shot water wheel with iron hub and rim, spokes and buckets of wood, timber-cogged driving wheels and three sets of millstones.

WINTERBURN

9050

Flasby with Winterburn

CHAPEL (now a house). Built 1703–4 for the Presbyterians. s flank of five bays with central Tudor-arched doorway and two tiers of two-light mullioned windows. An upper tier only to the N. C19 gabled vestry against the w end.

FRIARS HEAD, ¾ m. s. Fine and slightly mysterious house, probably built *c.* 1600 for Michael Lister 'esquyer' (†1618). Two tall storeys and attic. Symmetrical front of gritstone ashlar, the proportions of which are governed by a complex system of arithmetical ratios. Four close-set gabled projections with six-light transomed windows to each floor – plus single transomed lights to the sides – and to the attic three-light windows with truncated-ogee heads which are probably the earliest of their kind in the Pennine region. Porch accommodated in the second projection, with moulded three-centre-headed entrance. Ball finials to the gables, diagonally set chimneys. The back is much less formal, with two projecting wings and a staircase turret between them, and mullioned windows functionally disposed. Interior somewhat altered but the plan remains clear enough. Cross-passage, former kitchen to the l., with huge segment-headed fireplace, and housebody, surprisingly small, to the r. The room above the housebody and passage was the largest and presumably the great chamber, but has been subdivided and the position of its fireplace changed. Roof of upper-cruck type, with collars supporting upper king-posts (cf. Paget Hall, Gargrave).

33

WINTERBURN RESERVOIR, 1 m. NNE. *c.* 1885–93 by *Rofe & Fil-liter*, engineers of Leeds, to serve the Leeds and Liverpool Canal. The earthen dam has a monumental stone-built water ladder for the spillway, with crowstepped copings.

WOODHOUSE GROVE SCHOOL
Rawdon

1030

Founded by the Methodists in 1811. Its accommodation then was a small C18 country house and this forms the core of the present main building, a long two-storeyed ashlar range, facing s, with slightly taller projecting wings at each end. The middle five bays – the first and fifth slightly projecting, with pediments to the ground-floor windows – are the front block added to the house *c.* 1790; and the earlier part, mid-C18, remains behind this, its front facing E. Three bays, with ground- and first-floor Venetian windows flanking the centre. Some mid-C18 detail inside, including an enriched chimneypiece. The flanking parts of the range, including the wings, are of 1847–54 by *Thomas Shaw* of Leeds. They contained *inter alia* the dining hall and a new schoolroom. Central porch, with Ionic columns, added 1864.

To the NW are the STABLE BLOCK of the C18 house, part of which in 1811 became the first school chapel, and at right angles to it a former barn which became the first schoolroom. Both much altered, the stables of one-and-a-half storeys and five bays with three-bay pedimented centre, the barn with early C19 round-headed windows and a clock turret added in 1902. Further W, crowning a wooded hillock, is another relic of the country-house phase, the skeleton of a Gothick ornamental TOWER built *c.* 1799. Big arched window openings, battlements. NW of this, beside the road, the present CHAPEL, 1887 by *H. Isitt* of Bradford. Indistinguishable from an ordinary Gothic Nonconformist chapel of the period, with a thin NW spirelet. NE of the main building, linked to it by an institutional extension of 1900 etc. behind the mid-C18 house, a big lumpish L-shaped range mainly of 1953–65 by *J. Poulson*. Attached to the far end of this the THEATRE, 2002–4 by *Watson & Batty* of Guiseley. Eyecatching in pale brick, glass and steel, with a cylindrical glazed turret.

WOODKIRK

2020

ST MARY. Beside the Leeds to Dewsbury road, on the edge of suburbia: no village. Parochial church which also served a cell of Augustinian canons attached to Nostell Priory (West Riding

South). The conventual buildings, located by excavation in the 1960s, were to the N, apparently arranged round a cloister. Unbuttressed W tower of the early C13, heavily restored *c.* 1911: bell-openings of two pointed lights on an octagonal dividing shaft, within round-headed relieving arches, and a W lancet with nutmeg decoration to the hoodmould. The rest – aisleless nave and long aisleless chancel of the same height – all rebuilt *c.* 1831–4 by *Joseph Furness*, mason. Windows with intersected and Dec tracery, nave N wall suggesting a blocked three-bay arcade, not repeated on the interior face. Much restored double-chamfered tower arch, jambs of the chancel arch perhaps reused. – PULPIT. C17, with arched panels. – Good late medieval BENCH ENDS reused on the C19 choir stalls. Blank Perp tracery and carved poppyheads. – PANELLING in the vestry, made from C17 pews. – ROYAL ARMS of George I, painted on canvas. – STAINED GLASS. Chancel SE with medieval fragments, assembled in C19. – Three nave windows by *Ward & Hughes*, 1885–90.

WYKE
Bradford

1020

Suburban salient S of the city.

ST MARY, Green Lane. 1846–7 by *Mallinson & Healey*. Quite large, in unfussy E.E. style. Tall SW tower and broach spire, lancet windows. – STAINED GLASS. E window 1875 by *R. B. Edmundson*. Several others by *Warrington*, *c.* 1880–1900.

UNITED REFORMED CHAPEL (Congregational), Westfield Lane. 1824. Usual plain gabled front. Gallery forming a half-octagon, box pews throughout.

WYKE MANOR COMMUNITY COLLEGE, Towngate. Former Board School, 1902–3 by *Adkin & Hill*. Art Nouveau tower-chimney, with blocked masonry and undulating coping. Class-room block with shaped gables.

HIGH FERNLEY HOUSE, High Fernley Road, ½m. N of the church. Double pile of 1698 built by the gentry Richardson family of Bierley, much altered and reduced in size. Front originally triple-gabled but the l. third of the house demolished, fortuitously rendering what is left near-symmetrical, and the other two gables replaced by a parapet. Round-headed doorway, now central, with keystone, panelled pilasters, cornice on brackets and big oculus over (cf. Trench Farm-house, Baildon, 1697). Transomed window of nine lights to l., the others replaced by pairs of upright rectangles, the hood-moulds remaining above. At WOODSIDE FARM nearby, a rear wing with another oculus (and earlier timber framing inside).

At LOWER WYKE, ½m. S, the MORAVIAN CHAPEL, Chapel Fold. 1775, replacing a chapel of 1753. Plain rendered oblong. Classic early Nonconformist scheme with a four-bay front on the long axis, with two tall round-headed windows in the centre and round-headed doorways with smaller windows over to l. and r. Little louvred bellcote with pyramid roof and ball finial. Charming interior with handsome late C18 PULPIT between the central windows, galleries l. and r., each on a single Tuscan column, with box pews of 1824. Organ recess at back, *c.* 1895.

Adjoining to the l., continuing the same roof-line, the MIN-ISTER'S HOUSE, 1795; and behind the chapel to the N the SISTERS' HOUSE, 1782, later a school, three bays with a Venetian window to the attic in a gable over the centre. Further NE the SUNDAY SCHOOL, 1881, one storey, with round-headed windows.

Nearby the MANOR HOUSE, C17 Pennine farmhouse of several phases. Centre part, facing W, of 1614, with traces of timber framing inside. N wing 1687, rear and probably the S extension – the latter the parlour end of the house – 1694. Mullioned windows, and in the 1694 part a blocked upright oval. Extensive early C20 renovation.

YEADON

Small mill town 'noted for anything but its architectural beauty' (P. Slater, 1880), agglomerated with Guiseley and Rawdon (qq.v.).

ST ANDREW, Haw Lane. 1890–1 by *T. H. & F. Healey*. Arts and Crafts Perp, low and unassuming. Octagonal SW turret with timber belfry and ogee domelet. S aisle and double S transept. Kingpost roof trusses.

ST JOHN, Henshaw, S of the town centre. 1843–4 by *Walker Raw-storne*. Lancet style, formerly with a big W tower, cut down to roof level in 1971. Chancel 1893 by *T. H. & F. Healey*. – STAINED GLASS. Nave SE 1921 by *A. K. Nicholson*.

TOWN HALL. 1879–80 by *William Hill* of Leeds, the dominant building in the town. Crude design in C13 Gothic. Short symmetrical front, with central tower crowned by a spire-like hipped roof and flanking it a pair of semi-dormers under bizarre concave-sided pyramids. Another of these on each flank. First-floor auditorium with hammerbeam roof.

LEEDS AND BRADFORD AIRPORT, E of the town. TERMINAL BUILDING of several phases, the much altered core 1967–8 by *Norman & Dawbarn* (job architect *K. Poloczanski*). Crescent-shaped – concave side towards the approach road, convex to the runway – with the control tower above. Big extensions l. and r. 1985 onwards by *Leeds City Architect's Department* (City Architect *M. J. Thurmott*, project architect *J. Lindley*), and others.

GREEN LANE DYEWORKS, Green Lane. Mainly 1908 onwards. Tall cylindrical chimney of red brick.

LOW HALL, Gill Lane, w of St John's church. Early C17, comprehensively restored and modernized, and rear wing added, 1876. Two-storey porch with date of 1658, said to have been brought from Esholt Priory – in which case the date will be that of the transfer. Tudor-arched doorway, and a pretty canted oriel above. Mullioned windows l. and r., some with arched lights, all apparently renewed, that to the housebody of seven lights, others of five.

ADDENDA (2014)

p. 228, CLIFFORD: ST EDWARD KING AND CONFESSOR. In the N aisle two windows (Life of St Anne; Life of William of York) designed by *A. W. N. Pugin*, 1848.

p. 325, HAWORTH. The new spinning mill at Ebor Mill has been burnt down and the remains demolished.

p. 706, SKIPTON CASTLE. There is persuasive evidence that *Isaac de Caux*, who probably designed the Woburn Abbey grotto, worked at Skipton Castle in 1626; but given the disparity in sophistication between the two examples it seems probable that his employment there related not to the grotto but to the lost C17 garden.

p. 711, SKIPTON: BELLE VUE MILLS. The chimney has been demolished.

GLOSSARY

Numbers and letters refer to the illustrations (by John Sambrook) on pp. 772–779.

ABACUS: flat slab forming the top of a capital (3a).

ACANTHUS: classical formalized leaf ornament (4b).

ACCUMULATOR TOWER: *see* Hydraulic power.

ACHIEVEMENT: a complete display of armorial bearings.

ACROTERION: plinth for a statue or ornament on the apex or ends of a pediment; more usually, both the plinth and what stands on it (4a).

AEDICULE (*lit.* little building): architectural surround, consisting usually of two columns or pilasters supporting a pediment.

AGGREGATE: *see* Concrete.

AISLE: subsidiary space alongside the body of a building, separated from it by columns, piers, or posts.

ALMONRY: a building from which alms are dispensed to the poor.

AMBULATORY (*lit.* walkway): aisle around the sanctuary (q.v.).

ANGLE ROLL: roll moulding in the angle between two planes (1a).

ANSE DE PANIER: *see* Arch.

ANTAE: simplified pilasters (4a), usually applied to the ends of the enclosing walls of a portico *in antis* (q.v.).

ANTEFIXAE: ornaments projecting at regular intervals above a Greek cornice, originally to conceal the ends of roof tiles (4a).

ANTHEMION: classical ornament like a honeysuckle flower (4b).

APRON: raised panel below a window or wall monument or tablet.

APSE: semicircular or polygonal end of an apartment, especially of a chancel or chapel. In classical architecture sometimes called an *exedra*.

ARABESQUE: non-figurative surface decoration consisting of flowing lines, foliage scrolls etc., based on geometrical patterns. Cf. Grotesque.

ARCADE: series of arches supported by piers or columns. *Blind arcade* or *arcading*: the same applied to the wall surface. *Wall arcade*: in medieval churches, a blind arcade forming a dado below windows. Also a covered shopping street.

ARCH: Shapes *see* 5c. *Basket arch* or *anse de panier* (basket handle): three-centred and depressed, or with a flat centre. *Nodding*: ogee arch curving forward from the wall face. *Parabolic*: shaped like a chain suspended from two level points, but inverted. Special purposes. *Chancel*: dividing chancel from nave or crossing. *Crossing*: spanning piers at a crossing (q.v.). *Relieving or discharging*: incorporated in a wall to relieve superimposed weight (5c). *Skew*: spanning responds not diametrically opposed. *Strainer*: inserted in an opening to resist inward pressure. *Transverse*: spanning a main axis (e.g. of a vaulted space). *See also* Jack arch, Triumphal arch.

ARCHITRAVE: formalized lintel, the lowest member of the classical entablature (3a). Also the moulded frame of a door or window (often borrowing the profile of a classical architrave). For *lugged* and *shouldered* architraves *see* 4b.

ARCUATED: dependent structurally on the arch principle. Cf. Trabeated.

ARK: chest or cupboard housing the

tables of Jewish law in a synagogue.

ARRIS: sharp edge where two surfaces meet at an angle (3a).

ASHLAR: masonry of large blocks wrought to even faces and square edges (6d).

ASTRAGAL: classical moulding of semicircular section (3f).

ASTYLAR: with no columns or similar vertical features.

ATLANTES: *see* Caryatids.

ATRIUM (plural: atria): inner court of a Roman or C20 house; in a multi-storey building, a toplit covered court rising through all storeys. Also an open court in front of a church.

ATTACHED COLUMN: *see* Engaged column.

ATTIC: small top storey within a roof. Also the storey above the main entablature of a classical façade.

AUMBRY: recess or cupboard to hold sacred vessels for the Mass.

BAILEY: *see* Motte-and-bailey.

BALANCE BEAM: *see* Canals.

BALDACCHINO: free-standing canopy, originally fabric, over an altar. Cf. Ciborium.

BALLFLOWER: globular flower of three petals enclosing a ball (1a). Typical of the Decorated style.

BALUSTER: pillar or pedestal of bellied form. *Balusters*: vertical supports of this or any other form, for a handrail or coping, the whole being called a *balustrade* (6c). *Blind balustrade*: the same applied to the wall surface.

BARBICAN: outwork defending the entrance to a castle.

BARGEBOARDS (corruption of 'vergeboards'): boards, often carved or fretted, fixed beneath the eaves of a gable to cover and protect the rafters.

BAROQUE: style originating in Rome *c.*1600 and current in England *c.*1680–1720, characterized by dramatic massing and silhouette and the use of the giant order.

BARROW: burial mound.

BARTIZAN: corbelled turret, square or round, frequently at an angle.

BASCULE: hinged part of a lifting (or bascule) bridge.

BASE: moulded foot of a column or pilaster. For *Attic* base *see* 3b.

BASEMENT: lowest, subordinate storey; hence the lowest part of a classical elevation, below the *piano nobile* (q.v.).

BASILICA: a Roman public hall; hence an aisled building with a clerestory.

BASTION: one of a series of defensive semicircular or polygonal projections from the main wall of a fortress or city.

BATTER: intentional inward inclination of a wall face.

BATTLEMENT: defensive parapet, composed of *merlons* (solid) and *crenels* (embrasures) through which archers could shoot; sometimes called *crenellation*. Also used decoratively.

BAY: division of an elevation or interior space as defined by regular vertical features such as arches, columns, windows etc.

BAY LEAF: classical ornament of overlapping bay leaves (3f).

BAY WINDOW: window of one or more storeys projecting from the face of a building. *Canted*: with a straight front and angled sides. *Bow window*: curved. *Oriel*: rests on corbels or brackets and starts above ground level; also the bay window at the dais end of a medieval great hall.

BEAD-AND-REEL: *see* Enrichments.

BEAKHEAD: Norman ornament with a row of beaked bird or beast heads usually biting into a roll moulding (1a).

BELFRY: chamber or stage in a tower where bells are hung.

BELL CAPITAL: *see* 1b.

BELLCOTE: small gabled or roofed housing for the bell(s).

BERM: level area separating a ditch from a bank on a hill-fort or barrow.

BILLET: Norman ornament of small half-cylindrical or rectangular blocks (1a).

BLIND: *see* Arcade, Baluster, Portico.

BLOCK CAPITAL: *see* 1a.

BLOCKED: columns, etc. interrupted by regular projecting

blocks (*blocking*), as on a Gibbs surround (4b).

BLOCKING COURSE: course of stones, or equivalent, on top of a cornice and crowning the wall.

BOLECTION MOULDING: covering the joint between two different planes (6b).

BOND: the pattern of long sides (*stretchers*) and short ends (*headers*) produced on the face of a wall by laying bricks in a particular way (6e).

BOSS: knob or projection, e.g. at the intersection of ribs in a vault (2c).

BOWTELL: a term in use by the C15 for a form of roll moulding, usually three-quarters of a circle in section (also called *edge roll*).

BOW WINDOW: *see* Bay window.

BOX FRAME: timber-framed construction in which vertical and horizontal wall members support the roof (7). Also concrete construction where the loads are taken on cross walls; also called *cross-wall construction*.

BRACE: subsidiary member of a structural frame, curved or straight. *Bracing* is often arranged decoratively e.g. quatrefoil, herringbone (7). *See also* Roofs.

BRATTISHING: ornamental crest, usually formed of leaves, Tudor flowers or miniature battlements.

BRESSUMER (*lit.* breast-beam): big horizontal beam supporting the wall above, especially in a jettied building (7).

BRICK: *see* Bond, Cogging, Engineering, Gauged, Tumbling.

BRIDGE: *Bowstring*: with arches rising above the roadway which is suspended from them. *Clapper*: one long stone forms the roadway. *Roving*: *see* Canal. *Suspension*: roadway suspended from cables or chains slung between towers or pylons. *Stay-suspension* or *stay-cantilever*: supported by diagonal stays from towers or pylons. *See also* Bascule.

BRISES-SOLEIL: projecting fins or canopies which deflect direct sunlight from windows.

BROACH: *see* Spire and 1C.

BUCRANIUM: ox skull used decoratively in classical friezes.

BULL-NOSED SILL: sill displaying a pronounced convex upper moulding.

BULLSEYE WINDOW: small oval window, set horizontally (cf. Oculus). Also called *œil de bœuf*.

BUTTRESS: vertical member projecting from a wall to stabilize it or to resist the lateral thrust of an arch, roof, or vault (1c, 2c). A *flying buttress* transmits the thrust to a heavy abutment by means of an arch or half-arch (1c).

CABLE OR ROPE MOULDING: originally Norman, like twisted strands of a rope.

CAMES: *see* Quarries.

CAMPANILE: free-standing bell-tower.

CANALS: *Flash lock*: removable weir or similar device through which boats pass on a flush of water. Predecessor of the *pound lock*: chamber with gates at each end allowing boats to float from one level to another. *Tidal gates*: single pair of lock gates allowing vessels to pass when the tide makes a level. *Balance beam*: beam projecting horizontally for opening and closing lock gates. *Roving bridge*: carrying a towing path from one bank to the other.

CANTILEVER: horizontal projection (e.g. step, canopy) supported by a downward force behind the fulcrum.

CAPITAL: head or crowning feature of a column or pilaster; for classical types *see* 3; for medieval types *see* 1b.

CARREL: compartment designed for individual work or study.

CARTOUCHE: classical tablet with ornate frame (4b).

CARYATIDS: female figures supporting an entablature; their male counterparts are *Atlantes* (*lit.* Atlas figures).

CASEMATE: vaulted chamber, with embrasures for defence, within a castle wall or projecting from it.

CASEMENT: side-hinged window.

CASTELLATED: with battlements (q.v.).

CAST IRON: hard and brittle, cast in a mould to the required shape.

Wrought iron is ductile, strong in tension, forged into decorative patterns or forged and rolled into e.g. bars, joists, boiler plates; *mild steel* is its modern equivalent, similar but stronger.

CATSLIDE: *See* 8a.

CAVETTO: concave classical moulding of quarter-round section (3f).

CELURE OR CEILURE: enriched area of roof above rood or altar.

CEMENT: *see* Concrete.

CENOTAPH (*lit.* empty tomb): funerary monument which is not a burying place.

CENTRING: wooden support for the building of an arch or vault, removed after completion.

CHAMFER (*lit.* corner-break): surface formed by cutting off a square edge or corner. For types of chamfers and *chamfer stops see* 6a. *See also* Double chamfer.

CHANCEL: part of the E end of a church set apart for the use of the officiating clergy.

CHANTRY CHAPEL: often attached to or within a church, endowed for the celebration of Masses principally for the soul of the founder.

CHEVET (*lit.* head): French term for chancel with ambulatory and radiating chapels.

CHEVRON: V-shape used in series or double series (later) on a Norman moulding (1a). Also (especially when on a single plane) called *zigzag*.

CHOIR: the part of a cathedral, monastic or collegiate church where services are sung.

CIBORIUM: a fixed canopy over an altar, usually vaulted and supported on four columns; cf. Baldacchino. Also a canopied shrine for the reserved sacrament.

CINQUEFOIL: *see* Foil.

CIST: stone-lined or slab-built grave.

CLADDING: external covering or skin applied to a structure, especially a framed one.

CLERESTORY: uppermost storey of the nave of a church, pierced by windows. Also high-level windows in secular buildings.

CLOSER: a brick cut to complete a bond (6e).

CLUSTER BLOCK: *see* Multi-storey.

COADE STONE: ceramic artificial stone made in Lambeth 1769–c.1840 by Eleanor Coade (†1821) and her associates.

COB: walling material of clay mixed with straw. Also called *pisé*.

COFFERING: arrangement of sunken panels (coffers), square or polygonal, decorating a ceiling, vault, or arch.

COGGING: a decorative course of bricks laid diagonally (6e). Cf. Dentilation.

COLLAR: *see* Roofs and 7.

COLLEGIATE CHURCH: endowed for the support of a college of priests.

COLONNADE: range of columns supporting an entablature. Cf. Arcade.

COLONNETTE: small medieval column or shaft.

COLOSSAL ORDER: *see* Giant order.

COLUMBARIUM: shelved, niched structure to house multiple burials.

COLUMN: a classical, upright structural member of round section with a shaft, a capital, and usually a base (3a, 4a).

COLUMN FIGURE: carved figure attached to a medieval column or shaft, usually flanking a doorway.

COMMUNION TABLE: unconsecrated table used in Protestant churches for the celebration of Holy Communion.

COMPOSITE: *see* Orders.

COMPOUND PIER: grouped shafts (q.v.), or a solid core surrounded by shafts.

CONCRETE: composition of *cement* (calcined lime and clay), *aggregate* (small stones or rock chippings), sand and water. It can be poured into *formwork* or *shuttering* (temporary frame of timber or metal) on site (*in-situ* concrete), or *pre-cast* as components before construction. *Reinforced*: incorporating steel rods to take the tensile force. *Pre-stressed*: with tensioned steel rods. Finishes include the impression of boards left by formwork (*board-marked* or *shuttered*), and texturing with steel brushes (*brushed*) or hammers (*hammer-dressed*). *See also* Shell.

CONSOLE: bracket of curved outline (4b).

COPING: protective course of masonry or brickwork capping a wall (6d).

CORBEL: projecting block supporting something above. *Corbel course*: continuous course of projecting stones or bricks fulfilling the same function. *Corbel table*: series of corbels to carry a parapet or a wall-plate or wall-post (7). *Corbelling*: brick or masonry courses built out beyond one another to support a chimney-stack, window, etc.

CORINTHIAN: *see* Orders and 3d.

CORNICE: flat-topped ledge with moulded underside, projecting along the top of a building or feature, especially as the highest member of the classical entablature (3a). Also the decorative moulding in the angle between wall and ceiling.

CORPS-DE-LOGIS: the main building(s) as distinct from the wings or pavilions.

COTTAGE ORNÉ: an artfully rustic small house associated with the Picturesque movement.

COUNTERCHANGING: of joists on a ceiling divided by beams into compartments, when placed in opposite directions in alternate squares.

COUR D'HONNEUR: formal entrance court before a house in the French manner, usually with flanking wings and a screen wall or gates.

COURSE: continuous layer of stones, etc. in a wall (6e).

COVE: a broad concave moulding, e.g. to mask the eaves of a roof. *Coved ceiling*: with a pronounced cove joining the walls to a flat central panel smaller than the whole area of the ceiling.

CRADLE ROOF: *see* Wagon roof.

CREDENCE: a shelf within or beside a piscina (q.v.), or a table for the sacramental elements and vessels.

CRENELLATION: parapet with crenels (*see* Battlement).

CRINKLE-CRANKLE WALL: garden wall undulating in a series of serpentine curves.

CROCKETS: leafy hooks. *Crocketing* decorates the edges of Gothic features, such as pinnacles, canopies, etc. *Crocket capital*: *see* 1b.

CROSSING: central space at the junction of the nave, chancel, and transepts. *Crossing tower*: above a crossing.

CROSS-WINDOW: with one mullion and one transom (qq.v.).

CROWN-POST: *see* Roofs and 7.

CROWSTEPS: squared stones set like steps, e.g. on a gable (8a).

CRUCKS (*lit.* crooked): pairs of inclined timbers (*blades*), usually curved, set at bay-lengths; they support the roof timbers and, in timber buildings, also support the walls (8b). *Base*: blades rise from ground level to a tie- or collar-beam which supports the roof timbers. *Full*: blades rise from ground level to the apex of the roof, serving as the main members of a roof truss. *Jointed*: blades formed from more than one timber; the lower member may act as a wall-post; it is usually elbowed at wall-plate level and jointed just above. *Middle*: blades rise from half-way up the walls to a tie- or collar-beam. *Raised*: blades rise from half-way up the walls to the apex. *Upper*: blades supported on a tie-beam and rising to the apex.

CRYPT: underground or half-underground area, usually below the E end of a church. *Ring crypt*: corridor crypt surrounding the apse of an early medieval church, often associated with chambers for relics. Cf. Undercroft.

CUPOLA (*lit.* dome): especially a small dome on a circular or polygonal base crowning a larger dome, roof, or turret.

CURSUS: a long avenue defined by two parallel earthen banks with ditches outside.

CURTAIN WALL: a connecting wall between the towers of a castle. Also a non-load-bearing external wall applied to a C20 framed structure.

CUSP: *see* Tracery and 2b.

CYCLOPEAN MASONRY: large irregular polygonal stones, smooth and finely jointed.

CYMA RECTA and CYMA REVERSA: classical mouldings with double curves (3f). Cf. Ogee.

DADO: the finishing (often with panelling) of the lower part of a wall in a classical interior; in origin a formalized continuous pedestal. *Dado rail*: the moulding along the top of the dado.

DAGGER: *see* Tracery and 2b.

DALLE-DE-VERRE (*lit.* glass-slab): a late C20 stained-glass technique, setting large, thick pieces of cast glass into a frame of reinforced concrete or epoxy resin.

DEC (DECORATED): English Gothic architecture *c.* 1290 to *c.* 1350. The name is derived from the type of window tracery (q.v.) used during the period.

DEMI- or HALF-COLUMNS: engaged columns (q.v.) half of whose circumference projects from the wall.

DENTIL: small square block used in series in classical cornices (3c). *Dentilation* is produced by the projection of alternating headers along cornices or stringcourses.

DIAPER: repetitive surface decoration of lozenges or squares flat or in relief. Achieved in brickwork with bricks of two colours.

DIOCLETIAN OR THERMAL WINDOW: semicircular with two mullions, as used in the Baths of Diocletian, Rome (4b).

DISTYLE: having two columns (4a).

DOGTOOTH: E.E. ornament, consisting of a series of small pyramids formed by four stylized canine teeth meeting at a point (1a).

DORIC: *see* Orders and 3a, 3b.

DORMER: window projecting from the slope of a roof (8a).

DOUBLE CHAMFER: a chamfer applied to each of two recessed arches (1a).

DOUBLE PILE: *see* Pile.

DRAGON BEAM: *see* Jetty.

DRESSINGS: the stone or brickwork worked to a finished face about an angle, opening, or other feature.

DRIPSTONE: moulded stone projecting from a wall to protect the

lower parts from water. Cf. Hoodmould, Weathering.

DRUM: circular or polygonal stage supporting a dome or cupola. Also one of the stones forming the shaft of a column (3a).

DUTCH or FLEMISH GABLE: *see* 8a.

EASTER SEPULCHRE: tomb-chest used for Easter ceremonial, within or against the N wall of a chancel.

EAVES: overhanging edge of a roof; hence *eaves cornice* in this position.

ECHINUS: ovolo moulding (q.v.) below the abacus of a Greek Doric capital (3a).

EDGE RAIL: *see* Railways.

E.E. (EARLY ENGLISH): English Gothic architecture *c.* 1190–1250.

EGG-AND-DART: *see* Enrichments and 3f.

ELEVATION: any face of a building or side of a room. In a drawing, the same or any part of it, represented in two dimensions.

EMBATTLED: with battlements.

EMBRASURE: small splayed opening in a wall or battlement (q.v.).

ENCAUSTIC TILES: earthenware tiles fired with a pattern and glaze.

EN DELIT: stone cut against the bed.

ENFILADE: reception rooms in a formal series, usually with all doorways on axis.

ENGAGED or ATTACHED COLUMN: one that partly merges into a wall or pier.

ENGINEERING BRICKS: dense bricks, originally used mostly for railway viaducts etc.

ENRICHMENTS: the carved decoration of certain classical mouldings, e.g. the ovolo (qq.v.) with *egg-and-dart*, the cyma reversa with *waterleaf*, the astragal with *bead-and-reel* (3f).

ENTABLATURE: in classical architecture, collective name for the three horizontal members (architrave, frieze, and cornice) carried by a wall or a column (3a).

ENTASIS: very slight convex deviation from a straight line, used to prevent an optical illusion of concavity.

EPITAPH: inscription on a tomb.

EXEDRA: *see* Apse.

EXTRADOS: outer curved face of an arch or vault.

EYECATCHER: decorative building terminating a vista.

FASCIA: plain horizontal band, e.g. in an architrave (3c, 3d) or on a shopfront.

FENESTRATION: the arrangement of windows in a façade.

FERETORY: site of the chief shrine of a church, behind the high altar.

FESTOON: ornamental garland, suspended from both ends. Cf. Swag.

FIBREGLASS, or glass-reinforced polyester (GRP): synthetic resin reinforced with glass fibre. GRC: glass-reinforced concrete.

FIELD: see Panelling and 6b.

FILLET: a narrow flat band running down a medieval shaft or along a roll moulding (1a). It separates larger curved mouldings in classical cornices, fluting or bases (3c).

FLAMBOYANT: the latest phase of French Gothic architecture, with flowing tracery.

FLASH LOCK: see Canals.

FLÈCHE or SPIRELET (*lit.* arrow): slender spire on the centre of a roof.

FLEURON: medieval carved flower or leaf, often rectilinear (1a).

FLUSHWORK: knapped flint used with dressed stone to form patterns.

FLUTING: series of concave grooves (flutes), their common edges sharp (arris) or blunt (fillet) (3).

FOIL (*lit.* leaf): lobe formed by the cusping of a circular or other shape in tracery (2b). *Trefoil* (three), *quatrefoil* (four), *cinquefoil* (five), and *multifoil* express the number of lobes in a shape.

FOLIATE: decorated with leaves.

FORMWORK: see Concrete.

FRAMED BUILDING: where the structure is carried by a framework – e.g. of steel, reinforced concrete, timber – instead of by load-bearing walls.

FREESTONE: stone that is cut, or can be cut, in all directions.

FRESCO: *al fresco*: painting on wet plaster. *Fresco secco*: painting on dry plaster.

FRIEZE: the middle member of the classical entablature, sometimes ornamented (3a). *Pulvinated frieze* (*lit.* cushioned): of bold convex profile (3c). Also a horizontal band of ornament.

FRONTISPIECE: in C16 and C17 buildings the central feature of doorway and windows above linked in one composition.

GABLE: For types see 8a. *Gablet*: small gable. *Pedimental gable*: treated like a pediment.

GADROONING: classical ribbed ornament like inverted fluting that flows into a lobed edge.

GALILEE: chapel or vestibule usually at the W end of a church enclosing the main portal(s).

GALLERY: a long room or passage; an upper storey above the aisle of a church, looking through arches to the nave; a balcony or mezzanine overlooking the main interior space of a building; or an external walkway.

GALLETING: small stones set in a mortar course.

GAMBREL ROOF: see 8a.

GARDEROBE: medieval privy.

GARGOYLE: projecting water spout often carved into human or animal shape.

GAUGED or RUBBED BRICKWORK: soft brick sawn roughly, then rubbed to a precise (gauged) surface. Mostly used for door or window openings (5c).

GAZEBO (jocular Latin, 'I shall gaze'): ornamental lookout tower or raised summer house.

GEOMETRIC: English Gothic architecture *c.* 1250–1310. See also Tracery. For another meaning, see Stairs.

GIANT or COLOSSAL ORDER: classical order (q.v.) whose height is that of two or more storeys of the building to which it is applied.

GIBBS SURROUND: C18 treatment of an opening (4b), seen particularly in the work of James Gibbs (1682–1754).

GIRDER: a large beam. *Box*: of hollow-box section. *Bowed*: with its top rising in a curve. *Plate*: of I-section, made from iron or steel plates. *Lattice*: with braced framework.

GLAZING BARS: wooden or sometimes metal bars separating and supporting window panes.

GRAFFITI: *see* Sgraffito.

GRANGE: farm owned and run by a religious order.

GRC: *see* Fibreglass.

GRISAILLE: monochrome painting on walls or glass.

GROIN: sharp edge at the meeting of two cells of a cross-vault; *see* Vault and 2c.

GROTESQUE (*lit.* grotto-esque): wall decoration adopted from Roman examples in the Renaissance. Its foliage scrolls incorporate figurative elements. Cf. Arabesque.

GROTTO: artificial cavern.

GRP: *see* Fibreglass.

GUILLOCHE: classical ornament of interlaced bands (4b).

GUNLOOP: opening for a firearm.

GUTTAE: stylized drops (3b).

HALF-TIMBERING: archaic term for timber-framing (q.v.). Sometimes used for non-structural decorative timberwork.

HALL CHURCH: medieval church with nave and aisles of approximately equal height.

HAMMERBEAM: *see* Roofs and 7.

HAMPER: in C20 architecture, a visually distinct topmost storey or storeys.

HEADER: *see* Bond and 6e.

HEADSTOP: stop (q.v.) carved with a head (5b).

HELM ROOF: *see* IC.

HENGE: ritual earthwork.

HERM (*lit.* the god Hermes): male head or bust on a pedestal.

HERRINGBONE WORK: *see* 7ii. Cf. Pitched masonry.

HEXASTYLE: *see* Portico.

HILL-FORT: Iron Age earthwork enclosed by a ditch and bank system.

HIPPED ROOF: *see* 8a.

HOODMOULD: projecting moulding above an arch or lintel to throw off water (2b, 5b). When horizontal often called a *label*. For label stop *see* Stop.

HUSK GARLAND: festoon of stylized nutshells (4b).

HYDRAULIC POWER: use of water under high pressure to work machinery. *Accumulator tower*: houses a hydraulic accumulator which accommodates fluctuations in the flow through hydraulic mains.

HYPOCAUST (*lit.* underburning): Roman underfloor heating system.

IMPOST: horizontal moulding at the springing of an arch (5c).

IMPOST BLOCK: block between abacus and capital (1b).

IN ANTIS: *see* Antae, Portico and 4a.

INDENT: shape chiselled out of a stone to receive a brass.

INDUSTRIALIZED or SYSTEM BUILDING: system of manufactured units assembled on site.

INGLENOOK (*lit.* fire-corner): recess for a hearth with provision for seating.

INTERCOLUMNATION: interval between columns.

INTERLACE: decoration in relief simulating woven or entwined stems or bands.

INTRADOS: *see* Soffit.

IONIC: *see* Orders and 3c.

JACK ARCH: shallow segmental vault springing from beams, used for fireproof floors, bridge decks, etc.

JAMB (*lit.* leg): one of the vertical sides of an opening.

JETTY: in a timber-framed building, the projection of an upper storey beyond the storey below, made by the beams and joists of the lower storey oversailing the wall; on their outer ends is placed the sill of the walling for the storey above (7). Buildings can be jettied on several sides, in which case a *dragon beam* is set diagonally at the corner to carry the joists to either side.

JOGGLE: the joining of two stones to prevent them slipping by a notch in one and a projection in the other.

KEEL MOULDING: moulding used from the late C12, in section like the keel of a ship (1a).

KEEP: principal tower of a castle.

KENTISH CUSP: *see* Tracery and 2b.

KEY PATTERN: *see* 4b.

KEYSTONE: central stone in an arch or vault (4b, 5c).

KINGPOST: *see* Roofs and 7.

KNEELER: horizontal projecting stone at the base of each side of a gable to support the inclined coping stones (8a).

LABEL: *see* Hoodmould and 5b.

LABEL STOP: *see* Stop and 5b.

LACED BRICKWORK: vertical strips of brickwork, often in a contrasting colour, linking openings on different floors.

LACING COURSE: horizontal reinforcement in timber or brick to walls of flint, cobble, etc.

LADY CHAPEL: dedicated to the Virgin Mary (Our Lady).

LANCET: slender single-light, pointed-arched window (2a).

LANTERN: circular or polygonal windowed turret crowning a roof or a dome. Also the windowed stage of a crossing tower lighting the church interior.

LANTERN CROSS: churchyard cross with lantern-shaped top.

LAVATORIUM: in a religious house, a washing place adjacent to the refectory.

LEAN-TO: *see* Roofs.

LESENE (*lit.* a mean thing): pilaster without base or capital. Also called *pilaster strip*.

LIERNE: *see* Vault and 2c.

LIGHT: compartment of a window defined by the mullions.

LINENFOLD: Tudor panelling carved with simulations of folded linen. *See also* Parchemin.

LINTEL: horizontal beam or stone bridging an opening.

LOGGIA: gallery, usually arcaded or colonnaded; sometimes freestanding.

LONG-AND-SHORT WORK: quoins consisting of stones placed with the long side alternately upright and horizontal, especially in Saxon building.

LONGHOUSE: house and byre in the same range with internal access between them.

LOUVRE: roof opening, often protected by a raised timber structure, to allow the smoke from a central hearth to escape.

LOWSIDE WINDOW: set lower than the others in a chancel side wall, usually towards its W end.

LUCAM: projecting housing for hoist pulley on upper storey of warehouses, mills, etc., for raising goods to loading doors.

LUCARNE (*lit.* dormer): small gabled opening in a roof or spire.

LUGGED ARCHITRAVE: *see* 4b.

LUNETTE: semicircular window or blind panel.

LYCHGATE (*lit.* corpse-gate): roofed gateway entrance to a churchyard for the reception of a coffin.

LYNCHET: long terraced strip of soil on the downward side of prehistoric and medieval fields, accumulated because of continual ploughing along the contours.

MACHICOLATIONS (*lit.* mashing devices): series of openings between the corbels that support a projecting parapet through which missiles can be dropped. Used decoratively in post-medieval buildings.

MANOMETER or STANDPIPE TOWER: containing a column of water to regulate pressure in water mains.

MANSARD: *see* 8a.

MATHEMATICAL TILES: facing tiles with the appearance of brick, most often applied to timber-framed walls.

MAUSOLEUM: monumental building or chamber usually intended for the burial of members of one family.

MEGALITHIC TOMB: massive stone-built Neolithic burial chamber covered by an earth or stone mound.

MERLON: *see* Battlement.

METOPES: spaces between the triglyphs in a Doric frieze (3b).

MEZZANINE: low storey between two higher ones.

MILD STEEL: *see* Cast iron.

MISERICORD (*lit.* mercy): shelf on a carved bracket placed on the underside of a hinged choir stall seat to support an occupant when standing.

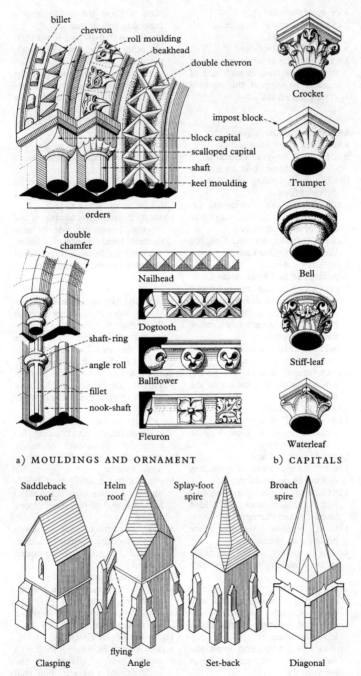

a) MOULDINGS AND ORNAMENT

b) CAPITALS

c) BUTTRESSES, ROOFS AND SPIRES

FIGURE 1: MEDIEVAL

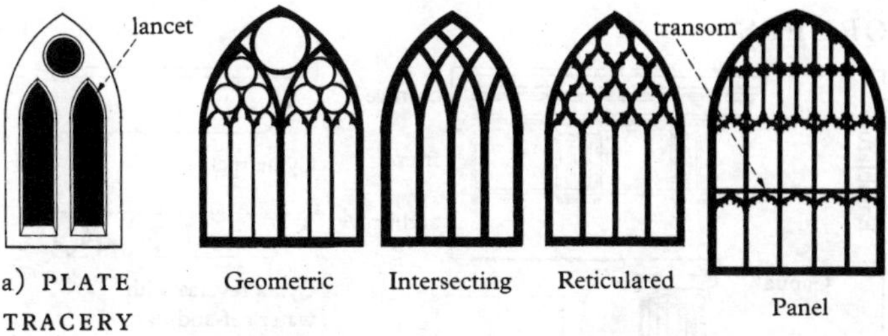

lancet

a) PLATE TRACERY

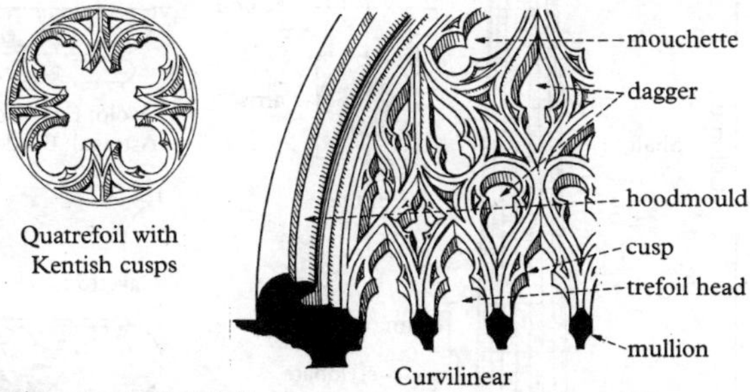

Geometric Intersecting Reticulated

transom

Panel

Quatrefoil with Kentish cusps

mouchette
dagger
hoodmould
cusp
trefoil head
mullion

Curvilinear

b) BAR TRACERY

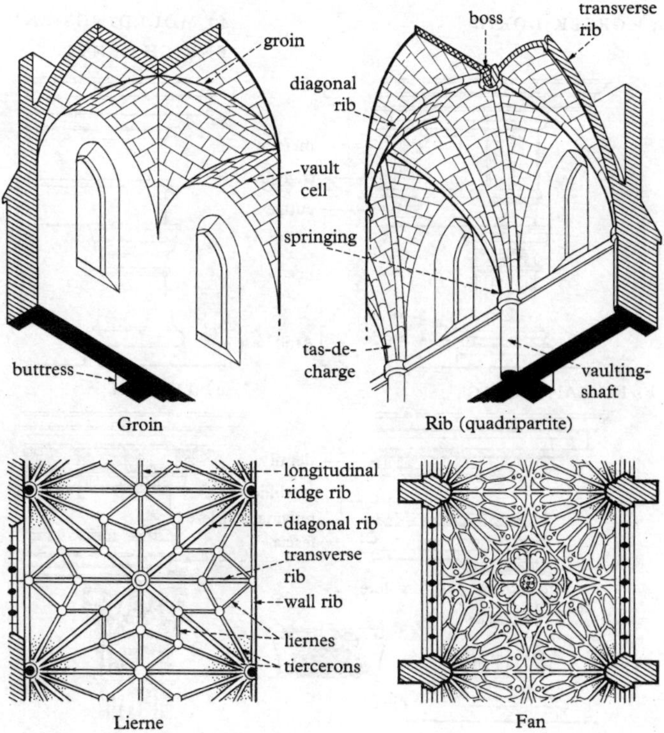

groin
diagonal rib
vault cell

buttress

Groin

boss transverse rib

springing

tas-de-charge

vaulting-shaft

Rib (quadripartite)

longitudinal ridge rib
diagonal rib
transverse rib
wall rib
liernes
tiercerons

Lierne

Fan

c) VAULTS

FIGURE 2: MEDIEVAL

ORDERS

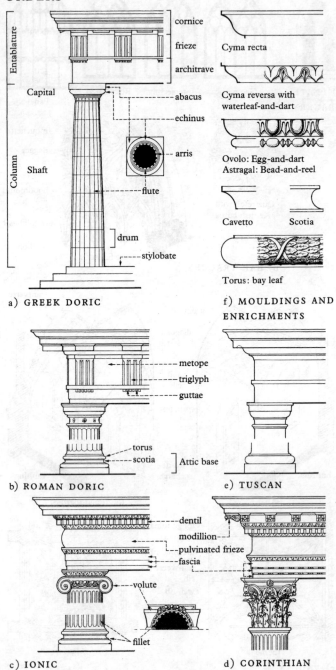

a) GREEK DORIC

b) ROMAN DORIC

c) IONIC

d) CORINTHIAN

e) TUSCAN

f) MOULDINGS AND ENRICHMENTS

FIGURE 3: CLASSICAL

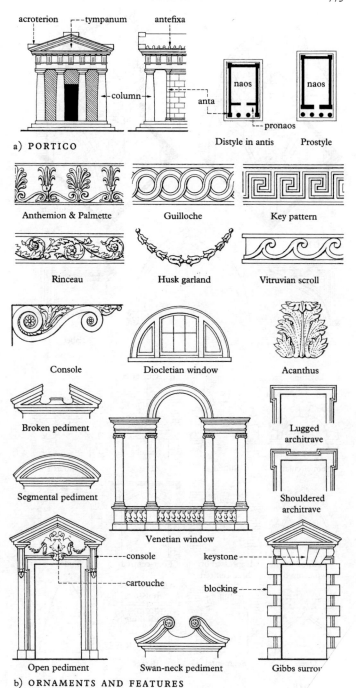

a) PORTICO

acroterion — tympanum — antefixa

column — anta — pronaos — naos — naos

Distyle in antis   Prostyle

Anthemion & Palmette   Guilloche   Key pattern

Rinceau   Husk garland   Vitruvian scroll

Console   Diocletian window   Acanthus

Broken pediment   Lugged architrave

Segmental pediment   Venetian window   Shouldered architrave

Open pediment — console — cartouche

Swan-neck pediment

keystone — blocking — Gibbs surround

b) ORNAMENTS AND FEATURES

FIGURE 4: CLASSICAL

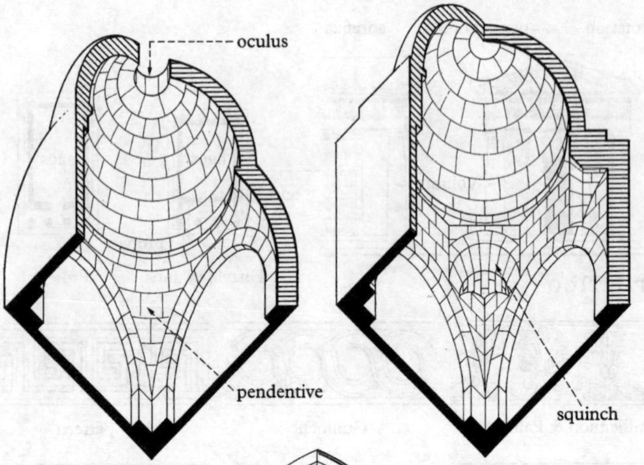

oculus

pendentive

squinch

a) DOMES

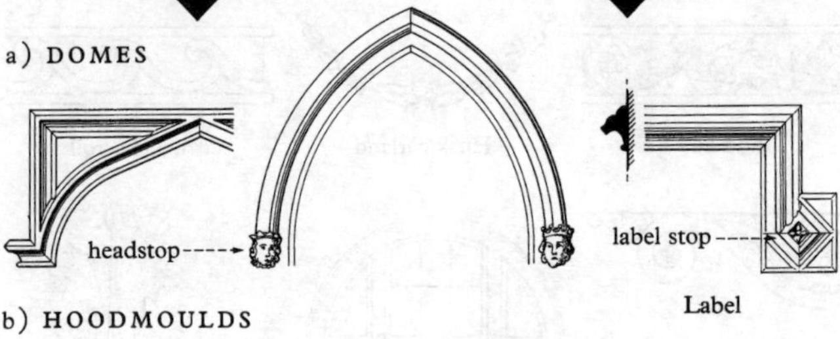

headstop

b) HOODMOULDS

label stop

Label

keystone

voussoir   impost

relieving arch

lintel

lintel

Semicircular   Stilted   Flat   Shouldered

spandrel

Pointed or two-centred   Depressed or three-centred   Four-centred   Tudor

gauged brick voussoirs

Ogee   Segmental   Basket   Parabolic

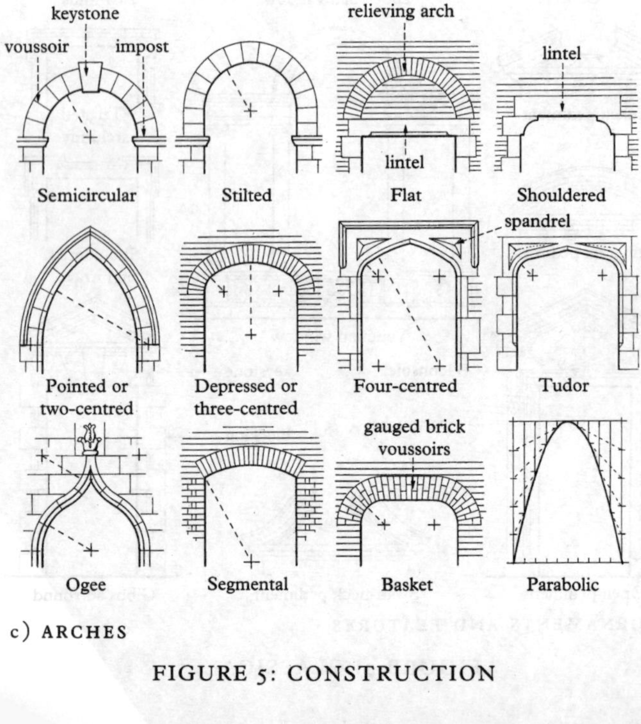

c) ARCHES

FIGURE 5: CONSTRUCTION

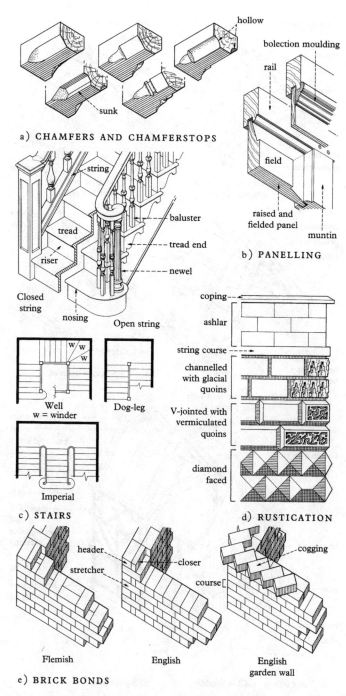

a) CHAMFERS AND CHAMFERSTOPS

b) PANELLING

c) STAIRS

d) RUSTICATION

e) BRICK BONDS

FIGURE 6: CONSTRUCTION

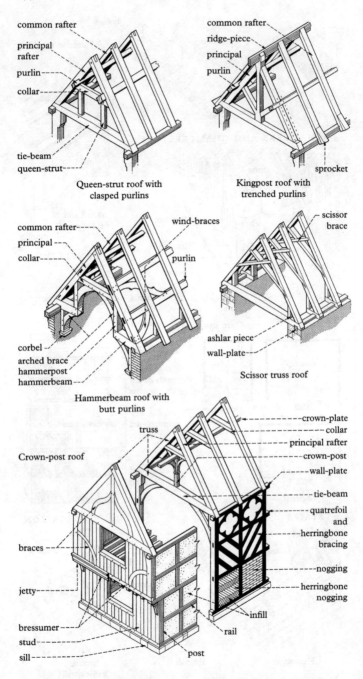

Queen-strut roof with clasped purlins

- common rafter
- principal rafter
- purlin
- collar
- tie-beam
- queen-strut

Kingpost roof with trenched purlins

- common rafter
- ridge-piece
- principal
- purlin
- sprocket

Hammerbeam roof with butt purlins

- common rafter
- principal
- collar
- wind-braces
- purlin
- corbel
- arched brace
- hammerpost
- hammerbeam

Scissor truss roof

- scissor brace
- ashlar piece
- wall-plate

Crown-post roof

- crown-plate
- collar
- principal rafter
- crown-post
- wall-plate
- tie-beam
- quatrefoil and herringbone bracing
- nogging
- herringbone nogging
- infill
- rail
- truss
- braces
- jetty
- bressumer
- stud
- sill
- post

Box frame: i) Close studding   ii) Square panel

FIGURE 7: ROOFS AND TIMBER-FRAMING

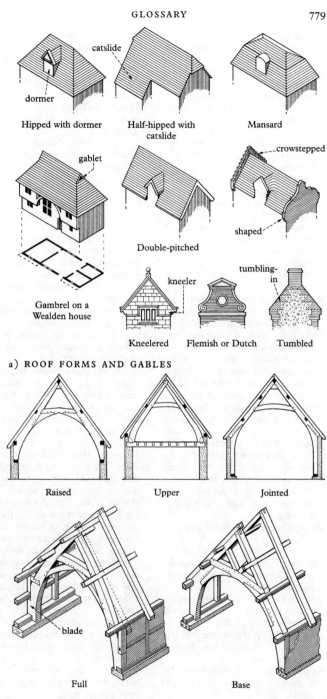

a) ROOF FORMS AND GABLES

Hipped with dormer

Half-hipped with catslide

Mansard

Double-pitched

Gambrel on a Wealden house

Kneelered

Flemish or Dutch

Tumbled

b) CRUCK FRAMES

Raised

Upper

Jointed

Full

Base

FIGURE 8: ROOFS AND TIMBER-FRAMING

MIXER-COURTS: forecourts to groups of houses shared by vehicles and pedestrians.

MODILLIONS: small consoles (q.v.) along the underside of a Corinthian or Composite cornice (3d). Often used along an eaves cornice.

MODULE: a predetermined standard size for co-ordinating the dimensions of components of a building.

MOTTE-AND-BAILEY: post-Roman and Norman defence consisting of an earthen mound (motte) topped by a wooden tower within a bailey, an enclosure defended by a ditch and palisade, and also, sometimes, by an internal bank.

MOUCHETTE: see Tracery and 2b.

MOULDING: shaped ornamental strip of continuous section; see e.g. Cavetto, Cyma, Ovolo, Roll.

MULLION: vertical member between window lights (2b).

MULTI-STOREY: five or more storeys. Multi-storey flats may form a *cluster block*, with individual blocks of flats grouped round a service core; a *point block*, with flats fanning out from a service core; or a *slab block*, with flats approached by corridors or galleries from service cores at intervals or towers at the ends (plan also used for offices, hotels etc.). *Tower block* is a generic term for any very high multi-storey building.

MUNTIN: see Panelling and 6b.

NAILHEAD: E.E. ornament consisting of small pyramids regularly repeated (1a).

NARTHEX: enclosed vestibule or covered porch at the main entrance to a church.

NAVE: the body of a church w of the crossing or chancel often flanked by aisles (q.v.).

NEWEL: central or corner post of a staircase (6c). Newel stair: see Stairs.

NIGHT STAIR: stair by which religious entered the transept of their church from their dormitory to celebrate night services.

NOGGING: see Timber-framing (7).

NOOK-SHAFT: shaft set in the angle of a wall or opening (1a).

NORMAN: see Romanesque.

NOSING: projection of the tread of a step (6c).

NUTMEG: medieval ornament with a chain of tiny triangles placed obliquely.

OCULUS: circular opening.

ŒIL DE BŒUF: see Bullseye window.

OGEE: double curve, bending first one way and then the other, as in an *ogee* or *ogival arch* (5c). Cf. Cyma recta and Cyma reversa.

OPUS SECTILE: decorative mosaic-like facing.

OPUS SIGNINUM: composition flooring of Roman origin.

ORATORY: a private chapel in a church or a house. Also a church of the Oratorian Order.

ORDER: one of a series of recessed arches and jambs forming a splayed medieval opening, e.g. a doorway or arcade arch (1a).

ORDERS: the formalized versions of the post-and-lintel system in classical architecture. The main orders are *Doric*, *Ionic*, and *Corinthian*. They are Greek in origin but occur in Roman versions. Tuscan is a simple version of Roman Doric. Though each order has its own conventions (3), there are many minor variations. The *Composite* capital combines Ionic volutes with Corinthian foliage. *Superimposed orders*: orders on successive levels, usually in the upward sequence of Tuscan, Doric, Ionic, Corinthian, Composite.

ORIEL: see Bay window.

OVERDOOR: painting or relief above an internal door. Also called a *sopraporta*.

OVERTHROW: decorative fixed arch between two gatepiers or above a wrought-iron gate.

OVOLO: wide convex moulding (3f).

PALIMPSEST: of a brass: where a metal plate has been reused by turning over the engraving on the back; of a wall painting: where one overlaps and partly obscures an earlier one.

PALLADIAN: following the examples and principles of Andrea Palladio (1508–80).

PALMETTE: classical ornament like a palm shoot (4b).

PANELLING: wooden lining to interior walls, made up of vertical members (*muntins*) and horizontals (*rails*) framing panels: also called *wainscot*. *Raised and fielded*: with the central area of the panel (*field*) raised up (6b).

PANTILE: roof tile of S section.

PARAPET: wall for protection at any sudden drop, e.g. at the wall-head of a castle where it protects the *parapet walk* or wall-walk. Also used to conceal a roof.

PARCLOSE: *see* Screen.

PARGETTING (*lit.* plastering): exterior plaster decoration, either in relief or incised.

PARLOUR: in a religious house, a room where the religious could talk to visitors; in a medieval house, the semi-private living room below the solar (q.v.).

PARTERRE: level space in a garden laid out with low, formal beds.

PATERA (*lit.* plate): round or oval ornament in shallow relief.

PAVILION: ornamental building for occasional use; or projecting subdivision of a larger building, often at an angle or terminating a wing.

PEBBLEDASHING: *see* Rendering.

PEDESTAL: a tall block carrying a classical order, statue, vase, etc.

PEDIMENT: a formalized gable derived from that of a classical temple; also used over doors, windows, etc. For variations *see* 4b.

PENDENTIVE: spandrel between adjacent arches, supporting a drum, dome or vault and consequently formed as part of a hemisphere (5a).

PENTHOUSE: subsidiary structure with a lean-to roof. Also a

separately roofed structure on top of a C20 multi-storey block.

PERIPTERAL: *see* Peristyle.

PERISTYLE: a colonnade all round the exterior of a classical building, as in a temple which is then said to be *peripteral*.

PERP (PERPENDICULAR): English Gothic architecture *c*. 1335–50 to *c*. 1530. The name is derived from the upright tracery panels then used (*see* Tracery and 2a).

PERRON: external stair to a doorway, usually of double-curved plan.

PEW: loosely, seating for the laity outside the chancel; strictly, an enclosed seat. *Box pew*: with equal high sides and a door.

PIANO NOBILE: principal floor of a classical building above a ground floor or basement and with a lesser storey overhead.

PIAZZA: formal urban open space surrounded by buildings.

PIER: large masonry or brick support, often for an arch. *See also* Compound pier.

PILASTER: flat representation of a classical column in shallow relief. *Pilaster strip*: *see* Lesene.

PILE: row of rooms. *Double pile*: two rows thick.

PILLAR: free-standing upright member of any section, not conforming to one of the orders (q.v.).

PILLAR PISCINA: *see* Piscina.

PILOTIS: C20 French term for pillars or stilts that support a building above an open ground floor.

PISCINA: basin for washing Mass vessels, provided with a drain; set in or against the wall to the S of an altar or free-standing (*pillar piscina*).

PISÉ: *see* Cob.

PITCHED MASONRY: laid on the diagonal, often alternately with opposing courses (*pitched and counterpitched* or *herringbone*).

PLATBAND: flat horizontal moulding between storeys. Cf. stringcourse.

PLATE RAIL: *see* Railways.

PLATEWAY: *see* Railways.

PLINTH: projecting courses at the

foot of a wall or column, generally chamfered or moulded at the top.

PODIUM: a continuous raised platform supporting a building; or a large block of two or three storeys beneath a multi-storey block of smaller area.

POINT BLOCK: *see* Multi-storey.

POINTING: exposed mortar jointing of masonry or brickwork. Types include *flush*, *recessed* and *tuck* (with a narrow channel filled with finer, whiter mortar).

POPPYHEAD: carved ornament of leaves and flowers as a finial for a bench end or stall.

PORTAL FRAME: C20 frame comprising two uprights rigidly connected to a beam or pair of rafters.

PORTCULLIS: gate constructed to rise and fall in vertical grooves at the entry to a castle.

PORTICO: a porch with the roof and frequently a pediment supported by a row of columns (4a). A portico *in antis* has columns on the same plane as the front of the building. A *prostyle* porch has columns standing free. Porticoes are described by the number of front columns, e.g. tetrastyle (four), hexastyle (six). The space within the temple is the *naos*, that within the portico the *pronaos*. *Blind portico*: the front features of a portico applied to a wall.

PORTICUS (plural: porticūs): subsidiary cell opening from the main body of a pre-Conquest church.

POST: upright support in a structure (7).

POSTERN: small gateway at the back of a building or to the side of a larger entrance door or gate.

POUND LOCK: *see* Canals.

PRESBYTERY: the part of a church lying E of the choir where the main altar is placed; or a priest's residence.

PRINCIPAL: *see* Roofs and 7.

PRONAOS: *see* Portico and 4a.

PROSTYLE: *see* Portico and 4a.

PULPIT: raised and enclosed platform for the preaching of sermons. *Three-decker*: with reading desk below and clerk's desk below that. *Two-decker*: as above, minus the clerk's desk.

PULPITUM: stone screen in a major church dividing choir from nave.

PULVINATED: *see* Frieze and 3c.

PURLIN: *see* Roofs and 7.

PUTHOLES or PUTLOG HOLES: in the wall to receive putlogs, the horizontal timbers which support scaffolding boards; sometimes not filled after construction is complete.

PUTTO (plural: putti): small naked boy.

QUARRIES: square (or diamond) panes of glass supported by lead strips (*cames*); square floor slabs or tiles.

QUATREFOIL: *see* Foil and 2b.

QUEEN-STRUT: *see* Roofs and 7.

QUIRK: sharp groove to one side of a convex medieval moulding.

QUOINS: dressed stones at the angles of a building (6d).

RADBURN SYSTEM: vehicle and pedestrian segregation in residential developments, based on that used at Radburn, New Jersey, USA, by Wright and Stein, 1928–30.

RADIATING CHAPELS: projecting radially from an ambulatory or an apse (*see* Chevet).

RAFTER: *see* Roofs and 7.

RAGGLE: groove cut in masonry, especially to receive the edge of a roof-covering.

RAGULY: ragged (in heraldry). Also applied to funerary sculpture, e.g. *cross raguly*: with a notched outline.

RAIL: *see* Panelling and 6b; also 7.

RAILWAYS: *Edge rail*: on which flanged wheels can run. *Plate rail*: L-section rail for plain unflanged wheels. *Plateway*: early railway using plate rails.

RAISED AND FIELDED: *see* Panelling and 6b.

RAKE: slope or pitch.

RAMPART: defensive outer wall of stone or earth. *Rampart walk*: path along the inner face.

REBATE: rectangular section cut out of a masonry edge to receive a shutter, door, window, etc.

REBUS: a heraldic pun, e.g. a fiery cock for Cockburn.

REEDING: series of convex mouldings, the reverse of fluting (q.v.). Cf. Gadrooning.

RENDERING: the covering of outside walls with a uniform surface or skin for protection from the weather. *Limewashing*: thin layer of lime plaster. *Pebbledashing*: where aggregate is thrown at the wet plastered wall for a textured effect. *Roughcast*: plaster mixed with a coarse aggregate such as gravel. *Stucco*: fine lime plaster worked to a smooth surface. *Cement rendering*: a cheaper substitute for stucco, usually with a grainy texture.

REPOUSSÉ: relief designs in metalwork, formed by beating it from the back.

REREDORTER (*lit.* behind the dormitory): latrines in a medieval religious house.

REREDOS: painted and/or sculptured screen behind and above an altar. Cf. Retable.

RESPOND: half-pier or half-column bonded into a wall and carrying one end of an arch. It usually terminates an arcade.

RETABLE: painted or carved panel standing on or at the back of an altar, usually attached to it.

RETROCHOIR: in a major church, the area between the high altar and E chapel.

REVEAL: the plane of a jamb, between the wall and the frame of a door or window.

RIB-VAULT: *see* Vault and 2c.

RINCEAU: classical ornament of leafy scrolls (4b).

RISER: vertical face of a step (6c).

ROACH: a rough-textured form of Portland stone, with small cavities and fossil shells.

ROCK-FACED: masonry cleft to produce a rugged appearance.

ROCOCO: style current *c.* 1720 and *c.* 1760, characterized by a serpentine line and playful, scrolled decoration.

ROLL MOULDING: medieval moulding of part-circular section (1a).

ROMANESQUE: style current in the CII and CI2. In England often called Norman. *See also* Saxo-Norman.

ROOD: crucifix flanked by the Virgin and St John, usually over the entry into the chancel, on a beam (*rood beam*) or painted on the wall. The *rood screen* below often had a walkway (*rood loft*) along the top, reached by a *rood stair* in the side wall.

ROOFS: Shape. For the main external shapes (hipped, mansard, etc.) *see* 8a. *Helm* and *Saddleback*: *see* IC. *Lean-to*: single sloping roof built against a vertical wall; lean-to is also applied to the part of the building beneath.
Construction. *See* 7.
Single-framed roof: with no main trusses. The rafters may be fixed to the wall-plate or ridge, or longitudinal timber may be absent altogether.
Double-framed roof: with longitudinal members, such as purlins, and usually divided into bays by principals and principal rafters. Other types are named after their main structural components, e.g. *hammerbeam, crown-post* (*see* Elements below and 7).
Elements. *See* 7.
Ashlar piece: a short vertical timber connecting inner wall-plate or timber pad to a rafter.
Braces: subsidiary timbers set diagonally to strengthen the frame. *Arched braces*: curved pair forming an arch, connecting wall or post below with tie- or collarbeam above. *Passing braces*: long straight braces passing across other members of the truss. *Scissor braces*: pair crossing diagonally between pairs of rafters or principals. *Wind-braces*: short, usually curved braces connecting side purlins with principals; sometimes decorated with cusping.
Collar or *collar-beam*: horizontal transverse timber connecting a pair of rafter or cruck blades (q.v.), set between apex and the wall-plate.
Crown-post: a vertical timber set centrally on a tie-beam and supporting a collar purlin braced to it longitudinally. In an open truss

lateral braces may rise to the collar-beam; in a closed truss they may descend to the tie-beam.

Hammerbeams: horizontal brackets projecting at wall-plate level like an interrupted tie-beam; the inner ends carry *hammerposts*, vertical timbers which support a purlin and are braced to a collar-beam above.

Kingpost: vertical timber set centrally on a tie- or collar-beam, rising to the apex of the roof to support a ridge-piece (cf. Strut).

Plate: longitudinal timber set square to the ground. *Wall-plate*: plate along the top of a wall which receives the ends of the rafters; cf. Purlin.

Principals: pair of inclined lateral timbers of a truss. Usually they support side purlins and mark the main bay divisions.

Purlin: horizontal longitudinal timber. *Collar purlin* or *crown plate*: central timber which carries collar-beams and is supported by crown-posts. *Side purlins*: pairs of timbers placed some way up the slope of the roof, which carry common rafters. *Butt* or *tenoned purlins* are tenoned into either side of the principals. *Through purlins* pass through or past the principal; they include *clasped purlins*, which rest on queenposts or are carried in the angle between principals and collar, and *trenched purlins* trenched into the backs of principals.

Queen-strut: paired vertical, or near-vertical, timbers placed symmetrically on a tie-beam to support side purlins.

Rafters: inclined lateral timbers supporting the roof covering. *Common rafters*: regularly spaced uniform rafters placed along the length of a roof or between principals. *Principal rafters*: rafters which also act as principals.

Ridge, ridge-piece: horizontal longitudinal timber at the apex supporting the ends of the rafters.

Sprocket: short timber placed on the back and at the foot of a rafter to form projecting eaves.

Strut: vertical or oblique timber between two members of a truss, not directly supporting longitudinal timbers.

Tie-beam: main horizontal transverse timber which carries the feet of the principals at wall level.

Truss: rigid framework of timbers at bay intervals, carrying the longitudinal roof timbers which support the common rafters.

Closed truss: with the spaces between the timbers filled, to form an internal partition.

See also Cruck, Wagon roof.

ROPE MOULDING: *see* Cable moulding.

ROSE WINDOW: circular window with tracery radiating from the centre. Cf. Wheel window.

ROTUNDA: building or room circular in plan.

ROUGHCAST: *see* Rendering.

ROVING BRIDGE: *see* Canals.

RUBBED BRICKWORK: *see* Gauged brickwork.

RUBBLE: masonry whose stones are wholly or partly in a rough state. *Coursed*: coursed stones with rough faces. *Random*: uncoursed stones in a random pattern. *Snecked*: with courses broken by smaller stones (snecks).

RUSTICATION: *see* 6d. Exaggerated treatment of masonry to give an effect of strength. The joints are usually recessed by V-section chamfering or square-section channelling (*channelled rustication*). *Banded rustication* has only the horizontal joints emphasized. The faces may be flat, but can be *diamond-faced*, like shallow pyramids, *vermiculated*, with a stylized texture like worm-casts, and *glacial* (frost-work), like icicles or stalactites.

SACRISTY: room in a church for sacred vessels and vestments.

SADDLEBACK ROOF: *see* IC.

SALTIRE CROSS: with diagonal limbs.

SANCTUARY: area around the main altar of a church. Cf. Presbytery.

SANGHA: residence of Buddhist monks or nuns.

SARCOPHAGUS: coffin of stone or other durable material.

SAXO-NORMAN: transitional Romanesque style combining Anglo-Saxon and Norman features, current *c.* 1060–1100.

SCAGLIOLA: composition imitating marble.

SCALLOPED CAPITAL: *see* 1a.

SCOTIA: a hollow classical moulding, especially between tori (q.v.) on a column base (3b, 3f).

SCREEN: in a medieval church, usually at the entry to the chancel; *see* Rood (screen) and Pulpitum. A *parclose screen* separates a chapel from the rest of the church.

SCREENS or SCREENS PASSAGE: screened-off entrance passage between great hall and service rooms.

SECTION: two-dimensional representation of a building, moulding, etc., revealed by cutting across it.

SEDILIA (singular: sedile): seats for the priests (usually three) on the S side of the chancel.

SET-OFF: *see* Weathering.

SETTS: squared stones, usually of granite, used for paving or flooring.

SGRAFFITO: decoration scratched, often in plaster, to reveal a pattern in another colour beneath. *Graffiti*: scratched drawing or writing.

SHAFT: vertical member of round or polygonal section (1a, 3a). *Shaft-ring*: at the junction of shafts set *en delit* (q.v.) or attached to a pier or wall (1a).

SHEILA-NA-GIG: female fertility figure, usually with legs apart.

SHELL: thin, self-supporting roofing membrane of timber or concrete.

SHOULDERED ARCHITRAVE: *see* 4b.

SHUTTERING: *see* Concrete.

SILL: horizontal member at the bottom of a window or door frame; or at the base of a timber-framed wall into which posts and studs are tenoned (7).

SLAB BLOCK: *see* Multi-storey.

SLATE-HANGING: covering of overlapping slates on a wall. *Tile-hanging* is similar.

SLYPE: covered way or passage leading E from the cloisters between transept and chapter house.

SNECKED: *see* Rubble.

SOFFIT (*lit.* ceiling): underside of an arch (also called *intrados*), lintel, etc. *Soffit roll*: medieval roll moulding on a soffit.

SOLAR: private upper chamber in a medieval house, accessible from the high end of the great hall.

SOPRAPORTA: *see* Overdoor.

SOUNDING-BOARD: *see* Tester.

SPANDRELS: roughly triangular spaces between an arch and its containing rectangle, or between adjacent arches (5c). Also nonstructural panels under the windows in a curtain-walled building.

SPERE: a fixed structure screening the lower end of the great hall from the screens passage. *Spere-truss*: roof truss incorporated in the spere.

SPIRE: tall pyramidal or conical feature crowning a tower or turret. *Broach*: starting from a square base, then carried into an octagonal section by means of triangular faces; and *splayed-foot*: variation of the broach form, found principally in the southeast, in which the four cardinal faces are splayed out near their base, to cover the corners, while oblique (or intermediate) faces taper away to a point (1c). *Needle spire*: thin spire rising from the centre of a tower roof, well inside the parapet: when of timber and lead often called a *spike*.

SPIRELET: *see* Flèche.

SPLAY: of an opening when it is wider on one face of a wall than the other.

SPRING or SPRINGING: level at which an arch or vault rises from its supports. *Springers*: the first stones of an arch or vaulting rib above the spring (2c).

SQUINCH: arch or series of arches thrown across an interior angle of a square or rectangular structure to support a circular or polygonal superstructure, especially a dome or spire (5a).

SQUINT: an aperture in a wall or through a pier usually to allow a view of an altar.

STAIRS: *see* 6c. *Dog-leg stair*: parallel flights rising alternately in opposite directions, without an open well. *Flying stair*: cantilevered from the walls of a stairwell, without newels; sometimes called a *Geometric* stair when the inner edge describes a curve. *Newel stair*: ascending round a central supporting newel (q.v.); called a *spiral stair* or *vice* when in a circular shaft, a *winder* when in a rectangular compartment. (Winder also applies to the steps on the turn.) *Well stair*: with flights round a square open well framed by newel posts. *See also* Perron.

STALL: fixed seat in the choir or chancel for the clergy or choir (cf. Pew). Usually with arm rests, and often framed together.

STANCHION: upright structural member, of iron, steel or reinforced concrete.

STANDPIPE TOWER: *see* Manometer.

STEAM ENGINES: *Atmospheric*: worked by the vacuum created when low-pressure steam is condensed in the cylinder, as developed by Thomas Newcomen. *Beam engine*: with a large pivoted beam moved in an oscillating fashion by the piston. It may drive a flywheel or be *non-rotative*. *Watt* and *Cornish*: single-cylinder; *compound*: two cylinders; *triple expansion*: three cylinders.

STEEPLE: tower together with a spire, lantern, or belfry.

STIFF-LEAF: type of E.E. foliage decoration. *Stiff-leaf capital see* 1b.

STOP: plain or decorated terminal to mouldings or chamfers, or at the end of hoodmoulds and labels (*label stop*), or stringcourses (5b, 6a); *see also* Headstop.

STOUP: vessel for holy water, usually near a door.

STRAINER: *see* Arch.

STRAPWORK: late C16 and C17 decoration, like interlaced leather straps.

STRETCHER: *see* Bond and 6e.

STRING: *see* 6c. Sloping member holding the ends of the treads and risers of a staircase. *Closed string*: a broad string covering the ends of the treads and risers. *Open string*: cut into the shape of the treads and risers.

STRINGCOURSE: horizontal course or moulding projecting from the surface of a wall (6d).

STUCCO: *see* Rendering.

STUDS: subsidiary vertical timbers of a timber-framed wall or partition (7).

STUPA: Buddhist shrine, circular in plan.

STYLOBATE: top of the solid platform on which a colonnade stands (3a).

SUSPENSION BRIDGE: *see* Bridge.

SWAG: like a festoon (q.v.), but representing cloth.

SYSTEM BUILDING: *see* Industrialized building.

TABERNACLE: canopied structure to contain the reserved sacrament or a relic; or architectural frame for an image or statue.

TABLE TOMB: memorial slab raised on free-standing legs.

TAS-DE-CHARGE: the lower courses of a vault or arch which are laid horizontally (2c).

TERM: pedestal or pilaster tapering downward, usually with the upper part of a human figure growing out of it.

TERRACOTTA: moulded and fired clay ornament or cladding.

TESSELLATED PAVEMENT: mosaic flooring, particularly Roman, made of *tesserae*, i.e. cubes of glass, stone, or brick.

TESTER: flat canopy over a tomb or pulpit, where it is also called a *sounding-board*.

TESTER TOMB: tomb-chest with effigies beneath a tester, either free-standing (tester with four or more columns), or attached to a wall (*half-tester*) with columns on one side only.

TETRASTYLE: *see* Portico.

THERMAL WINDOW: *see* Diocletian window.

THREE-DECKER PULPIT: *see* Pulpit.

TIDAL GATES: *see* Canals.

TIE-BEAM: *see* Roofs and 7.

TIERCERON: *see* Vault and 2c.

TILE-HANGING: *see* Slate-hanging.

TIMBER-FRAMING: *see* 7. Method of construction where the structural frame is built of interlocking timbers. The spaces are filled with non-structural material, e.g. *infill* of wattle and daub, lath and plaster, brickwork (known as *nogging*), etc. and may be covered by plaster, weatherboarding (q.v.), or tiles.

TOMB-CHEST: chest-shaped tomb, usually of stone. Cf. Table tomb, Tester tomb.

TORUS (plural: tori): large convex moulding usually used on a column base (3b, 3f).

TOUCH: soft black marble quarried near Tournai.

TOURELLE: turret corbelled out from the wall.

TOWER BLOCK: *see* Multi-storey.

TRABEATED: depends structurally on the use of the post and lintel. Cf. Arcuated.

TRACERY: openwork pattern of masonry or timber in the upper part of an opening. *Blind tracery* is tracery applied to a solid wall.

Plate tracery, introduced *c.* 1200, is the earliest form, in which shapes are cut through solid masonry (2a).

Bar tracery was introduced into England *c.* 1250. The pattern is formed by intersecting moulded ribwork continued from the mullions. It was especially elaborate during the Decorated period (q.v.). Tracery shapes can include circles, *daggers* (elongated ogee-ended lozenges), *mouchettes* (like daggers but with curved sides) and upright rectangular *panels*. They often have *cusps*, projecting points defining lobes or *foils* (q.v.) within the main shape: *Kentish* or *split-cusps* are forked (2b).

Types of bar tracery (*see* 2b) include *geometric(al)*: *c.* 1250–1310, chiefly circles, often foiled; *Y-tracery*: *c.* 1300, with mullions branching into a Y-shape; *intersecting*: *c.* 1300, formed by interlocking mullions; *reticulated*: early C14, net-like pattern of ogee-ended lozenges; *curvilinear*: C14, with uninterrupted flowing curves; *panel*: Perp, with straight-sided panels, often cusped at the top and bottom.

TRANSEPT: transverse portion of a church.

TRANSITIONAL: generally used for the phase between Romanesque and Early English (*c.* 1175–*c.* 1200).

TRANSOM: horizontal member separating window lights (2b).

TREAD: horizontal part of a step. The *tread end* may be carved on a staircase (6c).

TREFOIL: *see* Foil.

TRIFORIUM: middle storey of a church treated as an arcaded wall passage or blind arcade, its height corresponding to that of the aisle roof.

TRIGLYPHS (*lit.* three-grooved tablets): stylized beam-ends in the Doric frieze, with metopes between (3b).

TRIUMPHAL ARCH: influential type of Imperial Roman monument.

TROPHY: sculptured or painted group of arms or armour.

TRUMEAU: central stone mullion supporting the tympanum of a wide doorway. *Trumeau figure*: carved figure attached to it (cf. Column figure).

TRUMPET CAPITAL: *see* 1b.

TRUSS: braced framework, spanning between supports. *See also* Roofs and 7.

TUMBLING or TUMBLING-IN: courses of brickwork laid at right-angles to a slope, e.g. of a gable, forming triangles by tapering into horizontal courses (8a).

TUSCAN: *see* Orders and 3e.

TWO-DECKER PULPIT: *see* Pulpit.

TYMPANUM: the surface between a lintel and the arch above it or within a pediment (4a).

UNDERCROFT: usually describes the vaulted room(s), beneath the main room(s) of a medieval house. Cf. Crypt.

VAULT: arched stone roof (sometimes imitated in timber or plaster). For types see 2c.

Tunnel or *barrel vault*: continuous semicircular or pointed arch, often of rubble masonry.

Groin-vault: tunnel vaults intersecting at right angles. *Groins* are the curved lines of the intersections.

Rib-vault: masonry framework of intersecting arches (ribs) supporting *vault cells*, used in Gothic architecture. *Wall rib* or *wall arch*: between wall and vault cell. *Transverse rib*: spans between two walls to divide a vault into bays. *Quadripartite* rib-vault: each bay has two pairs of diagonal ribs dividing the vault into four triangular cells. *Sexpartite* rib-vault: most often used over paired bays, has an extra pair of ribs springing from between the bays. More elaborate vaults may include *ridge ribs* along the crown of a vault or bisecting the bays; *tiercerons*: extra decorative ribs springing from the corners of a bay; and *liernes*: short decorative ribs in the crown of a vault, not linked to any springing point. A *stellar* or *star* vault has liernes in star formation.

Fan-vault: form of barrel vault used in the Perp period, made up of halved concave masonry cones decorated with blind tracery.

VAULTING SHAFT: shaft leading up to the spring or springing (q.v.) of a vault (2c).

VENETIAN or SERLIAN WINDOW: derived from Serlio (4b). The motif is used for other openings.

VERMICULATION: *see* Rustication and 6d.

VESICA: oval with pointed ends.

VICE: *see* Stair.

VILLA: originally a Roman country house or farm. The term was revived in England in the C18 under the influence of Palladio and used especially for smaller, compact country houses. In the later C19 it was debased to describe any suburban house.

VITRIFIED: bricks or tiles fired to a darkened glassy surface.

VITRUVIAN SCROLL: classical running ornament of curly waves (4b).

VOLUTES: spiral scrolls. They occur on Ionic capitals (3c). *Angle volute*: pair of volutes, turned outwards to meet at the corner of a capital.

VOUSSOIRS: wedge-shaped stones forming an arch (5c).

WAGON ROOF: with the appearance of the inside of a wagon tilt; often ceiled. Also called *cradle roof*.

WAINSCOT: *see* Panelling.

WALL MONUMENT: attached to the wall and often standing on the floor. *Wall tablets* are smaller with the inscription as the major element.

WALL-PLATE: *see* Roofs and 7.

WALL-WALK: *see* Parapet.

WARMING ROOM: room in a religious house where a fire burned for comfort.

WATERHOLDING BASE: early Gothic base with upper and lower mouldings separated by a deep hollow.

WATERLEAF: *see* Enrichments and 3f.

WATERLEAF CAPITAL: Late Romanesque and Transitional type of capital (1b).

WATER WHEELS: described by the way water is fed on to the wheel. *Breastshot*: mid-height, falling and passing beneath. *Overshot*: over the top. *Pitchback*: on the top but falling backwards. *Undershot*: turned by the momentum of the water passing beneath. In a *water turbine*, water is fed under pressure through a vaned wheel within a casing.

WEALDEN HOUSE: type of medieval timber-framed house with a central open hall flanked by bays of two storeys, roofed in line; the end bays are jettied to the front, but the eaves are continuous (8a).

WEATHERBOARDING: wall cladding of overlapping horizontal boards.

WEATHERING or SET-OFF: inclined, projecting surface to keep water away from the wall below.

WEEPERS: figures in niches along the sides of some medieval tombs. Also called mourners.

WHEEL WINDOW: circular, with radiating shafts like spokes. Cf. Rose window.

WROUGHT IRON: *see* Cast iron.

INDEX OF ARCHITECTS, ARTISTS, PATRONS AND RESIDENTS

Names of architects and artists working in the area covered by this volume are given in *italic*. Entries for partnerships and group practices are listed after entries for a single name.

Also indexed here are the names/titles of families and individuals (not of bodies or commercial firms) recorded in this volume as having commissioned architectural work or owned or lived in properties in the area. The index includes monuments of such families and other individuals where they are of particular interest.

INDEX OF PLACES

Principal references are in **bold** type; demolished buildings are shown in *italic*.